C# and the .NET Platform, Second Edition

ANDREW TROELSEN

C# and the .NET Platform, Second Edition
Copyright ©2003 by Andrew Troelsen

ISBN : 1-59059-055-4

Printed and bound in the United States of America 3456789

Trademarked names may appear in this book. Rather than use a trademark symbol with every occurrence of a trademarked name, we use the names only in an editorial fashion and to the benefit of the trademark owner, with no intention of infringement of the trademark.

Technical Reviewers: Gregory A. Beamer, Gary Cornell, Eric Gunnerson, Joe Nalewabau, Kent Sharkey, Nick Symmonds, Pradeep Tapadiya

Editorial Directors: Dan Appleman, Gary Cornell, Simon Hayes, Martin Streicher, Karen Watterson, John Zukowski

Assistant Publisher: Grace Wong

Copy Editors: Anne Friedman and Ami Knox

Proofreader: Liz Berry

Production Goddess: Susan Glinert Stevens

Indexer: Ron Strauss

Artist and Cover Designer: Kurt Krames

Manufacturing Manager: Tom Debolski

Distributed to the book trade in the United States by Springer-Verlag New York, Inc., 175 Fifth Avenue, New York, NY, 10010 and outside the United States by Springer-Verlag GmbH & Co. KG, Tiergartenstr. 17, 69112 Heidelberg, Germany.

In the United States: phone 1-800-SPRINGER, email orders@springer-ny.com, or visit http://www.springer-ny.com. Outside the United States: fax +49 6221 345229, email orders@springer.de, or visit http://www.springer.de.

For information on translations, please contact Apress directly at 2560 Ninth Street, Suite 219, Berkeley, CA 94710. Phone 510-549-5930, fax 510-549-5939, email info@apress.com, or visit http://www.apress.com.

The source code for this book is available to readers at http://www.apress.com in the Downloads section.

I would like to dedicate this book to my father, Wally Troelsen. Thanks, Dad, for all of your support over the years and the years to come.

Luv ya,
Damn Kid

Contents at a Glance

Contents

Chapter 2 Building C# Applications 43

Part Two The C# Programming Language 91

Chapter 3 C# Language Fundamentals 93

Part Three   Programming with .NET Assemblies 393

Chapter 9   Understanding .NET Assemblies 395

Part Four   Leveraging the .NET Libraries 537

Chapter 13 Building a Better Window (Introducing Windows Forms) 607

Chapter 14 A Better Painting Framework (GDI+) 671

Chapter 15 Programming with Windows Forms Controls 743

Chapter 16 The System.IO Namespace 805

Chapter 17 Data Access with ADO.NET 843

About the Author

Andrew Troelsen is a partner, trainer, and consultant at Intertech-Inc., a .NET and J2EE developer education center (http://www.intertech-inc.com). He is a leading authority on both .NET and COM. His earlier five-star treatment of traditional COM in the best-selling *Developer's Workshop to COM and ATL 3.0* is mirrored in his latest book, *COM and .NET Interoperability*, and his award-winning treatment of C# in *C# and the .NET Platform*, as well as his five-star investigation of VB .NET in *Visual Basic .NET and the .NET Platform: An Advanced Guide*. He has a degree in mathematical linguistics and South Asian studies from the University of Minnesota and is a frequent speaker at numerous .NET-related conferences.

He currently lives in Minneapolis, Minnesota, with his wife Amanda, and spends his free time investigating .NET and waiting for the Wild to win the Stanley Cup, the Vikings to win the Super Bowl (before he retires would be nice), and the Timberwolves to grab numerous NBA championship titles.

Acknowledgments

COMPLETING THE SECOND EDITION of *C# and the .NET Platform* would have been completely impossible without the assistance and talent offered by numerous individuals. First of all, many thanks to my copy editors, Anne Friedman and Ami Knox. Both of you, as always, did an outstanding job massaging my raw manuscript into a polished product. (See you both on the next book?) Next, I must thank the numerous technical reviewers who took the time to read these chapters for any coding faux pas: Gregory A. Beamer, Gary Cornell, Eric Gunnerson, Joe Nalewabau, Kent Sharkey, Nick Symmonds, and Pradeep Tapadiya. Special thanks to Beth Christmas, Ron Strauss, Susan Glinert Stevens, and Liz Berry, whose combined efforts formatted, indexed, and finalized this text to completion. Of course, any remaining errors (spelling, coding, or otherwise) that may have snuck into this book are my sole responsibility.

I also must say a huge thanks to all of those at Apress who have made a publishing company that is a pleasure to work with. Thanks to Hollie Fisher (for many things), Doris Wong (for many more things), and Grace Wong, my chaka friend, for not totally blasting me into pieces when I abused the phrase "I'll get it to you today" one too many times.

Thanks to my friends and family who (once again) tolerated my lack of time and sometimes grumpy demeanor. More thanks to my friends at Intertech-Inc. (not Tom Salonek, who I still don't like much). Your support (directly and indirectly) is greatly appreciated. Finally, thanks to my wife Mandy and "all the kids" for their love and encouragement.

Introduction

I REMEMBER A TIME years ago when I proposed a book to Apress regarding a forthcoming software SDK named Next Generation Windows Services (NGWS). As you may already know, NGWS eventually became what we now know as the .NET platform. My research of the C# programming language and the .NET platform took place in parallel with the authoring of the text. It was a fantastic project; however, I must confess that it was more than a bit nerve-wracking writing about a technology that was undergoing drastic changes over the course of its development. It pains me to recall how many chapters had to be completely destroyed and rewritten during that time. Thankfully, after many sleepless nights, the first edition of *C# and the .NET Platform* was published in conjunction with the release of .NET Beta 2, circa the summer of 2001.

Since that point, I have been extremely happy and grateful to see that the first edition of this text was very well received by the press and, most importantly, the readers. Over the years, it was nominated as a Jolt award finalist (I lost . . . crap!) as well as the 2003 Referenceware programming book of the year (I won . . . cool!). Although the first edition of this book has enjoyed a good run, it became clear that a second edition was in order—not only to account for the changes brought about with the minor release of the .NET platform, but to expand upon and improve the existing content. As I write this frontmatter, version 1.1 of the .NET platform is just about official, and I am happy to say that *C# and the .NET Platform, Second Edition* is being released in tandem.

As in the first edition, this second edition presents the C# programming language and .NET base class libraries using a friendly and approachable tone. I have never understood the need some technical authors have to spit out prose that reads more like a GRE vocabulary study guide than a readable discourse. As well, this new edition remains focused on providing you with the information you need to build software solutions today, rather than spending too much time focusing on esoteric details that few individuals will ever actually care about. To this end, when I do dive under the hood and check out some more low-level functionality of the CLR (or blocks of CIL code), I promise it will prove enlightening (rather than simple eye candy).

We're a Team, You and I

Technology authors write for a demanding group of people (I should know, I'm one of them). You know that building software solutions using any platform is extremely detailed and is very specific to your department, company, client base, and subject matter. Perhaps you work in the electronic publishing industry, develop systems for the state or local government, work at NASA or a branch of the military. Speaking for myself, I have developed children's educational software, various n-tier systems, as well as numerous projects within the medical and financial world. The chances are almost 100 percent that the code you write at your place of employment has little to do with the code I write at mine (unless we happened to work together previously!).

Therefore, in this book, I have deliberately chosen to avoid creating examples that tie the example code to a specific industry or vein of programming. Rather, I choose to explain C#, OOP, the CLR, and the .NET base class libraries using industry-agnostic examples. Rather than having every blessed example fill a grid with data, calculate payroll, or whatnot, I'll stick to subject matter we can all relate to: automobiles (with some geometric structures and employees thrown in for good measure). And that's where you come in.

My job is to explain the C# programming language and the core aspects of the .NET platform the best I possibly can. As well, I will do everything I can to equip you with the tools and strategies you need to continue your studies at this book's conclusion. Your job is to take this information and apply it to your specific programming assignments.

I obviously understand that your projects most likely don't revolve around automobiles with pet names; however, that's what applied knowledge is all about! Rest assured, once you understand the concepts presented within this text, you will be in a perfect position to build .NET solutions that map to your own unique programming environment.

An Overview of the Second Edition

C# and the .NET Platform, Second Edition is logically divided into five distinct sections, each of which contains some number of chapters that somehow "belong together." If you read the first edition of this text, you will notice some similarities in chapter names; however, be aware that just about every page has been updated with new content. You will also notice that some topics in the first edition (such as .NET delegates) have been moved into an entire chapter of their very own. Of course, as you would hope, the second edition contains several brand new chapters (such as an exploration of .NET Remoting, and a much deeper examination of ASP.NET).

On the flip side, I did choose to *remove* some topics from the second edition to make room for new content. The most notable omission is the topic of COM and .NET interoperability, which in no way, shape, or form reflects the importance of this topic. In fact, I felt this topic was so important, that I wrote an entire book on the subject. If you require a detailed examination, check out *COM and .NET Interoperability* (Apress, 2002).

These things being said, here is a chapter-by-chapter breakdown of the text.

Part One: Introducing C# and the .NET Platform

Chapter 1: The Philosophy of .NET

This first chapter functions as the backbone for the remainder of this text. We begin by examining the world of traditional Windows development and uncover the short-comings with the previous state of affairs. The primary goal of this chapter, however, is to acquaint you with a number of .NET-centric building blocks such as the common language runtime (CLR), Common Type System (CTS), Common Language Specification (CLS), and the base class libraries. You also take an initial look at the C# programming language, the role of the .NET assembly, and various development utilities that ship with the .NET SDK.

Chapter 2: Building C# Applications

The goal of this chapter is to introduce you to the process of compiling and debugging C# source code files using various approaches. First, you learn to make use of the command-line compiler (csc.exe) and examine each of the corresponding command-line flags. Over the remainder of the chapter, you learn how to make use of the Visual Studio .NET IDE, navigate the official .NET help system (MSDN), and understand the role of XML-based source code comments.

Part Two: The C# Programming Language

Chapter 3: C# Language Fundamentals

This chapter examines the core constructs of the C# programming language. Here you come to understand basic class construction techniques, the distinction between value types and reference types, iteration and decision constructs, boxing and unboxing, and the role of everybody's favorite base class, System.Object. Also, Chapter 3 illustrates how the .NET platform places a spin on various commonplace programming constructs such as enumerations, arrays, and string processing.

Chapter 4: Object-Oriented Programming with C#

The role of Chapter 4 is to examine the details of how C# accounts for each "pillar" of object-oriented programming: encapsulation, inheritance, and polymorphism. In addition to examining the syntax used to build class hierarchies, you are exposed to various tools within Visual Studio .NET which may be used to decrease your typing time.

Chapter 5: Exceptions and Object Lifetime

Here you learn how to handle runtime anomalies using the official error handling mechanism of the .NET platform: structured exception handling. As you will see, exceptions are class types that contain information regarding the error at hand and can be manipulated using the "try", "catch", "throw", and "finally" keywords of C#. The latter half of this chapter examines how the CLR manages the memory consumed by allocated objects using an associated garbage collector. This discussion also examines the role of the IDisposable interface, which is a perfect lead-in to the next chapter.

Chapter 6: Interfaces and Collections

This material builds upon your understanding of object-based development by checking out the topic of interface-based programming. Here you learn how to define types that support multiple behaviors, how to discover these behaviors at runtime, and how to selectively hide select behaviors using *explicit interface implementation*. To showcase the usefulness of interface types, the remainder of this chapter examines the System.Collections namespace. As you will see, this region of the base class libraries contains numerous types that may be used out of the box, or serve as a foundation for the development of strongly typed collections.

Chapter 7: Callback Interfaces, Delegates, and Events

This chapter begins by examining how interface-based programming techniques can be used to build an event-based system. This will function as a point of contrast to the meat of Chapter 7: the delegate type. Simply put, a .NET delegate is an object that "points" to other methods in your application. Using this pattern, you are able to build systems that allow multiple objects to engage in a two-way conversation. After you examine the use of .NET delegates, you are then introduced to the C# "event" keyword, which is used to simplify the manipulation of raw delegate programming.

Chapter 8: Advanced C# Type Construction Techniques

The final chapter of this section completes your study of the C# programming language by introducing you to a number of advanced programming techniques. For example, here you learn how to overload operators and create custom conversion routines (both implicit and explicit), as well how to manipulate C-style pointers within a *.cs code file. This chapter also takes the time to explain how these C#-centric programming constructs can be accessed by other .NET programming languages (such as Visual Basic .NET), which is a natural lead-in to the topic of *.NET assemblies*.

Part Three: Programming with .NET Assemblies

Chapter 9: Understanding .NET Assemblies

From a very high level, an assembly can be considered the term used to describe a managed *.dll or *.exe file. However, the true story of .NET assemblies is far richer than that. Here you learn the distinction between single-file and multifile assemblies and how to build and deploy each entity. Next, this chapter examines how private and shared assemblies may be configured using XML-based *.config files and publisher policy *.dlls. Along the way, you investigate the internal structure of the Global Assembly Cache (GAC) and learn how to force Visual Studio .NET to display your custom assemblies within the Add Reference dialog box (trust me, this is one of the most common questions I am asked).

Chapter 10: Processes, AppDomains, Contexts, and Threads

Now that you have a solid understanding of assemblies, this chapter dives much deeper into the composition of a loaded .NET executable. The goal of Chapter 10 is to define several terms and illustrate the relationship between processes, application domains, contextual boundaries, and threads. Once these terms have been qualified, the remainder of this chapter is devoted to the topic of building multithread applications using the types of the System.Threading namespace. Be aware that the information presented here provides a solid foundation for understanding the .NET Remoting layer (examined in Chapter 12).

Chapter 11: Type Reflection, Late Binding, and Attribute-Based Programming

Chapter 11 concludes our examination of .NET assemblies by checking out the process of runtime type discovery via the System.Reflection namespace. Using these types, you are able to build applications that can read an assembly's metadata on the fly (think object browsers). Next, you learn how to dynamically activate and manipulate types at runtime using *late binding*. The final topic of this chapter explores the role of .NET attributes (both standard and custom). To illustrate the usefulness of each of these topics, the chapter concludes with the construction of an extendable Windows Forms application.

Part Four: Leveraging the .NET Libraries

Chapter 12: Object Serialization and the .NET Remoting Layer

Contrary to popular belief, XML Web services are not the only way to build distributed applications under the .NET platform. Here you learn about the managed equivalent of the (now legacy) DCOM architecture: .NET Remoting. Unlike DCOM, .NET supports the ability to *easily* pass objects between application and machine boundaries using marshal-by-value (MBV) and marshal-by-reference (MBR) semantics. Also, the runtime behavior of a distributed .NET application can be altered without the need to recompile the client and server code bases using XML configuration files.

Chapter 13: Building a Better Window (Introducing Windows Forms)

Despite the term *.NET*, the base class libraries provide numerous namespaces used to build traditional GUI-based desktop applications. Here you begin your examination of the System.Windows.Forms namespace and learn the details of building main windows (as well as MDI applications) that support menu systems, toolbars, and status bars. As you would hope, various aspects of the Visual Studio .NET IDE are examined over the flow of this material.

Chapter 14: A Better Painting Framework (GDI+)

This chapter examines how to dynamically render graphical data in the Windows Forms environment. In addition to learning how to manipulate fonts, colors, geometric images, and image files, you also examine *hit testing* and GUI-based drag-and-drop techniques. You learn about the new .NET resource format, which, as you may suspect by this point in the text, is based on XML data representation. By way of a friendly heads up, don't pass over this chapter if you are primarily concerned with ASP.NET. As you will see later in Chapter 18, GDI+ can be used to dynamically generate graphical data on the Web server.

Chapter 15: Programming with Windows Forms Controls

This final Windows-centric chapter examines numerous GUI widgets that ship with the .NET Framework. Not only do you learn how to program against the core Windows Forms controls, but you also learn about the related topics of dialog box development and Form inheritance, and how to build *custom* Windows Forms controls. If you have a background in ActiveX control development, you will be pleased to find that the process of building a custom GUI widget has been greatly simplified (especially with regard to design time support).

Chapter 16: The System.IO Namespace

As you can gather from its name, the System.IO namespace allows you to interact with a machine's file and directory structure. Over the course of this chapter, you learn how to programmatically create (and destroy) a directory system as well as move data into and out of various streams (file based, string based, memory based, and so forth). In addition, this chapter illustrates some more exotic uses of System.IO, such as monitoring a set of files for modification using the FileSystemWatcher type. We wrap up by building a complete Windows Forms application that illustrates the relationship between object serialization (described in Chapter 12) and file I/O operations.

Chapter 17: Data Access with ADO.NET

ADO.NET is an entirely new data access API that has practically nothing to do with classic (COM-based) ADO. Here you learn about the fundamental shift away from Universal Data Access (UDA) to a namespace-based data access mentality. As you will see, you are able to interact with the types of ADO.NET using a "connected" and "disconnected" layer. Over the course of this chapter, you have the chance to work with both modes of ADO.NET, and come to understand the role of data readers, DataSets, and DataAdapters. The chapter concludes with coverage of various data-centric wizards of Visual Studio .NET.

Part Five: Web Applications and XML Web Services

Chapter 18: ASP.NET Web Pages and Web Controls

This chapter begins your study of Web technologies supported under the .NET platform. ASP.NET is a completely new approach for building Web applications and has absolutely nothing to do with classic (COM-based) ASP. For example, server-side scripting code has been replaced with "real" object-oriented languages (such as C#, VB.NET, managed C++ and the like). This chapter introduces you to key ASP.NET topics such as working with (or without) code behind files, the role of ASP.NET Web controls (including the mighty DataGrid), validation controls, and interacting with the base class libraries from *.aspx files.

Chapter 19: ASP.NET Web Applications

This chapter extends your current understanding of ASP.NET by examining various ways to handle state management under .NET. Like classic ASP, ASP.NET allows you to easily create cookies, as well as application-level and session-level variables. However, ASP.NET also introduces a new state management technique: the application cache. Once you examine the numerous ways to handle state with ASP.NET, you then learn the role of the System.HttpApplication base class (lurking within the Global.asax file) and how to dynamically alter the runtime behavior of your Web application using the web.config file.

Chapter 20: XML Web Services

In this final chapter of this book, you examine the role of .NET XML Web services. Simply put, a *Web service* is an assembly that is activated using standard HTTP requests. The beauty of this approach is the fact that HTTP is the one wire protocol that is almost universal in its acceptance and is, therefore, an excellent choice for building platform- and language-neutral distributed systems. You also check out numerous surrounding technologies (WSDL, SOAP, and UDDI) which enable a Web service and external client to communicate in harmony.

Obtaining This Book's Source Code

All of the code examples contained within this book (minus small code snippets here and there) are available for free and immediate download from the Apress Web site. Simply navigate to http://www.apress.com and look up this title by name. Once you are on the homepage for *C# and the .NET Platform, Second Edition,* you may download a self-extracting .zip file. After you unzip the contents, you will find that the code has been logically divided by chapter. Do be aware that the following icon:

SOURCE CODE

is your cue that the example under discussion may be loaded into Visual Studio .NET for further examination and modification. To do so, simply open the *.sln file found in the correct subdirectory.

NOTE   All of the source code for this book as been compiled using Visual Studio .NET 2003. Sadly, *.sln files created with VS .NET 2003 cannot be open using VS .NET 2002. If you are still currently running Visual Studio .NET 2002, my advice is to simply create the appropriate project workspace, delete the auto-generated C# files, and copy the supplied *.cs files into the project using the Project | Add Existing Item menu selection.

Obtaining Updates for This Book

As you read over this text, you may find an occasional grammatical or code error (although I sure hope not). If this is the case, my apologies. Being human, I am sure that a glitch or two may be present, despite my best efforts. If this is the case, you can obtain the current errata list from the Apress Web site (located once again on the "homepage" for this book) as well as information on how to notify me of any errors you might find.

Contacting Me

If you have any questions regarding this book's source code, are in need of clarification for a given example, or simply wish to offer your thoughts regarding the .NET platform, feel free to drop me a line at the following e-mail address (to ensure your messages don't end up in my junk mail folder, please include "C# SE" in the title somewhere!): atroelsen@intertech-inc.com.

Please understand that I will do my best to get back to you in a timely fashion; however, like yourself, I get busy from time to time. If I don't respond within a week or two, do know I am not trying to be a jerk or don't care to talk to you. I'm just busy (or if I'm lucky, on vacation somewhere).

So then! Thanks for buying this text (or at least looking at it in the bookstore, trying to decide if you will buy it). I hope you enjoy reading this book and put your newfound knowledge to good use.

Take care,

Andrew Troelsen
Minneapolis, MN

Part One
Introducing C# and the .NET Platform

CHAPTER 1

The Philosophy of .NET

EVERY FEW YEARS OR SO, THE modern day programmer must be willing to perform a self-inflicted knowledge transplant to stay current with the new technologies of the day. The languages (C++, Visual Basic 6.0, Java), frameworks (MFC, ATL, STL), and architectures (COM, CORBA, EJB) that were touted as the silver bullets of software development, eventually become overshadowed by something better or at very least something new. Regardless of the frustration you can feel when upgrading your internal knowledge base, it is unavoidable. Microsoft's .NET platform represents the latest wave of (positive) changes coming from those kind folks in Redmond.

The point of this chapter is to lay the conceptual groundwork for the remainder of the book. It begins with a high-level discussion of a number of .NET-related atoms such as assemblies, the common intermediate language (CIL), and just-in-time (JIT) compilation. In addition to previewing some key features of the C# programming language, you will also come to understand the relationship between various aspects of the .NET Framework, such as the common language runtime (CLR), the Common Type System (CTS), and the Common Language Specification (CLS). As you would hope, many of these topics are explored in further detail throughout the remainder of this text.

This chapter also provides you with an overview of the functionality supplied by the .NET base class libraries, sometimes abbreviated as the "BCL" or alternatively as the "FCL" (being the Framework Class Library). Finally, you examine a number of helpful utilities (such as ildasm.exe and wincv.exe) that may be used to investigate the structure of these libraries at your leisure.

Understanding the Previous State of Affairs

Before examining the specifics of the .NET universe, it's helpful to consider some of the issues that motivated the genesis of this new platform. To get in the proper mindset, let's begin this chapter with a brief and painless history lesson to remember our roots and understand the limitations of the previous state of affairs (after all, admitting you have a problem is the first step toward finding a solution). After completing this quick tour of life as we knew it, we turn our attention to the numerous benefits provided by C# and the .NET platform.

Life As a C/Win32 API Programmer

Traditionally speaking, developing software for the Windows family of operating systems involved using the C programming language in conjunction with the Windows API (Application Programming Interface). While it is true that numerous applications have been successfully created using this time-honored approach, few of us would disagree that building applications using the raw API is a complex undertaking.

The first obvious problem is that C is a very terse language. C developers are forced to contend with manual memory management, ugly pointer arithmetic, and ugly syntactical constructs. Furthermore, given that C is a structured language, it lacks the benefits provided by the object-oriented approach (can anyone say *spaghetti code*?) When you combine the thousands of global functions and data types defined by the raw Win32 API to an already formidable language, it is little wonder that there are so many buggy applications floating around today.

Life As a C++/MFC Programmer

One vast improvement over raw C/API development is the use of the C++ programming language. In many ways, C++ can be thought of as an object-oriented *layer* on top of C. Thus, even though C++ programmers benefit from the famed "pillars of OOP" (encapsulation, inheritance, and polymorphism), they are still at the mercy of the painful aspects of the C language (e.g., manual memory management, ugly pointer arithmetic, and ugly syntactical constructs).

Despite its complexity, many C++ frameworks exist today. For example, the Microsoft Foundation Classes (MFC) provides the developer with a set of existing C++ classes that facilitate the construction of Windows applications. The main role of MFC is to wrap a "sane subset" of the raw Win32 API behind a number of classes, magic macros, and numerous code Wizards (i.e., AppWizard, ClassWizard, and so forth). Regardless of the helpful assistance offered by the MFC framework (as well as many other C-based windowing toolkits), the fact of the matter is C++ programming remains a difficult and error-prone experience, given its historical roots in C.

Life As a Visual Basic 6.0 Programmer

Due to a heartfelt desire to enjoy a simpler lifestyle, many programmers have shifted away from the world of C(++)-based frameworks to kinder, gentler languages such as Visual Basic 6.0 (VB). VB is popular due to its ability to build complex user interfaces, code libraries (e.g., COM servers), and data access logic with minimal fuss and bother. Even more than MFC, VB hides the complexities of the raw Win32 API from view using a number of integrated code Wizards, intrinsic data types, classes, and VB-centric functions.

The major downfall of VB (at least until the advent of VB .NET) is that it is not a fully object-oriented language, but rather "object aware." For example, VB 6.0 does not allow the programmer to establish "is-a" relationships between types (i.e., no classical inheritance) and has no support for parameterized class construction. Moreover, VB 6.0 doesn't support the ability to build multithreaded applications (unless you are willing to drop down to low-level API calls, which is complex at best and dangerous at worst).

Life As a Java/J2EE Programmer

Enter Java. The Java programming language is (almost) completely object oriented and has its syntactic roots in C++. As many of you are aware, Java's strengths are far greater than its support for platform independence. Java (as a language) cleans up the unsavory syntactical aspects of C++. Java (as a platform) provides programmers with a large number of predefined "packages" that contain various class and interface definitions.

Using these types, Java programmers are able to build "100% Pure Java" applications complete with database connectivity, messaging support, Web-enabled front ends, and a rich-user interface.

Although Java is a very elegant language, one potential problem is that using Java typically means that you must use Java front-to-back during the development cycle. In effect, Java offers little hope of language independence, as this goes against the grain of Java's primary goal (a single programming language for every need). In reality however, there are millions of lines of existing code out there in the world that would ideally like to commingle with newer Java code. Sadly, Java makes this task problematic.

Pure Java is simply not appropriate for many graphically or numerically intensive applications. For example, if you are building a graphics intensive product (such as a 3D-rendered video game), you will find Java's execution speed will leave something to be desired. A better approach for such programs would be to use a lower-level language (such as C++) where appropriate. Alas, while Java does provide a limited ability to access non-Java APIs, there is little support for true cross-language integration.

Life As a COM Programmer

The truth of the matter is, if you are not currently building Java-based solutions, the chances are very good that you have invested your time and energy understanding Microsoft's Component Object Model (COM). COM is an architecture that says in effect, "If you build your classes in accordance with the rules of COM, you end up with a block of *reusable binary code.*"

The beauty of a binary COM server is that it can be accessed in a language-independent manner. Thus, C++ programmers can build COM classes that can be used by VB. Delphi programmers can use COM classes built using C, and so forth. However, as you may be aware, COM's language independence is somewhat limited. For example, there is no way to derive a new COM type using an existing COM type (no support for classical inheritance). Rather, you must make use of the more cumbersome "has-a" relationship to reuse COM types.

Another benefit of COM is its location-transparent nature. Using constructs such as application identifiers (AppIDs), stubs, proxies, and the COM runtime environment, programmers can avoid the need to work with raw sockets, RPC calls, and other low-level details. For example, ponder the following Visual Basic 6.0 COM client code:

```
' This block of VB 6.0 code can activate a COM class written in
' any COM-aware language, which may be located anywhere
' on the network (including your local machine).
Dim c as MyCOMClass
Set c = New MyCOMClass       ' Location resolved using AppID.
c.DoSomeWork
```

Although COM is a very dominant object model, it is extremely complex under the hood (at least until you have spent many months exploring its plumbing...especially if you happen to be a C++ programmer). To help simplify the development of COM binaries, numerous COM-aware frameworks have come into existence. For example, the Active Template Library (ATL) provides another set of C++ -based classes, templates, and macros to ease the creation of classic COM types.

Many other languages (such as Visual Basic 6.0) also hide a good part of the COM infrastructure from view. However, language support alone is not enough to hide the complexity of classic COM. Even when you choose a relatively simply COM-aware language such as VB 6.0, you are still forced to contend with fragile registration entries and numerous deployment-related issues (collectively termed *DLL hell*).

Life As a Windows DNA Programmer

Finally, there is a little thing called the Internet. Over the last several years, Microsoft has been adding more Internet-aware features into its family of operating systems. It seems that the popularity of Web applications is ever expanding. Sadly, building a complete Web application using classic Windows DNA (Distributed iNternet Architecture) is also very complex.

Some of this complexity is due to the simple fact that Windows DNA requires the use of numerous technologies and languages (ASP, HTML, XML, JavaScript, VBScript, COM(+), as well as a data access API such as ADO). One problem is that many of these items are completely unrelated from a syntactic point of view. For example, JavaScript has a syntax much like C, while VBScript is a subset of Visual Basic proper. The COM servers that are created to run under the COM+ runtime have an entirely different look and feel from the ASP pages that invoke them. The result is a highly confused mishmash of technologies. Furthermore, and perhaps more important, each language and/or technology has its own type system (that typically looks nothing like the other type systems). An "int" in JavaScript is not the same as an "int" in C, which is different from an "Integer" in VB proper.

The .NET Solution

So much for the brief history lesson. The bottom line is that life as a Windows programmer has been tough. The .NET Framework is a rather radical and brute-force approach to making our lives easier. The solution proposed by .NET is "Change everything from here on out" (sorry, you can't blame the messenger for the message). As you will see during the remainder of this book, the .NET Framework is a completely new model for building systems on the Windows family of operating systems, and additional (non-Microsoft) operating systems now and in the future. To set the stage, here is a quick rundown of some core features provided courtesy of .NET:

- *Full interoperability with existing Win32 code.* This is (of course) a good thing. Existing COM binaries can commingle (i.e., interop) with newer .NET binaries and vice versa. Also, PInvoke (Platform Invocation) allows you to invoke invoke raw C-based functions (such as the Win32 API) from managed code.

- *Complete and total language integration.* Unlike classic COM, .NET supports cross-language inheritance, cross-language exception handling, and cross-language debugging.

- *A common runtime engine shared by all .NET-aware languages.* One aspect of this engine is a well-defined set of types that each .NET-aware language "understands."

- *A base class library* that provides shelter from the complexities of raw API calls, and offers a consistent object model used by all .NET-aware languages.

- *No more COM plumbing!* IClassFactory, IUnknown, IDispatch, IDL code, and the evil VARIANT-compliant data types (BSTR, SAFEARRAY, and so forth) have no place in a native .NET binary.

- *A truly simplified deployment model.* Under .NET, there is no need to register a binary unit into the system registry. Furthermore, the .NET runtime allows multiple versions of the same *.dll to exist in harmony on a single machine (using an approach termed "side-by-side execution").

The Building Blocks of the .NET Platform (CLR, CTS, and CLS)

Now that you have been given a peek into some of the benefits provided by .NET, let's preview three key (and interrelated) entities that make it all possible: the CLR, CTS, and CLS. From a programmer's point of view, .NET can be simply understood as a new runtime environment and a common base class library. The runtime layer is properly referred to as the common language runtime, or CLR. The primary role of the CLR is to locate, load, and manage .NET types on your behalf. The CLR also takes care of a number of low-level details such as automatic memory management, language integration, and ensuring type safety.

Another building block of the .NET platform is the Common Type System, or CTS. The CTS fully describes all possible data types and programming constructs supported by the runtime, specifies how these entities can interact with each other and details how they are represented in the .NET metadata format (more information on "metadata" later in this chapter).

Understand that a given .NET-aware language might not support each and every entity defined by the CTS. The Common Language Specification (CLS) is a set of rules that define a subset of common types and programming constructs that all .NET programming languages can agree on. Thus, if you build .NET types that only expose CLS-compliant features, you can rest assured that all .NET-aware languages could make use of your types. Conversely, if you make use of a data type or programming construct that is outside of the CLS, you cannot guarantee that every .NET programming language can interact with your binary code library.

The Role of the .NET Base Class Libraries

In addition to the CLR and CTS/CLS specifications, the .NET platform provides a base class library that is available to all .NET programming languages. Not only does this base class library encapsulate various primitives such as threads, file IO, graphical rendering and interaction with various hardware devices, but it also provides support for a number of services required by most real-world applications.

For example, the base class libraries define types that facilitate database manipulation, XML integration, programmatic security, and the construction of Web-enabled (as well as traditional desktop and console-based) front ends. From a conceptual point of view, you can visualize the relationship between the .NET runtime layer and the corresponding base class library as shown in Figure 1-1.

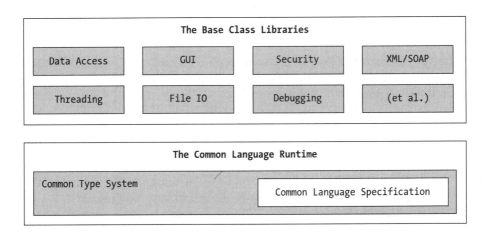

Figure 1-1. The CLR, CTS, CLS base class library relationship

What C# Brings to the Table

Given that .NET is such a radical departure from the current thoughts of the day, Microsoft has developed a new programming language (C#) specifically for this new platform. C# is a programming language that looks *very* similar (but not identical) to the syntax of Java. For example, like Java, a C# class definition is contained within a single-source code file (*.cs) rather than the C++-centric view of splitting a class definition into discrete header (*.h) and implementation (*.cpp) files. However, to call C# a Java rip-off is inaccurate. Both C# and Java are based on the syntactical constructs of C++. Just as Java is in many ways a cleaned-up version of C++, C# can be viewed as a cleaned-up version of Java—after all, they are all in the same family of languages.

The truth of the matter is that many of C#'s syntactic constructs are modeled after various aspects of Visual Basic and C++ itself. For example, like Visual Basic, C# supports the notion of formal class properties as well the declaration of methods that take a varying number of arguments (via parameter arrays). Like C++, C# allows you to overload operators on your custom types, as well as create structures (value types) and enumerations (as you may know, Java lacks all of these features).

Given that C# is a hybrid of numerous languages, the result is a product that is as syntactically clean (if not cleaner) than Java, just about as simple as Visual Basic 6.0, and provides just about as much power and flexibility as C++ (without the associated ugly bits). In a nutshell, the C# languages offers the following features (many of which are shared by other .NET-aware programming languages):

- No pointers required! C# programs typically have no need for direct pointer manipulation (although you are free to drop down to that level if you desire, as seen in Chapter 8).

- Automatic memory management. Given this, C# does not support a "delete" keyword.

- Formal syntactic constructs for enumerations, structures, and class properties.

- The C++-like ability to overload operators for a custom type, without the complexity (i.e., making sure to "return *this to allow chaining" is not your problem).

- Full support for interface-based programming techniques. However, unlike classic COM, the interface is *not* the only way to manipulate types between binaries. .NET supports true object references that can be passed between boundaries (by reference or by value).

- Full support for aspect-based programming techniques via attributes. This brand of development allows you to assign characteristics to types and their members (much like COM IDL) to further qualify the behavior of a given entity.

Perhaps the most important point to understand about the C# language shipped with the .NET platform is that it can only produce code that can execute within the .NET runtime (you could never use C# to build a classic COM server or a traditional Win32 API application). Officially speaking, the term used to describe the code targeting the .NET runtime is *managed code*. The binary unit that contains the managed code is termed an *assembly* (more details in just a bit).

Additional .NET-Aware Programming Languages

On a related language-centric note, understand that C# is not the only language targeting the .NET platform. When the .NET platform was first revealed to the general public during the 2000 Professional Developers Conference (PDC), several vendors announced they were busy building .NET-aware versions of their respective compilers. At the time of this writing, dozens of different languages are slated to undergo (or have undergone) .NET enlightenment. In addition to the five languages that ship with Visual Studio .NET Professional (C#, J#, Visual Basic .NET, "Managed C++," and JScript .NET), be on the lookout for .NET-aware compilers targeting Smalltalk (S#), COBOL, Pascal, Python, and Perl (as well as many others).

Although this book focuses (almost) exclusively on C#, Table 1-1 lists a number of .NET-enabled programming languages and where to learn more about them (do note that the exact URLs are subject to change).

Table 1-1. A Sampling of .NET-Aware Programming Languages

.NET-Centric Web Link	Meaning in Life
http://www.oberon.ethz.ch	Homepage for Active Oberon .NET
http://www.dyadic.com	Homepage for Dyalog APL .NET
http://www.adtools.com	For those interested in COBOL .NET
http://www.eiffel.com	For those interested in Eiffel .NET
http://research.microsoft.com/projects/ilx/fsharp.htm	Details of the F# language
http://lahey.com	For those interested in Fortran .NET
http://www.cs.inf.ethz.ch	For those interested in Oberon .NET
http://www.activestate.com	Details regarding Perl .NET and Python .NET
http://smallscript.org	Yes, even Smalltalk .NET (S#) is available

Also be aware that Table 1-1 is not exhaustive. Microsoft maintains a list of vendors who are currently building (or have built) .NET implementations for their respective compilers, so check http://msdn.microsoft.com/vstudio/partners/language for the most up-to-date listings (again, the exact URL is subject to change).

Life in a Multi-Language World

As developers first come to understand the language-agnostic nature of .NET, numerous questions arise. The most prevalent of these questions would have to be, "If all .NET languages compile down to managed code, why do we need more than one compiler?" There are a number of ways to answer this question. First, we programmers are a *very* particular lot when it comes to our choice of programming languages (myself included). Some of us prefer languages full of semicolons, curly brackets, and as few language keywords as possible. Others enjoy a language that offers more "human-readable" syntactic tokens (such as VB .NET). Still others may want to leverage their mainframe skills while moving to the .NET platform (via COBOL .NET).

Now, be honest: If Microsoft were to build a single "official" .NET language that was derived from the BASIC family of languages, can you really say all programmers would be happy with this choice? Or, if the single official managed language was based on C syntax, imagine all the folks out there who would ignore .NET altogether. Because the .NET runtime could care less where a block of managed code originated, .NET programmers can stay true to their syntactic preferences, and share the compiled assemblies among teammates, departments, and external organizations (regardless of which .NET language others choose to use).

Another excellent byproduct of integrating various .NET languages into a single unified software solution is the simple fact that all programming languages have their own sets of strengths and weaknesses. For example, some programming languages offer excellent intrinsic support for advanced mathematical processing. Others offer superior support for graphical rendering, financial calculations, logical calculations, interaction with mainframe computers and so forth. When you take the strengths of a particular programming language and then incorporate the benefits provided by the .NET platform, everybody wins.

Of course, in reality the chances are quite good that you will spend much of your time building software using your .NET language of choice (which is great!) However, as you may be expecting, once you learn the syntax of one .NET language, it is very easy to master another. This is also quite beneficial, especially to the consultants of the world. If your language of choice happens to be C#, but you are placed at a client site that has committed to VB .NET, you should be able to parse the existing code body almost instantly (honest!) while still continuing to leverage the .NET Framework. Enough said.

An Overview of .NET Binaries (aka Assemblies)

Regardless of which .NET language you choose to program with, understand that despite the fact that .NET binaries take the same file extension as classic COM binaries (*.dll or *.exe), they have absolutely no internal similarities. For example, *.dll .NET binaries do not export methods to facilitate communications with the classic COM runtime (given that .NET is *not* COM). Furthermore, .NET binaries are not described using IDL and are not registered into the system registry. Perhaps most important, unlike classic COM servers, .NET binaries do not contain platform-specific instructions, but rather platform-agnostic "intermediate language" (IL). Conceptually, Figure 1-2 shows the big picture of the story thus far.

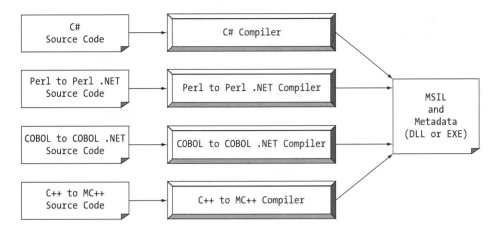

Figure 1-2. All .NET-aware compilers emit IL instructions and metadata.

NOTE   There is one point to be made regarding the acronym "IL." During the development of .NET, the official term for "IL" was Microsoft intermediate language (MSIL). However with the final release of .NET, the (new) official term is common intermediate language (CIL). Thus, as you read the .NET literature (including the first edition of this text), understand that IL, MSIL and CIL are all describing the same exact entity. In keeping with the current terminology, I will use the term CIL throughout this text from here on out.

When a *.dll or *.exe has been created using a .NET-aware compiler, the resulting module is bundled into an "assembly." You examine numerous details of .NET assemblies in Chapter 9. However to facilitate the discussion of the .NET runtime environment, you do need to examine some basic properties of this new file format.

As mentioned, an assembly contains CIL code, which is conceptually similar to Java byte code in that it is not compiled to platform-specific instructions until absolutely necessary. Typically "absolutely necessary" is the point at which a block of CIL instructions (such as a method implementation) are referenced for use by the .NET runtime engine.

In addition to CIL instructions, assemblies also contain metadata that describes in vivid detail the characteristics of every "type" living within the binary. For example, if you have a class named Car contained within a given assembly, the type metadata describes details such as Car's base class, which interfaces are implemented by Car (if any), as well as a full description of each member supported by the Car type.

In many respects, .NET metadata is a dramatic improvement to classic COM type information. As you may already know, classic COM binaries are typically described using an associated type library (which is little more than a binary version of IDL code). The problems with COM type information are that it is not guaranteed to be present, and the fact that IDL code has no way to catalog externally referenced servers that are required for the correct operation of the contained coclasses (a.k.a. 'COM class'). In contrast, .NET metadata is always present and is automatically generated by a given .NET-aware compiler.

Finally, in addition to CIL and type metadata, assemblies themselves are also described using metadata, which is officially termed a *manifest*. The manifest contains information about the current version of the assembly, culture information (used for localizing string and image resources), and a list of all externally referenced assemblies that are required for proper execution. You examine various tools that can be used to examine an assembly's underlying CIL, type metadata and manifest information later in this chapter.

Single File and Multifile Assemblies

In a great number of cases, there is a simple one-to-one correspondence between a .NET assembly and the underlying *.dll or *.exe binary. Thus, if you are building a .NET *.dll, it is safe to consider that the binary and the assembly are one and the same. Likewise, if you are building a .NET *.exe desktop application, the *.exe can simply be referred to as the assembly itself. As seen in Chapter 9 however, this is not completely accurate. Technically speaking, if an assembly is composed of a single *.dll or *.exe module, you have a "single file assembly." Single file assemblies contain all the necessary CIL, metadata and associated manifest in an autonomous, single, well-defined package.

Multifile assemblies, on the other hand, are composed of numerous .NET binaries, each of which is termed a *module*. When building a multifile assembly, one of these modules (termed the *primary module*) must contain the assembly manifest (and possibly CIL instructions and metadata for various types). The other related modules contain a module level manifest, CIL and type metadata. As you might suspect, the primary module documents the set of required secondary modules within the assembly manifest.

So, why would you choose to create a multifile assembly? When you partition an assembly into discrete modules, you end up with a more flexible deployment option. For example, if a user is referencing a remote assembly that needs to be downloaded onto his or her machine, the runtime will only download the required modules. Therefore, you are free to construct your assembly in such a way that less frequently required types (such as a type named HardDriveReformatter) are kept in a separate stand-alone module.

In contrast, if all your types were placed in a single file assembly, the end user may end up downloading a large chunk of data that is not really needed (which is obviously a waste of time). Thus, as you can see, an assembly is really a *logical grouping* of one or more related modules that are intended to be deployed and versioned as a single unit.

The Role of the Common Intermediate Language

Now that you have a better feel for .NET assemblies, let's examine the role of the common intermediate language (CIL) in a bit more detail. CIL is a language that sits above any particular platform-specific instruction set. Regardless of which .NET-aware language you choose (C#, Visual Basic .NET, Eiffel .NET, and so forth), the associated compiler emits CIL instructions. For example, the following C# namespace definition models a trivial calculator (which is only capable of returning the sum of 10 and 84…). Don't concern yourself with the exact syntax for the time being, but do notice the signature of the Add() method:

```
// We will examine namespaces later in the chapter...
using System;

namespace Calculator
{
    // This class contains the app's entry point.
    public class CalcApp
    {
        public static void Main()
        {
            Calc c = new Calc();
            int ans = c.Add(10, 84);
            Console.WriteLine("10 + 84 is {0}.", ans);
            Console.ReadLine();  // Wait for user key-press.
        }
    }
    // The C# calculator.
    public class Calc
    {
        // A single method.
        public int Add(int x, int y)
        { return x + y; }
    }
}
```

Once the C# compiler (csc.exe) compiles this source code file, you end up with a single file *.exe assembly that contains a manifest, CIL instructions, and metadata describing each aspect of the Calc and CalcApp classes. For example, if you peek inside this binary using ildasm.exe (examined a little later in this chapter) you find the Add() method is represented using CIL such as the following:

```
.method public hidebysig instance int32  Add(int32 x, int32 y) cil managed
{
  // Code size       8 (0x8)
  .maxstack  2
  .locals init ([0] int32 CS$00000003$00000000)
  IL_0000:  ldarg.1
  IL_0001:  ldarg.2
  IL_0002:  add
  IL_0003:  stloc.0
  IL_0004:  br.s       IL_0006
  IL_0006:  ldloc.0
  IL_0007:  ret
} // end of method Calc::Add
```

Don't worry if you are unable to make heads or tails of the resulting CIL for this method. The point to concentrate on is that the C# compiler emits CIL, not platform specific instructions.

Now, recall that this is true of all .NET-aware compilers. To illustrate, assume you created the Calc application using Visual Basic .NET, rather than C#:

```
' The VB .NET calculator...
Class Calc
    Public Function Add(ByVal x As Integer, ByVal y As Integer) As Integer
        ' Yes!  VB .NET (finally) supports a 'Return' keyword.
        Return x + y
    End Function
End Class

' A VB .NET 'Module' is a class that only contains
' static members.
Module CalcApp
    Sub Main()
        Dim ans As Integer
        Dim c As New Calc
        ans = c.Add(10, 84)
        Console.WriteLine("10 + 84 is {0}.", ans)
        Console.ReadLine()
    End Sub
End Module
```

If you examine the CIL for the Add() method, you find the same sort of instructions (slightly tweaked by the VB .NET compiler):

```
.method public instance int32  Add(int32 x, int32 y) cil managed
{
  // Code size       9 (0x9)
  .maxstack  2
  .locals init ([0] int32 Add)
  IL_0000:  nop
  IL_0001:  ldarg.1
  IL_0002:  ldarg.2
  IL_0003:  add.ovf
  IL_0004:  stloc.0
  IL_0005:  br.s       IL_0007
  IL_0007:  ldloc.0
  IL_0008:  ret
} // end of method Calc::Add
```

SOURCE CODE   The CSharpCalculator and VBCalculator applications are both included under the Chapter 1 subdirectory.

Benefits of CIL

At this point, you might be wondering exactly what benefits are gained by compiling source code into CIL (with the associated metadata) rather than directly to a specific instruction set. One benefit of compiling to CIL (with the associated metadata) is language integration. As you have already seen, each .NET-aware language produces the same underlying CIL. Therefore, all languages are able to interact within a well-defined binary arena.

Furthermore, given that CIL is platform agnostic, the .NET runtime is poised to become a platform-independent architecture, providing the same benefits Java developers have grown accustomed to (i.e., the potential of a single code base running on numerous operating systems). In fact, there is an international standard for a large subset of the .NET platform and implementations already exist on a few non-Windows operating systems. For example, you can run basic C# programs on both FreeBSD Unix and Apple (under OS X) platforms already. Unlike Java however, .NET allows you to build applications in a language-independent fashion. Thus, .NET has the potential to allow you to develop an application in any language and have it run on any platform.

NOTE   I'll comment a bit more on the platform-independent nature of .NET at the conclusion of this chapter.

The Role of .NET Type Metadata

COM programmers are without a doubt familiar with the Interface Definition Language (IDL). IDL is a "metalanguage" that is used to describe the types contained within a given COM server. IDL is compiled into a binary format (termed a type library) using the midl.exe compiler, which can then be used by a COM-aware language to manipulate the contained types.

In addition to describing the types within a COM binary, IDL has minimal support to describe characteristics about the COM binary itself, such as its current version (e.g., 1.0, 2.0, or 2.4) and intended locale (e.g., English, German, Urdu, Russian). The problem with COM metadata is that it may or may not be present and it is often the role of the programmer to ensure the underlying IDL accurately reflects the internal types.

The .NET Framework makes no use of IDL whatsoever. However, the spirit of describing the types residing within a particular binary lives on. In addition to the underlying CIL instructions, a .NET assembly contains full, complete and accurate metadata. Like COM IDL, .NET metadata describes each and every type (class, structure, enumeration, and so forth) defined in the binary, as well as the members of each type (properties, methods, events, and so on).

Furthermore, the .NET manifest (which as you recall is metadata describing the assembly itself) is far more complete than IDL, in that it also describes each externally referenced assembly that is required by the executing assembly to operate correctly. Because .NET metadata is so wickedly meticulous, assemblies are completely self-describing entities. So much so in fact, .NET binaries have no need to be registered into the system registry (more on that little tidbit later in the text).

A Quick Metadata Example

To illustrate the format of .NET metadata, let's take a look at the metadata that has been generated for the Add() method of the C# Calculator class you examined previously (the metadata generated for the VB .NET Add() method is similar). Using the ildasm.exe utility (examined at the end of this chapter) you can view your assembly's metadata by hitting the Ctrl+M keystroke. Within the resulting "MetaInfo" window, you will find a description of the Add() method looking something like the following::

```
Method #2
-----------------------------------------------------------
MethodName: Add (06000002)
Flags      : [Public] [HideBySig] [ReuseSlot]  (00000086)
RVA        : 0x00002064
ImplFlags  : [IL] [Managed]  (00000000)
CallCnvntn: [DEFAULT]
hasThis
ReturnType: I4
2 Arguments
    Argument #1:  I4
    Argument #2:  I4
2 Parameters
    (1) ParamToken : (08000001) Name : x flags: [none] (00000000)
    (2) ParamToken : (08000002) Name : y flags: [none] (00000000)
```

Here you can see that the Add() method, return type, and method arguments have been fully described by the C# compiler. Needless to say, metadata is used by numerous aspects of the .NET runtime environment, as well as by various development tools. For example, the IntelliSense feature provided by Visual Studio .NET is made possible by reading an assembly's metadata at design time. Metadata is also used by various object browsing utilities, debugging tools, and even the C# compiler itself. To be sure, metadata is the backbone of numerous .NET technologies such as .NET Remoting, reflection services, and object serialization.

The Role of the Assembly Manifest

Last but not least, recall that a valid .NET assembly will also contain metadata that describes the code library itself (technically termed a manifest). Like type metadata, it is always the job of the compiler to generate the assembly's manifest. For example, here are some relevant details of the CSharpCalculator assembly:

```
.assembly extern mscorlib
{
  .publickeytoken = (B7 7A 5C 56 19 34 E0 89 )
  .ver 1:0:3300:0
}
.assembly CSharpCalculator
{
  .hash algorithm 0x00008004
  .ver 1:0:932:40235
}
.module CSharpCalculator.exe
.imagebase 0x00400000
.subsystem 0x00000003
.file alignment 512
.corflags 0x00000001
```

In a nutshell, this manifest metadata documents the list of external assemblies that have been referenced by the CSharpCalculator.exe (via the .assembly extern directive) as well as various characteristics of the binary itself (via the .assembly, .ver, .module (etc.) directives).

Compiling CIL to Platform-Specific Instructions

Due to the fact that assemblies contain CIL instructions and metadata, rather than platform-specific instructions, the underlying CIL must be compiled on the fly before use. The entity that compiles the CIL into meaningful CPU instructions is termed a just-in-time (JIT) compiler that sometimes goes by the friendly name of "Jitter." The .NET runtime environment leverages a JIT compiler for each CPU targeting the CLR, each of which is optimized for the platform it is targeting.

For example, if you are building a .NET application that is to be deployed on a handheld device, the corresponding Jitter is well-equipped to run within a low-memory environment. On the other hand, if you are deploying your assembly to a back end server (where memory is seldom an issue), the related Jitter will be optimized to function in a high-memory environment. In this way, developers can write a single body of code that can be efficiently JIT-compiled and executed on machines with different architectures.

Furthermore, as a given Jitter compiles CIL instructions into corresponding machine code, it will cache the results in memory in a manner suited to the target OS. In this way, if a call is made to a method named Bar() defined within a class named Foo, the Bar() CIL instructions are compiled into platform-specific instructions on the first invocation and retained in memory for later use. Therefore, the next time Bar() is called, there is no need to recompile the CIL. As you will see in Chapter 9, the .NET SDK also provides a tool called ngen.exe that will compile CIL code to a native image at the time of installation.

Understanding the Common Type System

As already mentioned, a given assembly (single file or multifile) may contain any number of distinct "types." In the world of .NET, a type is simply a generic term used to collectively refer to an entity from the set {class, structure, interface, enumeration, delegate}.

When you build solutions using a .NET-aware language (such as C#), you will most likely interact with each of these types. For example, your assembly may define a single class that implements some number of interfaces. Perhaps one of the interface methods takes a custom enum type as an input parameter and returns a populated structure to the caller.

Recall that the Common Type System (CTS) is a formal specification that describes how a given type (class, structure, interface, etc.) must be defined in order to be hosted by the CLR. Also recall that the CTS defines a number of syntactic constructs (such as the use of unsigned types) that may or may not be supported by a given .NET-aware language. When you wish to build assemblies that can be used by all possible .NET-aware languages, you need to conform your exposed types to the rules of the CLS (defined shortly). For the time being, let's preview the formal definitions of all possible CTS types.

CTS Class Types

Every .NET-aware language supports, at the very least, the notion of a "class type," which is the cornerstone of object-oriented programming. A class may be composed of any number of members (such as constructors, operators, properties, methods, and events) and data points (fields). As you would expect, the CTS allows a given class to support virtual and abstract members that define a polymorphic interface for derived classes. On the limiting side of the equation, CTS classes may only derive from a single base class (multiple inheritance is not allowed for class types). Chapter 4 provides all the gory details of building CTS class types with C#, however, Table 1-2 documents a number of characteristics pertaining to class types.

Table 1-2. CTS Class Characteristics

Class Characteristic	Meaning in Life
Is the class "sealed" or not?	Sealed classes are types that cannot function as a base class to other types.
Does the class implement any interfaces?	An interface is a collection of abstract members that provide a contract between the object and object user. The CTS allows a class to implement any number of interfaces.
Is the class abstract or concrete?	Abstract classes cannot be directly created, but are intended to define common behaviors for derived types. Concrete classes can be created directly.
What is the "visibility" of this class?	Each class must be configured with a visibility attribute. Basically this trait defines if the class may be used by external assemblies, or only from within the containing assembly (e.g., a private helper class).

CTS Structure Types

The concept of a structure is also formalized under the CTS. If you have a C background, you should be pleased to know that these user-defined types (UDTs) have survived in the world of .NET (although they behave a bit differently under the hood). In general, a structure can be thought of as a lightweight class type having value semantics. For more details on the subtleties see Chapter 3. For example, CTS structures may define any number of *parameterized* constructors (the no-argument constructor is reserved). In this way, you are able to establish the value of each field during the time of construction. While structures are best suited for modeling geometric and mathematical types, the following type offers a bit more pizzazz (at the risk of offending the C++ purists):

```
// Create a C# structure.
struct Baby
{
    // Structures can contain fields.
    public string name;

    // Structures can contain constructors (with arguments).
    public Baby(string name)
    { this.name = name; }

    // Structures may take methods.
    public void Cry()
    { Console.WriteLine("Waaaaaaaaaaaah!!!"); }

    public bool IsSleeping() { return false; }
    public bool IsChanged() { return false; }
}
```

Here is our structure in action (assume this logic is contained in some Main() method):

```
// Welcome to the world Max Barnaby!!
Baby barnaBaby = new Baby("Max");
Console.WriteLine("Changed?: {0} ", barnaBaby.IsChanged());
Console.WriteLine("Sleeping?: {0} ", barnaBaby.IsSleeping());

// Show your true colors Max...
for(int i = 0; i < 10000; i++)
    barnaBaby.Cry();
```

As you will see, all CTS structures are derived from a common base class: System.ValueType. This base class configures a type to behave as a stack-allocated entity rather than a heap-allocated entity. Finally, be aware that the CTS permits structures to implement any number of interfaces; however, structures may not function as the base type to other classes or structures and are therefore explicitly "sealed."

CTS Interface Types

Interfaces are nothing more than a named collection of abstract member definitions, which may be supported (i.e., implemented) by a given class or structure. Unlike classic COM, .NET interfaces do *not* derive a common base interface such as IUnknown. In fact, interfaces are the only .NET type that do not derive from a common base type (not even System.Object). This point should be clear, given that interfaces typically express pure protocol and do not provide an implementation.

On their own, interfaces are of little use. However when a class or structure implements a given interface in its unique way, you are able to request access to the supplied functionality using an interface reference in a polymorphic manner. As well, when you create custom interfaces using a .NET-aware programming language, the CTS permits a given interface to derive from *multiple* base interfaces (unlike classic COM). As you might suspect, this allows us to build some rather exotic behaviors. Interface-based programming in will be fully detailed in Chapter 6.

CTS Enumeration Types

Enumerations are a handy programming construct that allows you to group name/value pairs under a specific name. For example, assume you are creating a video game application that allows the user to select one of three player types (Wizard, Fighter, or Thief). Rather than keeping track of raw numerical values to represent each possibility, you could build a custom enumeration:

```
// A C# enumeration.
public enum PlayerType
{ Wizard = 100, Fighter = 200, Thief = 300 } ;
```

By default, the storage used to hold each item is a System.Int32 (i.e., a 32-bit integer), however it is possible to alter this storage slot if need be (e.g., when programming for a low memory device such as a Pocket PC). Also, the CTS demands that enumerated types derive from a common base class, System.Enum. As you will see in Chapter 3, this base class defines a number of interesting members that allow you to extract, manipulate, and transform the underlying name/value pairs at runtime.

CTS Delegate Types

Delegates are the .NET equivalent of a type safe C style function pointer. The key difference is that a .NET delegate is a *class* that derives from System.MulticastDelegate, rather than a simple pointer to a raw memory address. These types are useful when you wish to provide a way for one entity to forward a call to another entity. Furthermore, delegates provide intrinsic support for multicasting (i.e., forwarding a request to multiple recipients) and asynchronous method invocations. As you will see in Chapter 7, delegates provide the foundation for the .NET event protocol.

CTS Type Members

Now that you have previewed each of the .NET types formalized by the CTS, realize that each may take any number of *members*. Formally speaking, a *type member* is constrained by the set {constructor, static constructor, nested type, operator, method, property, field, constant, event}.

The CTS defines the various "adornments" that may be associated with a given member. For example, each member has a given "visibility" trait (e.g., public, private, protected, and so forth). A member may be declared as "abstract" to enforce a polymorphic behavior on derived types as well as "virtual" to define a canned (but overridable) implementation. As well, most members may be configured as "static" (bound at the class level) or "instance" level (bound at the object level) entities. The construction of type members is examined over the course of the next several chapters.

Intrinsic CTS Data Types

The final aspect of the CTS to be aware of for the time being, is that it establishes a well-defined set of intrinsic data types used by all .NET-aware languages. Although a given language typically has a unique keyword used to declare an intrinsic data type, all languages ultimately resolve to the same type defined in mscorlib.dll. Consider Table 1-3, which documents how key CTS data types are expressed in various .NET languages.

Table 1-3. The Intrinsic CTS Data Types

.NET Base Type	Visual Basic .NET Keyword	C# Keyword	C++ with Managed Extensions Keyword
System.Byte	Byte	byte	char
System.SByte	Not supported	sbyte	signed char
System.Int16	Short	short	short
System.Int32	Integer	int	int or long
System.Int64	Long	long	__int64
System.UInt16	Not supported	ushort	unsigned short
System.UInt32	Not supported	uint	unsigned int or unsigned long
System.UInt64	Not supported	ulong	unsigned __int64
System.Single	Single	float	float
System.Double	Double	double	double
System.Object	Object	object	Object*
System.Char	Char	char	__wchar_t

Table 1-3. The Intrinsic CTS Data Types (Continued)

.NET Base Type	Visual Basic .NET Keyword	C# Keyword	C++ with Managed Extensions Keyword
System.String	String	string	String*
System.Decimal	Decimal	decimal	Decimal
System.Boolean	Boolean	bool	bool

As you can see, not all languages are able to represent the same intrinsic data types of the CTS using specific keywords. As you might imagine, it would be very helpful to create a well-known subset of the CTS that defines a common, shared set of programming constructs (and data types) for all .NET-aware languages. Enter the CLS.

Understanding the Common Language Specification

As you are aware, different languages express the same programming constructs in unique, language-specific terms. For example, in C#, string concatenation is denoted using the plus operator while in Visual Basic you typically make use of the ampersand. Even when two distinct languages express the same programmatic idiom (for example, a function with no return value) the chances are very good that the syntax will appear quite different on the surface:

```
' VB .NET function returning void (aka VB .NET subroutines).
Public Sub Foo()
     ' stuff...
End Sub

// C# function returning void.
public void Foo()
{
    // stuff...
}
```

As you have already seen, these minor syntactic variations are inconsequential in the eyes of the .NET runtime, given that the respective compilers (csc.exe or vbc.exe in this case) are configured to emit the same CIL instruction set. However, languages can also differ with regard to their overall level of functionality. For example, some languages (C#) allow you to overload operators for a given type while others (VB .NET) do not. Some languages may support the use of unsigned data types, which will not map correctly in other languages. What we need is to have a baseline to which all .NET-aware languages are expected to conform.

The CLS is a set of guidelines that describe in vivid detail, the minimal and complete set of features a given .NET-aware compiler must support to produce code that can be hosted by the CLR, while at the same time be accessed in a uniform manner by all languages that target the .NET platform. In many ways the CLS can be viewed as a physical *subset* of the full functionality defined by the CTS.

The CLS is ultimately a set of rules that compiler builders must conform to, if they intend their products to function seamlessly within the .NET universe. Each rule is assigned a simple name (e.g., "CLS Rule 6"), and describes how this rule affects those who build the compilers as well as those who (in some way) interact with them. For example, the crème de la crème of the CLS is the mighty Rule 1:

- **RULE 1:** CLS rules apply only to those parts of a type that are exposed outside the defining assembly.

Given this key rule you can (correctly) infer that the remaining rules of the CLS do not apply to the internal logic used to build the inner workings of a .NET type. Assume you are building a .NET application that exposes three classes, each of which defines a single function. Given the first rule of the CLS, the only aspects of the classes that must conform to the CLS are the member definitions (i.e., naming conventions, parameters, and return types). The internal implementations of each method may use any number of non-CLS techniques, as the outside world won't know the difference.

For example, if you were to add the following member to the C# Calc class type seen previously in this chapter, you would have just written a non-CLS-compliant method, as the parameters and return values make use of an unsigned data type:

```
public class Calc
{
    // CLS compliant!
    public int Add(int x, int y)
    { return x + y; }

    // Not CLS compliant!
    public ulong Add(ulong x, ulong y)
    { return x + y;}
}
```

However, if you were to update your CLS-compliant method as follows:

```
public class Calc
{
    // Still CLS compliant!
    public int Add(int x, int y)
    {
        // As this ulong is only used internally, we are still
        // CLS compliant.
        ulong theAnswer = (ulong)(x + y);
        Console.Write("Answer as ulong: {0}\n",
            theAnswer);
        return x + y;
    }
...
}
```

You have still conformed to the rules of the CLS, and can rest assured that all .NET languages are able to interact with this implementation of the Add() method.

Of course, in addition to Rule 1, the CLS defines numerous other rules. For example, the CLS describes how a given language must represent text strings, how enumerations should be represented internally (the base type used for storage), how to use static types, and so forth. Again, remember that in most cases these rules do not have to be committed to memory (unless you need to build a LISP .NET compiler!).

Ensuring CLS Compliance

As you will see over the course of this book, C# does define a number of constructs that are not CLS compliant. The good news, however, is that you are always free to inform the C# compiler to check your code for CLS compliance using a single .NET attribute (which must be placed outside the scope of any namespace or type definitions):

```
// Tell the C# compiler to check for CLS compliance.
[assembly: System.CLSCompliant(true)]
```

Chapter 11 dives into the details of attribute-based programming in detail. For the time being, simply understand that this line of code will instruct the C# compiler to check your code for complete CLS compliance. If any non-CLS-compliant syntactic tokens are discovered, you are issued a compiler error and a description of the offending code.

NOTE If you are interested in investigating each constraint imposed by the CLS, check out Partition I of the Common Language Infrastructure (CLI, not to be confused with CIL). By default, this Word document is located under <drive>:\Program Files\Microsoft Visual Studio .NET 2003\SDK\v1.1\ Tool Developers Guide\Docs. If you can't locate this path on your machine, simply do a search for a folder named "Tool Developers Guide".

Understanding the Common Language Runtime

In addition to the CTS and CLS specifications, the final TLA (three-letter-acronym) to contend with at the moment is the CLR. Programmatically speaking, the term *runtime* can be understood as a collection of external services that are required to execute a given compiled unit of code. For example, when developers make use of the Microsoft Foundation Classes (MFC) to create a new application, they are (painfully) aware that their binary is required to link with the rather hefty MFC runtime library (e.g., mfc42.dll). Other popular languages also have a corresponding runtime. Visual Basic 6.0 programmers are also tied to a runtime module or two (e.g., msvbvm60.dll). Java developers are tied to the Java Virtual Machine (e.g., JVM) and so forth.

The .NET platform offers yet another runtime system. The key difference between the .NET runtime and the various other runtimes I have just mentioned is the fact that the .NET runtime provides a single well-defined runtime layer that is shared by *all* languages and platforms that are .NET aware. As mentioned earlier in this chapter, the .NET runtime is officially termed the common language runtime, or simply CLR.

The crux of the CLR is physically represented by an assembly named mscoree.dll (aka, the Common Object Runtime Execution Engine). When an assembly is referenced for use, mscoree.dll is loaded automatically, which in turn loads the required assembly into memory. The runtime engine is responsible for a number of tasks. First and foremost, it is the entity in charge of resolving the location of an assembly and finding the requested type (e.g., class, interface, structure, etc.) within the binary by reading the contained metadata. The execution engine lays out the type in memory, compiles the associated CIL into platform-specific instructions, performs any (optional) security checks and then executes the code in question.

In addition to loading your custom assemblies and creating your custom types, the CLR will also interact with the types contained within the .NET base class libraries. Although the entire base class library has been broken into a number of discrete assemblies, the key binary is mscorlib.dll. This .NET assembly contains a large number of core types that encapsulate a wide variety of common programming tasks as well as the core data types used by all .NET languages. When you build .NET solutions, you always make use of this particular assembly, and perhaps numerous other .NET binaries (both system supplied and custom).

Figure 1-3 illustrates the workflow that takes place between your source code (which is making use of base class library types), a given .NET compiler, and the .NET execution engine.

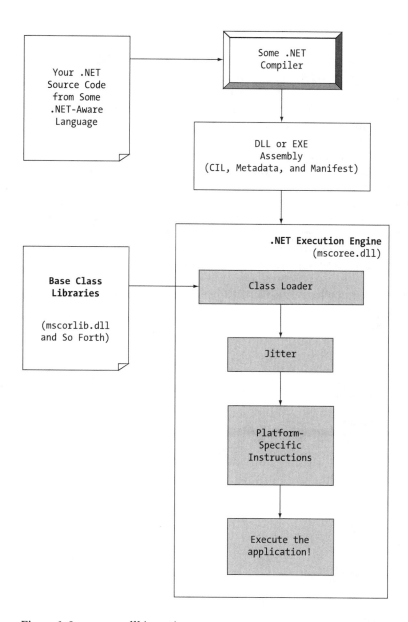

Figure 1-3. mscoree.dll in action

A Tour of the .NET Namespaces

Each of us understands the importance of code libraries. The point of libraries such as MFC, J2EE, or ATL is to give developers a well-defined set of existing code to leverage in their applications. For example, MFC defines a number of C++ classes that provide canned implementations of dialog boxes, menus, and toolbars. This is a good thing for the MFC programmers of the world, as they can spend less time reinventing the wheel, and more time building a custom solution. Visual Basic and Java offer similar notions: intrinsic types/global functions and packages, respectively.

Unlike MFC, Java, or Visual Basic 6.0, the C# language does not come with a pre-defined set of language-specific classes. Ergo, there is no C# class library. Rather, C# developers leverage existing types supplied by the .NET Framework. To keep all the types within this binary well organized, the .NET platform makes extensive use of the *namespace* concept.

The key difference between this approach and a language-specific library such as MFC, is that any language targeting the .NET runtime makes use of the *same* namespaces and *same* types as a C# developer. For example, the following three programs all illustrate the ubiquitous "Hello World" application, written in C#, VB .NET, and C++ with managed extensions (MC++):

```
// Hello world in C#
using System;
public class MyApp
{
    public static void Main()
    {
        Console.WriteLine("Hi from C#");
    }
}
```

```
' Hello world in VB .NET
Imports System
Public Module MyApp
    Sub Main()
        Console.WriteLine("Hi from VB .NET")
    End Sub
End Module
```

```
// Hello world in Managed C++ (MC++)
#using <mscorlib.dll>
using namespace System;
void main()
{
    Console::WriteLine(S"Hi from MC++");
}
```

Notice that each language is making use of the Console class defined in the System namespace. Beyond minor syntactic variations, these three applications look and feel very much alike, both physically and logically. As you can see, the .NET platform has brought a streamlined elegance to the world of software engineering.

Clearly, your primary goal as a .NET developer is to get to know the wealth of types defined in the numerous base class namespaces. The most fundamental namespace to get your hands around is named "System." This namespace provides a core body of types that you will need to leverage time and again as a .NET developer. In fact, you cannot build any sort of functional C# application without at least making a reference to the System namespace.

System is the root namespace for numerous other .NET namespaces. Simply put, namespaces are a way to group semantically related types (classes, enumerations, interfaces, delegates, and structures) under a single umbrella. For example, the System.Drawing namespace contains a number of types to assist you in rendering images onto a given graphics device. Other namespaces exist for data access, Web development, threading, and programmatic security (among many others). From a very high level, Table 1-4 offers a rundown of some (but certainly not all) of the .NET namespaces.

Table 1-4. A Sampling of .NET Namespaces

.NET Namespace	Meaning in Life
System	Within System you find numerous low-level classes dealing with primitive types, mathematical manipulations, garbage collection, as well as a number of commonly used exceptions and predefined attributes.
System.Collections	This namespace defines a number of stock container objects (ArrayList, Queue, etc.) as well as base types and interfaces that allow you to build customized collections.
System.Data System.Data.Common System.Data.OleDb System.Data.SqlClient	These namespaces are (of course) used for database manipulations (ADO.NET). You will see each of these later in this book.
System.Diagnostics	Here, you find numerous types that can be used by any .NET-aware language to programmatically debug and trace your source code.
System.Drawing System.Drawing.Drawing2D System.Drawing.Printing	Here, you find numerous types wrapping GDI+ primitives such as bitmaps, fonts, icons, printing support, and advanced graphical rendering support.
System.IO	This namespace includes file IO, buffering, and so forth.
System.Net	This namespace (as well as other related namespaces) contains types related to network programming (requests/responses, sockets, end points, etc.).

Table 1-4. A Sampling of .NET Namespaces (Continued)

.NET Namespace	Meaning in Life
System.Reflection System.Reflection.Emit	Defines types that support runtime type discovery and dynamic creation and invocation of custom types.
System.Runtime.InteropServices	Provides facilities to allow .NET types to interact with "unmanaged code" (e.g., C-based DLLs and classic COM servers) and vice versa.
System.Runtime.Remoting	This namespace (and other related namespaces) define types used to build solutions that incorporate the new .NET Remoting layer (which has nothing to do with classic DCOM whatsoever).
System.Security	Security is an integrated aspect of the .NET universe. In the security-centric namespaces you find numerous types dealing with permissions, cryptography, and so on.
System.Threading	You guessed it, this namespace deals with threading issues. Here you will find types such as Mutex, Thread, and Timeout.
System.Web	A number of namespaces are specifically geared toward the development of .NET Web applications, including ASP.NET and XML Web services.
System.Windows.Forms	Despite the name, the .NET platform does contain namespaces that facilitate the construction of more traditional main windows, dialog boxes, and custom widgets.
System.Xml	The XML-centric namespaces contain numerous types that represent core XML primitives and types used to interact with XML data.

Accessing a Namespace Programmatically

It is worth reiterating that a namespace is nothing more than a convenient way for us mere humans to logically understand and organize related types. For example, consider again the System namespace. From your perspective, you can assume that System.Console represents a class named *Console* that is contained within a namespace called *System*. However, in the eyes of the .NET runtime, this is not so. The runtime engine only sees a single entity named *System.Console*.

As you build your custom types, you have the option of organizing your items into a custom namespace. Again, a namespace is a logical naming scheme used by .NET languages to group related types under a unique umbrella. When you group your types into a namespace, you provide a simple way to circumvent possible name clashes between assemblies. For example, if you were building a new Windows Forms application that references two external assemblies, and each assembly contained a type named GoCart, you would be able to specify which GoCart class you are interested in by appending the type name to its containing namespace (i.e., "Intertech.CustomVehicles.GoCart" not "SlowVehicles.GoCart").

In C#, the "using" keyword simplifies the process of declaring types defined in a particular namespace. Here is how it works. Let's say you are interested in building a traditional desktop application. The main window renders a bar chart based on some information obtained from a back-end database and displays your company logo using a Bitmap type. While learning the types each namespace contains takes study and experimentation, here are some obvious candidates to reference in your program:

```
// Here are all the namespaces used to build this application.
using System;                  // General base class library types.
using System.Drawing;          // Rendering types.
using System.Windows.Forms;    // GUI widget types.
using System.Data;             // General data centric types.
using System.Data.OleDb;       // OLE DB data access types.
```

Once you have referenced some number of namespaces (and set a reference to the associated external assembly), you are free to create instances of the types they contain. For example, if you are interested in creating an instance of the Bitmap class (defined in the System.Drawing namespace), you can write:

```
// Explicitly list the namespaces used by this file...
using System;
using System.Drawing;
class MyClass
{
    public void DoIt()
    {
        // Create a 20×20 pixel bitmap.
        Bitmap bm = new Bitmap(20, 20);
        // Use the bitmap...
    }
}
```

Because your application is referencing System.Drawing, the compiler is able to resolve the Bitmap class as a member of this namespace. If you did not directly reference System.Drawing in your application, you would be issued a compiler error. However, you are free to declare variables using a "fully qualified name" as well:

```
// Not listing System.Drawing namespace!
using System;
class MyClass
{
    public void DoIt()
    {
        // Using fully qualified name.
        System.Drawing.Bitmap bm = new System.Drawing.Bitmap(20, 20);
        ...
    }
}
```

While defining a type using the fully qualified name provides greater readability, I think you'd agree that the C# using keyword reduces keystrokes. In this text, I will avoid the use of fully qualified names (unless there is a definite ambiguity to be resolved) and opt for the simplified approach of the C# using keyword. However, always remember that this technique is simply a shorthand notation for specifying a type's fully qualified name, and each approach results in the *exact* same underlying CIL.

Referencing External Assemblies

In addition to specifying a namespace via the C# using keyword, you also need to tell the C# compiler the name of the assembly containing the actual CIL definition for the referenced type. As mentioned, many core .NET namespaces live within mscorlib.dll. System.Drawing however, is contained in a separate binary named System.Drawing.dll. By default, the system-supplied assemblies are located under <drive>: \ %windir%\ Microsoft.NET\ Framework\ <version>, as seen in Figure 1-4.

Figure 1-4. The base class libraries

Depending on the development tool you are using to build your .NET types, you will have various ways to inform the compiler which assemblies you wish to include during the compilation cycle. You examine how to do so in the next chapter, so I'll hold off on the details for now.

Increasing Your Namespace Nomenclature

If you are beginning to feel a tad overwhelmed at the thought of gaining mastery over every nuance of the .NET universe, just remember that what makes a namespace unique is that the types it defines are all somehow *semantically related*. Therefore, if you have no need for a user interface beyond a simple console application, you can forget all about the System.Windows.Forms and System.Drawing namespaces (among others). If you are building a painting application, the database programming namespaces are most likely of little concern. Like any new set of prefabricated code, you learn as you go.

Over the chapters that follow, you are exposed to numerous aspects of the .NET platform and related namespaces. As it would be impractical to detail every type contained in every namespace in a single book (honestly, there are many thousands of types in .NET version 1.0 and even more with the release of version 1.1), you should be aware of the following techniques that can be used to learn more about the .NET libraries:

- .NET SDK online documentation (MSDN)

- The ildasm.exe utility

- The Class Viewer Web application

- The wincv.exe desktop application

- The Visual Studio .NET integrated Object Browser

I think it's safe to assume you know what to do with the supplied online Help (remember, F1 is your friend), however Chapter 2 points out some strategies used when navigating MSDN. In addition, it is important that you understand how to work with the ildasm.exe, the Class Viewer Web application, and wincv.exe utilities, each of which is shipped with the .NET SDK (the VS .NET Object Browser is examined in Chapter 2).

Using ildasm.exe

Recall that at one time in the evolution of .NET, CIL was simply named IL. Given this, the first tool under examination in this chapter is *not* named cildasm.exe, but ildasm.exe. The Intermediate Language Dissasembler utility (ildasm.exe) allows you to load up any .NET assembly and investigate its contents (including the associated manifest, CIL instruction set and type metadata) using a friendly GUI. The ildasm.exe is most likely found in <drive>:\Program Files\Microsoft Visual Studio .NET 2003\SDK\v1.1\Bin. Once you launch this tool, proceed to the "File | Open" menu command and navigate to the assembly you wish to explore. For the time being, open up mscorlib.dll (Figure 1-5). Note the path of the opened assembly is documented in the caption of the ildasm.exe utility.

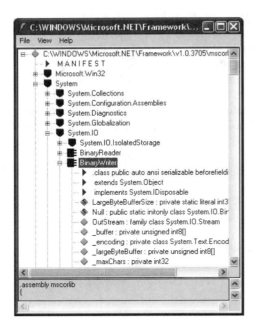

Figure 1-5. Your new best friend, ildasm.exe

As you can see, the structure of an assembly is presented in a familiar tree view format. While exploring a given type, notice that the members for a given type (methods, properties, nested classes, and so forth) are identified by a specific icon. Table 1-5 lists some of the more common iconic symbols and text dump abbreviations.

Table 1-5. ildasm.exe Tree View Icons

ildasm.exe TreeView Icon	Text Dump Abbreviation	Meaning in Life
▶	. (dot)	This icon signifies that additional information is available for a given type. Also marks the assembly manifest.
	[NSP]	Represents a namespace.
	[CLS]	Signifies a class type. Be aware that nested types are marked with the dollar sign notation (for example, <outer class>$<inner class>).
	[VCL]	Represents a structure type.
	[INT]	Represents an interface type.
	[MET]	Represents a method of a given type.

Table 1-5. ildasm.exe Tree View Icons (Continued)

ildasm.exe TreeView Icon	Text Dump Abbreviation	Meaning in Life
[STM icon]	[STM]	Represents a static method of a given type (note the "s" marker).
[FLD icon]	[FLD]	Represents a field (e.g., public data) defined by a given type.
[STF icon]	[STF]	Represents a static field defined by a given type (again note the "s" marker).
[PTY icon]	[PTY]	Signifies a property supported by the type.

Beyond allowing you to explore the types (and members of a specific type) contained in a given assembly, ildasm.exe also allows you to view the underlying CIL instructions for a given member. To illustrate, locate and double-click the default constructor icon for the System.IO.BinaryWriter class. This launches a separate window, displaying the CIL shown in Figure 1-6.

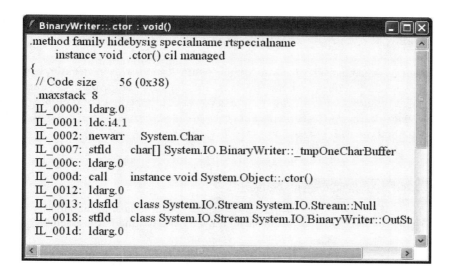

Figure 1-6. Viewing the underlying CIL

Dumping Namespace Information to File

The next point of interest with regard to ildasm.exe is the very useful ability to dump the relational hierarchy of an assembly into a text file. In this way, you can make hard copies of your favorite assemblies to read at your neighborhood coffeehouse (or brew pub). To do so, select "File | Dump TreeView" and provide a name for the resulting *.txt file. As you look over the dump, notice that the identifying icons have been replaced with their corresponding textual abbreviations (see the previous table). For example, ponder Figure 1-7.

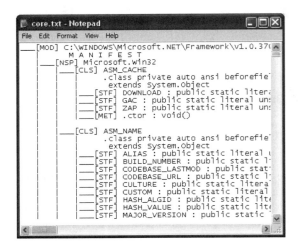

Figure 1-7. Dumping namespace information to file

Dumping CIL Instructions to File

On a related note, you are also able to dump the CIL instructions for a given assembly to file, using the "File | Dump" menu option. Once you configure your dump options, you are asked to specify a location for the *.IL file. Assuming you have dumped the contents of mscorlib.dll to file you can view its contents using notepad. For example, Figure 1-8 shows the CIL for a method you will come to know (and love) in Chapter 11, GetType().

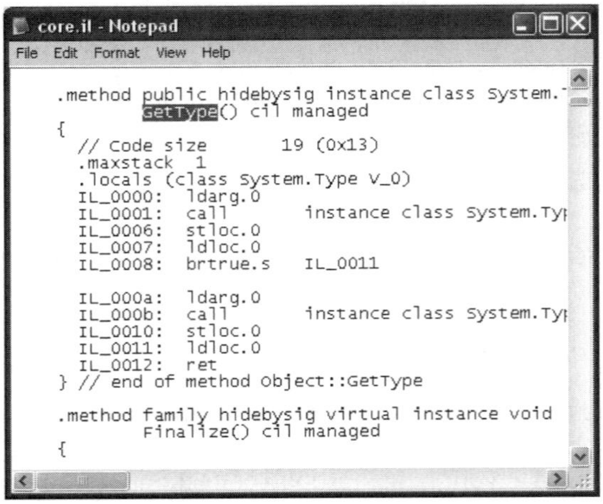

Figure 1-8. Dumping CIL to file

Ildasm.exe has additional options that can be discovered from the supplied online Help. Although I assume you will investigate these options on your own, as I mentioned earlier, one item of interest is the "Ctrl+M" keystroke. As you recall, .NET-aware compilers emit CIL *and* metadata that is used by the CLR to interact with a given type. Once you load an assembly into ildasm.exe, press Ctrl+M to view the generated type metadata. To offer a preview of things to come, Figure 1-9 shows the metadata for the TestApp.exe assembly you will create in Chapter 2.

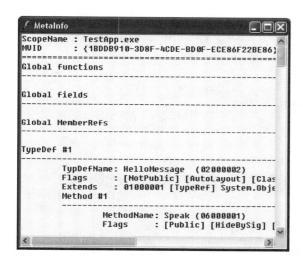

Figure 1-9. Viewing type metadata via ildasm.exe

Viewing Assembly Metadata

Finally, if you are interested in viewing the contents of the assembly's manifest (and I know you are), simply double click the MANIFEST icon (Figure 1-10).

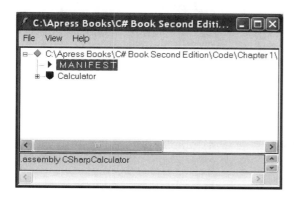

Figure 1-10. Double click here to view the assembly manifest.

If you have not realized it by now, ildasm.exe is in many ways the .NET equivalent of the OLE/COM Object Viewer utility. Oleview.exe is the tool of choice to learn about classic COM servers and examine the underlying IDL and registry settings behind a given binary. Ildasm.exe is the tool of choice to examine .NET assemblies, the underlying CIL and related metadata.

The Class Viewer Web Application

In addition to ildasm.exe, the Class Viewer Web application (shipped with the .NET SDK sample applications) is yet another way to explore the .NET namespaces. Once you have configured the samples provided with the .NET SDK (via the Start | All Programs | Microsoft .NET Framework SDK v1.1 | Samples and QuickStart Tutorials menu item), launch your browser of choice and navigate to `http://localhost/quickstart/aspplus/samples/classbrowser/vb/classbrowser.aspx` (do note that the exact location of this Web application may change in future releases of the .NET SDK). This enables you to examine the relationship of various types in a more Web-savvy manner (Figure 1-11).

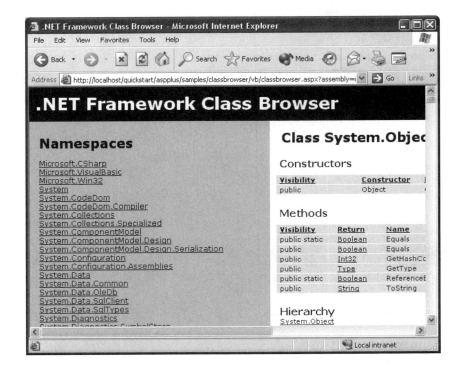

Figure 1-11. Viewing types using the ClassViewer Web application

The `wincv.exe` Desktop Application

The final tool to be aware of is wincv.exe (Windows Class Viewer). Again, by default this tool is installed in the same directory as ildasm.exe (most likely in <drive>:\Program Files\ Microsoft Visual Studio .NET 2003\SDK\V1.1\Bin directory). This Windows-based application allows you to browse the underlying C# type definition in the base class libraries. The use of this tool is quite simple: Type in the name of the item you wish to explore, and the underlying C# source code definitions are displayed on the right side. Figure 1-12 shows the member set for the System.Windows.Forms.ToolTip class.

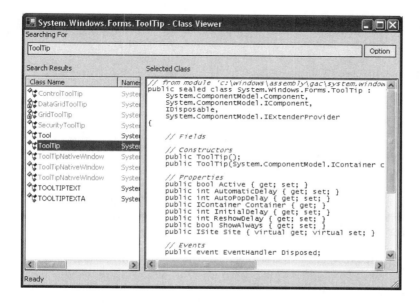

Figure 1-12. Working with wincv.exe

Cool! Now that you have a number of strategies that you can use to explore the entirety of the .NET universe, you are just about ready to examine how to build some C# applications. But first, let me comment on one final "minor" (read: "not-so-minor") detail.

Deploying the .NET Runtime

As you have most likely surmised, .NET assemblies can only be loaded and executed on a machine that has been configured to host the .NET runtime. As an individual who builds .NET software, this should never be an issue, as your development machine will be properly configured at the time you install the .NET SDK (or Visual Studio .NET). However, assume you have just created a fantastic .NET application and wish to copy it to a brand new machine. Of course, this *.exe will fail to run if the target computer does not have .NET installed.

Rather than opting for overkill and installing the full .NET SDK on each and every machine that may run your application, Microsoft has created a specific redistribution package named Dotnetfx.exe that can be freely shipped and installed along with your custom software. This installation program is included with the .NET SDK (or VS .NET), however, it is also freely downloadable (simply do a search on http://www.microsoft.com).

Dotnetfx.exe will correctly configure a "virgin machine" to execute .NET assemblies, as long as said machine is one of the following flavors of Microsoft Windows (of course, future versions of the Windows OS will have native .NET support):

- Microsoft Windows 98

- Microsoft Windows NT 4.0 (SP 6a or greater)

- Microsoft Windows Millennium Edition (aka Windows Me)

- Microsoft Windows 2000 (SP2 or greater)

- Microsoft Windows XP Home / Professional

Once installed, the target machine will now host the necessary base class libraries, mscoree.dll, and additional .NET infrastructure (such as the Global Assembly Cache). Do understand however, that if you are building a Web application using .NET technologies, the end user's machine does *not* need to be configured with the .NET redistribution kit (as the browser will simply display generic HTML).

Running .NET on Non-Microsoft Operating Systems

As mentioned at various places in this chapter, the .NET platform is already being ported to other operating systems. The key that makes this possible is yet another .NET specification termed the Common Language Infrastructure (CLI, which previously went under the code name "rotor"). Simply put, the CLI is the ECMA standard that describes the core libraries of the .NET universe. Microsoft has released an open-source implementation of the CLI (The Shared Source CLI) which can be compiled on Windows XP, FreeBSD Unix as well as the Macintosh (OS X and higher).

NOTE For more information regarding the Shared Source CLI, do a search for "Shared Source Common Language Infrastructure" on http://www.microsoft.com.

Although the role of this book is to confine the creation, deployment and execution of .NET applications to the Windows family of operating systems, Table 1-6 provides a few helpful links you may find interesting (understand the exact URL may change in the future).

Table 1-6. Select Links to the Platform-Agnostic Nature of .NET

.NET-Centric Web Link	Meaning in Life
http://msdn.microsoft.com/net/ecma	Details the standardization of C# and the .NET platform
http://www.go-mono.com	Homepage for the Mono project, which is a porting of C# and .NET to various flavors of Linux

Summary

The point of this chapter was to lay out the conceptual framework necessary for the remainder of this book. We began by examining a number of limitations and complexities found within the technologies prior to .NET, and followed up with an overview of how .NET and C# attempt to simplify the current state of affairs.

.NET basically boils down to a runtime execution engine (mscoree.dll) and base class library (mscorlib.dll and associates). The common language runtime (CLR) is able to host any .NET binary (aka "assembly") that abides by the rules of managed code. As you have seen, assemblies contain CIL instructions (in addition to type metadata and the assembly manifest) that are compiled to platform-specific instructions using a just-in-time (JIT) compiler. In addition, you explored the role of the Common Language Specification (CLS) and Common Type System (CTS) and examined a number of tools that allow you to check out the types within a given .NET namespace. We wrapped up with a brief examination of the process of configuring a given machine to host the .NET runtime. With this necessary preamble complete, you can now begin to build .NET assemblies using C#.

CHAPTER 2

Building C# Applications

C# IS ONE OF MANY possible languages which may be hosted by Visual Studio .NET (VS .NET). Unlike previous editions of Microsoft IDEs (Integrated Development Environments), the professional and enterprise versions of VS .NET may be used to build C#, J#, VB .NET and MC++ project types (including unmanaged frameworks such as MFC and ATL 4.0). Furthermore, if you download or purchase additional .NET-aware languages (such as COBOL .NET, Eiffel .NET and so forth), the chances are quite good that they will 'snap-in' to the existing VS .NET IDE out of the box.

This chapter offers a grand tour of the key features of the VS .NET IDE within the context of C#. Along the way, you will examine some common configuration options, preview various design time tools, examine the use of XML-based code documentation, and examine various "preprocessor" directives. We wrap up by examining a small subset of freeware .NET-related tools. To open this discussion however, we begin with an examination of the raw C# compiler itself—csc.exe.

The Role of the Command Line Compiler (csc.exe)

There are a number of techniques you may use to compile C# source code. In addition to VS .NET proper (as well as various third party .NET IDEs), you are also able to compile your .NET assemblies using the stand-alone compiler, csc.exe (as I'm sure you can gather, "csc" is short for C Sharp Compiler). This tool is included in the freely downloadable Microsoft .NET SDK (http://msdn.microsoft.com/net). Now, while it is true that you may never decide to build an entire application using the raw C# compiler, it is important to understand the basics of how to compile your *.cs files by hand. I can think of two reasons you should get a grip on the process:

- The most obvious reason is the simple fact that you might not have a full copy of Visual Studio .NET (but do have the free .NET SDK). If this is the case, you will need to make use of csc.exe as you move throughout this text.

- Another reason is this very important fact: Design time editors, code Wizards, and configuration dialogs do little more than save you typing time. The more you understand what happens "under the hood" the stronger your programming muscle becomes. As you use VS .NET to build applications, you are ultimately instructing the raw C# compiler how to manipulate your *.cs input files. In this light, it's edifying to see what takes place behind the scenes.

Another nice by-product of working with csc.exe in the raw, is that you become that much more comfortable manipulating other command line tools included with the .NET SDK. As you will see throughout this book, a number of important utilities are only accessible from the command prompt.

Configuring the C# Compiler

Before you can begin to make use of the C# command line compiler, you need to ensure that your development machine recognizes the existence of csc.exe. Ideally, csc.exe is configured correctly at the time you install the .NET SDK. However, in my experiences teaching various .NET classes, I have found out the hard way (typically during the first code demo) this is not always the case. If csc.exe is not configured correctly, you are forced to change to the directory containing csc.exe before you can compile your programs (which is a massive pain in the neck, given that you must type in the full path name to the *.cs files to be compiled).

To equip your development machine to compile *.cs files from any subdirectory, follow these steps (which assume a Windows XP installation; WinNT/Win2000 steps will slightly differ):

- Right-click the My Computer icon and select Properties from the pop-up menu.

- Select the Advanced tab and click the Environment Variables button.

- Double click the Path variable from the System Variables list box.

- Add the following line to the end of the current value (note each value in the Path variable is separated by a semicolon, as shown in Figure 2-1):

  ```
  <drive>:\%windir%\Microsoft.NET\Framework\v1.1.4322
  ```

Figure 2-1. Establishing the path to csc.exe

Of course, the exact path name may need to be adjusted based on your current version and location of the .NET SDK (so be sure to do a sanity check). Once you have added the correct Path setting, you may take a test run by closing any command windows open in the background (to commit the settings), then open a new command window and enter:

```
csc -?
```

If you set things up correctly, you should see a display of each option supported by the raw C# compiler.

Configuring Additional .NET Command Line Tools

Now, before we begin to investigate manipulating csc.exe, add the following additional Path variable to the System Variables list box (again, performing a sanity check to ensure path settings):

```
<drive>:\Program Files\Microsoft Visual Studio .NET\FrameworkSDK\Bin
```

As you will see later in this text, this path contains additional command line tools (such as sn.exe, al.exe, wsdl.exe and so forth) that are commonly used during .NET development. With these two path settings established, you should now be able to run any .NET utility directly from the command line. If you wish to confirm this new setting, close any open command window, open a new command window and enter the following command to view the flags for the assembly linker utility, al.exe:

```
al -?
```

NOTE Now that you have seen how to manually configure your .NET command line tools, I'll let you in on a shortcut. If you own a copy of VS .NET 2003, navigate to the Microsoft Visual Studio .NET 2003 | Visual Studio .NET Tools menu using the Window's Start button. There you will find a preconfigured command prompt (Visual Studio 2003 Command Prompt) that can be used to run .NET command line tools without the need to manually set your Path settings.

Building a C# Application Using csc.exe

Now that your development machine recognizes csc.exe, the next goal of this chapter is to build a simple single file assembly named TestApp.exe using the raw C# compiler. First, you need some source code. Open a text editor (notepad.exe is fine), and enter the following:

```
// The first C# app of the book...
using System;
class TestApp
{
    public static void Main()
    {
        Console.WriteLine("Testing! 1, 2, 3");
    }
}
```

Once you have finished, save the file (in a convenient location) as TestApp.cs. Now, let's get to know the core options of the C# compiler. The first point of interest is to understand how to specify the name and type of output file you are interested in obtaining (e.g., a console application named MyShell.exe, a code library named HelperTypes.dll, a Windows Forms application named MyRadWnd.exe, and so forth). Each possibility is represented by a specific flag passed into csc.exe as a command line parameter (Table 2-1).

Table 2-1. Output Options of the C# Compiler

File Output Option	Meaning in Life
/out	Used to specify the name of the output file (e.g., MyAssembly.dll, WordProcessingApp.exe, etc.) to be created. By default, the name of the output file is the same as the name of the input *.cs file containing the program's specified entry point (the static Main() method).
/target:exe	This option builds an *.exe console application. This is the default file output type, and thus may be omitted when building this application type.
/target:library	This option builds a single file *.dll assembly.
/target:module	This option builds a "module." Modules are elements of multifile assemblies (as seen later in Chapter 9).
/target:winexe	Although you are free to build Windows-based applications using the /target:exe flag, the /target:winexe flag prevents an annoying console window from appearing in the background.

Given these options, to compile TestApp.cs into a console application named TextApp.exe, you would use the following command set (note that the /target flag must come before the name of the C# file, not after):

```
csc /target:exe TestApp.cs
```

Also be aware that most of the C# compiler flags support an abbreviated version, such as "/t" rather than "/target" (you can view all abbreviations by entering csc -? at the command prompt):

```
csc /t:exe TestApp.cs
```

Furthermore, given that the /t:exe flag is the default output used by the C# compiler, you could also compile TestApp.cs simply by saying:

```
csc TestApp.cs
```

To try things for yourself, open a command window and change to the directory containing your TestApp.cs file. Then, enter the previous command and hit return. This builds TestApp.exe, which can now be run from the command line (see Figure 2-2).

Figure 2-2. The TestApp in action

The first thing that should strike you is the fact that you have just created a console application using C#! The reason I point this out is due to a common misconception (especially among management) that .NET is only useful during the development of Internet applications. Nothing could be further from the truth. As you will see over the course of this text, .NET provides support for developing any type of application you might envision (Web-based or otherwise).

While console applications are far less sexy than a Windows-based or HTML-based front end, they can prove useful when you need to build a program that requires a minimal graphical user interface.

NOTE   Given their simplicity, the initial chapters of this text make use of simple command window applications to ensure that you are able to focus on the syntax of C# rather than focusing on the complexities of building GUIs using Windows Forms or ASP.NET technologies.

Referencing External Assemblies

Next up, let's examine how to build an application that makes use of types defined in a separate .NET assembly. Speaking of which, just in case you are wondering how the C# compiler understood your reference to the System.Console type, realize that mscorlib.dll is automatically referenced during the compilation process (if for some strange reason you wish to disable this behavior, you may specify the /nostdlib flag).

To illustrate the process of referencing external assemblies, let's update the TestApp application to display a Windows Forms message box. Thus, open your TestApp.cs file and modify it as follows:

```
using System;
// Add this!
using System.Windows.Forms;
class TestApp
{
    public static void Main()
    {
        Console.WriteLine("Testing! 1, 2, 3");
        // Add this!
        MessageBox.Show("Hello...");
    }
}
```

Notice the reference to the System.Windows.Forms namespace (via the C# "using" directive introduced in Chapter 1). Recall that when you explicitly list the namespaces used within a given *.cs file, you avoid the need to make use of fully qualified names (which can lead to hand cramps).

In addition to using the "using" keyword, you must also inform csc.exe which assembly contains the referenced namespace. Given that we have made use of the System.Windows.FormsMessageBox class, you must specify the System.Windows.Forms.dll assembly using the /reference flag (which can be abbreviated to /r):

```
csc /r:System.Windows.Forms.dll testapp.cs
```

If you now rerun your application, you should see what appears in Figure 2-3.

Figure 2-3. Your first Windows Forms application

Compiling Multiple Source Files

The current incarnation of the TestApp.exe application was created using a single *.cs source code file (as well as a single external assembly). While it is perfectly permissible to have all of your .NET types defined in a single *.cs file, most projects are composed of multiple *.cs files to keep your code base a bit more flexible. To illustrate, assume you have authored an additional class contained in a new file named HelloMsg.cs.

```csharp
// The HelloMessage Class
using System;
using System.Windows.Forms;
class HelloMessage
{
    public void Speak()
    { MessageBox.Show("Hello..."); }
}
```

Now, update your initial TestApp class to make use of this new type, and comment out the previous Windows Forms logic:

```csharp
using System;
// Don't need this anymore.
// using System.Windows.Forms;
class TestApp
{
    public static void Main()
    {
        Console.WriteLine("Testing! 1, 2, 3");
        // Don't need this anymore either.
        // MessageBox.Show("Hello...");

        // Exercise the HelloMessage class!
        HelloMessage h = new HelloMessage();
        h.Speak();
    }
}
```

You can compile this multifile application by listing each *.cs file explicitly:

```
csc /r:System.Windows.Forms.dll testapp.cs hellomsg.cs
```

As an alternative, the C# compiler allows you to make use of the wildcard character (*) to inform csc.exe to include all *.cs files contained in the project directory as part of the current build. When you use this option, you will typically want to specify the name of the output file (/out) as well, to directly control the name of the resulting assembly:

```
csc /r:System.Windows.Forms.dll /out:TestApp.exe *.cs
```

When you run the program again, the output is identical. The only difference between the two applications is the fact that the current logic has been split among multiple files.

Referencing Multiple External Assemblies

Now, what if you need to reference numerous external assemblies? Simply list each assembly using a semicolon-delimited list (annoyingly, the VB .NET compiler [vbc.exe] uses a *comma* delimited list, so be mindful when using multiple .NET compilers). You don't need to specify multiple external assemblies for the current example, but some sample usage follows:

```
csc /r:System.Windows.Forms.dll;System.Drawing.dll /out:TestApp.exe *.cs
```

Working with Csc.exe Response Files

As you might guess, if you were to build a complex C# application at the command prompt, your life would be full of pain as you type in the flags that specify numerous referenced assemblies and *.cs input files. To help lessen your typing burden, the C# compiler honors the use of "response files."

C# response files contain all the instructions to be used during the compilation of your current build. By convention, these files end in a *.rsp (response) extension and can be used as an alternative to pounding out lines and lines of flags manually at the command prompt. To illustrate, assume that you have created a response file named TestApp.rsp that contains the following arguments (as you can see, comments are denoted with the "#" character):

```
# This is the response file
# for the TestApp.exe app
# of Chapter 2.
# External assembly references.
/r:System.Windows.Forms.dll
# output and files to compile (using wildcard syntax).
/target:exe /out:TestApp.exe *.cs
```

Now, assuming this file is saved in the same directory as the C# source code files to be compiled, you are able to build your entire application as follows (note the use of the @ symbol):

```
csc @TestApp.rsp
```

Again, the output of the compiler is identical.

If the need should arise, you are also able to specify multiple *.rsp files as input (for example: csc @FirstFile.rsp @SecondFile.rsp @ThirdFile.rsp). If you take this approach, do be aware that the compiler processes the command options as they are encountered! Therefore, command line arguments in a later *.rsp file can override options in a previous response file.

Also note that any flags listed explicitly on the command line will be overridden by the options in a given response file. Thus, if you were to enter:

```
csc /out:Foo.exe @TestApp.rsp
```

the name of the assembly would still be TestApp.exe (rather than Foo.exe), given the /out:TestApp.exe flag listed in the TestApp.rsp response file.

The Default Response File (csc.rsp)

The final point to be made regarding response files is that the C# compiler has an associated default response file (csc.rsp), which is located in the same directory as csc.exe itself. If you were to open this file using Notepad, you will find that numerous .NET assemblies have already been specified using the /r: flag (Figure 2-4).

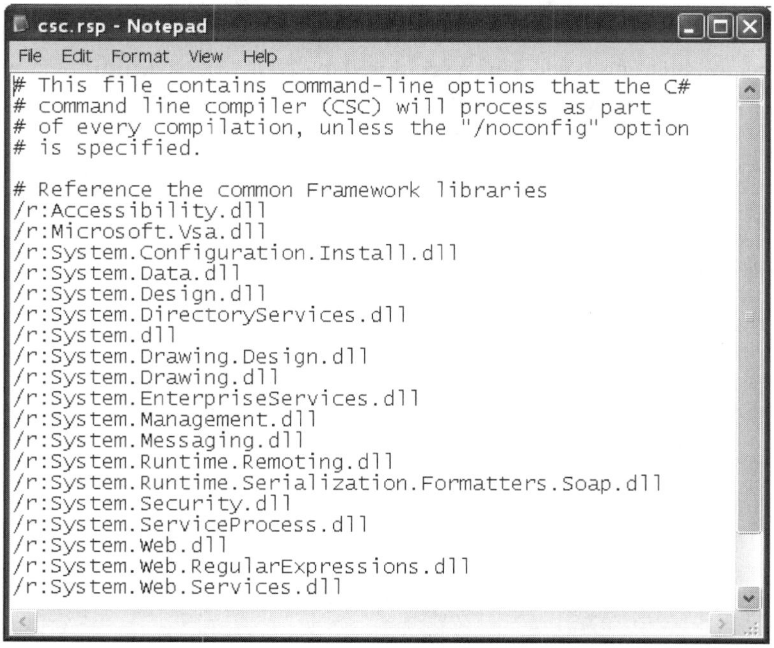

```
# This file contains command-line options that the C#
# command line compiler (CSC) will process as part
# of every compilation, unless the "/noconfig" option
# is specified.

# Reference the common Framework libraries
/r:Accessibility.dll
/r:Microsoft.Vsa.dll
/r:System.Configuration.Install.dll
/r:System.Data.dll
/r:System.Design.dll
/r:System.DirectoryServices.dll
/r:System.dll
/r:System.Drawing.Design.dll
/r:System.Drawing.dll
/r:System.EnterpriseServices.dll
/r:System.Management.dll
/r:System.Messaging.dll
/r:System.Runtime.Remoting.dll
/r:System.Runtime.Serialization.Formatters.Soap.dll
/r:System.Security.dll
/r:System.ServiceProcess.dll
/r:System.Web.dll
/r:System.Web.RegularExpressions.dll
/r:System.Web.Services.dll
```

Figure 2-4. Behold, the default response file

When you are building your C# programs using csc.exe, this file will be automatically referenced, even when you supply a custom *.rsp file (be aware that Visual Studio .NET does not make use of response files whatsoever, custom or csc.rsp). Given the presence of the default response file, it should be clear that the current TestApp.exe application (which contains a reference to the System.Windows.Forms.MessageBox class) could be successfully compiled using the following command line (note that I did not specify /r:System.Windows.Forms.dll as this reference will be added via csc.rsp):

```
csc /out:TestApp.exe *.cs
```

Finally, in the event that you wish to disable the automatic reading of csc.rsp, you can specify the /noconfig flag:

```
csc @TestApp.rsp /noconfig
```

Generating Bug Reports

The raw C# compiler provides a helpful flag named /bugreport. As you can gather by its name, this flag allows you to specify a file that will be populated (by csc.exe) with various statistics regarding your current build; including any errors encountered during the compilation process. Its use is self-explanatory:

```
csc /bugreport:bugs.txt *.cs
```

When you specify /bugreport, you will be prompted to enter corrective information for the possible error(s) at hand, which will be saved (along with other details) into the file you specify. To illustrate, let's inject a bug into the TestApp class:

```
public static void Main()
{
   ...
   HelloMessage h = new HelloMessage();
   // Note lack of semicolon below!
   h.Speak()   // <= Error!
}
```

When you recompile this file using the /bugreport flag, you are prompted to enter corrective action for the error at hand (Figure 2-5).

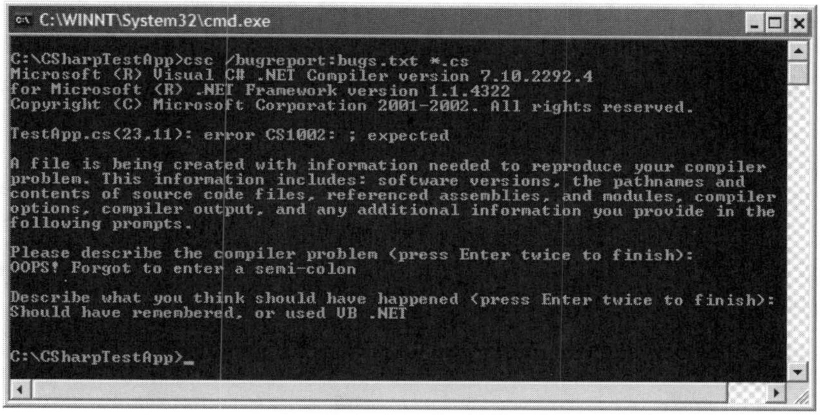

Figure 2-5. Documenting the bug

If you were to open the resulting *.txt file you would find a complete report regarding this compilation cycle (Figure 2-6).

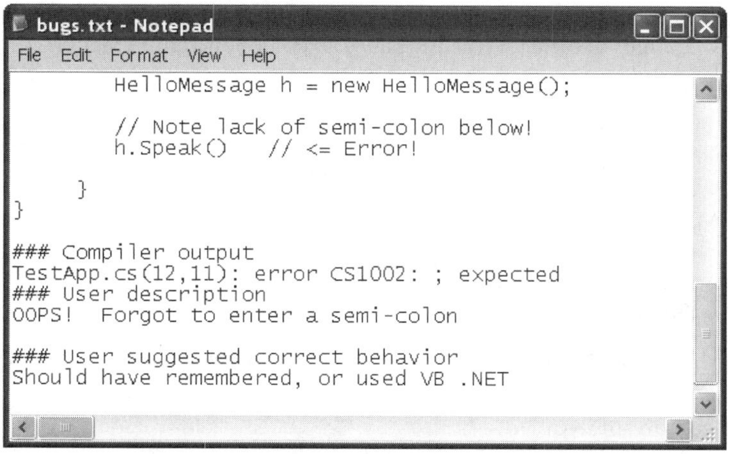

Figure 2-6. The entire bug report

Remaining C# Compiler Options

Obviously, the C# compiler has many other flags that can be used to control how the resulting .NET assembly is to be generated. For example, flags exist to build XML source code documentation files (explained shortly), create multifile assemblies, and embed .NET resource files. Although I will comment on additional command line flags where necessary during the remainder of this text, Table 2-2 documents the complete set of possible flags (listed alphabetically).

Table 2-2. Options of the C# Command Line Compiler

Command Line Flag of csc.exe	Meaning in Life
@	Allows you to specify a response file used during compilation
/? or /help	Prints out the list of all command line flags of csc.exe (which is basically the information in this table)
/addmodule	Used to specify the modules to add to a multifile assembly
/baseaddress	Used to specify the preferred base address at which to load a *.dll
/bugreport	Used to build text-based bug reports for the current compilation
/checked	Used to specify whether integer arithmetic that overflows the bounds of the data type will cause an exception at run time
/codepage	Used to specify the code page to use for all source code files in the compilation
/debug	Forces csc.exe to emit debugging information
/define	Used to define preprocessor symbols
/doc	Used to construct an XML documentation file
/filealign	Specifies the size of sections in the output file
/fullpaths	Specifies the absolute path to the file in compiler output
/incremental	Enables incremental compilation of source code files
/lib	Specifies the location of assemblies referenced via /reference
/linkresource	Used to create a link to a managed resource
/main	Specifies which Main() method to use as the program's entry point, if multiple Main() methods have been defined in the current *.cs file set
/nologo	Suppresses compiler banner information when compiling the file

Table 2-2. Options of the C# Command Line Compiler (Continued)

Command Line Flag of csc.exe	Meaning in Life
/nostdlib	Prevents the automatic importing of the core .NET library, mscorlib.dll
/noconfig	Prevents the use of *.rsp files during the current compilation
/nowarn	Suppress the compiler's ability to generate specified warnings
/optimize	Enable/disable optimizations
/out	Specifies the name of the output file
/recurse	Searches subdirectories for source files to compile
/reference	Used to reference an external assembly
/resource	Used to embed .NET resources into the resulting assembly
/target	Specifies the format of the output file
/unsafe	Compiles code that uses the C# "unsafe" keyword
/utf8output	Displays compiler output using UTF-8 encoding
/warn	Used to set warning level for the compilation cycle
/warnaserror	Used to automatically promote warnings to errors
/win32icon	Inserts an .ico file into the output file
/win32res	Inserts a Win32 resource into the output file

SOURCE CODE   The CSharpTestApp application is included under the Chapter 2 subdirectory.

The Command Line Debugger (cordbg.exe)

Before moving on to our examination of building C# applications using Visual Studio .NET, I would like to briefly point out that the .NET SDK does provide a command line debugger named cordbg.exe. This tool provides dozens of options that allow you to run your .NET assemblies under debug mode. You may view them by specifying the -? flag:

```
cordbg -?
```

Table 2-3 documents some (but certainly not all) of the command line flags recognized by cordbg.exe (with the alternative shorthand notation).

Table 2-3. A Handful of Useful cordbg.exe Flags

Command Line Flag of cordbg.exe	Meaning in Life
b[reak]	Set or display current breakpoints
del[ete]	Remove one or more breakpoints
ex[it]	Exit the debugger
g[o]	Continue debugging the current process until hitting next breakpoint
si	Step into the next line
o[ut]	Step out of the current function
so	Step over of the next line
p[rint]	Print all loaded variables (local, arguments, etc.)

As I assume that most of you will choose to make use of the VS .NET integrated debugger, I will not bother to comment on each flag of cordbg.exe. However, for those of you who are interested, here is a minimal walk-through of the basic process of debugging at the command line.

Debugging at the Command Line

Before you can debug your application using cordbg.exe, the first step is to generate symbolic debugging symbols for your current application by specifying the /debug flag of csc.exe. For example:

```
csc @testapp.rsp /debug
```

This generates a new file named (in this case) testapp.pdb. If you do not have an associated *.pdb file, it is still possible to make use of cordbg.exe; however, you will not be able to view your C# source code during the process (which is typically no fun whatsoever, unless you wish to complicate the process by reading raw CIL).

Once you have a valid *.pdb file, open a session with cordbg.exe by specifying your .NET assembly as a command line argument (the *.pdb file will be loaded automatically):

```
cordbg.exe testapp.exe
```

At this point, you are in debugging mode, and may apply any number of cordbg.exe flags at the "(cordbg)" command prompt (Figure 2-7).

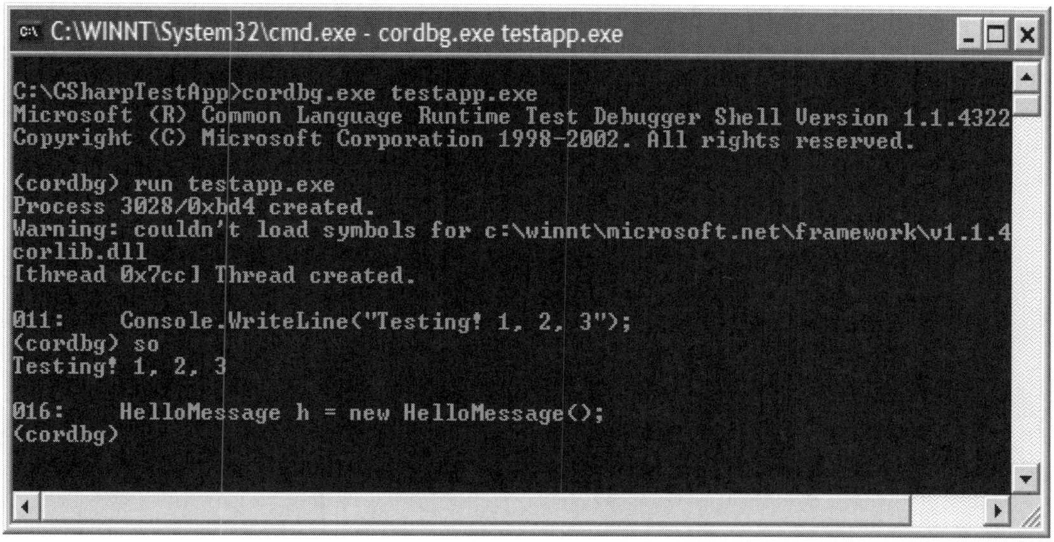

Figure 2-7. Debugging at the command line

When you are finished debugging your application and wish to exit debugging mode, simply type exit (or the shorthand "ex"). Again, unless you are a command-line warrior, I assume you will opt for the integrated VS .NET IDE debugger. If you are interested in further details of cordbg.exe, check out online Help.

Using the Visual Studio .NET IDE

Now that you have had the chance to work with the C# compiler in the raw, we can turn our attention to the use of Visual Studio .NET. As mentioned, this product allows you to build applications using any number of .NET-aware (and unaware) languages. Thus, you are able to use VS .NET when building C#, J#, VB .NET, MFC, ATL (4.0) or traditional C-based Win32 applications. The one thing you *cannot* do is build a traditional Visual Basic 6.0 application using VS .NET. If you want to create classic VB 6.0 COM servers (or any additional VB 6.0 project types) you need to make use of the Visual Basic 6.0 IDE (and yes, it is safe to have both IDEs installed on a single development machine).

Let's take some time to examine the core features of the Visual Studio .NET IDE (the operative word being *core*). My goal in this section is *not* to comment on each and every option of the IDE's menu system, document each of the integrated wizards, or offer exhaustive details for a given GUI configuration tool. I assume that you are more than capable of examining the IDE at your leisure. Nevertheless, let's check out some key traits you will tend to use on a daily basis (and of course, other key aspects of the development environment will be pointed out as necessary throughout this text).

The VS .NET Start Page

By default, the first thing you see when you launch Visual Studio .NET is the Start Page. For the present, you need only be concerned with the Projects and My Profile tabs (the remaining options allow you to connect to the Internet to view online resources, obtain product updates, and whatnot).

The Projects view (Figure 2-8) allows you to open existing projects as well as create a brand-new project workspace. Be aware that these options are also available via the File menu.

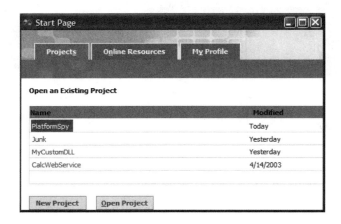

Figure 2-8. The Projects tab of the VS .NET Start Page

Now, if you were to click the My Profile tab, you would be shown something like what you see in Figure 2-9.

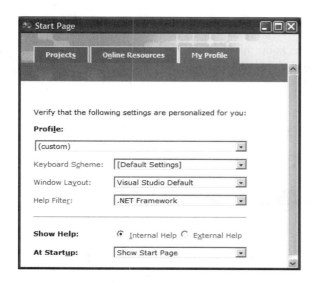

Figure 2-9. The My Profile tab of the VS .NET Start Page

Here, you are able to control how the VS .NET IDE should be configured each time you launch the tool. For example, the Keyboard Scheme drop-down list allows you to control which keyboard mapping should be used. If you want, you can opt to have your shortcut keys configured to mimic VB 6.0, Visual C++ 6.0, or the default VS .NET settings.

Other options allow you to configure how online Help should be filtered (and displayed), as well as how the core IDE windows (i.e., Properties, Toolbox, etc.) should dock themselves. To check things out first-hand, take a moment to select the various options found under the Window Layout drop-down list and find a look and feel you are comfortable with.

Finally, be aware that if you close the Start Page window (and want to get it back), access the Help | Show Start Page menu option. On a related note, if you do not want to see the Start Page, you can disable its automatic display using the At Startup drop-down list from the My Profile section.

Creating a VS .NET Project Solution

Our next stop on the tour is to get to know the various types of C# project workspaces. Open the New Project dialog box by clicking the New Project button from the Start Page, or by choosing the File | New | Project menu selection. As you can see from Figure 2-10, project types are grouped (more or less) by language (do note that you may not have each of the .NET-aware languages, or project options shown in Figure 2-10, based on your edition of VS .NET and/or the managed languages installed on your development machine).

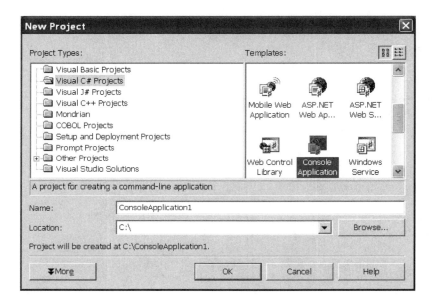

Figure 2-10. The New Project dialog box

Table 2-4 offers an explanation of the core C# project types (again, note that other project workspaces are possible based on the installation of optional .NET SDKs and your version of VS .NET).

Table 2-4. Core Project Workspace Types

Project Type	Meaning in Life
Windows Application	This project type represents a Windows Forms application.
Class Library	This option allows you to build a single file assembly (*.dll).

Table 2-4. Core Project Workspace Types (Continued)

Project Type	Meaning in Life
Windows Control Library	This type of project allows you to build a single file assembly (*.dll) that contains custom Windows Forms Controls (as you can guess, this is the .NET version of a COM-based ActiveX control).
ASP.NET Web Application	Select this option when you want to build an ASP.NET Web application.
ASP.NET Web Service	This option allows you to build a .NET Web Service. As shown later in this text, a Web Service is a block of code, reachable using HTTP requests.
Web Control Library	VS .NET also allows you to build customized Web controls. These GUI widgets are responsible for emitting HTML to a requesting browser.
Console Application	The good old command window. As mentioned, you spend the first number of chapters working with this type of project type, just to keep focused on the syntax and semantics of C#.
Windows Services	.NET allows you to build NT/2000 services. As you may know, these are background worker applications that are launched during the OS boot process.

NOTE   In addition to the items listed in Table 2-4, be aware that VS .NET 2003 also defines a number of project types that target mobile .NET development (previously only available using freely downloadable plug-ins).

Building a VS .NET Test Application

To illustrate the basic mechanics of this new IDE, let's build a new console application that mimics the functionality of the previous TestApp.exe assembly. To get started, create a brand-new C# Console Application project named VsTestApp. Once you hit OK, you will find a new folder has been created that contains a number of starter files and project subdirectories. Table 2-5 describes the key items:

Table 2-5. The Structure of a VS .NET Console Application

Generated Item	Meaning in Life
\bin\Debug	The \bin\Debug folder contains the debug version of your compiled .NET assembly. If you configure a release build, a new folder (\bin\Release) will be generated that contains a copy of your assembly, stripped of any debugging information. You can switch between debug and release builds using the "Build | Configuration Manager" menu selection.
\obj*	Under the \obj folder there are numerous subfolders used by VS .NET during the compilation process. You are always safe to ignore this folder set.
App.ico	An *.ico file used to specify the icon for the current program.
AssemblyInfo.cs	This file allows you to establish assembly-level attributes for your current project. This topic is examined in detail in Chapter 11 (so ignore it for now).
Class1.cs	This file is your initial class file.
*.csproj	This file represents a C# project that is loaded into a given solution.
*.sln	This file represents the current VS .NET solution (which by definition is a collection of individual projects).

Examining the Solution Explorer Window

VS .NET logically arranges a given project using a solution metaphor. Simply put, a "solution" is a collection of one or more "projects." Each project contains any number of source code files, external references, and resources that constitute the application as a whole. Do be aware that regardless of which project workspace type you create, the *.sln file can be opened using VS .NET to load each project in the workspace. Using the Solution Explorer window, you are able to view and open any such item (Figure 2-11). Notice the default name of your initial class is "Class1.cs."

Figure 2-11. The Solution Explorer

Notice as well that the Solution Explorer window provides a Class View tab, which shows the object-oriented view of your project (Figure 2-12). One nice feature of this perspective is that if you double click on a given icon, you are launched to the definition of the given type member.

Figure 2-12. Class View

As you would expect, when you right-click a given item, you activate a context-sensitive pop-up menu. The menu lets you access a number of tools that allow you to configure the current project settings and sort items in a variety of ways. For example, right-click the Solution node from Class View and check out Figure 2-13.

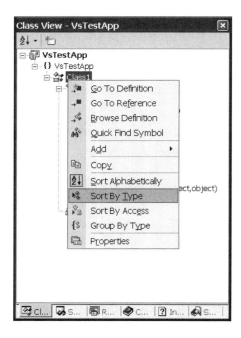

Figure 2-13. Type sorting options

Configuring a C# Project

Now, switch back to the Solution Explorer tab. Right-click the VsTestApp project node, and select Properties from the context menu. This launches the all-important Project Property Page (Figure 2-14).

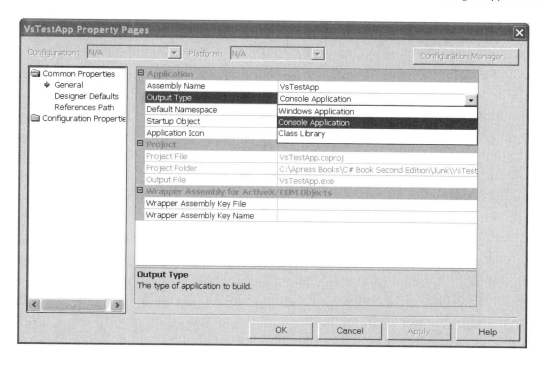

Figure 2-14. Configuring your C# project starts here.

This dialog box provides a number of intriguing settings, which map to various flags of the command line compiler. To begin, when you select the General node, you are able to configure the type of output file that should be produced by csc.exe (as you can guess, this is a GUI-based alternative to specifying the /target: flag).

You are also able to configure which item in your application should be marked as the "Startup object" (meaning, the class in the application that contains the Main() method). By default, this value is set to Not Set, which will be just fine unless your application happens to contain multiple class types that define a method named Main() (which will seldom, if ever, be the case). Finally, notice that the General node also allows you to configure the 'default' namespace for this particular project (when you create a new project with VS .NET, the default namespace is the same as your project name). You'll get to know the role of the default namespace in Chapter 3.

The Properties Window

Another important aspect of the IDE is the Properties window. This window allows you to interact with a number of characteristics for the item that has the current focus. This item may be an open source code file, a GUI widget, or the project itself. For example, to change the name of your initial *.cs file, select it from the Solution Explorer and configure the FileName property (Figure 2-15).

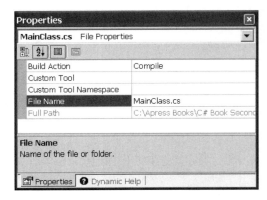

Figure 2-15. File names may be changed using the Properties window.

On a related note, if you wish to change the name of your initial class, select the Class1 icon from ClassView and edit the Properties window accordingly (Figure 2-16).

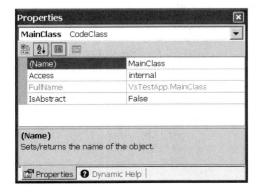

Figure 2-16. Class names can also be changed using the Properties window.

Adding Some Code

Now that you have configured your new C# project workspace, you can add source code. Within the Main() method, print a line to the command window and display a Windows Forms message box (don't forget to specify the correct C# using statements!):

```
using System;
using System.Windows.Forms;
namespace VsTestApp
{
    class MainClass
    {
        // See note below...
        [STAThread]
        static void Main(string[] args)
        {
            Console.WriteLine("Hello again!");
            MessageBox.Show("Yo!");
        }
    }
}
```

NOTE By default, VS .NET adorns the application's Main() method with the [STAThread] attribute. This informs the runtime that if (and only if) the application makes use of classic COM types, it should default to the single threaded apartment model (STA). If the application in question is not making use of COM types, the [STAThread] attribute is ignored and can be safely removed.

Referencing External Assemblies via VS .NET

As you typed in the previous code example, you may have noticed that the WriteLine() method was displayed through the expected IntelliSense, while the Show() method failed to reveal itself. This may seem odd, given that you specified the System.Windows.Forms namespace via the C# "using" keyword. However, unlike the raw C# compiler, VS .NET does not automatically load the default csc.rsp file to include key assembly references.

Therefore, in addition to specifying the namespaces you are using in a given *.cs file, VS .NET requires that you set a reference to the actual physical assembly (just like you learned to do with the command line C# compiler /r option). When you need to add external references (such as System.Windows.Forms.dll) into your current project, access the Project | Add Reference menu selection (or right-click the References node from the Solution Explorer window). Whichever way you go, you end up with the dialog box shown in Figure 2-17.

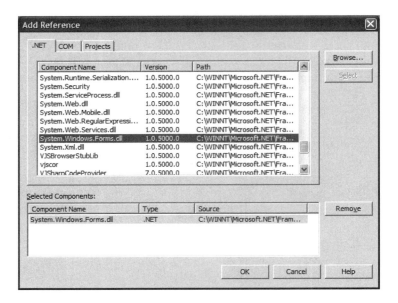

Figure 2-17. The Add References dialog box

Do understand that the assemblies listed here do *not* reflect all the .NET assemblies on your development machine! These are simply a predefined list of assemblies automatically recognized by VS .NET. During your examination of .NET assemblies (Chapter 9) you learn how to reference custom assemblies. In any case, once you have added the System.Windows.Forms.dll assembly you can compile and run your application.

Inserting New C# Type Definitions

When you want to add new custom types (such as a class, interface, or enumeration) to your current project you are always free to insert a blank *.cs file and manually flesh out the details of the new item. As an alternative, you are also free to use the Project | Add Class menu selection and modify the initial code accordingly. Pick your poison, and insert a new class named HelloClass. As you can see, you are given a skeletal definition of an empty class that is defined in the default namespace. Add a simple method named SayHi():

```
using System;
using System.Windows.Forms;

namespace VsTestApp
{
    public class HelloClass
    {
        public HelloClass() {}
        public void SayHi()
        {
            MessageBox.Show("Hello from HelloClass...");
        }
    }
}
```

Now, update your existing Main() method to create a new instance of this type, and call the SayHi() member:

```
static void Main(string[] args)
{
    Console.WriteLine("Hello again!");
    // Make a HelloClass type.
    HelloClass h = new HelloClass();
    h.SayHi();
}
```

Once you have done so, you are able to run your new VS .NET application using the Debug | Start Without Debugging menu option.

Outlining Your Code via VS .NET

One extremely helpful aspect of the IDE is the ability to show or hide blocks of code using the "+" and "-" icons. When you place your cursor over the ellipses icon (which represents a collapsed block of code) a pop-up window gives you a snapshot of the member implementation (Figure 2-18).

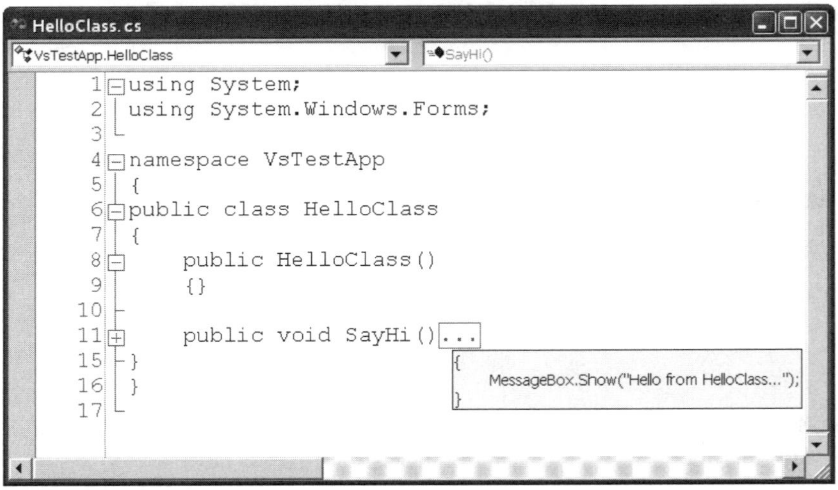

Figure 2-18. Collapsing the SayHi() method

Debugging with the Visual Studio .NET IDE

As you would expect, Visual Studio .NET contains an integrated debugger, which provides the same functionality of cordbg.exe using a friendly user interface. To illustrate the basics, begin by clicking in the far left gray column of an active code window to insert a breakpoint (Figure 2-19).

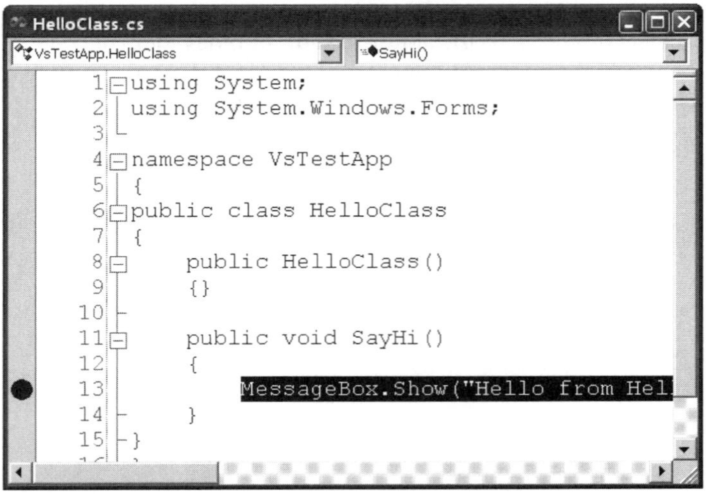

Figure 2-19. Setting breakpoints

When you initiate a debug session (via the Debug | Start menu selection), the flow of execution halts at each breakpoint. Using the Debug toolbar (or the corresponding keystroke commands), you can step over, step into, and step out of a given function. As you would expect, the integrated debugger hosts a number of debug-centric windows (e.g., Call Stack, Autos, Locals, Breakpoints, Modules, Exceptions, and so forth). To show or hide a particular window, simply access the Debug | Windows menu selection while in a debugging session.

"Running" Versus "Debugging"

One VS .NET debugging-related topic has to do with the distinction between running an application (via the Debug | Start Without Debugging menu selection) verses debugging an application (via the Debug | Start menu selection). When you run an application, you are instructing VS .NET to ignore all breakpoints, and most important, to automatically prompt for a keystroke before terminating the current console window.

On the other hand, if you debug a project that does not have any breakpoints set, the console application terminates so quickly that you will be unable to view the output! To ensure that the command window is alive regardless of the presence of a given breakpoint, one surefire technique is to simply add the following code at the end of the Main() method:

```
static void Main(string[] args)
{
    ...
    // Keep console window up until user hits return.
    Console.ReadLine();
}
```

 SOURCE CODE   The VsTestApp project is included under the Chapter 2 subdirectory.

Other Key Aspects of the VS .NET IDE

At this point, you should have a better feeling about the core features of the IDE. I'll assume you will keep exploring with the IDE as you read through the book. However, to paint a more complete picture, let's quickly check out additional features of VS .NET.

Examining the Server Explorer Window

One extremely useful aspect of Visual Studio .NET is the Server Explorer window (Figure 2-20), which can be accessed using the View menu.

Figure 2-20. The Server Explorer window

This window can be thought of as the command center of a distributed application you may be building. Using the Server Explorer, you can attach to and manipulate local and remote databases (and view any of the given database objects), examine the contents of a given message queue, and obtain general machine-wide information (such as seeing what services are running and viewing information in the Windows event log). You will see this view of the IDE in action at various places in the text.

XML-Related Editing Tools

Visual Studio .NET also provides numerous XML-related editors. As a simple example, if you insert a new XML file into your application (via the Project | Add New Item... menu selection), you are able to manipulate the underlying XML using GUI design-time tools (and related toolbars). Figure 2-21 shows an XML file you will generate during our discussion of ADO.NET.

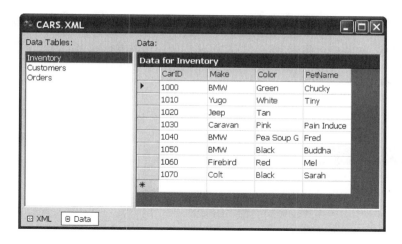

Figure 2-21. The integrated XML editor

The Object Browser Utility

In addition to the type browsing tools you examined in Chapter 1 (such as ildasm.exe and wincv.exe), the Visual Studio .NET IDE also supplies a utility that looks and feels much like the VB 6.0/J++ 6.0 Object Browser. If you access the View | Object Browser menu option, you will see the tool displayed in Figure 2-22.

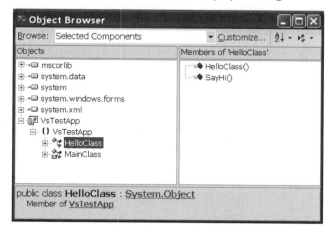

Figure 2-22. The integrated Object Browser

Obviously, the object browser allows you to view the namespaces, types, and type members of each assembly referenced by the current solution.

Database Manipulation Tools

Integrated database support is also part of the VS .NET IDE. Using the Server Explorer window, you can open and examine any database object from within the IDE. For example, Figure 2-23 shows a view of the Inventory table of the Cars database you build during our examination of ADO.NET.

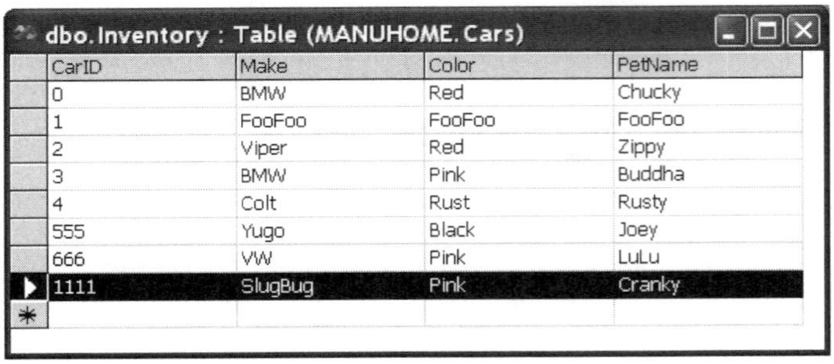
dbo.Inventory : Table (MANUHOME.Cars)
CarID | Make | Color | PetName
0 | BMW | Red | Chucky
1 | FooFoo | FooFoo | FooFoo
2 | Viper | Red | Zippy
3 | BMW | Pink | Buddha
4 | Colt | Rust | Rusty
555 | Yugo | Black | Joey
666 | VW | Pink | LuLu
1111 | SlugBug | Pink | Cranky

Figure 2-23. Integrated database editors

Integrated Help

The final aspect of the IDE you *must* be comfortable with from the outset is the fully integrated Help system. The .NET documentation is extremely good, very readable, and full of useful information. Given the huge number of predefined .NET types (which number well into the thousands) you must be willing to roll up your sleeves and dig into the provided documentation. If you resist, you are doomed to a long, frustrating, and painful existence.

To prevent this from happening, VS .NET provides the Dynamic Help window, which changes its contents (dynamically!) based on what item (window, menu, source code keyword, etc.) is currently selected. For example, if you place the cursor on Main() method, the Dynamic Help window displays what's shown in Figure 2-24.

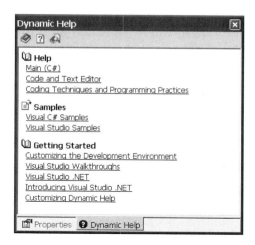

Figure 2-24. Visual Studio .NET Integrated Help

As you would expect, if you select on one of the suggested links (such as /main), you are shown the information that appears in Figure 2-25.

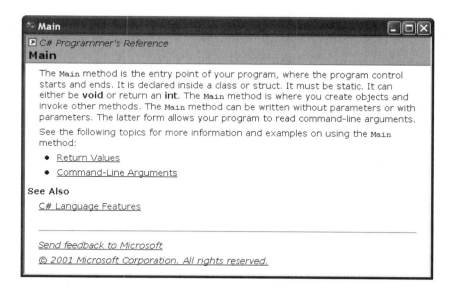

Figure 2-25. Remember, F1 is your friend.

Bookmark This Help Link!

In addition to context-sensitive online Help, you should also be aware of a very important subdirectory of the .NET MSDN Help system. If you look under the MSDN Library | .NET Development | .NET Framework SDK | .NET Framework | Reference | Class Library node of the MSDN library, you will find complete documentation of each and every namespace in the .NET base class libraries (Figure 2-26). Do be aware that the location of the Class Library node is subject to change in future (or previous) editions of MSDN.

Figure 2-26. Again, F1 is your friend.

As you would guess, each "book" defines the set of types in a given namespace, the members of a given type, and the parameters of a given member. Furthermore, when you view the Help page for a given type, you will be told the name of the assembly and namespace that contains the type in question (located at the end of said page). As you read the remainder of this book, I assume that you will dive into this *very, very* critical node to read up on additional details of the entity under examination.

Documenting Your Source Code via XML

The next goal of this chapter is to examine a technique honored by the C# compiler, which allows you to turn your source code documentation into a corresponding XML file. If you have a background in Java, you are most likely familiar with the javadoc utility. Using javadoc, you are able to turn Java source code into a corresponding HTML representation. The C# documentation model is slightly different, in that the "code comments to XML" conversion process is the job of the C# compiler (csc.exe) rather than a stand-alone utility.

So, why use XML to document our type definitions rather than HTML? The main reason is that XML is a very enabling technology. Given that XML separates the definition of data from the presentation of that data, we (as programmers) can apply any number of XML transformations to the raw XML. You could also programmatically read (and modify) the raw XML using types defined in the System.Xml.dll assembly.

When you wish to document your types in XML, your first step is to make use of a special comment syntax, the triple forward slash (///) rather than the C++ style double slash (//) or C-based comment syntax (/*... */). After the triple slash, you are free to use any well-formed XML elements, including the predefined set shown in Table 2-6.

Table 2-6. Stock XML Tags

Predefined XML Documentation Element	Meaning in Life
<c>	Indicates that text within a description should be marked as code
<code>	Indicates multiple lines should be marked as code
<example>	Used to mock up a code example for the item you are describing
<exception>	Used to document which exceptions a given class may throw
<list>	Used to insert a list into the documentation file
<param>	Describes a given parameter
<paramref>	Associates a given XML tag with a specific parameter
<permission>	Used to document access permissions for a member
<remarks>	Used to build a description for a given member
<returns>	Documents the return value of the member
<see>	Used to cross-reference related items
<seealso>	Used to build an "also see" section within a description
<summary>	Documents the "executive summary" for a given item
<value>	Documents a given property

As a concrete example, here is a very streamlined definition of a type named Car, adorned with some XML-based code comments (note the use of the <summary> and <param> tags):

```csharp
/// <summary>
///  This is a simple Car that illustrates
///  working with XML style documentation.
/// </summary>
public class Car
{
    /// <summary>
    /// Do you have a sunroof?
    /// </summary>
    private bool hasSunroof = false;

    /// <summary>
    /// The ctor lets you set the sunroofedness.
    /// </summary>
    /// <param name="hasSunroof"> </param>
    public Car(bool hasSunroof)
    {
        this.hasSunroof = hasSunroof;
    }

    /// <summary>
    /// This method allows you to open your sunroof.
    /// </summary>
    /// <param name="state"> </param>
    public void OpenSunroof(bool state)
    {
        if(state == true && hasSunroof == true)
            Console.WriteLine("Put sunscreen on that bald head!");
        else
            Console.WriteLine("Sorry...you don't have a sunroof.");
    }
    /// <summary>
    /// Entry point to application.
    /// </summary>
    public static void Main()
    {
        Car c = new Car(true);
        c.OpenSunroof(true);
    }
}
```

Once you have your XML documentation in place, you can specify the /doc flag as input to the raw C# compiler as follows:

```
csc /doc:XmlCarDoc.xml simplecar.cs
```

As you would hope, Visual Studio .NET also allows you to specify the name of an XML documentation file. To do so, open the Properties window for your current project (Figure 2-27).

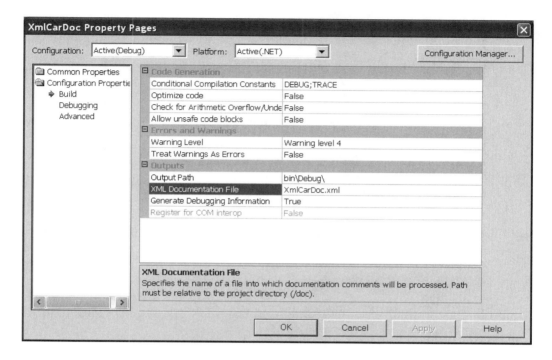

Figure 2-27. Specifying the XML documentation file via VS .NET

Using the Build option from the Configuration Properties folder, you will find an edit box (XML Documentation File) that allows you to specify the name of the file that will contain XML definitions for the types in your project (which is automatically regenerated when you rebuild your project).

Viewing the Generated XML File

If you were now to open the XmlCarDoc.xml file from within the Visual Studio.NET IDE, you would find the display you see in Figure 2-28.

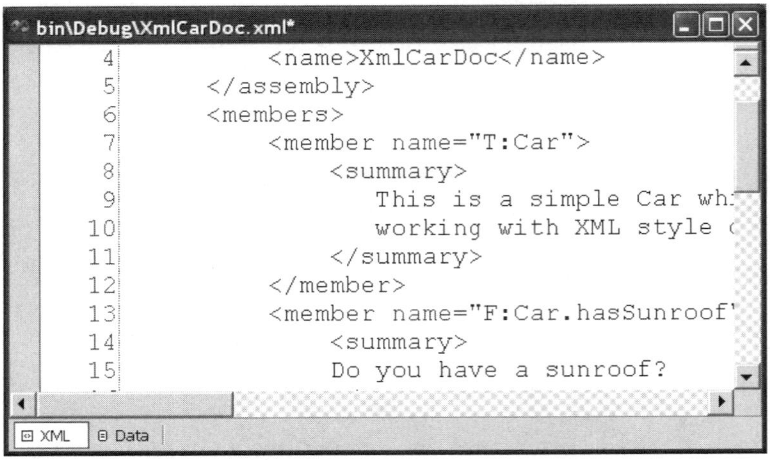

Figure 2-28. XmlCarDoc.xml

Be aware that assembly members are denoted with the <member> tag, fields are marked with an "F" prefix, types with "T" and members with "M." Some additional XML format characters are shown in Table 2-7.

Table 2-7. XML Format Characters

Format Character	Meaning in life
N	Item denotes a namespace.
T	Item represents a type (e.g., class, interface, struct, enum, delegate).
F	Item represents a field.
P	Item represents type properties (including indexes).
M	Item represents method (including constructors and overloaded operators).
E	Item denotes an event.
!	This represents an error string that provides information about the error. The C# compiler generates error information for links that cannot be resolved.

At this point you have a raw XML file that can be transformed using XSLT transformations or programmatically manipulated using the XML-centric .NET types. Although this approach gives you the biggest bang for the buck when it comes to customizing the look and feel of your source code comments, there is a simpler alternative.

Visual Studio .NET Documentation Support

If the thought of ending up with a raw XML file is a bit anticlimactic, be aware that VS .NET does offer another comment formatting option. Leveraging the same XML elements we have just examined, you may make use of the Tools | Build Comment Web Pages... menu option. When you select this item, you will be asked if you wish to build the entire solution or a specific project within the solution set, as seen in Figure 2-29.

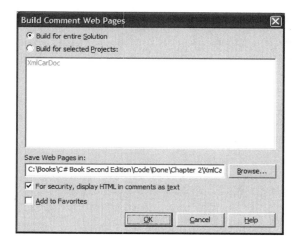

Figure 2-29. Configuration of your HTML-based documentation

This tool responds by creating a new folder in your project directory (CodeCommentReport) that holds a number of images and HTML files created, based on your XML documentation. At this point you can open the main HTML file and view your commented project. For example, check out Figure 2-30.

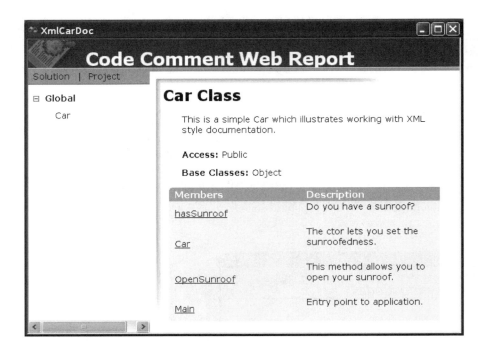

Figure 2-30. The generated XmlCarDoc online documentation

SOURCE CODE   The XmlDocCar project is located under the Chapter 2 subdirectory.

C# "Preprocessor" Directives

Like many other languages in the C family, C# supports the use of various symbols that allow you to interact with the compilation process. Before we dive headlong into the topic of C# preprocessor directives, let's get our terminology correct. The phrase *preprocessor directives* is not entirely accurate. In reality, this term is used only for consistency with the C and C++ programming languages. In C#, there is no separate preprocessing step. Rather, preprocessing directives are processed as part of the lexical analysis phase of the compiler. Nevertheless, the syntax of the "C# preprocessor" is identical to that of the other members of the C family. Specifically, C# supports the tokens you see in Table 2-8.

Table 2-8. C# Preprocessor Directives

C# Preprocessor Symbol	Meaning in Life
#define, #undef	Used to define and un-define conditional compilation symbols.
#if, #elif, #else, #endif	Used to conditionally skip sections of source code (based on specified compilation symbols).
#line	Used to control the line numbers emitted for errors and warnings.
#error, #warning	Used to issue errors and warnings for the current build.
#region, #endregion	Used to explicitly mark sections of source code. Under VS .NET, regions may be expanded and collapsed within the code window, other IDEs (including simple text editors) will ignore these symbols.

Specifying Code Regions

Perhaps some of the most interesting of all preprocessor directives are #region and #endregion. Using these tags, you are able to specify a block of code that may be hidden from view and identified by a friendly textual marker. As you can probably gather, the use of regions can help keep lengthy *.cs files more manageable. For example, you could create one region for a type's constructors, another for type properties, and yet another for internal helper classes. The following class has nested two internal helper types, which have been wrapped in a region block:

```
class ProcessMe
{
...
    // Nested types will be examined later.
    #region Stuff I Don't Care About
    public class MyHelperClass
    { // stuff...
    }
    public interface MyHelperInterface
    {// stuff...
    }
    #endregion
}
```

When you place your mouse cursor over a collapsed region, you are provided with a snapshot of the code lurking behind (Figure 2-31).

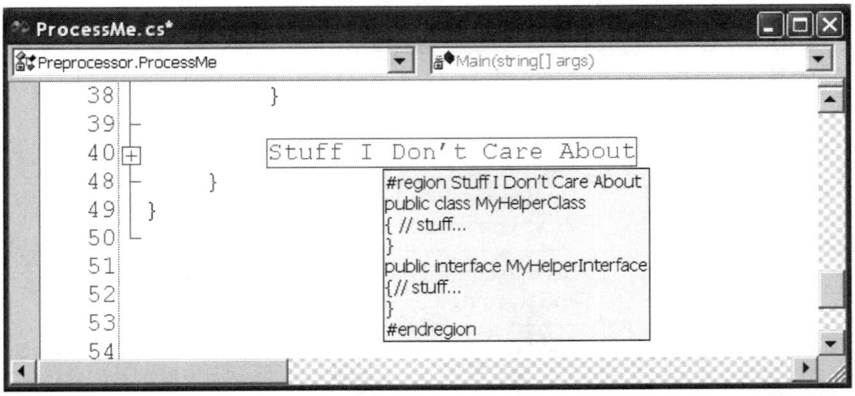

Figure 2-31. Regions at work

Conditional Code Compilation

The next helpful batch of preprocessor directives (#if, #elif, #else, #endif) allows you to conditionally compile a block of code, based on predefined symbols. The classic use of these directives is to include additional (typically diagnostic-centric) code only compiled under debug builds. Assume, for example, that when your current application is configured under a debug build, you wish to dump out a number of statistics to the console:

```
using System;
class ProcessMe
{
...
    static void Main(string[] args)
    {
        // Are we in debug mode?
        #if (DEBUG)
        Console.WriteLine("App directory: {0}",
            Environment.CurrentDirectory);
        Console.WriteLine("Box: {0}",
            Environment.MachineName);
        Console.WriteLine("OS: {0}",
            Environment.OSVersion);
        Console.WriteLine(".NET Version: {0}",
            Environment.Version);
        #endif
    }
}
```

Here, we are checking for a symbol named DEBUG. If it is present, we dump out a number of interesting statistics using some (quite helpful) static members of the System.Environment class (explained in the next section). If the DEBUG symbol is not defined, the code placed between #if and #endif will not be compiled into the resulting assembly, and effectively ignored.

The next logical question is where exactly is the DEBUG symbol defined? Well, if you wish to define this symbol on a file by file basis, you are able to make use of the #define preprocessor symbol as follows (do note that the #define directive *must* be listed before anything else in the *.cs source code file):

```
#define DEBUG
using System;
namespace Preprocessor
{
    class ProcessMe
    {
        static void Main(string[] args)
        {
            // Are we in debug mode?
            #if (DEBUG)
            // Same code as before...
            #endif
        }
    ...
    }
}
```

If you would rather configure the DEBUG symbol to apply for each *.cs file in your application, you can simply select a Debug build of the current project using the IDE's Standard toolbar (Figure 2-32) or using the Build | Configuration Manager menu selection.

Figure 2-32. Configuring debug or release builds

You are also able to define your own custom symbols. Again, using #define, you can define a specific symbol on a file by file basis. To create a project-wide symbol, make use of the Conditional Compilation Constants edit box located in the Project Properties window (Figure 2-33).

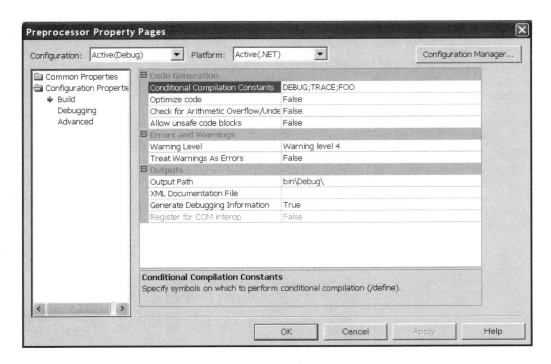

Figure 2-33. Setting project-wide symbols

Issuing Warnings and Errors

Next up we have the #warning and #error preprocessor directives. These directives allow you to instruct the C# compile to generate a warning or error on the fly. For example, assume that you wish to ensure that when a given symbol (such as DEBUG) is defined in the current project, a compiler warning is issued. This may be helpful to your teammates, as it would be a *huge* bummer to ship commercial software that is configured under a debug release:

```
static void Main(string[] args)
{
    // Are we in debug mode?
    #if (DEBUG)
    #warning Beware!  Debug is defined...configure release build.
    // Same code as before...
    #endif
}
```

On the next compile you will find your custom warning (or error, if using #error) is displayed in the Output window (assuming the DEBUG symbol is indeed defined).

Altering Line Numbers

The final directive, #line, will seldom be necessary for a vast majority of your projects. Basically, this directive allows you to alter the compiler's recognition of #line numbers during its recording of compilation warnings and errors. The #line directive allows you to specify the name of a file to dump said compiler anomalies. To reset the default line numbering, you may specify the default tag. By way of a simple example, ponder the following code:

```
// The warning below will be issued on line
// Set line number to 3000.
#line 3000
#warning "Custom warning on line 3000 (for no good reason)..."
// Resume default line numbering.
#line default
```

On a related note, understand that you are able to view the "real" line numbering for a given source code file by selecting the "Tools | Options" menu command and enabling the Line Numbers check box (Figure 2-34).

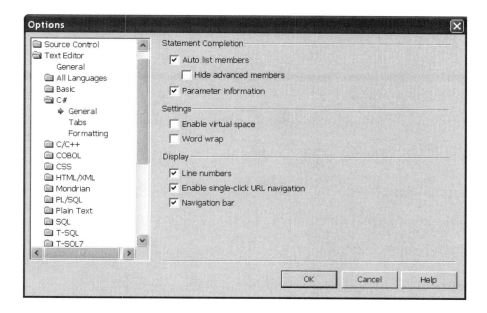

Figure 2-34. Viewing line numbers within VS .NET

SOURCE CODE   The Preprocessor project is located under the Chapter 2 subdirectory.

An Interesting Aside: The System.Environment Class

As illustrated in the previous example, the System.Environment class allows you to obtain a number of details regarding the context of the operating system hosting your .NET application using various static members. To illustrate, create a new Console Application project that dumps out a number of intriguing details regarding your current .NET development machine (I'm sure you can extrapolate the usefulness of this type for your custom projects):

```
// Here are some (but not all) of the interesting
// static members of the Environment class.
using System;

class PlatformSpy
{
    public static int Main(string[] args)
    {
        // Which OS version are we running on?
        Console.WriteLine("Current OS: {0} ", Environment.OSVersion);

        // Directory?
        Console.WriteLine("Current Directory: {0} ",
                        Environment.CurrentDirectory);

        // Here are the drives on this box.
        string[] drives = Environment.GetLogicalDrives();
        for(int i = 0; i < drives.Length; i++)
            Console.WriteLine("Drive {0} : {1} ",  i, drives[i]);

        // Which version of the .NET platform?
        Console.WriteLine("Current version of .NET: {0} ",
            Environment.Version);
        return 0;
    }
}
```

The output can be seen in Figure 2-35.

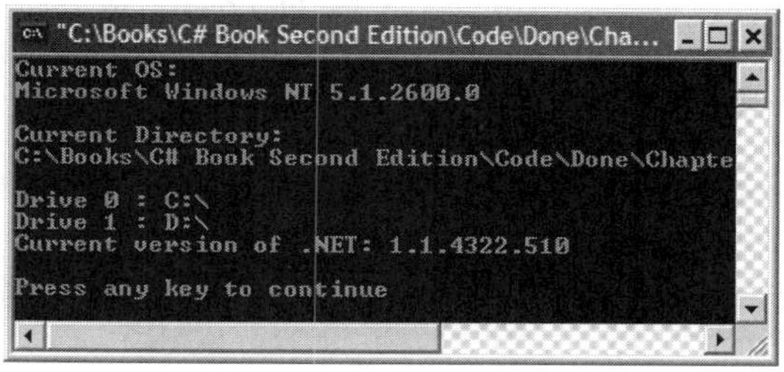

Figure 2-35. Obtaining various environment variables

SOURCE CODE The PlatformSpy example is located under the Chapter 2 subdirectory.

Building .NET Applications with Other IDEs

To close this chapter, I'd like to briefly investigate a few freeware (and in some cases *open-source*) IDEs that can be used to build .NET applications. If you are coming to .NET from a Java background, you are already well aware of the benefits of the open-source mindset. As strange as it may seem, the whole idea of tools for free (with source code to boot) is almost entirely new to those in the Microsoft camp. However, with the advent of the .NET platform, the tides are turning.

With the release of .NET, numerous companies and individuals (many of whom have no connection whatsoever to Microsoft proper) have created .NET development tools that can be freely downloaded from the Web; others may be purchased for a nominal fee. At the time of this writing, there are thousands of .NET-related sites and discussion boards, a mere two of which I will point out for your edification (if you wish to see other sites of interest, consult `http://www.gotdotnet.com`).

If you are interested in obtaining a free open-source .NET IDE that mimics the functionality of VS .NET, check out `http://www.icsharpcode.net` (as always, this Web link is subject to change). Here you will find a link to the SharpDevelop IDE, which was written completely in C# (in addition to the setup program, you may download the corresponding source code). This tool allows you to create and compile C# and VB .NET code files using various integrated wizards, design-time editors, and an integrated help system. If you do not own a copy of VS .NET, I wholeheartedly recommend you download this tool as you work through the remainder of this text (unless you are content working at the command line).

Also, you will want to check out `http://www.asp.net`. Here you can download the latest build of the Microsoft sponsored ASP.NET IDE named Web Matrix. Although we do not examine ASP.NET until later in this book, you should get your hands on Web Matrix ASAP for one very simple reason. This tool has the most complete .NET base class library browser I have yet encountered (ClassBrowser.exe), which is installed at the time you install Web Matrix. This single tool allows you to view the underlying CIL of a given member, namespace definitions, and metadata tokens of a given .NET assembly (including your custom assemblies that may be snapped in using the "File | Customize" menu item).

NOTE   Regardless of the fact that I do not describe in this text how to work with SharpDevelop or ASP.NET Web Matrix in this text, you will be well equipped to understand the use of these tools once you complete the chapters that follow.

So! As you have seen from these first two chapters, you have many new toys at your disposal. Now that you have a solid background on the philosophy of .NET and have seen various approaches used to compile your .NET projects, you are ready to begin your formal investigation of the C# language and the .NET platform.

Summary

The point of this chapter was to introduce you to the process of building C# applications. As you have seen, the ultimate recipient of your *.cs files is the C# compiler, csc.exe. You began by learning how to use csc.exe in the raw, and during the process examined a number of compiler options (including XML documentation, error reporting, preprocessor directives, and csc.exe response files).

The remainder of this chapter explored the key details of the Visual Studio.NET IDE. In effect, VS .NET is nothing more than an elaborate wrapper around the raw C# compiler. To this end, anything that can be done with VS .NET can be done with the raw C# compiler (and a bit of elbow grease). As mentioned, I will describe further features of VS .NET where appropriate.

Part Two
The C# Programming Language

C# Language Fundamentals

THE THRUST OF THIS CHAPTER IS to introduce you to the core aspects of the C# language, including intrinsic data types (both value-based and reference-based); decision and iteration constructs; boxing and unboxing mechanisms; the role of System.Object and basic class construction techniques. Along the way, you also learn how to manipulate CLR strings, arrays, enumerations, and structures using the syntax of C#.

To illustrate these language fundamentals, you will take a programmatic look at the .NET base class libraries, and build a number of sample applications making use of various .NET namespaces. The chapter closes by showing you how to organize your custom types into discrete user-defined namespaces (and explains why you might want to do so).

The Anatomy of a Basic C# Class

Like the Java language, C# demands that all program logic is contained within a type definition (recall that a *type* is a generic term referring to a member of the set {class, interface, structure, enumeration, delegate}). Unlike C(++), it is not possible to create global functions or global points of data. In its simplest form, a C# class can be defined as follows (also recall that the "using" keyword simplifies type declarations):

```
// By convention, C# files end with a *.cs file extension.
using System;
class HelloClass
{
    /* Main() can be declared as 'private'
    if you desire... */
    public static int Main(string[] args)
    {
        Console.WriteLine("Hello World!");
        return 0;
    }
}
```

Here, you have created a definition for an appropriately named type (HelloClass) that supports a single method named Main(). Every executable C# application must contain a class defining a Main() method, which is used to signify the entry point of the application.

> **NOTE** Although it is technically possible (albeit unlikely) for a single C#
> project to contain multiple classes defining a Main() method, you must
> specify which type contains the Main() method to be used as the appli-
> cation's entry point (via the csc.exe /main flag or, for VS .NET applications,
> via the "Startup Object" setting of the Project Properties window). If you
> fail to do so, you encounter a compile-time error.

As you can see, the signature of Main() is adorned with the public and static keywords (also note the capital "M" in Main(), which is obligatory as C# is case-sensitive).
Later in this chapter you are supplied with a formal definition of the "public" and
"static" keywords. Until then, understand that public methods are accessible from
other types, while static methods are scoped at the class level (not at an object level)
and can thus be invoked without the need to first create a new object variable.

In addition to the public and static keywords, our Main() method has a single
parameter, which happens to be an array of strings (string[] args). Although you are not
currently bothering to manipulate this array, it is possible that this parameter can contain
any number of command line arguments (you see how to access them momentarily).

The program logic of the HelloClass is within Main() itself. Here, you make use of the
Console class, which is defined within the System namespace. Among its set of
members is the static WriteLine(), which as you might assume, pumps a text string to
the standard console (more details on System.Console a bit later in this chapter):

```
// Pump some text to the console.
Console.WriteLine("Hello World!");
```

Because our Main() method has been defined as returning an integer data type, you
return zero (success) before exiting. Finally, as you can see from the HelloClass type
definition, C and C++ styles comments have carried over into the C# language.

Variations on the Main() Method

The previous iteration of Main() was defined to take a single parameter (an array of
strings) and return an integer data type. This is not the only possible form of Main(),
however. It is permissible to construct your application's Main() method using any of
the following signatures (assuming it is contained within a C# class definition):

```
// No return type, array of strings as argument.
public static void Main(string[] args)
{
    // Process command line arguments.
    // Make some objects.
}
```

```
// No return type, no arguments.
public static void Main()
{
    // Make some objects.
}

// Integer return type, no arguments.
public static int Main()
{
    // Make some objects.
    // Return a value to the system.
}
```

Obviously, your choice of how to construct Main() will be based on two questions: First, do you need to process any command line parameters? If so, they will be stored in the array of strings. Next, do you want to return a value to the system when Main() has completed? If so, you need to return an integer data type rather than void.

Processing Command Line Parameters

Assume that you now wish to update HelloClass to process any possible command line parameters (I examine the details behind the {0} notation in just a bit):

```
// This time, check if we have been sent any command line arguments.
using System;
class HelloClass
{
    public static int Main(string[] args)
    {
        Console.WriteLine("***** Command line args *****");
        for(int x = 0; x < args.Length; x++)
            Console.WriteLine("Arg: {0} ", args[x]);

        Console.WriteLine("Hello World!");
        return 0;
    }
}
```

Here, you are checking to see if the array of strings contains some number of items using the Length property of System.Array (as you see later in this chapter, all C# arrays actually alias the System.Array base type, and therefore have a common set of members). If you have at least one member in the array, you loop over each item and print the contents to the output window.

Supplying the arguments themselves is equally as simple, as illustrated in Figure 3-1.

Figure 3-1. Supplying and processing command line arguments

As an alternative to the standard for loop, you may iterate over incoming string arrays using the C# "foreach" keyword. This bit of syntax is fully explained later in this chapter, however here is some sample usage:

```
// Notice we have no need to check the size of the array when using 'foreach'.
public static int Main(string[] args)
{
    foreach(string s in args)
        Console.WriteLine("Arg: {0} ", s);
    ...
}
```

Finally, be aware that you are also able to access command line arguments using the static GetCommandLineArgs() method of the System.Environment type. The return value of this method is an array of strings. The first index identifies the current directory containing the application itself, while the remaining elements in the array contain the individual command line arguments. For example:

```
// Now using System.Environment.
string[] theArgs = Environment.GetCommandLineArgs();
Console.WriteLine("Path is: {0}", theArgs[0]);
// Skip the path to the *.exe.
for(int i=1; i < theArgs.Length; i++)
    Console.WriteLine("Again, the args are {0}", theArgs[i]);
```

Simulating Command Arguments a la VS .NET

In the real world, the end user defines the command line arguments used by a given application. However, during the development cycle you may wish to simulate possible command line flags. Using VS .NET, you are able to do so by accessing the Properties dialog for your current project. Simply set the "Command Line Arguments" textbox found under the Configuration | Debugging node (Figure 3-2).

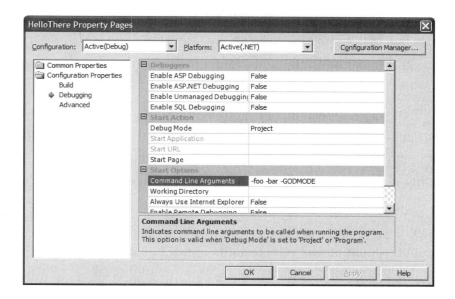

Figure 3-2. Setting command arguments via VS .NET

Needless to say, regardless of the technique you use to specify application arguments, you are the one in charge of determining which command line parameters your application will respond to, and what to do with them once the end user has supplied them.

Creating Objects: Constructor Basics

Now that you have the role of Main() under your belt, let's move on to the topic of object construction. All object-oriented languages make a clear distinction between *classes* and *objects*. A *class* is a definition of a user-defined type (UDT) that is often regarded as a blueprint for variables of this type. An *object* is simply a term describing a given instance of a particular class. In C#, the "new" keyword is the de facto way to create an object instance. Unlike other OO languages (such as C++), it is not possible to allocate a class type on the stack, and therefore if you attempt to use a class variable that has not been "new-ed" you are issued a compile time error. Thus the following illustrative C# logic is *illegal:*

```
// This is no good...
Using System;
class HelloClass
{
    public static int Main(string[] args)
    {
        // Error!  Use of unassigned local variable!  Must use 'new'.
        HelloClass c1;
        c1.SayHi();
        return 0;
    }
}
```

To illustrate the proper procedure for class instantiation, observe the following update:

```
// Make HelloClass types correctly using the C# 'new' keyword.
Using System;
class HelloClass
{
    public static int Main(string[] args)
    {
        // You can declare and create a new object in a single line...
        HelloClass c1 = new HelloClass();
        // ...or break declaration and creation into two lines.
        HelloClass c2;
        c2 = new HelloClass();
        return 0;
    }
}
```

The "new" keyword is in charge of allocating the correct number of bytes for the specified class and acquiring sufficient memory from the managed heap. Here, you have allocated two objects (c1 and c2) each of which points to a unique instance of the HelloClass type. Understand that C# object variables are actually a *reference* to the object in memory, not the actual object itself. Thus, in this light, c1 and c2 each reference a distinct HelloClass object allocated on the managed heap (Chapter 4 offers additional details regarding the .NET garbage collector and the managed heap).

As you may be aware, the previous code is making calls to the *default constructor* of the class. Every C# class is automatically endowed with a default constructor, which you are free to redefine if need be. Like C++ (and Java), default constructors never take arguments. Beyond allocating a new class instance, the default constructor ensures that all member data is set to an appropriate default value (this behavior is true for all constructors). Contrast this to C++, where uninitialized state data points to garbage (sometimes the little things mean a lot).

Typically, your custom classes provide additional constructors beyond the default. In doing so, you provide the object user with a simple way to initialize the state of an object at the time of creation. Here is the HelloClass type once again, with a custom constructor, a redefined default constructor, and some simple state data:

```
// HelloClass, with constructors.
using System;
class HelloClass
{
    // Constructors always assign state data to default values.
    public HelloClass()
    { Console.WriteLine("Default ctor called!"); }
    // This custom constructor assigns state data to a known value.
    public HelloClass (int x, int y)
    {
        Console.WriteLine("Custom ctor called!");
        intX = x;
        intY = y;
    }
```

```
    // Some public state data.
    public int intX, intY;

    // Program entry point.
    public static int Main(string[] args)
    {
        // Trigger default constructor.
        HelloClass c1 = new HelloClass();
        Console.WriteLine("c1.intX = {0}\nc1.intY = {1}\n",
            c1.intX, c1.intY);

        // Trigger parameterized constructor.
        HelloClass c2;
        c2 = new HelloClass(100, 200);
        Console.WriteLine("c2.intX = {0}\nc2.intY = {1}\n",
            c2.intX, c2.intY);
        return 0;
    }
}
```

As you can see, C# constructors are named identical to the class they are constructing, and do not take a return value (not even void). On examining the program's output you can see that the default constructor has indeed assigned the internal state data to the default values (zero), while the custom constructor has assigned the member data to values specified by the object user (see Figure 3-3).

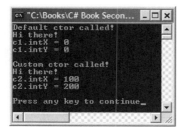

Figure 3-3. Simple constructor logic

Is That a Memory Leak?

If you have a background in C++, you may be alarmed by the previous code samples. Specifically, notice how the Main() method of the previous HelloClass type has no logic that explicitly destroys the c1 and c2 variables:

```
// Leaky method?
public static int Main(string[] args)
{
    HelloClass c1 = new HelloClass();
    Console.WriteLine("c1.intX = {0}\nc1.intY = {1}\n", c1.intX, c1.intY);
    HelloClass c2;
    c2 = new HelloClass(100, 200);
    Console.WriteLine("c2.intX = {0}\nc2.intY = {1}\n", c2.intX, c2.intY);
    // Hey! Did someone forget to delete these objects?
    return 0;
}
```

This is not a horrible omission, but the way of .NET. Like Visual Basic and Java developers, C# programmers never explicitly destroy an object. The .NET garbage collector frees the allocated memory automatically, and therefore C# does not support a "delete" keyword. Again, Chapter 4 examines the garbage collection process in more detail. Until then, just remember that the .NET runtime environment automatically destroys the objects you allocate.

The Composition of a C# Application

Currently, our HelloClass type has been constructed to perform two duties. First, the class defines the entry point of the application. Second, HelloClass maintains two custom data members and a few overloaded constructors. While this is all well and good, it may seem a bit strange (although perfectly legal) that the static Main() method creates an instance of the very class in which it was defined:

```
class HelloClass
{
...
    public static int Main(string[] args)
    {
        HelloClass c1 = new HelloClass();
        ...
    }
}
```

Many of my initial examples take this approach, just to keep focused on illustrating the task at hand. However, a more natural design would be to factor the HelloClass type into two distinct classes: HelloClass and HelloApp. In OO parlance, this is termed the "separation of concerns." Thus, you could reengineer the application as the following (notice you have added a new member named SayHi() to the HelloClass type):

```
class HelloClass
{
    public HelloClass(){ Console.WriteLine("Default ctor called!"); }
    public HelloClass (int x, int y)
    {
        Console.WriteLine("Custom ctor called!");
        intX = x; intY = y;
    }
    public int intX, intY;
    public void SayHi() { Console.WriteLine("Hi there!"); }
}

class HelloApp
{
    public static int Main(string[] args)
    {
        // Make some HelloClass objects and say howdy.
        HelloClass c1 = new HelloClass();
        c1.SayHi();
        ...
    }
}
```

When you build your C# applications, it becomes quite common to have one type functioning as the "application object" (the type that defines the Main() entry point) and numerous other types that constitute the application at large. On the other hand, it is permissible to create an application object that defines any number of members called from the type's Main() method. You will see examples of each approach during the remainder of this text.

NOTE   If you are coming to .NET from an MFC background, be aware that there is no intrinsic doc / view / frame / app model under .NET. If you desire such a paradigm, you must roll your own.

SOURCE CODE   The HelloThere project is located under the Chapter 3 subdirectory.

Default Assignments and Variable Scope

As seen in the previous example, all intrinsic .NET data types have a default value. When you create custom types, all member variables are automatically assigned to their appropriate default value. To illustrate, assume you have created a new Console application containing the following class type:

```
// C# automatically sets all member variables to a safe default value.
class DefaultValueTester
{
    // Here are a number of fields...
    public sbyte theSignedByte;
    public byte theByte;
    public short theShort;
    public ushort theUShort;
    public int theInt;
    public uint theUInt;
    public long theLong;
    public ulong theULong;
    public char theChar;
    public float theFloat;
    public double theDouble;
    public bool theBool;
    public decimal theDecimal;
    public string theStr;
    public object theObj;
    public static int Main(string[] args)
    {
        DefaultValueTester v = new DefaultValueTester();
        return 0;      // Set breakpoint here and check out the Locals window.
    }
}
```

If you were to now create an instance of the DefaultValueTester class and begin a debugging session, you would see that each member variable has been automatically assigned to a corresponding default value, as seen in Figure 3-4.

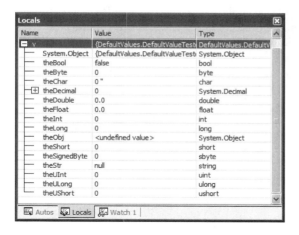

Figure 3-4. Viewing default values for member data

The story is very different, however, when you create variables within a method scope. When you define variables within a method scope, you *must* assign an initial value before you use them, as they do not receive a default assignment. For example, the following code results in a compiler error:

```
// Compiler error! Must assign localInt to an initial value before use.
public static void Main()
{
    int localInt;
    Console.WriteLine(localInt);
}
```

Fixing the problem is trivial. Simply make an initial assignment:

```
// Better. Everyone is happy.
public static void Main()
{
    int localInt = 0;
    Console.WriteLine(localInt);
}
```

There is one exception to the mandatory assignment of local variables. If the variable is functioning as an "output" parameter (examined a bit later in this chapter) the variable does not need to be assigned an initial value. The rationale for this is simple: Methods that define output parameters assign incoming variables within their function scope before the caller makes direct use of them.

 SOURCE CODE   The DefaultValues project is located under the Chapter 3 subdirectory.

The C# Member Variable Initialization Syntax

Class types tend to have numerous member variables. Given that a class may define various custom constructors, you can find yourself in the annoying position of having to write the same initialization code in each and every constructor implementation. This is particularly necessary if you do not wish to accept the default values assigned to your state data. For example, if you wish to ensure that an integer member variable always begins life with the value of 9, you could write:

```
// This is OK, but redundant...
class Test
{
    private int myInt;
    Test() { myInt = 9; }
    Test(string someStringParam)
    { myInt = 9; }
    Test(bool someBoolParam)
    { myInt = 9; }
      ...
}
```

An alternative would be to define a private helper function for your class type that is called by each constructor. While this will reduce the amount of repeat assignment code, you are now stuck with the following redundancy:

```
// This is still rather redundant...
class Test
{
    private int myInt;
    Test() { InitData(); }
    Test(string someStringParam)
    { InitData(); }
    Test(bool someBoolParam)
    { InitData(); }
    private void InitData()
    { myInt = 9; }
      ...
}
```

While both of these techniques are still valid, C# allows you to assign a type's member data to an initial value at the time of declaration [as you may be aware, other object-oriented languages (such as C++) do not allow you to initialize a member in this way]. Notice in the following code blurb that member initialization may be used with internal object references as well as numerical data types:

```
// This technique is useful when you don't want to accept default values
// and would rather not write the same initialization code in each constructor.
class Test
{
    private int myInt = 9;
    private string myStr = "My initial value.";
    private HotRod viper = new HotRod(200, "Chucky", Color.Red);
    ...
}
```

NOTE   Be aware that member assignment happens *before* constructor logic. Thus, if you assign a member to a value within the scope of a constructor, it effectively cancels out the previous member assignment.

In addition to each of these member variable initialization techniques, yet another option is to forward calls from one constructor to another "master" constructor. You will see this technique later in Chapter 4 during our discussion of the "this" keyword.

Basic Input and Output with the Console Class

Many of the example applications seen over the course of these first few chapters make use of the System.Console class. Console is one of many types defined in the System namespace. As its name implies, this class encapsulates input, output, and error stream manipulations. Thus, you are correct to assume that this type is mostly useful when creating console-based applications rather than Windows-based or Web-based applications.

Principal among the methods of System.Console are Read(), ReadLine() Write() and WriteLine(), all of which are defined as static. As you have seen, WriteLine() pumps a text string (including a carriage return) to the output stream. The Write() method pumps text to the output stream without a carriage return. ReadLine() allows you to receive information from the input stream up until the carriage return, while Read() is used to capture a single character from the input stream.

To illustrate basic IO using the Console class, consider the following program, which prompts the user for some bits of information and echoes each item to the standard output stream. The output can be seen in Figure 3-5.

```
// Make use of the Console class to perform basic IO.
using System;
class BasicIO
{
    public static void Main(string[] args)
    {
        // Echo some stats.
        Console.Write("Enter your name: ");
        string s;
        s = Console.ReadLine();
        Console.WriteLine("Hello, {0} ", s);
        Console.Write("Enter your age: ");
        s = Console.ReadLine();
        Console.WriteLine("You are {0}  years old", s);
    }
}
```

Figure 3-5. Basic IO using System.Console

Formatting Textual Output

During these first few chapters, you have also seen numerous occurrences of the tokens {0}, {1}, and the like. .NET introduces a new style of string formatting, slightly reminiscent of the C printf() function, without the cryptic "%d" "%s'" or "%c" flags. A simple example follows (see the output in Figure 3-6).

```
using System;
class BasicIO
{
    public static void Main(string[] args)
    {
        ...
        int theInt = 90;
        float theFloat = 9.99;
        BasicIO myIO = new BasicIO();
        // Format a string...
        Console.WriteLine("Int is: {0}\nFloat is: {1}\nYou Are: {2}",
                        theInt, theFloat, myIO.ToString());
    }
}
```

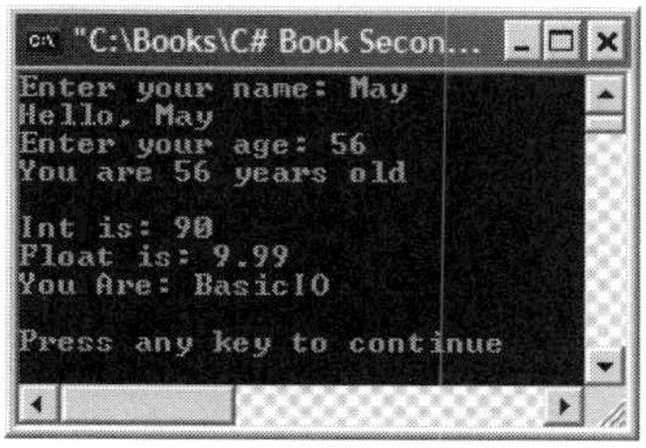

Figure 3-6. Simple format characters

The first parameter to WriteLine() represents a format string that contains optional placeholders designated by {0}, {1}, {2}, and so forth. The remaining parameters to WriteLine() are simply the values to be inserted into the respective placeholders (in this case, an integer, a float, and a string). Also be aware that WriteLine() has been overloaded to allow you to specify placeholder values as an array of objects. Thus, you can represent any number of items to be plugged into the format string as follows:

```
// Fill placeholders using an array of objects.
object[] stuff = {"Hello", 20.9, 1, "There", "83", 99.99933} ;
Console.WriteLine("The Stuff: {0} , {1} , {2} , {3} , {4} , {5} ", stuff);
```

It is also permissible for a given placeholder to repeat within a given string. For example, if you want to build the string "9Number9Number9" you would write:

```
// John says...
Console.WriteLine("{0}Number{0}Number{0}", 9);
```

> **NOTE**   If you have a mismatch between the number of curly-bracket placeholders and fill-arguments, you will receive a FormatException exception at runtime.

String Formatting Flags

If you require more elaborate formatting, each placeholder can optionally contain various format characters (in either uppercase or lowercase), as seen in Table 3-1.

Table 3-1. .NET String Format Characters

C# Format Character	Meaning in Life
C or c	Used to format currency. By default, the flag will prefix the local cultural symbol [a dollar sign ($) for US English], however, this can be changed using a System.Globalization.NumberFormatInfo object.
D or d	Used to format decimal numbers. This flag may also specify the minimum number of digits used to pad the value.
E or e	Exponential notation.
F or f	Fixed point formatting.
G or g	Stands for *general*. Used to format a number to fixed or exponential format.
N or n	Basic numerical formatting (with commas).
X or x	Hexadecimal formatting. If you use an uppercase X, your hex format will also contain uppercase characters.

These format characters are suffixed to a given placeholder using the colon token (for example, {0:C}, {1:d}, {2:X}, and so on). To illustrate, assume you have updated Main() with the following logic:

```
// Now make use of some format tags.
public static void Main(string[] args)
{
...
    Console.WriteLine("C format: {0:C}", 99989.987);
    Console.WriteLine("D9 format: {0:D9}", 99999);
    Console.WriteLine("E format: {0:E}", 99999.76543);
    Console.WriteLine("F3 format: {0:F3}", 99999.9999);
    Console.WriteLine("N format: {0:N}", 99999);
    Console.WriteLine("X format: {0:X}", 99999);
    Console.WriteLine("x format: {0:x}", 99999);
}
```

Be aware that the use of the C# formatting characters is not limited to the System.Console.WriteLine() method. For example, these same flags can be used within the context of the static String.Format() method. This can be helpful when you need to build a string containing numerical values in memory and display it at a later time:

```
// Use the static String.Format() method to build a new string.
string formStr;
formStr =
    String.Format("Don't you wish you had {0:C} in your account?",
    99989.987);
Console.WriteLine(formStr);
```

Figure 3-7 shows a test run.

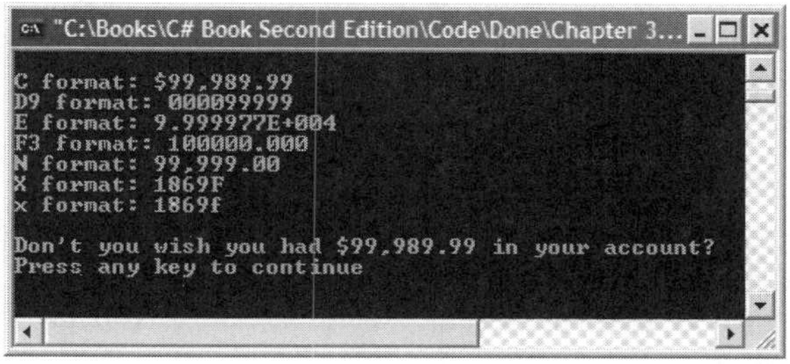

Figure 3-7. String format flags in action

SOURCE CODE The BasicIO project is located under the Chapter 3 subdirectory.

Understanding Value Types and Reference Types

Like any programming language, C# defines a number of intrinsic (aka "primitive") keywords that represent basic data types. As you would expect, there are types to represent whole numbers, strings, floating-point numbers, and Boolean values. If you are coming from a C++ background, you will be happy to know that these intrinsic types are fixed constants in the universe. Meaning, when you create a data point of type integer, all .NET-aware languages understand the fixed nature of this type, and all agree on the range it is capable of handling.

Specifically speaking, a .NET data type may be *value-based* or *reference-based*. Value-based types, which include all numerical data types (int, float, etc.) as well as enumerations and structures, are allocated *on the stack*. Given this factoid, value types can be quickly removed from memory once they fall out of the defining scope:

```
// Integers are value types!
public void SomeMethod()
{
    int i = 0;
    Console.WriteLine(i);
} // 'i' is popped off the stack here!
```

When you assign one value type to another, a member-by-member copy is achieved by default. In terms of simple data types (such as integers and floats), the only "member" to copy is the value of the variable itself.

```
// Assigning two intrinsic value types results in
// two independent variables on the stack.
public void SomeMethod()
{
    int i = 99;
    int j = i;
    // After the following assignment, i is still 99.
    j = 8732;
}
```

While the previous example is no major news flash, recall that custom .NET structures and enumerations also fall under the value-type category. To illustrate, assume you have the following C# structure (you examine structures in greater detail later in this chapter):

```
// Structures are value types!
struct FOO
{
    public int x, y;
}
```

Now, observe the following Main() logic (the output can be seen in Figure 3-8).

```
class ValRefClass
{
    // Exercise some value types.
    public static int Main(string[] args)
    {
        // The 'new' keyword is optional when creating structures
        // using the default constructor, however you must assign
        // all field data before use.
        FOO f1 = new FOO();
        f1.x = 100;
        f1.y = 100;
        Console.WriteLine("-> Assigning f2 to f1\n");
        FOO f2 = f1;
        // Here is F1.
        Console.WriteLine("F1.x = {0}", f1.x);
        Console.WriteLine("F1.y = {0}", f1.y);
        // Here is F2.
        Console.WriteLine("F2.x = {0}", f2.x);
        Console.WriteLine("F2.y = {0}", f2.y);
        // Change f2.x. This will NOT change f1.x.
        Console.WriteLine("-> Changing f2.x to 900");
        f2.x = 900;
        // Print again.
        Console.WriteLine("-> Here are the X's again...");
        Console.WriteLine("F2.x = {0}", f2.x);
        Console.WriteLine("F1.x = {0}\n", f1.x);
        return 0;
    }
}
```

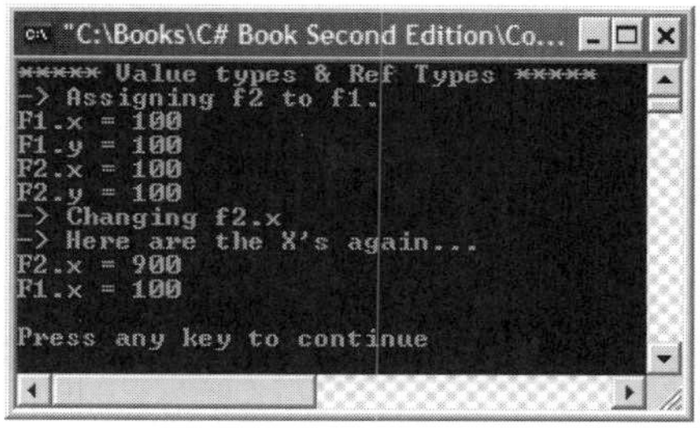

Figure 3-8. Assignment of value types results in a verbatim copy of each field.

Here you have created a structure of type FOO (named f1) that is then assigned to another FOO structure (f2). Because FOO is a value type, you have two copies of the FOO type on the stack, each of which can be independently manipulated. Therefore, when you change the value of f2.*x*, the value of f1.*x* is unaffected (just like the behavior seen in the previous integer example).

In stark contrast, reference types (classes) are allocated on the garbage-collected heap. These entities stay in memory until the .NET garbage collector destroys them. By default, assignment of reference types results in a new reference to the *same* object in memory. To illustrate, let's change the definition of the FOO type from a C# structure to a C# class:

```
// Classes are always reference types.
class FOO  // <= Now a class!
{
    public int x, y;
}
```

If you were to run our test program once again, you would notice the change in behavior (Figure 3-9). Here, you have two references pointing to the same object on the managed heap. Therefore, when you change the value of *x* using the f2 reference, f1.*x* reflects the same value.

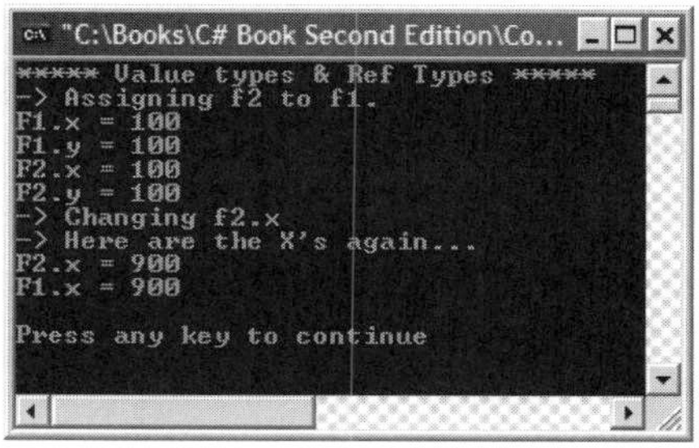

Figure 3-9. Assignment of reference types copies the reference.

Value Types Containing Reference Types

Now that you have a better feeling for the core differences between value types and reference types, let's see a more complex example. Assume you have the following reference (class) type:

```
class TheRefType
{
    public string x;
    public TheRefType(string s) {x = s;}
}
```

Now assume that you want to contain a variable of this reference type within a value type (structure) named InnerRef. In addition to this internal reference type, also assume that InnerRef defines a simple integer (value type) data member. Finally, to allow the outside world to set the value of the inner TheRefType, we also provide the following custom constructor (as explained in just a bit, the default constructor of a structure is reserved and cannot be redefined):

```
struct InnerRef
{
    public TheRefType refType;        // Reference type.
    public int structData;            // Value type.
    public InnerRef(string s)
    {
        refType = new TheRefType(s);
        structData = 9;
    }
}
```

At this point, you have contained a reference type within a value type. The million-dollar question would now be: what happens if you assign one InnerRef variable to another? Given what you already know about value types, you would be correct in assuming that the structData integer should be an independent entity for each InnerRef variable (as a copy was achieved). But what about the internal reference type? Will the object's state be fully copied, or will the *reference* to that object be copied? Ponder the following code and check out Figure 3-10 for the answer.

```
// Make value type that contains ref type.
Console.WriteLine("-> Making InnerRef type and setting structData to 666");
InnerRef valWithRef = new InnerRef("Initial value");
valWithRef.structData = 666;

// Now assign a new InnerRef
Console.WriteLine("-> Assigning valWithRef2 to valWithRef");
InnerRef valWithRef2;
valWithRef2 = valWithRef;
```

```
// Change the value of the internal reference type.
Console.WriteLine("-> Changing all values of valWithRef2");
valWithRef2.refType.x = "I am NEW!";
valWithRef2.structData = 777;

// Print everything.
Console.WriteLine("-> Values after change:");
Console.WriteLine("-> valWithRef.refType.x is {0}", valWithRef.refType.x);
Console.WriteLine("-> valWithRef2.refType.x is {0}", valWithRef2.refType.x);
Console.WriteLine("-> valWithRef.structData is {0}", valWithRef.structData);
Console.WriteLine("-> valWithRef2.structData is {0}", valWithRef2.structData);
```

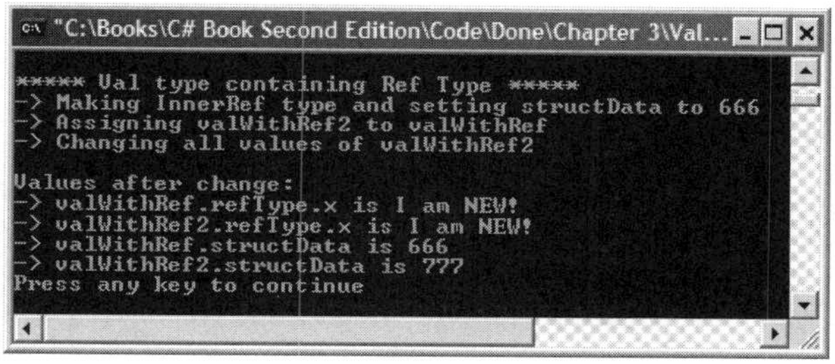

Figure 3-10. The internal references point to the same object!

As you can see, the state of the internal reference type (refType) was not fully copied into the new InnerRef variable. By default, when a value type contains other reference types, assignment results in a copy *of the references.* In this way, you have two independent structures, each of which contains a reference pointing to the same object in memory (i.e., a "shallow copy"). When you want to perform a "deep copy," where the state of internal references is fully copied into a new object, you need to implement the ICloneable interface (as you do in Chapter 6).

Value and Reference Types: Final Details

To wrap up our examination of value types and reference types, ponder the information in Table 3-2 that illustrates how each stands up against a number of intriguing questions (many of which are examined in greater detail throughout this text).

Table 3-2. Value Types and Reference Types Side by Side

Intriguing Question	Value Type	Reference Type
Where is this type allocated?	Allocated on the stack.	Allocated on the managed heap.
How is a variable represented?	Value type variables are local copies.	Reference type variables are pointing to the memory occupied by the allocated instance.
What is the base type?	Must directly derive from System.ValueType.	Can derive from any other type (except System.ValueType) as long as that type is not "sealed"... more later.
Can this type function as a base to other types?	No. Value types are always sealed and cannot be extended.	Yes. If the type is not sealed, it may function as a base to other types.
Default parameter passing behavior?	Variables are passed by value (i.e., a copy of the variable is passed into the called function).	Variables are passed by reference (e.g., the address of the variable is passed into the called function).
Able to override Object.Finalize()?	No. Value types are never placed onto the heap and therefore do not need to be finalized.	Yes...indirectly (more details in Chapter 4).
Can I define constructors for this type?	Yes, but the default constructor is reserved (i.e., your custom constructors must all have arguments).	But, of course!
When do variables of this type die?	When it falls out of the defining scope.	When the managed heap is garbage collected.

Despite their differences, value types and reference types both have the ability to implement interfaces, and may support any number of fields, methods, overloaded operators, constants, properties, and events.

 SOURCE CODE   The ValAndRef project is located under the Chapter 3 subdirectory.

The Master Node: System.Object

In C#, every data type (value or reference based) is ultimately derived from a common base class: System.Object. The Object class defines a common polymorphic behavior for every type in the .NET universe. In the previous HelloClass type definition, you did not explicitly indicate that Object was the base class, but this is assumed if you do not say otherwise:

```
// Implicitly deriving from System.Object.
class HelloClass {...}
```

If you wish to explicitly state System.Object as your base class, you are free to define your class definitions using either of the following notations:

```
// Here we are explicitly deriving from System.Object.
class HelloClass : System.Object {...}
// Same story here...
class HelloClass : object {...}
```

Like most .NET classes, System.Object defines a set of instance-level and class-level (static) members. Note that some of these items are declared "virtual," and can therefore be overridden by a derived class:

```
// The topmost class in the .NET world: System.Object
namespace System
{
    public class Object
    {
        public Object();
        public virtual Boolean Equals(Object obj);
        public virtual Int32 GetHashCode();
        public Type GetType();
        public virtual String ToString();
        protected virtual void Finalize();
        protected Object MemberwiseClone();
        public static bool Equals(object objA, object objB);
        public static bool ReferenceEquals(object objA, object objB);
    }
}
```

Table 3-3 offers a rundown of the functionality provided by each instance-level method.

Table 3-3. Core Members of System.Object

Instance Method of Object Class	Meaning in Life
Equals()	By default this method returns true only if the items being compared refer to the exact same item in memory. Thus, Equals() is used to compare object references, not the state of the object. Typically, this method is overridden to return "true" only if the objects being compared have the same internal state values (that is, value-based semantics). Be aware that if you override Equals(), you should also override GetHashCode().
GetHashCode()	Returns an integer that identifies a specific object instance. If you intend your custom types to be contained in a System.Collections.Hashtable type, you are well advised to override the default implementation of this member.
GetType()	This method returns a System.Type object that fully describes details of the type you are currently referencing. In short, this is a Runtime Type Identification (RTTI) method available to all objects (discussed in greater detail in Chapter 11).
ToString()	Returns a string representation of a given object, using the "<namespace.<class name." format (termed the "fully qualified name"). If the type has not been defined within a namespace, <class name. alone is returned. This method can be overridden by a subclass to return a tokenized string of name/value pairs that represent the object's internal state, rather than its fully qualified name.
Finalize()	For the time being, you can understand this protected method (when overridden) is invoked by the .NET runtime when an object is to be removed from the heap. We talk more about the CLR garbage collection services in Chapter 4.
MemberwiseClone()	This protected method exists to return a new object that is a member-by-member copy of the current object. Thus, if your object contains references to other objects, the *references* to these types are copied (i.e., a shallow copy). If the object contains value types, full copies of the values are achieved.

To illustrate some of the default behavior provided by the System.Object base class, consider the following class definition:

```
// Create some objects and exercise the inherited System.Object methods.
using System;
class ObjTest
{
    public static int Main(string[] args)
    {
        // Make an instance of ObjTest.
        ObjTest c1 = new ObjTest();
        // Pump info to console.
        Console.WriteLine("ToString: {0} ", c1.ToString());
        Console.WriteLine("Hash code: {0} ", c1.GetHashCode());
        Console.WriteLine("Base class: {0} ", c1.GetType().BaseType);
        // Make some other references to c1.
        ObjTest c2 = c1;
        object o = c2;
        // Are all 3 instances pointing to the same object in memory?
        if(o.Equals(c1) && c2.Equals(o))
            Console.WriteLine("Same instance!");
        return 0;
    }
}
```

Figure 3-11 shows a test run.

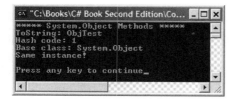

Figure 3-11. Default implementation of select System.Object members

First, notice how the default implementation of ToString() simply returns the name of the current type (ObjTest). In many situations, derived classes override this method to return a string representing the values of its internal state data (as you do in a moment). GetType() retrieves a System.Type object, which defines a property named BaseType (as you can guess, this will identify the fully qualified name of the type's base class). Now, examine the following block of code:

```
// Compare object references...
public static int Main(string[] args)
{
    // Make an instance of ObjTest.
    ObjTest c1 = new ObjTest();
    ...
    // Make some other references to c1.
    ObjTest c2 = c1;
    object o = c2;
    // Are all 3 instances pointing to the same object in memory?
    if(o.Equals(c1) && c2.Equals(o))
        Console.WriteLine("Same instance!");
    return 0;
}
```

The default behavior of Equals() is to compare two objects' variables using *reference semantics* not *value semantics*. Here, you create a new ObjTest variable named c1. At this point, a new ObjTest is placed on the managed heap. C2 is also of type ObjTest. However, you are not creating a *new* instance, but rather assigning this variable to reference c1. Therefore, c1 and c2 are both pointing to the same object in memory, as is the variable *o* (of type object, which was thrown in for good measure). Given that c1, c2 and *o* all point to the same object in memory, the equality test succeeds.

Overriding Some Default Behaviors of System.Object

Although the canned behavior of System.Object can fit the bill in a number of cases, it is quite common for your custom types to override some of these inherited methods. Chapter 4 provides a complete examination of OOP under C#, but in a nutshell, *overriding* is the process of redefining the behavior of an inherited virtual member in a derived class. As you have just seen, System.Object defines a number of virtual methods (such as ToString() and Equals()) that do define a canned implementation. However, if you want to build a custom implementation of these virtual members for a derived type, you make use of the C# "override" keyword.

To illustrate, assume you have a Person class that defines some state data representing an individual's name, social security number, and age:

```
// Remember! All classes implicitly derive from System.Object.
class Person
{
    public Person(string fname, string lname, string ssn, byte a)
    {
        firstName = fname;
        lastName = lname;
        SSN = ssn;
        age = a;
    }
```

```
    public Person(){}
    // The state of a person.
    public string firstName;
    public string lastName;
    public string SSN;
    public byte age;
}
```

Overriding ToString()

To begin, let's override System.Object.ToString() to return a textual representation of a person's state:

```
// Need to reference this namespace to access StringBuilder type.
using System.Text;
// A Person class implements ToString() as so:
class Person
{
    // Overriding System.Object.ToString().
    public override string ToString()
    {
        StringBuilder sb = new StringBuilder();
        sb.AppendFormat("[FirstName= {0}", this.firstName);
        sb.AppendFormat(" LastName= {0}", this.lastName);
        sb.AppendFormat(" SSN= {0}", this.SSN);
        sb.AppendFormat(" Age= {0}]", this.age);
        return sb.ToString();
    }
...
}
```

How you choose to format the string returned from System.Object.ToString() is largely a matter of personal choice. In this example, the name/value pairs have been contained within square brackets ([...]). Also notice that this example makes use of a new type, System.Text.StringBuilder (which is also a matter of personal choice). This type is described in greater detail later in the chapter. The short answer, however, is that this type is typically a more efficient alternative to System.String, given that you have direct access to the underlying buffer of character data.

Overriding Equals()

Let's also override the behavior of System.Object.Equals() to work with *value-based semantics*. Recall that by default, Equals() returns true only if the two references being compared are referencing the same object in memory. For our Person class, it may be helpful to implement Equals() to return true if the two variables being compared contain the same state values (e.g., name, SSN, and age):

```
// A Person class implements Equals() as so:
class Person
{
    public override bool Equals(object o)
    {
        // Does the incoming object instance have the same values as me?
        Person temp = (Person)o;
        if(temp.firstName == this.firstName &&
            temp.lastName == this.lastName &&
            temp.SSN == this.SSN &&
            temp.age == this.age)
                return true;
        else
                return false;
    }
...
}
```

Here you are examining the values of the incoming object against the values of our internal values (note the use of the "this" keyword, which refers to the current object). If the name, SSN, and age of each are identical, you have two objects with the exact same state data and therefore return true.

The prototype of System.Object.Equals() takes a single argument of type object. Thus, we are required to perform an explicit cast (further examined in Chapter 4) within the Equals() method to access the members of the Person type. Now, for the sake of argument, assume that an object user passed in a Car object to the Equals() method as so:

```
// Cars are not people!
Car c = new Car();
Person p = new Person();
p.Equals(c);
```

This is obviously a problem. In fact, if this was attempted, an InvalidCastException would be thrown by the runtime. Furthermore, what if the end user passed in a null object reference to the Equals() method as follows:

```
// Forgot to create the Person!
Person theGhost = null;
p.Equals(theGhost);
```

To design a more bullet-proof Equals() method, you would do well to check for a null value on the incoming parameter, as well as wrap the explicit cast logic within a try / catch statement. I'll examine structured exception handling in Chapter 4, so for the time being, let's assume that the world is a perfect place and the object user will only pass in like-minded (and allocated) types.

Overriding GetHashCode()

Before you see the output of this modified Person type, you have one final detail to attend to. When a class overrides the Equals() method, you should also override the default implementation of GetHashCode() (if you do not, you are issued a compiler warning). This method returns a numerical value used to identify an object in memory, and is commonly used with hash-based collections.

Under the hood, if you place a custom object into a System.Collections.Hashtable type, its Equals() and GetHashCode() members will be called behind the scenes to determine the correct type to return from the container. Given this factoid, your custom types should redefine the hashing algorithm used to identify itself within such a type.

There are many algorithms that can be used to create a hash code, some fancy, others not so fancy. In the simplest case, an object's hash value will be generated by taking its state data into consideration, and building a unique numerical identifier for the type. For our purposes, let's assume that the hash code of the string representing an individual's SSN is unique enough. System.String has a very solid implementation of GetHashCode(). Therefore if you have a string member that should be unique among objects (such as an SSN), this is an elegant solution:

```csharp
// Return a hash code based on the person's SSN.
public override int GetHashCode()
{
    return SSN.GetHashCode();
}
```

With this, here is our new Person class in action (check out Figure 3-12 for output):

```csharp
// Make a few people and play with the overridden Object methods.
public static int Main(string[] args)
{
    ...
    // NOTE:  We want these to be identical to test the Equals() method.
    Person p1 = new Person("Fred", "Jones", "222-22-2222", 98);
    Person p2 = new Person("Fred", "Jones", "222-22-2222", 98);

    // Equals() now uses value semantics.
    // As well, given that each object has the same SSN, they should have
    // the same hash-code (given the work performed by System.String).
    if(p1.Equals(p2) && p1.GetHashCode() = = p2.GetHashCode())
        Console.WriteLine("P1 and P2 have same state\ n");
    else
        Console.WriteLine("P1 and P2 are DIFFERENT\ n");
    // Change state of p2.
    Console.WriteLine("Changing the age of p2");
    p2.age = 2;
    // Test again.
    if(p1.Equals(p2) && p1.GetHashCode() = = p2.GetHashCode())
        Console.WriteLine("P1 and P2 have same state\ n");
    else
        Console.WriteLine("P1 and P2 are DIFFERENT\ n");
    // Get 'stringified' version of objects.
    Console.WriteLine("Stringified people!");
    Console.WriteLine(p1.ToString());
    Console.WriteLine(p2);          // ToString() called automatically
    return 0;
}
```

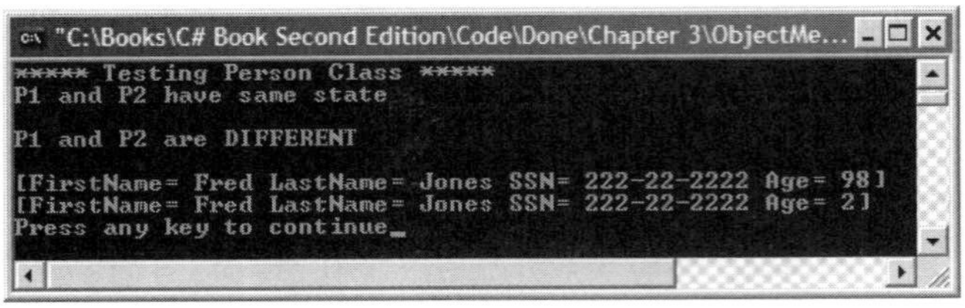

Figure 3-12. Overridden System.Object members in action

Static Members of System.Object

In addition to the instance-level members you have just examined, System.Object does define two static members (Object.Equals() and Object.ReferenceEquals()) that also test for value-based or reference-based equality. Consider the following code:

```
// Static members of System.Object.
Person p3 = new Person("Sally", "Jones","333", 4);
Person p4 = new Person("Sally", "Jones","333", 4);
// Do P3 and P4 have the same state? TRUE!
Console.WriteLine("P3 and P4 have same state: {0} ", object.Equals(p3, p4));
// Are they the same object in memory? FALSE!
Console.WriteLine("P3 and P4 are pointing to same object: {0} ",
    object.ReferenceEquals(p3, p4));
```

Here, you are able to simply send in two objects (of any type) and allow the System.Object class to determine the details automatically.

Excellent! At this point you have a solid understanding of the topmost base class in the .NET class hierarchy. Understand that every class, structure, enumeration, and delegate defined in the .NET base class libraries are always guaranteed to support the public members of System.Object (interface types however, do not derive from System.Object, or any base class for that matter). Next up, let's examine the C# intrinsic data types in a bit more detail.

SOURCE CODE   The ObjectMethods project is located under the Chapter 3 subdirectory.

The System Data Types (and C# Aliases)

As you may have begun to notice, every intrinsic C# data type is actually an alias to an existing type defined in the System namespace. Specifically, each C# data type aliases a well-defined *structure* type in the System namespace. Table 3-4 lists each system data type, its range, the corresponding C# alias, and the type's compliance with the Common Language Specification (CLS).

Table 3-4. System Types and C# Aliases

C# Alias	CLS Compliant?	System Type	Range	Meaning in Life
sbyte	No	System.SByte	-128 to 127	Signed 8-bit number.
byte	Yes	System.Byte	0 to 255	Unsigned 8-bit number.
short	Yes	System.Int16	-32,768 to 32,767	Signed 16-bit number.
ushort	No	System.UInt16	0 to 65,535	Unsigned 16-bit number.
int	Yes	System.Int32	-2,147,483,648 to 2,147,483,647	Signed 32-bit number.
uint	No	System.UInt32	0 to 4,294,967,295	Unsigned 32-bit number.
long	Yes	System.Int64	-9,223,372,036,854,775,808 to 9,223,372,036,854,775,807	Signed 64-bit number.
ulong	No	System.UInt64	0 to 18,446,744,073,709,551,615	Unsigned 64-bit number.
char	Yes	System.Char	U10000 to U1ffff	A single 16-bit Unicode character.
float	Yes	System.Single	1.5×10^{-45} to 3.4×10^{38}	32-bit floating point number.
double	Yes	System.Double	5.0×10^{-324} to 1.7×10^{308}	64-bit floating point number.
bool	Yes	System.Boolean	true or false	Represents truth or falsity.
decimal	Yes	System.Decimal	10^0 to 10^{28}	A 96-bit signed number.
string	Yes	System.String	Limited by system memory.	Represents a set of Unicode characters.
object	Yes	System.Object	Anything at all. All types (not including interfaces) derive from object. Therefore, everything is an object.	The base class of all types in the .NET universe.

The relationship between these core system types (as well as some other soon-to-be-discovered types) can be understood as shown in Figure 3-13.

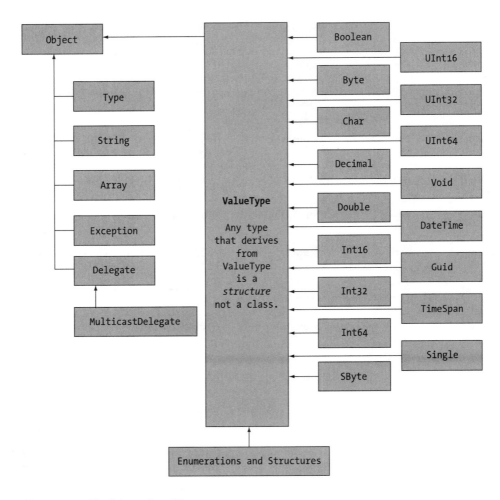

Figure 3-13. The hierarchy of System types

As you can see, each of these types ultimately derives from System.Object. Thus, because data types such as "int" are simply shorthand notations for the corresponding system type (in this case System.Int32), the following is perfectly legal syntax:

```
// Remember! A C# int is really an alias for System.Int32.
Console.WriteLine(12.GetHashCode());
Console.WriteLine(12.GetType().BaseType);
```

Also notice that although C# defines a number of data types, only a subset of the whole are compliant with the rules of the CLS. When you build custom types that must work seamlessly across all languages, you must stick to this well-defined subset. The basic rule of thumb is to avoid exposing unsigned types when defining any public member of a type definition (as seen in Chapter 1). By doing so, you ensure that your custom classes, interfaces, and structures can be understood by any language targeting the .NET runtime.

Experimenting with the System Data Types

As you have seen, C# data types alias a related structure in the System namespace (and thus derive from System.ValueType). Functionally, the only purpose of System.ValueType is to override the virtual methods defined by System.Object to work with value-based versus reference-based semantics. In fact, the signatures of the instance methods defined by System.ValueType are identical to those of System.Object:

```
// Behold the immediate base class for all .NET structures and enums.
public abstract class ValueType : object
{
    public virtual bool Equals(object obj);
    public virtual int GetHashCode();
    public Type GetType();
    public virtual string ToString();
}
```

Given your understanding of System.ValueType, it should be clear that when you compare two intrinsic data types for equality, you are using *value-based* semantics:

```
// Test value semantics.
System.Int32 intA = 1000;          // Same as: int intA = 1000;
System.Int32 intB = 1000;          // Same as  int intB = 1000;
// The test succeeds! The two instances contain the same value.
if(intA == intB)
    Console.WriteLine("Same value!");
```

The structures that represent the C# intrinsic data types (e.g., System.Int32, System.Char, System.Boolean, and so on) also support a set of helpful static members. While I assume you will consult online Help for full details, let's check out some select points of interest.

Basic Numerical Members

First of all, understand that the numerical types support MaxValue and MinValue properties that provide information regarding the minimum and maximum value a given type can hold. Assume you have created some variables of type System.UInt16, and exercised it as follows:

```
// Note that an implicit data type (ushort) has the same methods available as
// the corresponding wrapper (System.UInt16).
class MyDataTypes
{
    public static int Main(string[] args)
    {
        System.UInt16 myUInt16 = 30000;
        Console.WriteLine("Max for an UInt16 is: {0} ", UInt16.MaxValue);
        Console.WriteLine("Min for an UInt16 is: {0} ", UInt16.MinValue);
        Console.WriteLine("Value is: {0} ", myUInt16);
        Console.WriteLine("I am a: {0} ", myUInt16.GetType().ToString());
        // Now in System.UInt16 shorthand (e.g. a ushort).
        ushort myOtherUInt16 = 12000;
        Console.WriteLine("Max for an UInt16 is: {0} ", ushort.MaxValue);
        Console.WriteLine("Min for an UInt16 is: {0} ", ushort.MinValue);
        Console.WriteLine("Value is: {0} ", myOtherUInt16);
        Console.WriteLine("I am a: {0} ", myOtherUInt16.GetType().ToString());
        return 0;
    }
}
```

In addition to the MinValue / MaxValue properties, a given system type may define further useful members. For example, System.Double type allows you to obtain the values for Epsilon, and infinity values:

```
Console.WriteLine("-> double.Epsilon: {0}", double.Epsilon);
Console.WriteLine("-> double.PositiveInfinity: {0}", double.PositiveInfinity);
Console.WriteLine("-> double.NegativeInfinity: {0}", double.NegativeInfinity);
Console.WriteLine("-> double.MaxValue: {0}", double.MaxValue);
Console.WriteLine("-> double.MinValue: {0}",double.MinValue);
```

Members of System.Boolean

Next, consider the System.Boolean data type. Unlike C(++), the only valid assignment a C# bool can take is from the set {true | false}. You cannot assign makeshift values (e.g., -1, 0, 1) to a C# bool, which (to most programmers) is a welcome change. Given this point, it should be clear that System.Boolean does not support a MinValue/MaxValue property set, but rather TrueString/FalseString:

```
// No more ad-hoc Boolean types in C#!
bool b = 0;        // Illegal!
bool b2 = -1;      // Also illegal!
bool b3 = true;    // No problem.
bool b4 = false;   // No problem.
Console.WriteLine("-> bool.FalseString: {0}", bool.FalseString);
Console.WriteLine("-> bool.TrueString: {0}", bool.TrueString);
```

Members of System.Char

It is important to note that C# textual data is represented by the intrinsic C# string and char data types. Thus, no more nasty char*, wchar_t*, LPSTR, LPCSTR, BSTR or OLECHAR string types! I am sure you agree with me that string manipulation in the COM and Win32 universe was horrifying. Utterly and completely horrifying. On a happy note, .NET offers a very simplified view of string management, as all .NET-aware languages map textual data to the same underlying types (System.String and System.Char), both of which are Unicode under the hood.

The System.Char type (represented by the C# "char" keyword) provides you with a great deal of functionality beyond the ability to hold a single point of character data (which must be placed between single tick marks). More interestingly, using the static methods of System.Char, you are able to determine if a given character is numerical, alphabetical, a point of punctuation, or whatnot. To illustrate, check out the following:

```
// Test the truth or falsity of the following statements...
Console.WriteLine("-> char.IsDigit('K'): {0}", char.IsDigit('K'));
Console.WriteLine("-> char.IsDigit('9'): {0}", char.IsDigit('9'));
Console.WriteLine("-> char.IsLetter('10', 1): {0}", char.IsLetter("10", 1));
Console.WriteLine("-> char.IsLetter('p'): {0}", char.IsLetter('p'));
Console.WriteLine("-> char.IsWhiteSpace('Hello There', 5): {0}",
    char.IsWhiteSpace("Hello There", 5));
Console.WriteLine("-> char.IsWhiteSpace('Hello There', 6): {0}",
    char.IsWhiteSpace("Hello There", 6));
Console.WriteLine("-> char.IsLetterOrDigit('?'): {0}",
    char.IsLetterOrDigit('?'));
Console.WriteLine("-> char.IsPunctuation('!'): {0}",
    char.IsPunctuation('!'));
Console.WriteLine("-> char.IsPunctuation('>'): {0}",
    char.IsPunctuation('>'));
Console.WriteLine("-> char.IsPunctuation(','): {0}",
    char.IsPunctuation(','));
```

As you can see, each of these static members of System.Char has two calling conventions: a single character or a string with a numerical index that specified the position of the character to test.

Parsing Values from String Data

Finally, also understand that the .NET data types provide the ability to generate a variable of their underlying type given a textual equivalent (e.g., parsing). This technique can be extremely helpful when you wish to convert a bit of user input data (such as a listbox selection) into a numerical value. Ponder the following parsing logic:

```
bool myBool = bool.Parse("True");
Console.WriteLine("-> Value of myBool: {0}", myBool);
double myDbl = double.Parse("99.884");
Console.WriteLine("-> Value of myDbl: {0}", myDbl);
int myInt = int.Parse("8");
Console.WriteLine("-> Value of myInt: {0}", myInt);
char myChar = char.Parse("w");
Console.WriteLine("-> Value of myChar: {0}\n", myChar);
```

SOURCE CODE   The DataTypes project is located under the Chapter 3 subdirectory.

Converting Between Value Types and Reference Types: Boxing and Unboxing

Given that .NET defines two broad categories of types (value-based and reference-based), you may occasionally need to represent a variable of one category as a variable of the other category. C# provides a very simple mechanism to convert between value types and reference types, termed *boxing*. To illustrate, assume that you have created a simple value data type of type short:

```
// Make a simple value data point.
short s = 25;
```

If, during the course of your application, you wish to represent this value type as a reference type, you would "box" the value as follows:

```
// Box the value into an object reference.
object objShort = s;
```

Boxing can be formally defined as the process of explicitly converting a value type into a corresponding reference type. When you box a value, essentially all you are doing is allocating a new object on the heap and copying the internal value (in this case 25) into that instance. What is returned to you is a true-blue reference to the newly allocated object. Using this technique, .NET developers have no need to make use of a set of wrapper classes used to temporarily treat intrinsic data as heap-allocated objects (as is the case in Java).

The opposite operation is also permitted through *unboxing*. Unboxing is the term given to the process of converting the value held in the object reference back into a corresponding value type on the stack. The unboxing operation begins by verifying that the receiving data type is equivalent to the boxed type, and if so, copying the value out of the box into a local stack based variable. For example, the following unboxing operation works successfully, given that the underlying type of the objShort is indeed a "short":

```
// Now, unbox the reference back into a corresponding short.
short anotherShort = (short)objShort;
```

Again, it is critical that you unbox into an appropriate data type. Thus, the following unboxing logic generates an InvalidCastException exception (you examine casting and exception handling in detail in the next chapter, so hold tight for now):

```
// Bad unboxing!
public static int Main(string[] args)
{
...
    try
    {
        // The type contained in the box is NOT a string, but a short!
        string str = (string)objShort;
    }
    catch(InvalidCastException e)
    {
        Console.WriteLine("OOPS!\n{0} ", e.ToString());
    }
}
```

Some Practical (Un)boxing Examples

So, you may be thinking, when would you really need to manually box (or unbox) a data type? The previous example was purely illustrative in nature, as there was no good reason to box (and then unbox) the short data point. The truth of the matter is that you will seldom need to manually box data types, if ever. Much of the time, the C# compiler automatically boxes variables when appropriate.

For example, if you pass a value type into a method requiring an object parameter, boxing occurs behind the curtains. However, if you wish to invoke members of the underlying value type, you will be required to perform an explicit unboxing operation. To illustrate, ponder the following:

```
class Boxer
{
    // Helper f(x) to illustrate automatic boxing.
    public static void UseThisObject(object o)
    {
        Console.WriteLine(o.GetType());
        Console.WriteLine(o.ToString());
        Console.WriteLine("Value of o is: {0}", o);
        // Need to explicitly unbox to get at members of
        // System.Int32. (GetTypeCode() returns a value
        // representing the underlying "type of intrinsic type".
        Console.WriteLine(((int)o).GetTypeCode());
    }
    static void Main(string[] args)
    {
        int x = 99;
        UseThisObject(x);  // Automatic boxing.
    }
}
```

In addition to the automatic boxing performed when calling custom functions, boxing implicitly occurs when interacting with numerous types of the .NET base class libraries. For example, the System.Collections namespace (further examined in Chapter 6) defines a type named ArrayList. Like most collection types, ArrayList provides members that allow you to insert, index, and remove items. If you were to check the formal class definition using wincv.exe, you would find prototypes such as:

```
public class System.Collections.ArrayList : object,
    System.Collections.IList,
    System.Collections.ICollection,
    System.Collections.IEnumerable,
    ICloneable
{
...
    public virtual int Add(object value);
    public virtual void Insert(int index, object value);
    public virtual void Remove(object obj);
}
```

As you can see, these members take generic System.Object types as parameters. Given that everything ultimately derives from this common base class, the following code is perfectly legal:

```
ArrayList myInts = new ArrayList();
myInts.Add(88);
myInts.Add(3);
myInts.Add(9764);
```

However, given your understanding of value types and reference types, you might wonder exactly what was placed into the ArrayList type (references, copies of references, (copies of) structures, etc). Just like the previous Foo() method, it should be clear that each of the System.Int32 data types were indeed boxed before being stored into the ArrayList type. As well, just like the Foo() helper method, if you wish to interact with the members of the boxed type, you are required to unbox accordingly. Thus, assume the following static helper method:

```
public static void BoxAndUnboxInts()
{
    // Box ints into ArrayList.
    ArrayList myInts = new ArrayList();
    myInts.Add(88);
    myInts.Add(3);
    myInts.Add(9764);
    // Unbox first item.
    int firstItem = (int)myInts[0];
    Console.WriteLine("First item is {0}", firstItem);
}
```

(Un)Boxing Under the Hood

If you examine the underlying CIL using ildasm.exe for the BoxAndUnboxInts() method, you can clearly see exactly when the System.Int32 types are copied from the heap to the stack (and vice versa):

```
.method public hidebysig static void  BoxAndUnboxInts() cil managed
{
  // Code size       81 (0x51)
  .maxstack  3
  .locals init ([0] class [mscorlib]System.Collections.ArrayList myInts,
           [1] int32 firstItem)
  IL_0000:  newobj
    instance void [mscorlib]System.Collections.ArrayList::.ctor()
  IL_0005:  stloc.0
  IL_0006:  ldloc.0
  IL_0007:  ldc.i4.s    88
  IL_0009:  box         [mscorlib]System.Int32
  IL_000e:  callvirt
    instance int32 [mscorlib]System.Collections.ArrayList::Add(object)
  IL_0013:  pop
  IL_0014:  ldloc.0
  IL_0015:  ldc.i4.3
  IL_0016:  box         [mscorlib]System.Int32
  IL_001b:  callvirt
    instance int32 [mscorlib]System.Collections.ArrayList::Add(object)
  IL_0020:  pop
  IL_0021:  ldloc.0
  IL_0022:  ldc.i4      0x2624
  IL_0027:  box         [mscorlib]System.Int32
  IL_002c:  callvirt
    instance int32 [mscorlib]System.Collections.ArrayList::Add(object)
  IL_0031:  pop
  IL_0032:  ldloc.0
  IL_0033:  ldc.i4.0
  IL_0034:  callvirt
    instance object [mscorlib]System.Collections.ArrayList::get_Item(int32)
  IL_0039:  unbox       [mscorlib]System.Int32
  IL_003e:  ldind.i4
  IL_003f:  stloc.1
  IL_0040:  ldstr       "First item is {0}"
  IL_0045:  ldloc.1
  IL_0046:  box         [mscorlib]System.Int32
  IL_004b:  call        void [mscorlib]System.Console::WriteLine(string, object)
  IL_0050:  ret
}
```

Here, we have indirectly triggered a fourth CIL box operation at the point of printing out the value of the first item help in the ArrayList. The reason? System.Console.WriteLine() does not supply an overloaded variation that operates on raw System.Int32 types!

To be sure, boxing and unboxing types takes some processing time, and if used without restraint, could hurt the performance of your application. However, given this .NET technique, you are able to symmetrically operate on value-based and reference-based types. Without such a mechanism, we would be forced to be painfully aware of the underlying type of a given variable (which would also result in extraneous code, as we see in C and C++). In this light, I'd place my vote that (un)boxing is a positive trait of a mature runtime.

On a final boxing-related note, understand that if you were to pass custom structures or enumerations into a method taking generic System.Object parameters, you would also be required to unbox the parameter to interact with the specific members of the structure (or enum). This topic will be revisited later in this chapter when you formally examine the C# structure.

 SOURCE CODE   The Boxing project is included under the Chapter 3 subdirectory.

Defining Program Constants

Now that you can create (and transform) value-based and reference-based variables, you need to examine the logical opposite: Constants. C# offers the "const" keyword, to define variables with a fixed, unalterable value. Unlike C++, the C# "const" keyword cannot be used to qualify parameters or return values. Furthermore, it is important to understand that the value of a constant point of data is computed at *compile time*, and therefore a constant member cannot be assigned to an object reference (whose value is computed at runtime). Although it is possible to define local constants within a method scope, a more beneficial use of const is to create class-level constant definitions. For example:

```
// Some const data.
using System;
class MyConstants
{
    // When accessed by another type, these constants
    // must be referenced via the fully qualified name.
    public const int myIntConst = 5;
    public const string myStringConst = "I'm a const";
```

```
public static void Main()
{
    // Scoped constant.
    const string localConst = "I am a rock, I am an island";
    // Use const data.
    Console.WriteLine("myIntConst = {0}\nmyStringConst = {1}",
                      myIntConst, myStringConst );
    Console.WriteLine("Local constant: {0}", localConst);
}
}
```

If you create a utility class that contains nothing but constant data, you may wish to define a private constructor. In this way, you ensure the object user cannot make an instance of your class (which would be desirable given that the class has no real implementation):

```
// Private constructors prevent the creation of a given type.
class MyConstants
{
    public const int myIntConst = 5;
    public const string myStringConst = "I'm a const";
    // Don't let the user make this class,
    // as its only purpose is to define constant values.
    private MyConstants(){ }
}
```

The same result can be achieved by marking your "constant-only class" as an abstract type. You examine the use of this keyword in the next chapter, but here is the updated MyConstants definition:

```
// Abstract definition also prevents the creation of a given type.
abstract class MyConstants
{
    public const int myIntConst = 5;
    public const string myStringConst = "I'm a const";
}
```

In either case, if another object attempts to create an instance of MyConstants, a compiler error is generated. These techniques can be quite helpful given that C# does not allow you to define global level constants.

Referencing Constant Data Across Types

Given that we have moved our constant points of data into a new class definition, how are they accessed from within another type? If you attempt to simply reference them by their unqualified name (myIntConstant, myStringConstant) you will be issued a compiler error. Again, the reason has to do with the fact that under C#, global points of data are not allowed. Thus, any time you wish to access a constant defined outside of the defining class, you must make use of the fully-qualified name. On the other hand, if a given class wishes to access a constant it directly defined, you are able to directly refer to the item at hand:

```
public static void Main()
{
    const string localConst = "I am a rock, I am an island";
    // Use const data.
    Console.WriteLine("myIntConst = {0}\nmyStringConst = {1}\nLocalConst = {2}",
    MyConstants.myIntConst, MyConstants.myStringConst, localConst);
}
```

SOURCE CODE   The Constants project is located under the Chapter 3 subdirectory.

C# Iteration Constructs

Consider the next few pages a mid-chapter reprieve from the complexities of value/reference types, overriding members of System.Object, and boxing types on the heap (in other words, the next few sections are boring, but necessary to cover). As you are well aware, all programming languages provide ways to repeat blocks of code until a terminating condition has been met. Regardless of which language you are coming from, the C# iteration statements should pose no raised eyebrows and require little explanation. In a nutshell, C# provides the following four iteration constructs:

- for loop

- foreach/in loop

- while loop

- do/while loop

    C, C++, and Java programmers will no doubt be familiar with the "for," "while," and "do/while" loops, but may be unfamiliar with the "foreach" statement. Visual Basic programmers on the other hand, are in the fortunate position to be well aware of all four C# iteration statements, as VB already supports "For Each" syntax. Let's quickly examine each looping construct in turn.

The for Loop

When you need to iterate over a block of code a fixed number of times, the "for" statement is the construct of champions. In essence, you are able to specify how many times a block of code repeats itself, as well as the terminating condition. Without belaboring the point, here is a sample of the syntax:

```
// A basic for loop.
public static int Main(string[] args)
{
    // Note! 'i' is only visible within the scope of the for loop.
    for(int i = 0; i < 10; i++)
    {
        Console.WriteLine("Number is: {0} ", i);
    }
    // 'i' is not visible here.
    return 0;
}
```

All of your old C, C++, and Java tricks still hold when building a C# for statement. You can create complex terminating conditions, build endless loops, and make use of the "goto," "continue," and "break" keywords. I'll assume that you will bend this iteration construct as you see fit.

The foreach/in Loop

Visual Basic programmers have long seen the benefits of the For Each construct. The C# equivalent allows you to iterate over all items within an array. Here is a simple example using foreach to traverse an array of strings that represent possible titles for forthcoming publications. Once this array has been filled, you iterate over the contents looking for a pattern match (COM or .NET) using String.IndexOf():

```
// Digging into an array using foreach.
public static int Main(string[] args)
{
    string[] arrBookTitles = new string[] {  "Complex Algorithms",
                                    "COM for the Fearful Programmer",
                                    "Do you Remember Classic COM?",
                                    "C# and the .NET Platform",
                                    "COM for the Angry Engineer"  } ;
    int COM = 0, NET = 0;
    // Assume we are not looking for books on COM interop.
    foreach (string s in arrBookTitles)
    {
        if (-1 != s.IndexOf("COM"))
            COM++;
        else if(-1 != s.IndexOf(".NET"))
            NET++;
    }
```

```
    Console.WriteLine("Found {0}  COM references and {1}  .NET references.",
        COM, NET);
    return 0;
}
```

In addition to iterating over simple arrays, foreach is also able to iterate over system-supplied or user-defined collections. I'll hold off on the details until Chapter 6, as this aspect of the "foreach" keyword entails an understanding of interface-based programming and the system-supplied IEnumerator and IEnumerable interfaces.

The while and do/while Looping Constructs

You have already seen that the for statement is typically used when you have some fore-knowledge of the number of iterations you wish to perform (e.g., loop until $j > 20$). The while statement on the other hand is useful for those times when you are uncertain how long it might take for a terminating condition to be met.

To illustrate the while loop, here is a brief look at C# file manipulation (which is fully detailed in Chapter 16). The StreamReader class, defined within the System.IO namespace, encapsulates the details of reading from a given file. Notice that you are obtaining an instance of the StreamReader type as a return value from the static File.OpenText() method. Once you have opened the boot.ini file, you are able to iterate over each line in the file using StreamReader.ReadLine():

```
try    // Just in case we can't find the correct file...
{
  // Open the file named 'boot.ini'.
  StreamReader strReader = File.OpenText("C:\\boot.ini");

  // Read the next line and dump to the console.
  string strLine;
  while(null != (strLine = strReader.ReadLine()))
  {
      Console.WriteLine(strLine);
  }
  // Close the file.
  strReader.Close();
}
catch(FileNotFoundException e)
{
  Console.WriteLine(e.Message);
}
```

Closely related to the while loop is the do/while statement. Like a simple while loop, do/while is used when you need to perform some action for an undetermined number of times. The difference is that do/while loops are guaranteed to execute the corresponding block of code at least once (in contrast, it is possible that a simple while loop may never execute if the terminating condition is false from the onset).

```
// The do/while statement
string ans;
do
{
    Console.Write("Are you done? [yes] [no] : ");
    ans = Console.ReadLine();
}while(ans != "yes");
```

SOURCE CODE   The Iterations project is located under the Chapter 3
subdirectory.

C# Control Flow Constructs

Now that you can iterate over a block of code, the next related concept is how to control
the flow of program execution. C# defines two simple constructs to alter the flow of
your program, based on various contingencies. First you have our good friend, the
"if/else" statement. Unlike C and C++ however, the if/else statement only operates on
Boolean expressions (not ad-hoc values such as –1, 0 and so on). Given this, if/else
statements typically involve the use of the following C# operators (Table 3-5).

Table 3-5. C# Relational and Equality Operators

C# Equality/ Relational Operator	Example Usage	Meaning in Life
==	if(age == 30)	Returns true only if each expression is the same.
!=	if("Foo" != myStr)	Returns true only if each expression is different.

>
<=
>=
	if(bonus < 2000)
	if(bonus > 2000)
	if(bonus <= 2000)
	if(bonus >= 2000)
		Returns true if expression A is less than, greater than, less than or equal to, or greater than or equal to expression B.

C and C++ programmers need to be aware that the old tricks of testing a condition
for a value "not equal to zero" will not work in C#. Let's say you want to see if the string
you are working with is greater than zero. You may be tempted to write:

```
// This is illegal, given that Length returns an int, not a bool.
string thoughtOfTheDay = "You CAN teach an old dog new tricks";
if(thoughtOfTheDay.Length)      // Error!
{
    // Stuff...
}
```

If you wish to make use of the String.Length property to determine if you have an empty string, you need to modify your conditional expression as follows:

```
// No problem.
if( 0 != thoughtOfTheDay.Length)      // Better!  This resolves to {true | false}.
{
    // Stuff...
}
```

An "if" statement may be composed of complex expressions as well. As you would expect, if conditionals can contain *else* statements to perform more complex testing. The syntax is identical to C(++) and Java (and not too far removed from Visual Basic). To build such a beast, C# offers an expected set of conditional operators (Table 3-6).

Table 3-6. C# Conditional Operators

C# Conditional Operator	Example	Meaning in Life
&&	if((age = = 30) && (name = = "Fred"))	Conditional AND operator
||	if((age = = 30) || (name = = "Fred"))	Conditional OR operator
!	if(!myBool)	Conditional NOT operator

The other simple selection construct offered by C# is the *switch* statement. As I am sure you are aware, switch statements allow you to handle program flow based on a predefined set of choices. For example, the following application prompts the user for one of three possible values. Based on the user input, act accordingly:

```
// The good ol' switch statement.
class Selections
{
    public static int Main(string[] args)
    {
        Console.WriteLine("Welcome to the world of .NET");
        Console.WriteLine("1 = C#\n2 = Managed C++ (MC++)\n3 = VB.NET\n");
        Console.Write("Please select your implementation language:");
        string s = Console.ReadLine();
        int n = int.Parse(s);

        switch(n)
        {
            // C# demands that each case (including 'default') which
            // contains executable statements, must have
            // a terminating 'break' or 'goto' to avoid fall through.
            case 1:
                Console.WriteLine("Good choice!  C# is all about managed code.");
            break;
```

```
    case 2:
        Console.WriteLine("Let me guess, maintaining a legacy system?");
    break;
    case 3:
        Console.WriteLine("VB .NET:  It is not just for kids anymore...");
    break;
    default:
        Console.WriteLine("Well...good luck with that!");
    break;
    }
    return 0;
    }
}
```

NOTE   It is worth pointing out that the C# also supports switching on character data as well (it even supports a "null" case for empty strings).

SOURCE CODE   The Selections project is located under the Chapter 3 subdirectory.

The Complete Set of C# Operators

C# defines a number of operators in addition to those you have previously examined. By and large, these operators behave like their C(++) and Java counterparts. Table 3-7 lists the set of C# operators in order of precedence.

Table 3-7. The Full Set of C# Operators

Operator Category	Operators
Unary	+ - ! ~ ++x x++ --x x--
Multiplicative	* / %
Additive	+ -
Shift	<< >>
Relational	< > <= >= is as
Equality	== !=

Table 3-7. The Full Set of C# Operators (Continued)

Operator Category	Operators
Logical AND	&
Logical XOR	^
Logical OR	|
Conditional AND	&&
Conditional OR	||
Conditional	?:
Indirection / Address	* -> &
Assignment	= *= /= %= += -= <<= >>= &= ^= |=

The only operators that you may not be familiar with are the *is* and *as* operators. The *is* operator is used to verify at runtime if an object is compatible with a given type. One common use for this operator is to determine if a given object supports a particular interface, as you discover in Chapter 6. The *as* operator allows you to downcast between types (seen briefly in this chapter and formally in Chapter 4) or implemented interface.

Also note that the C# language does support the use of classic C(++) pointer manipulations, via the *, -> and & operators. If you choose to make use of these operators, you are bypassing the runtime memory management scheme and writing code in "unsafe mode." You learn about these operators in Chapter 8.

As for the remaining operators, I will make the assumption that many (if not all) of them are old hat to you. If you need additional information regarding the C# looping and decision constructs, consult the C# Language Reference using MSDN.

Defining Custom Class Methods

Now that we have concluded our mid-chapter reprieve, let's move on to more interesting topics and examine the details of defining custom methods for a C# class. First understand that, like points of data, every method you implement must be a member of a class or struct (global methods are not allowed in C#).

As you know, a method exists to allow the type to perform a unit of work. Like Main(), your custom methods may or may not take parameters, may or may not return values (of any intrinsic or user defined types). Also custom methods may be declared nonstatic (instance-level) or static (class-level) entities.

Method Access Modifiers

A method must specify its level of accessibility (see Table 3-8). C# offers the following method access modifiers (you examine the use of protected and internal methods in the next chapter during the discussion of class hierarchies):

Table 3-8. C# Accessibility Keywords

C# Access Modifier	Meaning in Life
public	Marks a method as accessible from an object instance, or any subclass.
private	Marks a method as accessible only by the class that has defined the method. If you don't say otherwise, private is assumed (it is the default visibility level).
protected	Marks a method as usable by the defining class, as well as any child class, but is private as far as the outside world is concerned.
internal	Defines a method that is publicly accessible by all types in an assembly (but not from outside the assembly).
protected internal	Defines a method whose access is limited to the current assembly or types derived from the defining class in the current assembly.

Here are the implications of each accessibility keyword:

```
// Visibility options.
class SomeClass
{
    // Accessible anywhere.
    public void MethodA(){}
    // Accessible only from SomeClass types.
    private void MethodB(){}
    // Accessible from SomeClass and any descendent.
    protected void MethodC(){}
    // Accessible from within the same assembly.
    internal void MethodD(){}
    // Assembly-protected access.
    protected internal void MethodE(){}
    // Unmarked members are private by default in C#.
    void MethodF(){}
}
```

As you may already know, methods that are declared public are directly accessible from an object instance via the dot operator. Private methods cannot be accessed by an object reference, but instead are called internally by the object to help the instance get its work done (that is, private helper functions). To illustrate, the Teenager class shown next defines two public methods, Complain() and BeAgreeable(), each of which returns a string to the object user. Internally, both methods make use of a private helper method named GetRandomNumber(), which manipulates a private member variable of type System.Random:

```
// Two public methods, each using an internal helper function.
using System;
class Teenager
{
    // The System.Random type generates random numbers.
    private Random r = new Random();
    public string Complain()
    {
        string[] messages = new string[5]{ "Do I have to?",
            "He started it!", "I'm too tired...",
            "I hate school!", "You are sooo wrong." } ;
        return messages[GetRandomNumber(5)];
    }
    public string BeAgreeable()
    {
        string[] messages = new string[3]{ "Sure!  No problem!",
            "Uh uh.", "I guess so." } ;
        return messages[GetRandomNumber(3)];
    }
    private int GetRandomNumber(short upperLimit)
    {
        // Random.Next() returns a random integer
        // between 0 and upperLimit.
        return r.Next(upperLimit);
    }
    public static void Main(string[] args)
    {
        // Let mike do his thing.
        Console.WriteLine("Grumpy Mike says:");
        Teenager mike = new Teenager();
        for(int i = 0; i < 10; i++)
            Console.WriteLine("-> {0}", mike.Complain());
        // Now be agreeable.
        Console.WriteLine("\nHappy Mike says:");
        Console.WriteLine("-> {0}", mike.BeAgreeable());
    }
}
```

Obviously the benefit of defining GetRandomNumber() as a private helper method is that various parts of the Teenager class can make use of its functionality. The only alternative would be to duplicate the random number logic within the Complain() and BeAgreeable() methods (which in this case would not be too traumatic, but assume

GetRandomNumber() contains 20 or 30 lines of code). Figure 3-14 shows a possible test run.

Figure 3-14. Random teenager chatter

NOTE The System.Random type is used to generate and manipulate random numbers. Random.Next() method returns a number between 0 and the specified upper limit. As you would guess, the Random type provides additional members, all of which are documented within MSDN.

SOURCE CODE The Teenager application is located under the Chapter 3 subdirectory.

Understanding Static Methods

As you have seen, methods can be declared "static." But, what exactly does it mean to be a static method? When a method is marked with the "static" keyword, it may be called directly from the class level, and does not require an object variable. For this very reason, Main() is declared static to allow the runtime to invoke this function without needing to allocate a new instance of the defining class. This is a good thing of course, or else you would need to create an object to create an object to create an object to (...).

You should also consider our good friend System.Console. As you have seen, you do not invoke the WriteLine() method from an object instance:

```
// No!  WriteLine() not instance level...
Console c = new Console();
c.WriteLine("I can't be printed...");
```

but instead simply prefix the type name to the static WriteLine() member.

```
// Yes!  WriteLine() is static...
Console.WriteLine("Thanks...");
```

Simply put, static members are methods that are deemed (by the class designer) to be so commonplace that there is no need to create an instance of the type. When you are designing your custom class types, you are also able to define any number of static and/or instance level members. To illustrate custom static methods, assume I have reconfigured the Complain() and BeAgreeable() methods of the Teenager class as follows:

```
// Teenagers complain so often, there is no need to create an initial object...
public static string Complain()
{
    string[] messages = new string[5]{  "Do I have to?",
        "He started it!", "I'm too tired...",
        "I hate school!", "You are sooo wrong." } ;
    return messages[GetRandomNumber(5)];
}
public static string BeAgreeable()
{
    string[] messages = new string[3]{  "Sure!  No problem!",
        "Uh uh.", "I guess so." };
    return messages[GetRandomNumber(3)];
}
```

This update also assumes that the System.Random and GetRandomNumber() helper function method have also been declared as static members of the Teenager class, given the rule that static members can only operate on other static members:

```
class Teenager
{
    private static Random r = new Random();
    private static int GetRandomNumber(short upperLimit)
    { return r.Next(upperLimit); }
...
}
```

These assumptions aside, the process of calling a static method is simple. Just append the member to the name of the defining class:

```
// Call the static Complain method of the Teenager class.
public static void Main(string[] args)
{
    for(int i = 0; i < 40; i++)
        Console.WriteLine("-> {0}", Teenager.Complain());
}
```

Again, by contrast, nonstatic (instance) methods are scoped at the object level. Thus, if Complain() was *not* marked static, you would need to create an instance of the Teenager class before you could hear about the gripe of the day:

```
// Must make an instance of Teenager class to call instance methods.
Teenager joe = new Teenager();
joe.Complain();
```

SOURCE CODE   The StaticTeenager application is located under the Chapter 3 subdirectory.

Defining Static Data

In addition to static methods, a C# class may also define static data (such as the previous Random member variable from the Teenager example). Typically, a class defines a set of nonstatic state data. This simply means that each object instance maintains a private copy of the underlying values. Thus, if you have a class defined as follows:

```
// We all love Foo.
class Foo
{
    public int intFoo;
}
```

you can create any number of objects of type Foo and assign the intFoo field to a value to each instance:

```
// Each Foo reference maintains a copy of the intFoo field.
Foo f1 = new Foo();
f1.intFoo = 100;
Foo f2 = new Foo();
f2.intFoo = 993;
Foo f3 = new Foo();
f3.intFoo = 6;
```

Static data, on the other hand, is shared among all object instances of the same type. Rather than each object holding a copy of a given field, a point of static data is allocated exactly once for all instances of the type. Assume you have a class named Airplane that contains a single point of static data. In the constructor of the Airplane class you increment this data point. Here is the initial definition:

```
// Note the use of static keyword.
class Airplane
{
    // This static data member is shared by all Airplane objects.
    private static int NumberInTheAir = 0;
    public Airplane()
    {
        NumberInTheAir++;
    }
    // Get value from an object instance.
    public int GetNumberFromObject() {  return NumberInTheAir; }
    // Get value from class level.
    public static int GetNumber() {  returnNumberInTheAir; }
}
```

Notice that the Airplane class defines two methods. The static GetNumber() returns the current number of airplane objects that have been allocated by the application. GetNumberFromObject() also returns the value of the static NumberInTheAir integer, however given that this method has not been defined as static, the object user must call this method from an instance of Airplane. To illustrate, observe the following usage:

```
// Make some airplanes are examine the static members.
class StaticApp
{
    public static int Main(string[] args)
    {
        // Make some planes.
        Console.WriteLine("Created two Airplane types");
        Airplane a1 = new Airplane();
        Airplane a2 = new Airplane();
        // How many are in flight?
        Console.WriteLine("Number of planes: {0} ",
            a1.GetNumberFromObject());
        Console.WriteLine("Number of planes: {0} ",
            Airplane.GetNumber());
        // More planes!
        Console.WriteLine("\nCreated two more Airplane types");
        Airplane a3 = new Airplane();
        Airplane a4 = new Airplane();
        // Now how many?
        Console.WriteLine("Number of planes: {0} ",
            a3.GetNumberFromObject());
        Console.WriteLine("Number of planes: {0} ",
            Airplane.GetNumber());
        return 0;
    }
}
```

Figure 3-15 shows the output.

Figure 3-15. Static data is shared among like objects.

As you can see, all instances of the Airplane class are sharing (i.e., viewing) the same integer. If one object changes the value (using either static or instance level members) all types 'see' the change. That's the point of static data: To allow all objects to share a given value at the class (rather than at the object) level.

SOURCE CODE   The StaticData project is located under the Chapter 3 subdirectory.

Method Parameter Modifiers

Methods tend to take parameters. If you have a COM background, you are certainly familiar with the use of the [in], [out], and [in, out] IDL attributes. Classic COM objects use these attributes to clearly identify the direction of travel (and memory allocation rules) for a given interface method parameter. While IDL is not used in the .NET universe, there is analogous behavior with the set of C# parameter modifiers shown in Table 3-9.

Table 3-9. C# Parameter Modifiers

Parameter Modifier	Meaning in Life
(none)	If a parameter is not marked with a parameter modifier, it is assumed to be an input parameter passed by value. This is analogous to the IDL [in] attribute.
out	This is analogous to an IDL [out] parameter. Output parameters are assigned by the called member.
ref	Analogous to the IDL [in, out] attribute. The value is assigned by the caller, but may be reassigned within the scope of the method call.
params	This parameter modifier allows you to send in a variable number of parameters as a single parameter. A given method can only have a single params modifier, and must be the final parameter of the method.

The Default Parameter Passing Behavior

The default manner in which a parameter is sent into a function is *by value*. Simply put, if you do not mark an argument with a parameter-centric keyword, a copy of the data is passed into the function (the story changes slightly when passing reference types by value, as you will see in just a bit). You have already been making use of by-value parameter passing, however, here is a simple example (with implications):

```
// Default param passing is by value.
public static int Add(int x, int y)
{
    int ans = x + y;
    // Caller will not see these changes.
    x = 99999;
    y = 88888;
    return ans;
}
```

Here, the two value type parameters have been sent by value into the Add() method. Therefore, if we change the values of the parameters within the scope of the member, the caller is blissfully unaware, given that we are changing the values of copies of the caller's System.Int32 data types:

```
// Call Add() using input params.
Console.WriteLine("***** Adding 2 ints *****");
int x = 9, y = 10;
Console.WriteLine("X: {0}, Y: {1}", x, y);
Console.WriteLine("Answer is: {0}", Add(x, y));
Console.WriteLine("X: {0}, Y: {1}", x, y);
```

As you would expect, the values of *x* and *y* remain identical before and after the call to Add().

The C# "out" Keyword

Next, we have the use of output parameters. Here is an alternative version of the Add() method that returns the sum of two integers using the C# "out" keyword (note the physical return value of this method is now void):

```
    // Output parameters are allocated by the callee.
    public static void Add(int x, int y, out int ans)
    {
        ans = x + y;
    }
```

Calling a method with output parameters also requires the use of the "out" keyword. Recall that when you are local, output variables are not required to be assigned before use (if you do so, the value is forgotten after the call). For example:

```
// No need to assign before use when a variable is used ala out.
int ans;
// Note use of out keyword in calling syntax.
Add(90, 90, out ans);
Console.WriteLine("90 + 90 = {0} ", ans);
```

Now in this case, we really have no good reason to return the value of our summation using an output parameter. However, the C# "out" keyword does serve a very useful purpose: It allows the caller to obtain multiple return values from a single method invocation. For example, assume we have the following member:

```
// Returning multiple output parameters.
public static void FillTheseValues(out int a, out string b, out bool c)
{
    a = 9;
    b = "Enjoy your string...";
    c = true;
}
```

The caller would be able to invoke the following method:

```
// Method with multiple output params.
Console.WriteLine("Calling method with multiple output params");
int i;
string str;
bool b;
FillTheseValues(out i, out str, out b);
Console.WriteLine("Int is: {0}", i);
Console.WriteLine("String is: {0}", str);
Console.WriteLine("Boolean is: {0}", b);
```

The C# "ref" Keyword

Now consider the use of the C# ref parameter modifier. Reference parameters are necessary when you wish to allow a method to operate on (and usually change the values of) various data points declared in the caller's scope (such as a sort routine). Note the distinction between output and reference parameters:

- Output parameters do not need to be initialized before they are sent to the callee. Reason? It is assumed the method fills the value on your behalf.

- Reference parameters *must* be initialized before being sent to the callee. Reason? You are passing a reference to an existing type. If you don't assign it to an initial value, that would be the equivalent to operating on a NULL pointer!

Let's check out the use of the "ref" keyword:

```
// Reference parameter.
public static void UpperCaseThisString(ref string s)
{
    // Return the uppercase version of the string.
    s = s.ToUpper();
}
public static void Main()
{
    ...
    // Use 'ref'.
    string s = "Can you really have sonic hearing for $19.00?";
    Console.WriteLine("Before: {0} ", s);
    UpperCaseThisString(ref s);
    Console.WriteLine("After: {0} ", s);
}
```

Here, the caller has assigned an initial value to a local string named "s." Once the call to UpperCaseThisString() returns, the caller will find "s" has been converted into uppercase, given the use of the "ref" keyword.

The C# "params" Keyword

The final parameter modifier is the "params" keyword, which is somewhat odd (but convenient) given that it allows you to send a varied number of arguments *as a single parameter*. Yes, this can be confusing. To clear the air, assume I have written a simple method defined as follows:

```
// This method has two physical parameters.
public static void DisplayArrayOfInts(string msg, params int[] list)
{
    Console.WriteLine(msg);
    for ( int i = 0 ; i < list.Length ; i++ )
        Console.WriteLine(list[i]);
}
```

This method has been defined to take two physical parameters: one of type string, and one as a parameterized array of integers. What this method is in fact saying is, "Send me a string as the first parameter and *any number of integers as the second.*" Given this, you can call ArrayOfInts() in any of the following ways:

```
// Use 'params' keyword.
int[] intArray = new int[3] {10,11,12} ;
DisplayArrayOfInts ("Here is an array of ints", intArray);
DisplayArrayOfInts ("Enjoy these 3 ints", 1, 2, 3);
DisplayArrayOfInts ("Take some more!", 55, 4, 983, 10432, 98, 33);
```

Looking at the previous code, you can see that the bolded items in a given invocation correspond to the second parameter (the array of integers).

Of course, you do not have to make use of simple numeric value types when using the params keyword. Assume we have yet another variation of the Person class, now defined as follows:

```
// Yet another person class.
class Person
{
    private string fullName;
    private byte age;
    public Person(string n, byte a)
    {
        fullName = n;
        age = a;
    }
    public void PrintInfo()
    { Console.WriteLine("{0} is {1} years old", fullName, age); }
}
```

Now assume a new method that leverages the "params" keyword. This time however, you specify an array of objects, which boils down to any number of *anything*. With the method implementation, you can test for an incoming Person type using the C# "is" keyword. If your current item is of type Person, call the PrintInfo() method. If you do not have a Person type, just dump the textual information of the type to the console:

```
// This method takes any number of any type.
public static void DisplayArrayOfObjects(params object[] list)
{
    for ( int i = 0 ; i < list.Length ; i++ )
    {
        if(list[i] is Person)  // Is the current item a Person type?
        {
            ((Person)list[i]).PrintInfo();  // If so, call some methods.
        }
        else
            Console.WriteLine(list[i]);
    }
    Console.WriteLine();
}
```

The calling logic is as follows:

```
// Pass a System.Int32, Person and System.String into our method.
Person p = new Person("Fred", 93);
DisplayArrayOfObjects(777, p, "I really am an instance of System.String");
```

As you can see, C# allows you to work with parameters on many different levels. For the C++ programmers of the world, you should be able to map C# output and reference parameters to pointer (or C++ reference) primitives without the ugly * and & operators.

Passing Reference Types By Reference (and By Value)

A majority of the previous static methods illustrated how value types may be sent into a function by value (no parameter keyword) or by reference (the "ref" keyword). However, what if we had two additional methods that allow the user to send in Person types by reference as well as by value? First, consider the following methods:

```
public static void SendAPersonByValue(Person p)
{
    // Change some data of 'p'.
    p.age = 666;
    // This will be forgotten after the call!
    p = new Person("Nikki", 999);
}
public static void SendAPersonByReference(ref Person p)
{
    // Change some data of 'p'.
    p.age = 555;
    // 'p' is now pointing to a new object on the heap!
    p = new Person("Nikki", 999);
}
```

Notice how the SendAPersonByValue() method attempts to reassign the incoming Person reference to a new object. However, given that this method is making use of the default parameter passing behavior (pass by value), the object to which the incoming reference is pointing to is preserved. However, if you were to check the age of the person after the call, you might be shocked to see s/he is now 666 years old! How can this be? The golden rule to keep in mind when passing reference types by value is the following:

- If a reference type is passed by value, the callee may change the values of the object's state data, but may not change the object it is referencing.

Strange, huh? To clarify, here is some calling code:

```
// Passing ref-types by value.
Console.WriteLine("***** Passing person by value *****");
Person fred = new Person("Fred", 12);
Console.WriteLine("Before by value call, Person is:");
fred.PrintInfo();
SendAPersonByValue(fred);
Console.WriteLine("After by value call, Person is:");
fred.PrintInfo();
```

Figure 3-16 shows the output of this call.

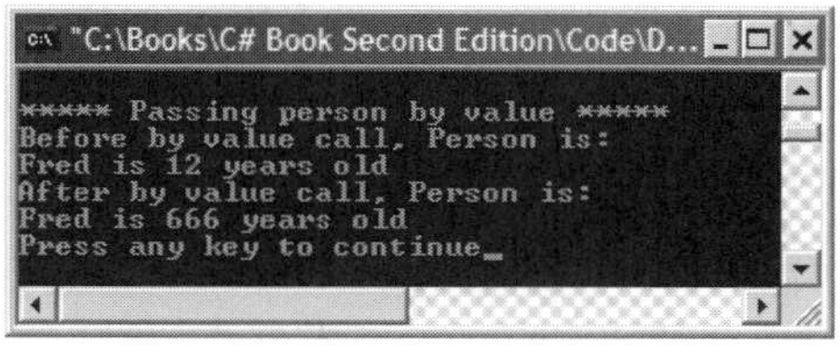

Figure 3-16. Passing reference types by value locks the reference in place.

This behavior seems to fly in the face of what it means to pass a parameter "by value." Given that we were able to change the state of the incoming Person, what was copied? The answer: a copy of the *reference* to the caller's object! Therefore, as the SendAPersonByValue() method is pointing to the same object as the caller, it is possible to alter the object's state data. What is *not* permissible is to reassign what the reference is pointing to (slightly akin to a constant pointer in C++).

In contrast, we have the SendAPersonByReference() method, which passes a reference type by reference. As you may expect, this allows complete flexibility of how the callee is able to manipulate the incoming parameter. Not only can the callee change the state of the object, but if it so chooses, it may reassign the pointer! Consider the following calling logic:

```
// Passing ref-types by ref.
Console.WriteLine("\n***** Passing person by reference *****");
Person mel = new Person("Mel", 23);
Console.WriteLine("Before by value call, Person is:");
mel.PrintInfo();
Console.WriteLine("After by ref call, Person is:");
SendAPersonByReference(ref mel);
Console.WriteLine("After by value call, Person is:");
mel.PrintInfo();
```

As you can see from Figure 3-17, the type named Fred returns after the call as a type named Nikki:

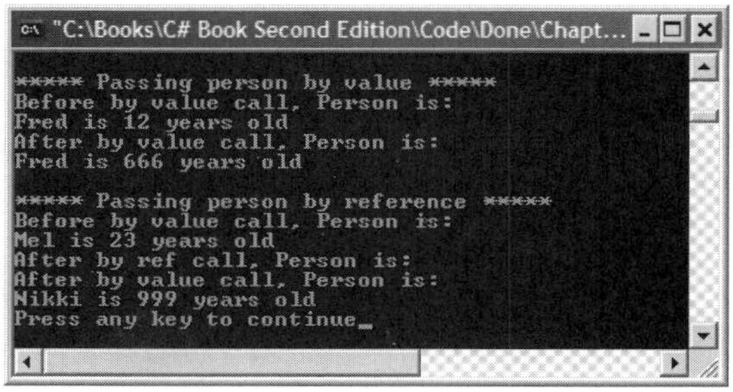

Figure 3-17. Passing reference types by reference allows the reference to be redirected.

The golden rule to keep in mind when passing reference types by reference is the following:

- If a class type is passed by reference, the callee may change the values of the object's state data *as well as the object it is referencing.*

That wraps up our examination of parameter passing behavior under C#. Next up: the role of System.Array.

 SOURCE CODE   The MethodsAndParams project is located under the Chapter 3 subdirectory.

Array Manipulation in C#

Mechanically, C# arrays look and feel much like their C, C++ counterparts. However, as you'll soon see, all C# arrays actually derive from the System.Array base class, and therefore share a common set of members (in the same vein as Java).

Formally speaking, an array is a collection of data points (of the same underlying type) that are accessed using a numerical index. Understand that CLS-compliant arrays always have a lower bound of zero (although it is possible to create a non-CLS compliant array with arbitrary lower bounds using the static CreateInstance() method of System.Array). As you might assume, arrays can contain any intrinsic type defined by C#, including arrays of objects, interfaces, or structures. In C#, arrays can be single or multidimensional, and must be declared with the square brackets ([]) placed *after* the data type of the array. For example:

```
// A string array containing 10 elements {0, 1, ..., 9}
string[] booksOnCOM;
booksOnCOM = new string[10];
// A 2 item string array, numbered {0, 1}
string[] booksOnPL1 = new string[2];
// 100 item string array, numbered {0, 1, ..., 99}
string[] booksOnDotNet = new string[100];
```

As you can see, the first example declares the type and size of the array on two separate lines. The final two examples illustrate that you are also able to declare and construct your array on a single line (just like any object). In either case, notice that you are required to make use of the "new" keyword when you are constructing an array of an initial fixed size. Thus, the following array declaration is illegal:

```
// Need 'new' keyword when you define a fixed size array.
int[4] ages = {30, 54, 4, 10} ;    // Error!
```

Understand that the previous three valid array declarations have simply allocated a type on the managed heap, which has some initial storage space. At this point, you have not literally filled with array with data. To do so, you would need to make use of the index operator as follows:

```
// A 2 item string array, numbered {0, 1}
string[] booksOnPL1 = new string[2];
booksOnPL1[0] = "PL1 for Dummies";
booksOnPL1[1] = "What have we done?! Essays on the PL1 programming language";
```

The same holds true if you create an array of custom objects:

```
// A 2 item Person array, numbered {0, 1}
Person[] theFolks = new Person[2];        // This creates the System.Array type.
theFolks[0] = new Person("Alex", 23);     // This creates a new Person in slot 0.
theFolks[1] = new Person("Liz", 32);      // This creates a new Person in slot 1.
```

Allocating and filling arrays using this longhand notation can become a bother, especially if the array in question contains numerous elements. Therefore, if you would rather let the compiler determine the size of the array, you are free to use the following shorthand notation:

```
// The size of this array will automatically be set to 4.
// Note the lack of the 'new' keyword and empty [].
int[] ages = {20, 22, 23, 0} ;
```

Again, the curly bracket notation ({}) is simply a time saver. Therefore, the following two arrays are identical:

```
// Initialize each member at declaration...
string[] firstNames = new string[5]{ "Steve", "Gina",
    "Swallow", "Baldy", "Gunner" } ;
```

```
// ...OR assign values member by member.
string[] firstNames = new string[5];
firstNames[0] = "Steve";
firstNames[1] = "Gina";
firstNames[2] = "Swallow";
firstNames[3] = "Baldy";
firstNames[4] = "Gunner";
```

Finally be aware that the members in a .NET array are automatically set to their respective default value. Thus, if you have an array of numerical types, each member is set to 0 (or 0.0 in the case of floating point numerics), arrays of objects begin life set to null, and Boolean types are set to false.

Arrays As Parameters (and Return Values)

Declaring and filling local arrays may be helpful from time to time. However, as you would hope, arrays can also be passed into and returned from custom functions. For example:

```
public static void PrintArray(int[] myInts)
{
    for(int i = 0; i < myInts.Length; i++)
        Console.WriteLine("Item {0} is {1}", i, myInts[i]);
}
public static string[] GetStringArray()
{
    string[] theStrings = {  "Hello", "from", "GetStringArray" };
    return theStrings;
}
```

Calling these static members is equally as straightforward:

```
int[] ages = {20, 22, 23, 0} ;
PrintArray(ages);
string[] strs = GetStringArray();
foreach(string s in strs)
    Console.WriteLine(s);
```

Working with Multidimensional Arrays

In addition to the single dimension arrays you have seen thus far, C# also supports two varieties of multidimensional arrays. The first of these is termed a *rectangular array*. This type is simply an array of multiple dimensions, where each row is of the same length. To declare and fill a multidimensional rectangular array, proceed as follows:

```
// A rectangular MD array.
int[,] myMatrix;
myMatrix = new int[6,6];
// Populate (6 * 6) array.
for(int i = 0; i < 6; i++)
    for(int j = 0; j < 6; j++)
        myMatrix[i, j] = i * j;
// Show (6 * 6) array.
for(int i = 0; i < 6; i++)
{
    for(int j = 0; j < 6; j++)
    { Console.Write(myMatrix[i, j] + "\t"); }
    Console.WriteLine();
}
```

The output is seen in Figure 3-18 (note the rectangular nature of the array).

```
***** A rectangular MD array *****
0       0       0       0       0       0
0       1       2       3       4       5
0       2       4       6       8       10
0       3       6       9       12      15
0       4       8       12      16      20
0       5       10      15      20      25
Press any key to continue_
```

Figure 3-18. A multidimensional array

The second type of multidimensional array is termed a *jagged* array. As the name implies, jagged arrays contain some number of inner arrays, each of which may have a unique upper limit. For example:

```csharp
// A jagged MD array (i.e., an array of arrays).
// Here we have an array of 5 different arrays.
    int[][] myJagArray = new int[5][];
// Create the jagged array.
for (int i = 0; i < myJagArray.Length; i++)
{
    myJagArray[i] = new int[i + 7];
}
// Print each row (remember, each element is defaulted to zero!)
for(int i = 0; i < 5; i++)
{
    Console.Write("Length of row {0}  is {1} :\t", i, myJagArray[i].Length);
    for(int j = 0; j < myJagArray[i].Length; j++)
    {
        Console.Write(myJagArray[i][j] + " ");
    }
    Console.WriteLine();
}
```

The output is seen in Figure 3-19 (note the jaggedness of the array).

```
***** A jagged MD array *****
Length of row 0 is 7:    0 0 0 0 0 0 0
Length of row 1 is 8:    0 0 0 0 0 0 0 0
Length of row 2 is 9:    0 0 0 0 0 0 0 0 0
Length of row 3 is 10:   0 0 0 0 0 0 0 0 0 0
Length of row 4 is 11:   0 0 0 0 0 0 0 0 0 0 0
Press any key to continue_
```

Figure 3-19. Jagged arrays

Now that you understand how to build and populate C# arrays, you can turn your attention to the ultimate base class of any array, System.Array.

The System.Array Base Class

The most striking difference between C and C++ arrays is the fact that every array you create is automatically derived from System.Array. This class defines a number of helpful methods that make working with arrays much more palatable. Table 3-10 gives a rundown of some (but not all) of the more interesting members.

Table 3-10. Select Members of System.Array

Member of Array Class	Meaning in Life
BinarySearch()	This static method is applicable only if the items in the (previously sorted) array implement the IComparer interface (see Chapter 6). If so, BinarySearch() finds a given item.
Clear()	This static method sets a range of elements in the array to empty values (0 for value items, null for object references).
CopyTo()	Used to copy elements from the source array into the destination array.
GetEnumerator()	Returns the IEnumerator interface for a given array. I address interfaces in Chapter 5, but for the time being, keep in mind that this interface is required by the "foreach" keyword.
GetLength() Length	The GetLength() method is used to determine the number of elements in a given dimension of the array. Length is a read-only property.
GetLowerBound() GetUpperBound()	As you can guess, these two methods can be used to determine the bounds of a given dimension.
GetValue() SetValue()	Retrieves or sets the value for a given index in the array. These methods have been overloaded to work with single and multidimensional arrays.
Reverse()	This static method reverses the contents of a one-dimensional array.
Sort()	Sorts a one-dimensional array of intrinsic types. If the elements in the array implement the IComparer interface, you can also sort your custom types (again, see Chapter 5).

Let's see some of these members in action. The following code makes use of the static Reverse() and Clear() methods (and the Length property) to pump out some information about the firstName string array to the console:

```
// Create some string arrays and exercise some System.Array members.
class Arrays
{
    public static int Main(string[] args)
    {
        // Array of strings.
        string[] firstNames = new string[5]{  "Steve", "Gina", "Swallow",
            "Baldy", "Gunner" } ;
        // Print out names in declared order.
        Console.WriteLine("Here is the array:");
        for(int i = 0; i < firstNames.Length; i++)
            Console.Write(firstNames[i] + "\t");
        // Flip things around using the static Reverse() method...
        Array.Reverse(firstNames);
        // ... and print them.
        Console.WriteLine("Here is the array once reversed:");
        for(int i = 0; i < firstNames.Length; i++)
            Console.Write(firstNames[i] + "\t");
        // Clear out all but young gunner.
        Console.WriteLine("Cleared out all but young Gunner...");
        Array.Clear(firstNames, 1, 4);
        for(int i = 0; i < firstNames.Length; i++)
            Console.Write(firstNames[i] + "\t\n");
        return 0;
    }
}
```

The complete output of our array example can be seen in Figure 3-20.

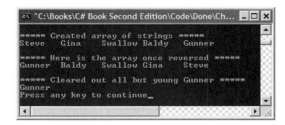

Figure 3-20. Fun with System.Array

 SOURCE CODE   The Arrays application is located under the Chapter 3 subdirectory.

String Manipulation in C#

As you have already seen, string is a keyword type in C#. However, like all intrinsic types, string actually aliases a type in the .NET library, which in this case is a class named System.String. System.String provides a number of methods you would expect from such a utility class, including methods that return the length, find substrings, convert to and from uppercase/lowercase, and so forth. Table 3-11 lists some (but by no means all) of the interesting members.

Table 3-11. Select Members of System.String

Member of String Class	Meaning in Life
Length	This property returns the length of the current string.
Concat()	This static method of the String class returns a new string that is composed of two discrete strings.
CompareTo()	Compares two strings.
Copy()	This static method returns a fresh new copy of an existing string.
Format()	Used to format a string using other primitives (i.e., numerical data, other strings) and the {0} notation examined earlier in this chapter.
Insert()	Used to insert a string within a given string.
PadLeft() PadRight()	These methods are used to pad a string with some character.
Remove() Replace()	Use these methods to receive a copy of a string, with modifications (characters removed or replaced).
ToUpper() ToLower()	Creates a copy of a given sting in uppercase or lowercase.

You should be aware of a few aspects of C# string manipulation. First, although string is a reference type, the equality operators (== and !=) are defined to compare the *values* of string objects, not the memory to which they refer. On a related note, understand that the addition operator (+) has been overloaded as a shorthand alternative to calling Concat():

```
// == and != are used to compare the values within strings.
// + is used for concatenation.
public static int Main(string[] args)
{
    // Alternative ways to declare a string.
    System.String strObj = "This is a TEST";
    string s = "This is another TEST";
    // Test for equality between the stings.
```

```
    if(s == strObj)
        Console.WriteLine("Same info...");
    else
        Console.WriteLine("Not the same info...");
    // Concatenation.
    string newString = s + strObj;
    Console.WriteLine("s + strObj = {0} ", newString);
    // System.String also defines a custom indexer to access each
    // character in the string.
    for(int k = 0; k < s.Length; k++)
        Console.WriteLine("Char {0}  is {1} ", k, s[k]);
    return 0;
}
```

When you run this program, you are able to verify that the two string objects (s and strObj) do not contain the same values, and therefore, the test for equality fails. When you examine the contents of newString, you will see it is indeed "This is another TESTThis is a TEST." Finally, notice that you can access the individual characters of a string using the index operator ([]).

Escape Characters and "Verbatim Strings"

Like C(++) and Java, C# strings can contain any number of escape characters:

```
// Escape characters (\t, \\ , \n, et al.)
string anotherString;
anotherString = "Every programming book needs \"Hello World\"";
Console.WriteLine("\t" + anotherString);
anotherString = "c:\\ CSharpProjects\\ Strings\\ string.cs";
Console.WriteLine("\t" + anotherString);
```

In case you are a bit rusty with the meaning behind these escape characters, Table 3-12 should refresh your memory.

Table 3-12. String Escape Characters

String Escape Character	Meaning in Life
\'	Inserts a single quote into a string literal.
\"	Inserts a double quote into a string literal.
\\	Inserts a backslash into a string literal. This can be quite helpful when defining file paths.
\a	Triggers a system alert.
\b	Triggers a backspace.
\f	Triggers a form feed.

Table 3-12. String Escape Characters (Continued)

String Escape Character	Meaning in Life
\n	Inserts a new line.
\r	Inserts a carriage return.
\t	Inserts a horizontal tab into the string literal.
\u	Inserts a Unicode character into the string literal.
\v	Inserts a vertical tab into the string literal.
\0	Represents a NULL character.

In addition to traditional escape characters, C# introduces the @-quoted string literal notation (termed a *verbatim string*). Using verbatim strings, you are able to bypass the use of cryptic escape characters and define your literals as follows:

```
// The following string is printed verbatim (e.g., all \markers are displayed!).
string finalString = @"\n\tString file: 'C:\CSharpProjects\Strings\string.cs'";
Console.WriteLine(finalString);
```

The output has been prefixed with "\n\t", as these escape characters are not processed in @-quoted strings. Also note that verbatim strings can be used to ignore white space that flows over multiple lines. Assume you have a mighty long string literal that would require the reader to scroll right for a rather long time. If you were to make use of @-prefixed strings, you would be able to author the following (more readable) code:

```
// White Space is preserved!
string myLongString = @"Stuff Stuff Stuff Stuff Stuff
    Stuff Stuff Stuff Stuff Stuff Stuff Stuff
    Stuff Stuff Stuff Stuff Stuff";
Console.WriteLine(myLongString);
```

Using System.Text.StringBuilder

One thing to be very aware of with regard to C# strings: The value of a string cannot be modified once established. Like Java, C# strings are immutable. In fact, if you examine the methods of System.String, you notice that the methods that *seem* to internally modify a string, in fact return a modified *copy* of the string. For example, when you send the ToUpper() message to a string object, you are not modifying the underlying buffer of the existing string object, but are returned a fresh copy of the buffer in uppercase form:

```
// Make changes to this string? Not really...
System.String strFixed = "This is how I began life";
Console.WriteLine(strFixed);
// Returns an uppercase copy of strFixed.
string upperVersion = strFixed.ToUpper();
Console.WriteLine(strFixed);
Console.WriteLine(upperVersion);
```

It can become slightly annoying (and inefficient) to work with copies of copies of strings. To help ease the pain, the System.Text namespace defines a class named StringBuilder. This class operates much more like an MFC CString or ATL CComBSTR, in that any modifications you make to the StringBuilder instance affect the underlying buffer (and are thus more efficient):

```
using System;
using System.Text;      // Recall, StringBuilder lives here!
class StringApp
{
    public static int Main(string[] args)
    {
        // Create a StringBuilder and change the underlying buffer.
        StringBuilder myBuffer = new StringBuilder("I am a buffer");
        myBuffer.Append(" that just got longer...");
        Console.WriteLine(myBuffer);
        return 0;
    }
}
```

Beyond appending to your internal buffer, the StringBuilder class allows you to replace and remove characters at will. Once you have established the state of your buffer, call ToString() to store the final result into a System.String data type:

```
using System;
using System.Text;
class StringApp
{
    public static int Main(string[] args)
    {
        StringBuilder myBuffer = new StringBuilder("I am a buffer");
        myBuffer.Append(" that just got longer...");
        Console.WriteLine(myBuffer);
        myBuffer.Append("and even longer.");
        Console.WriteLine(myBuffer);
        // Transfer the buffer to an uppercase fixed string.
        string theReallyFinalString = myBuffer.ToString().ToUpper();
        Console.WriteLine(theReallyFinalString);
        return 0;
    }
}
```

Now, do understand that in many cases, System.String will be your textual object of choice. For most applications, the overhead associated with returning modified copies of character data will be negligible. However, if you are building a text-intensive application (such as a word processor application) you will most likely find that using System.Text.StringBuilder will improve performance. As you might assume, StringBuilder contains additional methods and properties beyond those examined here. I leave it to you to drill into more specifics at your leisure.

 SOURCE CODE   The Strings project is located under the Chapter 3 subdirectory.

C# Enumerations

Often it is convenient to create a set of symbolic names for underlying numerical values. For example, if you are creating an employee payroll system, you may wish to use the constants VP, Manager, Grunt, and Contractor rather than raw numerical values such as {0, 1, 2, 3}. Like C(++), C# supports the notion of custom enumerations for this very reason. For example, here is the EmpType enumeration:

```
// A custom enumeration.
enum EmpType
{
    Manager,       //  = 0
    Grunt,         //  = 1
    Contractor,  //  = 2
    VP             //  = 3
}
```

The EmpType enumeration defines four named constants, corresponding to discrete numerical values. In C#, the numbering scheme sets the first element to zero (0) by default, followed by an n+1 progression. You are free to change this behavior as you see fit, thus:

```
// Begin number at 102.
enum EmpType
{
    Manager = 102,
    Grunt,         //  = 103
    Contractor,  //  = 104
    VP             //  = 105
}
```

Enumerations do not necessarily need to follow a sequential ordering. If (for some reason) it made good sense to establish your EmpType as seen next, the compiler continues to be happy:

```
// Elements of an enumeration need not be sequential!
enum EmpType
{
    Manager = 10,
    Grunt = 1,
    Contractor = 100,
    VP = 9
}
```

Under the hood, the storage type used for each item in an enumeration automatically maps to a System.Int32 by default. You are also free to change this to your liking. For example, if you want to set the underlying storage value of EmpType to be a byte rather than an int, you would write the following:

```
// This time, EmpType maps to an underlying byte.
enum EmpType : byte
{
    Manager = 10,
    Grunt = 1,
    Contractor = 100,
    VP = 9
}
```

NOTE   C# enumerations can be defined in a similar manner for any of the core numerical types (byte, sbyte, short, ushort, int, uint, long, or ulong).

Once you have established the range and storage type of your enumeration, you can use them in place of so-called "magic numbers." Assume you have a class defining a static public function, taking EmpType as the sole parameter:

```
using System;
class EnumClass
{
    public static void AskForBonus(EmpType e)
    {
        switch(e)
        {
        case EmpType.Contractor:
            Console.WriteLine("You already get enough cash...");
        break;
        case EmpType.Grunt:
            Console.WriteLine("You have got to be kidding...");
        break;
        case EmpType.Manager:
            Console.WriteLine("How about stock options instead?");
        break;
```

```
        case EmpType.VP:
            Console.WriteLine("VERY GOOD, Sir!");
        break;
        default: break;
        }
    }
    public static int Main(string[] args)
    {
        // Make a contractor type.
        EmpType fred;
        fred = EmpType.Contractor;
        AskForBonus(fred);
        return 0;
    }
}
```

The System.Enum Base Class

The interesting thing about C# enumerations is that they implicitly derive from System.Enum. This base class defines a number of methods that allow you to interrogate and transform a given enumeration. Table 3-13 documents some items of interest, all of which are static.

Table 3-13. Select static Members of System.Enum

Member of System.Enum	Meaning in Life
Format()	This method converts a value of a specified enumerated type to its equivalent string representation according to the specified format.
GetName() GetNames()	Retrieves the name (or array of names) for the constant in the specified enumeration that has the specified value.
GetUnderlyingType()	Returns the underlying type of the specified enumeration.
GetValues()	Retrieves an array of the values of the constants in a specified enumeration.
IsDefined()	Returns an indication whether a constant with a specified value exists in a specified enumeration.
Parse()	Converts the string representation of the name or numeric value of one or more enumerated constants to an equivalent enumerated object.

First, System.Enum defines a static method named GetUnderlyingType(), which resolves (pardon the redundancy) the underlying data type used to represent a given enumeration:

```
// Get underlying type (System.Byte for the current example).
Console.WriteLine(Enum.GetUnderlyingType(typeof(EmpType)));
```

Of greater interest is the ability to extract the named constant behind the numerical values. How many times have you had to perform transformational logic between a C++ enumeration and the underlying string value? Using the inherited ToString() method, the dirty work as been done on your behalf:

```
// Print out string version of 'fred'.
Console.WriteLine(fred.ToString());
```

If you require a more exotic format of your enumerations, you can make use of the static Enum.Format() method. For example, using the EmpType variable, you may extract the corresponding string, by specifying "G" as a parameter to Enum.Format(). You may also specify the hexadecimal value (x) or decimal value (d) of the underlying enum. System.Enum also defines a static method named GetValues(). This method returns an instance of System.Array, with each item in the array corresponding to a member of the specified enumeration. To illustrate these points, ponder the following:

```
// Get all statistics for the EmpType enumeration.
Array obj = Enum.GetValues(typeof(EmpType));
Console.WriteLine("This enum has {0}  members.", obj.Length);
// Now show the string name and associated value.
foreach(EmpType e in obj)
{
    Console.Write("String name: {0},", e.ToString());
    Console.Write(" int: ({0}),", Enum.Format(typeof(EmpType), e, "D"));
    Console.Write(" hex: ({0})\n", Enum.Format(typeof(EmpType), e, "X"));
}
```

As you can guess, this code block prints out the name/value pairs (in decimal and hexadecimal) for the EmpType enumeration.

Next, let's explore the IsDefined property. This allows you to determine if a given string name is a member of the current enumeration. For example, assume you wish to know if the value "SalesPerson" is part of the EmpType enumeration:

```
// Does EmpType have a SalePerson value?
if(Enum.IsDefined(typeof(EmpType), "SalesPerson"))
    Console.WriteLine("Yep, we have sales people.");
else
    Console.WriteLine("No, we have no profits...");
```

It is also possible to generate an enumeration from a string literal via the static Enum.Parse() method. Given that Parse() returns a generic System.Object, you will need to cast the return value into the correct enum type (more on casting in the next chapter):

```
// Prints: "Sally is a Manager"
EmpType sally = (EmpType)Enum.Parse(typeof(EmpType), "Manager");
Console.WriteLine("Sally is a {0}", sally.ToString());
```

As you might guess, this could be extremely helpful when you are prompting for user input, and wish to translate the textual data into an enumeration type for use in the program.

Last but not least, it is worth pointing out that C# enumerations support the use of various overloaded operators, which test against the assigned values. For example:

```
// Which of these two EmpType variables has the greatest numerical value?
EmpType Joe = EmpType.VP;
EmpType Fran = EmpType.Grunt;
if(Joe < Fran)
    Console.WriteLine("Joe's value is less than Fran's");
else
    Console.WriteLine("Fran's value is less than Joe's");
```

SOURCE CODE   The EnumExample project is located under the Chapter 3 subdirectory.

Defining Structures in C#

While you have already encountered structures earlier in this chapter, they do deserve a second look. Structures in general are a way to achieve the bare bones benefits of object orientation (i.e., encapsulation) while having the efficiency of stack-allocated data. Beyond this key point, C# structures behave very much like a custom class.

NOTE   Over the course of this chapter you may have noticed that I have defined all structures in capital letters. This is in no way a requirement, but is simply an old C style naming convention I can't seem to get rid of. As you explore the .NET base class libraries, you will *not* find structures defined in all caps.

As mentioned, structures can take constructors (provided they have arguments), can implement interfaces, and can contain numerous members. Furthermore, recall that C# structures do not have an identically named alias in the .NET library (that is, there is no System.Structure class), but are implicitly derived from System.ValueType to retrofit the virtual members of System.Object to work with value-based semantics. Here is a simple example:

```
// Our existing enumeration.
enum EmpType : byte
{
    Manager = 10, Grunt = 1,
    Contractor = 100, VP = 9
}
struct EMPLOYEE
{
    public EmpType title;   // One of the fields is our custom enum.
    public string name;
    public short deptID;
}
class StructTester
{
    public static int Main(string[] args)
    {
        // Create and format Fred.
        EMPLOYEE fred;
        fred.deptID = 40;
        fred.name = "Fred";
        fred.title = EmpType.Grunt;
        return 0;
    }
}
```

Here, you created an EMPLOYEE structure on the stack and manipulated each field using the dot operator. To be sure, if you do not denote a custom constructor, you are required to assign values to each field before making use of your stack-based variable.

To provide a more optimized construction of this type, you are free to define additional custom constructors. Recall that you *cannot* redefine the default constructor for a C# structure, as this is a reserved member. Given this fact, any custom constructors must take some number of parameters:

```
// Structs may define custom constructors (if they have args).
struct EMPLOYEE
{
    // Fields.
    public EmpType title;
    public string name;
    public short deptID;
    // Constructor.
    public EMPLOYEE(EmpType et, string n, short d)
    {
        title = et;
        name = n;
        deptID = d;
    }
}
```

With this, you can create a new employee as follows:

```
class StructTester
{
    public static int Main(string[] args)
    {
        // Must use 'new' to trigger a custom constructor.
        EMPLOYEE mary = new EMPLOYEE(EmpType.VP, "Mary", 10);
        ...
    }
}
```

NOTE Remember! The "new" keyword is only used for consistency between value-based and reference-based types. When you "new" a structure, you are still creating a stack-based entity.

Structures can, of course, be used as parameters to any member function. For example, assume the StructTester class defines a method named DisplayEmpStats():

```
// Extract interesting information from an EMPLOYEE structure.
public static void DisplayEmpStats(EMPLOYEE e)
{
    Console.WriteLine("Here is {0}\'s info:", e.name);
    Console.WriteLine("Department ID: {0} ", e.deptID);
    Console.WriteLine("Title: {0} ", e.title);
}
```

Here is a test run of using DisplayEmpStats():

```
// Let Mary & Fred strut their stuff.
public static int Main(string[] args)
{
    ...
    DisplayEmpStats(mary);
    DisplayEmpStats(fred);
    return 0;
}
```

(Un)boxing Custom Structures

As mentioned earlier in this chapter, boxing and unboxing provide a convenient way to flip between value types and reference types. As you recall, to convert a structure variable into an object reference, simply box the value:

```
// Create and box a new employee.
EMPLOYEE stan = new EMPLOYEE(EmpType.Grunt, "Stan", 10);
object stanInBox = stan;
```

Because stanInBox is a reference-based data type (which still holds the internal values of the original EMPLOYEE data type) you can unbox the reference as needed to gain access to the members of the EMPLOYEE structure:

```
// Because we have boxed our value data type into a structure,
// we can unbox and manipulate the contents.
public static void UnboxThisEmployee(object o)
{
    EMPLOYEE temp = (EMPLOYEE)o;
    Console.WriteLine(temp.name + " is alive!");
}
```

Here is the calling logic and output:

```
// Send boxed employee in for processing.
UnboxThisEmployee(stanInBox);
```

Recall that the C# compiler automatically box values where appropriate. Therefore, it would be permissible to directly pass stan (the EMPLOYEE type) into UnboxThisEmployee() directly:

```
// Stan is boxed automatically.
UnboxThisEmployee(stan);
```

However, because you have defined UnboxThisEmployee() to take an object parameter, you have no choice but to unbox this reference to access the fields of the EMPLOYEE structure.

 SOURCE CODE   The Structures project is located under the Chapter 3 subdirectory.

Defining Custom Namespaces

To this point, you have been building small test programs leveraging existing namespaces in the .NET universe (System in particular). When you build real-life applications, it can be very helpful to group your related types into custom namespaces. In C#, this is accomplished using the "namespace" keyword.

Assume you are developing a collection of geometric classes named Square, Circle, and Hexagon. Given their similarities, you would like to group them all together into a shared custom namespace. You have two basic approaches. First, you may choose to define each class within a single file (shapeslib.cs) as follows:

```
// shapeslib.cs
using System;
namespace MyShapes
{
    // Circle class.
    public class Circle{  // Interesting methods... }
    // Hexagon class.
    public class Hexagon{ // More interesting methods... }
    // Square class.
    public class Square{  // Even more interesting methods... }
}
```

Notice how the MyShapes namespace acts as the conceptual "container" of each type. Alternatively, you can split a single namespace into multiple C# files. To do so, simply wrap the given class definitions in the same namespace:

```
// circle.cs
using System;
namespace MyShapes
{
    // Circle class.
    class Circle{  // Interesting methods... }
}
```

```
// hexagon.cs
using System;
namespace MyShapes
{
    // Hexagon class.
    class Hexagon{  // More interesting methods... }
}
```

```
// square.cs
using System;
namespace MyShapes
{
    // Square class.
    class Square{  // Even more interesting methods... }
}
```

As you already know, when another application you are building wishes to use these fine objects from within its namespace, simply use the "using" keyword:

```
// Make use of objects defined in another namespace
using System;
using MyShapes;
namespace MyApp
{
    class ShapeTester
    {
```

```
        public static void Main()
        {
            // All defined in the MyShapes namespace.
            Hexagon h = new Hexagon();
            Circle c = new Circle();
            Square s = new Square();
        }
    }
}
```

Resolving Name Clashes Across Namespaces

A namespace can also be used to avoid nasty name clashes across multiple namespaces.
Assume the ShapeTester class wishes to make use of a new namespace termed
My3DShapes, which defines three additional classes capable of rendering a shape in
stunning 3D:

```
// Another shapes namespace...
using System;
namespace My3DShapes
{
    // 3D Circle class.
    class Circle{ }
    // 3D Hexagon class
    class Hexagon{ }
    // 3D Square class
    class Square{ }
}
```

If you update ShapeTester as was done here, you are issued a number of compile-
time errors, because both namespaces define identically named types:

```
// Ambiguities abound!
using System;
using MyShapes;
using My3DShapes;
namespace MyApp
{
    class ShapeTester
    {
        public static void Main()
        {
            // Which namespace do I reference?
            Hexagon h = new Hexagon();      // Compiler error!
            Circle c = new Circle();        // Compiler error!
            Square s = new Square();        // Compiler error!
        }
    }
}
```

As one would hope, these errors are caught at compile time. Resolving the ambiguity is simply a matter of using "fully qualified names:"

```
// We have now resolved the ambiguity.
public static void Main()
{
    My3DShapes.Hexagon h = new My3DShapes.Hexagon();
    My3DShapes.Circle c = new My3DShapes.Circle();
    MyShapes.Square s = new MyShapes.Square();
}
```

Defining Namespace Aliases

An alternative approach to resolving namespace ambiguity is accomplished through the use of aliases. For example:

```
using System;
using MyShapes;
using My3DShapes;
// Make an alias to a class defined in another namespace.
using The3DHexagon = My3DShapes.Hexagon;
namespace MyApp
{
    class ShapeTester
    {
        public static void Main()
        {
            My3DShapes.Hexagon h = new My3DShapes.Hexagon();
            My3DShapes.Circle c = new My3DShapes.Circle();
            MyShapes.Square s = new MyShapes.Square();
            // Create a 3D hex using a defined alias:
            The3DHexagon h2 = new The3DHexagon();
        }
    }
}
```

Nested Namespaces

When organizing your types, you are free to nest namespaces within other namespaces. The .NET base class libraries do so in numerous places to provide an even deeper level of type organization. For example, if you wish to create a higher-level namespace that contains the existing My3DShapes namespace, you can update your code as follows:

```
// The Chapter3Types.My3DShapes namespace contains 3 classes.
using System;
namespace Chapter3Types
{
    namespace My3DShapes
    {
        // 3D Circle class.
        class Circle{ }
        // 3D Hexagon class
        class Hexagon{ }
        // 3D Square class
        class Square{ }
    }
}
```

Do note that you are also able to define a nested namespace using the following shorthand (which as you may guess, helps decrease the use of the moving horizontal scrollbar within the VS .NET code window):

```
// The Chapter3Types.My3DShapes namespace contains 3 classes.
using System;
namespace Chapter3Types.My3DShapes
{
    // 3D Circle class.
    class Circle{ }
    // 3D Hexagon class
    class Hexagon{ }
    // 3D Square class
    class Square{ }
}
```

The "Default Namespace" of VS .NET IDE

On a final namespace-related note, it is worth pointing out that by default, when you create a new C# project using VS .NET, the name of the topmost namespace in your application will be identical to that of the name you gave your initial project. As you have seen, as you insert new types into your project using the various IDE Wizards, they will automatically be wrapped within this default namespace. If you wish to change the name of this default namespace after the fact, simply access the Default Namespace option of the project's Properties dialog (Figure 3-21).

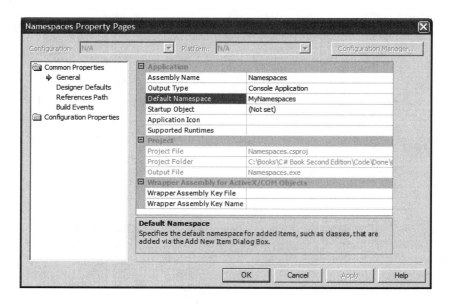

Figure 3-21. Configuring the default namespace

With this update, any new item inserted into the project will be wrapped within the Intertech.MyNamespaces namespace (and obviously, if another namespace wishes to use these types, the correct using directive must be applied).

SOURCE CODE   The Namespaces project is located under the Chapter 3 subdirectory.

Summary

This (very, very lengthy) chapter has exposed you to the numerous core aspects of the C# programming language. The focus was to examine the constructs that will be commonplace in any application you may be interested in building. First, every C# program must have a class defining a static Main() method, which serves as the program's entry point. Within the scope of Main(), you typically create any number of objects, which work together to breathe life into your application.

As you have seen, all intrinsic C# data types alias a corresponding type in the System namespace. Each system type has a number of members that provide a programmatic manner to obtain the range of the type. Furthermore, you have learned the basic process of building C# class types, and examined the various parameter passing conventions, value types and reference types, and the role of the mighty System.Object.

You also examined various aspects of the CLR that place an OO spin on common programming constructs, such as arrays, strings, structures, and enumerations. This chapter also illustrated the concept of boxing and unboxing. This simple mechanism allows you to easily move between value-based and reference-based data types. Finally, the chapter wrapped up by explaining how to build your own custom namespaces, and why you might want to do so.

So at this point, feel free to take a break and relax. When you are ready to pound out some further code, turn to Chapter 4 and see how C# contends with the mighty pillars of OOP.

Object-Oriented Programming with C#

IN THE PREVIOUS CHAPTER, you were introduced to a number of core constructs of the C# language and the .NET platform in general. Here, you will spend your time digging deeper into the details of object-based development. I begin by reviewing the famed "pillars of OOP" from a high level, and then examine exactly how C# contends with the notions of encapsulation, inheritance, and polymorphism. This will equip you with the knowledge you need in order to build custom class hierarchies using C#.

During this process, you examine some new constructs such as establishing type (rather than member) level visibility, building type properties, versioning type members, and designing "sealed" classes. Do be aware that the information presented here will serve as the foundation for more advanced class design techniques (such as over-loaded operators, events, and custom conversion routines) seen in later chapters.

By way of a friendly invitation, even if you are currently comfortable with the constructs of object-oriented programming, I would encourage you to pound out the code examples found within this chapter. As you will see, C# does place a new spin on many common OO techniques.

Formal Definition of the C# Class

If you have been "doing objects" in another programming language, you are no doubt aware of the role of class definitions. Formally, a class is nothing more than a custom user defined type (UDT) that is composed of data (sometimes termed *attributes*) and functions that act on this data (often called *methods* in OO speak). The power of object-based languages is that by grouping data and functionality in a single UDT, you are able to model your software types after real-world entities.

For example, assume you are interested in modeling a generic employee. At minimum, you may wish to build a class that maintains the name, current pay, and employee ID for each worker. In addition, the Employee class defines one method named GiveBonus(), which increases an individual's current pay by some amount, and another named DisplayStats(), which prints out the relevant statistics for this individual (Figure 4-1).

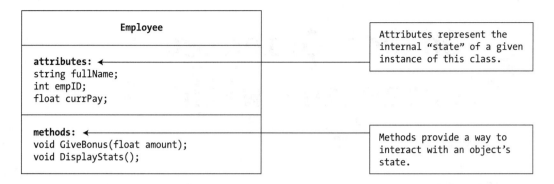

Figure 4-1. A simple class definition

As you recall from Chapter 3, C# classes can define any number of *constructors*. These special class methods provide a simple way for an object user to create an instance of a given class with an initial look and feel. As you know, every C# class is endowed with a freebie default constructor. The role of the default constructor is to ensure that all state data is set to an initial safe value. In addition to the default constructor, you are also free to define as many custom constructors as you feel are necessary. To get the ball rolling, here is our first crack at the Employee class:

```
// The initial Employee class definition.
class Employee
{
    // Private state data.
    private string fullName;
    private int empID;
    private float currPay;
    // Constructors.
    public Employee(){ }
    public Employee(string fullName, int empID, float currPay)
    {
        this.fullName = fullName;
        this.empID = empID;
        this.currPay = currPay;
    }
    // Bump the pay for this employee.
    public void GiveBonus(float amount)
    {  currPay += amount; }
    // Show current state of this object.
    public virtual void DisplayStats()
    {
        Console.WriteLine("Name: {0} ", fullName);
        Console.WriteLine("Pay: {0} ", currPay);
        Console.WriteLine("ID: {0} ", empID);
    }
}   // See note that follows!
```

NOTE   Unlike C++, C# class definitions do not end with a terminating semicolon (however, if you do add such a token, your *.cs file will still compile).

Notice the empty implementation of the default constructor for the Employee class:

```
class Employee
{
    // Remember! All member variables assigned to default values automatically.
    public Employee(){ }
...
}
```

Like C++ and Java, if you choose to include custom constructors in a class definition, the default constructor is *silently removed*. Therefore, if you wish to allow the object user to create an instance of your class as follows:

```
// Calls the default constructor.
Employee e = new Employee();
```

you must explicitly redefine the default constructor for your class. If you forget to do so, you will receive compile time errors. This point aside, triggering the logic behind a constructor is self-explanatory:

```
// Call some custom ctors (two approaches).
public static void Main()
{
    Employee e = new Employee("Joe", 80, 30000);
    e.GiveBonus(200);
    Employee e2;
    e2 = new Employee("Beth", 81, 50000);
    e2.GiveBonus(1000);
    e2.DisplayStats();
}
```

SOURCE CODE   The complete Employees example that we examine over the course of this chapter is included under the Chapter 4 subdirectory.

Understanding Method Overloading

Like other object-oriented languages, C# allows a type to "overload" various members. Simply put, when a class has a set of identically named members that differ by the number (or type) of parameters, the member in question is said to be *overloaded*. In the Employee class, you have overloaded the class constructor, given that you have provided two definitions that differ only by the parameter set:

```
class Employee
{
    public Employee(){ }
    public Employee(string fullName, int empID, float currPay){...}
...
}
```

Constructors, however, are not the only members that may be overloaded for a type. Assume you have a class named Triangle that supports an overloaded Draw() method. By doing so, you allow the object user to render the image using various input parameters:

```
class Triangle
{
    // The overloaded Draw() method.
    public void Draw(int x, int y, int height, int width);
    public void Draw(float x, float y, float height, float width);
    public void Draw(Point upperLeft, Point bottomRight);
    public void Draw(Rect r);
}
```

If C# did not support method overloading, you would be forced to create four uniquely named members, which as you can see, is far from ideal:

```
class Triangle
{
    // Yuck...
    public void DrawWithInts(int x, int y, int height, int width);
    public void DrawWIthFloats(float x, float y, float height, float width);
    public void DrawWithPoints(Point upperLeft, Point bottomRight);
    public void DrawWithRect(Rect r);
}
```

Finally, be aware that when you are overloading a class member, the return type alone is *not* unique enough. Thus, the following is illegal:

```
class Triangle
{
    ...
    // Error! Cannot overload methods
    // based solely on return values!
    public float GetX();
    public int GetX();
}
```

Self-Reference in C#

Next, note that the custom constructor of the Employee class makes use of the C# "this" keyword:

```
// Like C++ and Java, C# also supplies a 'this' keyword.
public Employee(string fullName, int empID, float currPay)
{
    // Assign the incoming params to my state data.
    this.fullName = fullName;
    this.empID = empID;
    this.currPay = currPay;
}
```

This particular C# keyword is used whenever you wish to make reference to the *current object*. Visual Basic programmers can equate the C# "this" keyword with the VB "Me" keyword. C++ and Java programmers should feel right at home, given that these languages have an identically named "this" keyword used for the same purpose.

The reason you make use of "this" in your custom constructor is to avoid clashes between the parameter names and names of your internal state variables. Of course, another approach would be to change the names for each parameter and avoid the name clash altogether (but I am sure you get the point).

NOTE Be aware that static member functions of a type cannot use the "this" keyword within its method scope. This fact should make perfect sense, as static member functions operate on the class (not object) level.

Forwarding Constructor Calls Using "this"

Another use of the C# "this" keyword is to force one constructor to call another during the time of construction. As suggested in Chapter 3, this is yet another way to avoid redundant member initialization logic. Consider the following example:

```
class Employee
{
    public Employee(string fullName, int empID, float currPay)
    {
        this.fullName = fullName;
        this.empID = empID;
        this.currPay = currPay;
    }
    // If the user calls this ctor, forward to the 3-arg version.
    public Employee(string fullName)
        : this(fullName, IDGenerator.GetNewEmpID(), 0.0F) { }
    ...
}
```

This iteration of the Employee class defines two custom constructors, the second of which requires a single parameter (the individual's name). However, to fully construct a new Employee, you want to ensure you have a proper Employee ID and rate of pay. Assume you have a custom class (IDGenerator) that defines a static method named GetNewEmpID() to generate a new ID for a given employee. Once you gather the correct set of start-up parameters, you forward the creation request to the alternate three-argument constructor. If you did not forward the call, you would need to add redundant code to each constructor:

```
// currPay automatically set to 0.0F...
public Employee(string fullName)
{
    this.fullName = fullName;
    this.empID = IDGenerator.GetNewEmpID();
}
```

Defining the "Default Public Interface" of a Type

Once you have established a class' internal state data and constructor set, your next step is to flesh out the details of the *default public interface* to the class. The term refers to the set of public members that are directly accessible from an object variable. From the class builder's point of view, the default public interface is any item declared in a class using the "public" keyword. In C#, the default interface of a class may be populated by any of the following members:

- *Methods:* Named units of work that model some behavior of a class.

- *Properties:* Accessor and mutator functions in disguise.

- *Public field data:* Although public data is typically a bad idea, C# supports it.

As you will see in Chapter 7, the default public interface of a class may also be configured to support custom events and delegates. Furthermore, as you will see later in this chapter, nested type definitions may also appear on a type's default public interface. For the time being, let's concentrate on the use of properties, methods, and field data.

Specifying Type Visibility: Public and Internal Types

Before we get too far along into this employee example, you must understand how to establish visibility levels for your custom types. In the previous chapter, you were introduced to the following class definition:

```
// Note the lack of access modifier on the class definition.
class HelloClass
{
    // Any number of methods with any number of parameters...
    // Default and/or custom constructors...
    // If this is the program's entry point, a static Main() method.
}
```

Recall that each member defined by a class must establish its level of visibility using the "public", "private", "protected", "internal", or "protected internal" keywords. In the same vein, C# types also need to specify their level of visibility. The distinction is that *method visibility* is used to constrain which members can be accessed from a given object, and *type visibility* is used to establish which parts of the system can create the types themselves.

A non-nested C# type can be marked by one of two visibility keywords: "public" or "internal" (as you will see later in this chapter, nested types can be marked as "private"). Public types may be created by any other objects within the same assembly as well as by other external assemblies. If you wish to allow HelloClass to be created by other .NET assemblies, you could redefine it as follows:

```csharp
// We are now creatable by types outside this assembly.
public class HelloClass
{
    // Any number of methods with any number of parameters...
    // Default or custom constructors...
    // If this is the program's entry point, a static Main() method.
}
```

By default, if you do not explicitly mark the visibility level of a class, it is implicitly set to "internal". Internal classes can only be created by types living within the same assembly, and are not accessible from outside the assembly's bounds. As you might suspect, internal items can be viewed as "helper types" used by an assembly's types to help the contained classes get their work done:

```csharp
// Internal classes can only be used by other types within the same assembly.
internal class HelloClassHelper
{
    ...
}
```

Classes are not the only UDT that can accept a visibility attribute. As you recall, a type is simply a generic term used to refer to classes, structures, enumerations, interfaces, and delegates. Any .NET type can be assigned public or internal visibility. For example:

```csharp
// Any type may be assigned public or internal visibility.
namespace HelloTypes
{
    // Cannot be used outside this assembly.
    internal struct X
    {
        private int myX;
        public int GetMyX() {  return myX; }
        public X(int x){  myX = x; }
    }

    // Cannot be used outside this assembly.
    internal enum Letters
    { a = 0, b = 1, c = 2 }
```

```
    // May be used outside this assembly.
    public class HelloClass
    {
        public static int Main(string[] args)
        {
            X theX = new X(26);
            Console.WriteLine("{0}\n{1}", theX.GetMyX(), Letters.b.ToString());
            return 0;
        }
    }
}
```

Logically, the previously defined types can be envisioned as seen in Figure 4-2.

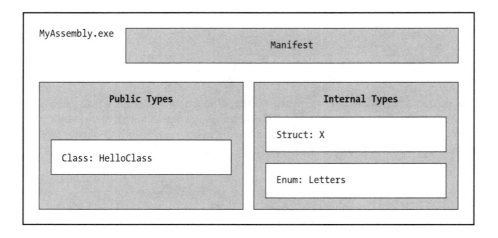

Figure 4-2. Internal and public types

Chapter 9 drills into the specifics of composing .NET assemblies. Until then, just understand that all of your nonnested types may be defined as public (accessible by other assemblies) or internal (not accessible by other assemblies).

Recapping the Pillars of OOP

C# is a newcomer to the world of object-oriented languages (OOLs). Java, C++, Object Pascal, and (to some extent) Visual Basic 6.0 are but a small sample of the popularity of the object paradigm. Regardless of exactly when a given OOL came into existence, all object-based languages contend with three core principals of object-oriented programming, often called the famed "pillars of OOP."

- *Encapsulation:* How well does this language hide an object's internal implementation?

- *Inheritance:* How does this language promote code reuse?

- *Polymorphism:* How does this language let you treat related objects in a similar way?

Before digging into the syntactic details of each pillar, it is important you understand the basic role of each. Therefore, here is a brisk, high-level rundown, just to clear off any cobwebs you may have acquired between project deadlines.

Encapsulation Services

The first pillar of OOP is called *encapsulation*. This trait boils down to the language's ability to hide unnecessary implementation details from the object user. For example, assume you have created a class named DBReader (database reader) that has two primary methods: Open() and Close():

```
// The database reader encapsulates the details of opening and closing a database...
DBReader f = new DBReader();
f.Open(@"C:\foo.mdf");
    // Do something with database...
f.Close();
```

The fictitious DBReader class has encapsulated the inner details of locating, loading, manipulating, and closing the data file. Object users love encapsulation, as this pillar of OOP keeps programming tasks simpler. There is no need to worry about the numerous lines of code that are working behind the scenes to carry out the work of the DBReader class. All you do is create an instance and send the appropriate messages (e.g., "open the file named foo.mdf located on my C drive").

Closely related to the notion of encapsulating programming logic is the idea of data hiding. As you know, an object's state data should ideally be specified as private. In this way, the outside world must ask politely in order to change or obtain the underlying value. This is a good thing, as publicly declared data points can easily become corrupted (hopefully by accident rather than intent!).

Inheritance: The "is-a" and "has-a" Relationships

The next pillar of OOP, inheritance, boils down to the languages' ability to allow you to build new class definitions based on existing class definitions. In essence, inheritance allows you to extend the behavior of a base (parent) class by inheriting core functionality into a subclass (also called a *child class* or *derived class*). Figure 4-3 shows a simple example.

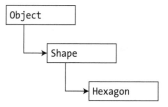

Figure 4-3. The "is-a" relationship

As you are aware, System.Object is always the topmost node in any .NET hierarchy. Here, the Shape class extends Object. You can assume that Shape defines some number of properties, fields, methods, and events that are common to all shapes. The Hexagon class extends Shape, and inherits the core functionality defined by Shape and Object, as well as defines additional hexagon-related details of its own (whatever those may be).

You can read this diagram as "A hexagon is-a shape that is-an object." When you have classes related by this form of inheritance, you establish "is-a" relationships between types. The "is-a" relationship is often termed *classical inheritance.*

There is another form of code reuse in the world of OOP: the containment/delegation model (also known as the "has-a" relationship). This form of reuse is not used to establish base/subclass relationships. Rather, a given class can define a member variable of another class and expose part or all of its functionality to the outside world.

For example, if you are modeling an automobile, you might wish to express the idea that a car "has-a" radio. It would be illogical to attempt to derive the Car class from a Radio, or vice versa. (A Car "is-a" Radio? I think not!) Rather, you have two independent classes working together, where the containing class creates and exposes the contained class' functionality (Figure 4-4).

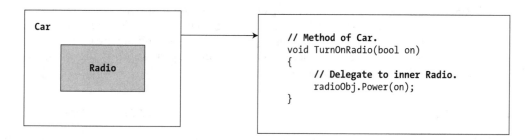

Figure 4-4. The "has-a" relationship

Here, the containing type (Car) is responsible for creating the inner object (Radio). If the Car wishes to make the Radio's behavior accessible from a Car instance, it must extend its own public interface with some set of functions that operate on the inner type. Notice that the object user has no clue that the Car class is making use of an inner object.

```
// The inner Radio is encapsulated by the outer Car class.
Car viper = new Car();
viper.TurnOnRadio(false);    // Forward request to inner Radio object.
```

Polymorphism: Classical and Ad Hoc

The final pillar of OOP is *polymorphism*. This trait captures a language's ability to treat related objects the same way. Like inheritance, polymorphism falls under two camps: classical and ad hoc. Classical polymorphism can only take place in languages that also support classical inheritance. If this is the case (as it is in C#), it becomes possible for a base class to define a set of members that can be *overridden* by a subclass. When subclasses override the behavior defined by a base class, they are essentially redefining how they respond to the same message.

To illustrate classical polymorphism, let's revisit the shapes hierarchy. Assume that the Shape class has defined a function named Draw(), taking no parameters and returning nothing. Given the fact that every shape needs to render itself in a unique manner, subclasses (such as Hexagon and Circle) are free to reinterpret this method to their own liking (Figure 4-5).

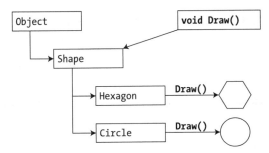

Figure 4-5. Classical polymorphism

Classical polymorphism allows a base class to enforce a given behavior on all descendents. From Figure 4-5, you can assume that any object derived from the Shape class has the ability to be rendered. This is a great boon to any language because you are able to avoid creating redundant methods to perform a similar operation (e.g., DrawCircle(), DrawRectangle(), DrawHexagon(), and so forth).

Next, you have *ad hoc polymorphism*. This flavor of polymorphism allows objects that are *not* related by classical inheritance to be treated in a similar manner, provided that every object has a method of the exact same signature (that is, method name, parameter list, and return type). Languages that support ad hoc polymorphism employ a technique called *late binding* to discover at runtime the underlying type of a given object. Based on this discovery, the correct method is invoked. As an illustration, first ponder Figure 4-6.

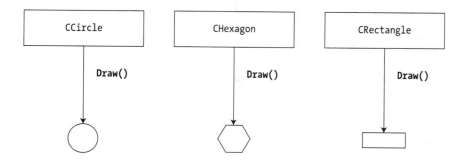

Figure 4-6. Ad hoc polymorphism

Notice how there is no common base class between the CCircle, CHexagon, and CRectangle classes. However, each class supports an identical Draw() method. To illustrate what this boils down to syntactically, consider the following Visual Basic 6.0 code. Until the advent of VB .NET, the Visual Basic language did not support classical polymorphism (or classical inheritance for that matter), forcing developers to make due with the following ad hoc functionality:

```
' Visual Basic 6.0 code below!
' First create an array of Object data types, setting each to an object reference.
Dim objArr(3) as Object
Set objArr(0) = New CCircle
Set objArr(1) = New CHexagon
Set objArr(2) = New CCircle
Set objArr(3) = New CRectangle
' Now loop over the array, asking each object to render itself.
Dim i as Integer
For i = 0 to 3
    objArr(i).Draw      ' Late binding...
Next i
```

In this code block, you begin by creating an array of generic Object data types (which is an intrinsic Visual Basic 6.0 type capable of holding any object reference, and has nothing to do with System.Object). As you iterate over the array at runtime, each shape is asked to render itself. Again, the key difference is that you have no common base class that contains a default implementation of the Draw() method.

NOTE A savvy VB programmer could make use of interface-based programming techniques (as opposed to ad hoc polymorphism) to build relationships among related classes, but that's another story. We'll examine the role of interfaces in Chapter 6.

To wrap up this brisk review of the pillars of OOP, recall that every object-oriented language needs to address how it contends with encapsulation, polymorphism, and inheritance. As you may already suspect, C# completely supports each pillar of object technology, including both flavors of inheritance ("is-a" and "has-a") as well as classical and ad hoc polymorphism. Now that you have the theory in your minds, the bulk of this chapter explores the exact C# syntax that represents each trait.

The First Pillar: C#'s Encapsulation Services

The concept of encapsulation revolves around the notion that an object's internal data should not be directly accessible from an object instance. Rather, if an object user wishes to alter the state of an object, it does so indirectly using accessor (get) and mutator (set) methods. In C#, encapsulation is enforced at the syntactic level using the "public", "private", "protected", and "protected internal" keywords. To illustrate, assume you have created the following class definition:

```
// A class with a single field.
public class Book
{
    public int numberOfPages;
...
}
```

When a class defines points of data, we typically term these items *fields*. The problem with public field data is that the items have no ability to "understand" if the current value to which they are assigned is valid with regard to the current business rules of the system. As you know, the upper range of a C# integer is quite large (2,147,483,647). Therefore, the compiler allows the following assignment:

```
// Humm...
public static void Main()
{
    Book miniNovel = new Book();
    miniNovel.numberOfPages = 30000000;
}
```

Although you do not overflow the boundaries of an integer data type, it should be clear that a mini-novel with a page count of 30,000,000 pages is a bit unreasonable. As you can see, public fields do not provide a way to trap logical upper (or lower) limits. If your current system has a business rule that states a mini-novel must be between 1 and 200 pages, you are at a loss to enforce this programmatically. Because of this, public fields typically have no place in a production-level class definition.

Encapsulation provides a way to preserve the integrity of state data. Rather than defining public fields (which can easily foster data corruption), you should get in the habit of defining *private data fields*, which are indirectly manipulated using one of two main techniques:

- Define a pair of traditional accessor and mutator methods.

- Define a named property.

Additionally, C# supports a special keyword, "readonly," that also delivers an additional form of data protection. Whichever technique you choose, the point is that a well-encapsulated class should hide its raw data and the details of how it operates from the prying eyes of the outside world. This is often termed *black box programming*. The beauty of this approach is that an object is free to change how a given method is implemented under the hood, without breaking any existing code making use of it (provided that the signature of the method remains constant).

Enforcing Encapsulation Using Traditional Accessors and Mutators

Let's return to the existing Employee class. If you want the outside world to interact with your private fullName data field, tradition dictates defining an *accessor* (get method) and *mutator* (set method). For example, if you wish to provide safe access to the Employee's internal fullName data member using accessors and mutators, you would write:

```
// Traditional accessor and mutator for a point of private data.
public class Employee
{
    private string fullName;
...
    // Accessor.
    public string GetFullName() {  return fullName; }
    // Mutator.
    public void SetFullName(string n)
    {
        // Remove any illegal characters (!, @, #, $, %),
        // check maximum length (or case rules) before making assignment.
        fullName = n;
    }
}
```

Understand, of course, that the compiler could care less what you call your accessor and mutator methods. Given the fact that GetFullName() and SetFullName() encapsulate a private string named fullName, this choice of method names seems to fit the bill. The calling logic is as follows:

```
// Accessor/mutator usage.
public static int Main(string[] args)
{
    Employee p = new Employee();
    p.SetFullName("Fred Flintstone");
    Console.WriteLine("Employee is named: {0}", p.GetFullName());

    // Error below! Can't access private data from an object instance.
    // p.fullName;
    return 0;
}
```

Another Form of Encapsulation: Class Properties

In addition to traditional accessor and mutator methods, .NET classes (as well as structures and interfaces) can also define *properties*. Visual Basic and COM programmers have long used properties to simulate publicly accessible points of data (that is, fields). Under the hood, however, properties resolve to a pair of hidden internal methods. Rather than requiring the user to call two discrete methods to get and set the state data, the user is able to call what appears to be a single named field. To illustrate, assume you have provided a property named EmpID that wraps the internal empID member variable of the Employee type. The calling logic would look like this:

```
// Representing a person's first name as a property.
public static int Main(string[] args)
{
    Employee p = new Employee();
    // Set the value.
    p.EmpID = 81;

    // Get the value.
    Console.WriteLine("Person ID is: {0} ", p.EmpID);
    return 0;
}
```

Type properties always map to "real" accessor and mutator methods. Therefore, as a class designer you are able to perform any internal logic necessary before making the value assignment (e.g., uppercase the value, scrub the value for illegal characters, check the bounds of a numerical value, and so on). Here is the C# syntax behind the EmpID property:

```
// Custom property for the EmpID data point.
public class Employee
{
...
    private int empID;
    // Property for the empID data point.
    public int EmpID
    {
        get { return empID;}
        set
        {
            // You are still free to investigate (and possibly transform)
            // the incoming value before making an assignment.
            empID = value;
        }
    }
}
```

A C# property is composed using a get block (accessor) and set block (mutator). The C# "value" keyword represents the right-hand side of the assignment. Like all things in C#, "value" is also an object. However, the underlying type of the object depends on which sort of data it represents. In this example, the EmpID property is operating on a private integer, which, as you recall, maps to a System.Int32:

```
// 81 is an instance of System.Int32, so 'value' is a System.Int32.
e3.EmpID = 81;
```

To prove the point, assume you have updated your set logic as follows:

```
// Property for the empID.
public int EmpID
{
    get { return empID;}
    set
    {
        #if DEBUG
        Console.WriteLine("value is an instance of: {0} ", value.GetType());
        Console.WriteLine("value as string: {0} ", value.ToString());
        #endif

        empID = value;
    }
}
```

You would see the output shown in Figure 4-7.

Figure 4-7. The value of "value" when setting EmpID to 81

> **NOTE**   Strictly speaking, the C# "value" token is not a keyword, but rather a placeholder that represents the implicit parameter used during a property assignment. Therefore, you are free to have member variables and local data points named "value".

Understand that properties (as opposed to traditional accessors and mutators) tend to make your types easier to manipulate, in that properties are able to respond to the intrinsic operators of C#. For example, assume that the Employee type had an internal private member variable representing the age of the employee. On his or her birthday, you wish to increment the age by one. Using traditional accessor and mutator methods, you would need to write:

```
Employee joe = new Employee();
joe.SetAge( joe.GetAge() + 1 );
```

However, using type properties, you are able to simply write:

```
Employee joe = new Employee();
joe.Age++;
```

This being said, for the examples that follow, assume you have configured the Employee type to support a property named Pay that interacts with the private currPay field:

```
// Property for the currPay.
public float Pay
{
    get {return currPay;}
    set {currPay = value;}
}
```

Internal Representation of C# Properties

Many programmers (especially those of the C++ ilk) tend to design traditional accessor and mutator methods using "get_" and "set_" prefixes (e.g., get_Name() and set_Name()). This naming convention itself is not problematic. However, it is important to understand that under the hood, a C# property is internally represented using these same prefixes. For example, if you open up the Employees.exe assembly using ildasm.exe, you see that each property actually resolves to two discrete (and hidden) methods (Figure 4-8).

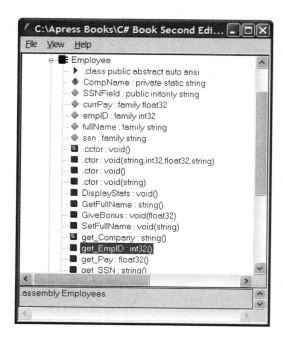

Figure 4-8. Properties map to hidden get_ and set_ methods.

Assume the Employee type now has a private member variable named empSSN to represent an individual's Social Security number, which is manipulated by a property named SSN. Given the previous property-related factoid, if you were to also define two methods named get_SSN() and set_SNN(), you would be issued compile time errors:

```
// Remember, a C# property really maps to a get_/set_ pair.
public class Employee
{
    // Assume this member is assigned by the class constructors.
    private string empSSN;
...
    public string SSN
    {
        get {  return empSSN; }        // Maps to get_SSN().
        set {  empSSN = value;}        // Maps to set_SSN().
    }

    // ERROR! Already defined under the hood by SSN property!
    public string get_SSN() {  return empSSN;}
    public void set_SSN(string val) {  empSSN = val;}
}
```

Finally, understand that the reverse of this situation is *not true*. Meaning, if you define two methods named get_X() and set_X() in a given class, you cannot write syntax that references a property named X:

```
// Assume Foo has two methods named get_X() and set_X() but not a
// literal C# property definition.
Foo f = new Foo();
f.X = 100;               // Error! ! Must be defined as C# property, not set_X().
Console.WriteLine(f.X);  // Error! ! Must also be a C# property, not get_X().
```

NOTE　The .NET base class libraries *always* favor type properties over traditional accessor and mutator methods. Therefore, if you wish to build custom types that integrate well with the .NET platform, avoid defining GetXXX() and SetXXX() methods.

Read-Only and Write-Only Properties

Recall that EmpID was established as a read/write property. When building custom properties, you may wish to configure a read-only property. To do so, simply build a property without a corresponding set block. Likewise, if you wish to have a write-only property, omit the get block. To illustrate, here is the SSN property, retrofitted as read-only (note that the constructor set has been modified to allow the caller to set the initial value of the private empSSN field):

```
public class Employee
{
...
    private string empSSN;
    public Employee(string FullName, int empID,
        float currPay, string ssn)
    {
        this.fullName = FullName;
        this.empID = empID;
        this.currPay = currPay;
        this.empSSN = ssn;
    }
    // Now as a read-only property.
    public string SSN { get { return empSSN; } }
}
```

Understanding Static Properties

C# also supports *static properties*. Recall that static members are bound to a given class, not an instance (object) of that class. For example, assume that the Employee type defines a point of static data to represent the name of the organization employing these workers. You may define a static (e.g., class level) property as follows:

```
// Static properties must operate on static data!
public class Employee
{
    private static string companyName;
    public static string Company
    {
        get { return companyName; }
        set { companyName = value;}
    }
    ...
}
```

Static properties are manipulated in the same manner as static methods, as seen here:

```
// Set and get the name of the company that employs these people...
public static int Main(string[] args)
{
    Employee.Company = "Intertech, Inc";
    Console.WriteLine("These folks work at {0} ", Employee.Company);
    ...
}
```

Understanding Static Constructors

As an interesting sidebar to the topic of static properties, consider the use of static constructors. This construct may seem strange given that the term *constructor* is typically understood as a method called to create a new *object*. Nevertheless, C# supports the use of static constructors that serve no other purpose than to assign initial values to static data. Syntactically, static constructors are odd in that they *cannot* take a visibility modifier (but must take the "static" keyword).

To illustrate, if you wished to ensure that the name of the static companyName field was always assigned to "Intertech, Inc" by default, you would write:

```
// Static constructors are used to initialize static data.
public class Employee
{
...
    private static string companyName;
    static Employee()
    { companyName = "Intertech, Inc"; }
}
```

If you were to invoke the Employee.Company property, there would be no need to assign an initial value within the Main() method, as the static constructor does so automatically:

```
// Automatically set to "Intertech, Inc" via the static constructor.
public static int Main(string[] args)
{
    Console.WriteLine("These folks work at {0} ", Employee.Company);
}
```

To wrap up this examination of C# properties, understand that these syntactic entities are used for the same purpose as a classical accessor/mutator pair. The benefit of properties is that the users of your objects are able to manipulate the internal data point using a single named item.

Pseudo-Encapsulation: Creating Read-Only Fields

Closely related to read-only properties is the notion of read-only *fields*. Read-only fields offer data preservation via the "readonly" keyword. By way of a simple example, assume you have a read-only field named SSNField that offers an alternative manner for the caller to obtain an employee's SSN (again note that you update the constructor to assign a value to this read-only field):

```
public class Employee
{
...
    // Read-only field (set in the ctors).
    public readonly string SSNField;
    public Employee(string FullName, int empID,
                    float currPay, string ssn)
    {
        this.fullName = FullName;
        this.empID = empID;
        this.currPay = currPay;
        this.empSSN = ssn;
```

```
        // Assign read-only field.
        SSNField = ssn;
    }
}
```

As you can guess, any attempt to make assignments to a field marked "readonly" results in a compiler error:

```
// Error! This code won't compile!
Employee brenner = new Employee();
brenner.SSNField = "666-66-6666";
```

Static Read-Only Fields

Static read-only fields are also permissible. This can be helpful if you wish to create a number of constant values bound to a given class. In this light, "readonly" seems to be a close cousin to the "const" keyword. The difference is that the value assigned to "const" must be resolved at compile time, and therefore cannot be assigned a new type instance (as this is computed at runtime). The value of read-only static fields, however, may be computed at *runtime*, and therefore may be assigned type instances as well as simply data types (int, float, string, etc.).

For example, assume a type named Car that needs to establish a set of tires at runtime. You can create a new class (Tire) consisting of a number of static read-only fields:

```
// The Tire class has a number of read-only fields.
public class Tire
{
    // Given that the state of the Tire type is determined at
    // runtime, we cannot use the 'const' keyword here!
    // ERROR: public const Tire GoodStone = new Tire(90);

    // In contrast, the 'readonly' keyword can be assigned
    // values which are computed at runtime.
    public static readonly Tire GoodStone = new Tire(90);
    public static readonly Tire FireYear = new Tire(100);
    public static readonly Tire ReadyLyne= new Tire(43);
    public static readonly Tire Blimpy = new Tire(83);
    private int manufactureID;
    public int MakeID
    { get {  return manufactureID; } }
    public Tire (int ID)
    { manufactureID = ID; }
}
```

Here is an example of working with these new types:

```
// Make use of a dynamically created read-only field.
public class Car
{
    // What sort of tires do I have?
    public Tire tireType = Tire.Blimpy;  // Returns a new Tire.
    ...
}

public class CarApp
{
    public static int Main(string[] args)
    {
        Car c = new Car();

        // Prints out "Manufacture ID of tires: 83"
        Console.WriteLine("Manufacture ID of tires: {0} ", c.tireType.MakeID);
        return 0;
    }
}
```

SOURCE CODE   The StaticReadOnlyData project is included under the Chapter 4 subdirectory.

The Second Pillar: C#'s Inheritance Support

Now that you have seen various techniques that allow you to create a single well-encapsulated class, it is time to turn your attention to building a family of related classes. As mentioned, inheritance is the aspect of OOP that facilitates code reuse. Inheritance comes in two flavors: classical inheritance (the "is-a" relationship) and the containment/delegation model (the "has-a" relationship). Let's begin by examining the classical "is-a" model.

When you establish "is-a" relationships between classes, you are building a dependency between types. The basic idea behind classical inheritance is that new classes may leverage (and extend) the functionality of other classes. To illustrate, assume that you wish to define two additional classes to model salespeople and managers. The hierarchy looks something like what you see in Figure 4-9.

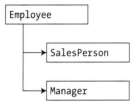

Figure 4-9. The employee hierarchy

As illustrated in Figure 4-9, you can see that a SalesPerson "is-a" Employee (as is a Manager—at least in a perfect world). In the classical inheritance model, base classes (such as Employee) are used to define general characteristics that are common to all descendents. Subclasses (such as SalesPerson and Manager) extend this general functionality while adding more specific behaviors to the class.

In C#, extending a class is accomplished using the colon operator on the class definition (:). Therefore, you can syntactically model these relationships as follows:

```
// Add two new subclasses to the Employees namespace.
namespace Employees
{
    public class Manager : Employee
    {
        // Managers need to know their number of stock options.
        private ulong numberOfOptions;
        public ulong NumbOpts
        {
            get { return numberOfOptions;}
            set { numberOfOptions = value; }
        }
    }

    public class SalesPerson : Employee
    {
        // Salespeople need to know their number of sales.
        private int numberOfSales;
        public int NumbSales
        {
            get { return numberOfSales;}
            set {  numberOfSales = value; }
        }
    }
}
```

Notice how each subclass has extended the base class behavior by adding a custom property that operates on an underlying private point of data. Because you have established an "is-a" relationship, SalesPerson and Manager have automatically inherited all public (and protected) members of the Employee base class. To illustrate:

```
// Create a subclass and access base class functionality.
public static int Main(string[] args)
{
    // Make a salesperson.
    SalesPerson stan = new SalesPerson();
    // These members are inherited from the Employee base class.
    stan.EmpID = 100;
    stan.SetFullName("Stan the Man");
    // This is defined by the SalesPerson subclass.
    stan.NumbSales = 42;
    return 0;
}
```

Needless to say, a child class cannot directly access private members defined by its parent class (as inheritance preserves encapsulation). Also, when the object user creates an instance of a subclass, encapsulation of private data is ensured:

```
// Error! ! Instance of child class cannot allow access to a base class' private data!
SalesPerson stan = new SalesPerson();
stan.currPay;  // <= error!
```

Controlling Base Class Creation

Currently, SalesPerson and Manager can only be created using a default constructor. With this in mind, assume you have added the following new five-argument constructor to the Manager type:

```
// Create a subclass using a custom constructor.
Manager chucky = new Manager("Chucky", 92, 100000, "333-23-2322", 9000);
```

If you look at the argument list, you can clearly see that most of these parameters should be stored in the member variables defined by the Employee base class. To do so, you could implement this new constructor as follows:

```
// If you do not say otherwise, a subclass constructor automatically calls the
// default constructor of its base class.
public Manager(string fullName, int empID,
            float currPay, string ssn, ulong numbOfOpts)
{
    // This point of data belongs with us!
    numberOfOptions = numbOfOpts;

    // Leverage the various members inherited from Employee
    // to assign the state data.
    EmpID = empID;
    SetFullName(fullName);
    SSN = ssn;
    Pay = currPay;
}
```

Although this is technically permissible, it is not optimal. First, like C++ and Java, unless you say otherwise, the default constructor of a base class is called automatically before the logic of the custom Manager constructor is executed. After this point, the current implementation accesses four public members of the Employee base class to establish its state. Thus, you have really made six hits (four inherited members and two constructor calls) during the creation of this derived object!

To help optimize the creation of a derived class, you will do well to implement your subclass constructors to *explicitly* call an appropriate custom base class constructor, rather than the default. In this way, you are able to reduce the number of calls to inherited initialization members (which saves time). Let's retrofit the custom constructor to do this very thing:

```
// This time, use the C# 'base' keyword to call a custom
// constructor on the base class.
public Manager(string fullName, int empID, float currPay,
               string ssn, ulong numbOfOpts)
    : base(fullName, empID, currPay, ssn)
{ numberOfOptions = numbOfOpts; }
```

Here, your constructor has been adorned with an odd bit of syntax. Directly after the closing parenthesis of the constructor's argument list there is a single colon followed by the C# "base" keyword. In this situation, you are explicitly calling the four-argument constructor defined by Employee and saving yourself unnecessary calls during the creation of the child class. The SalesPerson constructor looks almost identical:

```
// As a general rule, all subclasses should explicitly call an appropriate
// base class constructor.
public SalesPerson(string fullName, int empID,
                   float currPay, string ssn, int numbOfSales)
    : base(fullName, empID, currPay, ssn)
{ numberOfSales = numbOfSales; }
```

Also be aware that you may use the "base" keyword any time a subclass wishes to access a public or protected member defined by a parent class. Use of this keyword is not limited to constructor logic. You will see examples using the "base" keyword in this manner during our examination of polymorphism.

Regarding Multiple Base Classes

Speaking of base classes, it is important to keep in mind that C# demands that a given class have *exactly one* direct base class. Therefore, it is not possible to have a single type with two or more base classes (this technique is known as *multiple inheritance,* or simply MI). As you will see in Chapter 6, C# does allow a given type to implement any number of discrete interfaces. In this way, a C# class can exhibit a number of behaviors while avoiding the problems associated with classic MI. On a related note, it is permissible to configure a single *interface* to derive from multiple *interfaces* (again, more details to come in Chapter 6).

Keeping Family Secrets: The "protected" Keyword

As you already know, public items are directly accessible from any subclass, while private items cannot be accessed from any object beyond the object that has indeed defined the private data point. C# takes the lead of many other modern day object languages and provides an additional level of accessibility: protected.

When a base class defines protected data or protected methods, it is able to create a set of members that can be accessed directly by any descendent. If you wish to allow the SalesPerson and Manager child classes to directly access the data sector defined by Employee, you can update the original Employee class definition as follows:

```
// Protected state data.
public class Employee
{
    // Child classes can directly access this information. Object users cannot.
    protected string fullName;
    protected int empID;
    protected float currPay;
    protected string empSSN;
...
}
```

The benefit of defining protected members in a base class is that derived types no longer have to access the data using public methods or properties. The possible downfall, of course, is that when a derived type has direct access to its parent's internal data, it is very possible to accidentally break existing business rules (such as the mini-novel that exceeds the page count). To be sure, when you define protected members, you are creating a level of trust between the parent and child class, as the compiler will not catch any violation of your type's business rules.

Finally, understand that as far as the object user is concerned, protected data is regarded as private (as the user is "outside" of the family). Therefore, the following is illegal:

```
// Error! Can't access protected data from object instance.
Employee emp = new Employee();
emp.empSSN = "111-11-1111";
```

Preventing Inheritance: Sealed Classes

Classical inheritance is a wonderful thing. When you establish base class/subclass relationships, you are able to leverage the behavior of existing types. However, what if you wish to define a class that cannot (for whatever reason) be subclassed? For example, assume you have added yet another class to your employee namespaces that extends the existing SalesPerson type. Figure 4-10 shows the current update.

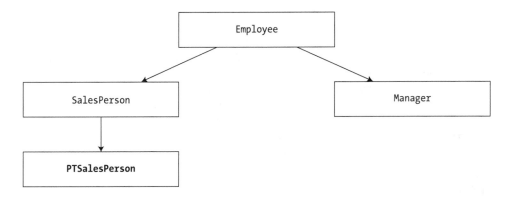

Figure 4-10. The extended employee hierarchy

PTSalesPerson is a class representing (of course) a part-time salesperson. For the sake of argument, let's say that you wish to ensure that no other developer is able to subclass from PTSalesPerson (after all, how much more part-time can you get than "part-time"?). To prevent others from extending a class, make use of the C# "sealed" keyword:

```
// Ensure that PTSalesPerson cannot act as a base class to others.
public sealed class PTSalesPerson : SalesPerson
{
    public PTSalesPerson(string fullName, int empID,
        float currPay, string ssn, int numbOfSales)
            : base(fullName, empID, currPay, ssn, numbOfSales)
    {
        // Interesting constructor logic...
    }
    // Other interesting members...
}
```

Because PTSalesPerson is sealed, it cannot serve as a base class to any other type. Thus, if you attempted to extend PTSalesPerson, you receive a compiler error:

```
// Compiler error! PTSalesPerson is sealed and cannot be extended!
public class ReallyPTSalesPerson : PTSalesPerson
{ ... }
```

By and large, the "sealed" keyword is most useful when creating standalone utility classes. As an example, the String class defined in the System namespace has been explicitly sealed (also note that the String type implements a set of interfaces that will be examined later in this text . . . so feel free to ignore this for the time being):

```
public sealed class string : object,
    IComparable, ICloneable,
    IConvertible, IEnumerable {...}
```

Therefore, you cannot create some new class deriving from System.String:

```
// Another error!
public class MyBetterString : string
{...}
```

Simply put, if you wish to build a class that leverages the functionality of a sealed class, your only option is to forego classical inheritance and make use of the containment/delegation model. (Speaking of which . . .)

Programming for Containment/Delegation

As noted a bit earlier in this chapter, inheritance comes in two flavors. We have just explored the classical "is-a" relationship. To conclude the exploration of the second pillar of OOP, let's examine the "has-a" relationship (also known as the *containment/ delegation* model). Leaving behind the employee hierarchy for the time being, assume you have created a simple C# class modeling a radio:

```
// This type will function as a contained class.
public class Radio
{
    public void TurnOn(bool on)
    {
        if(on)
            Console.WriteLine("Jamming...");
        else
            Console.WriteLine("Quiet time...");
    }
}
```

Now assume you are interested in modeling an automobile. The Car class maintains a set of state data (the car's pet name, current speed, and maximum speed), all of which may be set using a custom constructor. Also, the Car type has a Boolean member variable (carIsDead) that represents the state of the automobile's engine. Here is the initial definition:

```
// This class will function as the containing class.
public class Car
{
    private int currSpeed;
    private int maxSpeed;
    private string petName;
    bool carIsDead = false;
    public Car()
    { maxSpeed = 100;}
    public Car(string name, int max, int curr)
    {
        currSpeed = curr;
        maxSpeed = max;
        petName = name;
    }
```

```
public void SpeedUp(int delta)
{
    // If the car is already dead print error message...
    if(carIsDead)
        Console.WriteLine("{0} is out of order....", petName);
    else    // Car is not currently maxed out, so speed up.
    {
        currSpeed += delta;
        // Did we exceed the car's max speed?
        if(currSpeed >= maxSpeed)
        {
            Console.WriteLine("Sorry, {0} has overheated...", petName);
            carIsDead = true;
        }
        else
            Console.WriteLine("=> CurrSpeed = {0}", currSpeed);
    }
}
```

At this point, you have two independent classes. Obviously, it would be rather odd to establish an "is-a" relationship between the two entities. However, it should be clear that some sort of relationship between the two could be established. In short, you would like to express the idea that the Car "has-a" Radio. In OO parlance, a class that wishes to contain another class is termed the *containing* class. The inner class is often termed a *contained* class. To begin, you can update the Car class definition as follows:

```
// A Car has-a Radio.
public class Car
{
...
    // The contained Radio.
    private Radio theMusicBox;
}
```

Notice how the outer Car class has declared the Radio object as private. This, of course, is typically a good thing, as you have preserved encapsulation. However, the next obvious question is: How can the outside world interact with contained objects? It should be clear that it is the responsibility of the outer Car class to create the contained Radio class. Although the containing class may create any child objects whenever it sees fit, one common place to do so is in the type's constructor set:

```
// Containing classes are responsible for creating any child objects.
public class Car
{
...
    private Radio theMusicBox;
    public Car()
    {
        maxSpeed = 100;
        theMusicBox = new Radio();
    }
    public Car(string name, int max, int curr)
    {
        currSpeed = curr;
        maxSpeed = max;
        petName = name;
        theMusicBox = new Radio();
    }
}
```

Alternatively, rather than duplicate the same code in each custom constructor, you could make use of the C# initializer syntax (see Chapter 3) as follows:

```
// A Car has-a Radio.
public class Car
{
    private Radio theMusicBox = new Radio();
...
}
```

At this point, you have successfully contained another object. However, to expose the functionality of the inner class to the outside world requires delegation. *Delegation* is simply the act of adding members to the containing class that make use of the contained classes' functionality. For example:

```
// Containing classes extend their public interface to provide access to
// the contained classes.
public class Car
{
...
    public void CrankTunes(bool state)
    {
        // Delegate request to inner object.
        theMusicBox.TurnOn(state);
    }
}
```

In the following code, notice how the object user is able to interact with the hidden inner object indirectly, and is totally unaware of the fact that the Car class is making use of a private Radio instance:

```csharp
// Take this car for a test drive.
public class CarApp
{
    public static int Main(string[] args)
    {
        // Make a car (which makes the radio).
        Car c1;
        c1 = new Car("SlugBug", 100, 10);
        // Jam some tunes (which makes use of the radio).
        c1.CrankTunes(true);
        // Speed up (and watch engine die...)
        for(int i = 0; i < 10; i++)
            c1.SpeedUp(20);
        // Shut down (which again makes use of the radio).
        c1.CrankTunes(false);
        return 0;
    }
}
```

Figure 4-11 shows the output.

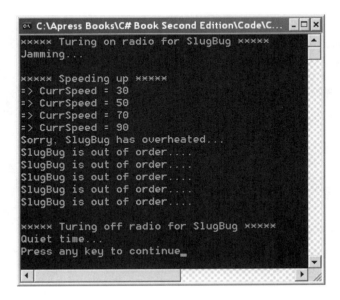

Figure 4-11. The contained Radio in action

SOURCE CODE   The Containment project is included under the Chapter 4 subdirectory.

Nested Type Definitions

Before examining the final pillar of OOP (polymorphism), let's explore a programming technique termed *nested types*. In C#, it is possible to define a type (enum, class, interface, struct, delegate) directly within the scope of class. When you have done so, the nested type is considered a member of the nesting class, and in the eyes of the runtime can be manipulated like any "normal" member (fields, properties, methods, events, etc.). The syntax used to nest a type is quite straightforward:

```
// C# allows classes to nest others.
public class MyClass
{
    // Members of outer class.
    ...
    public class MyNestedClass
    {
        // Members of inner class.
        ...
    }
}
```

Although the syntax is clean, understanding *why* you might do this is not readily apparent. Typically, a nested type is regarded only as a helper type of the nesting type, and is not intended for use by the outside world. This is slightly along the lines of the "has-a" relationship; however, in the case of nested types, you are in greater control of the inner type's visibility. In this light, nested types also help enforce encapsulation services. In general, when you are attempting to model the fact that type B makes no sense outside of the context of type A, nested classes do the trick.

NOTE   Be aware that when you read over the .NET literature (including online help samples) you may find that nested relationships are denoted in text using the dollar sign token ($). Thus, if you come across Car$Radio, you are able to interpret this as "the Radio class is nested within the Car class." As you will see during your examination of Windows Forms, the pattern of nesting types within other types is commonplace, so make a mental note of the $ token!

To illustrate how to nest types, let's redesign your current Car application by representing the Radio as a private nested type. By doing so, you are assuming the outside world does not need to directly create a Radio. In other words, you are attempting to programmatically capture the idea that a Radio type makes no sense outside of the Car to which it belongs. Here is the update:

```
// The Car is nesting the Radio. Everything else is as before.
public class Car
{
...
    // A nested, private radio that
    // cannot be created by the outside world.
    private class Radio
    {
        public void TurnOn(bool on)
        {
            if(on)
                Console.WriteLine("Jamming...");
            else
                Console.WriteLine("Quiet time...");
        }
    }
    // The outer class can make instances of nested types.
    private Radio theMusicBox = new Radio();
}
```

Notice that the Car type is able to create object instances of any nested item. Also notice that this class has been declared a private type. In C#, nested types may be declared private as well as public. Recall, however, that classes that are directly within a namespace (e.g., nonnested types) cannot be defined as private. As far as the object user is concerned, the Car type works as before. Because of the private, nested nature of the Radio, the following is now illegal:

```
// Can't do it outside the scope of the Car class!
Radio r = new Radio();
```

However, the caller is able to interact with the nested Radio type indirectly as follows:

```
Car c1= new Car("SlugBug", 100, 10);
// Jam some tunes.
c1.CrankTunes(true);
```

 SOURCE CODE   The Nested project is included under the Chapter 4 subdirectory.

The Third Pillar: C#'s Polymorphic Support

Switching back to the employees hierarchy, let's now examine the final pillar of OOP: polymorphism. Assume that the Employee base class now defines a method named GiveBonus() as follows:

```
// Employee defines a new method that gives a bonus to a given employee.
public class Employee
{
...
    public void GiveBonus(float amount)
    {
        currPay += amount;
    }
}
```

Because this method has been defined as public, you can now give bonuses to salespersons and managers (see Figure 4-12 for output):

```
// Give each child class a bonus.
Manager chucky = new Manager("Chucky", 92, 100000, "333-23-2322", 9000);
chucky.GiveBonus(300);
chucky.DisplayStats();
SalesPerson fran = new SalesPerson("Fran", 93, 3000, "932-32-3232", 31);
fran.GiveBonus(200);
fran.DisplayStats();
```

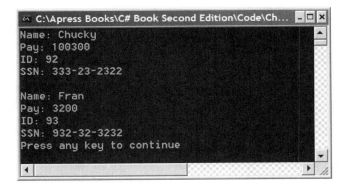

Figure 4-12. The current employee hierarchy does not honor polymorphism.

The problem with the current design is that the inherited GiveBonus() method operates identically for each subclass. Ideally, the bonus of a salesperson should take into account the number of sales. Perhaps managers should gain additional stock options in conjunction with a monetary bump in salary. Given this, you are suddenly faced with an interesting question: "How can related objects respond differently to the same request?"

Polymorphism is the final pillar of OOP, and it provides a way for a subclass to redefine how it responds to a method defined by its base class. To retrofit your current design, you need to revisit the use of the C# "virtual" and "override" keywords. When a base class wishes to define a method that may be overridden by a subclass, it must specify the method as virtual:

```
public class Employee
{
    // GiveBonus() has a default implementation, however
    // child classes are free to override this behavior.
    public virtual void GiveBonus(float amount)
    { currPay += amount; }
...
}
```

If a subclass wishes to redefine a virtual method, it is required to reimplement the method in question using the "override" keyword. For example:

```
public class SalesPerson : Employee
{
    // A salesperson's bonus is influenced by the number of sales.
    public override void GiveBonus(float amount)
    {
        int salesBonus = 0;
        if(numberOfSales >= 0 && numberOfSales <= 100)
            salesBonus = 10;
        else if(numberOfSales >= 101 && numberOfSales <= 200)
            salesBonus = 15;
        else
            salesBonus = 20;     // Anything greater than 200.
        base.GiveBonus (amount * salesBonus);
    }
...
}
```

```
public class Manager : Employee
{
    private Random r = new Random();
    // Managers get some number of new stock options, in addition to raw cash.
    public override void GiveBonus(float amount)
    {
        // Increase salary.
        base.GiveBonus(amount);
        // And give some new stock options...
        numberOfOptions += (ulong)r.Next(500);
    }
...
}
```

Notice how each overridden method is free to leverage the default behavior using the "base" keyword. In this way, you have no need to completely reimplement the logic behind GiveBonus(), but can reuse (and extend) the default behavior of the parent class.

Also assume that Employee.DisplayStats() has been declared virtual, and has been overridden by each subclass to account for displaying the number of sales (for salespeople) and current stock options (for managers). Now that each subclass can interpret what these virtual methods means to itself, each object instance behaves as a more independent entity (see Figure 4-13 for output):

```
// A better bonus system!
Manager chucky = new Manager("Chucky", 92, 100000, "333-23-2322", 9000);
chucky.GiveBonus(300);
chucky.DisplayStats();
SalesPerson fran = new SalesPerson("Fran", 93, 3000, "932-32-3232", 31);
fran.GiveBonus(200);
fran.DisplayStats();
```

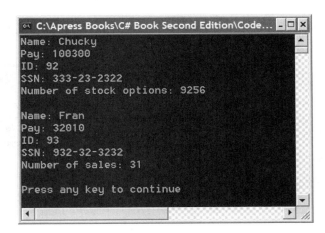

Figure 4-13. A better bonus system (thanks to polymorphism)

Excellent! At this point you are not only able to establish "is-a" and "has-a" relationships among related classes, but also have injected polymorphic activity into your employee hierarchy. As you may suspect, however, the story of polymorphism goes beyond simply overriding virtual methods.

Defining (and Understanding) Abstract Classes

Currently, the Employee base class has been designed to supply protected member variables for its descendents, as well as supply two virtual methods (GiveBonus() and DisplayStats()) that may be overridden by a given descendent. While this is all well and good, there is a rather odd byproduct of the current design: You can directly create instances of the Employee base class:

```
// What exactly does this mean?
Employee X = new Employee();
```

Now think this one through. The only real purpose of the Employee base class is to define default state data and behaviors for any given subclass. In all likelihood, you did not intend anyone to create a direct instance of this class. The Employee type itself is too general of a concept. For example, if I were to walk up to you and say, "I'm an Employee!", I would bet your very first question to me would be, "What *kind* of employee are you?" (a consultant, trainer, admin assistant, copy editor, White House aide, etc.).

Given that base classes tend to be rather nebulous entities, in this example, a far better design is to prevent the ability to directly create a new Employee instance. In C#, you can enforce this programmatically by using the "abstract" keyword:

```
// Update the Employee class as abstract to prevent direct instantiation.
abstract public class Employee
{ ...}
```

With this, if you now attempt to create an instance of the Employee class, you are issued a compile time error:

```
// Error! Can't create an instance of an abstract class.
Employee X = new Employee();
```

Enforcing Polymorphic Activity: Abstract Methods

Once a class has been defined as an abstract base class, it may define any number of *abstract members* (which is analogous to a C++ pure virtual function). Abstract methods can be used whenever you wish to define a method that *does not* supply a default implementation. By doing so, you enforce a polymorphic trait on each descendent, leaving them to contend with the task of providing the details behind your abstract methods.

The first logical question you might have is: Why would I ever want to do this? To understand the role of abstract methods, let's return to the shapes hierarchy seen earlier in this chapter (Figure 4-14).

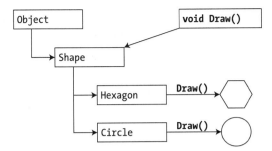

Figure 4-14. Our current shapes hierarchy

Much like the employee hierarchy, you should be able to tell that you don't want to allow the object user to create an instance of Shape directly, as it is too abstract of a concept. To prevent the direct creation of the Shape type, update your code as follows:

```
namespace Shapes
{
    public abstract class Shape
    {
        // Shapes can be assigned a friendly pet name.
        protected string petName;
        // Constructors.
        public Shape(){ petName = "NoName"; }
        public Shape(string s) {   petName = s;}
        // Draw() is virtual and may be overridden.
        public virtual void Draw()
        {
            Console.WriteLine("Shape.Draw()");
        }
        public string PetName
        {
            get { return petName;}
            set {   petName = value;}
        }
    }

    // Circle does NOT override Draw().
    public class Circle : Shape
    {
        public Circle() { }
        public Circle(string name): base(name) { }
    }
```

```
    // Hexagon DOES override Draw().
    public class Hexagon : Shape
    {
        public Hexagon(){ }
        public Hexagon(string name): base(name) { }
        public override void Draw()
        {
            Console.WriteLine("Drawing {0}  the Hexagon", petName);
        }
    }
}
```

Notice that the Shape class has defined a virtual method named Draw(). As you have just seen, subclasses are free to redefine the behavior of a virtual method using the "override" keyword (as in the case of the Hexagon class). The point of abstract methods becomes crystal clear when you understand that subclasses are not required to override virtual methods (as in the case of Circle). Therefore, if you create an instance of the Hexagon and Circle types, you'd find that the Hexagon understands how to draw itself correctly. The Circle, however, is more than a bit confused (see Figure 4-15 for output):

```
// The Circle object did not override the base class implementation of Draw().
public static int Main(string[] args)
{
    Hexagon hex = new Hexagon("Beth");
    hex.Draw();
    Circle cir = new Circle("Cindy");
    // Humm. Using base class implementation.
    cir.Draw();
...
}
```

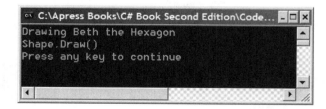

Figure 4-15. Virtual methods do not have to be overridden.

Clearly this is not a very intelligent design. To enforce that each child object defines what Draw() means to itself, you can simply establish Draw() as an abstract method of the Shape class, which by definition means you provide no default implementation whatsoever (again, like a C++ pure virtual function). Note that abstract methods can only be defined in abstract classes. If you attempt to do otherwise, you will be issued a compiler error:

```
// Force all kids to figure out how to be rendered.
public abstract class Shape
{
    ...
    // Draw() is now completely abstract (note semicolon).
    public abstract void Draw();
    public string PetName
    {
        get { return petName;}
        set {  petName = value;}
    }
}
```

Given this, you are now obligated to implement Draw() in your Circle class. If you do not, Circle is also assumed to be a noncreatable abstract type that must be adorned with the "abstract" keyword (which is obviously not very useful in this example):

```
// If we did not implement the abstract Draw() method, Circle would also be
// considered abstract, and could not be directly created!
public class Circle : Shape
{
    public Circle(){ }
    public Circle(string name): base(name) { }
    // Now Circle must decide how to render itself.
    public override void Draw()
    {
        Console.WriteLine("Drawing {0}  the Circle", PetName);
    }
}
```

With this update, you are now able to enforce some order in your shapes hierarchy. To illustrate the full story of polymorphism, consider the following code:

```
// Create an array of various Shapes.

public static int Main(string[] args)
{
    // Array of shapes.
    Shape[] s = {new Hexagon(), new Circle(), new Hexagon("Mick"),
                new Circle("Beth"), new Hexagon("Linda")};
    // Loop over the array and ask each object to draw itself.
    for(int i = 0; i < s.Length; i++)
        s[i].Draw();
...
}
```

Figure 4-16 shows the output.

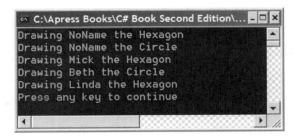

Figure 4-16. Better! Abstract members must be overridden.

This illustrates polymorphism at its finest. Recall that when you mark a class as abstract, you are unable to create a *direct instance* of that type. However, you can freely store references to any subclass within an abstract base variable. As you iterate over the array of Shape references, it is at runtime that the correct type is determined. At this point, the correct method is invoked.

Versioning Class Members

C# provides a facility that is the logical opposite of method overriding: method hiding. Assume you have added a brand new class named Oval to the current shapes hierarchy. Given that an Oval "is-a" type of Circle, you may wish to extend the shapes hierarchy as shown in Figure 4-17.

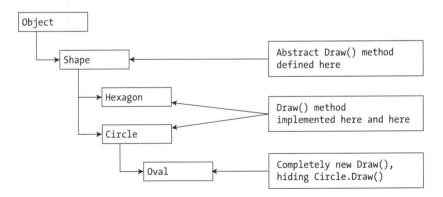

Figure 4-17. Versioning the Draw() method

Now, for the sake of this argument, assume that the Oval also defines a method named Draw(). This is good, as you can ensure that this class behaves like any other class in the hierarchy. However, what if you wish to *prevent* the Oval class from inheriting any previous drawing logic? Formally, this technique is termed *versioning* a class. Syntactically, this can be accomplished using the "new" keyword on a method-by-method basis. For example:

```
// This class extends Circle, but hides the inherited Draw() method.
public class Oval : Circle
{
    public Oval(){ base.PetName = "Joe";}
    // Hide any Draw() implementation above me.
    public new void Draw()
    {
        // Oval specific drawing algorithm.
    }
}
```

Because you used the "new" keyword in the definition of Draw(), you are guaranteed that if an object user makes an instance of the Oval class and calls Draw(), the most derived implementation is called. In effect, the "new" method breaks the relationship between the abstract Draw() method defined by the base class and the derived version:

```
// The Draw() defined by Oval will be called.
Oval o = new Oval();
o.Draw();
```

As an odd caveat, it is possible to trigger the base class implementation of a hidden method using an *explicit cast* (defined in the next section):

```
// The Draw() defined by Circle will be called!
Oval o = new Oval();
((Circle)o).Draw();          // Cast o to base class.
```

At this point, method hiding may seem to be little more than an interesting exercise in class design. However, this technique can be very useful when you are extending types defined within another .NET assembly. Imagine that you have purchased a .NET *.dll from a third-party vendor, and wish to derive a new class from a base class in the third-party library. Now, what if the base type defines a Draw() method that is somehow incompatible with your own Draw() method? To prevent object users from triggering a base class implementation, just use "new."

NOTE You can also apply the new keyword of a field of a derived type to hide an identically named data type defined up the inheritance chain.

SOURCE CODE The shapes hierarchy can be found under the Chapter 4 subdirectory.

Casting Between Types

At this point in the chapter, you have created a number of class hierarchies (employees, cars, and shapes). Next, you need to examine the laws of casting between class types. First, recall the employee hierarchy. The topmost member in your hierarchy is System.Object. Given the terminology of classical inheritance, everything "is-a" object. Furthermore, a part-time salesperson "is-a" salesperson, and so forth. Therefore, the following implicit cast operations are legal:

```
// A Manager 'is-a' object.
object frank = new Manager("Frank Zappa", 9, 40000, "111-11-1111", 5);
// A Manager 'is-a' Employee too.
Employee moonUnit = new Manager("MoonUnit Zappa", 2, 20000, "101-11-1321", 1);
// A PT salesperson 'is-a' salesperson.
SalesPerson jill = new PTSalesPerson("Jill", 834, 100000, "111-12-1119", 90);
```

The first law of casting between class types is that when two classes are related by an "is-a" relationship, it is always safe to reference a derived class using a base class reference. This leads to some powerful programming constructs. For example, if you have a class named TheMachine that supports the following static function:

```
public class TheMachine
{
    public static void FireThisPerson(Employee e)
    {
        // Remove from database...
        // Get key and pencil sharpener from fired employee...
    }
}
```

you can effectively pass any descendent from the Employee class into this method, given the "is-a" relationship:

```
// Streamline the staff.

TheMachine.FireThisPerson(moonUnit);        // Fire MoonUnit.
TheMachine.FireThisPerson(jill);            // Fire Jill.
```

The following logic works as there is an implicit cast from the base class type (Employee) to the derived type. However, what if you also wanted to fire Frank Zappa (currently held in a generic System.Object reference)? If you pass the object reference into the TheMachine.FireThisPerson() method as follows:

```
// A Manager 'is-a' object, but...
object frank = new Manager("Frank Zappa", 9, 40000, "111-11-1111", 5);
...
TheMachine.FireThisPerson(frank);      // Error!
```

you are issued a compiler error! The reason for the error is because of the fact that you cannot automatically treat a base type reference (in this case System.Object) as a derived type (in this case Employee) without first performing an *explicit cast*.

In C#, explicit casts are denoted by placing parentheses around the type you wish to cast to, followed by the type you are attempting to cast from. For example:

```
// Cast from the generic System.Object into a strongly
// typed Manager.
Manager mgr = (Manager)frank;
Console.WriteLine("Frank's options: {0}", mgr.NumbOpts);
```

If you would rather not declare a specific variable of "type to cast to", you are able to condense the previous code as follows:

```
// An 'inline' explicit cast.
Console.WriteLine("Frank's options: {0}",  ((Manager)frank).NumbOpts);
```

As far as passing the System.Object reference into the FireThisPerson() method, the problem can be rectified as follows:

```
// Better! Explicitly cast System.Object into an Employee.
TheMachine.FireThisPerson((Employee)frank);
```

Determining the "Type of" Employee

Given that the static TheMachine.FireThisPerson() method has been designed to take any possible type derived from Employee, one question on your mind may be how this method can dynamically determine which derived type was sent into the method. Furthermore, given that the incoming parameter is of type Employee, how can you gain access to the specialized members of the SalesPerson and Manager types?

The C# language provides three ways to determine if a given base class reference is actually referring to a derived type: explicit casting (previously examined), the "is" keyword, and the "as" keyword. The "is" keyword is helpful in that it will return a Boolean that signals if the base class reference is compatible with a given derived type. To illustrate how to make use of such techniques, ponder the following updated FireThisPerson() method:

```
public class TheMachine
{
    // Fire everyone >:-)
    public static void FireThisPerson(Employee e)
    {
        if(e is SalesPerson)
        {
            Console.WriteLine("Lost a sales person named {0}", e.GetFullName());
            Console.WriteLine("{0} made {1} sales...",
                e.GetFullName(), ((SalesPerson)e).NumbSales);
        }
        if(e is Manager)
        {
            Console.WriteLine("Lost a suit named {0}", e.GetFullName());
            Console.WriteLine("{0} had {1} stock options...",
                e.GetFullName(), ((Manager)e).NumbOpts);
        }
    }
}
```

Here, you make use of the "is" keyword to dynamically determine the type of
employee. To gain access to the NumbSales and NumbOpts properties, you make use
of an explicit cast. As an alternative, you could make use of the "as" keyword to obtain
a reference to the more derived type (if the types are incompatible, the reference is set
to null):

```
SalesPerson p = e as SalesPerson;
if(p != null)
    Console.WriteLine("# of sales: {0}", p.NumbSales);
```

NOTE As you will see in Chapter 6, these same techniques (explicit cast,
"is", and "as") can be used to obtain an interface reference from an
implementing type.

Numerical Casts

In addition to casting between objects, be aware that numerical conversions follow
more or less the same rules. If you are attempting to cast a "larger" numerical type to a
"smaller" type (such as an integer to a byte), you must also make an explicit cast that
informs the compiler you are willing to accept any possible data loss:

```
int x = 30000;
byte b = (byte)x;            // Loss of information here...
```

However, when you are storing a "smaller" numerical type into a "larger" type (such as a byte to an integer), the type is implicitly cast on your behalf, as there is no loss of data:

```
byte b = 30;
int x = b;            // No loss of information...
```

Cool! This concludes our examination of how C# contends with the famed pillars of OOP. To close this chapter, allow me to point out a few select tools of VS .NET that aid in the construction of custom types.

Generating Class Definitions Using Visual Studio .NET

Over the course of this chapter, you have seen how the C# programming language contends with the three pillars of OOP, by making use of the "Keyboard Wizard" (read: typing everything in by hand using a text editor). While you are always free to do this very thing, it is worth pointing out that Visual Studio .NET does provide a number of integrated tools that allow you to build initial class definitions using various GUI input dialog boxes.

To illustrate how to leverage VS .NET, assume you have created a brand new console application (named whatever you choose—I called mine ClassWithWizards) and wish to insert a new class definition to the project. Your first task is to select the Class View tab of the Solution Explorer window. From here, simply right-click the solution icon and select Add | Class (Figure 4-18).

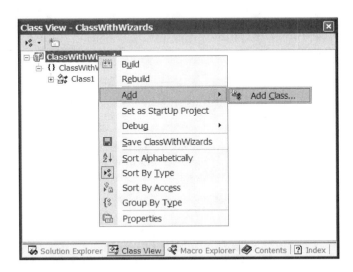

Figure 4-18. Adding a new class via VS .NET

The resulting dialog box will allow you to set up the initial class definition. As you can see from Figure 4-19, the Class Options link of the wizard allows you to define whether the class is sealed or abstract, public or internal, and any optional XML code documentation (see Chapter 2).

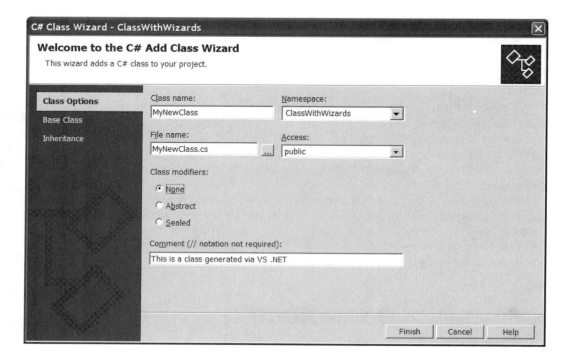

Figure 4-19. The Add Class Wizard

The Base Class link allows you to select the name of the new type's base class. Do note that the choice of base classes will depend on the set of classes defined in the currently selected namespace (Figure 4-20).

Finally, the (rather poorly named) Inheritance link (Figure 4-21) allows you to choose the set of interfaces (if any) the type will *implement* (not inherit).

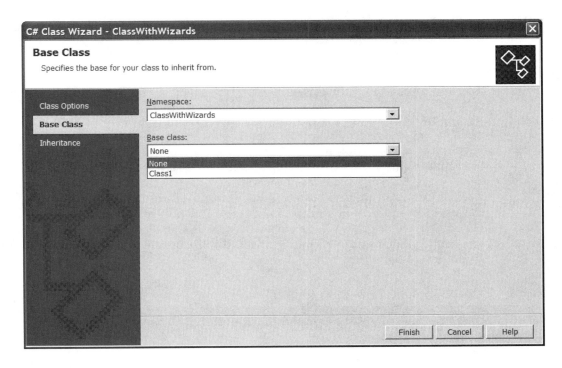

Figure 4-20. Specifying the base class

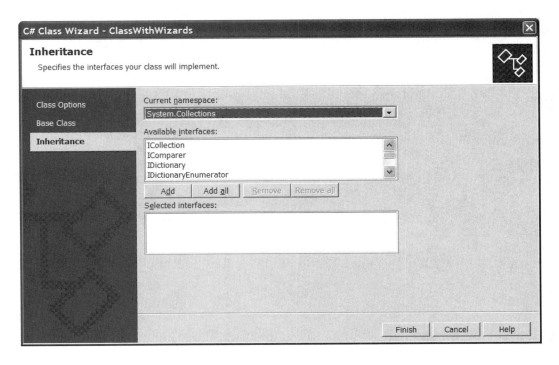

Figure 4-21. Implementing (not inheriting) select interfaces

Once you have defined your new class using this integrated wizard, you will find your new type is now part of your current project and is a member of the current default namespace.

Adding Members to Types Using Visual Studio .NET

VS .NET also supports the ability to add members to existing types using the Class View tab of the Solutions Explorer. To do so, simply right-click a type, and using the add menu, pick the member of your choice (field, property, method, or indexer, which will be defined in Chapter 8). Each possible option of the Add context menu will result in a unique dialog box. While I will assume you will check things out as you see fit, Figure 4-22 illustrates the result of electing to add a new method to an existing class. Do note that you are able to add any number of parameters to the member as well as configure a versioned, abstract, virtual, or static member. Of course, if your type is not defined as abstract, you cannot add an abstract member. Also, if your member is private, you cannot declare it using the "virtual" keyword.

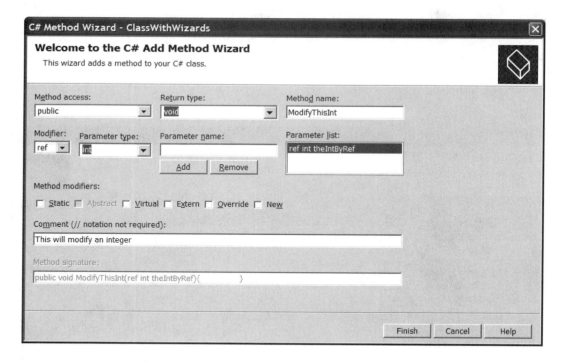

Figure 4-22. The Add Member Wizard

So, at this point you should have a solid understanding of C#'s handling of the pillars of OOP (as well as some insights as to how VS .NET can aid in the process of defining custom types). The next chapter will build upon this foundation by examining how to handle runtime anomalies using structured exception handling and showing how the CLR manages an object's lifetime.

Summary

If you already come to the universe of .NET from another object-oriented language, this chapter may have been more of a quick compare and contrast between your current language of choice and C#. On the other hand, those of you who are exploring OOP for the first time may have found many of the concepts presented here a bit confounding. Regardless of your background, rest assured that the information presented here is the foundation for any .NET application, and will be reiterated over the course of this text.

This chapter began with a review of the pillars of OOP: encapsulation, inheritance, and polymorphism. As you have seen, C# provides full support for each aspect of object orientation. Encapsulation services can be accounted for using traditional accessor/ mutator methods, type properties, or read-only public fields. Inheritance under C# could not be any simpler, given that the language does not provide a specific keyword, but rather makes use of the simple colon operator. Last but not least, you have polymorphism, which is supported via the "abstract", "virtual", and "new" keywords (as you recall, "new" can be applied to members as well!).

The chapter closed by illustrating some built-in tools of VS .NET that can be used to lessen reliance on the "keyboard wizard." Again, the mission of this text is *not* to examine every aspect of VS .NET; however, you will find numerous examples throughout the remainder of the book.

Exceptions and
Object Lifetime

IN THE PREVIOUS CHAPTER, you dug into the details of how C# supports encapsulation services, reuse of code (inheritance), and polymorphic activity among related classes. The point of this chapter is twofold. First, you will come to understand how to handle runtime anomalies in your code base through the use of structured exception handling. Not only will you learn about the C# keywords that allow you to handle such problems ("try", "catch", "throw", "finally"), but you will also come to understand the distinction between *application-level* and *system-level* exceptions. This discussion will also provide a lead-in to the topic of building custom exception types, as well as how to leverage the built-in exception handling functionality of Visual Studio .NET.

The second half of the chapter will examine the process of object lifetime management as handled by the CLR. As you will see, the .NET runtime destroys objects in a rather nondeterministic nature. Thus, you typically do not know *when* a given object will be deallocated from the managed heap, only that it *will* (eventually) come to pass. On this note, you will come to understand how the System.Object.Finalize() method and IDisposable interface can be used to interact with an object's lifetime management. Finally, we wrap up with an examination of the System.GC type, and illustrate a number of ways you are able to "get involved" with the garbage collection process.

Ode to Errors, Bugs, and Exceptions

Despite what our (often inflated) egos may tell us, no programmer is perfect. Writing software is a complex undertaking, and given this complexity, it is quite common for even the best software to ship with various "problems." Sometimes the problem is caused by "bad code" (such as overflowing the bounds of an array). Other times, a problem is caused by bogus user input that has not been accounted for in the application's code base (e.g., a phone number field assigned "Chucky"). Now, regardless of the cause of said problem, the end result is that your application does not work as expected. To help frame the upcoming discussion of structured exception handling, allow me to provide definitions for three common anomaly-centric terms:

- *Bugs:* This is, simply put, an error on the part of the programmer. For example, assume you are programming with unmanaged C++. If you make calls on a NULL pointer, overflow the bounds of an array, or fail to delete allocated memory (resulting in a memory leak), you have a bug.

- *Errors:* Unlike bugs, errors are typically caused by the end user of the application, rather than by those who created said application. For example, an end user who enters a malformed string into a text box that requires a Social Security number could very well generate an error if you fail to trap this faulty input in your code base.

- *Exceptions:* Exceptions are typically regarded as runtime anomalies that are difficult, if not impossible, to prevent. Possible exceptions include attempting to connect to a database that no longer exists, opening a corrupted file, or contacting a machine that is currently offline. In each of these cases, the programmer (and end user) has little control over these "exceptional" circumstances.

Given the previous definitions, it should be clear that .NET structured exception handling is a technique best suited to deal with runtime exceptions. However, as for the bugs and errors that have escaped your view, do be aware that the CLR will generate a corresponding exception that identifies the problem at hand. As you will see, the .NET base class libraries define exceptions such as OutOfMemoryException, IndexOutOfRangeException, FileNotFoundException, ArgumentOutOfRangeException, and so forth.

Before we get too far ahead of ourselves, let's formalize the role of structured exception handling and check out how it differs from traditional error handling techniques.

The Role of .NET Exception Handling

Error handling among Windows developers has grown into a confused mishmash of techniques over the years. Many programmers roll their own error handling logic within the context of a given application. For example, a development team may define a set of numerical constants that represent known error conditions, and make use of them as method return values. For example, ponder the following C code:

```c
/* A very C-style error trapping mechanism. */
#define E_FILENOTFOUND 1000

int SomeFunction()
{
    // Assume something happens in this f(x)
    // which causes the following return value.
    return E_FILENOTFOUND;
}

void Main()
{
    int retVal = SomeFunction();
    if(retVal == E_FILENOTFOUND)
    { printf("Can not find file...");}
}
```

This approach is less than ideal, given the fact that the constant E_FILENOTFOUND is little more than a raw numerical value, and is far from being a self-describing agent.

Ideally, you would like to encapsulate the name, message, and other helpful information regarding this error condition into a single, well-defined package (which is exactly what happens under structured exception handling).

In addition to this ad hoc technique, the Windows API defines hundreds of error codes that come by way of #defines, HRESULTs, and far too many variations on the simple Boolean (bool, BOOL, VARIANT_BOOL, and so on). Also, many C++ COM developers (and indirectly, many VB 6.0 COM developers) have made use of a small set of standard COM interfaces (e.g., ISupportErrorInfo, IErrorInfo, ICreateErrorInfo) to return meaningful error information to a COM client using a COM error object.

The obvious problem with these previous techniques is the tremendous lack of symmetry. Each approach is more or less tailored to a given technology, a given language, and perhaps even a given project. In order to put an end to this madness, the .NET platform provides exactly *one* technique to send and trap runtime errors: structured exception handling (SEH).

The beauty of this approach is that developers now have a well-defined approach to error handling, which is common to all languages targeting the .NET universe. Therefore, the way in which a C# programmer handles errors is conceptually similar to that of a VB .NET programmer, and a C++ programmer using managed extensions (MC++). As an added bonus, the syntax used to throw and catch exceptions across assemblies, AppDomains (defined in Chapter 10), and machine boundaries is identical.

Another bonus of .NET exceptions is the fact that rather than receiving a cryptic numerical value that identifies the problem at hand, exceptions are objects that contain a human-readable description of the problem, as well as a detailed snapshot of the call stack that eventually triggered the exception in the first place. Furthermore, you are able to provide the end user with help link information that points the user to a URL that provides detailed information regarding the error at hand.

The Atoms of .NET Exception Handling

Programming with structured exception handling involves the use of four key (and interrelated) elements:

- A type that represents the details of the exceptional circumstance

- A method that *throws* the exception to the caller

- A block of code that will invoke the exception-ready method

- A block of code that will process (or *catch*) the exception (should it occur)

As you will see, the C# programming language offers four keywords ("try", "catch", "throw", and "finally") that allow you to throw and handle exceptions. The type that represents the problem at hand is a class derived from System.Exception (or a descendent thereof). Given this fact, let's check out the role of this exception-centric base class.

The System.Exception Base Class

All system-supplied and custom exceptions ultimately derive from the System.Exception base class (which in turn derives from System.Object). As you can see from the following C# definition of this type, System.Exception also implements a standard interface named ISerializable; however, ignore this fact for the time being (given that this interface has more to do with .NET Remoting than SEH).

```csharp
public class Exception : object,
    ISerializable
{
    public Exception();
    public Exception(string message);
    public Exception(string message, Exception innerException);
    public string HelpLink { virtual get; virtual set; }
    public Exception InnerException { get; }
    public string Message { virtual get; }
    public string Source { virtual get; virtual set; }
    public string StackTrace { virtual get; }
    public MethodBase TargetSite { get; }
    public virtual bool Equals(object obj);
    public virtual Exception GetBaseException();
    public virtual int GetHashCode();
    public virtual void
        GetObjectData(SerializationInfo info, StreamingContext context);
    public Type GetType();
    public virtual string ToString();
}
```

As you can see, many of the members defined by System.Exception are read-only in nature. This is due to the simple fact that derived types will typically supply default values for each property (for example, the default message of the IndexOutOfRangeException type is "Index was outside the bounds of the array"). As you would expect, these default values can be altered and extended with custom information via constructor parameters. Table 5-1 describes the core members of System.Exception.

Table 5-1. Core Members of the System.Exception Type

System.Exception Property	Meaning in Life
HelpLink	This property returns a URL to a help file describing the error in gory detail.
InnerException	This read-only property can be used to obtain information about the previous exceptions that caused the current exception to occur. The previous exceptions are documented by passing them into the constructor of the most current exception.

Table 5-1. Core Members of the System.Exception Type (Continued)

System.Exception Property	Meaning in Life
Message	This read-only property returns the textual description of a given error. The error message itself is set as a constructor parameter.
Source	This property returns the name of the assembly that threw the exception.
StackTrace	This read-only property contains a string that identifies the sequence of calls that triggered the exception. As you might guess, this property is very useful during debugging.
TargetSite	This read-only property returns a MethodBase type, which describes numerous details about the method that threw the exception (ToString() will identify the method by name).

Throwing a Generic Exception

To illustrate the simplest use of System.Exception, let's revisit the Car class defined in Chapter 4, in particular, the SpeedUp() method. Here is current implementation:

```
// Currently, SpeedUp() reports errors using console IO.
public void SpeedUp(int delta)
{
    // If the car is dead, just say so...
    if(carIsDead)
        Console.WriteLine("{0} is out of order....", petName);
    else    // Not dead, speed up.
    {
        currSpeed += delta;
        if(currSpeed >= maxSpeed)
        {
            Console.WriteLine("{0} has overheated...", petName);
            carIsDead = true;
        }
        else
            Console.WriteLine("=> CurrSpeed = {0}", currSpeed);
    }
}
```

Now, let's retrofit SpeedUp() to throw an exception if the user attempts to speed up the automobile after it has met its maker (carIsDead == true). First, you want to create and configure a new instance of the System.Exception class, setting the value of the read-only Message property via the class constructor. When you wish to send the error object back to the caller, make use of the C# "throw" keyword. Here is the relevant code update:

```
// This time, throw an exception if the user speeds up a trashed automobile.
public void SpeedUp(int delta)
{
    if(carIsDead)
        throw new Exception("This car is already dead...");
    else
    { ... }
}
```

Before examining how to catch this exception, a few points of interest. First of all, when you are building a custom type, it is always up to you to decide exactly what constitutes an exception, and when it should be thrown. Here, you are making the assumption that if the program attempts to increase the speed of a car that has expired, a System.Exception type should be thrown to indicate the SpeedUp() method cannot continue (which may or may not be a valid assumption).

Alternatively, you could implement SpeedUp() to recover automatically without needing to throw an exception in the first place. By and large, exceptions should be thrown only when a more terminal condition has been met (for example, the inability to allocate a block of unmanaged memory, not finding a necessary file, failing to connect to a database, and whatnot). Deciding exactly what constitutes throwing an exception is a design issue you must always contend with. For our current purposes, assume that asking a doomed automobile to increase its speed justifies a cause for an exception.

Catching Exceptions

Because the SpeedUp() method now throws an exception, you need to be ready to handle the exception should it occur (you'll see what happens if you fail to catch an exception a bit later in this chapter). When you are calling a method that may throw an exception, you make use of a try/catch block. Once you have caught the exception type, you are able to invoke of the members of the System.Exception type. What you do with this information is largely up to you. You may wish to log this information to a given file, write the error to the Windows event log, or display the message to the end user. Here, you will simply dump the contents to the console window:

```
// Speed up the car safely...
public static int Main(string[] args)
{
    // Make a car.
    Car buddha = new Car("Buddha", 100, 20);
    // Speed up past the car's max speed to
    // trigger the exception.
    try
    {
        for(int i = 0; i < 10; i++)
            buddha.SpeedUp(10);
    }
```

```
    catch(Exception e)
    {
        Console.WriteLine("\n*** Error! ***");
        Console.WriteLine("Method: {0}", e.TargetSite);
        Console.WriteLine("Message: {0}", e.Message);
        Console.WriteLine("Source: {0}", e.Source);
    }
    // The error has been handled, continue on with the flow of this app...
    Console.WriteLine("\n***** Out of exception logic *****");
    return 0;
}
```

In essence, a try block is a section of code that is on the lookout for any exception that may be encountered during its scope. If an exception is detected, the flow of program execution is sent to the appropriate catch block. On the other hand, if the code within a try block does not trigger an exception, the catch block is skipped entirely, and all is right with the world. Figure 5-1 shows a test run of the handled error.

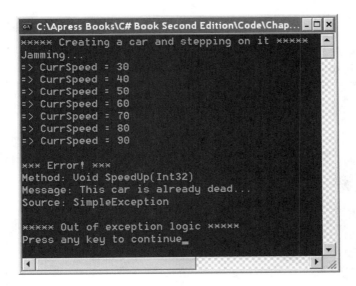

Figure 5-1. Dealing with the error using structured exception handling

As you can see, once an exception has been handled, the application is free to continue on from the point after the catch block. In some circumstances, a given exception may be critical enough to warrant the termination of the application. However, in a good number of cases, the logic within the exception handler will ensure the application will be able to continue on its merry way (although it may be slightly less functional, such as the case of not being able to connect to a remote data source).

The TargetSite Property

As you have just seen, the System.Exception.TargetSite property allows you to determine the name of the method that threw the current exception. Understand, however, that TargetSite does not simply return a vanilla-flavored string, but a strongly typed System.Reflection.MethodBase class. This abstract type can be used to gather numerous details regarding the offending method as well as the class that defines the offending method. To illustrate, assume the previous catch logic has been updated as follows:

```
catch(Exception e)
{
    Console.WriteLine("\n*** Error! ***");
    Console.WriteLine("Class defining member: {0}",
        e.TargetSite.DeclaringType);
    Console.WriteLine("Member type: {0}", e.TargetSite.MemberType);
    Console.WriteLine("Member name: {0}", e.TargetSite);
    Console.WriteLine("Message: {0}", e.Message);
    Console.WriteLine("Source: {0}", e.Source);
}
```

This time, you make use of the MethodBase.DeclaringType property to determine the fully qualified name of the class that threw the error (SimpleException.Car in this case) as well as the MethodBase.MemberType property to identify the type of member (such as a property versus a method) where this exception originated. Figure 5-2 shows the updated output.

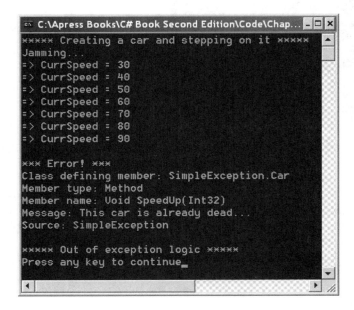

Figure 5-2. Obtaining detailed error information

As you may be aware, the ability to discover information regarding the structure of a type is a form of RTTI (runtime type identification). The .NET base class library supplies an entire namespace devoted to the topic of RTTI named System.Reflection (in fact, MethodBase is defined within System.Reflection). Chapter 11 will examine the details of .NET reflection services. For the time being, simply understand that the System.Exception.TargetSite property allows you to discover a number of details about the method that triggered the exception at hand.

The StackTrace Property

In addition to identifying the type and member that threw a given exception via TargetSite, the System.Exception.StackTrace property allows you to identify the series of calls that resulted in the exception. To illustrate, assume you have once again updated your catch logic:

```
catch(Exception e)
{
    ...
    Console.WriteLine("Stack: {0}", e.StackTrace);
}
```

If you were to run the program, you would find the following line printed to the console (assuming the application is located under the C:\MyApps\Exception directory):

```
Stack: at SimpleException.Car.SpeedUp(Int32 delta)
in c:\myapps\exceptions\car.cs:line 65
at Exceptions.App.Main()
in c:\myapps\exceptions\app.cs:line 21
```

As you can see, the System.String returned from StackTrace documents the sequence of calls that resulted in the throwing of this exception. Notice how the bottommost line number of this string identifies the first call in the sequence, while the topmost line number identifies the exact location of the offending member. Clearly, this information can be quite helpful during the debugging of a given application, as you are able to "follow the flow" of the error's origin.

The HelpLink Property

While the TargetSite and StackTrace properties allow programmers to gain an understanding of a given exception, this information is of little use to the end user. As you have already seen, the System.Exception.Message property can be used to obtain human-readable information that may be displayed to the current user. In addition, the HelpLink property can be set to point the user to a given URL or standard Win32 help file that contains more detailed information.

By default, the value managed by the HelpLink property is an empty string. If you wish to fill this property with a relevant value, you will need to do so before throwing the System.Exception type. Here is the relevant update to the SpeedUp() method:

```
if(carIsDead)
{
    Exception ex = new Exception("Error information can be found at:");
    ex.HelpLink = "http://www.CarsRUs.com";
    throw ex;
}
```

The catch logic, of course, would print out this help link information as follows:

```
catch(Exception e)
{
    ...
    Console.WriteLine("Help Link: {0}", e.HelpLink);
}
```

 SOURCE CODE   The SimpleException project is included under the Chapter 5 subdirectory.

CLR System-Level Exceptions (System.SystemException)

As mentioned, the .NET base class libraries already define a number of exception classes. For example, the System namespace defines numerous general exception types such as ArgumentOutOfRangeException, IndexOutOfRangeException, StackOverflowException, and so forth. Other namespaces define additional exceptions that reflect the behavior of that namespace (e.g., System.Drawing.Printing defines printing exceptions, System.IO defines IO-based exceptions, System.Data defines data-centric exceptions, and so forth).

Exceptions that are thrown by methods in the base class libraries are (appropriately) called *system exceptions*. System exceptions generally (but sadly not always) derive directly from a base class named System.SystemException, which in turn derives from System.Exception (which of course derives from System.Object):

```
public class SystemException : Exception,
    ISerializable
{
    public SystemException();
    public SystemException(string message);
    public SystemException(string message, Exception innerException);
    public string HelpLink { virtual get; virtual set; }
    public Exception InnerException { get; }
    public string Message { virtual get; }
    public string Source { virtual get; virtual set; }
    public string StackTrace { virtual get; }
    public MethodBase TargetSite { get; }
    public virtual bool Equals(object obj);
    public virtual Exception GetBaseException();
    public virtual int GetHashCode();
    public virtual void
        GetObjectData(SerializationInfo info, StreamingContext context);
    public Type GetType();
    public virtual string ToString();
}
```

Given that the System.SystemException type does not add any additional functionality beyond that of System.Exception, you might wonder why SystemException exists in the first place. The idea is that when an exception type derives from System.SystemException, you are able to determine that the .NET runtime is the entity that has thrown the exception, rather than the custom code base of the executing application. As you will see in just a bit, however, there is a lack of consistency within the .NET base class libraries regarding this pattern.

Locating System Exceptions

While it is nice to know that System.SystemException provides a way to identify the underlying source of the error, the next logical question would be "How do I know which exceptions may be thrown by a given base class library method?" The ultimate answer to that question is simple: Use online help. For example, if you were to look up the File.Open() method, you would find a table that describes the set of possible system exceptions that may be thrown should an error occur (Figure 5-3).

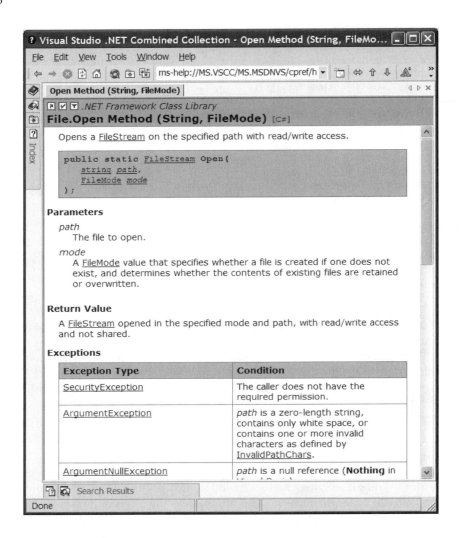

Figure 5-3. Identifying the exceptions thrown from a given method

For those coming to .NET from a Java mindset, understand that a method is *not* prototyped with the set of exceptions it may emit. Therefore you are *not* required to handle each and every possible exception that may be thrown from a given member. As you will see in just a bit, if you fail to handle a raised exception, the operating system will trigger a "last chance exception."

Custom Application-Level Exceptions (System.ApplicationException)

Now that you understand the proposed role of System.SystemException (to identify CLR exceptions), you may wonder if it is possible to build custom exceptions for use within your proprietary applications. The answer is a resounding "yes." In fact, the .NET base class library defines another System.Exception derived type named (appropriately enough) System.ApplicationException:

```
public class ApplicationException : Exception,
    ISerializable
{
    public ApplicationException();
    public ApplicationException(string message);
    public ApplicationException(string message, Exception innerException);
    public string HelpLink { virtual get; virtual set; }
    public Exception InnerException { get; }
    public string Message { virtual get; }
    public string Source { virtual get; virtual set; }
    public string StackTrace { virtual get; }
    public MethodBase TargetSite { get; }
    public virtual bool Equals(object obj);
    public virtual Exception GetBaseException();
    public virtual int GetHashCode();
    public virtual void
        GetObjectData(SerializationInfo info, StreamingContext context);
    public Type GetType();
    public virtual string ToString();
}
```

Like SystemException, ApplicationException does not add any additional functionality beyond the inherited members of System.Exception. Again, the only real role of System.ApplicationException is to identify the underlying source of the error. When you handle an exception deriving from System.ApplicationException, you can (ideally) assume the exception was raised by the code base of the executing application, rather than by the .NET base class libraries.

Figure 5-4 illustrates the relationship between these key exception-centric base classes.

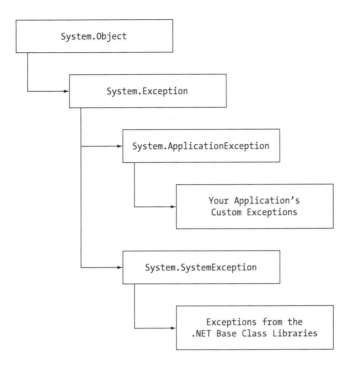

Figure 5-4. Application and system exceptions

Strictly speaking, when you create your own custom .NET exception types, you are not required to derive from System.ApplicationException. If you so choose, you are able to simply derive from the more generic System.Exception (and if you really wanted to, nothing would stop you from deriving from System.SystemException . . . but don't do so!). To understand the various possibilities, let's build a custom exception type.

Building Custom Exceptions, Take One

Although you could simply throw instances of System.Exception to signal a runtime error (as seen in the previous example), it is sometimes advantageous to build a custom class that encapsulates the unique details of your problem. For example, assume you wish to build a custom exception to represent the error of speeding up a doomed automobile.

The first approach we will look at involves defining a new class derived directly from System.Exception (by convention, all exception types end with an "Exception" suffix). Like any class, you are free to include any custom properties, methods, or fields that can be used from within the catch block of the calling logic. You are also free to override any virtual members defined by your parent class:

```
// This custom exception describes the details of the car-is-dead condition.
public class CarIsDeadException : System.Exception
{
    // This custom exception maintains the name of the doomed car.
    private string carName;
    public CarIsDeadException(){ }
    public CarIsDeadException(string carName)
    {
        this.carName = carName;
    }
    // Override the Exception.Message property.
    public override string Message
    {
        get
        {
            string msg = base.Message;
            if(carName != null)
                msg += carName + " has bought the farm...";
            return msg;
        }
    }
}
```

Here, the CarIsDeadException type maintains a private data member that holds the pet name of the car that threw the exception. You have also added two constructors to the class, and overridden the virtual Message property in order to include the pet name of the car in the description. Throwing this error from within SpeedUp() is straightforward:

```
// Throw the custom CarIsDeadException.
public void SpeedUp(int delta)
{
    // If the car is dead, just say so...
    if(carIsDead)
    {
        // Throw 'car is dead' exception.
        throw new CarIsDeadException(this.petName);
    }
    else      // Not dead, speed up.
    { ... }
}
```

Catching the custom exception is just as easy:

```
try
{... }
catch(CarIsDeadException e)
{
    Console.WriteLine("Method: {0}", e.TargetSite);
    Console.WriteLine("Message: {0}", e.Message);
}
```

So, now that you understand the basic process of defining a custom exception, you may wonder if you are required to do so. Typically, you only need to create custom exceptions when the error is tightly bound to the class issuing the error (for example, a File class that throws a number of file-related errors, a Car class that throws a number of car-related errors, and so forth). In doing so, you provide the caller with the ability to handle numerous exceptions on a name-by-name basis (as seen in just a bit).

Building Custom Exceptions, Take Two

Our current CarIsDeadException type has overridden the System.Exception.Message property in order to configure a custom error message. This class also has an overloaded constructor that accepts the pet name of the automobile that has currently met its maker. As you build custom exceptions, you are able to build the type as you see fit. However, the recommended approach is to build a relatively simple type that supplies three named constructors matching the following signature:

```
public class CarIsDeadException : System.Exception
{
    public CarIsDeadException(){ }
    public CarIsDeadException(string message)
        : base(message){ }
    // Just in case the CarIsDeadException is generated by
    // another exception, the previous exception can be passed in
    // as a constructor parameter.
    public CarIsDeadException(string message, Exception innerEx)
        : base(message, innerEx){ }
}
```

Notice that this time you have *not* provided a private string to hold the pet name, and have *not* overridden the Message property. Rather, you are simply passing all the relevant information to your base class. When you wish to throw an exception of this type, you would send in all necessary information as a constructor argument (the output would be identical):

```
public void SpeedUp(int delta)
{
    ...
    if(carIsDead)
    {
        // Pass pet name and message as ctor argument.
        throw new CarIsDeadException(this.petName + " has bought the farm!");
    }
    else      // Not dead, speed up.
    {... }
}
```

Using this design, this custom exception is little more than a uniquely named class, devoid of any unnecessary member variables (or overrides). Don't be surprised if most (if not all) of your custom exception classes follow this pattern. Many times, the role of a custom exception is not necessarily to provide additional functionality beyond what is inherited from the base class, but to provide a *strongly named type* that clearly identifies the nature of the error.

Building Custom Exceptions, Take Three

Recall the exceptions can be categorized as system-level or application-level types. If you wish to clearly mark the fact that the CarIsDeadException is a type thrown by the application itself (rather than the base class libraries), you are free to retrofit the type definition as follows:

```
public class CarIsDeadException : ApplicationException
{
    // Constructors for this custom exception.
    public CarIsDeadException(){ }
    public CarIsDeadException(string message)
        : base(message){ }
    public CarIsDeadException(string message, Exception innerEx)
        : base(message, innerEx){ }
}
```

Once you have done so, the logic that handles the CarIsDeadException is unchanged. Again, we'll look at the process of identifying the underlying nature of a generated exception in just a bit. Until then, let's check how to handle multiple exceptions.

Handling Multiple Exceptions

In its simplest form, a try block has a single corresponding catch block. In reality, you often run into a situation where the code within a try block could trigger numerous possible exceptions. For example, assume the car's SpeedUp() method not only throws an exception when you attempt to speed up a doomed automobile, but throws a system-level exception if you send in an invalid parameter (which for the sake of argument is any number less than zero):

```
// Test for bad parameter.
public void SpeedUp(int delta)
{
    // Bad param?  Throw system supplied exception!
    if(delta < 0)
        throw new ArgumentOutOfRangeException("Speed must be greater than zero!");
    if(carIsDead)
    {
        // Throw 'Car is dead' application exception.
        throw new CarIsDeadException(this.petName + " has bought the farm!");
    }
    ...
}
```

The calling logic would look like this:

```
// Here, we are on the lookout for multiple exceptions.
try
{
    for(int i = 0; i < 10; i++)
        buddha.SpeedUp(10);
}
catch(CarIsDeadException e)
{
    Console.WriteLine("Method: {0}", e.TargetSite);
    Console.WriteLine("Message: {0}", e.Message);
}
catch(ArgumentOutOfRangeException e)
{
    Console.WriteLine("Method: {0}", e.TargetSite);
    Console.WriteLine("Message: {0}", e.Message);
}
```

When you are constructing multiple catch blocks for a single try block, you must be aware that when an exception is thrown, it will be processed by the "nearest available" catch. To illustrate exactly what the "nearest available" catch means, assume you retrofitted the previous catch logic as follows:

```
// This code will not compile!
try
{
    for(int i = 0; i < 10; i++)
        buddha.SpeedUp(10);
}
catch(Exception e)
{...}
catch(CarIsDeadException e)
{...}
catch(ArgumentOutOfRangeException e)
{...}
```

This exception handling logic generates compile-time errors. The problem is due to the fact that the first catch block can handle *anything* derived from System.Exception (given the "is-a" relationship), including the CarIsDeadException and ArgumentOutOfRangeException types. Therefore, the final two catch blocks are unreachable!

The rule of thumb to keep in mind is to make sure your catch blocks are structured such that the very first catch is the most specific exception (i.e., the most derived type in a given exception inheritance chain) while the final catch is the most general (i.e., the base class of a given exception inheritance chain, in this case System.Exception).

Therefore, if you wish to provide a catch statement that will handle any errors beyond CarIsDeadException and ArgumentOutOfRangeException, you would write the following:

```
// Better.
try
{
    for(int i = 0; i < 10; i++)
        buddha.SpeedUp(10);
}
catch(CarIsDeadException e)
{...}
catch(ArgumentOutOfRangeException e)
{...}
catch(Exception e)  // This will handle any other exception.
{...}
```

Again, notice how this catch block explicitly specifies the exception type it is willing to catch. Given that you construct your final catch logic to handle System.Exception, you write an exception handling routine that can (in effect) work with any type deriving from System.Exception (given that all types defined in a catch block must derive from this base class).

Generic Catch Statements

C# (as well as numerous other languages targeting the .NET platform) also supports a generic catch block that does not explicitly define the type of exception. Thus, you could implement a catch block as follows:

```
// I handle any possible error thrown from a try block.
catch
{
    Console.WriteLine("Something bad happened...");
}
```

Obviously, this is not the most descriptive manner in which to handle runtime exceptions, given that you have no way to obtain meaningful information about the error that occurred (such as the method name, call stack, or custom message). Nevertheless, C# does allow for such a construct.

Rethrowing Exceptions

Also, beware that it is permissible to "rethrow" an error up the call stack to the previous caller. To do so, simply make use of the "throw" keyword within a catch block. This passes the exception up the chain of calling logic:

```
try
{
    // Speed up car logic...
}
catch(CarIsDeadException e)
{
    // Do any partial processing of this error and pass the buck.
    // Here, we are rethrowing the CarIsDeadException type.
    // HOWEVER, you are also free to throw a different exception if need be.
    throw e;
}
```

The Finally Block

Your try/catch logic may also be augmented with an optional finally block. The idea behind a finally block is to ensure that a block of code will *always* execute, even if an exception (of any type) interferes with the normal flow of execution. For example, assume you wish to always power down the car's radio before exiting Main(), regardless of any possible exception:

```
// Provide a manner to clean up.
public static int Main(string[] args)
{
...
    // Try to rev the engine hard!
    try
    {
        // Speed up car logic ...
    }
    catch(CarIsDeadException e)
    {...}
    catch(ArgumentOutOfRangeException e)
    {...}
    finally
    {
        // This will always occur. Exception or not.
        buddha.CrankTunes(false);
    }
    return 0;
}
```

If you did include a finally block, the radio would *not* be turned off if an exception is caught (which may or may not be problematic). In a more real-world scenario, if you need to clean up any allocated memory, close down a file, or detach from a data source (or whatever), you must add that code within a finally block to ensure proper cleanup. To this end, it is important to realize that the code contained within a finally block executes *all the time,* even if the logic within your try clause does not generate an exception. This is especially helpful if a given exception requires the termination of the current application.

The Last Chance Exception

Unlike ad hoc error handling techniques, .NET exceptions cannot be ignored. One obvious question that may be on your mind is what would happen if you do not handle an exception thrown your direction. For example, assume that the logic in Main() that increases the speed of the Car object has no error handling logic. The result of ignoring the generated error would be highly obstructive to the end user of your application, as the following "last chance exception" dialog box is displayed (Figure 5-5).

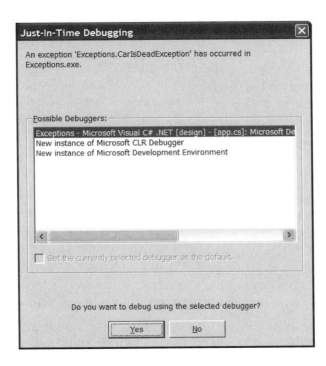

Figure 5-5. You have just entered no-man's land.

Now that you see the inherent goodness of catching an exception programmatically, you may wonder what to do with the exception once you have trapped it. Again, this is a design issue based on your current project. In your trivial Car example, you simply dumped your custom message and call stack to the console. A more realistic scenario may include freeing up acquired resources or writing to a log file. The exception-handling schema is simply a pattern to follow when sending, receiving, and processing runtime anomalies. How you do so is largely up to you.

SOURCE CODE   The CustomException project is included under the Chapter 5 subdirectory.

Dynamically Identifying Application- and System-Level Exceptions

In the previous example, you saw how to handle each exception by its specific class name. As an illustrative alternative, assume you wish to generalize your catch blocks in such a way that all application-level exceptions are handled apart from possible system-level exceptions:

```
// This time, make things a bit more general.
try
{
    for(int i = 0; i < 10; i++)
        buddha.SpeedUp(10);
}

// Any type derived from System.ApplicationException
// handled here.
catch(ApplicationException e)
{
    Console.WriteLine("Caught an app exception!");
    Console.WriteLine("Method: {0}", e.TargetSite);
    Console.WriteLine("Message: {0}", e.Message);
}
// Any type derived from System.SystemException
// handled here.
catch(SystemException e)
{
    Console.WriteLine("Caught a system-level exception");
    Console.WriteLine("Method: {0}", e.TargetSite);
    Console.WriteLine("Message: {0}", e.Message);
}
```

Although the ability to discover at runtime the underlying source of an exception might sound intriguing, you really gain nothing by doing so. Sadly, if you spend time digging through the .NET base class libraries, you will find that some base class library methods that should ideally throw a type derived from System.SystemException are in fact derived from System.ApplicationException or even the more generic System.Exception!

Thus, although the proposed idea issued by Microsoft was noble, you *cannot* always use the previous technique to universally determine the source of the exception. In your applications, you will do well to simply handle each possible exception on a name-by-name basis. However, if you are building a custom exception class, best practice dictates deriving directly from System.ApplicationException.

Debugging System Exceptions Using VS .NET

Visual Studio .NET provides a number of helpful tools that you can use to debug the exceptions that may be thrown by a given member during the development cycle. By default, when an exception is caught during a debugging session, the IDE will *not* automatically stop at the offending line of code.

To illustrate this default behavior, begin to debug your current CustomExceptions project without setting any breakpoints. You will find that the only visible display of the CarIsDeadException is the information printed to the console (via your catch block), which disappears so quickly you cannot see the error. Of course, you are free to set any number of manual breakpoints by hand; however, there is a better way.

VS .NET may be configured to automatically break whenever an exception occurs, without requiring you to set dozens of manual breakpoints at various catch blocks. When you wish to enable such support, begin by launching the Exceptions dialog box, using the Debug | Exceptions menu selection (Figure 5-6).

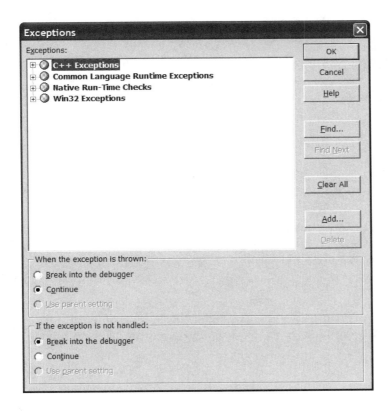

Figure 5-6. Preparing to enable VS .NET exception handling

As you can see, VS .NET is able to interact with various types of exceptions; the only category of interest is the common language runtime exceptions. If you open up the CLR Exceptions node, you will find a list of all the System.Exception-derived types that Visual Studio .NET is aware of. For example, if you open up the System node, you will find a list of all exception types listed in this namespace (Figure 5-7).

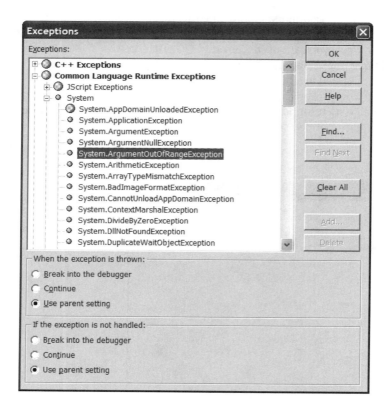

Figure 5-7. The CLR exception set

To enable automatic breaking for a specific exception, simply select the exceptions of interest. For example, to instruct VS .NET to automatically break when an ArgumentOutOfRange exception occurs, check the "Break into the debugger" option (Figure 5-8).

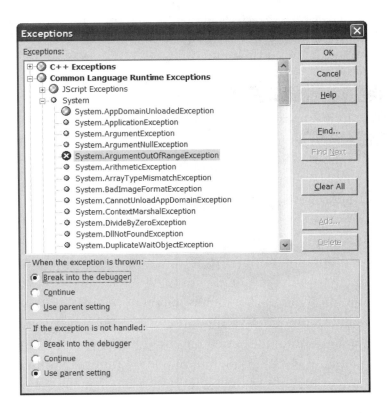

Figure 5-8. Specifying VS .NET exception support for a given exception

Handling Custom Exceptions Using VS .NET

In addition to handling system-level exceptions, you are also able to configure Visual Studio .NET to handle your custom application exceptions (such as the CarIsDeadException). To do so, first select the CLR Exceptions node and click the Add button. At this point, type in the fully qualified name of your custom exception type (Figure 5-9).

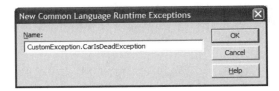

Figure 5-9. Enabling your custom application exceptions via VS .NET

At this point you are able to configure the custom exception as if it were a standard exception (Figure 5-10).

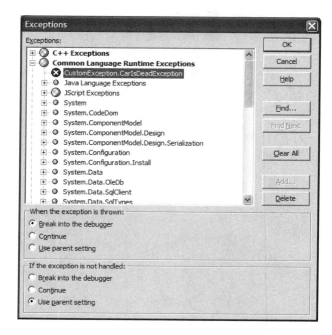

Figure 5-10. Handling your custom application exceptions via VS .NET

With this, you are now able to debug your application, and automatically step into the debugger when a given exception is raised.

So then, this wraps up the first topic of the chapter. As you read over the remainder of this text, you will be introduced to numerous other system-level exceptions. Next up, we will turn our attention to the topic of object lifetime.

NOTE To make the code examples used in this text as clean as possible, I will *not* catch every possible exception that may be thrown by a CLR type. Do be aware that your production-level projects should, of course, make liberal use of try/catch/finally blocks.

Understanding Object Lifetime

To close this chapter, we will switch topics completely and address *garbage collection*. Recall that unlike C++, C# programmers (and .NET programmers in general) never directly deallocate an object from memory (therefore there is no "delete" keyword in the C# language). Rather, .NET objects are allocated onto a region of memory termed the *managed heap*, where they will be automatically deallocated by the runtime at "some time in the future."

As you are building your C# applications, you are correct to assume that the managed heap will take care of itself without your direct intervention. In fact, the golden rule of .NET memory management is simple.

- **Rule:** The Zen of .NET memory management says this: Allocate an object onto the managed heap using the "new" keyword and forget about it.

Once "new-ed," the CLR removes the object when it is no longer needed. Next question: How does the runtime determine when an object is "no longer needed"? The short (i.e., incomplete) answer is that the runtime removes an object from the heap when it is unreachable by the current application. To illustrate, assume you have a new application that makes use of the Car type as follows:

```
// Create a local Car object.
public static int Main(string[] args)
{
    // Place an object onto the managed heap.
    Car c = new Car("Viper", 200, 100);
    ...
}   // If c is the only reference to the Car object,
    // it may be destroyed when Main() exits.
```

Notice that the Car variable (c) has been created within the scope of Main(). Thus, once the application shuts down, this reference is no longer valid, and therefore is a *candidate* for garbage collection. Understand, however, that you cannot guarantee that this object will be reclaimed from memory when Main() has completed. All you can assume at this point in the game is that when the CLR performs the next garbage collection, "c" is ready to be destroyed.

The CIL of "new"

Under the hood, when the C# compiler encounters the "new" keyword, it will emit a CIL "newobj" instruction to the code module. Thus, if you were to open up the previous assembly using ildasm.exe, you would find the following CIL:

```
.method public hidebysig static int32  Main(string[] args) cil managed
{
  .entrypoint
  // Code size       24 (0x18)
  .maxstack  4
  .locals init ([0] class GC.Car c,
           [1] int32 CS$00000003$00000000)
  IL_0000:  ldstr      "Viper"
  IL_0005:  ldc.i4     0xc8
  IL_000a:  ldc.i4.s   100
  IL_000c:  newobj instance void GC.Car::.ctor
    (string, int32, int32)
  IL_0011:  stloc.0
  IL_0012:  ldc.i4.0
  IL_0013:  stloc.1
  IL_0014:  br.s       IL_0016
  IL_0016:  ldloc.1
  IL_0017:  ret
} // end of method GCApp::Main
```

Before we examine the exact rules that determine when an object is removed from the managed heap, let's check out the role of the CIL newobj instruction in a bit more detail. First, understand that the managed heap is more than just a raw chunk of memory accessed by the CLR. The .NET garbage collector is quite a tidy housekeeper, given that it will compact empty blocks of memory (when necessary) for purposes of optimization. To aid in this endeavor, the managed heap maintains a pointer (commonly referred to as the *new object pointer*) that identifies exactly where the *next* object will be placed on the heap itself. These things being said, the newobj instruction informs the CLR to perform the following sequence of events:

- Calculate the total amount of memory required for the object about to be allocated. As you would expect, if this object contains other internal objects (i.e., the "has-a" relationship as well as nested type members), they are also factored into the equation. As well, the memory required for each base class is also taken into account (i.e., the "is-a" relationship).

- The CLR then examines the managed heap to ensure that there is indeed enough room to host the object to be allocated. If so, the type's constructor is called, and the caller is returned a reference to the type in memory, which just happens to be identical to the last position of the new object pointer.

- Finally, before returning the reference to the caller, the CLR will advance the new object pointer to point to the next available slot on the managed heap.

This process is illustrated in Figure 5-11.

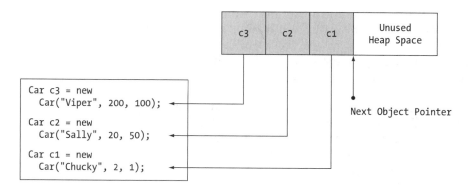

Figure 5-11. Reference types are allocated on the managed heap.

The Basics of Garbage Collection

As you are busy creating objects, the managed heap may eventually become full. When the newobj instruction is being processed, if the CLR determines that the managed heap does not have sufficient memory to allocate the requested type, it will perform a garbage collection in an attempt to free up memory. Thus, the next rule of garbage collection is quite simple.

- **Rule:** If the managed heap does not have sufficient memory to allocate a new object, a garbage collection will occur.

Now, assuming that the CLR performs a garbage collection, we need to return to the question regarding how the runtime is able to determine an object on the heap is "no longer needed." To understand the details, you need to be aware of the notion of *application roots*.

Simply put, a *root* is a storage location containing a reference to an object on the heap. Put even more succinctly, a root can be understood as a variable in your application that points to some area of memory on the managed heap. Strictly speaking, however, a root can fall into any of the following categories:

- References to global objects (while not allowed in C#, raw CIL does permit allocation of global objects)

- References to static objects

- References to local objects within a given method

- References to object parameters passed into a method

- Any CPU register that references a local object

When a garbage collection occurs, the runtime will investigate all objects on the managed heap to determine if it is still in use (aka "rooted") in the application. To do so, the CLR will build an *object graph*, which represents each object on the heap that is still reachable. We will explore object graphs in more detail later during our examination of object serialization (see Chapter 12). For the time being, simply understand that the CLR will ensure that all related objects are accounted for before a possible garbage collection through the construction of an object graph that documents all codependencies for the current object. One nice feature of this process is the fact that the runtime will *never* graph the same object twice, thus avoiding the nasty circular reference count found in classic COM programming.

Now then, once the garbage collector determines that a given root is no longer used by a given application, the object is marked for termination. When the entire heap has been searched for "severed roots," the underlying memory is reclaimed for each unreachable object. After the objects have been swept from memory, the memory on the heap is compacted, which in turn will cause the CLR to modify the set of application roots to refer to the correct memory location (this is done automatically and transparently). Finally, the new object pointer is readjusted to point to the next available slot.

NOTE   Be aware that the garbage collection process happens on a unique thread of execution (more on threading in Chapter 10).

Finalizing a Type

As you might have gathered from the previous discussion, the .NET garbage collection scheme is rather *nondeterministic* in nature. In other words, you are typically unable to determine exactly *when* an object will be deallocated from memory. Although this approach to memory management can simplify your coding efforts at some levels, you are left with the unappealing byproduct of your objects possibly holding onto *unmanaged resources* (raw HWNDs, raw Win32 file handles, etc.) longer than necessary. When you build .NET types that interact with unmanaged resources (a common task when working with platform invocation and COM interoperability), you will most likely wish to ensure that this resource is released in a timely manner rather than at the whim of the .NET garbage collector.

To account for such situations, one choice you have as a C# class designer is to override the virtual System.Object.Finalize() method (the default implementation does nothing). Believe it or not, most of the time you will not need to support a custom implementation of the Finalize() method. In fact, the only reason you will be required to do so is if your custom C# classes make use of unmanaged resources that are typically obtained by directly calling into the Win32 API. On the other hand, if your C# types do not make use of unmanaged resources but only make use of managed types, you are not required to implement a custom Finalize() method at all.

Nevertheless, assume you have a type that has acquired various unmanaged resources and wish to support a custom version of System.Object.Finalize() to ensure proper cleanup of the internal unmanaged resources. While this is all well and good, the odd thing is that the C# language does not allow you to directly override the Finalize() method using standard C# syntax:

```
public class FinalizedCar
{
    // Compile time error!
    protected override void Finalize(){ }
}
```

Rather, when you wish to configure your custom C# class types to override the Finalize() method, you make use of the following (C++-like) destructor syntax to achieve the same effect:

```
// This Car overrides System.Object.Finalize().
class FinalizedCar
{
    ~FinalizedCar()
    {Console.WriteLine("=> Finalizing car..."); }
}
```

The C# destructor-style syntax can be understood as a shorthand notation for the following code:

```
protected override void Finalize()
{
    try
    { Console.WriteLine("=> Finalizing car..."); }
    finally
    { base.Finalize(); }
}
```

In fact, if you were to check out the CIL that is generated for classes supporting the C# destructor method (via ildasm.exe), you will find that an override is indeed made for the virtual System.Object.Finalize() method. Also notice that the CIL code will automatically call the base class Finalize() method on your behalf:

```
.method family hidebysig virtual instance void
        Finalize() cil managed
{
    // Code size       20 (0x14)
    .maxstack  1
    .try
    {
        IL_0000:  ldstr      "=> Finalizing car..."
        IL_0005:  call       void [mscorlib]System.Console::WriteLine(string)
        IL_000a:  leave.s    IL_0013
    }  // end .try
```

```
  .finally
  {
    IL_000c:  ldarg.0
    IL_000d:  call instance void [mscorlib]System.Object::Finalize()
    IL_0012:  endfinally
  } // end handler
  IL_0013:  ret
}
```

(Indirectly) Invoking System.Object.Finalize()

As mentioned, the .NET runtime will trigger a garbage collection when it requires more memory than is currently available on the managed heap. Therefore, if you have created an application that is intended to run for lengthy periods of time (such as a background service), garbage collections may occur few and far between over the course of the application's lifetime.

It is important to note that finalization will automatically take place when an *application domain* is unloaded by the CLR. Application domains (or simply AppDomains) will be examined in greater detail later in this text. For the time being, simply assume that an AppDomain is the application itself. Thus, you can rest assured that a finalizable object will have its cleanup logic triggered upon application shutdown. This brings us to the next rule of garbage collection.

- **Rule:** When an AppDomain is unloaded, the Finalize() method is invoked for all finalizable objects.

To illustrate, ponder the following illustrative example:

```
namespace SimpleFinalize
{
    class FinalizedCar
    {
        ~FinalizedCar()
        { Console.WriteLine("=> Finalizing car..."); }
    }
    class FinalizeApp
    {
        static void Main(string[] args)
        {
            Console.WriteLine("***** Making object *****");
            FinalizedCar fc = new FinalizedCar();
            Console.WriteLine("***** Exiting main *****");
        }
    }
}
```

The output of this program can be seen in Figure 5-12. Notice that the finalization message is automatically printed to the console once the program exits. Of course, a proper finalizer would free up some set of unmanaged resources, but I think the point has been made.

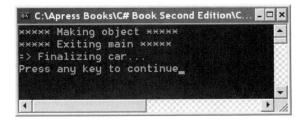

Figure 5-12. Finalizers are called automatically upon application shutdown.

The Finalization Process

Given that finalization is guaranteed to take place when your application exits, you may be tempted to support C#-style destructors on all of your types. But don't. First of all, always remember that the role of a finalizer is to ensure that a .NET object can clean up unmanaged resources. Thus, if you are building a type that does not make use of unmanaged entities, finalization is of little use. However, there is a more practical reason to avoid supporting a finalize method: Finalization takes time.

When you place an object onto the managed heap using the new operator, the runtime automatically determines if your object supports a custom Finalize() method. If so, the object is marked as *finalizable*, and a pointer to this object is stored on an internal queue named (of course) the finalization queue. Simply put, the finalization queue is a table maintained by the CLR that points to each and every object that must be finalized before it is removed from the heap.

When the garbage collector determines it is time to free an object from memory, it examines each entry cataloged on the finalization queue, and copies the object off the heap to yet another CLR-managed structure termed the *finalization reachable* table (often abbreviated as freachable, and pronounced "F-reachable"). At this point, a separate thread is spawned to invoke the Finalize() method for each object on the freachable table *at the next garbage collection.*

The bottom line is that when you build a custom type that overrides the System.Object.Finalize() method, the .NET runtime will ensure that this member is called once your object is removed from the managed heap. However, this comes at a cost in terms of application performance.

SOURCE CODE   The SimpleFinalize project is included under the Chapter 5 subdirectory.

Building an Ad Hoc Destruction Method

As you have seen, the process of finalizing an object is quite time consuming. Ideally, you should design your objects in such a way so they do not need to be marked as finalizable in the first place. However, when a type manipulates unmanaged resources, you do need to ensure they are released in a timely and predictable manner. While you could support a C# destructor (and incur the overhead of being finalized), there are better ways.

One alternative is to define a custom ad hoc method that you can assume all objects in your system implement. Let's call this method Dispose(). The assumption is that when the *object user* is finished using your type, it manually calls Dispose() before allowing the object reference to drop out of scope. In this way, your objects can perform any amount of cleanup necessary of unmanaged resources without incurring the hit of being placed on the finalization queue and without waiting for the garbage collector to trigger the class' finalization logic:

```
// Equipping our class with an ad hoc destruction method.
public Car
{
...
    // This is a custom method we expect the object user to call manually.
    public void Dispose()
    {   /* Clean up your internal unmanaged resources. */}
}
```

Of course, the name of this method is completely up to you. While Dispose() is a very common name, if you are building a class that manipulates a physical file, you may opt to call this member Close(). However, any name will do (ShutDown(), Kill(), DestroyMeNow(), and so forth).

 NOTE   To ensure that unmanaged resources are always cleaned up appropriately, the implementation of a Dispose() method should be safely callable multiple times without throwing an exception.

The IDisposable Interface

In order to provide symmetry among all objects that support an explicit destruction routine, the .NET class libraries define an interface named IDisposable that (surprise, surprise) supports a single member named Dispose():

```
public interface IDisposable
{
    public void Dispose();
}
```

Now, rest assured that the concepts behind interface-based programming are fully detailed in Chapter 6. Until then, understand that the recommended design pattern to follow is to implement the IDisposable interface for all types that wish to support an explicit form of resource deallocation. Thus, you may update the Car type as follows:

```
// Implementing IDisposable.
public Car : IDisposable
{
...
    // This is still a custom method we expect the object user to call
    // manually.
    public void Dispose()
    {
        // Clean up your internal unmanaged resources.
    }
}
```

Again, using this approach, you provide the object user with a way to manually dispose of acquired resources as soon as possible, and avoid the overhead of being placed on the finalization queue. The calling logic is straightforward:

```
namespace DisposeMe
{
    public class App
    {
        public static int Main(string[] args)
        {
            Car c1 = new Car("Car one", 40, 10);
            c1.Dispose();
            return 0;
        } // C1 is still on the heap and may be collected at this point.
    }
}
```

This example exposes yet another rule of working with garbage collected types.

- **Rule:** Always call Dispose() for any object you manually allocate to the heap. The assumption you should make is that if the class designer chose to support the Dispose() method (or a named alternative such as Close()), the type has some cleanup to perform.

As you may be guessing, it is possible for a single class to support a C#-style destructor as well as implement the IDisposable interface. You see this technique in just a moment.

Reusing the C# "using" Keyword

When you are handling a managed object that implements IDisposable, it will be quite common to make use of structured exception handling to ensure the type's Dispose() method is called in the event of a runtime exception:

```
public void SomeMethod()
{
    Car c = new Car();
    try
    {// Use the car. }
    catch
    { // Catch any exceptions here. }
    finally
    {
        // Always call Dispose(), error or not.
        c.Dispose();
    }
}
```

While this is a fine example of defensive programming, the truth of the matter is that few developers are thrilled by the prospects of wrapping each and every type within a try/catch/finally block just to ensure the type's Dispose() method is called. To achieve the same result in a much less obtrusive manner, C# supports a special bit of syntax that looks like this:

```
public void SomeMethod()
{
    using(Car c = new Car())
    {
        // Use the car.
        // Dispose() is called automatically when the
        // using block exits.
    }
}
```

Unfortunately, the "using" keyword now has a double meaning (specifying namespaces and triggering a Dispose() method). Nevertheless, when you are working with .NET types that support the IDisposable interface, this syntactical construct will ensure that the object "being used" will automatically have its Dispose() method called once the using block has exited. On the other hand, if you specify a type that does not implement IDisposable within the using declaration, you are issued a compile time error.

 SOURCE CODE   The DisposableCar project is included under the Chapter 5 subdirectory.

Garbage Collection Optimizations

Now that you have seen two approaches that may be used to ensure the proper cleanup of your custom types, let's dig a bit deeper into the functionality of the .NET garbage collector and check out the topic of object *generations*.

When the CLR is attempting to locate unreachable objects, is does *not* literally walk over each and every object placed on the managed heap looking for orphaned roots. Doing so would involve considerable time, especially in larger (i.e., real-world) applications.

To help optimize the collection process, each object on the heap is assigned to a given "generation." The idea behind generations is simple: The longer an object has existed on the heap, the more likely it is to stay there (for example, the object implementing an application's Main() method). Conversely, objects that have been recently placed on the heap are more likely to be dereferenced by the application rather quickly (such as an object created within a method scope). Given these assumptions, each object belongs to one of the following generations (as of .NET version 1.1):

- *Generation 0:* Identifies a newly allocated object that has never been marked for collection.

- *Generation 1:* Identifies an object that has survived a garbage collection sweep (i.e., it was marked for collection, but was not removed due to the fact that the heap had enough free space).

- *Generation 2:* Identifies an object that has survived more than one sweep of the garbage collector.

Now, when a collection occurs, the GC marks and sweeps all generation 0 objects first. If this results in the required amount of memory, the remaining objects are promoted to the next available generation. If all generation 0 objects have been removed from the heap, but more memory is still necessary, generation 1 objects are marked and swept, followed (if necessary) by generation 2 objects. In this way, the newer objects (i.e., local variables) are removed quickly while an older object (i.e., the object defining the Main() method) is assumed to be in use. In a nutshell, the GC is able to quickly free heap space using the generation as a baseline.

The System.GC Type

Like everything in the .NET universe, you are able to interact with the garbage collector using a base class library type, which in this case is System.GC. This type allows you to interact with the garbage collector using a small set of static members. Table 5-2 gives a rundown of some of the more interesting items.

Table 5-2. Select Members of the System.GC Type

System.GC Member	Meaning in Life
Collect()	Forces the GC to call the Finalize() method for every object on the managed heap. You can also (if you choose) specify the generation to sweep .
GetGeneration()	Returns the generation to which an object currently belongs.
MaxGeneration	This property returns the maximum of generations supported on the target system.
ReRegisterForFinalize()	Sets a flag indicating that a suppressed object should be reregistered as finalizable. This (of course) assumes the object was marked as nonfinalizable using SuppressFinalize().
SuppressFinalize()	Sets a flag indicating that a given object should not have its Finalize() method called.
GetTotalMemory()	Returns the estimated amount of memory (in bytes) currently being used by all objects in the heap, including objects that are soon to be destroyed. This method takes a Boolean parameter that is used to specify if a garbage collection should occur during the method invocation.

Building Finalizable and Disposable Types

To illustrate programmatic interaction with the .NET garbage collector, let's retrofit the automobile's destruction logic to support both an overridden Finalize() method as well as the IDisposable interface:

```
// Memory clean up.
public class Car : IDisposable
{
    ...
    ~Car()
    { // Clean up any internal unmanaged resouces.  }
    public void Dispose()
    {
        // Clean up any internal resources.
        ...
        // No need to finalize if user called Dispose(),
        // so suppress finalization.
        GC.SuppressFinalize(this);
    }
}
```

Notice that this iteration of the Car class supports both a C#-style destructor as well as the IDisposable interface. Here, your Dispose() method has been altered to call GC.SuppressFinalize(), which informs the system that it should no longer call the destructor for the specified object, as the end user has called Dispose() manually (and has therefore cleaned up any internal resources of the Car type).

To illustrate the interplay between explicit and implicit object deallocation, assume the following updated Main() method. Given that two of the Car types have been manually disposed by the object user, these types do not have their destructor logic triggered due to the call to GC.SuppressFinalize():

```
// Interacting with the GC.
public class GCApp
{
    public static int Main(string[] args)
    {
        // Add these cars to the managed heap.
        Car c1, c2, c3, c4;
        c1 = new Car("Car one", 40, 10);
        c2 = new Car("Car two", 70, 5);
        c3 = new Car("Car three", 200, 100);
        c4 = new Car("Car four", 140, 80);

        // Manually dispose some objects.
        c1.Dispose();
        c3.Dispose();
        return 0;
    }
}
```

The output can be seen in Figure 5-13.

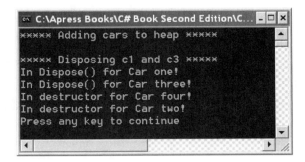

Figure 5-13. The interplay of finalization and disposal

SOURCE CODE   The FinalizedAndDisposedType project is included under the Chapter 5 subdirectory.

Forcing a Garbage Collection

Recall that the CLR will automatically trigger a garbage collection when the managed heap is full, which will happen "whenever." If you so choose, you are able to programmatically force the runtime to perform a garbage collection using the static GC.Collect() method. Now, understand that you should seldom (if ever) do so, given that the whole purpose of the managed heap is that it is maintained by forces outside of your control.

Nevertheless, assume you have an object-hungry application that is designed to run for a lengthy amount of time. To trigger a garbage collection, you could write the following:

```
// Force a garbage collection, and wait for
// each object to be finalized.
GC.Collect();
GC.WaitForPendingFinalizers();
```

Note that you call GC.WaitForPendingFinalizers() after forcing a garbage collection cycle. In this way, you can rest assured that all finalizable objects have had a chance to perform any necessary cleanup before continuing forward. Do note that this call will suspend the current thread during the process (which is a good thing, as it ensures you don't invoke methods on a type that is currently being destroyed!).

Programmatically Interacting with Generations

To close this chapter, let's revisit the topic of an object's generation. Programmatically speaking, you are able to investigate the generation an object currently belongs to using GC.GetGeneration(). Furthermore, GC.Collect() does allow you to specify which generation should be checked for valid application roots. Consider the following:

```
// Just how old are you?
public static int Main(string[] args)
{
    // Add these cars to the managed heap.
    Car c1, c2, c3, c4;
    c1 = new Car("Car one", 40, 10);
    c2 = new Car("Car two", 70, 5);
    c3 = new Car("Car three", 200, 100);
    c4 = new Car("Car four", 140, 80);

    // Display generations.
    Console.WriteLine("C1 is gen {0} ", GC.GetGeneration(c1));
    Console.WriteLine("C2 is gen {0} ", GC.GetGeneration(c2));
    Console.WriteLine("C3 is gen {0} ", GC.GetGeneration(c3));
    Console.WriteLine("C4 is gen {0} ", GC.GetGeneration(c4));

    // Dispose some cars manually.
    c1.Dispose();
    c3.Dispose();
```

```
// Collect all gen 0 objects?
GC.Collect(0);

// Display generations again (each will be promoted).
Console.WriteLine("C1 is gen {0} ", GC.GetGeneration(c1));
Console.WriteLine("C2 is gen {0} ", GC.GetGeneration(c2));
Console.WriteLine("C3 is gen {0} ", GC.GetGeneration(c3));
Console.WriteLine("C4 is gen {0} ", GC.GetGeneration(c4));
return 0;
}
```

The output is shown in Figure 5-14.

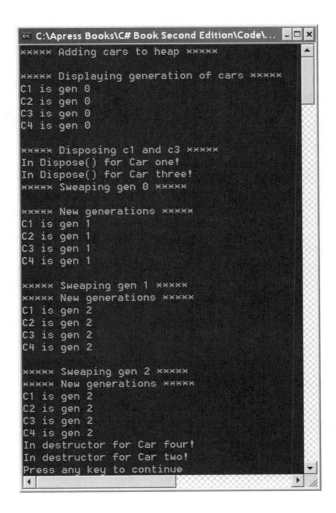

Figure 5-14. Influencing an object's current generation

Notice that when you request a collection of generation 0, each object is promoted to generation 1, given that these objects did not need to be removed from memory (as the heap was not exhausted). Also note that if you request a collection of generation 2 objects, the objects that have survived the current garbage collection remain at generation 2 (there is no generation greater than 2 as of .NET version 1.1).

All things considered, keep in mind that your interactions with the System.GC type should be slim to none. The whole point of having a managed heap is to move the responsibility of memory management from your hands into the hands of the runtime.

 SOURCE CODE   The Generations project is included under the Chapter 5 subdirectory.

Summary

This chapter examined two OOP-centric topics. First, you were shown how the .NET runtime makes use of structured exception handling to contend with runtime problems. Using a small set of keywords ("try", "catch", "throw", "finally"), C# programmers are able to raise and handle system-level and application-level exceptions.

Next, you were exposed to various aspects of object lifetime. Given that the CLR makes use of runtime garbage collections, the basic rule of thumb is to assume that the runtime will destroy an object when it is "no longer needed." However, if your C# types make use of unmanaged resources that need to be freed in a timely and predictable manner, you are free to override the virtual System.Object.Finalize() method and/or implement the IDisposable interface. Finally, you were exposed to the role of the System.GC type and checked out a subset of its functionality.

#### CHAPTER 6

Interfaces and Collections

THIS CHAPTER BUILDS on your current understanding of object-oriented development by introducing the topic of interface-based programming. Here you learn how to use C# to define and implement custom interfaces, and come to understand the benefits of building types that support multiple behaviors. Along the way, a number of related topics are also discussed, such as obtaining interface references, explicit interface implementation, and the construction of interface hierarchies.

The remainder of this chapter is spent examining some of the standard interfaces defined within the .NET base class libraries. As you will see, your custom types are free to implement these predefined interfaces to support a number of advanced behaviors such as object cloning, object enumeration, and object sorting. To wrap things up, you will check out the numerous predefined interfaces that are implemented by various collection classes (ArrayList, Stack, etc.) defined by the System.Collections namespace.

Defining Interfaces Using C#

COM programmers have lived and died by the notion of interface-based programming for years. In fact, one of the central tenets of COM is that the only way a client can communicate with a COM class is via an interface pointer (not a direct object reference). Although the .NET universe still honors the use of interfaces, they are not the only means by which two binaries can communicate (as the CLR supports true object references). Be aware, however, that this does not in any way imply that interfaces are obsolete! These syntactic entities are still the most elegant manner by which you can safely extend the functionality of a custom type without breaking existing code.

First, a formal definition: An interface is nothing more than a named collection of semantically related *abstract members*. The exact number of members defined by a given interface always depends on the exact *behavior* you are attempting to model. Yes, it's true. An interface expresses a behavior that a given class may support. At a syntactic level, an interface is defined using the C# "interface" keyword. Unlike other .NET types, interfaces never specify a base class (not even System.Object) and contain members that do *not* take an access modifier (given that interface methods are implicitly public, in order to allow the supporting type to implement the members). To get the ball rolling, here is a custom interface definition:

```
// This interface defines the behavior of 'having points'.
// Interfaces don't have base classes!
public interface IPointy
{
    byte GetNumberOfPoints();   // Implicitly public and abstract.
}
```

.NET interfaces (C# or otherwise) are also able to define any number of properties. For example, you could modify the IPointy interface to use a read/write property:

```
// The pointy behavior as a read / write property.
public interface IPointy
{
    // Remove 'get' or 'set' to build read/write only property.
    byte Points{ get; set;}
}
```

In either case, IPointy is an interface that expresses the behavior of "having points." As you can tell, this behavior might be useful in the shapes hierarchy developed in Chapter 4. The idea is simple: Some objects in the Shapes application have points (such as the Hexagon and Triangle) while others (such as the Circle) do not. If you configure the Hexagon and Triangle to support the IPointy interface, you can safely assume that each class supports a common behavior, and therefore a common set of methods.

NOTE   .NET interfaces may also contain event and indexer method definitions.

Implementing an Interface Using C#

When a C# class (or structure) chooses to extend its functionality by supporting a given interface, it does so using a comma-delimited list in the type definition. Be aware that the direct base class must be listed first. When your class type derives directly from System.Object, you are free to simply list the interface(s) supported by the class, as the C# compiler will extend your types from System.Object if you do not say otherwise. On a related note, given that structures always derive from System.ValueType, simply list each interface directly after the structure definition:

```
// This class derives from System.Object and
// implements a single interface.
public class SomeClass : ISomeInterface
{...}

// This class derives from a specific base class
// and implements a single interface.
public class AnotherClass : MyBaseClass, ISomeInterface
{...}

// This struct derives from System.ValueType and
// implements a single interface.
public struct SomeStruct : ISomeInterface
{...}
```

Understand that implementing an interface is an all-or-nothing proposition. The supporting class is not able to selectively choose which members it will implement. Given that the IPointy interface defines a single method, this is not too much of a burden. However, if you are implementing an interface that defines ten members, the type is now responsible for fleshing out the details of the ten abstract entities.

NOTE   Abstract base classes are permitted to support interfaces without implementing the interface members so long as they explicitly define them as abstract. By doing so, derived types will be responsible for implementing each member and thus become compatible with the interface in question.

Here is the implementation of the updated shapes hierarchy:

```
// A given class may implement as many interfaces as necessary,
// but may have exactly 1 base class.
public class Hexagon : Shape, IPointy
{
    public Hexagon(){ }
    public Hexagon(string name) : base(name){ }
    public override void Draw()
    {
        // Recall the Shape class defined the PetName property.
        Console.WriteLine("Drawing {0}  the Hexagon", PetName);
    }
    // IPointy Implementation.
    public byte GetNumberOfPoints()
    {  return 6; }
}
```

```
public class Triangle : Shape, IPointy
{
    public Triangle() { }
    public Triangle(string name) : base(name) { }
    public override void Draw()
    { Console.WriteLine("Drawing {0} the Triangle", PetName); }
    // IPointy Implementation.
    public byte GetNumberOfPoints()
    { return 3; }
}
```

Each class now returns the number of points to the outside world when asked to do so. To sum up the story so far, the following diagram illustrates IPointy-compatible objects using the popular *COM lollipop* notation. For those coming from a non-Microsoft view of the world, COM objects are graphically represented using a lollipop (aka jack) for each interface supported by a given class. For those who are familiar with the COM lifestyle, notice that the Hexagon and Triangle classes (see Figure 6-1) do *not* implement IUnknown and derive from a common base class (again illustrating the stark differences between COM and .NET).

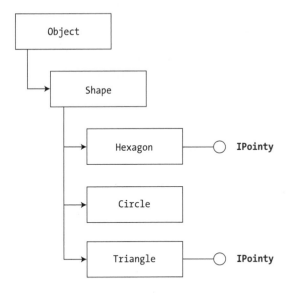

Figure 6-1. The updated shapes hierarchy

Contrasting Interfaces to Abstract Base Classes

Given your work in Chapter 4, you may be wondering why you need the "interface" keyword in the first place. After all, C# allows you to build base classes containing abstract methods. Like an interface, when a child class derives from an abstract base class, it is also under obligation to flesh out the details of the abstract methods. However, abstract base classes typically do far more than define a group of abstract methods. They are free to define public, private, and protected state data, as well as any number of concrete methods that can be accessed by the subclasses.

Interfaces on the other hand, are pure protocol. Interfaces *never* define data types, and *never* provide a default implementation of the methods. Every member of an interface (whether it is a property or method) is automatically abstract. Furthermore, given that C# (and .NET-aware languages in general) only supports single inheritance, the interface-based protocol allows a given type to support numerous behaviors, while avoiding the issues that arise when deriving from multiple base classes.

In a nutshell, interface-based programming provides yet another way to inject polymorphic behavior into a system: If multiple classes (or structures) implement the same interface in their unique ways, you have the power to treat each type in the same manner. As you will see a bit later in this chapter, interfaces are extremely polymorphic, given that types that are not related via classical inheritance can support identical behaviors.

Invoking Interface Members at the Object Level

Now that you have a set of types that support the IPointy interface, the next question is how you interact with the defined members. The most straightforward way to interact with functionality supplied by a given interface is to invoke the methods directly from the object level. For example:

```
Hexagon hex = new Hexagon();
Console.WriteLine("Points: {0}", hex.GetNumberOfPoints());
```

This approach works fine in this case, given that you are well aware that the Hexagon type has implemented the interface in question. Many times, however, you will not be able to determine at compile time which interfaces are supported by a given type. For example, assume you have a collection containing some number of types. Ideally, you would like to determine which interfaces are supported by a type at runtime to trigger the functionality on the fly.

Furthermore, in a number of circumstances (as seen over the course of this chapter) you will be required to obtain a valid interface reference *directly* before you are able to trigger said functionality. Given these two scenarios, let's check out a number of techniques that can be used to test for interface support and see how to obtain a stand-alone interface reference from an implementing type.

Obtaining Interface References: Explicit Casting

Assume you have created an instance of the Hexagon class, and wish to dynamically discover if it supports the pointy behavior. One approach is to make use of an explicit cast (as described in Chapter 4) in order to obtain an interface reference:

```
// Cast for the interface reference.
Hexagon hex = new Hexagon("Bill");
IPointy itfPt = (IPointy)hex;
Console.WriteLine(itfPt.GetNumberOfPoints());
```

If you do not require a stand-alone interface reference, you could shorten the previous code into a single step as follows:

```
// Same end result, less code.
Hexagon hex = new Hexagon("Bill");
Console.WriteLine(((IPointy)hex).GetNumberOfPoints());
```

In each of these cases, you are explicitly asking the Hexagon instance for access to the IPointy interface. If the object does support this interface, you are then able to exercise the behavior accordingly. However, what if you were to create an instance of Circle? Given that the Circle class does not support the IPointy interface, you are issued a runtime error if you attempt to invoke GetNumberOfPoints()! When you attempt to access an interface not supported by a given class using a direct cast, the runtime throws an InvalidCastException. To safely recover from this possibility, simply catch the exception:

```
// Safely cast for interface reference.
Circle c = new Circle("Lisa");
IPointy itfPt;
try
{
    itfPt = (IPointy)c;
    Console.WriteLine(itfPt.GetNumberOfPoints());
}
catch(InvalidCastException e)
{   Console.WriteLine("OOPS!  Not pointy..."); }
```

Obtaining Interface References: The "as" Keyword

The second way you can test for interface support (as well as obtain an interface from an object reference) is to make use of the "as" keyword, which was first introduced in Chapter 4 during our examination of explicit casting operations. For example:

```
// Second way to test for an interface:
Hexagon hex2 = new Hexagon("Peter");
IPointy itfPt2;
itfPt2 = hex2 as IPointy;
if(itfPt2 != null)
    Console.WriteLine(itfPt2.GetNumberOfPoints());
else
    Console.WriteLine("OOPS!  Not pointy...");
```

As you can see, the "as" syntax sets the interface variable to null if a given interface is not supported by the object (notice that you check your IPointy reference for null before continuing) rather than throwing an exception.

Obtaining Interface References: The "is" Keyword

Finally, you may also obtain an interface from an object using the "is" keyword. If the object in question is not IPointy compatible, the condition fails:

```
// Third way to test for an interface.
Triangle t = new Triangle();
if(t is IPointy)
    Console.WriteLine(t.GetNumberOfPoints());
else
    Console.WriteLine("OOPS!  Not pointy...");
```

Exercising the Shapes Hierarchy

In these examples, you could have avoided checking the outcome of asking for the IPointy reference, given that you knew ahead of time which shapes were IPointy compatible. However, what if you were to create an array of generic Shape references, each of which has been assigned to a given subclass? You may make use of any of the previous techniques to discover at runtime which items in the array support this behavior:

```
// Let's discover which shapes are pointy at runtime...
Shape[] s = { new Hexagon(), new Circle(), new Triangle("Joe"),
              new Circle("JoJo")} ;
for(int i = 0; i < s.Length; i++)
{
    // Recall the Shape base class defines an abstract Draw() member,
    // so all shapes know how to draw themselves.
    s[i].Draw();
    // Who's pointy?
    if(s[i] is IPointy)
        Console.WriteLine("-> Points: {0} ", ((IPointy)s[i]).GetNumberOfPoints());
    else
        Console.WriteLine("-> {0}\'s not pointy!", s[i].PetName);
}
```

The output follows in Figure 6-2.

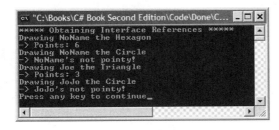

Figure 6-2. Dynamically determining implemented interfaces

Interfaces As Parameters

Given that interfaces are strongly typed entities, you may construct methods that take interfaces as parameters as well as method return values. To illustrate, assume you have defined another interface named IDraw3D as follows:

```
// The 3D drawing behavior.
public interface IDraw3D
{
    void Draw3D();
}
```

Next, assume that two of your three shapes (Circle and Hexagon) have been configured to support this new behavior:

```
// Circle supports IDraw3D.
public class Circle : Shape, IDraw3D
{
...
    public void Draw3D()
    { Console.WriteLine("Drawing Circle in 3D!"); }
}

// If your types support multiple interfaces, simply tack them
// to the end of the class definition.
public class Hexagon : Shape, IPointy, IDraw3D
{
...
    public void Draw3D()
    { Console.WriteLine("Drawing Hexagon in 3D!"); }
}
```

If you now define a method taking an IDraw3D interface as a parameter, you are able to effectively send in *any* object supporting IDraw3D. Consider the following:

```
// Make some shapes. If they can be rendered in 3D, do it!
public class ShapesApp
{
    // I'll draw anyone supporting IDraw3D!
    public static void DrawThisShapeIn3D(IDraw3D itf3d)
    {
        Console.WriteLine("-> Drawing IDraw3D compatible type");
        itf3d.Draw3D();
    }
```

```
    public static int Main(string[] args)
    {
        Shape[] s = { new Hexagon(), new Circle(),
                    new Triangle(), new Circle("JoJo")} ;
        for(int i = 0; i < s.Length; i++)
        {
            ...
            // Can I draw you in 3D?
            if(s[i] is IDraw3D)
                DrawThisShapeIn3D((IDraw3D)s[i]);
        }
        return 0;
    }
}
```

Notice that the triangle is never drawn, as it is not IDraw3D compatible (Figure 6-3).

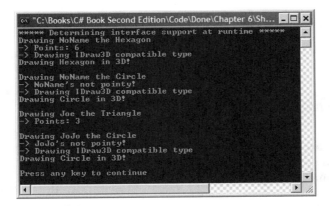

Figure 6-3. Interfaces as parameters

Understanding Explicit Interface Implementation

In our previous definition of IDraw3D, you were forced to name your method Draw3D() in order to avoid clashing with the abstract Draw() method defined in the Shapes base class:

```
// The 3D drawing behavior.
public interface IDraw3D
{ void Draw3D();  }
```

While there is nothing horribly wrong with this interface definition, a more natural method name would simply be Draw():

```
// The 3D drawing behavior.
public interface IDraw3D
{  void Draw(); }
```

If you were to create a new class that derives from Shape *and* implements IDraw3D, you would be in for some problematic behavior. Before seeing the problem firsthand, assume you have defined the following new class named Line:

```
// Problems...
public class Line : Shape, IDraw3D          // Both define a Draw() method!
{
    public override void Draw()
    {
        Console.WriteLine("Drawing a line...");
    }
}
```

The Line class compiles without a hitch. But, consider the following object user code:

```
// Calls Line.Draw()
Line myLine = new Line();
myLine.Draw();
```

```
// Also calls Line.Draw().
IDraw3D itfDraw3d= (IDraw3D) myLine;
itfDraw3d.Draw();
```

Given what you already know about the Shapes base class and IDraw3D interface, it looks as if you have acquired *two* abstract methods named Draw(). However, as the Line class offers a concrete implementation, the compiler is happy to call the same implementation from an interface or object reference. This is problematic in that you would like to have the IDraw3D.Draw() method render a type in stunning 3-D, while the overridden Shape.Draw() method draws in boring 2-D.

Now consider a related problem. What if you wish to ensure that the methods defined by a given interface are only accessible from an interface reference rather than an object reference? Currently, the members defined by the IPointy interface can be accessed using either an object reference or an IPointy reference.

The answer to both questions comes by way of explicit interface implementation. Using this technique, you are able to ensure that the object user can only access methods defined by a given interface using the correct interface reference, as well as circumvent possible name clashes. To illustrate, here is the updated Line class:

```
// Using explicit method implementation we are able
// to provide distinct Draw() implementations.
public class Line : Shape, IDraw3D
{
    // You can only call this method using an IDraw3D interface reference.
    void IDraw3D.Draw()
    { Console.WriteLine("Drawing a 3D line..."); }

    // You can only call this using a Line (or base class) reference.
    public override void Draw()
    { Console.WriteLine("Drawing a line..."); }
}
```

There are a few odds and ends to be aware of when using explicit interface implementation. First and foremost, you cannot make use of an access modifier when using this technique. For example, the following is illegal syntax:

```
// Nope! Illegal.
public class Line : Shape, IDraw3D
{
    public void IDraw3D.Draw()  // <= Error!
    {
        Console.WriteLine("Drawing a 3D line...");
    }
...
}
```

This should make sense. The whole reason to use explicit interface method implementation is to ensure that a given interface method is bound at the interface level. If you were to add the "public" keyword, this would suggest that the method is a member of the public sector of the class, which defeats the point! Given this design, the caller is unable to invoke IDraw3D.Draw() from an object level:

```
// This triggers the overridden Shape.Draw() method.
Line l = new Line();
l.Draw();
```

Now let's build upon the name clash issue. Explicit interface implementation can be very helpful whenever you are implementing a number of interfaces that happen to contain identical methods (even when there is no clashing abstract base class member). For example, assume you wish to create a class that implements all the following interfaces:

```
// Three interfaces each defining identical methods.
public interface IDraw
{ void Draw(); }
public interface IDraw3D
{ void Draw(); }
public interface IDrawToPrinter
{ void Draw(); }
```

If you wish to build a shape (using interface-based techniques) that supports basic rendering (IDraw), 3D rendering (IDraw3D), as well as printing services (IDrawToPrinter), the only way to provide unique behaviors for each method is to use explicit interface implementation:

```
// Not deriving from Shape, but still injecting a name clash.
public class SuperImage : IDraw, IDrawToPrinter, IDraw3D
{
    void IDraw.Draw()
    { // Basic drawing logic. }
    void IDrawToPrinter.Draw()
    { // Printer logic. }
    void IDraw3D.Draw()
    { // 3D support. }
}
```

SOURCE CODE   The Shapes project is located under the Chapter 6 subdirectory.

Interfaces As Polymorphic Agents

As you already know, an abstract base class (containing abstract members) allows us to define a specific behavior that is common across all members in the same class hierarchy. To really understand the usefulness of interfaces, assume that the GetNumberOfPoints() method was *not* defined by IPointy, but rather as an abstract member of the Shape class. If this were the case, Hexagon and Triangle would still be able to return the correct result. At the same time, Circle would also be obligated to contend with the GetNumberOfPoints() method as well. In this case, however, it might seem a bit inelegant to simply return 0. (After all, why bother asking a round object to return the number of points in the first place?)

The problem with defining GetNumberOfPoints() in the Shapes base class is that *all* derived types must contend with this member, regardless of the semantics. Thus, the first key point about interfaces is the fact that you can select which members in the hierarchy support custom behaviors.

Also understand that the same interface can be implemented by numerous types, even if they are not within the same class hierarchy in the first place! This can yield some very powerful programming constructs. For example, assume that you have developed a brand new class hierarchy modeling kitchen utensils and another modeling gardening equipment. Although each hierarchy of types is completely unrelated from a classical inheritance point of view, you can link them together using the common behavior supplied by the IPointy interface:

```
// This array can only contain types which
// implement the IPointy interface.
IPointy myPointyObjects[] = {new Hexagon(), new Knife(),
    new Triangle(), new Fork(), new PitchFork()};
```

At this point (no pun intended), you are able to iterate through the array and treat each object as an IPointy-compatible object, regardless of the overall diversity of the class hierarchies. In fact, you have already seen this situation pop up in Chapter 5. Recall that the IDisposable interface may be implemented by numerous .NET types, regardless of which assembly they reside in. At runtime, you are able to determine if the object supports this behavior (using an explicit cast or the "as"/"is" keywords) and call the Dispose() method.

NOTE   Given the language-agnostic nature of .NET, you are able to define an interface in one language (such as C#) and implement it in another (such as VB .NET). To do so requires a solid understanding of assemblies, which we will tackle in Chapter 9 (so just put this idea on the back burner for now).

Building Interface Hierarchies

To continue our investigation of creating custom interfaces, let's examine the issue of interface hierarchies. Just as a class can serve as a base class to other classes (which can in turn function as base classes to yet another class), it is possible to build derived relationships among interfaces. As you might expect, the topmost interface defines a general behavior, while the most derived interface defines more specific behaviors. To illustrate, ponder the following interface hierarchy:

```
// The base interface.
interface IDraw
{   void Draw();}
interface IDraw2 : IDraw
{   void DrawToPrinter(); }
interface IDraw3 : IDraw2
{   void DrawToMetaFile(); }
```

Understand, of course, that you can name your derived interfaces anything you choose. Here I demonstrate how to make use of a common COM-centric naming convention, which is to suffix a numerical qualifier to the derived type. The relationships between these custom interfaces can be seen in Figure 6-4.

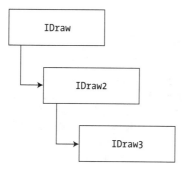

Figure 6-4. A versioned interface hierarchy

Now, if a class wished to support each behavior expressed in this interface hierarchy, it would derive from the *nth-most* interface (IDraw3 in this case). Any methods defined by the base interface(s) are automatically carried into the definition. For example:

```
// This class supports IDraw, IDraw2 and IDraw3.
public class SuperImage : IDraw3
{
    // We don't need to use explicit interface implementation
    // in this case, as there is no name clash. However, by
    // doing so, we will force the user to obtain the interface first.
    void IDraw.Draw()
    { // Basic drawing logic }
    void IDraw2.DrawToPrinter()
    { // Draw to printer. }
    void IDraw3.DrawToMetaFile()
    { // Draw to metafile. }
}
```

Here is some sample usage:

```
// Exercise the interfaces.
public class TheApp
{
    public static int Main(string[] args)
    {
        SuperImage si = new SuperImage();
        // Get IDraw.
        IDraw itfDraw = (IDraw)si;
        itfDraw.Draw();
```

```
            // Now get IDraw3.
            if(itfDraw is IDraw3)
            {
                    IDraw3 itfDraw3 = (IDraw3)itfDraw;
                    itfDraw3.DrawToMetaFile();
                    itfDraw3.DrawToPrinter();
            }
            return 0;
    }
}
```

Interfaces with Multiple Base Interfaces

As you build interface hierarchies, be aware that it is completely permissible to create an interface that derives from multiple base interfaces (unlike classic COM). Recall, of course, that it is *not* permissible to build a class that derives from multiple base classes. For example, assume you are building a new set of interfaces that model automobile behaviors:

```
interface IBasicCar
{  void Drive(); }
interface IUnderwaterCar
{  void Dive(); }
// Here we have an interface with TWO base interfaces.
interface IJamesBondCar : IBasicCar, IUnderwaterCar
{  void TurboBoost(); }
```

If you were to build a class that implements IJamesBondCar, you would now be responsible for implementing TurboBoost(), Dive(), and Drive():

```
public class JBCar : IJamesBondCar
{
    public JBCar(){ }
    // Again, we are not required to use explicit interface implementation,
    // as we have no name clashes.
    void IBasicCar.Drive(){ Console.WriteLine("Speeding up...");}
    void IUnderwaterCar.Dive(){ Console.WriteLine("Submerging...");}
    void IJamesBondCar.TurboBoost(){ Console.WriteLine("Blast off!");}
}
```

This specialized automobile can now be manipulated as you would expect:

```
JBCar j = new JBCar();
if(j is IJamesBondCar)
{
    ((IJamesBondCar)j).Drive();
    ((IJamesBondCar)j).TurboBoost();
    ((IJamesBondCar)j).Dive();
}
```

SOURCE CODE   The IFaceHierarchy project is located under the Chapter 6 subdirectory.

Implementing Interfaces Using VS .NET

Although interface-based programming is a very powerful programming technique, one drawback is the very simple fact that you are required to do a lot of manual typing. Given that interfaces are a named set of abstract members, you will be required to type in the stub code (and implementation) for *each* interface method on *each* class that supports the behavior.

As you would expect, VS .NET does support an integrated tool that helps make this task less burdensome. To illustrate, assume you have an interface defining the following four methods:

```
public interface IAmAnInterface
{
    void MethodA();
    void MethodC();
    void MethodD();
    void MethodE();
}
```

And also assume you have a class that supports IAmAnInterface:

```
public class SomeClass : IAmAnInterface
{
}
```

At this point, you are free to build stub code for each abstract method by hand. However, if you wish to leverage VS .NET, switch to Class View and find a class that already specifies support for the interface you wish to implement. Once you do, expand the Bases and Interfaces node, right-click the interface icon, and select Add | Implement Interface (Figure 6-5).

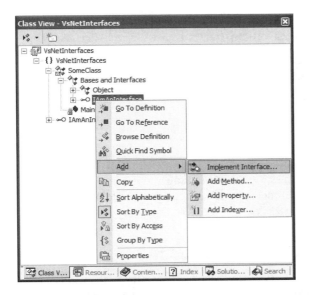

Figure 6-5. Implementing interfaces via VS .NET

Once you do, you will see that VS .NET has built automatic stub code wrapped in a #region/#endregion pair. Also recall from Chapter 4, that when you insert a new class definition into your VS .NET projects using Class View, you are able to specify the set of implemented interfaces at the time of creation (Figure 6-6). When you do so, you will still need to run the Implement Interface Wizard as shown previously.

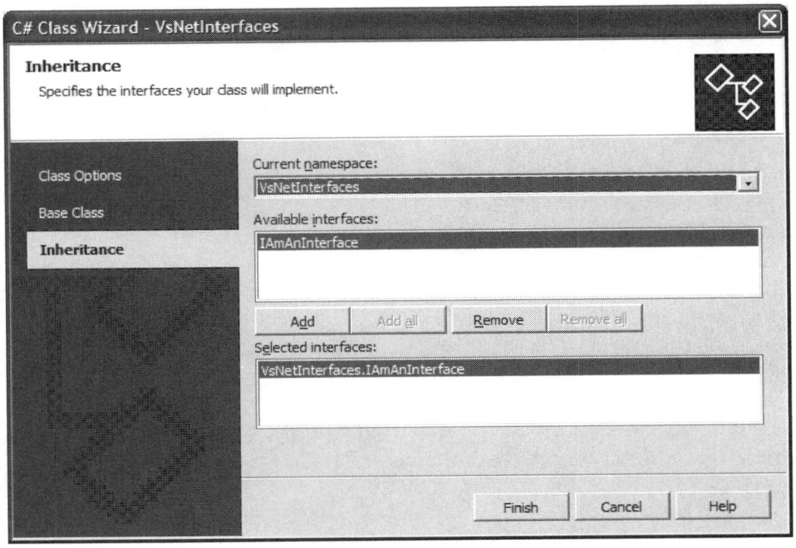

Figure 6-6. Specifying interfaces for new types

NOTE The Implement interface Wizard has existed since the first release of VS .NET. However, with VS .NET 2003, you are given an additional IDE support that makes implementing interfaces even simpler. When you type in the name of an interface to be supported by a class or structure, the IDE will automatically bring up a prompt for you to hit the Tab key. Once you do, each method will be stubbed out as if you ran the Implement Interface Wizard.

Now that you have drilled into the specifics of building and implementing custom interfaces, the remainder of the chapter examines a number of predefined interfaces defined in the .NET base class libraries.

Understanding the IConvertible Interface

Interfaces are used extensively throughout the .NET base class libraries, even in the most unsuspecting of places. Consider the IConvertible type, which allows you to dynamically convert between data types using interface-based programming techniques. Using this interface, you are able to cast between types on the fly using language-agnostic terms (in contrast to the language-specific C# casting operator).

Recall from Chapter 3 that a majority of the intrinsic data types of C# (bool, int, double, etc.) are simply aliases to true-blue structures in the System namespace. Like any .NET type, each of these structures may define any number of methods and may optionally implement any number of predefined interfaces. For example, if you were to view the formal C# definition of System.Boolean (using wincv.exe), you would find this type (as well as all intrinsic data type structures) implements the IComparable and IConvertible interfaces:

```
public struct Boolean : IComparable, IConvertible
{
    public static readonly string FalseString;
    public static readonly string TrueString;
    public virtual int CompareTo(object obj);
    public virtual bool Equals(object obj);
    public virtual int GetHashCode();
    public Type GetType();
    public virtual TypeCode GetTypeCode();
    public static bool Parse(string value);
    public virtual string ToString();
    public virtual string ToString(IFormatProvider provider);
}
```

For this current discussion, we are only concerned with the behavior of the IConvertible interface, which is defined as follows:

```
public interface IConvertible
{
    TypeCode GetTypeCode();
    bool ToBoolean(IFormatProvider provider);
    byte ToByte(IFormatProvider provider);
    char ToChar(IFormatProvider provider);
    DateTime ToDateTime(IFormatProvider provider);
    Decimal ToDecimal(IFormatProvider provider);
    double ToDouble(IFormatProvider provider);
    short ToInt16(IFormatProvider provider);
    int ToInt32(IFormatProvider provider);
    long ToInt64(IFormatProvider provider);
    SByte ToSByte(IFormatProvider provider);
    float ToSingle(IFormatProvider provider);
    string ToString(IFormatProvider provider);
    object ToType(Type conversionType, IFormatProvider provider);
    UInt16 ToUInt16(IFormatProvider provider);
    UInt32 ToUInt32(IFormatProvider provider);
    UInt64 ToUInt64(IFormatProvider provider);
}
```

Now, if you are doing a quick compare and contrast, you might feel that the previous definition of System.Boolean is in error, given that most of the members of IConvertable do not appear in the formal structure definition! The reason for this behavior may surprise you: If a type implements members of a given interface using explicit interface implementation, they are hidden from tools such as wincv.exe (and typically from online help!). Therefore, if you wish to gain access to each member of IConvertible interface, you must explicitly request access to the interface using any of the previously examined techniques:

```
// Obtain the IConvertible interface.
bool myBool = true;
IConvertible itfConv = (IConvertible)myBool;
```

NOTE   This illustrates yet another use of explicit interface implementation: to hide advanced behaviors. If you are building a type that supports an interface you suspect may be leveraged by only a small number of developers, this technique ensures the implemented members are not visible from the object level.

The IConvertible.ToXXXX() Members

At this point, you may attempt to call each member of the IConvertible interface. However, what exactly do these members do? First, this interface defines a number of methods of the form ToXXXX(), which as you can most likely tell, provide a way to convert from one type into another. As you may also be able to tell, it may not always be possible to convert between data types. For example, although it is natural to envision converting from an Int32 into a Double, it really makes no sense to convert from a Boolean into a DateTime.

Given the fact that when a type implements an interface, it must contend with *all* methods (even if they are not applicable), the system types will simply throw an InvalidCastException if the conversion is semantically ill formed:

```
// Obtain the IConvertible interface.
bool myBool = true;
IConvertible itfConv = (IConvertible)myBool;
try
{ itfConv.ToSingle(...); }
catch(InvalidCastException e)
{ Console.WriteLine(e); }
```

A Brief Word Regarding IFormatProvider

Notice that all of the ToXXXX() methods take a parameter of type IFormatProvider. Objects that implement this interface are able to format their contents based on culture-specific information (for example, returning a floating point number that is formatted in various currencies). Here is the formal definition:

```
public interface IFormatProvider
{
    object GetFormat(Type formatType);
}
```

If you were to build a custom type that should be formatted using various locals, implementing IFormatProvider would be a must. However, if you are simply attempting to call members of the base class libraries that require an IFormatProvider-compatible object, feel free to leverage the System.Globalization.CultureInfo type as follows:

```
IConvertible itfConvert = (IConvertible)theInt;
byte theByte = itfConvert.ToByte(CultureInfo.CurrentCulture);
Console.WriteLine("Type code int converted to byte is: {0}",
    theByte.GetTypeCode());
Console.WriteLine("Value of converted int: {0}", theByte);
```

IConvertible.GetTypeCode()

In addition to the ToXXXX() members, IConvertible defines a member named GetTypeCode(). This method, which is available to any class or structure implementing IConvertible, allows you to programmatically discover a value that represents the *type code* of the type, which is represented by the following enumeration:

```
public enum TypeCode
{
    Boolean, Byte, Char, DateTime,
    DBNull, Decimal, Double, Empty,
    Int16, Int32, Int64, Object,
    SByte, Single, String, UInt16,
    UInt32, UInt64
}
```

To be sure, IConvertible.GetTypeCode() is not a method you will need to call all that often in your day-to-day programming endeavors. However, when we look at dynamic assemblies and the System.Reflection.Emit namespace in Chapter 11, you will see the usefulness of determining the underlying identity of a given type.

The System.Convert Type

To wrap up this overview of the IConvertible type, it is worth pointing out that the System namespace defines a type named Convert, which echoes (and greatly extends) the functionality of the IConvertible interface. Contrary to what you might be thinking, System.Convert does *not* directly implement IConvertible; however, the same set of members are defined on its default public interface (with numerous overrides).

To list the formal definition of this type here in the text would be a dreadful waste of space, so I'll assume you will check it out at your leisure using wincv.exe. In a nutshell, each of these static methods allows you to pass in "the type you have" to get back "the type you want." without having to make use of language-specific casting syntax. Like the members of IConvertible, if the conversion makes no semantic sense, an InvalidCastException is thrown.

SOURCE CODE   The TypeConversions project is located under the Chapter 6 subdirectory.

Building a Custom Enumerator (IEnumerable and IEnumerator)

Next up, let's examine how you can implement the standard IEnumerable and IEnumerator interfaces on a custom type (and see why you might wish to do so). Assume you have developed a class named Cars that represents a collection of individual Car objects using a simple System.Array type. Here is the initial definition:

```
// Cars is a container of Car objects.
public class Cars
{
    private Car[] carArray;
    // Create some Car objects upon startup.
    public Cars()
    {
        carArray = new Car[4];
        carArray[0] = new Car("FeeFee", 200, 0);
        carArray[1] = new Car("Clunker", 90, 0);
        carArray[2] = new Car("Zippy", 30, 0);
        carArray[3] = new Car("Fred", 30, 0);
    }
}
```

Ideally, it would be convenient from the object user's point of view to iterate over the Cars type using the C# foreach construct, in order to obtain each internal Car:

```
// This seems reasonable...
public class CarDriver
{
    public static void Main()
    {
        Cars carLot = new Cars();
        // Hand over each car in the collection?
        foreach (Car c in carLot)
        {
            Console.WriteLine("Name: {0} ", c.PetName);
            Console.WriteLine("Max speed: {0} ", c.MaxSpeed);
        }
    }
}
```

Sadly, if you attempt to execute this code, the compiler would complain that the Cars class does not implement the GetEnumerator() method. This method is defined by the IEnumerable interface, which is found lurking within the System.Collections namespace:

```
// To obtain subtypes using the foreach syntax, the container
// must implement IEnumerable.
public interface IEnumerable
{
    IEnumerator GetEnumerator();
}
```

Thus, to rectify the problem, you may begin by updating the Cars definition as follows:

```
public class Cars : IEnumerable
{
    ...
```

```
    // IEnumerable defines a single method.
    public IEnumerator GetEnumerator()
    {
        // OK, now what?
    }
}
```

So far so good. However, as you can see, GetEnumerator() returns yet another interface named IEnumerator. IEnumerator can be obtained from an object to traverse over an internal collection of types. IEnumerator is also defined in the System.Collections namespace and defines the following three methods:

```
// IEnumerable.GetEnumerator() returns an object
// implementing IEnumerator.
public interface IEnumerator
{
    bool MoveNext ();        // Advance the internal position of the cursor.
    object Current { get;}   // Get the current item (read-only property).
    void Reset ();           // Reset the cursor to the beginning of the list.
}
```

Now, given that IEnumerable.GetEnumerator() returns an IEnumerator interface, you may update the Cars type as follows:

```
// Getting closer...
public class Cars : IEnumerable, IEnumerator
{
...
    // Implementation of IEnumerable.
    public IEnumerator GetEnumerator()
    {
        return (IEnumerator)this;
    }
}
```

The final detail is to flesh out the implementation of MoveNext(), Current, and Reset() for the Cars type. Here is one possible implementation of these members:

```
// An enumerable car collection!
public class Cars : IEnumerable, IEnumerator
{
    private Car[] carArray;
    // Current position in array.
    int pos = -1;
    public Cars()
    {  // Make some cars and add them to the array... }
```

```
    // IEnumerator implementation.
    public bool MoveNext()
    {
        if(pos < carArray.Length)
        {
            pos++;
            return true;
        }
        else
            return false;
    }
    public void Reset() {  pos = 0; }
    public object Current
    {  get {  return carArray[pos]; }  }
    // IEnumerable implementation.
    public IEnumerator GetEnumerator()
    {  return (IEnumerator)this; }
}
```

So then, what have you gained by equipping your class to support the IEnumerator and IEnumerable interfaces? First, your custom type can now be traversed using the foreach syntax.

```
// No problem!
foreach (Car c in carLot)
{
    Console.WriteLine("Name: {0} ", c.PetName);
    Console.WriteLine("Max speed: {0} ", c.MaxSpeed);
}
```

In addition, when you explicitly implement the members of IEnumerator, you provide the object user with an alternative of accessing the underlying objects in the container (which, as you may be able to tell depending on your background, looks a lot like manipulating the COM IEnumXXXX interface using raw C++):

```
// Access Car types using IEnumerator.
IEnumerator itfEnum;
itfEnum = (IEnumerator)carLot;
// Reset the cursor to the beginning.
itfEnum.Reset();
// Advance internal cursor by 1.
itfEnum.MoveNext();
// Grab current Car and crank some tunes.
object curCar = itfEnum.Current;
((Car)curCar).CrankTunes(true);
```

Tightening Up the Cars Class Implementation

The current implementation of the IEnumerator interface, while illustrative, is actually a bit on the verbose side. Given the fact that System.Array already implements

IEnumerator, you could shorten the coding of the Cars type quite a bit. Here is the complete update:

```
public class Cars : IEnumerable, // IEnumerator  Don't need this anymore!
{
    // This class maintains an array of cars.
    private Car[] carArray;
    public Cars()
    {
        carArray = new Car[4];
        carArray[0] = new Car("FeeFee", 200, 0);
        carArray[1] = new Car("Clunker", 90, 0);
        carArray[2] = new Car("Zippy", 30, 0);
        carArray[3] = new Car("Fred", 30, 0);
    }
    public IEnumerator GetEnumerator()
    {
        // Now just get back the IEnumerator from
        // the internal array!
        return carArray.GetEnumerator();
    }
}
```

Now that you are simply asking the carArray type for its implementation of GetEnumerator(), your custom container type is not required to provide a manual implementation of Move(), Current(), or Reset() (as well, you no longer have to maintain a current position index!). Do be aware that when you build custom container types in this fashion, you are no longer able to call the members of IEnumerator directly from the Cars type (which will seldom pose a problem).

SOURCE CODE   The ObjEnum project is located under the Chapter 6 subdirectory.

Building Cloneable Objects (ICloneable)

As you recall from Chapter 3, System.Object defines a member named MemberwiseClone(). This method is used to make a *shallow copy* of an object instance. Object users do not call this method directly (as it is protected); however, a given object instance may call this method itself during the *cloning* process. To illustrate, assume you have a simple class named Point:

```
// The classic Point example...
public class Point
{
    // Public for easy access.
    public int x, y;
    public Point(){ }
    public Point(int x, int y) { this.x = x; this.y = y;}
    // Override Object.ToString().
    public override string ToString()
    {  return "X: " + x + " Y: " + y; }
}
```

Given what you already know about reference types and value types (Chapter 3), you are aware that if you set one reference to another reference, you have two variables pointing to the same object in memory. Thus, the following assignment operation results in two references to the same Point object on the heap; modifications using either reference affect the same object on the heap:

```
// Two references to same object!
Console.WriteLine("Assigning points.");
Point p1 = new Point(50, 50);
Point p2 = p1;
p2.x = 0;
```

When you wish to equip your custom types to support the ability to return an identical copy of itself to the caller, you may implement the standard ICloneable interface. This type defines a single method named Clone():

```
public interface ICloneable
{
    object Clone();
}
```

Obviously, the implementation of the Clone() method varies between objects. However, the basic functionality tends to be the same: Copy the values of your member variables into a new object instance, and return it to the user. To illustrate, ponder the following update to the Point class:

```
// The Point class supports deep copy semantics a la ICloneable.
public class Point : ICloneable
{
    public int x, y;
    public Point(){ }
    public Point(int x, int y) { this.x = x; this.y = y;}
    // Return a copy of the current object.
    public object Clone()
    {  return new Point(this.x, this.y); }
    public override string ToString()
    {  return "X: " + x + " Y: " + y; }
}
```

In this way, you can create exact stand-alone copies of the Point type, as illustrated by the following code:

```
// Notice Clone() returns a generic object type.
// You must perform an explicit cast to obtain the derived type.
Point p3 = new Point(100, 100);
Point p4 = (Point)p3.Clone();
// Change p4.x (which will not change p3.x).
p4.x = 0;
// Print each object.
Console.WriteLine(p3);
Console.WriteLine(p4);
```

While the current implementation of Point fits the bill, you can streamline things just a bit. Because the Point type does not contain references to other internal reference types, you could simplify the Clone() method as follows:

```
public object Clone()
{
    // Copy each field of the Point member by member.
    return this.MemberwiseClone();
}
```

Be aware, however, that if the Point type did contain references to other internal reference types, MemberwiseClone() will copy the references as well (aka a shallow copy)! If you wish to support a true deep copy, you will need to create a new instance of the type, and manually assign the inner object reference to new (identical) objects. Let's see an example.

A More Elaborate Cloning Example

Now assume the Point class contains an internal class that represents a description of a given Point (time of creation and pet name). To represent the time this point came into being, the PointDesc class contains an object of type System.DateTime. Here is the implementation:

```
// This class describes a point.
public class PointDesc
{
    public string petName;
    public DateTime creationDate;
    public PointDesc(string petName)
    {
        this.petName = petName;
        // Inject a time lag to get
        // unique times.
        System.Threading.Thread.Sleep(2000);
        creationDate = DateTime.Now;
    }
    public string CreationTime()
    { return creationDate.ToString(); }
}
```

The initial updates to the Point class itself included modifying ToString() to account for these new bits of state data, as well as defining and creating the PointDesc reference type. To allow the outside world to establish a pet name for the Point, you also update the arguments passed into the overloaded constructor. Here is the first code update:

```
public class Point : ICloneable
{
    public int x, y;
    public PointDesc desc;
    public Point(){}
    public Point(int x, int y)
    {
        this.x = x; this.y = y;
        desc = new PointDesc("NoName");
    }
    public Point(int x, int y, string petname)
    {
        this.x = x;
        this.y = y;
        desc = new PointDesc(petname);
    }
    public object Clone()
    { return this.MemberwiseClone(); }
    public override string ToString()
    {
        return "X: " + x + " Y: " + y +
        " PetName: " + desc.PetName +
        " Time of creation: " + desc.CreationTime();
    }
}
```

Notice that you did not yet update your Clone() method. Therefore, when the object user asks for a clone, a shallow (member-by-member) copy is achieved. Thus, the Point returned from Clone() references the same string in the PointDesc as the original! To illustrate:

```
// Now Clone object.
Point p3 = new Point(100, 100, "Jane");
Point p4 = (Point)p3.Clone();
Console.WriteLine("Before modification:");
Console.WriteLine("p3: {0}", p3);
Console.WriteLine("p4: {0}", p4);
p4.desc.petName = "XXXXX";
Console.WriteLine("\nCloned p3 into p4 and changed p4.PetName:");
Console.WriteLine("p3: {0}", p3);
Console.WriteLine("p4: {0}\n", p4);
```

Figure 6-7 shows the output.

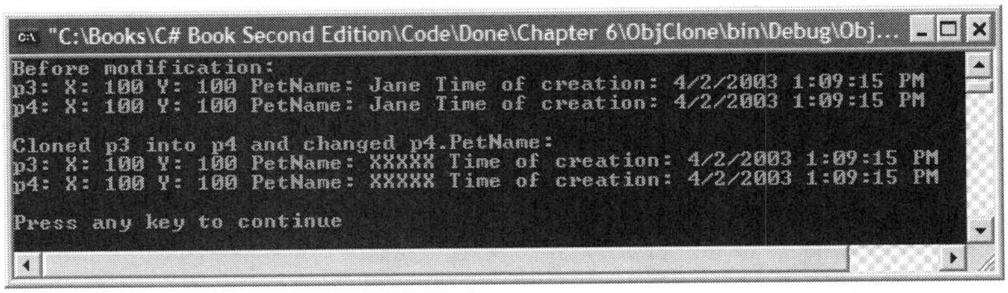

Figure 6-7. MemberwiseClone() copies references, not values.

In order for your Clone() method to make a complete deep copy of the internal reference types, you need to bypass the MemberwiseClone() call with something along the lines of the following:

```
// Now we need to adjust for the PointDesc type.
public object Clone()
{
    Point copyPt = new Point();
    copyPt.x = this.x;
    copyPt.y = this.y;
    PointDesc copyPtDesc = new PointDesc(this.desc.petName);
    copyPtDesc.petName = this.desc.petName;
    copyPtDesc.creationDate = this.desc.creationDate;
    copyPt.desc = copyPtDesc;
    return copyPt;
}
```

If you rerun the application once again (Figure 6-8), you see that the Point returned from Clone() does indeed reference its own copy of the PointDesc type (note the pet name is unique).

Figure 6-8. Now you have a true deep copy.

To summarize the cloning process, if you have a class or structure that contains nothing but value types, implement your Clone() method using MemberwiseClone(). However, if you have a custom type that maintains other reference types, you need to establish a new type that takes into account each internal class type.

SOURCE CODE The ObjClone project is located under the Chapter 6 subdirectory.

Building Comparable Objects (IComparable)

The IComparable interface (defined in the System namespace) specifies a behavior that allows an object to be sorted based on some internal key. Here is the formal definition:

```
// This interface allows an object to specify its
// relationship between other like objects.
interface IComparable
{
    int CompareTo(object o);
}
```

Let's assume you have updated the Car class to maintain an internal ID number. Object users might create an array of Car types as follows:

```
// Make an array of Car types.
Car[] myAutos = new Car[5];
myAutos[0] = new Car(123, "Rusty");
myAutos[1] = new Car(6, "Mary");
myAutos[2] = new Car(83, "Viper");
myAutos[3] = new Car(13, "NoName");
myAutos[4] = new Car(9873, "Chucky");
```

As you recall, the System.Array class defines a static method named Sort(). When you invoke this method on an array of intrinsic types (e.g., int, short), you are able to sort the items in the array from lowest to highest, as these intrinsic data types implement IComparable. However, what if you were to send an array of Car types into the Sort() method as follows:

```
// Sort my cars?
Array.Sort(myAutos);    // Nope, not yet...sorry!
```

If you run this test, you would find that an ArgumentException exception is thrown by the runtime, with the following message: "At least one object must implement IComparable." Therefore, when you build custom types, you can implement IComparable to allow arrays of your types to be sorted. When you flesh out the details of CompareTo(), it will be up to you to decide what the baseline of the ordering operation will be. For the Car type, the internal ID seems to be the most logical candidate:

```
// The iteration of the Car can be ordered
// based on the CarID.
public class Car : IComparable
{
...
    // IComparable implementation.
    int IComparable.CompareTo(object o)
    {
        Car temp = (Car)o;
        if(this.CarID > temp.CarID)
            return 1;
        if(this.CarID < temp.CarID)
            return -1;
        else
            return 0;
    }
}
```

As you can see, the logic behind CompareTo() is to test the incoming type against the current instance. The return value of CompareTo() is used to discover if this type is less than, greater than, or equal to the object it is being compared with (Table 6-1).

Table 6-1. CompareTo() Return Values

CompareTo() Return Value	Meaning in Life
Any number less than zero	This instance is less than object.
Zero	This instance is equal to object.
Any number greater than zero	This instance is greater than object.

Now that your Car type understands how to compare itself to like objects, you can write the following user code:

```
// Exercise the IComparable interface.
public class CarApp
{
    public static int Main(string[] args)
    {
        // Make an array of Car types.
        Car[] myAutos = new Car[5];
        myAutos[0] = new Car(123, "Rusty");
        myAutos[1] = new Car(6, "Mary");
        myAutos[2] = new Car(83, "Viper");
        myAutos[3] = new Car(13, "NoName");
        myAutos[4] = new Car(9873, "Chucky");
```

```
// Dump current array.
Console.WriteLine("Here is the unordered set of cars:");
foreach(Car c in myAutos)
    Console.WriteLine("{0} {1}", c.ID, c.PetName);
// Now, sort them using IComparable!
Array.Sort(myAutos);
// Dump sorted array.
Console.WriteLine("Here is the ordered set of cars:");
foreach(Car c in myAutos)
    Console.WriteLine("{0} {1}", c.ID, c.PetName);
return 0;
    }
}
```

Figure 6-9 illustrates a test run.

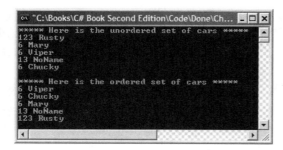

Figure 6-9. Comparing automobiles based on car ID

As a side note, if multiple items in the Car array have the same value assigned to the ID member variable, the sort simply lists them according to their occurrence in the sort (notice in Figure 6-9 there are three cars with the ID of 6).

Specifying Multiple Sort Orders (IComparer)

In this version of the Car type, you made use of the underlying ID to function as the baseline of the sort order. Another design might have used the pet name of the car as the basis of the sorting algorithm (to list cars alphabetically). Now, what if you wanted to build a Car that could be sorted by ID *as well as* by pet name? If this is the behavior you are interested in, you need to make friends with another standard interface named IComparer, defined within the System.Collections namespace as follows:

```
// A generic way to compare two objects.
interface IComparer
{
    int Compare(object o1, object o2);
}
```

Unlike the IComparable interface, IComparer is typically *not* implemented on the type you are trying to sort (i.e., the Car). Rather, you implement this interface on any number of helper objects, one for each sort order (pet name, ID, etc.). Currently, the Car type already knows how to compare itself against other cars based on the internal car ID. Therefore, to allow the object user to sort an array of Car types by pet name will require an additional helper class that implements IComparer. Here's the code:

```
// This helper class is used to sort an array of Cars by pet name.
using System.Collections;
public class SortByPetName : IComparer
{
    public SortByPetName(){ }
    // Test the pet name of each object.
    int IComparer.Compare(object o1, object o2)
    {
        Car t1 = (Car)o1;
        Car t2 = (Car)o2;
        return String.Compare(t1.PetName, t2.PetName);
    }
}
```

The object user code is able to make use of this helper class. System.Array has a number of overloaded Sort() methods, one that just happens to take an object implementing IComparer (Figure 6-10):

```
// Now sort by pet name.
Array.Sort(myAutos, new SortByPetName());
// Dump sorted array.
Console.WriteLine("Ordering by pet name:");
foreach(Car c in myAutos)
    Console.WriteLine("{0} {1}", c.ID, c.PetName);
```

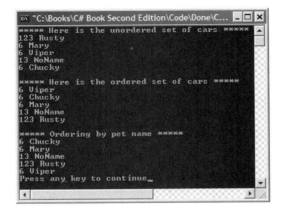

Figure 6-10. Sorting automobiles by pet name

Custom Properties, Custom Sort Types

It is worth pointing out that you can make use of a custom static property in order to help the object user along when sorting your Car types by pet name. Assume the Car class has added a static read-only property named SortByPetName() that returns the correct IComparer interface:

```
// We now support a custom property to return
// the correct IComparer interface.
public class Car : IComparable
{
    ...
    // Property to return the SortByPetName comparer.
    public static IComparer SortByPetName
    { get { return (IComparer)new SortByPetName(); } }
}
```

The object user code can now be modified as follows:

```
// This was a bit cumbersome.
// Array.Sort(myAutos, new SortByPetName());
// Cleaner!  Just ask the car for the correct sort object.
Array.Sort(myAutos, Car.SortByPetName);
```

SOURCE CODE The ObjComp project is located under the Chapter 6 subdirectory.

Exploring the System.Collections Namespace

The most primitive C# collection construct is System.Array. As you have already seen in Chapter 3, this class does provide quite a number of member functions that encapsulate a number of interesting services (e.g., reversing, sorting, cloning, and enumerating). In a similar vein, this chapter has also shown you how to build custom types with many of the same services using standard interfaces. To round out your appreciation of the various .NET interfaces, the final order of business is to investigate the various types defined within the System.Collections namespace.

The Interfaces of System.Collections

First of all, System.Collections defines a number of standard interfaces (many of which you have already implemented during the course of this chapter). Most of the classes defined within the System.Collections namespace implement these interfaces to provide access to their contents. Table 6-2 gives a breakdown of the core collection-centric interfaces.

Table 6-2. Interfaces of System.Collections

System.Collections Interface	Meaning in Life
ICollection	Defines generic characteristics (e.g., read-only, thread safe, etc.) for a collection class
IComparer	Allows two objects to be compared
IDictionary	Allows an object to represent its contents using name/value pairs
IDictionaryEnumerator	Used to enumerate the contents of an object supporting IDictionary
IEnumerable	Returns the IEnumerator interface for a given object
IEnumerator	Generally used to support foreach-style iteration of subtypes
IHashCodeProvider	Returns the hash code for the implementing type using a customized hash algorithm
IList	Provides behavior to add, remove, and index items in a list of objects

As you may suspect, many of these interfaces are related by an interface hierarchy, while others are stand-alone entities. Figure 6-11 illustrates the relationship between each type (recall that it is permissible for a single interface to derive from multiple interfaces).

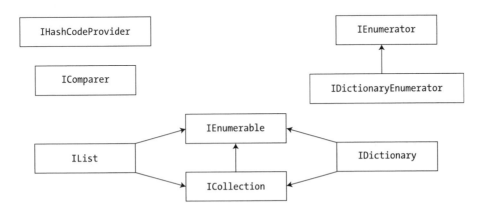

Figure 6-11. The System.Collections interface hierarchy

As you have already seen the behavior provided by IComparer, IEnumerable, and IEnumerator firsthand during this chapter, let's check out the remainder of these key interfaces of the System.Collections namespace, and then turn our attention to select class types.

The Role of ICollection

The ICollection interface is the most primitive interface of the System.Collections namespace in that it defines a behavior supported by a collection type. In a nutshell, this interface provides a small set of properties that allow you to determine (a) the number of items in the container, (b) the thread-safety of the container, as well as (c) the ability to copy the contents into a System.Array type. Formally, ICollection is defined as follows (again note that ICollection extends IEnumerable):

```
public interface ICollection : IEnumerable
{
    // IEnumerable member...
    int Count { get; }
    bool IsSynchronized { get; }
    object SyncRoot { get; }
    void CopyTo(Array array, int index);
}
```

The Role of IDictionary

IDictionary is a fairly simple interface, in that much of its functionality is obtained by its base interfaces ICollection and IEnumerable. Here is the formal definition:

```
public interface IDictionary :
    ICollection, IEnumerable
{
    // ICollection and IEnumerable members...
    bool IsFixedSize { get; }
    bool IsReadOnly { get; }
    object this[ object key ] { get; set; }
    ICollection Keys { get; }
    ICollection Values { get; }
    void Add(object key, object value);
    void Clear();
    bool Contains(object key);
    IDictionaryEnumerator GetEnumerator();
    void Remove(object key);
}
```

As you may already be aware, a *dictionary* is simply a collection that maintains a set of name/value pairs. For example, you could build a custom type that implements IDictionary such that you can store Car types (the values) that may be retrieved by ID or pet name (e.g., names). Given this functionality, you can see that the IDictionary interface defines a Keys and Values property as well as Add(), Remove(), and Contains() methods. The individual items may be obtained by the type indexer.

The Role of IDictionaryEnumerator

If you were paying attention, you may have noted that IDictionary.GetEnumerator() returns an instance of the IDictionaryEnumerator type. As you may be expecting, IDictionaryEnumerator is simply a strongly typed enumerator, given that it extends IEnumerator by adding the following functionality:

```
public interface IDictionaryEnumerator : IEnumerator
{
    // IEnumerator methods...
    DictionaryEntry Entry { get; }
    object Key { get; }
    object Value { get; }
}
```

Notice how IDictionaryEnumerator allows you to enumerate over items in the dictionary via the generic Entry property, which returns a System.Collections.DictionaryEntry class type. In addition, you are also able to traverse the name/value pairs using the Key/Value properties.

The Role of IHashCodeProvider

IHashCodeProvider is a very simple interface defining only one member:

```
public interface IHashCodeProvider
{
    int GetHashCode(object obj);
}
```

Types that implement this interface provide the ability to retrieve the hash code for a particular type (which may or may not leverage the type's implementation of System.Object.GetHashCode()).

The Role of IList

The final key interface of System.Collections is IList, which provides the ability to insert, remove, and index items into (or out of) a container:

```
public interface IList :
    ICollection, IEnumerable
{
    bool IsFixedSize { get; }
    bool IsReadOnly { get; }
    object this[ int index ] { get; set; }
    int Add(object value);
    void Clear();
    bool Contains(object value);
    int IndexOf(object value);
    void Insert(int index, object value);
    void Remove(object value);
    void RemoveAt(int index);
}
```

The Class Types of System.Collections

Now that you understand the basic functionality provided by each interface, Table 6-3 provides a rundown of the core collection classes, including a list of implemented interfaces.

Table 6-3. Classes of System.Collections

System.Collections Class	Meaning in Life	Key Implemented Interfaces
ArrayList	A dynamically sized array of objects.	IList, ICollection, IEnumerable, and ICloneable
Hashtable	Represents a collection of objects identified by a numerical key. Types stored in a Hashtable should always override System.Object.GetHashCode().	IDictionary, ICollection, IEnumerable, and ICloneable
Queue	Represents a standard first-in-first-out (FIFO) queue.	ICollection, ICloneable, and IEnumerable
SortedList	Like a dictionary; however, the elements can also be accessed by ordinal position (e.g., index).	IDictionary, ICollection, IEnumerable, and ICloneable
Stack	A last-in, first-out (LIFO) queue providing push, pop (and peek) functionality.	ICollection and IEnumerable

In addition to these key types, System.Collections defines some minor players (at least in terms of their day-to-day usefulness) such as BitArray, CaseInsensitiveComparer, and CaseInsensitiveHashCodeProvider. Furthermore, this namespace also defines a small set of abstract base classes (CollectionBase, ReadOnlyCollectionBase, and DictionaryBase) that can be used to build strongly typed containers.

As you begin to experiment with the System.Collections types, you will find they all tend to share common functionality (that's the point of interface-based programming). Thus, rather than listing out the members of each and every collection class, the next task of this chapter is to illustrate how to interact with three common collection types: ArrayList, Queue, and Stack. Once you understand the functionality of these types, gaining an understanding of the remaining collection classes should naturally follow (especially since each of the types is fully documented within online help).

Working with the ArrayList Type

The ArrayList type is bound to be your most frequently used collection type in that it allows you to dynamically resize the contents at your whim (in stark contrast to a simple System.Array type). To illustrate the basics of this type, ponder the following code:

```
// Create ArrayList and fill with some initial values.
ArrayList carArList = new ArrayList();
carArList.AddRange(new Car[] { new Car("Fred", 90, 10),
    new Car("Mary", 100, 50), new Car("MB", 190, 0)});
Console.WriteLine("Items in carArList: {0}", carArList.Count);
// Print out current values.
foreach(Car c in carArList)
{ Console.WriteLine("Car pet name: {0}", c.PetName); }
// Insert a new item.
carArList.Insert(2, new Car("TheNewCar", 0, 0));
Console.WriteLine("Items in carArList: {0}", carArList.Count);
// Get object array from ArrayList and print again.
object[] arrayOfCars = carArList.ToArray();
for(int i = 0; i < arrayOfCars.Length; i++)
{
    Console.WriteLine("Car pet name: {0}",
        ((Car)arrayOfCars[i]).PetName);
}
```

Here you are making use of the AddRange() method to populate your ArrayList with a set of Car types (as you can tell, this is basically a shorthand notation for calling Add() *n* number of times). Once you print out the number of items in the collection (as well as enumerate over each item to obtain the pet name), check out the call to Insert(). As you can see, Insert() allows you to plug a new item into the ArrayList at a specified index. Next, notice the call to the ToArray() method, which returns a generic array of System.Object types based on the contents of the original ArrayList. Figure 6-12 shows the output.

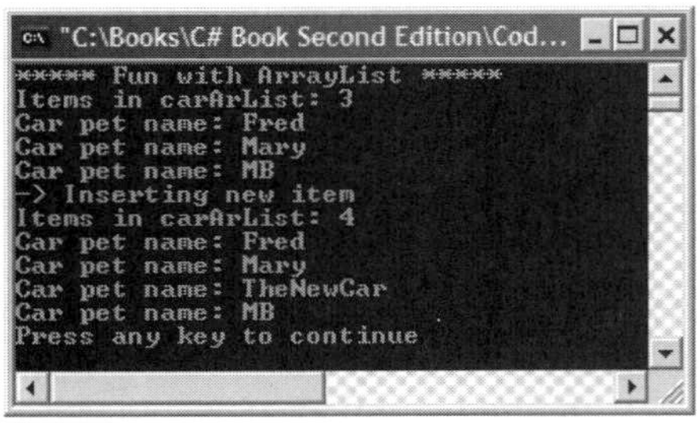

Figure 6-12. Fun with System.Collections.ArrayList

Working with the Queue Type

Queues are containers that ensure that items are accessed using a first-in, first-out manner. Sadly, we humans are subject to queues all day long: lines at the bank, lines at the movie theater, and lines at the morning coffee house. When you are modeling a scenario in which items are handled on a first-come, first-served basis, System.Collections.Queue is your type of choice. In addition to the functionality provided by the supported interfaces, Queue defines the key members shown in Table 6-4.

Table 6-4. Members of the Queue Type

Member of System.Collection.Queue	Meaning in Life
Dequeue()	Removes and returns the object at the beginning of the Queue
Enqueue()	Adds an object to the end of the Queue
Peek()	Returns the object at the beginning of the Queue without removing it

To illustrate these methods, we will leverage our automobile theme once again and build a Queue object that simulates a line of cars waiting to enter a car wash. First, assume the following static helper method:

```
public static void WashCar(Car c)
{
    Console.WriteLine("Cleaning {0}", c.PetName);
}
```

Now, ponder the following code:

```
// Make a Q with three items.
Queue carWashQ = new Queue();
carWashQ.Enqueue(new Car("FirstCar", 0, 0));
carWashQ.Enqueue(new Car("SecondCar", 0, 0));
carWashQ.Enqueue(new Car("ThirdCar", 0, 0));
// Peek at first car in Q.
Console.WriteLine("First in Q is {0}",
    ((Car)carWashQ.Peek()).PetName);
// Remove each item from Q.
WashCar((Car)carWashQ.Dequeue());
WashCar((Car)carWashQ.Dequeue());
WashCar((Car)carWashQ.Dequeue());
// Try to de-Q again?
try
{
    WashCar((Car)carWashQ.Dequeue());
}
catch(Exception e)
{ Console.WriteLine("Error!! {0}", e.Message);}
```

Here, you insert three items into the Queue type via its Enqueue() method. The call to Peek() allows you to view (but not remove) the first item currently in the Queue, which in this case is the car named FirstCar. Finally, the called to Dequeue() removes the item off the line and sends it into the WashCar() helper function for processing. Do note that if you attempt to remove items from an empty queue, a runtime exception is thrown. Figure 6-13 shows the output of the queue example.

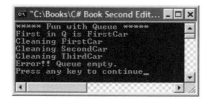

Figure 6-13. System.Collections.Queue at work

Working with the Stack Type

The System.Collections.Stack type represents a collection that maintains items using a last-in, first-out manner. As you would expect, Stack defines a member named Push() and Pop() (to place items onto or remove items from the stack), as well as a Peek() method. Due to the fact that I am hard-pressed to come up with a car-centric stack example (perhaps a junkyard automobile crusher?), the following stack example makes use of the standard System.String:

```
Stack stringStack = new Stack();
stringStack.Push("One");
stringStack.Push("Two");
stringStack.Push("Three");
// Now look at the top item, pop it and look again.
Console.WriteLine("Top item is: {0}", stringStack.Peek());
Console.WriteLine("Popped off {0}", stringStack.Pop());
Console.WriteLine("Top item is: {0}", stringStack.Peek());
Console.WriteLine("Popped off {0}", stringStack.Pop());
Console.WriteLine("Top item is: {0}", stringStack.Peek());
Console.WriteLine("Popped off {0}", stringStack.Pop());
try
{
    Console.WriteLine("Top item is: {0}", stringStack.Peek());
    Console.WriteLine("Popped off {0}", stringStack.Pop());
}
catch(Exception e)
{ Console.WriteLine("Error!! {0}", e.Message);}
```

Here, you build a stack that contains three string types (named according to their order of insertion). As you peek onto the stack, you will always see the item at the very top, and therefore the first call to Peek() reveals the third string. After a series of Pop() and Peek() calls, the stack is eventually empty, at which time additional Peek()/Pop() calls raise a system exception. The output can be seen in Figure 6-14.

Figure 6-14. System.Collections.Stack type at work

System.Collections.Specialized Namespace

In addition to the types defined within the System.Collections namespace, you should also be aware that the .NET base class libraries provide the System.Collections.Specialized namespace that defines another set of types that are more (pardon the redundancy) specialized. For example, the StringDictionary and ListDictionary types each provide a stylized implementation of the IDictionary interface. Table 6-5 documents the key types.

Table 6-5. Types of the System.Collections.Specialized Namespace

Member of System.Collections.Specialized	Meaning in Life
CollectionsUtil	Creates collections that ignore the case in strings.
HybridDictionary	Implements IDictionary by using a ListDictionary while the collection is small, and then switching to a Hashtable when the collection gets large.
ListDictionary	Implements IDictionary using a singly linked list. Recommended for collections that typically contain 10 items or less.
NameObjectCollectionBase	Provides the abstract (MustInherit in Visual Basic) base class for a sorted collection of associated String keys and Object values that can be accessed either with the key or with the index.
NameObjectCollectionBase. KeysCollection	Represents a collection of the String keys of a collection.
NameValueCollection	Represents a sorted collection of associated String keys and String values that can be accessed either with the key or with the index.
StringCollection	Represents a collection of strings.
StringDictionary	Implements a hashtable with the key strongly typed to be a string rather than an object.
StringEnumerator	Supports a simple iteration over a StringCollection.

 SOURCE CODE The CollectionTypes project can be found under the Chapter 6 subdirectory.

Building a Custom Container (Retrofitting the Cars Type)

To conclude this chapter, let's examine one possible way to build a stylized custom collection. As mentioned, the System.Collections namespace supplies some abstract base types that allow you to build strongly typed collections. However, rather than dealing with the implementation of various abstract members, you are able to build custom collections using simple containment/delegation techniques.

Previously in this chapter, you created the Cars type that was responsible for holding a number of Car objects. Internally, the set of Car objects was represented with an instance of System.Array, and because of this fact, you needed to write a good deal of extra code to allow the outside world to interact with your subobjects. Furthermore, the Car array is defined with a fixed upper limit.

A more intelligent design would be to represent the internal set of Car objects as an instance of System.Collections.ArrayList. Given that this class already has a number of methods to insert, remove, and enumerate its contents, the only duty of the Cars type is to supply a set of public functions that delegate to the inner ArrayList (in other words, the Cars type "has-a" ArrayList). As with any containment/delegation scenario, it is up to you to decide how much functionality of the inner object to expose to the object user. Here, then, is one possible implementation of the updated Cars type:

```
// This time use an ArrayList, not System.Array.
public class Cars : IEnumerable
{
    // This class maintains an array of cars.
    private ArrayList carList;
    // Make the ArrayList.
    public Cars() { carList = new ArrayList ();}
    // Expose select methods of the ArrayList to the outside world.
    // Insert a car.
    public void AddCar(Car c)
    {  carList.Add(c);}
    // Remove a car.
    public void RemoveCar(int carToRemove)
    {  carList.RemoveAt(carToRemove);}
    // Return number of cars.
    public int CarCount
    {  get{  return carList.Count;}  }
    // Kill all cars.
    public void ClearAllCars()
    {  carList.Clear(); }
    // Determine if the incoming car is already in the list.
    public bool CarIsPresent(Car c)
    {  return carList.Contains(c); }
    // Simply return the IEnumerator of the ArrayList.
    public IEnumerator GetEnumerator()
    {  return carList.GetEnumerator();}
}
```

This new implementation also makes using the Cars type a bit less of a burden for the object user:

```csharp
// Use the new Cars container class.
public static void Main()
{
    Cars carLot = new Cars();
    // Add some cars.
    carLot.AddCar( new Car("Jasper", 200, 80));
    carLot.AddCar( new Car("Mandy", 140, 0));
    carLot.AddCar( new Car("Porker", 90, 90));
    carLot.AddCar( new Car("Jimbo", 40, 4));
    // Get each one and print out some stats.
    Console.WriteLine("You have {0}  in the lot:\n", carLot.CarCount);
    foreach (Car c in carLot)
    {
        Console.WriteLine("Name: {0} ", c.PetName);
        Console.WriteLine("Max speed: {0} \n", c.MaxSpeed);
    }
    // Kill the third car.
    carLot.RemoveCar(3);
    Console.WriteLine("You have {0}  in the lot.\n", carLot.CarCount);
    // Add another car and verify it is in the collection.
    Car temp = new Car("Zippy", 90, 90);
    carLot.AddCar(temp);
    if(carLot.CarIsPresent(temp))
        Console.WriteLine("{0} is already in the lot.", temp.PetName);
    // Kill 'em all.
    carLot.ClearAllCars();
    Console.WriteLine("You have {0}  in the lot.\n", carLot.CarCount);
}
```

The output is shown in Figure 6-15.

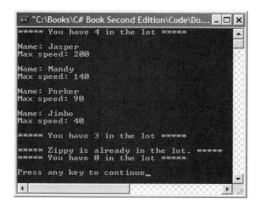

Figure 6-15. The updated Cars container

You may be wondering why you bothered to make the custom Cars type at all, given that the object user could create an ArrayList type directly. The reason is that ArrayList can contain *any* object reference. If you did not create a custom wrapper class such as Cars, the ArrayList instance could contain Cars, Boats, Airplanes, Strings, or any other type!

```
ArrayList ar = new ArrayList();
ar.Add(carLot);
ar.Add("Hello");
ar.Add(new JamesBondCar());
ar.Add(23);
```

Using the containment/delegation model, you are able to leverage the functionality of the ArrayList type, while maintaining control over what can be inserted into the container.

NOTE   Also be aware that many of the types of the System.Collections namespace can function as base classes to derived types. Thus, as an alternative, you are able to build strongly typed collections by deriving from the collection type of interest and overriding various virtual members.

SOURCE CODE   This updated Cars collection (ObjectEnumWithCollection) can be found under the Chapter 6 subdirectory.

This concludes our formal investigation of interface-based programming techniques. Be painfully aware, however, that you will encounter numerous .NET interfaces through the remainder of this text. As you will see, interfaces are used during ASP .NET development, Windows Forms development, multithreaded applications, and so forth. Unlike other development frameworks (such as MFC), interfaces are unavoidable when exploring the .NET universe.

Summary

If you are a COM programmer by trade, this chapter must have given you warm fuzzies. The interface is a collection of abstract members that may be implemented by a given class. Because an interface does not supply any implementation details, it is common to regard an interface as a behavior that may be supported by a given type. When two or more classes implement the same interface, you are able to treat each type the same way (aka interface-based polymorphism).

C# provides the interface keyword to allow you to define a new interface. As you have seen, a type can support as many interfaces as necessary using a comma-delimited list. Furthermore, it is permissible to build interfaces that derive from multiple base interfaces.

In addition to building your custom interfaces, the .NET libraries define a number of standard (i.e., framework-supplied) interfaces. This chapter focused on the interfaces defined within the System.Collections namespace. As you have seen, you are free to build custom types that implement these predefined interfaces to gain a number of desirable traits such as cloning, sorting, and enumerating.

Finally, you spent some time investigating the stock collection classes defined within the System.Collections namespace and examined a number of common interfaces used by the collection-centric types.

Callback Interfaces, Delegates, and Events

UP TO THIS POINT in the text, every sample application you have developed added various bits of code to Main(), which (in some way or another) sent messages *to* a given object. However, you have not yet examined how an object can *talk back* to the entity that created it. In most programs, it is quite common for objects in a system to engage in a "two-way conversation" through the use of events, callback interfaces, and other programming constructs. To prime the pump, I begin this chapter by examining how custom interfaces may be used to enable callback functionality (which may ring a bell if you are a COM developer).

The bulk of this chapter, however, examines various techniques provided by C# and the .NET Framework that enable the objects in your system to engage in bidirectional communications. First, you learn about the C# "delegate" keyword, which is little more than an object that "points to" other method(s) it is able to make calls on when told to do so.

Once you learn how to create and manipulate delegates (both synchronously and asynchronously), you then investigate the .NET event protocol, which is based on the delegation model. Although one typically views events within the context of a GUI-based application, this chapter will illustrate how non-GUI agents are able to fire events to their invokers (as shown later during our investigation of Windows Forms and ASP.NET, the process is identical to that of firing and handling GUI-centric events).

Understanding Callback Interfaces

As you have seen in the previous chapter, interfaces can be used to define common behaviors supported by various types in your system. In addition to using interfaces to establish polymorphic behaviors, interfaces are also commonly used as a *callback mechanism*. COM programmers may already be familiar with the notion of defining and implementing *callback interfaces*. This technique allows a COM client to receive events from a coclass using a custom COM interface, and is often used to bypass the overhead imposed by the official COM connection point architecture.

To illustrate the use of callback interfaces under .NET, let's update the now familiar Car type to inform the caller when it is about to explode (the current speed is 10 miles below the maximum speed), and has exploded (the current speed is at or above the maximum speed). These events will be represented by the following custom interface:

```
// The callback interface.
public interface IEngineEvents
{
    void AboutToBlow(string msg);
    void Exploded(string msg);
}
```

Event interfaces are not typically implemented directly by the client executable, but rather by a helper *sink object*, upon which the sender of the events (the Car type in this case) will make calls. Assume the client-side sink class is called CarEventSink. When the Car type sends the event notification to the sink, it will simply print out the incoming messages to the console:

```
// Car event sink.
public class CarEventSink : IEngineEvents
{
    private string name;    // Diagnostic member to identify sink.
    public CarEventSink(){}
    public CarEventSink(string sinkName)
    { name = sinkName; }
    public void AboutToBlow(string msg)
    { Console.WriteLine("{0} reporting: {1}", name, msg); }
    public void Exploded(string msg)
    { Console.WriteLine("{0} reporting: {1}", name, msg); }
}
```

Now that you have a sink object that implements the event interface, your next task is to pass a reference to this sink into the Car type. The Car holds onto the reference, and makes calls back on the sink when appropriate. In order to allow the Car to obtain a reference to the sink, you can assume some method has been added to the default public interface. In keeping with the COM paradigm, let's call this method Advise(). When the object user wishes to detach from the event source, it may call another custom method on the Car type (Unadvise() in COM-speak).

Furthermore, in order to allow the call to register multiple event sinks, let's assume that the Car maintains an ArrayList to represent each outstanding connection (analogous to the array of IUnknown* types used with classic COM connection points). Here are the relevant updates:

```
// This Car does not make any use of the
// C# delegate or event keyword, but can
// still send out events to the caller.
public class Car
{
    // The set of connected sinks.
    ArrayList itfConnections = new ArrayList();
    // Attach or disconnect from the source of events.
    public void Advise(IEngineEvents itfClientImpl)
    { itfConnections.Add(itfClientImpl); }
    public void Unadvise(IEngineEvents itfClientImpl)
    { itfConnections.Remove(itfClientImpl); }
...
}
```

Finally, to send the events, let's update the Car.SpeedUp() method to iterate over the list of connections and fire the correct notification when appropriate:

```
// Interface-based event protocol!
class Car
{
...
    public void SpeedUp(int delta)
    {
        // If the car is dead, send exploded event to each sink.
        if(carIsDead)
        {
            foreach(IEngineEvents e in itfConnections)
                e.Exploded("Sorry, this car is dead...");
        }
        else
        {
            currSpeed += delta;
            // Dude, you're almost dead!  Proceed with caution!
            if(10 == maxSpeed - currSpeed)
            {
                foreach(IEngineEvents e in itfConnections)
                    e.AboutToBlow("Careful buddy!  Gonna blow!");
            }
            if(currSpeed >= maxSpeed)
                carIsDead = true;
            else
                Console.WriteLine("\tCurrSpeed = {0} ", currSpeed);
        }
    }
}
```

To wrap things up all nice and tidy, here is some client-side code, now making use of a callback interface to listen to the Car events:

```
// Make a car and listen to the events.
public class CarApp
{
    public static int Main(string[] args)
    {
        Car c1 = new Car("SlugBug", 100, 10);
        // Make sink object.
        CarEventSink sink = new CarEventSink();
        // Pass the Car a reference to the sink.
        c1.Advise(sink);
        // Speed up (this will generate the events).
        for(int i = 0; i < 6; i++)
            c1.SpeedUp(20);
        // Detach from events.
        c1.Unadvise(sink);
        return 0;
    }
}
```

Figure 7-1 shows the end result of this interface-based event protocol.

Figure 7-1. An interface-based event protocol

Do note that the Unadvise() method can be very helpful in that it allows the caller to selectively detach from events at will. Here, you call Unadvise() before exiting Main(), although this is not technically necessary. However, assume that the application now wishes to register two sinks, dynamically remove a particular sink during the flow of execution, and continue processing the program at large:

```csharp
public static int Main(string[] args)
{
    // Make a car as usual.
    Car c1 = new Car("SlugBug", 100, 10);
    // Make sink objects.
    Console.WriteLine("***** Creating sinks *****");
    CarEventSink sink = new CarEventSink("First sink");
    CarEventSink myOtherSink = new CarEventSink("Other sink");
    // Hand sinks to Car.
    Console.WriteLine("\n***** Sending 2 sinks into Car *****");
    c1.Advise(sink);
    c1.Advise(myOtherSink);
    // Speed up (this will generate the events.)
    Console.WriteLine("\n***** Speeding up *****");
    for(int i = 0; i < 6; i++)
        c1.SpeedUp(20);
    // Detach first sink from events.
    Console.WriteLine("\n***** Removing first sink *****");
    c1.Unadvise(sink);
    // Speed up again (only 'other sink' will be called.)
    Console.WriteLine("\n***** Speeding up again *****");
    for(int i = 0; i < 6; i++)
        c1.SpeedUp(20);
    // Detach other sink from events.
    Console.WriteLine("\n***** Removing second sink *****");
    c1.Unadvise(myOtherSink);
    return 0;
}
```

Event interfaces will always have their place under any programming architecture. However, as you may be suspecting, the .NET platform supplies native support for enabling bidirectional communications. To understand this intrinsic event protocol, we begin by examining the role of the delegate type.

 SOURCE CODE The EventInterface project is located under the Chapter 7 subdirectory.

Understanding the .NET Delegate Type

Before formally defining .NET delegates, let's gain a bit of perspective. Historically speaking, the Windows API makes frequent use of C-style function pointers to create entities termed *callback functions* or simply *callbacks*. Using callbacks, programmers were able to configure one function to report back to (call back) another function in the application. Understand that C-style callback functions have nothing to do with traditional COM connection points or event interfaces (however, in many ways the same end result was achieved).

The problem with standard C-style callback functions is that they represent little more than a raw address in memory. Ideally, callbacks could be configured to include additional type-safe information such as the number of (and types of) parameters and the return value (if any) of the method pointed to. Sadly, this is not the case in traditional callback functions, and, as you may suspect, can therefore be a frequent source of bugs, hard crashes, and other runtime disasters.

Nevertheless, callbacks are useful entities. In the .NET Framework, callbacks are still possible, and their functionality is accomplished in a much safer and more object-oriented manner using *delegates*. In essence, a delegate is an object that points to another method in the application. Specifically speaking, a delegate maintains three important pieces of information:

- The *name* of the method on which it makes calls

- The *arguments* (if any) of this method

- The *return value* (if any) of this method

Once a delegate has been created and provided the aforementioned information, it may dynamically invoke the method it represents at runtime. As you will see, the .NET Framework automatically supports the use of synchronous and asynchronous delegates (both of which are seen over the course of this chapter).

Defining a Delegate in C#

When you want to create a delegate in C#, you make use of (surprise, surprise) the "delegate" keyword. Under the hood, the delegate keyword expands to a sealed class type deriving from System.MulticastDelegate. For example, if you write the following C# delegate definition:

```
public delegate void PlayAcidHouse(Person theDJ, int volume);
```

the C# compiler dynamically produces a new sealed class named PlayAcidHouse deriving from System.MulticastDelegate. This class is only capable of calling a method that takes two parameters (of type Person and System.Int32) and returns nothing. If you check out how this class type is represented in metadata format using ildasm.exe (Figure 7-2), you would see that the PlayAcidHouse type indeed derives from System.MulticastDelegate.

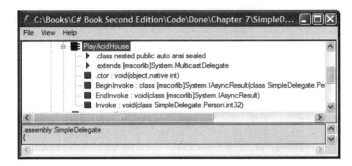

Figure 7-2. The C# "delegate" keyword represents a sealed type deriving from System.MulticastDelegate.

As you can see, the PlayAcidHouse class has been automatically endowed (thanks to the C# compiler) with three public methods. Invoke() is perhaps the core method, and it may be called to inform the delegate it is time to call the method it is currently pointing to. Notice that the parameters that are sent into Invoke() are identical to the declaration of the PlayAcidHouse delegate. BeginInvoke() and EndInvoke() provide the ability to call the current method asynchronously (Invoke(), on the other hand, makes synchronous method calls). Strangely enough, the synchronous Invoke() method is *not* directly callable from C#. As you will see in just a bit, Invoke() is called behind the scenes when you make use of the appropriate C# syntax.

Now, how exactly does the compiler know how to prototype the Invoke(), BeginInvoke(), and EndInvoke() methods? To understand the process, here is the crux of the generated PlayAcidHouse class type (the items in **bold** represent the auto-generated items):

```
sealed class PlayAcidHouse : System.MulticastDelegate
{
    public PlayAcidHouse(object target, uint functionAddress);
    public void Invoke(Person theDJ, int volume);
    public IAsyncResult BeginInvoke(Person theDJ, int volume,
        AsyncCallback cb, object state);
    public void EndInvoke(IAsyncResult result);
}
```

First, notice that the parameters that are defined for the Invoke() and BeginInvoke() members (in addition to the mandatory AsyncCallback and System.Object parameters of the BeginInvoke() method) are the same number of, and type of, the original C# delegate declaration. Likewise, the return value of Invoke() and EndInvoke() is identical to the original C# delegate declaration. And obviously, the name of the constructor is based on the name of the original C# delegate declaration.

Now assume you have defined another C# delegate type that represents a method returning a string and taking three Booleans:

```
public delegate string TakeSomeBools(bool a, bool b, bool c);
```

This time, the auto-generated class breaks down as follows:

```
sealed class TakeSomeBools : System.MulticastDelegate
{
    public TakeSomeBools(object target, uint functionAddress);
    public string Invoke(bool a, bool b, bool c);
    public IAsyncResult BeginInvoke(bool a, bool b, bool c,
        AsyncCallback cb, object state);
    public string EndInvoke(IAsyncResult result);
}
```

Finally, understand that delegates can also "point to" methods that contain out and ref parameters:

```
public delegate string TakeSomeBoolsByRefAndAsOut
    (out bool a, out bool b, ref bool c);
```

In this case, the signatures of the Invoke() and BeginInvoke() methods look as you would expect; however, check out the EndInvoke() method, which now pads the first set of parameters with the set of out/ref arguments from the delegate:

```
sealed class TakeSomeBoolsByRefAndAsOut : System.MulticastDelegate
{
    public TakeSomeBoolsByRefAndAsOut (object target, uint functionAddress);
    public string Invoke(out bool a, out bool b, ref bool c);
    public IAsyncResult BeginInvoke(out bool a, out bool b, ref bool c,
        AsyncCallback cb, object state);
    public string EndInvoke(out bool a, out bool b,
        ref bool c, IAsyncResult result);
}
```

I think you can see the general pattern: A C# delegate definition results in a sealed class with three auto-generated methods whose parameter and return types are based on the delegate's declaration. We will see exactly how we interact with Invoke(), BeginInvoke(), and EndInvoke() in just a bit, but first let's check out the System.MulticastDelegate base class.

Members of System.MulticastDelegate

So then, when you build a type using the C# "delegate" keyword, you indirectly declare a type that derives from System.MulticastDelegate. The MulticastDelegate type in turn derives from System.Delegate (as well as implements two standard interfaces). Here is the formal definition of MulticastDelegate:

```
public abstract class MulticastDelegate :
    Delegate, ICloneable, ISerializable
{
    public MethodInfo Method { get; }
    public object Target { get; }
    public virtual object Clone();
    public object DynamicInvoke(object[] args);
    public virtual bool Equals(object obj);
    public virtual int GetHashCode();
    public virtual Delegate[] GetInvocationList();
    public virtual void
        GetObjectData(SerializationInfo info, StreamingContext context);
    public Type GetType();
    public virtual string ToString();
}
```

And here is the definition of System.Delegate:

```
public abstract class Delegate : object,
    ICloneable, ISerializable
{
    public MethodInfo Method { get; }
    public object Target { get; }
    public virtual object Clone();
    public static Delegate Combine(Delegate a, Delegate b);
    public static Delegate Combine(Delegate[] delegates);
    public static Delegate
        CreateDelegate(Type type, System.Reflection.MethodInfo method);
    public static Delegate
        CreateDelegate(Type type, object target, string method);
    public static Delegate CreateDelegate(Type type, Type target, string method);
    public static Delegate CreateDelegate(Type type,
        object target, string method, bool ignoreCase);
    public object DynamicInvoke(object[] args);
    public virtual bool Equals(object obj);
    public virtual int GetHashCode();
    public virtual Delegate[] GetInvocationList();
```

```
    public virtual void GetObjectData(SerializationInfo info,
        StreamingContext context);
    public Type GetType();
    public static Delegate Remove(Delegate source, Delegate value);
    public virtual string ToString();
}
```

Together, these two base classes provide the necessary infrastructure for the derived type to wrap and invoke a method on the fly. Table 7-1 documents the key members to be aware of.

Table 7-1. Select Members of System.MultcastDelegate/System.Delegate

Inherited Member	Meaning in Life
Method	This property returns the name of a static method that is maintained by the delegate.
Target	If the method to be called is defined at the object level (rather than a static method), Target returns the name of the method maintained by the delegate. If the value returned from Target equals null, the method to be called is a static member.
Combine()	This static method adds a method to the list maintained by the delegate. In C#, you trigger this method using the overloaded += operator as a shorthand notation.
GetInvocationList()	This method returns an array of System.Delegate types, each representing a particular method that may be invoked.
Remove()	This static method removes a delegate from the list methods to call. In C#, you trigger this method using the overloaded -= operator as a shorthand notation.

As you may be able to infer from Table 7-1, delegates are capable of pointing to multiple methods. Under the hood, the System.Delegate type defines a linked list that is used to hold onto each method maintained by a given delegate. Additional methods can be added to this internal list using the static Combine() method (or using the C# overloaded += operator). To remove a method from the internal list, call the static Remove() method (or the C# overloaded -= operator). As you may know, the ability for a delegate to call multiple functions is termed *multicasting*. You see this technique action a bit later in this chapter.

The Simplest Possible Delegate Example

Delegates can tend to cause a great deal of confusion when encountered for the first time. Thus, to get the ball rolling, let's take a look at a very simple example. Here is the complete code, with analysis to follow:

```
namespace SimpleDelegate
{
    class DelegateApp
    {
        // This is the method that will be called
        // by the delegate.
        public static void PlainPrint(string msg)
        { Console.WriteLine("Msg is: {0}", msg); }
        // Define a delegate type.
        public delegate void AnyMethodTakingAString(string s);
        public static void Main()
        {
            // Make the delegate.
            AnyMethodTakingAString del;
            del = new AnyMethodTakingAString(PlainPrint);
            // AnyMethodTakingAString.Invoke() called here!
            del("Hello there...");
            // Dump info about the delegate.
            Console.WriteLine("I just called: {0}", del.Method);
        }
    }
}
```

Here, you begin by declaring a .NET delegate type using the C# "delegate" keyword. The AnyMethodTakingAString delegate represents an object that maintains a reference to some method that takes a single string parameter and returns nothing. When you want to assign the target (i.e., the method to call) of a given delegate, simply pass in the name of the method to the delegate's constructor. At this point, you are able to indirectly invoke the member using a syntax that looks like a direct function invocation:

```
// Make the delegate.
AnyMethodTakingAString del;
del = new AnyMethodTakingAString(PlainPrint);
del("Hello there...");
// Dump info about the delegate.
Console.WriteLine("I just called: {0}", del.Method);
```

Notice that when you print out the method maintained by the delegate (using the Method property), you see that each parameter is automatically mapped to the corresponding .NET system type (when you run this example, notice the presence of the System.Void type, which is a language-neutral way to denote a method with no return value).

Now recall that a delegate object could care less about the actual name of the method it is responsible for invoking. If you want, you could dynamically change the target method as follows:

```
class DelegateApp
{
    public static void PlainPrint(string msg)
    { Console.WriteLine("Msg is: {0}", msg); }
    public static void UpperCasePrint(string msg)
    { Console.WriteLine("Msg is: {0}", msg.ToUpper()); }
    public static void XXXXYYYYZZZZ888777aaa(string msg)
    { Console.WriteLine("Msg is: {0}", msg); }
    public delegate void AnyMethodTakingAString(string s);
    public static void Main()
    {
        AnyMethodTakingAString del;
        del = new AnyMethodTakingAString(PlainPrint);
        del("Hello there...");
        Console.WriteLine("->I just called: {0}\n", del.Method);
        // Reassign and invoke delegate.
        del= new AnyMethodTakingAString(UpperCasePrint);
        del("Hello there...");
        Console.WriteLine("->I just called: {0}\n", del.Method);
        // Reassign and invoke delegate.
        del= new AnyMethodTakingAString(XXXXYYYYZZZZ888777aaa);
        del("Hello there...");
        Console.WriteLine("->I just called: {0}\n", del.Method);
    }
}
```

The final output can be seen in Figure 7-3.

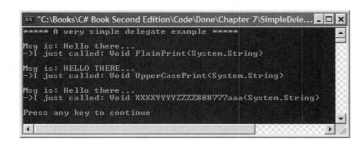

Figure 7-3. Dynamically "pointing to" various methods

If you attempt to assign the address of a method that did not match the delegate's declaration:

```
// Bad target!
public void BadTargetForDelegate(int x, System.AppDomain y)
{
    // Stuff...
}
...
// This is not a valid target! Error!
del = new AnyMethodTakingAString(BadTargetForDelegate);
del("Huh?!?");
```

you are (thankfully) issued the following compile time error (note the **bold** text that highlights the crux of the error):

```
C:\Books\C# Book Second Edition\Code\Chapter
7\SimpleDelegate\SimpleDel.cs(53): Method
'SimpleDelegate.DelegateApp.BadTargetForDelegate(int, System.AppDomain)'
does not match delegate 'void
SimpleDelegate.DelegateApp.AnyMethodTakingAString(string)'
```

Multicasting with .NET Delegates

The final point to be made with this simple delegate example is the fact that a single delegate object may be configured to point to numerous methods. When you wish to insert multiple methods into the invocation list maintained by the System.Delegate base class, you are able to make use of the overloaded += operator. The topic of operator overloading will be examined in detail in the next chapter, but for the time being simply understand that when you apply the += operator to a type derived from System.MulticastDelegate, the hidden Combine() method is triggered automatically (so be sure to check out the CIL via ildasm.exe).

```
// Now some multicasting.
AnyMethodTakingAString myMultiCaster;
myMultiCaster = new AnyMethodTakingAString(PlainPrint);
myMultiCaster += new AnyMethodTakingAString(UpperCasePrint);
myMultiCaster += new AnyMethodTakingAString(XXXXYYYYZZZZ888777aaa);
myMultiCaster("Here is a string");
```

SOURCE CODE   The SimpleDelegate project is located under the Chapter 7 subdirectory.

Building a More Elaborate Delegate Example

To illustrate a more advanced use of delegates, let's begin by updating the Car class to include two new Boolean member variables. The first is used to determine if your automobile is due for a wash (isDirty); the other represents if the car in question is in need of a tire rotation (shouldRotate). To enable the object user to interact with this new state data, Car also defines some additional properties and an updated constructor. Here is the story so far:

```
// Another updated Car class.
public class Car
{
...
    // NEW!  Are we in need of a wash? Need to rotate tires?
    private bool isDirty;
    private bool shouldRotate;

    // Extra params to set bools.
    public Car(string name, int max, int curr, bool dirty, bool rotate)
    {
        ...
        isDirty = dirty;
        shouldRotate = rotate;
    }
    public bool Dirty        // Get and set isDirty.
    {
        get{  return isDirty; }
        set{  isDirty = value; }
    }
    public bool Rotate       // Get and set shouldRotate.
    {
        get{  return shouldRotate; }
        set{  shouldRotate = value; }
    }
}
```

Now, assume you have declared the following delegate (which, again, is nothing more than an object-oriented wrapper around a function pointer) within your current namespace:

```
// This delegate is actually a class encapsulating a function pointer
// to 'some method', taking a Car as a parameter, and returning void.
public delegate void CarDelegate(Car c);
```

Here, you have created a delegate named CarDelegate. The CarDelegate type represents "some function" taking a Car as a parameter and returning void.

Delegates As Nested Types

Currently, your delegate is decoupled from its logically related Car type (given that you have simply declared the CarDelegate type within the defining namespace). While there is nothing horribly wrong with this approach, a more enlightened alternative would be to define the CarDelegate directly within the Car class:

```
// This time, define the delegate as part of the class definition.
public class Car
{
    // This is represented in CIL as
    // Car$CarDelegate (i.e., a nested type).
    public delegate void CarDelegate(Car c);
...
}
```

Given that the "delegate" keyword produces a new class deriving from System.MulticastDelegate, the CarDelegate is in fact a nested type definition! If you check ildasm.exe (see Figure 7-4), you will see the truth of the matter.

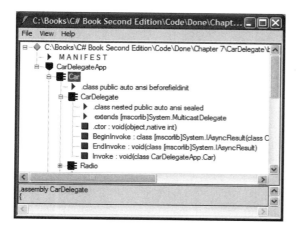

Figure 7-4. Remember! C# delegate types alias System.MulticastDelegate

Using the CarDelegate

Now that you have a type that points to "some function" taking a Car parameter and returning nothing, you can create other functions that take this delegate *as a parameter*. To illustrate, assume you have a new class named Garage. This type maintains a collection of Car types contained in an ArrayList. Upon creation, the ArrayList is filled with some initial Car types.

More importantly, the Garage class defines a public ProcessCars() method, which takes a single argument of type Car.CarDelegate. In the implementation of ProcessCars(), you pass each Car in your collection as a parameter to the "function pointed to" by the delegate.

To help keep your wits about you, ProcessCars() also makes use of two members defined by the System.MulticastDelegate class (Target and Method) to determine exactly which function the delegate is currently pointing to. Here, then, is the complete definition of the Garage class:

```
// The Garage class has a method that makes use of the CarDelegate.
Using System.Collections;
...
public class Garage
{
    // A list of all cars in the garage.
    ArrayList theCars = new ArrayList();
    // Create the cars in the garage.
    public Garage()
    {
        // Recall, we updated the ctor to set isDirty and shouldRotate.
        theCars.Add(new Car("Viper", 100, 0, true, false));
        theCars.Add(new Car("Fred", 100, 0, false, false));
        theCars.Add(new Car("BillyBob", 100, 0, false, true));
        theCars.Add(new Car("Bart", 100, 0, true, true));
        theCars.Add(new Car("Stan", 100, 0, false, true));
    }
    // This method takes a Car.CarDelegate as a parameter.
    // Therefore 'proc' is nothing more than a function pointer!
    public void ProcessCars(Car.CarDelegate proc)
    {
        // Diagnostics: Where are we forwarding the call?
        Console.WriteLine("***** Calling: {0}  *****",
            d.Method.ToString());
        // Diagnostics: Are we calling an instance method or a static method?
        if(proc.Target != null)
            Console.WriteLine("->Target: {0} ", proc.Target.ToString());
        else
            Console.WriteLine("->Target is a static method");
        // Real Work: Now call the method, passing in each car.
        foreach(Car c in theCars)
            proc(c);
    }
}
```

When the object user calls ProcessCars(), it will send in the name of the method that should handle this request. For the sake of argument, assume these are static members named WashCar() and RotateTires(). Consider the following usage:

```
// The garage delegates all work orders to these static functions
// (finding a good mechanic is always a problem...)
public class CarApp
{
    // A target for the delegate.
    public static void WashCar(Car c)
    {
        if(c.Dirty)
            Console.WriteLine("Cleaning a car");
        else
            Console.WriteLine("This car is already clean...");
    }
    // Another target for the delegate.
    public static void RotateTires(Car c)
    {
        if(c.Rotate)
            Console.WriteLine("Tires have been rotated");
        else
            Console.WriteLine("Don't need to be rotated...");

    }
    public static int Main(string[] args)
    {
        // Make the garage.
        Garage g = new Garage();
        // Wash all dirty cars.
        g.ProcessCars(new Car.CarDelegate(WashCar));
        // Rotate the tires.
        g.ProcessCars(new Car.CarDelegate(RotateTires));
        return 0;
    }
}
```

Notice (of course) that the two static methods are an exact match to the delegate type (void return value and a single Car argument). Also, recall that when you pass in the name of your function as a constructor parameter, you are adding this item to the internal linked list maintained by System.MulticastDelegate. Figure 7-5 shows the output of this test run. (Notice the output messages supplied by the Target and Method properties.)

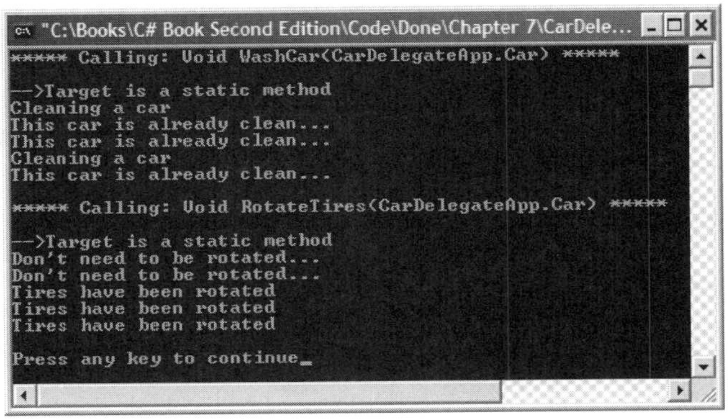

Figure 7-5. Passing the buck

Analyzing the Delegation Code

As you can see, the Main() method begins by creating an instance of the Garage type. This class has been configured to delegate all work to other named static functions. Now, when you write the following:

```
// Wash all dirty cars.
g.ProcessCars(new Car.CarDelegate(WashCar));
```

what you are effectively saying is "Add a pointer to the WashCar() function to the CarDelegate type, and pass this delegate to Garage.ProcessCars()." Like most real-world garages, the real work is delegated to another part of the system (which explains why a 30-minute oil change takes 2 hours). Given this, you can assume that ProcessCars() *actually* looks like the following under the hood:

```
// CarDelegate points to the WashCar function:
public void ProcessCars(Car.CarDelegate proc)
{
...
    foreach(Car c in theCars)
        proc(c);     // proc(c) => CarApp.WashCar(c)
}
```

Likewise, if you say:

```
// Rotate the tires.
g.ProcessCars(new Car.CarDelegate(RotateTires));
```

ProcessCars() can be understood as:

```
// CarDelegate points to the RotateTires function:
public void ProcessCars(Car.CarDelegate proc)
{
    foreach(Car c in theCars)
        proc(c);       // proc(c) => CarApp.RotateTires(c)
...
}
```

Also notice that when you are calling ProcessCars(), you must create a new instance of the custom delegate:

```
// Wash all dirty cars.
g.ProcessCars(new Car.CarDelegate(WashCar));
// Rotate the tires.
g.ProcessCars(new Car.CarDelegate(RotateTires));
```

This might seem odd at first, given that a delegate represents a function pointer. However, remember that this function pointer is represented by an instance of type System.MulticastDelegate, and therefore must be "new-ed."

Multicasting with the Car.CarDelegate

Recall that a multicast delegate is an object that is capable of calling any number of functions. In the current example, you do not make use of this feature. Rather, you make two calls to Garage.ProcessCars(), sending in a new instance of the CarDelegate each time. However, assume you have updated Main() to look like the following:

```
// Add two function pointers to the internal linked list.
public static int Main(string[] args)
{
    // Make the garage.
    Garage g = new Garage();
    // Create two new delegates.
    Car.CarDelegate wash = new Car.CarDelegate(WashCar);
    Car.CarDelegate rotate = new Car.CarDelegate(RotateTires);
    // The overloaded + operator can be applied to multicast delegates.
    // The result is a new delegate that maintains pointers to
    // both functions.
    g.ProcessCars(wash + rotate);
    return 0;
}
```

Here, you begin by creating two new CarDelegate objects, each of which points to a given function. When you call ProcessCars(), you are actually passing in a new delegate that holds each function pointer within the internal linked list (crazy huh?). Do note that the + operator is simply a shorthand for calling the static Delegate.Combine() method. Thus, you could write the following equivalent (but uglier) code:

```
// The + operator has the same effect as calling the Combine() method.
g.ProcessCars((Car.CarDelegate)Delegate.Combine(wash, rotate));
```

Furthermore, if you wish to hang onto the new delegate for later use, you could write the following instead:

```
// Create two new delegates.
Car.CarDelegate wash = new Car.CarDelegate(WashCar);
Car.CarDelegate rotate = new Car.CarDelegate(RotateTires);
// Store the new delegate for later use.
MulticastDelegate d = wash + rotate;
// Send the new delegate into the ProcessCars() method.
g.ProcessCars((Car.CarDelegate)d);
```

Regardless of how you configure a multicast delegate, understand that when you call Combine() (or use the overloaded + operator), you are adding a new function pointer to the internal list. If you wish to remove an item from this internal linked list, you can call the static Remove() method. The first parameter marks the delegate you wish to manipulate, while the second parameter marks the item to remove:

```
// The static Remove() method returns a Delegate type.
Delegate washOnly = MulticastDelegate.Remove(d, rotate);
g.ProcessCars((Car.CarDelegate)washOnly);
```

Before you view the output of this program, let's also update ProcessCars() to print out each function pointer stored in the linked list using Delegate.GetInvocationList(). This method returns an array of Delegate objects, which you iterate over using foreach:

```
// Now print out each member in the linked list.
public void ProcessCars(Car.CarDelegate proc)
{
    // Where are we passing the call?
    foreach(Delegate d in proc.GetInvocationList())
    {
        Console.WriteLine("***** Calling: {0} *****",
            d.Method.ToString());
    }
...
}
```

Instance Methods As Callbacks

Currently, the CarDelegate type is storing pointers to *static functions*. This is not a requirement of the delegate protocol (unlike C-based callbacks, which require static members). It is also possible to delegate a call to a method defined on any *object instance*. To illustrate, assume that the WashCar() and RotateTires() methods have now been moved into a new class named ServiceDept:

```
// We have now moved the static functions into a helper class.
public class ServiceDept
{
    // Not static!
    public void WashCar(Car c)
    {
        if(c.Dirty)
            Console.WriteLine("Cleaning a car");
        else
            Console.WriteLine("This car is already clean...");
    }
    // Still not static!
    public void RotateTires(Car c)
    {
        if(c.Rotate)
            Console.WriteLine("Tires have been rotated");
        else
            Console.WriteLine("Don't need to be rotated...");
    }
}
```

You could now update Main() as follows:

```
// Delegate to instance methods of the ServiceDept type.
public static int Main(string[] args)
{
    // Make the garage.
    Garage g = new Garage();
    // Make the service department.
    ServiceDept sd = new ServiceDept();
    // The garage delegates the work to the service department.
    Car.CarDelegate wash = new Car.CarDelegate(sd.WashCar);
    Car.CarDelegate rotate = new Car.CarDelegate(sd.RotateTires);
    MulticastDelegate d = wash + rotate;
    // Tell the garage to do some work.
    g.ProcessCars((Car.CarDelegate)d);
    return 0;
}
```

Figure 7-6 shows the final fruits of our labor.

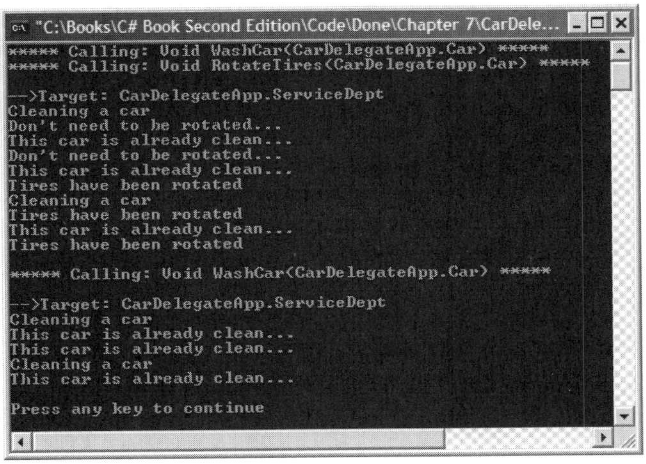

Figure 7-6. Passing the buck yet again

SOURCE CODE   The CarDelegate project is located under the Chapter 7 subdirectory.

Understanding Asynchronous Delegates

Now that you have some experience with the synchronous behavior of .NET delegate types, let's examine how to invoke methods asynchronously. First off, what exactly warrants an *asynchronous* method invocation? As you are fully aware, some programming operations take time. For example, if you build a word processing application that has the ability to print the current document, and that document happens to be 1000 pages in length, the computer's CPU has the potential to spin away for quite some time.

Now assume that this application has all of its programming logic taking place within the Main() method using a single *thread*. Simply put, a thread is a path of execution within a .NET application. Single-threaded applications are quite simple to program; however, in the case of the word processor application, the end user is far less than pleased. The reason has to do with the fact that while the application's single thread of execution is crunching out the 1000-page document, all other aspects of this program (such as menu activation, toolbar clicking, and keyboard input) are unresponsive.

When programmers wish to build applications that are able to simulate numerous tasks performing "at the same time," they will typically spawn additional threads to perform background tasks (e.g., printing documents) while the main thread is still able to respond to basic user-input needs.

So, what does threading have to do with .NET delegates? Well, to illustrate the potential problem with *synchronous* delegate invocations, ponder the following simple application:

```
using System;
using System.Threading;

namespace AsyncDelegate
{
    // A new delegate type.
    public delegate string NewCarDelegate(Car carToDetail);
    public class Car{...}
    class App
    {
        public static string DetailCar(Car c)
        {
            // Detailing a car takes 10 seconds.
            Console.WriteLine("Detailing car on thread {0}",
                Thread.CurrentThread.GetHashCode());
            Thread.Sleep(10000);
            return "Your car is ready!";
        }
        static void Main(string[] args)
        {
            Console.WriteLine("Main() is on thread {0}",
                Thread.CurrentThread.GetHashCode());
            NewCarDelegate d = new NewCarDelegate(DetailCar);
            Car myCar = new Car();
            Console.WriteLine(d(myCar));
            Console.WriteLine("Done invoking delegate");
        }
    }
}
```

First, notice that this example makes use of a new namespace named System.Threading. Chapter 10 will fully examine the details of multithreading within the .NET platform; however, to frame the use of asynchronous delegates, simply understand this namespace defines a type named Thread, which provides a static method named CurrentThread(). If you obtain the hash code for the current thread, you (in effect) obtain a unique identifier for the currently executing thread.

Here, you print out the hash code of the current thread within Main(), and then synchronously invoke the NewCarDelegate type. Once the flow of execution passes into the DetailCar() helper function, you print out the hash code of the active thread once again and put it to sleep (which is to say, stop all activity on said thread) for 10 seconds. Given this, you will not see the final message of Main() print to the console until approximately 10 seconds after the delegate's invocation.

When you run this example, note that the same hash code has been printed twice, signifying the fact that your application is performing all work on a single thread of execution. Now, in many cases, this behavior may be perfectly acceptable. However, given that the DetailCar() method takes 10 seconds to complete, your application appears to be hanging until the call has completed (just like the printing of the 1000-page document).

The question therefore is: How can you tell a delegate to invoke a method on a separate thread of execution and "report back" to the main thread once the method has completed? The good news is that every .NET delegate type is automatically equipped with this ability. The even better news is that you are *not* required to directly dive into the details of the System.Threading namespace to do so (although these entities can quite naturally work hand in hand).

Again, full details of multithreaded programming will be examined later in this text, but for the time being, let's check out how System.MulticastDelegate provides automatic support for asynchronous method invocations.

Invoking Methods Asynchronously

As you recall, when the C# compiler processes the "delegate" keyword, you dynamically receive two methods named BeginInvoke() and EndInvoke(). Thus, for the NewCarDelegate type, you are provided with the following members:

```
public IAsyncResult BeginInvoke(Car carToDetail,
    System.AsyncCallback callback, object state);
public string EndInvoke(IAsyncResult result);
```

Note that BeginInvoke() returns an IAsyncResult interface, while EndInvoke() requires an IAsyncInvoke type as parameter. This interface (defined in the System namespace) breaks down as follows:

```
public interface IAsyncResult
{
    object AsyncState { get; }
    WaitHandle AsyncWaitHandle { get; }
    bool CompletedSynchronously { get; }
    bool IsCompleted { get; }
}
```

In the simplest case, one is able to effectively ignore directly interacting with these members. All you have to do is cache the returned IAsyncResult type in a local variable in order to pass it to EndInvoke() when you are ready to obtain the result of the method invocation. Thus, to invoke DetailCar() asynchronously, you simply need to make the following updates:

```
static void Main(string[] args)
{
    Console.WriteLine("Main() is on thread {0}",
        Thread.CurrentThread.GetHashCode());
    NewCarDelegate d = new NewCarDelegate(DetailCar);
    Car myCar = new Car();
    IAsyncResult itfAR = d.BeginInvoke(myCar, null, null);
    Console.WriteLine("Done invoking delegate");
    // Do other work...
    string msg = d.EndInvoke(itfAR);  // Get the result.
    Console.WriteLine(msg);
}
```

Before viewing the output, a point must be made regarding Visual Studio .NET. As you were typing in the previous code updates, you may have noticed that IntelliSense failed to show you the BeginInvoke() and EndInvoke() members. The reason is due to the fact that these methods don't exist until the current assembly has been compiled! Recall that the C# compiler will autogenerate a type derived from System.MulticastDelegate at *compile time*. Thus, when you are invoking members asynchronously, always remember that you are smarter than any IDE. As long as you are mindful of the parameters and return value of the member you are invoking, you will be able to type in the code for BeginInvoke()/EndInvoke() accordingly. Now, check out Figure 7-7.

Figure 7-7. Asynchronous invocations increase program responsiveness.

Here, you can see that two threads of execution are working to perform the work of the program (automatically). In addition to the unique hash codes, you will also be able to see upon running the application that the "Done invoking delegate" message displays immediately, while the secondary thread is busy attending to its business (in this case, sleeping on the job for 10 seconds).

SOURCE CODE   The AsyncDelegate project is located under the Chapter 7 subdirectory.

Callbacks for Asynchronous Delegates

So far, so good. At this point, you are able to trigger a method via a custom delegate and obtain the result at some time in the future (e.g., when you call the EndInvoke() method). While this is all well and good, there may be times when you would rather not manually call EndInvoke() to obtain the results of your invocation, but would rather that the delegate *call you* when the method has been completed. In many ways, this functionality is quite similar to the callback interface pattern examined at the opening of this chapter. To understand the connection, let's break down the parameters to the BeginInvoke() method generated for the NewCarDelegate type:

```
public IAsyncResult BeginInvoke(
    Car carToDetail,                  // All delegate parameters are listed first.
    System.AsyncCallback callback,    // A standard delegate for the callback.
    // Allows the calling thread to pass information to the callback.
    object state
);
```

Note that the second parameter to BeginInvoke() is (get this) another delegate. In this case, System.AsyncCallback is a system-defined delegate that knows how to call methods that match the following prototype:

```
void SomeCallBackFunction(IAsyncResult itfAR)
```

When you wish to inform the delegate to call *you* back when the asynchronous invocation is complete, pass in an instance of the AsyncCallback type as the second parameter to BeginInvoke() and build a static (or instance-level) method to receive the call. Here is the complete code update, with analysis to follow (note the extra and required namespace reference):

```
using System;
using System.Threading;
using System.Runtime.Remoting.Messaging;

namespace AsyncCallbackDelegate
{
    // The delegate.
    public delegate string NewCarDelegate(Car carToDetail);
    public class Car{...}
    class App
    {
        public static void DetailCarCallBack(IAsyncResult itfAR)
        {
            Console.WriteLine("DetailCarCallBack on thread {0}",
                Thread.CurrentThread.GetHashCode());
            // Get message from DetailCar().
            AsyncResult res = (AsyncResult)itfAR;
            NewCarDelegate d = (NewCarDelegate)res.AsyncDelegate;
            Console.WriteLine(d.EndInvoke(itfAR));
        }
        public static string DetailCar(Car c)
        {
            // Detail car for 10 seconds.
            Console.WriteLine("Detailing car on thread {0}",
                Thread.CurrentThread.GetHashCode());
            Thread.Sleep(10000);
            return "Your car is ready!";
        }
    }
}
```

```
        static void Main(string[] args)
        {
            Console.WriteLine("Main() is on thread {0}",
                Thread.CurrentThread.GetHashCode());
            NewCarDelegate d = new NewCarDelegate(DetailCar);
            Car myCar = new Car();
            // Call asynchronously via callback.
            d.BeginInvoke(myCar, new AsyncCallback(DetailCarCallBack), null);
            Console.WriteLine("Done invoking delegate");
            // Keep console alive until call completes.
            Console.ReadLine();
        }
    }
}
```

First of all, notice that you now have a new helper function named DetailCarCallBack that will be invoked *by the delegate* when the DetailCar() method has completed. As well, notice that this time you are not caching the IAsyncResult type returned from BeginInvoke(), given that Main() is no longer required to call EndInvoke()!

Now, let's look at the implementation of DetailCarCallBack(). After printing out the hash code of the current thread (which logically should be the same number as the thread that is calling DetailCar()), you find the following lines of (technically optional) code:

```
public static void DetailCarCallBack(IAsyncResult itfAR)
{
    ...
    // Get message from DetailCar().
    AsyncResult res = (AsyncResult)itfAR;
    NewCarDelegate d = (NewCarDelegate)res.AsyncDelegate;
    Console.WriteLine(d.EndInvoke(itfAR));
}
```

Recall that the DetailCar() method returns a string message that informs the user that the operation has completed. In the previous interaction of this example, Main() directly called EndInvoke() to obtain the return value of the "method pointed to" by the NewCarDelegate. However, now that the delegate will call DetailCarCallBack() at some time in the future, this method needs to be the entity in charge of this task.

Here, you cast the incoming parameter into a System.Runtime.Remoting.Messaging.AsyncResult type and obtain the underlying delegate type (NewCarDelegate) via the AsyncDelegate property (this new namespace defines numerous types used when leveraging the .NET Remoting layer, as you will see later in this text). Once you have a handle to the delegate that is calling your callback method, you are able to indeed call EndInvoke() to obtain the textual message from DetailCar().

Cool! At this point you have dug into the details of synchronous and asynchronous delegate invocations. To be sure, there are additional techniques that may be used when asynchronously invoking a member, and you will see further examples where necessary. As you will see over the remainder of this text, this same asynchronous pattern is used when invoking file access methods, remote types, XML Web services, and whatnot.

SOURCE CODE   The AsyncCallbackDelegate project is located under the Chapter 7 subdirectory.

Understanding (and Using) Events

Delegates are fairly interesting constructs because you can resolve the name of a function to call at runtime, rather than at compile time. Admittedly, this syntactic orchestration can take a bit of getting used to. However, because the ability for one object to call back to another object is such a helpful construct, C# provides the "event" keyword to lessen the burden of using delegates in the raw.

The most prevalent use of the "event" keyword would be found in GUI-based applications, in which Button, TextBox, and Calendar widgets all report back to the containing Form when a given action (such as clicking a Button) has occurred. However, events are not limited to GUI-based applications. Indeed, they can be quite helpful when creating non–GUI-based projects (as you will now see).

Recall that the current implementation of Car.SpeedUp() (as of Chapter 4) throws an exception if the user attempts to increase the speed of an automobile that has already been destroyed. This is a rather brute force way to deal with the problem, given that the exception has the potential to halt the program's execution if the error is not handled in an elegant manner. A better design would be to simply inform the object user when the car has died using a custom event, and allow the caller to act accordingly.

Let's reconfigure the Car to send two events to those who happen to be listening. The first event (AboutToBlow) will be sent when the current speed is 10 miles below the maximum speed. The second event (Exploded) will be sent when the user attempts to speed up a car that is already dead. Establishing an event is a two-step process. First, you need to define a delegate, which will be used to hold onto the set of methods that will be called when the event occurs. Next, you define the events themselves using the C# "event" keyword, which as you can see is defined in terms of the related delegate. Here are the initial updates:

```
// This car can 'talk back' to the user.
public class Car
{
...
    // Is the car alive or dead?
    private bool carIsDead;
    // Holds the function(s) to call when the event occurs.
    public delegate void EngineHandler(string msg);
    // This car can send these events.
    public static event EngineHandler Exploded;
    public static event EngineHandler AboutToBlow;
...
}
```

Firing an event is as simple as specifying the event by name and sending out any specified parameters as defined by the related delegate. To illustrate, update the previous implementation of SpeedUp() to send each event accordingly (and remove the previous exception logic):

```
// Fire the correct event based on our current state of affairs.
public void SpeedUp(int delta)
{
    // If the car is dead, send exploded event.
    if(carIsDead)
    {
        if(Exploded != null)
            Exploded("Sorry, this car is dead...");
    }
    else
    {
        currSpeed += delta;
        // Almost dead?  Send about to blow event.
        if(10 == maxSpeed - currSpeed)
            if(AboutToBlow != null)
                AboutToBlow("Careful, approaching terminal speed!");
        // Still OK!  Proceed as usual.
        if(currSpeed >= maxSpeed)
            carIsDead = true;
        else
            Console.WriteLine("\tCurrSpeed = {0} ", currSpeed);
    }
}
```

With this, you have configured the car to send two custom events (under the correct conditions). You will see the usage of this new automobile in just a moment, but first, let's check the event architecture in a bit more detail.

NOTE Notice how you are checking the event against a null object reference before firing. This is to ensure that if the caller did not register to listen to a given event, it is not sent into sweet oblivion.

Events Under the Hood

A given event actually expands into two hidden public functions, one having an "add_" prefix, the other having a "remove_" prefix. For example, the Exploded event expands to the following methods:

```
// The following event expands in CIL code to:
// add_Exploded()
// remove_Exploded()
public static event EngineHandler Exploded;
```

In addition to defining hidden add_XXX() and remove_XXX() methods, each event also actually maps to a private class, which associates the corresponding delegate to a given event. In this way, when an event is raised, each method maintained by the delegate will be called. This is a convenient way to allow an object to broadcast the event to multiple *event sinks*. To illustrate, check out Figure 7-8, which shows the Car type as seen through the eyes of ildasm.exe.

Figure 7-8. Asynchronous invocations via callbacks

As you can see, each event (Exploded and AboutToBlow) is internally represented as the following members:

- A private class

- An add_XXX() method

- A remove_XXX() method

If you were to check out the CIL instructions behind add_AboutToBlow(), you would find the following (note the call to Delegate.Combine() is handled on your behalf):

```
.method public hidebysig specialname static
        void  add_AboutToBlow(class CarEvents.Car/EngineHandler 'value')
        cil managed synchronized
{
  // Code size       22 (0x16)
  .maxstack  2
  IL_0000:  ldsfld class CarEvents.Car/EngineHandler CarEvents.Car::AboutToBlow
  IL_0005:  ldarg.0
  IL_0006:  call class [mscorlib]System.Delegate
    [mscorlib]System.Delegate::Combine
  (class [mscorlib]System.Delegate, class [mscorlib]System.Delegate)
  IL_000b:  castclass  CarEvents.Car/EngineHandler
  IL_0010:  stsfld
    class CarEvents.Car/EngineHandler CarEvents.Car::AboutToBlow
  IL_0015:  ret
} // end of method Car::add_AboutToBlow
```

As you would expect, remove_AboutToBlow() will make the call to Delegate.Remove() automatically:

```
.method public hidebysig specialname static
        void  remove_AboutToBlow(class CarEvents.Car/EngineHandler 'value')
        cil managed synchronized
{
  // Code size       22 (0x16)
  .maxstack  2
  IL_0000:  ldsfld  class CarEvents.Car/EngineHandler CarEvents.Car::AboutToBlow
  IL_0005:  ldarg.0
  IL_0006:  call class [mscorlib]System.Delegate
    [mscorlib]System.Delegate::Remove
  (class [mscorlib]System.Delegate, class [mscorlib]System.Delegate)
  IL_000b:  castclass  CarEvents.Car/EngineHandler
  IL_0010:  stsfld      class CarEvents.Car/EngineHandler
    CarEvents.Car::AboutToBlow
  IL_0015:  ret
} // end of method Car::remove_AboutToBlow
```

The CIL instructions for the event itself make use of the [.addon] and [.removeon] directives to establish the correct add_XXX and remove_XXX methods (also note the private class is mentioned by name):

```
.event CarEvents.Car/EngineHandler AboutToBlow
{
  .addon void CarEvents.Car::add_AboutToBlow(class CarEvents.Car/EngineHandler)
  .removeon void CarEvents.Car::remove_AboutToBlow
    (class CarEvents.Car/EngineHandler)
} // end of event Car::AboutToBlow
```

So, now that you understand how to build a class that can send events, the next big question is how you can configure an object to receive these events.

Listening to Incoming Events

Assume you have now created an instance of the Car class and wish to listen to the events it is capable of sending. The goal is to create a method that represents the event sink that will be called by the related delegate. To bind this method to the event, you need to call the correct add_XXX() method to ensure that your method is added to the list of function pointers maintained by the EngineHandler delegate. However, you cannot call the CIL add_XXX() and remove_XXX() directly, but rather use the overloaded += and -= operators. Thus, when you wish to listen to an event, follow the pattern shown here:

```
// I'm listening...
// ObjectVariable.EventName += new ObjectVariable.DelegateName(functionToCall);
Car.Exploded += new Car.EngineHandler(OnBlowUp);
```

When you wish to detach from a source of events, use the -= operator:

```
// Shut up already!
// ObjectVariable.EventName -= new ObjectVariable.DelegateName(functionToCall);
Car.Exploded -= new Car.EngineHandler(OnBlowUp);
```

Here is the complete code:

```
// Make a car and listen to the events.
public class CarApp
{
    public static int Main(string[] args)
    {
        Car c1 = new Car("SlugBug", 100, 10);
        // Hook into events.
        Car.Exploded += new Car.EngineHandler(OnBlowUp);
        Car.AboutToBlow += new Car.EngineHandler(OnAboutToBlow);
        // Speed up (this will generate the events.)
        for(int i = 0; i < 10; i++)
            c1.SpeedUp(20);
        // Detach from events.
        Car.Exploded -= new Car.EngineHandler(OnBlowUp);
        Car.Exploded -= new Car.EngineHandler(OnAboutToBlow);
        // No response!
        for(int i = 0; i < 10; i++)
            c1.SpeedUp(20);
        return 0;
    }
    // OnBlowUp event sink.
    public static void OnBlowUp(string s)
    {
        Console.WriteLine("Message from car: {0} ", s);
    }
```

```
    // OnAboutToBlow event sink.
    public static void OnAboutToBlow(string s)
    {
        Console.WriteLine("Message from car: {0} ", s);
    }
}
```

If you wish to have multiple event sinks called by a given event, simply repeat the process:

```
// Multiple event sinks.
public class CarApp
{
    public static int Main(string[] args)
    {
        // Make a car as usual.
        Car c1 = new Car("SlugBug", 100, 10);

        // Hook into events.
        Car.Exploded += new Car.EngineHandler(OnBlowUp);
        Car.Exploded += new Car.EngineHandler(OnBlowUp2);
        Car.AboutToBlow += new Car.EngineHandler(OnAboutToBlow);

        // Speed up (this will generate the events.)
        for(int i = 0; i < 10; i++)
            c1.SpeedUp(20);
        ...
        // Detach from events when desired.
        Car.Exploded -= new Car.EngineHandler(OnBlowUp);
        Car.Exploded -= new Car.EngineHandler(OnBlowUp2);
        Car.Exploded -= new Car.EngineHandler(OnAboutToBlow);
        ...
    }
    // OnBlowUp event sink A.
    public static void OnBlowUp(string s)
    { Console.WriteLine("Message from car: {0} ", s); }
    // OnBlowUp event sink B.
    public static void OnBlowUp2(string s)
    { Console.WriteLine("AGAIN I say: {0} ", s); }
    // OnAboutToBlow event sink.
    public static void OnAboutToBlow(string s)
    { Console.WriteLine("Message from car: {0} ", s); }
}
```

Now, when the Exploded event is sent, the associated delegate calls OnBlowUp() as well as OnBlowUp2(), as shown in Figure 7-9.

Figure 7-9. Hooking into the engine events

NOTE   VS .NET 2003 further simplifies event handling. When you apply the + syntax to an object's event, you may use the Tab key to automatically generate the delegate target.

Objects As Event Sinks

At this point, you have the background to build objects that can participate in a two-way conversation. However, understand that you are free to build a helper object to respond to an object's event set, much in the same way that you created a helper class to be called by all delegates. For example, let's move your event sink methods out of the CarApp class and into a new class named CarEventSink:

```
// Car event sink
public class CarEventSink
{
    // OnBlowUp event handler.
    public void OnBlowUp(string s)
    { Console.WriteLine("Message from car: {0} ", s); }
    // OnBlowUp event handler version 2.
    public void OnBlowUp2(string s)
    { Console.WriteLine("AGAIN I say: {0} ", s); }
    // OnAboutToBlow handler.
    public void OnAboutToBlow(string s)
    { Console.WriteLine("Message from car: {0} ", s); }
}
```

The CarApp class is then a bit more self-contained, as the event sink methods have been pulled out of the CarApp definition and into their own custom type. Here is the update:

```
// Note the creation and use of the CarEventSink.
public class CarApp
{
    public static int Main(string[] args)
    {
        Car c1 = new Car("SlugBug", 100, 10);
        // Make the sink object.
        CarEventSink sink = new CarEventSink();
        // Hook into events using sink object.
        Car.Exploded += new Car.EngineHandler(sink.OnBlowUp);
        Car.Exploded += new Car.EngineHandler(sink.OnBlowUp2);
        Car.AboutToBlow += new Car.EngineHandler(sink.OnAboutToBlow);
        for(int i = 0; i < 10; i++)
            c1.SpeedUp(20);
        // Detach from events using sink object.
        Car.Exploded -= new Car.EngineHandler(sink.OnBlowUp);
        Car.Exploded -= new Car.EngineHandler(sink.OnBlowUp2);
        Car.Exploded -= new Car.EngineHandler(sink.OnAboutToBlow);
        return 0;
    }
}
```

The output is (of course) identical.

SOURCE CODE   The CarEvents project is located under the Chapter 7
subdirectory.

Summary

In this chapter, you have examined a number of ways in which multiple objects can
partake in a bidirectional conversation under .NET. First, you examined the use of
callback interfaces, which provide a way to have object B make calls on object A via an
interface reference. Do understand that this design pattern is *not* specific to .NET, but
may be employed in any language or platform that honors the use of interface types.

Next, you examined the C# "delegate" keyword, which is used to indirectly construct
a class derived from System.MulticastDelegate. As you have seen, a delegate is simply
an object that maintains a list of methods to call when told to do so. These invocations
may be made synchronously (using the Invoke() method) or asynchronously (via the
BeginInvoke() and EndInvoke() methods).

Finally, you examined the C# "event" keyword which, when used in conjunction
with a delegate type, can simplify the process of sending your event notifications to
awaiting callers. As seen via the resulting CIL, the .NET event model maps to hidden
calls on the System.Delegate/System.MulticastDelegate types. In this light, the C#
"event" keyword is purely optional in that it simply saves you some typing time.

CHAPTER 8

Advanced C# Type Construction Techniques

THIS CHAPTER WRAPS UP our investigation of the C# programming language by examining a number of advanced (but extremely useful) syntactic constructs. To begin, we will examine a small set of C# keywords that we have not yet formally examined. For example, you will learn how to programmatically account for overflow/underflow conditions using the "checked"/"unchecked" keywords as well as how to create an "unsafe" code context in order to directly manipulate pointer types using C#.

Next, you learn how to construct and use an *indexer method*. This C# mechanism enables you to build custom types that expose internal subtypes using the familiar bracket operator (i.e., []). If you have a C++ background, you will find that creating a C# indexer method is analogous to overloading the [] operator on a C++ class. Once you learn how to build an indexer method, you then examine how to overload various operators (+, −, <, >, and so forth) and create custom conversion functions (the C# equivalent to overloading the () operator under C++) for a type.

The Advanced Keywords of C#

Over the course of the previous seven chapters, you have seen a majority of the C# keywords in action. In addition to those already investigated, C# does have a set of lesser used, but still intriguing, keywords, specifically

- "checked"/"unchecked"

- "unsafe"/"stackalloc"/"fixed"/"volatile"/"sizeof"

- "lock"

The "lock" keyword will be examined later in this text during our formal examination of multithreaded programming (see Chapter 10). The remaining members of the preceding list ("checked", "unchecked", "unsafe", "stackalloc", "fixed", "volatile", and "sizeof") will be the focus of the first part of this chapter. To start, let's check out how C# provides automatic detection of arithmetic overflow (and underflow).

The "checked" Keyword

As you are well aware, each numerical data type has a fixed upper and lower limit (which may be obtained programmatically using the MaxValue/MinValue properties). Now, when you are performing arithmetic operations on a specific type, it is very possible that you may accidentally *overflow* the maximum storage of the type (assign a value that is greater than the maximum value) or *underflow* the minimum storage of the type (assign a value that is less than the minimum value). To keep in step with the CLR, I will refer to both of these possibilities collectively as "overflow." (As you will see, both overflow and underflow conditions result in a System.OverflowException type. There is no System.UnderflowException type in the base class libraries.)

To illustrate the issue, assume you have created two System.Byte types, each of which have been assigned a value that is safely below the maximum value (255). If you were to add the values of these types (casting the result as a byte) and print out the result, you would assume that the result would be the exact sum of each member:

```
namespace CheckedUnchecked
{
    class TheChecker
    {
        static void Main(string[] args)
        {
            // Overflow the max value of a System.Byte.
            Console.WriteLine("Max value of byte is {0}.", byte.MaxValue);
            Console.WriteLine("Min value of byte is {0}.", byte.MinValue);
            byte b1 = 100;
            byte b2 = 250;
            byte b3 = (byte)(b1 + b2);
            // b3 should hold the value 350, however...
            Console.WriteLine("b3 = {0}", b3);
        }
    }
}
```

If you were to view the output of this application, you might be surprised to find that b3 contains the value 94 (rather than the expected 350). The reason is simple. Given that a System.Byte can only hold a value between 0 and 255 (inclusive, for a grand total of 256 slots), b3 now contains the overflow value (350 – 256 = 94). As you have just seen, if you take no corrective course of action, overflow occurs without exception. At times, this hidden overflow may cause no harm whatsoever in your project. Other times, this loss of data is completely unacceptable.

To handle overflow or underflow conditions in your application, you have two possibilities. Your first choice is to leverage your wits and programming skills to handle all overflow conditions manually. Assuming you were indeed able to find each overflow condition in your program, you could resolve the previous overflow error as follows:

```
// Store sum in an integer to prevent overflow.
byte b1 = 100;
byte b2 = 250;
int answer = b1 + b2;
```

Of course, the problem with this technique is the simple fact that we *are* humans, and even our best attempts may result in errors that have escaped our eyes. Given this, C# provides the "checked" keyword. When you wrap a statement (or block of statements) within the scope of the "checked" keyword, the C# compiler will emit specific CIL instructions that test for overflow conditions that may result when adding, multiplying, subtracting, or dividing two numerical data types. If an overflow has occurred, the runtime will throw a System.OverflowException type. To illustrate, observe the following update:

```
class TheChecker
{
    static void Main(string[] args)
    {
        // Overflow the max value of a System.Byte.
        Console.WriteLine("Max value of byte is {0}.", byte.MaxValue);
        byte b1 = 100;
        byte b2 = 250;
        try
        {
            byte b3 = checked((byte)(b1 + b2));
            Console.WriteLine("b3 = {0}", b3);
        }
        catch(OverflowException e)
        { Console.WriteLine(e.Message); }
    }
}
```

Here, you wrap the addition of b1 and b2 within the scope of the "checked" keyword. If you wish to force overflow checking to occur over a block of code, you can interact with the "checked" keyword as follows:

```
try
{
    checked
    {
        byte b3 = (byte)(b1 + b2);
        byte b4, b5 = 100, b6 = 200;
        b4 = (byte)(b5 + b6);
        Console.WriteLine("b3 = {0}", b3);
    }
}
catch(OverflowException e)
{
    Console.WriteLine(e.Message);
}
```

In either case, the code in question will be evaluated for possible overflow conditions automatically, which will trigger an overflow exception.

Setting Project-Wide Overflow Checking

Now, if you are creating an application that should never allow silent overflow to occur, you may find yourself in the annoying position of wrapping numerous lines of code within the scope of the "checked" keyword. As an alternative, the C# compiler supports the /checked flag. When enabled, all of your arithmetic will be evaluated for overflow without the need to make use of the C# "checked" keyword. If overflow has been discovered, you will still receive a runtime exception. To enable this flag under VS .NET, activate the Check for Arithmetic Overflow/Underflow option from the project's property page (Figure 8-1).

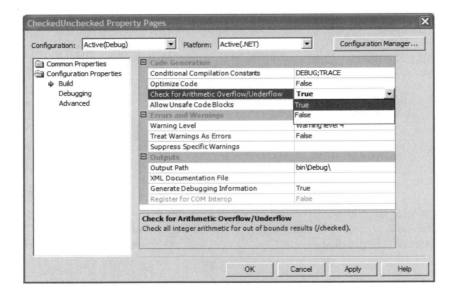

Figure 8-1. Enabling VS .NET overflow checking

As you may guess, this technique can be very helpful when creating a debug build. Once all of the overflow exceptions have been squashed out of the code base, you are free to disable the /checked flag for subsequent builds (which will increase the runtime execution of your application).

The "unchecked" Keyword

Now, assuming you have enabled this project-wide setting, what are you to do if you have a block of code where silent overflow *is* acceptable? Given that the /checked flag will evaluate *all* arithmetic logic, the C# language provides the "unchecked" keyword to disable the throwing of System.OverflowException on a case-by-case basis. The use of this keyword is identical to the "checked" keyword in that you can specify a single statement or a block of statements. For example:

```
// Assuming +checked is enabled,
// this block will not trigger
// a runtime exception.
unchecked
{
    byte b3 = (byte)(b1 + b2);
    Console.WriteLine("b3 = {0}", b3);
}
```

So, to summarize the C# "checked" and "unchecked" keywords, recall that the default behavior of the .NET runtime is to ignore arithmetic overflow. When you want to selectively handle discrete statements, make use of the "checked" keyword. If you wish to trap overflow errors throughout your application, enable the +checked flag. Finally, the "unchecked" keyword may be used if you have a block of code where overflow is acceptable (and thus should not trigger a runtime exception).

Regarding Underflow Conditions

Finally, recall that there is no System.UnderflowException type within the .NET base class libraries. Rather, in the event of an underflow condition, the runtime will again throw an OverflowException:

```
// Underflow conditions also trigger an OverflowException!
try
{
    byte a = 9, b = 9;
    byte c = (byte)(a + b + -100);  // c is less than zero!
}
catch(OverflowException e){Console.WriteLine(e);}
```

SOURCE CODE The CheckedUnchecked project can be found under the Chapter 8 subdirectory.

Working with "Unsafe" Code

Next up, we have three keywords that allow the C# programmer to bypass the CLR's memory management scheme in order to take matters into their own hands. In a nutshell, this allows C# programmers to make use of C(++) style pointers. Given this, C# does indeed provide additional operators specifically for this purpose (see Table 8-1).

Table 8-1. Pointer-Centric C# Operators

C# Pointer-Centric Operator	Meaning in Life
*	Used to create a *pointer variable,* a variable that represents a direct location in memory. Like C(++), this same operator is used to represent pointer indirection.
&	Used to obtain the address of a pointer.
->	This operator is used to access fields of a type that is represented by a pointer variable (the unsafe version of the C# dot operator).
[]	The [] operator (in an unsafe context) allows you to index the slot pointed to by a pointer variable (recall the interplay between a pointer variable and the [] operator in C(++)!).

Now, before we dig into the details, let me point out the fact that you will *seldom if ever* need to make use of the techniques we are about to examine. Although C# does allow you to drop down to the level of pointer manipulations, understand that the .NET runtime has absolutely no clue of your intentions. Thus, if you mismanage a pointer, you are the one in charge of dealing with the consequences. Given these warnings, when exactly would you need to work with unsafe code (and therefore the operators seen in Table 8-1)? There are two common situations:

- You are looking to optimize select parts of your application by bypassing the CLR. For example, you want to build a function that copies an array using pointer arithmetic.

- You are attempting to trigger the functionality of a C-based *.dll (such as the Win32 API or a custom C-based *.dll) and need to create pointer variables to call various methods.

Beyond these two reasons, there will never be a need to declare, dereference, or manipulate direct pointers using C#. In the event that you decide to make use of this C# language feature, you will also be required to inform csc.exe of your intent! If you are making use of csc.exe in the raw, be sure you supply the /unsafe flag. From VS .NET, you will need to access your project's Property page and enable the Allow Unsafe Code Blocks setting (Figure 8-2).

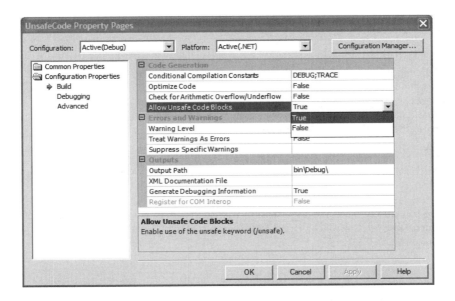

Figure 8-2. Enabling VS .NET unsafe compilation

Now let's ponder the basics. In the examples that follow, I'm assuming that you do have some background in C(++) pointer manipulations. If this is not true in your case, don't sweat it. Again, writing unsafe code will not be a common task for a huge majority of .NET applications.

The "Unsafe" Keyword

When you wish to work with pointers in C#, you must specifically declare a block of "unsafe" code using the "unsafe" keyword (as you might guess, any code that is not marked with the "unsafe" keyword is considered "safe" automatically, thus there is not a "safe" keyword in C#):

```
unsafe
{
    // Work with pointers here!
}
```

In addition to declaring a scope of unsafe code, you are able to build structures, classes, type members, and parameters that are "unsafe." Here are a few examples to gnaw on:

```
// This entire structure is 'unsafe' and can
// only be used in an unsafe context.
public unsafe struct Node
{
    public int Value;
    public Node* Left;
    public Node* Right;
}
// This struct is safe, but the Node* members
// are not. Technically, you may access 'Value' from
// outside a unsafe context, but not 'Left' and 'Right'.
public struct Node
{
    public int Value;
    // These can only be accessed in an unsafe context!
    public unsafe Node* Left;
    public unsafe Node* Right;
}
```

Methods (static or instance level) may be marked as unsafe as well. For example, assume that you know a given static method will make use of pointer logic. To ensure that this method can only be called from an unsafe context, you could define the method as follows:

```
unsafe public static void SomeUnsafeCode()
{
    // Work with pointers here!
}
```

This configuration would demand that the caller invoke SomeUnsafeCode() as so:

```
static void Main()
{
    unsafe{SomeUnsafeCode();}
}
```

Conversely, if you would rather not force the caller to wrap the invocation within an unsafe context, you could remove the "unsafe" keyword from the SomeUnsafeCode() method signature and opt for the following:

```
public static void SomeUnsafeCode()
{
    unsafe
    {
        // Work with pointers here!
    }
}
```

which would simplify the call to:

```
static void Main()
{
    SomeUnsafeCode();
}
```

Working with the * and & Operators

Once you have established an unsafe context, you are then free to build pointers to data types using the * operator as well as obtain the address of said pointer using the & operator. Using C#, the * operator is applied to the underlying type only, not as a prefix to each pointer variable name. For example, the following declares two variables, both of type int* (a pointer to an integer).

```
// No! This is incorrect under C#!
int *pi, *pj;
// Yes! This is the way of C#.
int* pi, pj;
```

Given this, check out the following example:

```
unsafe
{
    int myInt;
    // Define an int pointer, and
    // assign it the address of myInt.
    int* ptrToMyInt = &myInt;
    // Assign value of myInt using pointer indirection.
    *ptrToMyInt = 123;
    // Print some stats.
    Console.WriteLine("Value of myInt {0}", myInt);
    Console.WriteLine("Address of myInt {0:X}", (int)ptrToMyInt);
}
```

An Unsafe (and Safe) Swap Function

Of course, declaring pointers to local variables simply to assign their value (as shown in the previous example) is never required. To illustrate a more useful example of unsafe code, assume you wish to build a swap function using pointer arithmetic:

```
unsafe public static void UnsafeSwap(int* i, int* j)
{
    int temp = *i;
    *i = *j;
    *j = temp;
}
```

Very C-like, don't you think? However, given your work in Chapter 3, you should be aware that you could write the following safe version of your swap algorithm using the C# "ref" keyword:

```
public static void SafeSwap(ref int i, ref int j)
{
    int temp = i;
    i = j;
    j = temp;
}
```

The functionality of each method is identical, thus reinforcing the point that direct pointer manipulation is not a mandatory task under C#.

Field Access via Pointers (the -> Operator)

Now assume that you have a Point structure and wish to declare a pointer to a Point type. Like C(++), when you wish to invoke methods or trigger fields of a pointer type, you will need to make use of the pointer-field access operator (–>). As mentioned in Table 8-1, this is the unsafe version of the standard (safe) dot operator (.). In fact, using the pointer indirection operator (*), it is possible to dereference a pointer to (once again) apply the dot operator notation. Check out the following:

```
struct Point
{
    public int x;
    public int y;
    public override string ToString()
    { return "(" + x + "," + y + ")"; }
}
static void Main(string[] args)
{
    // Access members via pointer.
    unsafe
    {
        Point point;
        Point* p = &point;
        p->x = 100;
        p->y = 200;
        Console.WriteLine(p->ToString());
    }
    // Access members via pointer indirection.
    unsafe
    {
        Point point;
        Point* p = &point;
        (*p).x = 100;
        (*p).y = 200;
        Console.WriteLine((*p).ToString());
    }
}
```

The "stackalloc" Keyword

In an unsafe context, you may need to declare a local variable that allocates memory directly from the call stack (and is therefore not subject to .NET garbage collection). To do so, C# provides the "stackalloc" keyword, which is the C# equivalent to the _alloca function of the C runtime library. Here is a simple example:

```
unsafe
{
    char* p = stackalloc char[256];
    for (int k = 0; k < 256; k++)
        p[k] = (char)k;
}
```

Pinning a Type via the "fixed" Keyword

As seen in the previous example, allocating a chunk of memory within an unsafe context may be facilitated via the "stackalloc" keyword. By the very nature of this operation, the allocated memory is cleaned up as soon as the allocating method has returned (as the memory is acquired from the stack). However, assume a more complex example. During our examination of the –> operator, you created a value type named Point. Like all value types, the allocated memory is popped off the stack once the executing scope has terminated. For the sake of argument, assume Point was instead defined as a *reference* type:

```
class Point  // <= Now a class!
{
    public int x;
    public int y;
    public override string ToString()
    { return "(" + x + "," + y + ")"; }
}
```

As you are well aware, if the caller declares a variable of type Point, the memory is allocated on the garbage collected heap. The burning question then becomes: What if an unsafe context wishes to interact with this type (or any type on the heap)? Given that garbage collection can occur at any given moment (see Chapter 5), imagine the pain of accessing the members of Point at the very time in which a sweep of the heap is underway. Theoretically, it is possible that the unsafe context is attempting to interact with a member that is no longer accessible or has been repositioned on the heap after surviving a generational sweep (which is an obvious problem).

To lock a reference type variable in memory from an unsafe context, C# provides the "fixed" keyword. The fixed statement sets a pointer to a managed type and "pins" that variable during the execution of statement. Without "fixed", pointers to managed variables would be of little use, since garbage collection could relocate the variables unpredictably. (In fact, the C# compiler will not allow you to set a pointer to a managed variable except in a fixed statement.) Thus, if you were to create a Point type (now redesigned as a class) and wish to interact with its members, you must write the following code (or receive a compiler error):

```
unsafe public static void Main()
{
    Point pt = new Point();
    pt.x = 5;
    pt.y = 6;
    // pin pt in place so it will not
    // be moved or GC-ed.
    fixed (int* p = &pt.x)
    {
        // Use int* variable here!
    }
    // pt is now unpinned, and ready to be GC-ed.
    Console.WriteLine ("Point is: {0}", pt);
}
```

In a nutshell, the "fixed" keyword allows you to build a statement that locks a reference variable in memory, such that its address remains constant for the duration of the statement. To be sure, any time you interact with a reference type from within the context of unsafe code, pinning the reference is a must.

The "volatile" Keyword

The next (and arguably most exotic) C# keyword we will consider is "volatile". In effect, when you define a volatile variable, you are performing the converse operation of pinning a type in memory, in that you are telling the runtime that it is *completely* fine to allow an outside agent (such as the operating system, the hardware, or a concurrently executing thread) to modify the item in question at any time. Declaring such a variable is simple:

```
volatile int moveMeAnytime;
```

Basically, the "volatile" keyword may be used to define a type field that is accessed by multiple threads without using the lock statement (examined in Chapter 10) to serialize access. Using the "volatile" modifier ensures that one thread retrieves the most up-to-date value written by another thread. Again, we have not examined threads at this point in the game, so for the time being, simply understand that this C# keyword ensures that all threads will observe volatile write operations performed by a given thread in the order they were performed.

To be completely honest, you will more than likely never make use of this keyword, given that the System.Threading namespace provides you with numerous synchronization primitives that achieve the same effect. In fact, C# is one of the very few .NET-aware languages that provide a keyword such as "volatile".

The "sizeof" Keyword

The final advanced C# keyword to consider is "sizeof". Like C(++), the "sizeof" keyword is used to obtain the size in bytes for a value type (never reference types), and may only be applied from within an unsafe context. As you may imagine, this ability may prove helpful when interacting with unmanaged C-based APIs. Its usage is straightforward:

```
Console.WriteLine("The size of short is {0}.", sizeof(short));
Console.WriteLine("The size of int is {0}.", sizeof(int));
Console.WriteLine("The size of long is {0}.", sizeof(long));
```

As "sizeof" will evaluate the number of bytes for any System.ValueType-derived entity, you are able to obtain the size of custom structures as well:

```
struct MyValueType
{
    public short s;
    public int i;
    public long l;
}
Console.WriteLine("The size of MyValueType is {0}.",
    sizeof(MyValueType));
```

SOURCE CODE   The UnsafeCode project can be found under the Chapter 8 subdirectory.

A Catalog of C# Keywords

At this point in the text, you have used of a majority of C# keywords. Beyond the "lock" (see Chapter 10), "typeof" (see Chapter 11), and "extern" (used via P/Invoke operations) keywords, the remaining tokens of interest are "explicit" and "implicit", which will be examined a bit later in this chapter. For your convenience, Table 8-2 lists the complete set of keywords currently supported by C#, grouped by related functionality.

Table 8-2. A Summary of C# Keywords

C# Keyword	Meaning in Life
bool, byte, char, float, uint, ulong, ushort, decimal, int, sbyte, short, void, double, long, string, object	These C# keywords are simply aliases to structures in the System namespace. Collectively, they represent the core data types of the CTS (recall that unsigned types are not CLS compliant).
null	The "null" keyword is a literal that represents a null reference, one that does not refer to any object.
true, false	These keywords represent the possible values that can be assigned to a System.Boolean type.

Table 8-2. A Summary of C# Keywords (Continued)

C# Keyword	Meaning in Life
out, ref, params	These keywords are used to control how parameters are passed into (and out from) a type member.
public, private, internal, protected	These keywords are used to control the visibility of types and their members.
class, interface, struct, enum, delegate, event	These C# keywords are used to build custom CTS types and type members (e.g., the "event" keyword).
return	This keyword is used to designate the return value of a type member.
as, is	These keywords are used to determine at runtime if one type is compatible with another type.
do, while, foreach, in, for	These C# keywords represent the set of language iteration constructs.
if, else, switch, case, default, break	These C# keywords represent the set of language decision constructs.
goto, continue	These keywords work in conjunction with the decision and iteration constructs to further refine control flow.
try, catch, throw, finally	These keywords are used to handle runtime exceptions.
operator, explicit, implicit	These C# keywords are used to build types that support overloaded operators and custom conversion routines (keep reading . . .).
this, base	These keywords are used to reference the current object or a reference type's base class.
abstract, virtual, override	These C# keywords allow you to incorporate polymorphism into your class hierarchies.
namespace	This keyword defines a custom namespace that contains your custom types.
using	This single keyword can be used under two circumstances: • Namespace referencing • Automatic disposal of an object
new	This single keyword also has a dual identity: • Type allocation • Shadowing inherited members

Table 8-2. A Summary of C# Keywords (Continued)

C# Keyword	Meaning in Life
const	This keyword allows you to create a constant (e.g., unchangeable) point of data.
checked, unchecked	These C# keywords are used to control the overflow-checking context for arithmetic operations and conversions.
unsafe, fixed, stackalloc	These keywords are used when declaring (or using) an unsafe context, which is required when interacting with memory pointers using C#.
extern	While we have not made use of this keyword, "extern" allows you to qualify that a member is defined in an external C-based module (used during PInvoke operations).
sealed	This keyword is used to build class types that cannot be extended.
sizeof	The "sizeof" operator is used to obtain the size in bytes for a value type.
volatile	This keyword indicates that a field can be modified at any time, without error, in the program by something such as the operating system, the hardware, or a concurrently executing thread.
static	This keyword is used to define a member (or data point) that is shared by all instances of the defining type.
lock	We have not yet examined this C# keyword; however, as you will see during our examination of multithreaded programming, "lock" can be used to mark a block of code that is thread safe.
readonly	This keyword declares a field that can only be assigned values as part of the declaration or in a constructor in the same class.
typeof	Again, we have not formally investigated this keyword; however, as you will see during our examination of System.Reflection (Chapter 11), "typeof" allows you to obtain a System.Type variable that contains the metadata descriptors for the entity sent into the typeof operator.

Now that you have the bulk of the C# language keywords under your belt, we can direct our attention to the finer details of building C# types, beginning with the concept of an *indexer*.

Building a Custom Indexer

As programmers, we are very familiar with the process of accessing discrete items held within a standard array using the index (aka *bracket*) operator:

```
// Declare an array of integers.
int[] myInts = { 10, 9, 100, 432, 9874};
// Use the [] operator to access each element.
for(int j = 0; j < myInts.Length; j++)
    Console.WriteLine("Index {0}  = {1} ", j,  myInts[j]);
```

The previous code is by no means a major news flash. However, the C# language provides the capability to build custom classes that may be indexed just like an array of intrinsic types. It should be no big surprise that the method that provides the capability to access items in this manner is termed an *indexer*.

Before exploring how to create such a construct, let's begin by seeing one in action. Assume you have added support for an indexer method to the Cars container developed in Chapter 6. Observe the following usage:

```
// Indexers allow you to access items in an array-like fashion.
public class CarApp
{
    public static void Main()
    {
        // Assume the Cars type has an indexer method.
        Cars carLot = new Cars();
        // Make some cars and add them to the car lot.
        carLot[0] = new Car("FeeFee", 200, 0);
        carLot[1] = new Car("Clunker", 90, 0);
        carLot[2] = new Car("Zippy", 30, 0);
        // Now obtain and display each item.
        for(int i = 0; i < 3; i++)
        {
            Console.WriteLine("Car number {0} :", i);
            Console.WriteLine("Name: {0} ", carLot[i].PetName);
            Console.WriteLine("Max speed: {0} ", carLot[i].MaxSpeed);
        }
    }
}
```

As you can see, indexers behave much like a custom collection supporting the IEnumerator and IEnumerable interfaces. The only major difference is that rather than accessing the contents using interface references, you are able to manipulate the internal collection of automobiles just like a standard array.

Now for the big question: How do you configure the Cars class (or any class) to do so? The indexer itself is represented as a slightly mangled C# property. In its simplest form, an indexer is created using the this[] syntax:

```
// Add the indexer to the existing class definition.
public class Cars : IEnumerable
{
...
    // To contain the car types.
    private ArrayList carArray = new ArrayList();
    // The indexer returns a Car based on a numerical index.
    public Car this[int pos]
    {
        // Accessor returns an item in the array.
        get
        {
            if(pos < 0)
                throw new IndexOutOfRangeException("Out of range!");
            else
                return (Car)carArray[pos];
        }
        // Or simply call carArray.Add(value);
        set {carArray.Insert(pos, value);}
    }
}
```

Beyond the use of the "this" keyword, the indexer looks just like any other C# property declaration. Do be aware that indexers do not provide any array-like functionality beyond the use of the subscript operator. In other words, the object user cannot write code such as the following:

```
// Use System.Array.Length? Nope!
Console.WriteLine("Cars in stock: {0} ", carLot.Length);
```

To support this functionality, you would need to add your own Length property to the Cars type, and delegate accordingly:

```
public class Cars
{
    ...
    // Containment/delegation in action once again.
    public int Length() {  carArray.Count; }
}
```

At this point you have equipped a class to support an indexer method. As you can gather, this technique is yet another form of syntactic sugar given that the semantics of a type indexer can also be represented by simple public methods. For example, if the Cars type did not support an indexer, we would be able to allow the outside world to interact with the internal array list using a named property or traditional accessor/ mutator methods. Nevertheless, you will find that indexers can help make the manipulation of your types more natural. Also be aware that many key technologies within the .NET base class libraries (ADO.NET, ASP.NET, and so forth) already have numerous types that support array-like manipulations.

SOURCE CODE   The Indexer project is located under the Chapter 8 subdirectory.

A Variation of the Cars Indexer

The current Cars type defined an indexer that allowed the caller to identify the subitem it is interested in obtaining using a numerical index. Understand, however, that this is *not* a requirement of a type indexer. For example, assume you would rather contain the Car objects within a System.Collections.Specialized.ListDictionary, rather than an ArrayList. Given that ListDictionary types allow access to the contained types using a key token (such as a string), it could configure the Cars indexer as follows:

```
public class Cars
{
    // This class maintains a dictionary of cars.
    private ListDictionary carDictionary;
    public Cars(){ carDictionary = new ListDictionary(); }
    // The new indexer.
    public Car this[string name]
    {
        get { return (Car)carDictionary[name]; }
        set { carDictionary.Add(name, value); }
    }
}
```

The caller would now be able to interact with the internal cars as shown here:

```
public class CarApp
{
    public static void Main()
    {
        Cars carLot = new Cars();
        // Add to car dictionary.
        carLot["FeeFee"] = new Car("FeeFee", 200, 0);
        carLot["Clunker"] = new Car("Clunker", 90, 0);
        carLot["Zippy"] = new Car("Zippy", 30, 0);
        // Now get Zippy.
        Console.WriteLine("***** Getting Zippy using indexer *****");
        Car zippy = carLot["Zippy"];
        Console.WriteLine("{0}'s max speed is {1} MPH",
            zippy.PetName, zippy.MaxSpeed);
    }
}
```

SOURCE CODE   The DictionaryIndexer project is located under the
Chapter 8 subdirectory.

Indexers: Further Details

Also understand that indexers, like any member, may be overloaded. Thus, if it made
sense to allow the caller to access subitems using a numerical index *or* a string value,
you might define multiple indexers for a single type (as you will see, this is a very
common technique used within the ADO.NET class library).

Furthermore, if you want to get really exotic, you can also create an indexer that
takes multiple parameters. Assume you have a custom collection that stores subitems
in a two-dimensional array. If this is the case, you may configure an indexer method
as follows:

```
public class SomeContainer
{
    private int[,] my2DintArray = new int[10, 10];
    public int this[int row, int column]
    { /* get or set value from 2D array */ }
}
```

Finally, understand that indexers can be defined on a given .NET interface type to
allow implementing types to provide a custom implementation. Such an interface is
seen here:

```
public interface IAmAnInterfaceWithAnIndexer
{
    // This interface defines an indexer that returns
    // strings based on a numerical index.
    string this[int index] { get; set; }
}
```

Internal Representation of Type Indexers

Now that you have seen a number of variations on the C# indexer method, you may be
wondering how this member is represented in terms of raw CIL. If you were to open up
the numerical indexer of the Cars type, you would find that the C# compiler has created
a property named Item:

```
.property instance class Indexer.Car Item(int32)
{
  .get instance class Indexer.Car Indexer.Cars::get_Item(int32)
  .set instance void Indexer.Cars::set_Item(int32,
      class Indexer.Car)
} // end of property Cars::Item
```

Now, if you have a background in the Visual Basic programming language, you may be happy to see that the internal representation of a C# indexer is indeed a property named Item. The reason (for those who are not aware of various VB-isms) is that VB types that provide access to subtypes typically define a *default* method named Item. In the world of VB, a *default* item identifies the method to be called on a type if the caller does not explicitly specify it by name, but rather makes use of the index notation (which under VB is denoted as () rather than []). Given this factoid, understand that C# indexers are CLS compliant, and can be called from any .NET-aware programming language.

NOTE   FYI, unlike VB 6.0, VB .NET will only allow you to define a default property that has at least one parameter. Given this, the VB 6.0 "Set" keyword is now obsolete.

Using the C# Indexer from VB .NET

To illustrate the language-agnostic nature of C# indexers requires an understanding of .NET code libraries (e.g., custom *.dll assemblies). The next chapter will examine this process in great detail, so for the time being simply assume you have created a C# code library named IndexerCodeLibrary that contains the Cars, Radio, and Car types. If a VB .NET application were to set a reference to this external assembly, it would be able to interact with the contained types as follows:

```
' The VB .NET 'Imports' keyword is
' the same as the C# 'using' keyword.
Imports IndexerCodeLibrary
' A VB .NET 'Module' is simple a class containing nothing
' but static members.
Module CarApp
    Sub Main()
        Dim carLot As New Cars()
        ' Item is mapped to the default property in VB .NET,
        ' and can therefore be omitted. Thus, either of these calls
        ' are perfectly fine and legal.
        carLot.Item(0) = New Car("MB", 150, 40)
        carLot(1) = New Car("Daisy", 130, 40)
        Dim c As Car
        For Each c In carLot
            Console.WriteLine("Name: {0}, Max Speed: {1}", _
                c.PetName, c.MaxSpeed)
        Next
    End Sub
End Module
```

Although we have not yet drilled into the details of code libraries or cross-language programming (more details to come in Chapter 9), the code shown here should be quite easy on the eyes. Do note that VB .NET client applications have the option of specifying the Item property by name, given that VB .NET interprets any C# indexers as the *default property* of the type (e.g., it will be invoked even if the code base does not explicitly reference it by name).

SOURCE CODE   The IndexerCodeLibrary and VbNetIndexerClient projects are located under the Chapter 8 subdirectory.

Overloading Operators

So much for the topic of C# indexers. Next up, we will examine a technique that is not supported by all .NET-aware programming languages, but is useful nonetheless. C#, like any programming language, has a canned set of tokens that are used to perform basic operations on intrinsic types. For example, everyone knows that the + operator can be applied to two integers in order to yield a new integer:

```
// The + operator in action.
int a = 100;
int b = 240;
int c = a + b;  // c is now 340
```

This is no major news flash, but have you ever stopped and noticed how the same + operator can be applied to any intrinsic C# data type? For example:

```
// + operator with strings.
string s1 = "Hello";
string s2 = " world!";
string s3 = s1 + s2;  // s3 is now "Hello world!"
```

In essence, the + operator has been overloaded to function correctly on various individual data types. When the + operator is applied to numerical types, the result is the summation of the operands. However, when applied to string types, the result is string concatenation.

NOTE   Understand that unlike numerous types in the .NET base class libraries, the intrinsic data types of the System namespace have not literally overloaded the set of C# operators, as CIL provides specific op codes for the manipulation of numeric data types.

The C# language (like C++ and unlike Java) provides the capability for you to build custom classes and structures that also respond uniquely to the same set of basic tokens (such as the + operator). To illustrate, assume the following simple Point structure (and yes, you are able to overload operators on class types as well):

```csharp
// Just a simple everyday C# struct.
public struct Point
{
    private int x, y;
    public Point(int xPos, int yPos)
    {
        x = xPos;
        y = yPos;
    }
    public override string ToString()
    {
        return string.Format("X pos: {0} Y pos: {1}",
            this.x, this.y);
    }
}
```

Now, logically speaking, it makes sense to add Points together. On a related note, it would be helpful to subtract one Point from another. For example, if you created two Point objects with some initial startup values, you may like to do something like this:

```csharp
// Adding and subtracting two points.
public static int Main(string[] args)
{
    // Make two points
    Point ptOne = new Point(100, 100);
    Point ptTwo = new Point(40, 40);
    // Add the points to make a new point.
    Point bigPoint = ptOne + ptTwo;
    Console.WriteLine("Here is the big point: {0} ", bigPoint.ToString());
    // Subtract the points to make a new point.
    Point minorPoint = bigPoint - ptOne;
    Console.WriteLine("Just a minor point: {0} ", minorPoint.ToString());
    return 0;
}
```

Clearly, your goal is to somehow make your Point type react uniquely to the + and – operators. To allow a custom type to respond to these intrinsic tokens, C# provides the "operator" keyword, which can only be used in conjunction with *static* methods. To illustrate:

```
// A more intelligent Point type.
public struct Point
{
    private int x, y;
    public Point(int xPos, int yPos){  x = xPos; y = yPos; }
    // The Point type can be added...
    public static Point operator + (Point p1, Point p2)
    {
        Point newPoint = new Point(p1.x + p2.x, p1.y + p2.y);
        return newPoint;
    }
    // ...and subtracted.
    public static Point operator - (Point p1, Point p2)
    {
        // Figure new X (assume [0,0] base).
        int newX = p1.x - p2.x;
        if(newX < 0)
            throw new ArgumentOutOfRangeException();
        // Figure new Y (also assume [0,0] base).
        int newY = p1.y - p2.y;
        if(newY < 0)
            throw new ArgumentOutOfRangeException();
        return new Point(newX, newY);
    }
    public override string ToString()
    {
       return string.Format("X pos: {0} Y pos: {1}",
            this.x, this.y);
    }
}
```

Notice that the class now contains two strange looking methods called operator + and operator –. The logic behind operator + is simply to return a brand new Point based on the summation of the incoming Point arguments. Thus, when you write pt1 + pt2, under the hood you can envision the following hidden call to the static operator + method:

```
// p3 = Point.operator+ (p1, p2)
p3 = p1 + p2;
```

Likewise, p1 – p2 maps to the following:

```
// p3 = Point.operator- (p1, p2)
p3 = p1 - p2;
```

Overloading the Equality Operators

As you may recall, System.Object.Equals() can be overridden in order to perform value-based (rather than referenced-based) comparisons between objects. In addition to overriding Equals() and GetHashCode(), an object may choose to override the equality operators (= = and !=). To illustrate, here is the updated Point type:

```
// This incarnation of Point also overloads the == and != operators.
public struct Point
{
    public int x, y;
    public Point(int xPos, int yPos){ x = xPos; y = yPos;}
...
    public override bool Equals(object o)
    {
        if( ((Point)o).x = = this.x &&
            ((Point)o).y = = this.y)
                return true;
        else
                return false;
    }
    public override int GetHashCode()
    { return this.ToString().GetHashCode(); }
    // Now let's overload the == and != operators.
    public static bool operator ==(Point p1, Point p2)
    { return p1.Equals(p2); }
    public static bool operator !=(Point p1, Point p2)
    { return !p1.Equals(p2); }
}
```

Notice how the implementation of operator == and operator != simply makes a call to the overridden Equals() method to get the bulk of the work done. Given this, you can now exercise your Point class as follows:

```
// Make use of the overloaded equality operators.
public static int Main(string[] args)
{
...
    if(ptOne == ptTwo)      // Are they the same?
        Console.WriteLine("Same values!");
    else
        Console.WriteLine("Nope, different values.");
    if(ptOne != ptTwo)      // Are they different?
        Console.WriteLine("These are not equal.");
    else
        Console.WriteLine("Same values!");
}
```

As you can see, it is quite intuitive to compare two objects using the well-known == and != operators rather than making a call to Object.Equals(). As a rule of thumb, classes that override Object.Equals()/Object.GetHashCode() should always overload the == and != operators.

If you do overload the equality operators for a given class, keep in mind that C# demands that if you override operator ==, you *must* also override operator !=, just as when you override Equals() you will need to override GetHashCode(). This ensures that an object behaves in a uniform manner during comparisons and functions correctly if placed into a hash table (if you forget, the compiler will let you know).

SOURCE CODE   The OverLoadOps project is located under the Chapter 8 subdirectory.

Overloading the Comparison Operators

In Chapter 6, you learned how to implement the IComparable interface in order to compare the relative relationship between two like objects. Additionally, you may also overload the comparison operators (<, >, <=, and >=) for the same class. Like the equality operators, C# demands that < and > are overloaded as a set. The same holds true for the <= and >= operators. If the Car type you developed in Chapter 6 overloaded these comparison operators, the object user could now compare types as follows:

```
// Exercise the overloaded < operator for the Car class.
public class CarApp
{
    public static int Main(string[] args)
    {
        // Make an array of Car types.
        Car[] myAutos = new Car[5];
        myAutos[0] = new Car(123, "Rusty");
        myAutos[1] = new Car(6, "Mary");
        myAutos[2] = new Car(6, "Viper");
        myAutos[3] = new Car(13, "NoName");
        myAutos[4] = new Car(6, "Chucky");

        // Is Rusty less than Chucky?
        if(myAutos[0] < myAutos[4])
            Console.WriteLine("Rusty is less than Chucky!");
        else
            Console.WriteLine("Chucky is less than Rusty!");
        return 0;
    }
}
```

Assuming you have a Car type that implements IComparable, overloading the comparison operators is trivial. Here is the updated class definition:

```
// This class is also comparable using the comparison operators.
public class Car : IComparable
{
...
    public int CompareTo(object o)
    {
        Car temp = (Car)o;
        if(this.CarID > temp.CarID)
            return 1;
        if(this.CarID < temp.CarID)
            return -1;
        else
            return 0;
    }
    public static bool operator < (Car c1, Car c2)
    {
        IComparable itfComp = (IComparable)c1;
        return (itfComp.CompareTo(c2) < 0);
    }
    public static bool operator > (Car c1, Car c2)
    {
        IComparable itfComp = (IComparable)c1;
        return (itfComp.CompareTo(c2) > 0);
    }
    public static bool operator <= (Car c1, Car c2)
    {
        IComparable itfComp = (IComparable)c1;
        return (itfComp.CompareTo(c2) <= 0);
    }
    public static bool operator >= (Car c1, Car c2)
    {
        IComparable itfComp = (IComparable)c1;
        return (itfComp.CompareTo(c2) >= 0);
    }
}
```

 SOURCE CODE The ObjCompWithOps project is located under the Chapter 8 subdirectory.

The Internal Representation of Overloaded Operators

Like any C# programming element, overloaded operators are represented using specific CIL instructions. To begin examining what takes place behind the scenes, open up your OverLoadOps.exe assembly (created previously) using ildasm.exe. As you can see from Figure 8-3, the +, –, = =, and != operators are internally expressed via hidden methods, which in this case are named op_Addition(), op_Subtraction(), op_Equality(), and op_Inequality().

Figure 8-3. Internal CIL representation of overloaded operators

Now, if you were to examine the specific CIL instructions for the op_Addition method, you would find that the specialname flag has also been inserted by csc.exe:

```
.method public hidebysig specialname static
        valuetype OverLoadOps.Point  op_Addition(valuetype OverLoadOps.Point p1,
            valuetype OverLoadOps.Point p2) cil managed
{
...
}
```

The truth of the matter is that any operator that you may overload equates to a specially named method in terms of CIL. Table 8-3 documents the C#-operator-to-CIL mapping for the key C# operators.

Table 8-3. C#-Operator-to-CIL Special Name Roadmap

Intrinsic C# Operator	CIL Representation
--	op_Decrement()
++	op_Increment()
Unary–	op_UnaryNegation()
Unary +	op_UnaryPlus()
!	op_LogicalNot()

Table 8-3. C#-Operator-to-CIL Special Name Roadmap (Continued)

Intrinsic C# Operator	CIL Representation
True	op_True()
False	op_False()
~	op_OnesComplement()
Binary +	op_Addition()
Binary –	op_Subtraction()
Binary *	op_Multiply()
/	op_Division()
%	op_Modulus()
^	op_ExclusiveOr()
Binary &	op_BitwiseAnd()
|	op_BitwiseOr()
&&	op_LogicalAnd()
||	op_LogicalOr()
=	op_Assign()
<<	op_LeftShift()
>>	op_RightShift()
= =	op_Equality()
>	op_GreaterThan()
<	op_LessThan()
!=	op_Inequality()
>=	op_GreaterThanOrEqual()
<=	op_LessThanOrEqual()
->	op_MemberSelection()
>>=	op_RightShiftAssignment()
*=	op_MultiplicationAssignment()
->*	op_PointerToMemberSelection()
-=	op_SubtractionAssignment()
^=	op_ExclusiveOrAssignment()

Table 8-3. C#-Operator-to-CIL Special Name Roadmap (Continued)

Intrinsic C# Operator	CIL Representation
<<=	op_LeftShiftAssignment()
%=	op_ModulusAssignment()
+=	op_AdditionAssignment()
&=	op_BitwiseAndAssignment()
|=	op_BitwiseOrAssignment()
/=	op_DivisionAssignment()

Interacting with Overloaded Operators from Overloaded-Operator-Challenged Languages

The capability to overload operators is useful in that it enables the object user to work with your types (more or less) like any intrinsic data point. Now, understand that the capability to overload operators is *not a requirement* of the Common Language Specification; thus, not all .NET-aware languages support the construction of types that overload operators.

What then would happen if an overloaded-operator-challenged language wished to add two points together? To make it as simple as possible for such languages to trigger the same functionality as an overloaded operator, you will do well to provide a publicly named member for the same purpose. To illustrate, assume you have updated the Point type as follows:

```csharp
// Exposing overloaded operator semantics using simple
// member functions.
public struct Point
{
...
    // Operator + via AddPoints()
    public static Point AddPoints (Point p1, Point p2)
    { return new Point(p1.x + p2.x, p1.y + p2.y); }
    // Operator - via SubtractPoints()
    public static Point SubtractPoints (Point p1, Point p2)
    {
        // Figure new X.
        int newX = p1.x - p2.x;
        if(newX < 0)
            throw new ArgumentOutOfRangeException();
        // Figure new Y.
        int newY = p1.y - p2.y;
        if(newY < 0)
            throw new ArgumentOutOfRangeException();
        return new Point(newX, newY);
    }
}
```

Rather than having duplicate code within your overloaded operators and public members, to maximize your coding efforts, simply implement the overloaded operators to call the member function alternative (or vice versa). For example:

```
public struct Point
{
...
    // For overload-operator-aware languages.
    public static Point operator + (Point p1, Point p2)
    { return AddPoints(p1, p2); }
    // For overload-challenged languages.
    public static Point AddPoints (Point p1, Point p2)
    { return new Point(p1.x + p2.x, p1.y + p2.y); }
}
```

With this, the Point type is able to expose the same functionality using whichever technique a given language demands. C# users can apply the + and − operators and/or call AddPoints()/SubtractPoints(). Languages that cannot use overloaded operators (such as VB .NET) can make due with the public member functions.

Triggering the "Special Names" from VB .NET

On a related note, understand that it is also possible to directly call the specially named methods from operator-overload-lacking languages, given that they appear as public members on the type. Thus, if you were to bundle the logic of the previous OverLoadOps project into a C# code library (named OverLoadOpsCodeLibrary), a VB .NET client could interact with the + operator as follows:

```
Imports OverLoadOpsCodeLibrary
Module OverLoadedOpClient
    Sub Main()
        Dim p1 As Point
        p1.x = 200
        p1.y = 9
        Dim p2 As Point
        p2.x = 9
        p2.y = 983
        ' Not as clean as calling AddPoints(),
        ' but it gets the job done.
        Dim bigPoint = Point.op_Addition(p1, p2)
        Console.WriteLine("Big point is {0}", bigPoint)
    End Sub
End Module
```

As you can see, overloaded-operator-challenged .NET programming languages are able to directly invoke the internal CIL methods as if they were "normal" methods. While it is not pretty, it works. Therefore, even if you (or your teammates) do not take the time to create a more friendly named method (such as AddPoints()), the same functionality can be obtained using the underlying "special" methods.

SOURCE CODE   The OverLoadOpsCodeLibrary and VbNetOverLoadOpsClient projects are located under the Chapter 8 subdirectory.

Final Thoughts Regarding Operator Overloading

C# provides the capability to build types that can respond uniquely to various intrinsic, well-known operators. Now, before you go and retrofit all your classes to support such behavior, you must be sure that the operator(s) you are about to overload make some sort of logical sense in the world at large.

For example, let's say you overloaded the multiplication operator for the Engine class. What exactly would it mean to multiply two Engine objects? Not much. Overloading operators is generally only useful when building utility types. Strings, points, rectangles, fractions, and hexagons make good candidates for operator overloading. People, managers, cars, headphones, and baseball hats do not. Use this feature wisely.

Finally, be aware that you cannot overload each and every intrinsic C# operator. Table 8-4 outlines the "overloadability" of each item.

Table 8-4. Valid Overloadable Operators

C# Operator	Meaning in Life (Can This Operator Be Overloaded?)
+, −, !, ~, ++, − −, true, false	This set of unary operators can be overloaded.
+, −, *, /, %, &, |, ^, <<, >>	These binary operators can be overloaded.
= =, !=, <, >, <=, >=	The comparison operators can be overloaded. Recall, however, that C# will demand that "like" operators (i.e., < and >, <= and >=, = = and !=) are overloaded together.
[]	The [] operator cannot technically be overloaded. As you have seen earlier in this chapter, however, the indexer construct provides the same functionality.

And What of the += and −+ Operators?

If you are coming to C# from a C++ background, you may lament the loss of overloading the shorthand assignment operators (+=, −=, and so forth) as well as the explicit cast operator (()). Fear not. In terms of C#, the shorthand assignment operators are automatically simulated if a type overloads a given unary operator and the assignment operator. Thus, given that the Point structure has already overloaded the +, −, and == operators, you are able to write the following:

```
// Freebie!!
Point ptThree = new Point(90, 5);
ptThree += ptTwo;
Console.WriteLine("ptThree is now {0}", ptThree);
```

In a similar manner, given that the Point type has overloaded the – and assignment operators, you are also able to exercise a Point type as follows:

```
// Another freebie!!
Point ptFour = new Point(0, 500);
ptFour += ptThree;
Console.WriteLine("ptFour is now {0}", ptFour);
```

As for the apparent loss of overloading the explicit cast operator, C# offers an appealing alternative. . . .

Understanding Custom Type Conversions

To wrap up this chapter, we will examine a topic closely related to operator overloading: defining custom type conversion functions (as mentioned, this technique is functionally similar to overloading the () operator using C++). Before we dive into the details, let's quickly review the notion of explicit and implicit conversions between numerical data as well as related class types.

Recall: Numerical Conversions

In terms of the intrinsic numerical types (sbyte, int, float, etc.), an explicit conversion is required when you attempt to store a larger value into a smaller container, as this may result in a loss of data. Basically, this is your way to tell the compiler, "Leave me alone, I know what I am trying to do." As you recall, in an explicit conversion in C#, you make use of an explicit cast (via the () operator). Conversely, implicit conversions happen automatically when you attempt to place a smaller type into a destination type that will not result in a loss of data:

```
int a = 123;
long b = a;          // Implicit conversion from int to long
int c = (int) b;     // Explicit conversion from long to int
```

 NOTE   Also recall that the "checked"/"unchecked" keywords can be used to generate (or disable) runtime errors should a loss of data occur (as you have seen at the opening of this chapter).

Now, assume for a moment that C# did not honor the use of the () operator. This would be nasty, as you would be required to call various member functions in order to convert between types. For example:

```
int a = 123;
long b = a;
int c = ((IConvertible)b).ToInt32(CultureInfo.CurrentCulture);  // Yuck...
```

Recall: Conversions Among Related Class Types

As seen in Chapter 4, class types may be related by classical inheritance (the "is-a" relationship). In this case, the C# conversion process allows you to cast up and down the class hierarchy. For example, a derived class can always be implicitly cast into a given base type. However, if you wish to store a base class type in a derived variable, you must perform an explicit cast:

```
// Implicit cast between derived to base.
Base myBaseType;
myBaseType = new Derived();
// Must explicitly cast to store base reference
// in derived type.
Derived myDerivedType = (Derived)myBaseType;
```

This explicit cast works due to the fact that the Base and Derived classes are related by classical inheritance. However, what if you had two class types in different class hierarchies that require conversions? On a related note, consider structure types. Assume you have two .NET structures named Square and Rectangle. Given that structures cannot leverage classic inheritance, you have no natural way to cast between these seemingly related types.

While you could build custom methods (such as Square.ToRectangle() or Rectangle.ToSquare()), C# allows you to build custom conversion routines that allow your types to respond to the () operator. Therefore, if you configured the Square type correctly, you would be able to use the following syntax to explicitly convert between types:

```
// Convert a Square to a Rectangle.
Square sq;
sq.sideLength = 3;
Rectangle rect = (Rectangle)sq;
```

Creating Custom Conversion Routines

Now that you have a better feel about how it would look to interact with a type using a custom conversion routine, let's see how to equip the type itself. C# provides two keywords ("explicit" and "implicit") that are used to control how your types respond during an attempted conversion. To begin, assume you have the following structure definitions:

```csharp
public struct Rectangle
{
    public int width, height;
    public void Draw()
    { Console.WriteLine("Drawing a rect.");}
    // Rectangles can be explicitly converted
    // into squares using the () syntax.
    public static explicit operator Rectangle(Square s)
    {
        Rectangle r;
        r.height = s.sideLength;
        r.width = s.sideLength;
        return r;
    }
    public override string ToString()
    {
        return string.Format("[Width = {0}; Height = {1}]",
            width, height);
    }
}
public struct Square
{
    public int sideLength;
    public void Draw()
    { Console.WriteLine("Drawing a square.");}
    public override string ToString()
    {
        return string.Format("[SideLength = {0}]", sideLength);
    }
}
```

Notice that the Rectangle type defines an explicit conversion operator. Like the process of overloading an operator, conversion routines make use of the C# operator keyword (in conjunction with the "explicit" or "implicit" keyword), and must be defined as static. The incoming parameter is the entity you are converting *from* while the return value is the entity you are converting *to*:

```csharp
public static explicit operator Rectangle(Square s)
{...}
```

In any case, the assumption is that a square (being a geometric pattern in which all sides are of equal length) can be transformed into a rectangle, provided that the dimensions remain identical. Thus, you are free to convert a Square into a Rectangle in the following ways:

```csharp
// Create a 10 * 10 square.
Square sq;
sq.sideLength = 3;
Console.WriteLine("sq = {0}", sq);
// Convert Square to a new Rectangle.
Rectangle rect = (Rectangle)sq;
Console.WriteLine("rect = {0}", rect);
```

While it may not be all that helpful to convert your Square into a Rectangle within the same scope, assume you have a function that has been prototyped to take Rectangle types. Using your explicit conversion operation, you can safely pass in Square types for processing:

```
private static void DrawThisRect(Rectangle r)
{r.Draw();}
...
// Meanwhile, back in Main()...
DrawThisRect((Rectangle)sq);
```

Explicit Conversion Operators for the Square Type

Now that you can explicitly convert squares into rectangles, let's update the Square structure to support a few conversions of its own. Given that a square is symmetrical on each side, it might be helpful to provide an explicit conversion routine that allows the caller to cast from a System.Int32 type into a Square (which, of course, will have a side length equal to the incoming integer). Likewise, what if you were to update Square such that the caller can cast *from* a Square into a System.Int32? Here is the calling logic:

```
// Converting System.Int32 to Square.
Square sq2 = (Square)90;
Console.WriteLine("sq2 = {0}", sq2);
// Convert a Square to a System.Int32.
int side = (int)sq2;
Console.WriteLine("Side of sq2 = {0}", side);
```

And here is the update to the Square type:

```
public struct Square
{
    public int sideLength;
    public void Draw()
    { Console.WriteLine("Drawing a square.");}
    public override string ToString()
    {
        return string.Format("[SideLength = {0}]", sideLength);
    }
    public static explicit operator Square(int sideLength)
    {
        Square newSq;
        newSq.sideLength = sideLength;
        return newSq;
    }
    public static explicit operator int (Square s)
    {return s.sideLength; }
}
```

Wild, huh? To be honest, the need to convert from a Square into a System.Int32 may not be the most intuitive (or useful) operation. However, this does point out a very important fact regarding custom conversion routines: The compiler does not care what you convert to or from, as long as you have written syntactically correct code. Thus, as with overloading operators, just because you can create an explicit cast operation for a given type does not mean you should. Typically this technique will be most helpful when creating .NET structure types, given that they are unable to participate in classical inheritance (where casting comes for free).

Defining Implicit Conversion Routines

Thus far, you have equipped your Rectangle type to honor explicit conversions between Square types. However, what about the following implicit conversion?

```
// Attempt to make an implicit cast.
Square s3;
s3.sideLength= 83;
Rectangle rect2 = s3;
```

As you might expect, this code will not compile, given that you have not provided an implicit conversion routine for the Rectangle type. Now here is the catch: It is illegal to define explicit and implicit conversion functions on the same type, if they do not differ by their return type or parameter set. This might seem like a limitation; however, the second catch is that when a type defines an implicit conversion routine, it is legal for the caller to make use of the explicit cast syntax!

Confused? To clear things up, let's begin by modifying the existing conversion routine for the Rectangle to make use of the C# "implicit" keyword:

```
public static implicit operator Rectangle(Square s)
{
    Rectangle r;
    r.height = s.sideLength;
    r.width = s.sideLength;
    return r;
}
```

With this update, you are now able to convert between types as follows:

```
// Implicit cast OK!
Square s3;
s3.sideLength= 83;
Rectangle rect2 = s3;
Console.WriteLine("rect2 = {0}", rect2);
DrawThisRect(s3);
// Explicit cast syntax still OK!
Square s4;
s4.sideLength = 3;
Rectangle rect3 = (Rectangle)s4;
Console.WriteLine("rect3 = {0}", rect3);
```

Do be aware that it is permissible to define explicit and implicit conversion routines for the same type as long as their signatures differ. Thus, you would update the Square as follows:

```
public struct Square
{
    // Can call as:
    // Square sq2 = (Square)90;
    // or as:
    // Square sq2 = 90;
    public static implicit operator Square(int sideLength)
    {
        Square newSq;
        newSq.sideLength = sideLength;
        return newSq;
    }
    // Must call as:
    // int side = (Square)mySquare;
    public static explicit operator int (Square s)
    { return s.sideLength; }
}
```

SOURCE CODE The UserDefinedConversions project is located under the Chapter 8 subdirectory.

The Internal Representation of Custom Conversion Routines

Before moving on, you have one more conversion detail to contend with. Like overloaded operators, methods that are qualified with the "implicit" or "explicit" keywords have "special" names in terms of CIL: op_implicit and op_explicit, respectively (Figure 8-4).

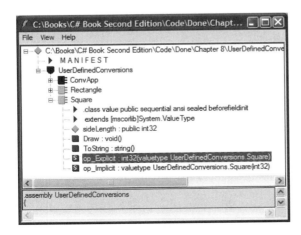

Figure 8-4. CIL representation of user-defined conversion routines

As you might imagine, you cannot guarantee that a given .NET language will be able to interact with a type's set of custom conversion functions, given that the () cast operator is a C#-ism. However, you would still be able to interact with these members using their underlying CIL representation:

```
Module UserConvApp
    Sub Main()
        Dim s As Square
        s.sideLength = 83
        Dim rect As Rectangle = Rectangle.op_Implicit(s)
        Console.WriteLine("rect = {0}", rect)
    End Sub
End Module
```

That wraps up our examination of defining custom conversion routines (and this chapter). Remember that this bit of syntax is simply a shorthand notation for "normal" member functions, and in this light is always optional.

SOURCE CODE   The UserConvLib and VbNetUserConvClient projects are located under the Chapter 8 subdirectory.

Summary

The purpose of this chapter was to round out your understanding of the C# programming language. We began by examining a small set of lesser know keywords (e.g., "sizeof", "checked", "unsafe", and so forth) and during the process came to learn how to work with raw pointer types.

The remainder of this chapter was spent investigating various advanced type construction techniques (indexer methods, overloaded operators, and custom conversion routines). As you have seen, each of these constructs can be triggered from languages other than C# (directly or indirectly).

Part Three
Programming with
.NET Assemblies

CHAPTER 9

Understanding .NET Assemblies

EACH OF THE APPLICATIONS DEVELOPED in the first eight chapters are along the lines of traditional "stand-alone" applications, given that all programming logic is contained within a single *.exe. One major aspect of .NET is the notion of binary reuse. Like COM, .NET provides the ability to access types located in external binaries in a language-independent manner. However, the .NET platform provides far greater language integration than classic COM. For example, the .NET platform supports cross-language inheritance (e.g., a Visual Basic .NET class deriving from a C# class). To understand how this is achieved requires a deeper understanding of assemblies.

Once you understand the logical and physical layout of an assembly, you then learn the distinction between "private" and "shared" assemblies, as well as single file and multifile assemblies. You also examine exactly how the .NET runtime resolves the location of an assembly and come to understand the role of the Global Assembly Cache (GAC) and application configuration files (*.config). As you will see, *.config files may be used by a client application to interact with the assembly binding process.

Problems with Classic COM Binaries

Binary reuse (i.e., portable code libraries) is not a new idea. To date, the most popular way in which a programmer can share types between binaries (and in some respects, across languages) is to build what can now be regarded as "classic COM servers." Although the construction and use of COM binaries is a well-established industry standard, these little blobs have caused each of us a fair share of headaches. Beyond the fact that COM demands a good deal of complex infrastructure (IDL, class factories, scripting support, and so forth), I am sure you have also pondered the following questions during your time developing with COM:

- Why is it so difficult to version my COM binary?

- Why is it so complex to distribute my COM binary?

The .NET Framework greatly improves on the current state of affairs and addresses the versioning and deployment problems head-on using a new binary format termed an assembly. However, before you come to understand how the assembly offers a clean solution to these issues, let's spend some time recapping the problems in a bit more detail.

Problem: COM Versioning

In COM, you build entities named *coclasses* that are little more than a custom UDT (user-defined type) implementing any number of COM interfaces (including the mandatory IUnknown). The coclasses are then packaged into a binary home, which is physically represented as a *.dll or *.exe file. Once all the (known) bugs have been squashed out of the code, the COM binary eventually ends up on some user's computer, ready to be accessed by other programs.

The versioning problem in COM revolves around the fact that the COM runtime offers no intrinsic support to ensure that the correct version of a binary server is loaded for the calling client. It is true that a COM programmer can modify the version of the type library, update the registry to reflect these changes, and even reengineer the client's code base to reference a particular library. But, the fact remains that these are tasks delegated to the programmer and typically require rebuilding the code base and redeploying the software. As many of you have learned the hard way, this is far from ideal.

Assume that you have jumped through the necessary hoops to try to ensure the COM client activates the correct version of a COM binary. Your worries are far from over, given that some other application may be installed on the target machine that overrides your carefully configured registry entries (and maybe even replaces a COM server or two with an earlier version during the process). Mysteriously, your client application may now fail to operate.

For example, if you have ten applications that all require the use of MyCOMServer.dll version 1.4, and another application installs MyCOMServer.dll version 2.0, all ten applications are at risk of breaking. This is because we cannot be assured of complete backward compatibility. In a perfect world, all versions of a given COM binary are fully compatible with previous versions. In practice however, keeping COM servers (and software in general) completely backward compatible is extremely difficult.

The lump sum of each of these versioning issues is lovingly referred to as "DLL Hell" (which, by the way, is not limited to COM DLLs; traditional C DLLs suffer the same hellish existence). As you'll see during the course of this chapter, the .NET Framework solves this nightmare by using a number of techniques including side-by-side execution and a very robust (yet very simple) versioning scheme.

In a nutshell, .NET allows multiple versions of the same binary to be installed on the same target machine. Therefore, under .NET, if client A requires MyDotNETServer.dll version 1.4 and client B demands MyDotNETServer.dll version 2.0, the correct version is loaded for the respective client automatically. You are also able to bind to a specific version using an application configuration file.

Problem: COM Deployment

The COM runtime is a rather temperamental service. When a COM client wishes to make use of a coclass, the first step is to load the COM libraries for a given thread by calling CoInitialize(). At this point, the client makes additional calls to the COM runtime (e.g., CoCreateInstance(), CoGetClassObject(), and so forth) to load a given binary into memory and create the required COM type. The result is that the COM client receives an interface reference that is then used to manipulate the coclass.

For the COM runtime to locate and load a binary, the COM server must be configured correctly on the target machine. From a high level, registering a COM server sounds so simple: build an installation program (or make use of a system-supplied registration tool) to trigger the correct logic in the COM binary (DllRegisterServer() for DLLs or WinMain() for EXEs) and call it a day. However, as you may know, a COM server requires a vast number of registration entries to be made. Typically, every COM class (CLSID), interface (IID), type library (LIBID), and application (AppID) must be documented within the system registry.

The key point to keep in mind is that the relationship between the binary image and the related registry entries is extremely loose, and therefore extremely fragile. In COM, the location of the binary image (e.g., C:\MyCOMServer.dll) is entirely separate from the massive number of registry entries that completely describe the component. Therefore, if the end user were to relocate (or rename) a COM server, the entire system breaks, as the registration entries are now out of sync.

The .NET platform makes the process of deploying an application extremely simple given the fact that .NET binaries (i.e., assemblies) are not registered in the system registry at all. Plain and simple. Deploying a .NET application can be (and most often is) as simple as copying the files that compose the application to some location on the machine, and running your program. In short, be prepared to bid a fond farewell to HKEY_CLASSES_ROOT.

An Overview of .NET Assemblies

Now that you understand the problems, let's check out the solution. .NET applications are constructed by piecing together any number of assemblies. Simply put, an assembly is nothing more than a versioned, self-describing binary (*.dll or *.exe) containing some collection of types (classes, interfaces, structures, etc.) and optional resources (images, string tables, and whatnot). One thing to be painfully aware of right now is that the internal organization of a .NET assembly is nothing like the internal organization of a classic COM server (regardless of the shared file extensions). For example, an in-process COM server exports four functions (DllCanUnloadNow(), DllGetClassObject(), DllRegisterServer() and DllUnregisterServer()),to allow the COM runtime to access its contents. .NET DLLs on the other hand do not.

Local COM servers define WinMain() as the sole entry point into the *.exe, which is implemented to test for various command line parameters to perform the same duties as a COM *.dll. Not so under the .NET protocol. Although .NET *.exe binaries do provide an entry point (identified using the .entrypoint CIL directive), the behind-the-scenes logic is entirely different.

Given that .NET binaries are a completely new binary format, the next logical question would be how managed assemblies are composed under the hood. Specifically speaking, a .NET binary consists of five major elements:

- A standard Windows file header

- A CLR header that marks the file as a managed module

- CIL code

- Type metadata

- The assembly manifest

The first two elements (the Win32 header and CLR header) are entities that you can safely ignore; however they do deserve some brief consideration. The Win32 header is just about identical to that of an unmanaged binary, and is simply used to identify that the module is usable by the Windows operating system. This header also identifies the type of application to be launched (console-based, GUI-based, or a *.dll module). If you were to open a .NET assembly using dumpbin.exe and specify the /headers flag, you would indeed file a block identifying the Win32 header information. To illustrate, Figure 9-1 shows the output of viewing the CarLibrary.dll assembly you will build a bit later in this chapter:

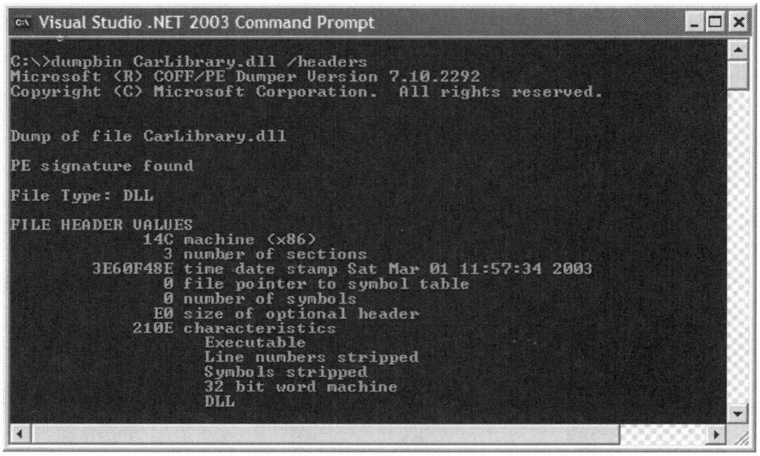

Figure 9-1. Assembly Win32 header file information

The CLR header is a block of information that all .NET files must support (and do support, courtesy of the C# compiler) to be loaded by the CLR. In a nutshell, this header defines numerous flags that enable the runtime to understand the layout of the managed file. For example, flags exist that identify the location of the metadata and resources within the file, the version of the runtime the assembly was built against, the value of the (optional) public key, and so forth.

For those who are interested, note that all of this information is represented by a C-style structure (IMAGE_COR20_HEADER) defined in <corhdr.h>. Although 99.99 percent (or greater) of .NET programmers will never need to interact with this UDT, for your edification, here is the layout of the structure in question:

```
// CLR 2.0 header structure.
typedef struct IMAGE_COR20_HEADER
{
    // Header versioning
    ULONG       cb;
    USHORT      MajorRuntimeVersion;
    USHORT      MinorRuntimeVersion;

    // Symbol table and startup information
    IMAGE_DATA_DIRECTORY      MetaData;
    ULONG       Flags;
    ULONG       EntryPointToken;

    // Binding information
    IMAGE_DATA_DIRECTORY      Resources;
    IMAGE_DATA_DIRECTORY      StrongNameSignature;

    // Regular fixup and binding information
    IMAGE_DATA_DIRECTORY      CodeManagerTable;
    IMAGE_DATA_DIRECTORY      VTableFixups;
    IMAGE_DATA_DIRECTORY      ExportAddressTableJumps;

    // Precompiled image info (internal use only - set to zero)
    IMAGE_DATA_DIRECTORY      ManagedNativeHeader;
} IMAGE_COR20_HEADER;
```

Header information aside, the key point is that an unmanaged binary contains instructions that target a specific platform and specific CPU and platform. In contrast, .NET binaries contain common intermediate language (CIL), which is platform- and CPU-agnostic. At runtime, the internal CIL is compiled on the fly (using a just-in-time compiler) to platform and CPU-specific instructions. This is a powerful extension of classic COM in that .NET assemblies are poised to be platform-neutral entities that are not necessarily tied to the Windows operating system (see Chapter 1).

In addition to CIL code, an assembly also contains metadata that completely describes each type defined within the current assembly as well as the set of external types referenced by this assembly. For example, if you created a class named JoyStick using some .NET-aware language, the corresponding compiler emits metadata describing all the fields, methods, properties, and events defined by this custom type. Also, if the application in question makes calls to Console.WriteLine(), the metadata records information about the external System.Console type. The .NET runtime uses this metadata to resolve the location of types (and their members) within the binary, create object instances, as well as to facilitate remote method invocations. We check out the details of the .NET metadata format in Chapter 11 during our examination of reflection services.

Finally, unlike traditional unmanaged Windows files or classic COM servers, an assembly must contain an associated *manifest* (also referred to as "assembly metadata"). The manifest documents each module within the assembly, establishes the version of the assembly, and also documents any *external* assemblies referenced by the current assembly (unlike a classic COM type library that does not document required external dependencies). Given all these elements, a .NET assembly is a completely self-describing entity.

Single File and Multifile Assemblies

Under the hood, a given assembly can be composed of multiple *modules*. A module is really nothing more than a generic name for a valid .NET file. In this light, an assembly can be viewed as a unit of versioning and deployment (often termed a "logical DLL"). In most situations, an assembly is in fact composed of a single module. In this case, there is a one-to-one correspondence between the (logical) assembly and the underlying (physical) binary, as shown in Figure 9-2.

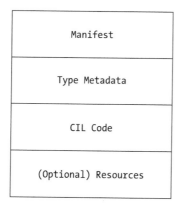

Figure 9-2. A single file assembly

When you create an assembly that is composed of multiple files, you gain a more efficient way to download content. For example, assume you have a remote client that is referencing a multifile assembly composed of three modules, one of which is automatically installed with the client. If the client references another of the remote modules, the .NET runtime will download the file on demand. If each module is 1 MB in size, I'm sure you can see the benefits.

Understand that multifile assemblies are not literally linked together into a new (larger) file. Rather, multifile assemblies are logically related by information contained in the corresponding manifest. On a related note, multifile assemblies contain a single manifest that may be placed in a stand-alone file, but is more typically bundled directly into the primary module. The big picture is seen in Figure 9-3.

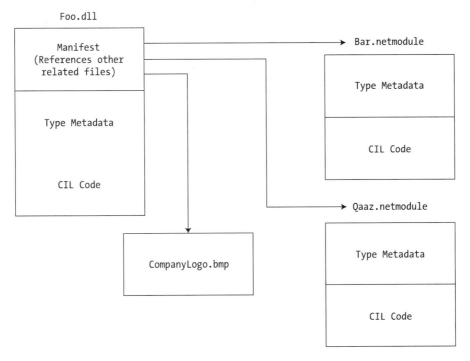

Figure 9-3. *A multifile assembly*

Two Views of an Assembly: Physical and Logical

As you begin to work with .NET binaries, it can be helpful to regard an assembly (both single file and multifile) as having two conceptual views. When you build an assembly, you are interested in the *physical* view. In this case, the assembly can be realized as some number of files that contain your custom types and resources (Figure 9-4).

Figure 9-4. *The physical view of a .NET assembly*

As an assembly consumer, you are typically interested in a logical view of the assembly (Figure 9-5). In this case, you can understand an assembly as a versioned collection of public types that you can use in your current application (recall that "internal" types can only be referenced by the assembly in which they are defined).

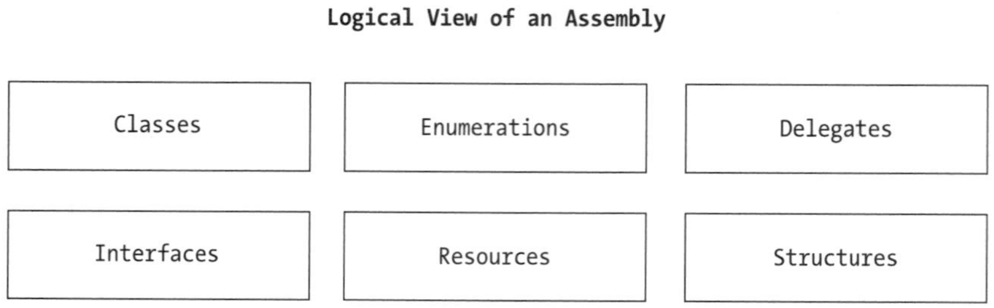

Logical View of an Assembly

Classes	Enumerations	Delegates

Interfaces	Resources	Structures

Figure 9-5. The logical view of a .NET assembly

For example, the kind folks in Redmond who developed System.Drawing.dll created a physical assembly for you to consume in your applications. Although System.Drawing.dll can be physically viewed as a binary *.dll, you logically regard this assembly as a collection of related types. Of course, ildasm.exe is the tool of choice when you are interested in discovering the logical layout of a given assembly.

The chances are good that you will play the role of both an assembly builder and assembly consumer, as is the case throughout this book. However, before digging into the code, let's briefly examine some of the core benefits of this new file format.

Assemblies Promote Code Reuse

Assemblies contain code that is executed by the .NET runtime. As you might imagine, the types and resources contained within an assembly can be shared and reused by multiple applications, much like a traditional COM binary. Unlike COM, it is possible to configure "private" assemblies as well (in fact, this is the default behavior). Private assemblies are intended for use only by a single application on a given machine. As you will see, private assemblies greatly simplify the deployment and versioning of your applications.

Like COM, binary reuse under the .NET platform honors the ideal of language independence. C# is one of numerous languages capable of building managed code, with even more languages to come. When a .NET-aware language adheres to the rules of the Common Language Specification (CLS), your choice of language becomes little more than a personal preference.

Therefore, it is not only possible to reuse types between languages, but to extend types across languages as well. In classic COM, developers were unable to derive COM object A from COM object B (even if both types were developed in the same language). In short, classic COM did not support classical inheritance (the "is-a" relationship). Later in this chapter you'll see an example of cross-language inheritance.

Assemblies Establish a Type Boundary

Assemblies are used to define a boundary for the types (and resources) they contain. In .NET, the identity of a given type is defined (in part) by the assembly in which it resides. Therefore, if two assemblies each define an identically named type (class, structure, or whatnot) they are considered independent entities in the .NET universe.

Assemblies Are Versionable and Self-Describing Entities

As mentioned, in the world of COM, the developer is in charge of correctly versioning a binary. For example, to ensure binary compatibility between MyComServer.dll version 1.0 and MyComServer.dll version 2.4, the programmer must use basic common sense to ensure interface definitions remain unaltered or run the risk of breaking client code. While a healthy dose of versioning common sense also comes in handy under the .NET universe, the central problem with the COM versioning scheme is that these programmer-defined techniques are *not* enforced by the runtime.

Another major headache with current versioning practices is that COM does not provide a way for a binary server to explicitly list the set of other binaries that must be present for it to function correctly. If an end user mistakenly moves, renames, or deletes a dependency, the solution fails.

Under .NET, an assembly's manifest is the entity in charge of explicitly listing all internal and external contingencies. Each assembly has a version identifier that applies to all types and all resources contained within each module of the assembly. Using a version identifier, the runtime is able to ensure that the correct assembly is loaded on behalf of the calling client, using a well-defined versioning policy (detailed later). An assembly's version identifier is composed of two basic pieces: A friendly text string (termed the *informational* version) and a numerical identifier (termed the *compatibility* version).

For example, assume you have created a new assembly with an informational string of "MyInterestingTypes." This same assembly would also define a compatibility number, such as 1.0.70.3. The compatibility version number always takes the same general format (four numbers separated by periods). The first and second numbers identify the major and minor version of the assembly (1.0 in this case). The third value (70) marks the build number, followed by the current revision number (3).

NOTE You are not required to provide a four-part version number. This is simply a convention suggested by Microsoft. If you wish, you may choose to version a binary using a major and minor numerical value (such as 1.0).

Assemblies Define a Security Context

An assembly may also contain security details. Under the .NET platform, security measures are scoped at the assembly level. For example, if AssemblyA wishes to use a class contained within AssemblyB, AssemblyB is the entity that chooses to provide access (or not). The security constraints defined by an assembly are explicitly listed within its manifest. While a treatment of .NET security measures is outside the mission of this text, simply be aware that access to an assembly's contents is verified using assembly metadata.

NOTE　If you are interested in investigating .NET security issues, check out *.NET Security* (Bock et al., Apress 2002).

Assemblies Enable Side-by-Side Execution

Perhaps the biggest advantage of the .NET assembly is the ability to install and load multiple versions of the same assembly on a single machine. In this way, clients are isolated from other incompatible versions of the same assembly.

Furthermore, it is possible to control which version of a (shared) assembly should be loaded using application configuration files. These files are little more than a simple text file describing (via XML syntax) the version, and specific location, of the assembly to be loaded on behalf of the calling application. You learn how to author application configuration files later in this chapter.

Building a Single File Test Assembly

Now that you have a better understanding of the benefits provided by .NET assemblies, let's build a minimal and complete code library using C#. Physically, this will be a single file assembly named CarLibrary. Logically, this binary will contain a handful of public types for consumption by other .NET binaries. To build a code library using the Visual Studio.NET IDE, you would select a new Class Library project workspace (Figure 9-6).

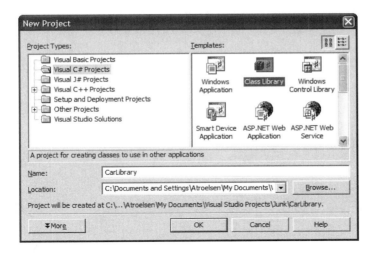

Figure 9-6. Creating a C# code library (e.g., a managed *.dll)

The design of our automobile library begins with an abstract base class named Car that defines a number of protected data members exposed through custom properties. This class has a single abstract method named TurboBoost() and makes use of a single enumeration (EngineState). Here is the initial definition of the CarLibrary namespace:

```
// The single file assembly.
using System;
namespace CarLibrary
{
    // Holds the state of the engine.
    public enum EngineState
    {
        engineAlive,
        engineDead
    }
    // The abstract base class in the hierarchy.
    public abstract class Car
    {
        // Protected state data.
        protected string petName;
        protected short currSpeed;
        protected short maxSpeed;
        protected EngineState egnState;
```

```
            public Car(){egnState = EngineState.engineAlive;}
            public Car(string name, short max, short curr)
            {
                egnState = EngineState.engineAlive;
                petName = name; maxSpeed = max; currSpeed = curr;
            }
            public string PetName
            {
                get {   return petName; }
                set {   petName = value; }
            }
            public short CurrSpeed
            {
                get {   return currSpeed; }
                set {   currSpeed = value; }
            }
            public short MaxSpeed
            {   get {   return maxSpeed; }   }
            public EngineState EngineState
            {   get {   return egnState; }   }
            public abstract void TurboBoost();
        }
    }
```

Now assume that you have two direct descendents of the Car type named MiniVan and SportsCar. Each implements the abstract TurboBoost() method in an appropriate manner:

```
using System;
using System.Windows.Forms;      // Needed for MessageBox definition.
namespace CarLibrary
{
    // The SportsCar
    public class SportsCar : Car
    {
        // Ctors.
        public SportsCar(){ }
        public SportsCar(string name, short max, short curr)
            : base (name, max, curr){ }
        // TurboBoost impl.
        public override void TurboBoost()
        {
            MessageBox.Show("Ramming speed!", "Faster is better...");
        }
    }
```

```
// The MiniVan
public class MiniVan : Car
{
    // Ctors.
    public MiniVan(){ }
    public MiniVan(string name, short max, short curr)
        : base (name, max, curr){ }
    // TurboBoost impl.
    public override void TurboBoost()
    {
        // Minivans have poor turbo capabilities!
        egnState = EngineState.engineDead;
        MessageBox.Show("Time to call AAA", "Your car is dead");
    }
}
}
```

Notice how each subclass implements TurboBoost() using the MessageBox class, which is defined in the System.Windows.Forms.dll assembly. For your assembly to make use of the types defined within this assembly, the CarLibrary project must include a reference to this binary using the "Project | Add Reference" menu selection (Figure 9-7).

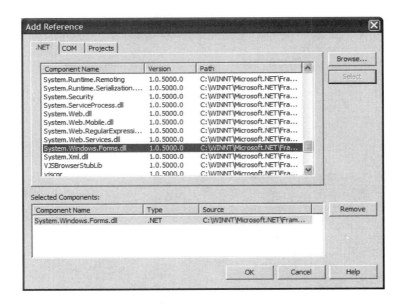

Figure 9-7. Referencing external .NET assemblies begins here.

In Chapter 13, the System.Windows.Forms namespace is described in detail. As you can tell by its name, this namespace contains numerous types to help you build desktop applications. For now, the MessageBox class is all you need to concern yourself with. If you are following along, go ahead and compile your new code library.

NOTE   The list of assemblies displayed in the Add Reference dialog box of VS .NET does *not* represent each and every assembly on your development machine, does *not* list your custom assemblies, and does *not* map to the Global Assembly Cache (GAC)! The items in the Add Reference list box are simply a suggested set that VS .NET has been configured to show automatically. When you are building applications that require the use of an assembly not listed within the Add Reference dialog, you need to click the Browse button to manually navigate to the *.dll in question.

A C# Client Application

Because each of our types has been declared "public," other binaries are able to make use of them. In a moment, you learn how to make use of these types from other .NET-aware languages such as VB .NET. Until then, let's create a C# client. Begin by creating a new C# Console Application project (CSharpCarClient). Next, set a reference to your CarLibrary.dll, using the Browse button of the Add Reference dialog to navigate to the location of your custom assembly.

Once you add a reference to your CarLibrary assembly, the Visual Studio .NET IDE responds by making a full copy of the referenced assembly and placing it into your Debug folder (assuming, of course, you have configured a debug build) (Figure 9-8). Obviously this is a huge change from classic COM, where the resolution of the binary is achieved using the system registry.

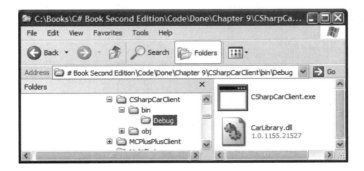

Figure 9-8. Local copies of (non-shared) assemblies are placed in your Debug folder.

Now that your client application has been configured to reference the CarLibrary assembly, you are free to create a class that makes use of these types. Here is a test drive (pun intended):

```
using System;
// Make use of the CarLib types!
using CarLibrary;

namespace CSharpCarClient
{
    public class CarClient
    {
        public static int Main(string[] args)
        {
            // Make a sports car.
            SportsCar viper = new SportsCar("Viper", 240, 40);
            viper.TurboBoost();
            // Make a minivan.
            MiniVan mv = new MiniVan();
            mv.TurboBoost();
            return 0;
        }
    }
}
```

This code looks just like the other applications developed thus far. The only point of interest is that the C# client application is now making use of types defined within a unique assembly (and therefore must specify the namespace name via the "using" keyword and set a reference to the CarLibrary.dll assembly). Go ahead and run your program. As you would expect, the execution of this program results in the display of two message boxes.

A Visual Basic .NET Client Application

When you install Visual Studio .NET, you receive four languages that are capable of building managed code: JScript.NET, C++ with managed extensions (MC++), C#, and Visual Basic .NET. A nice feature of Visual Studio .NET is that all languages share the same IDE. Therefore, VB .NET, ATL, C#, and MFC programmers all make use of a common development environment. Given this fact, the process of building a Visual Basic .NET application making use of the CarLibrary is simple. Assume a new VB .NET Windows Application project workspace named VBCarClient has been created (Figure 9-9).

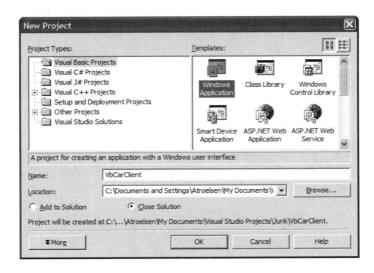

Figure 9-9. Selecting a VB .NET Windows Forms Application

Similar to Visual Basic 6.0, this project workspace provides a design time template used to build the GUI of the main window. However, VB .NET is a completely different animal. The template you are looking at is actually a subclass of the Form type, which is quite different from a traditional VB 6.0 Form.

Now, set a reference to the C# CarLibrary, again using the Add Reference dialog. Like C#, VB .NET requires you to list each namespace used within your project. However, VB .NET makes use of the "Imports" keyword rather than the C# "using" keyword. Thus, open the code window for your Form (simply right-click the design-time template and select "View Code") and add the following:

```
' Like C#, VB .NET needs to 'see' the namespaces used by a given file.
Imports CarLibrary
```

Switching back to the design-time template, construct a minimal and complete user interface to exercise your automobile types (Figure 9-10). Two buttons should fit the bill (simply select the Button widget from the Toolbox and draw it on the Form object).

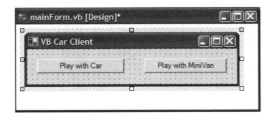

Figure 9-10. A painfully simple GUI

The next step is to add event handlers to capture the Click event of each Button object. To do so, simply double-click each button on the Form. The IDE responds by writing stub code that will be called when a particular button is clicked. Here is some sample code:

```
' A taste of VB .NET.
Private Sub btnMiniVan_Click(ByVal sender As Object,
  ByVal e As System.EventArgs) Handles btnMiniVan.Click
    Dim sc As New MiniVan()
    sc.TurboBoost()
End Sub
Private Sub btnCar_Click(ByVal sender As Object,
  ByVal e As System.EventArgs) Handles btnCar.Click
    Dim sc As New SportsCar()
    sc.TurboBoost()
End Sub
```

Although the goal of this book is not to turn you into a powerhouse VB .NET developer, here is one point of interest. Notice how each Car subclass is created using the "New" keyword. Unlike VB 6.0 however, classes now have true constructors! Therefore, the empty parentheses suffixed on the class name do indeed invoke a given constructor on the class. As you would expect, when you run the program, each automobile responds appropriately.

Cross-Language Inheritance

A very sexy aspect of .NET development is the notion of cross-language inheritance. To illustrate, let's create a new VB .NET class that derives from CarLibrary.SportsCar. Impossible you say? Well, if you were using Visual Basic 6.0 this would be the case. However with the advent of VB .NET, programmers are able to use the same object-oriented features found in C#, Java, and C++, including classical inheritance (i.e., the "is-a" relationship).

To illustrate, add a new class to your current VB .NET client application named PerformanceCar (using the "Project | Add Class" menu selection). In the code that follows, notice you are deriving from the C# Car type using the VB .NET "Inherits" keyword. As you recall, the Car class defined an abstract TurboBoost() method, which we implement using the VB .NET "Overrides" keyword:

```
' VB .NET supports each pillar of OOP!
Imports CarLibrary
' This VB type is deriving from the C# SportsCar.
Public Class PerformanceCar
  Inherits CarLibrary.SportsCar
    ' Implementation of abstract Car method.
    Public Overrides Sub TurboBoost()
        MessageBox.Show("Blistering speed", "VB PerformanceCar says")
    End Sub
End Class
```

If we update the existing Form to include an additional Button to exercise the performance car, we could write the following test code:

```
PrivateSub btnPreCar_Click(ByVal sender As Object,
  ByVal e As System.EventArgs) Handles btnPerfCar.Click
    Dim pc As New PerformanceCar()
    pc.PetName = "Hank"  ' Inherited property.
    ' Display base class.
    MessageBox.Show(pc.GetType().BaseType.ToString(),
       "Base class of Perf car")
    ' Custom Implementation of Car.TurboBoost()
    pc.TurboBoost()
End Sub
```

Notice that we are able to identify our base class programmatically (Figure 9-11).

Figure 9-11. Cross-language inheritance in action

 NOTE If you wish to check out the details of the VB .NET programming language, may I humbly recommend my offering in the VB .NET arena: *VB .NET and the .NET Platform: An Advanced Guide* (Apress 2002).

Building an MC++ Subclass

So far, you have a VB .NET class deriving from a C# class. To really drive the point of cross-language inheritance home, let's build a MC++ subclass that derives from the VB .NET class. Recall that C++ with Managed Extensions (MC++) is Microsoft's augmentation of the C++ language. For the C++ programming language to interact with the CLR, several new keywords were introduced. Understand that C++ programmers are *not* required to make use of these new .NET specific keywords when they build C++ projects using Visual Studio .NET (ATL, MFC, and Win32 projects are still possible). However, when a C++ programmer does want to inject .NET functionality into their programs, VS .NET does include several new project workspaces. To begin, close down your current project workspace and create a brand-new Managed C++ Console Application (see Figure 9-12).

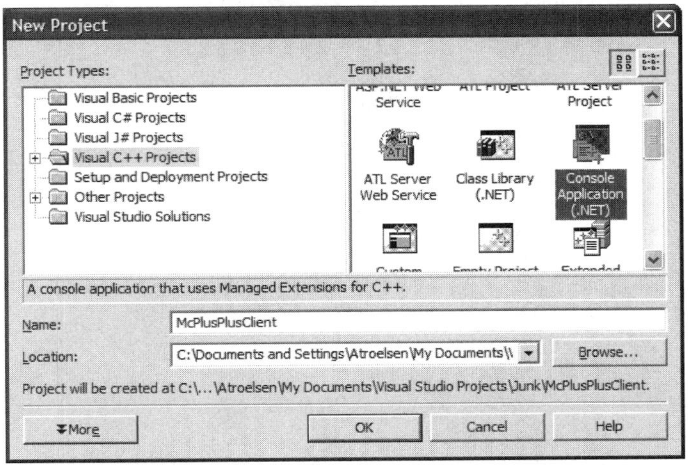

Figure 9-12. An MC++ project workspace

Of all the languages that are able to produce managed code, MC++ is by far the most cryptic. Therefore, if you do not have a background in C(++), don't fret over each and every line of syntax. The point to focus on is the fact that the MC++ JamesBondCar class is deriving from the VB .NET PerformanceCar (which in turn derives from the C# SportsCar). Here is the complete code; be sure to set a reference to the VBCarClient.exe and CarLibrary.dll assemblies using the Add Reference dialog (if you are not using VS .NET 2003, be sure to read the code comment in bold!):

```
#pragma once
#include "stdafx.h"

// '#using' is functionally equivalent to the 'Add References' dialog.
#using <mscorlib.dll>
#using <System.Windows.Forms.dll>

// Uncomment these lines (and adjust your path)
// if you are not using VS .NET 2003, as
// VS .NET 2002 did not have an Add Ref dialog!
//#using "C:\VbCarClient.exe"
//#using "C:\CarLibrary.dll"

// 'using namespace' is identical to the C# "using" keyword.
using namespace CSharpCarClient;
using namespace System;
```

```
// __gc (garbage collected) marks this class as managed by the CLR.
__gc class JamesBondCar : public PerformanceCar
{
public:
    JamesBondCar(void){}
    ~JamesBondCar(void){}
    virtual void TurboBoost()
    {
        Console::WriteLine("Diving, flying and drilling...");
    }
};
// This is the entry point for this application.
#ifdef _UNICODE
int wmain(void)
#else
int main(void)
#endif
{
    // Make a JamesBondCar.
    JamesBondCar* jbc = new JamesBondCar();
    jbc->PetName = S"Jello";
    jbc->TurboBoost();
    Console::Write("Car is called: ");
    Console::WriteLine(jbc->PetName);
    Console::WriteLine(jbc->GetType()->BaseType->ToString());
    return 0;
}
```

Before we move on, a few points of interest. First, when an MC++ developer wants to add a reference to an external assembly, he or she may use the Add Reference dialog (available under VS .NET 2003) or make use of the #using preprocessor directive that will import the assembly's metadata for use in the current application. Also notice that MC++ supports a "using" keyword, which is the functional equivalent to the VB .NET "Imports" and C# "using" keywords.

NOTE If you wish to check out the syntax and semantics of the MC++ programming language, I recommend getting a copy of *Essential Guide to Managed Extensions for C++* (Challa and Laksberg, Apress 2002).

SOURCE CODE The CarLibrary, CSharpCarClient, VbCarClient, and McPlusPlusClient projects are located under the Chapter 9 subdirectory.

Exploring the CarLibrary's Manifest

At this point, you have successfully created a single file code library and various client applications. Your next order of business is to gain a deeper understanding of how .NET assemblies are constructed under the hood. To begin, recall that every assembly contains an associated manifest. The manifest contains bits of metadata that specify the name and version of the assembly, as well as a listing of all internal and external modules that compose the assembly as a whole.

Additionally, a manifest may contain cultural information (used for internationalization), a corresponding "strong name" (required by shared assemblies), and optional resource information (you examine the .NET resource format in Chapter 17). Table 9-1 describes some of the key bits of functionality lurking within an assembly manifest.

Table 9-1. Key Elements of an Assembly Manifest

Manifest-Centric Information	Meaning in Life
Assembly name	A text string specifying the assembly's name.
Version number	A major and minor version number, and a revision and build number.
Strong name information	In part, the "strong name" of an assembly consists of a public key maintained by the publisher of the assembly.
List of all modules in the assembly	A hash of each module contained in the assembly (in the case of a single file assembly, there will only be a single module listing).
Information on referenced assemblies	A list of other assemblies that are statically referenced by the assembly.

.NET aware compilers (such as csc.exe) automatically create a manifest at compile time. To illustrate, go ahead and load the CarLibrary assembly into ildasm.exe. As you can see from Figure 9-13, this tool has read the metadata to display relevant information for each type (the MusicMedia enumeration will be added later in this chapter).

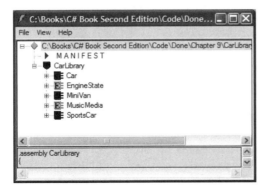

Figure 9-13. Your car library as seen via ildasm.exe

Now, open the manifest by double-clicking the MANIFEST icon. The first code block contained in a manifest is used to specify all external assemblies that are required by the current assembly to function correctly. As you recall, CarLibrary.dll made use of mscorlib.dll and System.Windows.Forms.dll, each of which is marked in the manifest using the [.assembly extern] tag:

```
.assembly extern mscorlib
{
  .publickeytoken = (B7 7A 5C 56 19 34 E0 89 )
  .ver 1:0:3300:0
}
.assembly extern System.Windows.Forms
{
  .publickeytoken = (B7 7A 5C 56 19 34 E0 89 )
  .ver 1:0:3300:0
}
```

Here, each [.assembly extern] block is colored by the [.publickeytoken] and [.ver] directives. The [.publickeytoken] instruction is only present if the assembly has been configured as a shared assembly (more details later). [.ver] is (of course) the numerical version identifier.

After enumerating each of the external references, the manifest then enumerates each module contained in the assembly. Given that the CarLibrary is a single file assembly, you will find exactly one [.module] tag. This manifest also lists a number of attributes (marked with the [.custom] tag) such as company name, trademark, and so forth, all of which are currently empty (more information on these attributes in Chapter 11):

```
.assembly CarLibrary
{
  // Ignore these attribute declarations for the time being...
  .custom instance void [mscorlib]
System.Reflection.AssemblyKeyNameAttribute::.ctor(string) = ( 01 00 00 00 00 )
  .custom instance void [mscorlib]
```

```
System.Reflection.AssemblyKeyFileAttribute::.ctor(string) = ( 01 00 00 00 00 )
  .custom instance void [mscorlib]
System.Reflection.AssemblyDelaySignAttribute::.ctor(bool) = ( 01 00 00 00 00 )
  .custom instance void [mscorlib]
System.Reflection.AssemblyTrademarkAttribute::.ctor(string) = ( 01 00 00 00 00 )
  .custom instance void [mscorlib]
System.Reflection.AssemblyCopyrightAttribute::.ctor(string) = ( 01 00 00 00 00 )
  .custom instance void [mscorlib]
System.Reflection.AssemblyProductAttribute::.ctor(string) = ( 01 00 00 00 00 )
  .custom instance void [mscorlib]
System.Reflection.AssemblyCompanyAttribute::.ctor(string) = ( 01 00 00 00 00 )
  .custom instance void [mscorlib]
System.Reflection.AssemblyConfigurationAttribute::.ctor(string)=( 01 00 00 00 00 )
  .custom instance void [mscorlib]
System.Reflection.AssemblyDescriptionAttribute::.ctor(string) = ( 01 00 00 00 00 )
  .custom instance void [mscorlib]
System.Reflection.AssemblyTitleAttribute::.ctor(string) = ( 01 00 00 00 00 )
    .hash algorithm 0x00008004
    .ver 1:0:454:30104
}
.module CarLibrary.dll
```

Here, you can see that the [.assembly] tag is used to mark the friendly name of your custom assembly (CarLibrary). Like external declarations, the [.ver] tag defines the compatibility version number for this assembly. To summarize the core CIL tokens found within the assembly manifest, ponder Table 9-2.

Table 9-2. Manifest CIL Tokens

Manifest Tag	Meaning in Life
.assembly	Marks the assembly declaration, indicating that the file is an assembly.
.file	Marks additional files in a multifile assembly.
.class extern	Classes exported by the assembly but declared in another module (only used with a multifile assembly).
.manifestres	Indicates the manifest resources (if any).
.module	Module declaration, indicating that the file is a module (i.e., a .NET binary with no assembly level manifest) and not the primary assembly.
.assembly extern	The assembly reference indicates another assembly containing items referenced by this module.
.publickey	Contains the actual bytes of the public key.
.publickeytoken	Contains a token of the actual public key.

Exploring the CarLibrary's Types

Recall that an assembly does not contain platform-specific instructions, but rather platform-agnostic CIL. When the .NET runtime loads an assembly into memory, the underlying CIL is compiled (using the JIT compiler) into instructions that can be understood by the target platform. .

If you double-click the TurboBoost() method of the SportsCar class, ildasm.exe will open a new window showing the raw CIL instructions (slightly reformatted for easy reading):

```
.method public hidebysig virtual instance void
       TurboBoost() cil managed
{
  // Code size       17 (0x11)
  .maxstack  2
  IL_0000:  ldstr      "Ramming speed!"
  IL_0005:  ldstr      "Faster is better..."
  IL_000a:  call       valuetype [System.Windows.Forms]
    System.Windows.Forms.DialogResult [System.Windows.Forms]
    System.Windows.Forms.MessageBox::Show(string, string)
  IL_000f:  pop
  IL_0010:  ret
} // end of method SportsCar::TurboBoost
```

Notice that the [.method] tag is used to identify (of course) a method defined by the SportsCar type. Public data defined by a type is marked with the [.field] tag. Recall that the Car class defined a set of protected data, such as currSpeed (note that the "family" tag signifies protected data).

```
.field family int16 currSpeed
```

Properties are also marked with the [.property] tag. Here is the CIL describing the public CurrSpeed property (note the read/write nature of a property is marked by .get and .set tags):

```
.property instance int16 CurrSpeed()
{
  .get instance int16 CarLibrary.Car::get_CurrSpeed()
  .set instance void CarLibrary.Car::set_CurrSpeed(int16)
} // end of property Car::CurrSpeed
```

If you now select the Ctrl+M keystroke, ildasm.exe displays the metadata for each type (Figure 9-14).

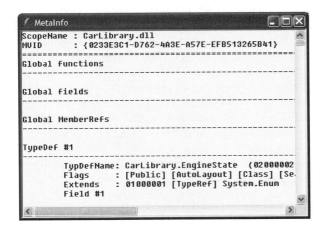

Figure 9-14. Type metadata for the types within carlibrary.dll

Using this metadata (which is examined in greater detail in Chapter 11), the .NET runtime is able to locate and construct object instances and to invoke methods. Various tools (such as Visual Studio .NET and the C# compiler itself) make use of metadata at design time to validate the number (and types) of parameters during compilation. To summarize the story of assemblies thus far, make sure the following points are clear in your mind:

- An assembly is a versioned, self-describing set of modules. Each module contains some number of types and optional resources. Type implementation is realized via CIL.

- Every assembly contains metadata that describes all types within a given module. The .NET runtime (as well as numerous .NET tools) reads the metadata to locate and create objects, validate method calls, activate IntelliSense, and so on.

- Every assembly contains a manifest that enumerates the set of all internal and external files required by the binary, version information, as well as other assembly-centric details.

Building a Multifile Assembly

Now that we have explored the internals of a single file assembly, let's turn our attention to the process of building a multifile assembly. Recall that a multifile assembly will contain a particular *.dll or *.exe file that contains the assembly manifest (often termed the *primary module*). Additionally, multifile assemblies contain any number of *.netmodule files that are loaded on demand when referenced by an external client. Do be aware that the use of *.netmodule is simply a naming convention. If you wish, your auxiliary modules could simply take a *.dll file extension.

At the time of this writing, Visual Studio .NET does not support a project workspace type that allows you to build stand-alone *.netmodule files. Therefore, you need to drop down to the level of the raw csc.exe compiler and specify the correct flags manually (be sure to read Chapter 2 if you happened to skip the discussion of csc.exe).

To keep things simple, let's build some rather basic types contained within a multifile assembly named AirVehicles. The primary airvehicles.dll module will contain CIL and metadata for a single class type named Helicopter. The related manifest (also contained in airvehicles.dll) catalogues an additional *.netmodule file named ufos.netmodule, which contains another class type named (of course) UFO. Although both class types are physically contained in separate binaries, you will group them into a unified namespace named AirVehicles. Finally, both classes are created using C# (although you could certainly mix and match languages if you desire).

To begin, open notepad.exe and create a trivial class definition named UFO within a file named ufo.cs:

```
using System;
namespace AirVehicles
{
    public class UFO
    {
        public void AbductHuman()
        {
            Console.WriteLine("Resistance is futile");
        }
    }
}
```

To compile this class into a .NET module, open a command prompt and issue the following command to the C# compiler (recall the /t: flag is a shorthand notation for /target, while module specifies you wish to build a *.netmodule binary, as opposed to the primary module):

```
csc.exe /t:module ufo.cs
```

If you now look in the folder containing the ufo.cs file, you should see a new file named ufo.netmodule (go ahead and take a peek). Next, create a new file (using notepad.exe) named helicopter.cs:

```
using System;
namespace AirVehicles
{
    public class Helicopter
    {
        public void TakeOff()
        {
            Console.WriteLine("Helicopter taking off!");
        }
    }
}
```

Given that AirVehicles.dll is the primary module of this multifile assembly, you will need to specify the /t: library flag. However, as you also want to encode the ufo.netmodule binary into the assembly manifest, you must also specify the /addmodule flag. The following command does the trick:

```
csc /t:library /addmodule:ufo.netmodule /out:airvehicles.dll helicopter.cs
```

Now, check out the directory containing these files. You should see something like what appears in Figure 9-15.

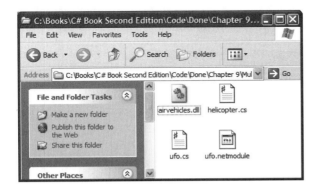

Figure 9-15. Your multifile assembly

Exploring the ufo.netmodule

Using ildasm.exe, open your ufo.netmodule file (see Figure 9-16).

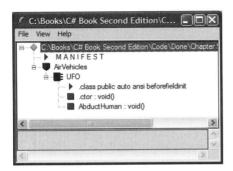

Figure 9-16. The ufo.netmodule

As you can see, *.netmodules contain a *module-level manifest;* however, its sole purpose in life is to list each external assembly referenced within the code base. Given that the UFO class did little more than make a call to System.Console.WriteLine(), you find the following:

```
.assembly extern mscorlib
{...}
.module ufo.netmodule
```

Exploring the airvehicles.dll

Now, using ildasm.exe, open the assembly manifest contained within airvehicles.dll. As you can see, you now have a [.file] reference to the ufo.netmodule (in addition to the various [.assembly extern] tags). The [.class extern] tag is used to mark each external type referenced by the current module.

```
.assembly extern mscorlib
{...}
.assembly airvehicles
{
...
  .hash algorithm 0x00008004
  .ver 0:0:0:0
}
.file ufo.netmodule
...
.class extern public AirVehicles.UFO
{
  .file ufo.netmodule
  .class 0x02000002
}
.module airvehicles.dll
```

Again, realize that the only entity that links together the airvehicles.dll and the ufo.netmodule is the assembly manifest. These two binary files have not been merged into a single, larger *.dll.

Using the Multifile Assembly

The consumers of a multifile assembly could care less that the assembly they are referencing is composed of numerous files. To illustrate, let's create a brand new VB .NET Console application (or if you prefer, a C# application). Set a reference to the primary module of this multifile assembly (AirVehicles.dll) and System.Windows.Forms.dll using the Add References dialog. Within the VB. NET Module type, create two subroutines that activate a given air vehicle. Within Main(), call each method, placing a message box call between each (in this way you are able to view the loading of the ufo.netmodule). Here is the complete VB .NET code:

```
Imports AirVehicles
Imports System.Windows.Forms

Module Module1
    Sub Main()
        UseHelicopter()
        MessageBox.Show("Click to load ufo.netmodule")
        UseUFO()
        MessageBox.Show("Done")
    End Sub
    Sub UseHelicopter()
        Dim h As New AirVehicles.Helicopter()
        h.TakeOff()
    End Sub
    Sub UseUFO()
        ' This will load the *.netmodule on demand.
        Dim u As New UFO()
        u.AbductHuman()
    End Sub
End Module
```

Now, start a debug session and once the first message box is displayed, open the Modules window (using the "Debug | Windows" menu selection). At this point, you should see that airvehicles.dll has been loaded (see Figure 9-17).

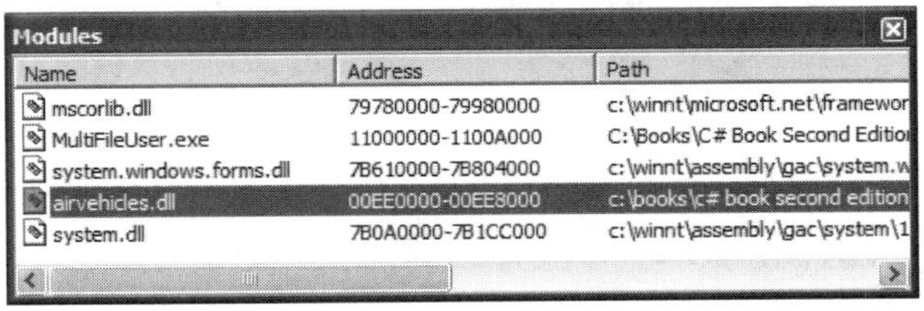

Figure 9-17. A single module of the multifile assembly

Now, dismiss the message box. You should now find that the related ufo.netmodule has been loaded on demand (see Figure 9-18).

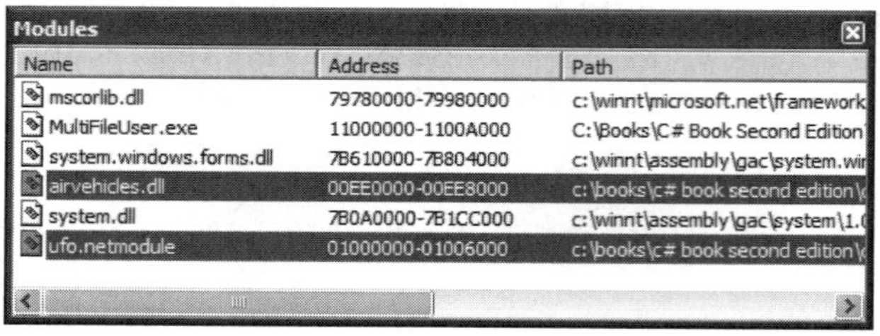

Modules			
Name	Address	Path	
mscorlib.dll	79780000-79980000	c:\winnt\microsoft.net\framework	
MultiFileUser.exe	11000000-1100A000	C:\Books\C # Book Second Edition	
system.windows.forms.dll	7B610000-7B804000	c:\winnt\assembly\gac\system.win	
airvehicles.dll	00EE0000-00EE8000	c:\books\c# book second edition\	
system.dll	7B0A0000-7B1CC000	c:\winnt\assembly\gac\system\1.(	
ufo.netmodule	01000000-01006000	c:\books\c# book second edition\	

Figure 9-18. *.netmodules are loaded on demand.

Again, remember that the point of multifile assemblies is to have a physical collection of files behave as a singly named (and versioned) unit. In and of themselves, *.netmodules do not have an individual version number, cannot be loaded directly by the .NET runtime, and cannot be used as a stand-alone entity. Individual *.netmodules can only be loaded by the primary module (e.g., the file that contains the assembly manifest).

At this point you should feel comfortable with the process of building both single file and multifile assemblies. To be completely honest, the chances are that 99.99 percent of your assemblies will be single file entities. Nevertheless, multifile assemblies can prove helpful when you wish to break a large physical binary into more modular units (and are quite useful for remote download scenarios).

NOTE   The .NET SDK supplies a command line tool named al.exe (assembly linker). This tool can also be used to build multifile assemblies, and can be quite helpful if you wish to build a multifile assembly using a compiler that does not support the equivalent of the csc.exe /addmodule flag. You will get to know "al" later in this chapter when you examine the construction of publisher policy assemblies.

Next up, you need to distinguish between private and shared assemblies. If you are coming into the .NET paradigm from a classic COM perspective, be prepared for some significant changes.

SOURCE CODE   The MultiFileAsm and MultiFileClient projects are included under the Chapter 9 subdirectory.

Understanding Private Assemblies

Formally speaking, every assembly is deployed as "private" or "shared." The good news is each variation has the same underlying structure (i.e., some number of modules and an associated manifest). Furthermore, each flavor of assembly provides the same kind of services (access to some number of public types). The real differences between a private and shared assembly boil down to naming conventions, versioning policies, and deployment issues. Let's begin by examining the traits of a private assembly, which is far and away the most common of the two options.

Private assemblies are a collection of modules that is only used by the application with which it has been deployed. For example, CarLibrary.dll is a private assembly used by the CSharpCarClient.exe and VbCarClient.exe applications. When you create and deploy a private assembly, the assumption is that the collection of types is only used by the "owning" application, and not shared with other applications on the system.

Private assemblies are required to be located within the same directory as the client application (termed the *application directory*) or a subdirectory thereof. For example, recall that when you set a reference to the CarLibrary.dll assembly (as you did in the CSharpCarClient.exe and VbCarClient.exe applications), the Visual Studio .NET IDE responded by making a full copy of the assembly that was placed in your project's application directory. This is the default behavior, as private assemblies are assumed to be the deployment option of choice.

Note the painfully stark contrast to classic COM— there is no need to register any items under HKEY_CLASSES_ROOT and no need to enter a hard-coded path to the binary using an InprocServer32 or LocalServer32 registry listing. The resolution and loading of the private CarLibrary.dll happens by virtue of the fact that the assembly is placed in the application directory. In fact, if you moved CSharpCarClient.exe and CarLibrary.dll to a new directory, the application would still run. To illustrate this point, copy these two files to your desktop and run the client (can you say "XCopy" installation?)

Uninstalling (or replicating) an application that makes exclusive use of private assemblies is a no-brainer. Delete (or copy) the application folder. Unlike classic COM, you do not need to worry about dozens of orphaned registry settings. More important, you do not need to worry that the removal of private assemblies will break any other applications on the machine.

Probing for Private Assemblies (The Basics)

Later in this chapter, you are exposed to some gory details regarding location resolution of an assembly. Until then, the following overview should help prime the pump. Formally speaking, the .NET runtime resolves the location of a private assembly using a technique termed *probing*, which is much less invasive than it sounds. Probing is the process of mapping an external assembly reference (i.e., [.assembly extern]) to the correct corresponding binary file. For example, when the runtime reads the following line from the CSharpCarClient manifest:

```
.assembly extern CarLibrary
{...}
```

a search is made in the application directory for a file named CarLibrary.dll. If a *.dll binary cannot be located, an attempt is made to locate an *.exe version (CarLibrary.exe). If neither of these files can be located in the application directory, the runtime throws an exception. However, as you will see in just a bit, XML configuration files (*.config) can be used to instruct the runtime to probe in other locations beyond the application directory.

The Identity of a Private Assembly

The identity of a private assembly consists of a friendly string name and numerical version, both of which are recorded in the assembly manifest. The friendly name is created based on the name of the binary module that contains the assembly's manifest. For example, if you examine the manifest of the CarLibrary.dll assembly, you find the following (your version will no doubt differ):

```
.assembly CarLibrary
{
...
    .ver 1:0:454:30104
}
```

However, given the nature of a private assembly, it should make sense that the .NET runtime does not bother to apply any version policies when loading the assembly. The assumption is that private assemblies do not need to have any elaborate version checking, given that the client application is the only entity that "knows" of its existence. As an interesting corollary you should understand that it is (very) possible for a single machine to have multiple copies of the same private assembly in various application directories.

Private Assemblies and XML Configuration Files

When the .NET runtime is instructed to bind to an assembly, the first step is to determine the presence of an application configuration file. These optional files contain XML elements that control the binding behavior of the launching application. By law, configuration files must have the same name as the launching application and take a *.config file extension.

As mentioned, configuration files can be used to specify any optional subdirectories to be searched when probing for private assemblies. As you have seen earlier in this chapter, a .NET application can be deployed simply by placing all assemblies into the same directory as the application directory. Often, however, you may wish to deploy an application such that the application directory contains a number of related subdirectories, in order to give some meaningful structure to the application as a whole.

You see this all the time in commercial software. For example, assume our main directory is called MyRadApplication, which contains a number of subdirectories (\Images, \Bin, \SavedGames, \OtherCoolStuff). Using application configuration files, you can instruct the runtime where it should probe while attempting to locate the set of private assemblies used by the launching application.

To illustrate, let's create a simple XML configuration file for the previous CSharpCarClient application. Our goal is to move the referenced assembly (CarLibrary) from the Debug folder into a new subdirectory named \MyLibraries. Go ahead and move this file now (Figure 9-19).

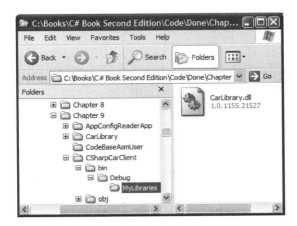

Figure 9-19. Relocating CarLibrary.dll into a specific subdirectory

Now, create a new configuration file named CSharpCarClient.exe.config (Notepad will do just fine) and save it into the *same* folder containing the CSharpCarClient.exe application, which will most likely be the Debug folder of the client project (be aware that XML is case sensitive!):

```
<configuration>
    <runtime>
        <assemblyBinding xmlns="urn:schemas-microsoft-com:asm.v1">
            <probing privatePath="MyLibraries"/>
        </assemblyBinding>
    </runtime>
</configuration>
```

Notice how *.config files always open with the root <configuration> element. The nested <runtime> element may specify an <assemblyBinding> element, which nests a further element named <probing>. The privatePath attribute is the key, as this is used to specify the list of subdirectories relative to the root.

Multiple subdirectories can be specified using a semicolon-delimited list. We have no need to do so at this time, but here is an example:

```
<probing privatePath="MyLibraries;MyOtherLibaries;MyLibraries\Tests"/>
```

Once you are done, save the file and launch the client by double-clicking the executable using the Windows Explorer. You should find that the CSharpCarClient application runs without a hitch. As a final test, change the name of your configuration file and attempt to run the program once again. The client application should now fail. Remember that configuration files must have the same name as the related client application. Because you have renamed this file, the .NET runtime assumes you do not have a configuration file, and thus attempts to probe for the referenced assembly directly in the application directory (which it cannot locate).

Configuration Files and VS .NET

While you are always able to create a property named XML configuration file by hand (a la Notepad), it is worth pointing out that VS .NET does provide a handy alternative. To illustrate, delete the current *.config file and insert a new "Application Configuration File" item using the Project | Add New Item menu selection.

Before you click the OK button, be sure the name of this new file is app.config (and nothing else). If you look in your Solution Explorer window, you will now find app.config has been inserted into your current project (Figure 9-20).

Figure 9-20. Working with the app.config file

At this point, add the necessary XML to your app.config file. Now, here is the cool thing. When you compile your project, VS .NET will automatically create a new properly named file (clientName.exe.config) and place it into your \Debug folder. The benefit is that if you rename your project, the *.config file is automatically updated.

You may also notice when you rebuild your project that VS .NET will re-copy the externally referenced CarLibrary.dll to the client's application directory (which sort of defeats the purpose of a client *.config file). To prevent VS .NET from copying externally referenced assemblies on each compile, select the *.dll in question from the Solution Explorer and set the Copy Local property to False (Figure 9-21).

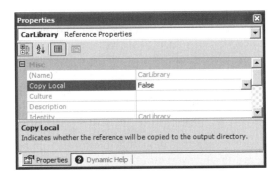

Figure 9-21. Preventing automatic re-copying of private assemblies

Probing for Private Assemblies (The Details)

To wrap up our discussion of private assemblies, let's formalize the specific steps involved in binding to a private assembly at runtime. First, a request to load an assembly may be either *explicit* or *implicit*. An implicit load request occurs whenever the manifest makes a direct reference to some external assembly. As you recall, external references are marked with the [.assembly extern] token:

```
// An implicit load request...
.assembly extern CarLibrary
{
    ...
}
```

An explicit load request occurs programmatically using System.Reflection.Assembly.Load(). The Assembly class is examined in Chapter 11, but be aware that the Load() method allows you to specify the name, version, public key token, and culture information syntactically. In its simplest form, the assembly name will do:

```
// An explicit load request...
Assembly asm = Assembly.Load("CarLibrary");
```

Collectively, the name, version, public key token, and cultural information is termed an assembly reference (or simply AsmRef). The entity in charge of locating the correct assembly based on an AsmRef is termed the assembly resolver, which is a facility of the CLR. If the resolver determines the AsmRef refers to a private assembly (i.e., no public key token is specified), the following steps are followed:

1. First, the assembly resolver attempts to locate the assembly in the client's application directory (looking for a *.dll file on the first pass, followed by an *.exe file).

2. If the AsmRef cannot be resolved in looking in the application directory, the assembly resolver will attempt to locate a configuration file in the application directory. If a configuration file exists, the runtime will attempt to locate the private assembly using the <probing> element.

3. If the assembly cannot be found within the application directory (or a specified subdirectory) the search stops here and a FileNotFound exception is raised.

Again, as you can see, the location of a private assembly is fairly simple to resolve. Next up, let's turn our attention to the construction of shared assemblies.

Understanding Shared Assemblies

Like a private assembly, a "shared" assembly is a collection of types and (optional) resources contained within some number of modules. The most obvious difference between shared and private assemblies is the fact that shared assemblies can be used by several clients on a single machine. By way of a simple example, consider all the applications created in this text which required you to set a reference to System.Windows.Forms.dll. If you were to look in the application directory of each of these clients, you would *not* find a private copy of this .NET binary. The reason is that System.Windows.Forms.dll has been deployed as a shared assembly. Clearly, if you need to create a machine-wide class library, this is the way to go.

As suggested in the previous paragraph, a shared assembly is not deployed within the same directory as the application making use of it. Rather, shared assemblies are installed into a machine-wide Global Assembly Cache, which lends itself to yet another colorful acronym in the programming universe: the GAC. The GAC itself is located under the <drive>: \ %windir%\ Assembly subdirectory (Figure 9-22).

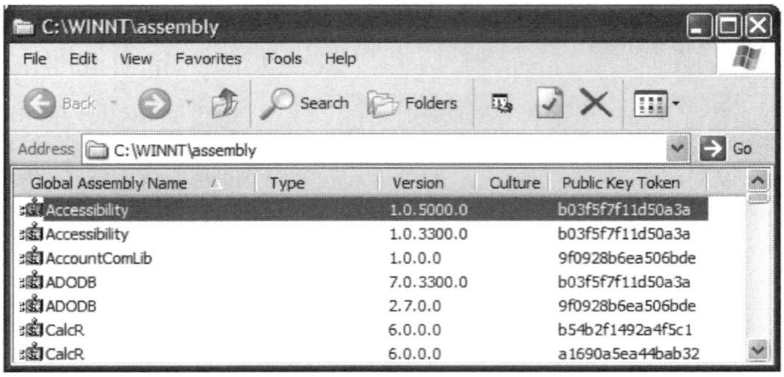

Figure 9-22. The Global Assembly Cache

Before you deploy an assembly to the GAC, you must assign it a "strong name." Simply put, a strong name is used to uniquely identify the publisher of a given .NET binary. This publisher could be an individual programmer, a department within a given company, or the entire company at large.

> **NOTE** Technically speaking, private assemblies may also be assigned a strong name. However, given that all shared assemblies *must* have a strong name, you are correct to assume that a vast majority of strongly named assemblies are intended to be shared.

Understanding Strong Names

A strong name is composed of the following bits of information:

- A friendly string name of the assembly (i.e., the name of the binary without its file extension)

- A version number of the assembly

- A public key (or a token derived from the full public key)

- A culture identity value (for localization)

In some ways, a strong name is the modern day .NET equivalent of the COM AppID. Unlike AppIDs (which were simply 128-bit numbers), strong names are based on public/private key cryptography. When you create a shared assembly, you must make use of a public/private key pair (which you do momentarily). This aspect of a strong name helps ensure that (a) the assembly has not been tampered with since it was shipped, (b) each assembly publisher has a unique identity, and (c) new versions of a specific assembly ship from the same publisher.

In a nutshell, public/private key cryptography requires two distinct, but interrelated, keys (termed the "public" key and the "private" key). In terms of .NET, this information is generated by a command line hook (sn.exe) and saved to a file, which by default takes a *.snk file extension (Strong Name Key). This file is referenced during the compilation of an assembly to embed the public key value in the shared assembly's manifest (identified with the [.publickey] tag).

The private key is obviously not listed in the manifest, but rather is used to digitally sign the contents of the assembly (in conjunction with a generated hash code). The resulting digital signature is stored in the assembly itself as an embedded blob within the CLR header. Again, the whole idea of making use of public/private key cryptograph is to ensure that no two companies, departments, or individuals have the same identity in the .NET universe. In any case, once the process of assigning a strong name is complete, the assembly may be installed into the GAC.

When a client application using a shared assembly is compiled, a token of the shared assembly's public key is recorded in the client manifest (denoted with the [.publickeytoken] tag). This public key token is a shorted form of the full public key, which boils down to a 64-bit hashing of the entire public key value.

Building a Shared Assembly

To illustrate the process of assigning a strong name to an assembly, let's walk through a complete example. Assume you have created a new C# Class Library named SharedAssembly, which contains the following class definition:

```csharp
public class VWMiniVan
{
    private bool isBustedByTheFuzz = false;

    public VWMiniVan()
    {
        MessageBox.Show("Using version 1.0.0.0!", "Shared Car");
    }
    public void Play60sTunes()
    {
        MessageBox.Show("What a loooong, strange trip it's been...");
    }
    public bool Busted
    {
        get {  return isBustedByTheFuzz; }
        set {  isBustedByTheFuzz = value; }
    }
}
```

To generate the key file, you need to make use of the sn.exe (strong name) utility. Although this tool has numerous command line options, all you need to concern yourself with for the moment is the "-k" flag, which instructs the tool to generate a new *.snk file that contains the public/private key information (Figure 9-23).

Figure 9-23. Using sn.exe to generate the public/private key pair file

NOTE Once you have a *.snk file, you may use this same file for all of the shared assemblies you create from here on out. Again, understand that this file contains information that provides you with a unique identity in the world of .NET. Obviously, this key file should be kept in a safe location.

The next step is to inform the C# compiler exactly where the *.snk file is located to record the public key in the assembly manifest. When you create a new C# project workspace, you will notice that one of your initial project files is named "AssemblyInfo.cs".

This file contains a number of attributes that describe the assembly itself (more information on attributes in the Chapter 11). One attribute that may appear within this file is named AssemblyKeyFile. Simply update the initial empty value with a string specifying the location of your *.snk file, for example:

```
[assembly: AssemblyKeyFile(@"C:\MyKey\myKey.snk")]
```

Given that the version of a shared assembly is of prime importance, let's also specify a fixed numerical value. In the same AssemblyInfo.cs file, you will find another attribute named AssemblyVersion. Initially the value is set to "1.0.*":

```
[assembly: AssemblyVersion("1.0.*")]
```

Every new C# projects begins life versioned at 1.0.*. Recall that a .NET version number is composed of the four parts (<major>.<minor>.<build>.<revision>). Until you say otherwise, VS .NET automatically increments the build and revision numbers (as marked by the "*" wildcard symbol) as part of each compilation. To enforce a fixed value for the assembly's build version, simply update accordingly:

```
[assembly: AssemblyVersion("1.0.0.0")]
```

Using these two assembly-level attributes, the C# compiler now merges the necessary information into the corresponding manifest to establish your strong name, which can be seen using ildasm.exe (note the [.publickey] and [.ver] tokens in Figure 9-24).

```
MANIFEST                                                    _ □ ✕
.publickey = (00 24 00 00 04 80 00 00 94 00 00 00 06 02 00 00
              00 24 00 00 52 53 41 31 00 04 00 00 01 00 01 00
              19 47 57 E8 59 06 CF E5 44 43 BD 0A 28 03 CE 90
              91 8C D8 E6 29 C8 B2 CC 86 79 EC B9 C0 88 0E A3
              CF 3A 41 07 2A 48 30 FC 79 37 5C BD 92 A4 5E 00
              B7 92 E5 8A 7B 97 4E DD 2A B5 58 6E DD 6B F3 FD
              1D 83 EA EE 1C 22 CD 35 C8 8D C4 C8 96 E3 B8 1D
              82 46 57 43 1D F1 B4 6B 91 E0 53 F7 59 93 00 51
              F4 07 57 77 8A 8D 06 CB FA 6A 44 90 9F 4D D7 49
              6F 63 28 12 31 2B 72 7A AE AF 8B CA D7 05 04 B1 )
.hash algorithm 0x00008004
.ver 1:0:0:0
}
```

Figure 9-24. A strongly named assembly documents the public key in the manifest.

SOURCE CODE   The SharedAssembly project is located under the Chapter 9 subdirectory.

Understanding Delayed Signing

In the previous example, you played the role of the sole assembly builder and consumer, and thus had direct access to the *.snk file. However, given the sensitive nature of a public/private key file, don't be surprised if your company refuses to give you access to the master *.snk file. This is an obvious problem, given that we (as developers) will often need to install an assembly into the GAC for testing purposes. To allow this sort of testing (while not passing around the true *.snk file), the individual holding the master *.snk file can extract the value of the public key from the public/private *.snk file using the –p command line flag of sn.exe, to produce a new pseudo *.snk file:

```
sn –p myKey.snk testPublicKey.snk
```

At this point, the testPublicKey.snk file can be distributed to individual developers for the creation and testing of shared assemblies. To inform the C# compiler that the assembly in question is making use of delayed signing, the developer must make sure to set the value of the AssemblyDelaySign attribute to true in addition to specifying the pseudo-key file as the parameter to the AssemblyKeyFile attribute. Here are the relevant updates to the project's AssemblyInfo.cs file:

```
[assembly: AssemblyDelaySign(true)]
[assembly: AssemblyKeyFile(@"C:\MyKey\testPublicKey.snk")]
```

Once an assembly has enabled delayed signing, the next step is to disable the signature verification process that happens automatically when an assembly is deployed to the GAC. To do so, specify the -vr flag (using sn.exe) to skip the verification process on the current machine:

```
sn.exe -vr TheAssembly.dll
```

Once all testing has been performed, the assembly in question can be shipped to the trusted individual who holds the "true" public/private key file to resign the binary to provide the correct digital signature. Again, sn.exe provides the necessary behavior, this time using the –r flag:

```
sn.exe –r TheAssembly.dll C:\MyKey\myKey.snk
```

Finally, to enable the signature verification process, the final step is to apply the –vu flag:

```
sn.exe –vu TheAssembly.dll
```

Understand, of course, that if you (or your company) only build a .NET assembly intended for internal use, you may never need to bother with the process of delayed signing. However, if you are in the business of building .NET assemblies that may be purchased by external parties, the ability to delay signing keeps things safe and sane for all involved.

Installing/Removing Shared Assemblies

The final step is to install SharedAssembly.dll into the GAC. The simplest way to install a shared assembly into the GAC is to drag-and-drop the *.dll onto the active window using the Windows Explorer. Also, the .NET SDK provides a command line utility named gacutil.exe (the /i flag is used to install the binary). Figure 9-25 shows the result of copying our SharedAssembly.dll into the GAC.

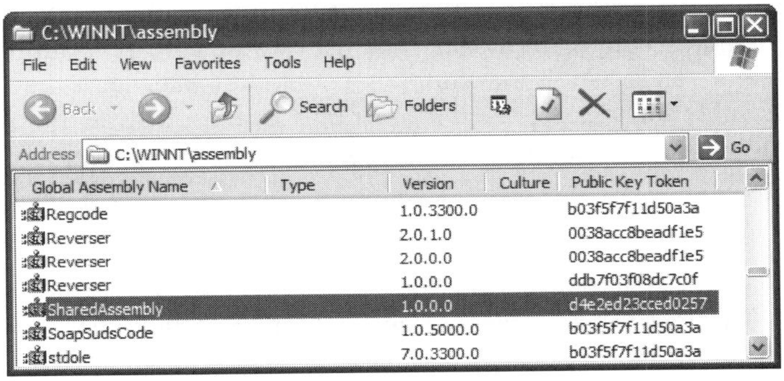

Figure 9-25. Our strongly named, shared assembly (version 1.0.0.0)

Once an assembly has been installed into the GAC, you may right-click a given assembly icon to pull up a property page for the binary, as well as delete the item from the GAC altogether (the GUI equivalent of supplying the /u flag when using gacutil.exe).

NOTE   Do be aware that you must have Administrative rights on the computer to interact with assemblies in the GAC. This is a good thing in that it prevents the casual user from accidentally breaking existing applications.

Using a Shared Assembly

Now let's make use of our shared assembly. Create a new C# Console application named SharedAssemblyClient. Like any external assembly, you will need to set a reference to the SharedAssembly binary using the Add Reference dialog. Understand, however, that you *do not* navigate to the GAC directory (\Assembly) when referencing shared binaries. The GAC is a runtime entity that is not intended to be accessed directly during the development cycle. Rather, navigate to the \Debug folder of the SharedAssembly project using the Browse button. At this point, exercise your VW MiniVan as you wish:

```
public class SharedAsmClient
{
    public static int Main(string[] args)
    {
        VWMiniVan v = new VWMiniVan();
        v.Play60sTunes();
        return 0;
    }
}
```

Once you have run your application, check out the client's application directory using the Windows Explorer. Recall, that when you reference a private assembly, the IDE automatically creates a local copy of the assembly for use by the client application. However, when you reference an assembly that contains a public key value (as is the case with the SharedAssembly.dll), VS .NET will not generate a local copy, given the assumption that assemblies supporting a public key are typically shared (and are therefore placed in the GAC).

SOURCE CODE   The SharedAssemblyClient application can be found under the Chapter 9 subdirectory.

Versioning Shared Assemblies

Like a private assembly, shared assemblies can also be configured using an application configuration file. Of course, as shared assemblies are placed in a well-known location (the GAC) we will not specify a <privatePath> element as we did for private assemblies (although if the client is using both shared and private assemblies, the <privatePath> element may still exist in the *.config file). To understand the role of *.config files and shared assemblies, we need to step back and take a closer look at the .NET versioning scheme.

As you have observed during this chapter, the AssemblyVersion attribute is used to specify a four part numerical version of an assembly (private or shared). Specifically speaking, these four numbers represent the major, minor, build, and revision numbers:

```
// Format: <Major version>.<Minor version>.<Build number>.<Revision>
// Valid values for each part of the version number are between 0 to 65535.
[Assembly: AssemblyVersion("1.0.0.0")]
```

When an assembly is compiled, this version is documented in the manifest. Likewise, when a client sets a reference to an external assembly, the version number is documented as well. For example, given that SharedAssembly.dll was set to version 1.0.0.0, the client application records this value in its own assembly using the [.assembly extern] tag:

```
.assembly extern SharedAssembly
{
  .publickeytoken = (82 FB C8 20 D1 60 F2 B8 )
  .ver 1:0:0:0
}
```

By default, the CLR will only load this external binary if indeed there is a shared assembly named SharedAssembly, version 1.0.0.0 with a public key token of the value 82 FB C8 20 D1 60 F2 B8 in the GAC. If any of these elements are not correct, the runtime will throw an exception (again remember that version checking only applies for strongly named assemblies).

Application configuration files can be used in conjunction with shared assemblies whenever you wish to instruct the CLR to bind to a *different* version of a specific assembly, effectively bypassing the value recorded in the client's manifest. This can be useful for a number of reasons. For example, imagine that you have shipped version 1.0.0.0 of an assembly and discover a major bug some time after the fact. One option of corrective action would be to rebuild the client application to reference the correct version of the bug-free assembly (say, 1.0.0.1) and redistribute both updated binaries to each and every target machine.

Another option is to ship the new code library and a *.config file that automatically instructs the runtime to bind to the new (bug-free) version. As long as the new version has been installed into the GAC, the original client runs without recompilation, redistribution, or fear of having to update your resume. Furthermore, other client applications that run just fine using the first version of the assembly can still make use of it.

Here's another example: You have shipped the first version of a bug-free assembly (1.0.0.0) and after a month or two, have added new logic to the current assembly (such as additional types or a refinement of existing types) to yield version 2.0.0.0. Obviously, previous client applications that were compiled against version 1.0.0.0 have no clue about these new types (given that their code base makes no reference to them).

New client applications, however, wish to make reference to the new functionality found in version 2.0.0.0. Under .NET, you are free to ship version 2.0.0.0 to the target machines, which will be run alongside the older version 1.0.0.0. Existing clients can dynamically be redirected to load version 2.0.0.0 (to gain access to the implementation refinements), using an application configuration file without needing to recompile and redeploy the client app.

Freezing the Current SharedAssembly

Before we build SharedAssembly.dll version 2.0.0.0, relocate your current assembly (version 1.0.0.0) into a distinct subdirectory (I called mine Version1) to symbolize the freezing of this version (Figure 9-26).

Figure 9-26. Freezing the current version of SharedAssembly.dll

Building SharedAssembly Version 2.0.0.0

Update your VWMiniVan class with a new member (which makes use of a custom enumeration) to allow the user to play some more modern musical selections. Also be sure to update the message displayed from within the constructor logic to reflect the fact that version 2.0.0.0 has been loaded:

```
// Insert your favorite bands here...
public enum BandName
{
    TonesOnTail, SkinnyPuppy, deftones, PTP
}

public class VWMiniVan
{
    public VWMiniVan()
    { MessageBox.Show("Using version 2.0.0.0!", "Shared Car"); }
...
```

```
// New functionality!
public void CrankGoodTunes(BandName band)
{
    switch(band)
    {
        case BandName.deftones:
            MessageBox.Show("So forget about me...");
            break;
        case BandName.PTP:
            MessageBox.Show("Tick tick tock...");
            break;
        case  BandName.SkinnyPuppy:
            MessageBox.Show("Water vapor, to air...");
            break;
        case  BandName.TonesOnTail:
            MessageBox.Show("Oooooh the rain. Oh the rain.");
            break;
    }
}
}
```

Before you compile, be sure to update this version of this assembly to 2.0.0.0:

```
// Update your AssemblyInfo.cs file as so...
[assembly: AssemblyVersion("2.0.0.0")]
```

If you look in your project's debug folder, you see that you have a new version of this assembly (2.0) while the previous version is safe in storage under the Version1 directory. Finally, let's install this new assembly into the GAC. Notice that you now have two versions of the same assembly (Figure 9-27).

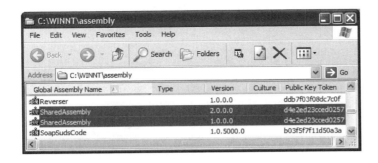

Figure 9-27. Side-by-side execution

Now that you have a distinctly versioned assembly recorded in the GAC, you can build application configuration files to control how a client binds to a specific version.

Specifying Custom Version Policies

When you wish to redirect a client to bind to an alternate shared assembly, you make use of the <dependentAssembly>, <assemblyIdentity>, and <bindingRedirect> elements. For example, the following configuration file forces version the client to use version 2.0.0.0 of the shared assembly, regardless of the fact that its manifest specifies version 1.0.0.0. (note that the GAC can be used to view the value of the public key token):

```
<configuration>
    <runtime>
        <assemblyBinding xmlns="urn:schemas-microsoft-com:asm.v1">
            <dependentAssembly>
                <assemblyIdentity name="sharedassembly"
                        publicKeyToken="d4e2ed23cced0257"
                        culture=""/>
                <bindingRedirect oldVersion= "1.0.0.0"
                    newVersion= "2.0.0.0"/>
            </dependentAssembly.
        </assemblyBinding>
    </runtime>
</configuration>
```

Here, the oldVersion attribute is used to specify the value stored in the client's manifest while the newVersion attribute marks the new version to load. To test this out yourself, create the previous configuration file and save it into the directory of the SharedAssemblyUser application (be sure you name this configuration file correctly). Now, run the program. You should see the message that displays version 2.0.0.0 has loaded. If you set the newVersion attribute to 1.0.0.0 (or simply delete the *.config file), you now see the message that version 1.0.0.0 has loaded.

What you have just observed is side-by-side execution. Because the .NET Framework allows you to place multiple versions of the same assembly into the GAC, you can easily configure custom version policies as you (or a system administrator) see fit.

GAC Internals

Now that you understand the overall role of the GAC, let's dig into its internal composition. When you view the GAC using the Windows Explorer, you find a number of icons displayed within a comfortable GUI shell. This GUI shell is provided courtesy of a COM server named shfusion.dll (if for some reason your machine's GAC is not displaying itself correctly, simply run regsvr32.exe and provide shfusion.dll as its sole argument).

To understand what the GAC really boils down to, open a command prompt and change to the following directory (where %windir% represents the name of your registered Window's directory and <drive> is, well, your drive):

```
<drive>:\%windir%\Assembly\GAC
```

Once you are in, issue a "dir" command from the command line. You will be presented with a list of a number of hidden subdirectories (Figure 9-28).

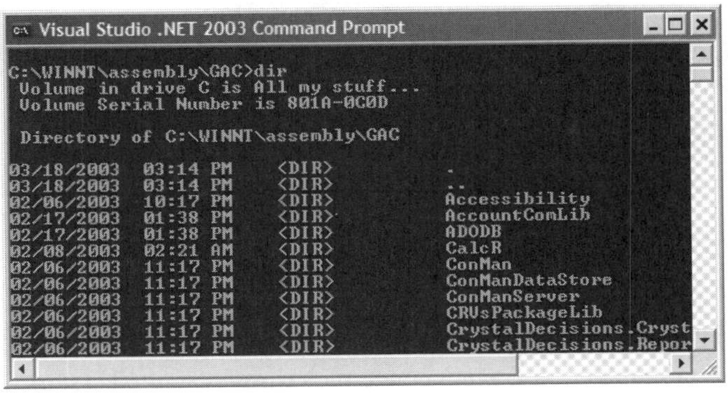

Figure 9-28. The hidden GAC subdirectory

Now, using the same command prompt, change to the \SharedAssembly subdirectory and again issue a "dir" command (Figure 9-29).

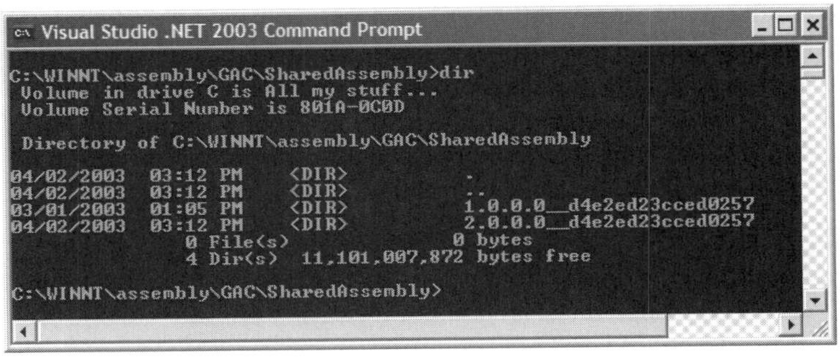

Figure 9-29. Inside the hidden \SharedAssembly subdirectory

As you can see, the GAC has created a subdirectory for each version of the SharedAssembly.dll assembly, each of which is contained within a uniquely named folder: <versionOfAssembly>__PublicKeyToken. If you were again to change the current directory to version 1.0.0.0 of SharedAssembly, you would indeed find a copy of the original single file assembly you created a la VS .NET (Figure 9-30).

```
cx  Visual Studio .NET 2003 Command Prompt                    _ □ ×

C:\WINNT\assembly\GAC\SharedAssembly\1.0.0.0__d4e2ed23cced0257>dir
 Volume in drive C is All my stuff...
 Volume Serial Number is 801A-0C0D

 Directory of C:\WINNT\assembly\GAC\SharedAssembly\1.0.0.0__d4e2ed23

03/01/2003  01:05 PM    <DIR>          .
03/01/2003  01:05 PM    <DIR>          ..
03/01/2003  01:05 PM            16,384 SharedAssembly.dll
03/01/2003  01:05 PM               311 __AssemblyInfo__.ini
               2 File(s)         16,695 bytes
               2 Dir(s)  11,100,332,032 bytes free

C:\WINNT\assembly\GAC\SharedAssembly\1.0.0.0__d4e2ed23cced0257>_
```

Figure 9-30. Behold! The GAC's internal copy of sharedassembly.dll

As you can see, the GAC is a shell that hides a number of subdirectories from view using various icons. Thus, understand that when you deploy strongly named assemblies to the GAC, the OS responds by creating a specific subdirectory behind the scenes. This is how the runtime is able to store multiple copies of a particular .NET assembly (while avoiding name-clashes).

Assembly-Centric Odds and Ends

At this point, you hopefully have a solid understanding of the distinction between a private and shared assembly, as well as an understanding of a number of ways to leverage configuration files to declaratively control how the CLR loads an external reference. To wrap up this chapter, I'd like to examine a set of unrelated (but very important) assembly-centric topics that you are sure to find useful.

Specifying <codeBase> Elements

Another aspect of application configuration files is the use of code bases. A given *.config file can support another XML element named <codeBase>, which is used by the assembly resolver to locate dependent assemblies located at arbitrary locations (including other machines). Understand, however, that if you wish to make use of <codeBase> to direct the runtime to look in a folder outside of the client's application directory, the referenced assembly should be equipped with a strong name.

NOTE While <codeBase> can be used to probe for assemblies that do not have a strong name, the assembly's location must be relative to the client's application's directory (and thus is little more than an alternative to the <privatePath> element).

To illustrate, create a new Console application (CodeBaseAsmUser) that makes use of the SharedAssembly.dll (version 2.0.0.0):

```
using System;
using SharedAssembly;
namespace CodeBaseAsmUser
{
    class CodeBaseUser
    {
        static void Main(string[] args)
        {
            VWMiniVan v = new VWMiniVan();
            v.CrankGoodTunes(BandName.deftones);
        }
    }
}
```

Given that sharedassembly.dll is located in the GAC, you are able to run the program "as-is." To illustrate the use of <codeBase>, create a new folder under your C drive (perhaps C:\MyAsms) and place a copy of SharedAssembly.dll 2.0.0.0 under the new directory. Next, create a configuration file (CodeBaseAsmUser.exe.config) that will force the assembly resolver to probe under C:\MyAsms as it attempts to locate each referenced assembly:

```
<configuration>
  <runtime>
    <assemblyBinding xmlns="urn:schemas-microsoft-com:asm.v1">
      <dependentAssembly>
        <assemblyIdentity name="SharedAssembly" publicKeyToken="82fbc820d160f2b8" />
        <codeBase version="2.0.0.0" href="file:///C:\MyAsms\SharedAssembly.dll" />
      </dependentAssembly>
    </assemblyBinding>
  </runtime>
</configuration>
```

As you can see, the <codeBase> element is nested within the <dependentAssembly> element, and specifies the version and location (via the "href" property) of the .NET binary. If you were now to delete version 2.0.0.0 of SharedAssembly.dll from the GAC, your client application would still run, as the assembly resolver was able to locate the dependent binary under your custom directory. Also, if you were now to delete the MyAsms folder from your machine, the client would fail. As you may have been able to gather, <codeBase> elements (if present) take precedent over the investigation of the GAC.

Let me offer a word of caution regarding this particular aspect of application configuration files. When you place custom assemblies at random locations on your development machine, you are in effect re-creating DLL hell, given that if you move or rename the folder containing your binaries, the current bind will fail.

As mentioned however, <codeBase> can be helpful when you are attempting to reference assemblies (single file or multifile) located on some other networked machine. For the sake of illustration, assume you have permission to access a folder located at www.intertech-inc.com. You could update your <codeBase> element as follows:

```
<codeBase version="2.0.0.0"
href="http://www.Intertech-inc.com/MyAsms/SharedAssembly.dll" />
```

In this case, you still have the possibility of breaking the client application. The bottom line is that <codeBase> elements should be used with care.

SOURCE CODE   The CodeBaseAsmUser application can be found under the Chapter 9 subdirectory.

Working with Publisher Policy Assemblies

The next configuration issue we examine is the use of publisher policy assemblies. As you have already seen, *.config files can be used by private assemblies to instruct the runtime to probe under various subdirectories when resolving the location of a given assembly. Shared assemblies can also make use of *.config files to dynamically bind to an assembly other than the version recorded in the client manifest. Do note that both of these approaches require that somebody (such as a system administrator) is required to create and edit a *.config file on each client machine.

Publisher policy allows the publisher of a given assembly (you, your department, your company, or what have you) to ship a special binary version of a *.config file that is installed into the GAC along with the assembly it is responsible for influencing. When this information is placed into the GAC, the client's application directory does not need to contain a specific *.config file. Given this, the redirecting of shared assemblies is less of a burden on the individual responsible for configuring individual .NET clients. All he or she needs to do is install the new binary *.config file shipped by the publisher into the GAC and walk away.

Given that the GAC can only store .NET *.dlls, the *.config file itself is not installed into the GAC. Rather, the publisher is responsible for creating a *.dll file based on the *.config (or *.xml) file using the command line tool, al.exe (assembly linker). Do note that VS .NET does not support the construction of publisher policy binaries.

The good news is that the syntax of a *.xml publisher policy configuration file is identical to that of an application-specific *.config file. Assume you wish to build a publisher policy assembly based on the XML contained in the previous SharedAsmUser.exe.config file. The command set is as follows:

```
al /link:SharedAssemblyUser.xml /out:policy.1.0.SharedAssembly.dll
/keyf:C:\MyKey\myKey.snk /v:1.0.0.0
```

As you can see, you do need to specify the input file containing the XML, the name of the output file (which must be in the format "policy.<major>.<minor>.assemblyToConfigure"), and the name of the file containing the public/private key pair (remember! Publisher policy files are shared, and therefore must have a strong name!). Once the al.exe tool has executed, the result is a new assembly that can be placed into the GAC to force all clients to bind to version 2.0.0.0 of the SharedAssembly.dll, without the use of a specific client application configure file (Figure 9-31).

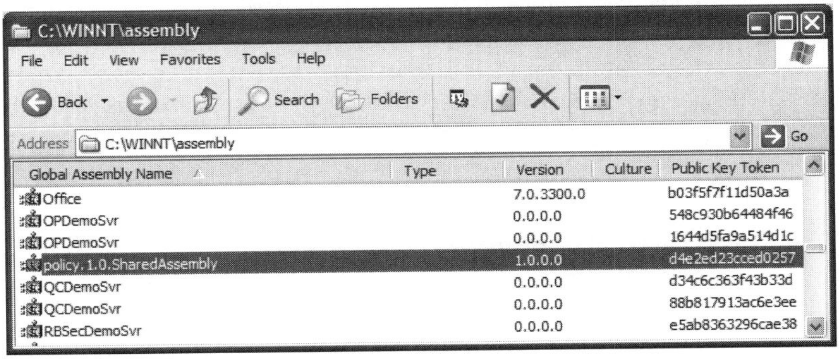

Figure 9-31. Our publisher policy assembly

Disabling Publisher Policy

It is possible to build a client configuration file that instructs the CLR to ignore the presence of any publisher policy files installed in the GAC. This may be helpful if a system administrator determines that a particular client executable is (somehow) broken when rebinding to the new version of the shared binary. To disable publisher policy on a client-by-client basis, simply build a (properly named) *.config file with the following XML:

```
<configuration>
  <runtime>
    <assemblyBinding xmlns="urn:schemas-microsoft-com:asm.v1">
      <publisherPolicy apply="no" />
    </assemblyBinding>
  </runtime>
</configuration>
```

Once this is done, the CLR will load the version of the assembly originally listed in the client's manifest.

The Machine-wide Configuration File

The configuration files you have been examining in this chapter each have a common theme. They only apply to a specific application (that is why they had the same name as the launching application). In addition, each .NET-aware machine has a file named "machine.config" that contains listings used to override any application-specific configuration files (as you might guess, reading this file is a great way to learn more *.config-centric tags).

Practically speaking, if you wish to automatically redirect the binding policy for all clients that make use of a given assembly, altering the machine.config file provides an easy alternative to distributing numerous application-specific *.config files to each application directory.

Although this file can be directly edited using notepad.exe, be very aware that if you were to alter this file incorrectly, you may cripple the ability of the runtime to function correctly. This scenario can be far more painful than a malformed application *.config file, given that bad XML in an application configuration file only affects a single application. On the other hand, bad XML in the machine.config file can entail reformatting your development machine.

The System.Configuration Namespace

It should come as no surprise that the .NET Framework provides a namespace that allows you to programmatically interact with *.config files. The System.Configuration namespace (defined within the System.dll assembly) provides a small set of types you may use to read data from a client's <appSettings> section of a configuration file. Specifically, the AppSettingsReader type will allow you to pull out values based on a string key token. For example, assume we have a *.config file for a Console application named AppConfigReaderApp, which maintains an ADO.NET connection string and a point of data named "timesToSayHello":

```xml
<configuration>
    <appSettings>
        <add key="appConStr" value="server=localhost;uid=sa;pwd=;database=Cars" />
        <add key="timesToSayHello" value="8" />
    </appSettings>
</configuration>
```

To read these values for use by the client application is as simple as calling the instance level GetValue() method of the AppSettingsReader type:

```csharp
class TheReader
{
    static void Main(string[] args)
    {
        AppSettingsReader ar = new AppSettingsReader();
        Console.WriteLine(ar.GetValue("appConStr", typeof(string)));
        int numbOfTimes = (int)ar.GetValue("timesToSayHello", typeof(int));
        for(int i = 0; i < numbOfTimes; i++)
            Console.WriteLine("Yo!");
    }
}
```

SOURCE CODE   The AppConfigReaderApp application can be found under the Chapter 9 subdirectory.

Using the .NET Administrative Tool

This chapter has illustrated how to create an XML application configuration file by hand. While seeing what happens under the hood is edifying, the process of crafting raw XML files is a bit on the verbose side and a rather error-prone endeavor. Given this, the .NET SDK ships with a tool named mscorcfg.msc (yet another MS snap-in utility) that will generate the correct XML automatically, based on your design-time configurations. To illustrate, open up the .NET admin tool (which by default is located under <drive>:\%windir%\Microsoft.NET\Framework\<version>) and check out the initial GUI (see Figure 9-32).

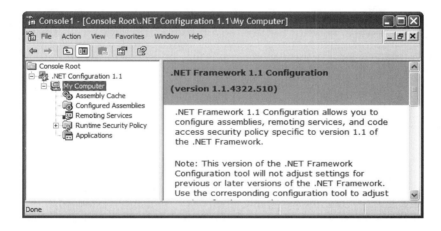

Figure 9-32. The .NET administration utility

As you can see, this tool has numerous options. While I'll assume you will check things out at your leisure, I would like to point out the use of the Applications node. By right-clicking this item, you are able to specify the name of a client application you wish to configure (as seen in the previous figure). Once you have added a client application (or two), you may select the Configured Assemblies node and activate the Configure an Assembly link. Once you pick the dependent assembly you wish to configure, you are able to specify binding policies for the client application (Figure 9-33). Once you hit OK, the underlying *.config file will be automatically generated.

*Figure 9-33. Declaratively building a *.config file*

If you wish to alter aspects of the machine.config file, simply make use of the options seen in the right-hand pane when you select the Configured Assemblies icon of the left tree-view.

The Ngen.exe Utility

The .NET SDK ships with an assembly-centric command line utility named ngen.exe. The role of ngen.exe is to compile CIL instructions to platform-specific code during the installation process, rather than an as needed basis (which is the default behavior).

While examining the contents of your machine's GAC, you may have noticed that some of the shared assemblies have been marked with the "Native Image" designation. When a shared assembly has been configured as "prejitted," the result is an assembly that can be loaded faster by the assembly resolver. Notice that I did not say the code within the assembly will necessarily execute any faster. The truth of the matter is, prejitted code is not guaranteed to run any faster than standard just-in-time compiled code, given that the CLR is still required to access the metadata found in the non-prejitted assembly in addition to the native instructions contained in the native image.

Given this, pre-Jitting CIL code is advantageous when you have an assembly that you suspect will be used by a great many applications on a given machine (or at least when you suspect the types within this assembly will be used frequently). Reason? Faster load times.

If you determine (through code profiling or an educated guess) that a particular assembly may benefit from the prejit process, you need to make use of the ngen.exe utility that ships with the .NET SDK, located (by default) under

C:\WINNT\Microsoft.NET\Framework\<version> (your version may differ). Ngen.exe requires you to specify the friendly name of the assembly to register. If the binary is in the GAC, there is no need to supply a literal path to the binary, as ngen.exe makes use of the same probing process as outlined during the course of this chapter. Thus:

```
ngen SomeAssembly
```

Like any of the tools that ship with the .NET SDK, ngen.exe has numerous options, so check out online Help for further details (simply search for ngen.exe using MSDN).

Regarding the VS .NET Add References Dialog Box

Finally, let's revisit the VS .NET Add Reference dialog box. Recall that the list of assemblies seen from the .NET tab does not represent each and every assembly on your machine and does not directly map to the items within the GAC. This list is nothing more than a set of suggestions. Although you are always free to simply use the Browse button to navigate to the location of an external .NET assembly, it is possible to configure your custom .NET assemblies to appear within the suggested list presented by VS .NET.

When you install VS .NET 2003 a directory will be created named PublicAssemblies, located by default under C:\Program Files\Microsoft Visual Studio .NET 2003\Common7\IDE. If you place a copy of your custom assembly within the PublicAssemblies folder, lo and behold, your *.dll will be listed automatically (Figure 9-34).

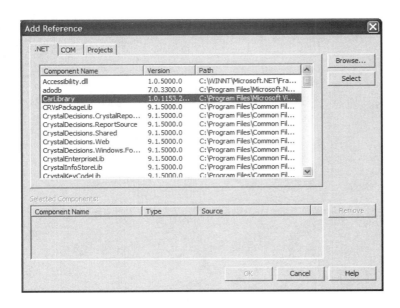

Figure 9-34. Suggesting CarLibrary.dll to VS .NET developers

Summary

This chapter drilled into the details behind the innocent-looking .NET DLLs and EXEs located on your development machine. You began the journey by examining the core concepts of the assembly: CLR headers, metadata, manifests, and CIL. As illustrated in this chapter, .NET supports the notion of cross-language inheritance, and to this end, you received a glimpse into the syntax of the VB .NET and MC++ programming language.

As you have seen, assemblies may be private or shared. In stark contrast to classic COM, private assemblies are the default. When you wish to configure a shared assembly, you are making an explicit choice, and need to generate a corresponding strong name. Recall that both private and shared assemblies can be configured declaratively using a client side *.config file, or alternatively, a publisher policy *.dll.

This chapter wrapped up by quickly examining a set of related assembly-centric details: the machine.config file, the .NET configuration utility (to simplify the process of building XML configuration files), ngen.exe (to prejit CIL code at the time of installation); and you learned how to inform VS .NET to display your custom .NET binaries within the Add References dialog.

CHAPTER 10

Processes, AppDomains, Contexts, and Threads

IN THE PREVIOUS CHAPTER, you examined the steps taken by the CLR to resolve the location of an externally referenced assembly. Here, you drill deeper into the constitution of a .NET executable host and come to understand the relationship between Win32 processes, application domains, contexts, and threads. In a nutshell, *application domains* (or simply, AppDomains) are logical subdivisions within a given process, which host a set of related .NET assemblies. As you will see, an application domain is further subdivided into contextual boundaries, which are used to group together like-minded .NET objects. Using the notion of context, the CLR is able to ensure that objects with special needs are handled appropriately.

Once you have come to understand the relationship between processes, application domains, and contexts, the remainder of this chapter examines how the .NET platform allows you to manually spawn multiple threads of execution for use by your program within its application domain. Using the types within the System.Threading namespace, the task of creating additional threads of execution has become extremely simple (if not downright trivial). Of course, the complexity of multithreaded development is not in the creation of threads, but in ensuring that your code base is well equipped to handle concurrent access to shared resources. Given this, the chapter closes by examining various synchronization primitives that the .NET Framework provides (which you will see is somewhat richer than raw Win32 threading primitives).

Reviewing Processes and Threads Under Traditional Win32

The concept of processes and threads has existed within Windows-based operating systems well before the release of the .NET platform. Simply put, *process* is the term used to describe the set of resources (such as external code libraries and the primary thread) as well as the necessary memory allocations used by a running application. For each *.exe loaded into memory, the operating system creates a separate and isolated memory partition (aka process) for use during its lifetime. Using this approach to application isolation, the result is a much more robust and stable runtime environment, given that the failure of one process does not effect the functioning of another.

Now, every Win32 process is assigned a unique process identifier (PID), and may be independently loaded and unloaded by the operating system as necessary (as well as programmatically using Win32 API calls). As you may be aware, the Processes tab of the

Task Manager utility (activated via the Ctrl+Shift+Esc keystroke combination) allows you to view statistics regarding the set of processes running on a given machine, including its PID and image name (Figure 10-1). (If you do not see a PID column, select the View | Select Columns menu and check the PID box.)

Figure 10-1. The Windows Task Manager

Every Win32 process has at least one main "thread" that functions as the entry point for the application. Formally speaking, the first thread created by a process' entry point is termed the *primary thread*. Simply put, a thread is a specific path of execution within a Win32 process. Traditional Windows applications define the WinMain() method as the application's entry point. On the other hand, console application provides the main() method for the same purpose.

Processes that contain a single primary thread of execution are intrinsically "thread-safe," given the fact that there is only one thread that can access the data in the application at a given time. However, a single-threaded process (especially one that is GUI-based) will often appear a bit unresponsive to the user if this single thread is performing a complex operation (such as printing out a lengthy text file, performing an exotic calculation, or attempting to connect to a remote server thousands of miles away).

Given this potential drawback of single-threaded applications, the Win32 API makes it is possible for the primary thread to spawn additional secondary threads (also termed *worker threads*) in the background, using a handful of Win32 API functions such as CreateThread(). Each thread (primary or secondary) becomes a unique path of execution in the process and has concurrent access to all shared points of data.

As you may have guessed, developers typically create additional threads to help improve the program's overall responsiveness. Multithreaded processes provide the illusion that numerous activities are happening at more or less the same time.

For example, an application may spawn a worker thread to perform a labor-intensive unit of work (again, such as printing a large text file). As this secondary thread is churning away, the main thread is still responsive to user input, which gives the entire process the potential of delivering greater performance. However, this may not actually be the case: using too many threads in a single process can actually *degrade* performance, as the CPU must switch between the active threads in the process (which takes time).

In reality, it is always worth keeping in mind that multithreading is most commonly an illusion provided by the operating system. Machines that host a single CPU do not have the ability to literally handle multiple threads at the same exact time. Rather, a single CPU will execute one thread for a unit of time (called a *time-slice*) based on the thread's priority level. When a thread's time-slice is up, the existing thread is suspended to allow another thread to perform its business. For a thread to remember what was happening before it was kicked out of the way, each thread is given the ability to write to Thread Local Storage (TLS) and is provided with a separate call stack, as illustrated in Figure 10-2.

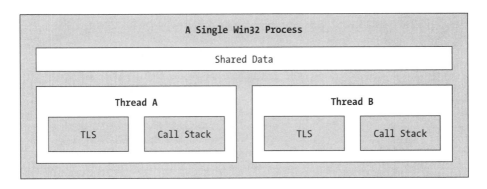

Figure 10-2. *The Win32 process / thread relationship*

NOTE   The newest Intel CPUs have an ability called hyperthreading that allows a single CPU to handle multiple threads simultaneously under certain circumstances. See http://www.intel.com/info/hyperthreading for more details.

Interacting with Processes Under the .NET Platform

Although processes and threads are nothing new, the manner in which we interact with these primitives under the .NET platform has changed quite a bit (for the better). To pave the way to understanding the world of building multithreaded assemblies, let's begin by checking out how processes have been altered to accommodate the needs of the CLR.

The System.Diagnostics namespace defines a number of types that allow you to programmatically interact with processes and various diagnostic-related types such as the system event log and performance counters. For the purposes of this chapter, we are only concerned with the process-centric types, defined in Table 10-1.

Table 10-1. Select Members of the System.Diagnostics Namespace

Process-Centric Types of the System.Diagnostics Namespace	Meaning in Life
Process	The Process class provides access to local and remote processes and also allows you to programmatically start and stop processes.
ProcessModule	This type represents a module (*.dll or *.exe) that is loaded into a particular process. Understand that the ProcessModule type can represent *any* module, COM-based, .NET-based, or traditional C-based binaries.
ProcessModuleCollection	Provides a strongly typed collection of ProcessModule objects.
ProcessStartInfo	Specifies a set of values used when starting a process via the Process.Start() method.
ProcessThread	Represents a thread within a given process. ProcessThread is a type used to diagnose a process' thread set, and is not used to spawn new threads of execution within a process. As you will see later in this chapter, duties of this sort are the role of the types within the System.Threading namespace.
ProcessThreadCollection	Provides a strongly typed collection of ProcessThread objects.

The System.Diagnostics.Process type allows you to identify the running processes on a given machine (local or remote). The Process class also provides members that allow you to programmatically start and terminate processes, establish a process' priority level, and obtain a list of active threads and/or loaded modules within a given process. Table 10-2 illustrates some (but not all) of the key members of System.Diagnostics.Process.

Table 10-2. Select Members of the Process Type

Member of System.Diagnostic.Process	Meaning in Life
ExitCode	This property gets the value that the associated process specified when it terminated. Do note that you will be required to handle the Exited event (for asynchronous notification) or call the WaitForExit() method (for synchronous notification) to obtain this value.
ExitTime	This property gets the time stamp associated with the process that has terminated (represented with a DateTime type).
Handle	Returns the handle associated to the process by the OS.
HandleCount	Returns the number of handles opened by the process.
Id	This property gets the process ID (PID) for the associated process.
MachineName	This property gets the name of the computer the associated process is running on.
MainModule	Gets the ProcessModule type that represents the main module for a given process.
MainWindowTitle MainWindowHandle	MainWindowTitle gets the caption of the main window of the process (if the process does not have a main window, you receive an empty string). MainWindowHandle gets the underlying handle (represented via a System.IntPtr type) of the associated window. If the process does not have a main window, the IntPtr type is assigned the value System.IntPtr.Zero.
Modules	Provides access to the strongly typed ProcessModuleCollection type, which represents the set of modules (*.dll or *.exe) loaded within the current process.
PriorityBoostEnabled	Determines if the OS should temporarily boost the process if the main window has the focus.
PriorityClass	Allows you to read or change the overall priority for the associated process.
ProcessName	This property gets the name of the process (which as you would assume is the name of the application itself).
Responding	This property gets a value indicating whether the user interface of the process is responding (or not).
StartTime	This property gets the time that the associated process was started (via a DateTime type).

Table 10-2. Select Members of the Process Type (Continued)

Member of **System.Diagnostic.Process**	**Meaning in Life**
Threads	This property gets the set of threads that are running in the associated process (represented via an array of ProcessThread types).
CloseMainWindow()	Closes a process that has a user interface by sending a close message to its main window.
GetCurrentProcess()	This static method returns a new Process type that represents the currently active process.
GetProcesses()	This static method returns an array of new Process components running on a given machine.
Kill()	Immediately stops the associated process.
Start()	Starts a process.

Enumerating Running Processes

To illustrate the process of manipulating Process types (pardon the redundancy), assume you have a C# console application named ProcessManipulator, which defines the following static helper method:

```
public static void ListAllRunningProcesses()
{
    // Get all the processes on the local machine.
    Process[] runningProcs = Process.GetProcesses(".");
    // Print out PID and name of each proc.
    foreach(Process p in runningProcs)
    {
        string info = string.Format("-> PID: {0}\tName: {1}",
            p.Id, p.ProcessName);
        Console.WriteLine(info);
    }
    Console.WriteLine("************************************\n");
}
```

Notice how the static Process.GetProcesses() method returns an array of Process types that represent the running processes on the target machine (the dot notation seen here represents the local computer).

Once you have obtained the array of Process types, you are able to trigger any of the members seen in Table 10-2. Here, simply dump the process identifier (PID) and the name of each process. Assuming the Main() method has been updated to call this helper function, you will see something like the output in Figure 10-3.

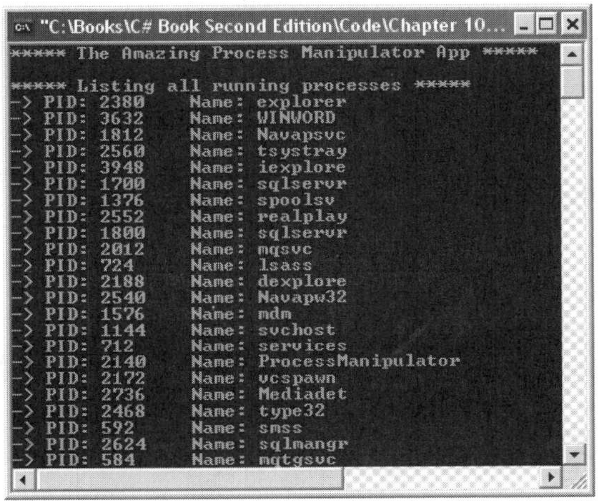

Figure 10-3. Enumerating running processes

Investigating a Specific Process

In addition to obtaining a full and complete list of all running processes on a given machine, the static Process.GetProcessById() method allows you to obtain a single Process type via the associated PID. As you would hope, if you request access to a nonexistent process ID, an ArgumentException exception is thrown:

```
// If there is no process with the PID of 987, a
// runtime exception will be thrown.
int pID = 987;
Process theProc;
try
{ theProc = Process.GetProcessById(pID); }
catch  // Generic catch for simplicitiy
{ Console.WriteLine("-> Sorry...bad PID!"); }
```

Investigating a Process' Thread Set

Now that you understand how to gain access to a Process type, you are able to program-matically investigate the set of all threads currently alive in the process at hand. This set of threads is represented by the strongly typed ProcessThreadCollection collection, which contains any number of individual ProcessThread types. To illustrate, assume the following additional static helper function has been added to your current application:

```csharp
public static void EnumThreadsForPid(int pID)
{
    Process theProc;
    try
    { theProc = Process.GetProcessById(pID); }
    catch
    {
        Console.WriteLine("-> Sorry...bad PID!");
        Console.WriteLine("*********************************\n");
        return;
    }
    // List out stats for each thread in the specified process.
    Console.WriteLine("Here are the thread IDs for: {0}",
        theProc.ProcessName);
    ProcessThreadCollection theThreads = theProc.Threads;
    foreach(ProcessThread pt in theThreads)
    {
        string info =
            string.Format("-> Thread ID: {0}\tStart Time {1}\tPriority {2}",
                pt.Id , pt.StartTime.ToShortTimeString(), pt.PriorityLevel);
        Console.WriteLine(info);
    }
    Console.WriteLine("*********************************\n");
}
```

As you can see, the Threads property of the System.Diagnostics.Process type provides access to the ProcessThreadCollection class. Here, we are printing out the assigned thread ID, start time, and priority level of each thread in the process specified by the client. Thus, if you update your program's Main() method to prompt the user for a PID to investigate:

```csharp
Console.WriteLine("***** Enter PID of process to investigate *****");
Console.Write("PID: ");
string pID = Console.ReadLine();
int theProcID = int.Parse(pID);
EnumThreadsForPid(theProcID);
```

you would find output along the lines of the Figure 10-4.

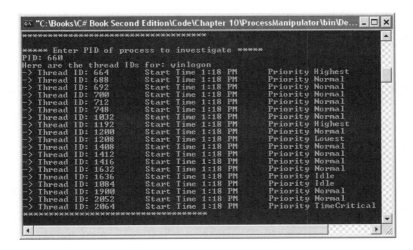

Figure 10-4. Enumerating the threads within a running process

The ProcessThread type has additional members of interest beyond Id, StartTime, and PriorityLevel. Table 10-3 documents some members of interest.

Table 10-3. Select Members of the ProcessThread Type

Member of System.Diagnostics.ProcessThread	Meaning in Life
BasePriority	Gets the base priority of the thread
CurrentPriority	Gets the current priority of the thread
Id	Gets the unique identifier of the thread
IdealProcessor	Sets the preferred processor for this thread to run on
PriorityLevel	Gets or sets the priority level of the thread
ProcessorAffinity	Sets the processors on which the associated thread can run
StartAddress	Gets the memory address of the function that the operating system called that started this thread
StartTime	Gets the time that the operating system started the thread
ThreadState	Gets the current state of this thread
TotalProcessorTime	Gets the total amount of time that this thread has spent using the processor
WaitReason	Gets the reason that the thread is waiting

Now before reading any further, be very aware that the ProcessThread type is *not* the entity used to create, suspend, or kill threads under the .NET platform. Rather, ProcessThread is a vehicle used to obtain diagnostic information for the active threads within a running process.

Investigating a Process' Module Set

Next up, let's check out how to iterate over the number of loaded modules that are hosted within a given process. Recall that a *module* is a generic name used to describe a given *.dll (or the *.exe itself) which is hosted by a specific process. When you access the ProcessModuleCollection via the Process.Module property, you are able to enumerate over *all modules* in a process; .NET-based, COM-based, or traditional C-based binaries. Ponder the following helper function:

```
public static void EnumModsForPid(int pID)
{
    Process theProc;
    try
    { theProc = Process.GetProcessById(pID); }
    catch
    {
        Console.WriteLine("-> Sorry...bad PID!");
        Console.WriteLine("***********************************\n");
        return;
    }
    Console.WriteLine("Here are the loaded modules for: {0}",
        theProc.ProcessName);
    try
    {
        ProcessModuleCollection theMods = theProc.Modules;
        foreach(ProcessModule pm in theMods)
        {
            string info = string.Format("-> Mod Name: {0}", pm.ModuleName);
            Console.WriteLine(info);
        }
    Console.WriteLine("***********************************\n");
    }
    catch{Console.WriteLine("No mods!");}
}
```

To illustrate one possible invocation of this function, let's check out the loaded modules for the process hosting your current console application (ProcessManipulator). To do so, run the application, identify the PID assigned to ProcessManipulator.exe, and pass this value to the EnumModsForPid() method (be sure to update your Main() method accordingly). Once you do, you may be surprised to see the list of *.dlls used for a simple console application (atl.dll, mfc42u.dll, oleaut32.dll and so forth.) Figure 10-5 shows a test run.

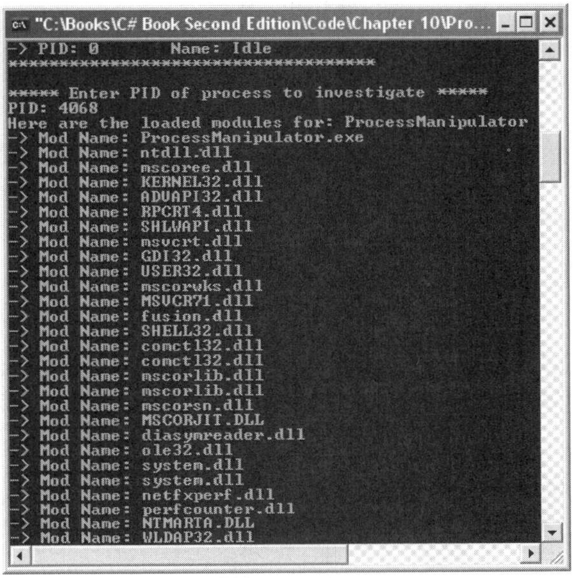

Figure 10-5. Enumerating the loaded modules within a running process

Starting and Killing Processes Programmatically

The final aspects of the System.Diagnostics.Process type examined here are the Start()
and Kill() methods. As you can gather by their names, these members provide a way to
programmatically launch and terminate a process. For example:

```
public static void StartAndKillProcess()
{
    // Launch Internet Explorer.
    Process ieProc = Process.Start("IExplore.exe",
        "www.intertech-inc.com");
    Console.Write("--> Hit enter to kill {0}...", ieProc.ProcessName);
    Console.ReadLine();
    // Kill the iexplorer.exe process.
    try { ieProc.Kill(); }
    catch{}   // In case user already killed it...
}
```

The static Process.Start() method has been overloaded a few times, however. At
minimum you will need to specify the friendly name of the process you wish to launch
(such as MS Internet Explorer). This example makes use of a variation of the Start()
method that allows you to specify any additional arguments to pass into the program's
entry point (i.e., the Main() method).

The Start() method also allows you to pass in a System.Diagnostics.ProcessStartInfo
type to specify additional bits of information regarding how a given process should

come into life. Here is the formal definition of ProcessStartInfo (see online Help for full details of this type):

```
public sealed class System.Diagnostics.ProcessStartInfo :
    object
{
    public ProcessStartInfo();
    public ProcessStartInfo(string fileName);
    public ProcessStartInfo(string fileName, string arguments);
    public string Arguments { get; set; }
    public bool CreateNoWindow { get; set; }
    public StringDictionary EnvironmentVariables { get; }
    public bool ErrorDialog { get; set; }
    public IntPtr ErrorDialogParentHandle { get; set; }
    public string FileName { get; set; }
    public bool RedirectStandardError { get; set; }
    public bool RedirectStandardInput { get; set; }
    public bool RedirectStandardOutput { get; set; }
    public bool UseShellExecute { get; set; }
    public string Verb { get; set; }
    public string[] Verbs { get; }
    public ProcessWindowStyle WindowStyle { get; set; }
    public string WorkingDirectory { get; set; }
    public virtual bool Equals(object obj);
    public virtual int GetHashCode();
    public Type GetType();
    public virtual string ToString();
}
```

Regardless of which version of the Process.Start() method you invoke, do note that you are returned a reference to the newly activated process. When you wish to terminate the process, simply call the instance level Kill() method.

 SOURCE CODE   The ProcessManipulator application is included under the Chapter 10 subdirectory.

Understanding the System.AppDomain Type

Now that you understand how to interact with a Win32 process from managed code, we need to examine more closely the new (but related) concept of a *.NET application domain*. As I mentioned briefly in the introduction, unlike a traditional (non-.NET) Win32 *.exe application, .NET assemblies are hosted in a logical partition within a process termed an application domain (aka AppDomain) and many application domains can be hosted inside a single OS process. This additional subdivision of a traditional Win32 process offers several benefits, some of which are:

- AppDomains are a key aspect of the OS-neutral nature of the .NET platform, given that this logical division abstracts away the differences in how an underlying operating system represents a loaded executable.

- AppDomains are far less expensive in terms of processing power and memory than a full blown process (for example, the CLR is able to load and unload application domains much quicker than a formal process).

- AppDomains provide a deeper level of isolation for hosting a loaded application. If one AppDomain within a process fails, the remaining AppDomains remain functional.

As suggested in the previous hit-list, a single process can host any number of AppDomains, each of which is fully and completely isolated from other AppDomains within this process (or any other process). Given this factoid, be very aware that applications that run in unique AppDomains are unable to share any information of any kind (global variables or static fields) unless they make use of the .NET Remoting protocol (examined in Chapter 12) to marshal the data.

NOTE   In some respects, .NET application domains are reminiscent of the "apartment" architecture of classic COM. Of course, .NET AppDomains are managed types whereas the COM apartment architecture is built on an unmanaged (and hideously complex) structure.

Understand that while a single process *may* host multiple AppDomains, this is not always the case. At the very least an OS process will host what is termed the default application domain. This specific application domain is automatically created by the CLR at the time the process launches. After this point, the CLR creates additional application domains on an as-needed basis. If the need should arise (which it most likely *will not* for a majority of your .NET endeavors), you are also able to programmatically create application domains at runtime within a given process using static methods of the System.AppDomain class. This class is also useful for low-level control of application domains. Key members of this class are shown in Table 10-4.

Table 10-4. Select Members of AppDomain

AppDomain Member	Meaning in Life
CreateDomain()	This static method creates a new AppDomain in the current process. Understand that the CLR will create new application domains as necessary, and thus the chance of you absolutely needing to call this member is slim to none (unless you happen to be building a custom CLR host).
GetCurrentThreadId()	This static method returns the ID of the active thread in the current application domain.
Unload()	Another static method that allows you to unload a specified AppDomain within a given process.
BaseDirectory	This property returns the base directory that the assembly resolver used to probe for dependent assemblies.
CreateInstance()	Creates an instance of a specified type defined in a specified assembly file.
ExecuteAssembly()	Executes an assembly within an application domain, given its file name.
GetAssemblies()	Gets the set of .NET assemblies that have been loaded into this application domain. Unlike the Process type, the GetAssemblies() method will only return the list of true-blue .NET binaries. COM-based or C-based binaries are ignored.
Load()	Used to dynamically load an assembly into the current application domain.

In addition, the AppDomain type also defines a small set of events that correspond to various aspects of an application domain's life-cycle (Table 10-5).

Table 10-5. Events of the AppDomain Type

Events of System.AppDomain	Meaning in Life
AssemblyLoad	Occurs when an assembly is loaded
AssemblyResolve	Occurs when the resolution of an assembly fails
DomainUnload	Occurs when an AppDomain is about to be unloaded
ProcessExit	Occurs on the default application domain when the default application domain's parent process exits
ResourceResolve	Occurs when the resolution of a resource fails
TypeResolve	Occurs when the resolution of a type fails
UnhandledException	Occurs when an exception is not caught by an event handler

Fun with AppDomains

To illustrate how to interact with .NET application domains programmatically, assume you have a new C# console application named AppDomainManipulator. The static PrintAllAssembliesInAppDomain() helper method makes use of AppDomain.GetAssemblies() to obtain a list of all .NET binaries hosted within the application domain in question.

This list is represented by an array of System.Reflection.Assembly types, and thus we are required to use the System.Reflection namespace (full details of this namespace and the Assembly type are seen in Chapter 11). Once we obtain the list of loaded assemblies, we iterate over the array and print out the friendly name and version of each module:

```
using System.Reflection;  // For the Assembly type.
...
public static void PrintAllAssembliesInAppDomain(AppDomain ad)
{
    Assembly[] loadedAssemblies = ad.GetAssemblies();
    Console.WriteLine("***** Here are the assemblies loaded in {0} *****\n",
        ad.FriendlyName);
    foreach(Assembly a in loadedAssemblies)
    {
        Console.WriteLine("-> Name: {0}", a.GetName().Name);
        Console.WriteLine("-> Version: {0}\n", a.GetName().Version);
    }
}
```

Now assume you have updated the Main() method to obtain a reference to the current application domain before invoking PrintAllAssembliesInAppDomain(), using the AppDomain.CurrentDomain property. To make things a bit more interesting, notice that the Main() method launches a message box to force the assembly resolver to load the System.Windows.Forms.dll and System.dll assemblies (so be sure to set a reference to these assemblies and update your "using" statements appropriately):

```
public static int Main(string[] args)
{
    Console.WriteLine("***** The Amazing AppDomain app *****\n");
    // Get info for current AppDomain.
    AppDomain defaultAD= AppDomain.CurrentDomain;
    MessageBox.Show("This call loaded System.Windows.Forms.dll and System.dll");
    PrintAllAssembliesInAppDomain(defaultAD);
    return 0;
}
```

Figure 10-6 shows the output.

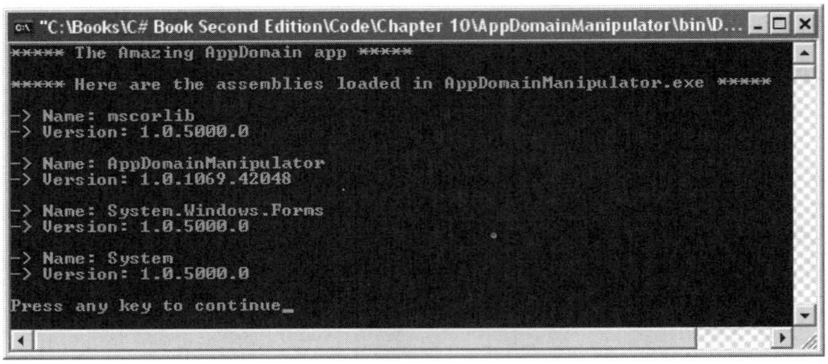

Figure 10-6. Enumerating assemblies within a given app domain (within a given process)

Programmatically Creating New AppDomains

Recall that a single process is capable of hosting multiple AppDomains. While it is true that you will seldom (if ever) need to manually create AppDomains directly (unless you happen to be creating a custom host for the CLR), you are able to do so via the static CreateDomain() method. As you would guess, this method has been overloaded a number of times. At minimum you will simply specify the friendly name of the new application domain as seen here:

```
public static int Main(string[] args)
{
...
    // Make a new AppDomain in the current process.
    AppDomain anotherAD = AppDomain.CreateDomain("SecondAppDomain");
    PrintAllAssembliesInAppDomain(anotherAD);
    return 0;
}
```

Now, if you run the application again (Figure 10-7), notice that the System.Windows.Forms.dll and System.dll assemblies are only loaded within the default application domain! This may seem counterintuitive if you have a background in traditional Win32 (as you might suspect that both application domains have access to the same assembly set). Recall, however, that an assembly loads into an *application domain,* not directly into the process itself.

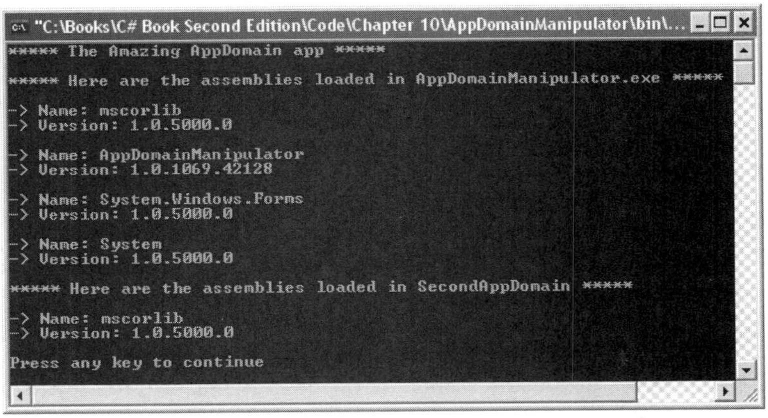

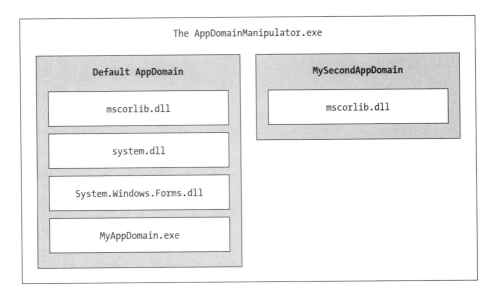

Figure 10-7. A single process with two application domains

Next, notice how the SecondAppDomain application domain automatically contains its own copy of mscorlib.dll, as this key assembly is automatically loaded by the CLR for each and every application domain. This begs the question, "How can I programmatically load an assembly into an application domain?" Answer? The AppDomain.Load() method (or alternatively, AppDomain.ExecuteAssembly()). I'll hold off on this topic until I discuss the process of dynamically loading assemblies in Chapter 11 during our examination of .NET reflection services.

To solidify the relationship between processes, application domains, and assemblies, Figure 10-8 diagrams the internal composition of the AppDomainManipulator.exe process you have just constructed.

The AppDomainManipulator.exe

Default AppDomain	MySecondAppDomain
mscorlib.dll	mscorlib.dll
system.dll	
System.Windows.Forms.dll	
MyAppDomain.exe	

Figure 10-8. The AppDomainManipulator.exe process under the hood

Programmatically Unloading AppDomains (and Hooking into Events)

It is important to point out that the CLR does not permit unloading individual .NET assemblies. However, using the AppDomain.Unload() method you are able to selectively unload a given application domain from its hosting process. When you do so, the application domain will unload each assembly in turn.

Recall that the AppDomain type defines a small set of events, one of which is DomainUnload. This is fired when a (non-default) AppDomain is unloaded from the containing process. Another event of interest is the ProcessExit event, which is fired when the default application domain is unloaded from the process (which obviously entails the termination of the process itself). Thus, if you wish to programmatically unload anotherAD from the AppDomainManipulator.exe process, and be notified when the application domain is torn down, you are able to write the following event logic:

```
public static void anotherAD_DomainUnload(object sender, EventArgs e)
{ Console.WriteLine("***** Unloaded anotherAD! *****\n"); }
...
// Hook into DomainUnload event.
anotherAD.DomainUnload +=
    new EventHandler(anotherAD_DomainUnload);
// Now unload anotherAD.
AppDomain.Unload(anotherAD);
```

If you wish to be notified when the default AppDomain is unloaded, modify your application to support the following event logic:

```
private static void defaultAD_ProcessExit(object sender, EventArgs e)
{ Console.WriteLine("***** Unloaded defaultAD! *****\n");  }
...
defaultAD.ProcessExit +=new EventHandler(defaultAD_ProcessExit);
```

SOURCE CODE   The AppDomainManipulator project is included under the Chapter 10 subdirectory.

Understanding Context (or How Low Can You Go?)

As you have just seen, AppDomains are logical partitions within a process used to host .NET assemblies. A given application domain may be further subdivided into numerous *context boundaries*. In a nutshell, a .NET context provides a way for a single AppDomain to partition .NET objects that have similar execution requirements. Using context, the CLR is able to ensure that objects that have special runtime requirements are handled appropriately and in a consistent manner by intercepting method invocations into and out of a given context. This layer of interception allows CLR to adjust the current method invocation to conform to the contextual settings of a given type.

Just as a process defines a default AppDomain, every application domain has a default context. This default context (sometimes referred to as *context 0*, given that it is always the first context created within an application domain) is used to group together .NET objects that have no specific or unique contextual needs. As you may expect, a vast majority of your .NET class types will be loaded into context 0. If the CLR determines a newly created object has special needs, a new context boundary is created within the hosting application domain. Figure 10-9 illustrates the process, AppDomain, context relationship.

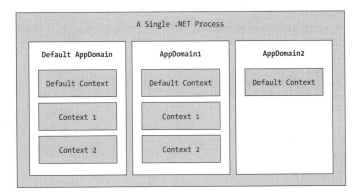

Figure 10-9. Processes, application domains, and context boundaries

Context-Agile and Context-Bound Types

.NET types that do not demand any special contextual treatment are termed *context-agile* objects. These objects can be accessed from anywhere within the hosting AppDomain without interfering with the object's runtime requirements. Building context-agile objects is a no-brainer, given that you simply do nothing (specifically, you do not adorn the type with any contextual attributes and do not derive from the System.ContextBoundObject base class):

```
// A context-agile object is loaded into context 0.
public class IAmAContextAgileClassType{}
```

On the other hand, objects that do demand contextual allocation are termed *context-bound* objects, and *must* derive from the System.ContextBoundObject base class. This base class solidifies the fact that the object in question can only function appropriately within the context in which it was created.

In addition to deriving from System.ContextBoundObject, a context-sensitive type will also be adorned with a special category of .NET attributes termed (not surprisingly) *context attributes*. All context attributes derive from the System.Runtime.Remoting.Contexts.ContextAttribute base class, which is defined as follows (note this class type implements two context-centric interfaces, IContextAttribute and IContextProperty):

```
public class System.Runtime.Remoting.Contexts.ContextAttribute :
    Attribute,
    System.Runtime.Remoting.Contexts.IContextAttribute,
    System.Runtime.Remoting.Contexts.IContextProperty
{
    public ContextAttribute(string name);
    public string Name { virtual get; }
    public object TypeId { virtual get; }
    public virtual bool Equals(object o);
    public virtual void Freeze(System.Runtime.Remoting.Contexts.Context newContext);
    public virtual int GetHashCode();
    public virtual void GetPropertiesForNewContext(
        System.Runtime.Remoting.Activation.IConstructionCallMessage ctorMsg);
    public Type GetType();
    public virtual bool IsContextOK(
      System.Runtime.Remoting.Contexts.Context ctx,
      System.Runtime.Remoting.Activation.IConstructionCallMessage ctorMsg);
    public virtual bool IsDefaultAttribute();
    public virtual bool IsNewContextOK(
        System.Runtime.Remoting.Contexts.Context newCtx);
    public virtual bool Match(object obj);
    public virtual string ToString();
}
```

The .NET base class libraries define numerous context attributes that describe specific runtime requirements (such as thread synchronization and URL activation). Given the role of .NET context, it should stand to reason that if a context-bound object were to somehow end up in an incompatible context, bad things are guaranteed to occur at the most inopportune times.

Creating a Context-Bound Object

So, what sort of bad things might occur if a context-bound object is placed into an incompatible context? The answer depends on the object's advertised contextual settings. Assume for example that you wish to define a .NET type that is automatically thread-safe in nature, even though you have not hard-coded thread-safe-centric logic within the method implementations. To do so, you may apply the System.Runtime.Remoting.Contexts.SynchronizationAttribute attribute as follows:

```
using System.Runtime.Remoting.Contexts;
...
// This context-bound type will only be loaded into a
// synchronized (and hence, thread safe) context.
[Synchronization]
public class MyThreadSafeObject : ContextBoundObject
{}
```

As you will see in greater detail later in this chapter, classes that are attributed with the [Synchronization] attribute are loaded into a thread-safe context. Given the special contextual needs of the MyThreadSafeObject class type, imagine the problems that would occur if an allocated object were moved from a synchronized context into a non-synchronized context. The object is suddenly no longer thread-safe and thus becomes a candidate for massive data corruption, as numerous threads are attempting to interact with the (now thread-volatile) reference object. This is obviously a huge problem, given that the code base has not specifically wrapped thread-sensitive resources with hard-coded synchronization logic.

Placing Context in Context

Now, the good news is that you do *not* have to concern yourself with the act of ensuring that your context-bound objects are loaded into the correct contextual setting. The .NET runtime will read the assembly metadata when constructing the type, and build a new context within the current application domain when necessary.

To be honest, the notion of .NET context is an extremely low-level facility of the CLR. So much so, that a key context-centric namespace, System.Runtime.Remoting.Context, only formally lists the SynchronizationAttribute class type within online Help (as of .NET version 1.1). The remaining members are considered usable only by the CLR, and are intended to be ignored (which you should do, given that many members of this namespace are subject to change in future releases of .NET).

Nevertheless, it is possible to make use of these hands-off types, simply as an academic endeavor. Thus, by way of a friendly heads-up, understand that the following example is purely illustrative in nature. As a .NET programmer, you can safely ignore these low-level primitives in 99.99 percent of your applications. If you wish to see the formal definition of the any of the following context-centric types, make use of the wincv.exe utility.

NOTE COM+ developers are already aware of the notion of context. Using COM IDL attributes and the Component Services utility, developers are able to establish contextual settings for a given COM+ type. Although .NET and COM+ both make use of contextual boundaries, understand that the underlying implementations of both systems are not the same and cannot be treated identically.

Fun with Context

To begin, assume you have a new console application named ContextManipulator. This application defines two context-agile types and a single context-bound type:

```
using System.Runtime.Remoting.Contexts;  // For Context type.
using System.Threading;  // For Thread type.
...
// These classes have no special contextual
// needs and will be loaded into the
// default context of the app domain.
public class NoSpecialContextClass
{
    public NoSpecialContextClass()
    {
        // Get context information and print out context ID.
        Context ctx = Thread.CurrentContext;
        Console.WriteLine("Info about context {0}", ctx.ContextID);
        foreach(IContextProperty itfCtxProp in ctx.ContextProperties)
            Console.WriteLine("-> Ctx Prop: {0}", itfCtxProp.Name);
    }
}
public class NoSpecialContextClass2
{
    public NoSpecialContextClass2()
    {
        // Get context information and print out context ID.
        Context ctx = Thread.CurrentContext;
        Console.WriteLine("Info about context {0}", ctx.ContextID);
        foreach(IContextProperty itfCtxProp in ctx.ContextProperties)
            Console.WriteLine("-> Ctx Prop: {0}", itfCtxProp.Name);
    }
}
// This class demands to be loaded in
// a synchronization context.
// RECALL! All context-bound types must derive from
// System.ContextBoundObject.
[Synchronization]
public class SynchContextClass : ContextBoundObject
{
    public SynchContextClass()
    {
        // Get context information and print out context ID.
        Context ctx = Thread.CurrentContext;
        Console.WriteLine("Info about context {0}", ctx.ContextID);
        foreach(IContextProperty itfCtxProp in ctx.ContextProperties)
            Console.WriteLine("-> Ctx Prop: {0}", itfCtxProp.Name);
    }
}
```

Notice that each of the class constructors obtains a
System.Runtime.Remoting.Contexts.Context type from the current thread of
execution, via the static Thread.CurrentContext property. Using this type, you
are able to print out statistics about the contextual boundary, such as its assigned
ID, as well as a set of descriptors obtained via the Context.ContextProperties property.

This instance-level property returns a (very) low-level interface named IContextProperty, which exposes each descriptor through the Name property.

Now, assume Main() has been updated to allocate an instance of each class type. As the objects come to life, the class constructors will dump out various bits of context-centric information (Figure 10-10):

```
static void Main(string[] args)
{
    Console.WriteLine("***** The Amazing Context Application *****\n");
    // Make each class type and print contextual info.
    NoSpecialContextClass noBigDealObj = new NoSpecialContextClass();
    Console.WriteLine();
    NoSpecialContextClass2 noBigDealObj2 = new NoSpecialContextClass2();
    Console.WriteLine();
    SynchContextClass synchObj = new SynchContextClass();
    Console.WriteLine();
}
```

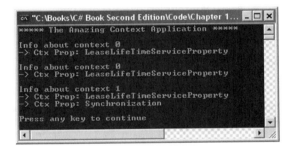

Figure 10-10. Investigating an object's context

Given that the NoSpecialContextClass and NoSpecialContextClass2 types have not been qualified with a specific context attribute, the CLR will have both loaded into context 0 (i.e., the default context). However, the SynchContextClass type is loaded into a unique contextual boundary within the current application domain, given the fact that this context-bound type was adorned with the [Synchronization] attribute.

 SOURCE CODE   The ContextManipulator project is included under the Chapter 10 subdirectory.

Summarizing Processes, AppDomains, and Context

So then, at this point in the game you have seen how the .NET runtime has altered the composition of a traditional Win32 process to function within the common language runtime (CLR). To summarize the key points, remember the following:

- A .NET process hosts one to many application domains. Each AppDomain is able to host any number of related .NET assemblies, and may be independently loaded and unloaded by the CLR (or programmatically via the System.AppDomain type).

- A given AppDomain consists of one to many contexts. Using a context, the CLR is able to group special needs objects into a logical container, to ensure that their runtime requirements are honored.

If the previous pages have seemed to be a bit too low-level for your liking, fear not. For the most part, the .NET runtime automatically deals with the details of processes, application domains, and contexts on your behalf. However, this background discussion has provided a solid foundation regarding how the CLR creates, processes, and destroys specific threads of execution (as well as increased your understanding of some underlying CLR concepts).

The Process/AppDomain/Context/Thread Relationship

As mentioned at the opening of this chapter, a thread is a path of execution within a loaded application. While many .NET applications can live happy and productive single-threaded lives, the primary thread may spawn secondary threads of execution to perform additional units of work. In just a moment, you will be introduced to the System.Threading namespace, which defines numerous types used to create multithreaded .NET applications. First however, we need to check out exactly "where" a thread lives within a .NET process.

The first thing you must understand is that under the .NET platform, there is *not* a direct one-to-one correlation between application domains and threads. In fact, a given AppDomain can have numerous threads executing within it at any given time. Furthermore, a particular thread is not confined to a single application domain during its lifetime. Threads are free to cross application domain boundaries as the thread scheduler and the CLR see fit.

Although active threads can be moved between application boundaries, a given thread can only execute within a single application domain at any point in time (in other words, it is impossible for a single thread to be doing work in more than one AppDomain). If you wish to gain access to the AppDomain that is currently hosting the Thread type, call the static Thread.GetDomain method:

```
// Thread.GetDomain() returns an AppDomain type.
Console.WriteLine(Thread.GetDomain().FriendlyName);
```

A single thread may also be moved into a particular context at any given time, and may be relocated within a new context at the whim of the CLR. If you wish to programmatically discover the current context a thread happens to be executing in, make use of the static Thread.CurrentContext property:

```
// CurrentContext returns a Context type.
Console.WriteLine(Thread.CurrentContext.ContextID);
```

As you would guess, the CLR is the entity that is in charge of moving threads into (and out of) application domains and contexts. As a .NET developer, you are able to remain blissfully unaware where a given thread ends up (or exactly when it is placed into its new boundary). Nevertheless, you should be aware of the underlying model.

The Problem of Concurrency and Thread Synchronization

One of the many joys (read: painful aspects) of multithreaded programming is that you have little control over how the underlying operating system makes use of its threads. For example, if you craft a block of code that creates a new thread of execution, you cannot guarantee that the thread executes immediately. Rather, such code only instructs the OS to execute the thread as soon as possible (which is typically when the thread scheduler gets around to it).

Furthermore, given that threads can be moved between application and contextual boundaries as required by the CLR, you must be mindful of which aspects of your application are *thread-volatile* and which operations are *atomic.* (Thread-volatile operations are the dangerous ones!) For example, assume a given thread is accessing a shared point of data (or type member), and begins to modify its contents. Now assume that this thread is instructed to suspend its activity (by the thread scheduler) to allow another thread to access the same point of data.

If the original thread was not completely finished with its current modification of the type, the second incoming thread may be viewing a partially modified object. At this point, the second thread is basically reading bogus values, which is sure to give way to extremely odd (and very hard to find) bugs (which are even harder to replicate and thus debug).

Atomic operations, on the other hand, are always safe in a multithreaded environment, and yet there are very few operations in .NET that are guaranteed to be atomic. Even a simple assignment statement to a double is not atomic! Unless the .NET Framework documentation specifically says an operation is atomic, you must assume it is thread-volatile and take precautions.

Given this, it should be clear that multithreaded application domains are in themselves quite volatile, as numerous threads can operate on the shared functionality at (more or less) the same time. To protect an application's resources from possible corruption, the .NET developer must make use of any number of threading primitives such as locks, monitors, and the [synchronization] attribute, to control access among the executing threads.

Although the .NET platform cannot make the difficulties of building robust multithreaded applications completely disappear, the process has been simplified considerably. Using types defined within the System.Threading namespace, you are able to spawn additional threads with minimal fuss and bother. Likewise, when it is time to lock down shared points of data, you will find additional types that provide the same functionality as the raw Win32 threading primitives (using a much cleaner object model).

Multithreaded Programming via Delegates

Before checking out the details of programming with threads under the .NET platform, it is worth reiterating that the whole point of creating additional threads is to increase the overall functionality of a given application to the *user*. Recall, however, that many common programming tasks that traditionally required manual creation of threads (e.g., remote method invocations, manipulating IO streams, and so forth) are automated using asynchronous delegates (first examined in Chapter 7).

As you have seen throughout various points in this text (and will see in future chapters), when you invoke a delegate asynchronously, the CLR automatically creates a worker thread to handle the task at hand. However, if you have an application-specific task to account for (such as printing a lengthy document or working with a GUI display), you will be required to manually manipulate threads if you wish to keep your primary thread responsive. This disclaimer aside, allow me to formally introduce the System.Threading namespace.

The System.Threading Namespace

Under the .NET platform, the System.Threading namespace provides a number of types that enable multithreaded programming. In addition to providing types that represent a specific CLR thread, this namespace also defines types that can manage a collection of threads (ThreadPool), a simple (non-GUI based) Timer class, and various types used to provide synchronized access to shared resources. Table 10-6 lists some (but not all) of the core members of this namespace.

Table 10-6. Select Types of the System.Threading Namespace

System.Threading Type	Meaning in Life
Interlocked	Provides atomic operations for objects that are shared by multiple threads.
Monitor	Provides the synchronization of threading objects using locks and wait/signals.
Mutex	Synchronization primitive that can be used for interprocess synchronization.
Thread	Represents a thread that executes within the CLR. Using this type, you are able to spawn additional threads in the originating AppDomain.
ThreadPool	This type manages related threads in a given process.

Table 10-6. Select Types of the System.Threading Namespace (Continued)

System.Threading Type	Meaning in Life
Timer	Provides a mechanism for executing a method at specified intervals.
ThreadStart	Delegate that specifies the method to call for a given Thread.
ThreadState	This enum specifies the valid states a thread may take (Running, Aborted, etc.).
TimerCallback	Delegate type used in conjunction with Timer types.
ThreadPriority	This enum specifies the valid levels of thread priority.

Examining the Thread Class

The most primitive of all types in the System.Threading namespace is Thread. This class represents an object-oriented wrapper around a given path of execution within a particular AppDomain. This type also defines a number of methods (both static and shared) that allow you to create new threads from the scope of the current thread, as well as suspend, stop, and destroy a particular thread. Consider the list of core static members given in Table 10-7.

Table 10-7. Key Static Members of the Thread Type

Thread Static Member	Meaning in Life
CurrentContext	This (read-only) property returns the context the thread is currently running.
CurrentThread	This (read-only) property returns a reference to the currently running thread.
GetDomain() GetDomainID()	Returns a reference to the current AppDomain (or the ID of this domain) in which the current thread is running.
Sleep()	Suspends the current thread for a specified time.

Thread also supports the object level members shown in Table 10-8.

Table 10-8. Select Instance Level Members of the Thread Type

Thread Instance Level Member	Meaning in Life
Abort()	This method instructs the CLR to terminate the thread ASAP.
IsAlive	This property returns a Boolean that indicates if this thread has been started.
IsBackground	Gets or sets a value indicating whether or not this thread is a background thread.
Name	This property allows you to establish a friendly textual name of the thread.
Priority	Gets or Sets the priority of a thread, which may be assigned a value from the ThreadPriority enumeration.
ThreadState	Gets the state of this thread, which may be assigned a value from the ThreadState enumeration.
Interrupt()	Interrupts the current thread.
Join()	Instructs a thread to wait for another thread to complete.
Resume()	Resumes a thread that has been previously suspended.
Start()	Instructs the CLR to execute the thread ASAP.
Suspend()	Suspends the thread. If the thread is already suspended, a call to Suspend() has no effect.

Gathering Basic Thread Statistics

Recall that the entry point of an executable assembly (i.e., the Main() method) runs on the primary thread of execution. To illustrate the basic use of the Thread type, assume you have a new console application named ThreadStats. The static Thread.CurrentThread property retrieves a Thread type that represents the currently executing thread. Thus, if you trigger this member within the scope of Main(), you are able to print out various statistics about the primary thread:

```
using System.Threading;
...
static void Main(string[] args)
{
    // Get some info about the current thread.
    Thread primaryThread = Thread.CurrentThread;
    // Get name of current AppDomain and context ID.
```

```
      Console.WriteLine("***** Primary Thread stats *****");
      Console.WriteLine("Name of current AppDomain: {0}",
          Thread.GetDomain().FriendlyName);
      Console.WriteLine("ID of current Context: {0}",
          Thread.CurrentContext.ContextID);
      Console.WriteLine("Thread Name: {0}", primaryThread.Name);
      Console.WriteLine("Apt state: {0}", primaryThread.ApartmentState);
      Console.WriteLine("Alive: {0}", primaryThread.IsAlive);
      Console.WriteLine("Priority Level: {0}", primaryThread.Priority);
      Console.WriteLine("Thread State: {0}", primaryThread.ThreadState);
      Console.WriteLine();
}
```

Naming Threads

When you run this application, notice how the name of the default thread is currently an empty string. Under .NET, it is possible to assign a human-readable string to a thread using the Name property. Thus, if you wish to be able to programmatically identify the primary thread via the moniker "ThePrimaryThread," you could write the following:

```
// Name the thread.
primaryThread.Name = "ThePrimaryThread";
Console.WriteLine("This thread is called: {0}", primaryThread.Name);
```

.NET Threads and Legacy COM Apartments

Also notice that every Thread type has a property named ApartmentState. Those of you who come from a background in classic COM may already be aware of apartment boundaries. In a nutshell, COM *apartments* were a unit of isolation used to group COM objects with similar threading needs. Under the .NET platform however, apartments are no longer used by managed objects. If you happen to be making use of COM objects from managed code (via the interoperability layer), you are able to establish the apartment settings that should be simulated to handle the coclass in question. To do so, the .NET base class libraries provide two attributes to mimic the single-threaded apartment (STAThreadAttribute, which is added by default to your application's Main() method when using the VS .NET IDE) and multithreaded-apartment (MTAThreadAttribute) of classic COM. In fact, when you create a new *.exe .NET application type, the primary thread is automatically established to function as an STA:

```
// This attribute controls how the primary thread should
// handle COM types.
[STAThread]
static void Main(string[] args)
{
    // COM objects will be placed into an STA.
}
```

If you wish to specify support for the MTA, simply adjust the attribute:

```
[MTAThread]
static void Main(string[] args)
{
    // COM objects will be placed into the MTA.
}
```

Of course, if you don't know (or care) about classic COM objects, you can simply leave the [STAThread] attribute on your Main() method. Doing so will keep any COM types thread-safe without further work on your part. If you don't make use of COM types within the Main() method, the [STAThread] attribute does nothing.

Setting a Thread's Priority Level

As mentioned, we programmers have little control over when the thread scheduler switches between threads. We can, however, mark a given thread with a priority level to offer a hint to the CLR regarding the importance of the thread's activity. By default, all threads have a priority level of normal. However this can be changed at any point in the thread's lifetime using the ThreadPriority property and the related ThreadPriority enumeration:

```
public enum System.Threading.ThreadPriority
{
    AboveNormal, BelowNormal,
    Highest, Lowest,
    Normal,  // Default value.
}
```

Always keep in mind that a thread with the value of ThreadPriority.Highest is not necessarily guaranteed to given the highest precedence. Again, if the thread scheduler is preoccupied with a given task (e.g., synchronizing an object, switching threads, moving threads, or whatnot) the priority level will most likely be altered accordingly. However, all things being equal, the CLR will read these values and instruct the thread scheduler how to best allocate time slices. All things still being equal, threads with an identical thread priority should each receive the same amount of time to perform their work.

NOTE   Again, you will seldom (if ever) need to directly alter a thread's priority level. In theory, it is possible to jack up the priority level on a set of threads, thereby preventing lower priority threads from executing at their required levels (so use caution).

Spawning Secondary Threads

When you wish to create additional threads to carry on some unit of work, you need to interact with the Thread class as well as a special threading-related delegate named ThreadStart. The general process is quite simple. First and foremost, you need to create a function (static or instance-level) to perform the additional work. For example, assume the current SimpleThreadApp project defines the following additional static method, which mimics the work seen in Main():

```
static void MyThreadProc()
{
    Console.WriteLine("***** Secondary Thread stats *****");
    Thread.CurrentThread.Name = "TheSecondaryThread";
    Thread secondaryThread = Thread.CurrentThread;
    Console.WriteLine("Name? {0}", secondaryThread.Name);
    Console.WriteLine("Apt state? {0}", secondaryThread.ApartmentState);
    Console.WriteLine("Alive? {0}", secondaryThread.IsAlive);
    Console.WriteLine("Priority? {0}", secondaryThread.Priority);
    Console.WriteLine("State? {0}", secondaryThread.ThreadState);
    Console.WriteLine();
}
```

NOTE   The target for the ThreadStart delegate cannot take any arguments and must return void.

Now, within Main(), create a new Thread class and specify a new ThreadStart delegate as a constructor parameter (note the lack of parentheses in the constructor when you give the method name). To inform the CLR that this new thread is ready to run, call the Start() method (but always remember that Start() doesn't actually start the thread). Starting a thread is a nondeterministic operation under the total control of the CLR—you can't do *anything* to force the CLR to execute your thread. It will do so on its own time and on its own terms:

```
[STAThread]
static void Main(string[] args)
{
...
    // Start a secondary thread.
    Thread secondaryThread = new Thread(new ThreadStart(MyThreadProc));
    secondaryThread.Start();
}
```

The output is seen in Figure 10-11.

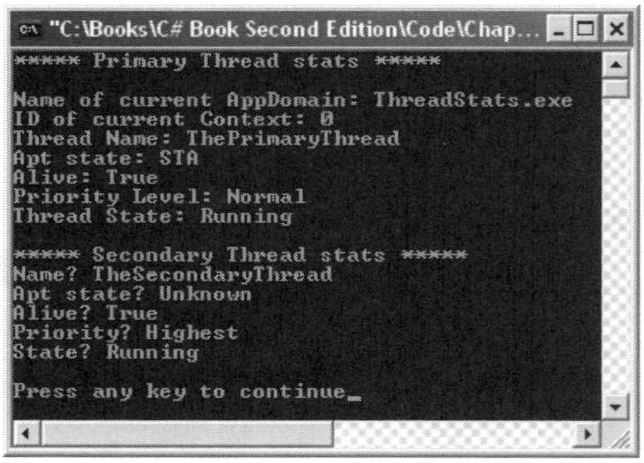

Figure 10-11. Your first multithreaded application

One question that may be on your mind is exactly when a thread terminates. By default, a thread terminates as soon as the function used to create it in the ThreadStart delegate has exited.

Foreground Threads and Background Threads

The CLR assigns a given thread to one of two broad categories:

- *Foreground threads:* Foreground threads have the ability to prevent the current application from terminating. The CLR will not shut down an application (which is to say, unload the hosting AppDomain) until all foreground threads have ended.

- *Background threads:* Background threads (sometimes called *daemon* threads) are viewed by the CLR as expendable paths of execution, which can be ignored at any point in time (even if it is currently laboring over some unit of work). Thus, if all foreground threads have terminated, any and all background threads are automatically killed.

It is important to note that foreground and background threads are *not* synonymous with primary and worker threads. By default, every thread you create via the Thread.Start() method is automatically a *foreground* thread. Again, this means that the AppDomain will not unload until all threads of execution have completed their units of work. In most cases, this is exactly the behavior you require.

For the sake of argument, however, assume that you wish to spawn a secondary thread that should behave as a background thread. Again, this means that the method pointed to by the Thread type (via the ThreadStart delegate) should be able to halt safely as soon as all foreground threads are done with their work. Configuring such a thread is as simple as setting the IsBackground property to true:

```
// Start a new background thread.
Thread secondaryThread = new Thread(new ThreadStart(MyThreadProc));
secondaryThread.Priority = ThreadPriority.Highest;
secondaryThread.IsBackground = true;
```

Now, to illustrate the distinction, assume that the MyThreadProc() method has been updated to print out 1000 lines to the console, pausing for 5 milliseconds between iterations using the Thread.Sleep() method (more on the Thread.Sleep() method later in this chapter):

```
static void MyThreadProc()
{
    ...
    for(int i = 0; i < 1000; i ++)
    {
        Console.WriteLine("Value of i is: {0}", i);
        Thread.Sleep(5);
    }
}
```

If you run the application again, you will find that the for loop is only able to print out a tiny fraction of the values, given that the secondary Thread object has been configured as a background thread. Given that the Main() method has spawned a primary foreground thread, as soon as the secondary thread has been started, it is ready for termination.

Now, you are most likely to simply allow all threads used by a given application to remain configured as foreground threads. If this is the case, all threads must finish their work before the AppDomain is unloaded from the hosting process. Nevertheless, marking a thread as a background type can be helpful when the worker-thread in question is performing noncritical tasks or helper tasks that are no longer needed when the main task of the program is over.

The VS .NET Threads Window

To wrap up our initial investigation of threads, it is worth pointing out that the Visual Studio .NET IDE provides a Threads window, which can be accessed from the Debug | Windows menu item during a debugging session. As you can see from Figure 10-12, this window allows you to view the set of currently executing threads in your .NET assembly.

Figure 10-12. The VS .NET Threads window

SOURCE CODE The ThreadStats project is included under the Chapter 10 subdirectory.

A More Elaborate Threading Example

Now that you have seen the basic process of creating a new thread of execution, we can turn to a more illustrative example. Create a new console application named SimpleMultiThreadApp. Next, define a helper class that supports a public method named DoSomeWork():

```
internal class WorkerClass
{
    public void DoSomeWork()
    {
        // Get hash code for this worker thread.
        Console.WriteLine("ID of worker thread is: {0} ",
            Thread.CurrentThread.GetHashCode());
        // Do the work.
        Console.Write("Worker says: ");
        for(int i = 0; i < 10; i++)
        {
            Console.WriteLine(i + ", ");
        }
        Console.WriteLine();
    }
}
```

Now assume the Main() method creates a new instance of WorkerClass. For the primary thread to continue processing its workflow, create and start a new Thread that is configured to execute the DoSomeWork() method of the WorkerClass type:

```
public class MainClass
{
    public static int Main(string[] args)
    {
        // Get hash code of the current thread.
        Console.WriteLine("ID of primary thread is: {0} ",
            Thread.CurrentThread.GetHashCode());
        // Make worker class.
        WorkerClass w = new WorkerClass();
        // Now make (and start) the worker thread.
        Thread workerThread =
                new Thread(new ThreadStart(w.DoSomeWork));
        workerThread.Start();
        return 0;
    }
}
```

If you run the application you would find each thread has a unique hash code (which is a good thing, as you should have two separate threads at this point).

Clogging Up the Primary Thread

Currently, our application creates a secondary thread to perform a unit of work (in this case, printing 10 numbers). The problem is the fact that printing 10 numbers takes no time at all, and therefore we are not really able to appreciate the fact that the primary thread is free to continue processing. Let's update the application to illustrate this very fact. First, let's tweak the WorkerClass to print out 30,000 numbers, to account for a more labor-intensive process:

```
internal class WorkerClass
{
    public void DoSomeWork()
    {
        ...
        // Do a lot of work.
        Console.Write("Worker says: ");
        for(int i = 0; i < 30000; i++)
        { Console.WriteLine(i + ", "); }
        Console.WriteLine();
    }
}
```

Next, update the MainClass such that it launches a Windows Forms message box directly after it creates the worker thread (don't forget to set a reference to System.Windows.Forms.dll):

```
public class MainClass
{
    public static int Main(string[] args)
    {
        // Create worker thread as before.
        ...

        // Now while worker thread is busy,
        // do some additional work on primary thread.
        MessageBox.Show("I'm buzy");
        return 0;
    }
}
```

If you were to now run the application, you would see that the message box is displayed and can be moved around the desktop while the worker thread is busy pumping numbers to the console (Figure 10-13).

Figure 10-13. Two threads each performing a unit of work

Now, contrast this behavior with what you might find if you had a single-threaded application. Assume the Main() method has been updated with logic that allows the user to enter the number of threads used within the current AppDomain (one or two):

```
public static int Main(string[] args)
{
    Console.Write("Do you want [1] or [2] threads? ");
    string threadCount = Console.ReadLine();
...
    // Make worker class.
    WorkerClass w = new WorkerClass();
    // Only make a new thread if the user said so.
    if(threadCount == "2")
    {
        // Now make the thread.
        Thread workerThread =
            new Thread(new ThreadStart(w.DoSomeWork));
        workerThread.Start();
    }
    else  // Execute this method on the single thread.
        w.DoSomeWork();
    // Do some additional work.
    MessageBox.Show("I'm buzy");
    return 0;
}
```

As you can guess, if the user enters the value "1" he or she must wait for all 30,000 numbers to be printed before seeing the message box appear, given that there is only a single thread in the AppDomain. However, if the user enters "2" he or she is able to interact with the message box while the secondary thread spins right along.

Putting a Thread to Sleep

The static Thread.Sleep() method can be used to currently suspend the current thread for a specified amount of time (specified in milliseconds). In particular, you can use this to pause a program. To illustrate, let's update the WorkerClass again. This time around, the DoSomeWork() method does not print out 30,000 lines to the console, but 10 lines. The trick is, between each call to Console.WriteLine(), this worker thread is put to sleep for approximately 2 seconds.

```
internal class WorkerClass
{
    public void DoSomeWork()
    {
        // Get some information about the worker thread.
        Console.WriteLine("ID of worker thread is: { 0} ",
            Thread.CurrentThread.GetHashCode());
        // Do the work (and take a nap).
        Console.Write("Worker says: ");
        for(int i = 0; i < 10; i++)
        {
            Console.WriteLine(i + ", ");
            Thread.Sleep(2000);
        }
        Console.WriteLine();
    }
}
```

Now run your application a few times and specify both threading options. You will find radically different behaviors based on your choice of thread number.

SOURCE CODE   The SimpleMultiThreadApp project is included under the Chapter 10 subdirectory.

Concurrency Revisited

Given this previous example, you might be thinking that threads are the magic bullet you have been looking for. Simply create threads for each part of your application and the result will be increased application performance to the user. You already know this is a loaded question, as the previous statement is not necessarily true. If not used carefully and thoughtfully, multithreaded programs are slower than single threaded programs.

Even more important is the fact that each and every thread in a given AppDomain has direct access to the shared data of the application. In the current example, this is not a problem. However, imagine what might happen if the primary and secondary threads were both modifying a shared point of data. As you know, the thread scheduler will force threads to suspend their work at random. Since this is the case, what if thread A is kicked out of the way before it has fully completed its work? Again, thread B is now reading unstable data.

To illustrate, let's build another C# console application named MultiThreadSharedData. This application also has a class named WorkerClass, which maintains a private

System.Int32 that is manipulated by the DoSomeWork() helper function. Also notice that this helper function also leverages a for loop to printout the value of this private integer, the iterator's value as well as the name of the current thread. Finally, to simulate additional work, each iteration of this logic places the current thread to sleep for approximately one second. Here is the type in question:

```
internal class WorkerClass
{
    private int theInt;
    public void DoSomeWork()
    {
        theInt++;
        for(int i = 0; i < 5; i++)
        {
            Console.WriteLine("theInt: {0}, i: {1}, current thread: {2}",
                theInt, i, Thread.CurrentThread.Name);
            Thread.Sleep(1000);
        }
    }
}
```

The Main() method is responsible for creating three uniquely named secondary threads of execution, each of which is making calls to the same instance of the WorkerClass type:

```
public class MainClass
{
    public static int Main(string[] args)
    {
        // Make the single worker object.
        WorkerClass w = new WorkerClass();
        // Create and name three secondary threads,
        // each of which makes calls to the same shared object.
        Thread workerThreadA =
            new Thread(new ThreadStart(w.DoSomeWork));
        workerThreadA.Name = "A";
        Thread workerThreadB =
            new Thread(new ThreadStart(w.DoSomeWork));
        workerThreadB.Name = "B";
        Thread workerThreadC =
            new Thread(new ThreadStart(w.DoSomeWork));
        workerThreadC.Name = "C";
        // Now start each one.
        workerThreadA.Start();
        workerThreadB.Start();
        workerThreadC.Start();
        return 0;
    }
}
```

Now before you see some test runs, let's recap the problem. The primary thread within this AppDomain begins life by spawning three secondary worker threads. Each worker thread is told to make calls on the DoSomeWork() method of a single WorkerClass instance. Given that we have taken no precautions to lock down the object's shared resources, there is a good chance that a given thread will be kicked out of the way before the WorkerClass is able to print out the results for the previous thread. Because we don't know exactly when (or if) this might happen, we are bound to get unpredictable results. For example, you might find the output shown in Figure 10-14.

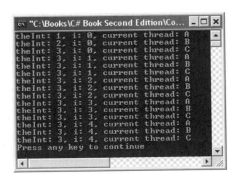

Figure 10-14. Possible output of the MultiThreadSharedData application

Now run the application a few more times. Figure 10-15 shows another possibility (note the ordering among thread names).

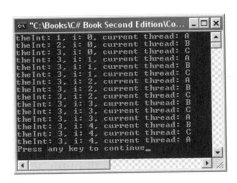

Figure 10-15. Another possible output of the MultiThreadSharedData application

Humm. There are clearly some problems here. As each thread is telling the WorkerClass to "do some work," the thread scheduler is happily swapping threads in the background. The result is inconsistent output. What we need is a way to programmatically enforce synchronized access to the shared resources.

489

As you would guess, the System.Threading namespace provides a number of synchronization-centric types. The C# programming language also provides a particular keyword for the very task of synchronizing shared data in multithreaded applications.

Synchronization Using the C# "lock" Keyword

The first approach to providing synchronized access to our DoSomeWork() method is to make use of the C# "lock" keyword. This intrinsic keyword allows you to lock down a block of code so that incoming threads must wait in line for the current thread to finish up its work completely. The "lock" keyword requires you to pass in a token (an object reference) that must be acquired by a thread to enter within the scope of the lock statement. When you are attempting to lock down an instance level method, you can simply pass in a reference to the current type:

```
internal class WorkerClass
{
    private int theInt;
    public void DoSomeWork()
    {
        lock(this)
        {
            theInt++;
            for(int i = 0; i < 5; i++)
            {
                Console.WriteLine("theInt: {0}, i: {1}, current thread: {2}",
                    theInt, i, Thread.CurrentThread.Name);
                Thread.Sleep(1000);
            }
        } // Lock token released here!
    }
}
```

Now, once a thread enters into a locked block of code, the token (in this case, a reference to the current object) is inaccessible by other threads until the lock is released. Thus, if threadA has obtained the lock token, and threadB or threadC are attempting to enter, they must wait until threadA relinquishes the lock.

NOTE　If you are attempting to lock down code in a static method, you obviously cannot use the "this" keyword. If this is the case, you can simply pass in the System.Type of the current class using the C# "typeof" operator (although any object reference will work).

If you now rerun the application, you can see that the threads are instructed to politely wait in line for the current thread to finish its business (Figure 10-16).

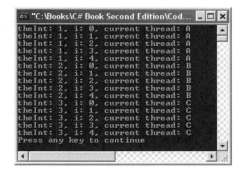

Figure 10-16. Consistent output of the MultiThreadSharedData application

SOURCE CODE The MultiThreadSharedData application is included under the Chapter 10 subdirectory.

Synchronization Using the System.Threading.Monitor Type

The C# lock statement is really just a shorthand notation for working with the System.Threading.Monitor class type. Under the hood, the previous locking logic (via the C# "lock" keyword) actually resolves to the following (which can be verified using ildasm.exe):

```
internal class WorkerClass
{
    private int theInt;
    public void DoSomeWork()
    {
        // Enter the monitor with token.
        Monitor.Enter(this);
        try
        {
            theInt++;
            for(int i = 0; i < 5; i++)
            {
                Console.WriteLine("theInt: {0}, i: {1}, current thread: {2}",
                    theInt, i, Thread.CurrentThread.Name);
                Thread.Sleep(1000);
            }
        }
```

```
        finally
        {
            // Error or not, you must exit the monitor
            // and release the token.
            Monitor.Exit(this);
        }
    }
}
```

If you run the modified application, you will see no changes in the output (which is good). Here, you make use of the static Enter() and Exit() members of the Monitor type, to enter (and leave) a locked block of code. Now, given that the "lock" keyword seems to require less code than making explicit use of the System.Threading.Monitor type, you may wonder about the benefits. The short answer is control.

If you make use of the Monitor type, you are able to instruct the active thread to wait for some duration of time (via the Wait() method), inform waiting threads when the current thread is completed (via the Pulse() and PulseAll() methods), and so on. As you would expect, in a great number of cases, the C# "lock" keyword will fit the bill. If you are interested in checking out additional members of the Monitor class, consult online Help.

Synchronization Using the System.Threading.Interlocked Type

Although it always is hard to believe until you look at the underlying CLR code, assignments and simple arithmetic operations are *not atomic*. For this reason, the System.Threading namespace also provides a type that allows you to operate on a single point of data atomically. The Interlocked class type defines the static members shown in Table 10-9.

Table 10-9. Members of the Interlocked Type

Member of the System.Threading.Interlocked Type	Meaning in Life
Increment()	Safely increments a value by one
Decrement()	Safely decrements a value by one
Exchange()	Safely swaps two values
CompareExchange()	Safely tests two values for equality, and if so, changes one of the values with a third

Although it might not seem like it from the onset, the process of atomically altering a single value is quite common in a multithreaded environment. Thus, rather than writing synchronization code such as the following:

```
int i = 9;
lock(this)
{ i++; }
```

you can simply write:

```
// Pass by reference the value you wish to alter.
int i = 9;
Interlocked.Increment(ref i);
```

Likewise, if you wish to assign the value of a previously assigned System.Int32 to the value 83, you can avoid the need to an explicit lock statement (or Monitor logic) and make use of the Interlocked.Exchange() method:

```
int i = 9;
Interlocked.Exchange(ref i, 83);
```

Finally, if you wish to test two values for equality to change the point of comparison in a thread-safe manner, you would be able to leverage the Interlocked.CompareExchange() method as follows:

```
// If the value of i is currently 83, change i to 99.
Interlocked.CompareExchange(ref i, 99, 83);
```

Synchronization Using the [Synchronization] Attribute

The final synchronization primitive examined here is the [Synchronized] attribute, which, as you recall, is a contextual attribute that can be applied to context-bound objects. When you apply this attribute on a .NET class type, you are effectively locking down *all* members of the object for thread safety:

```
using System.Runtime.Remoting.Contexts;
...
// This context-bound type will only be loaded into a
// synchronized (and hence, thread-safe) context.
[Synchronization]
public class MyThreadSafeObject : ContextBoundObject
{ /* all methods on class are now thread safe */}
```

In some ways, this approach can be seen as the lazy approach to writing thread-safe code, given that we are not required to dive into the details about which aspects of the type are truly manipulating thread-sensitive data. The major downfall of this approach, however, is that even if a given method is not making use of thread-sensitive data, the CLR will *still* lock invocations to the method. Obviously, this could degrade the overall functionality of the type, so use this technique with care.

Thread Safety and the .NET Base Class Libraries

Although this chapter has illustrated how you can build custom thread-safe types, you should also be aware that many of the types of the base class libraries have been pre-programmed to be thread-safe. In fact, when you look up a given type using online Help (such as System.Console) you will find information regarding its level of thread safety (Figure 10-17).

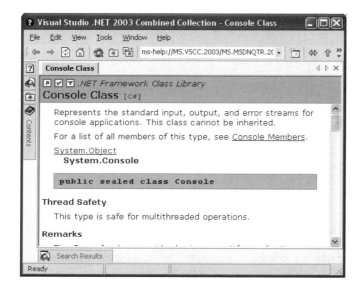

Figure 10-17. Many (but not all) .NET types are already thread-safe .

Sadly, many .NET types in the base class libraries are *not* thread-safe, and therefore, you will have to make use of the various locking techniques you have examined to ensure the object is able to survive multiple requests from the thread base.

Programming with Timer Callbacks

At this point you have seen a number of ways in which you are able to provide synchronized access to shared blocks of data. To be sure, there are additional types under the System.Threading namespace, which I will allow you to explore at your leisure. However, to wrap up our examination of thread programming, allow me to introduce two additional types, TimerCallback and Timer.

Many applications have the need to call a specific method during regular intervals of time. For example, you may have an application that needs to display the current time on a status bar via a given helper function. As another example, you may wish to have your application call a helper function every so often to perform noncritical background tasks such as checking for new e-mail messages. For situations such as these, the System.Threading.Timer type can be used in conjunction with a related delegate named TimerCallback.

To illustrate, assume you have a console application that will print the current time every second until the user hits a key to terminate the application. The first obvious step is to write the method that will be called by the Timer type:

```
class TimePrinter
{
    static void PrintTime(object state)
    {
        Console.WriteLine("Time is: {0}",
            DateTime.Now.ToLongTimeString());
    }
...
}
```

Notice how this method has a single parameter of type System.Object and returns void. This is not optional, given that the TimerCallback delegate can only call methods that match this signature. The value passed into the target of your TimerCallback delegate can be any bit of information whatsoever (in the case of the e-mail example, this parameter might represent the name of the MS Exchange server to interact with during the process). Also note that given that this parameter is indeed a System.Object, you are able to pass in multiple arguments using a System.Array type.

The next step would be to configure an instance of the TimerCallback type and pass it into the Timer object. In addition to a TimerCallback delegate, the Timer constructor also allows you to specify the optional parameter information to pass into the delegate target, the interval to poll the method, as well as the amount of time to wait before making the first call. For example:

```
static void Main(string[] args)
{
    Console.WriteLine("***** Working with Timer type *****\n");
    // Create the delegate for the Timer type.
    TimerCallback timeCB = new TimerCallback(PrintTime);
    // Establish timer settings.
    Timer t = new Timer(
        timeCB,      // The TimerCallback delegate type.
        null,        // Any info to pass into the called method (null for no info).
        0,           // Amount of time to wait before starting.
        1000);       // Interval of time between calls.
    Console.WriteLine("Hit key to terminate...");
    Console.ReadLine();
}
```

In this case, the PrintTime() method will be called roughly every second, and will pass in no additional information to said method. If you did wish to send in some information for use by the delegate target, simply substitute the null value of the second constructor parameter with the appropriate information. For example, ponder the following updates:

```
static void PrintTime(object state)
{
    Console.WriteLine("Time is: {0}, Param is: {1}",
        DateTime.Now.ToLongTimeString(), state.ToString());
}
...
Timer t = new Timer(timeCB, "Hi", 0, 1000);
```

Figure 10-18 shows the output.

```
"C:\Books\C# Book Second Edition\Code\Chapte...
***** Working with Timer type *****

Hit key to terminate...
Time is: 12:40:51 AM, Param is: Hi
Time is: 12:40:52 AM, Param is: Hi
Time is: 12:40:53 AM, Param is: Hi
Time is: 12:40:54 AM, Param is: Hi
Time is: 12:40:55 AM, Param is: Hi
Time is: 12:40:56 AM, Param is: Hi

Press any key to continue
```

Figure 10-18. The (very useful) console-based clock application

---

SOURCE CODE   The TimerApp application is included under the Chapter 10 subdirectory.

That wraps up our examination of multithreaded programming under .NET. To be sure, the System.Threading namespace defines numerous types beyond what I had the space to examine in this chapter. Nevertheless, at this point you should have a solid foundation to build on.

Summary

The point of this chapter was to expose the internal composition of a .NET executable image. As you have seen, the long-standing notion of a Win32 process has been altered under the hood to accommodate the needs of the CLR. A single process (which can be programmatically manipulated via the System.Diagnostics.Process type) is now composed on multiple application domains, which represent isolated and independent boundaries within a process. As you recall, a single process can host multiple application domains, each of which is capable of hosting and executing any number of related assemblies. Furthermore, a single application domain can contain any number of contextual boundaries. Using this additional level of type isolation, the CLR can ensure that special-need objects are handled correctly.

The remainder of this chapter examined the role of the System.Threading namespace. As you have seen, when an application creates additional threads of execution, the result is that the program in question is able to carry out numerous tasks at (what appears to be) the same time. Finally, the chapter examined various manners in which you can mark thread-sensitive blocks of code to ensure that shared resources do not become unusable units of bogus data.

CHAPTER 11

Type Reflection, Late Binding, and Attribute-Based Programming

As YOU HAVE SEEN, assemblies are the basic unit of deployment in the .NET universe. Tools such as Visual Studio .NET have integrated Object Browsers that allow you to examine the internal types of referenced assemblies (as well as the assembly you happen to be building). Furthermore, external tools such as ildasm.exe allow us to peek into the underlying CIL code, type metadata, and assembly manifest. In addition to this design-time investigation of .NET assemblies, you are also able to *programmatically* obtain this same information using the types defined within the System.Reflection namespace.

The remainder of the chapter examines a number of closely related topics. For example, you learn how a .NET client may employ late binding to activate and manipulate a given type, as well as how to insert custom metadata into your .NET assemblies through the use of system-supplied and custom attributes. Finally, to pull together all of the topics presented in this chapter, you learn how to build custom snap-in utilities that can be plugged into an extendable application.

The Necessity of Type Metadata

The ability to fully qualify the definition of types using metadata is a key element of the .NET runtime. Numerous .NET technologies such as serialization, remoting, and XML Web services (among other things) all hinge on the ability to discover the format of types at runtime. Furthermore, as you have already seen in the previous chapters, cross-language interoperability, compiler support, and an IDE's IntelliSense capabilities all rely on a concrete description of *type*. As mentioned numerous times thus far, a .NET type is any member from the set {class, interface, structure, enumeration, delegate}. .NET metadata is the vehicle used to describe the internal composition of said members.

Regardless of (or perhaps due to) its importance, metadata is not a new idea supplied by the .NET Framework. Java, CORBA, and COM all have similar concepts. For example, under COM, IDL (Interface Definition Language) is used to describe the internal COM types found within a given COM server. Like COM, .NET code libraries also support type metadata. Understand, of course, that the .NET type metadata does not have the same syntax as COM IDL! Rather, type metadata is internally documented as a more tabular (i.e., indexed) format.

As you are already aware, using ildasm.exe, you are able to view an assembly's type metadata using the "Ctrl+M" keyboard option (see Chapter 1). Thus, if you were to open any of the *.dll or *.exe assemblies created over the course of this book (such as CarLibrary.dll) using ildasm.exe and hit Ctrl+M, you would find the relevant metadata visible for viewing (Figure 11-1).

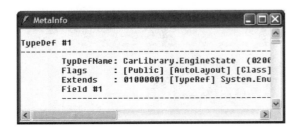

Figure 11-1. Viewing an assembly's metadata

As you can see, .NET type metadata is very verbose (for good reason) when contrasted to COM IDL. Using this assembly-embedded metadata, the .NET runtime is able to locate and load a given type for a calling client as well as obtain a complete description of each item. In fact, if I were to list the entire set of metadata generated for the CarLibrary.dll assembly, it would span several pages. Given that this act would be a woeful waste of your time (and paper), let's just glimpse into some key types of the CarLibrary.dll assembly.

Viewing (Partial) Metadata for the EngineState Enumeration

First, understand that each type contained within an assembly is documented using a "TypeDef #*n*" token (where TypeDef is short for *type definition*). If the type being described uses a type defined within a separate .NET assembly, the referenced type is documented using the "TypeRef #*n*" token (where TypeRef is short for *type reference*). A "TypeRef" token is a pointer (if you will) to the referenced type's full metadata definition. In a nutshell, .NET metadata is a set of tables that clearly mark all internal type definitions (TypeDefs) and referenced entities (TypeRefs), all of which can be viewed using ildasm.exe's metadata window.

As far as CarLibrary.dll goes, the first TypeDef we encounter (assuming that the CarLibrary.EngineState enumeration is the first type encountered by the C# compiler) is the following metadata description:

```
TypeDef #1
-------------------------------------------------------
    TypDefName: CarLibrary.EngineState  (02000002)
    Flags     : [Public] [AutoLayout] [Class] [Sealed] [AnsiClass]  (00000101)
    Extends   : 01000001 [TypeRef] System.Enum
...
```

```
Field #2
---------------------------------------------------------
Field Name: engineAlive (04000002)
Flags      : [Public] [Static] [Literal] [HasDefault]  (00008056)
DefltValue: (I4) 0
CallCnvntn: [FIELD]
Field type:  ValueClass CarLibrary.EngineState
...
```

Here, the "TypDefName" token is used to establish the name of the given type. The "Extends" metadata token is used to document the base class of a given .NET type (in this case, the referenced type, System.Enum). Each field of an enumeration is marked using the "Field #*n*" token. For brevity, I have simply listed the metadata for EngineState.engineAlive.

Viewing (Partial) Metadata for the Car Type

Each of our automobiles is also completely documented using the .NET metadata format. As you may expect, the complete metadata dump for a given type would be pages worth of data. To hit the highlights, here is a partial dump of the Car type that illustrates (a) how fields are defined in terms of .NET metadata, (b) how methods are documented via .NET metadata, and (c) how a single type property is mapped to two discrete member functions:

```
TypeDef #3
---------------------------------------------------------
    TypDefName: CarLibrary.Car  (02000004)
    Flags      : [Public] [AutoLayout] [Class] [Abstract] [AnsiClass]  (00100081)
    Extends    : 01000002 [TypeRef] System.Object
    Field #1
    ---------------------------------------------------------
        Field Name: petName (04000008)
        Flags      : [Family]  (00000004)
        CallCnvntn: [FIELD]
        Field type:  String
...
    Method #1
    ---------------------------------------------------------
        MethodName: .ctor (06000001)
        Flags      : [Public] [HideBySig] [ReuseSlot] [SpecialName]
        [RTSpecialName] [.ctor]  (00001886)
        RVA        : 0x00002050
        ImplFlags : [IL] [Managed]  (00000000)
        CallCnvntn: [DEFAULT]
        hasThis
        ReturnType: Void
        No arguments.
...
```

```
Property #1
-------------------------------------------------------
        Prop.Name : PetName (17000001)
        Flags     : [none] (00000000)
        CallCnvntn: [PROPERTY]
        hasThis
        ReturnType: String
        No arguments.
        DefltValue:
        Setter    : (06000004) set_PetName
        Getter    : (06000003) get_PetName
        0 Others
...
```

First, note that the Car class metadata marks the type's base class, and includes various flags that describe how this type was constructed (e.g., [public], [abstract], and whatnot). Methods (such as our Car's constructor) are described in regard to their parameters, return value, and name. Finally, note how properties are mapped to their internal getter and setter methods using the .NET metadata "Setter"/"Getter" tokens. As you would expect, the derived Car types (SportsCar and MiniVan) are described in a similar manner.

Examining a TypeRef

Recall that an assembly's metadata will not only describe the set of internal types (Car, EngineState, etc) but each external type referenced by the types themselves. For example, given that CarLibrary.dll has defined two enumerations, we find a TypeRef block for the System.Enum type:

```
TypeRef #1 (01000001)
-------------------------------------------------------
Token:              0x01000001
ResolutionScope:    0x23000001
TypeRefName:        System.Enum
      MemberRef #1
      -------------------------------------------------------
      Member: (0a00000f) ToString:
      CallCnvntn: [DEFAULT]
      hasThis
      ReturnType: String
        No arguments.
```

Documenting the Defining Assembly

The ildasm.exe metadata window also allows you to view the .NET metadata that describes the assembly itself using the "Assembly" token. As you can see from this (partial) listing, information documented within the Assembly table is (surprise, surprise) the same information that can be viewed via the MANIFEST icon:

```
Assembly
-------------------------------------------------------
      Token: 0x20000001
      Name : CarLibrary
      Public Key    :
      Hash Algorithm : 0x00008004
      Major Version: 0x00000001
      Minor Version: 0x00000000
      Build Number: 0x000003d6
      Revision Number: 0x00005da4
      Locale: <null>
      Flags : [SideBySideCompatible]   (00000000)
      CustomAttribute #1 (0c000001)
-------------------------------------------------------
      CustomAttribute Type: 0a000001
      CustomAttributeName:
      System.Reflection.AssemblyKeyNameAttribute ::
      instance void .ctor(class System.String)
      Length: 5
      Value : 01 00 00 00 00
      ctor args: ("")
```

Documenting Referenced Assemblies

In addition to the Assembly token and the set of TypeDef and TypeRef blocks, .NET metadata also makes use of "AssemblyRef #*n*" tokens to document each external assembly. Given that our CarLibrary.dll makes use of the MessageBox type, we find an AssemblyRef for System.Windows.Forms. For example:

```
AssemblyRef #2
-------------------------------------------------------
Token: 0x23000002
Public Key or Token: b7 7a 5c 56 19 34 e0 89
Name: System.Windows.Forms
Major Version: 0x00000001
Minor Version: 0x00000000
Build Number: 0x00000ce4
Revision Number: 0x00000000
Locale: <null>
HashValue Blob:
Flags: [none] (00000000)
```

Documenting String Literals

The final point of interest regarding .NET metadata is the fact that each and every string literal in your code base is documented under the "User Strings" token:

```
User Strings
-------------------------------------------------------
70000001 : (  8) L"Jamming "
70000013 : (13) L"Quiet time..."
7000002f : (14) L"Ramming speed!"
7000004d : (19) L"Faster is better..."
70000075 : (16) L"Time to call AAA"
70000097 : (16) L"Your car is dead"
700000b9 : (  9) L"Be quiet "
700000cd : (  2) L"!!"
```

Now, don't be too concerned with the exact syntax of each and every piece of .NET metadata. The bigger point to absorb is that .NET metadata is very descriptive and lists each internally defined (and externally referenced) type found within a given code base. The next question on your mind may be (in the best-case scenario), "How can I leverage this information" or (in a worse case scenario), "Why do I care?" To address both points of view, allow me to introduce .NET reflection services. Be aware that the pages that follow may be a bit of a head-scratcher until this chapter's endgame. So hang tight.

Understanding Reflection

In the .NET universe, *reflection* is the process of runtime type discovery. Using reflection services, you are able to load an assembly at runtime and discover the same sort of information presented by the ildasm.exe metadata window, using a friendly object model. For example, through reflection, you can obtain a list of all types contained within a given assembly (or *.netmodule), including the methods, fields, properties, and events defined by a given type. You can also dynamically discover the set of interfaces supported by a given class (or structure), the parameters of a method as well as other related details (base class details, namespace information, manifest data, and so forth).

To understand how to use reflection services to read .NET metadata, you need to come to terms with the Type class (defined in the System namespace) as well as a new namespace, System.Reflection. As you will see, the System.Type class contains a number of methods that allow you to extract valuable information about the current type you happen to be observing. The System.Reflection namespace contains numerous related types to facilitate late binding and dynamic loading of assemblies. To begin, let's investigate System.Type in some detail.

The System.Type Class

Many of the items defined within the System.Reflection namespace make use of the abstract System.Type class. This class provides a number of methods that can be used to discover the details behind a given item. The complete set of members is quite expansive; however, Table 11-1 offers a partial snapshot of the members supported by System.Type.

Table 11-1. Select Members of System.Type

Type Member	Meaning in Life
IsAbstract IsArray IsClass IsCOMObject IsEnum IsInterface IsPrimitive IsNestedPublic IsNestedPrivate IsSealed IsValueType	These properties (among others) allow you to discover a number of basic traits about the Type you are referring to (e.g., if it is an abstract method, an array, a nested class, and so forth).
GetConstructors() GetEvents() GetFields() GetInterfaces() GetMethods() GetMembers() GetNestedTypes() GetProperties()	These methods (among others) allow you to obtain an array representing the items (interface, method, property, etc.) you are interested in. Each method returns a related array (e.g., GetFields() returns a FieldInfo array, GetMethods() returns a MethodInfo array, etc.). Be aware that each of these methods has a singular form (e.g., GetMethod(), GetProperty()) that allows you to retrieve a specific item by name, rather than an array of all related items.
FindMembers()	Returns an array of MemberInfo types, based on search criteria.
GetType()	This static method returns a Type instance given a string name.
InvokeMember()	This method allows late binding to a given item.

Obtaining a Type Reference

There are numerous ways you can obtain an instance of the Type class. However, the one thing you cannot do is directly create a Type object using the "new" keyword, as Type is an abstract class. Regarding your first choice, as you recall, System.Object defines a method named GetType() that returns an instance of the Type class:

```
// Extract Type using a valid Foo instance.
Foo theFoo = new Foo();
Type t = theFoo.GetType();
```

In addition to the previous technique, you may also obtain a Type using (of all things) the Type class itself. To do so, call the static GetType() member and specify the textual name of the item you are interested in examining (and optionally, a System.Boolean to indicate case sensitivity):

```
// Get a Type using the static Type.GetType() method.
Type t = null;
t = Type.GetType("Foo");
```

Here, you are able to simply pass in the friendly name of the Type.GetType() method, assuming a type named Foo is within your same assembly. If this were not the case, Type.GetType() would require a string that describes the fully qualified name of the entity you are interested in examining, followed by the friendly name of the assembly containing the type (each of which is separated by a comma). Furthermore, the string passed into Type.GetType() may specify the plus token (+) to signify a nested type definition. Given this information, ponder the following type request:

```
// Get a nested type in a distinct assembly.
Type t =
    Type.GetType("MyNamespace.OuterType+NestedType, myOtherAsm");
```

Finally, you can also obtain an instance of Type using the C# typeof() operator:

```
// Get the Type using typeof.
Type t = typeof(Foo);
```

Notice that Type.GetType() and typeof() are helpful in that you do not need to first create an object instance to extract type information (which is obviously quite helpful when employing late binding), whereas the use of the inherited System.Object.GetType() method does. In any case, now that you understand how to obtain a Type reference, let's examine how you can exercise it.

Fun with the Type Class

To illustrate the usefulness of System.Type, assume you have a class named Foo that has been defined as follows (the implementation of the various methods is irrelevant for this example):

```
// These are the items we will discover at runtime.
namespace TheType
{
    // Two interfaces.
    public interface IFaceOne
    {   void MethodA(); }
    public interface IFaceTwo
    {   void MethodB(); }
    // Foo supports these 2 interfaces.
    public class Foo: IFaceOne, IFaceTwo
    {
        // Fields.
        public int myIntField;
        public string myStringField;
        // A method.
        public void myMethod(int p1, string p2){...}
        // A property.
        public int MyProp
        {
            get {  return myIntField; }
            set {  myIntField = value; }
        }
    }
```

```
            // IFaceOne and IFaceTwo methods.
            public void MethodA() {...}
            public void MethodB() {...}
        }
    }
```

Now, let's create a program that is able to discover the methods, properties, supported interfaces, and fields for a given Foo object (in addition to some other points of interest). The FooReader class defines a number of static methods that look more or less identical. First you have ListMethods(), which extracts each method from Foo using a Type object. Notice how Type.GetMethods() returns an array of MethodInfo types:

```
// Suck out all method names from Foo.
public static void ListMethods(Foo f)
{
    Console.WriteLine("***** Methods of Foo *****");
    Type t = f.GetType();
    MethodInfo[] mi = t.GetMethods();
    foreach(MethodInfo m in mi)
        Console.WriteLine("Method: {0} ", m.Name);
    Console.WriteLine("***********************\n");
}
```

The implementation of ListFields() is similar. The only notable difference is the call to Type.GetFields() and the resulting FieldInfo array:

```
// Suck out all fields from Foo.
public static void ListFields(Foo f)
{
    Console.WriteLine("***** Fields of Foo *****");
    Type t = f.GetType();
    FieldInfo[] fi = t.GetFields();
    foreach(FieldInfo field in fi)
        Console.WriteLine("Field: {0} ", field.Name);
    Console.WriteLine("***********************\n");
}
```

The ListVariousStats(), ListProps(), and ListInterfaces() methods should be self-explanatory at this point:

```
// Suck out some interesting statistics about Foo.
public static void ListVariousStats(Foo f)
{
    Console.WriteLine("***** Various stats about Foo *****");
    Type t = f.GetType();
    Console.WriteLine("Full name is: {0} ", t.FullName);
    Console.WriteLine("Base is: {0} ", t.BaseType);
    Console.WriteLine("Is it abstract? {0} ", t.IsAbstract);
    Console.WriteLine("Is it a COM object? {0} ", t.IsCOMObject);
    Console.WriteLine("Is it sealed? {0} ", t.IsSealed);
    Console.WriteLine("Is it a class? {0} ", t.IsClass);
    Console.WriteLine("********************************\n");
}
```

```
// Gather all properties.
public static void ListProps(Foo f)
{
    Console.WriteLine("***** Properties of Foo *****");
    Type t = f.GetType();
    PropertyInfo[] pi = t.GetProperties();
    foreach(PropertyInfo prop in pi)
        Console.WriteLine("Prop: {0} ", prop.Name);
    Console.WriteLine("***************************\n");
}
// Dump all interfaces supported by Foo.
public static void ListInterfaces(Foo f)
{
    Console.WriteLine("***** Interfaces of Foo *****");
    Type t = f.GetType();
    Type[] ifaces = t.GetInterfaces();
    foreach(Type i in ifaces)
        Console.WriteLine("Interface: {0} ", i.Name);
    Console.WriteLine("***************************\n");
}
```

The Main() method of the FooReader class simply calls each static method:

```
// Put Foo under the magnifying glass.
using System;
// Needed to gain definitions of MethodInfo, FieldInfo, etc.
using System.Reflection;
namespace TheType
{
    public class FooReader
    {
        // ...Static methods seen previously...
        public static int Main(string[] args)
        {
            // Make a new Foo object.
            Foo theFoo = new Foo();
            // Now examine everything.
            ListVariousStats(theFoo);
            ListMethods(theFoo);
            ListFields(theFoo);
            ListProps(theFoo);
            ListInterfaces(theFoo);
            return 0;
        }
    }
}
```

Here, I made use of Object.GetType() to gather information about the Foo class defined in the current namespace. Now assume you wish to obtain metadata information for a nested enumeration of the Foo type:

```
// Foo now supports a nested enum.
public class Foo: IFaceOne, IFaceTwo
{
    public enum MyNestedEnum{}
    ...
}
```

Recall that nested items can be identified using the "+" token. Thus, to obtain metadata information for MyNestedEnum, you could write the following:

```
// Get info on nested enum.
Type t = Type.GetType("TheType.Foo+MyNestedEnum");
Console.WriteLine("Enum name? {0}", t.Name);
Console.WriteLine("Is enum nested private? {0}", t.IsNestedPrivate);
Console.WriteLine("Is enum nested public? {0}", t.IsNestedPublic);
```

Obviously, System.Type provides additional members beyond the items seen thus far. One especially interesting member is named GetInterfaceMap(). Recall that explicit interface implementation allows you to map a given interface method to a particular class method. GetInterfaceMap() can be used to obtain these relationships at runtime. To illustrate, update the Foo type to make use of explicit interface implementation:

```
// Use explicit interface impl.
public class Foo: IFaceOne, IFaceTwo
{
    void IFaceOne.MethodA(){}
    void IFaceTwo.MethodB(){}
    ...
}
```

Now, create the following additional helper method:

```
public static void MapInterfaceMethodsToClassMethods(Foo f)
{
  Console.WriteLine("***** Explicit interface impl mappings *****");
  Type t = f.GetType();
  // Get all interfaces on type.
  Type[] iFaces = t.GetInterfaces();
  // Do the following for each interface on type.
  for(int i = 0; i < iFaces.Length; i ++)
  {
    Console.WriteLine("Info on Interface named: {0}", iFaces[i]);
    // Get method infos for name of method on the class.
    MethodInfo[] classMethodNames = t.GetInterfaceMap(iFaces[i]).TargetMethods;
    MethodInfo[] interfaceMethodNames =
      t.GetInterfaceMap(iFaces[i]).InterfaceMethods;
```

```
            for(int j = 0; j < classMethodNames.Length; j++)
            {
                Console.WriteLine("Interface method: {0}",
                    interfaceMethodNames[j].Name);
                Console.WriteLine("is implemented by class method: {0}",
                    classMethodNames[j].Name);
            }
            Console.WriteLine();
        }
    }
}
```

This example is a bit more involved. First, we obtain a list of each interface supported by the Foo type using GetInterfaces(), which is held in a System.Type array. Next, we loop through each member in the array and extract an array of MethodInfo types to represent the names class methods, and another MethodInfo array representing the names of the interface methods. Once we have all the necessary information, we simply print out the association to the console window. Figure 11-2 shows partial output of your first reflection application.

Figure 11-2. Reflecting on Foo

Interesting stuff, huh? While the System.Type class can be very helpful on its own, reflection becomes even more powerful when you make use of the Assembly class defined within the System.Reflection namespace.

SOURCE CODE   The TheType project can be found under the Chapter 11 subdirectory.

Investigating the System.Reflection Namespace

Like any namespace, System.Reflection contains a number of related types. Like any namespace, some types are of more immediate interest than others. Table 11-2 lists some of the core items you should be familiar with, many of which you have already seen in the previous Foo example.

Table 11-2. A Sampling of Members of the System.Reflection Namespace

System.Reflection Type	Meaning in Life
Assembly	This class (in addition to numerous related types) contains a number of methods that allow you to load, investigate, and manipulate an assembly.
AssemblyName	This class allows you to discover numerous details behind an assembly's identity (version information, culture information, and so forth).
EventInfo	Holds information for a given event.
FieldInfo	Holds information for a given field.
MemberInfo	This is the abstract base class that defines common behaviors for the EventInfo, FieldInfo, MethodInfo, and PropertyInfo types.
MethodInfo	Contains information for a given method.
Module	Allows you to access a given module within a multifile assembly.
ParameterInfo	Holds information for a given parameter.
PropertyInfo	Holds information for a given property.

Reflecting on a Private Assembly

The real workhorse of System.Reflection is the Assembly class. Using this type, you are able to dynamically load an assembly, invoke class members at runtime (late binding), as well as discover properties about the assembly itself. The first step to investigating the contents of a .NET binary is to load the assembly in memory. Assume you have a new console project named CarReflector, which has set a reference to the CarLibrary assembly created in Chapter 9. The static Assembly.Load() method can now be called by passing in the friendly string name:

```
using System;
using System.Reflection;
using System.IO;  // Needed for FileNotFoundException definition.
// Investigate the CarLibrary assembly.
namespace CarReflector
{
    public class CarReflector
    {
        public static int Main(string[] args)
        {
            // Use Assembly class to load the CarLibrary.
            Assembly a = null;
            try
            {
                a = Assembly.Load("CarLibrary");
            }
            catch(FileNotFoundException e)
            { Console.WriteLine(e.Message);}
            return 0;
        }
    }
}
```

Notice that the static Assembly.Load() method has been passed in the friendly name of the assembly we are interested in loading into memory (and thus assumes that the CarLibrary.dll is contained within the application directory of the executable). As you may suspect, this method has been overloaded a number of times to provide a number of ways in which you can bind to an assembly. One variation to be aware of is that the textual information sent into Assembly.Load() may contain additional string segments beyond the friendly name. Specifically, you may choose to specify a version number, culture value (for localized assemblies) and public key token value (for shared assemblies).

Collectively speaking, the set of items identifying an assembly is termed the "display name." The format of a display name is a comma-delimited string of name/value pairs that begins with the friendly name of the assembly, followed by optional qualifiers (that may appear in any order). Here is the template to follow (optional items have been placed in parentheses):

```
Name (,Culture = culture token) (,Version = major.minor.build.revision)
(,PublicKeyToken= public key token)
```

When crafting a display name, the convention PublicKeyToken=null, indicates that binding and matching against a non-strongly-named assembly is required. Additionally, the convention Culture= "" indicates matching against the default culture of the target machine. To illustrate:

```
// A fully specified AssemblyName for simply named assembly with default culture.
a = Assembly.Load(
  @"CarLibrary, Version=1.0.982.23972, PublicKeyToken=null, Culture=""");
```

Also be aware that the System.Reflection namespace supplies the AssemblyName type, which allows you to represent the above string information in a handy object variable. Typically, this class is used in conjunction with System.Version, which is an OO wrapper round an assembly's version number. Once you have established the display name, it can then be passed into the overloaded Assembly.Load() method:

```
// Our OO-Aware display name.
AssemblyName asmName;
asmName = new AssemblyName();
asmName.Name = "CarLibrary";
Version v = new Version("1.0.982.23972");
asmName.Version = v;
a = Assembly.Load(asmName);
```

NOTE The Assembly type also defines a static LoadFrom() method that allows you to load an assembly using a given code base (for example, C:\MyAsms).

Enumerating Types in a Referenced Assembly

Now that you have a reference to the CarLibrary assembly, you can discover the name of each type it contains using the static Assembly.GetTypes() method. Here is a helper method named ListAllTypes() that does this very thing (assume this method is called within Main() after loading the CarLibrary.dll):

```
// List all types within the assembly.
private static void ListAllTypes(Assembly a)
{
    Console.WriteLine("***** Types in Assembly *****");
    Console.WriteLine("->{0}\n", a.FullName);
    Type[] types = a.GetTypes();
    foreach(Type t in types)
        Console.WriteLine("Type: {0}", t);
    Console.WriteLine("****************************\n");
}
```

Enumerating Class Members

Let's now assume you are interested in discovering the full set of members supported by one of our automobiles. To do so, you can make use of the GetMembers() method defined by the Type class. As you recall, the Type class also defines a number of related methods (GetInterfaces(), GetProperties(), GetMethods(), and so forth) that allow you to request a specific kind of member. GetMembers() returns an array of MemberInfo types.

Here is an example that lists the type and signature of each method defined by the MiniVan:

```
// Another static method of the CarReflector class.
private static void ListAllMembers(Assembly a)
{
    Console.WriteLine("***** Members of MiniVan *****");
    Type miniVan = a.GetType("CarLibrary.MiniVan");
    MemberInfo[] mi = miniVan.GetMembers();
    foreach(MemberInfo m in mi)
        Console.WriteLine("{0}: {1} ",
            m.MemberType.ToString(), m);
    Console.WriteLine("*****************************\n");
}
```

Enumerating Method Parameters

Not only can you use reflection to gather information for the members of a type, you can also obtain information about the parameters of a given member. To illustrate, let's assume that the Car class has defined the following additional method:

```
// A new member of the Car class.
public void TurnOnRadio(bool state, MusicMedia mm)
{
    if(state)
        MessageBox.Show("Jamming with {0} ", mm.ToString());
    else
        MessageBox.Show("Quiet time...");
}
```

TurnOnRadio() takes two parameters, the second of which is a custom enumeration:

```
// Holds source of music.
public enum MusicMedia
{ musicCD, musicTape, musicRadio }
```

Extracting information for the parameters of TurnOnRadio() requires using MethodInfo.GetParameters(). This method returns a ParameterInfo array. Each item in this array contains numerous properties for a given parameter. Here is another static method of the CarReflector class, GetParams(), which displays various details for each parameter of the TurnOnRadio() method (see Figure 11-3 for partial output):

```
// Get parameter information for the TurnOnRadio() method.
private static void GetParams(Assembly a)
{
    Console.WriteLine("***** Here are the params for TurnOnRadio() *****");
    // Get a MethodInfo type.
    Type miniVan = a.GetType("CarLibrary.MiniVan");
    MethodInfo mi = miniVan.GetMethod("TurnOnRadio");
    // Show number of params.
    Console.WriteLine("Here are the params for {0} ", mi.Name);
    ParameterInfo[] myParams = mi.GetParameters();
    Console.WriteLine("Method has {0} params", myParams.Length);
    // Show some info for param.
    foreach(ParameterInfo pi in myParams)
    {
        Console.WriteLine("Param name: {0} ", pi.Name);
        Console.WriteLine("Position in method: {0} ", pi.Position);
        Console.WriteLine("Param type: {0} ", pi.ParameterType);
    }
    Console.WriteLine("*****************************\n");
}
```

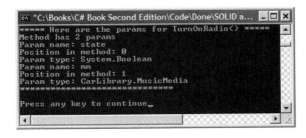

Figure 11-3. Reflecting on a private assembly

SOURCE CODE   The CarReflector project is included in the Chapter 11 subdirectory.

Reflecting on Shared Assemblies

The Assembly type can also be used to load a shared assembly (i.e., a GAC deployed .NET binary). To do so, your Load() method must specify a full display name for the assembly to be loaded. Assume you wish to load version 1.0.0.0 of the SharedAssembly.dll you created in Chapter 9. The following code prints out various statistics of this binary and then lists the names of each type (be sure to update the value of publickeytoken to use your own!):

```
namespace SharedAsmReflector
{
    public class SharedAsmReflector
    {
        private static void DisplayInfo(Assembly a)
        {
            Console.WriteLine("***** Info about Assembly *****");
            Console.WriteLine("Loaded from GAC? {0}", a.GlobalAssemblyCache);
            Console.WriteLine("Asm Name: {0}", a.GetName().Name);
            Console.WriteLine("Asm Version: {0}", a.GetName().Version);
            Console.WriteLine("Asm Culture: {0}",
                a.GetName().CultureInfo.DisplayName);
            Type[] types = a.GetTypes();
            foreach(Type t in types)
                Console.WriteLine("Type: {0}", t);
            Console.WriteLine("*****************************\n");
        }
        public static int Main(string[] args)
        {
            // Load from GAC (without error checking...)
            // Adjust your publickeytoken value!
            Assembly a = null;
            string displayName = "SharedAssembly," +
                "Version=1.0.0.0," +
                "PublicKeyToken=82fbc820d160f2b8," +
                @"Culture="""";
            a = Assembly.Load(displayName);
            DisplayInfo(a);
            return 0;
        }
    }
}
```

Of course, you may load any item installed in the GAC using a full display name, including standard .NET binaries. For example, to load System.Drawing.Design.dll from the GAC, you simply update the display name as follows (your version may differ):

```
// Load System.Drawing.Design.dll from GAC.
displayName = null;
displayName = "System.Drawing.Design," +
    "Version=1.0.5000.0," +
    "PublicKeyToken=b03f5f7f11d50a3a," +
    @"Culture=""";
a = Assembly.Load(displayName);
```

SOURCE CODE   The SharedAsmReflector project is included in the Chapter 11 subdirectory.

Sweet! At this point you understand how to use some of the core items defined within the System.Reflection namespace to discover a wealth of information at runtime. And, maybe you are already envisioning the code behind tools such as ildasm.exe and wincv.exe. Next up, let's check out how to create and interact with types on the fly via .NET late binding.

Understanding Dynamic Invocation (Late Binding)

The System.Reflection namespace provides additional functionality beyond runtime type discovery. .NET reflection services also provides the ability to exercise "late binding" to a type. Simply put, late binding is a technique in which you are able create a given type and invoke its members at runtime without having compile-time knowledge of its existence. Therefore, when you are building an application that binds late to a type in a given assembly, you have no reason to set a reference to the type (and therefore, the caller's manifest has no direct listing of the binary). Do be aware, however, that the CLR will still follow the same search heuristics when searching for the location of the dynamically referenced type (code bases, public key tokens, XML configuration files, and the like).

The value of late binding may not be immediately understood. It is true that if you can "bind early" to a type (e.g., set an assembly reference and use the C# "new" keyword) you should opt to do so. Early binding allows you to determine errors at compile time, rather than runtime. Nevertheless, late binding does have a place among tool builders, as well as COM/.NET interoperability. For example, using late binding, a .NET programmer is able to obtain a COM object's IDispatch reference. Let's examine how to dynamically invoke a method on the MiniVan class.

The Activator Class

The System.Activator class is the key to .NET late binding. Beyond the methods inherited from Object, Activator only defines a small set of members. Activator.CreateInstance() is one core method that creates an instance of a type at runtime. This method has been overloaded numerous times to provide a good deal of flexibility. The simplest variation of the CreateInstance() member takes a valid Type variable that describes the entity you wish to invoke:

```
// Create a type dynamically.
public class LateBind
{
    public static int Main(string[] args)
    {
        // Assume the CarLibrary is in the app directory.
        Assembly a = null;
        try
        { a = Assembly.Load("CarLibrary"); }
        catch(FileNotFoundException e)
        { Console.WriteLine(e.Message);}
        // Specify the fully qualified name of the Minivan type.
        Type miniVan = a.GetType("CarLibrary.MiniVan");
        // Create the Minivan on the fly.
        object obj = Activator.CreateInstance(miniVan);
    }
}
```

At this point, the "obj" variable is pointing to a MiniVan instance in memory that has been created indirectly using the Activator class. Now assume you wish to invoke the TurboBoost() method of the MiniVan. As you recall, this will set the state of the engine to "dead" and display an informational message box.

The first step is to obtain a MethodInfo type for the TurboBoost() method using Type.GetMethod(). From a MethodInfo type, you are then able to call the method it describes using Invoke(). MethodInfo.Invoke() requires you to send in all parameters that are to be given to the method represented by MethodInfo. These parameters are represented by an array of System.Object types (as the parameters for a given method could be any number of various entities). Given that TurboBoost() does not require any parameters, you can simply pass "null" (meaning "this method has no parameters"):

```
public static int Main(string[] args)
{
    // Use Assembly class to load the CarLibrary.
    ...
    // Get the MiniVan type.
    Type miniVan = a.GetType("CarLibrary.MiniVan");
    // Create the MiniVan on the fly.
    object obj = Activator.CreateInstance(miniVan);
```

```
    // Get info for TurboBoost.
    MethodInfo mi = miniVan.GetMethod("TurboBoost");
    // Invoke method ('null' for no parameters).
    mi.Invoke(obj, null);
    return 0;
}
```

At this point you are happy to see Figure 11-4.

Figure 11-4. Late bound method invocation

To illustrate invoking a method that does take some number of parameters, assume you added the following new method to the MiniVan type of the CarLibrary.dll assembly:

```
// Quiet down the troops...
public void TellChildToBeQuiet(string kidName, int shameIntensity)
{
    for(int i = 0 ; i < shameIntensity; i++)
        MessageBox.Show("Be quiet {0} !!", kidName);
}
```

TellChildToBeQuiet() takes two parameters. In this case, the array of parameters must be fleshed out as follows:

```
// Now a method with params.
object[] paramArray = new object[2];
paramArray[0] = "Fred";     // Child name.
paramArray[1] = 4;          // Shame Intensity.
mi = miniVan.GetMethod("TellChildToBeQuiet");
mi.Invoke(obj, paramArray);
```

If you run this program, you will see four message boxes popping up, shaming young Fredrick.

At this point you have seen the basic details regarding reflection services and late binding. As I am sure you might be guessing, System.Reflection defines additional functionality, which I will assume you will check out at your leisure.

SOURCE CODE   The LateBinding project is included in the Chapter 11
subdirectory.

Understanding Attributed Programming

The official metalanguage of the component object model (COM) is IDL. As you may
know, IDL is used to describe the set of types defined within a given classic COM
server. To describe these types in completely unambiguous terms, IDL makes use
of "attributes," which are simply IDL keywords placed in square brackets. A given
attribute block always applies to the very next thing. For example, when a COM programmer describes an interface, he or she is required to make use of the [uuid] and
[object] attributes (at minimum). Parameters can be specified using the [in], [out],
[in, out] ,and [out, retval] attributes. Here is an example of a classic COM interface,
making use of various IDL attributes:

```
[object, uuid(4CB8B79A-E991-4AA4-8DB8-DD5D8751407D),
oleautomation]
interface IRememberCOM : IUnknown
{
    [helpstring("If you send me a string, I will change it...")]
    HRESULT TextManipulation([in] BSTR myStr, [out, retval] BSTR* newStr);
} ;
```

Once a COM type has been assigned various attributes, it can be discovered at
runtime programmatically, or at design time using various tools. For example, notice
how the TextManipulation() method has been assigned a [helpstring] attribute, which
is used to document how a given item is to be used. If you examine this COM method
using the Visual Basic 6.0 Object Browser utility, you will see the custom [helpstring] is
automatically extracted and displayed (Figure 11-5).

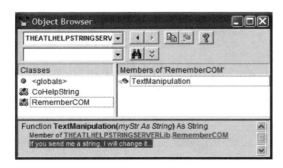

Figure 11-5. Attributes in action

Attributes have proven to be so helpful, that C# (as well as other .NET-aware languages) has integrated them as official aspects of the language. Using attributes, you are able to extend the metadata generated by a given compiler with your custom information.

As you explore the .NET namespaces, you will find that there are many predefined attributes that you are able to make use of in your applications. Furthermore, you are free to build custom attributes to further qualify the behavior of your types. Keep in mind that .NET attributes (predefined or custom) are actually *classes,* all of which extend System.Attribute (contrast this to IDL, in which attributes are nothing more than simple keywords).

Working with Existing Attributes

Like IDL, C# attributes are nothing more than annotations that can be applied to a given type (class, interface, structure, etc.), member (property, method, etc.), assembly, or module. As mentioned, the .NET library defines a number of predefined attributes in various namespaces. Many of the predefined attributes are most useful in the context of COM and .NET interoperability, debugging, and other "exotic" aspects of building managed code. Table 11-3 gives a snapshot of some (but by *absolutely* no means all) predefined attributes.

Table 11-3. A Tiny Sampling of Predefined System Attributes

Predefined .NET Attribute	Meaning in Life
CLSCompliant	Enforces that all types in the assembly conform to the Common Language Specification (CLS). This is the .NET equivalent of the IDL [oleautomation] attribute.
DllImport	Used to make calls to the native OS.
StructLayout	Used to configure the underlying representation of a structure.
Dispid	Specifies the DISPID for a member in a COM dispinterface.
Serializable	Marks a class or structure as being serializable.
NonSerialized	Specifies that a given field in a class or structure is not serializable.
WebMethod	Marks a method as being invokable via HTTP requests.

As an example, assume that you wish to assign the [Serializable] attribute to a given item. The Motorcycle class that follows has assigned an attribute to the class itself, as well as a field named temp. As you can see, C# attributes look very much like IDL attributes, in that they are enclosed within square brackets:

```
// This class can be saved to disk.
[Serializable]
public class Motorcycle
{
    bool hasRadioSystem;
    bool hasHeadSet;
    bool hasSissyBar;
    // But when you do, don't bother with this field.
    [NonSerialized]
    float weightOfCurrentPassengers;
}
```

Using ildasm.exe (Figure 11-6), you can see that these attributes are now specified within the type metadata (note the "serializable" and "notserialized" metadata tags).

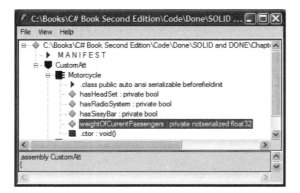

Figure 11-6. Attributes seen via ildasm.exe

Be aware that if you wish to apply more than one attribute to a single type, simply separate each using a comma-delimited list or make use of multiple bracketed attributes stacked on top (or beside) one another:

```
[AttOne, AttTwo, AttThree]
public class SomeClass{...}
...
[AttOne]
[AttTwo] [AttThree]
public class SomeOtherClass{...}
```

Now at this point, don't concern yourself with who or what is on the lookout for the presence of these attributes. Just understand that attributed programming allows you to extend an assembly's metadata with annotations.

Building Custom Attributes

C# (as well as other .NET-aware languages) allows you to build custom attributes. Recall that attributes are in fact a class derived from System.Attribute. Thus, when we applied the [Serializable] attribute to the Motorcycle class, we in fact applied an instance of the System.Serializable type. From a design point of view, an attribute is a class instance that can be applied to some other type. In the world of OOP, this approach is termed *aspect-oriented programming.*

The first step to building your custom attribute is to create a new class deriving from System.Attribute. The naming convention you should follow is to suffix "-Attribute" to the new type. Here is a basic custom attribute named VehicleDescriptionAttribute that allows a programmer to inject a string into the type metadata describing a particular automobile:

```
// A custom attribute.
public class VehicleDescriptionAttribute : System.Attribute
{
    private string description;
    public string Desc
    {
        get { return description; }
        set { description = value; }
    }
    public VehicleDescriptionAttribute(string desc)
    { description = desc;}
    public VehicleDescriptionAttribute(){ }
}
```

As you can see, VehicleDescriptionAttribute maintains a private internal string (description) that can be manipulated using a custom constructor and a named property (Desc). Now assume you wish to apply this attribute to a new class named Winnebago. Notice how the constructor signature determines the exact syntax of the attribute:

```
// This class using a custom attributes.
[VehicleDescriptionAttribute("A very long, slow but feature rich auto")]
public class Winnebago
{
    public Winnebago(){ }
    // Various methods...
}
```

Now, let's see your new type in action. The VehicleDescriptionAttribute attribute (or any attribute) makes use of parentheses to pass arguments to the constructor of the associated System.Attribute-derived class. As you have already seen, one of the constructors does indeed take a string parameter. Now, using ildasm.exe, you find your string message has been injected into the related metadata (Figure 11-7).

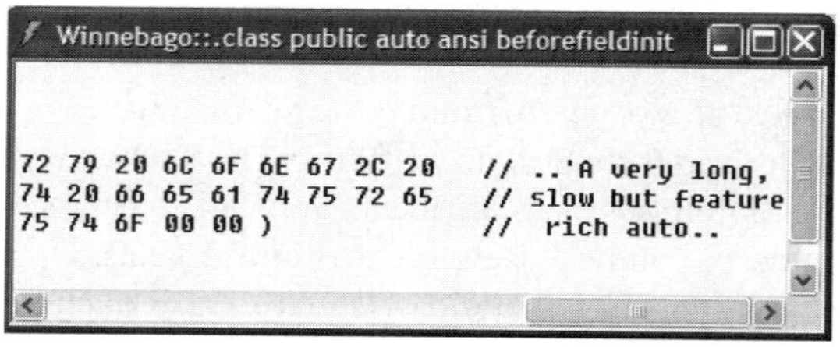

Figure 11-7. Metadata value

If you look at the CIL itself, you notice that custom attributes are marked using the CIL instruction ".custom."

```
.class public auto ansi beforefieldinit Winnebago
    extends [mscorlib]System.Object
{
    .custom instance
    void CustomAtt.VehicleDescriptionAttribute::.ctor(string)
...
} // end of class Winnebago
```

Attribute Shorthand Notation

The C# language does offer a shorthand notation for assigning an attribute to a given item. If the name of your custom attribute class does indeed have a "-Attribute" suffix, you are allowed to omit this same suffix in the code base:

```
// This shortcut only works if the class is named VehicleDescriptionAttribute.
[VehicleDescription("A very long, slow but feature rich auto")]
public class Winnebago
{
    public Winnebago(){ }
    // Various methods...
}
```

Be aware that this is a courtesy provided by C#. Not all .NET-enabled languages support this feature.

Restricting Attribute Usage

Currently, the custom attribute has no mechanism to prevent a developer from making illogical aspect specifications. For example, the following is syntactically correct, but semantically out of whack:

```
// Syntactically OK, but an odd use of this custom attribute...
public class Winnebago
{
    [VehicleDescriptionAttribute]       // Calls default ctor of attribute class.
    public void TurnOnRadio()
    {
    }
}
```

Ideally, it would be nice to enforce the fact that this particular custom attribute should only be allowed to modify a class (and perhaps a structure), but nothing else. If you wish to constrain your attributes in this way, you need to make use of the AttributeTargets enumeration:

```
// This enumeration is used to control how a custom attribute can be applied.
public enum AttributeTargets
{
    All, Assembly, Class, Constructor,
    Delegate, Enum, Event, Field,
    Interface, Method, Module, Parameter,
    Property, ReturnValue, Struct
}
```

These values are passed as a parameter to the AttributeUsage attribute. This predefined attribute is used by the C# compiler to enforce the correct application of a custom attribute. The first parameter is an OR-ing together of members from the AttributeTarget enumeration. The second (optional) parameter is typically a named argument (AllowMultiple), which specifies if the custom attribute can be used more than once on the same type. The final (optional) Boolean parameter determines if the attribute should be inherited by derived classes.

Thus, you can now configure the VehicleDescriptionAttribute to apply only to classes or structures as follows:

```
// This time, we are using the predefined AttributeUsage attribute
// to qualify our custom attribute!
[AttributeUsage(AttributeTargets.Class | AttributeTargets.Struct)]
public class VehicleDescriptionAttribute : System.Attribute
{
...
}
```

With this, if a developer attempted to apply the [VehicleDescription] attribute on anything other than a class or structure, they are issued a compile-time error.

NOTE Always get in the habit of explicitly marking the usage flags for any custom attribute you may create, as not all .NET programming languages honor the use of unqualified attributes!

Assembly- (and Module-) Level Attributes

It is also possible to apply attributes on all types within a given module, or all modules within a given assembly using the [assembly:] and [module:] tags. For example, assume you wish to ensure that every type defined within your assembly is compliant with the CLS.

```
// Enforce CLS compliance!
using System;
[assembly:System.CLSCompliantAttribute(true)]
namespace MyAttributes
{
    [VehicleDescriptionAttribute("A very long, slow but feature rich auto")]
    public class Winnebago
    {
        public Winnebago(){ }
    }
}
```

If we now add a bit of code that falls outside the CLS specification:

```
// Ulong types don't jive with the CLS.
public class Winnebago
{
    public Winnebago(){ }
    public ulong notCompliant;
}
```

you are issued a compiler error. To be sure, if you are building a .NET assembly that is to be used by numerous .NET languages, the [CLSCompliant] attribute is extremely helpful.

 NOTE   The .NET [CLSCompliant] attribute can be applied to any item defined by the AttributeUsage enumeration. Thus, if you only wish to selectively mark specific items as CLS compliant, you may do so.

Notice that the [assembly:] syntax is used to inform the compiler that the CLSCompliant attribute must be applied to the assembly level, and not (for example) a single type within the assembly. One fact to be aware of is that the [assembly:] and [module:] modifiers must be placed *outside* a namespace definition.

Visual Studio .NET AssemblyInfo.cs File

Visual Studio .NET projects define a file called AssemblyInfo.cs. This file is a handy place to put attributes that are to be applied at the assembly level. Table 11-4 lists some assembly-level attributes to be aware of.

Table 11-4 Select Assembly-level Attributes

Assembly-level Attribute	Meaning in Life
AssemblyCompanyAttribute	Holds basic company information.
AssemblyConfigurationAttribute	Build information, such as "retail" or "debug."
AssemblyCopyrightAttribute	Holds any copyright information for the product or assembly.
AssemblyDescriptionAttribute	A friendly description of the product or modules that make up the assembly.
AssemblyInformationalVersionAttribute	Additional or supporting version information, such as a commercial product version number.
AssemblyProductAttribute	Product information.
AssemblyTrademarkAttribute	Trademark information.
AssemblyCultureAttribute	Information on what cultures or languages the assembly supports.
AssemblyKeyFileAttribute	Specifies the name of the file containing the key pair used to sign the assembly (i.e. establish a shared name).
AssemblyKeyNameAttribute	Specifies the name of the key container. Instead of placing a key pair in a file, you can store it in a key container in the CSP. If you choose this option, this attribute will contain the name of the key container.
AssemblyOperatingSystemAttribute	Information on which operating system the assembly was built to support.
AssemblyProcessorAttribute	Information on which processors the assembly was built to support.
AssemblyVersionAttribute	Specifies the assembly's version information, in the format <major.minor.build.revision>.

Reflecting on Attributes at Runtime

As you have seen, it is possible to obtain attributes at runtime using the Type class. The logic behind doing so should be no surprise at this point:

```
// Reflecting on the custom attributes...
public class AttReader
{
    public static int Main(string[] args)
    {
        // Get the Type of Winnebago.
        Type t = typeof(Winnebago);
        // Get all attributes in the assembly.
        object[] customAtts = t.GetCustomAttributes(false);
        // List all info.
        Console.WriteLine("***** Value of VehicleDescriptionAttribute *****\n");
        foreach(VehicleDescriptionAttribute v in customAtts)
            Console.WriteLine("-> {0}\n", v.Desc);
        return 0;
    }
}
```

As the name implies, Type.GetCustomAttributes() returns an array (of System.Object types) that represent all the attributes applied to the member represented by the Type. From this array you are able to determine a specific attribute on the fly. What you do with this information is (of course) up to you.

NOTE   Be aware that the static Attribute.GetCustomAttribute() method allows you to obtain information for a specific attribute, rather than an array of all attributes on a given type.

SOURCE CODE   The CustomAtt and AttReader applications are included under the Chapter 11 subdirectory.

Putting Reflection, Late Binding, and Custom Attributes in Perspective

At this point, you may really be wondering if you will ever need to make use of reflection, late binding, or custom attributes. To be sure, these topics (while fascinating) can seem a bit on the academic side of programming (which may or may not be a bad thing, depending on your point of view). To help map these topics to a real-world situation, we need a solid example.

Assume for the moment that you are on a programming team that is building an application that has the following requirement:

- The product must be extendible by the use of additional third party tools.

So, what the heck does *that* mean? Well, consider Visual Studio .NET. When the VS .NET team was constructing this application, it left various hooks that allow other software vendors to snap in custom modules into the environment. Obviously the VS .NET team had no way to set references to external .NET assemblies it had not programmed (thus, no early binding)! However, to provide an open-ended model, the VS .NET team had to provide a mechanism by which other individuals (including yourself) could plug in new behaviors.

Extendability is an awesome benefit, as third-party vendors can build (and profit from) custom software modules. We benefit as developers as well, in that we are not required to by a brand-new (full price) IDE simply to gain augmentative functionality. So, how is it that tools such as VS .NET (and numerous other applications) have been programmed for extendability?

As you would guess, there are many ways to skin the proverbial cat. First, a tool built for extendability must provide some input vehicle to allow the user to specify the module to plug in (a dialog box, command line flag, or whatnot).

Second, the application in question must be able to determine if the module in question supports the correct functionality to be plugged into the environment. This advertisement of functionality could be provided via a specific interface or custom attribute. The key, however, is to make the entity as generic as possible. Given that attributes are nothing but advertisements, they seem like the most logical choice.

Finally, if the extendible application is able to determine the type in question is compatible with its needs, it will need to obtain an interface reference (again, think about the polymorphic nature of interface-types) to trigger the real functionality of the snap-in. Once the snap-in has been loaded and used, the assembly may be cached for further use or discarded (at the whim of the extendible application).

Simply put, if the extendible application has been preprogrammed to query for specific interfaces (and/or attributes), it is able to determine at runtime if the item in question is worthy of activation. Once this verification test has been passed, the type in question may support additional interfaces that provide a polymorphic fabric to their functionality. This same generalized approach is the exact approach taken by the VS .NET team, and despite what you may be thinking, is not at all difficult!

Building a Custom Snap-In Consumer

In the sections that follow, I will walk through a complete example that illustrates the process of building an extendible Windows Forms application that can be augmented by the functionality of additional snap-in *.dll assemblies. What I will *not* do at this point is comment on the process of programming Windows Forms applications (Chapters 13–15 will tend to that chore). So, if you are not familiar with the process of building Windows Forms applications, feel free to simply open up the supplied sample code and follow along (or build a console-based alternative). To serve as a roadmap, our extendible application entails the following assemblies:

- *CommonSnappableTypes.dll:* This assembly contains type definitions that will be implemented by each snap-in as well as referenced by the extendible Windows Forms application.

- *CSharpSnapIn.dll*: A simple snap-in written in C#, which leverages the types of CommonSnappableTypes.dll.

- *VbNetSnapIn.dll*: A simple snap-in written in VB .NET, which leverages the types of CommonSnappableTypes.dll.

- *MyPluggableApp.exe*: This Windows Forms application will be the entity that may be extended by the functionality of each snap-in. Again, remember! This application will make use of reflection, late binding, and custom attributes to dynamically gain the functionality of assemblies it has no foreknowledge about.

Building the Common Snappable Types

Our first order of business is to create an assembly that contains the types that a given snap-in must leverage to be plugged into our expandable Windows Forms application. If you are following along, create a new C# code library (CommonSnappableTypes) that defines the following two types:

```
namespace CommonSnappableTypes
{
    public interface IUseMyFunctionality
    { void DoIt(); }

    [AttributeUsage(AttributeTargets.Class)]
    public class SnappableAttribute : System.Attribute
    { public SnappableAttribute(){} }
}
```

Here, the CommonSnappableTypes.dll assembly offers a public interface (IUseMyFunctionality) that provides a polymorphic interface for all snap-ins that can be consumed by the extendible Windows Forms application. Of course, as this example is purely illustrative in nature, we supply a single method named DoIt(). To map this to a more real world example, imagine an interface (or set of interfaces) that allows the snapper to generate scripting code, render an image onto the application's toolbox, or integrate into the main menu.

The SnappableAttribute type is a custom attribute that will be applied on any class type that wishes to be snapped in to the container. Again, the theory here is that if (and only if) a type has been adorned with the [Snappable] attribute, it will support the functionality of the IUseMyFunctionality type.

Building the C# Snap-In

Next up, we need to create a concrete type that supports the [Snappable] attribute and implements the IUseMyFunctionality interface. Again, to focus on the overall design of an extendible application, a trivial type is in order. Assume the following class type is defined in a new C# code library named CSharpSnapIn. Given that the contained class type must make use of the types defined in CommonSnappableTypes, be sure to set a reference to this binary (as well as System.Windows.Forms.dll to display a noteworthy message). This being said, here is the code:

```
using System;
using CommonSnappableTypes;
using System.Windows.Forms;
namespace CSharpSnapIn
{
    // This type is Snappable into other containers.
    [Snappable]
    public class TheCSharpSnapIn : IUseMyFunctionality
    {
        public TheCSharpSnapIn(){}
        void IUseMyFunctionality.DoIt()
        {
            MessageBox.Show("You have just used the C# snap in!");
        }
    }
}
```

Note that the TheCSharpSnapIn type has been marked with the [SnappableAttribute] type to flag itself as a type that can be plugged into the extendible application you have yet to build. Given that it has advertised its support for snap-in-ability, you also implement the IUseMyFunctionality.

Building the VB .NET Snap-In

Now, to simulate the role of a third-party vendor who prefers VB .NET over C#, create a new VB .NET code library (VbNetSnapIn) that references the same external assemblies as the previous CSharpSnapIn project. The code is (again) straightforward:

```
Imports System.Windows.Forms
Imports CommonSnappableTypes
<SnappableAttribute()> Public Class VbNetSnapIn
    Implements IUseMyFunctionality
    Public Sub DoIt() Implements IUseMyFunctionality.DoIt
        MessageBox.Show("You have just used the VB .NET snap in!")
    End Sub
End Class
```

Not too much to say here! This assembly contains another class type that is [Snappable] and implements the functionality of the IUseMyFunctionality interface. Do notice that VB .NET applies attributes using angled brackets (< >) rather than square brackets ([ ]).

Building the Extendable Windows Forms Application

Now, on to the good stuff! The final piece of the extendability puzzle is to create the Windows Forms application that allows the user to select a snap-in using a standard Windows Open dialog box (represented by the System.Windows.Forms.OpenFileDialog type). Before I dive into the details, set a reference to the CommonSnappableTypes.dll assembly, but *not* the CSharpSnapIn.dll or VbNetSnapIn.dll binaries! Remember the goal of this application is to make use of late binding and reflection to determine the "snapability" of independent binaries created by third-party vendors (thus, there is no hope of early binding).

Again, I won't bother to examine all the details of Windows Forms development at this point in the game. However, assuming you have placed a MainMenu type onto the Form template, we will launch an Open File dialog via a custom "Tools | Snap In Something..." menu item (Figure 11-8).

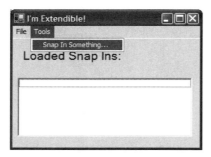

Figure 11-8. Input for a snap-in module

Behind the Click event handler for this menu item (which may be created simply by double-clicking the menu item from the design-time editor), our goal is to extract the path to the selected file, and using this path, perform the following tasks:

- Check to see if the user-selected assembly has any types marked with the [Snappable] attribute (by reflecting over custom attributes).

- For each type that does support the [Snappable] aspect, obtain the IUseMyFunctionality interface and call the DoIt() method (via late binding).

Here is the relevant code behind the Form type:

```
public class MainForm: System.Windows.Forms.Form
{
    ...
    // The " Tools | Snap In Something..." event handler.
    private void mnuToolsSnapIn_Click(object sender, System.EventArgs e)
    {
        if(myOpenFileDialog.ShowDialog() == DialogResult.OK)
        {
            string pathToAsm = myOpenFileDialog.FileName;
            if(TryToUseSnapIn(pathToAsm) == false)
                MessageBox.Show("This snap-in is bogus!");
        }
    }
    private bool TryToUseSnapIn(string path)
    {
        // Load the specified assembly.
        bool foundSnapIn = false;
        Assembly theSnapInAsm = Assembly.LoadFrom(path);
        // Get all types in assembly.
        Type[] theTypes = theSnapInAsm.GetTypes();
        // Get custom attributes for each type, and
        // see if one of them is [Snappable]
        for(int i = 0; i < theTypes.Length; i++)
        {
            object[] theAtts = theTypes[i].GetCustomAttributes(false);
            for(int j = 0; j < theAtts.Length; j++)
            {
                if(theAtts[j] is SnappableAttribute)
                {
                    // It is snappable!
                    // Get the IUseMyFunctionality interface.
                    foundSnapIn = true;
                    object o =
                        theSnapInAsm.CreateInstance(theTypes[i].FullName);
                    IUseMyFunctionality itfUseMe;
                    itfUseMe = o as IUseMyFunctionality;
                    if(itfUseMe != null)
                    {
                        itfUseMe.DoIt();
                        lstBoxSnapIns.Items.Add(theTypes[i].FullName);
                    }
                }
            }
        }
        return foundSnapIn;
    }
}
```

This really does summarize all the information presented over the course of this chapter. Note how the application is able to determine a bogus assembly (i.e., an assembly that contains no type that is [Snappable]–aware) via the Boolean value returned from TryToUseSnapIn() helper function. Within this helper method, we first leverage the Assembly.LoadFrom() method to load the binary based on the user specified path. Next, we iterate over each type and check to see if the item has been adorned with the [Snappable] attribute. If so, we set our Boolean flag and trigger the IUseMyFunctionality.DoIt() implementation of the given snap-in (to return the correct value to the caller). Finally, for good measure, we log the name of the snap-in within the Form's ListBox type. Figure 11-9 shows the result.

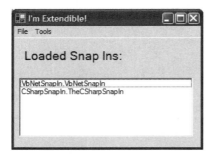

Figure 11-9. Snapping in external assemblies

While this is a far cry from building real-world extendible applications, you should have a better understanding how such a program may be constructed. In a nutshell, building an extendible application demands the creation of an assembly that defines types implemented by the third-party snap-in vendor and queried for by the extendible application itself. If you wish, you can think of the CommonSnappableTypes.dll as the middleman that bridges the gap between snap-ins and snappee.

SOURCE CODE The CommonSnappableTypes, CSharpSnapIn, VbNetSnapIn, and MyPluggableApp applications are included under the Chapter 11 subdirectory.

NOTE If you are interested in learning how to build custom snap-ins for VS .NET, check out *Writing Add-ins for Visual Studio .NET* (Smith, Apress 2002).

Summary

Reflection is a very interesting aspect of a robust OO environment. In the world of .NET, the keys to reflection services revolve around the System.Type class and the System.Reflection namespace. As you have seen, reflection is the process of placing a type under the magnifying glass at runtime to understand the "who, what, where, why, and how" of a given item.

Late binding is the process of creating a type and invoking its members without foreknowledge of the specific names of said members. As shown during our extendible application example, this is a very powerful technique used by tool builders as well as tool consumers.

This chapter also examined the role of attribute-based programming. When you adorn your types with attributes, the result is the augmentation of the underlying assembly metadata. While you may never find yourself in the position of *absolutely* having to build custom attributes, you are bound to find the predefined attributes invaluable, especially when building a bridge between your classic COM servers and .NET assemblies, or leveraging .NET serialization services and the .NET Remoting layer.

Part Four
Leveraging the .NET Libraries

Object Serialization and the .NET Remoting Layer

DEVELOPERS WHO ARE NEW to the .NET platform naturally assume that .NET is all about building Internet-centric applications (given the term ".NET"). As you have already seen however, this is simply not the case. In fact, the construction of Web-centric programs is simply one tiny (but quite well-touted) aspect of the .NET platform. In this same vein of misinformation, many new .NET developers tend to assume that XML Web services are the only way to interact with remote objects. Again, this is not true. The .NET platform provides numerous namespaces devoted to the creation of traditional distributed applications, which have nothing to do whatsoever with XML Web services (or Web applications). In short, using .NET you are able to build peer-to-peer distributed applications that have nothing to do with HTTP or XML (if you so choose). As you will see over the course of this chapter, the .NET Remoting architecture is a managed replacement for classic DCOM.

The first goal of this chapter is to describe a critical remoting-centric topic: object serialization. Simply put, serialization is the act of persisting an object's state data to a given location (e.g., a memory stream, physical file, etc.). Deserialization, on the other hand, is the process of reading the persisted data from said location and recreating a new type based on the preserved stateful values. As you might imagine, the ability to serialize types is critical when attempting to copy an object to a remote machine (e.g., marshal-by-value). Understand, however, that serialization is quite useful in its own right, and will likely play a role in many of your .NET applications (distributed or not).

Once you have seen the .NET serialization protocol in action, the next goal is to examine the low-level grunge used by the CLR to move information between application boundaries. Along the way, you will come to understand the numerous terms used when discussing .NET Remoting, such as proxies, channels, marshaling by reference (as opposed to by value), server-activated (versus client-activated) objects, and so forth. With these background elements complete, the remainder of this chapter offers numerous code examples that illustrate the process of building distributed systems using the .NET platform.

Object Persistence in the .NET Framework

Object serialization is one of the key underlying technologies used by the .NET Remoting layer. Simply put, *serialization* is the term describing the process of converting the state of an object to a linear sequence of data. This data sequence contains all necessary information needed to reconstruct (or *deserialize*) the state of the object for use later. The .NET serialization services are quite sophisticated: When a given object is serialized to a stream, any associated object references required by the root object are automatically serialized as well. For example, when a derived class is serialized, each serializable object in the chain of inheritance is able to write its own custom state data into the data stream. Furthermore, if a given type contains serializable member variables, the member variables themselves also automatically participate in the serialization process.

Once a set of objects has been saved to a stream, the data pattern can be relocated as necessary. For example, imagine you have serialized an object graph into a memory location using the System.IO.MemoryStream type. This stream could be forwarded to a remote computer, the Windows clipboard, burned to a CD, or simply written to a physical file. The object itself does not care where it is stored. All that matters is the fact that this stream of 1s and 0s (or, depending on your choice of formatter, XML elements) correctly represents the state of the serialized objects.

NOTE   The System.IO namespace defines numerous types that allow you to read (and write) information to (and from) files, memory locations, and character buffers. Chapter 16 examines this namespace in detail; however, by necessity, you will be introduced to some System.IO types during this chapter's examination of object serialization.

The Role of Object Graphs

As mentioned, when a type is serialized by the CLR, the runtime will account for each related object. The chain of related objects serialized to a stream is collectively referred to as an *object graph*. Object graphs provide a simple way to document how a set of objects refer to each other and are *not* intended to directly model classic OO relationships (such as the "is-a" or "has-a" relationship), although they do map to this paradigm quite well. To establish the relations among objects in a graph, each object is assigned a unique numerical value, followed by a graph of all related items. Keep in mind that the numbers assigned to the members in an object graph are arbitrary and have no real meaning to the outside world.

As a simple example, assume you have created a set of classes that model some automobiles (of course). You have a topmost type named Car, which "has-a" Radio. Another class named JamesBondCar extends the basic Car type. An object graph that models these relationships is shown in Figure 12-1.

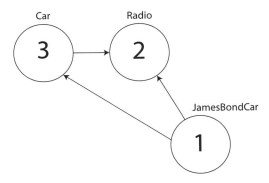

Figure 12-1. A simple object graph

In Figure 12-1 you can see that the Car class refers to the Radio class (given the "has-a" relationship). The JamesBondCar refers to the Car (given the "is-a" relationship) as well as the Radio (as it inherits this protected member variable). Given that we have assigned an arbitrary value to each member in the object graph, we could represent the relationship documented in the previous diagram with the following formula:

```
[Car 3, ref 2], [Radio 2], [JamesBondCar 1, ref 3, ref 2]
```

If we parse this formula, you can see that the Car type has a dependency on item 2 (the Radio). Also, the JamesBondCar has a dependency on item 3 (the Car) as well as item 2 (the Radio). Item 2, the Radio, is a lone wolf. If you serialize an instance of JamesBondCar to a stream, the object graph ensures that the Radio and Car types also participate in the process. The beautiful thing about the default serialization process is that the graph representing the relationships among your objects is established automatically behind the scenes.

Configuring Objects for Serialization

To make an object available to .NET serialization services, all you need to do is decorate each class with the [Serializable] attribute. That's it (really). If you determine that a given class has some member data that should not participate in the serialization scheme, you can mark such fields with the [NonSerialized] attribute. This can be helpful if you have member variables in a serializable class that do not need to be "remembered" (e.g., constants, transient data, and so on). For example, here is the Radio class, which has been marked as serializable (except for a single member variable):

```
// The Radio class can participate in the .NET serialization scheme.
[Serializable]
public class Radio
{
    // This member will not be persisted.
    [NonSerialized]
    private int objectIDNumber = 9;
    // Other serialized state data
    ...
    public Radio(){ }
    public void On(bool state)
    {
        if(state == true)
            MessageBox.Show("Music is on...");
        else
            MessageBox.Show("No tunes...");
    }
}
```

As you would guess, these attributes are embedded within the type's metadata, as you can see using ildasm.exe (Figure 12-2).

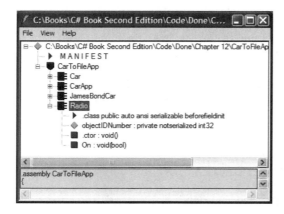

Figure 12-2. The Serializable and NonSerialized attributes

To finish the coding of this car hierarchy, here are the definitions for the Car base class and JamesBondCar subtype, each marked with the [Serializable] attribute:

```
// The Car class is serializable!
[Serializable]
public class Car
{
    protected string petName;
    protected int maxSpeed;
    protected Radio theRadio = new Radio();
```

```csharp
    public Car(string petName, int maxSpeed)
    {
        this.petName = petName;
        this.maxSpeed = maxSpeed;
    }
    public Car() { }
    public String PetName
    {
        get {  return petName; }
        set {  petName = value; }
    }
    public int MaxSpeed
    {
        get {  return maxSpeed; }
        set {  maxSpeed = value; }
    }
    public void TurnOnRadio(bool state)
    {  theRadio.On(state); }
}

// The JamesBondCar class is also serializable!
[Serializable]
public class JamesBondCar : Car
{
    // Made public for easy access.
    // Feel free to make use of type properties.
    public bool isFlightWorthy;
    public bool isSeaWorthy;
    public JamesBondCar(){ }
    public JamesBondCar(string petName, int maxSpeed,
                        bool canFly, bool canSubmerge)
        : base(petName, maxSpeed)
    {
        this.isFlightWorthy = canFly;
        this.isSeaWorthy = canSubmerge;
    }
    public void Fly()
    {
        if(isFlightWorthy)
            MessageBox.Show("Taking off!");
        else
            MessageBox.Show("Falling off cliff!");
    }
    public void GoUnderWater()
    {
        if(isSeaWorthy)
            MessageBox.Show("Diving....");
        else
            MessageBox.Show("Drowning!!!");
    }
}
```

Choosing a Serialization Formatter

Once you have configured your types to participate in the .NET serialization scheme, your next step is to choose which format should be used when persisting your object graph. The System.Runtime.Serialization.Formatters namespace contains two additional nested namespaces (*.Binary and *.Soap) that provide two out-of-the-box formatters. As you can guess, the BinaryFormatter type serializes your object graph to a stream using a compact binary format. The SoapFormatter type represents your graph as a SOAP (Simple Object Access Protocol) message that is expressed using XML data representation.

The System.Runtime.Serialization.Formatters.Binary.BinaryFormatter type is defined within mscorlib.dll. Therefore, to serialize your objects using a binary format, all you need to do is specify the following C# using directive:

```
// Persist object graph using a binary format!
using System.Runtime.Serialization.Formatters.Binary;
```

However, the System.Runtime.Serialization.Formatters.Soap.SoapFormatter type is defined in a *separate assembly*. To format your object graph into a SOAP message, you must set a reference to System.Runtime.Serialization.Formatters.Soap.dll and make the following C# using directive:

```
// Persist object graph using a SOAP format!
using System.Runtime.Serialization.Formatters.Soap;
```

Regardless of which formatter you choose to make use of, do be aware that .NET formatters supply a common set of functionality through the implementation of the IFormatter and IRemotingFormatter interfaces. IFormatter defines the key Serialize() and Deserialize() methods, which do the grunt work to move your object graphs into and out of a specific stream (represented by the System.IO.Stream abstract base class). Here is the formal definition of IFormatter:

```
public interface System.Runtime.Serialization.IFormatter
{
    SerializationBinder Binder { get; set; }
    StreamingContext Context { get; set; }
    ISurrogateSelector SurrogateSelector { get; set; }
    object Deserialize(System.IO.Stream serializationStream);
    void Serialize(System.IO.Stream serializationStream, object graph);
}
```

The IRemotingFormatter interface (which is leveraged internally by the .NET Remoting layer) overloads the Serialize() and Deserialize() members, into a manner more appropriate for remoting-centric persistence. Note that IRemotingFormatter derives from the more general IFormatter interface:

```
public interface System.Runtime.Remoting.Messaging.IRemotingFormatter
: System.Runtime.Serialization.IFormatter
{
    object Deserialize(System.IO.Stream serializationStream,
        System.Runtime.Remoting.Messaging.HeaderHandler handler);
    void Serialize(System.IO.Stream serializationStream, object graph,
        System.Runtime.Remoting.Messaging.Header[] headers);
}
```

Serialization Using a Binary Formatter

To illustrate how easy it is to persist an instance of our JamesBondCar to a physical file, let's make use of the BinaryFormatter type. Again, the two key methods of the BinaryFormatter type to be aware of are Serialize() and Deserialize() (Table 12-1).

Table 12-1. BinaryFormatter Members

BinaryFormatter Member	Meaning in Life
Deserialize()	Deserializes a stream of bytes to an object graph
Serialize()	Serializes an object or graph of related objects to a stream

In addition to the Deserialize() and Serialize() methods, the BinaryFormatter type defines a small number of properties that configure specific details regarding the (de)serialization process. By and large, the default configuration of BinaryFormatter is all you need to concern yourself with; however we will check out additional details as needed over the course of this chapter.

Now, assume you have created an instance of JamesBondCar, modified some state data, and want to persist your spy-mobile in a *.dat file. The first task is to create the *.dat file itself. This can be achieved using the static System.IO.File.Create() method, which returns an instance of the System.IO.FileStream type (again, file IO will be examined in Chapter 16). Given that the BinaryFormatter.Serialize() method requires a Stream-derived type as its first parameter, be sure to maintain this variable. Here is the complete serialization code:

```
using System.Runtime.Serialization.Formatters.Binary,
using System.IO;
public static void Main()
{
    // Make a car and change some state data.
    JamesBondCar myAuto = new JamesBondCar("Fred", 50, false, true);
    myAuto.TurnOnRadio(true);
    myAuto.GoUnderWater();
```

```
    // Create a file stream to hold the object's state.
    FileStream myStream = File.Create("CarData.dat");
    // Move the object graph into the file stream using a binary format.
    BinaryFormatter myBinaryFormat = new BinaryFormatter();
    myBinaryFormat.Serialize(myStream, myAuto);
    myStream.Close();
}
```

As you can see, the BinaryFormatter.Serialize() method is the member responsible for composing the object graph and moving the byte sequence to some Stream-derived type. In this case, the stream happens to be a physical file. However, you could also serialize your object types to any Stream-derived type (such as a memory location, given that MemoryStream is a descendent of the Stream type). If you open the *.dat file, you can peek inside the byte sequence (Figure 12-3).

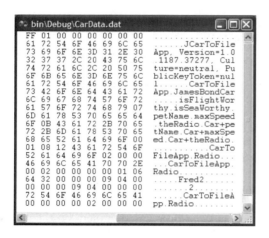

Figure 12-3. JamesBondCar serialized using a BinaryFormatter

Now suppose you want to read the persisted JamesBondCar back to an object variable. Once you have programmatically opened the correct *.dat file (via the File.OpenRead() method), simply call Deserialize(). Be aware that Deserialize() returns a generic System.Object type, and therefore you need to impose an explicit cast, as shown here:

```
// Read in the Car from the binary stream.
myStream = File.OpenRead("CarData.dat");
JamesBondCar carFromDisk =
    (JamesBondCar)myBinaryFormat.Deserialize(myStream);
Console.WriteLine("{0} is alive!", carFromDisk.PetName);
carFromDisk.TurnOnRadio(true);
myStream.Close();
```

Notice that when you call Deserialize(), you pass the Stream-derived type that represents the location of the persisted objects (again a file stream in this case). Now if that is not painfully simple, I'm not sure what is. In a nutshell, mark each class you wish to persist to a stream with the [Serializable] attribute. After this point, use the BinaryFormatter type to move your object graph to and from a binary stream.

Serialization Using a SOAP Formatter

The other available formatter you may use when serializing your types is SoapFormatter. Remember you must set a reference to System.Runtime.Serialization.Formatters.Soap.dll to use this type! The following block of code extends the previous serialization example to persist the JamesBondCar using the SoapFormatter type:

```
using System.Runtime.Serialization.Formatters.Soap;
...
// Save the same car using a soap format.
FileStream myStream = File.Create("CarSoapData.xml");
SoapFormatter mySoapFormat = new SoapFormatter();
mySoapFormat.Serialize(myStream, myAuto);
myStream.Close();
// Read in the Car from the XML file.
myStream = File.OpenRead("CarSoapData.xml");
JamesBondCar carFromSoap =
            (JamesBondCar)mySoapFormat.Deserialize(myStream);
Console.WriteLine("{0} is alive!", carFromSoap.PetName);
myStream.Close();
```

As you can see, the SoapFormatter type has the same public interface as the BinaryFormatter. As before, use Serialize() and Deserialize() to move the object graph in and out of the stream. If you open the resulting *.xml file (Figure 12-4), you can locate the XML tags that mark the stateful values of the current JamesBondCar (as well as the relationship maintained by the graph).

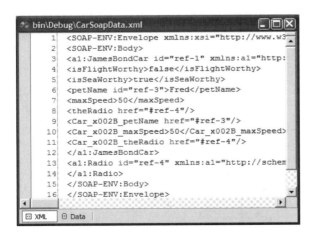

Figure 12-4. JamesBondCar serialized using a SoapFormatter

Serialization Using an XML Formatter

In addition to the SOAP and binary formatters, the System.Xml.dll assembly provides a third formatter (System.Xml.Serialization.XmlFormatter) that can be used to persist the state of a given object using pure XML (as opposed to XML data expressed via a SOAP message). Assuming your application has set a reference to System.Xml.dll (and you have a C# "using" directive specifying the System.Xml.Serialization namespace), you are able to serialize and deserialize your JamesBondCar as pure XML:

```
// Now save car using a pure XML format.
Console.WriteLine("\n***** Saving car to CarXmlData.xml file *****");
myStream = File.Create("CarXmlData.xml");
XmlSerializer myXmlFormat =
    new XmlSerializer(typeof(JamesBondCar), "Cars");
myXmlFormat.Serialize(myStream, myAuto);
myStream.Close();
// Read in the Car from the XML file.
Console.WriteLine("\n***** Reading car from Xml file *****");
myStream = File.OpenRead("CarXmlData.xml");
JamesBondCar carFromXml =
    (JamesBondCar)myXmlFormat.Deserialize(myStream);
Console.WriteLine("{0} is alive!", carFromXml.PetName);
carFromSoap.TurnOnRadio(true);
myStream.Close();
```

As you can see, the process is more or less identical to working with the BinaryFormatter and SoapFormatter types. The key difference is that the XmlFormatter type requires you to specify type information of the item to be serialized as well as the name of the XML namespace of the *.xml file via a constructor parameter.

 NOTE   The XmlFormatter demands that all serialized types in the object graph support a default constructor (so be sure to add it back if you define custom constructors).

If you were to look within the newly generated CarXmlData.xml file you would find the following:

```
<?xml version="1.0"?>
<JamesBondCar
xmlns:xsd="http://www.w3.org/2001/XMLSchema"
xmlns:xsi="http://www.w3.org/2001/XMLSchema-instance"
xmlns="Cars">
    <PetName>Fred</PetName>
    <MaxSpeed>50</MaxSpeed>
    <isFlightWorthy>false</isFlightWorthy>
    <isSeaWorthy>true</isSeaWorthy>
</JamesBondCar>
```

SOURCE CODE   The CarToFile application is located under the
Chapter 12 subdirectory.

Customizing the Serialization Process

Now that you understand how the .NET platform makes use of serialization services to
persist an object to a given stream, you are just about ready to check out the details of
the .NET Remoting layer. Before moving on however, let's dig a bit deeper into the .NET
serialization process.

In a vast majority of cases, you will configure a type as serializable by applying the
[Serializable] attribute. This attribute enables a given formatter to encode the type into
the client-supplied stream. While this is typically exactly the behavior you desire, the
System.Runtime.Serialization namespace provides several ways to customize the .NET
serialization process.

The types within this namespace allow you to build custom formatters, as well as
extend the default serialization processes provided by the [Serializable] attribute.
Table 12-2 describes some (but not all) of the core types to be aware of.

Table 12-2. System.Runtime.Serialization Namespace Core Types

Types of the System.Runtime.Serialization Namespace	Meaning in Life
Formatter	An abstract base class that provides base functionality for runtime serialization formatters.
ObjectIDGenerator	Generates IDs for objects in an object graph.
ObjectManager	Keeps track of objects as they are being deserialized.
SerializationBinder	An abstract base class that provides functionality to serialize a type to a stream.
SerializationInfo	Used by objects that have custom serialization behavior. SerializationInfo holds together all the data needed to serialize or deserialize an object. In essence, this class is a "property bag" that allows you to establish name/value pairs to represent the state of an object.

In addition to these types, there are two key interfaces used during the serialization
process: IFormatter (mentioned previously) and ISerializable. Regardless of which
formatter you choose (including any custom formatter you might dream up), the formatter is in charge of transmitting all of the information required to persist the object
during the serialization process. Specifically, the necessary information includes:

- The fully qualified name of the object (e.g., MyNamespace.MyClasses.Foo)

- The name of the assembly containing the object (e.g., myAsm.dll)

- The object's stateful information, contained within a SerializationInfo type

During the deserialization process, the formatter uses this same information to build an identical copy of the object, using the information extracted from the underlying stream. The big picture can be visualized as shown in Figure 12-5.

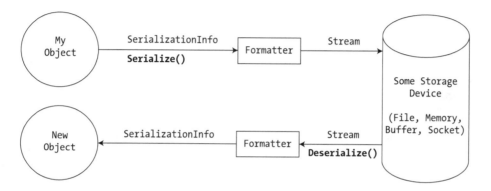

Figure 12-5. The serialization process

When you wish to "get involved" with the serialization process, your first step is to implement the standard ISerializable interface on the class requiring custom serialization. This interface is quite simple, given that it only defines a single method, GetObjectData():

```
// When you wish to tweak the serialization process,
// implement ISerializable.
public interface ISerializable
{
    public virtual  void GetObjectData(SerializationInfo info,
        StreamingContext context);
}
```

The GetObjectData() method is called automatically by a given formatter during the serialization process. The implementation of this method populates the incoming SerializationInfo parameter with a series of name/value pairs. If you check out this type using wincv.exe, you essentially find numerous variations on the overloaded AddValue() method, in addition to a small set of properties that allow the type to get and set the type's name, defining assembly, and member count. Here is a partial snapshot:

```
public sealed class SerializationInfo : object
{
    public SerializationInfo(Type type,
        System.Runtime.Serialization.IFormatterConverter converter);
    public string AssemblyName { get; set; }
    public string FullTypeName { get; set; }
    public int MemberCount { get; }
    public void AddValue(string name, short value);
    public void AddValue(string name, UInt16 value);
    public void AddValue(string name, int value);
...
}
```

In addition to implementing the ISerializable interface, all objects that make use of custom serialization must provide a special constructor taking the following signature:

```
// You must supply a custom constructor with this signature
// to allow the runtime engine to set the state of your object.
[Serializable]
class SomeClass : ISerializable
{
    private SomeClass (SerializationInfo si, StreamingContext ctx) {...}
...
}
```

Notice that the visibility of this constructor is set as *private*. This is permissible given that the formatter will have access to this member regardless of its visibility. These special constructors tend to be marked as private to ensure that the casual object user would never create an object in this manner.

As you can see, the first parameter of this constructor is an instance of the SerializationInfo type (seen previously). The second parameter of special constructor is a StreamingContext type, which contains information regarding the source or destination of the bits. The most informative member of this type is the State property, which represents a value from the StreamingContextStates enumeration (Table 12-3).

Table 12-3. StreamingContextStates Enumeration Members

StreamingContextStates Member Name	Meaning in Life
All	Specifies that the serialized data can be transmitted to or received from any of the other contexts.
Clone	Specifies that the object graph is being cloned.
CrossAppDomain	Specifies that the source or destination context is a new AppDomain.
CrossMachine	Specifies that the source or destination context is a different machine.

Table 12-3. StreamingContextStates Enumeration Members (Continued)

StreamingContextStates Member Name	Meaning in Life
CrossProcess	Specifies that the source or destination context is a different process on the same machine.
File	Specifies that the source or destination context is a file.
Other	Specifies that the serialization context is unknown.
Persistence	Specifies that the source or destination context is a persisted store. This could include databases, files, or other backing stores. Users should assume that persisted data is more long lived than the process that created the data and not serialize objects in such a way that deserialization requires accessing any data from the current process.
Remoting	Specifies that the source or destination context is remoting to an unknown location. Users cannot make any assumptions as to whether this is on the same machine.

A Simple Example of Custom Serialization

Let me reiterate that you typically do not need to bypass the default serialization mechanism provided by the .NET runtime. However, by way of a simple illustration, here is an updated version of the Car type (named CustomCarType) that has been configured to take part of custom serialization. You are not doing anything too radical in the implementation of GetObjectState() or the custom constructor. Other than persisting the name of the petName field using all capital letters (just to simulate something custom), each method dumps out information regarding the current serialization context and manipulates the incoming SerializationInfo type:

```
[Serializable]
public class CustomCarType : ISerializable
{
    public string petName;
    public int maxSpeed;
    public CustomCarType(string s, int i) {  petName = s; maxSpeed = i;}
    // Return state info to the formatter.
    public void GetObjectData(SerializationInfo si, StreamingContext ctx)
    {
        // What context is the stream?
        Console.WriteLine("[GetObjectData] Context State: {0} ",
                        ctx.State.ToString());
        si.AddValue("CapPetName", petName.ToUpper());
        si.AddValue("maxSpeed", maxSpeed);
    }
}
```

```
    // Rehydrate a new object based on incoming SerializationInfo type.
    private CustomCarType(SerializationInfo si, StreamingContext ctx)
    {
        // What context is the stream?
        Console.WriteLine("[ctor] Context State: {0} ", ctx.State.ToString());
        petName = si.GetString("CapPetName");
        maxSpeed = si.GetInt32("maxSpeed");
    }
}
```

Now that the type has been configured with the correct infrastructure, you will be happy to see that the caller's serialization and deserialization process remains unaltered (see Figure 12-6 for output):

```
public static int Main(string[] args)
{
    CustomCarType myAuto = new CustomCarType("Sid", 50);
    Stream myStream = File.Create("CarData.dat");
    // ISerializable interface obtained!
    BinaryFormatter myBinaryFormat = new BinaryFormatter();
    myBinaryFormat.Serialize(myStream, myAuto);
    myStream.Close();
    myStream = File.OpenRead("CarData.dat");
    // Special constructor called!
    CustomCarType carFromDisk =
        (CustomCarType)myBinaryFormat.Deserialize(myStream);
    Console.WriteLine("{0} is alive!", carFromDisk.petName);
    return 0;
}
```

Figure 12-6. Custom serialization

SOURCE CODE   The CustomSerialization project is included under the Chapter 12 subdirectory.

So at this point you should have a solid handle on the .NET serialization process. Understand that this technology is useful in a variety of circumstances, even when you are not building a distributed application. For example, you could save application-specific data, user preferences, or whatnot with these same techniques. As you would expect however, the .NET Remoting layer makes substantial use of these serialization primitives. Next question: what exactly is *remoting*?

Defining .NET Remoting

As you recall from your reading in Chapter 10, an *application domain* is a logical boundary for a .NET assembly, which is itself contained within a Process type. Understanding these concepts is critical when discussing distributed computing under .NET, given that *remoting* is nothing more than the act of two pieces of software communicating across application domains. The two application domains in question could be physically configured in any of the following manners:

- Two application domains in the same process (and thus on the same machine)

- Two application domains in separate processes on the same machine

- Two application domains in separate processes on different machines

Given these three possibilities, you can see that remoting does not necessarily need to involve two (or more) networked computers. In fact, each of the examples presented in this chapter can be successfully run on a single, stand-alone machine (but don't worry, you'll see how to distribute your applications across machine boundaries as well).

Regardless of the distance between two software entities, it is common to refer to each agent using the terms client and server. Simply put, the *client* is a piece of software that attempts to interact with a remote object. The *server* is the software agent that provides remote access to select objects. As you will see over the course of this chapter, a .NET server application is quite a different beast from that of classic DCOM.

The .NET Remoting Namespaces

Before we dive too deep into the details of the .NET Remoting layer, we need to check out the functionality provided by the remoting-centric namespaces. The .NET base class libraries provide numerous namespaces that allow you to build distributed applications. The bulk of the types found within these namespaces are contained within mscorlib.dll, however, the System.Runtime.Remoting.dll assembly does complement and extend the basic type set. The truth of the matter, however, is that many of these types are of little use to you unless you do wish to extend the default remoting architecture. Over the course of this chapter, you are required to make use of many of the core types within the namespaces seen in Table 12-4. Be sure to check out online Help if you wish to view every possible entity.

Table 12-4. The .NET Remoting Namespaces

Remoting-Centric Namespace	Meaning in Life
System.Runtime.Remoting	This is the core namespace you must use when building any sort of application using the .NET Remoting layer.
System.Runtime.Remoting.Activation	This relatively small namespace defines a handful of types that allow you to fine-tune the process of activating a remote object.
System.Runtime.Remoting.Channels	This namespace contains types that represent channels and channel sinks.
System.Runtime.Remoting.Channels.Http	This namespace contains types that use the HTTP protocol to transport messages and objects to and from remote locations.
System.Runtime.Remoting.Channels.Tcp	This namespace contains types that use the TCP protocol to transport messages and objects to and from remote locations.
System.Runtime.Remoting.Contexts	This namespace allows you to configure the details of an object's context.
System.Runtime.Remoting.Lifetime	This namespace contains types that manage the lifetime of remote objects.
System.Runtime.Remoting.Messaging	This namespace contains types used to create and transmit message object.
System.Runtime.Remoting.Metadata	This namespace contains types that can be used to customize the generation and processing of SOAP formatting.
System.Runtime.Remoting.Metadata.W3cXsd2001	Closely related to the previous namespace, this namespace contains types that represent the XML Schema Definition (XSD) defined by the World Wide Web Consortium (W3C) in 2001.
System.Runtime.Remoting.MetadataServices	This namespace contains the types used by the Soapsuds.exe command line tool to convert .NET metadata to and from XML schema for the remoting infrastructure.
System.Runtime.Remoting.Proxies	This namespace contains types that provide functionality for proxy objects.
System.Runtime.Remoting.Services	This namespace defines a number of common base classes (and interfaces) that are typically only leveraged by other intrinsic remoting agents.

Understanding the .NET Remoting Framework

When clients and servers exchange information across application boundaries, the CLR makes use of several low-level primitives to ensure the entities in question are able to communicate with each other as transparently as possible. Meaning, as a .NET programmer, you are *not* required to provide reams and reams of grungy networking code to invoke a method on a remote object. Likewise, the server process is *not* required to manually pluck a network packet out of the queue and reformat the message into terms the remote object can understand. As you would hope, the CLR will take care of such details automatically using a default set of remoting types (although you are certainly able to get involved with the process if you so choose).

Now, if you are coming to .NET Remoting from a classic DCOM background, do understand that the .NET Remoting layer is not quite as transparent as DCOM. Much of the reason has to do with the simple fact that .NET assemblies are not registered in the system registry, and therefore you lose any concept of an AppID value, which makes the use of dcomcnfg.exe obsolete in the .NET universe.

Although .NET does expose a wee-bit more network-centric details to the developer, the upside is that there is no need to manually author IDL code to describe your remotable types (given the advent of .NET metadata), and you can forget all about implementing IMarshal, IPropertyBag, or making use of ADO Recordsets to marshal objects by value. Under .NET, marshaling a type by value (e.g., placing a copy of the remote type into the caller's app domain) is as simple as applying the [Serializable] attribute.

Basically, the .NET Remoting layer revolves around a careful orchestration that takes place between four key players:

- Proxies

- Messages

- Channels

- Formatters

Let's check out each entity in turn, and see how their combined functionality facilitates remote method invocations.

Understanding Proxies and Messages

Clients and server objects do not communicate via a direct connection, but rather through the use of a middleman termed a *proxy*. Like Java RMI, CORBA and DCOM, the role of a .NET proxy is to fool the client into believing it is communicating with a local object in the *same application domain*. To facilitate this illusion, a proxy has the identical interface (i.e., members, properties, fields, and whatnot) as the remote type it represents. As far as the client is concerned, a given proxy *is* the remote object, and can be operated on as if it were a true-blue local entity. Under the hood however, the proxy is forwarding calls to the remote type.

Formally speaking, the proxy invoked directly by the client is termed the *transparent proxy*. This CLR auto-generated entity is in charge of ensuring that the client has provided the correct number of (and type of) parameters to invoke the remote method.

Given this, you can regard the transparent proxy as a fixed interception layer that *cannot* be modified or extended programmatically.

Assuming the transparent proxy is able to verify the incoming arguments, this information is packaged up into another CLR generated type termed the *message object*. By definition, all message objects implement the System.Runtime.Remoting.Messaging.IMessage interface:

```
public interface IMessage
{
    IDictionary Properties { get; }
}
```

As you can see, the IMessage interface defines a single property (named Properties) that provides access to a collection used to hold the client-supplied arguments. Once this message object has been populated by the CLR, it is then passed into a closely related type termed the *real proxy*.

The real proxy is the entity that literally passes the message object into the channel (described momentarily). Unlike the transparent proxy, the real proxy *can* be extended by the programmer, and is represented by a base class type named (of course) RealProxy. Again, it is worth pointing out that the CLR will always generate a default implementation of the client-side real proxy, which will serve your needs most (if not all) of the time. Nevertheless, to gain some insight into the functionality provided by the abstract RealProxy base class, ponder the formal definition type:

```
public abstract class RealProxy : object
{
    public virtual ObjRef CreateObjRef(Type requestedType);
    public virtual bool Equals(object obj);
    public virtual IntPtr GetCOMIUnknown(bool fIsMarshalled);
    public virtual int GetHashCode();
    public virtual void GetObjectData(SerializationInfo info,
            StreamingContext context);
    public Type GetProxiedType();
    public static object GetStubData(RealProxy rp);
    public virtual object GetTransparentProxy();
    public Type GetType();
    public IConstructionReturnMessage InitializeServerObject(
        IConstructionCallMessage ctorMsg);
    public virtual IMessage Invoke(IMessage msg);
    public virtual void SetCOMIUnknown(IntPtr i);
    public static void SetStubData(RealProxy rp, object stubData);
    public virtual IntPtr SupportsInterface(ref Guid iid);
    public virtual string ToString();
}
```

Again, unless you are interested in building a custom implementation of the client-side real proxy, the only member of interest is RealProxy.Invoke(). Under the hood, the CLR-generated transparent proxy passes the formatted message object into the RealProxy type via its Invoke() method.

Understanding Channels

Once the proxies have validated and formatted the client-supplied arguments into a message object, this IMessage-compatible type is passed from the real proxy into a channel object. As in other remoting architectures, channels are the entities in charge of transporting a message to the remote object, and if necessary, ensuring that any method return values are passed from the remote object back to the client. Unlike classic DCOM however, .NET channels are not limited to the ORPC (Object Remote Procedure Call) wire protocol. In fact, the .NET base class libraries provide two channel implementations out of the box:

- The TCP channel

- The HTTP channel

The TCP channel is represented by the TcpChannel class type, and is used to pass messages using the TCP/IP network protocol. TcpChannel is helpful in that the formatted packets are quite lightweight, given that the messages are converted into a tight binary format using a related binary formatter. The result is that use of the TcpChannel type tends to result in faster remote access. On the downside, TCP channels are not firewall friendly, and may require the services of a system administrator to allow messages to pass across machine boundaries (which does indeed echo the same limitations of classic DCOM).

In contrast, the HTTP channel is represented by the HttpChannel class type, which converts message objects into a SOAP format using a related soap formatter. As you have seen, SOAP is XML-based and thus tends to result in beefier payloads than those used by the TcpChannel type. Given this, using the HttpChannel can result in slightly slower remote access. On the plus side, HTTP is far more firewall friendly, given that most firewalls allow textual packets to be passed over port 80.

Regardless of which channel type you chose to use, understand that both the HttpChannel and TcpChannel type implement the IChannel, IChannelSender, and IChannelReciever interfaces (and yes, if you were to build your own custom channel type, you make use of these same interfaces). The IChannel interface (as you will see in just a bit) defines a small set of members that provide common functionality to all channel types. The role of IChannelSender is to define a common set of members for channels that are able to send information *to* a specific receiver. On the other hand, IChannelReceiver defines a set of members that allow a channel to receive information *from* a given sender. The HttpChannel and TcpChannel types (as you would hope) are able to send and receive network packets, and therefore implement all three channel-centric interfaces.

To allow the client and server applications to register their channel of choice, you will make use of the ChannelServices.RegisterChannel() method, which (surprise, surprise) takes a type implementing IChannel. To preview things to come, the following code snippet illustrates how a server-side application domain can register an HTTP channel on port 32469 (you see the client's role in just a bit):

```
// Create and register a server side HttpChannel on port 32469.
HttpChannel c = new HttpChannel(32469);
ChannelServices.RegisterChannel(c);
```

Revisiting the Role of .NET Formatters

The final piece of the .NET Remoting puzzle is the role of formatter objects. A given channel object (TcpChannel or HttpChannel) leverages a specific internal formatter, whose job it is to translate the message object into protocol specific terms. As you would guess, the TcpChannel type makes use of the System.Runtime.Serialization.Formatters.Binary.BinaryFormatter type, while the HttpChannel type uses the functionality provided by the System.Runtime.Serialization.Formatters.Soap.SoapFormatter type. Given your work at the beginning of this chapter, you should already have some insights as to how a given channel will format the incoming messages.

Once the formatted message has been generated, it is passed into the channel, where it will eventually reach its destination application domain, at which time the message is formatted from protocol-specific terms back to .NET-specific terms at which point an entity termed the *dispatcher* invokes the correct method on the remote object.

All Together Now!

If your head is spinning from reading the previous sections, fear not! The transparent proxy, real proxy, message object, and dispatcher can typically be completely ignored, provided you are happy with the default plumbing (which is the case most of the time). As you will see, the process of specifying the channel object (and related formatter) is as simple as a single line of code. Furthermore, the .NET runtime is the entity in charge of orchestrating the creation and handshaking that takes place to invoke methods on objects located in distinct application domains. To help solidify the sequence of events, ponder Figure 12-7, which illustrates the basic process of two objects communicating across distinct application domains.

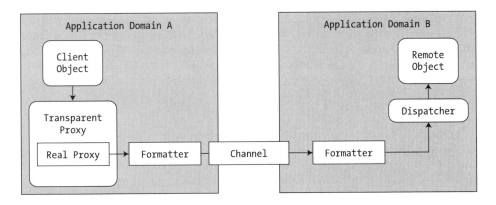

Figure 12-7. A high-level view of the default .NET Remoting architecture

A Brief Word Regarding the Extension of the Default Plumbing

A key aspect of the .NET Remoting layer (which is markedly different from that of classic DCOM) is the fact that most of the default remoting layers can be extended or completely replaced at the whim of the developer. Thus, if you truly want (or possibly need) to build a custom message dispatcher, custom formatter, or custom real proxy, you are free to do so.

You are also able to inject *additional* levels of indirection by plugging in custom types that stand between a given layer (for example, a custom sink used to perform preprocessing or post-processing of a given message). Now, to be sure, you may never need to retrofit the core .NET Remoting layer in such ways. However the fact remains that the .NET platform does provide the namespaces to allow you to do so.

NOTE   This chapter does not address the topic of extending the default .NET Remoting layer. If you wish to learn how to do so, check out *Advanced .NET Remoting* (Rammer, Apress 2002).

Terms of the .NET Remoting Trade

Like any new paradigm, .NET Remoting brings a number of TLAs (three-letter-acronyms) into the mix. Thus, before you see your first code example, we do need to define a number of terms used when describing the composition of a .NET Remoting application. As you would guess, this terminology is used to describe a number of details regarding common questions that arise during the construction of a distributed application: How do we pass a type across application domain boundaries? When exactly is a remote type activated ? How do we manage the lifetime of a remote object? (and so forth). Once you have an understanding of the related terminology, the act of building a distributed .NET application will be far less perplexing. Do understand that the acronyms that follow are mapped to specific code examples over the course of the chapter.

Object Marshaling Choices (MBR or MBV?)

Under the .NET platform, you have two options regarding how a remote object is marshaled to the client. First question: What the heck is *marshaling?* Simply put, marshaling is a term that describes how a remote object is passed between application domains. When you are designing a remotable object, you may choose to employ marshal-by-reference (MBR, for short) or marshal-by-value (MBV, for short) semantics. The distinction is as follows:

- *MBR objects*: The caller receives a proxy to the remote object

- *MBV objects*: The caller receives a full copy of the object in its own application domain

If you configure an MBR object type, the CLR ensures that the transparent and real proxies are created in the client's application domain, while the MBR object itself remains in the server's application domain. As the client invokes methods on the remote type, the .NET Remoting plumbing (examined previously) takes over the show and will package, pass, and return information between application domain boundaries. To be sure, MBR objects have a number of traits above and beyond their physical location. As you will see, MBR objects have various configuration options regarding their activation options and lifetime management.

MBV objects, on the other hand, are *local copies* of remote objects (which as you can guess make use of the .NET serialization protocol examined at the beginning of this chapter). MBV objects have far fewer configuration settings, given that their lifetime is directly controlled by the client. Like any .NET object, once a client has released all references to an MBV type, it is a candidate for garbage collection. Given that MBV types are local copies of remote objects, as a client invokes members on the type no network activity occurs during the process.

To solidify the distinction between MBR and MBV objects, think back to Chapter 3 when you examined the role of the C# "ref" keyword. Recall that by default, parameters are passed into a method *by value*. Thus, if the receiving function attempts to reassign the value of the incoming parameters, the caller is unaware of the modification. On the other hand, if method parameters are modified using the "ref" keyword, a reference to the value type is passed into the method, and thus any modifications are realized after the call.

The same basic behavior applies in the world of .NET Remoting. If a remote object has been configured as an MBV type, the caller receives a full copy of the remote object within the application's domain, again using the same object serialization technique presented at the start of this chapter.

If a remote object has been configured to be an MBR type, the client does not receive a local copy of the type. Rather, the remote object is bound to the application domain in which it was created, forcing the caller to interact with the remote type via the intervening proxy layer.

Now, understand that it will be quite common for a single server to provide access to numerous MBR and MBV types. As you may also suspect, MBR types tend to support methods that return various MBV types, which gives way to the familiar factory pattern (e.g., an object that creates and returns other related objects). Next question: How do we configure our custom class types as MBR or MBV entities?

Configuring an MBV Object

To configure an object as an MBV type, you have two options, which happen to be the exact same choices you have when configuring a local .NET object for serialization. Recall that the simplest (and typically most common) approach is to mark your type with the [Serializable] attribute:

```
[Serializable]
public class MyCustomMBVClass
{...}
```

The other, more exotic, approach is to implement the ISerializable interface. Using this technique, you are able to customize the serialization process to fit your needs (as illustrated previously in this chapter).

Configuring an MBR Object

MBR objects are not marked as such using a .NET attribute, but rather derive (directly or indirectly) from the System.MarshalByRefObject base class:

```
public class MyCustomMBRClass : MarshalByRefObject
{...}
```

So, what exactly does the MarshalByRefObject base class bring to the table? Here is the formal definition:

```
public abstract class MarshalByRefObject : object
{
    public virtual ObjRef CreateObjRef(Type requestedType);
    public virtual bool Equals(object obj);
    public virtual int GetHashCode();
    public virtual object GetLifetimeService();
    public Type GetType();
    public virtual object InitializeLifetimeService();
    public virtual string ToString();
}
```

Beyond the expected functionality provided by System.Object, Table 12-5 describes the role of the remaining members.

Table 12-5. Key Members of System.MarshalByRefObject

System.MarshalByRefObject Member	Meaning in Life
CreateObjRef()	Creates an object that contains all the relevant information required to generate a proxy used to communicate with a remote object
GetLifetimeServices()	Retrieves the current lifetime service object that controls the lifetime policy for this instance
InitializeLifetimeServices()	Obtains a lifetime service object to control the lifetime policy for this instance

As you can tell, the gist of MarshalByRefObject is to define members that can be overridden to programmatically control the lifetime of the MBR object (more on lifetime management later in this chapter).

NOTE Just because you have configured a type as an MBV or MBR entity does not mean it is only useable within a remoting application, just that it *may* be used in a remoting application. For example, the System.Windows.Forms.Form type is a descendent from MarshalByRefObject, and thus if it is accessed remotely, is realized as an MBR type. If not, it is just another local object in the client's application domain.

NOTE As a corollary to the previous note, understand that if a .NET type is not serializable and does not include MarshalByRefObject in its inheritance chain, the type in question can only be activated and used in the originating application domain (meaning, they are context bound types).

Final Notes Regarding MBR/MBV Objects

The .NET Remoting layer has a number of intrinsic optimizations that help ensure that when a client interacts with remotable objects, network traffic is kept to a minimum. To provide some insights to these internal tweaks, ponder the following points:

- *Treatment of static members*: Static type members are never invoked remotely, but are triggered within the client-side application domain.

- *Treatment of object fields and accessor methods*: For object-level fields and accessor methods, the system inserts a check at runtime to see whether the object is a proxy. If it is not a proxy, field access is direct. Otherwise, the proxy provides accessors to the caller.

- *Treatment of System.Object members*: Provided that a remote type has not overridden the virtual methods of System.Object, methods always execute in the client's application domain. However, if the remote type overrides Equals() or ToString(), a network round-trip will occur.

Now that you understand the distinct traits of MBR and MBV types, let's check out some issues that are specific to MBR types (MBV types need not apply).

Activation Choices for MBR Types (WKO or CAO?)

Another remoting-centric choice you face as a .NET programmer has to do with exactly *when* an MBR object is activated and *when* it should be a candidate for garbage collection on the server. This might seem like a strange choice to make, as you might naturally assume that MBR objects are created when the client requests it and die when the client is done. While it is true that the client is the entity in charge of instructing the remoting layer it wishes to communicate with a remote type, the server application domain may (or may not) create the type at the exact moment the client's code base requests it. The reason for this seemingly strange behavior has to do with the optimization. Specifically, every MBR type may be configured to be activated using one of two techniques:

- As a Well Known Object (WKO)

- As a Client Activated Object (CAO)

NOTE   A potential point of confusion is that fact that the acronym WKO is also called a server-activated object in the .NET literature. In fact, you may see the SAO acronym in various .NET-centric articles and books. As you read online Help and find the terms WKO, server-activated object, or SAO, understand that these three terms are one and the same. Given that WKO seems to be the moniker of choice at present, I make use of this acronym in this chapter.

WKO objects are MBR types whose lifetimes are directly controlled by the server's application domain. The client-side application activates the remote type using a friendly, well-known string name (hence the term, WKO). The server's application domain allocates WKO types only when the client makes the first method call on the object (via the transparent proxy), *not* when the client's code base makes use of the "new" keyword or via the static Activator.GetObject() method. To illustrate:

```
// Get a proxy to remote object. This line does NOT create the WKO type!
object remoteObj = Activator.GetObject( /* params seen later... */ );
// Invoke a method on remote WKO type. This WILL create the WKO object
// and invoke the ReturnMessage() method.
RemoteMessageObject simple = (RemoteMessageObject)remoteObj;
Console.WriteLine("Server says: {0}", simple.ReturnMessage());
```

The rationale for this behavior? This approach saves a network round-trip solely for the purpose of creating the object. As another interesting corollary, WKO types can *only be created via the type's default constructor*. This should make sense, given that the remote type's constructor is only triggered when the client makes the initial member invocation. Thus, the runtime has no other option than to invoke the type's default constructor.

> **NOTE**   Always remember all WKO types must support a default constructor!

If you wish to allow the client to create a remote MBR object using a custom constructor, the server must configure the object as a client-activated object (CAO). CAO objects are entities whose lifetime is controlled by the client's application domain. When accessing a CAO type, a round-trip to the server occurs at the time the client makes use of the "new" keyword (using any of the type's constructors) or via the Activator type.

Stateful Configuration of WKO Types (Singleton or Single Call?)

The final .NET design choice to consider with regard to MBR types has to do with how the server should handle multiple requests to a WKO type. CAO types need not apply, given that there is always a one-to-one correspondence between a client and a remote CAO type (given that they are stateful).

Your first option is to configure a WKO type to function as a singleton type. As the name implies, the CLR will create a single instance of the remote type that will take requests from any number of clients, and is a natural choice if you need to maintain stateful information among multiple remote callers. Given the fact that multiple clients could invoke the same method at the same time, the CLR places each client invocation on a new thread. It is *your* responsibility, however, to ensure that your objects are thread-safe using the same techniques seen in Chapter 10.

In contrast, a single call object is a WKO type that exists only during the context of a single method invocation. Thus, if there are 20 clients making use of a WKO type configured with single call semantics, the server will create 20 distinct objects (one for each client), all of which are candidates for garbage collection directly after the method invocation. As you can guess, single call objects are far more scalable than singleton types, given that they are invariably stateless entities.

The server is the entity in charge of determining the stateful configuration of a given WKO type. Programmatically, these options are expressed via the System.Runtime.Remoting.WellKnownObjectMode enumeration:

```
public enum WellKnownObjectMode
{
    SingleCall,
    Singleton
}
```

Summarizing the Traits of MBR Object Types

As you have seen, the configuration options of an MBV object are a no-brainer: apply the [Serializable] attribute to allow copies of the type to be returned to the client's application domain. At this point, all interaction with the MBV type takes place in the client's locale. When the client is finished using the MBV type, it is a candidate for garbage collection, and all is well with the world.

MBR types, however, have a number of possible configuration choices. As you have seen, a given MBR type can be configured with regard to its time of activation, statefullness, and lifetime management. To summarize the array of possibilities, Table 12-6 documents how WKO and CAO types stack up against the traits you have just examined.

Table 12-6. Configuration Options for MBR Types

MBR Object Trait	WKO Behavior (aka Server-Activated Object)	CAO Behavior
Instantiation options	WKO types can only be activated using the default constructor of the type, which is triggered when the client makes the first method invocation.	CAO types can be activated using any constructor of the type. The remote object is created at the point the caller makes use of constructor semantics (or via the Activator type).
State management	WKO types can be configured as singleton or single call entities. Singleton types can service multiple clients, and are therefore stateful. Single call types are alive only during a specific client-side invocation, and are therefore stateless.	The lifetime of a CAO type is dictated by the caller, and therefore, CAO types are stateful entities.
Lifetime management	Singleton WKO types make use of a lease-based management scheme (described later in this chapter). Single call WKO types are a candidate for garbage collection after the current method invocation.	CAO types make use of a lease-based management scheme (described later in this chapter).

Basic Deployment of a .NET Remoting Project

Enough acronyms! At this point you are almost ready to build your first .NET Remoting application. Before you do, however, I need to discuss one final detail—deployment. When you are building a .NET Remoting application, you are almost certain to end up with three distinct .NET assemblies that will constitute the entirety of your remote application (yes, three, not two). The first two assemblies I am sure you can already account for:

- *The client*: This assembly is the entity that is interested in obtaining access to a remote object. Like any .NET application, the client may be a Windows Forms application, a console application or an ASP.NET Web application.

- *The server*: This assembly is the entity that receives channel requests from the remote client and hosts the remote objects. Be aware that the server application is often termed the *listener* application. The server may be a custom console application, a custom Windows Service (as you will see), or MS IIS.

So then, where does the third assembly fit in? Well, in reality, the server application is typically a host to a third assembly that defines and implements the remote objects. For convenience, I'll call this assembly the 'general assembly'. This decoupling of the assembly containing the remote objects and server host is quite important, in that both the client and the server assemblies typically set a reference to the general assembly in order to obtain the metadata definitions of the remotable types.

In the simplest case, the general assembly is placed into the application directory of the client and server. The only possible drawback to this approach is the fact that the client has a reference to an assembly that contains CIL code that is never used (which may be a problem if you wish to ensure that the remote clients cannot examine your custom proprietary code). Specifically, the only reason the client requires a reference to the general assembly is to obtain the metadata descriptions of the remotable types. There are several ways to overcome this glitch, for example:

- Construct your remote objects to make use of interface-based programming techniques. In this way, you can build an additional assembly that contains nothing but interface definitions for the remote types. Given this, the client is able to set a reference to a .NET binary that contains nothing but interface definitions.

- Make use of the soapsuds.exe command line application. Using this tool, you are able to generate an assembly that contains nothing but metadata descriptions of the remote types. You'll check out the use of soapsuds.exe later in this chapter.

- Manually build an assembly that contains nothing but metadata descriptions of the remote types (from scratch or by altering the assembly generated via soapsuds.exe).

To keep things simple over the course of this chapter, you will build and deploy general assemblies that contain the required metadata as well as the CIL implementation.

NOTE   If you wish to examine how to implement general assemblies using each of these alternatives, check out *Distributed .NET Programming in C#* (Barnaby, Apress 2002).

Building Our First Distributed Application

There is nothing more satisfying than building a distributed application using a new platform. To illustrate how quickly you are able to get up and running with the .NET Remoting layer, let's build a simple example. As mentioned, the entirety of this example consists of three .NET assemblies:

- A general assembly named SimpleRemotingAsm.dll

- A client assembly named SimpleRemoteObjectClient.exe

- A server assembly named SimpleRemoteObjectServer.exe

The first iteration of this example makes use of various remoting-centric types (RemotingConfiguration and ChannelServices) that are examined in further detail in just a bit.

Building the General Assembly

First, let's create the general assembly (SimpleRemotingAsm.dll), which will be referenced by both the server and client binaries. SimpleRemotingAsm.dll defines a single MBR type named RemoteMessageObject, which supports two public members: DisplayMessage() prints a client supplied message to the server's console window, while ReturnMessage() returns a textual message to the client. Here is the complete code of this new C# class library:

```
namespace SimpleRemotingAsm
{
    // This is a type that will be
    // marshaled by reference (MBR) if accessed remotely.
    public class RemoteMessageObject: MarshalByRefObject
    {
        // The ctor prints a message just to
        // confirm it has been activated.
        public RemoteMessageObject()
        { Console.WriteLine("RemoteMessageObject ctor called!");}
        // This method takes an input string
        // from the caller.
        public void DisplayMessage(string msg)
        { Console.WriteLine("Message is: {0}", msg);}
        // This method returns a value to the caller.
        public string ReturnMessage()
        { return "Hello from the server!"; }
    }
}
```

The major point of interest is the fact that the type derives from the System.MarshalByRefObject base class, which ensures that the derived class will be accessible via a client-side proxy (e.g., an MBR object type). Also note I have added a Console.WriteLine() call in the type's constructor, to see exactly when the type is created. That's it. Go ahead and build your new SimpleRemotingAsm.dll assembly.

Building the Server Assembly

Recall that server assemblies are essentially hosts for general assemblies that contain the remotable objects. Thus, create a console-based *.exe assembly named SimpleRemoteObjectServer. The role of this binary is to open a channel for the incoming requests and register RemoteMessageObject as a WKO type. Set a reference to the System.Runtime.Remoting.dll and SimpleRemotingAsm.dll assemblies, and update Main() as follows:

```
using System;
using System.Runtime.Remoting;
using System.Runtime.Remoting.Channels;
using System.Runtime.Remoting.Channels.Http;
using SimpleRemotingAsm;

namespace SimpleRemoteObjectServer
{
    class SimpleObjServer
    {
        static void Main(string[] args)
        {
            Console.WriteLine("***** SimpleRemoteObjectServer started! *****");
            Console.WriteLine("Hit enter to end.");
            // Register a new HttpChannel
            HttpChannel c = new HttpChannel(32469);
            ChannelServices.RegisterChannel(c);
            // Register a WKO type, using singleton activation.
            RemotingConfiguration.RegisterWellKnownServiceType(
                typeof(SimpleRemotingAsm.RemoteMessageObject),
                "RemoteMsgObj.soap",
                WellKnownObjectMode.Singleton);
            Console.ReadLine();
        }
    }
}
```

Main() begins by creating a new HttpChannel type using an arbitrary port ID. This port is opened on registering the channel via the static ChannelServices.RegisterChannel() method. Once the channel has been registered, the remote server assembly is now equipped to process incoming messages via port number 32469.

NOTE The number you assign to a port is typically up to you (or your system administrator). Do be aware, however, that port IDs below 1024 are reserved for use.

Next, to register the SimpleRemotingAsm.RemoteMessageObject type as a WKO requires the use of the RemotingConfiguration.RegisterWellKnownServiceType() method. Here you are informing the CLR that this object is to be realized as a WKO type named RemoteMsgObj.soap. This second parameter to the static RegisterWellKnownServiceType() is a simple string (of your choosing) that will be used to identify the object across application domain boundaries (hence the notion of a well-known object).

The final parameter is a member of the WellKnownObjectMode enumeration, which you have specified as WellKnownObjectMode.Singleton. Recall that singleton WKO types ensure that a single instance of the RemoteMessageObject will service all incoming requests. Cool! Build your server assembly and move onto the client-side code.

Building the Client Assembly

Now that you have a listener that is hosting your remotable object, the final step is to build an assembly that will request access to its services. Again, let's use a simple console application. Set a reference to System.Runtime.Remoting.dll and SimpleRemotingAsm.dll. Implement Main() as follows:

```
using System;
using System.Runtime.Remoting;
using System.Runtime.Remoting.Channels;
using System.Runtime.Remoting.Channels.Http;
using SimpleRemotingAsm;

namespace SimpleRemoteObjectClient
{
    class SimpleObjClient
    {
        static void Main(string[] args)
        {
            Console.WriteLine("***** SimpleRemoteObjectClient started! *****");
            Console.WriteLine("Hit enter to end.");
            // Create a new HttpChannel
            HttpChannel c = new HttpChannel();
            ChannelServices.RegisterChannel(c);
             // Get a proxy to remote WKO type.
            object remoteObj = Activator.GetObject(
                typeof(SimpleRemotingAsm.RemoteMessageObject),
                "http://localhost:32469/RemoteMsgObj.soap");
            // Now use the remote object.
            RemoteMessageObject simple = (RemoteMessageObject)remoteObj;
            simple.DisplayMessage("Hello from the client!");
            Console.WriteLine("Server says: {0}", simple.ReturnMessage());
            Console.ReadLine();
        }
    }
}
```

A few notes about this client app. First, note that the client is also required to register an HTTP channel, but the client does not specify a port ID as this is dynamically assigned by the .NET Remoting layer. Given that the client is interacting with a registered WKO type, you are limited to triggering the type's default constructor. To do so, make use of the Activator.GetObject() method, specifying two parameters. The first is the type information that describes the remote object you are interested in interacting with. Read that last sentence again. Given that the Activator.GetObject() method requires the object's metadata description, it should make more sense why the client is *also* required to reference the general assembly! Again, at the end of the chapter you examine various ways to clean up this aspect of your client-side assembly.

The second parameter to Activator.GetObject() is termed the activation URL. Unlike classic DCOM which identified remote objects using a numerical GUID, .NET makes use of a friendlier, more readable string name. Activation URLs that describe a WKO type can be generalized into the following format:

```
ProtocolScheme://ComputerName:Port/ObjectUri
```

Finally, note that the Activator.GetObject() method returns a generic System.Object type, and thus you must make use of an explicit cast to gain access to the members of the RemoteMessageObject.

Testing the Remoting Application

To test your application, begin by launching the server application, which will open an HTTP channel and register your remote object for access. Next, launch an instance of the client application. If all is well, your server window should appear as follows (Figure 12-8) while the client application presents what you see in Figure 12-9.

Figure 12-8. The server's output

Figure 12-9. The client's output

Understanding the ChannelServices Type

As you have seen, when a server application wishes to advertise the existence of a remote type, it makes use of the System.Runtime.Remoting.Channels.ChannelServices type. ChannelServices provides a small set of static methods that aid in the process of remoting channel registration, resolution, and URL discovery. Table 12-7 documents the members in question.

Table 12-7. Select Members of the ChannelServices Type

Member of ChannelServices	Meaning in Life
RegisteredChannels	This property gets or sets a list of currently registered channels, each of which is represented by the IChannel interface.
AsyncDispatchMessage()	Asynchronously dispatches the given message to the server-side chain(s) based on the URI embedded in the message.
CreateServerChannelSinkChain()	Creates a channel sink chain for the specified channel.
DispatchMessage()	Dispatches incoming remote calls.
GetChannel()	Returns a registered channel with the specified name.
GetChannelSinkProperties()	Returns an IDictionary of properties for a given proxy.
GetUrlsForObject()	Returns an array of all the URLs that can be used to reach the specified object.
RegisterChannel()	Registers a channel with the channel services.
SyncDispatchMessage()	Synchronously dispatches the incoming message to the server-side chain(s) based on the URI embedded in the message.
UnregisterChannel()	Unregisters a particular channel from the registered channels list.

In addition to the aptly named RegisterChannel() and UnregisterChannel() methods, ChannelServices defines the RegisteredChannels property. This member returns an array of IChannel interfaces, that each represent a handle to each channel registered in a given application domain. The definition of the IChannel interface is quite straightforward:

```
public interface IChannel
{
    string ChannelName { get; }
    int ChannelPriority { get; }
    string Parse(string url, ref String objectURI);
}
```

As you can see, each channel is given a friendly string name as well as a priority level. To illustrate, if you were to update the SimpleRemoteObjectClient application with the following logic:

```
// List all registered channels.
IChannel[] channelObjs = ChannelServices.RegisteredChannels;
foreach(IChannel i in channelObjs)
{
    Console.WriteLine("Channel name: {0}", i.ChannelName);
    Console.WriteLine("Channel Priority: {0}", i.ChannelPriority);
}
```

You would find the client side console now looks like Figure 12-10.

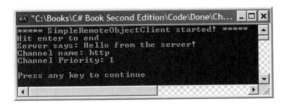

Figure 12-10. Enumerating client-side channels

The majority of the remaining methods of ChannelServices are used to interact with custom sink types, which may be plugged into the .NET Remoting layer.

Understanding the RemotingConfiguration Type

Another key remoting-centric type is RemotingConfiguration, which as the name suggests, is used to configure various aspects of a remoting application. Currently, you have seen this type in use on the server side (via the call to the RegisterWellKnownServiceType() method). Table 12-8 lists additional static members of interest, some of which you see in action over the remainder of this chapter:

Table 12-8. Members of the RemotingConfiguration Type

Member of RemotingConfiguration	Meaning in Life
ApplicationId	Gets the ID of the currently executing application
ApplicationName	Gets or sets the name of a remoting application
ProcessId	Gets the ID of the currently executing process
Configure()	Reads the configuration file and configures the remoting infrastructure
GetRegisteredActivatedClientTypes()	Retrieves an array of object types registered on the client as types that will be activated remotely
GetRegisteredActivatedServiceTypes()	Retrieves an array of object types registered on the service end that can be activated on request from a client
GetRegisteredWellKnownClientTypes()	Retrieves an array of object types registered on the client end as well-known types
GetRegisteredWellKnownServiceTypes()	Retrieves an array of object types registered on the service end as well-known types
IsActivationAllowed()	Returns a Boolean value indicating whether the specified Type is allowed to be client activated
IsRemotelyActivatedClientType()	Checks whether the specified object type is registered as a remotely activated client type
IsWellKnownClientType()	Checks whether the specified object type is registered as a well-known client type
RegisterActivatedClientType()	Registers an object Type on the client end as a type that can be activated on the server
RegisterActivatedServiceType()	Registers an object Type on the service end as one that can be activated on request from a client
RegisterWellKnownClientType()	Registers an object Type on the client end as a well-known type (single call or singleton)
RegisterWellKnownServiceType()	Registers an object Type on the service end as a well-known type (single call or singleton)

Recall that the .NET Remoting layer distinguishes between two types of MBR objects: WKO (aka server activated) and CAO (aka client activated). Furthermore, WKO types can be configured to make use of singleton or single call activations. Using the functionality of the RemotingConfiguration type, you are able to dynamically obtain such information at runtime. For example, if you update the Main() method of your SimpleRemoteObjectServer application with the following:

```
static void Main(string[] args)
{
...
    // Set a friendly name for this server app.
    RemotingConfiguration.ApplicationName = "First server app!";
    Console.WriteLine("App Name: {0}",
        RemotingConfiguration.ApplicationName);
    // Get an array of WellKnownServiceTypeEntry types
    // that represent all the registered WKOs.
    WellKnownServiceTypeEntry[] WKOs =
        RemotingConfiguration.GetRegisteredWellKnownServiceTypes();
    // Now print their statistics.
    foreach(WellKnownServiceTypeEntry wko in WKOs)
    {
        Console.WriteLine("Asm name containing WKO: {0}", wko.AssemblyName);
        Console.WriteLine("URL to WKO: {0}", wko.ObjectUri);
        Console.WriteLine("Type of WKO: {0}", wko.ObjectType);
        Console.WriteLine("Mode of WKO: {0}", wko.Mode);
    }
}
```

you will find a list of all WKO types registered by this server application domain. As you iterate over the array of WellKnownServiceTypeEntry types, you are able to print out various points of interest regarding each WKO. Given that our server's application only registered a single type (SimpleRemotingAsm.RemoteMessageObject), we find the following output (Figure 12-11).

Figure 12-11. Server-side statistics

The other major method of the RemotingConfiguration type is Configure(). As you see in just a bit, this static member allows the client- and server-side application domains to make use of remoting configuration files.

Revisiting the Activation Mode of WKO Types

Recall that WKO types can be configured to function under singleton or single call activation. Currently, our server application has registered our WKO to employ singleton activation semantics:

```
// Singletons can service multiple clients.
RemotingConfiguration.RegisterWellKnownServiceType(
    typeof(SimpleRemotingAsm.RemoteMessageObject),
    "RemoteMsgObj.soap",
    WellKnownObjectMode.Singleton);
```

Again, singleton WKOs are capable of receiving requests from multiple clients. Thus, singleton objects maintain a one-to-many relationship between themselves and the remote clients. To test this behavior for yourself, run the server application (if it is not currently running) and launch three separate client applications. If you look at the output for the server, you will find a single call to the RemoteMessageObject's default constructor (Figure 12-12).

Figure 12-12. Singleton WKOs are shared among remote clients.

Now to test the behavior of single call objects, modify the server to register the WKO to support single call activation:

```
// Single call types maintain a 1-to-1 relationship
// between client and WKO.
RemotingConfiguration.RegisterWellKnownServiceType(
    typeof(SimpleRemotingAsm.RemoteMessageObject),
    "RemoteMsgObj.soap",
    WellKnownObjectMode.SingleCall);
```

Once you have recompiled and run the server application, again launch three clients. This time you can see that a new RemoteMessageObject is created for each client request (Figure 12-13).

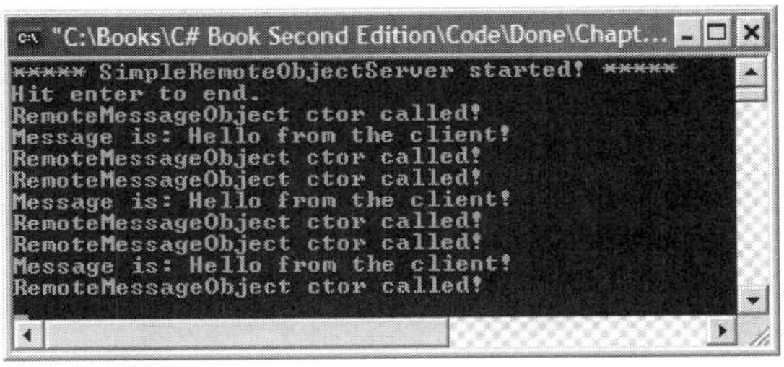

Figure 12-13. Single call WKOs maintain a one-to-one relationship with their remote clients.

SOURCE CODE   The SimpleRemotingAsm, SimpleRemoteObjectServer, and SimpleRemoteObjectClient projects are located under the Chapter 12 directory.

Deploying the Server to a Remote Machine

So far so good! At this point, you have just crossed an application and process boundary on a single machine. If you are connected to an additional machine, let's extend this example to allow the client to interact with the RemoteMessageObject type across a machine boundary. To do so, follow these steps:

1. On your server machine, create and share a folder to hold your server-side assemblies.

2. Copy the SimpleRemoteObjectServer.exe and SimpleRemotingAsm.dll assemblies to this server-side share point.

3. Open your SimpleRemoteObjectClient project workspace and retrofit the activation URL to specify the name of the remote machine. For example:

```
// Get a proxy to remote object.
object remoteObj = Activator.GetObject(
    typeof(SimpleRemotingAsm.RemoteMessageObject),
    "http://YourRemoteBoxName:32469/RemoteMsgObj.soap");
```

4. Execute the SimpleRemoteObjectServer.exe application on the server machine.

5. Execute the SimpleRemoteObjectClient.exe application on the client machine.

6. Sit back and grin.

NOTE Activation URLs may specify a machine's IP address in place of its friendly name.

Leveraging the TCP Channel

Currently, your remote object is accessible via the HTTP network protocol. As mentioned, this protocol is quite firewall-friendly, however the resulting SOAP packets are a bit on the bloated side (given the nature of XML data representation). To lighten the payload, we can update the client and server assemblies to make use of the TCP channel, and therefore make use of the BinaryFormatter type behind the scenes. Here are the relevant updates to the server assembly:

NOTE When you are defining an object to be URI-accessible via a TCP endpoint, it is common (but not required) to make use of the *rem" extension (i.e., remote).

```
// Server adjustments!
using System.Runtime.Remoting.Channels.Tcp;
...
static void Main(string[] args)
{
...
    // Create a new TcpChannel
    TcpChannel c = new  TcpChannel(32469);
    ChannelServices.RegisterChannel(c);
    // Register a 'well-known' object in single call mode.
    RemotingConfiguration.RegisterWellKnownServiceType(
        typeof(SimpleRemotingAsm.RemoteMessageObject),
        "RemoteMsgObj.rem",
        WellKnownObjectMode.SingleCall);
    Console.ReadLine();
}
```

Notice that we are now registering a System.Runtime.Remoting.Channels.Tcp.TcpChannel type to the .NET Remoting layer. Also note that the object URI has been altered to support a more generic name (RemoteMsgObj.rem) rather than the SOAP centric *.soap extension. The client-side updates are equally as simple:

```
// Client adjustments!
using System.Runtime.Remoting.Channels.Tcp;
...
static void Main(string[] args)
{
...
    // Create a new TcpChannel
    TcpChannel c = new TcpChannel();
    ChannelServices.RegisterChannel(c);
    // Get a proxy to remote object.
    object remoteObj = Activator.GetObject(
        typeof(SimpleRemotingAsm.RemoteMessageObject),
        "tcp://localhost:32469/RemoteMsgObj.rem");
    // Use object.
    RemoteMessageObject simple = (RemoteMessageObject)remoteObj;
    simple.DisplayMessage("Hello from the client!");
    Console.WriteLine("Server says: {0}", simple.ReturnMessage());
    Console.ReadLine();
}
```

The only point to be aware of here is that the client's activation URL now must specify the tcp:// channel qualifier rather than http://. Beyond that, the bulk of the code base is identical to the previous HttpChannel logic.

 SOURCE CODE The TCPSimpleRemoteObjectServer and TCPSimpleRemoteObjectClient projects are located under the Chapter 12 directory (both projects use the SimpleRemotingAsm.dll created previously).

Remoting Configuration Files

At this point you have successfully built a distributed application (leveraging two computers) using the .NET Remoting layer. One issue you may have noticed in these first examples is that fact that the client and the server applications have a good deal of hard-coded logic within their respective binaries. For example, the server specifies a fixed port ID, fixed activation mode, and fixed channel type. The client, on the other hand, hard-codes the name of the remote object it is attempting to interact with.

As you might agree, it is wishful thinking to assume that initial design notes remain unchanged once an application is deployed. Ideally, details such as port ID and object activation mode (and whatnot) could be altered on the fly without needing to recompile and redistribute the client or server code bases. Under the .NET Remoting scheme, all the aforementioned issues can be circumvented using the remoting configuration file.

As you recall from Chapter 9, *.config can be used to provide hints to the CLR regarding the loading of externally referenced assemblies. The same *.config files can be used to inform the CLR of a number of remoting-related details, on both the client side and the server side.

When building a remoting *.config file, the <system.runtime.remoting> element is used to hold various remoting-centric details. Do be aware that if you are building an application that already has a *.config file that specifies assembly resolution details, you are free to add remoting elements within the same file. Thus, a single *.config file that contains remoting and binding information would look something like this:

```
<configuration>
    <system.runtime.remoting>
        <! -- configure client / server remoting settings here -- >
    </system.runtime.remoting>
    <runtime>
        <! -- binding assembly settings here -- >
    </runtime>
</configuration>
```

If your configuration file has no need to specify assembly binding logic, you can omit the <runtime> element and make use of the following skeleton *config file:

```
<configuration>
    <system.runtime.remoting>
        <! -- configure client / server remoting settings here -- >
    </system.runtime.remoting>
</configuration>
```

Building Server-Side *.config Files

Server-side configuration files allow you to declare the objects that are to be reached via remote invocations as well as channel and port information. Basically, using the <service>, <wellknown>, and <channels> elements, you are able to replace the following server-side logic:

```
// Hard coded HTTP server logic.
HttpChannel c = new HttpChannel(32469);
ChannelServices.RegisterChannel(c);
RemotingConfiguration.RegisterWellKnownServiceType(
    typeof(SimpleRemotingAsm.RemoteMessageObject),
    "RemoteMsgObj.soap",
    WellKnownObjectMode.Singleton);
```

with the following *.config file:

```
<configuration>
  <system.runtime.remoting>
    <application>
      <service>
        <wellknown
          mode="Singleton"
          type="SimpleRemotingAsm.RemoteMessageObject, SimpleRemotingAsm"
          objectUri="RemoteMsgObj.soap"/>
      </service>
      <channels>
          <channel ref="http"/>
      </channels>
    </application>
  </system.runtime.remoting>
</configuration>
```

Notice that much of the relevant server-side remoting information is wrapped within the scope of the <service> (not *server*) element. The child <wellknown> element makes use of three attributes (mode, type, and objectUri) to specify the well-known object to register with the .NET Remoting layer. The child <channels> element contains any number of <channel> elements that allow you to define the type of channel (in this case HTTP) to open on the server. TCP channels would simply make use of the "tcp" string token in place of "http".

As the SimpleRemoteObjectServer.exe.config file contains all the necessary information, the server-side Main() method cleans up considerably. All you are required to do is make a single call to RemotingConfiguration.Configure(), and specify the name of your configuration file.

```
static void Main(string[] args)
{
    // Register a 'well-known' object using a *.config file.
    RemotingConfiguration.Configure("SimpleRemoteObjectServer.exe.config");
    Console.WriteLine("Server started!  Hit enter to end");
    Console.ReadLine();
}
```

Building Client-Side *.config Files

Clients are also able to leverage remoting-centric *.config files. Unlike a server-side configuration file, client-side configuration files make use of the <client> element to identify the name of the well-known object the caller wishes to interact with. In addition to providing the ability to dynamically change the remoting information without a need to recompile the code base, client-side *.config files allow you to create the proxy type directly using the C# "new" keyword, rather than the Activator.GetObject() method. Thus, if you have the following client-side *.config file:

```
<configuration>
   <system.runtime.remoting>
      <application>
         <client displayName = "SimpleRemoteObjectClient">
            <wellknown
               type="SimpleRemotingAsm.RemoteMessageObject, SimpleRemotingAsm"
               url="http://localhost:32469/RemoteMsgObj.soap"/>
         </client>
         <channels>
            <channel ref="http"/>
         </channels>
      </application>
   </system.runtime.remoting>
</configuration>
```

You are able to update the client's Main() method as follows:

```
static void Main(string[] args)
{
    RemotingConfiguration.Configure("SimpleRemoteObjectClient.exe.config");
    // Using *config file, the client is able to directly 'new' the type.
    RemoteMessageObject simple = new RemoteMessageObject();
    simple.DisplayMessage("Hello from the client!");
    Console.WriteLine("Server says: {0}", simple.ReturnMessage());
    Console.WriteLine("Client started!  Hit enter to end");
    Console.ReadLine();
}
```

Of course, when you run the application, the output is identical. If the client wishes to make use of the TCP channel, the "url" property of the <wellknown> element and <channel> ref property must make use of the "tcp"" token in place of "http."

SOURCE CODE   The SimpleRemoteObjectServerWithConfig and SimpleRemoteObjectClientWithConfig projects are located under the Chapter 12 subdirectory (both of which make use of the SimpleRemotingAsm.dll created previously).

Working with MBV Objects

Our first remoting applications allowed client-side access to a single WKO type. Recall that WKO types are (by definition) MBR types, and therefore client access takes place via an intervening proxy. In contrast, MBV types are local copies of a server-side type, which are typically returned from a public member of an MBR type. Although you already know how to configure an MBV type (mark a class with the [Serializable] attribute), we have not yet seen an example of MBV types in action. To illustrate the interplay of MBR and MBV types, let's see another example which will involve three assemblies:

- The general assembly named CarGeneralAsm.dll

- The client assembly named CarProviderClient.exe

- The server assembly named CarProviderServer.exe

As you might assume, the code behind the client and server applications is more or less identical to the previous example, especially since these applications will again make use of *.config files. Nevertheless, let's step through the process of building each assembly one at a time.

Building the Cars General Assembly

At the beginning of this chapter (during our examination of object serialization), you created a type named JamesBondCar. The CarGeneralAsm.dll code library will reuse this type (in addition to the dependent Radio and Car types), so begin by using the Project | Add Existing Item... menu command, and include these *.cs files into this new Class Library project. Given that each of these types have already been marked with the [Serializable] attribute, they are ready to be marshaled by value to a remote client.

All we need now is an MBR type which provides access to the JamesBondCar type. To make things a bit more interesting, however, our MBR object (CarProvider) will maintain an ArrayList of JamesBondCar types. CarProvider will also define two members, which allow the caller to obtain a specific JamesBondCar, as well as receive the entire ArrayList of types. Here is the complete code for our new class type:

```
namespace CarGeneralAsm
{
    // This type is an MBR object which provides
    // access to related MBV types.
    public class CarProvider : MarshalByRefObject
    {
        private ArrayList theJBCars = new ArrayList();
        // Add some cars to the array list.
        public CarProvider()
        {
            Console.WriteLine("Car provider created");
            theJBCars.Add(new JamesBondCar("QMobile", 140, true, true));
            theJBCars.Add(new JamesBondCar("Flyer", 140, true, false));
            theJBCars.Add(new JamesBondCar("Swinner", 140, false, true));
            theJBCars.Add(new JamesBondCar("BasicJBC", 140, false, false));
        }
        // Get all the JamesBondCars.
        public ArrayList GetAllAutos()
        { return theJBCars; }
        // Get one JamesBondCar.
        public JamesBondCar GetJBCByIndex(int i)
        { return (JamesBondCar)theJBCars[i]; }
    }
}
```

Notice the GetAllAutos() method returns the internal ArrayList type. The obvious question is how this member of the System.Collections namespace is marshaled back to the caller. If you look up this type using online Help, you may be surprise to find that ArrayList has been decorated with the [Serializable] attribute:

```
[Serializable]
public class ArrayList : IList, ICollection,
IEnumerable, ICloneable{...}
```

Therefore, the entire contents of the ArrayList type will be marshaled by value to the caller (provided the contained types are also serializable)! This brings up a very good point regarding .NET Remoting and members of the base class libraries. In addition to the custom MBV and MBR types you may create yourself, do understand that any type in the base class libraries which is decorated with the [Serializable] attribute is able to function as an MBV type in the .NET Remoting architecture. Likewise, any type which derives (directly or indirectly) from MarshalByRefObject will function as an MBR type.

Building the Server Assembly

The server host assembly (CarProviderServer.exe) has the following logic within Main():

```
using System;
using System.Runtime.Remoting;
using System.Runtime.Remoting.Channels;
using System.Runtime.Remoting.Channels.Http;
using CarGeneralAsm;

namespace CarProviderServer
{
    class CarServer
    {
        static void Main(string[] args)
        {
            RemotingConfiguration.Configure("CarProviderServer.exe.config");
            Console.WriteLine("Car server started!  Hit enter to end");
            Console.ReadLine();
        }
    }
}
```

The related *.config file is just about identical to the previous server side *.config file you created in the previous example. The only point of interest is to define an object URI value which makes sense for the CarProvider type (pick your channel of choice):

```
<configuration>
    <system.runtime.remoting>
        <application>
            <service>
                <wellknown mode="Singleton"
                    type="CarGeneralAsm.CarProvider, CarGeneralAsm"
                    objectUri="carprovider.soap" />
            </service>
            <channels>
                <channel ref="http" port="32469" />
            </channels>
        </application>
    </system.runtime.remoting>
</configuration>
```

Building the Client Assembly

Last but not least, we have the client application which will make use of the
MBR CarProvider type in order to obtain discrete JamesBondCars types as well
as the ArrayList type. Once we obtain a type from the CarProvider, we'll send them
into the UseCar() helper function from processing:

```
using System;
using System.Runtime.Remoting;
using System.Runtime.Remoting.Channels;
using System.Runtime.Remoting.Channels.Http;
using CarGeneralAsm;
using System.Collections;

namespace CarProviderClient
{
    class CarClient
    {
        private static void UseCar(JamesBondCar c)
        {
            Console.WriteLine("-> Name: {0}", c.PetName);
            Console.WriteLine("-> Max speed: {0}", c.MaxSpeed);
            Console.WriteLine("-> Sea worthy? : {0}", c.isSeaWorthy);
            Console.WriteLine("-> Flight worthy? : {0}", c.isFlightWorthy);
            Console.WriteLine();
            c.TurnOnRadio(true);
        }
```

```
        static void Main(string[] args)
        {
            RemotingConfiguration.Configure("CarProviderClient.exe.config");
            // Make the car provider.
            CarProvider cp = new CarProvider();
            // Get first JBC.
            JamesBondCar qCar = cp.GetJBCByIndex(0);
            // Get all JBCs.
            ArrayList allJBCs = cp.GetAllAutos();
            // Use first car.
            UseCar(qCar);
            // Use all cars in ArrayList
            foreach(JamesBondCar j in allJBCs)
                UseCar(j);
            Console.WriteLine("Client started!  Hit enter to end");
            Console.ReadLine();
        }
    }
}
```

The client side *.config is also what you would expect. Simply update the activation URL:

```
<configuration>
    <system.runtime.remoting>
        <application>
            <client displayName = "CarClient">
                <wellknown
                    type="CarGeneralAsm.CarProvider, CarGeneralAsm"
                    url="http://localhost:32469/carprovider.soap"/>
            </client>
            <channels>
                <channel ref="http"/>
            </channels>
        </application>
    </system.runtime.remoting>
</configuration>
```

Now, run your server and client applications (in that order, of course) and observe the output. Your client-side console window will whirl through the JamesBondCars and print out the statistics of each type. Recall that as you interact with the ArrayList and JamesBondCar types you are operating on their members within the client's application domain, as they have both been marked with the [Serializable] attribute.

To prove that point, update the UseCar() helper function to call the TurnOnRadio() method on the incoming JamesBondCar. Now, run the server and client applications once again. Notice that the message box appears on the client machine! Had the Car, Radio, and JamesBondCar types been configured as MBR types, the server would be the machine displaying the message box prompts. If you wish to verify this, derive each type from MarshalByRefObject, and recompile all three assemblies (to ensure VS .NET copies the latest CarGeneralAsm.dll into the client's and server's application directory).

When you run the application once again, the message boxes appear on the remote machine.

SOURCE CODE   The CarGeneralAsm, CarProviderServer, and CarProviderClient projects are located under the Chapter 12 subdirectory.

Understanding Client-Activated Objects (CAO)

All of our current remoting examples have made use of so-called well-known objects (which again, sometimes go by the term server-activated objects). Recall that WKOs have the following characteristics:

- WKOs can be configured either as singleton or single call.

- WKOs can only be activated using the type's default constructor.

- WKOs are instantiated on the server on the first client-side member invocation.

CAO types on the other hand, can be instantiated using any constructor on the type and are created at the point the client makes use of the C# "new" keyword or Activator type. Furthermore, the lifetime of CAO types is monitored by the .NET leasing mechanism. Do be aware that when you configure a CAO type, the .NET Remoting layer will generate a specific CAO remote object to service each client. Again, the big distinction is the fact that CAOs are always alive (and therefore stateful) beyond a single method invocation.

To illustrate the construction, hosting, and consumption of CAO types, let's retrofit our previous automobile-centric general assembly. Assume that our MBR CarProvider class has defined an additional constructor that allows the client to pass in an array of JamesBondCar types that will be used to populate the internal ArrayList:

```
public class CarProvider : MarshalByRefObject
{
    private ArrayList theJBCars = new ArrayList();
    public CarProvider(JamesBondCar[] theCars)
    {
        Console.WriteLine("Car provider created with custom ctor");
        theJBCars.AddRange(theCars);
    }
...
}
```

In order to allow the caller to activate the CarProvider using our new constructor syntax, we need to build a server application that registers CarProvider as a CAO type rather than a WKO type. This may be done programmatically (a la the

RemotingConfiguration.RegisterActivatedServiceType() method) or using a server-side
*.config file. If you wish to hard-code the name of the CAO object within the host
server's code base, all you need to do is pass in the type information of the type(s)
(after creating and registering a channel) as follows:

```
// Hard code the fact that CarProvider is a CAO type.
RemotingConfiguration.RegisterActivatedServiceType(
    typeof(CAOCarGeneralAsm.CarProvider));
```

If you would rather leverage the *.config file, replace the <wellknown> element with
the <activated> element as follows:

```
<configuration>
    <system.runtime.remoting>
        <application>
            <service>
                <activated type = "CAOCarGeneralAsm.CarProvider,
                    CAOCarGeneralAsm"/>
            </service>
            <channels>
                <channel ref="http" port="32469" />
            </channels>
        </application>
    </system.runtime.remoting>
</configuration>
```

Finally, we need to update the client application, not only by way of the *.config file
(or programmatically in the code base) to request access to the remote CAO, but to
indeed trigger the custom constructor of the CarProvider type. Here are the relevant
updates to the client side Main() method:

```
static void Main(string[] args)
{
    // Read updated *.config file.
    RemotingConfiguration.Configure("CAOCarProviderClient.exe.config");
    // Create array of types to pass to provider.
    JamesBondCar[] cars =
    {
        new JamesBondCar("One", 100, false, false),
        new JamesBondCar("Two", 100, false, false),
        new JamesBondCar("Three", 100, false, false)
    };
    // Now trigger the custom ctor.
    CarProvider cp = new CarProvider(cars);
...
}
```

The updated client side *.config file also makes use of the <activated> element, as
opposed to <wellknown>. In addition, however, the <client> element now requires the
url property to define the location of the registered CAO. Recall that when the server

registered the CarProvider as a WKO, the client specified such information within the <wellknown> element.

```
<configuration>
    <system.runtime.remoting>
        <application>
            <client displayName = "CarClient"
                    url = "http://localhost:32469">
                <activated type = "CAOCarGeneralAsm.CarProvider, CAOCarGeneralAsm" />
            </client>
            <channels>
                <channel ref="http"/>
            </channels>
        </application>
    </system.runtime.remoting>
</configuration>
```

If you would rather hard-code the client's request to the CAO type, you can make use of the RegistrationServices.RegisterActivatedClientType() method as follows:

```
static void Main(string[] args)
{
    // Use hard coded values.
    RemotingConfiguration.RegisterActivatedClientType(
        typeof(CAOCarGeneralAsm.CarProvider),
        "http://localhost:32469");
...
}
```

If you were to now execute the updated server and client assemblies, you would be pleased to find that you are able to pass your custom array of JamesBondCar types to the remote CarProvider via the overloaded constructor.

SOURCE CODE The CAOCarGeneralAsm, CAOCarProviderServer, and CAOCarProviderClient projects are located under the Chapter 12 subdirectory.

The Lease-Based Lifetime of CAO/WKO-Singleton Objects

As you have seen, WKO types configured with single-call activation are only alive for the duration of the current method call. Given this fact, WKO single-call types are stateless entities. As soon as the current invocation has completed, the WKO single-call type is a candidate for garbage collection.

On the other hand, CAO types and WKO types which have been configured to use singleton activation are both, by their nature, stateful entities. Given these two object configuration settings, the question which must be asked is: How does the server process know when to destroy these MBR objects? Clearly, it would be a huge bother if the server machine garbage collected MBR objects that were currently in use by a remote client. If the server machine waits too long to release its set of MBR types, this may place undo stress on the system, especially if the MBR object(s) in question maintain valuable system resources (database connections, unmanaged types, and whatnot).

Unlike classic DCOM, the .NET Remoting layer obviously does not make use of an interface-based reference counting mechanism (or occasional pings) to control object lifetime. Rather, the lifetime of a CAO or WKO-singleton MBR type is governed by a lease time that is tightly integrated with the .NET garbage collector. If the lease time of a CAO or WKO-singleton MBR type expires, the object is ready to be garbage collected on the next collection cycle. Like any .NET type, if the remote object has overridden System.Object.Finalize() (via the C# destructor syntax), the .NET runtime will indeed trigger the finalization logic.

The Default Leasing Behavior

CAO and WKO-singleton MBR types have what is known as a default lease, which lasts for 5 minutes. If the runtime detects 5 minutes of inactivity have passed for a CAO or WKO-singleton MBR type, the assumption is that the client is no longer making use of the entity (or perhaps is no longer running), and therefore the remote object may be garbage collected. Of course, this does not imply that a given CAO or WKO-singleton object is *automatically* marked for garbage collection after 5 minutes! The truth of the matter is that there are many ways to alter the timing of the default lease.

First and foremost, anytime the remote client invokes a member of the remote CAO or WKO-singleton MBR type, the lease is renewed back to its 5 minute limit. In addition to the automatic client-invocation-centric renew policy, the .NET runtime provides three additional alternatives:

- *.config files can be authored that override the default lease settings for a given remote object.

- Server-side lease sponsors can be used to act on behalf of a remote object whose lease time has expired.

- Client-side lease sponsors can be used to act on behalf of a remote object whose lease time has expired.

We will check out these options over the next several sections, but for the time being let's come to understand the default lease settings of a remote type. Recall that the MarshalByRefObject base class defines a member named GetLifetimeService(). This method returns a reference to an internally implemented object that supports the System.Runtime.Remoting.Lifetime.ILease interface. As you would guess, the ILease interface can be used to interact with the leasing behavior of a given CAO or WKO-singleton type. Here is the formal definition:

```
public interface ILease
{
    TimeSpan CurrentLeaseTime { get; }
    LeaseState CurrentState { get; }
    TimeSpan InitialLeaseTime { get; set; }
    TimeSpan RenewOnCallTime { get; set; }
    TimeSpan SponsorshipTimeout { get; set; }
    void Register(System.Runtime.Remoting.Lifetime.ISponsor obj);
    void Register(System.Runtime.Remoting.Lifetime.ISponsor obj,
        TimeSpan renewalTime);
    TimeSpan Renew(TimeSpan renewalTime);
    void Unregister(System.Runtime.Remoting.Lifetime.ISponsor obj);
}
```

The ILease interface not only allows you to obtain information regarding the current lease (via CurrentLeaseTime, CurrentState, and InitialLeaseTime) but also provides the ability to build lease sponsors (more later). Table 12-9 documents the role of each ILease member.

Table 12-9. Members of the ILease Interface

Member of ILease	Meaning in Life
CurrentLeaseTime	Gets the amount of time remaining before the object deactivates if it does not receive further method invocations.
CurrentState	Gets the current state of the lease, represented by the LeaseState enumeration.
InitialLeaseTime	Gets or sets the initial amount of time for a given lease. The initial lease time of an object is the amount of time following the initial activation before the lease expires if no other method calls occur.
RenewOnCallTime	Gets or sets the amount of time by which a call to the remote object increases the CurrentLeaseTime.
SponsorshipTimeout	Gets or sets the amount of time to wait for a sponsor to return with a lease renewal time.
Register()	Overloaded. Registers a sponsor for the lease.
Renew()	Renews a lease for the specified time.
Unregister()	Removes a sponsor from the sponsor list.

To illustrate the characteristics of the default lease of a CAO or WKO-singleton remote object, assume that our current CAOCarGeneralAsm project has defined a new type named LeaseInfo. LeaseInfo supports a static member named LeaseStats() which dumps select statistics regarding the current lease for the CarProvider type to the server side console window (be sure to specify a "using" directive for the System.Runtime.Remoting.Lifetime namespace to inform the compiler where the ILease type is defined):

```
internal class LeaseInfo
{
    public static void LeaseStats(ILease itfLease)
    {
        Console.WriteLine("***** Lease Stats *****");
        Console.WriteLine("Lease state: {0}", itfLease.CurrentState);
        Console.WriteLine("Initial lease time: {0}:{1}",
            itfLease.InitialLeaseTime.Minutes,
            itfLease.InitialLeaseTime.Seconds);
        Console.WriteLine("Current lease time: {0}:{1}",
            itfLease.CurrentLeaseTime.Minutes,
            itfLease.CurrentLeaseTime.Seconds);
        Console.WriteLine("Renew on call time: {0}:{1}",
            itfLease.RenewOnCallTime.Minutes,
            itfLease.RenewOnCallTime.Seconds);
        Console.WriteLine();
    }
}
```

Now that we have this helper type in place, assume LeaseInfo.LeaseStats() is called within the GetJBCByIndex() and GetAllAutos() methods of the CarProvider type. Once we recompile the server and client assemblies (again, simply to ensure VS .NET copies the latest and greatest version of the CarGeneralAsm.dll to the client and server application directories), run the application once again. Your server's console window will now look something like so (Figure 12-14).

Figure 12-14. The default lease information for CarProvider

As you can see, by default, a type's initial lease time is 5 minutes. If and when a method invocation is made on the object after its activation, the RenewOnCallTime property represents the minimum value the CurrentLeaseTime is incremented by, up to the InitialLeaseTime.

Altering the Default Lease Characteristics

Obviously the default lease characteristics of a CAO/ WKO-singleton type may not be appropriate for each and every CAO or WKO-singleton remote object. If you wish to alter these default settings, you have two approaches:

- As you would guess, you are able to adjust the default lease settings using a *.config file.

- You are also able to programmatically alter the settings of a type's default lease by overriding members of the MarshalByRefObject base class.

While each of these options will indeed alter the default lease settings, there is a key difference. When you make use of a server side *.config file, the lease settings affect *all* objects hosted by the server process! In contrast, when you override select members of the MarshalByRefObject type, you are able to change lease settings on an object-by-object basis.

To illustrate changing the default lease settings via a remoting *.config file, assume you have updated the server-side XML data with the following additional <lifetime> element:

```
<configuration>
    <system.runtime.remoting>
        <application>
            <lifetime leaseTime = "15M" renewOnCallTime = "5M"/>
            <service>
                <activated type = "CarGeneralAsm.CarProvider, CarGeneralAsm"/>
            </service>
            <channels>
                <channel ref="http" port="32469" />
            </channels>
        </application>
    </system.runtime.remoting>
</configuration>
```

Notice how the leaseTime and renewOnCallTime properties have been marked with the M suffix, which you might guess stands for the number of minutes to set for each lease-centric unit of time. If you wish, your <lifetime> element may also suffix the numerical values with MS (milliseconds), S (seconds), H (hours), or even D (days). Figure 12-15 shows the result of the updated *.config file:

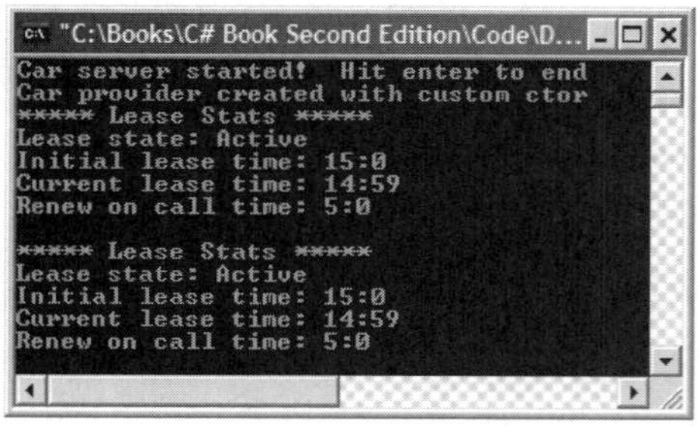

*Figure 12-15. Altering lease timing via a server-side *.config file*

Now recall that when you update the server's *.config file you have effectively changed the leasing characteristics for each CAO/WKO-singleton object hosted by the server. As an alternative, you may choose to programmatically override the InitializeLifetime() method in a specific remote type. Thus, assume you have *not* updated the server's configuration file, but rather updated the CarProviderType as follows:

```
public class CarProvider : MarshalByRefObject
{
    public override object InitializeLifetimeService()
    {
        // Obtain the current lease info.
        ILease itfLeaseInfo =
            (ILease) base.InitializeLifetimeService();
        // Adjust settings.
        itfLeaseInfo.InitialLeaseTime = TimeSpan.FromMinutes(50);
        itfLeaseInfo.RenewOnCallTime = TimeSpan.FromMinutes(10);
        return itfLeaseInfo;
    }
...
}
```

Here, the CarProvider has altered its InitialLeaseTime value to 50 minutes and its RenewOnCallTime value to 10. Again, the benefit of overriding InitializeLifetimeServices() is the fact that you can configure each remote type individually. Finally, on an odd note, if you wish to disable lease-based lifetime for a given CAO/WKO-singleton object type, you may override InitializeLifetimeServices() and simply return null. If you do so, you have basically configured an MBR type that will *never* die as long as the hosting server application is alive and kicking.

Server-Side Lease Adjustment

As you have just seen, when an MBR type overrides InitializeLifetimeServices(), it is able to change its default leasing behavior at the time of activation. However, for the sake of argument, what if a remote type desires to change its current lease *after* its activation cycle? For example, assume the CarProvider has a new method whose implementation requires a lengthy operation (such as connecting to a remote database and reading a large set of records). Before beginning the task, you may programmatically adjust your lease such that if you have less than 1 minute, you renew the lease time to 10 minutes. To do so, you can make use of the inherited MarshalByRefObject.GetLifetimeService() and ILease.Renew() methods as follows:

```
// Server-side lease adjustment.
// Assume this new method of the CarProvider type.
public void DoLengthyOperation()
{
    ILease itfLeaseInfo = (ILease)this.GetLifetimeService();
    if(itfLeaseInfo.CurrentLeaseTime.TotalMinutes < 1.0)
        itfLeaseInfo.Renew(TimeSpan.FromMinutes(10));
    // Do task...
}
```

Client-Side Lease Adjustment

On an additional ILease-related note, it is possible for the client's application domain to adjust the current lease properties for a CAO/WKO-singleton type it is communicating with across the wire. To do so, the client makes use of the static RemotingServices.GetLifetimeService() method. As a parameter to this member, the client passes in the reference to the remote type as follows:

```
// Client-side lease adjustment.
CarProvider cp = new CarProvider(cars);
ILease itfLeaseInfo = (ILease)RemotingServices.GetLifetimeService(cp);
if(itfLeaseInfo.CurrentLeaseTime.TotalMinutes < 10.0)
    itfLeaseInfo.Renew(TimeSpan.FromMinutes(1000));
```

This approach can be helpful if the client's application domain is about to enter a lengthy process on the same thread of execution that is using the remote type. For example, if a single threaded application is about to print out a 100-page document, the chances are quite good that a remote CAO/WKO-singleton type may time out during the process. The other (more elegant) solution, of course, is to spawn a secondary thread of execution, but I think you get the general idea.

Server-Side (and Client-Side) Lease Sponsorship

The final topic regarding the lease-based lifetime of a CAO/WKO-singleton object type considered here is the notion of lease sponsorship. As you have just seen, every CAO/WKO-singleton entity has a default lease, which may be altered in a number of ways on both the server side as well as the client side. Now, regardless of the type's lease configuration, eventually an MBR object times will be up. At this point, the runtime will garbage-collect the entity...well almost.

The truth of the matter is that before an expired type is truly marked for garbage collection, the runtime will check to see if the MBR object in question has any registered lease sponsors. Simply put, a sponsor is a type that implements the ISponsor interface, which is defined as follows:

```
public interface System.Runtime.Remoting.Lifetime.ISponsor
{
    TimeSpan Renewal(ILease lease);
}
```

If the runtime detects that an MBR object has a sponsor, it will *not* garbage-collect the type, but rather call the Renewal() method of the sponsor object to (once again) add time to the current lease. On the other hand, if the MBR has no sponsor, the object's time is truly up.

Assuming that you have created a custom class that implements ISponsor, and thus implements Renewal() to return a specific unit of time (via the TimeSpan type), the next question is how exactly to associate the type to a given remote object. Again, this operation may be performed by either the server's application domain or the client's application domain.

To do so, the interested party obtains an ILease reference (via the inherited GetLifetimeService() method on the server or using the static RemotingServices.GetLifetimeService() method on the client) and calls Register():

```
// Server-side sponsor registration.
CarSponsor mySponsor = new CarSponsor();
ILease itfLeaseInfo = (ILease)this.GetLifetimeService();
itfLeaseInfo.Register(mySponsor);
```

```
// Client-side sponsor registration.
CarSponsor mySponsor = new CarSponsor();
CarProvider cp = new CarProvider(cars);
ILease itfLeaseInfo = (ILease)RemotingServices.GetLifetimeService(cp);
itfLeaseInfo.Register(mySponsor);
```

In either case, if a client or server wishes to revoke sponsorship, it may do so using the ILease.Unregister() method. For example:

```
// Remove the sponsor for a given object.
itfLeaseInfo.Unregister(mySponsor);
```

NOTE Client-side sponsored objects, in addition to implementing ISponsor must also derive from MarshalByRefObject, given that the client must pass the sponsor to the remote application domain!

So, as you can see, the lifetime management of stateful MBR types is quite different from classic DCOM. On the plus side, you have a *ton* of control regarding when a remote type is destined to meet its maker. However, as you may be able to gather, there is the chance that a remote type may be removed from memory without the client's knowledge. Should a client attempt to invoke members on a type that has already been removed from memory the runtime will throw a System.Runtime.Remoting.RemotingException, at which point the client may simply create a brand-new instance of the remote type or simply take an alternative course of action.

SOURCE CODE   The CAOCarGeneralAsmLease, CAOCarProviderServerLease, and CAOCarProviderClientLease projects are located under the Chapter 12 subdirectory.

Alternative Hosts for Remote Objects

Over the course of this chapter, you have constructed numerous console-based server hosts, which provide access to some set of remote objects. If you have a background in classic DCOM, this step may have seemed a bit odd. Under the world of DCOM, it was not unusual to build a single server-side COM server that contained the remote objects and was also in charge of receiving incoming ORCP requests from some remote client. This single *.exe DCOM application would quietly load in the background without presenting a looming command window.

When you are building a .NET server assembly, the chances are quite good that the remote machine does not need to display any sort of UI. Rather, all you really wish to do is build a server-side entity that opens the correct channel(s) and registers the remote object(s) for client-side access. Moreover, when you build a simple console host, you (or someone) is required to manually run the server-side *.exe assembly, due to the fact that the .NET Remoting will not automatically run a server-side *.exe when called by a remote client. Given these two issues, the question then becomes: How can you build an invisible listener that loads automatically (in one way or another)?

Unlike classic DCOM, you are unable to simply pass your command windows a command line parameter that instructs the process to appear invisibly in the background. Rather, .NET programmers have two major choices at their disposal, when they wish to build a transparent host for various remote objects:

- Build a .NET Windows Service application to host the remote objects

- Allow IIS to host your remote objects

Hosting Remote Objects Using a Windows Service

Perhaps the ideal host for remote objects is a Windows service, given that it (a) can be configured to load automatically on system start-up, (b) runs as an invisible background process, and (c) can be run under discrete user accounts. As you would expect, building a custom Windows Service using the .NET platform is extremely simple when contrasted to the raw Win32 API. To illustrate, let's create a Windows Service project (named CarWinService) that will be in charge of hosting the remote types contained within the CarGeneralAsm.dll. To begin, create a new Windows Service project workspace (Figure 12-16).

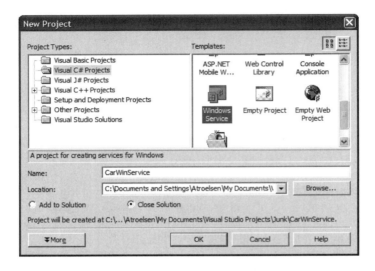

Figure 12-16. Creating a new Windows Service project workspace

As you can see, VS .NET responds by generating a new class (named Service1 by default) which derives from System.ServiceProcess.ServiceBase. Given that Service1 is a rather nondescript name for your custom service, your first order of business is to change the values of the (Name) and ServiceName properties to CarService using the IDE's Properties window. The distinction between these two settings is that the (Name) value is used to define the name used to refer to our type in the code base, while the ServiceName property marks the name to display to Windows Service-centric configuration tools (such as MMC, seen shortly).

The generated class type defines three methods of interest, two of which (OnStart() and OnStop()) are base class overrides:

- *Main():* This method is the entry point of the Windows Service process.

- *OnStart():* This method is called each time the service is started.

- *OnStop():* This method is called when the service is stopped.

First, let's take a peek at the Main() method. Before you do, be sure you set a reference to the CarProviderAsm.dll and System.Remoting.dll assemblies, and specify the following additional "using" directives:

```
using System.Runtime.Remoting;
using System.Runtime.Remoting.Channels.Http;
using System.Runtime.Remoting.Channels;
```

Implementing Main()

The Main() method of a ServiceBase-derived type is in charge of running each service defined in the project by passing an array of ServiceBase types into the static Service.Run() method. Given that you have renamed your custom service from Service1 to CarService, be sure to update the autogenerated array:

```
static void Main()
{
    System.ServiceProcess.ServiceBase[] ServicesToRun;
    ServicesToRun = new System.ServiceProcess.ServiceBase[]
        { new CarService() };
    System.ServiceProcess.ServiceBase.Run(ServicesToRun);
}
```

Implementing OnStart()

I would guess you can already assume what sort of logic should happen when your custom service is started on a given machine. Recall that the role of CarService is to perform the same tasks as your custom console-based service. Thus, if you wish to register CarService as a WKO singleton type which is available via HTTP, you could add the following code to the OnStart() method (as you would hope, you may make use of the RemotingConfiguration type to load up a server side remoting *.config file, rather than hard-coding your implementation, when hosting remote objects using a Windows Service).

```
using System.Diagnostics; // For the EventLog type.
...
protected override void OnStart(string[] args)
{
    // Create a new HttpChannel
    HttpChannel c = new HttpChannel(32469);
    ChannelServices.RegisterChannel(c);
    // Register as single call WKO.
    RemotingConfiguration.RegisterWellKnownServiceType(
        typeof(CarGeneralAsm.CarProvider),
        "CarProvider.soap",
        WellKnownObjectMode.SingleCall);
    // Log our successful start-up.
    EventLog.WriteEntry("CarGeneralAsm",
        "CarWinService started successful!",
        EventLogEntryType.Information);
}
```

Note that once the type has been registered, log a custom message to the Windows event log (via the System.Diagnostics.EventLog type) that informs the host machine of our successful start-up.

Implementing OnStop()

Technically speaking, our CarService does not demand any sort of shutdown logic. For illustrative purposes let's post another event to the EventLog to log the termination of your custom Windows Service:

```
protected override void OnStop()
{
    EventLog.WriteEntry("CarGeneralAsm",
        "CarWinService stopped",
        EventLogEntryType.Information);
}
```

As you would guess, you may choose to make use of the TcpChannel type as opposed to the HttpChannel, post the CarProvider MBR type as a CAO object (rather than WKO), and so forth. Now that the service is complete, the next task is to install this service on the remote machine.

Adding a Service Installer

Before you can install your service on a given machine, you need to add an additional type into your current CarWinService project. Specifically speaking, any Windows service (written using .NET or the raw Win32 API) requires a number of registry entries to be made to allow the OS to interact with the service itself. Rather than requiring us to make these entries manually, you can simply add an Installer type to a Windows Service project, which will configure your ServiceBase-derived type correctly when installed onto the target machine. To add an installer for the CarService, open the design-time service editor (by double-clicking the CarService.cs file from the Solutions Explorer), and click the Add Installer link that now appears on the bottom of the Properties window (Figure 12-17).

Figure 12-17. Including an installer for the custom Windows Service

This selection will add a new component that derives from the System.Configuration.Install.Installer base class. While there are numerous ways to configure your installer (both programmatically and declaratively), the default settings are all you need to install your CarWinService.exe on a given machine. Now, compile your project.

Installing the CarService

To install CarService.exe on a given machine (local or remote) requires two steps:

1. Move the compiled service assembly (and any necessary external assemblies) to the remote machine (obviously).

2. Run the Installutil.exe command line tool, specifying your service as an argument.

Assuming step one is complete, open a command window, navigate to the location of the CarWinService.exe assembly, and issue the following command:

```
Installutil carwinservice.exe
```

Once this Windows Service has been properly installed, you are now able to start and configure it using the Services applet, located under the Administrative Tools folder of your system's Control Panel. Once you have located your CarService (Figure 12-18), click the Start link to load and run the binary.

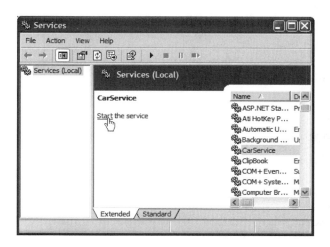

Figure 12-18. The Windows Services Applet

Once the service is started, you are able to run your client application as before.

Now that you have seen how to host your remote objects using a custom Windows Service, let's see how to host remote types using IIS.

> **SOURCE CODE**   The CarWinService project is located under the
> Chapter 12 subdirectory.

Hosting Remote Objects Using IIS

Hosting a remote assembly under the care of IIS is even simpler than building a
Windows Service, given that IIS is already preprogrammed to allow incoming HTTP
requests via port 80. Now, given the fact that IIS is a *Web* server, it should stand to
reason that IIS is only able to host remote objects using the HttpChannel type (unlike a
Windows Service that can also leverage the TcpChannel type). Assuming this is not
perceived as a limitation, follow the steps below to leverage the remoting support of IIS:

1. On your hard drive, create a new folder to hold your CarGeneralAsm.dll.
   Within this folder, create a subdirectory named \Bin. Now, copy the
   CarGeneralAsm.dll to this subdirectory (for example: C:\IISHostCarService\Bin).
   Do be aware that you are also able to install your general assembly into the
   GAC of the web-server machine as an alternative to placing a copy under the
   \Bin folder.

2. Open the Internet Information Services applet on the host machine (located
   under the Administrative Tools folder under your system's Control Panel).

3. Right-click the "Default Web Site" node and select "New | Virtual Directory".

4. Create a virtual directory that maps to the root folder you just created
   (C:\IISCarService). The remaining default settings presented by the New
   Virtual Directory Wizard are fine.

5. Finally, create a new configuration file named "web.config" (and *only*
   web.config) to control how this virtual directory should register the remote
   type (see the following). Make sure this file is saved under the root folder
   (in this example, C:\IISCarService).

```
<configuration>
    <system.runtime.remoting>
        <application>
            <service>
                <wellknown mode="Singleton"
                    type="CarGeneralAsm.CarProvider, CarGeneralAsm"
                    objectUri="carprovider.soap" />
            </service>
            <channels>
                <channel ref="http"/>
            </channels>
        </application>
    </system.runtime.remoting>
</configuration>
```

Now that your CarGeneralAsm.dll has been configured to be reachable via HTTP requests under IIS, you can update your client-side *config file as follows (using the name of your IIS host, of course):

```
<configuration>
    <system.runtime.remoting>
        <application>
            <client displayName = "CarClient">
                <wellknown
                    type="CarGeneralAsm.CarProvider, CarGeneralAsm"
                    url="http://NameTheRemoteIISHost/IISCarHost/carprovider.soap"/>
            </client>
            <channels>
                <channel ref="http"/>
            </channels>
        </application>
    </system.runtime.remoting>
</configuration>
```

Cool! At this point, you are able to run your client application as before.

Asynchronous Remoting

Next, let's examine how to invoke members of a remote type asynchronously. In Chapter 7 you were first introduced to the topic of asynchronous method invocations, given the support provided by the System.MulticastDelagete type. As you would expect, if a client assembly wishes to call a remote object asynchronously, the first step is to define a custom delegate to represent the remote method in question. At this point, the caller can make use of any of the techniques seen in Chapter 7 to invoke and receive the method return value.

By way of a simple illustration, create a new console application (AsyncWKOCarProviderClient) and set a reference to the first iteration of the CarGeneralAsm.dll assembly. Now, update the Main() method to look like this:

```
class AsyncCarClient
{
    // The delegate for the GetAllAutos() method.
    internal delegate ArrayList GetAllAutosDelegate();
    static void Main(string[] args)
    {
        Console.WriteLine("Client started!  Hit enter to end");
        RemotingConfiguration.Configure
            ("AsyncWKOCarProviderClient.exe.config");
        // Make the car provider.
        CarProvider cp = new CarProvider();
        // Make the delegate.
        GetAllAutosDelegate getCarsDel =
            new GetAllAutosDelegate(cp.GetAllAutos);
        // Call GetAllAutos() asynchronously.
        IAsyncResult ar = getCarsDel.BeginInvoke(null, null);
```

```
                    // Simulate client side activity.
                    while(!ar.IsCompleted)
                    { Console.WriteLine("Client working..."); }
                    // All done!  Get return value from delegate.
                    ArrayList allJBCs = getCarsDel.EndInvoke(ar);
                    // Use all cars in ArrayList.
                    foreach(JamesBondCar j in allJBCs)
                        UseCar(j);
                    Console.ReadLine();
            }
    }
```

Notice how the client application first declares a delegate that matches the signature of the GetAllAutos() method of the remote CarProvider type. When the delegate is created, you pass in the name of the method to call (GetAllAutos), as always. Next, you trigger the BeginInvoke() method, cache the resulting IAsyncResult interface, and simulate some work on the client side (recall that the IAsyncResult.IsCompleted property allows you to monitor if the associated method has completed processing). Finally, once the client's work has completed, you obtain the ArrayList returned from the CarProvider.GetAllAutos() method by invoking the EndInvoke() member, and pass each JamesBondCar into a static helper function named UseCar():

```
public static void UseCar(JamesBondCar j)
{
    Console.WriteLine("Can car fly? {0}", j.isFlightWorthy);
    Console.WriteLine("Can car swim? {0}", j.isSeaWorthy);
}
```

Again, the beauty of the .NET delegate type is the fact that the logic used to invoke remote methods asynchronously is identical to the process of local method invocations.

SOURCE CODE   The AsyncWKOCarProviderClient project is located under the Chapter 12 subdirectory.

The Role of the [OneWayAttribute] Type

To wrap things up, let's consider a .NET attribute that allows the remote client to automatically invoke a method asynchronously, without requiring the use of formal delegates. Imagine that your CarProvider has a new method named AddCar(), which takes a JamesBondCar input parameter and returns nothing. The key point is that it returns *nothing*. As you might assume given the name of the System.Runtime.Remoting.Messaging.OneWayAttribute class, the .NET Remoting layer passes the call to the remote one-way method but does *not* bother to set up the infrastructure used to return a given value (hence, the name *one-way*). Here is the update:

```
// Home of the [OneWay] attribute.
using System.Runtime.Remoting.Messaging;
namespace CarGeneralAsm
{
    public class CarProvider : MarshalByRefObject
    {
        private ArrayList theJBCars = new ArrayList();
...
        // The client can 'fire and forget' when calling this method.
        [OneWay]
        public void AddCar(JamesBondCar newJBC)
        { theJBCars.Add(newJBC);}
    }
}
```

Callers would invoke this method directly as always:

```
// Make the car provider.
CarProvider cp = new CarProvider();
// Add a new car.
cp.AddCar(new JamesBondCar("Zippy", 200, false, false));
```

From the client's point of view, the call to AddCar() is completely asynchronous, as the CLR will ensure that a background thread is used to remotely trigger the method. Given that AddCar() has been decorated with the [OneWay] attribute, the client is unable to obtain any return value from the call. Because AddCar() returns void, this is not an issue. In addition to this restriction, also be aware that if you have a [OneWay] method that defines output or reference parameters (via the "out" or "ref" keyword), the caller will *not* be able to obtain the callee's modification(s). Furthermore, if the [OneWay] method happens to throw an exception (of any type), the caller is completely oblivious to this fact. In a nutshell, remote objects can mark select methods as [OneWay] to allow the caller to employ a fire-and-forget mentality.

Final Thoughts...

That wraps up our investigation of the .NET Remoting layer. I'd bet that you still have many questions bouncing around at this point (which, sadly, I just don't have the physical space to cover in this text). For example:

- How can I prevent the client-side assembly from referencing general assemblies containing CIL to protect proprietary code?

- How can I incorporate message queuing (MSMQ) in a .NET application?

- How can I leverage component services (aka COM+ services) in a .NET application?

- How can I augment (or replace) the default .NET Remoting layer?

- What about security issues?

If you are interested in learning more about the .NET Remoting layer (and related topics such as MSMQ a la .NET), check out *Distributed .NET Programming in C#* (Barnaby, Apress 2002). If you are interested in learning the ins-and-outs of building secure .NET applications (local, remote, or otherwise) pick up a copy of *.NET Security* (Bock et al., Apress 2002). And as a friendly reminder, if you need to dive deep into the topic of bypassing the default remoting layer, check out *Advanced .NET Remoting* (Rammer, Apress 2002).

Summary

In this chapter, you examined how to configure distinct .NET assemblies to share types between application boundaries. As you have seen, a remote object may be configured as an MBV or MBR type. This choice ultimately controls how a remote type is realized in the client's application domain (a copy or transparent proxy). Given this distinction, the chapter opened by examining the MBV-centric topic of object serialization.

If you have configured a type to function as an MBR entity, you are suddenly faced with a number of related choices (WKO vs. CAO, single call vs. singleton, and so forth), each of which was addressed during this chapter. As well, you also examined the process of tracking the lifetime of a remote object via the use of leases and lease sponsorship. Finally, you revisited the role of the .NET delegate type in order to understand how to asynchronously invoke a remote method (which, as luck would have it, is identical to the process of asynchronously invoking a local type).

#### CHAPTER 13

Building a Better Window (Introducing Windows Forms)

IF YOU HAVE READ THROUGH the previous chapters, you should have a solid handle on the C# programming language as well as the foundation of the .NET architecture. While you could take your newfound knowledge and begin building the next generation of console applications (boring!) you are more likely to be interested in building an attractive graphical user interface (GUI) to allow the outside world to interact with your system.

This chapter introduces you to the System.Windows.Forms namespace. Here, you learn how to build a highly stylized main window (e.g., a Form-derived class). In the process, you learn about a number of window-related types, including MenuItem, ToolBar, StatusBar, and Application. This chapter also introduces how to capture and respond to user input (i.e., handling mouse and keyboard events) within the context of a GUI environment. Along the way, you will construct a final example that illustrates the construction of MDI applications a la Windows Forms.

A Tale of Three GUI Namespaces

The .NET platform (as of version 1.1) provides three GUI toolkits, known as "Windows Forms," "Web Forms," and "Mobile Forms." The System.Windows.Forms namespaces contain a number of types that allow you to build traditional desktop applications, as well as Windows-based applications that target handled computing devices (such as the Pocket PC). As you would expect, Windows Forms hides the raw windowing primitives from view, allowing you to focus on the functionality of your application using the familiar .NET type system.

Web Forms, on the other hand, is a GUI toolkit used during ASP.NET development. The bulk of the Web Form types are contained in the System.Web.UI.WebControls namespace. Using these types, you are able to build browser-independent front ends based on various industry standards (HTML, HTTP, and so forth). You will get to know the ASP.NET Web controls in Chapter 18.

Finally, .NET version 1.1 ships with a new GUI-centric namespace, System.Web.UI.MobileControls, which allow you to build UIs that target mobile devices (such as cellular phones). Not surprisingly, the programming model of Mobile control applications mimics the functionality found within ASP.NET.

NOTE Coverage of mobile .NET technologies (including Pocket PC programming) is outside the scope of this text. If you are interested, check out *Mobile .NET* (Ferguson, Apress 2001).

It is worth pointing out that while Windows Forms, Web Forms, and Mobile Forms technologies define a number of similarly named types (e.g., Button, CheckBox, etc.) with similar members (Text, BackColor, etc.), they do not share a common implementation and cannot be treated identically. Nevertheless, as you become comfortable with the Windows Forms namespace, you should find the process of learning the details of other .NET GUI toolkits far more palatable.

Overview of the System.Windows.Forms Namespace

Like any namespace, System.Windows.Forms is composed of a number of classes, structures, delegates, interfaces, and enumerations. Over the next couple of chapters, you drill into the specifics of a good number of these types. While it is redundant to list every member of the Windows Forms family (as they are all documented in online Help) Table 13-1 lists some (but by no means all) of the core classes found within System.Windows.Forms.

Table 13-1. A Subset of Types Within the System.Windows.Forms Namespace

Windows Forms Class	Meaning in Life
Application	This class represents the guts of a Windows Forms application. Using the members of Application, you are able to process windows messages, start and terminate a Windows Forms application, and so forth.
ButtonBase, Button, CheckBox, ComboBox, DataGrid, GroupBox, ListBox, LinkLabel, PictureBox	These classes (in addition to many others) represent types that correspond to various GUI widgets. You examine many of these items in detail in Chapter 15.
Form	This type represents a main window, dialog box, or MDI child window of a Windows Forms application.
ColorDialog, OpenFileDialog, SaveFileDialog, FontDialog, PrintPreviewDialog, FolderBrowserDialog	As you might expect, Windows Forms defines a number of canned dialog boxes. If these don't fit the bill, you are free to build your own custom dialogs.
Menu, MainMenu, MenuItem, ContextMenu	These types are used to build top most and context-sensitive (pop-up) menu systems.
Clipboard, Help, Timer, Screen, ToolTip, Cursors	Various utility types used to facilitate interactive GUIs.
StatusBar, Splitter, ToolBar, ScrollBar	Various types used to adorn a Form with common child controls.

Interacting with the Windows Forms Types

When you build a Windows Forms application, you may choose to write all the relevant code by hand (using Notepad perhaps) and send the resulting *.cs files into the C# compiler using the /target:winexe flag. Taking time to build some Windows Forms applications by hand is not only a great learning experience, but also helps you understand the code generated by various GUI wizards.

Another option is to build Windows Forms projects using the Visual Studio .NET IDE. To be sure, the IDE does supply a number of great wizards, starter templates, and configuration tools that make working with Windows Forms extremely simple. The problem with wizards, of course, is that if you do not understand what the generated code is doing on your behalf, you cannot gain a true mastery of the underlying technology.

Given this fact, you begin by creating your initial Windows Forms examples in the raw (complete with menus, status bars, and toolbars). Over the course of the chapter however, I'll illustrate the use of various wizards supplied by the Visual Studio .NET. Hopefully, this will also drive the point home that when you do leverage VS .NET to build your Windows Forms applications, you are *not* creating source code that will tie you to a particular IDE.

Prepping the Project Workspace

To begin understanding Windows Forms programming, let's build a simple main window by hand. The first order of business is to create a new *empty* C# project workspace named "MyRawWindow" using the VS .NET IDE. Next, insert a new C# class definition (resist the temptation to insert a new Windows Form class!) from the "Project | Add New Item..." menu option. Name this class MainWindow.

When you build a main window by hand, you need to use the Form and Application types (at minimum), both of which are contained in the System.Windows.Forms.dll assembly. A Windows Forms application also needs to reference System.dll, given that some types in the Windows Forms assembly make use of types in the System.dll assembly. Add references to these assemblies now (Figure 13-1).

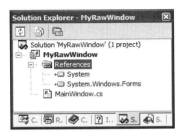

Figure 13-1. The minimal set of assembly references

Building a Main Window (By Hand)

In the world of Windows Forms, the Form class is used to represent any window in your application. This includes a topmost main window in an SDI (Single Document Interface) application, modeless and modal dialogs, as well as the parent and child windows of an MDI (Multiple Document Interface) application. When you are interested in creating a new main window, you have two mandatory steps:

- Derive a new custom class from System.Windows.Forms.Form.

- Configure the application's Main() method to call Application.Run(), passing an instance of your new Form-derived type as an argument.

With these steps in mind, you are able to update your initial class definition as follows:

```
using System;
using System.Windows.Forms;
namespace MyRawWindow
{
    public class MainWindow : Form
    {
        public MainWindow(){ }
        // Run this application and identify the main window.
        public static int Main(string[] args)
        {
            Application.Run(new MainWindow());
            return 0;
        }
    }
}
```

Here, I have defined with Main() method the scope of the class that represents the main window. If you prefer, you may wish to create a second class (I named mine, TheApp) which is responsible for the task of launching the main window:

```
namespace MyRawWindow
{
    public class MainWindow : Form
    {
        public MainWindow(){}
    }
    public class TheApp
    {
        public static int Main(string[] args)
        {
            Application.Run(new MainWindow());
            return 0;
        }
    }
}
```

In either case, Figure 13-2 shows a test run.

Figure 13-2. A simple main window a la Windows Forms

If you notice how your MyRawWindow application has been launched, you should notice an annoying command window looming in the background. This is because you have not yet configured the build settings to generate a Windows *.exe application. To supply the /t:winexe flag from within the IDE, open the Project Properties window (just right-click the project icon from the Solution Explorer) and expand the "Common Properties | General" node. Finally, configure the "Output Type" property as "Windows Application" (Figure 13-3). When you recompile, the annoying command window will be gone and your application will run as a true-blue Windows app.

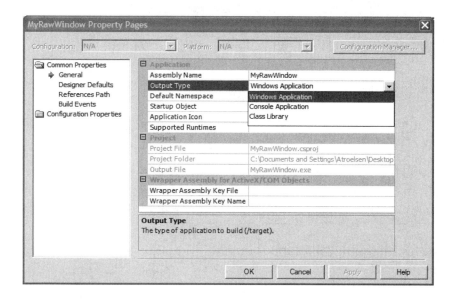

Figure 13-3. Specifying /t:winexe within VS .NET

So, at this point we have a minimizable, maximizable, resizable, and closable main window (with a default system-supplied icon to boot!). To be sure, it is a great boon to the Win32 programmers of the world to forego the need to manually configure a WndProc function, establish a WinMain() entry point, and twiddle the bits of a WNDCLASSEX structure. Granted, your MainWindow does not do too much at this point, however, you'll enhance its functionality throughout the chapter.

SOURCE CODE   The MyRawWindow application can be found under the Chapter 13 subdirectory.

Building a VS .NET Windows Forms Project Workspace

The benefit of building Windows Forms applications using Visual Studio .NET is that the integrated tools can take care of a number of mundane coding details by delegating them to a number of wizards, configuration windows, and so forth. To illustrate how to make use of such assistance, close your current workspace. Now, select a new C# Windows Application project type (see Figure 13-4).

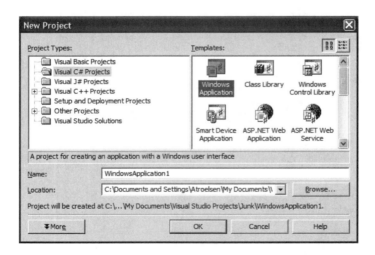

Figure 13-4. The Windows Forms project workspace

When you click OK, you will find that you are automatically given a new class derived from System.Windows.Forms.Form [with a properly configured Main() method] and have references set to each required assembly (as well as some additional assemblies that you may or may not make use of).

You will also see that you are given a design-time template that can be used to assemble the user interface of your Form (Figure 13-5). Understand that as you update this design-time template, you are indirectly adding code to the associated Form-derived class (named Form1 by default).

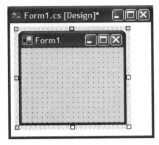

Figure 13-5. The Form Designer

Using the Solution Explorer window, you are able to alternate between this design-time template and the underlying C# code. To view the code that represents your current design, simply right-click the *.cs file and select "View Code". You can also open the code window by double-clicking anywhere on the design time Form; however, this has the (possibly undesirable) effect of writing an event handler for the Form's Load event (more on event processing later in this chapter).

Once you open the code window, you will see a class that looks very much like the following (XML-based code comments removed for clarity):

```
namespace VSWinApp
{
    public class Form1 : System.Windows.Forms.Form
    {
        private System.ComponentModel.Container components = null;
        public Form1()
        { InitializeComponent(); }
        protected override void Dispose( bool disposing )
        {
            if( disposing )
            {
                if (components != null)
                {
                    components.Dispose();
                }
            }
            base.Dispose( disposing );
        }
```

```
#region Windows Form Designer generated code
private void InitializeComponent()
{
    this.components = new System.ComponentModel.Container();
    this.Size = new System.Drawing.Size(300,300);
    this.Text = "Form1";
}
#endregion
[STAThread]
static void Main()
{
    Application.Run(new Form1());
}
}
}
```

As you can see, this class listing is essentially the same code as the previous raw Windows Forms example. Your type still derives from System.Windows.Forms.Form, and the Main() method still calls Application.Run(). The major change is a new method named InitializeComponent(), which is wrapped by the #region and #endregion preprocessor directives (as described in Chapter 2).

The Role of InitializeComponent() and Dispose()

The InitializeComponent() method is updated automatically by the Form Designer to reflect the modifications you make to the Form and its controls using the Visual Studio .NET IDE. For example, if you were to use the Properties window to modify the Form's Text and BackColor properties (Figure 13-6), you would find that InitializeComponent() has been modified accordingly:

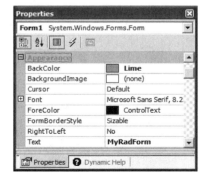

Figure 13-6. The Properties window provides design time editing support.

```
#region Windows Form Designer generated code
private void InitializeComponent()
{
    this.AutoScaleBaseSize = new System.Drawing.Size(5, 13);
    this.BackColor = System.Drawing.Color.Lime;
    this.ClientSize = new System.Drawing.Size(292, 273);
    this.Text = "My Rad Form";
}
#endregion
```

The Form-derived class calls InitializeComponent() within the scope of the default constructor:

```
public Form1()
{
    // Required for Windows Form Designer support
    InitializeComponent();
}
```

Do be very aware that this helper method is simply a well-known member that VS .NET understands. If you moved all the code within this method into the Form's constructor, your application would run identically. Unlike other windowing toolkits, the wizard-generated code does not tie you to a particular IDE (VS .NET or otherwise).

The final point of interest is the overridden Dispose() method. This method is called automatically when your Form is about to be destroyed, and is a safe place to free any allocated resources.

The System.Windows.Forms.Application Class

The Application class defines members that allow you to control various low-level behaviors of a Windows Forms application. For example, the Application class defines a set of events that allow you to respond to events such as application shutdown and idle processing. For the most part, you do not need to directly interact with this type (beyond calling Run() to show your main window); however, let's check out some of its behavior. To begin, ponder the following core methods (all of which are static) listed in Table 13-2.

Table 13-2. Methods of the Application Type

Method of the Application Class	Meaning in Life
AddMessageFilter() RemoveMessageFilter()	These methods allow your application to intercept messages for any necessary preprocessing. When you add a message filter, you must specify a class that implements the IMessageFilter interface (as you do shortly).
DoEvents()	Provides the ability for an application to process messages currently in the message queue, during a lengthy operation (such as a looping construct). Think of DoEvents() as a quick and dirty way to simulate multithreaded behaviors.
Exit()	Terminates the application.
ExitThread()	Exits the message loop on the current thread and closes all windows owned by the current thread.
OLERequired()	Initializes the OLE libraries. Consider this the .NET equivalent of manually calling OleInitialize().
Run()	Begins running a standard application message loop on the current thread.

The Application class also defines a number of static properties, many of which are read-only. As you examine the following table, realize that each property represents some "application-level" trait such as company name, version number, and so forth. In fact, given what you already know about .NET attributes (see Chapter 11), many of these properties should look vaguely familiar (Table 13-3).

Table 13-3. Core Properties of the Application Type

Property of Application Class	Meaning in Life
CommonAppDataRegistry	Retrieves the registry key for the application data that is shared among all users
CompanyName	Retrieves the company name associated with the current application
CurrentCulture	Gets or sets the locale information for the current thread
CurrentInputLanguage	Gets or sets the current input language for the current thread

Table 13-3. Core Properties of the Application Type (Continued)

Property of Application Class	Meaning in Life
ProductName	Retrieves the product name associated with this application
ProductVersion	Retrieves the product version associated with this application
StartupPath	Retrieves the path for the executable file that started the application

Notice that some properties, such as CompanyName and ProductName, provide a handy way to retrieve assembly-level metadata. As you recall from Chapter 11, an assembly may be described using a number of attributes. Thus, if you specify a value for the AssemblyCompany attribute, you may obtain this information using Application.CompanyName without the making direct use of the types defined within System.Reflection.

Finally, the Application class defines the events shown in Table 13-4.

Table 13-4. Events of the Application Type

Application Event	Meaning in Life
ApplicationExit	Occurs when the application is just about to shut down.
Idle	Occurs when the application's message loop has finished processing and is about to enter an idle state (meaning there are no messages to process at the current time).
ThreadExit	Occurs when a thread in the application is about to terminate. If the main thread for an application is about to be shut down, this event will be raised before the ApplicationExit event.

Fun with the Application Class

To illustrate some of the functionality of the Application class (as well as preview Windows Forms event handling), let's enhance our current raw MainWindow to perform the following tasks:

- Display some basic information about this application on startup.

- Respond to the ApplicationExit event.

- Perform some preprocessing of the WM_LBUTTONDOWN message.

To begin, assume that you have extended your manifest using a number of attributes that mark the name of this fine application and the company that created it.

Thus, insert a new file named assemblyinfo.cs which contains the following assembly-level attributes:

```
// Some attributes regarding this assembly.
[assembly:AssemblyCompany("Intertech, Inc.")]
[assembly:AssemblyProduct("A Better Window")]
```

The constructor of our Form-derived class can obtain this information using properties of the Application, which are displayed using the Show() method of the MessageBox type:

```
using System;
using System.Windows.Forms;

namespace AppClassExample
{
    public class MainForm : Form
    {
    ...
        public MainForm()
        { GetStats(); }
        private void GetStats()
        {
            // Read some metadata from the manifest.
            string info = string.Format("Company: {0}\n",
                Application.CompanyName);
            info += string.Format("App Name: {0}\n",
                Application.ProductName);
            info += string.Format("I live here: {0}",
                Application.StartupPath);
            MessageBox.Show(info);
        }
    }
}
```

When you run this application, you see a message box that displays various bits of information (Figure 13-7).

Figure 13-7. Reading attributes via the Application type

Responding to the ApplicationExit Event

Next, let's configure this Form to respond to the ApplicationExit event. When you wish to respond to events from within a Windows Forms application, you will be happy to find that the same event logic detailed in Chapter 7 is used to handle GUI-based events. Therefore, if you wish to intercept the ApplicationExit event, you simply register an event handler using the += operator:

```
public class MainForm : Form
{
    ...
    public MainForm()
    {
        ...
        // Intercept the ApplicationExit event.
        Application.ApplicationExit += new EventHandler(Form_OnExit);
    }
    // Event handler.
    private void Form_OnExit(object sender, EventArgs evArgs)
    {
        MessageBox.Show("See ya!", "This app is dead...");
    }
}
```

Notice that the signature of the ApplicationExit event handler must conform to a delegate of type System.EventHandler:

```
// Many GUI-based events make use of this delegate (EventHandler)
// which requires two parameters:
public delegate void EventHandler(object sender, EventArgs e);
```

As you will see, the EventHandler delegate is the most common type used to handle events under Windows Forms, however, alternatives do exist for other events. The first parameter of the EventHandler delegate is of type System.Object, which represents the object sending the event. The EventArgs parameter (or a descendent thereof) contains relevant information for the current event.

While the EventArgs parameter will always work in conjunction with the EventHandler delegate, it also functions as the base class to more specific event argument types. For example, if you have an event handler that responds to a mouse event, the MouseEventArgs parameter will contain mouse related details such as the (*x, y*) position of the cursor. Keyboard event handlers make use of the KeyEventArgs type. In any case, if you run the application, you will be able to respond to the termination of this application.

Preprocessing Messages with the Application Class

The final step of this example is to perform some preprocessing logic of the WM_LBUTTONDOWN message. As you may know, this standard Windows message is sent when the left mouse button has been clicked within the client area of a given Form (or any GUI widget that is equipped to respond to this event). Now, be very aware that you will find a much simpler way to intercept standard mouse events a bit later in this chapter. The point of this step is simply to illustrate how to perform custom preprocessing logic before a given event is fully dispatched to its handler.

When you wish to filter messages in the .NET framework, your first task is to create a new class that implements the IMessageFilter interface. This is extremely simple, given that IMessageFilter defines only one method, PreFilterMessage(). Return "true" to filter the message and prevent it from being dispatched or "false" to allow the message to continue on its way.

Within the scope of your implementation, you may examine the incoming Message.Msg field to extract the numerical value of the Windows message (in this case, WM_LBUTTONDOWN, which is the value 513). For example:

```
using Microsoft.Win32;      // Contains Win32 specific types.
...
// Create a message filter.
public class MyMessageFilter : IMessageFilter
{
    public bool PreFilterMessage(ref Message m)
    {
        // Intercept the left mouse button down message.
        if (m.Msg == 513)        // WM_LBUTTONDOWN = 513.
        {
            MessageBox.Show("WM_LBUTTONDOWN is: " + m.Msg);
            return true;
        }
        return false;      // All other messages are ignored...
    }
}
```

Once you have created the class that will be filtering the incoming messages, you must register a new instance of this type using the static AddMessageFilter() method. Here is the update to your existing MainForm class:

```
public class MainForm : Form
{
    private MyMessageFilter msgFilter = new MyMessageFilter();
    ...
    public MainForm()
    {
        ...
        // Add message filter.
        Application.AddMessageFilter(msgFilter);
    }
    // Event handler
    private void Form_OnExit(object sender, EventArgs evArgs)
    {
        MessageBox.Show("See ya!", "This app is dead...");
        // Remove message filter.
        Application.RemoveMessageFilter(msgFilter);
    }
}
```

When you run this application, you see a message that informs you of the numerical value of the Win32 WM_LBUTTONDOWN message when you click the left mouse button anywhere in the application.

As you can tell, filtering messages is not a task you need to perform all that often (if ever). Nevertheless, it is nice to know that Windows Forms allows you to drop down to this level of detail if you so choose.

SOURCE CODE   The AppClassExample project can be found under the Chapter 13 subdirectory.

The Anatomy of a Form

Now that you understand the role of the Application type, our next task is to examine the functionality of the Form class itself. As you have seen, when you create a new window (or dialog box) you need to define a new class deriving from System.Windows.Forms.Form. This class gains a great deal of functionality from the types in its inheritance chain. Figure 13-8 illustrates the big picture.

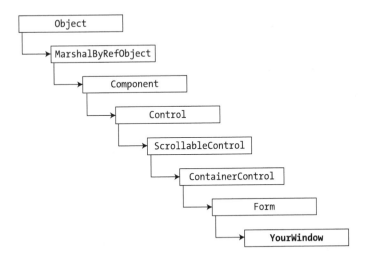

Figure 13-8. The derivation of a custom Form

Before we get to the real meat of the Form's inheritance chain, understand that like any type in the .NET universe, Form ultimately derives from System.Object (which should be no surprise to you at this point). As you recall from Chapter 12,

MarshalByRefObject defines the behavior to remote this type by reference, rather than by value. Thus, if you remotely interact with a Form across the wire, you are manipulating a reference to the Form on the remote machine (not a local copy of the Form on the client machine).

Detailing each and every member of each class in the Form's inheritance chain would require a small book in itself. However, it is important to understand the core behavior supplied by each base class. I assume that you will spend time examining the full details behind each class at your leisure.

The Component Class

The first base class of immediate interest is Component. The Component type provides a canned implementation of the IComponent interface. This predefined interface defines a property named Site, which returns (surprise, surprise) an ISite interface. Furthermore, IComponent inherits a single event from the IDisposable interface named Disposed:

```
public interface IComponent : IDisposable
{
    // The Site property.
    public ISite Site { get; set; }
    // The Disposed event.
    public  event EventHandler Disposed;
}
```

The ISite interface defines a number of methods that allow a Control to interact with the hosting container:

```
public interface ISite : IServiceProvider
{
    // Properties of the ISite interface.
    public IComponent Component { get; }
    public IContainer Container { get; }
    public  bool DesignMode { get; }
    public  string Name {  get; set; }
}
```

By and large, the properties defined by the ISite interface are only of interest to you if you are attempting to build a widget that can be manipulated at design time (such as a custom Windows Forms control).

In addition to the Site property, Component also provides an implementation of the Dispose() method (as seen earlier in this chapter). Recall that the Dispose() method is called when a component is no longer required. When a Form has been closed, the Dispose() method is called automatically for the Form and for all widgets contained within that form.

The Control Class

The next base class of interest is System.Windows.Forms.Control, which establishes the common behaviors required by any GUI-centric type. The core members of System.Windows.Forms.Control allow you to configure the size and position of a control, extract the underlying HWND (i.e., a numerical handle for a given window), as well as capture keyboard and mouse input. Table 13-5 defines some of the properties to be aware of.

Table 13-5. Core Properties of the Control Type

Control Property	Meaning in Life
Top, Left, Bottom, Right, Bounds, ClientRectangle, Height, Width	Each of these properties specifies various attributes about the current dimensions of the Control-derived object. Bounds returns a Rectangle that specifies the size of the control. ClientRectangle returns a Rectangle that corresponds to the size of the client area of the control.
Created, Disposed, Enabled, Focused, Visible	These properties each return a Boolean that specifies the state of the current Control.
Handle	Returns a numerical value (integer) that represents the HWND of this Control.
ModifierKeys	This static property checks the current state of the modifier keys (shift, control, and alt) and returns the state in a Keys type.
MouseButtons	This static property checks the current state of the mouse buttons (left, right, and middle mouse buttons) and returns this state in a MouseButtons type.
Parent	Returns a Control object that represents the parent of the current Control.
TabIndex, TabStop	These properties are used to configure the tab order of the Control.
Text	The current text associated with this Control.

The Control base class also defines a number of methods that allow you to interact with any Control-derived type. A partial list of some of the more common members appears in Table 13-6.

Table 13-6. Select Members of the Control Type

Control Method	Meaning in Life
GetStyle() SetStyle()	These methods are used to manipulate the style flags of the current Control using the ControlStyles enumeration.
Hide() Show()	These methods indirectly set the state of the Visible property.
Invalidate()	Forces the Control to redraw itself by forcing a paint message into the message queue. This method is overloaded to allow you to specify a specific Rectangle to refresh, rather than the entire client area.
OnXXXX()	The Control class defines numerous methods which can be overridden by a subclass to respond to various events (e.g., OnMouseMove(), OnKeyDown(), OnResize(), and so forth). As you see later in this chapter, when you wish to intercept a GUI-based event, you have two approaches. One approach is to simply override one of the existing event handlers. Another is to add a custom event handler to a given delegate.
Refresh()	Forces the Control to invalidate and immediately repaint itself and any children.
SetBounds(), SetLocation(), SetClientArea()	Each of these methods is used to establish the dimensions of the Control-derived object.

Setting a Form's Styles

Let's examine two interesting methods of the Control type: GetStyle() and SetStyle(), both of which interact with the ControlStyles enumeration. Win32 programmers are no doubt familiar with the WNDCLASSEX structure, and the dozens of oddball styles that can be used to fill the various fields. While Windows Forms hides this Windows "goo" from view, you are able to modify the default styles of your Form if need be. To illustrate, check out the related ControlStyles enumeration:

```
public enum ControlStyles
{
    AllPaintingInWmPaint, CacheText,
    DoubleBuffer, ContainerControl,
    EnableNotifyMessage, FixedHeight,
    FixedWidth, Opaque,
    ResizeRedraw, Selectable,
    StandardClick, StandardDoubleClick,
    SupportsTransparentBackColor,
    UserMouse, UserPaint
}
```

The values of the ControlStyle enumeration may OR-ed together if you wish to specify multiple styles. And, as you would expect, a Form has a default style set (I assume you will check out online Help for full details of each value).

Assume you have a Form containing a single Button type. In the Click event handler of this Button, you can check if the Form supports a given style using GetStyle():

```
// Shows false!
private void btnGetStyles_Click(object sender, System.EventArgs e)
{
    MessageBox.Show(GetStyle(ControlStyles.ResizeRedraw).ToString(),
        "Do you have ResizeRedraw?");
}
```

To set the bit of a given style (by specifying true or false) you could write:

```
public StyleForm()
{
    ...
    SetStyle(ControlStyles.ResizeRedraw, true);
}
```

The ResizeRedraw is one value you typically want to add to a given Form. By default this style is not active and thus, a Form will not automatically redraw its client area when resized. This means, if you have intercepted a Paint event (which you will do a bit later) and resize the Form, your drawing logic is not refreshed! If you wish to ensure that the Paint event fires whenever the user resizes the Form, be sure to specify the ResizeRedraw style using SetStyle().

Another (equally valid) alternative to ensure correct repainting is to intercept the Form's Resize event and call Invalidate() directly:

```
private void StyleForm_Resize(object sender, System.EventArgs e)
{
    Invalidate();  // This forces a repaint (more details later...)
}
```

Typically, you would want to intercept the Resize() event when you have
additional work to do beyond triggering a paint session. If you do not, setting the
ControlStyles.ResizeRedraw will do the trick.

Now, to illustrate the effect of setting Form styles, assume you have handled the
Form's Paint event and coded a block of GDI+ rendering logic that draws a dashed black
line around the client area rectangle (GDI+ is detailed in the next chapter, so don't
sweat the details):

```
// GDI+ requires setting a reference to System.Drawing.dll!
using System.Drawing;      // Needed for Color, Brush, and Font types.
...
private void MainForm_Paint(object sender, System.Windows.Forms.PaintEventArgs e)
{
    // A custom dash...
    Pen customDashPen = new Pen(Color.Black, 10);
    float[] myDashes = {5.0f, 2.0f, 1.0f, 3.0f};
    customDashPen.DashPattern = myDashes;
    e.Graphics.DrawRectangle(customDashPen, ClientRectangle);
}
```

If the ResizeRedraw bit is set to "false," you find the ugliness shown in Figure 13-9 as
you resize the Form.

Figure 13-9. ControlStyles.ResizeRedraw = false

If you set it to "true" you have correct rendering (Figure 13-10).

Figure 13-10. ControlStyles.ResizeRedraw = true

SOURCE CODE The FormStyles project is under the Chapter 13 subdirectory.

Control Events

The Control class also defines a number of events that can logically be grouped into two major categories: Mouse events and keyboard events (Table 13-7).

Table 13-7. Events of the Control Type

Control Event	Meaning in Life
Click, DoubleClick, MouseEnter, MouseLeave, MouseDown, MouseUp, MouseMove, MouseHover, MouseWheel	The Control class defines numerous events triggered in response to mouse input.
KeyPress, KeyUp, KeyDown	The Control class also defines numerous events triggered in response to keyboard input.

Fun with the Control Class

To be sure, the Control class does define additional properties, methods, and events beyond the subset you have just examined. However, to illustrate some of these core members, let's build a new Form type (also called MainForm) that provides the following functionality:

- Set the initial size of the Form to some arbitrary dimensions.

- Override the Dispose() method.

- Respond to the MouseMove and MouseUp events (using two approaches).

- Capture and process keyboard input.

To begin, assume you have a new C# class derived from Form. First, update the default constructor to set the top, left, bottom, and right coordinates of the Form using various properties of the Control class. To confirm these changes, make use of the Bounds property, and display the string version of the current dimensions. Do be aware that Bounds returns a Rectangle type that is defined in the System.Drawing namespace. Therefore be sure to set an assembly reference (to System.Drawing.dll) if you are building this Form by hand (Visual Studio .NET Windows Forms projects do so automatically):

```
// Need this for Rectangle definition.
using System.Drawing;
...
public class MainForm : Form
{
    public static int Main(string[] args)
    {
        Application.Run(new MainForm());
        return 0;
    }

    public MainForm()
    {
        Top = 100;
        Left = 75;
        Height = 100;
        Width = 500;
        MessageBox.Show(Bounds.ToString(), "Current rect");
    }
}
```

When you run this application, you are able to confirm the coordinates of your Form via the Bounds property.

Now, let's retrofit your class to override the inherited Dispose() method (this is done automatically when using VS .NET). As you recall from earlier in this chapter, the Application object defines an event named ApplicationExit. If you configure your Form to intercept this event, you are effectively informed of the destruction of the application. As a (much) simpler alternative, you can achieve the same effect by simply overriding the Dispose() method. Do note that you should call your base class' Dispose() method before exiting:

```
protected override void Dispose( bool disposing )
{
    MessageBox.Show("Disposing this Form");
    if( disposing )
    {
        if (components != null)
        {
            components.Dispose();
        }
    }
    base.Dispose( disposing );
}
```

Responding to Mouse Events: Take One

Next, you need to intercept the MouseUp event. The goal is to display the (x, y) position at which the MouseUp event occurred. When you wish to respond to events from within a Windows Forms application, you have two general approaches. The first approach should be familiar to you at this point in the game: Use delegates. The second approach is to override the appropriate base class method. Let's examine each technique, beginning with standard delegation. Here is the updated MainForm:

```
public class MainForm : Form
{
    public static int Main(string[] args)
    {
        Application.Run(new MainForm());
        return 0;
    }
    public MainForm()
    {
        ...
        // Listen for the MouseUp event...
        this.MouseUp += new MouseEventHandler(OnMouseUp);
    }
    // Method called in response to the MouseUp event.
    public void OnMouseUp(object sender, MouseEventArgs e)
    {
        this.Text = string.Format("Current Pos: ({0}, {1})", e.X, e.Y);
    }
...
}
```

Now, recall that GUI-based delegates take an EventArgs (or derivative thereof) as the second parameter. When you process mouse events, the second parameter is of type MouseEventArgs. This type (defined in the System.Windows.Forms namespace) defines a number of interesting properties that may be used to gather various statistics regarding the state of the mouse, as seen in Table 13-8.

Table 13-8. Properties of the MouseEventArgs Type

MouseEventArgs Property	Meaning in Life
Button	Gets which mouse button was pressed, as defined by the MouseButtons enumeration
Clicks	Gets the number of times the mouse button was pressed and released
Delta	Gets a signed count of the number of detents the mouse wheel has rotated
X	Gets the *x*-coordinate of a mouse click
Y	Gets the *y*-coordinate of a mouse click

The implementation of the OnMouseUp() method simply extracts the (x, y) position of the cursor and displays this information in the Form's caption via the inherited Text property.

To make things even more interesting, we could also capture a MouseMove event, and display the same (*x, y*) position data in the caption of the Form. In this way, the current location of the cursor is tracked whenever the mouse cursor is moved within the client area:

```
public class MainForm : Form
{
...
    public MainForm()
    {
        ...
        // Track mouse movement and MouseUp event.
        this.MouseUp += new MouseEventHandler(OnMouseUp);
        this.MouseMove += new MouseEventHandler(OnMouseMove);
    }
    public void OnMouseUp(object sender, MouseEventArgs e)
    {
        // Now we will just show a message when clicked.
        MessageBox.Show("Stop clicking me!");
    }
    public void OnMouseMove(object sender, MouseEventArgs e)
    {
        this.Text = string.Format("Current Pos: ({0}, {1})", e.X, e.Y);
    }
}
```

Determining Which Mouse Button Was Clicked

One thing to be aware of is that the MouseUp (or MouseDown) event is sent whenever *any* mouse button is clicked. If you wish to determine exactly *which* button was clicked (left, right, or middle) you need to examine the Button property of the MouseEventArgs class. The value of Button is constrained by the MouseButtons enumeration. For example:

```
public void OnMouseUp(object sender, MouseEventArgs e)
{
    // Which mouse button was clicked?
    if(e.Button == MouseButtons.Left)
        MessageBox.Show("Left click!");
    if(e.Button == MouseButtons.Right)
        MessageBox.Show("Right click!");
    if (e.Button == MouseButtons.Middle)
        MessageBox.Show("Middle click!");
}
```

Responding to Mouse Events: Take Two

The previous mouse event logic followed the standard .NET delegate pattern. The other approach to capture events in a Control-derived type is to override the correct base class method, which in this case would be OnMouseUp() and OnMouseMove().

The Control type defines a number of protected virtual methods that will be called automatically when the corresponding event is triggered. If you were to update your Form using this technique, you have no need to manually specify a custom event handler (or write the necessary event handling logic):

```
public class MainForm : Form
{
    ...
    public MainForm()
    {
        ...
        // No need to do this when overriding!
        // this.MouseUp += new MouseEventHandler(OnMouseUp);
        // this.MouseMove+= new MouseEventHandler(OnMouseMove);
    }
    protected override void OnMouseUp(/*object sender,*/ MouseEventArgs e)
    {
        // Which mouse button was clicked?
        if(e.Button == MouseButtons.Left)
            MessageBox.Show("Left click!");
        if(e.Button == MouseButtons.Right)
            MessageBox.Show("Right click!");
        if(e.Button == MouseButtons.Middle)
            MessageBox.Show("Middle click!");
        base.OnMouseUp(e);
    }
    protected override void OnMouseMove(/*object sender,*/ MouseEventArgs e)
    { this.Text = string.Format("Current Pos: ({0}, {1})", e.X, e.Y); }
}
```

Notice how the signature of each method takes a single parameter of type MouseEventArg, rather than two parameters that conform to the MouseEventHandler delegate. If you run the program again, you see no change whatsoever (which is good).

Recall that these virtual methods defined by your base types are simply the default event handlers that will be called if you do not explicitly handle a given event. Typically you only need to override an "OnXXXX()" method if you have additional work to perform before calling your parent's implementation. The preferred approach (and the one used by Visual Studio .NET) is to handle the event directly as you did in the first mouse example, and make use of the .NET event syntax. Given this, I will refrain from overriding base class GUI event handlers during the remainder of this text.

Responding to Keyboard Events

Processing keyboard input is almost identical to responding to mouse activity. The following code captures the KeyUp event and displays the textual name of the character that was pressed in a message box. Here, you capture this event using the delegation technique (there is a method named OnKeyUp() that can be overridden as an alternative):

```
public class MainForm : Form
{
...
    public MainForm()
    {
        ...
        // Listen to KeyUp Event.
        this.KeyUp += new KeyEventHandler(OnKeyUp);
    }
    public void OnKeyUp(object sender, KeyEventArgs e)
    {
        MessageBox.Show(e.KeyCode.ToString(), "Key Pressed!");
    }
}
```

As you can see, the KeyEventArgs type maintains an enumeration named KeyCode that holds the ID of the key press. In addition, the KeyEventArgs type, defines the useful properties listed in Table 13-9.

Table 13-9. Properties of the KeyEventArgs Type

KeyEventArgs Property	Meaning in Life
Alt	Gets a value indicating whether the Alt key was pressed
Control	Gets a value indicating whether the Ctrl key was pressed
Handled	Gets or sets a value indicating whether the event was handled
KeyCode	Gets the keyboard code for a System.Windows.Forms.Control.KeyDown or System.Windows.Forms.Control.KeyUp event
KeyData	Gets the key data for a System.Windows.Forms.Control.KeyDown or System.Windows.Forms.Control.KeyUp event
Modifiers	Indicates which modifier keys (Ctrl, Shift, and/or Alt) were pressed
Shift	Gets a value indicating whether the Shift key was pressed

Figure 13-11 shows a possible key press.

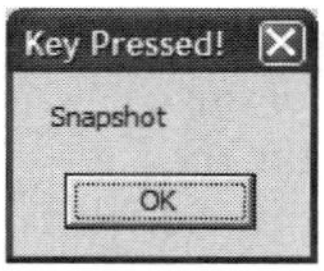

Figure 13-11. Intercepting key presses

SOURCE CODE   The ControlBehaviors project is included under the Chapter 13 subdirectory.

The Control Class Revisited

The Control class defines further behaviors to configure background and foreground colors, background images, font characteristics, drag-and-drop functionality and support for pop-up context menus. This class provides docking and anchoring behaviors for the derived types (which you examine in Chapter 15). Perhaps the most important duty of the Control class is to establish a mechanism to render images, text, and various geometric patterns onto the client area via a registered Paint event handler. To begin, observe these additional properties of the Control class, as seen in Table 13-10.

Table 13-10. Additional Control Properties

Control Property	Meaning in Life
AllowDrop	If AllowDrop is set to true then this control allows drag-and-drop operations and events to be used.
Anchor	The anchor property determines which edges of the control are anchored to the container's edges.
BackColor, BackgroundImage, Font, ForeColor, Cursor	These properties configure how the client area should be displayed.
ContextMenu	Specifies which context menu (e.g., pop-up menu) will be shown when the user right-clicks the control.
Dock	The dock property controls which edge of the container this control docks to. For example, when docked to the top of the container, the control is displayed flush at the top of the container, extending the length of the container.
Opacity	Determines the opacity of the control, in percentages (0.0 is completely transparent, 1.0 is completely opaque).
Region	This property configures a Region object that specifies the outline/silhouette/boundary of the control.
RightToLeft	This is used for international applications where the language is written from right to left.

The Control class also defines a number of additional methods and events used to configure how the Control should respond to drag-and-drop operations and respond to painting operations (Table 13-11).

Table 13-11. Additional Control Methods

Control Method/Event	Meaning in Life
DoDragDrop() OnDragDrop() OnDragEnter() OnDragLeave() OnDragOver()	These methods are used to monitor drag-and-drop operations for a given Control descendent.
ResetFont() ResetCursor() ResetForeColor() ResetBackColor()	These methods reset various UI attributes of a child control to the corresponding value of the parent.
OnPaint()	Inheriting classes should override this method to handle the Paint event.
DragEnter DragLeave DragDrop DragOver	These events are sent in response to drag-and-drop operations.
Paint	This event is sent whenever the Control has become "dirty" and needs to be repainted.

More Fun with the Control Class

To illustrate some of these additional Control members, the following class sets the background color of the Form object to "Tomato" (you just have to love the names of these colors), the opacity to 50 percent (to generate a semi-transparent main window), and configures the mouse cursor to display an hourglass icon. More important, let's handle the Paint event in order to render a text string into the Form's client area. Here is the update:

```
using System;
using System.Windows.Forms;
using System.Drawing;    // Needed for Color, Brush, and Font types.

public class MainForm : Form
{
    ...
```

```
public MainForm()
{
    // Set some properties that we have inherited from Control.
    BackColor = Color.Tomato;
    Opacity = 0.5d;
    this.Cursor = Cursors.WaitCursor;
    // Handle the Paint event.
    this.Paint += new PaintEventHandler(MainForm_Paint);
}
private void MainForm_Paint(object sender, PaintEventArgs e)
{
    Graphics g = e.Graphics;
    g.DrawString("What a head trip...",
        new Font("Times New Roman", 20),
        new SolidBrush(Color.Black), 40, 10);
}
}
```

If you run this application you will see that the Form is indeed transparent!

Painting Basics

The most important aspect of this application is the handling of the Paint event. Notice that the delegate defines a method that takes a parameter of type PaintEventArgs. This type defines two properties to help you configure the current paint session for the Control as seen in Table 13-12.

Table 13-12. Additional Control Properties

PaintEventArgs Property	Meaning in Life
ClipRectangle	Gets the rectangle in which to paint
Graphics	Gets the Graphics object used during a paint session

The critical property of PaintEventArgs is Graphics, which is called to retrieve a Graphics object to use during the painting session. You examine this class (and GDI+ in general) in greater detail in Chapter 14. For now, do understand that the Graphics class defines a number of members that allow you to render text, geometric shapes and images onto a Control-derived type.

Finally, in this example you also configured the Cursor property to display an hourglass symbol whenever the mouse cursor is within the bounding rectangle of this Control. The Cursors type can be assigned to any member of the Cursors enumeration (e.g., Arrow, Cross, UpArrow, Help, and so forth):

```
public MainForm()
{
    ...
    this.Cursor = Cursors.WaitCursor;
}
```

SOURCE CODE   The MoreControlBehaviors project is included under the Chapter 13 subdirectory.

The ScrollableControl Class

ScrollableControl is used to define a small number of members that allow your widget to support vertical and horizontal scrollbars. The most intriguing members of the ScrollableControl type would have to be the AutoScroll property and the related AutoScrollMinSize property. For example, assume you wish to ensure that if the end user resizes your Form, horizontal and vertical scrollbars are automatically inserted if the size of the client area is less than or equal to 300×300 pixels. Programmatically, your task is simple:

```
// Note that you need to reference the System.Drawing namespace
// to gain access to the Size type.
this.AutoScroll = true;
this.AutoScrollMinSize = new System.Drawing.Size (300, 300);
```

The ScrollableControl class takes care of the rest. For example, if you had a Form that contained a number of child objects (buttons, labels, or whatnot), you would find that the scrolling logic ensures the entire Form real estate is viewable. For the current example, simply render a large block of text onto a Label object (see Figure 13-12).

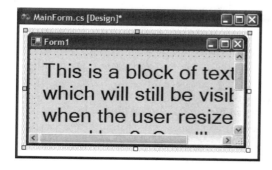

Figure 13-12. Scroll Form GUI

At runtime, the Form will automatically display vertical and horizontal scrollbars when any part of the Label is not visible. The ScrollableControl class does define a number of additional members beyond AutoScroll and AutoScrollMinSize, but not many. Also be aware that when you wish to take greater control over the scrolling process, you are able to create and manipulate individual ScrollBar types (such as HScrollBar and VScrollBar). I'll leave it to you to check out the remaining members using online Help.

SOURCE CODE   The ScrollForm project is included under the Chapter 13 subdirectory.

ContainerControl Class

ContainerControl defines support to manage the focus of a given GUI item. In practice, the behavior defined by System.Windows.Forms.ContainerControl is much more useful when you are building a Form that contains a number of child controls, and wish to allow the user to use the Tab key to alternate focus. Using a small set of members, you can programmatically obtain the currently selected control, force another to receive focus, and so forth. Table 13-13 gives a rundown of some of the more interesting members.

Table 13-13. Members of the ContainerControl Type

ContainerControl Member	Meaning in Life
ActiveControl ParentForm	These properties allow you to obtain and set the active control, as well as retrieve a reference to the Form that is hosting the item.
ProcessTabKey()	This method allows you to programmatically activate the Tab key to set focus to the next available control.

On a related note, recall that all descendents of System.Windows.Forms.Control inherit the TabStop and TabIndex properties. As you might be able to guess, these items are used to set the tab order of controls maintained by a parent container, and are used in conjunction with the members supplied by the ContainerControl class. You revisit the issue of tab order during the discussion of programming controls (Chapter 15).

The Form Class

This brings us to the Form class itself, which is typically the direct base class for your custom Form types. In addition to the large set of members inherited from the Control, ScrollableControl, and ContainerControl classes, the Form type adds even greater functionality. Let's start with the core properties (Table 13-14).

Table 13-14. Properties of the Form Type

Form Property	Meaning in Life
AcceptButton	Gets or sets the button on the Form that is clicked when the user presses the Enter key.
ActiveMDIChild IsMDIChild IsMDIContainer	Each of these properties is used within the context of an MDI application.
AutoScale	Gets or sets a value indicating whether the Form will adjust its size to fit the height of the font used on the form and scale its controls.
BorderStyle	Gets or sets the border style of the Form. Used in conjunction with the FormBorderStyle enumeration.
CancelButton	Gets or sets the button control that will be clicked when the user presses the Esc key.
ControlBox	Gets or sets a value indicating whether the Form has a control box.
Menu MergedMenu	Gets or sets the (merged) menu for the Form.
MaximizeBox MinimizedBox	Used to determine if this Form will enable the maximize and minimize boxes.
ShowInTaskbar	Should this Form be seen on the Windows taskbar?
StartPosition	Gets or sets the starting position of the Form at run time, as specified by the FormStartPosition enumeration.
WindowState	Configures how the Form is to be displayed on startup. Used in conjunction with the FormWindowState enumeration.

The truth of the matter is that the Form class does not define a great deal of additional methods. The bulk of a Form's functionality comes from the base classes you have already examined. However, Table 13-15 gives a partial list of some additional methods to be aware of.

Table 13-15. Key Methods of the Form Type

Method of the Form Type	Meaning in Life
Activate()	Activate a given Form and give it focus.
Close()	Closes a Form.
CenterToScreen()	Places the Form on the dead center of the screen.
LayoutMDI()	Arranges each child Form (as specified by the LayoutMDI enumeration) within the parent Form.

Table 13-15. Key Methods of the Form Type (Continued)

Method of the Form Type	Meaning in Life
OnResize()	May be overridden to respond to Resize events.
ShowDialog()	Displays a Form as a Modal dialog. More on dialog box programming at a later time.

Finally, the Form class does define a number of Events (Table 13-16).

Table 13-16. Select Events of the Form Type

Form Event	Meaning in Life
Activate	Sent when a Form is brought to the front of the active application.
Closed, Closing	These events are used to determine when the Form is about to close, or has closed.
MDIChildActive	Sent when a child window is activated.

Fun with the Form Class

At this point, you should feel quite comfortable with the functionality provided by the Form class and each of its parent classes. Here is a main window (MainForm) that makes use of various members in the inheritance chain:

```
public class MainForm: Form
{
    ...
    public MainForm ()
    {
        // Configure the initial look and feel of this form.
        BackColor = Color.LemonChiffon;    // Background color.
        Text = "My Fantastic Form";        // Form's caption.
        Size = new Size(200, 200);         // 200 * 200.
        CenterToScreen();                  // Center Form to the screen.
        // Handle events.
        this.Resize += new EventHandler(this.Form1_Resize);
        this.Paint += new PaintEventHandler(this.Form1_Paint);
    }
    private void MainForm_Resize(object sender, System.EventArgs e)
    {
        Invalidate();
    }
```

```
// Reference System.Drawing to render this string.
private void MainForm_Paint(object sender, PaintEventArgs e)
{
    Graphics g = e.Graphics;
    g.DrawString("Windows Forms is for building GUIs!",
                new Font("Times New Roman", 20),
                new SolidBrush(Color.Black),
                this.DisplayRectangle);         // Display in client rect.
}
}
```

Here, a Form object that begins life centered on the screen has been created. In addition, the Resize event has been handled. Simply call Invalidate() to force the client area to be refreshed. In this way, the text string rendered on the client area always fits within the bounding rectangle Form's client area (note the use of the DisplayRectangle property).

SOURCE CODE   The SimpleFormApp can be found under the Chapter 13 subdirectory.

The Life-Cycle of a Windows Form Type

If you have programmed user interfaces using GUI toolkits such as Java Swing, MFC or the raw Win32 API, you are aware that Window types have a number of events which fire during its lifetime. The same holds true for System.Windows.Forms.Form-derived types. Table 13-17 documents lifetime-centric Form level events.

Table 13-17. Form Life Time Events

Form Lifetime Event	Meaning in Life
Activated	Occurs whenever the Form is *activated*, meaning the Form has been given the current focus on the desktop.
Closing	Occurs when a Form is about to be closed completely. As you will see, this method allows you to prompt the user with the obligatory "Are you *sure* you wish to close this form" message.
Closed	This occurs when the Form is truly closing down and is about to be disposed.
Deactivate	Occurs whenever the Form is *deactivated*, meaning the Form has lost current focus on the desktop.

Table 13-17. Form Life Time Events (Continued)

Form Lifetime Event	Meaning in Life
Load	Occurs after the Form has been allocated into memory, but is not yet visible on the screen.
Dispose	As you have already seen, the Dispose() method is called automatically to allow the type to perform any clean up.

Of course, the true life of a Form begins when the Application.Run() method triggers the type's constructor. Once the object has been allocated on the heap, the first event that fires is Load. Within Load, you are free to configure the look and feel of Form (to augment the work preformed by the InitializeComponent() method), prepare any contained child controls (such as ListBoxes, TreeViews, and whatnot), or simply allocate resources used during the Form's operation (database connections, handles to remote objects, or whatnot).

Once the Load event has fired, the next event is Activate. As mentioned, this event fires when the Form receives focus as the active window on the desktop. The logical counterpart to the Activate event is (of course) Deactivate, which fires when the Form loses focus as the active window. As you can guess, the Activate and Deactivate events can fire numerous times over the life of a given Form type.

When the user has chosen to close the Form in question, two close-centric events fire: Closing and Closed. The Closing event is fired first, and is an ideal place to prompt the end user with the much hated "Are you *sure* you wish to close this application?" dialog box. As you are aware, this type of confirmation is quite helpful when you wish to ask the user if s/he wishes to save the current application-centric data. The Closing event works in conjunction with System.ComponentModel.CancelEventHandler delegate, which maps to methods that take a System.ComponentModel.CancelEventArgs type as its second argument (the first, as always is a System.Object). If you set the CancelEventArgs.Cancel property to "true," you prevent the Form from being destroyed and instruct it to return to normal operation. For example:

```
// Assume you have handled the Closing event in the Form.
private void MainForm_Closing(object sender,
    System.ComponentModel.CancelEventArgs e)
{
    DialogResult dr = MessageBox.Show("Do you REALLY want to close this app?",
        "Closing event!", MessageBoxButtons.YesNo);
    if(dr == DialogResult.No)
        e.Cancel = true;
    else
        e.Cancel = false;
}
```

Here, we display a message box that contains Yes and No buttons, and capture which button was clicked via the returned DialogResult type (more on this type and dialog boxes in general in Chapter 15). If the user clicks the No button, we set the

CancelEventArgs.Cancel property to true, thereby preventing the Form from shutting down.

Assuming the user does want to close the Form completely, the next event of the Form's life cycle is Closed. Here, you are able to clean up any acquired resources, write to log files, or what have you. Last but not least, the Dispose() method will be called to allow the Form to clean up any contained widgets.

A Form Lifetime Example

To solidify the sequence of events that take place during a Form's lifetime, assume you have a new application that handles the Load, Activated, Deactivate, Closing, and Close events:

```
public MainForm()
{
    InitializeComponent();
    this.Closing += new
        System.ComponentModel.CancelEventHandler(this.MainForm_Closing);
    this.Load += new System.EventHandler(this.MainForm_Load);
    this.Closed += new System.EventHandler(this.MainForm_Closed);
    this.Activated += new System.EventHandler(this.MainForm_Activated);
    this.Deactivate += new System.EventHandler(this.MainForm_Deactivate);
}
```

In each registered event handler, we are going to update a private System.String member variable (named lifeTimeInfo) with a simple message that displays the name of the event that has just been intercepted:

```
private void MainForm_Load(object sender, System.EventArgs e)
{ lifeTimeInfo += "Load event\n"; }
private void MainForm_Activated(object sender, System.EventArgs e)
{ lifeTimeInfo += "Activate event\n"; }
private void MainForm_Closing(object sender,
    System.ComponentModel.CancelEventArgs e)
{
    ...
    lifeTimeInfo += "Closing event\n";
}
private void MainForm_Deactivate(object sender, System.EventArgs e)
{ lifeTimeInfo += "Deactivate event\n"; }
private void MainForm_Closed(object sender, System.EventArgs e)
{ lifeTimeInfo += "Closed event\n"; }
```

Finally, in Dispose(), display your string using a MessageBox type:

```
protected override void Dispose( bool disposing )
{
    MessageBox.Show(lifeTimeInfo, "Life time events");
    ...
}
```

Now, run your application and shift the Form into and out of focus a few times (to trigger the Activate and Deactivate events). Once you shut down the Form, you will see a message box looking something like Figure 13-13.

Figure 13-13. Form events

SOURCE CODE   The FormLifeTime project can be found under the Chapter 13 subdirectory.

Handing Form Level Events a la VS .NET

Although you are always free to handle Form-level events by authoring the necessary logic by hand, it is worth pointing out that VS .NET offers design-time support as well. If you examine the IDE's Property Window, you will notice a small lightning bolt icon. Once selected, you will find the set of events for whatever GUI widget you select from the drop-down list box mounted on the top of the Window. Simply locate the name of the event you wish to handle and type in the name to be used as an event handler (or simply double-click the event to generate a default name).

For example, Figure 13-14 illustrates how you could handle the Load event for a given Form.

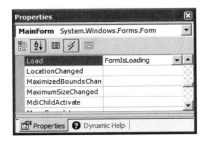

Figure 13-14. Form events

If you were now to look at the code behind your Form, you would find that the InitializeComponent() method has been updated to handle the given event, and a empty event handler has been generated automatically. As you might guess, this same technique can be used to autogenerate events for any GUI widget (as you will see over the course of this text).

NOTE The default name used to generate an event handler is formed as *ClassName_EventName* therefore, it is always a good idea to name your GUI types appropriately before autogenerating events (unless you like manually renaming auto-generated code).

NOTE Every GUI widget has a default event, which simply refers to the event that will be handled if you double-click the item at design time. For example, a Form's default event is Load, and if you double-click any-where on a Form type, the IDE will automatically write code to handle this event.

Building Menus with Windows Forms

Now that you understand the composition and lifecycle of the Form class, the next task is to learn how to establish a menu system to provide some degree of user interaction. The System.Windows.Forms namespace provides a number of types that facilitate the building of main menus (e.g., menus mounted at the top of a Form), as well as context-sensitive pop-up menus (e.g., "right-click" menus). To begin, let's examine what it would take to build a topmost menu that allows the user to exit the application using a standard "File | Exit" menu command.

The first class to be aware of is System.Windows.Forms.Menu, which functions as the base class for all other menu-related classes (MainMenu, MenuItem, and ContextMenu). Be aware that System.Windows.Forms.Menu is an abstract class, and therefore you cannot create a direct instance of this type. Rather, you create instances of one (or more) of the derived types. The Menu class defines basic menu-centric behaviors such as providing access to an individual menu item, cloning menus, merging menus (for MDI applications), and so forth. Figure 13-15 shows the relationship between these core types.

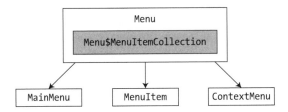

Figure 13-15. Menu-centric types of Windows Forms

Note that the Menu class defines a nested class named MenuItemCollection, which is inherited by the MainMenu, MenuItem, and ContextMenu subclasses. As you would expect, this collection holds onto a set of related menu items, which is accessed using the Menu.MenuItems property (more details in a moment). The Menu base class defines the core members shown in Table 13-18.

Table 13-18. Members of the Menu Type

Menu Member	Meaning in Life
Handle	This property provides access to the underlying Win32 HMENU handle that represents this Menu.
IsParent	This property specifies whether this menu contains any items or is the topmost item.
MdiListItem	This property returns the MenuItem that contains the list of MDI child windows.
MenuItems	Another property. Returns an instance of the nested Menu.MenuItemCollection type, which represents the submenus owned by the Menu derived class.
GetMainMenu()	Returns the MainMenu item that contains this menu.
MergeMenu()	Merges another menu's items with this one's as specified by their mergeType and mergeOrder properties. Used to merge an MDI container's menu with that of its active MDI child.
CloneMenu()	Sets this menu to be an identical (deep) copy of another menu.

Menu$MenuItemCollection Type

Perhaps the most immediately important member of the Menu class is the MenuItems property, which returns an instance of the nested Menu$MenuItemCollection type (recall that the the '$' notation is just a convention to represent a nested type, and has nothing at all to do with C# or .NET code). Recall that nested classes can be helpful when you wish to establish a logical relationship between related types. Here, the Menu$MenuItemCollection type represents the set of all submenus owned by a Menu-derived object.

For example, if you created a MainMenu to represent the topmost "File" menu, you would add MenuItems (for example, Open, Save, Close, Save As) into the collection. As you would expect, Menu$MenuItemCollection defines members to add and remove MenuItem types, obtain the current count of MenuItems, as well as access a particular member in the collection. Table 13-19 lists some (but not all) of the core members.

Table 13-19. The Nested MenuItemCollection Type

Menu$MenuItemCollection Member	Meaning in Life
Count	Returns the number of MenuItems in the collection.
Add() AddRange() Remove()	Inserts (or removes) a new MenuItem into the collection. (Add adds/ remove removes. Add does not remove.) Be aware that the Add() method has been overloaded numerous times to allow you to specify shortcut keys, delegates, and whatnot. AddRange() is helpful in that it allows you to add an array of MenuItems in a single call.
Clear()	Removes all items from the collection.
Contains()	Used to determine if a given MenuItem is inside the collection.

Building Your Menu System

Now that you understand the functionality of the abstract Menu class (and the nested MenuItemCollection type), you can build your simple File menu. The process begins by creating a MainMenu object. The MainMenu class represents the collection of topmost menu items (e.g., File, Edit, View, Tools, Help, and so forth) which appear on a Form type. Thus:

```
public class MainForm : Form
{
    // The Form's main menu.
    private MainMenu mainMenu = new MainMenu();
...
}
```

Once you have created a MainMenu object, use the Menu$MenuItemCollection.Add() method to insert the topmost item (the "File" menu). Menu$MenuItemCollection.Add() returns a MenuItem object that represents the newly inserted File menu.

To insert the subitems (e.g., Exit), you insert MenuItem types into the Menu$MenuItemCollection maintained by the File MenuItem. Finally (and most important), when you are finished populating the MainMenu type, attach it to the owning Form using the inherited Menu property. If you fail to do so, your menu system will not be visible! Here are the relevant code updates:

```
public class MainForm : Form
{
    // The Form's main menu.
    private MainMenu mainMenu = new MainMenu();
    public MainForm()
    {
        // Create the 'File' Menu and add it to the MenuItemCollection.
        MenuItem miFile = mainMenu.MenuItems.Add("&File");
        // Now make the Exit MenuItem and add it to the File MenuItem.
        // This version of Add() takes:
        // 1) A new MenuItem.
        // 2) A new delegate (EventHandler).
        // 3) An optional shortcut key.
        miFile.MenuItems.Add(new MenuItem("E&xit",
                            new EventHandler(this.FileExit_Clicked),
                            Shortcut.CtrlX));
        // Attach main menu to the Form object.
        this.Menu = mainMenu;
    }
    ...
}
```

Notice that if you embed an ampersand within the string name of a menu item, this marks which letter should be underlined to designate the Alt key access combination. Thus, when you specify "&File," you allow the user to activate the File menu by selecting "Alt+F."

When you added the Exit submenu item, you specified an optional shortcut flag. The System.Windows.Forms.Shortcut enumeration is fully detailed in online Help. As you might guess, this enumeration provides fields that specify traditional shortcut keys (Ctrl+C, Ctrl+V, F1, F2, Ins) as well as more exotic combinations.

Here then, is the current code for the simple menu application. Just for kicks, notice how you are able to set the BackColor property of the Form using the MainMenu.GetForm() method:

```
// The Simple Menu Application.
public class MainForm : Form
{
    // The Form's main menu.
    private MainMenu mainMenu = new MainMenu();
    // Run the application.
    public static void Main(string[] args)
    {
        Application.Run(new MainForm());
    }
```

```
// Construct the form.
public MainForm()
{
    // Configure the initial look and feel of this form.
    Text = "Simple Menu";
    CenterToScreen();
    // Create the 'File | Exit' Menu.
    MenuItem miFile = mainMenu.MenuItems.Add("&File");
    miFile.MenuItems.Add(new MenuItem("&Exit",
                         new EventHandler(this.FileExit_Clicked),
                         Shortcut.CtrlX));
    // Attach main menu to the Form object.
    this.Menu = mainMenu;
    // MainMenu.GetForm() returns a reference to the owning Form.
    // To illustrate...
    mainMenu.GetForm().BackColor = Color.Black;
}
// File | Exit Menu item handler
private void FileExit_Clicked(object sender, EventArgs e)
{
    this.Close();      // Just close the application...
}
}
```

Adding Another Topmost Menu Item

Now, what if you wish to add another topmost menu named "Help" that contains a single subitem named "About" (Figure 13-16)?

Figure 13-16. A more elaborate main menu

The code models the "File | Exit" menu logic almost exactly: Begin by adding a new MenuItem ("Help") to the MainMenu object. From here, add a new subitem ("About"):

```
public class MainForm : Form
{
    private MainMenu mainMenu = new MainMenu();
...
    public MainForm()
    {
        // Create the 'File | Exit' Menu.
        MenuItem miFile = mainMenu.MenuItems.Add("&File");
        miFile.MenuItems.Add(new MenuItem("E&xit",
            new EventHandler(this.FileExit_Clicked),
            Shortcut.CtrlX));
        // Now create a 'Help | About' menu.
        MenuItem miHelp = mainMenu.MenuItems.Add("Help");
        miHelp.MenuItems.Add(new MenuItem("&About",
            new EventHandler(this.HelpAbout_Clicked),
            Shortcut.CtrlA));
        ...
    }
    // Help | About Menu handler
    private void HelpAbout_Clicked(object sender, EventArgs e)
    {
        MessageBox.Show("The amazing menu app...");
    }
}
```

 SOURCE CODE The SimpleMenu application is located under the Chapter 13 subdirectory.

Creating a Pop-Up Menu

Let's now examine the process of building a context-sensitive pop-up (i.e., right-click) menu. The ContextMenu class represents the pop-up menu itself. Like the process of building a MainMenu, your goal is to add individual MenuItems to the MenuItemCollection to represent the possible selectable subitems. The following class makes use of a pop-up menu to allow the user to configure the font size of a string rendered to the client area:

```
namespace MainForm
{
    // Helper enum for font size.
    internal enum TheFontSize
    {
        FontSizeHuge = 30,
        FontSizeNormal = 20,
        FontSizeTiny = 8
    }

    public class MainForm : Form
    {
        // Current size of font.
        private TheFontSize currFontSize
            = TheFontSize.FontSizeNormal;
        // The Form's popup menu.
        private ContextMenu popUpMenu = new ContextMenu();
        public static void Main(string[] args)
        {  Application.Run(new MainForm()); }
        private void MainForm_Resize(object sender, System.EventArgs e)
        { Invalidate(); }
        public MainForm()
        {
            // Now add the subitems & attach context menu.
            popUpMenu.MenuItems.Add("Huge",
                new EventHandler(PopUp_Clicked));
            popUpMenu.MenuItems.Add("Normal",
                new EventHandler(PopUp_Clicked));
            popUpMenu.MenuItems.Add("Tiny",
                new EventHandler(PopUp_Clicked));
            this.ContextMenu = popUpMenu;
            // Handle events.
            this.Resize += new System.EventHandler(this.MainForm_Resize);
            this.Paint += new PaintEventHandler(this.MainForm_Paint);
        }
        // PopUp_Clicked | X Menu item handler
        private void PopUp_Clicked(object sender, EventArgs e)
        {
            // Figure out the string name of the selected item.
            MenuItem miClicked = null;
            if (sender is MenuItem)
                miClicked = (MenuItem)sender;
            else
                return;
            string item = miClicked.Text;
            if(item == "Huge")
                currFontSize = TheFontSize.FontSizeHuge;
            if(item == "Normal")
                currFontSize = TheFontSize.FontSizeNormal;
            if(item == "Tiny")
                currFontSize = TheFontSize.FontSizeTiny;
            Invalidate();
        }
```

```
    private void MainForm_Paint(object sender, PaintEventArgs e)
    {
        Graphics g = e.Graphics;
        g.DrawString("Please click on me...",
            new Font("Times New Roman", (float)currFontSize),
            new SolidBrush(Color.Black),
            this.DisplayRectangle);
    }
  }
}
```

Notice that as you add the subitems to the ContextMenu, you have assigned the *same* event handler to each MenuItem type. When a given item is clicked, the flow of logic brings us to the PopUp_Clicked() method. Using the "sender" argument, you are able to determine the textual name of the MenuItem and take an appropriate course of action (which works just fine, assuming you are not interested in localizing the application).

Also notice that once you have created a ContextMenu, you associate it to the Form using the Control.ContextMenu property. Be aware that *any* control can be assigned a context menu. For example, you could create a Button object on a dialog box that responds to a particular context menu. In this way, the menu would only be displayed if the mouse button were clicked while within the bounding rectangle of the button.

Adorning Your Menu System

The MenuItem class also defines a number of members that allow you to check, enable, and hide a given menu item. Table 13-20 gives a rundown of some of the interesting properties of MenuItem.

Table 13-20. More Details of the MenuItem Type

MenuItem Member	Meaning in Life
Checked	Gets or sets a value indicating whether a check mark appears beside the text of the menu item
DefaultItem	Gets or sets a value indicating whether the menu item is the default
Enabled	Gets or sets a value indicating whether the menu item is enabled
Index	Gets or sets the menu item's position in its parent menu
MergeOrder	Gets or sets the relative position of the menu item when its menu is merged with another
MergeType	Gets or sets a value that indicates the behavior of this menu item when its menu is merged with another
OwnerDraw	Gets or sets a value indicating whether code that you provide draws the menu item or Windows draws the menu item

Table 13-20. More Details of the MenuItem Type (Continued)

MenuItem Member	Meaning in Life
RadioCheck	Gets or sets a value that indicates whether the menu item, if checked, displays a radio-button mark instead of a check mark
Shortcut	Gets or sets the shortcut key associated with the menu item
ShowShortcut	Gets or sets a value that indicates whether the shortcut key that is associated with the menu item is displayed next to the menu item caption
Text	Gets or sets the text of the menu item

To illustrate further use of the MenuItem type, let's extend the previous pop-up menu to display a check mark next to the currently selected menu item. Setting a check mark on a given menu item is not at all difficult (just set the Checked property to true). However, tracking which menu item should be checked does require some additional logic. One possible approach is to define distinct MenuItem objects that map to each possible submenu item and an additional MenuItem that represents the currently selected item:

```
public class MainForm : Form
{
    ...
    // Used to keep track of the current checked item.
    private MenuItem currentCheckedItem;    // Marks the item checked.
    private MenuItem checkedHuge;
    private MenuItem checkedNormal;
    private MenuItem checkedTiny;
...
}
```

The next step is to associate each of these MenuItems to the correct submenu. Thus, you would update the constructor as follows:

```
// Construct the form.
public MainForm()
{
    ...
    // Set each MenuItem to the correct submenu.
    checkedHuge = this.ContextMenu.MenuItems[0];
    checkedNormal = this.ContextMenu.MenuItems[1];
    checkedTiny = this.ContextMenu.MenuItems[2];
    // Now check the 'Normal' menu item.
    currentCheckedItem = checkedNormal;
    currentCheckedItem.Checked = true;
}
```

At this point, you have a way to programmatically identify each subitem, as well as the currently checked item (which has been initially set to checkedNormal). The last step is to update the PopUp_Clicked() event handler to check the correct MenuItem in response to the user selection (see Figure 13-17 for a test run):

```
private void PopUp_Clicked(object sender, EventArgs e)
{
    // Uncheck the currently checked item.
    currentCheckedItem.Checked = false;
...
    // Based on selection, establish the current checked menu item.
    if(item == "Huge")
    {
        currFontSize = TheFontSize.FontSizeHuge;
        currentCheckedItem = checkedHuge;
    }
    if(item == "Normal")
    {
        currFontSize = TheFontSize. FontSizeNormal;
        currentCheckedItem = checkedNormal;
    }
    if(item == "Tiny")
    {
        currFontSize = TheFontSize. FontSizeTiny;
        currentCheckedItem = checkedTiny;
    }
    // Now check it.
    currentCheckedItem.Checked = true;
    Invalidate();
}
```

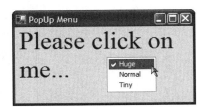

Figure 13-17. Check-marking a menu item

SOURCE CODE   The PopUpMenu project is contained under the Chapter 13 subdirectory.

Building a Menu Using Visual Studio .NET

Indeed, knowledge is power. On the other hand, now that you understand how you can write raw C# code to create and configure a menu system, let's examine how Visual Studio .NET can offer some design-time assistance. To begin, assume that you have created a new C# Windows Application project workspace.

Using the Toolbox window, double-click the MainMenu icon. Once you do, you see a new icon appear at the icon tray of the design-time template. Furthermore, you see a design-time representation of your menu attached to the top of your Form. To add new menu items, simply double-click a slot and type away! Consider Figure 13-18.

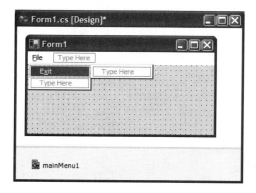

Figure 13-18. The integrated menu editor of VS .NET

As far as handling events for a given item (as well as configuring a number of other properties), select the MenuItem you wish to configure using the VS .NET Properties window (Figure 13-19).

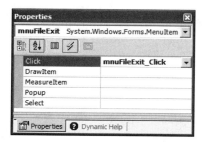

Figure 13-19. Handing menu-centric events using VS .NET

Once you enter the name of our event handler, the Visual Studio .NET IDE automatically generates stub code for the event handler:

```
private void mnuFileExit_Clicked (object sender, System.EventArgs e)
{
    // Respond to File | Exit selection...
}
```

Be aware, that as you modify your menus at design time, the IDE is updating the InitializeComponent() helper function, as well as adding member variables to represent the types you are manipulating at design time. If you examine the code, things (I hope) look very familiar.

NOTE   VS .NET also supports design-time configuration of pop-up menus. Simply drag a ContextMenu item onto your Form and edit the selections using the menu editor. Once this has been done, assign this object to the ContextMenu property of the widget you wish to leverage this pop-up.

Understanding Status Bars

In addition to a menu system, many Forms also maintain a status bar. Status bars may be divided into any number of "panes." Panes hold some textual (or graphical) information such as menu help strings, or other application-specific information. The StatusBar type derives directly from System.Windows.Forms.Control. In addition to the inherited members, StatusBar defines the core properties shown in Table 13-21.

Table 13-21. Select StatusBar Properties

StatusBar Property	Meaning in Life
BackgroundImage	Gets or sets the image rendered on the background of the StatusBar control
Font	Gets or sets the font the StatusBar control will use to display information
ForeColor	Gets or sets the foreground color of the control
Panels	Returns a nested StatusBarPanelCollection type that contains each Panel maintained by the StatusBar (much like the menu pattern)
ShowPanels	Gets or sets a value indicating whether panels should be shown
SizingGrip	Gets or sets a value indicating whether a sizing grip will be rendered on the corner of the StatusBar control

Once you create a StatusBar, your next task is to add any number of panels (represented by the StatusBarPanel class) into the nested StatusBar$StatusBarPanelCollection. Be aware that the constructor of StatusBarPanel automatically configures the new panel with a default look and feel (therefore, if you are happy with this initial configuration, your programming task is made even simpler). Table 13-22 lists of the core members of the StatusBarPanel type.

Table 13-22. Properties of the StatusBarPanel Type

StatusBarPanel Property	Meaning in Life
Alignment	Determines the alignment of text in the pane. The default value is HorizontalAlignment.Left.
AutoSize	Determines if this pane should automatically resize (and how). Default value is StatusBarPanelAutoSize.None.
BorderStyle	Configures border style. Default value is StatusBarPanelBorderStyle.Sunken.
Icon	Is there an icon in the pane? A null reference is the default (e.g., no icon).
MinWidth	Default is 10.
Style	What does this pane contain? Default is StatusBarPanelStyle.Text, but there may be other types as specified by the StatusBarPanelStyle enumeration.
Text	Caption of pane. The default is an empty string.
ToolTipText	Any tool-tip? An empty string is the default.
Width	Default is 100.

Building a Status Bar

To illustrate, let's construct a StatusBar object that is divided into two panes. The first pane is used to show helpful prompts describing the functionality of each menu selection. The second pane displays the current system time. And let's place a small icon on the far left side of the first pane (just to keep things interesting). Check out Figure 13-20.

Figure 13-20. A custom status bar

Assume you have updated the SimpleMenu application created earlier in this chapter, to support this status bar. Like any Control-derived type, the StatusBar needs to be added to the Form's Controls collection (more details on this collection in Chapter 15). As you might guess, this collection contains an entry for any GUI widget mounted on the client area, including StatusBars types. Here is the status bar logic:

```
public class MainForm : Form
{
    // Member data for the status bar, and each pane.
    private StatusBar statusBar = new StatusBar();
    private StatusBarPanel sbPnlPrompt = new StatusBarPanel();
    private StatusBarPanel sbPnlTime = new StatusBarPanel();
    public MainForm ()
    {
        ...
        BuildStatBar();      // Helper function.
    }

    private void BuildStatBar()
    {
        // Configure the status bar.
        statusBar.ShowPanels = true;
        statusBar.Size = new System.Drawing.Size(212, 20);
        statusBar.Location = new System.Drawing.Point(0, 216);
        // AddRange() allows you to add a set of panes at once.
        statusBar.Panels.AddRange(new StatusBarPanel[]
            { sbPnlPrompt, sbPnlTime} );
        // Configure prompt panel.
        sbPnlPrompt.BorderStyle = StatusBarPanelBorderStyle.None;
        sbPnlPrompt.AutoSize = StatusBarPanelAutoSize.Spring;
        sbPnlPrompt.Width = 62;
        sbPnlPrompt.Text = "Ready";
        // Configure time pane.
        sbPnlTime.AutoSize = StatusBarPanelAutoSize.Spring;
        sbPnlTime.Width = 120;
        // Add an icon.
        try
        {
            // This icon must be in the same app directory.
            // Chapter 14 will illustrate how to embed
            // resources into your assembly!
            Icon i = new Icon("status.ico");
            sbPnlPrompt.Icon = i;
        }
        catch(Exception e)
        {
            MessageBox.Show(e.Message);
        }
        // Now add this new status bar to the Form's Controls collection.
        this.Controls.Add(statusBar);
    }
}
```

Working with the Timer Type

Recall that the second pane should display the current time. The first step to take to achieve this design goal is to add a Timer member variable to the Form. If you have a Visual Basic background, you should understand this object quite well. Win32/C++ programmers also understand the notion of timers given the WM_TIMER message. Regardless of your background, a Windows Forms Timer object is simply a type that calls some method (specified by the Tick event) at a given interval (specified by the Interval property). Table 13-23 lists some core members.

Table 13-23. The Timer Type

Timer Member	Meaning in Life
Enabled	This property enables or disables the Timer's ability to fire the Tick event. You may also use Start() and Stop() to achieve the same effect.
Interval	Sets the number of milliseconds between ticks.
Start() Stop()	Like the Enabled property, these methods control the firing of the Tick event.
OnTick()	This member may be overridden in a custom class deriving from Timer.
Tick	The Tick event adds a new event handler to the underlying MulticastDelegate.

Thus, you can update our class as follows:

```
public class MainForm : Form
{
...
    private Timer timer1 = new Timer();
    public MainForm ()
    {
        // Configure the timer.
        timer1.Interval = 1000;
        timer1.Enabled = true;
        timer1.Tick += new EventHandler(timer1_Tick);
        ...
    }
    // This method will be called (roughly) every second.
    private void timer1_Tick(object sender, EventArgs e)
    {
        DateTime t = DateTime.Now;
        string s = t.ToLongTimeString();
        // Change text of pane to current time.
        sbPnlTime.Text = s;
    }
}
```

Notice that the Timer event handler makes use of the DateTime type. Here, you simply find the current system time using the Now property, and use it to set the Text property of the correct StatusBarPanel object.

Displaying Menu Selection Prompts

Finally, you must configure the first pane to hold menu help strings. As you know, most applications send a small bit of text information to the first pane of a status bar whenever the end user selects a menu item (e.g., "This terminates the application").

Assume the menu system for this application is identical to the Simple Menu application. This time, however, you need to respond to the Select event of each subitem. When the user selects "File | Exit" or "Help | About" you tell the first StatusBarPanel object to display a given text message. Note, you also handle the MenuComplete event (described in the **bold** code comment below). Here is the update:

```
public class MainForm: Form
{
    ...
    public MainForm ()
    {
        ...
        // The MenuComplete event is sent when the user clicks off
        // the menu. We want to capture this event in order to
        // set the text of the first pane to "Ready". If we did not,
        // the StatusBarPanel text would always be based on the last menu
        // selected!
        this.MenuComplete += new EventHandler(StatusForm_MenuDone);
        BuildMenuSystem();
    }
    private void FileExit_Selected(object sender, EventArgs e)
    { sbPnlPrompt.Text = "Terminates this app"; }
    private void HelpAbout_Selected(object sender, EventArgs e)
    { sbPnlPrompt.Text = "Displays app info"; }
    private void StatusForm_MenuDone(object sender, EventArgs e)
    {
        sbPnlPrompt.Text = "Ready";          // See big comment in ctor...
    }
    // Helper functions.
    private void BuildMenuSystem()
    {
        // First make the main menu.
        mainMenu = new MainMenu();
        // Create the 'File' Menu.
        MenuItem miFile = mainMenu.MenuItems.Add("&File");
        miFile.MenuItems.Add(new MenuItem("E&xit",
                        new EventHandler(this.FileExit_Clicked),
                        Shortcut.CtrlX));
        // Handle the Select event for the Exit menu item.
        miFile.MenuItems[0].Select += new EventHandler(FileExit_Selected);
        // Now create a 'Help | About' menu.
```

```
            MenuItem miHelp = mainMenu.MenuItems.Add("Help");
            miHelp.MenuItems.Add(new MenuItem("&About",
                              new EventHandler(this.HelpAbout_Clicked),
                              Shortcut.CtrlA));
            // Handle the Select event for the About menu item.
            miHelp.MenuItems[0].Select +=
                    new EventHandler(HelpAbout_Selected);
            // Attach main menu to the Form object.
            this.Menu = mainMenu;
        }
    ...
}
```

Excellent! As you may guess, the Visual Studio IDE also provides some design-time assistance to facilitate the building of status bar objects. In just a bit, you examine how to build a toolbar using tools provided by the IDE. Once you understand this process, you should have no problems designing status bars using the design-time tools.

 SOURCE CODE   The StatusBarApp project is included under the Chapter 13 subdirectory.

Building a Tool Bar

The final Form level GUI item to examine in this chapter is the ToolBar type. As you know, tool bars typically provide an alternate means to activate a given menu item. Thus, if the user would rather click a Save button, this has the same effect as selecting "File | Save." In the Windows Forms namespace, a handful of types are defined to allow you to build such a beast. Let's start with the ToolBar class itself. Note the core properties as seen in Table 13-24.

Table 13-24. Properties of the ToolBar Type

ToolBar Property	Meaning in Life
BorderStyle	The kind of border around this control, as specified by the BorderStyle enumeration.
Buttons	The collection of buttons belonging to the toolbar (e.g., ToolBar$ToolBarButtonCollection).
ButtonSize	Determines the size of a button in the ToolBar.
ImageList	Returns the ImageList control that maintains the images for this ToolBar.
ImageSize	The method to return the size of the images within the toolbar's image list.

Table 13-24. Properties of the ToolBar Type (Continued)

ToolBar Property	Meaning in Life
ShowToolTips	Indicates whether or not the ToolBar will show tool tips for each button.
Wrappable	ToolBar buttons can optionally "wrap" to the next line when the ToolBar becomes too narrow to include all buttons on the same line.

When a Form maintains a ToolBar (or two), the goal is to create some number of individual ToolBarButton objects and add them to the ToolBar$ToolBarButtonCollection type. Each button may contain text, images, or both. To keep things simple, let's build a toolbar containing two buttons displaying text prompts only. Table 13-25 presents some important members of the ToolBarButton.

Table 13-25. Properties of the ToolBarButton Type

ToolBarButton Property	Meaning in Life
DropDownMenu	ToolBarButtons can optionally specify a pop-up menu that is shown whenever the drop-down button is pressed. This property lets you control just which menu is shown. Note that this is only shown if the Style property is set to DropDownButton.
ImageIndex	Returns the index of the image that this ToolBarButton is using. The index comes from the parent ToolBar's ImageList.
Style	Returns the style of the ToolBar button. This will form the ToolBarButtonStyle enumeration.
Text	The caption that will be displayed in this ToolBar button.
ToolTipText	If the parent ToolBar has the ShowToolTips property turned on, then this property describes the text that will be displayed for this button.
Visible	Indicates whether the button is visible or not. If the button is not visible, it will not be shown and will be unable to receive user input.

Your custom toolbar will contain two buttons, echoing the behavior supplied by the Save and Exit menu items. Here is the code update:

```
public class MainForm: Form
{
    // State data for the toolbar and two buttons.
    private ToolBarButton tbSaveButton = new ToolBarButton();
    private ToolBarButton tbExitButton = new ToolBarButton();
    private ToolBar toolBar = new ToolBar();
```

```
        public MainForm()
        {
            ...
            BuildToolBar();    // Helper function.
        }
        private void BuildToolBar()
        {
            // Configure each button.
            tbSaveButton.Text = "Save";
            tbSaveButton.ToolTipText = "Save";
            tbExitButton.Text = "Exit";
            tbExitButton.ToolTipText = "Exit";
            // Configure ToolBar and add buttons.
            toolBar.BorderStyle = System.Windows.Forms.BorderStyle.Fixed3D;
            toolBar.ShowToolTips = true;
            toolBar.Buttons.AddRange( new ToolBarButton[]
                { tbSaveButton, tbExitButton} );
            toolBar.ButtonClick += new
                ToolBarButtonClickEventHandler(ToolBar_Clicked));
            // Add the new bar to the Controls collection.
            this.Controls.Add(toolBar);
        }
        // Button click handler.
        private void ToolBar_Clicked(object sender, ToolBarButtonClickEventArgs e)
        {
            MessageBox.Show(e.Button.ToolTipText);
        }
    ...
}
```

When you run the application, things will look quite bland (after all, how many toolbars display only text)? You will add some images in just a moment, but first let's analyze some code. The BuildToolBar() helper function begins by configuring some basic properties for each ToolBarButton. Next, add them to the ToolBar collection using the AddRange() method (rather than calling Add() multiple times). To handle the Click events for a given button, you must handle the ButtonClick event.

```
toolBar.ButtonClick += new ToolBarButtonClickEventHandler(ToolBar_Clicked);
```

The ToolBarButtonClickEventHandler delegate can only call methods taking a second parameter of type ToolBarButtonClickEventArgs. This type may be examined to determine which button sent the event, using the Button property:

```
private void ToolBar_Clicked(object sender, ToolBarButtonClickEventArgs e)
{
    // Just show the corresponding tool bar text.
    MessageBox.Show(e.Button.ToolTipText);
}
```

Adding Images to Your Toolbar Buttons

Real Toolbar buttons contain images. When you wish to configure your buttons to do so, the first step is to have the Form create an ImageList type. This class represents a set of images that are consumed by some other type (like a ToolBar). If you have ever created a toolbar using Visual Basic 6.0, you should feel right at home with this aspect of Windows Forms. Let's update your existing ToolBarForm to make use of two icons for display purposes, in addition to simple text strings. Here is the relevant update:

```
public class MainForm: Form
{
    // Contains the images used by the toolbar.
    private ImageList toolBarIcons = new ImageList();
    ...
    private void BuildToolBar()
    {
        // Configure save button.
        tbSaveButton.ImageIndex = 0;
        tbSaveButton.ToolTipText = "Save";
        // Configure exit button.
        tbExitButton.ImageIndex = 1;
        tbExitButton.ToolTipText = "Exit";
        // Create ToolBar and add buttons.
        toolBar.ImageList = toolBarIcons;

        ...
        // Load images (again, the icons need to be in the app dir).
        toolBarIcons.ImageSize = new System.Drawing.Size(32, 32);
        toolBarIcons.Images.Add(new Icon("filesave.ico"));
        toolBarIcons.Images.Add(new Icon("fileexit.ico"));
        toolBarIcons.ColorDepth = ColorDepth.Depth16Bit;
        toolBarIcons.TransparentColor = System.Drawing.Color.Transparent;

        ...
    }
}
```

Notice the following points:

- You must tell each ToolBarButton which image to use, via the ImageIndex property.

- You add new images to the ImageList class using the Images.Add() method.

- The ToolBar itself must be told which ImageList it is associated with using the ImageList property.

If you now run the application (Figure 13-21), you will see a much more pleasing end result (if you wish these buttons to look more standard, simply adjust the size to 16 × 16):

Figure 13-21. A custom tool bar

SOURCE CODE The SimpleToolBar project is included under the Chapter 13 subdirectory.

Building ToolBars at Design Time

As you would guess, VS .NET has design-time support for constructing toolbar entities. The first step is to drag a ToolBar from the Toolbox window onto your design-time template. Design-time configuration of the ToolBar is accomplished using the Properties Window. For example, if you wish to add buttons to the ToolBar type, double-click the Buttons property. This opens a dialog that allows you to add, remove, and configure the individual ToolBarButton items (Figure 13-22).

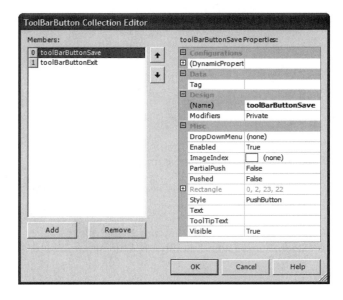

Figure 13-22. Toolbars a la VS .NET

Adding an ImageList at Design Time

Notice how this same dialog also allows you to assign an iconic image to each button using the ImageIndex property. However, this property is useless until you add an ImageList type to your current project. To add an ImageList member to a Form at design time, return to the Toolbox window and double-click the icon. At this point, you can use the Properties window to add the individual images using the Images property. Once you have added each image file to the ImageList, inform the ToolBar which ImageList it is to make use of using the Properties window (Figure 13-23).

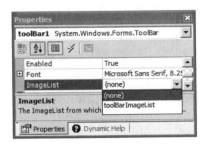

Figure 13-23. Assigning an ImageList via VS .NET

At this point, return to the ToolBar button editor and map a given image in the ImageList to each button (Figure 13-24).

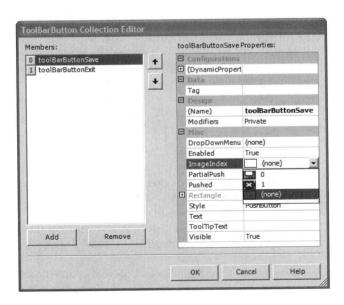

Figure 13-24. Assigning images to ToolBar buttons

Cool! Now that you understand how to make use of the Visual Studio .NET IDE to configure a ToolBar type, I assume you will continue to explore similar design-time configurations. For example, using (more or less) the same process, you can design a fully functional status bar with minimal coding on your part.

Building an MDI Application

To wrap up your initial look at Windows Forms, I'll close this chapter by examining how to configure a Form to function as a parent to any number of child windows (i.e., an MDI container). MDI applications allow the user to have multiple windows open at a single time, with each window representing a given "document" of the application. By way of an example, VS .NET is an MDI application in that you are able to have multiple documents open from within an instance of the application.

When you are building MDI applications using Windows Forms, your first task is to (of course) create a brand-new Windows Application. The initial Form of the application typically hosts a menuing system that allows the user to create new documents (such as File | New) as well as arrange existing open windows (cascade, vertical tile, and horizontal tile).

The child windows are interesting in that you typically have a prototypical Form that functions as a basis for each child window. Given that Forms are class types, any private data defined in the child Form will be unique to a given instance. For example, if you were to create an MDI word processing application, you might create a child Form that maintained a collection of Strings to represent a given line of text. If the user created five new child windows, each Form would maintain its own copy of the underlying collection and could be treated individually.

Additionally, MDI applications allow you to "merge menus." As mentioned previously, parent windows typically have a menu system that allows the user to spawn and organize additional child windows. However, what if the child window also maintains a menuing system? If the user maximizes a particular child window, you need to merge the child's menu system within the parent Form to allow the user to activate items from each menu system. The Windows Forms namespace defines a number of properties, methods, and events that allow you to programmatically merge menu systems. In addition, there is a "default merge" system, which works in a good number of cases. I leave it as a task for the interested reader to investigate this aspect of MDI applications.

Building the Parent Form

To illustrate the basics of building an MDI application, begin by creating a brand-new Windows Application named MDIApp. Almost all of the MDI infrastructure can be assigned to your initial Form using various design-time tools. To begin, locate the IsMdiContainer property in the Property window and set it to True. If you look at the design-time Form, you see that the client area has been modified to visually represent a container of child windows.

Next up, place a new MainMenu widget on your main Form. This menu specifies three topmost MenuItems named "File," "Window," and "Arrange Windows." The File menu contains two subitems named "New" and "Exit." The Window does not contain any subitems, as you will programmatically add new items as the user creates additional child windows. Finally, the Arrange Window menu defines three subitems named "Cascade," "Vertical," and "Horizontal." Figure 13-25 offers a high-level design-time view.

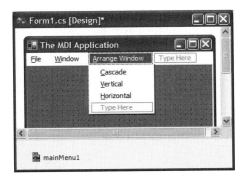

Figure 13-25. The parent window's menu system

Given that you already dove into the muck of coding raw menu logic during this chapter, simply use the IDE to generate event handlers for each submenu. You'll implement the File | New handler in the next section—however, here is the code behind the remaining menu selections (remember, the Window menu does not have any subitems just yet):

```
// Handle close event and arrange all child windows.
private void mnuFileExit_Click(object sender, System.EventArgs e)
{ this.Close(); }
private void mnuArrangeCascade_Click(object sender, System.EventArgs e)
{ LayoutMdi(MdiLayout.Cascade); }
private void mnuArrangeVert_Click(object sender, System.EventArgs e)
{ LayoutMdi(MdiLayout.TileVertical); }
private void mnuArrangeHorizontal_Click(object sender, System.EventArgs e)
{ LayoutMdi(MdiLayout.TileHorizontal); }
```

The main point of interest here is the use of the LayoutMdi() method and the corresponding MdiLayout enumeration. The code behind each menu select handler should be quite clear. When the user selects a given arrangement, you tell the parent Form to automatically reposition any and all child windows.

Before you move on to the child Form, you need to add one design-time property to the topmost Window menu item. The MdiList property may be set to true for a given topmost menu, to inform the hosting Form to automatically list the name of each child window as a possible menu selection. Enable this behavior for the topmost Windows menu item. By default, this list is the value of the child's Text property followed by a numerical suffix (i.e., Form1, Form2, Form3, and so on).

Building the Child Form

Now that you have the shell of an MDI container Form, you need to create an additional Form that functions as the prototype for a given child window. Begin by inserting a new Form type into your current project (using the Project | Add Windows Form... menu selection) named KidPrototypeForm, and handle the Click event. In the generated event handler, randomly set the background color of the client area. In addition, print out the "stringified" value of the new Color object into the child's caption bar. The following logic should do the trick:

```
private void KidPrototypeForm_Click(object sender, System.EventArgs e)
{
    // Get three random numbers
    int r, g, b;
    Random ran = new Random();
    r = ran.Next(0, 255);
    g = ran.Next(0, 255);
    b = ran.Next(0, 255);
    Color currColor = Color.FromArgb(r, g, b);
    this.BackColor = currColor;
    this.Text = currColor.ToString();
}
```

Spawning Child Windows

Your final order of business is to flesh out the details behind the parent Form's "File New" event handler. Now that you have defined a child Form, the logic is simple: Create and show a new instance of the ChildForm type. Furthermore, you need to set the value of the child Form's MdiParent property to point to the containing Form (in this case, your main window). Note that the child Form may also access the MdiParent property directly whenever it needs to manipulate (or communicate with) its parent window. Here is the update:

```
private void mnuFileNew_Click(object sender, System.EventArgs e)
{
    // Make a new child window.
    KidPrototypeForm newChild = new KidPrototypeForm();
    // Set the Parent Form of the Child window.
    newChild.MdiParent = this;
    // Display the new form.
    newChild.Show();
}
```

Now, to take this application out for a test drive, begin by creating a set of new child windows and click on each one to establish a unique background color (see Figure 13-26).

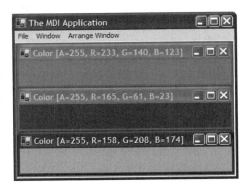

Figure 13-26. Spawning child windows

As you can see, if you access the Arrange Window menu items, you can instruct the parent Form to vertically tile, horizontally tile, or cascade the child Forms.

 SOURCE CODE   The SimpleMdiApp project can be found under the Chapter 13 subdirectory.

Summary

This chapter introduced the fine art of building a user interface with the types contained in the System.Windows.Forms namespace. It began by examining the basic steps you must take to build a custom Form. This entailed a discussion of the Application object, and its various members. As you have seen, the Form type gains a majority of its functionality from a rather long chain of base types.

During the course of this chapter, you learned how to build topmost menus (and pop-up menus) and how to respond to a number of menu events. You also came to understand how to further enhance your Form objects using toolbars and status bars. Finally, this chapter illustrated how to construct MDI applications using Windows Forms.

CHAPTER 14

A Better Painting Framework (GDI+)

THE PREVIOUS CHAPTER introduced you to the fine art of building a traditional main window using various types contained within the System.Windows.Forms namespace. Now that you can assemble a Form to represent the shell of your GUI-based applications, the next task is to understand the details of rendering graphical data (including stylized text and image data) onto the Form's client area.

We begin by taking a high-level view of the numerous drawing-related namespaces, and examine the process of responding to (and initiating) paint sessions. You will also discover various ways of obtaining (and configuring) a Graphics object. Once you understand the general layout of the GDI+ landscape, the remainder of this chapter covers how to manipulate colors, fonts, geometric shapes, and graphical images. This entails understanding related types such as Brush, Pen, Color, Point, and Rectangle (among others). This chapter also explores a number of GDI+-centric programming techniques such as nonrectangular hit testing and GUI drag-and-drop logic.

The chapter concludes by exploring the new .NET resource format. While *technically* not part of GDI+ proper, it does involve the manipulation of graphical data (which in my opinion is "GDI+-enough" to be presented here). Here, you learn how to embed your application's external resources directly into a .NET assembly to ship a more portable binary image. During the process, you explore the System.Resources namespace and learn how to perform read/write operations on the underlying *.resx and *.resources files by hand, as well as pull resources from an assembly at runtime using the System.Resources.ResourceManager type.

NOTE   If you are a Web programmer by trade, you may think that GDI+ is of no use to you. However, as you will see later in this text during our examination of ASP.NET, GDI+ is not limited to traditional desktop applications and is extremely relevant for Web applications.

Survey of the GDI+ Namespaces

The .NET Framework provides a number of namespaces devoted to two-dimensional graphical rendering. In addition to the basic functionality you would expect to find in a graphics package (color, font, pen, brush, and image manipulation), you also find types that enable geometric transformations, antialiasing, palette blending, and document printing support. Collectively speaking, these namespaces make up the .NET facility we call GDI+, which is a vast improvement over the traditional Win32 Graphical Device Interface (GDI) API. Table 14-1 gives a high-level view of each major player.

Table 14-1. The Core GDI+ Namespaces

GDI+Namespace	Meaning in Life
System.Drawing	This is the key GDI+ namespace, which defines numerous types for basic rendering (fonts, pens, basic brushes, etc.) as well as the almighty Graphics type.
System.Drawing.Drawing2D	This namespace provides types used for more advanced two-dimensional graphics functionality (e.g., gradient brushes, pen-caps, geometric transforms, etc.).
System.Drawing.Imaging	This namespace defines types that allow you to directly manipulate graphical images (e.g., change the palette, extract image metadata, manipulate metafiles, and so forth).
System.Drawing.Printing	This namespace defines types that allow you to render images to the printed page, interact with the printer itself, and format the overall appearance of a given print job.
System.Drawing.Text	This (rather small) namespace allows you to manipulate collections of fonts. For example, as you see in this chapter, the InstalledFontCollection type allows you to dynamically discover the set of installed fonts on the target machine.

Configuring a GDI+ Project Workspace

When you wish to make use of GDI+, you must set a reference to the System.Drawing.dll assembly. This single binary contains definitions of the types for each of the core GDI+ namespaces. Be aware that if you select a new Windows Application Project Workspace using VS .NET, this reference is set on your behalf automatically. Other project types, however, may require you to set this assembly reference explicitly. In any case, once you have set this reference, just make use of the C# "using" keyword and you are ready to render:

```
// Don't forget to reference System.Drawing.dll!
using System.Drawing;
```

To begin the GDI+ journey, let's examine the functionality defined by the System.Drawing namespace.

Overview of the System.Drawing Namespace

A vast majority of the types used when programming GDI+ applications are found within the System.Drawing namespace. As you would expect, there are classes that represent images, brushes, pens, and fonts. Furthermore, System.Drawing defines a number of related types such as Color, Point, and Rectangle. Table 14-2 lists some (but not all) of the core types.

Table 14-2. Core Types of the System.Drawing Namespace

System.Drawing Type	Meaning in Life
Bitmap	Encapsulates a given image file (*.bmp or otherwise) and defines a number of methods to manipulate the underlying graphical data.
Brush Brushes SolidBrush SystemBrushes TextureBrush	Brush objects are used to fill the interiors of graphical shapes such as rectangles, ellipses, and polygons. These types represent a number of brush variations, with Brush functioning as the abstract base class to the remaining types. Additional Brush types are defined in the System.Drawing.Drawing2D namespace.
Color SystemColors ColorTranslator	As you have already seen in the previous chapter, the Color structure defines a number of static fields that can be used to configure the color of fonts, brushes, and pens. The ColorTranslator type allows you to build a new .NET Color type from other color representations (Win32, the OLE_COLOR type, HTML color constants, etc.).
Font FontFamily	The Font type encapsulates the characteristics of a given font (i.e., type name, bold, italic, point size, and so forth). FontFamily provides an abstraction for a group of fonts having a similar generic design but with certain variations in styles.
Graphics	This core class represents a valid drawing surface, as well as a number of methods to render text, images, and geometric patterns. Consider this type the .NET equivalent of a Win32 HDC.
Icon SystemIcons	These classes represent custom icons, as well as the set of standard system supplied icons.
Image ImageAnimator	Image is an abstract base class that provides functionality for the Bitmap, Icon, and Cursor types. ImageAnimator provides a way to iterate over a number of Image-derived types at some specified interval.
Pen Pens SystemPens	Pens are objects used to draw lines and curves. The Pens type defines a number of static properties that return a new Pen of a given color.

Table 14-2. Core Types of the System.Drawing Namespace (Continued)

System.Drawing Type	Meaning in Life
Point PointF	These structures represent an (*x, y*) coordinate mapping to an underlying integer or float (respectively).
Rectangle RectangleF	These structures represent a rectangular dimension (again mapping to an underlying integer or float).
Size SizeF	These structures represent a given height/width (again mapping to an underlying integer or float).
StringFormat	This type is used to encapsulate various features of textual layout (i.e., alignment, line spacing, etc.).
Region	Describes the interior of a geometric image composed of rectangles and paths.

Many of these core types make substantial use of a number of related enumerations, most of which are also defined within the System.Drawing namespace. As you can guess, many of these enumerations are used to configure the look and feel of brushes and pens. For example, ponder the types listed in Table 14-3.

Table 14-3. Enumerations in the System.Drawing Namespace

System.Drawing Enumeration	Meaning in Life
ContentAlignment	Specifies how to align content on a drawing surface (center, left, right, and so forth)
FontStyle	Specifies style information applied to text (bold, italic, etc.)
GraphicsUnit	Specifies the unit of measure for the given item (much like the Win32 mapping mode constants)
KnownColor	Specifies friendly names for the known system colors
StringAlignment	Specifies the alignment of a text string relative to its layout rectangle
StringFormatFlags	Specifies the display and layout information for text strings (e.g., NoWrap, LineLimit, and so on)
StringTrimming	Specifies how to trim characters from a string that does not completely fit into a layout shape
StringUnit	Specifies the units of measure for a text string

If you currently have a background using graphic toolkits found in other frameworks (such as Java or MFC) you should feel right at home with the functionality provided by the .NET System.Drawing namespace. Next up, let's examine the set of basic utility types that are commonly used in GDI+ programming.

Examining the System.Drawing Utility Types

Many of the drawing methods defined by the System.Drawing.Graphics class require you to specify the position or area in which you wish to render a given item. For example, the DrawString() method requires you to specify the location to render the text string on the Control-derived type. Given that DrawString() has been overloaded a number of times, this positional parameter may be specified using an (*x*, *y*) coordinate or the dimensions of a "box" to draw within. Other GDI+ type methods may require you to specify the width and height of a given item, or the internal bounds of a geometric image.

To specify such information, the System.Drawing namespace defines the Point, Rectangle, Region, and Size types. Obviously, a Point represents some (*x*, *y*) coordinate. Rectangle types capture a pair of points representing the upper left and lower right bounds of a rectangular region. Size types are similar to Rectangles, however these structures represent a given dimension using a given length and width. Regions provide a way to represent and manipulate nonrectangular drawing surfaces.

The member variables used by the Point, Rectangle, and Size types are internally represented as an integer data type. If you need a finer level of granularity, you are free to make use of the corresponding PointF, RectangleF, and SizeF types, which (as you might guess) map to an underlying float. Regardless of the underlying data representation, each type has an identical set of members, including a number of overloaded operators. A quick run-through follows.

Point(F) Type

The first utility type you should be aware of is System.Drawing.Point(F). As you recall, you created a custom Point type earlier in this text, which in many ways was a slimmed-down version of the official GDI+ Point type. A breakdown of each member is shown in Table 14-4.

Table 14-4. Key Members of the Point(F) Types

Point and PointF Member	Meaning in Life
+ − == !=	Allows you to manipulate the underlying (*x*, *y*) point using common overloaded operators.
X Y	These properties allow you to get and set the underlying (*x*, *y*) values.
Ceiling()	This static method convents a PointF type into a Point by rounding off the underlying floats into integers.

Table 14-4. *Key Members of the Point(F) Types (Continued)*

Point and PointF Member	Meaning in Life
IsEmpty	This property returns true if *x* and *y* are both set to zero.
Offset()	This method translates a given Point type by a given amount.

Although this type is most commonly used when working with GDI+ and user interface applications, do be aware that you may make use of any utility type from any application. To illustrate, here is a console application that makes use of the System.Drawing.Point type (be sure to set a reference to System.Drawing.dll).

```
using System;
using System.Drawing;

namespace UtilTypes
{
    public class UtilTester
    {
        public static int Main(string[] args)
        {
            // Create and offset a point.
            Point pt = new Point(100, 72);
            Console.WriteLine(pt);
            pt.Offset(20, 20);
            Console.WriteLine(pt);
            // Overloaded Point operators.
            Point pt2 = pt;
            if(pt == pt2)
                WriteLine("Points are the same");
            else
                WriteLine("Different points");
            // Change pt2's X value.
            pt2.X = 4000;
            // Now show each X value:
            Console.WriteLine("First point: {0} ", pt);
            Console.WriteLine("Second point: {0} ", pt2);
            return 0;
        }
    }
}
```

Rectangle(F) Type

Rectangles, like Points, are useful in any application (GUI-based or otherwise). Some core members to be aware of are listed in Table 14-5.

Table 14-5. Key Members of the Rectangle(F) Types

Rectangle and RectangleF Member	Meaning in Life
== !=	Allows you to test if two rectangles have identical values (or not).
Inflate() Intersect() Union()	These static methods allow you to expand a rectangle, as well as create new rectangles that are a result of an intersection or union operation.
Top Left Bottom Right	These properties set the dimensions of a new Rectangle type.
Height Width	Configures the height and width of a given Rectangle.
Contains()	This method can be used to determine if a given Point (or Rectangle) is within the bounds of the current Rectangle. Great for hit testing a point within a rectangle.
X Y	These properties return the *x* or *y* coordinate of the Rectangle's upper left corner.

One of the more useful methods of the Rectangle type is Contains(). This method allows you to determine if a given Point or Rectangle is within the current bounds of another Rectangle object. Later in this chapter, you see how to make use of this method to reform hit testing of GDI+ images. Until then, here is a simple example:

```
public static int Main(string[] args)
{
    ...
    // Point is initially outside of rectangle's bounds.
    Rectangle r1 = new Rectangle(0, 0, 100, 100);
    Point pt3 = new Point(101, 101);
    if(r1.Contains(pt3))
        Console.WriteLine("Point is within the rect!");
    else
        Console.WriteLine("Point is not within the rect!");
```

```
    // Now place point in rectangle's area.
    pt3.X = 50;
    pt3.Y = 30;
    if(r1.Contains(pt3))
        Console.WriteLine("Point is within the rect!");
    else
        Console.WriteLine("Point is not within the rect!");
    return 0;
}
```

Size(F) and Region Types

The Size and SizeF types are quite simple to manipulate, and require little comment. These types each define Height and Width properties and a handful of overloaded operators (Table 14-6).

Table 14-6. Key Members of the Size(F) Types

Size and SizeF Member	Meaning in Life
+ − = = !=	Operators to manipulate Size types.
Height Width	These properties are used to manipulate the current dimension of a Size type.

The Region Class

Finally we have the Region class. This type represents the interior of a geometric shape. Given this last statement, it should make sense that the constructors of the Region class require you to send an instance of some existing geometric pattern. For example, assume you have created a (100 ×100) pixel rectangle. If you wish to gain access to the rectangle's interior region, you could write the following:

```
// Get the interior of this rectangle.
Rectangle r = new Rectangle(0, 0, 100, 100);
Region rgn = new Region(r);
```

Once you do have the interior dimensions of a given shape, you may manipulate it using the core members shown in Table 14-7.

Table 14-7. Members of the Region Class

Region Member	Meaning in Life
Complement()	Updates this Region to the portion of the specified graphics object that does not intersect with this Region.
Exclude()	Updates this Region to the portion of its interior that does not intersect with the specified graphics object.
GetBounds()	Returns a RectangleF that represents a rectangular region that bounds this Region.
Intersect()	Overloaded. Updates this Region to the intersection of itself with the specified graphics object.
IsEmpty() MakeEmpty()	Tests whether this Region has an empty interior on the specified drawing surface (or sets the current Region empty).
IsInfinite() MakeInfinite()	Tests whether this Region has an infinite interior on the specified drawing surface (or sets the current Region infinite).
Transform()	Transforms this Region by the specified Matrix.
Translate()	Offsets the coordinates of this Region by the specified amount.
Union()	Updates this Region to the union of itself and the specified graphics object.
Xor()	Updates this Region to the union minus the intersection of itself with the specified graphics object.

I'm sure you get the general idea behind these coordinate primitives. You will have a chance to work with each of them during the course of this chapter (and any time you program against GDI+). Now then, on to some more interesting material!

 SOURCE CODE The UtilTypes project is included under the Chapter 14 subdirectory.

Regarding the Disposal of System.Drawing Types

Before diving into specific GDI+ topics, it is important to point out that a number of types within the System.Drawing.dll assembly implement the IDisposable interface. As you recall from Chapter 5, this interface defines a single method named Dispose(), which may be called by the object user to release any internally managed resources of the type.

When you make use of GDI+, your best bet is to explicitly call Dispose() on any type you have explicitly created via the C# "new" keyword (when you are finished interacting with it) to ensure that the type cleans up any internally allocated memory as soon as possible. On the other hand, when operating on a GDI+ type passed as a member parameter or received via a method invocation, you should not call Dispose(), because another part of the system may still require the type. To illustrate:

```
private void mainForm_Paint(object sender, PaintEventArgs e)
{
    // Get a Graphics object from param (don't dispose!).
    Graphics g = e.Graphics;
    // Make a SolidBrush (you new-ed it, dispose when done)
    SolidBrush br = new SolidBrush(...);
    br.Dispose();
}
```

Recall, however, that if you fail (or forget) to call Dispose() on an IDisposable compatible type, the garbage collector will eventually clean up the allocated memory. The only downfall to this lazy approach is the fact that you do not know exactly when the .NET garbage collector will kick in. If your application happens to be installed on a machine with large amounts of memory, the lazy approach may be just fine. However, as you can never be completely sure about the hardware of the hosting machine, it is best to dispose of all GDI+ objects you create ASAP.

NOTE   For simplicity, I will abide by the lazy approach in this chapter and will not directly call Dispose() on the types created in this chapter's example applications.

Understanding Paint Sessions

As you have seen in the previous chapter, the Control class defines a virtual method named OnPaint(). When a Form (or any descendent of Control) wishes to render graphical information, you may override this method and extract a Graphics object from the incoming PaintEventArgs parameter:

```
public class MainForm : Form
{
    public MainForm()
    {
        CenterToScreen();
        this.Text = "Basic Paint Form";
    }
    public static void Main(string[] args)
    {
        Application.Run(new MainForm());
    }
    protected override void OnPaint(PaintEventArgs e)
    {
        Graphics g = e.Graphics;
        g.DrawString("Hello GDI+", new Font("Times New Roman", 20),
                    new SolidBrush(Color.Black), 0, 0);
        // If overriding OnPaint(), be sure to call base class implementation.
        base.OnPaint(e);
    }
}
```

Recall that when responding to GUI-based events, you actually have two options at your disposal. In the previous code you overrode the OnPaint() method directly. The other approach is to directly handle the raw Paint event using the associated PainEventHandler delegate:

```
public class MainForm : Form
{
    public MainForm()
    {
        // The VS .NET Property Window would rig this
        // up in InitializeComponent()
        this.Paint += new
            System.Windows.Forms.PaintEventHandler(MainForm_Paint);
    }
    // Note the signature of the event handler...
    public void MainForm_Paint(object sender, PaintEventArgs e)
    {
        Graphics g = e.Graphics;
        ...
    }
}
...
```

Regardless of how you respond to the Paint event, be aware that whenever a window becomes "dirty" a paint message is placed into the application's message queue. As you are most likely aware, a window is "dirty" whenever it is resized, covered by another window (partially or completely) or is minimized and then restored. Eventually, the flow of logic is routed to the method that handles repainting the window. In these cases, the .NET Framework ensures that when your Form needs to be redrawn, the Paint handler is called automatically.

Invalidating Your Client Area

During the flow of your GDI+ application, you may need to explicitly inform a window that it needs to redraw itself (in other words, you need to place a paint message into the queue programmatically). For example, you may have a program that allows the user to select from a number of bitmap images using a custom dialog. Once the dialog is dismissed, you need to draw the newly selected image onto the client area. Obviously, if you waited for the window to become "naturally dirty," the user would not see the change take place until it was resized or covered by another window. When you need to force a window to repaint itself programmatically, call Invalidate(). For example:

```
public class MainForm: Form
{
...
    private void MainForm_Paint(object sender, PaintEventArgs e)
    {
        Graphics g = e.Graphics;
        // Assume logic to render a bitmap...
    }
    private void GetNewBitmap()
    {
        // Show dialog and get new image...
        // Repaint the client area.
        Invalidate();
    }
}
```

Do be aware that the Invalidate() method has been overloaded a number of times to allow you to specify a specific rectangular region to repaint, rather than the entire client area (which is the default). If you only wish to update the extreme upper left rectangle of the client area, you could write:

```
// Repaint a given rectangular area of the Form.
private void UpdateUpperArea()
{
    Rectangle myRect = new Rectangle(0, 0, 75, 150);
    Invalidate(myRect);
}
```

Obtaining a Graphics Type Outside a Paint Handler

On a related note, you may find yourself in the position of needing to render some image *outside* the scope of a standard Paint event handler. For example, assume you wish to draw a small circle at the (x, y) position where the mouse has been clicked. The first step (of course) is to locate a valid Graphics object, which can be obtained using the static Graphics.FromHwnd() method. Notice that you are passing your current Handle as the sole parameter (recall that the Handle property is inherited from the Control class):

```
private void MainForm_MouseDown(object sender, MouseEventArgs e)
{
    // Grab a Graphics object via Hwnd.
    Graphics g = Graphics.FromHwnd(this.Handle);
    // Now draw a 10*10 circle at mouse click.
    g.DrawEllipse(new Pen(Color.Green), e.X, e.Y, 10, 10);
}
```

While this logic renders a circle outside an OnPaint() event handler, it is very important to understand that if the form is invalidated (and thus redrawn), each of the circles are erased! This should make sense, given that this rendering only happens within the context of a mouse click.

A better approach is to have the MouseUp logic add a new point to an internal collection (such as an ArrayList) of Point objects, followed by a call to Invalidate(). At this point, the OnPaint() method can simply iterate over the collection and draw each item:

```
public class MainForm : System.Windows.Forms.Form
{
    // Used to hold all the points.
    private ArrayList myPts = new ArrayList();
    ...
    private void MainForm_MouseDown(object sender, MouseEventArgs e)
    {
        // Add to points collection.
        myPts.Add(new Point(e.X, e.Y));
        Invalidate();
    }
    private void MainForm_Paint(object sender, PaintEventArgs e)
    {
        Graphics g = e.Graphics;
        g.DrawString("Hello GDI+", new Font("Times New Roman", 20),
                    new SolidBrush(Color.Black), 0, 0);
        // Draw all points in ArrayList.
        foreach(Point p in myPts)
            g.DrawEllipse(new Pen(Color.Green), p.X, p.Y, 10, 10);
    }
}
```

Obtaining a Graphics Type from Windows Forms Controls

As you have seen, the Graphics.FromHwnd() method provides a handy way to obtain a Graphics object for a Form outside a registered paint handler. However, this same method can also be used to extract a Graphics type from any System.Windows.Forms.Control-derived type. For example, assume you have two Button types on a single Form. The first button (named btnRenderToOtherButton) has the following Click event handler:

```
private void btnRenderToOtherButton_Click(object sender, System.EventArgs e)
{
    // Get graphics object for Button on Form.
    Graphics buttonGraphics =
        Graphics.FromHwnd(btnRenderedButton.Handle);
    // Make an interesting brush.
    // (must 'use' System.Drawing.Drawing2D namespace to get HatchBrush!)
    HatchBrush b = new HatchBrush(HatchStyle.Cross,
        Color.Purple, Color.Gold);
    // Render brush patter on the left side of button.
    buttonGraphics.FillRectangle(b, 0, 0, 50, btnRenderedButton.Height);
}
```

When you click this button, the appearance of the other button (named btnRenderedButton) is updated with a custom rectangular region established using a System.Drawing.Drawing2D.HatchBrush type (more on brush types later in this chapter). Figure 14-1 shows a test run of this initial GDI+ application.

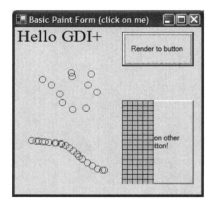

Figure 14-1. A simple GDI+ application

Do be aware, however, that if you click the newly rendered button, the graphical data will vanish (as the widget is repainted to its default look and feel). If you wish to build a stylized widget that always renders itself in a unique manner, you may wish to build a custom Windows Forms control (see Chapter 15).

SOURCE CODE   The BasicPaintForm project is included under the Chapter 14 subdirectory.

Understanding the Graphics Class

Now that you have seen various ways to obtain a Graphics object, you need to understand exactly how to manipulate it. The System.Drawing.Graphics object is your gateway to GDI+ rendering functionality. This class represents a valid device context (e.g., HDC) coupled with a slew of methods that allow you to render text, images (icons, bitmaps, and so on), as well as numerous geometric patterns. Table 14-8 gives a partial list of intriguing members.

Table 14-8. Members of the Graphics Class

Graphics Methods	Meaning in Life
FromHdc() FromHwnd() FromImage()	These static methods provide a way to obtain a valid Graphics object from a given image (e.g., icon, bitmap, etc.) or GUI widget.
Clear()	Fills a Graphics object with a specified color, erasing the current drawing surface in the process.
DrawArc() DrawBezier() DrawBeziers() DrawCurve() DrawEllipse() DrawIcon() DrawLine() DrawLines() DrawPie() DrawPath() DrawRectangle() DrawRectangles() DrawString()	These methods are used to render a given image or geometric pattern.
FillEllipse() FillPath() FillPie() FillPolygon() FillRectangle()	These methods are used to fill the interior of a given geometric shape.
MeasureString()	Returns a Size structure that represents the bounds of a given block of text.

As well as providing a number of rendering methods, the Graphics class defines additional members that control the details of the current rendering operation. In more concrete terms, the Graphics type allows you to configure the state of the Graphics object using the property set in Table 14-9.

Table 14-9. Stateful Properties of the Graphics Class

Graphics Property	Meaning in Life
Clip ClipBounds VisibleClipBounds IsClipEmpty IsVisibleClipEmpty	These properties allow you to set the clipping options used with the current Graphics object.
Transform	Allows you to transform "world coordinates" (more details later).
PageUnit PageScale DpiX DpiY	These properties allow you to configure the point of origin for your rendering operations, as well as configure the unit of measurement.
SmoothingMode PixelOffsetMode TextRenderingHint	These properties allow you to configure the smoothness of geometric objects and text. These are set with corresponding enumerations defined in the System.Drawing and System.Drawing.Drawing2D namespaces.
CompositingMode CompositingQuality	The CompositingMode property determines whether drawing overwrites the background or is blended with the background. The value is set with the corresponding CompositingMode enumeration defined in the System.Drawing.Drawing2D namespace. The CompositingQuality property specifies the complexity of the blending process.
InterpolationMode	Specifies how data is interpolated between endpoints, using a related enumeration.

During the course of this chapter you will check out how to configure a number of these stateful properties.

The GDI+ Coordinate Systems

Next up, you need a bit of background regarding the underlying coordinate system. GDI+ defines three distinct coordinate systems (Table 14-10), which are used by the runtime to determine the location and size of the element to be rendered.

Table 14-10. The GDI+ Coordinate Systems

GDI+ Coordinate System	Meaning in Life
World Coordinates	World coordinates represent an abstraction of the size of a given GDI+ type, irrespective of the unit of measurement. For example, if you draw a rectangle using the dimensions of (0, 0, 100, 100), you have specified a rectangle 100 × 100 "things" in size. As you may guess, the default thing is a pixel, but this can be configured to be another unit of measure (inch, centimeter, etc.).
Page Coordinates	Page coordinates represent an offset applied to the original world coordinates. This is helpful in that you are not the one in charge of manually applying offsets in your code (should you need them). For example, if you have a Form that needs to maintain a 100 × 100 pixel border, you can specify a (100 ×100) page coordinate to allow all rendering to begin at point (100 × 100). In your code base however, you are able to specify simple world coordinates (thereby avoiding the need to manually calculate the offset).
Device Coordinates	Device coordinates represent the result of applying page coordinates to the original world coordinates. This coordinate system is used to determine exactly where the GDI+ type will be rendered on the Control-derived type.

When you are programming with GDI+, you tend to think in terms of "world coordinates." Simply put, this coordinate system is the baseline used to determine the size and location of a GDI+ type:

```
// Render a rectangle by specifying world coordinates.
myGraphicsObject.DrawRectangle(10, 10, 100, 100);
```

Under the hood of GDI+, your world coordinates are automatically mapped in terms of page coordinates, and are then mapped into device coordinates. In many cases, you will never directly make use of page or device coordinates unless you wish to apply some sort of graphical transformation. Given that the previous line of code did not specify any transformational page coordinate logic, the world, page, and device coordinates are identical.

If you do wish to apply various transformations before rendering your GDI+ logic, you will make use of various members of the Graphics type (such as the TranslateTransform() method) to specify various "page coordinates" to your existing world coordinate system before the rendering operation. The result is the set of device coordinates that will be used to render the GDI+ type to the target device:

```
// Specify page coordinate offsets (10 * 10).
myGraphicsObject.TranslateTransform(10, 10);
// Render a rectangle by specifying world coordinates.
// However! Given the previous offset,
// this rectangle is really drawn at (20 ,20)
// and is 110 * 110 pixels in size.
myGraphicsObject.DrawRectangle(10, 10, 100, 100);
```

In this case, the rectangle is actually rendered with a upper left point of (20, 20) and a lower right point of (110, 110).

The Default Unit of Measure

As suggested in the last example, the default unit of measure is pixel-based and places the origin in the upper left corner with the *x*-axis increasing to the right and the *y*-axis increasing downward (Figure 14-2).

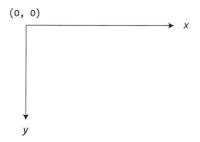

Figure 14-2. The default coordinate system of GDI+

Again, if you render a Rectangle as follows:

```
private void MainForm_Paint(object sender, PaintEventArgs e)
{
    // Set up world coordinates using the default unit of measure.
    Graphics g = e.Graphics;
    g.DrawRectangle(new Pen(Color.Red, 5), 10, 10, 100, 100);
}
```

you would see a square rendered 10 pixels down and in from the top left client edge of the Form, which spans 90 pixels in both directions (Figure 14-3). Given that you have not applied any page transformations, the world, page, and device coordinate values are identical.

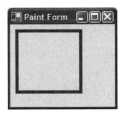

Figure 14-3. Rendering via pixel units

In most cases, the default measurement system will most likely be your unit of choice. However, like most things in the .NET Framework, you are able to configure the GDI+ mapping mode to your liking.

Specifying an Alternative Unit of Measure

If you do not wish to render images using a pixel-based unit of measure, you are able to change this default setting by setting the PageUnit property of the Graphics object to alter the units used by the page coordinate system. The PageUnit property can be assigned any member of the GraphicsUnit enumeration (Table 14-11).

Table 14-11. The GraphicsUnit Enumeration

GraphicsUnit Value	Description
Display	Specifies 1/75 inch as the unit of measure
Document	Specifies the document unit (1/300 inch) as the unit of measure
Inch	Specifies the inch as the unit of measure
Millimeter	Specifies the millimeter as the unit of measure
Pixel	Specifies a device pixel as the unit of measure
Point	Specifies a printer's point (1/72 inch) as the unit of measure

For example, if you update your previous rendering code as follows:

```
private void MainForm_Paint(object sender, PaintEventArgs e)
{
    // Draw a rectangle in inches...not pixels.
    Graphics g = e.Graphics;
    g.PageUnit = GraphicsUnit.Inch;
    g.DrawRectangle(new Pen(Color.Red, 5), 0, 0, 100, 100);
}
```

you find a *radically* different rectangle (Figure 14-4).

Figure 14-4. Rendering via inch units

The reason that 95% (or so) of the Form's client area is now filled in is due to the fact that you have configured a Pen with a five inch nib! The rectangle itself is 100 × 100 *inches* in size! In fact, the small gray box you see located in the lower right corner is the upper left interior of the rectangle! As you would guess, if you specify alternative values to the Graphics.PageUnit property, you would find the rectangle rendered in various units of measurement.

Specifying an Alternative Point of Origin

Recall that when you make use of the default coordinate and measurement system, point (0, 0) is at the extreme upper left of the client area. Again, this is typically what you desire. However, what if you wish to alter the location where rendering begins? For example, let's assume that your application always needs to reserve a 100-pixel boundary around the Form's client area (for whatever reason). You need to ensure that all GDI+ operations take place somewhere within this internal region.

One approach you could take is to offset all your rendering code manually. This, of course, is a huge bother, in that you would need to constantly apply some offset value to each and every rendering operation. It would be far better (and simpler) if you could set a property that says, in effect, "Although *I* might say render a rectangle with a point of origin at (0, 0), make sure *you* begin at point (100, 100)." This would simplify your life a great deal, as you can continue to specify your plotting points without modification.

In GDI+, you can adjust the point of origin by setting the transformation value using the TranslateTransform() method of the Graphics class, which allows you to specify a page coordinate system that will be applied to your original world coordinate specifications. For example:

```
private void MainForm_Paint(object sender, PaintEventArgs e)
{
    Graphics g = e.Graphics;
    // Set page coordinate to (100, 100).
    g.TranslateTransform(100, 100);
    // World origin is still (0, 0, 100, 100),
    // however device origin is now (100, 100, 200, 200).
    g.DrawRectangle(new Pen(Color.Red, 5), 0, 0, 100, 100);
}
```

Here, we have set our world coordinate values (0, 0, 100, 100). However, the page coordinate values have specified an offset of (100, 100). Given this, the device coordinates map to (100, 100, 200, 200). Thus, although the call to DrawRectangle() looks as if you are rendering a rectangle on the upper left of the Form, the following rendering has taken place (Figure 14-5).

Figure 14-5. The result of applying page offsets

To help you experiment with some of the ways to alter the default GDI+ mapping system, the companion code contains a sample application named CoorSystem. Using two topmost menu items, you are able to alter the point of origin as well as the unit of measurement (Figure 14-6).

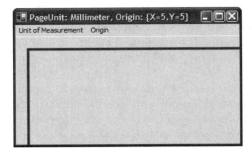

Figure 14-6. Altering coordinate and measurement modes

Now that you have a better understanding of the underlying transformations used to determine where to render a given GDI+ type onto a target device, the next order of business is to examine details of color manipulation.

SOURCE CODE   The CoorSystem project is included under the Chapter 14 subdirectory.

Establishing an Active Color

Many of the rendering methods defined by the Graphics class require you to specify the color that should be used during the drawing process. The System.Drawing.Color structure represents an alpha-red-green-blue (ARGB) color constant. Most of the Color type's functionality comes by way of a number of static read-only properties, which return a new (correctly configured), Color type:

```
// One of many predefined colors...
Color c = Color.PapayaWhip;
```

There are other ways you can create a Color type. Regardless of the method you use, you are then able to extract relevant information using any of the members listed in Table 14-12 (in addition to the set of static read-only properties).

Table 14-12. Members of the Color Type

Color Member	Meaning in Life
FromArgb()	Returns a new Color object based on numerical red, green, and blue values.
FromKnownColor()	Returns a new Color object based on a member of the KnownColor enumeration.
FromName()	Returns a new Color object based on a string name (e.g., "Red").
A, R, G, B	These properties return the value assigned to the alpha, red, green, and blue aspect of a Color object.
IsNamedColor() Name	These members can be applied to a Color object to determine if the current ARGB values have a predefined name (e.g., "Red") and if so, retrieve it via the Name property.
GetBrightness() GetHue() GetSaturation()	GDI+ Color types have an associated Hue-Saturation-Brightness (HSB) value. These methods retrieve the specifics.
ToArgb() ToKnownColor()	Returns the ARGB value of the Color type, or the KnownColor enumeration value based on a valid Color object.

Examining the ColorDialog Class

On a related note, the System.Windows.Forms namespace provides a predefined dialog box class (ColorDialog) that can be used to prompt the end user for his or her color selection (Figure 14-7).

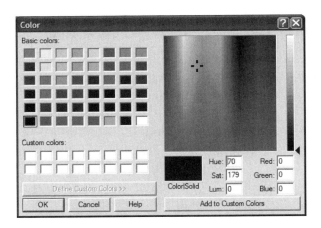

Figure 14-7. The stock .NET color dialog

Working with this dialog is simple: using a valid instance of the ColorDialog type, call ShowDialog() to display the dialog modally. Once the user has closed the dialog, you can extract the corresponding Color object using the ColorDialog.Color property.

For example, assume you wish to allow the user to configure the background color of the Form's client area using the ColorDialog. To keep things simple, let's assume that when the user clicks anywhere on the client area, you show the ColorDialog object and act accordingly. Here is the code:

```
public class ColorDlgForm : System.Windows.Forms.Form
{
    // The ColorDialog.
    private ColorDialog colorDlg;
    public ColorDlgForm()
    {
        colorDlg = new ColorDialog();
        Text = "Click on me to change the color";
        this.MouseUp +=
            new MouseEventHandler(this.ColorDlgForm_MouseUp);
    }
...
    private void ColorDlgForm_MouseUp(object sender, MouseEventArgs e)
    {
        if (colorDlg.ShowDialog() != DialogResult.Cancel)
        {
            currColor = colorDlg.Color;
            this.BackColor = currColor;
            // Show current color.
            string strARGB = colorDlg.Color.ToString();
            MessageBox.Show(strARGB, "Color is:");
        }
    }
}
```

Although there has not yet been a formal discussion of how to manipulate dialog boxes, the previous code should not raise too many eyebrows. Notice that you are able to determine which button has been clicked (OK or Cancel) by testing the return value of ShowDialog() against the DialogResult enumeration. You will see additional stock dialog boxes used in this chapter. Later, in Chapter 15, you learn how to build custom dialogs to gather (and validate) user input.

SOURCE CODE   The ColorDlg application is included under the Chapter 14 subdirectory.

Manipulating Fonts

Next, let's examine the specifics of the Font class (and related types). The System.Drawing.Font type represents a given font installed on the user's machine. While the Font class defines a number of overloaded constructors, here are some common options:

```
// Create a Font of a given type name and size.
Font f = new Font("Times New Roman", 12);
// Create a Font with a given name, size, and style set.
Font f2 = new Font("WingDings", 50, FontStyle.Bold | FontStyle.Underline);
```

Here, f2 has been created using a set of FontStyle flags. The members of this enumeration allow you to configure a number of properties of the Font object such as bold or italic (if you require more than one FontStyle, simply OR each item together). Table 14-13 lists your choices.

Table 14-13. The FontStyle Enumeration

FontStyle Enumeration Member	Meaning in Life
Bold	Bold text
Italic	Italic text
Regular	Normal text
Strikeout	Text with a line through the middle
Underline	Underlined text

Once you have configured the look and feel of your Font object, the next obvious task is to pass it as a parameter to the Graphics.DrawString() method. Although DrawString() has also been overloaded a number of times, each variation typically requires the same basic information: a string to draw, the font to draw it in, a brush used for rendering, and a location to place it. For example:

```
// One version: void DrawString(String, Font, Brush, Point);
g.DrawString("My string", new Font("Pop", 25),
            new SolidBrush(Color.Black), new Point(0,0));
// Another version: void DrawString(String, Font, Brush, float, float);
g.DrawString("Another string", new Font("Times New Roman", 16),
            new SolidBrush(Color.Red), 40, 40);
```

In each of these examples, you have made use of a SolidBrush type (of a particular color). It is possible to configure a number of brush types. For the time being, a solid brush fits the bill; you see more exotic brush types a bit later in this chapter. Once you have created a valid Font type, you are able to extract its current settings using a number of properties (e.g., Bold, Italic, Unit, Height, Size, FontFamily, and so forth).

Working with Font Families

The System.Drawing namespace also defines the FontFamily type, which abstracts a group of typefaces having a similar basic design but having certain style variations (such as point size). A family of fonts, like Verdana, can include several fonts that differ in style and size. For example, 12-point Verdana bold and 24-point Verdana italic are different fonts within the Verdana font family.

The constructor of the FontFamily type takes a string representing the name of the font family you are attempting to capture. Once you create the generic family, you are then able to create a more specific Font object (in the following code, assume "g" is an object of type Graphics):

```
// Make a family of fonts.
FontFamily myFamily = new FontFamily("Verdana");
// Pass family into ctor of Font.
Font myFont = new Font(myFamily, 12);
g.DrawString("Hello?", myFont, Brushes.Blue, 10, 10);
```

Of greater interest is the ability to gather statistics regarding a given family of fonts. For example, let's say you were building a text-processing application and wish to determine the average width of a character in a particular FontFamily. What if you wish to know the ascending and descending values for a given character? To answer such questions, the FontFamily type defines the key members shown in Table 14-14. Note that each requires you to specify the font style using the FontStyle enumeration.

Table 14-14. Members of the FontFamily Type

FontFamily Member	Meaning in Life
GetCellAscent()	Returns the ascender metric for the members in this family
GetCellDescent()	Returns the descender metric for members in this family
GetLineSpacing()	Returns the distance between two consecutive lines of text for this FontFamily with the specified FontStyle
GetName()	Returns the name of this FontFamily in the specified language
IsStyleAvailable()	Indicates whether the specified FontStyle is available

To illustrate, here is a Paint handler that prints a number of characteristics of the Verdana font family:

```
private void MainForm_Paint(object sender, PaintEventArgs e)
{
    Graphics g = e.Graphics;
    FontFamily myFamily = new FontFamily("Verdana");
    Font myFont = new Font(myFamily, 12);
    int y = 0;
    int fontHeight = myFont.Height;      // Get pixel height of font.
```

```
        // Show units of measurement for FontFamily members.
        this.Text = "Measurements are in GraphicsUnit." + myFont.Unit.ToString();
        g.DrawString("The Verdana family.", myFont, Brushes.Blue, 10, y);
        y += 20;
        // Print our family ties...
        g.DrawString("Ascent for bold Verdana: " +
                    myFamily.GetCellAscent(FontStyle.Bold),
                    myFont, Brushes.Black, 10, y + fontHeight);
        y += 20;
        g.DrawString("Descent for bold Verdana: " +
                    myFamily.GetCellDescent(FontStyle.Bold),
                    myFont, Brushes.Black, 10, y + fontHeight);
        y += 20;
        g.DrawString("Line spacing for bold Verdana: " +
                    myFamily.GetLineSpacing(FontStyle.Bold),
                    myFont, Brushes.Black, 10, y + fontHeight);
        y += 20;
        g.DrawString("Height for bold Verdana: " +
                    myFamily.GetEmHeight(FontStyle.Bold),
                    myFont, Brushes.Black, 10, y + fontHeight);
        y += 20;
}
```

Figure 14-8 shows the result.

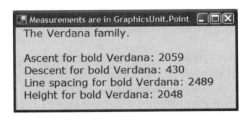

Figure 14-8. Gathering statistics of the Verdana font family

Note that these members of the FontFamily type return values using
GraphicsUnit.Point (not Pixel) as the unit of measure, which corresponds to
1/72 inch. You are free to transform these values to other units of measure as you see fit.

Understanding Font Metrics

If you have not worked with Fonts using this level of detail before, here are a few words
regarding character measurements. The dimensions of a given Font are all based on the
baseline value, which is the imaginary line on which each character "sits." Some characters
(such as "j," "y," or "g") have a portion that drops below this baseline. This is called the
descending value. The *ascending value* represents the amount a given character rises

above the baseline. The *leading value* represents the difference between the height and ascent, where height is the total distance between the leading and descending values.

To keep all these items fixed in your mind, ponder Figure 14-9 (the baseline is identified by the thicker line toward the bottom).

Figure 14-9. Font metrics

 SOURCE CODE   The FontFamily application is included under the Chapter 14 subdirectory.

Building a Font Application

Now, let's build a more complex application that allows the user to manipulate a Font object maintained by a main Form. The application will allow the user to select the current font face from a predefined set using the "Configure | Font Face" menu selection.

Let's also allow the user to indirectly control the size of the Font object using a Windows Forms Timer object. If the user activates the Timer using the "Configure | Swell?" menu item, the size of the Font object increases at a regular interval (to a maximum upper limit). In this way, the text appears to swell and thus provides a simple animation of "breathing" text.

Finally, add a final menu item under the Configure menu named "List All Fonts," which will be used to list all fonts installed on the end-user's machine. Figure 14-10 shows the menu UI logic (the File menu simply allows the user to exit the application).

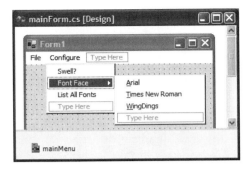

Figure 14-10. Menu layout of the FontApp project

To begin implementing our application, update the main Form with a Timer member variable (named timer), a string to represent the current font face (named fontFace), and an integer (named swellValue) to represent the amount to adjust the font size. In addition to configuring the basic look and feel of the Form, configure your timer to emit a Tick event every 100 milliseconds:

```
public class FontForm : System.Windows.Forms.Form
{
    private Timer timer;
    private int swellValue;
    private string fontFace  = " WingDings";      // The default font face.
    public FontForm()
    {
        // The menu system has been designed using the IDE...
        InitializeComponent();
        timer = new Timer();
        Text = "Font App";
        Width = 425;
        Height = 150;
        BackColor = Color.Honeydew;
        CenterToScreen();
        // Configure the Timer.
        timer.Enabled = true;
        timer.Interval = 100;
        timer.Tick += new EventHandler(FontForm_OnTimer);
    }
}
```

In the Tick event handler, increase the value of the swellValue data member, and refresh your client area via the Invalidate() method. Recall that the swellValue integer will be added to the current font size to provide a simple animation (assume swellValue has a maximum upper limit of 50). To help reduce the flicker that can occur when redrawing the entire client area, you only refresh the minimum dirty rectangular region:

```
private void FontForm_OnTimer(object sender, EventArgs e)
{
    // Increase current swellValue by 5.
    swellValue += 5;
    // If this value is greater than or equal to 50, reset to zero.
    if(swellValue >= 50)
        swellValue = 0;
    // Just invalidate the 'minimal dirty rectangle to help reduce flicker.
    Invalidate(new Rectangle(0, 0, ClientRectangle.Width, 100));
}
```

Now that the upper 100 pixels of your client area are refreshed with each tick of the Timer, you better have something to render! In the Form's Paint handler, create a Font object based on the user-defined font face (as selected from the appropriate menu item) and current swellValue (as dictated by the timer). Once you have your Font object fully configured, render a message into the center of the dirty rectangle:

```
private void FontForm_Paint(object sender, PaintEventArgs e)
{
    Graphics g = e.Graphics;
    // The font size can be between 12 and 62,
    // based on the current swellValue.
    Font theFont = new Font(fontFace, 12 + swellValue);
    string message = "Hello GDI+";
    // Display message in the center of the rect.
    float windowCenter = this.DisplayRectangle.Width/2;
    SizeF stringSize = g.MeasureString(message, theFont);
    float startPos = windowCenter - (stringSize.Width/2);
    g.DrawString(message, theFont, new SolidBrush(Color.Blue), startPos, 10);
}
```

As you would guess, if a user selects a specific font face, the Clicked handler for each menu selection is in charge of updating the fontFace string variable and invalidating the client area. The sample code for this example takes this a bit further to ensure that the user's font of preference is identified with a check mark. Given that the previous chapter has already pounded out the details of menu manipulations, I'll assume you will implement these details as you see fit.

The menu handler for the Swell menu item will be used to allow the user to stop or start the swelling of the text (i.e., enable or disable the animation). Thus, configure the Clicked handler to enable or disable the Timer as follows:

```
private void ConfigSwell_Clicked(object sender, EventArgs e)
{
    timer.Enabled = !timer.Enabled;
    mainMenu.MenuItems[1].MenuItems[0].Checked = timer.Enabled;
}
```

Enumerating Installed Fonts (a la System.Drawing.Text)

Next, let's expand the FontApp to programmatically discover the set of installed fonts on the target machine. Doing so gives you a chance to explore another namespace of GDI+, System.Drawing.Text. This namespace contains a (small) handful of useful types that can be used to discover and manipulate the set of fonts installed on the target machine. The highlights are shown in Table 14-15.

Table 14-15. The Text Type

System.Drawing.Text Type	Meaning in Life
InstalledFontCollection	Represents the set of all fonts installed on the target system.
PrivateFontCollection	Encapsulates a collection of specific Font types.
LineSpacing	This enumeration specifies the spacing between lines of text in a text string that spans more than a single line.
TextRenderingHint	Another enumeration that allows you to specify the quality of the current text rendering operation. For example, the Text value represents a fast (but low quality) rendering. AntiAliased marks better quality but a slower rendering cycle.

When the user selects the "Configure | List All Fonts" menu item, the corresponding Clicked handler creates an instance of the InstalledFontCollection class. This class maintains an array named FontFamily, which represents the set of all fonts on the target machine, and may be obtained using the InstalledFontCollection.Families property. Using the FontFamily.Name property, you are able to extract the font face (e.g., Times New Roman, Arial, etc.) for each font.

Here, you have added a private string data member named installedFonts to hold each font face. The logic in the "List Installed Fonts" menu handler creates an instance of the InstalledFontCollection type, reads the name of each string, and adds the new font face to the private installedFonts data member:

```
public class FontForm : System.Windows.Forms.Form
{
    // Holds the list of fonts.
    private string installedFonts;
    // Menu handler to get the list of installed fonts.
    private void mnuConfigShowFonts_Clicked(object sender, EventArgs e)
    {
        InstalledFontCollection fonts = new InstalledFontCollection();
        for(int i = 0; i < fonts.Families.Length; i++)
            installedFonts += fonts.Families[i].Name + "   ";
```

```
        // This time, we need to invalidate the entire client area,
        // as we will paint the installedFonts string on the lower half
        // of the client rectangle.
        Invalidate();
    }
...
}
```

The final task is to render the installedFonts string to the client area, directly below the screen real estate that is used for your swelling text:

```
private void FontForm_Paint(object sender, PaintEventArgs e)
{
    Graphics g = e.Graphics;
    Font theFont = new Font(fontFace, 12 + swellValue);
    string message = "Hello GDI+";
    // Display message in the center of the window!
    float windowCenter = this.DisplayRectangle.Width/2;
    SizeF stringSize = e.Graphics.MeasureString(message, theFont);
    float startPos = windowCenter - (stringSize.Width/2);
    g.DrawString(message, theFont, new SolidBrush(Color.Blue), startPos, 10);
    // Show installed fonts in the rectangle below the swell area.
    Rectangle myRect = new Rectangle(0, 100,
        ClientRectangle.Width, ClientRectangle.Height);
    // Paint this area of the Form black.
    g.FillRectangle(new SolidBrush(Color.Black), myRect);
    g.DrawString(installedFonts, new Font("Arial", 12),
                new SolidBrush(Color.White), myRect);
}
```

Recall that the size of the "dirty rectangle" has been mapped to the upper 100 pixels of the client rectangle. Because your Tick handler only invalidates a portion of the Form, the remaining area is not redrawn when the Tick event has been sent (to help optimize the rendering of the client area).

As a final touch, to ensure proper redrawing let's handle the Resize event to ensure that if the user resizes the Form, the lower part of client rectangle is redrawn correctly:

```
private void FontForm_Resize(object sender, System.EventArgs e)
{
    Rectangle myRect = new Rectangle(0, 100,
        ClientRectangle.Width, ClientRectangle.Height);
    Invalidate(myRect);
}
```

With that, Figure 14-11 shows the result.

Figure 14-11. The FontApp application in action

SOURCE CODE   The FontApp application is included under the Chapter 14 subdirectory.

The FontDialog Class

As you might assume, there is a default font dialog box (FontDialog), as seen in Figure 14-12.

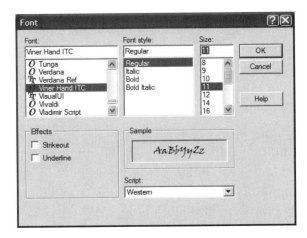

Figure 14-12. The stock .NET Font dialog

Like the ColorDialog type examined earlier in this chapter, when you wish to work with the FontDialog, simply call the ShowDialog() method. Using the Font property, you may extract the characteristics of the current selection for use in the application. To illustrate, here is a new Form that mimics the logic of the previous ColorDlgForm (i.e., click the form to launch the File dialog and render GDI+ logic onto the form's client area).

```
public class FontDlgForm : System.Windows.Forms.Form
{
    private FontDialog fontDlg;
    private Font currFont;
    private void FontDlgForm_Paint(object sender, PaintEventArgs e)
    {
        Graphics g = e.Graphics;
        g.DrawString("Testing...", currFont,
            new SolidBrush(Color.Black), 0, 0);
    }
    public FontDlgForm()
    {
        CenterToScreen();
        fontDlg = new FontDialog();
        fontDlg.ShowHelp = true;
        Text = "Click on me to change the font";
        currFont = new Font("Times New Roman", 12);
        ...
    }
    // Event handler for MouseUp event.
    private void FontDlgForm_MouseUp(object sender, MouseEventArgs e)
    {
        if (fontDlg.ShowDialog() != DialogResult.Cancel)
        {
            currFont = fontDlg.Font;
            Invalidate();
        }
    }
}
```

SOURCE CODE   The FontDlgForm application is included under the Chapter 14 subdirectory.

Survey of the System.Drawing.Drawing2D Namespace

Now that you have manipulated Font types, the next task is to examine how to manipulate Pen and Brush objects to render geometric patterns. While you could do so making use of nothing more than the types found in the System.Drawing namespace, you should be aware that many of the more "sexy" pen and brush configurations (for example, the HatchBrush type used at the beginning of this chapter) require types defined within the System.Drawing.Drawing2D namespace.

This additional GDI+ namespace (which is substantially smaller than System.Drawing) provides a number of classes that allow you to modify the line cap (triangle, diamond, etc.) used for a given pen, build textured brushes, as well as work with vector graphic manipulations. Some core types to be aware of, grouped by related functionality, are shown in Table 14-16.

Table 14-16. The Classes of System.Drawing.Drawing2D

System.Drawing.Drawing2D Class	Meaning in Life
AdjustableArrowCap CustomLineCap	Pen caps are used to paint the beginning and end points of a given line. These types represent an adjustable arrow-shaped and user-defined cap.
Blend ColorBlend	Used to define a blend pattern (and colors) used in conjunction with a LinearGradientBrush.
GraphicsPath GraphicsPathIterator PathData	A GraphicsPath object represents a series of connected lines and curves. This class allows you to insert just about any type of geometrical pattern (arcs, rectangles, lines, strings, polygons, etc.) into the path. PathData holds the graphical data that makes up a path.
HatchBrush LinearGradientBrush PathGradientBrush	Exotic brush types.

Also be aware that the System.Drawing.Drawing2D namespace defines another set of enumerations that are used in conjunction with these core types. Table 14-17 gives a quick rundown.

Table 14-17. The Enumerations of System.Drawing.Drawing2D

System.Drawing.Drawing2D Enumeration	Meaning in Life
DashStyle	Specifies the style of dashed lines drawn with a Pen
FillMode	Specifies how the interior of a closed path is filled
HatchStyle	Specifies the different patterns available for HatchBrush objects
LinearGradientMode	Specifies the direction to apply a linear gradient
LineCap	Specifies the current cap styles used by a Pen
PenAlignment	Specifies the alignment of a Pen in relation to the line being drawn
PenType	Specifies the type of fill a Pen uses to fill lines
QualityMode SmoothingMode RenderingHint	Specifies the overall quality used to render a graphic image

Establishing the Rendering Quality

Notice that some of the enumerations defined in the System.Drawing.Drawing2D namespace (such as QualityMode and SmoothingMode) allow you to configure the overall quality of the current rendering operation. When you obtain a Graphics object, it has a default rendering mode, which is a middle-of-the-road combination of speed and overall quality. Let's examine one way to tweak a Graphics object to override these default values.

The SmoothingMode enumeration (Table 14-18) is typically used to control how the GDI+ objects being rendered with the current Graphics object are antialiased (or not).

Table 14-18. Various SmoothingMode Values

SmoothingMode Value	Meaning in Life
AntiAlias	Specifies antialiased rendering. The AntiAlias mode uses shades of gray or color to smooth the edges of lines and curves, and is effective on CRT screens as well as LCD screens.
HighQuality	Specifies high-quality, lower-performance rendering. The high-quality mode uses more sophisticated techniques that take advantage of the subpixel resolution of LCD screens. A single pixel on an LCD screen is divided into three stripes that are set to various shades to produce the line or curve that appears the smoothest to the human eye.
HighSpeed	Specifies low-quality, high-performance rendering. The high-speed mode does not smooth the item being rendered; pixels are either on or off.

When you wish to override the default rendering quality for a current GDI+ rendering operation, make use of the SmoothingMode property of the Graphics object:

```
private void MainForm_Paint(object sender, PaintEventArgs e)
{
    Graphics g = e.Graphics;
    // Set quality of GDI+ object rendering.
    g.SmoothingMode = SmoothingMode.AntiAlias;
    ...
}
```

Be aware that the SmoothingMode property is only used to control the quality of rendering GDI+ objects, not textual information. If you wish to modify the rendering quality for Font types, you need to set the TextRenderingHint property using the related System.Drawing.Text.TextRenderingHint enumeration:

```
public enum System.Drawing.Text.TextRenderingHint
{
    AntiAlias, AntiAliasGridFit,
    ClearTypeGridFit, SingleBitPerPixel,
    SingleBitPerPixelGridFit, SystemDefault
}
```

Working with Pens

GDI+ Pen objects are used to draw lines (not too much of a stretch there!). However, a pen in and of itself is of little value. When you need to render a geometric shape onto a Control-derived type, you send a pass valid Pen type to any number of render methods defined by the Graphics class. In general, the DrawXXXX() methods are used to render some set of lines to a graphics surface, and are typically used with Pen objects. The Graphics class also defines a number of FillXXXX() methods that render an image using some sort of Brush-derived type (more on those in just a minute).

Although you have seen many drawing members earlier in the chapter, here they are again (Table 14-19) in a bit more detail (be aware that each of these methods have been overloaded a number of times).

Table 14-19. Drawing Members of the Graphics Class

Drawing Method of Graphics Type	Meaning in Life
DrawArc()	This method renders an arc given a pen, and an ellipse on which to base the angle of the arc.
DrawBezier() DrawBeziers()	Given four points, this method draws a cubic Bezier curve (or a number of Beziers).
DrawCurve()	Draws a curve defined by an array of points.
DrawEllipse()	Draws the outline of an ellipse within the scope of a bounding rectangle.

Table 14-19. Drawing Members of the Graphics Class (Continued)

Drawing Method of Graphics Type	Meaning in Life
DrawLine() DrawLines()	Given a Point (or an array of Point types), these methods connect the dots (if you will).
DrawPath()	Using the GraphicsPath type defined in the System.Drawing.Drawing2D namespace, this method renders a collection of lines/curves as specified by the path.
DrawPie()	Draws the outline of a pie section defined by an ellipse and two radial lines.
DrawPolygon()	Draws the outline of a polygon defined by an array of Point types.
DrawRectangle() DrawRectangles()	Renders a box, or a whole bunch of boxes, based on top-left-bottom-right coordinates. This can be specified using Rectangle types, integers, or floating point numbers.

Now that you better understand the core methods used to render geometric images, you can examine the Pen class itself. This class defines a small set of constructors that allow you to determine the initial color and width of the pen nib (you can also construct a new Pen based on an existing Brush object...more later). Most of a Pen's functionality comes by way of its supported properties. Table 14-20 gives a partial list.

Table 14-20. Pen Properties

Pen Property	Meaning in Life
Brush	Determines the Brush used by this Pen.
Color	Determines the Color type used by this Pen.
CompoundArray	Gets or sets an array of custom dashes and spaces.
CustomStartCap CustomEndCap	Gets or sets a custom cap style to use at the beginning or end of lines drawn with this Pen. Cap styles are simply the term used to describe how the initial and final stroke of the Pen should look and feel. These properties allow you to build custom caps for your Pen types.
DashCap	Gets or sets the cap style used at the beginning or end of dashed lines drawn with this Pen.
DashOffset	Gets or sets the distance from the start of a line to the beginning of a dash pattern.
DashPattern	Gets or sets an array of custom dashes and spaces. The dashes are made up of line segments.
DashStyle	Gets or sets the style used for dashed lines drawn with this Pen.

Table 14-20. Pen Properties (Continued)

Pen Property	Meaning in Life
LineJoin	Gets or sets the join style for the ends of two overlapping lines drawn with this Pen.
PenType	Gets the style of lines drawn with this Pen.
StartCap EndCap	Gets or sets the predefined cap style used at the beginning or end of lines drawn with this Pen. Set the cap of your Pen using the LineCap enumeration defined in the System.Drawing.Drawing2D namespace.
Width	Gets or sets the width of this Pen.

Remember that in addition to the Pen type, GDI+ also provides a Pens collection. Using a number of static properties, you are able to retrieve a Pen (or a given color) on the fly, rather than creating a custom Pen by hand. Be aware, however, that the Pen types returned will always have a width of 1. If you require a more exotic pen, you will need to build a Pen type by hand.

First, let's render some geometric images using simple Pen types. Assume we have a main Form object, which is capable of responding to paint requests. The implementation is as follows:

```
private void MainForm_Paint(object sender, PaintEventArgs e)
{
    Graphics g = e.Graphics;
    // Make a big blue pen.
    Pen bluePen = new Pen(Color.Blue, 20);
    // Get a stock pen from the Pens type.
    Pen pen2 = Pens.Firebrick;
    // Render some shapes with the pens.
    g.DrawEllipse(bluePen, 10, 10, 100, 100);
    g.DrawLine(pen2, 10, 130, 110, 130);
    g.DrawPie(Pens.Black, 150, 10, 120, 150, 90, 80);
    // Draw a purple dashed polygon as well...
    Pen pen3 = new Pen(Color.Purple, 5);
    pen3.DashStyle = DashStyle.DashDotDot;
    g.DrawPolygon(pen3, new Point[]{new Point(30, 140),
        new Point(265, 200), new Point(100, 225),
        new Point(190, 190), new Point(50, 330),
        new Point(20, 180)}  );
    // And a rectangle containing some text...
    Rectangle r = new Rectangle(150, 10, 130, 60);
    g.DrawRectangle(Pens.Blue, r);
    g.DrawString("Hello out there...How are ya?",
                new Font("Arial", 12), Brushes.Black, r);
}
```

Notice that the Pen that is used to render your polygon makes use of the DashStyle enumeration (defined in System.Drawing.Drawing2D). This is the .NET equivalent of the raw Win32 pen style flags (e.g., PS_SOLID). Table 14-21 lists your choices.

Table 14-21. Dash Styles

DashStyle Value	Meaning in Life
Custom	Specifies a user-defined custom dash style
Dash	Specifies a line comprised of dashes
DashDot	Specifies a line comprised of an alternating pattern of dash-dot-dash-dot
DashDotDot	Specifies a line comprised of an alternating pattern of dash-dot-dot-dash-dot-dot
Dot	Specifies a line comprised of dots
Solid	Specifies a solid line

In addition to the preconfigured DashStyles, you are also able to define custom dash types using the DashPattern property of the Pen type: (see Figure 14-13 for complete output).

```
// Draw custom dash pattern all around the boarder of the form.
Pen customDashPen = new Pen(Color.BlueViolet, 5);
float[] myDashes = { 5.0f, 2.0f, 1.0f, 3.0f} ;
customDashPen.DashPattern = myDashes;
g.DrawRectangle(customDashPen, ClientRectangle);
```

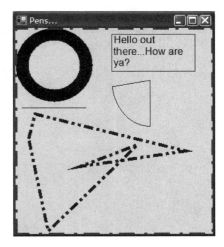

Figure 14-13. Working with Pen types

SOURCE CODE The PenApp project is included under the Chapter 14 subdirectory.

Working with Pen Caps

If you examined the output of the previous pen example, you should have noticed that the beginning and end of each line was rendered using a standard pen protocol (an end cap composed of 90 degree angles). Using the LineCap enumeration however, you are able to build Pens that exhibit a bit more flair. The core values of this enumeration are seen in Table 14-22.

Table 14-22. LineCap Values

LineCap Values	Meaning in Life
ArrowAnchor	Specifies an arrow-shaped cap
DiamondAnchor	Specifies a diamond anchor cap
Flat	Specifies a flat line cap
Round	Specifies a round line cap
RoundAnchor	Specifies a round anchor cap
Square	Specifies a square line cap
SquareAnchor	Specifies no line cap
Triangle	Specifies a triangular line cap

To illustrate, the following Pens application draws a series of lines using each of the LineCap styles. First, the result can be seen in Figure 14-14.

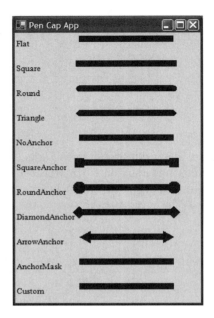

Figure 14-14. Working with pen caps

The code simply loops through each member of the LineCap enumeration, and prints out the name of the item (e.g., ArrowAnchor) and then configures and draws a line with the current cap:

```
private void MainForm_Paint(object sender, PaintEventArgs e)
{
    Graphics g = e.Graphics;
    Pen thePen = new Pen(Color.Black, 10);
    int yOffSet = 10;
    // Get all members of the LineCap enum.
    Array obj = Enum.GetValues(typeof(LineCap));
    // Draw a line with a LineCap member.
    for(int x = 0; x < obj.Length; x++)
    {
        // Get next cap and configure pen.
        LineCap temp = (LineCap)obj.GetValue(x);
        thePen.StartCap = temp;
        thePen.EndCap = temp;
        // Print name of LineCap enum.
        g.DrawString(temp.ToString(), new Font("Times New Roman", 10),
                new SolidBrush(Color.Black), 0, yOffSet);
        // Draw a line with the correct cap.
        g.DrawLine(thePen, 100, yOffSet, Width - 50, yOffSet);
        yOffSet += 40;
    }
}
```

SOURCE CODE   The PenCapApp project is included under the Chapter 14 subdirectory.

Working with Solid Brushes

So much for drawing lines. GDI+ Brush-derived types are used to fill the space between the lines, with a given color, pattern, or image. Recall that the Brush class is an abstract type, and cannot be directly created. Rather, this type serves as a base class to the other related brush types (for example, SolidBrush, HatchBrush, LinearGradientBrush, and so forth). In addition to the aforementioned Brush-derived types, the System.Drawing namespace also defines two types that return a configured brush using a number of static properties: Brushes and SystemBrushes. Using a properly configured brush, you are able to call any number of methods [such as DrawString()], as well as the following set of FillXXXX() methods (Table 14-23).

Table 14-23. Fill Methods of the Graphics Type

Fill Method of Graphics Class	Meaning in Life
FillClosedCurve()	Fills the interior of a closed curve defined by an array of points
FillEllipse()	Fills the interior of an ellipse defined by a bounding rectangle
FillPath()	Fills the interior of a path
FillPie()	Fills the interior of a pie section
FillPolygon()	Fills the interior of a polygon defined by an array of points
FillRectangle() FillRectangles()	Fills the interior of a rectangle (or a number of rectangles) with a Brush
FillRegion()	Fills the interior of a Region

Also recall, that you are able to build a custom Pen type by making use of a given brush. In this way, you are able to build some brush of interest (for example, a brush that paints a bitmap image) and render geometric patterns with configured Pen. To illustrate, here is a small sample program that makes use of the SolidBrush and Brushes types [the output of this program (Figure 14-15) should look familiar...]

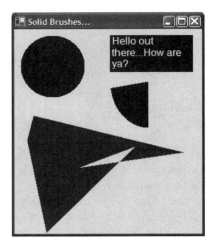

Figure 14-15. Working with Brush types

If you can't tell, this application is little more than the original Pens application, making use of the FillXXXX() methods and SolidBrush types, rather than pens and the related DrawXXXX() methods. Here is the implementation of the paint handler:

```
private void MainForm_Paint(object sender, PaintEventArgs e)
{
    Graphics g = e.Graphics;
    // Make a blue SolidBrush.
    SolidBrush blueBrush = new SolidBrush(Color.Blue);
    // Get a stock brush from the Brushes type.
    SolidBrush pen2 = (SolidBrush)Brushes.Firebrick;
    // Render some shapes with the brushes.
    g.FillEllipse(blueBrush, 10, 10, 100, 100);
    g.FillPie(Brushes.Black, 150, 10, 120, 150, 90, 80);
    // Draw a purple polygon as well...
    SolidBrush brush3= new SolidBrush(Color.Purple);
    g.FillPolygon(brush3, new Point[]{ new Point(30, 140),
        new Point(265, 200), new Point(100, 225),
        new Point(190, 190), new Point(50, 330),
        new Point(20, 180)} );
    // And a rectangle with some text...
    Rectangle r = new Rectangle(150, 10, 130, 60);
    g.FillRectangle(Brushes.Blue, r);
    g.DrawString("Hello out there...How are ya?",
                new Font("Arial", 12), Brushes.White, r);
}
```

SOURCE CODE   The SolidBrushApp project is included under the Chapter 14 subdirectory.

Working with Hatch Style Brushes

The System.Drawing.Drawing2D namespace defines another Brush-derived type named HatchBrush. This type allows you to fill a region using a (very large) number of predefined patterns, represented by the HatchStyle enumeration. Here are some (but not all) of the hatch values (Table 14-24).

Table 14-24. Values of the HatchStyle Enumeration

HatchStyle Enumeration Value	Meaning in Life
BackwardDiagonal	Creates a brush consisting of backward diagonal lines
Cross	Creates a brush consisting of horizontal and vertical crossing lines
DiagonalCross	Creates a brush consisting of diagonal crossing lines
ForwardDiagonal	Creates a brush consisting of forward diagonal lines
Hollow	Configures a "hollow" brush that doesn't paint anything
Horizontal	Creates a brush consisting of horizontal lines
Pattern	Creates a Brush with a pattern consisting of a custom bitmap
Solid	Creates a solid colored brush (as an alternative to using the SolidBrush type directly)
Vertical	A brush consisting of vertical lines

In addition, when constructing a HatchBrush, you need to specify the foreground and background colors to use during the fill operation. To illustrate, let's rework the logic seen previously from the PenCapApp example. The output renders a filled oval for the first ten hatch values (Figure 14-16).

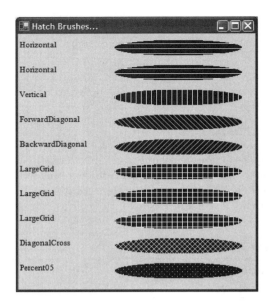

Figure 14-16. The hatch styles

Here is the code behind the Form:

```
private void MainForm_Paint(object sender, PaintEventArgs e)
{
    Graphics g = e.Graphics;
    int yOffSet = 10;
    // Get all members of the HatchStyle enum.
    Array obj = Enum.GetValues(typeof(HatchStyle));
    // Draw an oval with first 10 HatchStyle values.
    for(int x = 0; x < 10; x++)
    {
        // Configure Brush.
        HatchStyle temp = (HatchStyle)obj.GetValue(x);
        HatchBrush theBrush = new HatchBrush(temp,
            Color.White, Color.Black
        // Print name of HatchStyle enum.
        g.DrawString(temp.ToString(), new Font("Times New Roman", 10),
                new SolidBrush(Color.Black), 0, yOffSet);
        // Fill a rectangle with the correct brush.
        g. FillEllipse(theBrush, 150, yOffSet, 200, 25);
        yOffSet += 40;
    }
}
```

SOURCE CODE   The BrushStyles application is included under the Chapter 14 subdirectory.

Working with Textured Brushes

Next, we have the TextureBrush type. This type allows you to attach a bitmap image to a brush, which can then be used in conjunction with a fill operation. In just a few pages, you will learn about the details of the GDI+ Image class. For the time being, understand that a TextureBrush is assigned an Image reference for use during its lifetime. The image itself is typically found stored in some local file (*.bmp, *.gif, *.jpg) or embedded into a .NET assembly.

Let's build a sample application that makes use of the TextureBrush type. One brush is used to paint the entire client area with the image found in a file named "clouds.bmp," while the other brush is used to paint text with the image found within "soap bubbles.bmp" (yes, you can use TextureBrush types to render text as well!). The output is shown in Figure 14-17.

Figure 14-17. Bitmaps as brushes

The code is very simple. To begin, your Form-derived class maintains two abstract Brush types, which are assigned to a new TextureBrush in the constructor. Notice that the constructor of the TextureBrush type requires a type derived from Image:

```
public class MainForm : System.Windows.Forms.Form
{
    // Note!  These *.bmp files must be in the same folder
    // as the application (or specify hard coded paths).
    // We'll fix this limitation later in this chapter.

    // Data for the image brush.
    private Brush texturedTextBrush;
    private Brush texturedBGroundBrush;
    public MainForm()
    {
        ...
        // Load image for background brush.
        Image bGroundBrushImage = new Bitmap("Clouds.bmp");
        texturedBGroundBrush = new TextureBrush(bGroundBrushImage);
        // Now load image for text brush.
        Image textBrushImage = new Bitmap("Soap Bubbles.bmp");
        texturedTextBrush = new TextureBrush(textBrushImage);
    }
    ...
}
```

Now that you have two TextureBrush types to render with, the paint handler should be a no-brainer:

```
private void MainForm_Paint(object sender, PaintEventArgs e)
{
    Graphics g = e.Graphics;
    Rectangle r = ClientRectangle;
    // Paint the clouds on the client area.
    g.FillRectangle(texturedBGroundBrush, r);
    // Some big bold text with a textured brush.
    g.DrawString("Bitmaps as brushes!  Way cool...",
                new Font("Arial", 60,
                FontStyle.Bold | FontStyle.Italic),
                texturedTextBrush,
                r);
}
```

Not bad at all huh? For those of you who have spent time achieving the same effects using the raw Win32 API (or even MFC for that matter), you should be quite pleased with the minimal amount of work required to achieve rather complex results. Now, before moving on to a discussion of image manipulation, there is one final brush type to consider.

 SOURCE CODE   The TexturedBrushes application is included under the Chapter 14 subdirectory.

Working with Gradient Brushes

Last but not least, there is the LinearGradientBrush type, which can be used whenever you want to blend two colors together in a gradient pattern. Working with this type is just as simple as working with the other brush types. The only point of interest is that when building a LinearGradientBrush, you need to specify the direction of the blend, using a value from the LinearGradientMode enumeration (Table 14-25).

Table 14-25. LinearGradientMode Enumeration

LinearGradientMode Value	Meaning in Life
BackwardDiagonal	Specifies a gradient from upper right to lower left
ForwardDiagonal	Specifies a gradient from upper left to lower right
Horizontal	Specifies a gradient from left to right
Vertical	Specifies a gradient from top to bottom

To test each type, let's make use of the System.Enum class yet again, and draw a series of rectangles using a LinearGradientBrush. The output is seen in Figure 14-18.

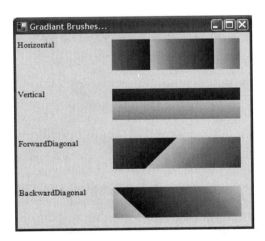

Figure 14-18. Gradient brushes at work

Now the code, which I assume requires little comment at this point:

```
private void MainForm_Paint(object sender, PaintEventArgs e)
{
    Graphics g = e.Graphics;
    Rectangle r = new Rectangle(10, 10, 100, 100);
    // A gradient brush.
    LinearGradientBrush theBrush = null;
    int yOffSet = 10;
    // Get all members of the LinearGradientMode enum.
    Array obj = Enum.GetValues(typeof(LinearGradientMode));
    // Draw an oval with a LinearGradientMode member.
    for(int x = 0; x < obj.Length; x++)
    {
        // Configure Brush.
        LinearGradientMode temp = (LinearGradientMode)obj.GetValue(x);
        theBrush = new LinearGradientBrush(r, Color.GreenYellow,
                                        Color.Blue, temp);
        // Print name of LinearGradientMode enum.
        g.DrawString(temp.ToString(), new Font("Times New Roman", 10),
                new SolidBrush(Color.Black), 0, yOffSet);
        // Fill a rectangle with the correct brush.
        g. FillRectangle(theBrush, 150, yOffSet, 200, 50);
        yOffSet += 80;
    }
}
```

SOURCE CODE   The GradientBrush application is included under the Chapter 14 subdirectory.

Rendering Images

At this point you have examined how to manipulate three of the four major GDI+ types (fonts, pens, and brushes). The final type you examine in this chapter is the Image class, and related subtypes. The abstract System.Drawing.Image type defines a number of methods and properties that hold various bits of information regarding the underlying pixel set it represents. For example, the Image class supplies the Width, Height, and Size properties to retrieve the dimensions of the image. Other properties allow you to gain access to the underlying palette. The Image class defines the core members shown in Table 14-26.

Table 14-26. Members of the Image Type

Image Member Name	Meaning in Life
FromFile()	This static method creates an Image from the specified file.
FromHbitmap()	This static method creates a Bitmap from a Windows handle.
FromStream()	This static method creates an Image from the specified data stream.
Height Width Size PhysicalDimensions HorizontalResolution VerticalResolution	These properties return information regarding the dimensions of this Image.
Palette	This property returns a ColorPalette data type that represents the underlying palette used for this Image.
GetBounds()	Returns a Rectangle that represents the current size of this Image.
Save()	Saves the data held in an Image-derived type to file.

Given that the abstract Image class cannot be directly created, you typically make a direct instance of the Bitmap type. For example, assume you have some Form-derived class that renders three bitmaps into the client area. To begin, you may create three private Image data members, each of which is assigned to a given *.bmp file on startup (again, be sure these files are located in the application directory):

```
public class MainForm : System.Windows.Forms.Form
{
    // The images.
    private Bitmap bMapImageA;
    private Bitmap bMapImageB;
    private Bitmap bMapImageC;
    public MainForm()
    {
        ...
        // Fill the images with bitmaps.
        bMapImageA = new Bitmap("imageA.bmp");
        bMapImageB = new Bitmap("imageB.bmp");
        bMapImageC = new Bitmap("imageC.bmp");
    }
    ...
}
```

Rendering these items from within the context of a paint handler is easy as could be, given that the Graphics class has a member named (appropriately enough) DrawImage(). This method has been overloaded numerous times to provide various ways to place the image onto the drawing surface. For example, you may specify optional ImageAttributes and GraphicsUnit enumerations. For your purposes, all you need to do is specify the location at which to render each image (which may be defined using Point, Rectangles, integers, or floats):

```
protected void OnPaint (object sender, System.Windows.Forms.PaintEventArgs e)
{
    Graphics g = e.Graphics;
    // Render all three images.
    g.DrawImage(bMapImageA, 10, 10, 90, 90);
    g.DrawImage(bMapImageB, 10, 110, 90, 90);
    g.DrawImage(bMapImageC, 10, 210, 90, 90);
}
```

The result can be seen in Figure 14-19.

Figure 14-19. Rendering images

Also be aware that regardless of the name given to the Bitmap type, you are able to load in images stored in any number of file formats. For example:

```
// The Bitmap type can hold work with any number of file formats!
Bitmap myBMP = new Bitmap("CoffeeCup.bmp");
Bitmap myGIF = new Bitmap("Candy.gif");
Bitmap myJPEG = new Bitmap("Clock.jpg");
Bitmap myPNG = new Bitmap("Speakers.png");
Bitmap myTIF = new Bitmap("FooFighters.tif");
// Now render each onto the Graphics context.
g.DrawImage(myBMP, 10, 10);
g.DrawImage(myGIF, 220, 10);
g.DrawImage(myJPEG, 280, 10);
g.DrawImage(myPNG, 150, 200);
g.DrawImage(myTIF, 300, 200);
```

SOURCE CODE   The Images application is included under the Chapter 14 subdirectory.

Dragging, Hit Testing, and the PictureBox Control

While you are free to render Bitmap images directly onto a Control-derived type (such as a Form), you will find that you gain far greater control and functionality if you instead choose to create a PictureBox type to hold your image on your behalf. There are numerous reasons to do so. First, because the PictureBox type derives from Control, you inherit a great deal of functionality, such as the ability to capture a number of events for a particular image, assign a tool tip or context menu, and numerous other details. While you could achieve similar behaviors using a raw Bitmap, you would be required to add a fair amount of boilerplate code.

To illustrate the usefulness of the PictureBox type, let's create an application that illustrates the ability to capture MouseUp, MouseDown, and MouseMove events from a graphical image contained in a PictureBox.

If users click the mouse somewhere within the bounds of the image, they are in "dragging" mode and can move the image around the Form. To make things more interesting, let's monitor where they release the image. If it is within the bounds of a GDI+-rendered rectangle, we take some additional course of action (seen shortly). As you may know, the process of testing for mouse Click events within the context of a region of the screen is termed "hit testing."

When it comes to the functionality provided by the PictureBox type, there is little to say, as all of the necessary functionality comes from the Control base class. Given that you have already explored a number of the members for these types, you can quickly turn your attention to the process of assigning an image to the PictureBox member variable:

```
public class MainForm : System.Windows.Forms.Form
{
    // This holds an image of a smiley face.
    private PictureBox happyBox;
    public MainForm()
    {
        // Configure the PictureBox.
        happyBox = new PictureBox();
        happyBox.SizeMode = PictureBoxSizeMode.StretchImage;
        happyBox.Location = new System.Drawing.Point(64, 32);
        happyBox.Size = new System.Drawing.Size(50, 50);
        happyBox.Cursor = Cursors.Hand;
        happyBox.Image = new Bitmap("happy.bmp");
        // Now add to the Form's Controls collection.
        Controls.Add(happyBox);
    }
    ...
}
```

The only point of interest is the SizeMode property, which makes use of the PictureBoxSizeMode enumeration. This type is used to control how the associated image should be rendered within the bounding rectangle of the PictureBox. Here, you assigned StretchImage, indicating that you wish to skew the image over the entire client area. Other possible values appear in Table 14-27.

Table 14-27. The PictureBoxSizeMode Enumeration

PictureBoxSizeMode Member Name	Meaning in Life
AutoSize	The PictureBox is sized equal to the size of the image that it contains.
CenterImage	The image is displayed in the center if the PictureBox is larger than the image. If the image is larger than the PictureBox, the picture is placed in the center of the PictureBox and the outside edges are clipped.
Normal	The image is located in the upper left corner of the PictureBox. If the PictureBox is smaller than the image, it will be clipped.

Now that you have configured the initial look and feel of the PictureBox, you need to hook up some handlers for the MouseMove, MouseUp, and MouseDown events. This is simple, as PictureBox "is-a" Control. Thus, you can update your constructor logic as follows:

```
// Add handlers for the following events.
happyBox.MouseDown += new MouseEventHandler(happyBox_MouseDown);
happyBox.MouseUp += new MouseEventHandler(happyBox_MouseUp);
happyBox.MouseMove += new MouseEventHandler(happyBox_MouseMove);
```

The logic behind MouseDown stores the incoming (*x*, *y*) location of the mouse click for later use, and sets a Boolean member variable (isDragging) to true, to indicate that a drag operation is in process.

```
// Mouse event handler to initiate dragging the pictureBox around.
private void happyBox_MouseDown(object sender, MouseEventArgs e)
{
    isDragging = true;
    // Save the (x, y) of the mouse down click,
    // because we need it as an offset when dragging the image.
    oldX = e.X;
    oldY = e.Y;
}
```

The MouseMove handler simply relocates the position of the PictureBox (using the Top and Left properties) by offsetting the current cursor location with the (*x*, *y*) position captured when the mouse went down.

```
// If the user clicks the image and moves the mouse,
// redraw the image at the new location.
private void happyBox_MouseMove(object sender, MouseEventArgs e)
{
    if (isDragging)
    {
        // Need to figure new Y value based on where the mouse
        // down click happened.
        happyBox.Top = happyBox.Top + (e.Y - oldY);
        // Same deal for X (use oldX as a base line).
        happyBox.Left = happyBox.Left + (e.X - oldX);
    }
}
```

Finally, MouseUp sets the isDragging Boolean to false, to signal the end of the drag operation. Recall however, that this application has one extra point of logic. If the MouseUp event occurs when the PictureBox is contained within a GDI+ Rectangle object, you can assume the user has won the game (albeit a rather lame game...). That said, here is the remainder of the Form's logic:

```
// When the mouse goes up, they are done dragging.
// See if they dropped the image in the rectangle...
private void happyBox_MouseUp(object sender, MouseEventArgs e)
{
    isDragging = false;
    // Is the mouse within the area of the drop rect?
    if(dropRect.Contains(happyBox.Bounds))
        MessageBox.Show("You win!", "What an amazing test of skill...");
}

// Assume we have a private Rectangle configured as follows:
// Rectangle dropRect = new Rectangle(100, 100, 150, 150);
private void MainForm_Paint(object sender, PaintEventArgs e)
{
    // Draw the drop box.
    Graphics g = e.Graphics;
    g.FillRectangle(Brushes.AntiqueWhite, dropRect);
    // Display instructions.
    g.DrawString("Drag the happy guy in here...",
        new Font("Times New Roman", 25), Brushes.Red, dropRect);
}
```

As a reminder, it is worth pointing out that the Rectangle type defines the Contains() method that has been overloaded to test for contained Rectangle, Point, or two integer values. This member can be quite helpful when calculating if a mouse click has occurred within a given rectangular region (as seen in the MouseUp event handler). When you run the application, you are presented with what appears in Figure 14-20.

Figure 14-20. The amazing happy-dude game

If you have what it takes to win the game, you are rewarded with the kudos shown in Figure 14-21.

Figure 14-21. *You have nerves of steel...*

SOURCE CODE   The DraggingImages application is included under the Chapter 14 subdirectory.

More Hit Testing Details

Validating a hit test against a Control-derived type (such as a PictureBox) is very simple, as each can respond to mouse events directly. However, what if you wish to perform a hit test on a geometric shape such as a region rendered on the screen using a raw GDI+ object? To illustrate, let's revisit the previous Images application, and add some additional functionality.

The goal is to determine when the user clicks a given image (which as you recall was *not* rendered within a PictureBox control). Once you discover which image was clicked, adjust the Text property of the Form, and highlight the image with a 5-pixel outline.

The first step is to intercept the MouseDown event for the Form itself. When the event occurs, you need to programmatically figure out if the incoming (x, y) coordinate is somewhere within the bounds of the Rectangles used to represent the dimension of each Image. If the user does click a given image, you set a private Boolean member variable (isImageClicked) to true, and indicate which image was selected via another member variable (of type integer):

```
public class MainForm : System.Windows.Forms.Form
{
    ...
    // Did they click an image?
    private bool isImageClicked = false;
    private int imageClicked;
    protected void OnMouseDown (object sender, MouseEventArgs e)
    {
        // Get (x, y) of mouse click.
        Point mousePt = new Point(e.X, e.Y);
        // See if the mouse is anywhere in the 3 regions...
        if(rectA.Contains(mousePt))
        {
            isImageClicked = true;
            imageClicked = 0;
            this.Text = "You clicked image A";
        }
```

```
        else if(rectB.Contains(mousePt))
        {
            isImageClicked = true;
            imageClicked = 1;
            this.Text = "You clicked image B";
        }
        else if(rectC.Contains(mousePt))
        {
            isImageClicked = true;
            imageClicked = 2;
            this.Text = "You clicked image C";
        }
        else    // Not in any shape, set defaults.
        {
            isImageClicked = false;
            this.Text = "Images";
        }
        // Redraw the client area.
        Invalidate();
    }
    ...
}
```

Notice that the final conditional check sets the isImageClicked member variable to false, indicating that the user did not click one of your three images. This is important, as you want to erase the outline of the previously selected image. Once all items have been checked, invalidate the client area. Here is the updated Paint handler:

```
private void MainForm_Paint(object sender, PaintEventArgs e)
{
    Graphics g = e.Graphics;
    // Render all three images.
    ...
    // Draw outline (if clicked...)
    if(isImageClicked == true)
    {
        Pen outline = new Pen(Color.Red, 5);
        switch(imageClicked)
        {
            case 0:
                g.DrawRectangle(outline, rectA);
                break;
            case 1:
                g.DrawRectangle(outline, rectB);
                break;
            case 2:
                g.DrawRectangle(outline, rectC);
                break;
            default:
                break;
        }
    }
}
```

Hit Testing Nonrectangular Images

Now, what if you wish to perform a hit test in a nonrectangular region, rather than a simple square? Assume you updated your application to render an oddball geometric shape that will also sport an outline when clicked (Figure 14-22).

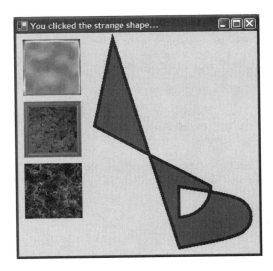

Figure 14-22. Hit-testing polygons

This geometric image was rendered on the Form using the FillPath() method of the Graphics type. This method takes an instance of a GraphicsPath object, which was mentioned earlier during your examination of the System.Drawing.Drawing2D namespace. The GraphicsPath object encapsulates a series of connected lines, curves, and (interestingly enough) strings. Adding new items to a GraphicsPath instance is achieved using a number of related "add" methods (Table 14-28).

Table 14-28. Add-Centric Methods of the GraphicsPath Class

GraphicsPath "Add" Method	Meaning in Life
AddArc()	Appends an elliptical arc to the current figure
AddBezier() AddBeziers()	Adds a cubic Bezier curve (or set of Bezier curves) to the current figure
AddClosedCurve()	Adds a closed curve to the current figure
AddCurve()	Adds a curve to the current figure
AddEllipse()	Adds an ellipse to the current figure

Table 14-28. Add-Centric Methods of the GraphicsPath Class (Continued)

GraphicsPath "Add" Method	Meaning in Life
AddLine() AddLines()	Appends a line segment to the current figure
AddPath()	Appends the specified GraphicsPath to the current figure
AddPie()	Adds the outline of a pie shape to the current figure
AddPolygon()	Adds a polygon to the current figure
AddRectangle() AddRectangles()	Adds one (or more) rectangle to the current figure
AddString()	Adds a text string to the current figure

Assume that you have added a private GraphicsPath member variable to your current Images application. In the Form's constructor, build the set of items that represent your path as follows:

```
public MainForm : System.Windows.Forms.Form
{
    GraphicsPath myPath = new GraphicsPath();

    public MainForm()
    {
        // Create an interesting region.
        myPath.StartFigure();
        myPath.AddLine(new Point(150, 10), new Point(120, 150));
        myPath.AddArc(200, 200, 100, 100, 0, 90);
        Point point1 = new Point(250, 250);
        Point point2 = new Point(350, 275);
        Point point3 = new Point(350, 325);
        Point point4 = new Point(250, 350);
        Point[] points = { point1, point2, point3, point4} ;
        myPath.AddCurve(points);
        myPath.CloseFigure();
        ...
    }
}
```

Notice the calls to StartFigure() and CloseFigure(). When you call StartFigure(), you are able to insert a new item into the current path you are building. A call to CloseFigure() closes the current figure and begins a new figure (if you require one). If the figure contains a sequence of connected lines and curves (as in the case of the myPath instance), the loop is closed by connecting a line from the endpoint to the starting point.

There are more members for System.Drawing.Drawing2D.GraphicsPath, but let's keep focused on the hit-testing logic. The next step would be to update your existing MouseDown event handler to test for the presence of the cursor's (x, y) position within the bounds of the GraphicsPath. Like a Region type, this can be discovered using the IsVisible() member:

```
protected void OnMouseDown (object sender, MouseEventArgs e)
{
    // Get (x, y) of mouse click.
    Point mousePt = new Point(e.X, e.Y);
    ...
    else if(myPath.IsVisible(mousePt))
    {
        isImageClicked = true;
        imageClicked = 3;
        this.Text = "You clicked the strange shape...";
    }
...
}
```

Finally, you can update the Paint handler as follows:

```
private void MainForm_Paint(object sender, PaintEventArgs e)
{
    Graphics g = e.Graphics;
    ...
    // Draw the graphics path.
    g.FillPath(Brushes.AliceBlue, myPath);
    // Draw outline (if clicked...)
    if(isImageClicked == true)
    {
        Pen outline = new Pen(Color.Red, 5);
        switch(imageClicked)
        {
            ...
            case 3:
                g.DrawPath(outline, myPath);
                break;
            default:
                break;
        }
    }
}
```

 SOURCE CODE   The (updated) Images project is included under the Chapter 14 subdirectory.

Understanding the .NET Resource Format

Up to this point, each application that made use of external resources (such as bitmaps) assumed that they were located in a separate stand-alone file within the application directory. For example, the Images application rendered three bitmap images, which as you recall were loaded directly from file:

```
// Fill the images with bitmaps.
bMapImageA = new Bitmap("imageA.bmp");
bMapImageB = new Bitmap("imageB.bmp");
bMapImageC = new Bitmap("imageC.bmp");
```

This logic of course demands that the application directory does indeed contain three files named "imageA.bmp," "imageB.bmp," and "imageC.bmp" (see Figure 14-23).

Figure 14-23. An application with three external resources

If any of these files are deleted, renamed, or relocated outside the application directory, the program fails to execute (give it a try just for verification's sake). Now, as you recall from Chapter 9, an assembly is a collection of types and *optional resources*. The time has now come to learn how to bundle external resources (such as image files and strings) into the assembly itself. In this way, your .NET binary is truly self-contained. In a nutshell, bundling external resources into a .NET assembly involves the following steps:

- Create an *.resx file that establishes name/value pairs for each resource in your application using XML data representation.

- Use the resgen.exe utility to convert your XML-based *.resx file into a binary equivalent (a *.resources file).

- Using the /resource: flag of the C# compiler, embed the binary *.resources file into your assembly.

As you might suspect, all these steps are followed automatically when using the Visual Studio .NET IDE. You'll examine how the IDE can assist you in just a bit. For now, let's take the time to work with the .NET resource format in the raw.

System.Resources Namespace

The key to understanding the .NET resource format is to know the types defined within the System.Resources namespace. This set of types provides the programmatic means to manipulate both *.resx (XML-based) and *.resources (binary) files. Table 14-29 provides a rundown of the core types.

Table 14-29. Members of the System.Resources Namespace

System.Resources Type	Meaning in Life
IResourceReader IResourceWriter	These interfaces are implemented by types that understand how to read and write .NET resources (in various formats). You do not need to implement these interfaces yourself unless you are interested in building a custom resource reader/writer.
ResourceReader ResourceWriter	These classes provide an implementation of the IResourceReader and IResourceWriter interfaces. Using the ResourceReader and ResourceWriter types, you are able to read from and write to binary *.resources files.
ResXResourceReader ResXResourceWriter	These classes also provide an implementation of the IResourceReader and IResourceWriter interfaces. Using the ResXResourceReader and ResXResourceWriter types, you are able to read from, and write to, XML *.resx files. This file may be turned into a binary equivalent (the *.resources file) using the resgen.exe utility.
ResourceManager	Provides easy access to culture-specific resources (BLOBs and string resources) at runtime.

*Programmatically Creating an *.resx File*

As mentioned, an *.resx file is a block of XML data that assigns name/value pairs for each resource in your application. The ResXResourceWriter class provides a set of members that allow you to create the *.resx file, add binary and string-based resources, and commit them to storage. To illustrate, assume you have a simple application you have built a la notepad and csc.exe, whose job in life is to build an *.resx file containing an entry for the happy.bmp image seen earlier in this chapter, and a single string resource. The GUI is as simple as possible (Figure 14-24).

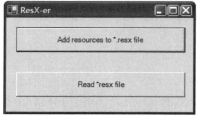

Figure 14-24. The ResX application

The Click event handler for the "Add resources" button does the grunt work of adding the happy.bmp and string resource to the *.resx file. Here is the code:

```
protected void btnMakeResxFile_Click (object sender, System.EventArgs e)
{
    // Make an resx writer & specify the file to write to.
    ResXResourceWriter w =
        new ResXResourceWriter("ResXForm.resx");
    // Add happy dude & string.
    Image i = new Bitmap("happy.bmp");
    w.AddResource("happyDude", i);
    w.AddResource("welcomeString", "Hello new resource format!");
    // Commit it.
    w.Generate();
    w.Close();
}
```

The member of interest is ResXResourceWriter.AddResource(). This method has been overloaded a few times to allow you to insert binary data (as you did with the happy.bmp image), as well as textual data (as you have done for your test string). Notice that each version takes two parameters: the name of a given resource in the *.resx file and the data itself. The Generate() method commits the information to file.

Understand that you are not the one in charge of writing the raw XML that describes your resources. Rather, the logic within the ResXResourceWriter class is responsible for building the XML description of the inserted items. To prove the point, compile and run your application, load the new *.resx file using VS .NET, and peek inside the contents (Figure 14-25).

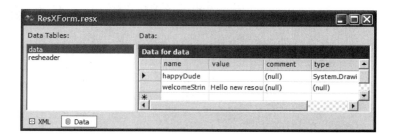

*Figure 14-25. Viewing the *.resx file a la VS .NET*

If you switch to the XML view, you should be able to identify happyDude and welcomeString by name. The XML syntax that is used to represent your name/value pairs follows [note the (partial) binary representation of the happy dude bitmap...]:

```
< data name="happyDude" mimetype="text/microsoft-urt/binary-serialized/base64" >
<value>
AAEAAAD/////AQAAAAAAAAMAgAAA

   ...
AAAAAAAAAAAAAAAAAAAA=
</value>
</data>
<data name="welcomeString">
<value>Hello new resource format!</value>
</data>
```

Programmatically Reading an *.resx File

To illustrate how you can load and investigate an *.resx file programmatically let's examine the code behind the "Read *resx" button. This time, make use of a ResXResourceReader type. Once the correct file has been opened, ask the reader for a reference to its IDictionaryEnumerator interface, and loop over each name/value pair:

```
protected void btnReadResxFile_Click (object sender, System.EventArgs e)
{
    // Make an resx reader.
    ResXResourceReader r = new ResXResourceReader("ResXForm.resx");
    // Grab the IDictionaryEnumerator interface and show everything.
    IDictionaryEnumerator en = r.GetEnumerator();
    while (en.MoveNext())
    {
        MessageBox.Show("Value:" + en.Value.ToString(),
                        "Key: " + en.Key.ToString());
    }
    r.Close();
}
```

When you click the button, you see a pair of message boxes pop up, as the ResXResourceReader type loops through the XML file for each named value.

Building the *.resources File

Now that you understand how to build and manipulate an *.resx file, you can make use of the resgen.exe utility to produce the binary equivalent. Again, VS .NET will do so automatically, but just for the love of learning, here is the raw command:

```
resgen resxform.resx resxform.resources
```

Of course, you must open a command prompt in the directory containing the *.resx file before running resgen.exe. Once you do, however, you are able to open the new *.resources file and check out the binary format (Figure 14-26).

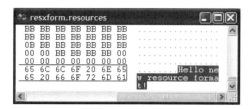

Figure 14-26. The binary *.resources file

Binding the *.resources File into a .NET Assembly

Cool! At this point you are able to add this *.resources file as a command-line argument to the C# compiler. Recall that doing so also requires you to reference each external assembly (e.g., System.Drawing.dll):

```
csc /resource:resxform.resources *.cs
```

If you were to now open your new assembly using ildasm.exe, you would find the entry shown in Figure 14-27 in the assembly's metadata.

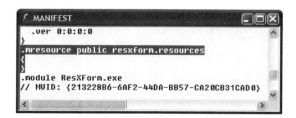

Figure 14-27. The embedded resources

As you can see, the manifest has recorded the name of the binary resources that are now contained in the owning assembly. In just a bit you will see how to programmatically read this information from an assembly to make use of it in your application.

SOURCE CODE   The ResXWriterReader.cs file is included under the Chapter 14 subdirectory.

Working with ResourceWriters

The previous example made use of the ResXResourceReader and ResXResourceWriter types to generate an XML file that contains name/value pairs for each application resource. The resulting *.resx file was then run through the resgen.exe utility. Finally the *.resources file was bound into the owning assembly using the /resource flag. The truth of the matter is that you do not need to build an *.resx file (although having an XML representation of your resources can come in handy, and is readable).

If you do not require an *.resx file, you can make use of the ResourceWriter type to directly create a binary *.resources file. To illustrate, assume you have created a new application named ResourceTest (again using Notepad and csc.exe). The Main() method of the ResourceGenerator class uses the ResourceWrite type to directly generate the myResources.resources file:

```
class ResourceGenerator
{
    static void Main(string[] args)
    {
        // Make a new *.resources file.
        ResourceWriter rw;
        rw = new ResourceWriter("myResources.resources");
        // Add 1 image and 1 string.
        rw.AddResource("happyDude", new Bitmap("happy.bmp"));
        rw.AddResource("welcomeString", "Welcome to .NET resources.");
        rw.Generate();
    }
}
```

At this point, compile and run the application to generate the *.resource file. Now, we can bind the contained binary data to the owning assembly as before:

```
csc /resource:myresources.resources *.cs
```

If you wish to read the raw name/value data from the binary *.resources file, you are free to make use of the ResourceReader class. This is almost identical to working with the ResXResourceWriter type.

Working with ResourceManagers

Rather than working with the ResourceReader class directly, you will most likely use the ResourceManager type. The reason is simple: It is easier to work with! Using the

ResourceManager, you are able to extract binary and textual data from an assembly for use in your application.

To illustrate, assume you have added a new class to the current project named MyResourceReader. This type uses a ResourceManager type to pull the happyDude and welcomeString resources from the assembly and dump them into a PictureBox and Label object using the GetObject() and GetString() members. Be very aware however, that the double quoted strings you send into these methods are *case sensitive*. Here is the code:

```
class MyResourceReader
{
    public static void ReadMyResources()
    {
        // Open the resources file.
        ResourceManager rm = new ResourceManager("myResources",
                Assembly.GetExecutingAssembly());
        // Load image resource.
        PictureBox p = new PictureBox();
        Bitmap b = (Bitmap)rm.GetObject("happyDude");
        p.Image = (Image)b;
        p.Height = b.Height;
        p.Width = b.Width;
        p.Location = new Point(10, 10);
        // Load string resource.
        Label label1 = new Label();
        label1.Location = new Point(50, 10);
        label1.Font = new Font( label1.Font.FontFamily, 12, FontStyle.Bold);
        label1.AutoSize = true;
        label1.Text = rm.GetString("welcomeString");
        // Build a Form to show the resources.
        Form f = new Form();
        f.Height = 100;
        f.Width = 370;
        f.Text = "These resources are embedded in the assembly!";
        // Add controls and show Form.
        f.Controls.Add(p);
        f.Controls.Add(label1);
        f.ShowDialog();
    }
}
```

Before you run the application, be sure to update Main() to call the ReadMyResources() method:

```
static void Main(string[] args)
{
    ...
    MyResourceReader.ReadMyResources();
}
```

When you run this application, you should find what appears in Figure 14-28.

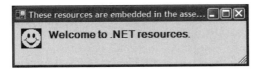

Figure 14-28. Reading (and using) embedded resources

SOURCE CODE   The ResourceTest project is included under the Chapter 14 subdirectory.

Automatic Resource Configuration a la Visual Studio .NET

To wrap things up, let's look at how the Visual Studio .NET IDE gets you up and running with the correct resource file configuration automatically. When you create a new Windows Forms project workspace using Visual Studio .NET, the IDE automatically defines an *.resx file for each Form in your application. Furthermore, when you insert new resources to a given Form, the name/value pairs contained in the *.resx file are updated on your behalf. You can view a Form's *.resx file by selecting the "Show all files" option from the Solution Explorer window (Figure 14-29).

*Figure 14-29. The underlying *.resx file for MainForm.cs*

Once you select this file, check out the Properties window. You will see that the build action for this file has been configured as "Embedded Resource" (Figure 14-30).

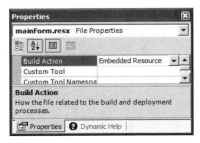

Figure 14-30. Under VS .NET, *.resx files are automatically embedded into your assembly.

This option compiles the *.resx file to produce the corresponding *.resources file, which is then embedded into your assembly. To illustrate updating *.resx files using VS .NET, create a new C# Windows Application workspace named ResLoader. The Form contains two PictureHolder types, one of which has its Image property set to the happy.bmp file, the other of which is empty. In addition, a single button type will be used to dynamically read this happy dude from file, and place it into the empty PictureHolder. The GUI is shown in Figure 14-31.

Figure 14-31. GUI of the ResLoader application

As you insert resources (such as a bitmap) into the project, the IDE responds by creating an instance of the ResourceManager type within the scope of your InitializeComponent() method:

```
private void InitializeComponent()
{
    // Note you need to specify the name of the Form that
    // maintains the embedded resources.
    System.Resources.ResourceManager resources =
        new System.Resources.ResourceManager (typeof(MainForm));
    ...
    pictureBox1.Image =
        (System.Drawing.Image) resources.GetObject ("pictureBox1.Image");
}
```

Needless to say, you are free to add a private ResourceManager member variable (or local variables) for use throughout your application. To illustrate, here is the code behind the button's Click event:

```
// Be sure to specify 'using System.Resources'
private void btnLoadRes_Click(object sender, System.EventArgs e)
{
    // Make a ResourceManager
    ResourceManager resources = new ResourceManager (typeof(MainForm));
    // Read happy dude from assembly and place it
    // into the second PictureBox object.
    this.pictureBox2.Image =
        ((System.Drawing.Bitmap)(resources.GetObject("pictureBox1.Image")));
    // All done!
    resources.ReleaseAllResources();
}
```

If you were to run the application and click the button, you would find that the image has been extracted from the assembly and placed into the second PictureBox (Figure 14-32).

Figure 14-32. Loading resources with the ResourceManager type

SOURCE CODE The ResLoader project is included under the Chapter 14 subdirectory.

That wraps up our look at GDI+. As you can guess, this .NET technology allows you to perform numerous other graphical manipulations. At this point you should have a solid understanding of the technology. You revisit GDI+ later in this text when you examine ASP.NET (as odd as that may seem). Until then, the next chapter addresses the use of Windows Forms widgets.

NOTE If you are interested in exploring GDI+ further (including printing support), be sure to check out *GDI+ Programming in C# and VB .NET* (Symmonds, Apress 2002).

Summary

GDI+ is the name given to a number of related .NET namespaces, each of which is used to render graphic images to a Control-derived type. The chapter began by examining the core types defined within the System.Drawing namespace (including a number of useful utility types), and examined various manners to intercept paint events.

The bulk of this chapter was spent examining how to work with core GDI+ object types such as colors, fonts, graphics images, pens, and brushes in conjunction with the almighty Graphics type. Along the way, you examined some GDI+-centric details such as hit-testing, and how to drag and drop images.

This chapter wrapped up by examining the new .NET resource format. As you have seen, an application does not *need* to bundle its external resources into the containing assembly, however, if your application does so, your binary image is far more portable. The *.resx file is used to describe a set of name/value pairs (a la XML). This file is fed into the resgen.exe utility, resulting in a binary format (*.resources) that can then be embedded into the owning assembly. The System.Resouces.ResourceManager type is your key to programmatically obtaining this information at runtime.

#### CHAPTER 15

Programming with Windows Forms Controls

THIS CHAPTER IS CONCERNED with providing a roadmap of the suite of GUI widgets defined in the System.Windows.Forms namespace. You have already had a chance to work with some Form-level control types such as MainMenu, MenuItem, StatusBar, and ToolBar (see Chapter 13); however, in this chapter, you will be examining various types that tend to exist within the boundaries of a Form's client area (e.g., Buttons, TextBoxes, Panels, and the like).

In addition to giving you a formal grounding in the Windows Forms Control set, this chapter also details a number of related topics, such as establishing the tab order for your widgets, as well as configuring the *docking* and *anchoring* behaviors for your family of GUI types. The chapter then investigates the process of building custom dialog boxes, including techniques for responding to (and validating) user input.

Next, you'll examine a new facility offered by the .NET Windows Forms architecture: Form inheritance. As you will see, it is now possible to establish "is-a" relationships between related Forms (which should make the MFC developers of the world insanely happy). Finally, we wrap things up with an examination of the process of building custom Windows Forms controls (which should make the ATL developers of the world insanely happy).

Understanding the Windows Forms Control Hierarchy

The System.Windows.Forms namespace contains a number of types that represent common GUI widgets that allow you to respond to user input in a Windows Forms application. Because .NET is a system of types built on standard OO principles, these controls are arranged in a hierarchy of related types. Figure 15-1 illustrates the big picture (note that System.Windows.Forms.Control is the common base class for all Windows Forms widgets.)

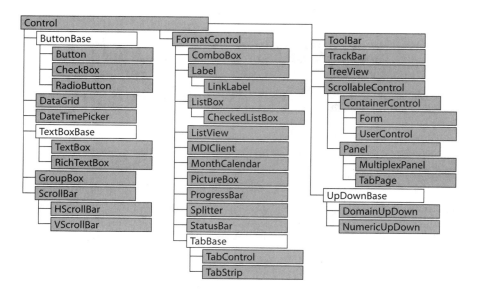

Figure 15-1. The Windows Forms control hierarchy

As you learned in Chapter 13, the System.Windows.Forms.Control type is the base class that provides a minimal and complete set of behaviors for all descending widgets. This includes the ability to process mouse and keyboard events, establish the physical dimensions of the widget using various properties (Height, Width, Left, Right, Location, and so on), manipulate background and foreground colors, establish the active font, and so forth. Also, the Control base type also defines members that control a widget's anchoring and docking behaviors (as seen later in this chapter).

As you read through this chapter, remember that the widgets examined in this chapter gain a good deal of their functionality from the System.Windows.Forms.Control base class. In this chapter we'll focus (more or less) on a given type's unique members.

Adding Controls to Forms (IDE-Free)

Regardless of which type of control you choose to place on a Form, you will follow a similar set of steps. First of all, you must define member variables that represent the GUI widgets maintained by the Form. Next, inside the Form's constructor (or within a helper method, called by the constructor), you'll configure the look and feel of each control using the exposed properties, methods, and events. Finally (and most important), once the control has been set to its initial state, it must be added into the Form's internal controls collection using the inherited Controls property. If you forget this final step, your widgets will *not* be visible at runtime! To illustrate this process in the raw, consider the MyForm class:

```
// Don't forget to add a reference to System.Windows.Forms.dll!
using System.Windows.Forms;
class MyForm : Form
{
```

```
      // Define a widget data member.
      private TextBox firstNameBox = new TextBox();
      public MyForm()
      {
          this.Text = "Controls in the raw";
          // Configure the widget.
          firstNameBox.Text = "Chucky";
          firstNameBox.Size = new Size(150, 50);
          firstNameBox.Location = new Point(10, 10);
          // Add new widget to the Form's Controls collection.
          this.Controls.Add(firstNameBox);
      }
...
}
```

The *Control$ControlCollection* Type

While the process of adding a new widget to a Form is quite simple, I'd like to discuss the Controls property in a bit more detail. This property returns a reference to a nested class named ControlCollection defined by the Control class (recall that a nested type can be denoted using the "$" token, e.g., Control$ControlCollection). The Control$ControlCollection type maintains an entry for each widget placed on the Form. You can obtain a reference to this collection anytime you wish to "walk the list" of child widgets:

```
// Get access to the Control$ControlCollection type for this Form.
Control.ControlCollection coll = this.Controls;
```

Once you have a reference to this collection, you can call any of the members described in Table 15-1. Be aware that by default controls are placed in the ControlCollection type using an $(n + 1)$ insertion policy.

Table 15-1. Nested ControlCollection Members

Control$ControlCollection Member	Meaning in Life
Add() AddRange()	Used to insert a new Control-derived type (or array of types) in the collection
Clear()	Removes all entries in the collection
Count	Returns the number of items in the collection
GetChildIndex() SetChildIndex()	Returns the index value for a specified item in the collection
GetEnumerator()	Returns the IEnumerator interface for this collection
Remove() RemoveAt()	Used to remove a control from the collection

To illustrate programmatic manipulation of this very important collection, assume you have now configured and added a new Button widget to the Form's collection (Figure 15-2).

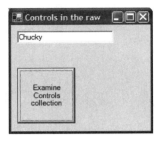

Figure 15-2. The Form's UI

Also assume you have written an event handler for the Button's Click event. In the implementation of this method, you loop over each item in the Controls collection and print out some relevant information regarding the contained members:

```csharp
class MyForm : Form
{
    private TextBox firstNameBox = new TextBox();
    private Button btnShowControls = new Button();
    public MyForm()
    {
        // Configure new TextBox.
        ...
        // Configure and add a new Button.
        btnShowControls.Text = "Examine Controls collection";
        btnShowControls.Size = new Size(90, 90);
        btnShowControls.Location = new Point(10, 70);
        btnShowControls.Click +=
            new EventHandler(btnShowControls_Clicked);
        this.Controls.Add(btnShowControls);
    }
    protected void btnShowControls_Clicked(object sender, EventArgs e)
    {
        Control.ControlCollection coll = this.Controls;
        string ctrs = "";
        foreach(Control c in coll)
        {
            if(c != null)
                ctrs += string.Format("Index: {0}, Text: {1}\n",
                        coll.GetChildIndex(c, false), c.Text);
        }
        MessageBox.Show(ctrs, "Index and Text values for each control");
    }
    ...
}
```

Notice how the call to GetChildIndex() allows you to obtain the numerical index of a given widget in the collection (the second Boolean parameter is used to control if an exception is raised in the case that the requested control is not found). If you run the application and click the Form's Button, you are presented with the information shown in Figure 15-3.

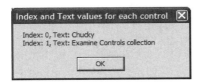

Figure 15-3. Interacting with a Form's Controls collection

Given that System.Windows.Forms.Control-derived types maintain a nested Control.ControlsCollection type, it stands to reason that you can dynamically add, hide, disable, or remove items using this collection at any point in a Form's lifetime (which can prove quite helpful if you need to dynamically generate new controls on the fly or restrict which controls should be displayed based on user preferences/ permissions).

Furthermore, also understand that it is completely possible to dynamically insert (or remove) Windows widgets into any descendent of System.Windows.Forms.Control (for example, adding RadioButton types to a GroupBox, TextBox types to a Panel, and so forth). We will see examples of this technique over the course of this chapter.

SOURCE CODE   The ControlsByHand project is included under the Chapter 15 subdirectory.

Adding Controls to Forms (via VS .NET)

Although you are always free to write Windows Forms code "in the raw," you will probably choose to use the Visual Studio .NET IDE instead. When you drop a widget from the Toolbox onto the form designer, the IDE responds by automatically adding the correct member variable to the Form-derived class on your behalf. Of course, you will typically want to change the name of this new variable (via the Properties window) to represent its overall functionality (e.g., "btnSubmitQuery" rather than the default "button1"). As you design the look and feel of the widget using the IDE's Properties window (Figure 15-4), the underlying code changes are added to the InitializeComponent() member function.

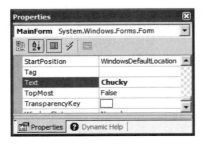

Figure 15-4. Design time property configuration

Be aware that this window allows you to configure not only the property set of a given GUI item, but the set of events as well (available by clicking the "lightning bolt" icon). Simply select the widget from the drop-down list and type in the name of the method to be called for the events you are interested in responding to (Figure 15-5).

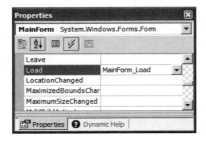

Figure 15-5. Design time event handling

If you examine the code generated in the InitializeComponent() method, you will find that the type has been configured based on your selections and inserted into the Control$ControlCollection automatically. For example, assume you have configured a TextBox type as follows:

```
private void InitializeComponent()
{
    this.firstNameBox = new System.Windows.Forms.TextBox();
    this.firstNameBox.Location = new System.Drawing.Point(32, 40);
    this.firstNameBox.TabIndex = 0;
    this.firstNameBox.Text = "Chucky";
    this.firstNameBox.TextChanged += new
        System.EventHandler(this.firstNameBox_TextChanged);
    this.AutoScaleBaseSize = new System.Drawing.Size(5, 13);
    this.ClientSize = new System.Drawing.Size(292, 273);
    this.Controls.AddRange(new System.Windows.Forms.Control[]
        { this.firstNameBox} );
    ...
}
```

Note that here you use VS .NET to handle the TextChanged event for the TextBox, and are thus provided with an empty event handler as well as the correct event registration syntax (an obvious benefit of this approach is that you are not the one in charge of determining the correct delegate used to handle a particular event):

```
protected void firstNameBox_TextChanged (object sender, System.EventArgs e)
{
    // Do whatever you need to do...
}
```

As you can see, the VS .NET IDE simply saves you some typing. The remainder of this chapter focuses on a number of behaviors offered by numerous GUI widgets by examining the "raw" code behind the scenes. If you decide to use the VS .NET IDE, be sure to examine the code generated inside the InitializeComponent() method to gain a true understanding of Windows Forms programming. Now that you understand the process of configuring and inserting types into a Form's Control collection, we can turn our attention to the specifics of various Windows Forms widgets.

The TextBox Control

The TextBox control is the first item under investigation. This GUI widget holds some blurb of text or possibly multiple lines of text. TextBox controls can also be configured as read-only and may support scroll bars. The immediate base class of TextBox is TextBoxBase, which provides many common behaviors for the TextBox and RichTextBox descendents. Table 15-2 describes some of the core properties provided by the TextBoxBase type.

Table 15-2. Members of the TextBoxBase Type

TextBoxBase Property	Meaning in Life
AcceptsTab	Indicates if pressing the Tab key in a multiline TextBox control tabs within the control itself, rather than moving the focus to the next control in the tab order.
AutoSize	Determines if the size of the control automatically adjusts when the assigned font is changed.
BackColor ForeColor	Get or set the background/foreground color of the control.
HideSelection	Gets or sets a value indicating whether the selected text in the TextBox control remains highlighted when the control loses focus.
MaxLength	Configures the maximum number of characters that can be entered into the TextBox control.
Modified	Gets or sets a value that indicates that the TextBox control has been modified by the user since the control was created or its contents were last set.

Table 15-2. Members of the TextBoxBase Type (Continued)

TextBoxBase Property	Meaning in Life
Multiline	Specifies if this TextBox can contain multiple lines of text.
ReadOnly	Marks this TextBox as read-only.
SelectedText SelectionLength SelectionStart	Contain the currently selected text (or some number of characters) in the control. SelectionStart gets or sets the starting point of text selected in the text box.
WordWrap	Indicates whether a multiline TextBox control automatically wraps words to the beginning of the next line when necessary.

The TextBoxBase type also defines a number of methods that allow the derived types to handle clipboard operations (via the Cut(), Copy(), and Paste() methods), undo operations (Undo(), of course), and carry out related functionality (Clear(), AppendText(), and so on).

As far as the events defined by TextBoxBase, the item of interest for this example is TextChanged (the Windows Forms equivalent of the raw EN_CHANGE message). As you may know, this event is fired whenever the content in a TextBoxBase-derived type is modified.

In addition to the behavior inherited by TextBoxBase, the TextBox type grabs a good deal of functionality from the Control base class. In fact, the properties defined by TextBox alone are quite limited, as you can see in Table 15-3.

Table 15-3. TextBox Properties

TextBox Property	Meaning in Life
AcceptsReturn	Gets or sets a value indicating whether pressing Enter in a multiline TextBox control creates a new line of text in the control or activates the default Button for the Form
CharacterCasing	Gets or sets whether the TextBox control modifies the case of characters as they are typed
PasswordChar	Gets or sets the character used to mask characters in a single-line TextBox control used to enter passwords
ScrollBars	Gets or sets which scroll bars should appear in a multiline TextBox control
TextAlign	Gets or sets how text is aligned in a TextBox control, using the HorizontalAlignment enumeration

Fun with TextBoxes

To illustrate some of the more exotic aspects of the TextBox, let's build a multiline text area that has been configured to accept Return and Tab keystrokes and supports a vertical scroll bar. Here is the configuration code (assume you have already defined a Form-level member variable of type TextBox named multiLineBox):

```
// Your first TextBox.
multiLineBox.Location = new System.Drawing.Point (152, 8);
multiLineBox.Text = "Type some stuff here (and hit the return and tab keys...)";
multiLineBox.Multiline = true;
multiLineBox.AcceptsReturn = true;
multiLineBox.ScrollBars = ScrollBars.Vertical;
multiLineBox.TabIndex = 0;
multiLineBox.AcceptsTab = true;
```

Notice that the ScrollBars property is assigned a value from the ScrollBars enumeration, which defines the following values:

```
public enum System.Windows.Forms.ScrollBars
{
    Both, Horizontal, None, Vertical
}
```

Now assume you have placed a Button on the Form and added an event handler for the Button's Click event. The implementation of this method simply places the TextBox's text in a message box:

```
protected void btnGetMultiLineText_Click (object sender, System.EventArgs e)
{
    MessageBox.Show(multiLineBox.Text, "Here is your text");
}
```

Next, add some additional TextBoxes to the Form, this time focusing on the masking capabilities of the widget. The second TextBox (capsOnlyBox) forces all keystrokes to be converted to uppercase. The third TextBox (passwordBox) forces all keystrokes to be converted to a password character (which I have chosen to be "$," signifying how your financial life as a .NET developer should pan out).

An additional Button (btnPasswordDecoderRing) supports a Click event handler that extracts the real keystrokes typed in the passwordBox TextBox widget, as shown here:

```
protected void btnPasswordDecoderRing_Click (object sender, System.EventArgs e)
{
    MessageBox.Show(passwordBox.Text, "Your password is:");
}
```

Here is the relevant code that configures these new TextBox types:

```
// The 'Caps Only!' widget.
// Note that CharacterCasing is established by an associated enumeration,
// which can be assigned Upper, Lower, or Normal.
capsOnlyBox.Location = new System.Drawing.Point (14, 176);
capsOnlyBox.CharacterCasing = System.Windows.Forms.CharacterCasing.Upper;
capsOnlyBox.Size = new System.Drawing.Size (120, 20);
// The password TextBox
passwordBox.Location = new System.Drawing.Point (160, 176);
passwordBox.PasswordChar = '$';
```

The final GUI can be seen in Figure 15-6.

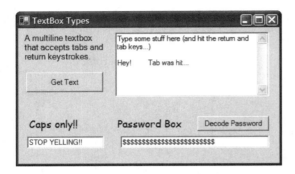

Figure 15-6. The many faces of the TextBox type

As mentioned, TextBoxBase has an additional derived type named RichTextBox. This class is a type that supports the display and manipulation of (highly) formatted text. For example, using this type you can configure support for multiple font selections, bulleted text, and so forth. I assume interested readers will consult online help for further details.

SOURCE CODE   The TextBoxes application is included under the Chapter 15 subdirectory.

The Mighty Button Type

Of all user interface widgets, the Button can be regarded as the simplest, but most well-respected GUI input device. The role of the System.Windows.Forms.Button type is to provide a simple vehicle for user input, typically in response to a mouse click or key press. The Button class immediately derives from an abstract type named ButtonBase, which provides a number of key behaviors for all Button-related types (CheckBox, RadioButton, and Button). Table 15-4 describes some (but by no means all) of the core properties of ButtonBase.

Table 15-4. ButtonBase Properties

ButtonBase Property	Meaning in Life
FlatStyle	Gets or sets the flat style appearance of the Button control, using members of the FlatStyle enumeration.
Image	Configures which (optional) image is displayed somewhere within the bounds of a ButtonBase-derived type. Recall that the Control class also defines a BackgroundImage property, which is used to render an image over the entire surface area of a widget.
ImageAlign	Sets the alignment of the image on the Button control, using the ContentAlignment enumeration.
ImageIndex ImageList	Work together to set the image list index value of the image displayed on the Button control from the corresponding ImageList control.
IsDefault	Specifies whether the Button control is the default Button (i.e., receives focus in response to pressing of the Enter key).
TextAlign	Gets or sets the alignment of the text on the Button control, using the ContentAlignment enumeration.

The Button class itself defines almost no additional functionality beyond that inherited by the ButtonBase base class, with the key exception of the DialogResult property. As you will see later in this chapter, a dialog box makes use of this property to return a value representing which Button was clicked (e.g., OK, Cancel, and so on) when the dialog box is terminated.

Configuring the Content Position

Most people assume that the text contained in a Button is always placed on the middle of the Button, equidistant from all sides. While this can be a well-established standard, the TextAlign property of the ButtonBase type makes it extremely simple to position text at just about any location. To set the position of your Button's caption, use the System.Drawing.ContentAlignment enumeration (which happens to be the same enumeration used to configure the location of any optional Button image):

```
public enum System.Drawing.ContentAlignment
{
    BottomCenter, BottomLeft,
    BottomRight, MiddleCenter,
    MiddleLeft, MiddleRight,
    TopCenter, TopLeft,
    TopRight
}
```

Fun with Buttons

To illustrate working with this most primitive of user input widgets, the following application uses the FlatStyle, ImageAlign, and TextAlign properties. The most interesting aspect of the underlying code is in the Click event handler for the btnStandard type (which would be the Button in the middle of the Form). The implementation of this method cycles through each member of the ContentAlignment enumeration and changes the Button's caption text and caption location based on the current value.

Also, the fourth Button on the Form (btnImage) supports a background image and a small bull's-eye icon, which is also dynamically relocated based on the current value of the ContentAlignment enumeration. Here is the relevant code:

```
public class ButtonForm: System.Windows.Forms.Form
{
    // You have four Buttons on this Form.
    private System.Windows.Forms.Button btnImage;
    private System.Windows.Forms.Button btnStandard;
    private System.Windows.Forms.Button btnPopup;
    private System.Windows.Forms.Button btnFlat;
    // Hold the current alignment value.
    ContentAlignment currAlignment = ContentAlignment.MiddleCenter;
    int currEnumPos = 0;
    ...
    protected void btnStandard_Click (object sender, System.EventArgs e)
    {
        // Get all possible values of the ContentAlignment enum.
        Array values = Enum.GetValues(currAlignment.GetType());
        // Bump the current position in the enum.
        // & check for wraparound.
        currEnumPos++;
        if(currEnumPos >= values.Length)
            currEnumPos = 0;
        // Change the current enum value.
        currAlignment =
            (ContentAlignment)ContentAlignment.Parse(currAlignment.GetType(),
            values.GetValue(currEnumPos).ToString());
        // Paint enum name on Button.
        btnStandard.Text = currAlignment.ToString();
        btnStandard.TextAlign = currAlignment;
        // Now assign the location of the icon on btnImage...
        btnImage.ImageAlign = currAlignment;
    }
    ...
}
```

The output can be seen in Figure 15-7.

Figure 15-7. The many faces of the Button type

 SOURCE CODE   The Buttons application is included under the Chapter 15 directory.

Working with CheckBoxes

The other two ButtonBase-derived types of interest are CheckBox (which can support up to three possible states) and RadioButton (which can be either selected or not selected). Like the Button, these types also receive most of their functionality from the Control base class. However, each class defines some additional functionality. First, consider the core properties of the CheckBox widget described in Table 15-5.

Table 15-5. CheckBox Properties

CheckBox Property	Meaning in Life
Appearance	Configures the appearance of a CheckBox control, using the Appearance enumeration.
AutoCheck	Gets or sets a value indicating whether the Checked or CheckState value and the CheckBox's appearance are automatically changed when it is clicked.
CheckAlign	Gets or sets the horizontal and vertical alignment of a CheckBox on a CheckBox control, using the ContentAlignment enumeration (see the Button type for a full description).

Table 15-5. CheckBox Properties (Continued)

CheckBox Property	Meaning in Life
Checked	Returns a Boolean value representing the state of the CheckBox (checked or unchecked). If the ThreeState property is set to true, the Checked property returns true for either checked or indeterminately checked values.
CheckState	Gets or sets a value indicating whether the CheckBox is checked, using a CheckState enumeration, rather than a Boolean value. This is very helpful when working with tristate CheckBoxes.
ThreeState	Configures whether the CheckBox supports three states of selection (as specified by the CheckState enumeration), rather than two.

Working with RadioButtons and GroupBoxes

The RadioButton type really requires little comment, given that it is (more or less) just a slightly redesigned CheckBox. In fact, the members of a RadioButton are almost identical to those of the CheckBox type. The only notable difference is the CheckedChanged event, which is fired when the Checked value changes. Also, the RadioButton type does not support the ThreeState property, as a RadioButton must be on or off.

Typically, multiple RadioButton objects are logically and physically grouped together to function as a whole. For example, if you have a set of four RadioButton types representing the color choice of a given automobile, you may wish to ensure that only one of the four types can be checked at a time. Rather than writing code programmatically to do so, use the GroupBox control. Like the RadioButton, there is little to say about the GroupBox control, given that it receives all of its functionality from the Control base class.

Fun with RadioButtons (and CheckBoxes)

To illustrate working with the CheckBox, RadioButton, and GroupBox types, let's create a new Windows Forms Application named CarConfig, which will be extended throughout this chapter. The main Form allows users to enter in (and confirm) information about a new vehicle they intend to purchase. The order summary is displayed in a Label type once the Confirm Order button has been clicked. Figure 15-8 shows the user interface.

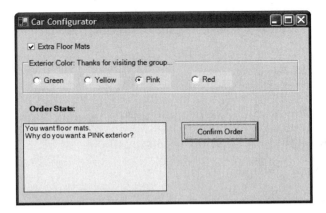

Figure 15-8. The initial UI of the CarConfig Form

Assume you have initialized a number of private member variables representing each GUI widget. First, you have your CheckBox, constructed as shown here:

```
// Create your CheckBox.
checkFloorMats.Location = new System.Drawing.Point (16, 16);
checkFloorMats.Text = "Extra Floor Mats";
checkFloorMats.Size = new System.Drawing.Size (136, 24);
checkFloorMats.FlatStyle = FlatStyle.Popup;
// Add to Control collection.
this.Controls.Add (this.checkFloorMats);
```

Programmatically speaking, when you wish to place a widget under the ownership of a related GroupBox, you want to add each item to the GroupBox's Controls collection (in the same way you add widgets to the Form's Controls collection). To make things a bit more interesting, respond to the Enter and Leave events sent by the GroupBox object as shown here:

```
// Yellow RadioButton.
radioYellow.Location = new System.Drawing.Point (96, 24);
radioYellow.Text = "Yellow";
radioYellow.Size = new System.Drawing.Size (64, 23);
// Green, Red, and Pink RadioButtons configured in a similar vein.
...
// Now build the group of radio items.
groupBox1.Location = new System.Drawing.Point (16, 56);
groupBox1.Text = "Exterior Color";
groupBox1.Size = new System.Drawing.Size (264, 88);
groupBox1.Leave += new System.EventHandler (groupBox1_Leave);
groupBox1.Enter += new System.EventHandler (groupBox1_Enter);
groupBox1.Controls.Add (this.radioPink);
groupBox1.Controls.Add (this.radioYellow);
groupBox1.Controls.Add (this.radioRed);
groupBox1.Controls.Add (this.radioGreen);
```

Understand, of course, that you do not *need* to capture the Enter or Leave events for a GroupBox. However, to illustrate, the event handlers update the caption text of the GroupBox as shown here:

```
// Figure out when the focus is in your group.
protected void groupBox1_Leave (object sender, System.EventArgs e)
{
    groupBox1.Text = "Exterior Color: Thanks for visiting the group...";
}
protected void groupBox1_Enter (object sender, System.EventArgs e)
{
    groupBox1.Text = "Exterior Color: You are in the group...";
}
```

The final GUI widgets on this Form (the Label and Button types) also need to be configured and inserted in the Form's Controls collection. The Label is used to display the order confirmation, which is formatted in the Click event handler of the order Button, as shown here:

```
protected void btnOrder_Click (object sender, System.EventArgs e)
{
    // Build a string to display information.
    string orderInfo = "";
    if(checkFloorMats.Checked)
        orderInfo += "You want floor mats.\n";
    if(radioRed.Checked)
        orderInfo += "You want a red exterior.\n";
    if(radioYellow.Checked)
        orderInfo += "You want a yellow exterior.\n";
    if(radioGreen.Checked)
        orderInfo += "You want a green exterior.\n";
    if(radioPink.Checked)
        orderInfo += "Why do you want a PINK exterior?\n";
    // Send this string to the Label.
    infoLabel.Text = orderInfo;
}
```

Notice that both the CheckBox and RadioButton support the Checked property, which allows you to investigate the state of the widget. Recall that if you have configured a tristate CheckBox, you will need to check the state of the widget using the CheckState property.

Examining the CheckedListBox Control

Now that you have explored the basic Button-centric widgets, let's move on to the set of list selection-centric types, specifically, CheckedListBox, ListBox, and ComboBox. The CheckedListBox widget allows you to group together related CheckBox options in a scrollable list control. Assume you have added such a control to your CarConfig application that allows the user to configure a number of options for regarding the automobile's sound system (Figure 15-9).

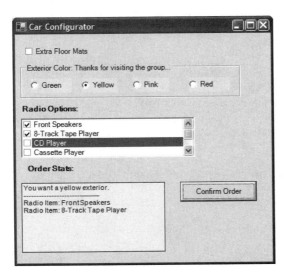

Figure 15-9. The CheckedListBox type

Like the controls examined thus far, the CheckedListBox type gains most of its functionality from the Control base class type. Also, the CheckedListBox type inherits additional functionality from its direct base class, ListBox (examined later in this chapter).

To insert new items in a CheckedListBox, call Add() for each item or use the AddRange() method and send in an array of objects (strings, to be exact) that represent the full set of checkable items. Here is the configuration code (be sure to check out online help for details about these new properties):

```
// Configure the CheckedListBox.
checkedBoxRadioOptions.Location = new System.Drawing.Point (16, 48);
checkedBoxRadioOptions.Cursor = Cursors.Hand;
checkedBoxRadioOptions.Size = new System.Drawing.Size (256, 64);
checkedBoxRadioOptions.CheckOnClick = true;
// Add items to the CheckedListBox.
checkedBoxRadioOptions.Items.AddRange(new object[6]
    { "Front Speakers", "8-Track Tape Player",
    "CD Player", "Cassette Player",
    "Rear Speakers", "Ultra Base Thumper"} );
// As always, add the new widget to the Controls collection.
this.Controls.Add (this.checkedBoxRadioOptions);
```

Now update the logic behind the Click event for the Order Button. Ask the CheckedListBox which of its items are currently selected and add them to the orderInfo string. Here are the relevant code updates:

```
protected void btnOrder_Click (object sender, System.EventArgs e)
{
    // Build a string to display information.
    string orderInfo = "";
    ...
    // For each item in the CheckedListBox:
    for(int i = 0; i < checkedBoxRadioOptions.Items.Count; i++)
    {
        // Is the current item checked?
        if(checkedBoxRadioOptions.GetItemChecked(i))
        {
            // Get text of checked item and append to orderinfo string.
            orderInfo += "Radio Item: ";
            orderInfo += checkedBoxRadioOptions.Items[i].ToString();
            orderInfo += "\n";
        }
    }
    ...
}
```

The final note regarding the CheckedListBox type is that it supports the use of multiple columns through the inherited MultiColumn property. Thus, if you make the following update:

```
checkedBoxRadioOptions.MultiColumn = true;
checkedBoxRadioOptions.ColumnWidth = 130;
```

You see the multicolumn CheckedListBox shown in Figure 15-10.

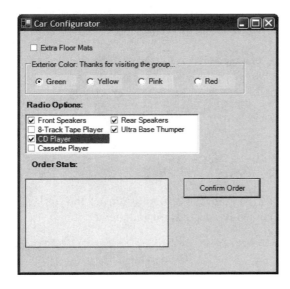

Figure 15-10. Multicolumn CheckedListBox type

ListBoxes and ComboBoxes

As mentioned, the CheckedListBox type inherits most of its functionality from the ListBox type. To illustrate using the ListBox type, let's add another feature to the current CarConfig application: the ability to select the make (BMW, Yugo, and so on) of the automobile. Figure 15-11 shows the desired UI.

Figure 15-11. The ListBox type

As always, begin by creating a member variable to manipulate your type (in this case a ListBox type). Next, configure the look and feel and insert the new widget in the Form's Controls collection, as shown here:

```
// Configure the list box.
carMakeList.Location = new System.Drawing.Point (168, 48);
carMakeList.Size = new System.Drawing.Size (112, 67);
carMakeList.BorderStyle = System.Windows.Forms.BorderStyle.FixedSingle;
carMakeList.ScrollAlwaysVisible = true;
carMakeList.Sorted = true;
// Populate the listBox using the AddRange() method.
carMakeList.Items.AddRange( new object[9] { "BMW", "Caravan", "Ford",
    "Grand Am", "Jeep", "Jetta", "Saab", "Viper", "Yugo"} );
// Add new widget to Form's Control collection.
this.Controls.Add (this.carMakeList);
```

The update to the btnOrder_Click() event handler is also simple, as shown here:

```
protected void btnOrder_Click (object sender, System.EventArgs e)
{
    // Build a string to display information.
    string orderInfo = "";
    ...
    // Get the currently selected item (not index of the item).
    if(carMakeList.SelectedItem != null)
        orderInfo += "Make: " + carMakeList.SelectedItem + "\n";
    ...
}
```

Fun with ComboBoxes

Like a ListBox, a ComboBox allows the user to make a selection from a well-defined set of possibilities. However, the ComboBox type is unique in that the user can also insert additional items. Recall that ComboBox derives from ListBox (which then derives from Control). To illustrate its use, add yet another GUI widget to the CarConfig application that allows a user to enter the name of a preferred salesperson. If the salesperson in question is not on the list, the user can enter a custom name. The GUI update is shown in Figure 15-12.

Figure 15-12. The ComboBox type

This modification begins with configuring the ComboBox itself. As you can see here, the logic looks identical to that for the ListBox:

```
// ComboBox configuration.
comboSalesPerson.Location = new System.Drawing.Point (152, 16);
comboSalesPerson.Size = new System.Drawing.Size (128, 21);
comboSalesPerson.Items.AddRange( new object[4]
    { "Baby Ry-Ry", "SPARK!", "Danny Boy",
    "Karin 'Baby' Johnson"} );
this.Controls.Add (this.comboSalesPerson);
```

The update to the btnOrder_Click() event handler is again simple, as shown here:

```
protected void btnOrder_Click (object sender, System.EventArgs e)
{
    // Build a string to display information.
    string orderInfo = "";
    ...
    // Use the Text property to figure out the user's salesperson.
    if(comboSalesPerson.Text != "")
        orderInfo += "Sales Person: " + comboSalesPerson.Text + "\n";
    else
        orderInfo += "You did not select a sales person!" + "\n";
    ...
}
```

The MonthCalendar Control

The System.Windows.Forms namespace provides an extremely useful widget that allows the user to select a date (or range of dates) using a friendly user interface: the MonthCalendar control. To showcase this new control, update the existing CarConfig application to allow the user to enter in the new vehicle's delivery date. Figure 15-13 shows the updated (and slightly rearranged) Form.

Figure 15-13. The MonthCalendar type

To begin understanding this new type, examine the core MonthCalendar properties described in Table 15-6.

Table 15-6. MonthCalendar Properties

MonthCalendar Property	Meaning in Life
BoldedDates	The array of DateTime objects that determine dates are shown in bold.
CalendarDimensions	The number of columns and rows of months displayed in the MonthCalendar control.
FirstDayOfWeek	The first day of the week for the MonthCalendar control.
MaxDate	The maximum allowable date that can be selected. (The default is no maximum date.)
MaxSelectionCount	The maximum number of days that can be selected in a MonthCalendar control.
MinDate	The minimum allowable date that can be selected. (The default is no minimum date.)

Table 15-6. MonthCalendar Properties (Continued)

MonthCalendar Property	Meaning in Life
MonthlyBoldedDates	The array of DateTime objects that determine which monthly days to bold.
SelectionEnd	Indicates the end date of the selected range of dates.
SelectionRange	Retrieves the selection range for a MonthCalendar control.
SelectionStart	Indicates the start date of the selected range of dates.
ShowToday ShowTodayCircle	Indicate whether the MonthCalendar control displays the today date at the bottom of the control, as well as circle the current date.
ShowWeekNumbers	Indicates whether the MonthCalendar control displays the week numbers (1–52) to the left of each row of days.
TodayDate	The date shown as Today in the MonthCalendar control. By default, Today is the current date at the time the MonthCalendar control is created.
TodayDateSet	Indicates whether or not the TodayDate property has been explicitly set by the user. If TodayDateSet is true, TodayDate returns whatever the user has set it to.

Although the MonthCalendar control offers a fair bit of functionality, it is very simple to programmatically capture the range of dates selected by the user. The default behavior of this type is to always select (and circle) today's date automatically. To obtain the currently selected date programmatically, you can update the Click event handler for the order Button, as shown here:

```
protected void btnOrder_Click (object sender, System.EventArgs e)
{
    // Build a string to display information.
    string orderInfo = "";
    ...
    // Get ship date.
    DateTime d = monthCalendar.SelectionStart;
    string dateStr = string.Format("{0}/{1}/{2}", d.Month, d.Day, d.Year);
    orderInfo += "Car will be sent: " + dateStr;
    ...
}
```

Notice that you can ask the MonthCalendar control for the currently selected date by using the SelectionStart property. This property returns a DateTime reference, which you store in a local variable. Using a handful of properties of the DateTime type, you can extract out the information you need in a custom format. (Note that this type returns the clock time as well, which you are not interested in.)

At this point I assume the user will specify exactly one day on which to deliver the new auto. However, what if you want to allow the user to select a range of possible shipping dates? In that case all the user needs to do is drag the cursor across the range of possible shipping dates (Figure 15-14).

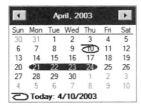

Figure 15-14. Selecting multiple dates

You already have seen that you can obtain the start of the selection using the SelectionStart property. The end of the selection can be determined using the SelectionEnd property. Here is the code update:

```
protected void btnOrder_Click (object sender, System.EventArgs e)
{
    // Build a string to display information.
    string orderInfo = "";
    ...
    // Get ship date range....
    DateTime startD = monthCalendar.SelectionStart;
    DateTime endD = monthCalendar.SelectionEnd;
    string dateStartStr = string.Format("{0}/{1}/{2}", startD.Month, startD.Day,
    startD.Year);
    string dateEndStr = string.Format("{0}/{1}/{2}", endD.Month, endD.Day, endD.Year);
    // The DateTime type supports overloaded operators!
    if(dateStartStr != dateEndStr)
    {
        orderInfo += "Car will be sent between "
        + dateStartStr + " and\n" + dateEndStr;
    }
    else    // They picked a single date.
        orderInfo += "Car will be sent on "  + dateStartStr;
    ...
}
```

More on the DateTime Type

In the current example, you extracted a DateTime type from the MonthCalendar widget using the SelectionStart and SelectionEnd properties. After this point, you used the Month, Day, and Year properties to build a custom format string. While this is permissible, it is not optimal, given that the DateTime type has a number of built-in formatting options (Table 15-7).

Table 15-7. DateTime Members

DateTime Member	Meaning in Life
Date	Retrieves the date of the instance with the time value set to midnight.
Day Month Year	Extract the day, month, and year of the current DateTime type.
DayOfWeek	Retrieves the day of the week represented by this instance.
DayOfYear	Retrieves the day of the year represented by this instance.
Hour Minute Second Millisecond	Extract various time-related details from a DateTime variable.
MaxValue MinValue	Represent the minimum and maximum DateTime value.
Now Today	These *static* members retrieve a DateTime type representing the current date and time (Now) or date (Today).
Ticks	Retrieves the 100-nanosecond tick count for this instance.
ToLongDateString() ToLongTimeString() ToShortDateString() ToShortTimeString()	Convert the current value of the DateTime type to a string representation.

Using these members, you can replace the previous formatting you programmed by hand with the following (you will see no change in the program's output):

```
string dateStartStr = startD.Date.ToShortDateString();
string dateEndStr = endD.Date.ToShortDateString();
```

Setting the Form's Default Input Button

Many user input Forms (especially dialog boxes) have a particular Button that will automatically respond to the user hitting the Enter key. For the CarConfig Form, if you wish to ensure that when the user hits the Enter key, simply make use of the Form's AcceptButton property:

```
this.AcceptButton = this.btnOrder;
```

Configuring the Tab Order

Next up, let's address the issue of tab order. As you know, when a Form or dialog box contains multiple GUI widgets, users expect to be able to shift focus using the Tab key. Configuring the tab order for your set of controls requires that you understand two key properties: TabStop and TabIndex.

The TabStop property can be set to true or false, based on whether or not you wish this GUI item to be reachable using the Tab key. Assuming the TabStop property has been set to true for a given widget, the TabOrder property is then set to establish its order of activation in the tabbing sequence (which is zero based). Consider this example:

```
// Configure tabbing properties.
radioRed.TabIndex = 2;
radioRed.TabStop = true;
```

The Tab Order Wizard

The Visual Studio .NET IDE supplies a Tab Order Wizard, accessed using the View | Tab Order menu selection. Once activated, your design time Form displays the current TabIndex value for each widget. To change these values, click each item in the order you choose (Figure 15-15).

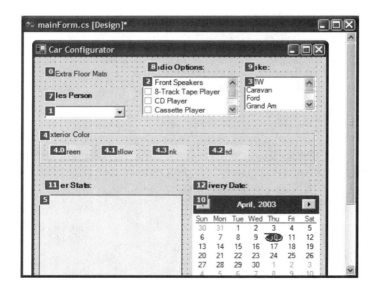

Figure 15-15. The VS .NET Tab Order Wizard

To exit this Tab Order Wizard, simply hit the Esc key.

Assigning ToolTips to Controls

To finish up the CarConfig Form, we have one final point of interest. Most modern user interfaces support tool tips. In the System.Windows.Forms namespace, the ToolTip type represents this functionality. These widgets are simply small floating windows that display a helpful message when the cursor hovers over a given item. Table 15-8 describes the core members of the ToolTip type.

Table 15-8. ToolTip Members

ToolTip Member	Meaning in Life
Active	Configures if the tool tip is activated or not. For example, perhaps you have a menu item that disables all tool tips for advanced users. This property allows you to turn off the pop-up text.
AutomaticDelay	Gets or sets the time (in milliseconds) that passes before the ToolTip appears.
AutoPopDelay	The period of time (in milliseconds) that the ToolTip remains visible when the cursor is stationary in the ToolTip region. The default value is 10 times the AutomaticDelay property value.
GetToolTip()	Returns the tool tip text assigned to a specific control.
InitialDelay	The period of time (in milliseconds) that the cursor must remain stationary in the ToolTip region before the ToolTip text is displayed. The default is equal to the AutomaticDelay property.
ReshowDelay	The length of time (in milliseconds) that it takes subsequent ToolTip instances to appear as the cursor moves from one ToolTip region to another. The default is 1/5 of the AutomaticDelay property value.
SetToolTip()	Associates a tool tip to a specific control.

To illustrate, add a tool tip to the CarConfig's Calendar type. Begin by creating a new member variable of type ToolTip. Next, configure the set of properties for the new item. Notice that you make a call to SetToolTip(), which configures not only the text to be displayed, but also the widget to which it is assigned:

```
// Create and associate a tool tip to the calendar
calendarTip.Active = true;
calendarTip.SetToolTip (monthCalendar,
    "Please select the date (or dates)\n when we can deliver your new car!");
```

Adding ToolTips at Design Time

If you wish to leverage the Visual Studio .NET IDE to build your tool tips, begin by adding a ToolTip widget to your Form using the Toolbox window. At this point, you can configure the ToolTip using the Properties window. To associate the new tip with a given widget, select the widget that should activate the tip and set the "ToolTip on" property (Figure 15-16).

Figure 15-16. Associating a ToolTip to a given widget

SOURCE CODE   The CarConfig project is included under the Chapter 15 directory.

The TrackBar Control

The TrackBar control allows users to select from a range of values, using a scroll bar–like input mechanism. In many respects a TrackBar is functionally similar to a traditional scroll bar. When working with this type, you need to set the minimum and maximum range, the minimum and maximum change increments, and the starting location of the slider's thumb. Each of these aspects can be set using the properties described in Table 15-9.

Table 15-9. TrackBar Properties

TrackBar Property	Meaning in Life
LargeChange	The number of ticks by which the TrackBar changes when an event considered a large change occurs (e.g., clicking the mouse button while the cursor is on the sliding range and using the Page Up or Page Down key).
Maximum Minimum	Configure the upper and lower bounds of the TrackBar's range.
Orientation	The orientation for this TrackBar. Valid values are from the Orientation enumeration (i.e., horizontally or vertically).
SmallChange	The number of ticks by which the TrackBar changes when an event considered a small change occurs (e.g., using the arrow keys).
TickFrequency	Indicates how many ticks are drawn. For a TrackBar with an upper limit of 200, it is impractical to draw all 200 ticks on a control 2 inches long. If you set the TickFrequency property to 5, the TrackBar draws 20 total ticks (each tick represents 5 units).
TickStyle	Indicates how the TrackBar control draws itself. This affects both where the ticks are drawn in relation to the movable thumb and how the thumb itself is drawn (using the TickStyle enumeration).
Value	Gets or sets the current location of the TrackBar. Use this property to obtain the numeric value contained by the TrackBar for use in your application.

Now you can build an application that makes use of three TrackBars. Each widget has an upper range of 255 and a lower range of 0. As the user slides each thumb, the application intercepts the Scroll event and dynamically builds a new Color type based on the value of each slider. In this way, the user is able to view the underlying RGB value (and see the color) for a given selection. (Of course, the System.Windows.Forms namespace already provides a ColorDialog type for this purpose.)

First you need to configure each TrackBar. Assume your Form contains three private TrackBar member variables (redTrackBar, greenTrackBar, and blueTrackBar). Here is the relevant code for blueTrackBar (the remaining bars look almost identical, with the exception of the name of the Scroll event handler):

```
// Here is the blue TrackBar.
blueTrackBar.TickFrequency = 5;
blueTrackBar.Location = new System.Drawing.Point (104, 200);
blueTrackBar.TickStyle = System.Windows.Forms.TickStyle.TopLeft;
blueTrackBar.Maximum = 255;
blueTrackBar.Scroll += new System.EventHandler (this.blueTrackBar_Scroll);
```

Note that the default minimum value of the TrackBar is 0 and thus does not need to be explicitly set. In the event handlers for each TrackBar, you make a call to an internal private helper function named UpdateColor(), which does the real grunt work, as shown here:

```
protected void blueTrackBar_Scroll (object sender, System.EventArgs e)
{
    UpdateColor();
}
```

UpdateColor() is responsible for two major tasks. First you read the current value of each TrackBar and send this state data to a new Color variable (using the FromArgb() member). Once you have the newly configured color, you update a Form-level member variable of type PictureBox (named colorBox), which in this case does not hold an actual bitmap image, but simply maintains the current background color. Finally, the UpdateColor() method formats this information in a string placed on the Form's color display label (lblCurrColor), as shown here:

```
private void UpdateColor()
{
    // Get the new color.
    Color c = Color.FromArgb(redTrackBar.Value,
                    greenTrackBar.Value, blueTrackBar.Value);
    // Change the color in the PictureBox.
    colorBox.BackColor = c;
    // Set color label.
    lblCurrColor.Text =
        string.Format("Current color is: ({0}, {1}, {2})",
        redTrackBar.Value, greenTrackBar.Value,
        blueTrackBar.Value);
}
```

The final detail is to set the initial values of each slider when the Form comes to life and render the current color, as shown here:

```
public TrackForm()
{
    InitializeComponent();
    CenterToScreen();
    // Set initial position of each slider.
    redTrackBar.Value = 100;
    greenTrackBar.Value = 255;
    blueTrackBar.Value = 0;
    UpdateColor();
}
```

Working with Panel Controls

As you have seen earlier in this chapter, the GroupBox control can be used to logically bind a number of controls (such as RadioButtons) to function as a collective. Closely related to the GroupBox is the Panel control. Panels are also used to group related controls in a logical unit. One difference is that the Panel type derives from the ScrollableControl class, and thus it can support scroll bars, which is not possible with a GroupBox.

Panels can be used to conserve screen real estate. For example, if you have a group of controls that take up the entire bottom half of a Form, you can contain them in a Panel that is half the size and set the AutoScroll property to true. In this way, the user can use the scroll bar(s) to view the hidden items. To illustrate, let's update the previous TrackBar application. This time, each TrackBar is contained in a single Panel. Figure 15-17 shows the update.

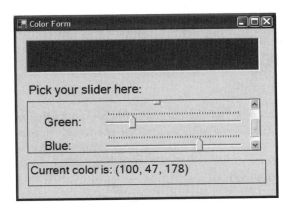

Figure 15-17. Working with Panel types

The underlying code looks almost identical to that of manipulating a GroupBox. Begin by declaring a Panel data member (panel1) and add each item using the Controls property, as shown here:

```
// Configure the panel.
panel1.AutoScroll = true;
panel1.Controls.Add (this.label2);
panel1.Controls.Add (this.blueTrackBar);
panel1.Controls.Add (this.label3);
panel1.Controls.Add (this.greenTrackBar);
panel1.Controls.Add (this.redTrackBar);
panel1.Controls.Add (this.label1);
```

 SOURCE CODE The Tracker application can be found under the Chapter 15 directory.

The UpDown Controls: DomainUpDown and NumericUpDown

Windows Forms provide two widgets that function as *spin controls* (also known as *up/down controls*). Like the ComboBox and ListBox types, these new items also allow the user to choose an item from a range of possible selections. The difference is that when using a DomainUpDown or NumericUpDown control, the information is selected using a small pair of up and down arrows. For example, check out Figure 15-18.

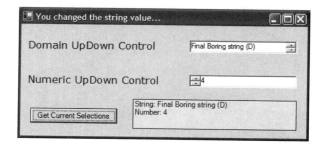

Figure 15-18. Working with UpDown types

Given your work with previous (and similar) types, you should find working with the UpDown widgets painless. The DomainUpDown widget allows the user to select from a set of string data. NumericUpDown allows selections from a range of numeric data points. Each widget derives from a common direct base class: UpDownBase. Table 15-10 describes some important properties of this class.

Table 15-10. UpDownBase Properties

UpDownBase Property	Meaning in Life
InterceptArrowKeys	Gets or sets a value indicating whether the user can use the Up Arrow and Down Arrow keys to select values
ReadOnly	Gets or sets a value indicating whether the text can only be changed by the use of the up or down arrows and not by typing in the control to locate a given string
Text	Gets or sets the current text displayed in the spin control
TextAlign	Gets or sets the alignment of the text in the spin control
UpDownAlign	Gets or sets the alignment of the up and down arrows on the spin control, using the LeftRightAlignment enumeration

The DomainUpDown control adds a small set of properties (Table 15-11) that allow you to configure and manipulate the textual data in the widget.

Table 15-11. DomainUpDown Properties

DomainUpDown Property	Meaning in Life
Items	Allows you to gain access to the set of types stored in the widget
SelectedIndex	Returns the zero-based index of the currently selected item
SelectedItem	Returns the selected item itself (not its index)
Sorted	Configures whether or not the strings should be alphabetized
Wrap	Controls if the collection of items continues to the first or last item if the user continues past the end of the list

The NumericUpDown type is just as simple (Table 15-12).

Table 15-12. NumericUpDown Properties

NumericUpDown Property	Meaning in Life
DecimalPlaces ThousandsSeparator Hexadecimal	Used to configure how the numerical data is to be displayed.
Increment	Sets the numerical value to increment the value in the control when the up or down arrow is clicked. The default is to advance the value by 1.
Minimum Maximum	Sets the upper and lower limits of the value in the control.
Value	Returns the current value in the control.

Here is the code behind the sample application:

```
// Configure DomainUpDown widget.
domainUpDown.Sorted = true;
domainUpDown.Wrap = true;
domainUpDown.Items.AddRange( new object[4] { "Another Boring String named B",
    "Boring String A", "BORING String C", "Final Boring string (D)"} );
domainUpDown.SelectedIndex = 2;
// Configure NumericUpDown widget.
numericUpDown.Maximum = new decimal (5000);
numericUpDown.ThousandsSeparator = true;
numericUpDown.UpDownAlign = LeftRightAlignment.Left;
```

The Click event handler for the Form's Button type simply asks each type for its current value and places it in the appropriate Label as a formatted string, as shown here:

```
protected void btnGetSelections_Click (object sender, System.EventArgs e)
{
    // Get info from updowns...
    lblCurrSel.Text =
        string.Format("String: {0}\nNumber: {1}",
        domainUpDown.Text, numericUpDown.Value);
}
```

Of course, the DomainUpDown and NumericUpDown types support a number of events. If you ever need to capture when the selection changes, you can use SelectedItemChanged (for DomainUpDown types) or ValueChanged (for NumericUpDown types). Here is an example:

```
// Intercept the SelectedItemChanged event.
domainUpDown.SelectedItemChanged
    += new EventHandler (domainUpDown_SelectedItemChanged);
...
// Handle the event.
protected void domainUpDown_SelectedItemChanged (object sender,
                                                 System.EventArgs e)
{
    this.Text = "You changed the string value...";
}
```

SOURCE CODE   The UpAndDown application is included under the Chapter 15 directory.

Working with the ErrorProvider

Most Windows Forms applications will need to validate user input in one way or another. This is especially true with dialog boxes, as you should inform users if they make a processing error before continuing forward. (I'll examine dialog box programming later in this chapter.)

The ErrorProvider type can be used to provide a visual cue of user input error. For example, assume you have a Form containing a TextBox and Button widget. If the user enters more than five characters in the TextBox, the error information shown in Figure 15-19 is displayed.

Figure 15-19. The ErrorProvider in action

Here, you have detected that the user entered more than five characters and responded by placing a small error icon (!) next to the TextBox object. When the user places the cursor over this icon, the descriptive error text appears as a pop-up. Also, this ErrorProvider is configured to cause the icon to blink a number of times to strengthen the visual cue (which, of course, you can't see without running the application).

If you wish to support this type of input validation, the first step is to understand the properties of the Control class (Table 15-13).

Table 15-13. Control Properties

Control Property	Meaning in Life
CausesValidation	Indicates whether selecting this control causes validation on the controls requiring validation
Validated	Occurs when the control is finished performing its validation logic
Validating	Occurs when the control is validating user input (e.g., when the control loses focus)

Every GUI widget can set the CausesValidation property to true or false. (The default is false.) If you set this bit of state data to true, the control forces the other controls on the Form to validate themselves when it receives focus (provided the CausesValidation property is also set to true).

Once a validating control has received focus, the Validating and Validated events are fired for each control. It is in the scope of the Validating event handler in which you configure a corresponding ErrorProvider. Optionally, the Validated event can be handled to determine when the control has finished its validation cycle.

To begin, assume you have set the CausesValidation property to true for the Button and TextBox and have added a member variable of type ErrorProvider. Here is the configuration code:

```
// Configure the error provider.
errorProvider1.DataMember = "";
errorProvider1.DataSource = null;
errorProvider1.ContainerControl = null;
errorProvider1.BlinkStyle = System.Windows.Forms.ErrorBlinkStyle.AlwaysBlink;
errorProvider1.BlinkRate = 500;
```

The ErrorProvider type has a small set of members. The most important item for your purposes is the BlinkStyle property, which can be set to any of the values of the ErrorBlinkStyle enumeration described in Table 15-14.

Table 15-14. ErrorBlinkStyle Properties

ErrorBlinkStyle Property	Meaning in Life
AlwaysBlink	Causes the error icon to blink when the error is first displayed or when a new error description string is set for the control and the error icon is already displayed
BlinkIfDifferentError	Causes the error icon to blink only if the error icon is already displayed, but a new error string is set for the control
NeverBlink	Indicates the error icon never blinks

The ErrorProvider also has additional members beyond BlinkStyle and BlinkRate. For example, if you wish to associate a custom icon to the error, you can do so using the Icon property. Nevertheless, once you have configured how the ErrorProvider looks and feels, you bind the error to the TextBox within the scope of its Validating event handler, as shown here:

```
protected void txtInput_Validating (object sender, CancelEventArgs e)
{
    // Check if the text length is greater than 5.
    if(txtInput.Text.Length > 5)
    {
        errorProvider1.SetError( txtInput, "Can't be greater than 5!");
    }
    else // Things are OK, don't show anything.
        errorProvider1.SetError(txtInput, "");
}
```

SOURCE CODE   The ErrorProvider application is included under the Chapter 15 directory.

Configuring a Control's Anchoring Behavior

When you are creating a Form containing widgets, you need to decide whether the Form should be resizable. Typically speaking, main windows are resizable, whereas dialog boxes are not. To configure the resizability of your Form, adjust the FormBorderStyle property to any of the values described in Table 15-15.

Table 15-15. FormBorderStyle Properties

FormBorderStyle Property	Meaning in Life
Fixed3D	A nonresizable, three-dimensional border
FixedDialog	A thick, nonresizable dialog box–style border
FixedSingle	A nonresizable, single-line border
FixedToolWindow	A tool window border that is not resizable
None	No border at all
Sizable	A resizable border
SizableToolWindow	A resizable tool window border

Assume that you have configured your Form to be resizable. This brings up some interesting questions regarding the contained controls. For example, if the user makes the Form smaller than the rectangle needed to display each control, should the controls adjust their size (and possibly location) to morph correctly with the Form?

In the Windows Forms worldview, the Anchor property is used to define a relative fixed position in which the control should always be rendered. Every Control-derived type has an Anchor property, which can be set to any of the values from the AnchorStyles enumeration described in Table 15-16.

Table 15-16. AnchorStyles Values

AnchorStyles Value	Meaning in Life
Bottom	The control is anchored to the bottom edge of its container.
Left	The control is anchored to the left edge of its container.
None	The control is not anchored to any edges of its container.
Right	The control is anchored to the right edge of its container.
Top	The control is anchored to the top edge of its container.

To anchor a widget at the upper left corner, you are free to "OR" styles together (e.g., AnchorStyles.Top | AnchorStyles.Left). Again, the idea behind the Anchor property is to configure which edges of the control are anchored to the edges of its container. For example, if you configure a Button with the following Anchor value:

```
// Anchor this widget relative to the right position.
myButton.Anchor = AnchorStyles.Right;
```

you are ensured that as the Form is resized, this Button maintains its position relative to the right side of the Form.

Configuring a Control's Docking Behavior

Another aspect of Windows Forms programming is establishing the docking behavior of your controls. If you so choose, you can set a widget's Dock property to configure which side (or sides) of a Form the widget should be attached to. The value you assign to a control's Dock property is honored, regardless of the Form's current dimensions. Table 15-17 describes possible options.

Table 15-17. DockStyle Values

DockStyle Value	Meaning in Life
Bottom	The control's bottom edge is docked to the bottom of its containing control.
Fill	All the control's edges are docked to all the edges of its containing control and sized appropriately.
Left	The control's left edge is docked to the left edge of its containing control.
None	The control is not docked.
Right	The control's right edge is docked to the right edge of its containing control.
Top	The control's top edge is docked to the top of its containing control.

So, for example, if you want to ensure that a given widget is always docked on the left side of a Form, you would write the following:

```
// This item is always located on the left of the Form, regardless
// of the Form's current size.
myButton.Dock = DockStyle.Left;
```

Using the topmost menu system, you can select from a set of AnchorStyles and DockStyles values and observe the change in behavior of the Button type (Figure 15-20).

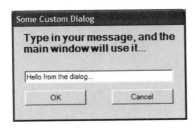

Figure 15-22. The dialog box Form

When the user clicks the OK Button, the end result is that the string is extracted from the TextBox maintained by the custom dialog box and painted in the parent Form's client area. Moreover, if the user reactivates the dialog box, the parent Form assigns the previous text message to the dialog box's TextBox (Figure 15-23).

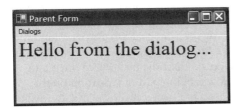

Figure 15-23. Obtaining information from the dialog box

The code representing the custom dialog box should be of no surprise, given that a dialog box is nothing more than a Form with minor modifications. Here is the relevant code:

```
// The dialog box.
public class SomeCustomForm : System.Windows.Forms.Form
{
    private System.Windows.Forms.Button btnCancel;
    private System.Windows.Forms.Button btnOK;
    private System.Windows.Forms.Label label1;
    private System.Windows.Forms.TextBox txtMessage;
    public SomeCustomForm()
    {
        InitializeComponent();
        this.StartPosition = FormStartPosition.CenterParent;
    }
    ...
```

```
private void InitializeComponent()
{
    ...
    // OK Button configuration.
    btnOK.DialogResult = System.Windows.Forms.DialogResult.OK;
    btnOK.Size = new System.Drawing.Size (96, 24);
    btnOK.Text = "OK";
    // Cancel Button configuration.
    btnCancel.DialogResult = System.Windows.Forms.DialogResult.Cancel;
    btnCancel.Size = new System.Drawing.Size (96, 24);
    btnCancel.Text = "Cancel";
    // Form configured to function as dialog box.
    this.Text = "Some Custom Dialog";
    this.MaximizeBox = false;
    this.ControlBox = false;
    this.MinimizeBox = false;
}
}
```

The first point of interest is in the constructor of the Form. Notice that you are setting the StartPosition property on startup. Earlier, you directly called CenterToScreen() to ensure that the Form was centered correctly. Using the StartPosition property (and the FormStartPosition enumeration), you can gain a finer level of granularity. Usually you should use FormStartPosition.CenterParent to ensure that the location of the dialog box is centered with regard to the parent (regardless of the parent's location on the screen), as shown here:

```
// Place dialog box centered to parent.
public SomeCustomForm()
{
    InitializeComponent();
    this.StartPosition = FormStartPosition.CenterParent;
}
```

Another important aspect of dialog box programming is to assign the termination Buttons to a value defined by the DialogResult enumeration. As you know, most dialog boxes define an OK button that says, in effect, "I am happy with my selections. Please use them in the program." Furthermore, most dialog boxes have a Cancel button that allows the user to back out of a selection. To configure how the dialog box's button should respond with respect to dialog box processing, use the DialogResult property, as shown here:

```
private void InitializeComponent()
{
    ...
    // OK Button configuration.
    btnOK.DialogResult = System.Windows.Forms.DialogResult.OK;
    // Cancel Button configuration.
    btnCancel.DialogResult = System.Windows.Forms.DialogResult.Cancel;
}
```

Validating Form Data with the DialogResult Property

What exactly does it mean to assign a Button's DialogResult value? First of all, when a Button has been set to DialogResult.OK or DialogResult.Cancel, the Form *automatically* closes (meaning it is invisible but still in memory). Also, you can query this property back in the code that launched this dialog box to see which Button the user selected, as shown here:

```
protected void mnuModalBox_Click (object sender, System.EventArgs e)
{
    // Style props set in Form.
    SomeCustomForm myForm = new SomeCustomForm();
    // Passing in a reference to the launching dialog box is optional.
    myForm.ShowDialog(this);
    if(myForm.DialogResult == DialogResult.OK)
    {
        // User hit OK, do whatever.
    }
    DoSomeMoreWork();
}
```

The DialogResult enumeration specifies the following values:

```
public enum System.Windows.Forms.DialogResult
{
    Abort, Cancel, Ignore, No,
    None, OK, Retry, Yes
}
```

Grabbing Data from a Dialog Box

Now that you can configure, launch, and test for a dialog box's Button click, you need to understand how to obtain the information from the dialog box. Your current dialog box allows the user to enter a custom string, which is used in the parent Form. Thus, the first step you need to take is to add some number of member variables that represent the data the dialog box is responsible for, as shown here:

```
public class SomeCustomForm : System.Windows.Forms.Form
{
    public SomeCustomForm()
    {
        InitializeComponent();
        this.StartPosition = FormStartPosition.CenterParent;
    }
    // The dialog box's state data (and a way to get it).
    private string strMessage;
    public string Message
    {
        get{ return strMessage;}
        // The set function allows the owner to send
        // in a startup string that you place in the
        // TextBox.
        set
        {
            strMessage = value;
            txtMessage.Text = strMessage;
        }
    }
...
}
```

Now, to transfer the value in the TextBox to this private member variable requires that you intercept the Click event for the OK Button. Remember that the DialogResult.OK assignment already ensures that your Form is hidden when this Button is clicked. This time, however, you need to do some additional work, as shown here:

```
protected void btnOK_Click (object sender, System.EventArgs e)
{
    // OK Button clicked! Configure new message.
    strMessage = txtMessage.Text;
}
```

That's it! Of course, if you had a more elaborate dialog box (such as the CarConfig Form), you would no doubt need a number of custom properties to represent the full set of user selections. To complete your example dialog box application, you can update the code that launched this dialog box to extract the internal message and use it in the program. Here is the complete menu selection logic:

```
protected void mnuModalBox_Click (object sender, System.EventArgs e)
{
    // Style props set in Form.
    SomeCustomForm myForm = new SomeCustomForm();
    // Assume this Form has a string variable named 'dlgMsg'.
    myForm.ShowDialog(this);
    myForm.Message = dlgMsg;
```

```
    if(myForm.DialogResult == DialogResult.OK)
    {
        dlgMsg = myForm.Message;
        Invalidate();
    }
    DoSomeMoreWork();
}
```

The extracted string is then painted on the client area using standard GDI+ logic, as shown here:

```
protected void mainForm_Paint (object sender, PaintEventArgs e)
{
    // Paint the message obtained from the dialog box.
    Graphics g = e.Graphics;
    g.DrawString(dlgMsg, new Font("times New Roman", 24),
        Brushes.Blue, this.ClientRectangle);
}
```

SOURCE CODE   The SimpleDialog application is included under the Chapter 15 directory.

Understanding Form Inheritance

As you are aware, inheritance is the pillar of OOP that allows one class to extend the functionality of another class. Typically, when you speak of inheritance, you envision one non-GUI type (e.g., SportsCar) deriving from another non-GUI type (Car). However, in the world of Windows Forms, it is possible for one Form to derive from another Form and in the process inherit the base class' widgets and implementation. Form-level inheritance is a very powerful technique, as this allows you to build a base Form that provides core-level functionality for a family of related dialog boxes. If you were to bundle these base-level Forms into a .NET assembly, other members of your team could extend these types using the .NET language of their choice.

For the sake of illustration, assume you have placed the CarConfigForm.cs file in a new C# code library application named CarConfigLib (be sure to add a reference to System.Windows.Forms.dll). Once you compile this *.dll, create a new Windows Application project workspace. To derive one Form from another, the first step is to set a reference to the external assembly (in this case, CarConfigLib.dll). Next, specify the base Form using standard C# syntax, as shown here:

```
// The namespace of the base Form.
using CarConfig;

// Your new Form is really a subclass of CarConfigForm!
public class DerivedForm : CarConfig.CarConfigForm
{ ...}
```

If you now save and reopen the DerivedForm type, you will see that the new class has inherited all the widgets! Like any inheritance scenario, be aware that any controls in the base Form that have been declared as private may not be repositioned by the derived type. However, if you were to update the logic in the CarConfigLib.dll to specify protected members, the derived type is free to reposition these items using the design time template.

At this point, you are free to extend this derived Form any way you choose. For test purposes, simply add a new MainMenu that allows the user to exit this application (Figure 15-24).

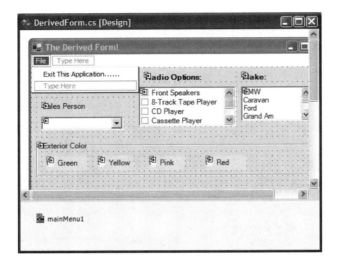

Figure 15-24. Building the derived Form

The Click event handler simply shuts down the application, as shown here:

```
private void mnuFileExit_Click(object sender, System.EventArgs e)
{
    this.Close();
}
```

It is worth pointing out that the Visual Studio .NET IDE provides an integrated wizard (named the Inheritance Picker) to create derived Forms. To access its functionality, activate the Project | Add Inherited Form menu item. Once you provide a name for your new class, you are asked to specify the name of the assembly that contains the base class Form. At that point, the IDE will automatically create a new class type derived from the specified base Form.

SOURCE CODE   The MyDerivedForm and CarConfigLib applications are
included under the Chapter 15 directory.

At this point in the game, you should have a firm understanding of the core set of
Windows Forms controls. As you would expect, the remaining widgets expose their
unique set of properties, methods and events, which I assume you will examine at your
leisure. To close this chapter, we'll now spend some time learning the process of building
custom Windows Forms controls.

Building Custom Windows Forms Controls

If you have a background in classic COM, you are no doubt aware of the use of ActiveX
controls. These coclasses are simply types that implement a (huge) number of (quite
complex) COM interfaces that provide behaviors for rendering graphical content, persisting the state of the coclass, and enabling control/host container communication
(among other duties). While ActiveX controls can now be regarded as a legacy technology,
their spirit lives on under .NET.

As you are already well aware, a *class* is a type that serves as a blueprint for discrete
variables of this type. In .NET, your custom classes can derive from other types, implement
any number of interfaces, serve as the basis for additional types, and typically support
any number of properties, methods, and events. In addition to this (obvious) definition,
generic classes are unique in that they do not support any design time manipulation.
For example, if you have a simple C# class named Car, you are unable to interact with
its members using the VS .NET Properties window. Furthermore, when you are programming with generic class types, you do not drag the item onto a Form-derived type
as you would a Windows Forms Button widget. In essence, a simple class is a non-GUI
type that is directly manipulated through code.

A *control* is also a class type, meaning it derives from a parent class (typically
System.Windows.Forms.Control) and inherits a good deal of functionality in the
process. Each of the GUI widgets you have examined during this chapter is considered
a control type. Like a simple class, controls support a set of public members and can be
manipulated directly by code. In addition, however, controls do support a GUI, and are
typically configured using various design time tools (such as the VS .NET Properties
window) and are "drawn" onto the owning host using the Toolbox. To be sure, like
any intrinsic Windows Forms controls, your custom controls inherit the same set of
behaviors from each class in the inheritance chain.

Next you have *user controls*. Like a control type, user controls also support a runtime
GUI and are fully configurable at design time. The key difference is that user controls
do not derive directly from System.Windows.Forms.Control. Rather, user controls
derive from System.Windows.Forms.UserControl, which in turn derives directly from
ContainerControl. Recall that ContainerControl (and its base class ScrollableControl)
provide additional members that allow you to configure scrolling, tab order, and focus
logic. When you wish to build a reusable GUI widget that maintains numerous related

widgets that need to work together as a whole, you will want to derive your custom class directly from UserControl (in fact, this is the default base class from which your custom controls derive). However, if you are not interested in building a widget that hosts interrelated composite controls, you are free to change the wizard-generated code to derive directly from Control itself.

Finally, you have *components*. Components can best be thought of as a middle-of-the-road alternative between a simple class and a full-fledged (user) control. Like a simple class, components do not support a runtime user interface. However, components can be selected from the VS .NET Toolbox window and configured using the integrated Property window at design time. For example, check out the Components tab in Figure 15-25.

Figure 15-25. The Components tab

As you can see, these intrinsic components are not necessarily GUI in nature, but they do lend themselves well to a design time environment. If you drop a component (such as the EventLog) onto your hosting Form-derived type, you will notice that the design time representation is placed in the designer's icon tray (as well as a member variable in the Form-derived type being created). Once you select the component, you are able to set various properties using the Properties window.

Programmatically speaking, what marks a type as a component is the fact that it implements the System.ComponentModel.IComponent interface. Most of the time, however, you will not directly flesh out the details of this interface by hand, but rather derive your type from System.ComponentModel.Component (and thus receive the canned implementation).

Building a Custom UserControl

During the next several pages, you construct a custom UserControl named CarControl. To begin, fire up Visual Studio .NET and select a new Windows Control Library workspace named CarControlLibrary (Figure 15-26). When you are finished, rename the initial C# class to CarControl (note that the base class of your type is UserControl).

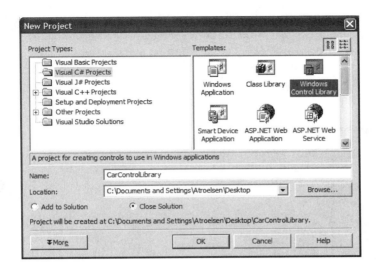

Figure 15-26. Creating a new Windows Control Library workspace

Before we get far along, let's establish the big picture of where you are going with this example. The CarControl type is responsible for animating through a series of bitmaps that will change based on the internal state of the automobile. If the car's current speed is safely under the car's maximum speed limit, the CarControl loops through three bitmap images that render an automobile driving safely along. If the current speed is ten miles below the maximum speed, the CarControl loops through four images, with the fourth image showing the car breaking down. Finally, if the car has surpassed its maximum speed, the CarControl loops over five images, where the fifth image represents a doomed automobile.

Creating the Images

Given our design notes, the first order of business is to create a set of five *.bmp files for use by the animation loop. If you wish to create custom images, begin by activating the Project | Add New Item menu selection and insert five new Bitmap resources. If you would rather not showcase your artistic abilities, feel free to use the images that accompany this sample application (keep in mind, I in *no way* consider myself a graphic artist). The first of these three images (Lemon1.bmp, Lemon2.bmp, and Lemon3.bmp) illustrates a car navigating down the road in a safe and orderly fashion. The final two bitmap images (AlmostDead.bmp and Dead.bmp) represent a car approaching its maximum upper limit and its ultimate demise.

Building the Design Time GUI

The next step is to open the design time editor for the CarControl type. As you can see, you are presented with a Form-like designer that represents the client area of the control under construction. Using the Toolbox window, add an ImageList type (to hold each of the bitmaps), a Timer type (to control the animation cycle), and a PictureBox (to hold the current image). Don't worry about configuring the size or location of the PictureBox type, as you will programmatically position this widget within the bounds of the CarControl. Figure 15-27 shows the story thus far.

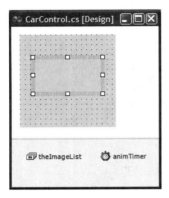

Figure 15-27. Creating the design time GUI

Now, using the Properties window, configure the ImageList's Images collection by adding each bitmap to the list. Be aware that you will want to add these items sequentially (Lemon1.bmp, Lemon2.bmp, Lemon3.bmp, AlmostDead.bmp, Dead.bmp) to ensure a linear animation loop. As you recall from Chapter 14, when you incorporate resources (such as bitmaps) into your VS .NET solutions, the underlying *.resx file is automatically updated. Therefore, the images will be embedded into your assembly with no extra work on your behalf.

Also be aware that the default width and height of *.bmp files inserted using VS .NET are 47×47 pixels. Thus, the ImageSize of the ImageList should also be set to 47×47 (or else you will have some skewed rendering). Finally, configure the state of your Timer type such that the Interval property is set to 200 and is initially disabled.

Implementing the CarControl

With this GUI prep work out of the way, you can now turn to implementation of the type members. To begin, create a new public enumeration named AnimFrame, which has a member representing each item maintained by the ImageList. As you will see, you make use of this enumeration to determine the current frame to render into the PictureBox:

```
// Helper enum for images.
public enum AnimFrames
{
    Lemon1, Lemon2,
    Lemon3, AlmostDead, Dead
}
```

The CarControl type maintains a good number of private data points to represent the animation logic. Here is the rundown of each member:

```
public class CarControl : System.Windows.Forms.UserControl
{
    // State data.
    private System.ComponentModel.IContainer components;
    private AnimFrames currFrame = AnimFrames.Lemon1;
    private AnimFrames currMaxFrame = AnimFrames.Lemon3;
    private bool IsAnim;
    private int currSp = 50;
    private System.Windows.Forms.PictureBox pictureBox;
    private int maxSp = 100;
    private System.Windows.Forms.Timer animTimer;
    private string carPetName= "NoName";
    private Rectangle bottomRect = new Rectangle();
    private System.Windows.Forms.ImageList theImageList;
...
}
```

As you can see, you have data points that represent the current and maximum speed, the pet name of the automobile, and two members of type AnimFrame. The currFrame variable is used to specify which member of the ImageList is to be rendered. The currMaxFrame variable is used to mark the current upper limit in the ImageList (recall that the CarControl loops through three to five images based on the current speed). The IsAnim data point is used to determine if the car is currently in animation mode. Finally, you have a Rectangle member (bottomRect) that is used to represent the bottom region of the CarControl type. Later, you render the pet name of the automobile into this piece of screen real estate.

To divide the CarControl into two rectangular regions, create a private helper function named StretchBox(). The role of this member is to calculate the correct size of the bottomRect member as well as to ensure that the PictureBox widget is stretched out over the upper two thirds (or so) of the CarControl type.

```
private void StretchBox()
{
    // Configure picture box.
    pictureBox.Top = 0;
    pictureBox.Left = 0;
    pictureBox.Height = this.Height - 50;
    pictureBox.Width = this.Width;
    pictureBox.Image =
        theImageList.Images[(int)AnimFrames.Lemon1];
    // Figure out size of bottom rect.
    bottomRect.X = 0;
    bottomRect.Y = this.Height - 50;
    bottomRect.Height = this.Height - pictureBox.Height;
    bottomRect.Width = this.Width;
}
```

Once you have carved out the dimensions of each rectangle, call StretchBox() from the default constructor.

Defining the Custom Events

The CarControl type supports two events that are fired back to the host Form based on the current speed of the automobile. The first event, AboutToBlow, is sent out when the CarControl's speed approaches the upper limit. BlewUp is sent to the container when the current speed is greater than the allowed maximum. Each of these events leverages a custom delegate (CarEventHandler) that can hold the address of any method returning void and taking a single System.String as its sole parameter. You'll fire these events in just a moment, but for the time being, add the following members to the public sector of the CarControl:

```
// Car events / custom delegate.
public delegate void CarEventHandler(string msg);
public event CarEventHandler AboutToBlow;
public event CarEventHandler BlewUp;
```

Defining the Custom Properties

Like any class type, custom controls may define a set of properties to allow the outside world to interact with the state of the widget. For your current purposes, you are only interested in defining three properties. First, you have Anim. This property enables or disables the Timer type:

```
// Used to configure the internal Timer type.
public bool Anim
{
    get {return IsAnim;}
    set
    {
        IsAnim = value;
        animTimer.Enabled = IsAnim;
    }
}
```

The PetName property is as you would expect, and requires no comment. Do notice, however, that when the user sets the pet name, you make a call to Invalidate() to render the name of the CarControl into the bottom rectangular area of the widget (you do this step in just a moment):

```
// Configure pet name.
public string PetName
{
    get{return carPetName;}
    set
    {
        carPetName = value;
        Invalidate();
    }
}
```

Next, you have the Speed property. In addition to simply modifying the currSp data member, Speed is also the entity that fires the AboutToBlow and BlewUp events based on the current speed of the CarControl. Here is the complete logic:

```
// Adjust currSp, currMaxFrame and fire our events.
public int Speed
{
    get{return currSp;}
    set
    {
        currSp = value;
        currFrame = currMaxFrame;
        // About to explode?
        if ((maxSp - currSp) <= 10)
        {
            AboutToBlow("Slow down dude!");
            currMaxFrame = AnimFrames.AlmostDead;
        }
        // Maxed out?
        if (currSp >= maxSp)
        {
            currSp = maxSp;
            BlewUp("Ug...you're toast...");
            currMaxFrame = AnimFrames.Dead;
        }
    }
}
```

As you can see, if the current speed is 10 miles below the maximum upper speed, you fire the AboutToBlow event and adjust the upper frame limit to AnimFrame.AlmostDead. If the user has pushed the limits of your automobile, you fire the BlewUp event and set the upper frame limit to AnimFrame.Dead.

Controlling the Animation

The next detail to attend to is ensuring that the Timer type advances the current frame to render within the PictureBox. Again, recall that the number of frames to loop through depends on the current speed of the automobile. You only want to bother adjusting the image in the PictureBox if the Anim property has been set to true. Begin by handling the Tick event for the Timer type, and flesh out the details as follows:

```
private void animTimer_Tick(object sender, System.EventArgs e)
{
    if(IsAnim)
        pictureBox.Image = theImageList.Images[(int)currFrame];
    // Bump frame.
    string s = Enum.Format(typeof(AnimFrames), currFrame, "D");
    int i = int.Parse(s);
    int nextFrame = i + 1;
    currFrame = (AnimFrames)nextFrame;
    if (currFrame > currMaxFrames)
        currFrame = AnimFrames.Lemon1;
}
```

Rendering the Pet Name

Before you can take your control out for a spin, you have one final detail to attend to: displaying the car's moniker. To do this, handle the Paint event for your CarControl, and within the handler, render the CarControl's pet name into the bottom rectangular region of the client area:

```
private void CarControl_Paint(object sender,
    System.Windows.Forms.PaintEventArgs e)
{
    // Render the petname on the bottom of the control.
    Graphics g = e.Graphics;
    g.FillRectangle(Brushes.GreenYellow, bottomRect);
    g.DrawString(PetName, new Font("Times New Roman", 15),
        Brushes.Black, bottomRect);
}
```

At this point, the initial crack at the CarControl is complete. Go ahead and build your project.

Testing the CarControl Type

Like all .NET types, you are now able to make use of your custom control from any language targeting the CLR. For your current purposes, build a C# tester application. Begin by closing down the current workspace and creating a new Windows Forms project named CarCtrlClient. To allow your current project to reference auxiliary controls, right-click your Toolbox window and select the Add/Remove Items menu selection. Using the Browse button on the .NET Framework Components tab, navigate to your MyControlLib library, and then select the CarControl type. At this point you will find a new icon on the Toolbox named, of course, CarControl.

Begin building your GUI by placing a CarControl onto the Form designer. Notice that the Anim, PetName, and Speed properties are all exposed through the Properties window. Also be aware that the control is "alive" at design time. Thus, if you set the Anim property to true at design time, you will find your car is animating on the Form designer.

Once you have configured the initial state of your CarControl, add additional GUI widgets that allow the user to increase and decrease the speed of the automobile, and view the incoming events and speed (Label widgets should do nicely for these purposes). One possible GUI design is shown in Figure 15-28.

Figure 15-28. The client-side GUI

The logic behind the Buttons will simply adjust the current speed by 10 MPH, and display the current speed of the CarControl in the Label widget. For example:

```
private void btnSpeedUp_Click(object sender, System.EventArgs e)
{
    carControl1.Speed += 10;
    lblCurrSp.Text =
        string.Format("Speed is: {0}", carControl1.Speed.ToString());
}
```

```
private void btnSlowDown_Click(object sender, System.EventArgs e)
{
    // NOTE!  We did not account for a negative current speed,
    // so your car may drive in reverse!
    carControl1.Speed -= 10;
    lblCurrSp.Text =
        string.Format("Speed is: {0}", carControl1.Speed.ToString());
}
```

Next, handle the Load event for the Form-derived type and activate the CarControl's animation:

```
private void mainForm_Load(object sender, System.EventArgs e)
{
    carControl1.Anim = true;
    lblCurrSp.Text =
        string.Format("Speed is: {0}", carControl1.Speed.ToString());
}
```

The final aspect of this client-side design is to capture the incoming events from the CarControl widget. Like all other Windows Forms GUI types, you are able to handle events using the Properties window. Handle the AboutToBlow and BlewUp events, and write some informative message to the output Label:

```
// Client-side event handlers.
private void carControl1_AboutToBlow(string msg)
{
    lblEventMsg.Text = msg;
}
private void carControl1_BlewUp(string msg)
{
    lblEventMsg.Text = msg;
}
```

At this point, you are able to run your client application and interact with the CarControl. As you can see, building and using custom controls is a fairly straight-forward task, given what you already know about OOP, GDI+, and Windows Forms.

While you do have enough information to continue exploring the process of .NET Windows Control development, there is one additional programmatic aspect to contend with: design time functionality. Before I describe exactly what this boils down to, you need to understand the role of a key design time–centric namespace.

Select Members of the System.ComponentModel Namespace

The System.ComponentModel namespace defines a number of such types that allow you to describe how your custom controls and components should display themselves at design time. For example, you can opt to supply a textual description of each property, define a default event, or group related members into a custom category (for display purposes within the Properties window). When you are interested in making the sorts of modifications previously mentioned, you will want to make use of the following core attributes (Table 15-18).

Table 15-18. Select Members of System.ComponentModel

System.ComponentModel Attribute	Applied to	Meaning in Life
BrowsableAttribute	Properties and events	Specifies whether a property or an event should be displayed in the property browser. By default, all custom properties and events can be browsed.
CategoryAttribute	Properties and events	Specifies the name of the category in which to group a property or event.
DescriptionAttribute	Properties and events	Defines a small block of text to be displayed at the bottom of the property browser when the user selects a property or event.
DefaultPropertyAttribute	Properties	Specifies the default property for the component. This property is selected in the property browser when a user clicks the control.
DefaultValueAttribute	Properties	Sets a simple default value for a property that will be applied when the control is reset to its default state.
LocalizableAttribute	Properties	Specifies that a property may be localized. Any properties that have this attribute are automatically persisted into the resources file when a user chooses to localize a Form.
DefaultEventAttribute	Events	Specifies the default event for the component. When a user double-clicks the control type, stub code is automatically written for the default event.

Enhancing the Design Time Appearance of CarControl

To illustrate the use of some of these new attributes, assume you want to create a custom category (called "Car Configuration") to which each property and event of the CarControl belong. Also, let's supply a friendly description for each member and default value for each property. To do so, simply update each of the properties and events of the CarControl type to support the [Category], [DefaultValue], and [Description] attributes. For example:

```
using System.ComponentModel;
...
public class CarControl : System.Windows.Forms.UserControl
{
    ...
    [Category("Car Configuration"),
    Description("Sent when the car is approaching terminal speed.")]
    public event CarEventHandler AboutToBlow;
    ...
    [Category("Car Configuration"),
    Description("Pet name for your auto."),
    DefaultValue("No Name")]
    public string PetName {...}
}
```

Now, let me make a comment on what it means to assign a default value to a property, because I can guarantee you it is not what you would (naturally) assume. Simply put, the [DefaultValue] attribute does *not* ensure that the underlying value of the data point wrapped by a given property will be automatically initialized to the default value. Thus, although you specify a default value of "No Name" to the PetName property, the carPetName member variable will not be set to "No Name" unless you do so via the type's constructor or via member initialization syntax:

```
private string carPetName= "NoName";
```

Rather, the [DefaultValue] attribute comes into play when the programmer "resets" the value of a given property using the Properties window. To reset a property using VS .NET, select the property of interest, right-click the description pane, and click "Reset". Also note the description appears in the lower pane of the Properties window (Figure 15-29).

Figure 15-29. Resetting a property to the default value

The [Category] attribute will only be realized if the programmer selects the categorized view of the Properties window (as opposed to the default alphabetical view) as seen in Figure 15-30.

Figure 15-30. The custom category

Defining a Default Property and Default Event

In addition to describing and grouping like members into a common category, you may also want to configure your controls (or components) to support default behaviors. A given control may support a default property. When you define the default property for a class using the [DefaultProperty] attribute as follows:

```
// Mark the default property for this control.
[DefaultProperty("Anim")]
public class CarControl
    : System.Windows.Forms.UserControl
{...}
```

you ensure that when the user selects this control at design time, the Anim property is automatically highlighted in the Properties window. Likewise, when you configure your control to have a default event:

```
// Mark the default event and property for this control.
[DefaultEvent("BlewUp"), DefaultProperty("Anim")]
public class CarControl
    : System.Windows.Forms.UserControl
{...}
```

you ensure that when the user double-clicks the widget at design time, stub code is automatically written for the default event.

Specifying a Custom Toolbox Bitmap

Another design time technique that is supported by a polished custom control is to specify a custom toolbox bitmap image. Currently, when the user selects the CarControl, the VS .NET IDE will make show this type on the ToolBox using the default "gear" icon. If you wish to specify a custom image, your first step is to insert a new *.bmp file into your project (CarControl.bmp) that is configured to be 16×16 pixels in size (established via the Width and Height properties).

Once you have created the image as you see fit (and set the Build Action value to Embedded Resource to ensure the image data is contained within the assembly), your final task is to make use of the [ToolboxBitmap] attribute, which is applied at the type level. The first argument is the type information for the control itself, while the second argument is the friendly name of the *.bmp file.

```
[ToolboxBitmap(typeof(CarControl), "CarControl")]
[DefaultEvent("BlewUp"), DefaultProperty("Anim")]
public class CarControl : System.Windows.Forms.UserControl
{...}
```

Once you do so, you will find that when the programmer adds the widget to the toolbox, your custom image will be displayed on the VS .NET Toolbox.

So, that wraps up our examination of the process of building custom Windows Forms controls. Obviously, complete coverage of this topic (especially programming for design time support) would require a book all of its own. If you are interested in additional details regarding developing custom Windows Forms controls, pick up a copy of *User Interfaces in C#: Windows Forms and Custom Controls* (MacDonald, Apress 2002).

SOURCE CODE   The CarControl and CarControlTestForm projects are included under the Chapter 15 directory.

Summary

This chapter rounded off your current understanding of Windows Forms by examining the programming of numerous GUI widgets from the simple (Button) to the more exotic (MonthCalendar). As you have seen, each and every Windows Forms control type derives from System.Windows.Forms.Control, which defines a number of members available to derived types (including the all important Control.ControlCollection type). This chapter also explored the various anchoring and docking behaviors that can be used to enforce a specific layout of your GUI types, regardless of the size of the owning Form.

In the latter half of this chapter, you learned how to build custom dialog boxes using Windows Forms and examined a number of issues related to dialog boxes. Next, you learned how to derive a new Form from an existing Form type using Form inheritance. Using this technique, you are able to build a set of generic GUIs that can be extended by derived types. Finally, this chapter introduced you to the process of building custom Windows Forms controls using the .NET platform.

CHAPTER 16

The System.IO Namespace

WHEN YOU ARE CREATING full-blown desktop applications, the ability to save information between user sessions is imperative. This chapter examines a number of IO-related topics as seen through the eyes of the .NET Framework. The first order of business is to explore the core types defined in the System.IO namespace and come to understand how to programmatically modify a machine's directory and file structure. Once you can do so, the next task is to explore various ways to read from and write to character-based, binary-based, string-based, and memory-based data stores.

Finally, to showcase some of these concepts using a cohesive example, I conclude this chapter with a complete Windows Forms application, which allows the end user to manage a collection of Car types that can be persisted to (and recovered from) a file using various types of the System.IO namespace and .NET object serialization services (first seen in Chapter 12). As an interesting bonus, the application in question also previews the use of the System.Windows.Forms.DataGrid widget (used extensively during the examination of ADO.NET).

Exploring the System.IO Namespace

In the framework of .NET, the System.IO namespace is the region of the base class libraries devoted to file-based (and memory-based) input and output services. Like any namespace, System.IO defines a set of classes, interfaces, enumerations, structures, and delegates, most all of which are contained in mscorlib.dll. In addition to the types contained within mscorlib.dll, the System.dll assembly defines additional members of the System.IO namespace (given that all VS .NET projects automatically set a reference to both assemblies, you should be ready to go).

As you will see during this chapter, a key set of types within the System.IO namespace focuses on the manipulation of physical directories and files. However, additional types provide support to read data from and write data to string buffers as well as to raw memory locations. To give you a roadmap of the functionality in System.IO, Table 16-1 outlines the core (nonabstract) classes.

Table 16-1. Key Members of the System.IO Namespace

Creatable IO Type	Meaning in Life
Directory DirectoryInfo File FileInfo	These types are all used to manipulate the properties for a given directory or physical file as well as create new files and extend the current directory structure. The Directory and File types expose their functionality primarily as *static methods*. The DirectoryInfo and FileInfo types expose similar functionality from a valid *object variable*.
FileSystemWatcher	This type allows you to monitor the external modification to a given external file.
Path	Performs operations on System.String types that contain file or directory path information in a platform-neutral manner.
StreamWriter StreamReader	These types are used to store (and retrieve) textual information to (or from) a file. These types do not support random file access.
StringWriter StringReader	Like the StreamReader/StreamWriter types, these classes also work with textual information. However, the underlying storage is a string buffer rather than a physical file.
FileStream	Allows for random file access (e.g., seeking capabilities) with data represented as a stream of bytes.
MemoryStream	Random access to streamed data, stored in memory, rather than a physical file.
BufferedStream	Provides temporary storage for a stream of bytes that may be committed to storage at a later time.
BinaryReader BinaryWriter	These types allow you to store and retrieve primitive data types (integers, Booleans, strings, and whatnot) as a binary value.

In addition to these creatable types, System.IO defines a number of enumerations, as well as a set of abstract classes (Stream, TextReader, TextWriter, and so forth) that define a shared polymorphic interface to all descendents. You will read about many of these types in this chapter.

The Directory(Info) and File(Info) Types

System.IO provides four types that allow you to manipulate individual files, as well as interact with a machine's directory structure. The first two types, Directory and File, expose creation, deletion, copying, and moving operations using various static members. The closely related FileInfo and DirectoryInfo types expose similar functionality as instance-level methods (and therefore must be "new-ed"). In Figure 16-1, notice that the Directory and File types directly extend System.Object, while DirectoryInfo and FileInfo derive from the abstract FileSystemInfo type. Generally speaking, FileInfo and DirectoryInfo are better choices for recursive operations, as the Directory and File class members tend to return strings rather than file objects.

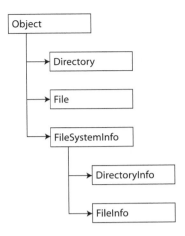

Figure 16-1. The File- and Directory-centric types

The Abstract FileSystemInfo Base Class

The DirectoryInfo and FileInfo types receive many behaviors from the abstract FileSystemInfo type. By and large, the members of the FileSystemInfo class can be used to discover general characteristics (such as time of creation, various attributes, and so forth) about a given file or directory. Table 16-2 lists some core properties of interest.

Table 16-2. FileSystemInfo Properties

FileSystemInfo Property	Meaning in Life
Attributes	Gets or sets the attributes associated to the current file that are represented by the FileAttributes enumeration.
CreationTime	Gets or sets the time of creation for the current file or directory.
Exists	Can be used to determine if a given file or directory exists.
Extension	Used to retrieve a file's extension.
FullName	Gets the full path of the directory or file.
LastAccessTime	Gets or sets the time the current file or directory was last accessed.
LastWriteTime	Gets or sets the time when the current file or directory was last written to.
Name	Returns the name of a given file; is a read-only property. For directories, gets the name of the last directory in the hierarchy if possible; otherwise, retrieves the fully qualified name.

The FileSystemInfo type also defines the Delete() method. This is implemented by derived types to delete a given file or directory from the hard drive. As well, Refresh() can (and should) be called prior to obtaining attribute information to ensure that the statistics regarding the current file (or directory) are not outdated.

NOTE   Always get in the habit of calling Refresh() before reading data from types derived from FileSystemInfo, as the chances are quite good that the contents of the item will be altered after the initial construction.

Working with the DirectoryInfo Type

The first creatable type you must understand is the DirectoryInfo class. This class contains a set of members used for creating, moving, deleting, and enumerating over directories and subdirectories. In addition to the functionality provided by its FileSystemInfo base class, DirectoryInfo offers the members in Table 16-3.

Table 16-3. Key Members of the DirectoryInfo Type

DirectoryInfo Members	Meaning in Life
Create() CreateSubdirectory()	Create a directory (or subdirectories) given a path name.
Delete()	Deletes a directory and all its contents.
GetDirectories()	Returns an array of strings that represent all subdirectories in the current directory.
GetFiles()	Gets the files in the specified directory (as an array of FileInfo types).
Parent	This property retrieves the parent directory of the specified path.
MoveTo()	Moves a directory and its contents to a new path.

You begin working with the DirectoryInfo type by specifying a particular directory path (e.g., "C:\," "D:\WinNT," "\CompanyServer\Utils," "A:\," or what have you) as a constructor parameter. If you want access to the application directory (i.e., the directory of the executing application), use the "." notation. Here are some examples:

```
// Create a new directory bound to the current directory.
DirectoryInfo dir1 = new DirectoryInfo(".");
// Create a new directory bound to C:\Foo\Bar, note the use of the symbol @.
DirectoryInfo dir2 = new DirectoryInfo(@"C:\Foo\Bar");
```

If you attempt to map to a nonexistent directory, you are thrown a System.IO.DirectoryNotFoundException. Assuming that an exception has not been thrown, you can investigate the underlying directory contents using any of the properties inherited from FileSystemInfo. To illustrate, the following class creates a new DirectoryInfo type mapped to "C:\WinNT" (adjust your letter drive and path if need be) and dumps out a number of interesting statistics (see Figure 16-2 for output):

```
class MyDirectory
{
    public static void Main(String[] args)
    {
        DirectoryInfo dir = new DirectoryInfo(@"C:\WinNT");
        // Dump directory information.
        Console.WriteLine("***** Directory Info *****");
        Console.WriteLine("FullName: {0} ", dir.FullName);
        Console.WriteLine("Name: {0} ", dir.Name);
        Console.WriteLine("Parent: {0} ", dir.Parent);
        Console.WriteLine("Creation: {0} ", dir.CreationTime);
        Console.WriteLine("Attributes: {0} ", dir.Attributes.ToString());
        Console.WriteLine("Root: {0} ", dir.Root);
        Console.WriteLine("***********************\n");
    }
}
```

Figure 16-2. %windir% directory information

The FileAttributes Enumeration

As shown in the previous code sample, the Attributes property obtains various traits for the current directory or file, all of which are represented by the FileAttributes enumeration. Table 16-4 describes some core values.

Table 16-4. Select FileAttributes Values

FileAttributes Enumeration Value	Meaning in Life
Archive	Represents the archive status of the file or directory. Applications use this attribute to mark files for backup or removal.
Compressed	The file or directory is compressed.
Directory	The item is a directory (rather than a file).
Encrypted	The file or directory is encrypted.
Hidden	The file or directory is hidden and thus is not included in an ordinary directory listing.
Normal	The file or directory is normal and has no other attributes set. This attribute is valid only if used alone.
Offline	The file or directory is offline. The data of the file is not immediately available.
ReadOnly	The file or directory is read only.
System	The file is a system file. The file is part of the operating system or is used exclusively by the operating system.

Enumerating Files with the DirectoryInfo Type

You can extend the current MyDirectory class to use some methods of the DirectoryInfo type. First, use the GetFiles() method to read all *.bmp files located under the "C:\WinNT" directory. This method returns an array of FileInfo types that you can iterate over using the foreach construct and thus use recursively if needed (full details of the FileInfo type are explored later in this chapter):

```
class MyDirectory
{
    public static void Main(String[] args)
    {
        DirectoryInfo dir = new DirectoryInfo(@"C:\WinNT");
        ...
        // Get all files with a *.bmp extension.
        FileInfo[] bitmapFiles = dir.GetFiles("*.bmp");

        // How many were found?
        Console.WriteLine("Found {0}  *.bmp files\n", bitmapFiles.Length);
```

```
        // Now print out info for each file.
        foreach (FileInfo f in bitmapFiles)
        {
            Console.WriteLine("**************************\n");
            Console.WriteLine("File name: {0} ", f.Name);
            Console.WriteLine("File size: {0} ", f.Length);
            Console.WriteLine("Creation: {0} ", f.CreationTime);
            Console.WriteLine("Attributes: {0} ", f.Attributes.ToString());
            Console.WriteLine("**************************\n");
        }
    }
}
```

Once you run the application, you see a listing something like that shown in Figure 16-3. (Your bitmaps may vary!)

Figure 16-3. Bitmap file information

Creating Subdirectories with the DirectoryInfo Type

You can programmatically extend a directory structure using the DirectoryInfo.CreateSubdirectory() method. This method can create a single subdirectory, as well as multiple nested subdirectories. To illustrate, here is a block of code that extends the directory structure of "C:\WinNT" with some custom subdirectories:

```
class MyDirectory
{
    public static void Main(String[] args)
    {
        DirectoryInfo dir = new DirectoryInfo(@"C:\WinNT");
        ...
        try
        {
```

```
                // Create \MyFoo off root.
                dir.CreateSubdirectory("MyFoo");
                // Create \MyBar\MyQaaz off root.
                dir.CreateSubdirectory(@"MyBar\MyQaaz");
            }
            catch(IOException e) {  Console.WriteLine(e.Message);}
        }
    }
```

If you examine your %windir% directory using Windows Explorer, you will see the new subdirectories are present and accounted for (Figure 16-4).

Figure 16-4. Creating subdirectories

Although you are not required to capture the return value of the CreateSubdirectory() method, be aware that a DirectoryInfo type representing the newly created item is passed back on successful execution:

```
// CreateSubdirectory() returns a DirectoryInfo item representing the new item.
try
{
    DirectoryInfo d = dir.CreateSubdirectory("MyFoo");
    Console.WriteLine("Created: {0} ", d.FullName);
    d = dir. CreateSubdirectory(@"MyBar\MyQaaz");
    Console.WriteLine("Created: {0} ", d.FullName);
}
catch(IOException e) {  Console.WriteLine(e.Message); }
```

The Static Members of the Directory Class

Now that you have seen the DirectoryInfo type in action, you can learn about the Directory type. By and large, the members of the Directory mimic the same functionality provided by the instance-level members defined by DirectoryInfo, with a few notable exceptions (GetLogicalDrives() for one). They also generally return strings rather than objects. Due to the common public interface of each type, I assume you will consult online help to view each member of the Directory class.

This final iteration of the MyDirectory class lists the names of all drives mapped to the current computer and uses the static Directory.Delete() method to remove the \MyFoo and \MyBar\MyQaaz subdirectories previously created:

```
class MyDirectory
{
    public static void Main(String[] args)
    {
        DirectoryInfo dir = new DirectoryInfo(@"C:\WinNT");

        // Now call some static members of the Directory class.
        // List all drives on current computer.
        string[] drives = Directory.GetLogicalDrives();
        Console.WriteLine("Here are your drives:");
        foreach(string s in drives)
        {
            Console.WriteLine("->{0} ", s);
        }
        // Delete what was created.
        Console.Write("Going to delete\n->" + dir.FullName +
            "\\MyBar\\MyQaaz.\nand\n->" + dir.FullName +
            "\\MyFoo.\n" +"Press a key to continue!");
        Console.Read();
        try
        {
            Directory.Delete(@"C:\WinNT\MyFoo");
            // The second parameter specifies if you
            // wish to blow away any internal subdirectories.
            Directory.Delete(@"C:\WinNT\MyBar", true);
        }
        catch(IOException e)
        {
            Console.WriteLine(e.Message);
        }
    }
}
```

Great! At this point you have investigated some core behaviors of the Directory and DirectoryInfo types. Next, you need to learn how to create, open, close, and destroy the files that populate a given directory.

SOURCE CODE   The MyDirectoryApp project is located under the Chapter 16 subdirectory.

The FileInfo Class

The role of the FileInfo class is to obtain a number of details regarding existing files on your hard drive (time created, size, file attributes, and so forth) as well as aid in the creation, copying, moving, and destruction of files. In addition to the set of functionality inherited by FileSystemInfo, Table 16-5 describes some core members unique to the FileInfo class.

Table 16-5. FileInfo Core Members

FileInfo Member	Meaning in Life
AppendText()	Creates a StreamWriter type (described later) that appends text to a file
CopyTo()	Copies an existing file to a new file
Create()	Creates a new file and returns a FileStream type (described later) to interact with the created file
CreateText()	Creates a StreamWriter type that writes a new text file
Delete()	Deletes the file to which a FileInfo instance is bound
Directory	Gets an instance of the parent directory
DirectoryName	Gets the full path to a file
Length	Gets the size of the current file or directory
MoveTo()	Moves a specified file to a new location, providing the option to specify a new filename
Name	Gets the name of the file
Open()	Opens a file with various read/write and sharing privileges
OpenRead()	Creates a read-only FileStream
OpenText()	Creates a StreamReader type (described later) that reads from an existing text file
OpenWrite()	Creates a read/write FileStream type

First, you should be aware that many methods defined by FileInfo return a specific stream-centric type (FileStream, StreamWriter, StreamReader, and so forth) that allows you to begin reading and writing data to (or reading from) the associated file in a variety of ways. We'll check out these types later in this chapter; however, until then, the following code block illustrates the most generic (and least flexible) way to create a file programmatically:

```
public class FileManipulator
{
    public static int Main(string[] args)
    {
        // Make a new file on the C: drive.
        FileInfo f = new FileInfo(@"C:\Test.txt");
        FileStream fs = f.Create();
        // Print some basic traits of the test.txt file.
        Console.WriteLine("Creation: {0} ", f.CreationTime);
        Console.WriteLine("Full name: {0} ", f.FullName);
        Console.WriteLine("Full atts: {0} ", f.Attributes.ToString());
        Console.Write("Press a key to delete file");
        Console.Read();
        // Close the file stream and delete the file.
        fs.Close();
        f.Delete();
        return 0;
    }
}
```

Notice that the FileInfo.Create() method returns a FileStream type that allows you to close the new file before removing it from the hard drive. (You will see additional uses of FileStream later in the chapter.) When you run this application, you will be able to find your newly created *.txt file under the C drive.

Examining the FileInfo.Open() Method

The FileInfo.Open() method can be used to open existing files as well as create new files with far more precision than FileInfo.Create(). To illustrate, ponder the following logic:

```
// Open (or create) a file with read/write attributes (no sharing),
// and store file handle in a FileStream object.
FileInfo f2 = new FileInfo(@"C:\HelloThere.ini");
FileStream s = f2.Open(FileMode.OpenOrCreate, FileAccess.ReadWrite,
                       FileShare.None);
...
s.Close();
f2.Delete();
```

This version of the overloaded Open() method requires three parameters. The first parameter specifies the general flavor of the open request (e.g., make a new file, open an existing file, append to a file, and so on), which is specified using the FileMode enumeration (Table 16-6).

Table 16-6. FileMode Enumeration Values

FileMode Enumeration Value	Meaning in Life
Append	Opens the file if it exists and seeks to the end of the file. If the specified file does not exist, a new file is created. Be aware that FileMode.Append can only be used in conjunction with FileAccess.Write.
Create	Specifies that the operating system should create a new file. Be very aware that if the file already exists, it is overwritten!
CreateNew	Specifies that the operating system should create a new file. If the file already exists, an IOException is thrown.
Open	Specifies that the operating system should open an existing file.
OpenOrCreate	Specifies that the operating system should open a file if it exists; otherwise, a new file should be created.
Truncate	Specifies that the operating system should open an existing file. Once opened, the file should be truncated so that its size is zero bytes.

The second parameter, a value from the FileAccess enumeration, is used to determine the read/write behavior of the underlying stream (Table 16-7).

Table 16-7. FileAccess Enumeration Values

FileAccess Enumeration Value	Meaning in Life
Read	Specifies read-only access to the file (i.e., data can only be obtained from the file)
ReadWrite	Specifies read and write access to the file (i.e., data can be added to or obtained from the file)
Write	Specifies write access to the file (i.e., data can only be added to the file)

Finally, you have the third parameter (FileShare), which specifies how the currently open file is to be shared among other file handlers (Table 16-8).

Table 16-8. FileShare Enumeration Values

FileShare Enumeration Value	Meaning in Life
None	Declines sharing of the current file. Any request to open the file (by this process or another process) fails until the file is closed.
Read	Allows subsequent opening of the file for reading. If this flag is not specified, any request to open the file for reading (by this process or another process) fails until the file is closed.
ReadWrite	Allows subsequent opening of the file for reading or writing. If this flag is not specified, any request to open the file for writing or reading (by this process or another process) fails until the file is closed.
Write	Allows subsequent opening of the file for writing. If this flag is not specified, any request to open the file for writing (by this process or another process) fails until the file is closed.

The FileInfo.OpenRead() and FileInfo.OpenWrite() Members

In addition to the Open() method, the FileInfo class also has members named OpenRead() and OpenWrite(). As you would imagine, these methods return a properly configured read-only or write-only FileStream type:

```
// Get a FileStream object with read-only permissions.
FileInfo f3 = new FileInfo(@"C:\boot.ini");
FileStream readOnlyStream = f3.OpenRead();
...
readOnlyStream.Close();
// Now get a FileStream object with write-only permissions.
FileInfo f4 = new FileInfo(@"C:\config.sys");
FileStream writeOnlyStream = f4.OpenWrite();
...
writeOnlyStream.Close();
```

The FileInfo.OpenText(), FileInfo.CreateText(), and FileInfo.AppendText() Members

Another "open-centric" member of the FileInfo type is OpenText(). Unlike Open(), OpenRead(), and OpenWrite(), the OpenText() method returns an instance of the StreamReader type, rather than a FileStream-derived type:

```
// Get a StreamReader object.
FileInfo f5 = new FileInfo(@"C:\bootlog.txt");
StreamReader sreader = f5.OpenText();
...
sreader.Close();
```

The final two methods of interest at this point are CreateText() and AppendText(), both of which return a StreamWriter reference, as shown here:

```
// Get some StreamWriters.
FileInfo f6 = new FileInfo(@"D:\AnotherTest.txt");
f6.Open(FileMode.Create, FileAccess.ReadWrite);
StreamWriter swriter = f6.CreateText();
...
swriter.Close();
FileInfo f7 = new FileInfo(@"D:\FinalTest.txt");
f7.Open(FileMode.Create, FileAccess.ReadWrite);
StreamWriter swriterAppend = f7.AppendText();
...
swriterAppend.Close();
```

At this point, you have a good feel for the functionality provided by the FileInfo type. (You will see exactly what to do with the FileStream, StreamReader, and StreamWriter types shortly.)

NOTE Be aware that the File type provides almost identical functionality using a number of static members. You will see the File type in action where appropriate, but be sure to check out online help for an exhaustive listing of each member.

The Abstract Stream Class

In the world of IO manipulation, a *stream* represents a chunk of data. The abstract System.IO.Stream class defines a number of members that provide support for synchronous and asynchronous interactions with the storage medium (e.g., an underlying file or memory location). Figure 16-5 shows the basic stream hierarchy.

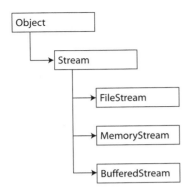

Figure 16-5. Stream-derived types

Stream descendents represent data as a raw stream of bytes (rather than text-based data). Also, some Streams-derived types support seeking, which refers to the process of obtaining and adjusting the current position in the stream. To begin understanding the functionality provided by the Stream class, take note of the core members described in Table 16-9.

Table 16-9. Abstract Stream Members

Stream Member	Meaning in Life
CanRead CanSeek CanWrite	Determine whether the current stream supports reading, seeking, and/or writing.
Close()	Closes the current stream and releases any resources (such as sockets and file handles) associated with the current stream.
Flush()	Updates the underlying data source or repository with the current state of the buffer and then clears the buffer. If a stream does not implement a buffer, this method does nothing.
Length	Returns the length of the stream, in bytes.
Position	Determines the position in the current stream.
Read() ReadByte()	Reads a sequence of bytes (or a single byte) from the current stream and advances the current position in the stream by the number of bytes read.
Seek()	Sets the position in the current stream.
SetLength()	Sets the length of the current stream.
Write() WriteByte()	Write a sequence of bytes (or a single byte) to the current stream and advance the current position in this stream by the number of bytes written.

Working with FileStreams

The FileStream class provides implementations for the abstract Stream members in a manner appropriate for file-based streaming. It is a fairly primitive stream; it can read or write bytes or arrays of bytes. Like the DirectoryInfo and FileInfo types, FileStream provides the ability to open existing files as well as create new files. FileStreams are typically configured using the FileMode, FileAccess, and FileShare enumerations. For example, the following logic creates a new file (test.dat) in the application directory:

```
// Create a new file in the working directory.
FileStream myFStream = new FileStream("test.dat",
    FileMode.OpenOrCreate, FileAccess.ReadWrite);
```

Let's experiment with the synchronous read/write capabilities of the FileStream type. To write a stream of bytes to a file, make calls to the inherited WriteByte() or Write() method, both of which advance the internal file pointer automatically. To read the bytes back from a file, simply call Read() or ReadByte(). Here is an example:

```
// Write bytes to the *.dat file.
for(int i = 0; i < 256; i++)
    myFStream.WriteByte((byte)i);
// Reset internal position.
myFStream.Position = 0;
// Read bytes from the *.dat file.
for(int i = 0; i < 256; i++)
    Console.Write(myFStream.ReadByte());
myFStream.Close();
```

SOURCE CODE   The BasicFileApp project is included under the Chapter 16 subdirectory.

Working with MemoryStreams

The MemoryStream type works much like FileStream, with the obvious difference that you are now writing to memory rather than a physical file. Given that each of these types derives from Stream, you can update the previous FileStream logic to use a MemoryStream type with minor adjustments:

```
// Create a memory stream with a fixed capacity.
MemoryStream myMemStream = new MemoryStream();
myMemStream.Capacity = 256;
// Write bytes to stream.
for(int i = 0; i < 256; i++)
    myMemStream.WriteByte((byte)i);
// Reset internal position.
myMemStream.Position = 0;
// Read bytes from stream.
for(int i = 0; i < 256; i++)
    Console.Write(myMemStream.ReadByte());
myMemStream.Close();
```

The output of this logic is identical to that of the previous FileStream example. The only difference is where you store the information (to file or memory). In addition to the inherited members, MemoryStream supplies other members. For example, the previous code used the Capacity property to specify how much memory to carve out for the streaming operation. Table 16-10 shows the core MemoryStream type members.

Table 16-10. MemoryStream Core Members

MemoryStream Member	Meaning in Life
Capacity	Gets or sets the number of bytes allocated for this stream
GetBuffer()	Returns the array of unsigned bytes from which this stream was created
ToArray()	Writes the entire stream contents to a byte array, regardless of the Position property
WriteTo()	Writes the entire contents of this MemoryStream to another stream-derived type (such as a file)

Notice the possible interplay between the MemoryStream and FileStream types. Using the WriteTo() method, you can easily transfer data stored in memory to a file. Furthermore, you can also retrieve the memory stream as a byte array:

```
// Dump memory data to file.
FileStream dumpFile = new FileStream("Dump.dat", FileMode.Create,
    FileAccess.ReadWrite);
myMemStream.WriteTo(dumpFile);
// Dump memory data to a byte array.
byte[] bytesinMemory = myMemStream.ToArray();
myMemStream.Close();
```

Working with BufferedStreams

The final Stream-derived type to consider here is BufferedStream. This type can be used as a temporary location to read or write information, which can later be committed to permanent storage. For example, assume you have opened a data file and need to write out a large series of bytes. While you could stuff each item directly to file using FileStream.Write(), you may wish to help optimize the process by storing the new items in a BufferedStream type and making a final commit when each addition has been accounted for. In this way, you can reduce the number of times you must hit the physical file. Here is an example:

```
// Build a buffer attached to a valid FileStream.
BufferedStream myFileBuffer = new BufferedStream(dumpFile);
// Add some bytes to the buffer.
byte[] str = { 127, 0x77, 0x4, 0x0, 0x0, 0x16};
myFileBuffer.Write(str, 0, str.Length);
// Commit changes to file.
myFileBuffer.Close();     // Automatically flushes.
```

SOURCE CODE The Streamer project illustrates working with the FileStream, MemoryStream, and BufferedStream types, and is located under the Chapter 16 subdirectory.

Working with StreamWriters and StreamReaders

The StreamWriter and StreamReader classes are useful whenever you need to read or write character-based data (e.g., strings). Both of these types work by default with Unicode characters; however, this can be changed by supplying a properly configured System.Text.Encoding object reference. To keep things simple, let's assume that the default Unicode encoding fits the bill. (Be sure to check out the System.Text namespace for other possibilities.)

StreamReader derives from an abstract type named TextReader, as does the related StringReader type (discussed later in this chapter). The TextReader base class provides a very limited set of functionality to each of these descendents, specifically the ability to read and peek into a character stream.

The StreamWriter type (as well as StringWriter, also examined later in this chapter) derives from an abstract base class named TextWriter. This class defines members that allow derived types to write textual data to a given character stream. The relationship between each of these new IO-centric types is shown in Figure 16-6.

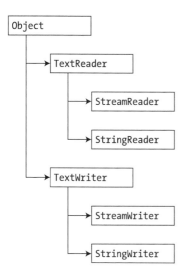

Figure 16-6. Readers and writers

To understand the writing capabilities of the StreamWriter class, you need to examine the base class functionality inherited from the TextWriter type. This abstract class defines the members described in Table 16-11.

Table 16-11. Core Members of TextWriter

TextWriter Member Name	Meaning in Life
Close()	Closes the writer and frees any associated resources. In the process, the buffer is automatically flushed.
Flush()	Clears all buffers for the current writer and causes any buffered data to be written to the underlying device, but does not close the writer.
NewLine	Used to make the new line constant for the derived writer class. The default line terminator is a carriage return followed by a line feed ("\r\n").
Write()	Writes a line to the text stream, without a new line constant.
WriteLine()	Writes a line to the text stream, with a new line constant.

The last two members of the TextWriter class probably look familiar to you. If you recall, the System.Console type has similar members that write textual data to the standard output device. (In fact Console.In inherits from TextWriter and Console.Out from TextReader.) Here, TextWriter moves the information to a specified file.

The derived StreamWriter class provides an appropriate implementation for the Write(), Close(), and Flush() methods, as well as defines the additional AutoFlush property. This property, when set to true, forces StreamWriter to flush all data every time you perform a write operation. Be aware that you can gain better performance by setting AutoFlush to false, provided you always call Close() when you are done writing with a StreamWriter.

Writing to a Text File

Now for an example of working with the StreamWriter type. The following class creates a new file named thoughts.txt using the FileInfo class. Using the CreateText() method, you can obtain a valid StreamWriter. At this point, you add some textual data to the new file, as shown here:

```csharp
public class MyStreamWriterReader
{
    public static int Main(string[] args)
    {
        // Make a file in the application directory.
        FileInfo f = new FileInfo("Thoughts.txt");
        // Get a StreamWriter and write some stuff.
        StreamWriter writer = f.CreateText();
        writer.WriteLine("Don't forget Mother's Day this year...");
        writer.WriteLine("Don't forget Father's Day this year...");
        writer.WriteLine("Don't forget these numbers:");
        for(int i = 0; i < 10; i++)
            writer.Write(i + " ");
        writer.Write(writer.NewLine);   // Insert a carriage return.
        // Closing automatically flushes!
        writer.Close();
        Console.WriteLine("Created file and wrote some thoughts...");
    }
}
```

If you locate this new file, you should be able to double-click it to open it a la Notepad. Figure 16-7 shows the content of your new file.

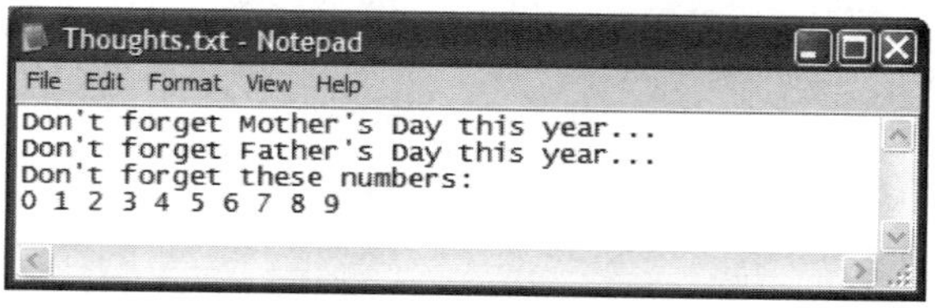

Figure 16-7. The contents of your *.txt file

As you can see, the StreamWriter has indeed written your data to a file. Do be aware that the Write() and WriteLine() methods have each been overloaded numerous times to provide a number of ways to add textual and numeric data (which defaults to Unicode encoding).

Reading from a Text File

Now you need to understand how to programmatically read data from a file using the corresponding StreamReader type. As you probably recall, this class derives from TextReader, which offers the functionality described in Table 16-12.

Table 16-12. TextReader Core Members

TextReader Member Name	Meaning in Life
Peek()	Returns the next available character without actually changing the position of the reader
Read()	Reads data from an input stream
ReadBlock()	Reads a maximum of count characters from the current stream and writes the data to a buffer, beginning at index
ReadLine()	Reads a line of characters from the current stream and returns the data as a string (a null string indicates EOF)
ReadToEnd()	Reads all characters from the current position to the end of the TextReader and returns them as one string

If you now extend the current MyStreamWriterReader class to use a StreamReader, you can read in the textual data from the thoughts.txt file, as shown here:

```
public class MyStreamWriterReader
{
    public static int Main(string[] args)
    {
        // Writing logic as before.
        ...
        // Now read it all back in using a StreamReader.
        Console.WriteLine("Here are your thoughts:\n");
        StreamReader sr = File.OpenText("Thoughts.txt");
        string input = null;
        while ((input = sr.ReadLine()) != null)
            Console.WriteLine (input);
        sr.Close();
        return 0;
    }
}
```

Running the program, you would see the output shown in Figure 16-8.

Figure 16-8. Reading from a file

Here, you obtained a valid StreamReader using the static File.OpenText() method. The read logic makes use of StreamReader.Peek() to ensure that you have an additional character ahead of the reader's current position. If so, you read the next line and pump it to the console. To obtain the contents of the entire file, you could avoid the "peeking" and simply call ReadToEnd(), as shown here:

```
// Be sure to add a reference to System.Windows.Forms.dll
// and specify a proper 'using' directive to access the
// MessageBox type.
string allOfTheData = sr.ReadToEnd();
MessageBox.Show(allOfTheData, "Here it is:");
sr.Close();
```

As you can see, the StreamReader and StreamWriter types provide a custom implementation of the abstract members defined by their respective base classes. Just remember that these two types are concerned with moving text-based data to and from a specified file.

SOURCE CODE   The StreamWriterReaderApp project is included under the Chapter 16 subdirectory.

Working with StringWriters

Using the StringWriter and StringReader types, you can treat textual information as a stream of in-memory characters. This can prove helpful when you wish to append character-based information to an underlying buffer. To gain access to the underlying buffer from an instance of a StringWriter type, you can call the overridden ToString() method (to receive a System.String type) or the GetStringBuilder() method, which returns an instance of System.Text.StringBuilder.

To illustrate, reengineer the previous example to write the character information to a StringWriter instance rather than a generated file. As you should notice, the two programs are nearly identical, given that both StringWriter and StreamWriter inherit the same base class functionality, as shown here:

```
public class MyStringWriterReader
{
    public static int Main(string[] args)
    {
        // Get a StringWriter and write some stuff.
        StringWriter writer = new StringWriter();
        writer.WriteLine("Don't forget Mother's Day this year...");
        writer.WriteLine("Don't forget Father's Day this year...");
        writer.WriteLine("Don't forget these numbers:");
        for(int i = 0; i < 10; i++)
            writer.Write(i + " ");
        writer.Write(writer.NewLine);      // Insert a carriage return.
        writer.Close();
        Console.WriteLine("Stored thoughts in a StringWriter...");
        // Get a copy of the contents (stored in a string) and pump
        // to console.
        Console.WriteLine("Contents: {0} ", writer.ToString());
        return 0;
    }
}
```

Running this program, of course, dumps out textual data to the console. To gain access to the underlying StringBuilder maintained by the StringWriter, simply add the following logic:

```
// For StringBuilder type!
using System.Text;
...
public class MyStringWriterReader
{
    public static int Main(string[] args)
    {
        // Previous logic...

        ...
        // Get the internal StringBuilder.
        StringBuilder str = writer.GetStringBuilder();
        string allOfTheData = str.ToString();
        Console.WriteLine("StringBuilder says:\n{0}  ", allOfTheData);
        // Insert item to buffer at position 20.
        str.Insert(20, "INSERTED STUFF");
        allOfTheData = str.ToString();
        Console.WriteLine("New StringBuilder says:\n{0}  ", allOfTheData);
```

```
        // Remove the inserted string.
        str.Remove(20, "INSERTED STUFF".Length);
        allOfTheData = str.ToString();
        Console.WriteLine("Original says:\n{0} ", allOfTheData);
        return 0;
    }
}
```

Here, you can write some character data to a StringWriter type and extract and manipulate a copy of the contents using the GetStringBuilder() member function.

Working with `StringReaders`

Next is the StringReader type, which (as you would expect) functions identically to the related StreamReader class. In fact, the StringReader class does nothing more than override the inherited members to read from a block of character data, rather than a file, as shown here:

```
// Now dump using a StringReader.
StringReader sr = new StringReader(writer.ToString());
string input = null;
while ((input = sr.ReadLine()) != null)
{
    Console.WriteLine (input);
}
sr.Close();
```

Figure 16-9 shows the output.

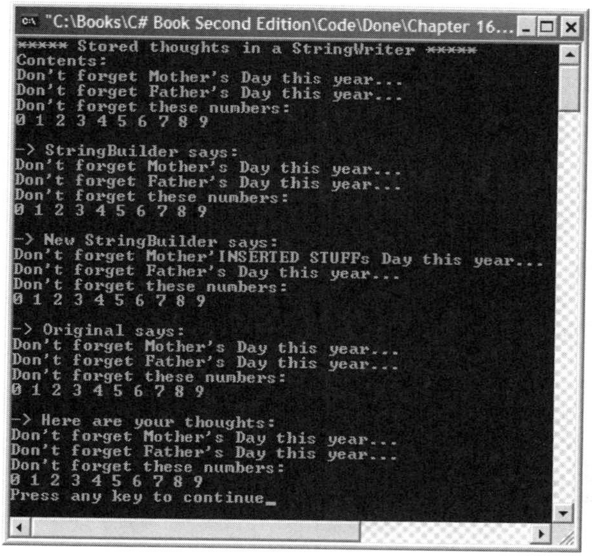

Figure 16-9. Manipulating the StringBuilder

If you were paying attention to the previous sample applications, you may have noticed one limitation of the TextReader and TextWriter descendents. None of these types has the ability to provide random access to its contents (e.g., seeking). For example, StreamReader has no members that allow you to reset the internal file cursor or jump over some number of characters and begin reading from that point. To gain this sort of functionality, you need to use various descendents of the Stream type.

SOURCE CODE   The StringReaderWriterApp is included under the Chapter 16 subdirectory.

Working with Binary Data (BinaryReaders and BinaryWriters)

The final two core classes provided by the System.IO namespace are BinaryReader and BinaryWriter, both of which derive directly from System.Object. These types allow you to read and write discrete data types to an underlying stream. The BinaryWriter class defines a highly overloaded method named (of course) Write() to place a data type in the corresponding stream. The BinaryWriter class also provides some other familiar-looking members (Table 16-13).

Table 16-13. BinaryWriter Core Members

BinaryWriter Member	Meaning in Life
BaseStream	Represents the underlying stream used with the binary reader
Close()	Closes the binary stream
Flush()	Flushes the binary stream
Seek()	Sets the position in the current stream
Write()	Writes a value to the current stream

The BinaryReader class complements the functionality offered by BinaryWriter with the members described in Table 16-14.

Table 16-14. BinaryReader Core Members

BinaryReader Member	Meaning in Life
BaseStream	Enables access to the underlying stream.
Close()	Closes the binary reader.
PeekChar()	Returns the next available character without actually advancing the position in the stream.
Read()	Reads a given set of bytes or characters and stores them in the incoming array.
ReadXXXX()	The BinaryReader class defines numerous ReadXXXX methods that grab the next type from the stream (ReadBoolean(), ReadByte(), ReadInt32(), and so forth).

The following class writes a number of character types to a new *.dat file created and opened using the FileStream class. Once you have a valid FileStream, pass this object to the constructor of the BinaryWriter type. Understand that the constructor of BinaryWriter takes any Stream-derived type (for example, FileStream, MemoryStream, or BufferedStream). Once the data has been written, a corresponding BinaryReader reads each byte back, as shown here:

```
public class ByteTweaker
{
    public static int Main(string[] args)
    {
        Console.WriteLine("Creating a file and writing binary data...");
        FileStream myFStream
            = new FileStream("temp.dat", FileMode.OpenOrCreate,
                FileAccess.ReadWrite);
        // Write some binary info.
        BinaryWriter binWrit = new BinaryWriter(myFStream);
        binWrit.Write("Hello as binary info...");
        int myInt = 99;
        float myFloat = 9984.82343F;
        bool myBool = false;
        char[] myCharArray = { 'H', 'e', 'l', 'l', 'o'} ;
        binWrit.Write(myInt);
        binWrit.Write(myFloat);
        binWrit.Write(myBool);
        binWrit.Write(myCharArray);
        // Reset internal position.
        binWrit.BaseStream.Position = 0;
        // Read the binary info as raw bytes.
        Console.WriteLine("Reading binary data...");
        BinaryReader binRead = new BinaryReader(myFStream);
        int temp = 0;
        while(binRead.PeekChar() != -1)
```

```
        {
            Console.Write(binRead.ReadByte());
            temp = temp + 1;
            if(temp ==  5)
            {
                // Add a blank line every 5 bytes.
                temp = 0;
                Console.WriteLine();
            }
        }
        // Clean things up.
        binWrit.Close();
        binRead.Close();
        myFStream.Close();
    }
}
```

SOURCE CODE   The BinaryReaderWriter application is included under the Chapter 16 subdirectory.

"Watching" Files and Directories

Now that you have a better handle on the use of various readers and writers, next we'll check out the role of the FileSystemWatcher class. This type can be quite helpful when you wish to programmatically monitor (or "watch") files on your system. Specifically, the FileSystemWatcher type can be instructed to monitor files for any of the actions specified by the NotifyFilters enumeration (while many of these members are self-explanatory, check online help for further details):

```
public enum System.IO.NotifyFilters
{
    Attributes, CreationTime,
    DirectoryName, FileName,
    LastAccess, LastWrite,
    Security, Size,
}
```

The first step you will need to take to work with the FileSystemWatcher type is to set the Path property to specify the name (and location) of the directory that contains the files to be monitored, as well as the Filter property that defines the file extension of the files to be monitored. Next, you will set the NotifyFilter property using members of the System.IO.NotifyFilters enumeration.

At this point, you may choose to handle the Changed, Created, and Deleted events, all of which work in conjunction with the FileSystemEventHandler delegate. As well, the Renamed event may also be handled via the RenamedEventHandler type. Last but not least, set the EnableRaisingEvents property to true to begin spying on your file set.

To illustrate, assume you have created a new directory on your C drive named ParanoidFolder that contains two *.txt files (named whatever you wish). The following console application will monitor the *.txt files within the ParanoidFolder, and print out messages in the event that the files are created, deleted, modified, or renamed:

```
public class TheWatcher
{
    public static void Main()
    {
        // Establish which directory to watch
        // (assume of course you have this directory...)
        FileSystemWatcher watcher = new FileSystemWatcher();
        watcher.Path = @"C:\ParanoidFolder";
        // Set up the things to be on the look out for.
        watcher.NotifyFilter = NotifyFilters.LastAccess | NotifyFilters.LastWrite
            | NotifyFilters.FileName | NotifyFilters.DirectoryName;
        // Only watch text files.
        watcher.Filter = "*.txt";
        // Add event handlers.
        watcher.Changed += new FileSystemEventHandler(OnChanged);
        watcher.Created += new FileSystemEventHandler(OnChanged);
        watcher.Deleted += new FileSystemEventHandler(OnChanged);
        watcher.Renamed += new RenamedEventHandler(OnRenamed);
        // Begin watching the directory.
        watcher.EnableRaisingEvents = true;
        // Wait for the user to quit the program.
        Console.WriteLine(@"Press 'q' to quit app.");
        while(Console.Read()!='q');
    }

    // Event handlers (note the signature of the delegate targets!)
    private static void OnChanged(object source, FileSystemEventArgs e)
    {
        // Specify what is done when a file is changed, created, or deleted.
        Console.WriteLine("File: {0} {1}!", e.FullPath, e.ChangeType);
    }
    private static void OnRenamed(object source, RenamedEventArgs e)
    {
        // Specify what is done when a file is renamed.
        Console.WriteLine("File: {0} renamed to\n{1}", e.OldFullPath, e.FullPath);
    }
}
```

Now, to test this program, run the application and open up the Windows Explorer. Try renaming your files, creating a new *.txt file, deleting a *.txt file, or whatnot. You will see the console application print out various bits of information regarding the state of the text files (Figure 16-10).

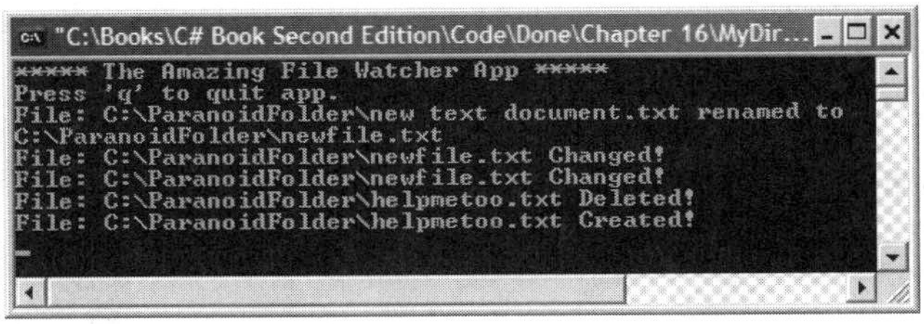

Figure 16-10. Watching some *.txt files

SOURCE CODE   The MyDirectoryWatcher application is included under the Chapter 16 subdirectory.

A Brief Word Regarding Asynchronous IO

You have already seen the asynchronous support provided by the .NET Framework during our examination of delegates (Chapter 7) and the .NET Remoting layer (Chapter 12). Needless to say, numerous types in the System.IO namespace support asynchronous operations. Specifically, any type deriving from the abstract System.IO.Stream type inherits BeginRead(), BeginWrite(), EndRead(), and EndWrite() methods. As you would expect, each of these methods works in conjunction with the IAsyncResult type:

```
public abstract class System.IO.Stream :
    MarshalByRefObject,
    IDisposable
{
...
    public virtual IAsyncResult BeginRead(byte[] buffer, int offset,
        int count, AsyncCallback callback, object state);
    public virtual IAsyncResult BeginWrite(byte[] buffer, int offset,
        int count, AsyncCallback callback, object state);
    public virtual int EndRead(IAsyncResult asyncResult);
    public virtual void EndWrite(IAsyncResult asyncResult);
}
```

The process of working with the asynchronous behavior of Stream-derived types is identical to working with asynchronous delegates and asynchronous remote method invocations. In reality, you may never need to read or write to a Stream derivative asynchronously, unless perhaps you are building a .NET-aware photo-editing application (where the image files can be quite large indeed). Nevertheless, should the need arise, just remember Stream-derived types automatically support this behavior.

A Windows Forms Car Logger Application

Speaking of Chapter 12 (see the preceding section), as you can surely surmise, the types of the System.IO namespace work naturally with the .NET object serialization model. Given this, the remainder of this chapter walks you through a minimal and complete Windows Forms application named CarLogApp. The CarLogApp allows the end user to create an inventory of Car types (contained in an ArrayList), which are displayed in yet another Windows Forms control, the DataGrid (Figure 16-11). To keep focused on the serialization logic, this grid is read-only.

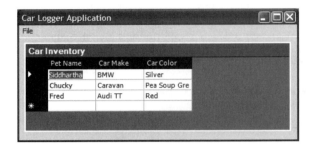

Figure 16-11. The car logger application

The topmost File menu provides a number of choices that operate on the underlying ArrayList. Table 16-15 describes the possible selections.

Table 16-15. File Menu Options of the CarLogApp Project

File Submenu Item	Meaning in Life
Make New Car	Displays a custom dialog box that allows the user to configure a new Car and refreshes the DataGrid.
Clear All Cars	Empties the ArrayList and refreshes the DataGrid.
Open Car File	Allows the user to open an existing *.car file and refreshes the DataGrid. This file is the result of a BinaryFormatter.
Save Car File	Saves all cars displayed in the DataGrid to a *.car file.
Exit	Exits the application.

I will not bother to detail the menu construction logic, as you have already seen these steps during the formal discussion of Windows Forms. The first task is to define the Car type itself. This is the class that represents not only a unique row in the DataGrid, but also an item in the serialized object graph. There are numerous iterations of the

Car class throughout this book, so this version is brutally bland (recall the role of the [Serializable] attribute!):

```
[Serializable]
public class Car
{
    // Make public for easy access.
    public string petName, make, color;
    public Car(string petName, string make, string color)
    {
        this.petName = petName;
        this.color = color;
        this.make = make;
    }
}
```

Next, you need to add a few members to the main Form class. The overall UI of the DataGrid type is configured using a small set of properties, all of which have been assigned using the Properties window of the Visual Studio .NET IDE. The most important property for this example is the ReadOnly member (set to true), which prevents the user from editing the cells in the DataGrid. The remaining configurations establish the type's color scheme and physical dimensions (which you can explore at your leisure).

In addition, the main Form maintains a private ArrayList type, which holds each of the Car references. The Form's constructor adds a number of default cars to allow the user to view some initial items in the grid. Once these Car types have been added to the collection, you call a helper function named UpdateGrid(), as shown here:

```
public class mainForm : System.Windows.Forms.Form
{
    // ArrayList for object serialization.
    private ArrayList arTheCars = null;
    ...
    public mainForm()
    {
        InitializeComponent();
        CenterToScreen();
        // Add some cars.
        arTheCars = new ArrayList();
        arTheCars.Add(new Car("Siddhartha", "BMW", "Silver"));
        arTheCars.Add(new Car("Chucky", "Caravan", "Pea Soup Green"));
        arTheCars.Add(new Car("Fred", "Audi TT", "Red"));
        // Display data in grid.
        UpdateGrid();
    }
    ...
}
```

The UpdateGrid() method is responsible for creating a System.Data.DataTable type that contains a row for each Car in the ArrayList. Once the DataTable has been populated, you then bind it the DataGrid type. Chapter 17 examines the ADO.NET types (such as the DataTable) in much greater detail, so here the focus is on the basics for the time being. Here is the code:

```
private void UpdateGrid()
{
    if(arTheCars != null)
    {
        // Make a DataTable object named Inventory.
        DataTable inventory = new DataTable("Inventory");
        // Create DataColumn objects that map to the fields of the Car type.
        DataColumn make = new DataColumn("Car Make");
        DataColumn petName = new DataColumn("Pet Name");
        DataColumn color = new DataColumn("Car Color");
        // Add columns to data table.
        inventory.Columns.Add(petName);
        inventory.Columns.Add(make);
        inventory.Columns.Add(color);
        // Iterate over the array list to make rows.
        foreach(Car c in arTheCars)
        {
            DataRow newRow;
            newRow = inventory.NewRow();
            newRow["Pet Name"] = c.petName;
            newRow["Car Make"] = c.make;
            newRow["Car Color"] = c.color;
            inventory.Rows.Add(newRow);
        }
        // Now bind this data table to the grid.
        carDataGrid.DataSource = inventory;
    }
}
```

Begin by creating a new DataTable type named Inventory. In the world of ADO.NET, a DataTable is an in-memory representation of a single table of information. While you might assume that a DataTable would be created as a result of some SQL query, you can also use this type as a stand-alone entity.

Once you have a new DataTable, you need to establish the set of columns that should be listed in the table. The System.Data.DataColumn type represents a single column. Given that this iteration of the Car type has three public fields (make, color, and pet name), create three DataColumns and insert them in the table using the DataTable.Columns property.

Next, you need to add each row to the table. Recall that the main Form maintains an ArrayList that contains some number of Car types. Given that ArrayList implements the IEnumerable interface, you can fetch each Car from the collection, read each public field, and compose and insert a new DataRow in the table. Finally, the new DataTable is bound to the GUI DataGrid widget using the DataSource property.

Now then! If you run the application at this point, you will find that the grid is indeed populated with the default set of automobiles. This is a good start, but you can do better.

Implementing the Add New Car Logic

The CarLogApp project defines another Form-derived type (AddCarDlg) that functions as a modal dialog box (Figure 16-12). From a GUI point of view, this type is composed of a TextBox (to hold the pet name) and two ListBox types (to allow the user to select the color and make).

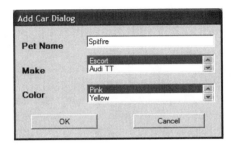

Figure 16-12. The Add a Car dialog box

As far as the code behind the Form, the OK button has been assigned the DialogResult property DialogResult.OK. As you recall, this value marks a Button type to function as a standard OK button. Also, this Form maintains a public Car type (for easy access), which is configured when the user clicks the OK button. The remainder of the code is nothing more than some GUI control prep work. The relevant logic is as follows:

```
public class AddCarDlg : System.Windows.Forms.Form
{
    // Make public for easy access.
    public Car theCar = null;
    ...
    protected void btnOK_Click (object sender, System.EventArgs e)
    {
        // Configure a new Car when user clicks OK button.
        theCar = new Car(txtName.Text, listMake.Text, listColor.Text);
    }
}
```

The main Form displays this dialog box when the user selects the Make New Car menu item. Here is the code behind that object's Clicked event:

```
protected void menuItemNewCar_Click (object sender, System.EventArgs e)
{
    // Show the dialog and check for OK click.
    AddCarDlg d = new AddCarDlg();
    if(d.ShowDialog() == DialogResult.OK)
    {
        // Add new car to array list.
        arTheCars.Add(d.theCar);
        UpdateGrid();
    }
}
```

No surprises here. You just show the Form as a modal dialog box, and if the OK button has been clicked, you read the public Car member variable, add it to the ArrayList, and refresh your grid.

The Serialization Logic

The core logic behind the Save Car File and Open Car File Click event handlers should pose no problems at this point. When the user chooses to save the current inventory, you create a new file and use a BinaryFormatter to serialize the object graph. However, just to keep things interesting, the user can establish the name and location of this file using a System.Windows.Forms.SaveFileDialog type. This type is yet another standard dialog box and is illustrated in Figure 16-13.

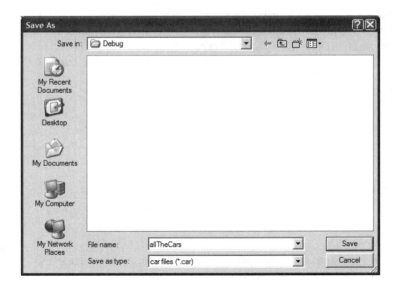

Figure 16-13. The standard File Save dialog box

Notice that the SaveFileDialog is listing a custom file extension (*.car). While I leave the task of investigating the complete functionality of the SaveFileDialog in your capable hands, it is worth pointing out that this has been assigned using the Filter property. This property takes an OR-delimited string that represents the text to be used in the drop-down File name and Save as type combo boxes. Here is the full implementation:

```
protected void menuItemSave_Click (object sender, System.EventArgs e)
{
    // Configure look and feel of save dialog box.
    SaveFileDialog mySaveFileDialog = new SaveFileDialog();
    mySaveFileDialog.InitialDirectory = ".";
    mySaveFileDialog.Filter = "car files (*.car)|*.car|All files (*.*)|*.*";
    mySaveFileDialog.FilterIndex = 1;
    mySaveFileDialog.RestoreDirectory = true;
    mySaveFileDialog.FileName = "carDoc";
    // Do you have a file?
    if(mySaveFileDialog.ShowDialog() == DialogResult.OK)
    {
        Stream myStream = null;
        if((myStream = mySaveFileDialog.OpenFile()) != null)
        {
            // Save the cars!
            BinaryFormatter myBinaryFormat = new BinaryFormatter();
            myBinaryFormat.Serialize(myStream, arTheCars);
            myStream.Close();
        }
    }
}
```

Also note that the OpenFile() member of the SaveFileDialog type returns a Stream that represents the specified file selected by the end user. As seen in Chapter 13, this is the very thing needed by the BinaryFormatter type.

The logic behind the Open Car File Click event handler looks very similar. This time you create an instance of the System.Windows.Forms OpenFileDialog type, configure accordingly, and obtain a Stream reference based on the selected file. Next you dump the contents of the ArrayList and read in the new object graph using the BinaryFormatter.Deserialize() method, as shown here:

```
protected void menuItemOpen_Click (object sender, System.EventArgs e)
{
    // Configure look and feel of open dialog box.
    OpenFileDialog myOpenFileDialog = new OpenFileDialog();
    myOpenFileDialog.InitialDirectory = ".";
    myOpenFileDialog.Filter = "car files (*.car)|*.car|All files (*.*)|*.*";
    myOpenFileDialog.FilterIndex = 1;
    myOpenFileDialog.RestoreDirectory = true;
```

```
// Do you have a file?
if(myOpenFileDialog.ShowDialog() == DialogResult.OK)
{
    // Clear current array list.
    arTheCars.Clear();
    Stream myStream = null;
    if((myStream = myOpenFileDialog.OpenFile()) != null)
    {
        // Get the cars!
        BinaryFormatter myBinaryFormat = new BinaryFormatter();
        arTheCars = (ArrayList)myBinaryFormat.Deserialize(myStream);
        myStream.Close();
        UpdateGrid();
    }
}
}
```

At this point, the application can save and load the entire set of Car types held in the ArrayList using a BinaryFormatter. The final menu items are self-explanatory, as shown here:

```
protected void menuItemClear_Click (object sender, System.EventArgs e)
{
    arTheCars.Clear();
    UpdateGrid();
}
protected void menuItemExit_Click (object sender, System.EventArgs e)
{
    Application.Exit();
}
```

This wraps up our exploration of the System.IO namespace. Over the course of this chapter you have seen how to read and write data to binary, character-based, and memory streams. In the next chapter you will come to understand how to interact with XML-based data readers (and writers).

SOURCE CODE   The CarLogApp project is included under the Chapter 16 subdirectory.

Summary

This chapter began by examining the use of the Directory(Info) and File(Info) types. As you have seen, these classes allow you to manipulate a physical file or directory on your hard drive.

Next you examined a number of types derived from the abstract Stream class, including FileStream, MemoryStream, and BufferedStream. Given that each of these types has (more or less) the same public interface, you can easily swap them in and out of your code to alter the ultimate location of your byte array. When you are interested in persisting textual data, the StreamReader and StreamWriter types usually fit the bill.

We wrapped things up by investigating how the types of the System.IO namespace can be used in conjunction with .NET object serialization services to persist custom types to a given location.

CHAPTER 17

Data Access
with ADO.NET

U<small>NLESS YOU ARE</small> a video game developer by trade, you are probably interested in database manipulation. As you would expect, the .NET platform defines a number of types (in a handful of related namespaces) that allow you to interact with local and remote data stores. Collectively speaking, these namespaces are known as ADO.NET, which as you will see is a major overhaul of the classic ADO object model.

This chapter begins by examining some core types defined in the System.Data namespace—specifically DataColumn, DataRow, and DataTable. These classes allow you to define and manipulate a local in-memory table of data. Next, you spend a good deal of time learning about the centerpiece of ADO.NET, the DataSet. As you will see, the DataSet is an in-memory representation of a *collection* of interrelated tables. During this discussion, you will learn how to programmatically model table relationships, establish custom views based on a given DataTable, and submit queries against your in-memory DataSet.

After examining how to manually build and manipulate a DataSet by hand, you'll examine how to obtain a populated DataSet from a Database Management System (DBMS) such as MS SQL Server, Oracle, or MS Access. During the process, you will examine the role of .NET data providers and come to understand the use of ADO.NET data adapters, command objects, and command builders.

In contrast to the intrinsically disconnected world of DataSets and data adapters, this chapter also examines the *connected layer* of ADO.NET and the related data reader types. As you will see, the data reader is ideal when you simply wish to obtain a result set from a data store for display purposes. We wrap things up with an overview of various database-centric wizards of Visual Studio .NET, and come to see how these integrated tools can be used to lessen the amount of ADO.NET code you would otherwise need to write by hand.

The Need for ADO.NET

The very first thing you must understand when approaching ADO.NET is that it is *not* simply the latest and greatest version of classic ADO. While it is true that there is some symmetry between the two systems (e.g., each has the concept of *connection* and *command* objects), some familiar types (e.g., the Recordset) no longer exist. Furthermore, there are a number of new ADO.NET types that have no direct equivalent under classic ADO (such as the data adapter). In a nutshell, ADO.NET is a brand new database access technology focused on facilitating the development of disconnected (and connected) systems using the .NET platform.

Unlike classic ADO, which was primarily designed for tightly coupled client/server systems, ADO.NET greatly extends the notion of the primitive ADO disconnected Recordset with a new creature named the DataSet. This type represents a *local* copy of any number of related tables. Using the DataSet, the client is able to manipulate and update its contents while disconnected from the data source and submit the modified data back for processing using a related *data adapter*.

Another major difference between classic ADO and ADO.NET is that ADO.NET has full support for XML data representation. In fact, the data obtained from a data store is internally represented, and transmitted, as XML. Given that XML is often transported between layers using standard HTTP, ADO.NET is not limited by firewall constraints.

As you might be aware, classic ADO makes use of the COM marshaling protocol to move data between tiers. While this was appropriate in some situations, COM marshaling poses a number of limitations. For example, most firewalls are configured to reject COM RPC packets, which made moving data between machines tricky.

Perhaps the most fundamental difference between classic ADO and ADO.NET is that ADO.NET is a managed library of code and therefore plays by all the same rules as any managed library. The types that comprise ADO.NET use the CLR memory management protocol, adhere to the same programming model, and work with many languages. Therefore, the types (and their members) are accessed in the same manner, regardless of which .NET-aware language you use.

The Two Faces of ADO.NET

The ADO.NET libraries can be used in two conceptually unique manners: connected or disconnected. When you are making use of the connected layer, you will make use of a .NET data reader. As you will see later in this chapter, data readers provide a way to pull records from a data store using a forward-only, read-only approach (much like a fire hose cursor). As a given data reader pulls over records based on your SQL query, you are directly connected to the data store and stay that way until you explicitly close the connection. In addition to simply reading data via a data reader, the connected layer of ADO.NET allows you to insert, update, or remove records using a related command object.

The disconnected layer, on the other hand, allows you to obtain a set of DataTable types (typically contained within a DataSet) that serves as a local client-side copy of information. When you obtain a DataSet using a data adapter type, the connection is automatically terminated immediately after the fill request (as you would guess, this approach helps quickly free up connects for other callers). At this point, the client application is able to manipulate the DataSet's contents without incurring any network traffic. If the client wishes to push the changes back to the data store, the data adapter (in conjunction with a set of SQL queries) is used once again to update the data source, at which point the connection is again closed immediately.

In some respects, this approach may remind you of the classic ADO disconnected Recordset. The key difference is that a disconnected Recordset represents a single set of record data, whereas ADO.NET DataSets can model a collection of related tables. In fact, it is technically possible to obtain a client-side DataSet that represents all of the tables found within the remote database. However, as you would expect, a DataSet will more commonly contain a reasonable subset of information.

The Role of ADO.NET Data Providers

Rather than providing a single set of objects to communicate to a variety of data stores, ADO.NET makes use of multiple *data providers*. Simply put, a data provider is a set of types (within some .NET assembly) that understand how to communicate with a specific data source. Although the names of these types will differ among data providers, each provider will have (at minimum) a set of class types that implement some key interfaces defined in the System.Data namespace, specifically IDbCommand, IDbDataAdapter, IDbConnection, and IDataReader. As you would guess, these interfaces define the behaviors a managed provider must support to provide connected and disconnected access to the underlying data store (see Figure 17-1).

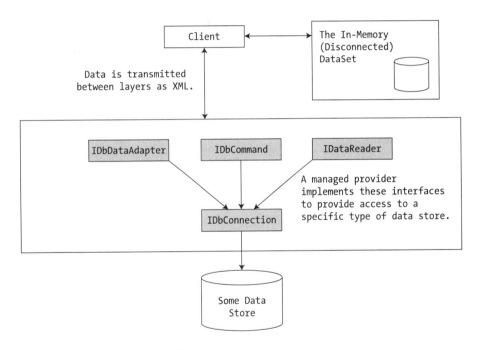

Figure 17-1. ADO.NET data providers provide access to a given DBMS.

To better understand the core functionality of any data provider, let's check out the formal definition of each interface type (of course, numerous details are to follow).

NOTE In version 1.0 of the .NET platform, data providers were termed *managed providers*. Therefore, if you are reading earlier .NET literature (including the first edition of this text), understand that these two terms are completely synonymous with each other.

The Role of the IDbConnection and IDbTransaction Interfaces

First we have the IDbConnection type, which is implemented by a data provider's connection object. This interface defines a set of members used to connect to (and disconnect from) a specific data store, as well as allowing you to obtain the data provider's transactional object, which (surprise, surprise) implements the System.Data.IDbTransaction interface:

```
public interface System.Data.IDbConnection : IDisposable
{
    string ConnectionString { get; set; }
    int ConnectionTimeout { get; }
    string Database { get; }
    ConnectionState State { get; }
    System.Data.IDbTransaction BeginTransaction();
    System.Data.IDbTransaction BeginTransaction(System.Data.IsolationLevel il);
    void ChangeDatabase(string databaseName);
    void Close();
    System.Data.IDbCommand CreateCommand();
    void Open();
}
```

As you can see, the overloaded BeginTransaction() method provides access to an IDbTransaction-compatible type. Using the members defined by this interface, you are able to programmatically interact with a transactional session and the underlying data store:

```
public interface System.Data.IDbTransaction : IDisposable
{
    IDbConnection Connection { get; }
    IsolationLevel IsolationLevel { get; }
    void Commit();
    void Rollback();
}
```

The Role of the IDbCommand, IDbDataParameter, and IDataParameter Interfaces

Next up, we have the IDbCommand interface, which will be implemented by a data provider's command object. Like other data access object models, command objects allow programmatic manipulation of SQL statements, stored procedures, and parameterized queries (note that each parameter object implements the IDbDataParameter type). In addition, command objects also provide access to the data provider's data reader type via the overloaded ExecuteReader() method:

```
public interface System.Data.IDbCommand :  IDisposable
{
    string CommandText { get; set; }
    int CommandTimeout { get; set; }
    CommandType CommandType { get; set; }
    IDbConnection Connection { get; set; }
    IDataParameterCollection Parameters { get; }
    IDbTransaction Transaction { get; set; }
    UpdateRowSource UpdatedRowSource { get; set; }
    void Cancel();
    System.Data.IDbDataParameter CreateParameter();
    int ExecuteNonQuery();
    System.Data.IDataReader ExecuteReader();
    System.Data.IDataReader ExecuteReader(System.Data.CommandBehavior behavior);
    object ExecuteScalar();
    void Prepare();
}
```

Notice that the Parameters property returns a strongly typed collection that implements IDataParameterCollection. This interface provides access to a set of IDbDataParameter-compliant data types (e.g., parameter objects):

```
public interface System.Data.IDbDataParameter :
    System.Data.IDataParameter
{
    byte Precision { get; set; }
    byte Scale { get; set; }
    int Size { get; set; }
}
```

IDbDataParameter extends the IDataParameter interface to obtain the following additional behaviors:

```
public interface System.Data.IDataParameter
{
    DbType DbType { get; set; }
    ParameterDirection Direction { get; set; }
    bool IsNullable { get; }
    string ParameterName { get; set; }
    string SourceColumn { get; set; }
    DataRowVersion SourceVersion { get; set; }
    object Value { get; set; }
}
```

As you will see, the functionality of the IDbDataParameter and IDataParameter interfaces allow you to represent parameters within a SQL query (as well as stored procedures) via specific ADO.NET parameter objects, rather than hard-coded strings.

The Role of the IDbDataAdapter and IDataAdapter Interfaces

Recall that data adapters are used to push and pull DataSets to and from a given data store. Given this, the IDbDataAdapter interface defines a set of properties that are used to maintain the SQL statements for the related SELECT, INSERT, UPDATE, and DELETE operations:

```
public interface System.Data.IDbDataAdapter : System.Data.IDataAdapter
{
    IDbCommand DeleteCommand { get; set; }
    IDbCommand InsertCommand { get; set; }
    IDbCommand SelectCommand { get; set; }
    IDbCommand UpdateCommand { get; set; }
}
```

In addition to these four properties, an ADO.NET data adapter also picks up the behavior defined in the base interface, IDataAdapter. This interface defines the key function of a data adapter type: the ability to push and pull DataSets between the caller and underlying data store using the Fill() and Update() methods. Also, the IDataAdapter interface allows you to map database column names to a more human-readable display name via the TableMappings property:

```
public interface System.Data.IDataAdapter
{
    MissingMappingAction MissingMappingAction { get; set; }
    MissingSchemaAction MissingSchemaAction { get; set; }
    ITableMappingCollection TableMappings { get; }
    int Fill(System.Data.DataSet dataSet);
    System.Data.DataTable[] FillSchema(System.Data.DataSet dataSet,
        System.Data.SchemaType schemaType);
    System.Data.IDataParameter[] GetFillParameters();
    int Update(System.Data.DataSet dataSet);
}
```

The Role of the IDataReader and IDataRecord Interfaces

The next key interface to be aware of is IDataReader, which (obviously) represents the common behaviors supported by a given data reader type. When you obtain an IDataReader-compatible type from an ADO.NET data provider, you are able to iterate over the result set using a forward-only, read-only manner.

```
public interface System.Data.IDataReader : IDisposable,
    System.Data.IDataRecord
{
    int Depth { get; }
    bool IsClosed { get; }
    int RecordsAffected { get; }
    void Close();
    System.Data.DataTable GetSchemaTable();
    bool NextResult();
    bool Read();
}
```

Finally, as you can see, IDataReader extends IDataRecord, which defines an additional set of members that allow you to extract out a strongly typed value from the stream, rather than casting the generic System.Object retrieved from the data reader's overloaded indexer method:

```
public interface System.Data.IDataRecord
{
    int FieldCount { get; }
    object this[ string name ] { get; }
    object this[ int i ] { get; }
    bool GetBoolean(int i);
    byte GetByte(int i);
    long GetBytes(int i, long fieldOffset, byte[] buffer,
        int bufferoffset, int length);
    char GetChar(int i);
    long GetChars(int i, long fieldoffset, char[] buffer,
        int bufferoffset, int length);
    System.Data.IDataReader GetData(int i);
    string GetDataTypeName(int i);
    DateTime GetDateTime(int i);
    Decimal GetDecimal(int i);
    double GetDouble(int i);
    Type GetFieldType(int i);
    float GetFloat(int i);
    Guid GetGuid(int i);
    short GetInt16(int i);
    int GetInt32(int i);
    long GetInt64(int i);
    string GetName(int i);
    int GetOrdinal(string name);
    string GetString(int i);
    object GetValue(int i);
    int GetValues(object[] values);
    bool IsDBNull(int i);
}
```

Now, to be sure, a data provider will supply you with other types beyond the classes that implement the key IDataReader, IDbCommand, IDbConnection, and IDbDataAdapter interfaces. Likewise, the classes in question will certainly define additional members beyond the set specified by the related interface type.

Nevertheless, at this point you should have a better idea of the common functionality found among all .NET data providers. Recall that even though the exact names of the implementing types will differ among data providers, you are able to program against these types in a similar manner, given the beauty of interface-based polymorphism:

```
System.Data.OleDb.OleDbConnection c;          // Implements IDbConnection!
System.Data.Odbc.OdbcConnection c2;           // Implements IDbConnection!
System.Data.Oracle.OracleConnection c3;       // Implements IDbConnection!
System.Data.SqlServerCe.SqlCeConnection c4;   // Implements IDbConnection!
System.Data.SqlClient.SqlConnection c5;       // Implements IDbConnection!
```

NOTE Explicit interface implementation (see Chapter 6) is not used by the types implementing these ADO.NET-centric interfaces. Therefore, you can call the interface methods directly from an object reference.

Understanding the ADO.NET Namespaces

.NET version 1.1 ships with five data providers out of the box, each of which is logically represented by a specific .NET namespace. In addition, ADO.NET defines some common namespaces that are used by all data provider implementations. Table 17-1 gives a quick rundown of each data-centric .NET namespace.

Table 17-1. ADO.NET Namespaces

ADO.NET Namespace	Meaning in Life
System.Data	This core namespace defines types that represent tables, rows, columns, constraints, and DataSets. This namespace does not define types to connect to a data source. Rather, it defines the types that represent the data itself.
System.Data.Common	This namespace contains types shared between data providers. Many of these types function as base classes to the concrete types defined by a given data provider.

Table 17-1. ADO.NET Namespaces (Continued)

ADO.NET Namespace	Meaning in Life
System.Data.OleDb	This namespace defines the types that allow you to connect to an OLE DB–compliant data source. Typically you will use this namespace only if you need to communicate with a data store that does not have a custom data provider.
System.Data.Odbc	This namespace defines the types that constitute the ODBC data provider.
System.Data.OracleClient	This namespace defines the types that constitute the Oracle data provider.
System.Data.SqlClient	This namespace defines the types that constitute the SQL data provider.
System.Data.SqlServerCe	This namespace defines the types that constitute the SQL CE data provider.
System.Data.SqlTypes	Represents native data types used by Microsoft SQL Server. Although you are always free to use the corresponding CLR data types, the SqlTypes are optimized to work with SQL Server.

The System.Data, System.Data.Common, System.Data.OleDb, System.Data.SqlClient, System.Data.Odbc, and System.Data.SqlTypes namespaces are all contained within the System.Data.dll assembly. However, the types of the System.Data.OracleClient namespaces are contained within a separate assembly named System.Data.OracleClient.dll, while the SqlCe types are placed within System.Data.Sqlservice.dll. Thus, like any .NET endeavor, be sure to set the correct external references (and C# "using" statements) for your current project.

The Types of System.Data

Of all the ADO.NET namespaces, System.Data is the lowest common denominator. You simply cannot build ADO.NET applications without specifying this namespace in your data access applications. This namespace contains types that are shared among all ADO.NET data providers, regardless of the underlying data store. In a nutshell, System.Data contains types that represent the data you obtain from a data store, but not the types that make the literal connection. In addition to a number of database-centric exceptions (NoNullAllowedException, RowNotInTableException, MissingPrimaryKeyException, and the like), these types are little more than OO representations of common database primitives (tables, rows, columns, constraints, and so on). Table 17-2 lists some of the core types, grouped by related functionality.

Table 17-2. Key Members of the System.Data Namespace

System.Data Type	Meaning in Life
DataColumnCollection DataColumn	DataColumnCollection is used to represent all of the columns used by a given DataTable.DataColumn represents a specific column in a DataTable.
ConstraintCollection Constraint	The ConstraintCollection represents all constraints (foreign key constrains, unique constraints) assigned to a given DataTable. Constraint represents an OO wrapper around a single constraint assigned to one or more DataColumns.
DataRowCollection DataRow	These types represent a collection of rows for a DataTable (DataRowCollection) and a specific row of data in a DataTable (DataRow).
DataRowView DataView	DataRowView allows you to carve out a predefined "view" from an existing row. The DataView type represents a customized view of a DataTable that can be used for sorting, filtering, searching, editing, and navigation.
DataSet	Represents an in-memory cache of data that may consist of multiple related DataTables.
ForeignKeyConstraint UniqueConstraint	ForeignKeyConstraint represents an action restriction enforced on a set of columns in a primary key/foreign key relationship. The UniqueConstraint type represents a restriction on a set of columns in which all values must be unique.
DataRelationCollection DataRelation	This collection represents all relationships (e.g., DataRelation types) between the tables in a DataSet.
DataTableCollection DataTable	The DataTableCollection type represents all of tables (e.g., DataTable types) for a particular DataSet.

To get the ball rolling, the first half of this chapter discusses how to manipulate these items by hand. Once you understand how to build a DataSet in the raw, you should have no problem manipulating a DataSet populated by a data provider using a related data adapter. Just as importantly, once you understand how to manually create and tweak a DataSet by hand, you will have no problems altering the wizard-generated code of VS .NET.

Examining the DataColumn Type

The DataColumn type represents a single column maintained by a DataTable. Collectively speaking, the set of all DataColumn types bound to a given DataTable represents the foundation of a table's schema information. For example, assume you have a table named Employees with three columns (EmpID, FirstName, and LastName). Programmatically, you would use three ADO.NET DataColumn objects to represent them in memory.

As you will see in just a moment, the DataTable type maintains an internal collection (which is accessed using the Columns property) to maintain its DataColumn types.

If you have a background in relational database theory, you know that a given column in a data table can be assigned a set of constraints (e.g., configured as a primary key, assigned a default value, configured to contain read-only information, and so on). Also, every column in a table must map to an underlying data type (int, varchar, and so forth). For example, the Employees table's schema may demand that the EmpID column maps to an integer, while FirstName and LastName map to an array of characters. The DataColumn class has numerous properties that allow you to configure these very things. Table 17-3 provides a rundown of some core properties.

Table 17-3. Properties of the DataColumn

DataColumn Property	Meaning in Life
AllowDBNull	Used to indicate if a row can specify null values in this column. The default value is true.
AutoIncrement AutoIncrementSeed AutoIncrementStep	These properties are used to configure the auto-increment behavior for a given column. This can be helpful when you wish to ensure unique values in a given DataColumn (such as a primary key). By default, a DataColumn does not support auto-incrementation.
Caption	Gets or sets the caption to be displayed for this column (for example, what the end user sees in a DataGrid).
ColumnMapping	This property determines how a DataColumn is represented when a DataSet is saved as an XML document using the DataSet.WriteXml() method.
ColumnName	Gets or sets the name of the column in the Columns collection (meaning how it is represented internally by the DataTable). If you do not set the ColumnName explicitly, the default values are Column with (n+1) numerical suffixes (i.e., Column1, Column2, Column3, and so forth).
DataType	Defines the data type (Boolean, string, float, and so on) stored in the column.
DefaultValue	Gets or sets the default value assigned to this column when inserting new rows. This is used if not otherwise specified.
Expression	Gets or sets the expression used to filter rows, calculate a column's value, or create an aggregate column.
Ordinal	Gets the numerical position of the column in the Columns collection maintained by the DataTable.
ReadOnly	Determines if this column can be modified once a row has been added to the table. The default is false.

Table 17-3. Properties of the DataColumn (Continued)

DataColumn Property	Meaning in Life
Table	Gets the DataTable that contains this DataColumn.
Unique	Gets or sets a value indicating whether the values in each row of the column must be unique or if repeating values are permissible. If a column is assigned a primary key constraint, the Unique property should be set to true.

Building a DataColumn

To illustrate the basic use of the DataColumn, assume you need to model a column named FirstName, which internally maps to an array of characters. For the sake of argument, let's say this column (for whatever reason) must be read-only. Assuming you wish to build your DataColumn in the Click event handler of a Button type within a Windows Forms application, you would write the following logic:

```
protected void btnColumn_Click (object sender, System.EventArgs e)
{
    // Build the FirstName column.
    DataColumn colFName = new DataColumn();
    // Set a bunch of values.
    colFName.DataType = Type.GetType("System.String");
    colFName.ReadOnly = true;
    colFName.Caption = "First Name";
    colFName.ColumnName = "FirstName";
    // Display DataColumn's values.
    string temp = "Column type: " + colFName.DataType + "\n" +
                  "Read only? " + colFName.ReadOnly + "\n" +
                  "Caption: " + colFName.Caption + "\n" +
                  "Column Name: " + colFName.ColumnName + "\n" +
                  "Nulls allowed? " + colFName.AllowDBNull;
    MessageBox.Show(temp, "Column properties");
}
```

This gives the result shown in Figure 17-2.

Figure 17-2. Exercising a DataColumn type

Do be aware that the DataColumn provides several overloaded constructors. Given this, you can specify a number of characteristics directly at the time of creation (as opposed to discrete properties), as shown here:

```
// Build the FirstName column (take two).
DataColumn colFName = new DataColumn("FirstName",
    Type.GetType("System.String"));
colFName.ReadOnly = true;
colFName.Caption = "First Name";
```

Adding a DataColumn to a DataTable

The DataColumn type does not typically exist as a stand-alone entity, but is instead inserted into a related DataTable. To illustrate, create a new DataTable type (fully detailed later in the chapter). Next, insert each DataColumn in the DataTable.DataColumnCollection type using the Columns property. Here is an example:

```
// Build the FirstName column.
DataColumn myColumn = new DataColumn();
...
// Create a new DataTable.
DataTable myTable = new DataTable("MyTable");
// The Columns property returns a DataColumnCollection type.
// Use the Add() method to insert the column in the table.
myTable.Columns.Add(myColumn);
```

Configuring a DataColumn to Function As a Primary Key

One common rule of database development is that a table should have at least one column that functions as the primary key. A primary key constraint is used to uniquely identify a record (row) in a given table. In keeping with the current Employees example, assume you now wish to build a new DataColumn type to represent the EmpID field. This column will be the primary key of the table and thus should have the AllowDBNull and Unique properties configured as shown here:

```
// This column is functioning as a primary key.
DataColumn colEmpID = new DataColumn(EmpID, Type.GetType("System.Int32"));
colEmpID.Caption = "Employee ID";
colEmpID.AllowDBNull = false;
colEmpID.Unique = true;
```

Once the DataColumn has been correctly set up to function as a primary key, the next step is to assign this DataColumn to the DataTable's PrimaryKey property. You will see how to do in just a bit during the discussion of the DataTable, so put this on the back burner for the time being.

Enabling Auto-Incrementing Fields

One aspect of the DataColumn you may choose to configure is its ability to auto-increment. Simply put, auto-incrementing columns are used to ensure that when a new row is added to a given table, the value of this column is assigned automatically, based on the current step of the incrementation. This can be helpful when you wish to ensure that a column has no repeating values (such as a primary key). This behavior is controlled using the AutoIncrement, AutoIncrementSeed, and AutoIncrementStep properties.

To illustrate, build a DataColumn that supports auto-incrementation. The seed value is used to mark the starting value of the column, where the step value identifies the number to add to the seed when incrementing, as shown here:

```
// Create a data column.
DataColumn myColumn = new DataColumn();
myColumn.ColumnName = "Foo";
myColumn.DataType = System.Type.GetType("System.Int32");
// Set the auto-increment behavior.
myColumn.AutoIncrement = true;
myColumn.AutoIncrementSeed = 500;
myColumn.AutoIncrementStep = 12;
```

Here, the Foo column has been configured to ensure that as rows are added to the respective table, the value in this field is incremented by 12. Because the seed has been set at 500, the first five values should be 500, 512, 524, 536, and 548.

To prove the point, insert this DataColumn in a DataTable. Then add a number of new rows to the table, which of course automatically bumps the value in the Foo column, as shown here:

```
protected void btnAutoCol_Click (object sender, System.EventArgs e)
{
    // Make a data column that maps to an int.
    DataColumn myColumn = new DataColumn();
    myColumn.ColumnName = "Foo";
    myColumn.DataType = System.Type.GetType("System.Int32");
    // Set the auto-increment behavior.
    myColumn.AutoIncrement = true;
    myColumn.AutoIncrementSeed = 500;
    myColumn.AutoIncrementStep = 12;
    // Add this column to a new DataTable.
    DataTable myTable = new DataTable("MyTable");
    myTable.Columns.Add(myColumn);
    // Add 20 new rows.
    DataRow r;
    for(int i =0; i < 20; i++)
    {
        r = myTable.NewRow();
        myTable.Rows.Add(r);
    }
```

```
    // Now list the value in each row.
    string temp = "";
    DataRowCollection rows = myTable.Rows;
    for(int i = 0;i < myTable.Rows.Count; i++)
    {
        DataRow currRow = rows[i];
        temp += currRow["Foo"] + " ";
    }
    MessageBox.Show(temp, "These values brought ala auto-increment");
}
```

If you run the application (and click the corresponding Button), you see the message shown in Figure 17-3.

Figure 17-3. Auto-incrementation of a DataColumn

Configuring a Column's XML Data Representation

While many of the remaining DataColumn properties are rather self-explanatory (provided you are comfortable with database terminology), I would like to discuss the ColumnMapping property. The DataColumn.ColumnMapping property is used to configure how this column should be represented in XML, if the owning DataSet dumps its contents using the WriteXml() method. The value of the ColumnMapping property is configured using the MappingType enumeration (Table 17-4).

Table 17-4. Values of the MappingType Enumeration

MappingType Enumeration Value	Meaning in Life
Attribute	The column is mapped to an XML attribute.
Element	The column is mapped to an XML element (the default).
Hidden	The column is mapped to an internal structure.
SimpleContent	The column is mapped to text.

The default value of the ColumnMapping property is MappingType.Element. Assume that you have instructed the owning DataSet to write its contents to a new file stream as XML. Using this default setting, the EmpID column would appear as shown here:

```
<Employee>
      <EmpID>500</EmpID>
</Employee>
```

However, if the DataColumn's ColumnMapping property is set to
MappingType.Attribute, you see the following XML representation:

```
<Employee EmpID = "500"/>
```

This chapter examines the ADO.NET/XML integration in greater detail when discussing
the DataSet. Nevertheless, at this point, you understand how to create a stand-alone
DataColumn type. Now for an examination of the related DataRow type.

SOURCE CODE   The DataColumn application is included under the
Chapter 17 subdirectory.

Examining the DataRow Type

As you have seen, a collection of DataColumn objects represents the schema of a table.
A DataTable maintains its columns using the internal DataColumnCollection type. In
contrast, a collection of DataRow types represents the actual data in the table. Thus, if
you have 20 listings in a table named Employees, you can represent these entries using
20 DataRow types. Using the members of the DataRow class, you are able to insert,
remove, evaluate, and manipulate the values in the table.

Working with a DataRow is a bit different from working with a DataColumn, because
you cannot create a direct instance of this type, but rather obtain a reference from a
given DataTable. For example, assume you wish to insert a new row in the Employees
table. The DataTable.NewRow() method allows you to obtain the next slot in the table,
at which point you can fill each column with new data via the type indexer, as shown here:

```
// Build a new Table.
DataTable empTable = new DataTable("Employees");
// Add EmpID, FirstName and LastName columns to table...
...
// Build a new Employee record.
DataRow row = empTable.NewRow();
row["EmpID"] = 102;
row["FirstName"] = "Joe";
row["LastName"] = "Blow";
// Add it to the Table's DataRowCollection.
empTable.Rows.Add(row);
```

Notice how the DataRow class defines an indexer that can be used to gain access to a given DataColumn by numerical position as well as column name. Also notice that the DataTable maintains another internal collection (DataRowCollection) to hold each row of data. The DataRow type defines the core members, grouped by related functionality, in Table 17-5.

Table 17-5. Key Members of the DataRow Type

DataRow Member	Meaning in Life
HasErrors GetColumnsInError() GetColumnError() ClearErrors() RowError	The HasErrors property returns a Boolean value indicating if there are errors in a columns collection. If so, the GetColumnsInError() method can be used to obtain the offending members, GetColumnError() can be used to obtain the error description, while the ClearErrors() method removes each error listing for the row. The RowError property allows you to configure a textual description of the error for a given row.
ItemArray	This property gets or sets all of the values for this row using an array of objects.
RowState	This property is used to pinpoint the current "state" of the DataRow using values of the RowState enumeration.
Table	Use this property to obtain a reference to the DataTable containing this DataRow.
AcceptChanges() RejectChanges()	Commit (or reject) all the changes made to this row since the last time AcceptChanges() was called.
BeginEdit() EndEdit() CancelEdit()	Begin, end, or cancel an edit operation on a DataRow object.
Delete()	This method marks this row to be removed when the AcceptChanges() method is called.
IsNull()	Gets a value indicating whether the specified column contains a null value.

Understanding the DataRow.RowState Property

Most of the methods of the DataRow class only make sense in the context of an owning DataTable. You will see the process of inserting, removing, and updating rows in just a moment; first, however, you should get to know the RowState property. This property is useful when you need to programmatically identify the set of all rows in a table that have changed, have been newly inserted, and so forth. This property may be assigned any value from the DataRowState enumeration (Table 17-6).

Table 17-6. Values of the DataRowState Enumeration

DataRowState Enumeration Value	Meaning in Life
Added	The row has been added to a DataRowCollection, and AcceptChanges() has not been called.
Deleted	The row has been deleted, via the Delete() method of the DataRow.
Detached	The row has been created but is not part of any DataRowCollection. A DataRow is in this state immediately after it has been created and before it is added to a collection, or if it has been removed from a collection.
Modified	The row has been modified, and AcceptChanges() has not been called.
Unchanged	The row has not changed since AcceptChanges() was last called.

To illustrate the various states a DataRow may have, the following class documents the changes to the RowState property as a new DataRow is created, inserted in, and removed from a DataTable:

```
public class DRState
{
    public static void Main()
    {
        Console.WriteLine("***** The RowState property *****");
        // Build a single column DataTable
        DataTable myTable = new DataTable("Employees");
        DataColumn colID = new DataColumn("empID",
            Type.GetType("System.Int32"));
        myTable.Columns.Add(colID);
        // The DataRow.
        DataRow myRow;
        // Create a new (detached) DataRow.
        Console.WriteLine("Made new DataRow");
        myRow = myTable.NewRow();
        Console.WriteLine("->Row state: {0}\n", myRow.RowState.ToString());
        // Now add it to table.
        Console.WriteLine("Added DataRow to DataTable");
        myTable.Rows.Add(myRow);
        Console.WriteLine("->Row state: {0}\n", myRow.RowState.ToString());
        // Trigger an accept.
        Console.WriteLine("Called AcceptChanges() on DataTable");
        myTable.AcceptChanges();
        Console.WriteLine("->Row state: {0}\n", myRow.RowState.ToString());
```

```
        // Modify it.
        Console.WriteLine("Modified DataRow");
        myRow["empID"] = 100;
        Console.WriteLine("->Row state: {0}\n", myRow.RowState.ToString());
        // Now delete it.
        Console.WriteLine("Deleted DataRow");
        myRow.Delete();
        Console.WriteLine("->Row state: {0}\n", myRow.RowState.ToString());
        myRow.AcceptChanges();
    }
}
```

The output can be seen in Figure 17-4.

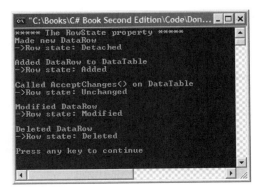

Figure 17-4. Examining row state

As you can see, the ADO.NET DataRow is smart enough to remember its current state of affairs. Given this, the owning DataTable is able to identify which rows have been modified. This is a key feature of the DataSet, given that when it comes time to send updated information to the data store, only the modified data is submitted. Clearly this behavior helps optimize trips between the layers of your system.

SOURCE CODE   The DataRowState is included under the Chapter 17 subdirectory.

Details of the DataTable

The DataTable is an in-memory representation of a tabular block of data. While you can manually compose a DataTable programmatically, you will more commonly obtain a DataTable dynamically using a DataSet and a given data provider. Table 17-7 describes some core properties of the DataTable type.

Table 17-7. Key Members of the DataTable

DataTable Property	Meaning in Life
CaseSensitive	This property indicates whether string comparisons within the table are case-sensitive (or not). The default value is "false".
ChildRelations	This property returns the collection of child relations (DataRelationCollection) for this DataTable (if any).
Columns	As you have seen, this property returns the collection of columns that belong to this table.
Constraints	Gets the collection of constraints maintained by the table (ConstraintCollection).
DataSet	Gets the DataSet that contains this table (if any).
DefaultView	Gets a customized view of the table that may include a filtered view, or a cursor position.
MinimumCapacity	Gets or sets the initial number of rows in this table (the default is 25).
ParentRelations	Gets the collection of parent relations for this DataTable.
PrimaryKey	Gets or sets an array of columns that function as primary keys for the data table.
Rows	As you have seen, this property returns the collection of rows that belong to this table.
TableName	Gets or sets the name of the table. This same property may also be specified as a constructor parameter.

To help visualize the key components of a DataTable, consider Figure 17-5. Be aware that this is *not* a traditional class hierarchy that illustrates the "is-a" relation between these types (e.g., the DataRow *does not* derive from DataRowCollection). Rather, this diagram points out the logical "has-a" relationships between the DataTable's core items (e.g., the DataRowCollection has a number of DataRow types).

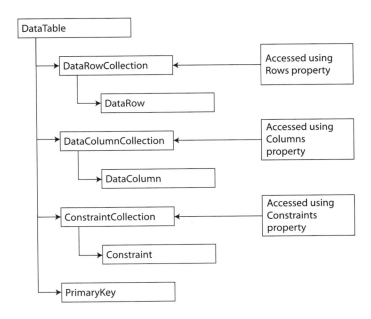

Figure 17-5. The structure of an ADO.NET DataTable

Building a Complete DataTable

Now that you have been exposed to the basics, let's see a complete example of creating and manipulating an in-memory data table. Assume you are interested in building a DataTable representing the current inventory in a database named Cars. The Inventory table will contain four columns: CarID, Make, Color, and PetName. Also, the CarID column will function as the table's primary key (PK) and support auto-incrementation. The PetName column will allow null values. (Sadly, not everyone loves their automobiles as much as we might.) Figure 17-6 shows the overall schema.

CarID (PK)	Make	Color	PetName
0	BMW	Green	Chucky
1	Yugo	White	Tiny
2	Jeep	Tan	(null)
3	Caravan	Pink	Pain Inducer

Figure 17-6. The DataTable under construction

The process begins by creating a new DataTable type. When you do so, you specify the friendly name of the table as a constructor parameter (as shown next). This friendly name can be used to reference this table from the containing DataSet:

```
// Create a new DataTable.
DataTable inventoryTable = new DataTable("Inventory");
```

The next step is to programmatically insert each column using the Add() method of the DataColumnCollection (accessed using the DataTable.Columns property). The following logic adds the CarID, Make, Color, and PetName columns to the current DataTable (recall that the underlying data type of each column is set using the DataType property):

```
// DataColumn var.
DataColumn myDataColumn;
// Create CarID column and add to table.
myDataColumn = new DataColumn();
myDataColumn.DataType = Type.GetType("System.Int32");
myDataColumn.ColumnName = "CarID";
myDataColumn.ReadOnly = true;
myDataColumn.AllowDBNull = false;
myDataColumn.Unique = true;
// Set the auto-increment behavior.
myDataColumn.AutoIncrement = true;
myDataColumn.AutoIncrementSeed = 1000;
myDataColumn.AutoIncrementStep = 10;
inventoryTable.Columns.Add(myDataColumn);
// Create Make column and add to table.
myDataColumn = new DataColumn();
myDataColumn.DataType = Type.GetType("System.String");
myDataColumn.ColumnName = "Make";
inventoryTable.Columns.Add(myDataColumn);
// Create Color column and add to table.
myDataColumn = new DataColumn();
myDataColumn.DataType = Type.GetType("System.String");
myDataColumn.ColumnName = "Color";
inventoryTable.Columns.Add(myDataColumn);
// Create PetName column and add to table.
myDataColumn = new DataColumn();
myDataColumn.DataType = Type.GetType("System.String");
myDataColumn.ColumnName = "PetName";
myDataColumn.AllowDBNull = true;
inventoryTable.Columns.Add(myDataColumn);
```

Before you add the rows, you will do well to take the time to set the table's primary key. To do so, set the DataTable.PrimaryKey property to whichever column necessary. Because more than a single column can function as a table's primary key, be aware that the PrimaryKey property requires an array of DataColumn types. For the Inventory table, assume the CarID column is the only aspect of the primary key, as shown here:

```
// Make the ID column the primary key column.
DataColumn[] PK = new DataColumn[1];
PK[0] = inventoryTable.Columns["CarID"];
inventoryTable.PrimaryKey = PK;
```

Last but not least, you need to add valid data to the table. Assuming you have an appropriate ArrayList maintaining Car types, you can fill the table as shown here:

```
// Iterate over the array list to fill rows (remember, the ID is
// auto-incremented).
foreach(Car c in arTheCars)
{
    DataRow newRow;
    newRow = inventoryTable.NewRow();
    newRow["Make"] = c.make;
    newRow["Color"] = c.color;
    newRow["PetName"] = c.petName;
    inventoryTable.Rows.Add(newRow);
}
```

To display your new local in-memory table, assume you have a Windows Forms application with a main Form displaying a DataGrid. As you saw in Chapter 11, the DataSource property is used to bind a DataTable to the GUI. The output is shown in Figure 17-7.

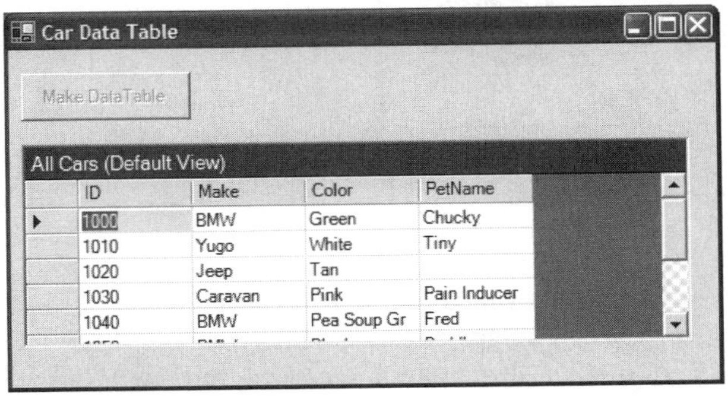

Figure 17-7. The visual representation of the DataTable

Here, you added rows by specifying the string name of the column to modify. However, you may also specify the numerical index of the column, which can be very helpful when you need to iterate over each column. Thus, the previous code could be updated as shown here (and still achieve the same end result):

```
foreach(Car c in arTheCars)
{
        // Specify columns by index.
        DataRow newRow;
        newRow = inventoryTable.NewRow();
        newRow[1] = c.make;
        newRow[2] = c.color;
        newRow[3] = c.petName;
        inventoryTable.Rows.Add(newRow);
}
```

Manipulating a DataTable: Deleting Rows

What if you wish to remove a row from a data table? One approach is to call the Delete() method of the DataRowCollection type. Simply specify the index (or DataRow) representing the row to remove. Assume you update your GUI as shown in Figure 17-8.

Figure 17-8. Removing rows from the DataTable

If you look at the previous screen shot, you will notice that you specified the second row in the DataTable, and therefore CarID 1020 has been marked as deleted. The following logic behind the new Button's Click event handler removes the specified row from your in-memory DataTable:

```
// Remove this row from the DataRowCollection.
protected void btnRemoveRow_Click (object sender, System.EventArgs e)
{
    try
    {
        inventoryTable.Rows[(int.Parse(txtRemove.Text))].Delete();
        inventoryTable.AcceptChanges();
    }
    catch(Exception ex)
    {
        MessageBox.Show(ex.Message);
    }
}
```

The Delete() method might have been better named MarkedAsDeletable() given that the row is not literally removed until the DataTable.AcceptChanges() method has been called. In effect, the Delete() method simply sets a flag that says "I am ready to die when my table tells me." Also understand that if a row has been marked for deletion, a DataTable may reject the delete operation via RejectChanges(), as shown here:

```
// Mark a row as deleted, but reject the changes.
protected void btnRemoveRow_Click (object sender, System.EventArgs e)
{
    inventoryTable.Rows[(int.Parse(txtRemove.Text))].Delete();
    // Do more work
    ...
    inventoryTable.RejectChanges();      // Restore previous RowState value.
}
```

Manipulating a DataTable: Applying Filters and Sort Orders

You may wish to see a small subset of a DataTable's data, as specified by some sort of filtering criteria. For example, what if you wish to only see a certain make of automobile from the in-memory Inventory table? The Select() method of the DataTable class provides this very functionality. Update your GUI once again, this time allowing users to specify a string that represents the make of the automobile they are interested in viewing (Figure 17-9). The result will be placed into a Windows Forms message box.

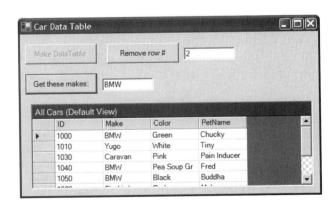

Figure 17-9. Specifying a filter

The Select() method has been overloaded a number of times to provide different selection semantics. At its most basic level, the parameter sent to Select() is a string that contains some conditional operation. To begin, observe the following logic for the Click event handler of your new Button:

```
protected void btnGetMakes_Click (object sender, System.EventArgs e)
{
    // Build a filter based on user input.
    string filterStr = "Make='" + txtMake.Text + "'";

    // Find all rows matching the filter.
    DataRow[] makes = inventoryTable.Select(filterStr);
    // Show what we got!
    if(makes.Length == 0)
        MessageBox.Show("Sorry, no cars...", "Selection error!");
    else
    {
        string strMake = null;
        for(int i = 0; i < makes.Length; i++)
        {
            DataRow temp = makes[i];
            strMake += temp["PetName"] + "\n";
        }
        MessageBox.Show(strMake, txtMake.Text + " type(s):");
    }
}
```

Here, you first build a simple filter criteria based on the value in the associated TextBox. If you specify BMW, your filter is Make = 'BMW'. When you send this filter to the Select() method, you get back an array of DataRow types that represent each row that matches the filter criteria (Figure 17-10).

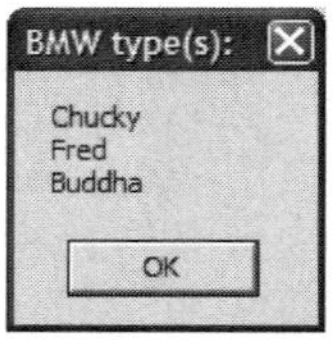

Figure 17-10. Filtered data

A filter string can be composed of any number of relational operators. For example, what if you wanted to find all cars with an ID greater than 1030? You could write the following (see Figure 17-11 for output):

```
// Now show the pet names of all cars with ID greater than 1030.
DataRow[] properIDs;
string newFilterStr = "ID > '1030'";
properIDs = inventoryTable.Select(newFilterStr);
string strIDs = null;
for(int i = 0; i < properIDs.Length; i++)
{
    DataRow temp = properIDs[i];
    strIDs += temp["PetName"]
            + " is ID " + temp["ID"] + "\n";
}
MessageBox.Show(strIDs, "Pet names of cars where ID > 1030");
```

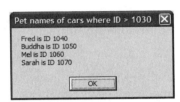

Figure 17-11. Specifying a range of data

As you can see, filtering logic is standard SQL syntax. To prove the point, assume you wish to obtain the results of the previous Select() invocation alphabetically based on pet name. In terms of SQL, this translates into a sort based on the PetName column. Luckily, the Select() method has been overloaded to send in a sort criterion, as shown here:

```
makes = inventoryTable.Select(filterStr, "PetName");
```

If you want the results in descending order, call Select(), as shown here:

```
// Return results in descending order.
makes = inventoryTable.Select(filterStr, "PetName DESC");
```

In general, the sort string contains the column name followed by "ASC" (ascending, which is the default) or "DESC" (descending). If need be, multiple columns can be separated by commas.

Manipulating a DataTable: Updating Rows

The final aspect of the DataTable you should be aware of is the process of updating an existing row with new values. One approach is to first obtain the row(s) that match a given filter criterion using the Select() method. Once you have the DataRow(s) in question, modify them accordingly. For example, assume you have a new Button that (when clicked) searches the DataTable for all rows where Make is equal to BMW. Once you identify these items, you change the Make from "BMW" to "Colt":

```
// Find the rows you want to edit with a filter.
protected void btnChange_Click (object sender, System.EventArgs e)
{
    // Build a filter.
    string filterStr = "Make='BMW'";
    string strMake = null;
    // Find all rows matching the filter.
    DataRow[] makes = inventoryTable.Select(filterStr);
    // Change all Beemers to Colts!
    for(int i = 0; i < makes.Length; i++)
    {
        DataRow temp = makes[i];
        strMake += temp["Make"] = "Colt";
        makes[i] = temp;
    }
}
```

The DataRow class also provides the BeginEdit(), EndEdit(), and CancelEdit() methods, which allow you to edit the content of a row while temporarily suspending any associated validation rules. In the previous logic, each row was validated with each assignment. (Also, if you capture any events from the DataRow, they fire with each modification.) When you call BeginEdit() on a given DataRow, the row is placed in edit mode. At this point you can make your changes as necessary and call either EndEdit() to commit these changes or CancelEdit() to roll back the changes to the original version. For example:

```
// Assume you have obtained a row to edit.
// Now place this row in edit mode.
rowToUpdate.BeginEdit();
// Send the row to a helper function, which returns a Boolean.
if( ChangeValuesForThisRow( rowToUpdate) )
{
    rowToUpdate.EndEdit();      // OK!
}
else
{
    rowToUpdate.CancelEdit();  // Forget it.
}
```

Although you are free to manually call these methods on a given DataRow, these members are automatically called when you edit a DataGrid widget that has been bound to a DataTable. For example, when you select a row to edit from a DataGrid, that row is automatically placed in edit mode. When you shift focus to a new row, EndEdit() is called automatically. To test this behavior, assume you have manually updated each car to be of a given Make using the DataGrid (Figure 17-12).

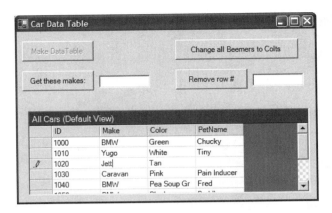

Figure 17-12. Editing rows in a DataGrid

If you now request all BMWs, the message box correctly returns *all* rows, as the underlying DataTable associated to the DataGrid has been automatically updated (Figure 17-13).

Figure 17-13. The updated set of BMW autos

Understanding the DataView Type

In database nomenclature, a *view object* is a stylized representation of a table. For example, using Microsoft SQL Server, you could create a view for your current Inventory table that returns a new table only containing automobiles of a given color. In ADO.NET, the DataView type allows you to programmatically extract a subset of data from the DataTable.

One great advantage of holding multiple views of the same table is that you can bind these views to various GUI widgets (such as the DataGrid). For example, one DataGrid might be bound to a DataView showing all autos in the Inventory, while another may be configured to display only green automobiles. On a related note, the DataTable type provides the DefaultView property that returns the default DataView for the table.

To illustrate, update the user interface of the current Windows Forms application to support two additional DataGrid types. One of these grids only shows the rows from the Inventory that match the filter Make='Colt'. The other grid only shows red automobiles (i.e., Color='Red'). Figure 17-14 shows the GUI update.

Figure 17-14. Creating multiple views for a single DataTable

To begin, you need to create two member variables of type DataView:

```
public class mainForm : System.Windows.Forms.Form
{
    // Views of the DataTable.
    DataView redCarsView;       // I only show red cars.
    DataView coltsView;         // I only show Colts.
...
}
```

Next, assume you have a new helper function named CreateViews(), which is called directly after the DataTable has been fully constructed, as shown here:

```
protected void btnMakeDataTable_Click (object sender, System.EventArgs e)
{
    // Make the data table.
    MakeTable();
    // Make views.
    CreateViews();
    ...
}
```

Here is the implementation of this new helper function. Notice that the constructor of each DataView has been passed the DataTable that will be used to build the custom set of data rows:

```
private void CreateViews()
{
    // Set the table that is used to construct these views.
    redCarsView = new DataView(inventoryTable);
    coltsView = new DataView(inventoryTable);
    // Now configure the views using a filter.
    redCarsView.RowFilter = "Color = 'red'";
    coltsView.RowFilter = "Make = 'colt'";
    // Bind to grids.
    RedCarViewGrid.DataSource = redCarsView;
    ColtsViewGrid.DataSource = coltsView;
}
```

As you can see, the DataView class supports a property named RowFilter, which contains the string representing the filtering criteria used to extract matching rows. Once you have your view established, set the grid's DataSource property accordingly. That's it! Because DataGrids are smart enough to detect changes to their underlying data source, if you click the Make Beemers Colts button, the ColtsViewGrid is updated automatically.

In addition to the RowFilter property, Table 17-8 describes some other members of the DataView class.

Table 17-8. Members of the DataView Type

DataView Member	Meaning in Life
AddNew()	Adds a new row to the DataView
AllowDelete AllowEdit AllowNew	Configure whether the DataView allows deleting, inserting, or updating of its rows
Delete()	Deletes a row at the specified index
RowFilter	Gets or sets the expression used to filter which rows are viewed in the DataView
Sort	Gets or sets the sort column or columns and sort order for the table
Table	Gets or sets the source DataTable

SOURCE CODE   The CarDataTable project is included under the Chapter 17 subdirectory.

Understanding the Role of the DataSet

You have been examining how to build a DataTable to represent a single table of data held in memory. Although DataTables can be used as stand-alone entities, they are more typically contained in a DataSet. Simply put, a DataSet is an in-memory representation of any number of tables (which may be just a single DataTable) as well as any (optional) relationships between these tables and any (optional) constraints. To gain a better understanding of the relationship among these core types, consider the logical hierarchy shown in Figure 17-15.

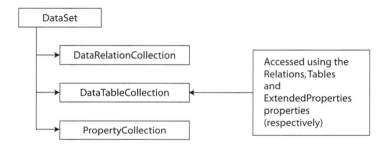

Figure 17-15. The anatomy of a DataSet

The Tables property of the DataSet allows you to access the DataTableCollection that contains the individual DataTables. Another important collection used by the DataSet is the DataRelationCollection. Given that a DataSet is a disconnected version of a database schema, it can programmatically represent the parent/child relationships between its tables.

For example, a relation can be created between two tables to model a foreign key constraint using the DataRelation type. This object can then be added to the DataRelationCollection through the Relations property. At this point, you can navigate between the connected tables as you search for data. You will see how this is done a bit later in the chapter.

The ExtendedProperties property provides access to the PropertyCollection type, which allows you to associate any extra information to the DataSet as name/value pairs. This information can literally be anything at all, even if it has no bearing on the data itself. For example, you can associate your company's name to a DataSet, which can then function as in-memory metadata, as shown here:

```
// Make a DataSet and add some metadata.
DataSet ds = new DataSet("MyDataSet");
ds.ExtendedProperties.Add("CompanyName", "Intertech, Inc");
// Print out the metadata.
Console.WriteLine(ds.ExtendedProperties["CompanyName"].ToString());
```

Other examples of extended properties might include an internal password that must be supplied to access the contents of the DataSet, a number representing a data refresh rate, and so forth. Be aware that the DataTable itself also supports the ExtendedProperties property.

Members of the DataSet

Before exploring too many other programmatic details, take a look at the public interface of the DataSet. The properties defined by the DataSet are centered on providing access to the internal collections, producing XML data representations and providing detailed error information. Table 17-9 describes some core properties of interest.

Table 17-9. Properties of the Mighty DataSet

DataSet Property	Meaning in Life
CaseSensitive	Indicates whether string comparisons in DataTable objects are case sensitive (or not).
DataSetName	Represents the friendly name of this DataSet. Typically this value is established as a constructor parameter.
DefaultViewManager	Establishes a custom view of the data in the DataSet.
EnforceConstraints	Gets or sets a value indicating whether constraint rules are followed when attempting any update operation.
HasErrors	Gets a value indicating whether there are errors in any of the rows in any of the tables of this DataSet.
Relations	Gets the collection of relations that link tables and allows navigation from parent tables to child tables.
Tables	Provides access to the collection of tables maintained by the DataSet.

The methods of the DataSet mimic some of the functionality provided by the aforementioned properties. In addition to interacting with XML streams, other methods exist to allow you to copy the contents of your DataSet, as well as establish the beginning and ending points of a batch of updates. Table 17-10 describes some core methods.

Table 17-10. Methods of the Mighty DataSet

DataSet Method	Meaning in Life
AcceptChanges()	Commits all the changes made to this DataSet since it was loaded or the last time AcceptChanges() was called.
Clear()	Completely clears the DataSet data by removing every row in each table.
Clone()	Clones the structure of the DataSet, including all DataTables, as well as all relations and any constraints.
Copy()	Copies both the structure and data for this DataSet.
GetChanges()	Returns a copy of the DataSet containing all changes made to it since it was last loaded, or since AcceptChanges() was called.
GetChildRelations()	Returns the collection of child relations that belong to a specified table.
GetParentRelations()	Gets the collection of parent relations that belong to a specified table.
HasChanges()	Overloaded. Gets a value indicating whether the DataSet has changes, including new, deleted, or modified rows.
Merge()	Overloaded. Merges this DataSet with a specified DataSet.
ReadXml() ReadXmlSchema()	These methods allow you to read XML data from a valid stream (file-based, memory-based, or network-based) into the DataSet.
RejectChanges()	Rolls back all the changes made to this DataSet since it was created, or the last time DataSet.AcceptChanges was called.
WriteXml() WriteXmlSchema()	These methods allow you to write out the contents of a DataSet into a valid stream.

Now that you have a better understanding of the role of the DataSet (and some idea what you can do with one), let's run through some specifics. Once this discussion of the ADO.NET DataSet is complete, the remaining bulk of this chapter will focus on how to obtain DataSet types from external sources (such as a relational database) using the types defined by the System.Data.SqlClient and System.Data.OleDb namespaces.

Building an In-Memory DataSet

To illustrate the use of a DataSet, create a new Windows Forms application that maintains a single DataSet, containing three DataTable objects named Inventory, Customers, and Orders. The columns for each table will be minimal but complete, with one column marking the primary key for each table. Most importantly, you can model the parent/child relationships between the tables using the DataRelation type. Your goal is to build the database shown in Figure 17-16 in memory.

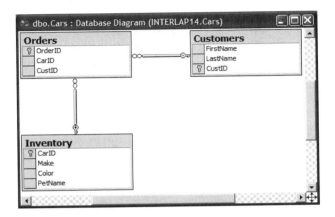

Figure 17-16. The Cars database

Here, the Inventory table is the parent table to the Orders table, which maintains a foreign key (CarID) column. Also, the Customers table is the parent table to the Orders table. (Again note the foreign key, CustID.) As you will soon see, when you add DataRelation types to your DataSet, they may be used to navigate between the tables to obtain and manipulate the related data.

To begin, assume you have added a set of member variables to your main Form, representing the individual DataTables and containing DataSet, as shown here:

```
public class mainForm : System.Windows.Forms.Form
{
    // Inventory DataTable.
    private DataTable inventoryTable = new DataTable("Inventory");
    // Customers DataTable.
    private DataTable customersTable = new DataTable("Customers");
    // Orders DataTable.
    private DataTable ordersTable = new DataTable("Orders");
    // Our DataSet!
    private DataSet carsDataSet = new DataSet("CarDataSet");
...
}
```

Now, to keep things as OO as possible, build some (very) simple wrapper classes to represent a Car and Customer in the system. Note that the Customer class maintains a field that identifies the car a customer is interested in buying, as shown here:

```
public class Car
{
    // Make public for easy access.
    public string petName, make, color;
    public Car(string petName, string make, string color)
    {
        this.petName = petName;
        this.color = color;
        this.make = make;
    }
}

public class Customer
{
    public Customer(string fName, string lName, int currentOrder)
    {
        this.firstName= fName;
        this.lastName = lName;
        this.currCarOrder = currentOrder;
    }
    // Make public for easy access.
    public string firstName, lastName;
    public int currCarOrder;
}
```

The main Form maintains two ArrayList types that hold a set of cars and customers, which are populated with some sample data in the scope of the Form's constructor. Next, the constructor calls a number of private helper functions to build the tables and their relationships. Finally, this method binds the Inventory and Customer DataTables to their corresponding DataGrid widgets. Notice that the following code binds a given DataTable in the DataSet using the SetDataBinding() method:

```
// Your list of Cars and Customers.
private ArrayList arTheCars, arTheCustomers;

public mainForm()
{
    // Fill the car array list with some cars.
    arTheCars = new ArrayList();
    arTheCars.Add(new Car("Chucky", "BMW", "Green"));
    ...
    // Fill the other array list with some customers.
    arTheCustomers = new ArrayList();
    arTheCustomers.Add(new Customer("Dave", "Brenner", 1020));
    ...
    // Make data tables (using the same techniques seen previously).
    MakeInventoryTable();
    MakeCustomerTable();
    MakeOrderTable();
    // Add relation (seen in just a moment).
    BuildTableRelationship();
```

```
    // Bind to grids (Param1 = DataSet, Param2 = name of table in DataSet).
    CarDataGrid.SetDataBinding(carsDataSet, "Inventory");
    CustomerDataGrid.SetDataBinding(carsDataSet, "Customers");
}
```

Each DataTable is constructed using the techniques examined earlier in this chapter. To keep focused on the DataSet logic, I will not repeat every detail of the table-building logic here. However, be aware that each table is assigned a primary key that is auto-incremented. Here is some partial table-building logic (check out the source code for complete details):

```
private void MakeOrderTable()
{
...
    // Add table to the DataSet.
    carsDataSet.Tables.Add(customersTable);
    // Create OrderID, CustID, CarID columns and add to table...
    // Make the ID column the primary key column...
    // Add some orders.
    for(int i = 0; i < arTheCustomers.Count; i++)
    {
        DataRow newRow;
        newRow = ordersTable.NewRow();
        Customer c = (Customer)arTheCustomers[i];
        newRow["CustID"] = i;
        newRow["CarID"] = c.currCarOrder;
        carsDataSet.Tables["Orders"].Rows.Add(newRow);
    }
}
```

The MakeInventoryTable() and MakeCustomerTable() helper functions behave almost identically (again, check source code for full details).

Expressing Relations Using the DataRelation Type

The really interesting work happens in the BuildTableRelationship() helper function. Once a DataSet has been populated with a number of tables, you can *optionally* choose to programmatically model their parent/child relationships. Be aware that this is not mandatory. You can have a DataSet that does little else than hold a collection of DataTables in memory (even a single DataTable). However, when you do establish the interplay between your DataTables, you can navigate between them on the fly, maintain data integrity, and collect any sort of information you may be interested in obtaining, all while disconnected from the data source.

The System.Data.DataRelation type is an OO wrapper around a table-to-table relationship. When you create a new DataRelation type, specify a friendly name, followed by the parent table (for example, Inventory) and the related child table (Orders). For a relationship to be established, each table must have an identically named column (CarID) of the same data type (Int32 in this case). In this light, a

DataRelation is basically bound by the same rules as a relational database. Here is the complete implementation of the BuildTableRelationship() helper function:

```
private void BuildTableRelationship()
{
    // Create a DataRelation obj.
    DataRelation dr = new DataRelation("CustomerOrder",
        carsDataSet.Tables["Customers"].Columns["CustID"],     // Parent.
        carsDataSet.Tables["Orders"].Columns["CustID"]);       // Child.
    // Add to the DataSet.
    carsDataSet.Relations.Add(dr);
    // Create another DataRelation obj.
    dr = new DataRelation("InventoryOrder",
        carsDataSet.Tables["Inventory"].Columns["CarID"],      // Parent.
        carsDataSet.Tables["Orders"].Columns["CarID"]);        // Child.
    // Add to the DataSet.
    carsDataSet.Relations.Add(dr);
}
```

As you can see, a given DataRelation is held in the DataRelationCollection maintained by the DataSet. The DataRelation type offers a number of properties that allow you to obtain a reference to the child and/or parent table that is participating in the relationship, specify the name of the relationship, and so on, and these are listed in Table 17-11.

Table 17-11. Properties of the DataRelation Type

DataRelation Property	Meaning in Life
ChildColumns ChildKeyConstraint ChildTable	Obtain information about the child table in this relationship as well as the table itself
DataSet	Gets the DataSet to which the relations' collection belongs
ParentColumns ParentKeyConstraint ParentTable	Obtain information about the parent table in this relationship as well as the table itself
RelationName	Gets or sets the name used to look up this relation in the parent data set's DataRelationCollection

Navigating Between Related Tables

To illustrate how a DataRelation allows you to move between related tables, extend your GUI to include a new Button type and a related TextBox. The end user is able to enter the ID of a customer and obtain all the information about that customer's order, which is placed in a simple message box (Figure 17-17). The Button's Click event handler is as shown here (error checking removed for clarity):

```
protected void btnGetInfo_Click (object sender, System.EventArgs e)
{
    string strInfo = "";
    DataRow drCust = null;
    DataRow[] drsOrder = null;
    // Get the specified CustID from the TextBox.
    int theCust = int.Parse(this.txtCustID.Text);
    // Now based on CustID, get the correct row in Customers table.
    drCust = carsDataSet.Tables["Customers"].Rows[theCust];
    strInfo += "Cust #" + drCust["CustID"].ToString() + "\n";
    // Navigate from customer table to order table.
    drsOrder =   drCust.GetChildRows(carsDataSet.Relations["CustomerOrder"]);
    // Get order number.
    foreach(DataRow r in drsOrder)
        strInfo += "Order Number: " + r["OrderID"] + "\n";
    // Now navigate from order table to inventory table.
    DataRow[] drsInv =
        drsOrder[0].GetParentRows(carsDataSet.Relations["InventoryOrder"]);
    // Get Car info.
    foreach(DataRow r in drsInv)
    {
        strInfo += "Make: " + r["Make"] + "\n";
        strInfo += "Color: " + r["Color"] + "\n";
        strInfo += "Pet Name: " + r["PetName"] + "\n";
    }
    MessageBox.Show(strInfo, "Info based on cust ID");
}
```

Figure 17-17. Navigating data relations

As you can see, the key to moving between data tables is to use a handful of methods defined by the DataRow type. Let's break this code down step by step. First, you obtain the correct customer ID from the text box and use it to grab the correct row in the Customers table (using the Rows property, of course), as shown here:

```
// Get the specified CustID from the TextBox.
int theCust = int.Parse(this.txtCustID.Text);
// Now based on CustID, get the correct row in the Customers table.
DataRow drCust = null;
drCust = carsDataSet.Tables["Customers"].Rows[theCust];
strInfo += "Cust #" + drCust["CustID"].ToString() + "\n";
```

Next, you navigate from the Customers table to the Orders table, using the CustomerOrder data relation. Notice that the DataRow.GetChildRows() method allows you to grab rows from your child table, and once you do, you can read information out of the table, as shown here:

```
// Navigate from customer table to order table.
DataRow[] drsOrder = null;
drsOrder =   drCust.GetChildRows(carsDataSet.Relations["CustomerOrder"]);
// Get order number.
foreach(DataRow r in drsOrder)
strInfo += "Order Number: " + r["OrderID"] + "\n";
```

Your final step is to navigate from the Orders table to its parent table (Inventory), using the GetParentRows() method. At this point, you can read information from the Inventory table using the Make, PetName, and Color columns, as shown here:

```
// Now navigate from order table to inventory table.
DataRow[] drsInv =
    drsOrder[0].GetParentRows(carsDataSet.Relations["InventoryOrder"]);
foreach(DataRow r in drsInv)
{
    strInfo += "Make: " + r["Make"] + "\n";
    strInfo += "Color: " + r["Color"] + "\n";
    strInfo += "Pet Name: " + r["PetName"] + "\n";
}
```

As a final example of navigating relations programmatically, the following code prints out the values in the Orders table that is obtained indirectly using the InventoryOrders relationship:

```
protected void btnGetChildRels_Click (object sender, System.EventArgs e)
{
    // Ask the CarsDataSet for the child relations of the inv. table.
    DataRelationCollection relCol;
    DataRow[] arrRows;
    string info = "";
    relCol = carsDataSet.Tables["inventory"].ChildRelations;
    info += "\tRelation is called: " + relCol[0].RelationName + "\n\n";
    // Now loop over each relation and print out info.
    foreach(DataRelation dr in relCol)
    {
        foreach(DataRow r in inventoryTable.Rows)
        {
            arrRows = r.GetChildRows(dr);
            // Print out the value of each column in the row.
            for (int i = 0; i < arrRows.Length; i++)
```

```
    {
            foreach(DataColumn dc in arrRows[i].Table.Columns )
            {
                info += "\t" + arrRows[i][dc];
            }
            info += "\n";
        }
    }
    MessageBox.Show(info,
        "Data in Orders Table obtained by child relations");
    }
}
```

Figure 17-18 shows the output.

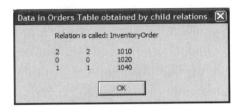

Figure 17-18. Navigating parent/child relations

Hopefully, this last example has you convinced of the usefulness of the DataSet type. Given that a DataSet is completely disconnected from the underlying data source, you can work with an in-memory copy of data and navigate around each table to make any necessary updates, deletes, or inserts. Once this is done, you can submit your changes to the data store for processing. Of course you don't yet know how to get connected! There is one final item of interest regarding the DataSet before addressing this issue.

Reading and Writing XML-Based DataSets

A major design goal of ADO.NET was to apply a liberal use of XML infrastructure. Using the DataSet type, you can write an XML representation of the contents of your tables, relations, and other schematic details to a given stream (such as a file). To do so, simply call the WriteXml() method, as shown here:

```
protected void btnToXML_Click (object sender, System.EventArgs e)
{
    // Write your entire DataSet to a file in the app directory.
    carsDataSet.WriteXml("cars.xml");
    MessageBox.Show("Wrote CarDataSet to XML file in app directory");
    btnReadXML.Enabled = true;
}
```

If you now open your new file in the Visual Studio .NET IDE (Figure 17-19), you will see that the entire DataSet has been transformed to XML.

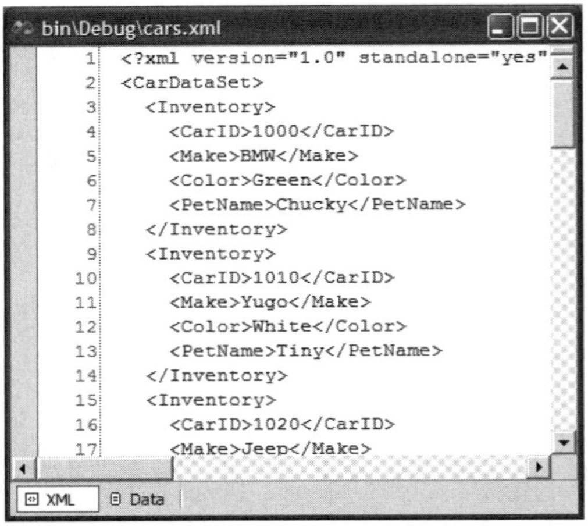

Figure 17-19. The Cars database as XML

To test the ReadXml() method of the DataSet, perform a little experiment. The CarDataSet application has a Button that will clear out the current DataSet completely (including all tables and relations). After the in-memory representation has been gutted, instruct the DataSet to read in the cars.xml file, which as you would guess restores the entire DataSet, as shown here:

```
protected void btnReadXML_Click (object sender, System.EventArgs e)
{
    // Kill current DataSet.
    carsDataSet.Clear();
    carsDataSet.Dispose();
    MessageBox.Show("Just cleared data set...");
    carsDataSet = new DataSet("CarDataSet");
    carsDataSet.ReadXml( "cars.xml" );
    MessageBox.Show("Reconstructed data set from XML file...");
    btnReadXML.Enabled = false;
    // Bind to grids.
    CarDataGrid.SetDataBinding(carsDataSet, "Inventory");
    CustomerDataGrid.SetDataBinding(carsDataSet, "Customers");
}
```

Figure 17-20 shows your final product.

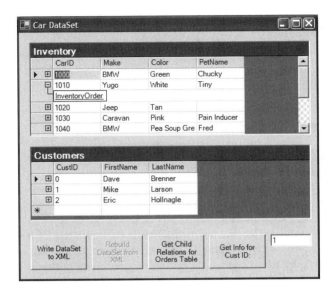

Figure 17-20. The final GUI update

In addition to the ability to persist the contents of a DataSet as XML, be aware that the WriteXmlSchema() and ReadXmlSchema() methods may also be used to generate and read an *.xsd file that represents the overall structure of the DataSet type. Once you have the data and structure of a DataSet persisted to file, you are able to manipulate the contents using the types of the System.Xml.dll assembly (see Chapter 18). Furthermore, once you have generated your schema file from a given DataSet, you are able to view and/or tweak the type definitions using VS .NET (Figure 17-21).

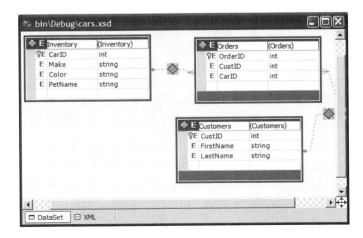

Figure 17-21. The Cars XML schema file

SOURCE CODE   The CarDataSet application is included under the
Chapter 17 subdirectory.

Building a Simple Test Database

Now that you understand how to create and manipulate a DataSet in memory, you can
get down to the business of making a data connection and seeing how to obtain a populated DataSet from a specific data provider. In keeping with the automotive theme
used throughout this text, I have included two versions of a sample Cars database that
models the Inventory, Orders, and Customers tables examined during the chapter.

The first version is a SQL script that builds the tables (including their relationships)
and is intended for users of SQL Server 7.0 (and greater). To create the Cars database,
begin by opening the Query Analyzer utility that ships with SQL Server. Next, connect
to your machine and open the cars.sql file. Before you run the script, be sure that the
path listed in the SQL file points to *your installation* of MS SQL Server. Thus, be sure
you edit the following DDL (in bold) as necessary (be aware that SQL Server 2000 has a
unique directory structure. I'm still using SQL 7.0 . . . don't ask):

```
CREATE DATABASE [Cars]  ON (NAME = N'Cars_Data', FILENAME
=N' C:\MSSQL7\Data \Cars_Data.MDF' ,
SIZE = 2, FILEGROWTH = 10%)

LOG ON (NAME = N'Cars_Log', FILENAME
= N' C:\MSSQL7\Data\Cars_Log.LDF' ,
SIZE = 1, FILEGROWTH = 10%)
GO
```

Now run your script. Once you do, open up the SQL Server Enterprise Manager. You
should see the Cars database with all three interrelated tables (with some sample data
to boot) as well as a single stored procedure.

The second version of the Cars database is for users of MS Access. Under the Access
DB folder you will find the cars.mdb file, which contains the same information and
underlying structure as the SQL Server version. During the remainder of this chapter,
I will assume that you are connecting to the SQL Server Cars database rather than the
Access equivalent. In just a bit, however, you will see how to configure an ADO.NET
connection object to hook into an *.mdb file.

Selecting a Data Provider

As mentioned earlier in this chapter, .NET 1.1 ships with five data providers. The first of these is the OleDb data provider, which is composed of the types defined in the System.Data.OleDb namespace. The OleDb provider allows you to access data located in any data store that supports the classic OLE DB protocol. Thus, like with classic ADO, you may use the ADO.NET data provider to access SQL Server, Oracle, or MS Access databases. Because the types in the System.Data.OleDb namespace must communicate with unmanaged code (e.g., the OLE DB providers), you need to be aware that a number of .NET to COM translations occur behind the scenes, which can affect performance. By and large, this namespace is useful when you are attempting to communicate with a data source that does not have a specific data provider assembly.

The SQL data provider offers direct access to MS SQL Server data stores, and *only* SQL Server data stores (version 7.0 and greater). The System.Data.SqlClient namespace contains the types used by the SQL provider and provides the same functionality as the OleDb provider. In fact, for the most part, both namespaces have similarly named items. The key difference is that the SQL provider does not use the OLE DB or classic ADO protocols and thus offers numerous performance benefits.

If you are interested in making use of the System.Data.Oracle, System.Data.Odbc, or System.Data.SqlServerCe namespaces, I will assume you will check out the details as you see fit. However, as you would hope, once you are comfortable with one data provider, you can easily manipulate other providers. Recall that while the exact names of the types will differ between namespaces (for example, OleDbConnection vs. SqlConnection vs. OdbcConnection), semantically related types can be treated in a polymorphic manner given the IDbCommand, IDbConnection, IDbDataAdapter, and IDataReader interfaces et al.

To begin, we'll examine how to connect to a data source using the OleDb data provider, therefore don't forget to specify the proper using directives (recall this data provider is contained within the System.Data.dll assembly):

```
// Using the OleDb data provider.
using System.Data;
using System.Data.OleDb;
```

Once we have checked out how to interact with a data store using the OleDb data provider, we will see how to make use of the types within the System.Data.SqlClient namespace.

The Types of the System.Data.OleDb Namespace

Table 17-12 provides a walkthrough of the core types of the System.Data.OleDb namespace. Note that each type sports an "OleDb-" prefix.

Table 17-12. Key Types of the System.Data.OleDb Namespace

System.Data.OleDb Type	Meaning in Life
OleDbCommand	Represents a SQL query command to be made to a data source.
OleDbConnection	Represents an open connection to a data source.
OleDbDataAdapter	Represents a set of data commands and a database connection used to fill and update the contents of a DataSet.
OleDbDataReader	Provides a way of reading a forward-only stream of data records from a data source.
OleDbErrorCollection OleDbError OleDbException	OleDbErrorCollection maintains a collection of warnings or errors returned by the data source, each of which is represented by an OleDbError type. When an error is encountered, an exception of type OleDbException is thrown.
OleDbParameterCollection OleDbParameter	Much like classic ADO, the OleDbParameterCollection collection holds onto the parameters sent to a stored procedure in the database. Each parameter is of type OleDbParameter.

Working with the Connected Layer of ADO.NET

The first step to take when working with the OleDb data provider is to establish a session with the data source using the OleDbConnection type (which, as you recall, implements the IDbConnection interface). Much like the classic ADO Connection object, OleDbConnection types are provided with a formatted connection string, containing a number of name/value pairs separated by semicolons. This information is used to identify the name of the machine you wish to connect to, required security settings, the name of the database on that machine, and, most importantly, the name of the OLE DB provider. (See online help for a full description of each name/value pair.)

The connection string may be set using the OleDbConnection.ConnectionString property or including it as a constructor argument. Assume you wish to connect to the Cars database on your local machine using the SQL OLE DB provider. The following logic does the trick:

```
// Build a connection string.
OleDbConnection cn = new OleDbConnection();
cn.ConnectionString = "Provider=SQLOLEDB.1;" +
    "User ID=sa;Pwd=;Initial Catalog=Cars;" +
    "Data Source=(local);";
```

As you can infer from the preceding code comments, the Initial Catalog name refers to the database you are attempting to establish a session with (Pubs, Northwind, Cars, and so on). The Data Source name identifies the name of the machine that maintains the database (for simplicity, I have assumed no specific password is required for local system administrators). The final point of interest is the Provider segment, which specifies the name of the OLE DB provider that will be used to access the data store. Table 17-13 describes some possible values.

Table 17-13. Core OLE DB Providers

Provider Segment Value	Meaning in Life
Microsoft.JET.OLEDB.4.0	You want to use the Jet OLE DB provider to connect to an Access database.
MSDAORA	You want to use the OLE DB provider for Oracle.
SQLOLEDB	You want to use the OLE DB provider for MS SQL Server. Once you have configured the connection string, the next step is to open a session with the data source, do some work, and release your connection to the data source, as shown in the code snippet following this table.

```
// Build a connection string.
OleDbConnection cn = new OleDbConnection();
cn.ConnectionString = "Provider=SQLOLEDB.1;" +
    "User ID=sa;Pwd=;Initial Catalog=Cars;" +
    "Data Source=(local);";
cn.Open();
    // Do some interesting work here...
cn.Close();
```

In addition to the ConnectionString, Open(), and Close() members, the OleDbConnection class provides a number of members that let you configure attritional settings regarding your connection, such as timeout settings and transactional information. Table 17-14 gives a partial rundown.

Table 17-14. Members of the OleDbConnection Type

OleDbConnection Member	Meaning in Life
BeginTransaction() CommitTransaction() RollbackTransaction()	Used to programmatically commit, abort, or roll back a transaction.
Close()	Closes the connection to the data source.
ConnectionString	Gets or sets the string used to open a session with a data store.
ConnectionTimeout	This read-only property returns the amount of time to wait while establishing a connection before terminating and generating an error (the default value is 15 seconds). If you wish to change this default, specify a "Connect Timeout" segment in the connection string (e.g., Connect Timeout=30).
Database	Gets the name of the database maintained by the connection object.
DataSource	Gets the location of the database maintained by the connection object.
Open()	Opens a database connection with the current property settings.
GetOleDbSchemaTable()	Obtains schema information from the data source.
Provider	Gets the name of the provider maintained by the connection object.
State	Gets the current state of the connection, represented by the ConnectionState enumeration.

As you can see, the properties of the OleDbConnection type are typically read-only in nature, and are only useful when you wish to obtain the characteristics of a connection at runtime. When you wish to override default settings, you must alter the construction string itself. For example, ponder the following code, which changes the default connection timeout setting from 15 seconds to 30 seconds (via the Connect Timeout segment of the connection string):

```
OleDbConnection cn = new OleDbConnection();
cn.ConnectionString = "Provider=SQLOLEDB.1;" +
    "User ID=sa;Pwd=;Initial Catalog=Cars;" +
    "Data Source=(local);Connect Timeout=30";
cn.Open();
Console.WriteLine("***** Info about your connection *****");
Console.WriteLine("Database location: {0}", cn.DataSource);
Console.WriteLine("Database name: {0}", cn.Database);
Console.WriteLine("Provider: {0}", cn.Provider);
Console.WriteLine("Timeout: {0}", cn.ConnectionTimeout);
```

```
Console.WriteLine("Connection state: {0}", cn.State.ToString());
cn.Close();
Console.WriteLine("Connection state: {0}", cn.State.ToString());
```

Notice that this connection is explicitly opened and closed each time before making a call to the State property. As mentioned in the previous table, this property may take any value of the ConnectionState enumeration:

```
public enum System.Data.ConnectionState
{
    Broken, Closed,
    Connecting, Executing,
    Fetching, Open
}
```

While it may be enticing to ponder the notion of asking a connection type if it is currently in the process of querying data (e.g., ConnectionState.Executing), do understand that with the current release of the .NET Framework, the only valid ConnectionState values are ConnectionState.Open and ConnectionState.Closed (the remaining members of this enum are reserved for future use and are basically no-ops as of .NET 1.1). Also, understand that it is always safe to close a connection whose connection state is currently ConnectionState.Closed.

Connecting to an Access Database

Much like classic ADO, the process of connecting to an Access database using ADO.NET requires little more than retrofitting your construction string. First, set the Provider segment to the JET engine, rather than SQLOLEDB. Beyond this adjustment, set the data source segment to point to the path of your *.mdb file, as shown here:

```
// Be sure to update the data source segment if necessary!
OleDbConnection cn = new OleDbConnection();
cn.ConnectionString = "Provider=Microsoft.JET.OLEDB.4.0;" +
                      @"data source = C:\cars.mdb";
 cn.Open();
```

Once the connection has been made, you can read and manipulate the contents of your data table.

Obtaining Database Schema Information Using Connection Types

Connection objects can also be used to obtain schema information from a given database through the GetOleDbSchemaTable() method. As you are most likely aware, "schema information" is little more than metadata that describes the database itself, rather than the tabular data it is maintaining. The GetOleDbSchemaTable() method takes two parameters, the first of which is a member of the OleDbSchemaGuid class type. This type exposes a number of read-only fields that map to the sort of metadata you are interested in obtaining (table names, stored procedure names, views, and whatnot).

The second parameter is an array of System.Object types that represents what (if any) restrictions should be placed on the schema information returned by the call. Be aware that the exact format of this array of System.Object types will vary based on the specified value of the OleDbSchemaGuid parameter. Upon completion, the GetOleDbSchemaTable() method returns a DataTable type that contains the schema information.

Rather than pound out all of the possible parameter combinations (as they are documented within online help), the following example illustrates how you can make use of an OleDbConnection type to obtain basic schema information regarding each table in the Cars database:

```
DataTable dtSchemaInfo = cn.GetOleDbSchemaTable(OleDbSchemaGuid.Tables,
    new object[] {null, null, null, "TABLE"});
// Print the DataTable.
for(int curRow = 0; curRow < dtSchemaInfo.Rows.Count; curRow++)
{
    for(int curCol= 0; curCol< dtSchemaInfo.Columns.Count; curCol++)
    {
        Console.Write(dtSchemaInfo.Rows[curRow][curCol].ToString().Trim()+ " ");
    }
    Console.WriteLine();
}
```

As you will see, it is also possible to obtain schema details for a specific table in a database using data reader types (more details to come).

Building a SQL Command via OleDbCommand

Now that you better understand the role of the OleDbConnection type, the next order of business is to check out how to submit SQL queries to the database in question. The OleDbCommand type (which as you recall implements the IDbCommand interface) is an OO representation of a SQL query, table name, or stored procedure that is specified using the CommandType property. This property may take any value from the CommandType enum:

```
public enum System.Data.CommandType
{
    StoredProcedure,
    TableDirect,
    Text    // Default value.
}
```

If the command type does indeed represent a SQL query, the CommandText property can be used to get or set the query text. When creating an OleDbCommand type, you may establish the SQL query as a constructor parameter or directly via the CommandText property.

Also, when you are creating an OleDbCommand type, you will need to specify the OleDbConnection to be used. Again, you may do so as a constructor parameter or via the Connection property. To illustrate, ponder the two (functionally equivalent) ways to build an OleDbCommand type that associates a SQL SELECT statement with an OleDbConnection variable named "cn":

```
// Specify SQL command and connection as constructor parameters.
string strSQL1 = "Select Make from Inventory where Color='Red'";
OleDbCommand myCommand1 = new OleDbCommand(strSQL1, cn);
// Specify SQL command and connection via properties.
string strSQL2 = "Select Make from Inventory where Color='Red'";
OleDbCommand myCommand2 = new OleDbCommand();
myCommand.Connection = cn;
myCommand.CommandText = strSQL2;
```

Realize that at this point, you have not literally submitted the SQL query to the Cars database, but rather prepped the state of the command type for future use. Table 17-15 highlights some additional members of the OleDbCommand type.

Table 17-15. Members of the OleDbCommand Type

OleDbCommand Member	Meaning in Life
CommandText	Gets or sets the SQL command text or the provider-specific syntax to run against the data source.
CommandTimeout	Gets or sets the time to wait while executing the command before terminating the attempt and generating an error. The default is 30 seconds.
CommandType	Gets or sets how the CommandText property is interpreted via the CommandType enumeration. The default value is CommandType.Text, which represents a SQL query.
Connection	Gets or sets the OleDbConnection used by this instance of the OleDbCommand.
Parameters	Gets the collection of OleDbParameter types used for a parameterized query.
Cancel()	Cancels the execution of a command.
ExecuteReader()	Returns an instance of an OleDbDataReader, which provides forward-only, read-only access to the underlying data.
ExecuteNonQuery()	This method issues the command text to the data store, without returning an OleDbDataReader type.
ExecuteScalar()	A lightweight version of the ExecuteNonQuery() method, designed specifically for singleton queries (such as obtaining a record count).
Prepare()	Creates a prepared (or compiled) version of the command on the data source.

Working with the OleDbDataReader

Once you have established the active connection and SQL command, the next step is to truly submit the query to the data source. As you would guess, there are a number of ways to do so. The OleDbDataReader type (which implements IDataReader) is the simplest and fastest way to obtain information from a data store. This class represents a read-only, forward-only stream of data returned one record at a time. Given this, it should stand to reason that data readers are useful only when submitting SQL selection statements to the underlying data store.

The OleDbDataReader is useful when you need to iterate over large amounts of data very quickly and have no need to work an in-memory DataSet representation. For example, if you request 20,000 records from a table to store in a text file, it would be rather memory intensive to hold this information in a DataSet. A better approach would be to create a data reader that spins over each record as rapidly as possible. Be aware, however, that DataReaders (unlike data adapter types) maintain an open connection to their data source until you explicitly close the session.

To illustrate, the following example issues a simple SQL query against the Cars database, using the ExecuteReader() method of the OleDbCommand type. Using the Read() method of the returned OleDbDataReader, you dump each member to the standard IO stream:

```
public class OleDbDR
{
    static void Main(string[] args)
    {
        // Make a connection.
        OleDbConnection cn = new OleDbConnection();
        cn.ConnectionString = "Provider=SQLOLEDB.1;" +
            "User ID=sa;Pwd=;Initial Catalog=Cars;" +
            "Data Source=(local);Connect Timeout=30";
        cn.Open();
...
        // Create a SQL command.
        string strSQL = "SELECT Make FROM Inventory WHERE Color='Red'";
        OleDbCommand myCommand = new OleDbCommand(strSQL, cn);
        // Obtain a data reader a la ExecuteReader().
        OleDbDataReader myDataReader;
        myDataReader = myCommand.ExecuteReader();
        // Loop over the results.
        Console.WriteLine("***** Red cars obtained from a DataReader *****");
        while (myDataReader.Read())
        {
            Console.WriteLine("-> Red car: " +
                myDataReader["Make"].ToString());
        }
        // Don't forget this!
        myDataReader.Close();
        cn.Close();
    }
}
```

The result is the listing of all red automobiles in the Cars database (Figure 17-22).

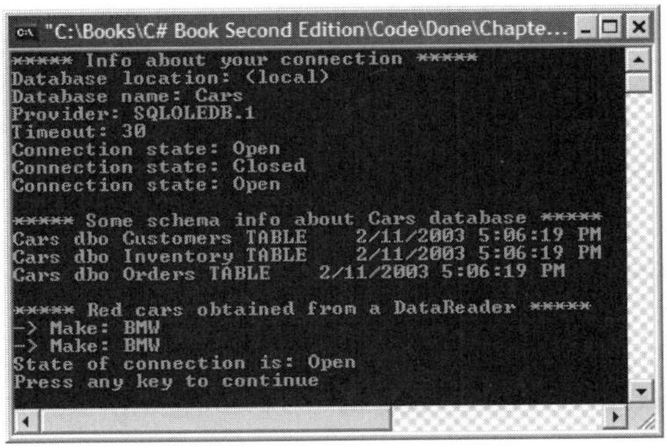

Figure 17-22. Reading records with the OleDbDataReader

Recall that DataReaders are forward-only, read-only streams of data. Given this, there is no way to navigate around the contents of the OleDbDataReader. All you can do is read the current record in memory and use it in your application:

```
// Get the value in the 'Make' column.
Console.WriteLine("Red car: {0} ", myDataReader["Make"].ToString());
```

When you are finished using the DataReader, make sure to terminate the session using the appropriately named method, Close().

In addition to the Read() and Close() methods, there are a number of other methods that allow you to obtain a strongly typed value from a specified column in a given format (e.g., GetBoolean(), GetByte(), and so forth). Thus, if you know that the column you are attempting to access has been typed as a Boolean data type, you can avoid an explicit cast by making a call to GetBoolean(). Finally, understand that the FieldCount property returns the number of columns in the current record.

Specifying the Data Reader's Command Behavior

As you may have noticed, the OleDbCommand.ExecuteReader() method has been overloaded. One version of this member takes a value from the CommandBehavior enumeration. This type supports the following values:

```
public enum System.Data.CommandBehavior
{
    CloseConnection, Default,
    KeyInfo, SchemaOnly,
    SequentialAccess,
    SingleResult, SingleRow,
}
```

One value of interest is CommandBehavior.CloseConnection. If you specify this value, the underlying connection maintained by the connection object will be automatically closed once you close the data reader type (check out online help for details on the remaining values):

```
// Auto close the connection.
OleDbDataReader myDataReader;
myDataReader =
    myCommand.ExecuteReader(CommandBehavior.CloseConnection);
...
myDataReader.Close();
// No need to do this anymore! cn.Close();
Console.WriteLine("State of connection is: {0}", cn.State);
```

Obtaining Multiple Result Sets Using a OleDbDataReader

Data reader types are able to obtain multiple result sets from a single command object. For example, if you are interested in obtaining all rows from the Inventory table as well as all rows from the Customers table, you are able to specify both SQL SELECT statements using a semicolon delimiter:

```
string theSQL = "SELECT * From Inventory;SELECT * from Customers";
```

Once you obtain the data reader, you are able to iterate over each result set via the NextResult() method. Do be aware that you are always returned the first result set automatically. Thus, if you wish to read over the rows of each table, you would be able to build the following iteration construct:

```
do
{
    while(myDataReader.Read())
    {
        // Read the info of the current result set.
    }
}while(myDataReader.NextResult());
```

Obtaining Schema Information Using a OleDbDataReader

A final point to be made regarding ADO.NET data reader types is that they also provide a manner to obtain schema information. However, unlike the connection types (which allow you to obtain schema information for the entire database), the OleDbDataReader.GetTableSchema() method returns a DataTable that describes the characteristics of the table specified by the SQL SELECT statement:

```
DataTable dt = myDataReader.GetSchemaTable();
```

Inserting, Updating, and Deleting Records Using OleDbCommand

As you have just seen, the ExecuteReader() method allows you to examine the results of a SQL SELECT statement using a forward-only, read-only flow of information. However, when you wish to submit SQL commands that result in the modification of a given table, you make use of the OleDbCommand.ExecuteNonQuery() method. This single method will perform inserts, updates, and deletes based on the format of your command text. Be very aware that when you are making use of the OleDbCommand.ExecuteNonQuery() method, you are operating within the connected layer of ADO.NET, meaning this method has nothing to do with obtaining populated DataSet types via a data adapter.

To illustrate modifying a data source via ExecuteNonQuery(), assume you wish to insert a new record into the Inventory table of the Cars database. Once you have configured your connection type, the remainder of your task is as simple as authoring the correct SQL:

```
class UpdateWithCommandObj
{
    static void Main(string[] args)
    {
        // Open a connection to Cars db.
        OleDbConnection cn = new OleDbConnection();
        cn.ConnectionString = "Provider=SQLOLEDB.1;" +
            "User ID=sa;Pwd=;Initial Catalog=Cars;" +
            "Data Source=(local);Connect Timeout=30";
        cn.Open();
        // SQL INSERT statement.
        string sql = "INSERT INTO Inventory" +
            "(CarID, Make, Color, PetName) VALUES" +
            "('777', 'Honda', 'Silver', 'NoiseMaker')";
        // Insert the record.
        OleDbCommand cmd = new OleDbCommand(sql, cn);
        try
        { cmd.ExecuteNonQuery(); }
        catch(Exception ex)
        { Console.WriteLine(ex.Message); }
        cn.Close();
    }
}
```

Updating or removing a record is just as easy:

```
// UPDATE existing record.
sql = "UPDATE Inventory SET Make = 'Hummer' WHERE CarID = '777'";
cmd.CommandText = sql;
try
{cmd.ExecuteNonQuery();}
catch(Exception ex)
{Console.WriteLine(ex.Message);}

// DELETE a record.
sql = "Delete from Inventory where CarID = '777'";
cmd.CommandText = sql;
try
{cmd.ExecuteNonQuery();}
catch(Exception ex)
{Console.WriteLine(ex.Message);}
```

Although you do not bother to obtain the value returned from the ExecuteNonQuery() method, do understand that this member returns a System.Int32 that represents the number of affected records:

```
try
{
    Console.WriteLine("Number of rows effected: {0}", cmd.ExecuteNonQuery());
}
```

Finally, do be aware that the ExecuteNonQuery() method of a given command object is the only way to issue Data Definition Language (DDL) commands to a data source (e.g., CREATE, ALTER, DROP, and so forth).

SOURCE CODE   The UpdateDBWithCommandObj application is included under the Chapter 17 subdirectory.

Working with Parameterized Queries

The previous insert, update, and delete logic worked as expected; however, you are able to tighten things up just a bit. As you may know, a *parameterized query* can be useful when you wish to treat SQL parameters as objects, rather than as a value within a hard-coded string. Typically, parameterized queries execute much faster than a literal block of text, in that they are parsed exactly once (rather than each time the SQL string is assigned to the CommandText property).

Like classic ADO, ADO.NET command objects maintain a collection of discrete parameter types. While it is initially more verbose to configure the parameters used for a given SQL query, the end result is a more convenient manner to tweak SQL statements programmatically. When you wish to map a textual parameter to a member in the command object's parameters collection, simply create a new OleDbParameter type and add it to the OleDbCommand's internal collection using the Parameters property. In addition, make use of the "@" symbol in the string itself. While you are free to make use of this technique whenever a SQL query is involved, it is most helpful when you wish to trigger a stored procedure.

Executing a Stored Procedure Using OleDbCommand

A *stored procedure* is a named block of SQL code stored at the database. Stored procedures can be constructed to return a set of rows (or native data types) to the calling component and may take any number of optional parameters. The end result is a unit of work that behaves like a typical function, with the obvious differences of being located on a data store rather than a binary business object.

Let's add a simple stored procedure to the existing Cars database called GetPetName, which takes an input parameter of type integer. (If you ran the supplied SQL script, this stored proc is already defined.) This is the numerical ID of the car for which you are interested in obtaining the pet name, which is returned as an output parameter of type char. Here is the syntax:

```
CREATE PROCEDURE GetPetName
     @carID int,
     @petName char(20) output
AS
SELECT @petName = PetName from Inventory where CarID = @carID
```

Now that you have a stored procedure in place, let's see the code necessary to execute it. Begin as always by creating a new OleDbConnection, configure your connection string, and open the session. Next, create a new OleDbCommand type, making sure to specify the name of the stored procedure and set the CommandType property accordingly, as shown here:

```
// Open connection to data store.
OleDbConnection cn = new OleDbConnection();
cn.ConnectionString = "Provider=SQLOLEDB.1;" +
     "User ID=sa;Pwd=;Initial Catalog=Cars;" +
     "Data Source=(local);Connect Timeout=30";
cn.Open();
// Make a command object for the stored proc.
OleDbCommand myCommand = new OleDbCommand("GetPetName", cn);
myCommand.CommandType = CommandType.StoredProcedure;
```

Specifying Parameters Using the OleDbParameter Type

The next task is to establish the parameters used for the call. To illustrate the syntax of parameterized queries, you will use the OleDbParameter type. This class maintains a number of properties that allow you to configure the name, size, and data type of the parameter, as well as its direction of travel. Table 17-16 describes some key properties of the OleDbParameter type.

Table 17-16. Key Members of the OleDbParameter Type

OleDbParameter Property	Meaning in Life
DataType	Establishes the type of the parameter, in terms of .NET
DbType	Gets or sets the native data type from the data source, represented as a CLR data type
Direction	Gets or sets whether the parameter is input-only, output-only, bidirectional, or a return value parameter
IsNullable	Gets or sets whether the parameter accepts null values
OleDbType	Gets or sets the native data type from the data source represented by the OleDbType enumeration
ParameterName	Gets or sets the name of the OleDbParameter
Precision	Gets or sets the maximum number of digits used to represent the Value property
Scale	Gets or sets the number of decimal places to which the Value property is resolved
Size	Gets or sets the maximum parameter size of the data
Value	Gets or sets the value of the parameter

Given that you have one input and one output parameter, you can configure your types as follows. Note that you then add these items to the OleDbCommand type's ParametersCollection (which is, again, accessed via the Parameters property):

```
// Create the parameters for the call.
OleDbParameter theParam = new OleDbParameter();
// Input param.
theParam.ParameterName = "@carID";
theParam.OleDbType = OleDbType.Integer;
theParam.Direction = ParameterDirection.Input;
theParam.Value = 1;  // Car ID = 1.
myCommand.Parameters.Add(theParam);
// Output param.
theParam = new OleDbParameter();
theParam.ParameterName = "@petName";
theParam.OleDbType = OleDbType.Char;
theParam.Size = 20;
theParam.Direction = ParameterDirection.Output;
myCommand.Parameters.Add(theParam);
```

The final step is to issue the command using (once again)
OleDbCommand.ExecuteNonQuery(). Notice that the Value property of the
OleDbParameter type is accessed to obtain the returned pet name, as shown here:

```
// Execute the stored procedure!
myCommand.ExecuteNonQuery();
// Display the result.
Console.WriteLine("Stored Proc Info:");
Console.WriteLine("Car ID: {0}", myCommand.Parameters["@carID"].Value);
Console.WriteLine("PetName: {0}", myCommand.Parameters["@petName"].Value);
```

SOURCE CODE   The OleDbStoredProc project is included under the
Chapter 17 subdirectory.

The Disconnected Layer and the OleDbDataAdapter Type

At this point you should understand how to connect to a data source using the
OleDbConnection type, issue a command (using the OleDbCommand and
OleDbParameter types), and iterate over a result set using the OleDbDataReader.
As you have just seen, these types allow you to obtain and alter data using the connected layer of ADO.NET. However, when you are using these techniques, you are not
receiving your data via DataSets, DataTables, DataRows, or DataColumns. Given that
you spend a good deal of time in this chapter getting to know these types, you are right
in assuming that there is more to the story of data access than the forward-only, read-
only world of the data reader.

To shift gears, we now need to examine the role of the OleDbDataAdapter type and
understand how it is our vehicle to obtaining a populated DataSet. In a nutshell, data
adapters pull information from a data store and populate a DataTable or DataSet type
using the OleDbDataAdapter.Fill() method. As you can see, this method has been
overloaded a number of times (FYI, the integer return type holds the number of
records returned):

```
// Fills the data set with records from a given source table.
public int Fill(DataSet yourDS, string tableName);

// Fills the data set with the records located between
// the given bounds from a given source table.
public int Fill(DataSet yourDS, int startRecord,
                int maxRecord, string tableName);
```

The OleDbDataAdapter.Fill() method has also been overloaded to return to you a populated DataTable type, rather than a full-blown DataSet:

```
public int Fill(System.Data.DataTable dataTable);
```

 NOTE   It is also worth pointing out that one version of the Fill() method will automatically populate a classic ADO Recordset type with the contents of a given ADO.NET DataTable.

Before you can call this method, you obviously need a valid OleDbDataAdapter object reference. The constructor has also been overloaded a number of times, but in general you need to supply the connection information and the SQL SELECT statement used to populate the DataTable/DataSet type at the time Fill() is called. Once the initial SQL Select has been established via the constructor parameter, it may be obtained (and modified) via the SelectCommand property:

```
// Whenever you call Fill(), the SQL statement
// contained within the SelectCommand property
// will be used to populate the DataSet.
myDataAdapter.Fill(myDS, "Inventory");
```

The OleDbDataAdapter type not only fills the tables of a DataSet on your behalf, but also is in charge of maintaining a set of core SQL statements used to push updates back to the data store. When you call the Update() method of a given data adapter, it will read the SQL contained within the DeleteCommand, InsertCommand, and UpdateCommand properties to push the changes within a given DataTable back to the data source:

```
// Whenever you call Update(), the SQL statements
// contained within the InsertCommand,
// DeleteCommand, and UpdateCommand properties
// will be used to update the data source
// given a DataTable in the DataSet.
myDataAdapter.Update(myDS, "Inventory");
```

Now, if you have a background in classic ADO, you should already be able to see the huge conceptual change at hand: Under ADO.NET, *you* are the individual in charge of specifying the SQL commands to use during the updating of a given database.

In addition to these four key properties (SelectCommand, UpdateCommand, DeleteCommand, and InsertCommand), Table 17-17 describes some additional members of the OleDbDataAdapter type.

Table 17-17. Core Members of the OleDbDataAdapter

OleDbDataAdapter Member	Meaning in Life
DeleteCommand InsertCommand SelectCommand UpdateCommand	Used to establish SQL commands that will be issued to the data store when the Fill() and Update() methods are called. Each of these properties is set using an OleDbCommand type.
Fill()	Fills a given table in the DataSet with some number of records based on the current SELECT command.
GetFillParameters()	Returns all parameters used when performing the select command.
Update()	Calls the respective INSERT, UPDATE, or DELETE statements for each inserted, updated, or deleted row for a given table in the DataSet.

Filling a DataSet Using the OleDbDataAdapter Type

To understand the functionality of the data adapter types, let's begin by learning how to use a data adapter to fill a DataSet programmatically. The following code populates a DataSet (containing a single table) using an OleDbDataAdapter:

```
public static int Main(string[] args)
{
    // Open a connection to Cars db.
    OleDbConnection cn = new OleDbConnection();
    cn.ConnectionString = "Provider=SQLOLEDB.1;" +
        "User ID=sa;Pwd=;Initial Catalog=Cars;" +
        "Data Source=(local);Connect Timeout=30";
    cn.Open();
    // Create data adapter using the following SELECT.
    string sqlSELECT = "SELECT * FROM Inventory";
    OleDbDataAdapter dAdapt = new OleDbDataAdapter(sqlSELECT, cn);
    // Create and fill the DataSet (connection closed automatically).
    DataSet myDS = new DataSet("CarsDataSet");
    dAdapt.Fill(myDS, "Inventory");
    // Private helper function.
    PrintTable(myDS);
    return 0;
}
```

Notice that unlike your work during the first half of this chapter, you did *not* manually create a DataTable type and add it to the DataSet. Also, you did *not* call ExecuteReader() from a command object to stream over the result set. Rather, you specified the Inventory table as the second parameter to the Fill() method, which functions as the friendly name of the newly populated table. Do be aware that if you do not specify a friendly name, the data adapter will simply name the table "Table":

```
    // This DataSet has a single table called 'Table'.
    dAdapt.Fill(myDS);
```

Internally, Fill() builds the DataTable, given the name of the table in the data store using the SELECT command. In this iteration, the connection between the given SQL SELECT statement and the OleDbDataAdapter was established as a constructor parameter:

```
// Create a SELECT command as string type.
string sqlSELECT = "SELECT * FROM Inventory";
OleDbDataAdapter dAdapt = new OleDbDataAdapter(sqlSELECT, cn);
```

As an alternative, you can associate the OleDbCommand to the OleDbDataAdapter, using the SelectCommand property, as shown here:

```
// Create a SELECT command object.
OleDbCommand selectCmd = new OleDbCommand("SELECT * FROM Inventory", cn);
// Make a data adapter and associate commands.
OleDbDataAdapter dAdapt = new OleDbDataAdapter();
dAdapt.SelectCommand = selectCmd;
```

The PrintTable() helper method is little more than some formatting razzle-dazzle:

```
public static void PrintTable(DataSet ds)
{
    // Get Inventory table from DataSet.
    Console.WriteLine("Here is what we have right now:\n");
    DataTable invTable = ds.Tables["Inventory"];
    // Print the Column names.
    for(int curCol= 0; curCol< invTable.Columns.Count; curCol++)
    {
        Console.Write(invTable.Columns[curCol].ColumnName.Trim() + "\t");
    }
    Console.WriteLine();
    // Print each cell.
    for(int curRow = 0; curRow < invTable.Rows.Count; curRow++)
    {
        for(int curCol= 0; curCol< invTable.Columns.Count; curCol++)
        {
            Console.Write(invTable.Rows[curRow][curCol].ToString().Trim()
                    + "\t");
        }
        Console.WriteLine();
    }
}
```

Altering Column Names Using the OleDbDataAdapter Type

The default behavior of a data adapter type is to map column names from the data source to the DataColumn collection without modification. However, oftentimes you wish to map the underlying column name (e.g., LName) to a more friendly display name (e.g., Last Name). When you wish to do so, you will need to establish specific column mappings for the table you will be filling with the corresponding data adapter. To do so, you must first obtain the data adapter's underlying System.Data.Common.DataTableMapping type (and thus need to specify that you are using the System.Data.Common namespace). Once you have a reference to this entity, you are able to establish unique column names for a specific table. For example, the following code alters the display names for the CarID, Make, and PetName columns of the Inventory table:

```
// Must reference this namespace
// to get definitions of DataTableMapping!
using System.Data.Common;
...
// Establish column mappings for the Inventory table
// by adding new DataColumnMapping types
// to the DataTableMapping type.
DataTableMapping tblMapper =
    dAdapt.TableMappings.Add("Table", "Inventory");
tblMapper.ColumnMappings.Add("CarID", "ID");
tblMapper.ColumnMappings.Add("Make", "Brand");
tblMapper.ColumnMappings.Add("PetName", "Friendly name of Car");
// Create and fill the DataSet.
dAdapt.Fill(myDS);
```

Here, you explicitly alter the internal DataColumnMappingCollection type before making the call to Fill(). Furthermore, note that you specify the friendly name of the table to interact with at the time you add in your unique table mapping, rather than at the time you call the Fill() method (recall that by default, the name of the newly populated DataTable is simply "Table").

If you run this application, you will now find the output shown in Figure 17-23.

Figure 17-23. Mapping database column names to unique display names

SOURCE CODE   The FillSingleTableDSWithAdapter project is under the Chapter 17 subdirectory.

Working with the SQL Data Provider

Before you see the details of inserting, updating, and removing records using a data adapter, I would like to introduce the SQL data provider. As you recall, the OleDb provider allows you to access any OLE DB–compliant data store, but incurs overhead via the COM interoperability layer lurking in the background.

When you know that the data source you need to manipulate is MS SQL Server, you will find performance gains if you use the System.Data.SqlClient namespace directly. Collectively, these classes constitute the functionality of the SQL data provider, which should look very familiar, given your work with the OleDb provider (Table 17-18).

Table 17-18. Core Types of the System.Data.SqlClient Namespace

System.Data.SqlClient Type	Meaning in Life
SqlCommand	Represents a Transact-SQL query to execute at a SQL Server data source.
SqlConnection	Represents an open connection to a SQL Server data source.
SqlDataAdapter	Represents a set of data commands and a database connection used to fill the DataSet and update the SQL Server data source.
SqlDataReader	Provides a way of reading a forward-only stream of data records from a SQL Server data source.
SqlErrors SqlError SqlException	SqlErrors maintains a collection of warnings or errors returned by SQL Server, each of which is represented by a SQLError type. When an error is encountered, an exception of type SQLException is thrown.
SqlParameterCollection SqlParameter	SqlParametersCollection holds onto the parameters sent to a stored procedure held in the database. Each parameter is of type SQLParameter.

Given that working with these types is almost identical to working with the OleDb data provider, you should already know what to do with them, as they have a similar public interface. To help you get comfortable with this new set of types, the remainder of the examples use the SQL data provider (don't forget to specify you are using the System.Data.SqlClient namespace!)

The System.Data.SqlTypes Namespace

On a quick related note, when you use the SQL data provider, you also have the luxury of using a number of managed types that represent native SQL server data types. Table 17-19 gives a quick rundown.

Table 17-19. Types of the System.Data.SqlTypes Namespace

System.Data.SqlTypes Wrapper	Native SQL Server
SqlBinary	binary, varbinary, timestamp, image
SqlInt64	bigint
SqlBit	bit
SqlDateTime	datetime, smalldatetime
SqlNumeric	decimal
SqlDouble	float
SqlInt32	int
SqlMoney	money, smallmoney
SqlString	nchar, ntext, nvarchar, sysname, text, varchar, char
SqlNumeric	numeric
SqlSingle	real
SqlInt16	smallint
System.Object	sql_variant
SqlByte	tinyint
SqlGuid	uniqueidentifier

Inserting Records Using the SqlDataAdapter

Now that you have flipped from the OleDb provider to the realm of the SQL provider, you can return to the task of understanding the role of data adapters. Let's examine how to insert new records into a given table using the SqlDataAdapter (which is nearly identical to using the OleDbDataAdapter, OdbcDataAdapter, and OracleDataAdapter types). As always, begin by creating an active connection, as shown here:

```
public class MySqlDataAdapter
{
    public static void Main()
    {
        // Create a connection and adapter (with select command).
        SqlConnection cn = new
            SqlConnection("server=(local);User ID=sa;Pwd=;database=Cars");
        SqlDataAdapter dAdapt = new
            SqlDataAdapter("SELECT * FROM Inventory", cn);
        // Kill record inserted on the last run of this app.
        cn.Open();
        SqlCommand killCmd = new
            SqlCommand("Delete from Inventory where CarID = '1111'", cn);
        killCmd.ExecuteNonQuery();
        cn.Close();
    }
}
```

You can see that the connection string has been cleaned up quite a bit. In particular, notice that you do not need to define a Provider segment (as the SQL data provider only talks to SQL server!). Next, note that you create a new SqlDataAdapter and specify the value of the SelectCommand property as a constructor parameter (just like with the OleDbDataAdapter).

The deletion logic is really more of a good housekeeping chore for the current application. Here, you create a new SqlCommand type that will destroy the record you are about to enter (to avoid a primary key violation).

If you wish to make use of parameterized queries, the next step is a bit more involved. Your goal is to create a new SQL statement that will function as the SqlDataAdapter's InsertCommand. First, create the new SqlCommand and specify a standard SQL insert, followed by SqlParameter types describing each column in the Inventory table, as shown here (and yes, you could avoid the use of the parameter objects if you wish and directly hard code the INSERT statement):

```
public static void Main()
{
    ...
    // Build the insert command!
    dAdapt.InsertCommand = new SqlCommand("INSERT INTO Inventory" +
        "(CarID, Make, Color, PetName) VALUES" +
        "(@CarID, @Make, @Color, @PetName)", cn)";
    SqlParameter workParam = null;
    // CarID.
    workParam = dAdapt.InsertCommand.Parameters.Add(new
        SqlParameter("@CarID", SqlDbType.Int));
    workParam.SourceColumn = "CarID";
    workParam.SourceVersion = DataRowVersion.Current;
    // Make.
    workParam = dAdapt.InsertCommand.Parameters.Add(new
        SqlParameter("@Make", SqlDbType.VarChar));
    workParam.SourceColumn = "Make";
    workParam.SourceVersion = DataRowVersion.Current;
```

```
    // Color.
    workParam = dAdapt.InsertCommand.Parameters.Add(new
            SqlParameter("@Color", SqlDbType.VarChar));
    workParam.SourceColumn = "Color";
    workParam.SourceVersion = DataRowVersion.Current;
    // PetName.
    workParam = dAdapt.InsertCommand.Parameters.Add(new
            SqlParameter("@PetName", SqlDbType.VarChar));
    workParam.SourceColumn = "PetName";
    workParam.SourceVersion = DataRowVersion.Current;
}
```

Now that you have formatted each of the parameters, the final step is to fill the DataSet and add your new row (note that the PrintTable() helper function has carried over to this example):

```
public static void Main()
{
    ...
    // Fill data set with initial data.
    DataSet myDS = new DataSet();
    dAdapt.Fill(myDS, "Inventory");
    PrintTable(myDS);
    // Add new row to the DataTable.
    DataRow newRow = myDS.Tables["Inventory"].NewRow();
    newRow["CarID"] = 1111;
    newRow["Make"] = "SlugBug";
    newRow["Color"] = "Pink";
    newRow["PetName"] = "Cranky";
    myDS.Tables["Inventory"].Rows.Add(newRow);
    // Send back to database and reprint.
    try
    {
        dAdapt.Update(myDS, "Inventory");
        myDS.Dispose();
        myDS = new DataSet();
        dAdapt.Fill(myDS, "Inventory");
        PrintTable(myDS);
    }
    catch(Exception e){  Console.Write(e.ToString()); }
}
```

When you run the application, you see the output shown in Figure 17-24.

Figure 17-24. Inserting new records using a data adapter

SOURCE CODE   The InsertRowsWithSqlAdapter project can be found under the Chapter 17 subdirectory.

Updating Existing Records Using the SqlDataAdapter

Now that you can insert new rows, let's look at how you can update existing rows, which you might guess will look quite similar to the process of inserting new rows (as well as the process of deleting existing rows). Again, start the process by obtaining a connection and creating a new SqlDataAdapter. Next, set the value of the UpdateCommand property, using the same general approach as when setting the value of the InsertCommand. Here is the relevant code in Main():

```
public static void Main()
{
    // Create a connection and adapter (same as previous code).
    ...
    // Establish the UpdateCommand.
    dAdapt.UpdateCommand = new SqlCommand
        ("UPDATE Inventory SET Make = @Make, Color = " +
        "@Color, PetName = @PetName " +
        "WHERE CarID = @CarID" , cn);
    // Build parameters for each column in Inventory table.
    // Same as before, but now you are populating the ParameterCollection
    // of the UpdateCommand:
    SqlParameter workParam = null;
    workParam = dAdapt.UpdateCommand.Parameters.Add(new
        SqlParameter("@CarID", SqlDbType.Int));
    workParam.SourceColumn = "CarID";
    workParam.SourceVersion = DataRowVersion.Current;
    // Do the same for PetName, Make, and Color params
    ...
    // Fill initial data set.
    DataSet myDS = new DataSet();
    dAdapt.Fill(myDS, "Inventory");
    PrintTable(myDS);
    // Change columns in second row to 'FooFoo'.
    DataRow changeRow = myDS.Tables["Inventory"].Rows[1];
    changeRow["Make"] = "FooFoo";
    changeRow["Color"] = "FooFoo";
    changeRow["PetName"] = "FooFoo";
    // Send back to database and reprint.
    try
    {
        dAdapt.Update(myDS, "Inventory");
        myDS.Dispose();
        myDS = new DataSet();
        dAdapt.Fill(myDS, "Inventory");
        PrintTable(myDS);
    }
    catch(Exception e)
    { Console.Write(e.ToString()); }
}
```

Figure 17-25 shows the output.

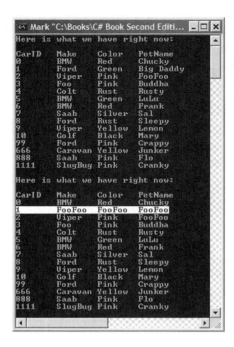

Figure 17-25. Updating existing records using a data adapter

As you may be guessing, if you wish to inform a data adapter how it should handle rows marked as deleted, you need to build yet another command type and assign it to the data adapter's DeleteCommand property. While having absolute control over the SQL used to insert, update, and delete records does allow a great deal of flexibility, you may agree that it can be a bit of a bother to constantly build verbose SQL commands by hand. You are, however, provided with some helper types.

SOURCE CODE   The UpdateRowsWithSqlAdapter project is found under the Chapter 17 subdirectory.

Auto-Generating SQL Commands Using CommandBuilder Types

Each ADO.NET data provider that ships with .NET 1.1 provides a *command builder* type. Using this type, you are able to automatically obtain command objects that contain the correct INSERT, DELETE, and UPDATE command types based on the initial SELECT statement. For example, the SqlCommandBuilder automatically generates the values contained within the SqlDataAdapter's InsertCommand, UpdateCommand,

and DeleteCommand properties based on the initial SelectCommand. The obvious benefit is that you have no need to build all the SqlCommand and SqlParameter types by hand.

An obvious question at this point is *how* a command builder is able to build these SQL commands on the fly. The short answer is *metadata*. At runtime, when you call the Update() method of a data adapter, the related command builder will read the database's schema data to autogenerate the underlying INSERT, DELETE, and UPDATE logic. If you are interested in seeing these SQL statements first-hand, you may call the SqlCommandBuilder.GetInsertCommand(), GetUpdateCommand(), and GetDeleteCommand() methods.

Consider the following example, which deletes a row in a DataSet using the auto-generated SQL statements. Furthermore, this application will print out the underlying command text of each command object:

```
static void Main(string[] args)
{
    DataSet theCarsInventory = new DataSet();
    // Make connection.
    SqlConnection cn = new
        SqlConnection("server=(local);User ID=sa;Pwd=;database=Cars");
    // Autogenerate INSERT, UPDATE, and DELETE commands
    // based on exiting SELECT command.
    SqlDataAdapter da = new SqlDataAdapter("SELECT * FROM Inventory", cn);
    SqlCommandBuilder invBuilder = new SqlCommandBuilder(da);
    // Print out values of the generated command objects.
    Console.WriteLine("SELECT command: {0}",
        da.SelectCommand.CommandText);
    Console.WriteLine("UPDATE command: {0}",
        invBuilder.GetUpdateCommand().CommandText);
    Console.WriteLine("INSERT command: {0}",
        invBuilder.GetInsertCommand().CommandText);
    Console.WriteLine("DELETE command: {0}",
        invBuilder.GetDeleteCommand().CommandText);
    // Fill data set.
    da.Fill(theCarsInventory, "Inventory");
    PrintTable(theCarsInventory);
    // Delete a row and update database.
    try
    {
        theCarsInventory.Tables["Inventory"].Rows[6].Delete();
        da.Update(theCarsInventory, "Inventory");
    }
    catch(Exception e)
    {
        Console.WriteLine(e.Message);
    }
    // Refill and reprint Inventory table.
    theCarsInventory = new DataSet();
    da.Fill(theCarsInventory, "Inventory");
    PrintTable(theCarsInventory);
}
```

Based on the initial SQL SELECT statement, the SqlCommandBuilder type generates the following UPDATE, INSERT, and DELETE parameterized queries:

```
UPDATE Inventory SET CarID = @p1 , Make = @p2 , Color = @p3 , PetName = @p4
WHERE ( (CarID = @p5) AND
((@p6 = 1 AND Make IS NULL) OR (Make = @p7)) AND
((@p8 =1 AND Color IS NULL) OR (Color = @p9)) AND
((@p10 = 1 AND PetName IS NULL) OR (PetName = @p11)) )
INSERT INTO Inventory( CarID , Make , Color , PetName ) VALUES
( @p1 , @p2 , @p3 , @p4 )
DELETE FROM  Inventory WHERE ( (CarID = @p1) AND
((@p2 = 1 AND Make IS NULL) OR (Make = @p3)) AND
((@p4 = 1 AND Color IS NULL) OR (Color = @p5)) AND
((@p6 = 1 AND PetName IS NULL) OR (PetName = @p7)) )
```

Now, while you may love the idea of getting something for nothing, do understand that command builders do come with some very critical restrictions. Specifically, a command builder is only able to auto-generate SQL commands for use by a data adapter if all of the following conditions are true:

- The SELECT command only interacts with a single table (e.g., no joins).

- The single table has been attributed with a primary key.

- The column(s) representing the primary key is accounted for in your SQL SELECT statement.

To wrap up our examination of the raw details of ADO.NET, allow me to provide two Windows Forms applications that tie together the topics discussed thus far. After this point, I'll wrap up with an overview of the data-centric tools provided by VS .NET and discuss *strongly typed DataSets*.

SOURCE CODE   The MySqlCommandBuilder project is found under the Chapter 17 subdirectory.

A Complete ADO.NET Windows Forms Example

Now assume you have a new Windows Forms example that allows the user to edit the values in a DataGrid (e.g., add new records, and update and delete existing records). When finished, the user may submit the modified DataSet back to the database using a Button type. First, assume the following constructor logic:

```
public class mainForm : System.Windows.Forms.Form
{
    private SqlConnection cn = new
        SqlConnection("server=(local);uid=sa;pwd=;database=Cars");
    private SqlDataAdapter dAdapt;
    private SqlCommandBuilder invBuilder;
    private DataSet myDS = new DataSet();
    private System.Windows.Forms.DataGrid dataGrid1;
    private System.Windows.Forms.Button btnUpdateData;
    ...
    public mainForm()
    {
        InitializeComponent();
        // Create the initial SELECT SQL statement.
        dAdapt = new SqlDataAdapter("SELECT * FROM Inventory", cn);
        // Autogenerate the INSERT, UPDATE,
        // and DELETE statements.
        invBuilder = new SqlCommandBuilder(dAdapt);
        // Fill and bind.
        dAdapt.Fill(myDS, "Inventory");
        dataGrid1.DataSource = myDS.Tables["Inventory"].DefaultView;
    }
...
}
```

At this point, the SqlDataAdapter has all the information it needs to submit changes back to the data store. Now assume that you have the following logic behind the Button's Click event:

```
private void btnUpdateData_Click(object sender, System.EventArgs e)
{
    try
    {
        dataGrid1.Refresh();
        dAdapt.Update(myDS, "Inventory");
    }
    catch(Exception ex)
    {
        MessageBox.Show(ex.Message);
    }
}
```

As usual, you call Update() and specify the table within the DataSet you wish to update. If you take this out for a test run, you see something like Figure 17-26 (be sure you exit out of edit mode on the DataTable before you submit your results!).

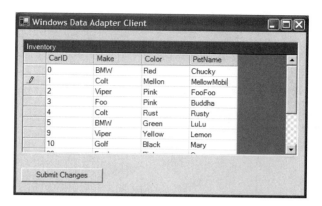

Figure 17-26. All good things do come . . .

 SOURCE CODE   The WinFormsExample project is included under the Chapter 17 subdirectory.

Filling a Multitabled DataSet (and Adding DataRelations)

Let's come full circle and build an additional Windows Forms example that mimics the application you created during the first half of this chapter. The GUI is simple enough. In Figure 17-27 you can see three DataGrid types that hold the data retrieved from the Inventory, Orders, and Customers tables of the Cars database. In addition, the single Button pushes any and all changes back to the data store.

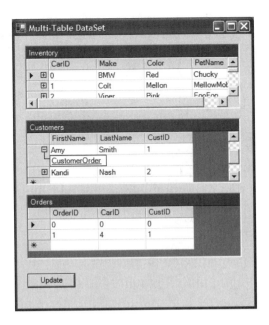

Figure 17-27. Viewing related DataTables

To keep things even simpler, you will use auto-generated commands for each of the three SqlDataAdapters (one for each table). First, here is the Form's state data:

```
public class mainForm : System.Windows.Forms.Form
{
    private System.Windows.Forms.DataGrid custGrid;
    private System.Windows.Forms.DataGrid inventoryGrid;
    private System.Windows.Forms.Button btnUpdate;
    private System.Windows.Forms.DataGrid OrdersGrid;
...
    // Here is the connection.
    private SqlConnection cn = new
            SqlConnection("server=(local);uid=sa;pwd=;database=Cars");
    // Our data adapters (for each table).
    private SqlDataAdapter invTableAdapter;
    private SqlDataAdapter custTableAdapter;
    private SqlDataAdapter ordersTableAdapter;
    // Command builders (for each table).
    private SqlCommandBuilder invBuilder = new SqlCommandBuilder();
    private SqlCommandBuilder orderBuilder = new SqlCommandBuilder();
    private SqlCommandBuilder custBuilder = new SqlCommandBuilder();
    // The dataset.
    DataSet carsDS = new DataSet();
...
}
```

The Form's constructor does the grunge work of creating your data-centric member variables and filling the DataSet. Also note that there is a call to a private helper function, BuildTableRelationship(), as shown here:

```
public mainForm()
{
    InitializeComponent();

    // Create adapters.
    invTableAdapter = new SqlDataAdapter("Select * from Inventory", cn);
    custTableAdapter = new SqlDataAdapter("Select * from Customers", cn);
    ordersTableAdapter = new SqlDataAdapter("Select * from Orders", cn);
    // Autogenerate commands.
    invBuilder = new SqlCommandBuilder(invTableAdapter);
    orderBuilder = new SqlCommandBuilder(ordersTableAdapter);
    custBuilder = new SqlCommandBuilder(custTableAdapter);
    // Add tables to DS.
    invTableAdapter.Fill(carsDS, "Inventory");
    custTableAdapter.Fill(carsDS, "Customers");
    ordersTableAdapter.Fill(carsDS, "Orders");
    // Build relations between tables.
    BuildTableRelationship();
}
```

The BuildTableRelationship() helper function does just what you would expect. Recall that the Cars database expresses a number of parent/child relationships. The code looks identical to the logic seen earlier in this chapter, as shown here:

```
private void BuildTableRelationship()
{
    // Create a DR obj.
    DataRelation dr = new DataRelation("CustomerOrder",
        carsDS.Tables["Customers"].Columns["CustID"],
        carsDS.Tables["Orders"].Columns["CustID"]);
    // Add relation to the DataSet.
    carsDS.Relations.Add(dr);
    // Create another DR obj.
    dr = new DataRelation("InventoryOrder",
        carsDS.Tables["Inventory"].Columns["CarID"],
        carsDS.Tables["Orders"].Columns["CarID"]);
    // Add relation to the DataSet.
    carsDS.Relations.Add(dr);
    // Fill the grids!
    inventoryGrid.SetDataBinding(carsDS, "Inventory");
    custGrid.SetDataBinding(carsDS, "Customers");
    OrdersGrid.SetDataBinding(carsDS, "Orders");
}
```

Now that the DataSet has been filled and disconnected from the data source, you can manipulate each table locally. To do so, simply insert, update, or delete values from any of the three DataGrids. When you are ready to submit the data back for processing, click the Form's Update button. The code behind the Click event should be clear at this point, as shown here:

```
private void btnUpdate_Click(object sender, System.EventArgs e)
{
    try
    {
        invTableAdapter.Update(carsDS, "Inventory");
        custTableAdapter.Update(carsDS, "Customers");
        ordersTableAdapter.Update(carsDS, "Orders");
    }
    catch(Exception ex)
    {
        MessageBox.Show(ex.Message);
    }
}
```

Once you update, you will find each table in the Cars database correctly altered.

SOURCE CODE   The WinFormsMultiTableDataSet project is included under the Chapter 17 subdirectory.

Bring In the Wizards!

To wrap up this chapter, I'd like to offer a guided tour of select integrated data-centric wizards provided by VS .NET. Now, let me preface the following sections by saying that the goal here is *not* to detail each and every option of each and every wizard. Doing so would require at least two additional (large) chapters. Rather, I will illustrate the use of a number of key tools in order to prime the pump for further exploration on your own terms. If you wish to follow along, create a brand new C# Windows Forms application named WinFormsVsNetWizardsApp.

Revisiting the Solutions Explorer

Back in Chapter 2, you were introduced to the Server Explorer utility of VS .NET. As you recall, this tool allows you to interact with a number of server-side services (such as MS SQL Server) using a familiar tree-view GUI. This view of the world can be quite helpful when working with ADO.NET, given that you are able to add any number of connections to your design time view. To do so, simply right-click the Data Connections node and select Add Connection (Figure 17-28).

Figure 17-28. Adding a new data connection

At this point you are provided with the Data Link Properties dialog box, which allows you to specify the name and location of the database you wish to communicate with. For this example, connect to your local Cars database (Figure 17-29).

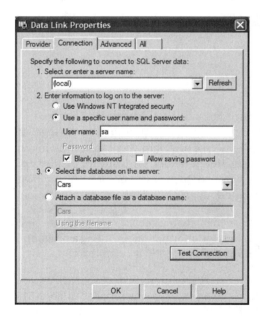

Figure 17-29. Configuring the new data connection

Once you have added a SQL connection, you are then able to view the underlying data source (Figure 17-30). As you would guess, each database item (tables, views, stored procedures, and whatnot) can be opened from within VS .NET by simply double-clicking the item of interest. To take things out for a test drive, double-click the Inventory table and GetPetName stored procedure.

Figure 17-30. Interacting with the Cars database via VS .NET

NOTE   Many of the advanced (read: really cool and helpful) features of the Solution Explorer (such as the ability to create, edit, and delete various database objects) require Visual Studio .NET Enterprise Edition or higher.

Creating a SQL Connection at Design Time

As you have seen earlier in this chapter, the System.Data.SqlClient.SqlConnection type defines a ConnectionString property, which contains information regarding a programmatic connection to a given data source. While it is not too difficult to build a connection string by hand, the IDE provides a number of tools to assist you in this regard. To illustrate one such approach, activate the Data tab from the Toolbox window (Figure 17-31), and place a SqlConnection component onto your design time Form.

Figure 17-31. Design time connection configuration

Once you have done so, select this item from the Icon Tray, and using the Properties window, select the name of your Cars connection from the ConnectionString property drop-down list. At this point, you should be pleased to see that a valid connection string has been created and configured on your behalf (within the #region code block):

```
public class Form1 : System.Windows.Forms.Form
{
    private System.Data.SqlClient.SqlConnection sqlConnection1;
...
    private void InitializeComponent()
    {
        this.sqlConnection1 = new System.Data.SqlClient.SqlConnection();
        this.sqlConnection1.ConnectionString = " <your connection string info>";
...
    }
}
```

You are now able to program against you new SqlConnection type using all of the techniques presented in this chapter. Command objects can be dragged onto the Forms designer in a similar manner. Once you do, you may edit your SQL queries using an integrated query editor (activated via the CommandText property).

Building a Data Adapter at Design Time

The VS .NET IDE also provides an integrated wizard that takes care of the grunge work that is necessary to build SELECT, UPDATE, INSERT, and DELETE commands for a given data adapter type (as you have seen, writing this code by hand can be a bit on the tedious side). To illustrate, delete your current SqlConnection component and place a SqlDataAdapter component onto your Icon Tray. This action will launch the Data Adapter Configuration Wizard. Once you click past the initial Welcome screen, you will be asked which data connection should be used to configure the data adapter (Figure 17-32). Again, pick your Cars connection.

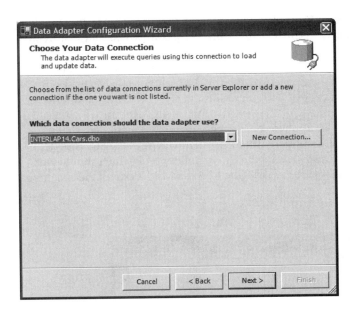

Figure 17-32. Specifying the connection for the new SqlDataAdapter

The next step allows you to configure how the data adapter should submit data to the data store (Figure 17-33).

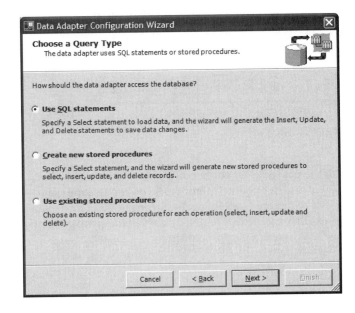

Figure 17-33. Specifying data store updates

As you can see from Figure 17-37, you have three choices. If you want to move data between the data store and the DataSet using stored procedures, you may instruct the wizard to generate new INSERT, UPDATE, and DELETE functions based on an initial SELECT statement or, as an alternative, choose prefabricated stored procedures. Your final option is to have the wizard build SQL queries. I'll assume you will check out the generated stored procedures at your leisure, so simply select Use SQL Statements for the time being.

The next step of the tool asks you to specify the SQL SELECT statement that will be used to build the set of SQL queries. Although you may type in the SQL SELECT statement by hand, you can also activate the Query Builder tool (which should look familiar to many Visual Basic developers). Figure 17-34 shows the crux of this integrated SQL editor.

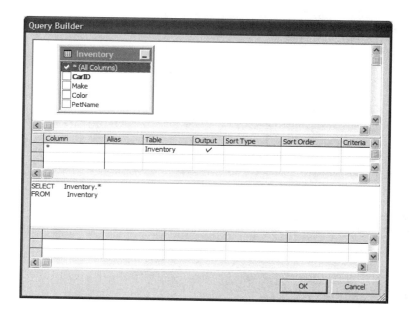

Figure 17-34. Creating the initial SELECT logic

Once you are finished with the data adapter configuration tool, open your code window and check out the InitializeComponent() method. As you can see, the new SqlCommand data members are configured automatically. I won't bother to list each aspect of the generated code, as you have already manually written the same syntax by hand during the chapter. However, here is a partial snapshot:

```
public class Form1 : System.Windows.Forms.Form
{
    private System.Data.SqlClient.SqlConnection sqlConnection1;
    private System.Data.SqlClient.SqlDataAdapter sqlDataAdapter1;
    private System.Data.SqlClient.SqlCommand sqlSelectCommand1;
    private System.Data.SqlClient.SqlCommand sqlInsertCommand1;
    private System.Data.SqlClient.SqlCommand sqlUpdateCommand1;
    private System.Data.SqlClient.SqlCommand sqlDeleteCommand1;
    private void InitializeComponent()
    {
        this.sqlDataAdapter1.DeleteCommand = this.sqlDeleteCommand1;
        this.sqlDataAdapter1.InsertCommand = this.sqlInsertCommand1;
        this.sqlDataAdapter1.SelectCommand = this.sqlSelectCommand1;
        this.sqlDataAdapter1.TableMappings.AddRange
        (new System.Data.Common.DataTableMapping[] {
        new System.Data.Common.DataTableMapping("Table", "Inventory",
            new System.Data.Common.DataColumnMapping[] {
            new System.Data.Common.DataColumnMapping("CarID", "CarID"),
            new System.Data.Common.DataColumnMapping("Make", "Make"),
            new System.Data.Common.DataColumnMapping("Color", "Color"),
...

        //
        // sqlInsertCommand1
        //
        this.sqlInsertCommand1.CommandText =
        "INSERT INTO Inventory(CarID, Make, Color, PetName)" +
        "VALUES (@CarID, @Make, @Color," +
        " @PetName); SELECT CarID, Make, Color, PetName FROM " +
        "Inventory WHERE (CarID = @CarID)";
        this.sqlInsertCommand1.Connection = this.sqlConnection1;
        this.sqlInsertCommand1.Parameters.Add(
        new System.Data.SqlClient.SqlParameter("@CarID",
            System.Data.SqlDbType.Int, 4, "CarID"));
...
    }
}
```

Hopefully, things look quite familiar. Once you have generated the basic look and feel of your data adapter, you may continue to alter its behavior using the Properties window. For example, if you were to select the TableMappings property, you could assign display names to each column of the underlying data table (Figure 17-35).

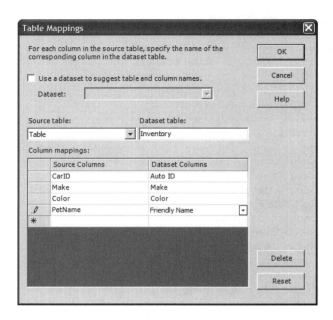

Figure 17-35. Altering column display names at design time

Using the Configured Data Adapter

At this point you are free to make use of any of the tricks you have learned about during the chapter to obtain and manipulate a DataSet. By way of a simple test, place a DataGrid widget onto the main Form, and show the contents of the Inventory table via a Button Click event:

```
private void btnLoadInventory_Click(object sender, System.EventArgs e)
{
    DataSet myDS = new DataSet();
    sqlConnection1.Open();
    sqlDataAdapter1.Fill(myDS);
    dataGrid1.DataSource = myDS.Tables["Inventory"];
}
```

Design Time Connections and Data Adapters, Take Two

The previous example illustrated how you can gain design time assistance for connection and data adapter types, by dragging and dropping the related components from the Data tab of the Toolbox onto the forms designer. If you are looking for the optimal short cut, try the following: First, delete all items from the Form's icon tray. Next, switch to the Server Explorer view and select the Inventory icon of the Cars database from the Data Connections node. Now, drag the Inventory table icon directly onto the Form. Once you do, you will be given SqlConnection and SqlDataAdapter types that are automatically preconfigured to communicate with the Cars database!

Understand that everything shown via the Server Explorer is "drag-and-droppable." To check things out further, select the GetPetName stored procedure and drag it onto the Form. As you can see, the result is a new SqlCommand type that is preconfigured to trigger the underlying stored proc:

```
this.sqlCommand1.CommandText = "dbo.[GetPetName]";
this.sqlCommand1.CommandType = System.Data.CommandType.StoredProcedure;
this.sqlCommand1.Connection = this.sqlConnection1;
this.sqlCommand1.Parameters.Add(
    new System.Data.SqlClient.SqlParameter("@RETURN_VALUE",
    System.Data.SqlDbType.Int, 4,
    System.Data.ParameterDirection.ReturnValue, false,
    ((System.Byte)(0)), ((System.Byte)(0)), "",
    System.Data.DataRowVersion.Current, null));
this.sqlCommand1.Parameters.Add(
    new System.Data.SqlClient.SqlParameter("@carID",
    System.Data.SqlDbType.Int, 4));
this.sqlCommand1.Parameters.Add(
    new System.Data.SqlClient.SqlParameter("@petName",
    System.Data.SqlDbType.VarChar, 20,
    System.Data.ParameterDirection.Output, false,
    ((System.Byte)(0)), ((System.Byte)(0)), "",
System.Data.DataRowVersion.Current, null));
```

Again, once the wizards have generated the initial code, you are free to tweak and change things to your liking. By way of example, select one of the SqlCommand types and check out the Parameters property of the Properties window. As you would guess, the resulting dialog editor allows you to edit parameter objects at design time.

Working with DataSets at Design Time

In the previous code samples, you directly created and allocated a DataSet type in your code base. As you would guess, VS .NET also offers design time support for the mighty DataSet. In fact, VS .NET allows you to generate two types of DataSets:

- *Untyped DataSets:* This corresponds to the DataSets examined thus far in the chapter. Untyped DataSets are simply variables of type System.Data.DataSet.

- *Typed DataSets:* This option allows you to generate a new .NET class type that derives from the DataSet class. Using this wrapper class, you can interact with the underlying data using object-oriented property syntax, rather than having to directly interact with the Rows and Columns collections.

If you wish to add an uptyped DataSet to your project, use the Data tab of the VS .NET Toolbox and place a new DataSet onto your design time template. When you do so, you will find that a new member variable of type DataSet has been added and allocated to a new instance, which can then be manipulated in your code.

Working with Typed DataSets at Design Time

Now, let's wrap up this chapter by checking out the role of *typed DataSets*. First of all, understand the typed DataSets perform the same function as an untyped DataSet (they contain a client-side cache of data) and are populated and updated via a corresponding data adapter. The key difference is, simply put, ease of use. For example, when you use untyped DataSets, you are required to drill into the internal structure of the DataTable type using the Rows and Columns properties. While nothing is horribly wrong with this approach, it would be nice to build a wrapper class that hides the internal complexities from view. For example, rather than writing this:

```
// A basic untyped DataSet.
lblCarID.Text = myDS.Tables["Inventory"].Rows[0]["CarID"];
```

you can write the following:

```
// A typed DataSet.
lblCarID.Text = myDS.Inventory[0].CarID;
```

In a nutshell, strongly typed DataSets are classes that derive from DataSet, and define numerous properties that interact with the underlying structure on your behalf.

To generate a strongly typed DataSet using VS .NET, right-click the related data adapter and select Generate DataSet (Figure 17-36).

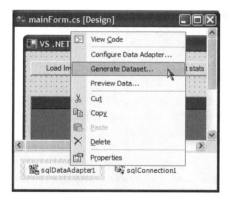

Figure 17-36. Creating a typed DataSet at design time

From the dialog box simply supply a name (such as CarsDataSet) and reconfirm the tables to wrap. At this point, you can make use of your new DataSet-derived type as follows:

```
private void btnLoadInventory_Click(object sender, System.EventArgs e)
{
    sqlConnection1.Open();
    sqlDataAdapter1.Fill(carsDataSet1);
    dataGrid1.DataSource = carsDataSet1.Inventory;
}
```

Note that you no longer need to make use of the Tables property to gain access to the contained Inventory table. Using a strongly typed DataSet, you simply reference the Inventory property.

Under the Hood of the Typed DataSets

Activate the Solution Explorer and click the Show all Files button. You will find that your strongly typed DataSet is represented by two related files. First you have an XML schema file (*.xsd) that represents the overall structure of the DataSet in terms of XML. Behind this schema file is a related *.cs class file (Figure 17-37).

Figure 17-37. Typed DataSets have a related "code behind" file

If you switch over to Class View, you will find that the newly generated CarsDataSet class defines a number of nested classes to represent the rows and tables it is responsible for maintaining (Figure 17-38).

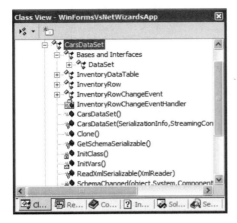

Figure 17-38. The DataSet-derived type maintains a set of nested classes.

While I will assume you will check out the generated code at your leisure, it is worth pointing out that strongly typed DataSets are automatically configured as serializable, which, as you recall from Chapter 12, allows you to persist the state data to some storage medium (as well as marshal the type by value):

```
[Serializable()]
...
public class CarsDataSet : DataSet {...}
```

If you were to check out the nested InventoryDataTable type, you would see that in addition to deriving from System.Data.DataTable, this new type is enumerable, and contains a number of private DataColumn types that are exposed via class properties (which are in turn exposed via the strongly typed DataRow-derived class). Thus, if you wish to access the stats of the first row in the Inventory table, you can write the following:

```
private void btnGetStats_Click(object sender, System.EventArgs e)
{
    string info = "Color: " + carsDataSet1.Inventory[0].Color;
    info += "\n" + "Make: " + carsDataSet1.Inventory[0].Make;
    info += "\n" + "Pet Name: " +
        carsDataSet1.Inventory[0].Friendly_Name_of_Car;
    MessageBox.Show(info, "First Car Info");
}
```

Again, the bonus is that the exposed properties are already mapped into CLR data types based on the underlying schema information. It is worth pointing out that while strongly typed DataSets are quite programmer friendly, the additional layers of indirection could be a potential performance drain. When you want to ensure your ADO.NET DataSets are operated on as quickly as possible, simple untyped DataSets tend to offer better performance.

Well, that wraps things up for this chapter. Obviously there is much more to say about ADO.NET than I had time to present here. If you are looking for a solid complement to this chapter, I recommend checking out *A Programmer's Guide to ADO.NET in C#* by Mahesh Chand (Apress, 2002).

Summary

ADO.NET is a new data access technology developed with the disconnected *n*-tier application firmly in mind. The System.Data namespace contains most of the core types you need to programmatically interact with rows, columns, tables, and views. As you have seen, the System.Data.SqlClient and System.Data.OleDb namespaces define the types you need to establish an active connection.

The centerpiece of ADO.NET is the DataSet. This type represents an in-memory representation of any number of tables and any number of optional interrelationships, constraints, and expressions. The beauty of establishing relations on your local tables is that you are able to programmatically navigate between them while disconnected from the remote data store.

Here you examined the role of the data adapter (OleDbDataAdapter and SqlDataAdapter). Using this type (and the related SelectCommand, InsertCommand, UpdateCommand, and DeleteCommand properties), the adapter can resolve changes in the DataSet with the original data store. Also, you learned about the connected layer of ADO.NET, and came to understand the role of data reader types.

We wrapped things up by checking out a subset of the tools available from VS .NET. As you have seen, the numerous integrated wizards do indeed help you with mundane and repetitive coding details. Like any code generation tool, you may find that a given wizard does not bring you all the way home. However, given your work throughout this chapter, you should be able to tweak the wizard-generated code to suit your needs.

Part Five
Web Applications and
XML Web Services

CHAPTER 18

ASP.NET Web Pages and Web Controls

UNTIL NOW, all of the example applications in this text have focused on Windows Forms and console-based front ends. In the next two chapters, you explore how the .NET platform facilitates the construction of browser-based presentation layers. To begin, you'll quickly review a number of key Web-centric atoms (HTTP, HTML, client-side, and server-side code bases) as well as the role of commercial Web servers (such as Microsoft IIS). During this process, you will create a simple Web application using HTML and classic ASP. Of course, if you are already "Web aware," feel free to skim or skip these initial sections entirely. On the other hand, if you come to ASP.NET with limited Web development experience, this primer will provide a valuable frame of reference for the chapters that follow.

With this Web primer complete, the remainder of this chapter will concentrate upon the composition of ASP.NET pages and the related topic of ASP.NET Web controls. As you will see, ASP.NET provides a far superior programming model than classic (COM-based) ASP. For example, you can now partition your presentation logic and business logic into discrete files using a technique called *code behind*. Also be very aware that ASP.NET demands that you to use "real" programming languages for your server-side logic (such as C#, VB .NET, MC++, etc.), rather than interpreted scripting languages (such as VBScript). Given this last point, it is critical to understand that you simply *cannot* build ASP.NET applications without solid knowledge of OOP, interfaces, and attributes.

The Role of HTTP

Web applications are very different animals than traditional desktop applications (to say the least). The first obvious difference is that a production-level Web application will always involve at least two networked machines (of course, during development it is entirely possible to have a single machine play the role of both client and server). Given this fact, the machines in question must agree upon a particular wire protocol to determine how to send and receive data. The wire protocol that connects the computers in question is the Hypertext Transfer Protocol (HTTP).

When a client machine launches a Web browser (such as Netscape Navigator or Microsoft Internet Explorer), an HTTP request is made to access a particular resource (such as an *.aspx file or *.htm file) located on a server machine. HTTP is a text-based protocol that is built upon a standard request/response paradigm. For example, if you navigate to http://www.intertech-inc.com, the browser software leverages a Web technology termed *Domain Name System* (DNS), which converts the registered URL into a four-part numerical value (aka an IP address). At this point, the browser opens a socket connection (typically via port 80), and sends the HTTP request to the default page at the Intertech-inc.com Web site.

Once the hosting Web server receives the incoming HTTP request, the specified resource may contain logic that scrapes out any client-supplied input values (such as values within a text box) in order to format a proper HTTP response. Web programmers may leverage any number of technologies (CGI, ASP, ASP.NET, Java Servlets, etc.) to dynamically generate the content to be emitted into the HTTP response. At this point, the client-side browser renders the HTML emitted from the Web server. Figure 18-1 illustrates the basic HTTP request/response cycle.

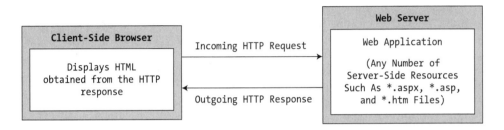

Figure 18-1. The HTTP request and response cycle

Another aspect of Web development that is markedly different from traditional desktop programming is the fact that HTTP is a *stateless* wire protocol. As soon as the Web server emits a response to the client browser, everything about the previous interaction is forgotten. Therefore, as a Web developer, it is up to you take specific steps to "remember" information (such as items in a shopping cart) about the clients who are currently logged onto your site. As you will see in the next chapter, ASP.NET provides numerous ways to handle state, many of which are commonplace to any Web platform (session variables, cookies, and application variables) as well as some new techniques (such as view state and the application cache).

Understanding Web Applications and Web Servers

Now that you better understand the role of HTTP and the underlying request/response cycle of the Web, we need to qualify some further terminology. To begin, a *Web application* can be understood as a collection of files (*.htm, *.asp, *.aspx, image files, and so on) and related components (.NET or classic COM binaries) stored within a particular directory (and optional subdirectories) on a given Web server. As you will see in the next chapter, Web applications have a specific life cycle and provide numerous events (such as initial startup or final shutdown) that you can hook into.

A *Web server* is a software product in charge of hosting your Web applications and typically provides a number of related services such as integrated security, File Transfer Protocol (FTP) support, mail exchange services, and so forth. Internet Information

Server (IIS) is Microsoft's enterprise-level Web server product, and as you would guess, has intrinsic support for classic ASP as well as ASP.NET Web applications.

NOTE   It is perfectly fine to have a single installation of IIS host classic ASP and ASP.NET Web applications. Because both Web platforms make use of distinct file extensions (for example, *.asp versus *.aspx), IIS will load the correct host process based on the incoming HTTP request.

When you build ASP.NET Web applications, you will be required to interact with IIS. Be aware, however, that IIS is *not* automatically selected when you install the Windows OS 2000 or XP Professional Edition (you can't run ASP.NET on the "Home" editions of Windows). Therefore, depending on the configuration of your development machine, you may be required to manually install IIS before proceeding through this chapter. To do so, simply access the Add/Remove Program applet from the Control Panel folder and select "Add/Remove Windows Components."

NOTE   Ideally, your development machine will have IIS installed *before* you install the .NET Framework. If you install IIS *after* you install the .NET Framework, none of your ASP.NET Web applications will execute correctly (you will simply get back a blank page). Luckily, you can reconfigure IIS to host .NET applications by running the aspnet_regiis.exe command line tool (using the /i flag).

Assuming you have IIS properly installed on your workstation, you can interact with IIS from the Administrative Tools folder (located in the Control Panel folder). For the purposes of this chapter, we are only concerned with the Default Web Site node (Figure 18-2).

Figure 18-2. The IIS applet

Working with IIS Virtual Directories

A single IIS installation is able to host numerous Web applications, each of which resides in a *virtual directory*. Each virtual directory is mapped to a physical directory on the local hard drive. Therefore, if you create a new virtual directory named CarsAreUs, the outside world can navigate to this site using a URL such as http://www.CarsAreUs.com (assuming your site's IP address has been registered with the world at large). Under the hood, the virtual directory maps to a physical root directory such as C:\TheCarsSite, which contains the set of files (and optional subdirectories) that constitutes the Web application.

When you create ASP.NET Web applications using VS .NET, you will automatically receive a new virtual directory for the current project. However, as you would guess, you are able to manually create a virtual directory by hand. For the sake of illustration, assume you wish to create a simple Web application named Cars. The first step is to create a new folder on your machine to hold the collection of files that constitute this new site (for example, C:\CarsWebSite).

Next, you need to create a new virtual directory to host the Cars site. Simply right-click the Default Web Site node of IIS and select New | Virtual Directory from the context menu. This menu selection launches an integrated wizard. Skip past the welcome screen and give your Web site a name (Cars). Next, you are asked to specify the physical folder on your hard drive that contains the various files and images that represent this site (in this case, C:\CarsWebSite).

The final step of the wizard prompts you for some basic traits about your new virtual directory (such as read/write access to the files it contains, the ability to view these files from a Web browser, the ability to launch executables [e.g., CGI applications], and so on). For this example, the default selections are just fine (be aware that you can always modify your selections after running this tool using various "right-click" Property dialog boxes integrated within IIS). When you are finished, you will see that your new virtual directory has been registered with IIS (Figure 18-3).

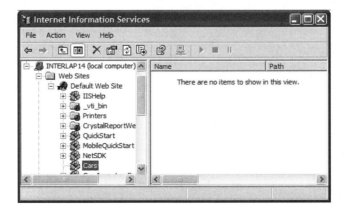

Figure 18-3. The Cars virtual directory

The Role of HTML

Once you have configured a virtual directory to host your Web application, you need to create the content itself. Recall that *Web application* is simply the term given to the set of files that constitute the functionality of the site. To be sure, a vast number of these files will contain syntactic tokens defined by the Hypertext Markup Language (HTML). HTML is a standard markup language used to describe how literal text, images, external links, and various HTML-based GUI widgets are rendered by the client-side browser.

This particular aspect of Web development is one of the major reasons that many programmers dislike building Web-based programs. While it is true that modern IDEs (including Visual Studio .NET) and Web development platforms (such as ASP.NET) hide much of the raw HTML tokens from view, you will do well to have a working knowledge of HTML as you work with ASP.NET. While this chapter will most certainly not cover all aspects of HTML (by any means), let's check out some basics.

The Basic Structure of an HTML Document

An HTML file consists of a set of tags that describe the look and feel of a given Web page. As you would expect, the basic structure of an HTML document tends to remain the same. For example, *.htm files (or alternatively, *.html files) open and close with <html> and </html> tags, typically define a <body> section, and so forth. Keep in mind that HTML is *not* case sensitive. Therefore, in the eyes of the hosting browser, <HTML>, <html>, and <Html> are identical.

To illustrate some HTML basics, open Visual Studio .NET, insert an empty HTML file using the File | New | File menu selection, and save this file under your physical directory as default.htm. If you examine the new *.htm file created by the IDE, you will find something like the following:

```
<!DOCTYPE HTML PUBLIC "-//W3C//DTD HTML 4.0 Transitional//EN">
<html>
    <head>
        <title></title>
        <meta name="GENERATOR" content="Microsoft Visual Studio .NET 7.1">
        <meta name="vs_targetSchema"
        content="http://shemas.microsoft.com/intellisense/ie5">
    </head>
    <body>
    </body>
</html>
```

The <html> and </html> tags are used to mark the beginning and end of your document. As you may guess, Web browsers use these tags to understand where to begin applying the rendering formats specified in the body of the document.

The <head> and </head> tags are used to hold any metadata about the document itself. Here the HTML header uses some <meta> tags that describe the origin of this file (VS .NET) and general bits of information. These tags will have no effect for the examples in this text, so feel free to delete them. Finally, note that a <title> tag is set (currently empty) that may be modified as follows:

```
<html>
    <head>
        <title>This Is the Cars Web Site</title>
    </head>
    <body>
    </body>
</html>
```

As you would guess, the <title> tags are used to specify the text string that should be placed in the title bar of the Web browser application.

HTML Form Development

The real action of an *.html file occurs within the scope of the <form> elements. Nestled within these tags are any number of additional tags used to render various user input widgets. Simply put, an *HTML form* is simply a named group of related UI elements used to gather user input, which is then transmitted to the Web application via HTTP. Do not confuse an HTML form with the entire display area shown by a given browser. In reality, an HTML form is more of a *logical grouping* of widgets placed in the <form> and </form> tag set:

```
<body>
    <form name = MainForm id = MainForm>
        <!--Add UI elements here -->
    </form>
</body>
```

This form has been assigned the ID and friendly name of "MainForm". Typically, the opening <form> tag supplies an action attribute that specifies the URL to which to submit the form data, as well as the method of transmitting that data itself (POST or GET). You will examine this aspect of the <form> tag in just a bit. For the time being, let's look at the sort of items that can be placed in an HTML form. The Visual Studio .NET IDE provides an HTML tab on the Toolbox dialog box that allows you to select each HTML-based UI widget (Figure 18-4).

Figure 18-4. The HTML Controls Toolbox

Table 18-1 gives a rundown of some of the more common HTML GUI widgets.

Table 18-1. Common HTML GUI Types

HTML GUI Widget	Meaning in Life
Button	A button that does not support the type attribute used to trigger a SUBMIT or RESET. This sort of button can be used to trigger a block of client-side script code or any other logic that does not require a trip to the Web server.
Checkbox Radio Button Listbox Dropdown	Standard UI selection elements.
Image	Allows you to specify an image to render onto the form.
Reset Button	This button element has its type attribute set to RESET. This instructs the browser to clear out the values in each UI element on the page to their default values.
Submit Button	This button element has its type attribute set to SUBMIT, which sends the form data to the recipient of a request.
Text Field Text Area Password Field	These UI elements are used to hold a single line (or multiple lines) of text. The Password Field renders input data using an asterisk (*) character mask.

NOTE   As shown later in this chapter, the System.Web.UI.HtmlControls namespace defines managed .NET types that correspond to these raw HTML widgets.

Building an HTML-Based User Interface

Before you add the HTML widgets to the HTML <form>, it is worth pointing out that VS .NET allows you to edit the overall look and feel of the *.html file itself using the integrated Properties window. For example, if you were to select DOCUMENT (Figure 18-5), you would be able to set the background color of the page (in addition to other details).

Figure 18-5. Editing an HTML document via VS .NET

Now, update the <body> of the default.html file to display some literal text that prompts the user to enter a user name and password and choose a background color of your liking (be aware that you can enter and format textual content directly onto the HTML designer):

```
<html>
    <head>
        <title>This Is the Cars Web Site</title>
    </head>
    <body BGCOLOR="#66ccff">
    <!-- Prompt for user input-->
    <h1 align="center">The Cars Login Page</h1>
    <p align="center">
    <br> Please enter your <i>user name</i> and <i>password</i>.</p>
    <!-- Build a form to get user info -->
    <form name="MainForm" ID="Form1">
    </form>
    </body>
</html>
```

Here, the <h1> tag defines the heading (or size) of the text to display.
 denotes a line break, <p> marks a paragraph, and <i> will italicize the text in question.

Now let's build the HTML form itself. In general, each HTML widget is described using a name attribute (used to identify the item programmatically) and a type attribute (used to specify which UI element you are interested in placing in the <form> declaration). Depending on which UI widget you manipulate, you will find additional attributes specific to that particular item. As you would expect, each UI element and its attributes can be modified using the Properties window.

The UI you will build here will contain two text fields (one of which is a Password widget), as well as two button types (one for submitting the form data and the other to reset the form data to the default values):

```
<!-- Build a form to get user info -->
<form name="MainForm" ID=" MainForm">
  <P align="center">User Name:
  <input id="txtUserName" type="text" NAME="txtUserName"></P>
  <P align="center">Password:
    <input name="txtPassword" type="password" ID="txtPassword"></P>
  <P align="center">
   <input name="btnSubmit" type="submit" value="Submit" ID="btnSubmit">
   <input name="btnReset" type="reset" value="Reset" ID="btnReset">
  </P>
</form>
```

Notice that you have assigned relevant names and IDs to each widget (txtUserName, txtPassword, btnSubmit, and btnReset). Of greater importance, note that each input button has an extra attribute named type, which marks these buttons as UI items that automatically clear all fields to their initial values (type = Reset) or send the form data to the recipient (type = Submit). Figure 18-6 illustrates your creation thus far.

Figure 18-6. The initial crack at the default.htm page

The Role of Client-Side Scripting

Now that you have a better understanding of how to construct an HTML form, the next issue is to examine the role of client-side scripting. A given *.html file may contain blocks of script code that will be emitted in the response stream and processed by the requesting browser. There are two major reasons that client-side scripting is used:

- To validate user input before posting back to the Web server

- To interact with the Document Object Model (DOM) of the target browser

Regarding the first point, understand that the inherent evil of a Web application is the need to make frequent round-trips (aka *postbacks*) to the server machine to update the HTML rendered into the browser. While postbacks are unavoidable, you should always be mindful of ways to minimize travel across the wire. One technique that saves round-trips is to use client-side scripting to validate user input before submitting the form data to the Web server. If an error is found (such as not specifying data within a required field), you can prompt the user of the error without incurring the cost of posting back to the Web server. (After all, nothing is more annoying to the user than posting back on a slow connection, only to receive instructions to address input errors!)

In addition to validating user input, client-side scripts can also be used to interact with the underlying object model (termed the Document Object Model, or DOM) of the browser itself. Most commercial browsers expose a set of objects that can be leveraged to control how the browser should behave. One major annoyance is the fact that different browsers tend to expose similar, but not identical, object models. Thus, if you emit a block of client-side script code that interacts with the DOM, it may not work identically on all browsers.

NOTE   ASP.NET provides the HttpRequest.Browser property, which allows you to determine at runtime the capacities of the browser that sent the current request.

There are many scripting languages that can be used to author client-side script code. Two of the more popular are VBScript and JavaScript. VBScript is a subset of the Visual Basic 6.0 programming language. Be aware that Microsoft Internet Explorer (IE) is the only Web browser that has built-in support for client-side VBScript support. Thus, if you wish your HTML pages to work correctly in any commercial Web browser, do *not* use VBScript for your client-side scripting logic.

The other popular scripting language is JavaScript. Be very aware that JavaScript is in no way, shape, or form a subset of the Java language. While JavaScript and Java have a somewhat similar syntax, JavaScript is not a full-fledged programming language, and thus is far less powerful than Java itself. The good news is that all modern day Web browsers support JavaScript, which makes it a natural candidate for client-side scripting logic.

NOTE   To further confuse the issue, recall that JScript .NET is a full-blown managed language that can be used to build valid .NET assemblies and is not used to author client-side script code!

A Client-Side Scripting Example

To illustrate the role of client-side scripting, we will first examine how to intercept events sent from client-side HTML GUI widgets. Assume you have added an additional HTML Button (btnHelp) type to your default.html page that allows the user to view help information. To capture the Click event for this button, activate the HTML view and select your button from the left drop-down list. Using the right drop-down list box, select the onclick event (Figure 18-7).

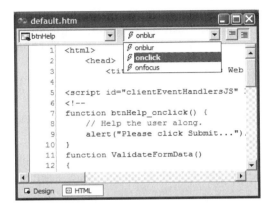

Figure 18-7. Capturing HTML widget events a la VS .NET

Once you do so, VS .NET will create an empty JavaScript function that will be called when the user clicks the button. Within this stub, simply make use of the alert() method to display a client-side message box:

```
<html>
    <head>
    <title>This Is the Cars Web Site</title>
    <script id="clientEventHandlersJS" language="javascript">
    <!--
    function btnHelp_onclick() {
        // Help the user along.
        alert("Please click Submit...");
    }
    //-->
    </script>
    </head>
    <body BGCOLOR="#66ccff">
...
    <!-- Prompt for user input -->
...
```

```
            <form name="MainForm" ID="Form1">
            <P align="center"><INPUT id="btnHelp" type="button" value="Help"
            name="btnHelp" onclick="return btnHelp_onclick()"> </P>
            </form>
        </body>
</html>
```

As you can see, a <script> block has been added to your HTML header, with JavaScript specified as the language of choice. Note that the scripting block has been wrapped within HTML style comments (<!-- -->). The reason is simple. If your page ends up on a browser that does not support JavaScript, the code will be treated as a comment block and ignored. Of course your page may be less functional, but the upside is that your page will not blow up when rendered by the browser. Also, notice that the attribute set for the HTML button has a new attribute named onclick, which is assigned to the name of the correct JavaScript function.

Validating the default.htm Form Data

Now, let's update the default.htm page to support some client-side validation logic. The goal is to ensure that when the user clicks the Submit button, you call a JavaScript function that checks each text box for empty values. If this is the case, you pop up an alert that instructs the user to enter the required data. First, handle an onclick event for the Submit button to a JavaScript method named ValidateFormData(). Within the logic of this method, check each text box for empty strings, as shown here:

```
<script id="clientEventHandlersJS" language = javascript>
...
function ValidateFormData()
{
    // If they forget either item, pop up a message box.
    if((MainForm.txtUserName.value == "") ||
    (MainForm.txtPassword.value == ""))
    {
        alert("You must supply a user name and password!");
        return false;
    }
    return true;
}
//-->
</script>
...
<input id = btnSubmit onclick = "return ValidateFormData()" type = submit
  value = Submit name = btnSubmit>
```

At this point, you can open your browser of choice and navigate to the default.html page hosted by your Cars virtual directory and test out your client-side script logic:

```
http://localhost/Cars/default.htm
```

Submitting the Form Data (GET and POST)

Now that you have a simple HTML page, you need to examine how to transmit the form data back to the Web server for processing. When you build an HTML form, you typically supply an action attribute on the opening <form> tag to specify the recipient of the incoming form data. Possible receivers include mail servers, other HTML files, an Active Server Page (classic or .NET), and so forth. For this example, you use a classic ASP file named ClassicAspPage.asp. Update your default.html file by specifying the following attribute in the opening <form> tag, as shown here:

```
<form name="MainForm" ID="MainForm"
  action="http://localhost/Cars/ClassicAspPage.asp" method = "GET">
    ...
</form>
```

This extra attribute specifies that when the Submit button for this form is clicked, the form data should be sent to the ClassicAspPage.asp file located within the Cars virtual directory on the current machine (i.e., localhost). When you specify method = "GET" as the mode of transmission, the form data is appended to the query string as a set of name/value pairs separated by ampersands. For example:

```
http://localhost/Cars/ClassicASPPage.asp?txtUserName=
Andrew&txtPassword=thisismypassword&btnSubmit=Submit
```

The other method of transmitting form data to the Web server is to specify method = "POST":

```
< form name="MainForm" ID="MainForm"
  action="http://localhost/Cars/ClassicAspPage.asp" method = "POST">
    ...
</form>
```

In this case, the form data is not appended to the query string, but instead is written to a separate line within the HTTP header. Using POST, the form data is not directly visible to the outside world and is therefore a wee bit more secure (more importantly, POST data is not limited by character length). For the time being, make use of HTTP GET to send the form data to the receiving *.asp page.

Building a Classic Active Server Page

A classic Active Server Page is a hodgepodge of HTML and server-side script code. If you have never worked with classic ASP, understand that the goal of ASP is to dynamically build HTML on the fly using server-side script logic and a small set of classic COM objects and related COM libraries. For example, you may have a server-side VBScript (or JavaScript) block that reads a table from a data source using classic ADO and returns the rows as a generic HTML table.

For this example, the ASP page uses the intrinsic ASP Request COM object to read the values of the incoming form data (appended to the query string) and echo them back to the caller (not terribly exciting, but it makes the point). The server-side script logic will make use of VBScript (as denoted by the "language" directive).

To do so, create a new HTML file using Visual Studio .NET and save this file under the name ClassicAspPage.asp into the folder to which your virtual directory has been mapped. Next, update your *.asp file with the following HTML and scripting logic:

```
<%@ language="VBScript" %>
<html>
<head>
    <title>The Cars Page</title>
</head>
 <body>
    <h1 align="center">Here is what you sent me:</h1>
    <P align="center"> <b>User Name: </b>
    <%= Request.QueryString("txtUserName") %> <br>
    <b>Password: </b>
    <%= Request.QueryString("txtPassword") %> <br>
    </P>
</body>
</html>
```

The first thing to be aware of is that an *.asp file begins and ends with the standard <html>, <head>, and <body> tag pairs. Here, you use the classic ASP Request COM object, which like any COM type supports a number of properties, methods, and events. You call the Request.QueryString() method to examine the values contained in each HTML widget submitted via method = "GET".

Also note that the <%= ...%> notation is a shorthand way of saying "Insert the following directly into the HTTP response." To gain a finer level of flexibility, you could interact with the ASP Response COM object within a full script block (denoted using the <%, %> notation). You have no need to do so here; however, here is a simple example:

```
<!-- Send back the info they gave us -->
<center>
...
    <%
        Dim pwd
        pwd = Request.QueryString("txtPassword")
        Response.Write (pwd)
    %>
</center>
```

Obviously, the Request and Response objects of classic ASP provide a number of additional members beyond Write() and QueryString(). Furthermore, classic ASP also defines a small number of additional COM objects (Session, Server, Application, and so on) that you can use while constructing your Web application.

NOTE   Under ASP.NET, these COM objects are effectively dead. However, you will see that the System.Web.UI.Page base class defines identically named properties that provide similar functionality.

To test the ASP logic, simply load the default.htm page from a browser and submit the form data. Once the script is processed on the Web server, you are returned a brand new (dynamically generated) HTML display (Figure 18-8).

Figure 18-8. The dynamically generated HTML

Responding to POST Submissions

Currently, your default.htm file specifies HTTP GET as the method of sending the form data to the target *.asp file. Using this approach, the values contained in the various GUI widgets are appended to the end of the query string. It is important to note that the ASP Request.QueryString() method is *only* able to extract data submitted via the GET method.

If you would rather submit form data to the Web resource using HTTP POST, the Request.Form collection can be used to read the values on the server. For example:

```
<body>
    <h1 align="center">Here is what you sent me:</h1>
    <P align="center">
        <b>User Name: </b>
        <%= Request.Form("txtUserName") %> <br>
        <b>Password: </b>
        <%= Request.Form("txtPassword") %> <br>
    </P>
</body>
```

That wraps up the Web development primer. Hopefully those of you who are new to Web development have a better understanding of what goes on behind the scenes. Now, before we check out how the .NET platform improves upon the current state of affairs, let's take a brief moment to bash (which is to say "critique") classic ASP.

SOURCE CODE   The default.html and ClassicAspPage.asp files are included under the ClassicAspCars subdirectory.

The Problem(s) with Classic ASP

While many successful Web applications have been created using classic ASP, this architecture is not without its downside. Perhaps the biggest downfall of classic ASP is the same point that makes it a powerful platform: server-side scripting languages. Scripting languages such as VBScript and JavaScript are interpreted, typeless entities that do not lend themselves to robust OO programming techniques. For example, under classic ASP, there was no concept of classical inheritance, attributes, strongly typed data, or classical polymorphism (although the interface-driven nature of classic COM did allow for interface-based polymorphism).

Another problem with classic ASP is the fact that an *.asp page does not yield very modularized code. Given that ASP is a blend of HTML and script in a *single* page, most ASP Web applications are a confused mix of two very different programming techniques. While it is true that classic ASP allows you to partition reusable code into distinct include files, the underlying object model does not support true separation of concerns. In an ideal world, a Web framework would allow the presentation logic (i.e., HTML tags) to exist independently from the business logic (i.e., functional code).

A final issue to consider here is the fact that classic ASP demands a good deal of boilerplate, redundant script code that tends to repeat between projects. Almost all Web applications need to validate user input, repopulate the state of HTML widgets before emitting the HTTP response, generate an HTML table of data, and so forth.

Some Benefits of ASP.NET

ASP.NET addresses each of the limitations of classic ASP (and brings a number of new bells and whistles to the game). First and foremost, ASP.NET files (*.aspx) do not use server-side scripting languages. As mentioned earlier, ASP.NET allows you to use real programming languages such as C#, MC++, and Visual Basic .NET (or any other .NET-aware language). Because of this, you can apply all of the technique you have learned throughout this book directly to your Web development efforts. As you would expect, *.aspx pages can make use of the .NET class libraries as well as the functionality provided by any of your custom assemblies. Like always, simply access the Add References dialog box and find the assembly in question.

NOTE   While it is true that you can literally use *any* .NET assembly, it should make sense that the types within System.Windows.Forms.dll are of no use within a Web application. Surprisingly, System.Drawing.dll is extremely useful when programming with ASP.NET, given that you can use GDI+ to dynamically generate an image file on the Web server (as seen at the end of this chapter).

Next, ASP.NET applications provide numerous ways to decrease the amount of code you need to write to begin with. For example, through the use of server-side Web controls, you can build a browser-based front end using various GUI widgets that emit raw HTML tags automatically. Other Web controls are used to perform automatic validation of your GUI items, which decreases (if not eliminates) the amount of client-side JavaScript you are responsible for authoring. To add to the current laundry list of benefits, ponder the additional aspects of ASP.NET:

- ASP.NET supports a technique termed *code behind*, which allows you to separate your presentation logic from your business logic.

- ASP.NET makes use of true compiled .NET assemblies, not interpreted scripting languages, which results in much faster execution.

- ASP.NET Web controls allow programmers to build the GUI of a Web app in a manner similar to building a traditional desktop application.

- ASP.NET Web controls automatically maintain their state during postbacks using a hidden form field named __VIEWSTATE.

- ASP.NET Web applications are completely object oriented. You no longer need to examine the Form or QueryString collections to obtain the values submitted by the client (although these techniques are still supported).

- ASP.NET Web applications can be easily configured using standard IIS settings *or* using a Web application configuration file (web.config).

- ASP.NET Web applications are extremely simple to deploy given that .NET assemblies are not registered into the system registry.

To begin seeing these and other benefits in action, let's get to know the ASP.NET namespaces, all of which are contained within the System.Web.dll assembly.

The ASP.NET Namespaces

The .NET base class libraries contain numerous namespaces focused on Web-based technologies. Generally speaking, these namespaces can be grouped into three major categories: core Web atoms (e.g., types that allow you to interact with the HTTP request and response, configuration types, e-mail, and security types), UI widgets (WebForm and HTML controls), and XML Web services (examined in Chapter 20). Table 18-2 documents the ASP.NET-centric namespaces.

Table 18-2. ASP.NET Namespaces

Web-Centric Namespace	Meaning in Life
System.Web	System.Web defines core types that enable browser/Web server communication (such as request and response capabilities, cookie manipulation, and file transfer).
System.Web.Caching	This namespace contains types that facilitate caching support for a Web application.
System.Web.Configuration	This namespace contains types that allow you to programmatically interact with the project's Web.config file.
System.Web.Mail	Defines the types that allow you to integrate e-mail functionality.
System.Web.SessionState	Defines the types that allow you to maintain stateful information on a per-user basis (e.g., session state variables).
System.Web.Security	Defines types that allow you to programmatically secure your site.
System.Web.UI System.Web.UI.WebControls System.Web.UI.HtmlControls	These namespaces define a number of types that allow you to build a GUI front end for your Web application.

The Core Types of System.Web

The System.Web namespace defines the minimal and complete set of types that allow you to build an ASP.NET Web application. Table 18-3 is a quick rundown of some items of interest, many of which are examined in greater detail throughout this chapter.

Table 18-3. Core Types of the System.Web Namespace

System.Web Type	Meaning in Life
HttpApplication	The HttpApplication class defines the members common to all ASP.NET applications. As you will see, the global.asax file defines a class derived from HttpApplication.
HttpApplicationState	The HttpApplicationState class enables developers to share global information across multiple sessions in an ASP.NET application.
HttpBrowserCapabilities	Enables the server to compile information on the capabilities of the browser that sent the HTTP request.
HttpCookie	Provides a type-safe way to access multiple HTTP cookies.
HttpRequest	Provides an object-oriented way to enable browser-to-server communication.
HttpResponse	Provides an object-oriented way to enable server-to-browser communication.

Creating an ASP.NET Web Application by Hand

ASP.NET Web applications typically make use of a technique termed *code behind*, which allows you to separate your programming code from your HTML presentation logic. While this is certainly the recommended approach, it is still technically possible to avoid using a code behind file and directly embed .NET code within the *.aspx file. However, be very aware that if you choose to build your ASP.NET pages in this manner, you are essentially re-creating a major issue found with classic ASP (the hodgepodge of script blocks and HTML presentation tags in a single server-side file).

Nevertheless, let's walk through an example of building a single-paged Web application that does not make use of code behind, and learn some basic features of ASP.NET in the process. Create a new virtual directory named CarsInventoryPage that maps to a specific directory on your hard drive. Next, create a new file named CarsInventoryPage.aspx and save it in the physical directory you just created.

Coding the *.aspx File

For this example (and this example only), you will avoid the use of a code behind file, and therefore your server-side programming logic will be embedded directly within the *.aspx file. The goal of this page is simple: Open a connection to the Cars database (created in Chapter 17) and display the current inventory. To do so, you will make use of three ASP.NET WebForm controls (a Label, DataGrid, and Button type) and a block of server-side C# code. Here is the complete page, with analysis to follow:

```
<%@ Page language="c#"%>
<%@ Import Namespace = "System.Data.SqlClient" %>
<HTML>
<HEAD>
    <title>This is the cars inventory page</title>
    <script language="C#" runat="server">
    void GetTheData(object sender, EventArgs e)
    {
        SqlConnection sqlConn =
            new SqlConnection("Data Source=.;Initial Catalog=Cars;UID=sa;PWD=");
        sqlConn.Open();
        SqlCommand cmd =
            new SqlCommand("Select * From Inventory", sqlConn);
        inventoryGrid.DataSource = cmd.ExecuteReader();
        inventoryGrid.DataBind();
        sqlConn.Close();
    }
    </script>
</HEAD>
<body>
    <form id="Form1" method="post" runat="server">
    <asp:Label id="Label1" runat="server">
     Click on the button below to fill the DataGrid
    </asp:Label></p>
    <asp:Button id="btnGetData" OnClick="GetTheData" runat="server"
    Text="Get the Data!">
    </asp:Button></p>
    <asp:DataGrid id=" inventoryGrid" runat="server" BorderColor="#CC9966"
        BorderStyle="None" BorderWidth="1px" BackColor="White" CellPadding="4">
    </asp:DataGrid>
    </form>
</body>
</HTML>
```

The <%@Page%> Directive

The first thing to be aware of is that a given *.aspx file will typically open with a set of page-level directives. ASP.NET directives are always denoted with <%@ XXX %> markers, and may be qualified with various attributes to inform the ASP.NET runtime how to process the information.

Every *.aspx file must have at minimum a <%@Page%> directive that is used to define the managed language used within the page (via the language directive). Also, the <%@Page%> directive may also define the name of the related code behind file (if any), enable tracing, and so forth. Table 18-4 documents some of the more interesting <%@Page%>-centric attributes.

Table 18-4. Some (But Not All) of the @Page Attributes

Attribute of the @Page Directive	Meaning in Life
ClassName	This attribute allows you to define a specific name for the auto-generated class type.
CodeBehind	This attribute is used to specify the name of the related code behind file.
EnableViewState	Indicates whether view state is maintained across page requests (more details later). True if view state is maintained; otherwise, false. The default value is true.
Inherits	Defines a code behind class for the page to inherit. Can be any class derived from the Page class. Used to specify the name of the class in the code behind file from which this type derives.
Trace	Indicates whether tracing is enabled (true or false).

The <%@Import%> Directive

In addition to the <%@Page%> directive, a given *.aspx file may specify further directives. In this example, you make use of the <%@Import%> directive (in conjunction with the Namespace attribute) to explicitly state that this page is using types within the System.Data.SqlClient namespace. As you would guess, if you need to make use of additional .NET namespaces, you simply specify multiple <%@Import%> directives.

NOTE   The <%@Import%> directive is only necessary if you are not making use of code behind. When you do make use of code behind, you will reference external namespaces using the C# "using" keyword.

Given your current knowledge of .NET, you may wonder how this *.aspx file avoided specifying the System.Data or System namespaces. The reason is due to the fact that all *.aspx pages automatically have access to a small set of key .NET namespaces:

- System

- System.Collections

- System.Configuration

- System.IO

- System.Text

- System.Text.RegularExpressions

- All of the System.Web-centric namespaces

ASP.NET does define a number of other directives that may appear in an *.aspx file above and beyond <%@Page%> and <%@Import%>; however, I'll reserve comment for the time being.

The "Script" Block

Even though server-side scripting is dead under ASP.NET, code that is embedded within an *.aspx file is scoped within <script> tags. Note that it is *critical* that all of your server-side code blocks are defined to execute at the server, using the runat="server" attribute:

```
<script language="C#" runat="server">
void GetTheData(object sender, EventArgs e)
{
    ...
}
```

The signature of this helper method should look strangely familiar. Recall from our examination of Windows Forms that a given event handler must match the pattern defined by a related .NET delegate. And, just like Windows Forms, when you wish to handle a server-side button click, the delegate in question is System.EventHandler (which, as you recall, can only call methods that take a System.Object as the first parameter and a System.EventArgs as the second).

Within the scope of the GetTheData() method, you make use of standard ADO.NET logic to bind the records returned by the DataReader to a variable of DataGrid. Now, if you have a background in classic ASP, I am pleased to inform you that your days of nested for-loops and table-centric HTML tags are over. Rather than manually building the HTML table by hand, ASP.NET DataGrids automatically emit the correct tag set automatically.

The ASP.NET Widget Declarations

The final point of interest is the declaration of the Button, Label, and DataGrid WebForm controls. Like classic ASP and raw HTML, ASP.NET Web widgets are scoped within <form> elements. This time, however, the opening <form> element is marked with the runat="server" attribute. This again is critical, as this tag informs the ASP.NET runtime that before the HTML is emitted into the response stream, the contained ASP.NET widgets have a chance to render their HTML appearance.

ASP.NET Web controls are declared with <asp> and </asp> tags, and are also marked with the runat="server" attribute. Within the opening tag, you will specify the name of the WebForm control (such as Label, Button, DataGrid) and any number of name/value pairs that will be used at runtime to render the correct HTML. Now, as you will see in the next example, these name/value pairs correspond directly to properties of the corresponding class type. For example, when you declare a DataGrid and specify BackColor="White", you have basically set the BackColor property of the System.Web.UI.WebControls.DataGrid type. In any case, ponder the following declarations:

```
<form id="Form1" method="post" runat="server"> <P>
    <asp:Label id="Label1" runat="server">
    Click on the button below to fill the DataGrid
    </asp:Label><p/>
    <asp:Button id="btnGetData" OnClick="GetTheData" runat="server"
    Text="Get the Data!">
    </asp:Button><p/>
    <asp:DataGrid id="DataGrid1" runat="server"
    BorderColor="#CC9966" BorderStyle="None"
        BorderWidth="1px" BackColor="White" CellPadding="4">
    </asp:DataGrid>
</form>
```

Finally, notice that the Button type has made use of the OnClick attribute to specify the name of the server-side function that will be called when the user clicks the Button widget. At this point, you can open a browser and navigate to the CarsInventoryPage.aspx page:

```
http://localhost/FirstAspNetWebApp/CarsInventoryPage.aspx
```

The results are seen in Figure 18-9.

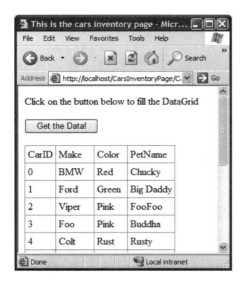

Figure 18-9. Your first ASP.NET Web application

The ASP.NET Compilation Cycle

One question that may be on your mind at this point is how exactly your block of C# code was executed by the ASP.NET runtime. As you are already well aware, the CLR can only interact with CIL code that is contained within a .NET assembly (obviously, your *.aspx file is not a .NET binary, but a simple text file). Behind the scenes, when the initial HTTP request comes in for a given *.aspx file, the runtime will parse all of the code within the <script> blocks and generate a brand new *dynamic* assembly. This image is then persisted to file, and stored under a very specific location (sometimes called the *shadow directory*) on the Web server machine:

```
<drive>:\<%windir%>\Microsoft .NET\Framework\<version>\Temporary ASP.NET Files
```

Under this directory, you will find a subdirectory that reflects the name of the hosting virtual directory. From here, you will need to drill down through some further auto-generated folders (which are named based on various hash algorithms) until you find the name of the compiled *.dll assembly. Again, the name of your .NET assembly will be unique (Figure 18-10).

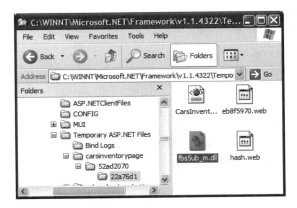

Figure 18-10. The location of the dynamically created assembly

Like any .NET assembly, you are able to open up the binary using ildasm.exe and check out the underlying CIL, manifest, and metadata. Looking at Figure 18-11, you can see that your immediate base class is System.Web.UI.Page.

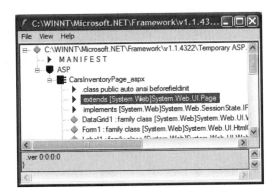

Figure 18-11. *.aspx files become classes that extend System.Web.UI.Page.

After the assembly has been created upon the initial HTTP request, it will be reused for all subsequent requests, and thus will not have to be recompiled. Understanding this factoid should help explain why the first request of an *.aspx page takes the longest, and subsequent hits to the same page are extremely efficient.

Now, open up your CarsInventoryPage.aspx file in Notepad and make some sort of code update, such as changing the Text value for the Button type:

```
<asp:Button id="btnGetData" OnClick="GetTheData"
runat="server" Text="Get the Data NOW!">
</asp:Button>
```

If you save this file and request the page once again, you will indeed find a time lag. Also, if you were to look at the shadow directory, you will find *another* auto-generated *.dll. Because the runtime is smart enough to detect changes to *.aspx files, it becomes painfully simple to update a running Web application. All you need to do is place the updated *.aspx files into the directory of the Web applications and the ASP.NET runtime will take care of the rest. Clients who are currently using the older version of the .NET assembly are completely unaware of the change as they still make use of the previous version. However, new clients will automatically receive the latest and greatest assembly. Figure 18-12 illustrates the ASP.NET compilation cycle.

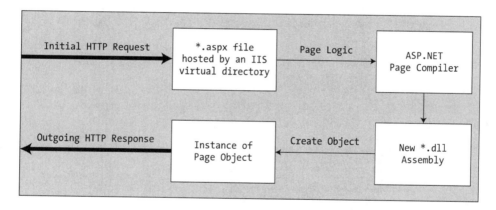

Figure 18-12. The ASP.NET compilation cycle

NOTE   This is a huge improvement to classic ASP, where updating ASP files typically involved re-registering COM servers and rebooting the Web server.

Controlling the Generated Class Name

As you have seen, the ASP.NET compilation cycle will automatically generate a class derived from System.Web.UI.Page when the initial HTTP request comes through. By default, the name of this class will be based on the filename of the *.aspx file; however, this can be changed by using the ClassName attribute of the @Page directive:

```
<%@ Page language="c#" ClassName="CarsInventory"%>
```

If you were now to open this auto-generated *.dll using ildasm.exe, you would find that the name of your derived class is indeed CarsInventory, rather than CarsInventoryPage_aspx.

Cool! At this point you have seen that you can indeed embed your C# code directly within a *.aspx file. However, this is *evil* and I will not take this approach for the remainder of this text. Speaking of "evil things," you may agree that it is a bit of a drag to manually build a virtual directory by hand. Given both of these issues, let's check out how VS .NET will not only build a virtual directory automatically, but also automatically configure ASP.NET pages to make use of an associated code behind file.

SOURCE CODE   The CarsInventoryPage.aspx file is included under the CarsInventoryPage subdirectory.

Creating an ASP.NET Web Application via VS .NET

Visual Studio .NET simplifies the process of building ASP.NET Web applications in a number of ways. To illustrate, let's now re-create the previous Web page using the functionality of VS .NET. First, create a new C# Web Application project workspace named BetterAspNetCarApp (Figure 18-13).

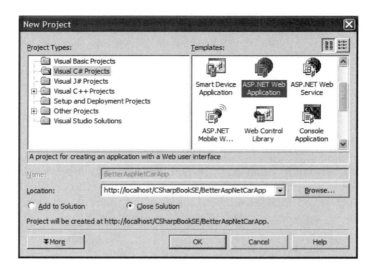

Figure 18-13. Creating an ASP.NET application project with VS .NET

Before you click the OK button, take a minute to notice that the Location text box maps not to a specific folder on your hard drive, but rather to the URL of the machine hosting this Web application. The Visual Studio .NET solution files (*.sln) are stored under the "My Documents\Visual Studio Projects" subfolder. Once the new project workspace has been created, you will notice that a design time template has been opened automatically (Figure 18-14).

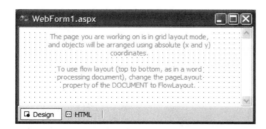

Figure 18-14. Your design time template

Much like a Windows Forms application, this template represents the visual appearance of the *.aspx file you are constructing. The difference, of course, is that you are using HTML-based WebForm controls rather than Win32-based Windows Forms controls. Note that the default name for this page is WebForm1; however, using the VS .NET Properties window, you are free to change this to a more fitting name (such as BetterAspNetCarApp.aspx).

NOTE   The GUI of an *.aspx page may be authored in two manners. If the pageLayout property of the DOCUMENT object is set to GridLayout (the default), you will be able to use absolute position of your GUI widgets. While this is very Windows Forms–like, be aware that older browsers may not support absolute positioning of HTML elements. If you wish to build a GUI that will be displayed correctly in all browsers, you should switch the pageLayout property to FlowLayout.

Next, click the Show All Files button and check out the Solution Explorer window (Figure 18-15). You have been given a number of new files and external assembly references.

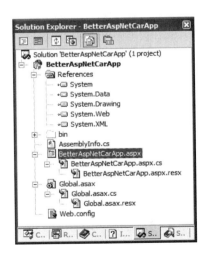

Figure 18-15. Initial files of an ASP.NET application

You will get to know the role of these files over the course of this chapter; for now, Table 18-5 hits the highlights.

Table 18-5. Initial Project Files

Generated Files of an ASP.NET Web Application Project	Meaning in Life
assemblyinfo.cs	Like any VS .NET project, this file is used to hold common assembly-level attributes.
*.aspx *.aspx.cs *.aspx.resx	Every ASP.NET page in your application is represented by three related files. The *.aspx file is used to define the WebForm controls used by the page. The *.aspx.cs file is the code behind file that will hold your related C# code. Finally, if your page makes use of any .NET resource, they will be defined in the *.aspx.resx file.
Global.aspx Global.aspx.cs Global.aspx.resx	As explained later in this chapter, your ASP.NET Web applications may optionally define a class type that derives from the HttpApplication type. These files set up this scenario.
Web.config	ASP.NET Web applications also make use of *.config files. Unlike a desktop application, however, this file will always be named web.config regardless of the name of the Web application.

Next, if you open IIS, you see that a new virtual directory (BetterAspNetCarApp) has been automatically created on your behalf. As you can see, each file in the workspace has been included in this virtual directory. The physical folder to which this virtual directory is mapped can be located under a subdirectory of <drive>:\Inetpub\wwwroot\<NameOfYourApp>.

Examining the Initial *.aspx File

If you examine the structure of your *.aspx file (by switching to the HTML view on the IDE's designer), you will find a skeleton declaration of an ASP.NET Web page. Note that the <%@Page%> directive now makes use of the Codebehind and Inherits attributes:

```
<%@ Page language="c#" Codebehind="BetterAspNetCarApp.aspx.cs"
AutoEventWireup="false"
Inherits="BetterAspNetCarApp.WebForm1" %>
<!DOCTYPE HTML PUBLIC "-//W3C//DTD HTML 4.0 Transitional//EN" >
```

```
<HTML>
    <HEAD>
    <title>WebForm1</title>
    <meta name="GENERATOR" Content="Microsoft Visual Studio .NET 7.1">
    <meta name="CODE_LANGUAGE" Content="C#">
    <meta name="vs_defaultClientScript" content="JavaScript">
    <meta name="vs_targetSchema"
    content="http://schemas.microsoft.com/intellisense/ie5">
    </HEAD>
    <body MS_POSITIONING="GridLayout">
        <form id="Form1" method="post" runat="server">
        </form>
    </body>
</HTML>
```

Recall that the Codebehind attribute is used to define the name of the source code file that contains the "real" code used by this page, while the Inherits attribute specifies the name of the class in the file that functions as your immediate base class.

Examining the Code Behind File

Now, ensure that the Show all Files option has been selected and open up this page's code behind file (BetterAspNetCarApp.aspx.cs):

```
using System;
using System.Collections;
using System.ComponentModel;
using System.Data;
using System.Drawing;
using System.Web;
using System.Web.SessionState;
using System.Web.UI;
using System.Web.UI.WebControls;
using System.Web.UI.HtmlControls;

namespace BetterAspNetCarApp
{
    public class WebForm1 : System.Web.UI.Page
    {
        private void Page_Load(object sender, System.EventArgs e) { }
        override protected void OnInit(EventArgs e)
        {
            InitializeComponent();
            base.OnInit(e);
        }
        private void InitializeComponent()
        {
            this.Load += new System.EventHandler(this.Page_Load);
        }
    }
}
```

First, because you are making use of a code behind file, you have no need to use the <%@Imports%> directive, but can opt for the C# "using" keyword. Next, notice how the class specified by the Inherits attribute of the <%@Page%> directive has a base class of System.Web.UI.Page. Also, your page has been wired up to handle two lifetime events: Init and Load (more information on a page's life cycle later in this chapter).

Coding the BetterAspNetCarApp Web Application

Rather than manually defining all of the Web widgets used by this *.aspx file (as you did in the previous example), you can make use of the VS .NET designer and the Web Forms tab of the IDE's Toolbox (Figure 18-16).

Figure 18-16. The ASP.NET Web Controls Toolbox

Create a GUI that mimics the previous *.aspx file. Notice that you are able to leverage the IDE's Properties window to automatically add the name/value pairs used for the control's ASP declaration. Handling the Button's Click event is also simplified when using VS .NET. Like a Windows Forms application, simply activate the event view from the Properties window, and type in the name of the event handler function. As you would expect, your code behind file has been updated to handle this event using standard C# event syntax. In addition, notice that the class defined in the code behind file has member variables that correspond to the ASP.NET Web widgets declared in the *.aspx file.

At this point, all you need to do is implement the event handler to bind the data from the Inventory table to the DataGrid widget:

```
using System.Data.SqlClient;
...
public class WebForm1 : System.Web.UI.Page
{
    // Widget member variables.
    protected System.Web.UI.WebControls.Button btnGetTheData;
    protected System.Web.UI.WebControls.DataGrid inventoryGrid;

    private void Page_Load(object sender, System.EventArgs e) {}
    override protected void OnInit(EventArgs e)
    {
        InitializeComponent();
        base.OnInit(e);
    }
    private void InitializeComponent()
    {
        this.btnGetTheData.Click +=
            new System.EventHandler(this.btnGetTheData_Click);
        this.Load += new System.EventHandler(this.Page_Load);
    }
    private void btnGetTheData_Click(object sender, System.EventArgs e)
    {
        SqlConnection sqlConn =
            new SqlConnection("Data Source=.;Initial Catalog=Cars;UID=sa;PWD=");
        sqlConn.Open();
        SqlCommand cmd =
            new SqlCommand("Select * From Inventory", sqlConn);
        inventoryGrid.DataSource = cmd.ExecuteReader();
        inventoryGrid.DataBind();
        sqlConn.Close();
    }
}
```

You can now take your ASP.NET application out for a test drive. Of course, the output is identical to the CarsInventoryPage Web application.

The Role of the \bin Directory

When you use VS .NET as the starting point for your ASP.NET Web applications, you will find that the virtual directory has a subdirectory named \bin. Each time you compile your current project, VS .NET will store the latest and greatest copy of the *.dll assembly within this folder. However, as you may be guessing, this is not the *.dll loaded by the CLR. As always, when the initial HTTP request comes in, the runtime will copy this precompiled *.dll into the shadow directory for subsequent use.

NOTE One nice by-product of the "precompilation" cycle is that the name of the *.dll assembly in the shadow directory is the same as the item in the \bin folder (rather than the auto-generated filename seen in the previous example).

SOURCE CODE The BetterAspNetCarApp files are included under the Chapter 18 subdirectory.

The Composition of an ASP.NET Page

Recall that the <%@Page%> directive is used to specify the name of the code behind file, as well as the name of the class in said file that becomes your base class:

```
<%@ Page language="c#" Codebehind="BetterAspNetCarApp.aspx.cs"
AutoEventWireup="false"  Inherits="BetterAspNetCarApp.WebForm1" %>
```

As you can see, the value of the Inherits attribute is the fully qualified name of the System.Web.UI.Page-derived type (which by default will be named WebForm1). Because the Inherits attribute works in conjunction with the file specified by the Codebehind attribute, be aware that if you wish to change the name of the class in your code behind as follows:

```
public class CarInventoryPage : System.Web.UI.Page
{ ... }
```

you will need to update the value of the related *.aspx file's Inherits attribute identically:

```
<%@ Page language="c#" Codebehind="BetterAspNetCarApp.aspx.cs"
AutoEventWireup="false" Inherits="BetterAspNetCarApp.CarInventoryPage" %>
```

When you first begin to work with code behind, one slightly odd concept to wrap your head around is that when you are writing code in the *.aspx file, you can reference the custom methods and properties defined in the designated code behind file. Assume you have built a simple function that obtains the current time and date:

```
public class SomeWebForm: System.Web.UI.Page
{
    ...
    public string GetDateTime()
    {   return DateTime.Now.ToString(); }
}
```

To reference this method in your *.aspx code, you can write the following:

```
<body>
    <!-- Get the time from the C# class -->
    <% Response.Write(GetDateTime()); %>
    ...
    <form method="post" runat="server" ID=Form1>
    </form>
</body>
```

Here, the C# code block is not only triggering the GetDateTime() method in the code behind file, but also making use of the inherited Response property defined by the System.Web.UI.Page base class. To build a more compact *.aspx file, you could make reference to the inherited Page members directly in your code behind class. Thus, you could also write the following:

```
public class SomeWebForm : System.Web.UI.Page
{
...
    public void GetDateTime()
    {
        Response.Write("It is now " + DateTime.Now.ToString());
    }
}
```

And then simply call:

```
<!-- Get the time -->
<% GetDateTime(); %>
```

Again, if you wish to follow the standard philosophy of ASP.NET, you will attempt to avoid making use of server-side code logic within your *.aspx files. However, in the event that you do wish to trigger a method in your code behind file, do attempt to build methods that can be invoked as cleanly as possible (as seen here). In this way, all of your "real" code is safe within your *.aspx.cs file while the GUI widgets defined in the *.aspx file can be scrapped as needed.

The Derivation of an ASP.NET Page

Each *.aspx file is ultimately represented by a class deriving from System.Web.UI.Page. Like any base class, this type provides a polymorphic interface to all derived types. However, the Page type is not the only member in your inheritance hierarchy. Figure 18-17 documents the full chain of inheritance for a custom page.

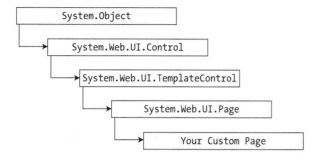

Figure 18-17. The derivation of an ASP.NET page

Key Members of the System.Web.UI.Page Type

The first parent class of interest is Page itself. Here you will find numerous properties that mimic the classic COM objects of classic ASP. Table 18-6 describes some (but by no means all) of the core properties.

Table 18-6. Properties of the Page Type

System.Web.UI.Page Property	Meaning in Life
Application	Gets the HttpApplicationState object provided by the runtime
Cache	Indicates the Cache object in which to store data for the page's application
IsPostBack	Gets a value indicating whether the page is being loaded in response to a client postback, or if it is being loaded and accessed for the first time
Request	Gets the HttpRequest object that provides access data from incoming HTTP requests
Response	Gets the HttpResponse object that allows you to send HTTP response data back to a client browser
Server	Gets the HttpServerUtility object supplied by the HTTP runtime
Session	Gets the System.Web.SessionState.HttpSessionState object, which provides information about the current request's session
Trace	Provides access to the System.Web.TraceContext type, which allows you to log custom messages during debugging sessions

Interacting with the Incoming HTTP Request

As you have seen earlier in this chapter, the basic flow of a Web session begins with a client logging onto a site, filling in user information, and clicking a Submit button to post back the HTML form data to a given Web page for processing. In most cases, the opening tag of the form statement specifies an action and method attribute that indicates the file on the Web server that will be sent the data in the various HTML widgets, and the method of sending this data (GET or POST). Here is an example:

```
<form name=MainForm action="http://localhost/default.aspx" method=get ID=Form1>
```

Unlike classic ASP, ASP.NET does not support an object named Request. However, all ASP.NET pages do inherit the System.Web.UI.Page.Request *property*, which provides access to the raw HTTP request. Under the hood, this property manipulates an instance of the HttpRequest class type. Table 18-7 lists some core members that, not surprisingly, mimic the same members found within the classic COM Request object.

Table 18-7. Members of the HttpRequest Type

System.Web.HttpRequest Member	Meaning in Life
ApplicationPath	Gets the virtual path to the currently executing server application.
Browser	Provides information about incoming client's browser capabilities.
Cookies	Gets a collection of client's cookie variables.
FilePath	Indicates the virtual path of the current request. This property is read-only.
Files	Gets the collection of client-uploaded files (multipart MIME format).
Filter	Gets or sets a filter to use when reading the current input stream.
Form	Gets a collection of Form variables.
Headers	Gets a collection of HTTP headers.
HttpMethod	Indicates the HTTP data transfer method used by the client (GET, POST).
IsSecureConnection	Indicates whether the HTTP connection is secure (that is, HTTPS).
QueryString	Gets the collection of QueryString variables.
RawUrl	Gets the current request's raw URL.
RequestType	Indicates the HTTP data transfer method used by the client (GET, POST).
ServerVariables	Gets a collection of Web server variables.
UserHostAddress	Gets the IP host address of the remote client.
UserHostName	Gets the DNS name of the remote client.

Again, for those of you who have experience with classic ASP, it is important to point out that there is no object named Request (or Response). Thus, when you author a block of ASP.NET code such as the following:

```
<b>You Are: </b><%= Request.ServerVariables["HTTP_USER_AGENT"] %>
```

what you are really doing is accessing the ServerVariables property on the underlying HttpRequest type, as shown here:

```
<b>You Are: </b>
<%
    HttpRequest r;
    r = this.Request;
    Response.Write(r.ServerVariables["HTTP_USER_AGENT"]);
%>
```

Obtaining Browser Statistics

The first interesting aspect of HttpRequest is the Browser property, which provides access to an underlying HttpBrowserCapabilities object. HttpBrowserCapabilities in turn exposes a set of members that allow you to programmatically investigate various statistics regarding the browser that sent the incoming HTTP request. To illustrate, assume you have a new ASP.NET Web application that contains a single *.aspx file. When the user clicks the Button Web control, the server-side event handler will create a System.String that contains various statistics about the client-side browser and display the results on a Label Web control. The Button Click event handler is as follows:

```
private void btnGetBrowserStats_Click(object sender, System.EventArgs e)
{
    string theInfo = "";
    theInfo += String.Format("<li>Is the client AOL? {0}",
        Request.Browser.AOL);
    theInfo +=
        String.Format("<li>Does the client support ActiveX? {0}",
        Request.Browser.ActiveXControls);
    theInfo += String.Format("<li>Is the client a Beta? {0}",
        Request.Browser.Beta);
    theInfo +=
        String.Format("<li>Dose the client support Applets? {0}",
        Request.Browser.JavaApplets);
    theInfo +=
        String.Format("<li>Does the client support Cookies? {0}",
        Request.Browser.Cookies);
    theInfo +=
        String.Format("<li>Does the client support VBScript? {0}",
        Request.Browser.VBScript);
    lblOutput.Text = theInfo;
}
```

Here you are testing for a number of browser capabilities. As you would guess, it is (very) helpful to discover a browser's support for ActiveX controls, Java Applets, and client-side VB Script code. If the calling browser does not support a given Web technology, your *.aspx page would be able to take an alternative course of action.

Simplified Access to Server Variables

Another aspect of HttpRequest is a simplified manner to obtain *server variables*. In classic ASP, you accessed server variables using a parameterized property of the Request object. Using this collection required you to memorize numerous string literals such as this one:

```
string agent = Request.ServerVariables["HTTP_USER_AGENT"];
```

While you are still able to access server variables using this classic ASP-like mindset, ASP.NET provides strongly typed properties of the HttpRequest type for an identical purpose. To illustrate, update your current *.aspx file to include a new Button type. In the Click event handler, scrape out various server-side characteristics. For example:

```
private void btnGetRequestStats_Click(object sender, System.EventArgs e)
{
    string theInfo = "";
    theInfo += String.Format("<li>Path of Virtual directory? {0}",
        Request.ApplicationPath);
    theInfo += String.Format("<li>Byte length of request? {0}",
        Request.ContentLength);
    theInfo += String.Format("<li>Virtual path? {0}",
        Request.FilePath);
    theInfo += String.Format("<li>Http method? {0}",
        Request.HttpMethod);
    theInfo += String.Format("<li>Raw URL? {0}",
        Request.RawUrl);
    theInfo += String.Format("<li>IP address? {0}",
        Request.UserHostAddress);
    theInfo += String.Format("<li>DNS name? {0}",
        Request.UserHostName);
    lblOutput.Text = theInfo;
    // Now save all stats to file.
    Request.SaveAs(@"C:\temp\requestDump.txt", true);
}
```

Notice that the final line of this server-side event handler makes a call to HttpRequest.SaveAs(). This method allows you to dump out all the characteristics regarding the current HTTP request to a physical file on the Web server (which may optionally include header information, specified via the second System.Boolean parameter). As you would guess, this functionality can be quite helpful during debugging.

NOTE   Be aware that if your Web application makes use of any file IO logic (such as the HttpRequest.SaveAs() method), the target file must be configured for writing.

Access to Incoming Form Data

The final aspect of the HttpResponse type we will examine here is the use of the Form and QueryString properties. These two properties allow you to examine the incoming form data using name/value pairs, and function identically to classic ASP. Recall from our discussion of classic ASP at the onset of this chapter that if the data is submitted using HTTP GET, the form data is accessed using the QueryString property, whereas data submitted via HTTP POST is obtained using the Form property.

While you could most certainly make use of the HttpRequest.Form and HttpRequest.QueryString properties to access client-supplied form data on the Web server, these old school techniques are (for the most part) unnecessary. Given that ASP.NET now supplies you with server-side Web controls, you are able to treat HTML form widgets as true objects. Therefore, rather than obtaining the value within a text box as follows:

```
string firstName = Request.Form["txtFirstName"];
```

you can simply ask the server-side widget directly:

```
string firstName = txtFirstName.Text;
```

Not only does this approach lend itself to solid OO principals, but you do not need to concern yourself with how the form data was submitted (GET or POST) before obtaining the values. Of course, this is not to say that you will *never* need to make use of the Form or QueryString properties in ASP.NET, but rather to say that the need to do so has greatly diminished.

 SOURCE CODE   The FunWithHttpRequest files are included under the Chapter 18 subdirectory.

Interacting with the Outgoing HTTP Response

Now that you have a better understanding how a System.Web.UI.Page-derived type can interact with the incoming HTTP request, the next step is to see how to interact with the outgoing HTTP response. In ASP.NET, the Response property of the Page class provides access to an internal HttpResponse type. This type defines a number of properties that allow you to format the HTTP response sent back to the client browser. Table 18-8 lists some core properties (many of which should look familiar if you have a classic ASP background).

Table 18-8. Properties of the HttpResponse Type

System.Web.HttpResponse Property	Meaning in Life
Cache	Returns the caching semantics of the Web page (e.g., expiration time, privacy, vary clauses)
ContentEncoding	Gets or sets the HTTP character set of the output stream
ContentType	Gets or sets the HTTP MIME type of the output stream
Cookies	Gets the HttpCookie collection sent by the current request
IsClientConnected	Gets a value indicating whether the client is still connected to the server
Output	Enables custom output to the outgoing HTTP content body
OutputStream	Enables binary output to the outgoing HTTP content body
StatusCode	Gets or sets the HTTP status code of output returned to the client
StatusDescription	Gets or sets the HTTP status string of output returned to the client
SuppressContent	Gets or sets a value indicating that HTTP content will not be sent to the client

Also, consider the methods of the HttpResponse type described in Table 18-9.

Table 18-9. Methods of the HttpResponse Type

System.Web.HttpResponse Method	Meaning in Life
AppendToLog()	Adds custom log information to the IIS log file.
Clear()	Clears all headers and content output from the buffer stream.
Close()	Closes the socket connection to a client. This method can be helpful when you wish to terminate further control rendering.
End()	Sends all currently buffered output to the client, then closes the socket connection.
Flush()	Sends all currently buffered output to the client.
Redirect()	Redirects a client to a new URL.
Write()	Writes values to an HTTP output content stream.
WriteFile()	Overloaded. Writes a file directly to an HTTP content output stream.

Emitting HTML Content

Perhaps the most well-known aspect of the HttpResponse type is the ability to write content directly to the HTTP output stream. The HttpResponse.Write() method behaves identically to the classic ASP Response.Write() method (simply pass in any HTML tags and/or raw text literals). The HttpResponse.WriteFile() method takes this functionality one step further in that you can specify the name of a physical file on the Web server whose contents should be rendered to the output stream (quite helpful to quickly emit the contents of an existing *.html file):

```
private void SomePageLevelHelperFunction()
{
    Response.Write("<b>My name is:</b><br>");
    Response.Write(this.ToString());
    Response.Write("<br><br><b>Here was your last request:</b><br>");
    Response.WriteFile(@"C:\temp\requestDump.txt");
}
```

The role of this helper function (which you can assume is called by some server-side event handler) is quite simple. The only point of interest is the fact that the HttpResponse.WriteFile() method is now emitting the contents of the *.txt file created previously using the HttpRequest.SaveAs() method (to be safe, of course, you would want to wrap this method invocation within a try/catch statement just in case the requestDump.txt file is missing).

Again, while you can always take this "old school" approach and render HTML tags and content using the Write() method, this approach is far less common under ASP.NET than with classic ASP. The reason is (once again) due to the advent of server-side Web controls. For example, if you wish to render a block of textual data to the browser, your task is as simple as assigning a given System.String to the Text property of a Label widget.

Redirecting Users

Another aspect of the HttpResponse type is the ability to redirect the user to a new URL:

```
private void PassTheBuck()
{
    Response.Redirect("http://Intertech-Inc.com");
}
```

If this helper function were called via a server-side event handler, the user would automatically be redirected to the specified URL.

NOTE The HttpResponse.Redirect() method will always entail a trip back to the client browser. If you simply wish to transfer control to a *.aspx file in the same virtual directory, the HttpServerUtility.Transfer() method (accessed via the inherited Server property) will be more efficient.

So much for our investigation regarding how a given *.aspx file may interact with the incoming HTTP request and outgoing HTTP response. I'll assume you will check out the remaining members of the HttpRequest and HttpResponse types at your leisure.

The Life Cycle of an ASP.NET Web Page

Like a Windows Forms application, every ASP.NET Web page has a fixed life cycle. When the ASP.NET runtime receives an incoming request for a given *.aspx file, the associated System.Web.UI.Page derived type is allocated into memory using the type's default constructor. After this point, the framework will automatically fire three core events: Init, Load, and Unload. By default, a VS .NET–generated code behind page will be prewired to handle the Init event (via the overloaded OnInit() method) as well as the Load event (via the standard C# event syntax and the System.EventHandler delegate):

```
public class MainPage: System.Web.UI.Page
{
    private void Page_Load(object sender, System.EventArgs e)
    { }
    // Override the base class event handler.
    override protected void OnInit(EventArgs e)
    {
        InitializeComponent();
        base.OnInit(e);
    }
    private void InitializeComponent()
    {
        // Rig-up the Load event!
        this.Load += new System.EventHandler(this.Page_Load);
    }
}
```

Once the Load event has been handled, the next major event to fire is whatever page-specific event handler caused the postback to occur in the first place (such as a Button Click or what have you). Once your page-specific event handling has completed, the framework will fire the Unload event, which is *not* handled automatically. To do so, you may use the VS .NET Properties window (simply select the name of your Web Form from the drop-down list with the designer active) or update InitializeComponent() manually.

NOTE   The Init, Load, and Unload events are common to all ASP.NET Web controls, given that they are defined in the System.Web.UI.Control base class.

Now, although you are aware of the set of key events that fire during a page's lifetime, you are most likely wondering what type of code will end up in each handler. Table 18-10 offers some insights.

Table 18-10. The Role of the Init, Load, and Unload Events

Page Event	Meaning in Life
Init	The base class' implementation of the OnInit() method is in charge of handling the view state for your ASP.NET Web controls (defined later in this chapter). Given this fact, be very aware that within the scope of the overridden Init event handler you *should not* add any code that directly interacts with the stateful values of a control (e.g., the value within a TextBox) as you cannot guarantee an accurate read. Typically, this event is of greatest use to WebForm control builders. You can, however, assign values to any non-GUI-centric variables within the scope of OnInit() as well as establish the event handlers for your page's widgets.
Load	Once the Load event fires, you can safely interact with any Web-widgets on your page. Common tasks include connecting to a database to fill a DataGrid, populating a ListBox with entries, and other GUI prep work.
Unload	When this event fires, your System.Web.UI.Page-derived type is on its way to the garbage collector. Here you should close any page-wide data connections, file handles, and other resources.

The Error Event

Another event that may occur during your page's life cycle is Error, which also works in conjunction with the System.EventHandler delegate. This event will be fired if a method on the Page-derived type triggered an exception that was not explicitly handled. Assume you have a server-side event handler for a Button Click event that attempts to open a file that is nonexistent. Also assume that you failed to test this file manipulation using standard structured exception handling. If you have rigged up the page's Error event, you have one final chance to deal with the problem. Ponder the following code:

```
public class MainPage : System.Web.UI.Page
{
    protected System.Web.UI.WebControls.Button btnTriggerError;
...
    private void InitializeComponent()
    {
        this.btnTriggerError.Click +=
            new System.EventHandler(this.btnTriggerError_Click);
        this.Error += new System.EventHandler(this.MainPage_Error);
        this.Load += new System.EventHandler(this.Page_Load);
    }

    private void btnTriggerError_Click(object sender, System.EventArgs e)
    {
        // Ack!  Unhandled exception here (assume bad path)!
        Response.WriteFile(@"C:\Foo.bar");
    }

    private void MainPage_Error(object sender, System.EventArgs e)
    {
        // Obtain the error and report to user.
        Exception ex = Server.GetLastError();
        Response.Write(ex.Message);
        Server.ClearError();
    }
}
```

When the Error event is fired, you are able to obtain the underlying System.Exception using the HttpServerUtility.GetLastError() method exposed from the inherited Server property. In this case, I am simply spitting back the error's description to the response stream. Do note, however, that before exiting this generic error handler, I am explicitly calling HttpServerUtility.ClearError(). This is almost always what you will want to do, as it informs the runtime that you have dealt with the issue at hand and require no further processing. To see the distinction, Figure 18-18 shows the output if you *do* call HttpServerUtility.ClearError(), while Figure 18-19 shows the result of *not* calling HttpServerUtility.ClearError().

Figure 18-18. The result of calling ClearError()

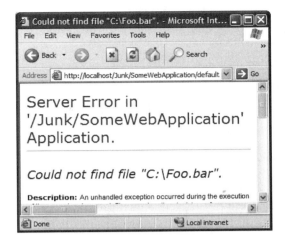

Figure 18-19. The result of not calling ClearError()

Understanding the Role of the IsPostBack Property

Closely related to the set of page-level events is a specific inherited property named IsPostBack. As defined at the beginning of this chapter, a *postback* is the term given to the act of return to a particular Web page while still in session with the server. Given this definition, you are most likely already to determine that the IsPostBack property will return true if the current HTTP request has been sent by a currently logged-on user and false if this is the user's first interaction with the page.

Typically, the need to determine whether or not the current HTTP request is indeed a postback is most helpful when you wish to perform a block of code only the first time the user accesses a given page. For example, you may wish to populate an ADO.NET DataSet when the user first accesses an *.aspx file and cache the object for later use. When the caller returns to the page, you can avoid the need to hit the database unnecessarily (of course, some pages may require that the DataSet is always updated upon each request, but that is another issue). We will see this property in action at various points during the remainder of this chapter, but here is a simple example:

```
private void Page_Load(object sender, System.EventArgs e)
{
    // Only read the DB the
    // very first time the user
    // comes to this page.
    if(!IsPostBack)
    {
        // Populate DataSet and cache it!
    }
    // Use precached DataSet.
}
```

At this point you should feel quite confident with the architecture of an ASP.NET Page type and the role of the System.Web.UI.Page base class. Now that you have such a foundation, we can turn our attention to the role of ASP.NET Web controls.

Understanding the ASP.NET Web Controls

One major benefit of ASP.NET is the ability to assemble the user interface of your Web pages using the GUI types defined in the System.Web.UI.WebControls namespace. These controls (which go by the names *server controls*, *Web controls*, or *Web Form controls*) are *extremely* helpful in that they automatically generate the necessary HTML tags for the requesting browser and expose a set of events that may be processed on the Web server. Furthermore, because each ASP.NET control has a corresponding class in the System.Web.UI.WebControls namespace, it can be programmatically manipulated from your *.aspx file (within a <script> block) as well as within the associated class defined in the code behind file.

As you would suspect, each of the ASP.NET Web controls are arranged within a class hierarchy, as seen in Figure 18-20.

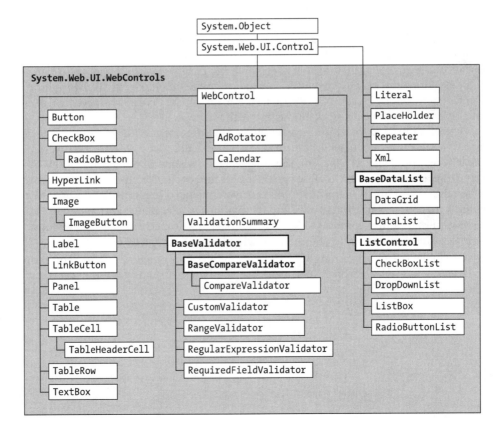

Figure 18-20. The ASP.NET Web controls

As you have seen, when you configure a given Web control using the VS .NET Properties window, your edits are written directly to the *.aspx file as a series of name/value pairs. In this regard, Web Form development is a bit different from that of Windows Forms development, given that under the Windows Forms model, modifications made on the Properties window appear within the InitializeComponent() helper method. As you have also seen, like a Windows Forms application, the InitializeComponent() method defined in your code behind file is still used to rig up events to specific event handlers.

To illustrate, if you add a new TextBox widget (named myTextBox) to the designer of a given *.aspx file and change the BorderStyle, BorderWidth, BackColor, and BorderColor properties using VS .NET, the opening <asp:textbox> tag is modified as follows:

```
<asp:textbox id=myTextBox runat="server" BorderStyle="Ridge" BorderWidth="5px"
BackColor="PaleGreen" BorderColor="DarkOliveGreen" >
</asp:TextBox>
```

In the code behind file, you will find a member variable whose name is identical to the ID element defined in the *.aspx file. Using this member variable, you are able to interact with the same properties as you would expect:

```
public class MainPage : System.Web.UI.Page
{
    // Note that the name of the member variable Is identical to
    // the ID value of the *.aspx declaration.
    protected System.Web.UI.WebControls.TextBox myTextBox;
...
    private void SomeHelperFunction()
    {
        // Interact with Web widget.
        myTextBox.BackColor = Color.Red;
        Response.Write(String.Format("Border color Is: {0}",
            myTextBox.BorderColor.ToString()));
    }
}
```

As seen in Figure 18-20, all of the ASP.NET server-side controls ultimately derive from a common base class named System.Web.UI.WebControls.WebControl. WebControl in turn derives from System.Web.UI.WebControls.Control (which derives from System.Object). Control and WebControl each define a number of properties common to all server-side controls. To help gain an understanding of your inherited functionality, let's check out the core functionality provided by each of these key base classes. But first, let's formalize what it means to handle a server-side event.

Qualifying the Role of Server-Side Event Handling

Given the current state of the World Wide Web, it is impossible to avoid the fundamental nature of browser/Web server interaction. Whenever these two entities communicate, there is always an underlying, stateless, HTTP request-and-response cycle. While ASP.NET server controls do a great deal to shield you from the details of the raw HTTP protocol, always remember that treating the Web as an event-driven entity is just a magnificent smoke-and-mirror show provided by the CLR, and is not semantically identical to a Windows-based user interface.

Given this, be aware that although the System.Windows.Forms and System.Web.UI.WebControls namespaces define numerous types with the same simple name (Button, TextBox, and so on), they do not expose the same set of events. For example, there is no way to handle a server-side MouseMove event when the user moves the cursor over a Web Form Button type. Obviously this is a good thing. (Who wants to post back to the server each time the mouse moves?) When you need to handle such logic, you will need to simply emit the correct client-side JavaScript. Furthermore, many Web widget events expose an event that may seem to be identical in nature to the Windows Forms equivalent (such as the Change event of a TextBox), but acts quite differently under the hood.

The bottom line is that a given ASP.NET Web control will expose a limited set of events, all of which ultimately correspond to a postback to the Web server. For example, a System.Web.UI.WebControl.Button type exposes a Click event that results in a postback to a specific method on the hosting Page-derived type. The System.Web.WebControl.TextBox type defines a Changed event that will entail a postback when the user tabs off the current control to a new control.

The AutoPostBack Property

It is also worth pointing out that many of the ASP.NET Web controls support a property named AutoPostBack (specifically, the CheckBox, RadioButton, and TextBox controls as well as any widget that derives from the abstract ListControl type). By default, this property is set to false, which as you would guess disables the automatic posting of server-side events (even if you have indeed rigged up the event in the code behind file). In many cases, this is the exact behavior you require.

However, if you do wish to cause any of these widgets to post back to a server-side event handler, simply set the value of AutoPostBack to true. This technique can be helpful if you wish to have the state of one widget automatically populate another widget.

To illustrate, create a Web application that contains a single TextBox and a single ListBox control. Now, handle the TextChanged event of the TextBox, and within the server-side event handler, populate the ListBox with the current value in the TextBox (got that?):

```
private void txtPostBackBox_TextChanged(object sender, System.EventArgs e)
{
    lstCharacters.Items.Add(txtPostBackBox.Text);
}
```

If you run the application as is, you will find that as you type in the TextBox, nothing happens. Furthermore, if you were to type in the TextBox and tab to the next control, nothing happens. The reason is that the AutoPostBack property of the TextBox is set to false by default. If you set this property to true:

```
<asp:TextBox id="txtPostBackBox"
style="Z-INDEX: 101; LEFT: 16px; POSITION: absolute; TOP: 48px"
runat="server" AutoPostBack="True">
</asp:TextBox>
```

you will find that when you tab off the TextBox, the ListBox is automatically populated with the current value via the server-side event handler. Beyond the need to populate the items of one widget based on the value of another widget, you will typically not need to alter the state of a widget's AutoPostBack property.

Key Members of the System.Web.UI.Control Type

The System.Web.UI.Control base class defines various properties, methods, and events that allow a given page to interact with its set of contained controls, enable (or disable) view state, and interact with the event set of a widget's lifetime. Table 18-11 documents some of the key properties, methods, and events to be aware of.

Table 18-11. Select Members of System.Web.UI.Control

Interesting Member of System.Web.UI.Control	Meaning in Life
Controls	This property gets a ControlCollection object that represents the child controls for a specified server control in the UI hierarchy.
EnableViewState	This property gets or sets a value indicating whether the server control persists its view state, and the view state of any child controls it contains, to the requesting client.
ID	This property gets or sets the programmatic identifier assigned to the server control.
Page	This property gets a reference to the Page instance that contains the server control.
Parent	This property gets a reference to the server control's parent control in the page control hierarchy.
Visible	This property gets or sets a value that indicates whether a server control is rendered as UI on the page.
DataBind()	Binds a data source to the invoked server control and all its child controls.
HasControls()	Determines if the server control contains any child controls.
DataBinding	This event occurs when the server control binds to a data source.
Init	Recall that this event occurs when the server control is initialized, which is the first step in its life cycle.
Load	Recall that this event occurs when the server control is loaded into the Page object.
Unload	Recall that this event occurs when the server control is unloaded from memory.

Fun with the Control Base Class: Enumerating Contained Controls

The first aspect of System.Web.UI.Control we will examine is the fact that all controls inherit a property named Controls that works in conjunction with the closely related HasControls() method. Much like a Windows Forms application, the Controls property provides access to a strongly typed collection of Web Form control types. Like any collection, you have the ability to add, insert, and remove items dynamically at runtime.

To illustrate, assume you have a new ASP.NET Web Application project and an *.aspx file that maintains a Panel type that contains three other types (say, a TextBox, HyperLink, and Button). Here are the widget's declarations:

```
<asp:Panel id="thePanel" style="Z-INDEX: 101; LEFT: 8px; POSITION: absolute;
TOP: 8px" runat="server" Width="500px" Height="110px" BorderStyle="Ridge">
    <P>This panel contains three controls</P>
    <P> <asp:TextBox id="TextBox1" runat="server"></asp:TextBox>
    <asp:Button id="Button1" runat="server" Text="Button"></asp:Button>
    <asp:HyperLink id="HyperLink1" runat="server">HyperLink</asp:HyperLink></P>
</asp:Panel>
```

Next, place a Label widget outside the scope of the Panel to hold the page's output. The associated UI can be seen in Figure 18-21.

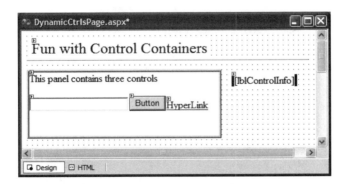

Figure 18-21. Panel with contained controls

Now, assume in your Page_Load() event, you wish to obtain a list of all the controls contained within the Panel (with the assistance of a private helper function) and display the results on a Label type. Ponder the following code update:

```
public class PanelPage : System.Web.UI.Page
{
...
    private void Page_Load(object sender, System.EventArgs e)
    {
        // Show the controls on a panel.
        ListControlsOnPanel();
    }

    public void ListControlsOnPanel()
    {
        string theInfo;
        theInfo = String.Format("Has controls? {0}<br>",
            thePanel.HasControls());
        ControlCollection myCtrls = thePanel.Controls;
        foreach(Control c in myCtrls)
        {
            if(c.GetType() != typeof(System.Web.UI.LiteralControl))
            {
                theInfo += "**************************<br>";
                theInfo += String.Format("Control Name? {0}<br>",
                    c.ToString());
                theInfo += String.Format("ID? {0}<br>", c.ID);
                theInfo += String.Format("Control Visible? {0}<br>",
                    c.Visible);
                theInfo += String.Format("ViewState? {0}<br>",
                    c.EnableViewState);
            }
        }
        lblControlInfo.Text = theInfo;
    }
...
}
```

Here, the ListControlsOnPanel() helper function iterates over each WebControl maintained on the Panel and performs a check to see if the current type is a System.Web.UI.LiteralControl. This type is used to represent literal HTML tags and content (such as <br>, text literals, and so on). If you do not make this sanity check, you might be surprised to find a total of seven types in the scope of the panel (given the *.aspx declaration seen previously). Assuming the type is not literal HTML content, you then print out some various statistics about the widget. Figure 18-22 shows the output.

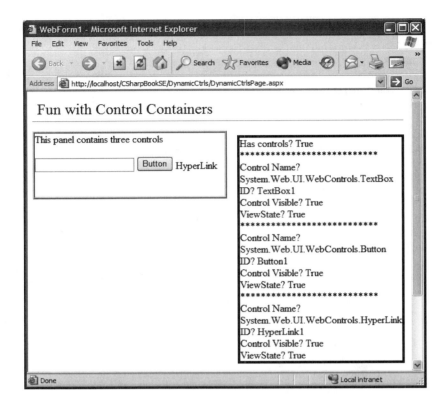

Figure 18-22. Enumerating contained widgets

Fun with the Control Base Class: Dynamically Adding (and Removing) Controls

Now, what if you wish to modify the contents of a Panel at runtime? The process should look very familiar to you, given your work with Windows Forms earlier in this text. Let's update the page to support one button that dynamically adds five new TextBox types to the Panel, and another that clears out the entire control set. The Click event handlers for each are shown here:

```
private void btnAddTextBoxes_Click(object sender, System.EventArgs e)
{
    for(int i = 0; i < 5; i++)
    {
        // Assign a name so we can get
        // the text value out later
        // using the HttpRequest.QueryString()
        // method.
```

```
        TextBox t = new TextBox();
        t.ID = string.Format("newTextBox{0}", i);
        thePanel.Controls.Add(t);
    }
    ListControlsOnPanel();
}
private void btnRemoveAllItems_Click(object sender, System.EventArgs e)
{
    thePanel.Controls.Clear();
    ListControlsOnPanel();
}
```

Notice that you assign a unique ID to each TextBox (e.g., newTextBox1, newTextBox2, and so on) in order to obtain their contained text programmatically using the HttpRequest.Form collection (seen momentarily). Given that you *dynamically* add these items to the Panel, you cannot obtain their values using page-level member variables, as they have no formal declaration in the *.aspx file!

To obtain the values within these dynamically generated TextBoxes, update your UI with an additional Button and Label type. Within the Click event handler for the Button, loop over each item contained within the HttpRequest.NameValueCollection type (accessed via HttpRequest.Form) and concatenate the textual information to a locally scoped System.String. Once you have exhausted the collection, assign this string to the Text property of the new Label widget named lblTextBoxText:

```
private void btnGetTextBoxValues_Click(object sender, System.EventArgs e)
{
    // Just in case the panel is empty
    string textBoxValues = "";
    for(int i = 0; i < Request.Form.Count; i++)
    {
        textBoxValues +=
        string.Format("<li>{0}</li><br>", Request.Form[i]);
    }
    lblTextBoxText.Text = textBoxValues;
}
```

When you run the application, you will find that you are able to view the context of each text box, including a rather long (unreadable) string. This string contains the view state for each widget on the page and will be examined later in the text. Also, you will notice that once the request has been processed, the ten new text boxes disappear. Again, the reason has to do with the stateless nature of HTTP. If you wish to maintain these dynamically created TextBoxes between postbacks, you would need to persist these objects using ASP.NET state programming techniques (examined in the next chapter).

NOTE The process of dynamically adding, deleting, and modifying the items in a Panel should drive the point home that one key initiative of ASP.NET was to make the process of building a Web application look and feel much like the process of building a Windows application. Although very intriguing, a simpler approach would be to place all possible widgets in the Panel at design time, and then set the Visible property to false for the items you do not wish to display.

In any case, at this point you have seen how all ASP.NET Web controls inherit a Controls property that is used to access internal child controls. Using this collection, you are able to dynamically add, delete, and modify items on the fly.

SOURCE CODE The DynamicCtrls files are included under the Chapter 18 subdirectory.

Key Members of the System.Web.UI.WebControl Type

As you can tell, the Control type provides a number of non–GUI-related behaviors. On the other hand, the WebControl base class provides a graphical polymorphic interface to all Web widgets as suggested in Table 18-12.

Table 18-12. Properties of the WebControl Base Class

WebControl Property	Meaning in Life
BackColor	Gets or sets the background color of the Web control
BorderColor	Gets or sets the border color of the Web control
BorderStyle	Gets or sets the border style of the Web control
BorderWidth	Gets or sets the border width of the Web control
Enabled	Gets or sets a value indicating whether the Web control is enabled
CssClass	Allows you to assign a cascading style sheet to a Web widget
Font	Gets font information for the Web control
ForeColor	Gets or sets the foreground color (typically the color of the text) of the Web control

Table 18-12. Properties of the WebControl Base Class (Continued)

WebControl Property	Meaning in Life
Height Width	Get or set the height and width of the Web control
TabIndex	Gets or sets the tab index of the Web control
Tool	Gets or sets the tool tip for the Web control to be displayed when the cursor is over the control

I'd bet that almost all of these properties are self-explanatory, so rather than drill through the use of all these properties, let's shift gears a bit and check out a number of ASP.NET Web Form controls in action.

Select Examples of ASP.NET WebForm Controls

The types in the System.Web.UI.WebControls can be broken down into four broad categories:

- Simple controls

- (Feature) Rich controls

- Data-centric controls

- Input validation controls

The *simple controls* are so named because they are ASP.NET Web controls that map to standard HTML widgets (buttons, lists, hyperlinks, image holders, tables, and so forth). Next we have a small set of controls named the *rich controls* for which there is no direct HTML equivalent (such as the Calendar and AdRotator). The *data-centric controls* are widgets that are typically populated via a given data connection. The best (and most complex) example of such a control would be the ASP.NET DataGrid. Other members of this category include "repeater" controls and the lightweight DataList. Finally, the *validation controls* are server-side widgets that automatically emit client-side JavaScript, for the purpose of form field validation.

In the pages that follow, I will *not* walk through each and every member of each and every control within the System.Web.UI.WebControls namespace. Given your work with Windows Forms controls earlier in this book, you should feel right at home when you manipulate these widgets. Just remember that while Windows Forms types encapsulate the raw Win32 API from view, Web Form controls encapsulate the generation of raw HTML tags. If you wish to follow along, create a new ASP.NET Web application named FunWithControls.

Working with the ListBox Control

To begin, let's examine some of the intrinsic simple controls. These types basically map to a standard HTML widget counterpart. For example, if you wish to display a static list of items for the end user, you can construct a ListBox type using a set of related ListItems:

```
<asp:ListBox id=ListBox1 runat="server" Width="86" Height="69">
    <asp:ListItem Value="BMW">BMW</asp:ListItem>
    <asp:ListItem Value="Jetta">Jetta</asp:ListItem>
    <asp:ListItem Value="Colt">Colt</asp:ListItem>
    <asp:ListItem Value="Grand Am">Grand Am</asp:ListItem>
</asp:ListBox>
```

When the controls are processed by the ASP.NET runtime, the resulting HTML returned to the browser looks something like this:

```
<select name="ListBox1" id="ListBox1" size="5" style="height:69px;width:86px;">
    <option value="BMW">BMW</option>
    <option value="Jetta">Jetta</option>
    <option value="Colt">Colt</option>
    <option value="Grand Am">Grand Am</option>
</select>
```

NOTE   Understand that when you declare an ASP.NET Web control within the scope of an *.aspx file (using ListItem types), you have basically defined a fixed set of items. If you wish to dynamically populate a list, add the items using the ListBox.Items.Add() method within the code behind file.

Working with Radio Buttons

Radio button types tend to work as a group in which only one item in the group can be selected at a given time. For example, if you are interested in creating a set of mutually exclusive radio buttons, your goal is to ensure that the GroupName of each ASP.NET RadioButton is set to the same friendly name:

```
<asp:RadioButton id=RadioHome runat="server"
Text="Contact me at home" GroupName="ContactGroup">
</asp:RadioButton>
<p><asp:RadioButton id=RadioWork runat="server"
 Text="Contact me at work" GroupName="ContactGroup">
</asp:RadioButton>
<p><asp:RadioButton id=RadioDontBother runat="server"
Text="Don't bother me..." GroupName="ContactGroup">
</asp:RadioButton>
```

Unlike a Windows Forms application, ASP.NET RadioButton types are not grouped together by virtue of being placed within a containing GroupBox. In fact, RadioButtons that share the same GroupName do not even need to be placed in a similar location on the page. However, if you do wish to simulate such a GUI, you can choose to make use of the RadioButtonList type, which like a ListBox maintains a set of ListItem types:

```
<asp:RadioButtonList id="carRadioButtonList"
style="Z-INDEX: 102; LEFT: 24px; POSITION: absolute; TOP: 24px"
runat="server" Width="96px" BorderStyle="Solid"
BorderWidth="1px" BorderColor="Black">
    <asp:ListItem Value="Colt">Colt</asp:ListItem>
    <asp:ListItem Value="BWM">BWM</asp:ListItem>
    <asp:ListItem Value="Audi TT">Audi TT</asp:ListItem>
    <asp:ListItem Value="Viper">Viper</asp:ListItem>
</asp:RadioButtonList>
```

When you make use of a RadioButtonList, the items are automatically mutually exclusive. Also, if you enable the AutoPostBack behavior and handle the SelectedIndexChanged event, you are able to obtain the value of the currently selected ListItem using the SelectedValue property:

```
private void carRadioButtonList_SelectedIndexChanged(object sender,
System.EventArgs e)
{
    // NOTE!  If you would rather obtain the specific ListItem widget,
    // make use of the SelectedItem property.
    lblCarSelection.Text = carRadioButtonList.SelectedValue;
}
```

Of course, even if you do not enable the AutoPostBack property for the widget, you are still able to obtain the selected value in another server-side event handler.

Creating a Scrollable, Multiline TextBox

Another common widget is a multiline text box. As you would expect, configuring a text box to function in this way is simply a matter of adding the correct attribute set to the opening <asp:TextBox> tag. Consider this example:

```
<asp:TextBox id=TextBox1 runat="server" Width="183" Height="96"
TextMode="MultiLine" BorderStyle="Ridge">
</asp:TextBox>
```

When you set the TextMode attribute to MultiLine, the TextBox automatically displays a vertical scroll bar when the content is larger than the display area.

NOTE   If you wish to build a password-style TextBox, simply set the TextMode property to Password.

Building a Simple HTML Table

The final simple control we will examine here is the Table type. This widget can be useful when you wish to emit an HTML table that is not based on a database connection (and would rather not emit all the HTML table tags by hand). First, if you have a table that will always maintain the exact same information, you can build the table completely at design time within the *.aspx file. Notice how the ASP.NET Table widget is composed of a set of rows, each of which contains a set of cells. Also note that the rows and cells of a Table are represented by the TableRow and TableCell types, respectively:

```
<asp:Table id="salesPeople"
style="Z-INDEX: 108; LEFT: 32px; POSITION: absolute; TOP: 304px"
runat="server" Width="216px">
    <asp:TableRow>
        <asp:TableCell Text="Sale Person"></asp:TableCell>
        <asp:TableCell Text="Employee ID"></asp:TableCell>
    </asp:TableRow>
    <asp:TableRow>
        <asp:TableCell Text="West Cost"></asp:TableCell>
        <asp:TableCell Text="2"></asp:TableCell>
    </asp:TableRow>
    <asp:TableRow>
        <asp:TableCell Text="McCabe Jr."></asp:TableCell>
        <asp:TableCell Text="1"></asp:TableCell>
    </asp:TableRow>
    <asp:TableRow>
        <asp:TableCell Text="McCabe Sr."></asp:TableCell>
        <asp:TableCell Text="3"></asp:TableCell>
    </asp:TableRow>
</asp:Table>
```

If your Table needs to be dynamically generated, you can simply place an empty ASP.NET Table widget and build it programmatically in the code behind file. For example the Button Click event handler creates the table seen in Figure 18-23 (assume you have added an ASP.NET Table widget named myAutoGenTable to your designer).

```
private void btnBuildTable_Click(object sender, System.EventArgs e)
{
    // Auto-generate the table
    for(int i = 0; i < 3; i++)
    {
        TableRow r = new TableRow();
        for(int j = 0; j < 3; j++)
        {
            TableCell c = new TableCell();
            c.Text = string.Format("Row {0}, Column {1}",
                i+1, j+1);
             r.Cells.Add(c);
        }
        myAutoGenTable.Rows.Add(r);
    }
}
```

Figure 18-23. A dynamically generated HTML table

The Feature-Rich Controls

Rich controls are also widgets that emit HTML to the HTTP response stream. The difference between these types and the set of intrinsic controls is that they have no direct HTML counterpart. Table 18-13 describes two rich controls.

Table 18-13. Rich WebControl Widgets

WebForm Rich Control	Meaning in Life
AdRotator	This control allows you to randomly display text/images using a corresponding XML configuration file.
Calendar	This control returns HTML that represents a GUI-based calendar.

Working with the Calendar Control

The Calendar control is a widget for which there is no direct HTML equivalent. Nevertheless, this type has been designed to return a batch of HTML tags that simulate such an entity. For example, suppose you place a Calendar control on your WebForm as shown here:

```
<asp:Calendar id=Calendar1 runat="server"></asp:Calendar>
```

Once you run this page, you find that a *huge* amount of raw HTML has been emitted to the browser. Like its Windows Forms counterpart, the ASP.NET Calendar control is highly customizable. One member of interest is the SelectionMode

995

property. By default, the Calendar control only allows the end user to select a single day (e.g., SelectionMode = "Day"). You can change this behavior by assigning this property to any of the following alternatives:

- *None:* No selection can be made (e.g., the Calendar is just for display purposes).

- *DayWeek:* User may select a single day or an entire week.

- *DayWeekMonth:* User may select a single day, an entire week, or an entire month.

For example, if you choose DayWeekMonth, the returned HTML renders an additional leftmost column (to allow the end user to select a given week) as well as a selector in the upper left of the widget (to allow the end user to select the entire month).

Working with the AdRotator

Although classic ASP also provided an AdRotator control, the ASP.NET variation has been substantially upgraded. The role of this widget is to randomly display a given advertisement at some position in the browser. When you place a server-side AdRotator widget on your design time template, the display is a simple placeholder. Functionally, this control cannot do its magic until you set the AdvertisementFile property to point to the XML file that describes each ad.

The format of the advertisement file is quite simple. For each ad you wish to show, create a unique <Ad> element. At minimum, each <Ad> element specifies the image to display (ImageUrl), the URL to navigate to if the image is selected (TargetUrl), mouseover text (AlternateText), and the weight of the ad (Impressions). For example, assume you have a file (ads.xml) that defines two possible ads, as shown here:

```
<Advertisements>
    <Ad>
        <ImageUrl>SlugBug.jpg</ImageUrl>
        <TargetUrl>http://www.Cars.com</TargetUrl>
        <AlternateText>Your new Car?</AlternateText>
        <Impressions>80</Impressions>
    </Ad>
    <Ad>
        <ImageUrl>car.gif</ImageUrl>
        <TargetUrl>http://www.CarSuperSite.com</TargetUrl>
        <AlternateText>Like this Car?</AlternateText>
        <Impressions>80</Impressions>
    </Ad>
</Advertisements>
```

Once you set the AdvertisementFile property correctly (and ensure that the images and XML file are in the correct virtual directory), one of these two ads is randomly displayed when users navigate to the site, as shown here:

```
<asp:AdRotator id=myAdRotator runat="server" Width="470"
 Height="60" AdvertisementFile="ads.xml">
</asp:AdRotator>
```

When you run this application and post back to the page, you will randomly be presented with one of two *.jpg files. Be aware that the Height and Width properties of the AdRotator are used to establish the size of your ads. In this example, each ad is the default 60 × 470 pixels. If your ads are larger (or smaller) than the AdRotator's size, you will get skewed images.

Assigning Tab Order and Style Sheets

Before examining how to make use of the ASP.NET validation controls, let's check out the issue of tab order and style sheets to an ASP.NET Web control. Like a Windows Forms application, all ASP.NET Web widgets support a TabIndex property. What is unique about assigning tab order to ASP.NET Web controls is that tab index 0 is reserved for the browser's URL input field! Therefore, be sure to begin numbering your TabIndex at number 1 to ensure the user can tab around your Web widgets correctly.

Next, recall that all ASP.NET Web controls inherit a property named CssStyle. Using this property, you are able to easily configure the UI of multiple widgets on your page by assigning an existing cascading style sheet. If you are unfamiliar with this aspect of HTML, simply consider a style sheet as a named set of name/value pairs that describe a UI template.

For example, assume you have an *.aspx file that defines a style sheet named CustomInputUI:

```
<style>
    .CustomInputUI { FONT: 10pt verdana; COLOR: green }
</style>
```

Once this style sheet is in place, you can automatically configure your widgets to support a 10-pt, green font using the Verdana font face. For example:

```
<asp:TextBox id="myTextBox" runat="server"
CssClass="CustomInputUI">
</asp:TextBox>
```

SOURCE CODE   The files for the FunWithControls project are included under the Chapter 18 subdirectory.

The Mighty DataGrid

The ADO.NET DataGrid is by far and away the most complex of all Web widgets. Up until this point, you have used the grid in read-only mode; however, the DataGrid type may be configured to support paging, sorting, in-place editing, and so forth. To demonstrate some of the more exotic aspects of this control, fire up VS .NET and create a new Web application (DataGridApp). The only widget you need on the initial *.aspx file is a DataGrid type. Now, within the Page_Load() event handler, fill the grid with the current items in the Inventory table of the Cars database by calling a helper function named UpdateGrid():

```
public class DataGridPage: System.Web.UI.Page
{
    protected System.Web.UI.WebControls.DataGrid myDataGrid;
    private void Page_Load(object sender, System.EventArgs e)
    {
        if(!IsPostBack)
        {
            UpdateGrid();
        }
    }

    private void UpdateGrid()
    {
        DataSet myDS = new DataSet();
        SqlConnection c = new
            SqlConnection("Server=localhost;UID=sa;PWD=;Database=Cars");
        c.Open();
        SqlCommand s = new SqlCommand("Select * from Inventory", c);
        SqlDataAdapter d = new SqlDataAdapter(s);
        d.Fill(myDS, "Inventory");
        myDataGrid.DataSource = myDS.Tables["Inventory"];
        myDataGrid.DataBind();
    }
...
}
```

At this point, you should be able to run your Web app and find a populated DataGrid. Currently, the *.aspx definition of the DataGrid is very simple:

```
<asp:DataGrid id="myDataGrid"
style="Z-INDEX: 103; LEFT: 16px; POSITION: absolute; TOP: 56px"
runat="server">
</asp:DataGrid>
```

In the next several sections, you will enhance the grid in a number of ways. As you would expect, most of these updates can be automated using VS .NET. If you select your DataGrid widget on the designer, you will notice a link on the Properties window named Property Builder. While this tool will automatically build the correct *.aspx definitions, I'll concentrate on the raw *.aspx definition just to ensure you understand what makes the grid tick under the hood.

Altering Column Names

The first aspect of the DataGrid we will examine is the process of assigning custom display names for each of the grid's columns. By default, column display names will map directly to the column names found in the table (which may or may not be a problem). When you wish to provide user-friendly names for each column, you will need to create a <Columns> definition within the scope of the DataGrid itself. The <Columns> definition will contain a set of <BoundColumn> controls that map data fields to custom header text. Also, you need to ensure that the AutoGenerateColumns attribute of the DataGrid is set to false. Ponder the following:

```
<asp:DataGrid id="myDataGrid"
style="Z-INDEX: 103; LEFT: 16px; POSITION: absolute; TOP: 56px"
runat="server" AutoGenerateColumns="False">
    <Columns>
    <asp:BoundColumn DataField="CarID" HeaderText="Auto Identifier">
    </asp:BoundColumn>
    <asp:BoundColumn DataField="Make" HeaderText="Make of Auto">
    </asp:BoundColumn>
    <asp:BoundColumn DataField="Color" HeaderText="Color of Auto">
    </asp:BoundColumn>
    <asp:BoundColumn DataField="PetName" HeaderText="The Pet Name">
    </asp:BoundColumn>
    </Columns>
</asp:DataGrid>
```

As you can tell, the DataField attribute of the <BoundColumn> type specifies the name of the column as found in the database, while the HeaderText attribute holds the friendly name to display in the grid. If you wish, update the overall GUI of the grid to suit your liking. In any case, your grid now looks something like Figure 18-24.

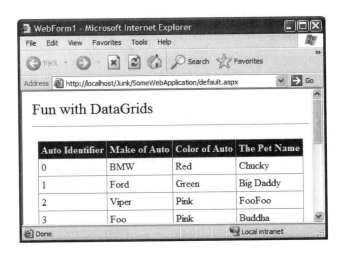

Figure 18-24. A DataGrid with friendly column names

> **NOTE** The Property Builder Wizard will generate all of these updates using the Columns tab. For this example, simply add four BoundColumn types and uncheck the "Create columns automatically at run time" option.

Enabling Paging

The next aspect of the DataGrid we will examine is its default paging ability. By default, a DataGrid will display all records returned from a SQL query, regardless of how many records are present. Of course, if you have a table that contains 200 records, you typically would *not* want to have them displayed at the same time. Rather, you may wish to configure the DataGrid to only show 10 records at a time, and allow the user to post back to the Web server (via "left" and "right" links or numerical identifiers) to fetch the next (or previous) 10 items.

The DataGrid supports this functionality right out of the box. The first step in doing so is to set the PageSize and AllowPaging attributes on the DataGrid type. Once this is done, you will need to add a <PagerStyle> element within the scope of the grid's definition. Consider the following example (<Columns> elements have been removed for clarity):

```
<asp:DataGrid id="myDataGrid" style="Z-INDEX: 103; LEFT: 16px;
POSITION: absolute; TOP: 56px"
runat="server" AutoGenerateColumns="False" Width="424px"
PageSize="5" AllowPaging="True">
...
<PagerStyle Mode="NumericPages" HorizontalAlign="Center"
ForeColor="#330099" BackColor="#FFFFCC">
</PagerStyle>
</asp:DataGrid>
```

Here, the <PagerStyle> element has been set up to support numerical paging (1, 2, 3) rather than "<" and ">" links.

The final step is to handle the grid's PageIndexChanged event (like any widget, this may be done via VS .NET). This event will fire when the user clicks the link set maintained by the DataGrid. The implementation of this event handler is as follows:

```
private void myDataGrid_PageIndexChanged(object source,
System.Web.UI.WebControls.DataGridPageChangedEventArgs e)
{
    // Set the grid's current page index to the new page index.
    myDataGrid.CurrentPageIndex = e.NewPageIndex;
    UpdateGrid();
}
```

Notice how the incoming DataGridPageChangedEventArgs type supplies the NewPageIndex property. As you would expect, this will be used to compute the next batch of records to display. Once you assign this value to the grid's CurrentPageIndex property, you will need to repopulate your grid via your helper UpdateGrid() function. Figure 18-25 shows the new GUI.

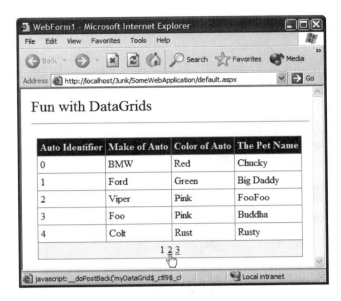

Figure 18-25. A DataGrid default paging support

As you will see in the next chapter, ASP.NET provides numerous ways to cache objects (such as DataSets) in memory. Thus, if you were to store the DataSet in a session variable, you would not need to directly query the database within the PageIndexChanged event handler, but simply assign the cached object to the DataGrid's DataSource property.

NOTE   The Property Builder Wizard will generate all of these updates using the Paging tab.

Enabling In-Place Editing

The final feature of the DataGrid we will examine here is the ability for the grid to support in-place activation. This is a very helpful feature, given that it allows the Web user to select a row for editing and push the changes back to the Web server for processing.

The first task is to add a new member to the <Columns> element named <EditCommandColumn>. This single element will be used to render back the necessary Edit, Cancel, and Update links to be displayed in the browser:

```
<Columns>
...
    <asp:EditCommandColumn
    ButtonType="LinkButton" UpdateText="Update"
    CancelText="Cancel" EditText="Edit">
    </asp:EditCommandColumn>
</Columns>
```

Notice that this element has been configured to display three hyperlinks that allow the user to activate a row for editing and submit or cancel the changes. In addition to updating the <Columns> element, let's update the DataGrid's definition of the CarID column to be read-only (to prevent the user from changing the value of this primary key):

```
<Columns>
...
    <asp:BoundColumn DataField="CarID" ReadOnly="True"
    HeaderText="Auto Identifier">
    </asp:BoundColumn>
</Columns>
```

The final *.asxp modification you will typically want to make is to set the DataGrid.DataKeyField property to the value of the table's primary key. As you will see, this can be helpful when handling the updates on the Web server, given that the grid has foreknowledge of the correct primary key:

```
<asp:DataGrid id="myDataGrid" ...
DataKeyField="CarID">
```

With this GUI prep work complete, the next task is to handle three server-side events for each possibility (CancelCommand, EditCommand, and UpdateCommand).

The implementation of the EditCommand handler will simply inform the DataGrid which row is currently being edited by assigning it the selected item via the incoming DataGridCommandEventArg type:

```
private void myDataGrid_EditCommand(object source,
System.Web.UI.WebControls.DataGridCommandEventArgs e)
{
    // Tell grid which row is active.
    myDataGrid.EditItemIndex = e.Item.ItemIndex;
    UpdateGrid();
}
```

The code within the CancelCommand event handler is also equally as simple. Here, you will inform the grid to exit the edit mode by assigning the EditItemIndex property to -1 (alas, a "magic number" is used here. Sadly, we don't have a strongly typed enumeration).

```
private void myDataGrid_CancelCommand(object source,
System.Web.UI.WebControls.DataGridCommandEventArgs e)
{
    // Disable edit mode.
    myDataGrid.EditItemIndex = -1;
    UpdateGrid();
}
```

The real work takes place within the implementation of the UpdateCommand event handler. When the user clicks the Update link, the incoming DataGridCommandEventArgs parameter will contain the values within each cell of the row currently under edit mode. Your task is to access the internal controls collection to obtain these values, format a SQL update statement, and submit the changes. In the code that follows, notice that you are accessing each cell *in order*, thus cell 0 is the CarID (which you obtain via the DataKeys collection), cell 1 is the Make, and so on. Before exiting this event handler, be sure to tell the DataGrid to exit out of edit mode using the magic number -1:

```
private void myDataGrid_UpdateCommand(object source,
System.Web.UI.WebControls.DataGridCommandEventArgs e)
{
    // Get new info from the cells of the row being edited.
    int theCarID;
    TextBox newMake, newColor, newPetName;
    theCarID = (int)myDataGrid.DataKeys[e.Item.ItemIndex];
    newMake = (TextBox)e.Item.Cells[1].Controls[0];
    newColor = (TextBox)e.Item.Cells[2].Controls[0];
    newPetName = (TextBox)e.Item.Cells[3].Controls[0];
    // Build a SQL string based on cell info.
    string sqlUpdate = string.Format(
    "Update Inventory Set Make='{0}', Color='{1}', PetName='{2}' Where CarID='{3}'",
        newMake.Text.Trim(), newColor.Text.Trim(),
        newPetName.Text.Trim(), theCarID);
    // Submit SQL to DB using a command object.
    SqlConnection c = new
      SqlConnection("Server=localhost;UID=sa;PWD=;Database=Cars");
    c.Open();
    SqlCommand s = new SqlCommand(sqlUpdate,c);
    s.ExecuteNonQuery();
    c.Close();
    // Exit out of edit mode.
    myDataGrid.EditItemIndex = -1;
    UpdateGrid();
}
```

That's it! At this point, if you run your application, you will find that you are able to select a row for editing, and then commit or cancel the changes (Figure 18-26).

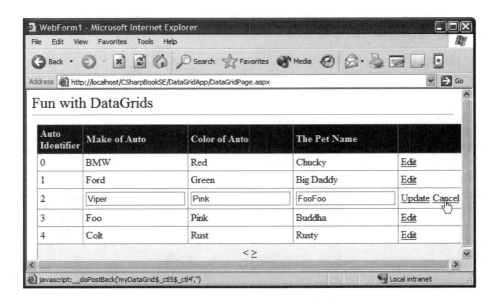

Figure 18-26. An editable DataGrid

As you would guess, the ASP.NET DataGrid has support for other bells and whistles such as deleting a row, programmatically add a new row, sorting ability, and whatnot. At this point, however, you should have a solid handle on some of the key features of this Web control.

SOURCE CODE   The files for the DataGridApp project are included under the Chapter 18 subdirectory.

Data-Centric Controls and Data Binding

As you have seen, the DataGrid control provides the DataSource and DataBind() members to allow you to render the contents of a given ADO.NET DataTable or DataReader type. This is obviously a great boon to the enterprise developer. However, WebForm controls (as well as Windows Forms controls) also allow you to bind other sources of data to a given widget.

For example, assume that you have a well-known set of values represented by a simple string array. Using the same technique as for binding to DataGrid types, you can attach an array to a GUI type. For example, if you place an ASP.NET ListBox control (with the ID of petNameList) on your *.aspx page, you can update the Page_Load() event handler as shown here:

```
protected void Page_Load(object sender, EventArgs e)
{
    if (!IsPostBack)
    {
        // Create an array of data to bind to the list box.
        string[] carPetNames =
        {
            "Viper", "Hank", "Ottis", "Alphonzo", "Cage", "TB"
        };
        petNameList.DataSource = carPetNames;
        petNameList.DataBind();
    }
}
```

Recall that all .NET arrays map to the System.Array type. Also recall that System.Array implements the IEnumerable interface. The fact is that any type that implements IEnumerable can be bound to a GUI widget. Therefore, if you update your simple string array to an instance of the ArrayList type, the output is identical, as shown here:

```
protected void Page_Load(object sender, EventArgs e)
{
    if (!IsPostBack)
    {
        // Now use an array list.
        ArrayList carPetNames = new ArrayList();
        carPetNames.Add("Viper");
        carPetNames.Add("Ottis");
        carPetNames.Add("Alphonzo");
        carPetNames.Add("Cage");
        carPetNames.Add("TB");
        petNameList.DataSource = carPetNames;
        petNameList.DataBind();
    }
}
```

The Role of the Validation Controls

The final group of WebForm controls we will examine are termed *validation controls*. Unlike the other WebForm controls we have been examining, validator controls are not used to emit HTML, but client-side JavaScript for the purpose of form validation. As illustrated at the beginning of this chapter, client-side form validation is quite useful in that you can ensure that various constraints are in place before posting back to the Web server, thereby avoiding expensive round-trips. Table 18-14 gives a rundown of the ASP.NET validation controls.

Table 18-14. The ASP.NET Validation Controls

WebForm Validation Control	Meaning in Life
CompareValidator	Validates that the value of an input control is equal to a given value of another input control.
CustomValidator	Allows you to build a custom validation function that validates a given control.
RangeValidator	Determines that a given value is in a predetermined range.
RegularExpressionValidator	Checks if the value of the associated input control matches the pattern of a regular expression.
RequiredFieldValidator	Ensures that a given input control contains a value (and is thus not empty).
ValidationSummary	Displays a summary of all validation errors of a page in a list, bulleted list, or single paragraph format. The errors can be displayed inline and/or in a pop-up message box.

All of the validator controls ultimately derive from a common base class named System.Web.UI.WebControls.BaseValidator, and therefore have a set of common features. Table 18-15 documents the key members.

Table 18-15. Common Properties of the ASP.NET Validators

Member of the BaseValidator Type	Meaning in Life
ControlToValidate	Gets or sets the input control to validate
Display	Gets or sets the display behavior of the error message in a validation control
EnableClientScript	Gets or sets a value indicating whether client-side validation is enabled
ErrorMessage	Gets or sets the text for the error message
ForeColor	Gets or sets the color of the message displayed when validation fails

Working with the ASP.NET Validators

To illustrate the basics of working with validation controls, let's create a new C# Web Application project workspace named ValidatorCtrls. To begin, place a single Button and four TextBox types (with four corresponding and descriptive Labels) onto your page.

Next, place a RequiredFieldValidator, RangeValidator, RegularExpressionValidator, and CompareValidator type adjacent to each respective field (Figure 18-27).

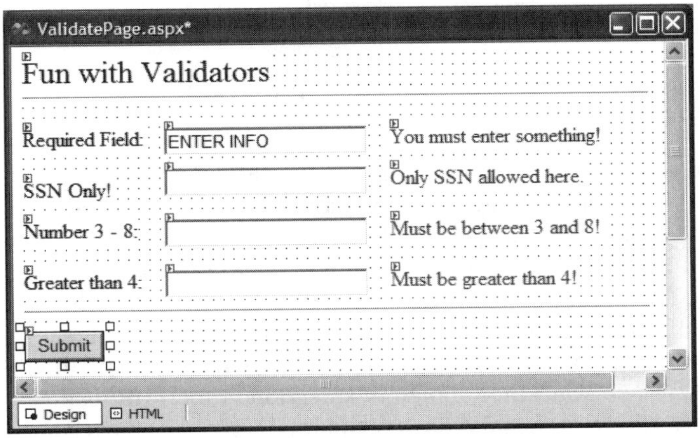

Figure 18-27. The items to be validated

Configuring the RequiredFieldValidator is very straightforward. Simply set the ErrorMessage and ControlToValidate properties accordingly using the VS .NET Properties window. The resulting *.aspx definition is as follows:

```
<asp:RequiredFieldValidator id="RequiredFieldValidator1"
style="Z-INDEX: 104; LEFT: 288px; POSITION: absolute; TOP: 64px"
runat="server" ErrorMessage="You must enter something!"
ControlToValidate="txtReqField">
</asp:RequiredFieldValidator>
```

One nice thing about the RequiredFieldValidator is that it supports an InitialValue property. You can use this property to ensure that the user enters any value other than the initial value in the related TextBox. For example, when the user first posts to a page, you may wish to configure a TextBox to have the string "ENTER INFO". Now, if you did not set the InitialValue property of the RequiredFieldValidator, the runtime would assume that the string "ENTER INFO" is valid. Thus, to ensure a required TextBox is valid only when the user enters anything other than "ENTER INFO", configure your widgets as follows:

```
<asp:RequiredFieldValidator id="RequiredFieldValidator1"
style="Z-INDEX: 104; LEFT: 288px; POSITION: absolute; TOP: 64px"
runat="server" ErrorMessage="You must enter something!"
ControlToValidate="txtReqField" InitialValue="ENTER INFO">
</asp:RequiredFieldValidator>
<asp:TextBox id="txtReqField" style="Z-INDEX: 105; LEFT: 116px;
POSITION: absolute; TOP: 64px"
runat="server">ENTER INFO</asp:TextBox>
```

The RegularExpressionValidator can be used when you wish to apply a pattern against the characters entered within a given input field. To ensure that a given TextBox contains a valid U.S. SSN, you could define the widget as follows:

```
<asp:RegularExpressionValidator id="RegularExpressionValidator1"
style="Z-INDEX: 109; LEFT: 152px; POSITION: absolute; TOP: 246px"
runat="server" ErrorMessage="Not an SSN!"
ControlToValidate="txtMustBeSSN" ValidationExpression="\d{3}-\d{2}\d{4}">
</asp:RegularExpressionValidator>
```

Notice how the RegularExpressionValidator defines a ValidationExpression property. If you have never worked with regular expressions before, all you need to be aware of for this example is that they are used to match a given string pattern. Here, the expression "\d{3}-\d{2}\d{4}" is capturing a standard U.S. Social Security number of the form xxx-xx-xxxx. This particular regular expression is fairly self-explanatory; however, assume you wish to test for a valid Japanese phone number. The correct expression now becomes much more complex: "(0\d{1,4}-|\(0\d{1,4}\) ?)?\d{1,4}-\d{4}". The good news is that when you select the ValidationExpression property using the Properties window of VS .NET, you can pick from a predefined set of possible regular expressions (Figure 18-28).

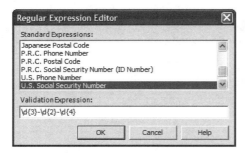

Figure 18-28. Creating a regular expression via VS .NET

NOTE If you are really into regular expressions, you will be happy to know that the .NET platform supplies an entire namespace (System.Text.RegularExpressions) devoted to the programmatic manipulation of such patterns.

In addition to a MinimumValue and MaximumValue property, RangeValidators have a property named Type. Because you are interested in testing the user-supplied input against a range of whole numbers, you need to specify "Integer" (which is *not* the default!).

```
<asp:RangeValidator id="RangeValidator1"
style="Z-INDEX: 112; LEFT: 288px; POSITION: absolute; TOP: 136px"
runat="server" ErrorMessage="Must be between 3 and 8!"
ControlToValidate="txtNumberRange" MaximumValue="8"
MinimumValue="3" Type="Integer">
</asp:RangeValidator>
```

The RangeValidator can also be used to test if a given value is between a currency value, date, floating point number, or string data (the default setting).

Finally, notice that the CompareValidator supports an Operator property:

```
<asp:CompareValidator id="CompareValidator1"
style="Z-INDEX: 115; LEFT: 288px; POSITION: absolute; TOP: 176px"
runat="server" ErrorMessage="Must be greater than 4!"
ControlToValidate="txtGreaterThanFour" Type="Integer"
ValueToCompare="4" Operator="GreaterThan">
</asp:CompareValidator>
```

Given that the role of this validator is to compare the value in the text box against another value using a binary operator, it should be no surprise that the Operator property may be set to values such as LessThan, GreaterThan, Equal, NotEqual, and so forth. Also, note that the ValueToCompare is used to establish a value to compare against.

NOTE   The CompareValidator can also be configured to compare a value within another WebForm control (rather than a hard-coded value) using the ControlToValidate property.

To finish up the code for this page, handle the Click event for the Button type and inform the user s/he has succeeded in the validation logic:

```
private void btnPostBack_Click(object sender, System.EventArgs e)
{
    Response.Write("You passed validataion!");
    Response.End();
}
```

Now, navigate to this page using your browser of choice. At this point, you should not see any noticeable changes. However, when you attempt to click the Submit button after entering bogus data, your error message is suddenly visible, as shown in Figure 18-29.

The following is the browser screenshot content:

WebForm1 - Microsoft Internet Explorer

File   Edit   View   Favorites   Tools   Help

Back   Search   Favorites   Media

Address   http://localhost/CSharpBookSE/ValidatorCtrls/ValidatePage.aspx   Go

Fun with Validators

Required Field: Hello there...

SSN Only!   huh?   Only SSN allowed here.

Number 3 - 8:   1   Must be between 3 and 8!

Greater than 4:

Submit

Done   Local intranet

Figure 18-29. Bad data ...

Once you enter valid data, the error messages are removed and postback occurs.

If you look at the HTML rendered by the browser, you see that the validator controls generate a client-side JavaScript function that makes use of a specific library of JavaScript functions (contained in the WebUIValidation.js file) that is automatically downloaded to the user's machine. Once the validation has occurred, the form data is posted back to the server, where the ASP.NET runtime will perform the *same* validation tests on the Web server (just to ensure that no along-the-wire tampering has taken place).

On a related note, if the HTTP request was sent by a browser that does not support client-side JavaScript, all validation will occur on the server. In this way, you can program against the validator controls without being concerned with the target browser; the returned HTML page redirects the error processing back to the Web server.

NOTE   It is permissible to assign more than one validator to a single widget. For example, if you wish to ensure that the user enters a *mandatory* phone number, you can associate a RequiredFieldValidator and RegularExpressionValidator to the same input field.

Performing Custom Validation

Although the ASP.NET validators we have just examined will take care of most (if not all) of your form-level validation, there may be a time in which you want to craft some custom validation logic (either server-side or client-side). Sometimes, for example, validation requires you to read from a remote data source, and therefore a postback to the Web server is mandatory. When you have a validation need that will always entail a round trip, you could choose to manually build a postback handler; however, the CustomValidator can simplify matters.

By way of illustration, assume you have a new TextBox field that can only be validated on the Web server (Figure 18-30).

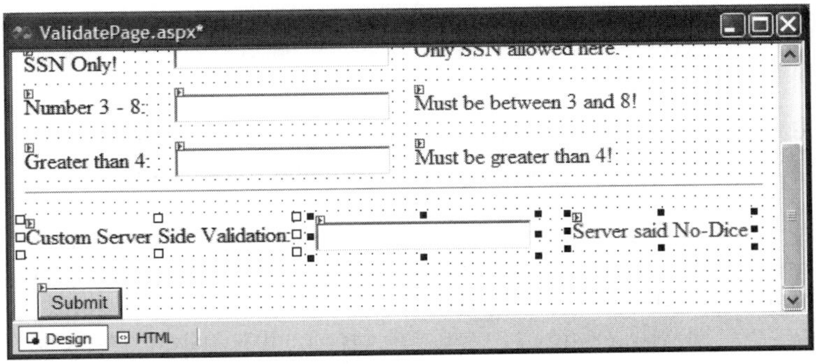

Figure 18-30. Custom server-side validation GUI prep

Here is the complete *.aspx declaration:

```
<asp:CustomValidator id="CustomValidator1"
style="Z-INDEX: 119; LEFT: 400px; POSITION: absolute; TOP: 232px"
runat="server" ErrorMessage="Server said No-Dice"
ControlToValidate="txtServerSideVal">
</asp:CustomValidator>
```

When the user attempts to post back, the runtime will automatically trigger a server-side event handler for the CustomValidator.ServerValidate event. Given this, the next step to establish custom server-side validation is to handle this event in the System.Web.UI.Page-derived type using the VS .NET Properties window. For this example, you will simply generate a random number to see if the validation succeeds. Notice that this method will set the IsValid property of the incoming ServerValidateEventArgs type accordingly:

```
public class ValidatePage : System.Web.UI.Page
{
...
    private void InitializeComponent()
    {
        this.CustomValidator1.ServerValidate +=
            new System.Web.UI.WebControls.ServerValidateEventHandler
            (this.CustomValidator1_ServerValidate);
        ...
    }
```

```
    private void CustomValidator1_ServerValidate(object source,
        System.Web.UI.WebControls.ServerValidateEventArgs args)
    {
        Random r = new Random();
        int i = r.Next(50);
        if(i > 45)
            args.IsValid = true;
        else
            args.IsValid = false;
    }
...
}
```

If you run this example, you will now find that your server-side event handler will run automatically. If the randomly generated number is greater than 45, validation succeeds!

In addition to building a server-side validation routine, the CustomValidator type may also be configured to function on the client side. For example, assume that you have a widget that will be validated based on a number of complex conditions and interactions with the browser's DOM. In this case, you can create a custom JavaScript or VBScript function that will be called automatically on the client. The key is to set the ClientValidationFunction property that points to the name of the script code emitted to the browser. For example:

```
<HTML>
<HEAD>
<title>Fun with Validators</title>
<script language = vbscript>
Sub SomeVBScriptFunction(s, e)
    ' Write the client-side VBScript code.
    ' Set the IsValid property of 'e'
End Sub
</script>
...
    <asp:CustomValidator id="CustomValidator1"
    runat="server" ErrorMessage="CustomValidator"
    ClientValidationFunction="SomeVBScriptFunction">
    </asp:CustomValidator>
</HTML>
```

Notice how the signature of the client-side VBScript function matches the pattern of the related delegate, using the typeless world of VBScript. Nevertheless, your client-side validation function will still need to set the IsValid property of the incoming second argument to inform the runtime if validation succeeded.

Creating Validation Summaries

The final validation-centric topic we will examine here is the use of the ValidationSummary widget. Currently, each of your validators displays its error message at the exact place in which it was positioned at design time. In many cases, this may be exactly what you are looking for. However, on a complex form with numerous input widgets, you may not want to have random blobs of red text pop up. Using the ValidationSummary type, you can instruct all of your validation types to display their error messages at a specific location on the page.

The first step is to simply place a ValidationSummary on your *.aspx file. You may optionally set the HeaderText property of this type as well as the DisplayMode, which by default will list all error messages as a bulleted list.

```
<asp:ValidationSummary id="ValidationSummary1"
style="Z-INDEX: 123; LEFT: 152px; POSITION: absolute; TOP: 320px"
runat="server" Width="353px"
HeaderText="Here are the stupid things you have done.">
</asp:ValidationSummary>
```

Next, you need to set the Display property to None for each of the individual validators (e.g., RequiredFieldValidator, RangeValidator, etc.) on the page. This will ensure that you do not see duplicate error messages for a given validation failure (one in the summary pane and another at the validator's location).

Once you do so, you will find the output shown in Figure 18-31.

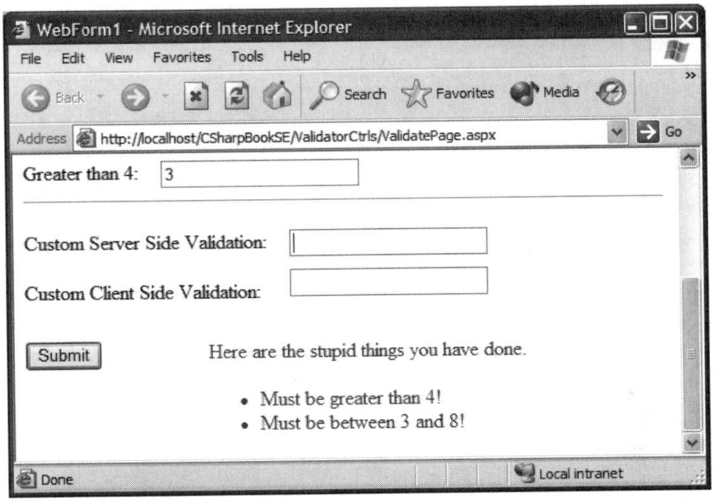

Figure 18-31. Using a validation summary

Last but not least, if you would rather have the error messages displayed using a client-side MessageBox, set the ShowMessageBox property to true and the ShowSummary property to false.

SOURCE CODE   The ValidatorCtrls project is included under the
Chapter 18 subdirectory.

Understanding the Role of ASP.NET HTML Controls

In addition to the GUI widgets found within System.Web.UI.WebControls, ASP.NET
also defines another GUI-centric namespace: System.Web.UI.HtmlControls. Like the
official Web controls, the members of the HtmlControls namespace are organized
within a class hierarchy (Figure 18-32).

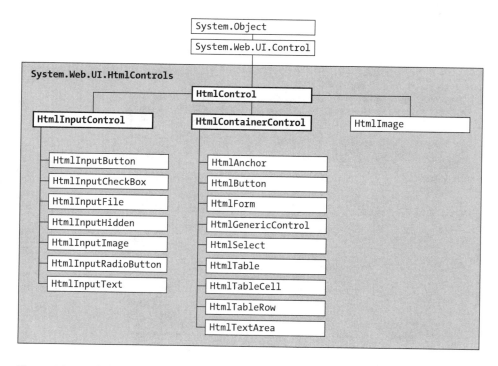

Figure 18-32. The System.Web.UI.HtmlControls hierarchy

Given the fact that you are able to build complete ASP.NET Web applications using
nothing but the official WebForm controls, you may wonder exactly why you have been
given two widget namespaces. The main reason has to do with the process of migrating
legacy *.html files to the world of ASP.NET. Simply put, ASP.NET allows you to treat a
simple HTML widget (which could be generated via toolkits such as ColdFusion or

FrontPage) as a full-blown object, capable of server-side event handling and programmatic manipulation.

For example, create a new ASP.NET Web application and build a GUI using the HTML Toolbox tab (not the WebControls tab!) that consists of an HTML Button, HTML Label, and HTML TextBox. The initial *.aspx definition looks like the following (notice the *lack* of runat="server"):

```
<INPUT id="btnHtmlButton" style="Z-INDEX: 101; LEFT: 24px;
POSITION: absolute; TOP: 56px"
type="button" value="Set The Label with value in TextBox">
<DIV id="lblHtmlLabel" style="DISPLAY: inline; Z-INDEX: 102;
LEFT: 200px; WIDTH: 70px; POSITION:
absolute; TOP: 24px; HEIGHT: 15px"
ms_positioning="FlowLayout">Label</DIV>
<INPUT id="txtHtmlTextBox" style="Z-INDEX: 103;
LEFT: 24px; POSITION: absolute; TOP: 24px"
type="text">
```

If you were to now look in the associated code behind file, you would *not* find member variables that represent these widgets, given that they have not been configured as server-side controls. To do so, select all of the widgets on the ASP.NET designer, right-click, and select Run as Server Control. Once you do, the *.aspx file will be updated as follows:

```
<INPUT id="btnHtmlButton" style="Z-INDEX: 101; LEFT: 24px;
POSITION: absolute; TOP: 56px"
type="button" value="Set The Label with value in TextBox" runat="server">
<DIV id="lblHtmlLabel" style="DISPLAY: inline; Z-INDEX: 102;
LEFT: 200px; WIDTH: 70px; POSITION:
absolute; TOP: 24px; HEIGHT: 15px"
ms_positioning="FlowLayout" runat="server">Label</DIV>
<INPUT id="txtHtmlTextBox" style="Z-INDEX: 103; LEFT: 24px;
POSITION: absolute; TOP: 24px"
type="text" runat="server">
```

More interestingly, the code behind file now has three member variables that represent these server-side widgets:

```
public class HtmlServerSideWidgetsPage : System.Web.UI.Page
{
    protected System.Web.UI.HtmlControls.HtmlInputButton btnHtmlButton;
    protected System.Web.UI.HtmlControls.HtmlGenericControl lblHtmlLabel;
    protected System.Web.UI.HtmlControls.HtmlInputText txtHtmlTextBox;
...
}
```

At this point, your HTML-based widgets may be programmed against as if they were ASP.NET Web controls. However, be very aware that the names of the properties, methods, and events exposed from the HtmlControl family will look and feel much more "HTML-like." Thus, if you were to handle the ServerClick event of the HtmlInputButton type in order to assign the value of the HtmlGenericControl (aka Label) based on the value in the HtmlInputText (aka TextBox), you would find the following code:

```
public class HtmlServerSideWidgetsPage : System.Web.UI.Page
{
    protected System.Web.UI.HtmlControls.HtmlInputButton btnHtmlButton;
    protected System.Web.UI.HtmlControls.HtmlGenericControl lblHtmlLabel;
    protected System.Web.UI.HtmlControls.HtmlInputText txtHtmlTextBox;
...
    private void InitializeComponent()
    {
        this.btnHtmlButton.ServerClick +=
            new System.EventHandler(this.btnHtmlButton_ServerClick);
...
    }
    private void btnHtmlButton_ServerClick(object sender, System.EventArgs e)
    {
        lblHtmlLabel.InnerText = txtHtmlTextBox.Value;
    }
}
```

If you do not have a ton of legacy *.html files, you may never need to interact with the System.Web.UI.HtmlControls namespace. In fact, beyond this example, I will not comment on them further. However, if you are interested, consult online help for additional details.

NOTE   In the same spirit of Windows Forms, understand that it is possible to build custom ASP.NET Web controls. Although I don't have time to examine this topic here, look up "Developing ASP.NET Server Controls" from MSDN for more details.

And Now for Something Completely Different: GDI+ on the Web Server

Next, I'd like to examine a very intriguing topic that you will most likely make use of when building your ASP.NET pages: the use of GDI+ on the Web server. Although it may seem unlikely, ASP.NET Web development can be greatly enhanced by making use of the types within System.Drawing.dll.

To take things out for a test drive, fire up VS .NET and create a new ASP.NET Web application named GdiPlusApp. The initial *.aspx file will allow the user to specify a number of traits regarding the image to be rendered on the Web server and emitted to the requesting browser. Specifically, the user may define a top, left, bottom, and right coordinate position used to render an ellipse within a 200×200 pixel Image ASP.NET Web control. Also, the user in question may specify a custom System.String to be rendered in the dynamically rendered image, and select a known color used to paint in the background of the Image type. To begin, update the UI of your *.aspx file as shown in Figure 18-33.

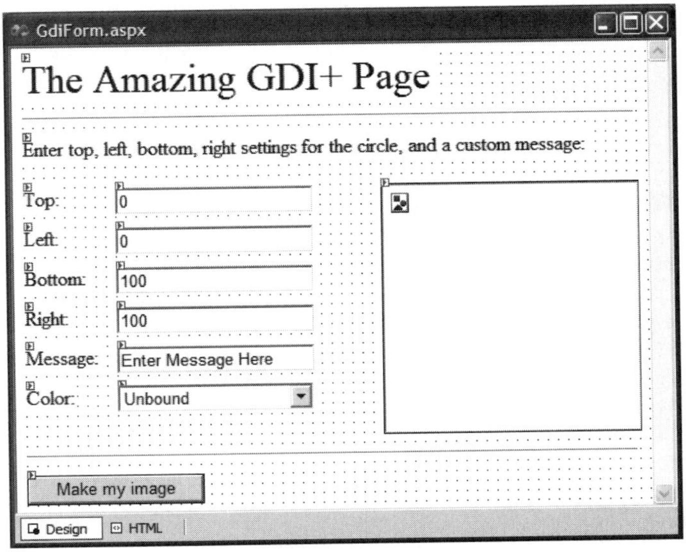

Figure 18-33. The GDI+ page UI

Within the Page_Load() event handler, make use of the static Enum.GetNames() method to fill the ListBox with all members of the KnownColor enumeration. Also, set the Visible property of the Image widget to false (that way, the user won't see an empty Image placeholder when first logging on):

```
private void Page_Load(object sender, System.EventArgs e)
{
    if(!IsPostBack)
    {
        imgTheImage.Visible = false;
        // Load the list box with all colors.
        Array theColors = Enum.GetNames(typeof(KnownColor));
        lstColors.DataSource = theColors;
        lstColors.DataBind();
    }
}
```

All of the true GDI+ action takes place in the Button Click event handler. Note in the code that follows that you must specify a C# "using" directive for the System.Drawing.Imaging namespace, given that this defines the ImageFormat enumeration. Ponder the following:

```
private void btnMakeImage_Click(object sender, System.EventArgs e)
{
    try
    {
        // Get color from list box to make the SolidBrush.
        KnownColor c = (KnownColor)Enum.Parse(typeof(KnownColor),
            lstColors.SelectedValue);
        SolidBrush br = new SolidBrush(Color.FromKnownColor(c));
        // Make a Bitmap and get Graphics object.
        Bitmap myBitmap = new Bitmap(200, 200);
        Graphics g = Graphics.FromImage(myBitmap);
        // Render image based on user prefs.
        g.FillRectangle(br, 0, 0, 200, 200);
        g.DrawEllipse(Pens.Blue,
            int.Parse(txtLeft.Text),
            int.Parse(txtTop.Text),
            int.Parse(txtRight.Text),
            int.Parse(txtBottom.Text));
        g.DrawString(txtMessage.Text,
            new Font("Times New Roman", 12, FontStyle.Bold),
            Brushes.Black, 50, 50);
        // Save image to temp.
        myBitmap.Save(@"C:\Temp\test.gif", ImageFormat.Gif);
        myBitmap.Dispose();
        g.Dispose();
        imgTheImage.ImageUrl = @"C:\Temp\test.gif";
        imgTheImage.Visible = true;
    }
    catch  // User forgot to supply a value...
    {
        Response.Write("Yo! Fill in data and try again...");
        Response.End();
    }
}
```

As you can see, this GDI+ logic is identical to the process of rendered GDI+ logic for a Windows Forms application. The key difference, of course, is that you are rendering your drawing logic to an in-memory Bitmap type. Once you have finished rendering the graphical data, save the image to file, assign it to the ImageUrl property of the Image widget, and set the Visible property to true. If you run this page, you will be pleased to see that you can view your dynamically rendered image (Figure 18-34).

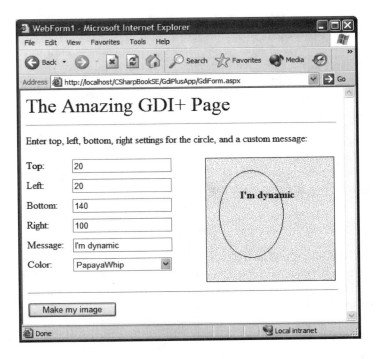

Figure 18-34. Serving up dynamic images

As you can assume, this is a very powerful technique. For example, imagine a Web page that has the ability to dynamically render a pie chart or bar graph based on a database read. If you are up for the challenge, try your hand at building a class type that reads the Inventory table of the Cars database (to make it more interesting, place this type in a standalone *.dll assembly so other ASP.NET Web applications can access this functionality).

SOURCE CODE   The GdiPlusApp project is included under the Chapter 18 subdirectory.

Debugging and Tracing ASP.NET Pages

Cool! You now have a solid understanding of how ASP.NET Web pages are composed. To close this chapter, let's check out the various ways that you can debug your Web apps. If you have worked with Visual Interdev, you understand the pain associated with debugging classic ASP applications. The good news is that when you are building ASP.NET Web projects, you can use the same debugging techniques as you would with any other sort of Visual Studio .NET project type. Thus, you can set breakpoints in your code behind file (as well as embedded "script" blocks in an *.aspx file), start a debug session (press F5), and step through your code.

Also, you can enable tracing support for your *.aspx files by specifying the trace attribute in your opening script block, as shown here:

```
<%@ Page language="c#" Codebehind="MyWebForm.aspx.cs"
AutoEventWireup="false" Inherits="MyNamespace.MyWebForm" trace = "true"  %>
```

When you do so, the returned HTML contains trace information regarding the previous HTTP response. To insert your own trace messages into the mix, you can use the Trace type. Any time you wish to log a custom message (from a script block or C# source code file), simply call the Write() method (Figure 18-35):

```
private void MyPageLevelHelperFunction()
{
    Trace.Write("App Category", "Inside helper function...");
}
```

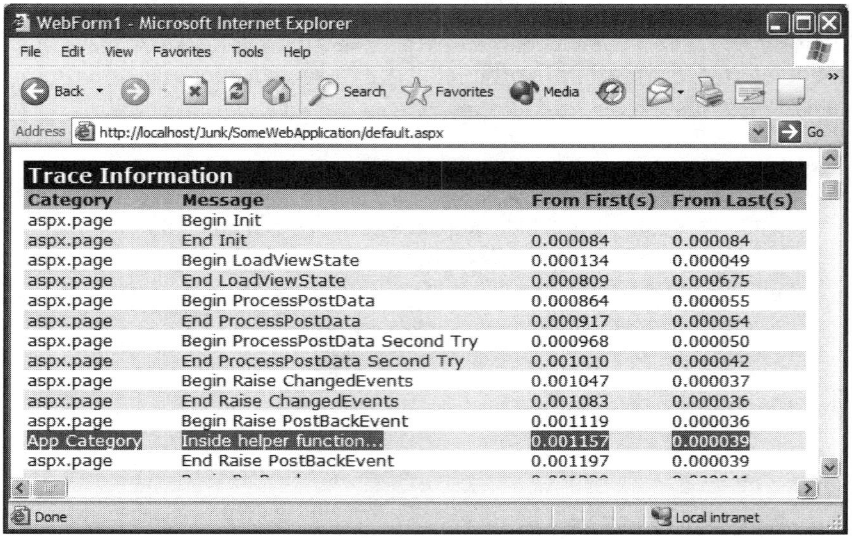

Figure 18-35. Logging custom trace messages

Summary

Building Web applications requires a different frame of mind than is used to assemble traditional desktop applications. In this chapter, you began with a quick and painless review of some core Web atoms, including HTML, HTTP, the role of client-side scripting, and server-side scripts using classic ASP.

The bulk of this chapter was spent examining the architecture of an ASP.NET page. As you have seen, each *.aspx file in your project has an associated System.Web.UI.Page-derived class. Using this code behind approach, ASP.NET allows you to build more reusable and OO-aware systems. Next, this chapter examined the use of Web Form controls. As you have seen, these GUI widgets are in charge of emitting HTML tags to the client side. The validation controls are server-side widgets that are responsible for rendering client-side JavaScript to perform form validation, without incurring a round-trip to the server. We wrapped up with an example of interacting with the .NET base class libraries, and examined how to dynamically render an image using GDI+.

CHAPTER 19

ASP.NET Web Applications

THE PREVIOUS CHAPTER concentrated on the composition and behavior of ASP.NET pages and the Web controls they contain. This chapter builds on these basics by examining the role of the HttpApplication type. As you will see, when you derive a type from HttpApplication, you are able to intercept numerous events that allow you to treat your Web applications as a cohesive unit, rather than a set of stand-alone *.aspx files.

In addition to investigating the HttpApplication type, this chapter also addresses the all-important topic of state management. Here you will learn the role of view state, session, and application-level variables, as well as a new state-centric entity provided by ASP.NET termed the *application cache*. Once you have a solid understanding of the state management techniques offered by the .NET platform, the chapter wraps up with a discussion of the role of the web.config file, and you come to learn various configuration-centric techniques.

The Issue of State

At the beginning of the last chapter, it was pointed out that HTTP is a stateless wire protocol. This very fact makes Web development extremely different from the process of building a stand-alone desktop application, Windows Service, or console-based UI. For example, when you are building a Windows Forms application, you can rest assured that any member variables defined in the main Form will exist in memory until the user explicitly shuts down the executable:

```
public class MyMainWindow : Form
{
    // State data!
    private string iAmHereUntilFormShutDown;
...
}
```

In the world of the World Wide Web however, you are not afforded the same luxurious assumption. To prove the point, assume you have a new ASP.NET Web application (named SimpleStateExample) that has a single *.aspx file. Within the code behind the file, define a page-level string variable named userFavoriteCar:

```
public class SimpleStatePage: Page
{
    // State data?
    private string userFavoriteCar;
    ...
}
```

Also, assume that you have constructed the following Web UI as seen in Figure 19-1.

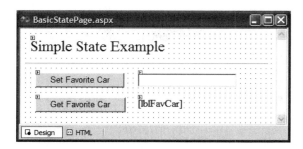

Figure 19-1. The UI for the simple state page

The server-side Click event handler for the Set button will allow the user to assign the string variable using the value within the TextBox:

```
private void btnSetFavCar_Click(object sender, System.EventArgs e)
{
    // Store fav car in member variable.
    userFavoriteCar = txtFavCar.Text;
}
```

while the Click event handler for the Get button will display the current value of the member variable within the page's Label widget:

```
private void btnShowFavCar_Click(object sender, System.EventArgs e)
{
    // Show value of member variable.
    lblFavCar.Text = userFavoriteCar;
}
```

Now, if you were building a Windows Forms application, you would be right to assume that once the user sets the initial value, it would be remembered throughout the life of the desktop application. Sadly, when you run this Web application, you will find that each time you post back to the Web server, the value of the userFavoriteCar string variable is set back to the initial empty value, and therefore the Label's text is continuously empty.

Again, given that HTTP has no clue how to automatically remember data once the HTTP response has been sent, it stands to reason that the Page object is destroyed instantly. Therefore, when the client posts back to the *.aspx file, a *new* Page object is constructed that will reset any page-level member variables. This is clearly a major dilemma. Imagine how painful online shopping would be if every time you posted back to the Web server, any and all information you previously entered (such as the items you wish to purchase) was discarded. When you wish to remember information regarding the users who are logged onto your site, you need to make use of various state management techniques.

NOTE   This issue is in no way limited to ASP.NET. Java Servlets, CGI applications, classic ASP, and PHP applications all must contend with the thorny issue of state management.

To remember the value of the userFavoriteCar string type between post backs, we are required to store the value of this string type within a session variable. You will examine the exact details of session state in the pages that follow. For the sake of completion, however, here are the necessary updates for the current page (note that we are no longer using the private string member variable, therefore feel free to comment out or remove the definition altogether):

```
private void btnSetFavCar_Click(object sender, System.EventArgs e)
{
    // Store fav car in member variable.
    // userFavoriteCar = txtFavCar.Text;
    Session["UserFavCar"] = txtFavCar.Text;
}
private void btnGetFavCar_Click(object sender, System.EventArgs e)
{
    // Show value of member variable.
    // lblFavCar.Text = userFavoriteCar;
    lblFavCar.Text =  (string)Session["UserFavCar"];
}
```

If you were to now run the application, the value of your favorite automobile would be preserved across post backs, thanks to the HttpSessionState object manipulated with the inherited Session property.

SOURCE CODE   The SimpleStateExample files are included under the Chapter 19 subdirectory.

ASP.NET State Management Techniques

ASP.NET provides several mechanisms that you can use to maintain stateful information in your Web applications. Specifically, you have the following options:

- Make use of ASP.NET view state.

- Define application-level variables.

- Make use of the application cache.

- Define session-level variables.

- Interact with cookie data.

We'll examine the details of each approach in turn, beginning with the topic of ASP.NET view state.

Understanding the Role of ASP.NET View State

The term *view state* has been thrown out numerous times here and in the previous chapter without a formal definition, so let's demystify this term once and for all. Under classic ASP, Web developers were required to manually repopulate the values of the incoming form widgets during the process of constructing the outgoing HTTP response. For example, if the incoming HTTP request contained five text boxes with specific values, the *.asp file needed to extract the current values (via the Form or QueryString collections of the Request object) and manually place them back into the HTTP response stream (needless to say, this was a drag). If the developer failed to do so, the caller was presented with a set of five empty text boxes!

Under ASP.NET, we are no longer required to manually scrape out and repopulate the values contained within the HTML widgets because the ASP.NET runtime will automatically embed a hidden form field (named __VIEWSTATE), which will flow between the browser and a specific page. The data assigned to this field is a 64-base encoded string that contains a set of name/value pairs that represent the values of each GUI widget on the page at hand.

The System.Web.UI.Page base class' Init event handler is the entity in charge of reading the incoming values found within the __VIEWSTATE field to populate the appropriate member variables in the derived class (which is why it is risky at best to access the state of a Web widget within the scope of a page's Init event handler).

Also, just before the outgoing response is emitted back to the requesting browser, the __VIEWSTATE data is used to repopulate the form's widgets, to ensure that the current values of the HTML widgets appear as they did prior to the previous post back.

Clearly, the best thing about this aspect of ASP.NET is that it just happens without any work on your part. Of course, you are always able to interact with, and alter, this default functionality if you so choose. To understand how to do this, let's see a concrete view state example.

Demonstrating View State

First create a new ASP.NET Web application called ViewStateApp. On your initial *.aspx page, add a single ASP.NET ListBox Web control and a single Button type. Handle the Click event for the Button to provide a way for the user to post back to the Web server:

```
private void btnDoPostBack_Click(object sender, System.EventArgs e)
{
    // No-op. This is just here to allow a post back.
}
```

Now, using the VS .NET Properties window, access the Items property and add four ListItems to the ListBox. The result looks like this:

```
<asp:ListBox id="myListBox"
style="Z-INDEX: 102; LEFT: 8px; POSITION: absolute; TOP: 64px" runat="server">
    <asp:ListItem Value="Item One">Item One</asp:ListItem>
    <asp:ListItem Value="Item Two">Item Two</asp:ListItem>
    <asp:ListItem Value="Item Three">Item Three</asp:ListItem>
    <asp:ListItem Value="Item Four">Item Four</asp:ListItem>
</asp:ListBox>
```

Note that we have hard-coded the items in the ListBox directly within the *.aspx file. As you already know, all <asp:> definitions found within an HTML form will automatically render back their HTML representation before the final HTTP response (provided they have the runat="server" attribute).

Now, recall from the previous chapter that the <%@Page%> directive has an optional attribute called enableViewState that by default is set to "true." To disable this behavior, simply update the <%@Page%> directive as follows:

```
<%@ Page language="c#" Codebehind="ViewStateForm1.aspx.cs"
AutoEventWireup="false" Inherits="ViewStateApp.WebForm1"
enableViewState="false"%>
```

So, what exactly does it mean to disable view state? The answer is "it depends." Given how we defined the term, you would think that if we disable view state for an *.aspx file, the values within our ListBox would not be remembered between post backs to the Web server. However, if you were to run this application as is, you might be surprised to find that the information in the ListBox is retained regardless of how many times you post back to the page. In fact, if you examine the source HTML returned to the browser, you may be further surprised to see that the hidden __VIEWSTATE field is *still present*:

```
<form name="Form1" method="post" action="ViewStateForm1.aspx" id="Form1">
<input type="hidden" name="__VIEWSTATE"
value="dDwtMjAxOTQ3NDgxNDs7Ps4WZe4amXU/eOtWIWDyPHpPqK7b" />
```

The reason that the view state string is still visible is the fact that the *.aspx file has explicitly defined the ListBox items within the scope of the HTML <form> tags. Thus, the ListBox items will be autogenerated each time the Web server responds to the client.

However, assume that our ListBox is dynamically populated within the code behind file rather than within the HTML <form> definition. First, remove the <asp:ListItem> declarations from the current *.aspx file:

```
<asp:ListBox id="myListBox"
style="Z-INDEX: 102; LEFT: 8px; POSITION: absolute; TOP: 64px" runat="server">
</asp:ListBox>
```

Next, fill the list items within the Load event handler within your code behind file:

```
private void Page_Load(object sender, System.EventArgs e)
{
    if(!IsPostBack)
    {
        // Fill ListBox dynamically!
        myListBox.Items.Add("Item One");
        myListBox.Items.Add("Item Two");
        myListBox.Items.Add("Item Three");
        myListBox.Items.Add("Item Four");
    }
}
```

If you post to this updated page, you will find that the first time the browser requests the page, the values in the ListBox are present and accounted for. However, on post back, the ListBox is suddenly *empty*. The first rule of ASP.NET view state is that its effect is only realized when you have widgets whose values are dynamically generated through code. If you hard-code values within the *.aspx file's <form> tags, the state of these items is always remembered across post backs (even when you set enableViewState to false for a given page).

Furthermore, view state is most useful when you have a dynamically populated Web widget that always needs to be repopulated for each and every post back (such as an ASP.NET DataGrid, which is always filled using a database hit). If you did not disable view state for pages that contain such widgets, the entire state of the grid is represented within the hidden __VIEWSTATE field. Given that complex pages may contain numerous ASP.NET Web controls, you can imagine how large this string would become. As the payload of the HTTP request/response cycle could become quite heavy, this may become a problem for the dial-up Web surfers of the world. In cases such as these, you may find faster throughput if you disable view state for the page.

If the idea of disabling view state for the entire *.aspx file seems a bit too aggressive, recall that every descendent of the System.Web.UI.Control base class inherits the EnableViewState property, which makes it very simple to disable view state on a control-by-control basis:

```
<asp:DataGrid id="myHugeDynamicallyFilledDataGrid"
style="Z-INDEX: 105; LEFT: 24px; POSITION: absolute; TOP: 200px"
runat="server" EnableViewState="false">
</asp:DataGrid>
```

NOTE   Be aware that ASP.NET pages reserve a small part of the __VIEWSTATE string for internal use. Given this, you will find that the __VIEWSTATE field will still appear in the client-side browser even when the entire page (and all the controls) have disabled view state.

Adding Custom View State Data

In addition to the EnableViewState property, the System.Web.UI.Control base class also provides an inherited property named ViewState. Under the hood, this property provides access to a System.Web.StateBag type, which represents all the data contained within the __VIEWSTATE field. Using the indexer of the StateBag type, you can embed custom information within the hidden __VIEWSTATE form field using a set of name/value pairs. By way of a simple example:

```
private void btnAddToVS_Click(object sender, System.EventArgs e)
{
    ViewState["CustomViewStateItem"] = "Some user data";
    lblVSValue.Text = (string)ViewState["CustomViewStateItem"];
}
```

Because the System.Web.StateBag type has been designed to operate on any type-derived System.Object, when you wish to access the value of a given key, you will need to explicitly cast it into the correct underlying data type (in this case, a System.String). Beware, however, that values placed within the __VIEWSTATE field cannot literally be *any* object. Specifically, the only valid types are strings, integers, Booleans, ArrayList, Hashtable, or an array of these types.

So, given that *.aspx pages may insert custom bits of information into the __VIEWSTATE string, the next logical question is when you would want to do so. Most of the time, custom view state data is best suited for user-specific preferences. For example, you may establish a point of view state data that specifies how a user wishes to view the UI of a DataGrid (such as a sort order). View state data is not well suited for full-blown user data such as items in a shopping cart, cached DataSets, or whatnot. When you need to store this sort of complex information, you are required to work with session data. Before we get to that point, we need to understand the role of the Global.asax file.

SOURCE CODE   The ViewStateApp files are included under the Chapter 19 subdirectory.

The Role of the Global.asax File

At this point, an ASP.NET application may seem to be little more than a set of *.aspx files and their respective Web controls. While you could build a Web application by simply linking a set of related Web pages, you will most likely need a way to interact with the Web application as a whole. To this end, your ASP.NET Web applications may choose to include an optional class type that derives from System.Web.HttpApplication. Simply put, this class is just about as close to a traditional double-clickable *.exe as we can get in the world of ASP.NET.

By default, ASP.NET Web projects created with VS .NET receive a Global.asax file and an associated code behind file (Global.asax.cs). If you open the Global.asax file within VS .NET, you will see that the designer is little more than a glorified component tray (Figure 19-2).

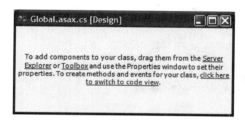

Figure 19-2. The Global.asax designer

While you technically could place GUI-based widgets onto this designer, they would be of little use as they are not rendered back into the HTTP response stream. Rather, this component tray is used to hold any application-level widgets you wish to define within your HttpApplication-derived class (SqlConnections, SqlCommands, EventLogs, and so forth). Like a Form- or Page-derived type, items placed on the Global.asax component tray will result in a member variable in the associated code behind file.

If you open the code behind file for an unaltered Global.asax, you see the following definition for a class named Global that derives from System.Web.HttpApplication:

```
public class Global : System.Web.HttpApplication
{
    protected void Application_Start(Object sender, EventArgs e){}
    protected void Session_Start(Object sender, EventArgs e){}
    protected void Application_BeginRequest(Object sender, EventArgs e){}
    protected void Application_EndRequest(Object sender, EventArgs e){}
    protected void Session_End(Object sender, EventArgs e){}
    protected void Application_End(Object sender, EventArgs e){}
    protected void Application_Error(Object sender, EventArgs e){}
    protected void Application_AuthenticateRequest(Object sender, EventArgs e){}
}
```

The members defined inside the Global class are in reality event handlers that allow you to interact with application-level (and session-level) events. Table 19-1 documents the role of each member.

Table 19-1. Core Types of the System.Web Namespace

Event Handler of the Global Type	Meaning in Life
Application_Start()	This event handler is called the very first time the Web application is launched. Thus, this event will fire exactly once over the lifetime of a Web app. This is an ideal place to define application-level data used throughout your Web application.
Application_End()	Called when the application is shutting down. This will occur when the last user times out or if you manually shut down the app via IIS.
Session_Start()	Fired when a new user logs onto your application. Here you may establish any user-specific data points.
Session_End	Fired when a user's session has terminated.
Application_BeginRequest() Application_EndRequest()	These events are fired each and every time an HTTP request begins and ends, and allow you to interact with (and possibly modify) the current request data. Once the EndRequest() event handler has completed, the response is sent.
Application_AuthenticateRequest()	Called when ASP.NET is just about to perform any authentication on the current request. This can be handy if you want to perform any customized authentication actions in addition to the standard ASP.NET logic (not covered here).
Application_Error()	This is a global error handler that will be called when an unhandled exception is thrown by the Web application.

Your Global class may define numerous other event handlers. However, the members seen in Table 19-1 fit the bill for this chapter (see online Help for further details).

The Global Last Chance Exception Event Handler

First up, let me point out the role of the Application_Error() event handler. Recall that a specific page may handle the Error event to process any unhandled exception that occurred within the scope of the page itself. In a similar light, the Application_Error() event handler is the final place to handle an exception that was not handled by a specific page. As with the page level Error event, you are able to access the specific System.Exception using the inherited Server property:

```
protected void Application_Error(Object sender, EventArgs e)
{
    Exception ex = Server.GetLastError();
    Response.Write(ex.Message);
    Server.ClearError();
}
```

Given that the Application_Error() event handler is the last chance exception handler for your Web application, the odds are that you would rather not report the error to the user, but rather log this information to the Web server's event log. For example:

```
using System.Diagnostics;
...
protected void Application_Error(Object sender, EventArgs e)
{
    // Log last error to event log.
    Exception ex = Server.GetLastError();
    EventLog ev = new EventLog("Application");
    ev.WriteEntry(ex.Message, EventLogEntryType.Error);
    Server.ClearError();
    Response.Write("This app has bombed. Sorry!");
}
```

The HttpApplication Base Class

The Global class derives from the System.Web.HttpApplication base class, which supplies the same sort of functionality as the System.Web.UI.Page type. Table 19-2 documents the key members of interest.

Table 19-2. Key Members Defined By the System.Web.HttpApplication Type

Select Properties of the HttpApplication Type	Meaning in Life
Application	This property allows you to interact with application-level variables, using the exposed HttpApplicationState type.
Request	This property allows you to interact with the incoming HTTP request (via HttpRequest).
Response	This property allows you to interact with the incoming HTTP response (via HttpResponse).
Server	This property gets the intrinsic server object for the current request (via HttpServerUtility).
Session	This property allows you to interact with session-level variables, using the exposed HttpSessionState type.

Understanding the Application/Session Distinction

Under ASP.NET, application state is represented by the HttpApplicationState type. This class enables you to share global information across all users who are logged onto your ASP.NET application. Not only can application data be shared by all users on your site, but if one user changes the value of an application-level data point, the change is seen by all others on their next post back.

On the other hand, session state is used to remember information for a specific user (again, such as items in a shopping cart). Physically, a user's session state is represented by the HttpSessionState type. When a new user logs onto an ASP.NET Web application, the runtime will automatically assign that user a new session ID, which by default will expire after 20 minutes of inactivity. Thus, if 20,000 users are logged onto your site, you have 20,000 distinct HttpSessionState objects, each of which is assigned a unique session ID. The relationship between a Web application and Web sessions is shown in Figure 19-3.

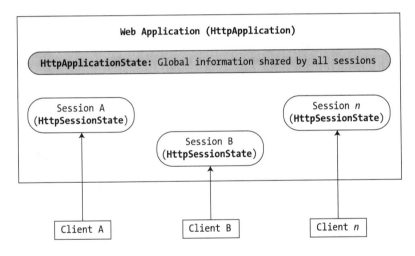

Figure 19-3. The Application/Session state distinction

As you may know, under classic ASP, application- and session-state data is represented using distinct COM objects (e.g., Application and Session). Under ASP.NET, Page-derived types as well as the HttpApplication type make use of identically named *properties* (i.e., Application and Session), which expose the underlying HttpApplicationState and HttpSessionState types.

Maintaining Application-Level State Data

The HttpApplicationState enables developers to share global information across multiple sessions in an ASP.NET application. For example, you may wish to maintain an application-wide connection string that can be used by all pages, a common DataSet used by multiple pages, or any other piece of data that needs to be accessed on an application-wide scale. Table 19-3 describes some core members of this type.

Table 19-3. Members of the HttpApplicationState Type

HttpApplicationState Member	Meaning in Life
AllKeys	This property returns an array of System.String types that represent all the names in the HttpApplicationState type.
Count	This property gets the number of item objects in the HttpApplicationState type.
Add()	This method allows you to add a new name/value pair into the HttpApplicationState type. Do note that this method is typically *not* used in favor of the indexer of the HttpApplicationState class.
Clear()	Deletes all items in the HttpApplicationState type. This is functionally equivalent to the RemoveAll() method.
Lock() Unlock()	These two methods are used when you wish to alter a set of application variables in a thread-safe manner.
Remove() RemoveAt()	Removes a specific item (by string name) within the HttpApplicationState type. RemoveAt() removes the item via a numerical indexer.

When you need to create data members that can be shared among all active sessions, you need to establish a set of name/value pairs. In most cases, the most natural place to do so is within the Application_Start() event handler of the HttpApplication-derived type. For example:

```
protected void Application_Start(Object sender, EventArgs e)
{
    // Set up some application variables.
    Application["SalesPersonOfTheMonth"] = "Chucky";
    Application["CurrentCarOnSale"] = "Colt";
    Application["MostPopularColorOnLot"] = "Black";
}
```

During the lifetime of your Web application (which is to say, until the Web application is manually shut down or until the final user times out), any user (on any page) may access these values as necessary. Assume you have a page that will display the current discount car within a Label via a button click:

```
private void btnShowAppVariables_Click(object sender, System.EventArgs e)
{
    // Must cast the returned System.Object
    // to a System.String!
    lblAppVariables.Text =
        (string)Application["CurrentCarOnSale"];
}
```

Like the ViewState property, notice how we must cast the value returned from the HttpApplicationState type into the correct underlying type. Now, given that the HttpApplicationState type can hold *any* type, it should stand to reason that you can place custom types (or any .NET type) within your site's application state.

To illustrate this technique, create a new ASP.NET Web application named AppState. Assume you would rather maintain the three current application variables within a strongly typed object named CarLotInfo:

```
public class CarLotInfo
{
    public CarLotInfo(string s, string c, string m)
    {
        salesPersonOfTheMonth = s;
        currentCarOnSale = c;
        mostPopularColorOnLot = m;
    }
    // Public for easy access.
    public string salesPersonOfTheMonth;
    public string currentCarOnSale;
    public string mostPopularColorOnLot;
}
```

With this helper class in place, we could modify the Application_Start() event handler as follows:

```
protected void Application_Start(Object sender, EventArgs e)
{
    // Place a custom object in the application data sector.
    Application["CarSiteInfo"] =
        new CarLotInfo("Chucky", "Colt", "Black");
}
```

and then access the information using the public field data within a server-side event handler:

```
private void btnShowAppVariables_Click(object sender, System.EventArgs e)
{
    CarLotInfo appVars =
        ((CarLotInfo)Application["CarSiteInfo"]);
    string appState =
        string.Format("<li>Car on sale: {0}</li>",
        appVars.currentCarOnSale);
    appState +=
        string.Format("<li>Most popular color: {0}</li>",
        appVars.mostPopularColorOnLot);
    appState +=
        string.Format("<li>Big shot SP: {0}</li>",
        appVars.salesPersonOfTheMonth);
    lblAppVariables.Text = appState;
}
```

If you were now to run this page, you would find that a list of each application variable is displayed on the page's Label type.

Modifying Application Data

You may programmatically update or delete any or all members using members of the HttpApplicationState type during the execution of your Web application. For example, to delete a specific item, simply call the Remove() method. If you wish to destroy all application-level data, call RemoveAll():

```
// Remove a single item via string name.
Application.Remove("SomeItemIDontNeed");
// Destroy all application data!
Application.RemoveAll();
```

If you wish to simply change the value of an existing application-level variable, you only need to make a new assignment to the data item in question. Assume your page now supports a new Button type that allows your user to change the current hotshot salesperson. The Click event handler is as you would expect:

```
private void btnSetNewSP_Click(object sender, System.EventArgs e)
{
    // Set the new Salesperson.
    ((CarLotInfo)Application["CarSiteInfo"]).salesPersonOfTheMonth
        = txtNewSP.Text;
}
```

If you ran the Web application, you would now find the application-level variable has been updated. Furthermore, given that application variables are accessible from all user sessions, if you were to launch three or four instances of your Web browser, you would find that if one instance changes the current hotshot salesperson, each of the other browsers will display the new value on post back.

Understand that if you have a situation where a set of application-level variables must be updated as a unit, you risk the possibility of data corruption (given that it is technically possible that an application-level data point may be changed while another user is attempting to access it!). While you could take the long road and manually lock down the logic using threading primitives of the System.Threading namespace, the HttpApplicationState type has two methods (Lock() and Unlock()) that automatically ensure thread safety:

```
// Safely access related application data.
Application.Lock();
    Application["SalesPersonOfTheMonth"] = "Maxine";
    Application["CurrentBonusedEmployee"] = Application["SalesPersonOfTheMonth"];
Application.Unlock();
```

NOTE   Much like the C# lock statement, if an exception occurs after the call to Lock() but before the call to Unlock(), the piece of application-level data that was being altered will automatically be freed.

Intercepting Web Application Shutdown

The HttpApplicationState type is designed to maintain the values of the items it contains until one of two situations occurs: the last user on your site times out (or manually logs out) or someone manually shuts down the Web via IIS. In each case, the Application_Exit() method of the HttpApplication-derived type will automatically be called. Within this event handler you are able to perform whatever sort of clean-up code is necessary:

```
protected void Application_End(Object sender, EventArgs e)
{
    // Write current application variables
    // to a database or whatever else you need to do...
}
```

SOURCE CODE   The AppState files are included under the Chapter 19 subdirectory.

Working with the Application Cache

ASP.NET provides a second and more flexible manner to handle application-wide data. As you recall, the values within the HttpApplicationState object remain in memory as long as your Web application is alive and kicking. Sometimes, however, you may wish to maintain a piece of application data only for a specific period of time. For example, you may wish to cache an ADO.NET DataSet that is only valid for 5 minutes. After that time, you may want to obtain a fresh DataSet to account for possible user modifications. While it is technically possible to build this infrastructure using HttpApplicationState and some sort of hand-crafted monitor, your task is greatly simplified using the ASP.NET application cache.

As suggested by its name, the ASP.NET System.Web.Caching.Cache object (which is accessible via the Context.Cache property) allows you to define an object that is accessible by all users (from all pages) for a fixed amount of time. In its simplest form, interacting with the cache looks identical to interacting with the HttpApplicationState type:

```
// Add an item to the cache.
// This item will *not* expire.
Context.Cache["SomeStringItem"] = "This is the string item";
string s = (string)Context.Cache["SomeStringItem"];
```

NOTE   If you wish to access the Cache from within the Global class, you are required to use the Context object. However, if you are within the scope of a System.Web.UI.Page-derived type, you can make use of the Cache object directly.

Now, understand that if you have no interest in automatically updating (or removing) an application-level data point (as seen here), the Cache object is of little benefit, as you can directly use the HttpApplicationState type. However, when you do wish to have a data point destroyed after a fixed point of time—and optionally be informed when this occurs—the Cache type is extremely helpful.

The System.Web.Caching.Cache class defines only a small number of members beyond the type's indexer. For example, the Add() method can be used to insert a new item into the cache that is not currently defined (if the specified item is already present, Add() does nothing). The Insert() method will also place a member into the cache. If, however, the item is currently defined, Insert() will replace the current item with the new type. Given that this is most often the behavior you will desire, I'll focus on the Insert() method exclusively.

Fun with Data Caching

Let's see an example. To begin, create a new ASP.NET Web application named CacheState. Like an application-level variable maintained by the HttpApplicationState type, the Cache may hold any System.Object-derived type, and is often populated within the Application_Start() event handler. For this example, the goal is to automatically update the contents of a DataSet every 15 seconds. The DataSet in question will contain the current set of records from the Inventory table of the Cars database created during our discussion of ADO.NET. Given these stats, update your Global class type as so (code analysis to follow):

```
public class Global : System.Web.HttpApplication
{
...
    // Define a static level Cache member variable.
    private static Cache theCache;

    protected void Application_Start(Object sender, EventArgs e)
    {
        // First assign the static 'theCache' variable.
        theCache = Context.Cache;

        // When the application starts up,
        // read the current records in the
        // Inventory table of the Cars DB.
        SqlConnection cn = new SqlConnection
          ("data source=localhost;initial catalog=Cars; user id ='sa';pwd=''");
        SqlDataAdapter dAdapt =
            new SqlDataAdapter("Select * From Inventory", cn);
        DataSet theCars = new DataSet();
        dAdapt.Fill(theCars, "Inventory");

        // Now store DataSet in the cache.
        theCache.Insert("AppDataSet",
            theCars, null,
            DateTime.Now.AddSeconds(15),
            Cache.NoSlidingExpiration,
            CacheItemPriority.Default,
            new CacheItemRemovedCallback(UpdateCarInventory));
    }

    // The target for the CacheItemRemovedCallback delegate.
    static void UpdateCarInventory(string key, object item,
        CacheItemRemovedReason reason)
    {
        // Populate the DataSet.
        SqlConnection cn = new SqlConnection
        ("data source=localhost;initial catalog=Cars; user id ='sa';pwd=''");
        SqlDataAdapter dAdapt =
            new SqlDataAdapter("Select * From Inventory", cn);
        DataSet theCars = new DataSet();
        dAdapt.Fill(theCars, "Inventory");
        // Now store in the cache.
        theCache.Insert("AppDataSet",
            theCars, null,
            DateTime.Now.AddSeconds(15),
            Cache.NoSlidingExpiration,
            CacheItemPriority.Default,
            new CacheItemRemovedCallback(UpdateCarInventory));
    }
...
}
```

First, notice that the Global class type has defined a static level Cache member variable. The reason is that we have also defined a static-level function (UpdateCarInventory()) that needs to access the Cache (recall that static members do not have access to inherited members, therefore, we can't use the Context property!)

Inside the Application_Start() event handler, we fill a DataSet and place the object within the application cache. As you would guess, the Context.Cache.Insert() method has been overloaded a number of times. Here we have supplied a value for each possible parameter:

```
// Now store in the cache.
theCache.Add("AppDataSet",          // Name used to identify item in the cache.
    theCars,                        // Object to put In the cache.
    null,                           // Any dependencies for this object?
    DateTime.Now. AddSeconds(15),   // How long item will be in cache.
    Cache.NoSlidingExpiration,      // Fixed or sliding time?
    CacheItemPriority.Default,      // Priority level of cache item.
    // Delegate for CacheItemRemove event
    new CacheItemRemovedCallback(UpdateCarInventory));
```

The first two parameters simply make up the name/value pair of the item. Parameter three allows you to define a CacheDependency type (which is null in this case, as we do not have any other entities in the cache that are dependent on the DataSet).

 NOTE The ability to define a CacheDependency type is quite interesting. For example, you could establish a dependency between a member and an external file. If the contents of the file were to change, the type can be automatically updated. Check out online Help for further details.

The next three parameters are used to define the amount of time the item will be allowed to remain in the application cache as well as its level of priority. Here, we specified the read-only Cache.NoSlidingExpiration field, which informs the cache that the specified time limit (15 seconds) is absolute. Finally, and most important for this example, we created a new CacheItemRemovedCallback delegate type, and passed in the name of the method to call when the DataSet is purged. As you can see from the signature of the UpdateCarInventory() method, the CacheItemRemovedCallback delegate can only call methods that match the following signature:

```
static void UpdateCarInventory(string key, object item,
    CacheItemRemovedReason reason)
{ ... }
```

So, at this point, when the application starts up, the DataSet is populated and cached. Every 15 seconds the DataSet is purged, updated and reinserted into the cache. To see the effects of doing this, we need to create a Page that allows for some degree of user interaction.

Modifying the *.aspx File

Update the UI of your initial *.aspx file as shown in Figure 19-4.

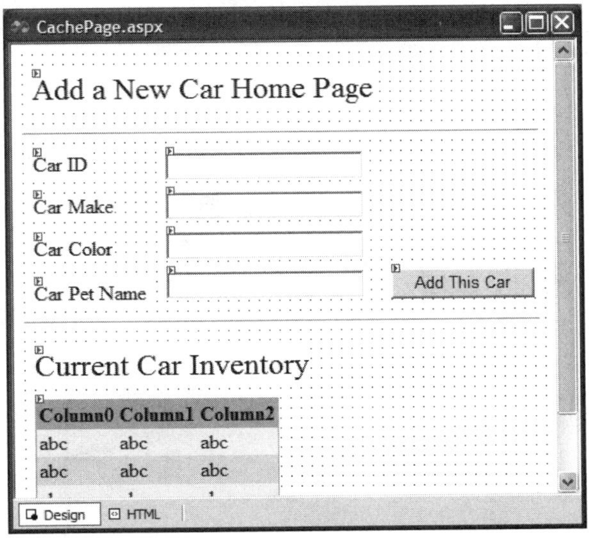

Figure 19-4. The cache application GUI

In the page's Load event handler, configure your DataGrid to display the current contents of the cached DataSet the first time the user posts to the page:

```
private void Page_Load(object sender, System.EventArgs e)
{
    if(!IsPostBack)
    {
        carsDataGrid.DataSource =  (DataSet)Cache["AppDataSet"];
        carsDataGrid.DataBind();
    }
}
```

In the Click event handler of the Add this Car button, insert the new record into the Cars database using an ADO.NET SqlCommand object. Once the record has been inserted, call a helper function named RefreshGrid(), which will update the UI via an ADO.NET SqlDataReader. Here are the methods in question:

```
private void btnAddNewCar_Click(object sender, System.EventArgs e)
{
    // Update the Inventory table
    // and call RefreshGrid().
    SqlConnection cn = new SqlConnection();
    cn.ConnectionString =
        "User ID=sa;Pwd=;Initial Catalog=Cars;" +
        "Data Source=(local)";
    cn.Open();
    string sql;
    SqlCommand cmd;
    // Insert new Car.
    sql = string.Format
        ("INSERT INTO Inventory(CarID, Make, Color, PetName) VALUES" +
        "('{0}', '{1}', '{2}', '{3}')",
        txtCarID.Text, txtCarMake.Text,
        txtCarColor.Text, txtCarPetName.Text);
    cmd = new SqlCommand(sql, cn);
    cmd.ExecuteNonQuery();
    cn.Close();
    RefreshGrid();
}
private void RefreshGrid()
{
    // Populate grid.
    SqlConnection cn = new SqlConnection();
    cn.ConnectionString =
        "User ID=sa;Pwd=;Initial Catalog=Cars;Data Source=(local)";
    cn.Open();
    SqlCommand cmd = new SqlCommand("Select * from Inventory", cn);
    carsDataGrid.DataSource = cmd.ExecuteReader();
    carsDataGrid.DataBind();
    cn.Close();
}
```

Now, to test the use of the cache, launch two instances of your Web browser and navigate to this *.aspx page. At this point, you should see that both DataGrids display identical information. From one instance of the browser, add a new Car. Obviously, this results in an updated DataGrid viewable from the browser that initiated the post back.

From browser two, click the Refresh button. You should *not* see the new item, given that the Page.Load event handler is reading directly from the cache. (If you did see the value, the 15 seconds had already expired. Either type faster or increase the amount of time the DataSet will remain in the cache ;-) Wait a few seconds, and click the Refresh button from browser two one more time. Now you *should* see the new item, given that the DataSet in the cache has expired, and the CacheItemRemovedCallback delegate target method has automatically updated the cached DataSet.

As you can see, the major benefit of the Cache type is that you can ensure that when a member is removed, you have a chance to respond. In this example, you certainly could avoid using the Cache, and simply have the Page_Load() event handler always read directly from the Cars database. Nevertheless, the point should be clear: The cache allows you to automatically refresh data using .NET delegates.

NOTE   Unlike the HttpApplicationState type, the Cache class does not support Lock() and Unlock() methods. If you need to update interrelated items, you will need to directly make use of the types within the System.Threading namespace or the C# "lock" keyword.

SOURCE CODE   The CacheState files are included under the Chapter 19 subdirectory.

Maintaining Session Data

So much for our examination of application-level state data. Next we check out the role of per-user data stores. As mentioned earlier, a *session* is little more than a given user's interaction with a Web application, which is represented via the HttpSessionState type. To maintain stateful information for a particular user, the HttpApplication-derived type and any System.Web.UI.Page-derived types may access the Session property. The classic example of the need to maintain per-user data would be an online shopping cart. Again, if 10 people all log onto an online store, each individual will maintain a unique set of items that they (may) intend to purchase.

When a new user logs onto your Web application, the .NET runtime will automatically assign the user a unique session ID, which is used to identify the user in question. Each session ID is assigned a custom instance of the HttpSessionState type to hold on to user-specific data. Inserting or retrieving session data is syntactically identical to manipulating application data, for example:

```
// Add / retreive a session variable for current user.
Session["DesiredCarColor"] = "Green";
string c = (string) Session["DesiredCarColor"];
```

The HttpApplication-derived type allows you to intercept the beginning and end of a session via the Session_Start() and Session_End() event handlers. Within Session_Start(), you can freely create any per-user data items, while Session_End() allows you to perform any work you may need to do when the user's session has terminated:

```
public class Global : System.Web.HttpApplication
{
    protected void Session_Start(Object sender, EventArgs e)
    { /* Prep user data here! */}
        protected void Session_End(Object sender, EventArgs e)
    { /* Terminate user data here! */ }
...
}
```

Like the HttpApplicationState type, the HttpSessionState may hold any System.Object-derived type, including your custom classes. For example, assume you have a new Web application (SessionState) that defines a helper class named UserShoppingCart:

```
public class UserShoppingCart
{
  public string desiredCar;
  public string desiredCarColor;
  public float downPayment;
  public bool isLeasing;
  public DateTime dateOfPickUp;
  public override string ToString()
  {
    return string.Format
      ("Car: {0}<br>Color: {1}<br>$ Down: {2}<br>Lease: {3}<br>Pick-up Date: {4}",
      desiredCar, desiredCarColor, downPayment, isLeasing,
      dateOfPickUp.ToShortDateString());
  }
}
```

Within the Session_Start() event handler, you can now assign each user a new instance of the UserShoppingCart class:

```
protected void Session_Start(Object sender, EventArgs e)
{
    Session["UserShoppingCartInfo"]
        = new UserShoppingCart();
}
```

As the user traverses your Web pages, you are able to pluck out the UserShoppingCart instance and fill the fields with user-specific data. For example, assume we have a simple *.aspx page that defines a set of input widgets that correspond to each field of the UserShoppingCart type and a Button used to set the values (Figure 19-5).

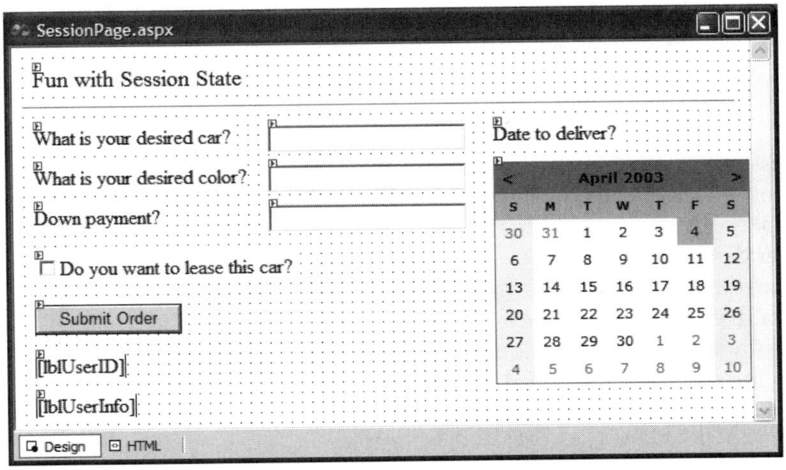

Figure 19-5. The cache application GUI

The server-side Click event handler is straightforward (scrape out values from TextBoxes and display the shopping cart data on a Label type):

```
private void btnSubmit_Click(object sender, System.EventArgs e)
{
    // Set current user prefs.
    UserShoppingCart u =
        (UserShoppingCart)Session["UserShoppingCartInfo"];
    u.dateOfPickUp = myCalendar.SelectedDate;
    u.desiredCar = txtCarMake.Text;
    u.desiredCarColor = txtCarColor.Text;
    u.downPayment = float.Parse(txtDownPayment.Text);
    u.isLeasing = chkIsLeasing.Checked;
    lblUserInfo.Text = u.ToString();
    Session["UserShoppingCartInfo"] = u;
}
```

Within Session_End(), you may wish to persist the fields of the UserShoppingCart to a database or whatnot. In any case, if you were to launch two or three instances of your browser of choice, you would find that each user is able to build a custom shopping cart that maps to his or her unique instance of HttpSessionState.

Additional Members of HttpSessionState

The HttpSessionState class defines a number of other members of interest beyond the type indexer. First, the SessionID property will return the current user's unique ID:

```
lblUserID.Text = string.Format("Here is your ID: {0}",
    Session.SessionID);
```

The Remove() and RemoveAll() method may be used to clear items out of the user's instance of HttpSessionState:

```
Session.Remove["SomeItemWeDontNeedAnymore"];
```

The HttpSessionState type also defines a set of members that control the expiration policy of the current session. Again, by default each user has 20 minutes of inactivity before the HttpSessionState object is destroyed. Thus, if a user enters your Web application (and therefore obtains a unique session ID), but does not return to the site within 20 minutes, the runtime assumes the user is no longer interested, and destroys all session data for that user. You are free to change this default 20-minute expiration value on a user-by-user basis using the TimeOut property. The most common place to do so is within the scope of your Global.Session_Start() method:

```
protected void Session_Start(Object sender, EventArgs e)
{
    // Each user has 5 minutes of inactivity.
    Session.Timeout = 5;
    Session["UserShoppingCartInfo"]
        = new UserShoppingCart();
}
```

NOTE If you do not need to tweak each user's Timeout value, you are able to alter the 20-minute default for all users via the Timeout attribute of the <sessionState> element within the web.config file (examined at the end of this chapter).

The benefit of the Timeout property is that you have the ability to assign specific timeout values discretely for each user. For example, imagine you have created a Web application that allows users to pay cash for a given membership level. You may say that Gold members time out within one hour while Wood members only get 30 seconds. This possibility begs the question: How can you remember user-specific information (such as the current membership level) across Web visits? One possible answer is through the user of the HttpCookie type (speaking of cookies...)

SOURCE CODE The SessionState files are included under the Chapter 19 subdirectory.

Understanding Cookies

The final state management technique examined here is the act of persisting data within a text file (formally called a *cookie*) on the user's machine. When a user logs onto a given site, the browser checks to see if the user's machine has a previously persisted file for the URL in question, and if so, appends the information to the outgoing HTTP request.

The receiving server-side Web page could then read the cookie data to create a GUI that may be based on the current user preferences. I am sure you noticed that when you visit one of your favorite Web sites, it somehow just knows the sort of content you wish to see. For example, when I log onto http://www.ministryofsound.com, I am automatically shown content that reflects my musical tastes. The reason (in part) has to do with a cookie stored on my computer that contains information regarding the type of music I tend to play.

The exact location of your cookie files will depend on which browser you happen to be using. For those of us using Microsoft IE, cookies are stored by default under <root>\Documents and Settings\<loggedOnUser>\Cookies (Figure 19-6).

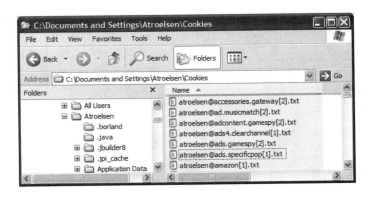

Figure 19-6. Cookie data as persisted under Microsoft IE

The contents of a given cookie file will obviously vary among URLs; however, keep in mind that they are ultimately text files. Thus, cookies are a horrible choice when you wish to maintain sensitive information about the current user (such as a credit card number, password, or whatnot). Even if you take the time to encrypt the data, a crafty hacker could decrypt the value and use it for purely evil pursuits. In any case, cookies do play a role in the development of Web applications, so let's check out how ASP.NET handles this particular state management technique.

Creating Cookies

First of all, understand that ASP.NET cookies can be configured to either be persistent or temporary. A *persistent* cookie is typically regarded as the classic definition of cookie data, in that the set of name/value pairs are physically saved to the user's hard drive.

Temporary cookies (also termed *session cookies*) contain the same data as a persistent cookie, however, the name/value pairs are never saved to the user's machine, but rather exist *only* within the HTTP header. Once the user logs off your site, all data contained within the session cookie is destroyed.

The System.Web.HttpCookie type is the class that represents the server side of the cookie data (persistent or temporary). When you wish to create a new cookie, you access the Response.Cookies property. Once the new HttpCookie is inserted into the internal collection, the name/value pairs flow back to the browser within the HTTP header.

To check out cookie behavior firsthand, create a new ASP.NET Web application (CookieStateApp) and create the user interface displayed in Figure 19-7.

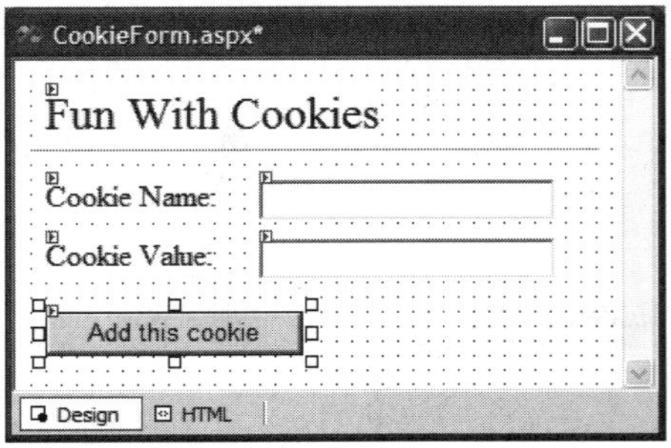

Figure 19-7. The UI of the CookiesStateApp

Within the Button's Click event handler, build a new HttpCookie and insert it into the Cookie collection exposed from the HttpRequest.Cookies property. Be very aware that the data will *not* persist itself to the user's hard drive unless you explicitly set an expiration date using the HttpCookie.Expires property. Thus, the following implementation will create a temporary cookie that is destroyed when the user shuts down the browser:

```
private void btnInsertCookie_Click(object sender, System.EventArgs e)
{
    // Make a new (temp) cookie.
    HttpCookie theCookie =
        new HttpCookie(txtCookieName.Text,
        txtCookieValue.Text);
    Response.Cookies.Add(theCookie);
}
```

However the following generates a persistent cookie that will expire on March 24, 2004:

```
private void btnInsertCookie_Click(object sender, System.EventArgs e)
{
    // Make a new (persistent) cookie.
    HttpCookie theCookie =
        new HttpCookie(txtCookieName.Text,
        txtCookieValue.Text);
    theCookie.Expires = DateTime.Parse("03/24/2004");
    Response.Cookies.Add(theCookie);
}
```

If you were to run this application and insert some cookie data, the browser automatically persists this data to disk. When you open this text file, you will see something like what is shown in Figure 19-8.

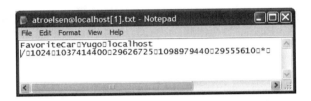

Figure 19-8. The persistent cookie data

Reading Incoming Cookie Data

Recall that the browser is the entity in charge of accessing persisted cookies when navigating to a previously visited page. To interact with the incoming cookie data under ASP.NET, access the HttpRequest.Cookies property. To illustrate, if you were to update your current UI with the means to obtain current cookie data via a Button widget, you could iterate over each name/value pair and present the information within a Label widget:

```
private void btnShowCookies_Click(object sender, System.EventArgs e)
{
    string cookieData = "";
    foreach(string s in Request.Cookies)
    {
        cookieData +=
            string.Format("<li><b>Name</b>: {0}, <b>Value</b>: {1}</li>",
            s, Request.Cookies[s].Value);
    }
    lblCookieData.Text = cookieData;
}
```

If you now run the application and click your new button, you will find that the cookie data has indeed been sent by your browser (Figure 19-9).

Figure 19-9. Viewing cookie data

So! At this point in the chapter you have examined numerous ways to remember information about your users. As you have seen, view state and application, cache, session, and cookie data are manipulated in more or less the same way (via a class indexer). As you have also seen, the HttpApplication type is often used to intercept and respond to events that occur during your Web application's lifetime. Next up: the role of the web.config file.

SOURCE CODE   The CookieStateApp files are included under the Chapter 19 subdirectory.

Configuring Your ASP.NET Web Application Using web.config

During your examination of .NET assemblies you learned that client applications can leverage an XML-based configuration file to instruct the CLR how it should handle binding requests, assembly probing, and other runtime details. The same holds true for ASP.NET Web applications, with the notable exception that Web-centric configuration files are *always* named web.config (unlike *.exe config files that are named based on the related client executable).

When you create a new ASP.NET Web app using VS .NET, you will be given a web.config file that resides in the root of the application's virtual directory. If you open this file and examine its contents, you find that its overall structure looks something like the following:

```xml
<?xml version="1.0" encoding="utf-8" ?>
<configuration>
  <system.web>
    <compilation
        defaultLanguage="c#"
        debug="true"/>
    <customErrors
    mode="RemoteOnly"/>
    <authentication mode="Windows" />
    <authorization>
        <allow users="*" />
    </authorization>
    <trace
        enabled="false"
        requestLimit="10"
        pageOutput="false"
        traceMode="SortByTime"
        localOnly="true"/>
    <sessionState
        mode="InProc"
        stateConnectionString="tcpip=127.0.0.1:42424"
        sqlConnectionString="data source=127.0.0.1;Trusted_Connection=yes"
        cookieless="false"
        timeout="20"/>
    <globalization
        requestEncoding="utf-8"
        responseEncoding="utf-8"/>
  </system.web>
</configuration>
```

Like any *.config file, web.config defines the root level <configuration> element. Nested within the root is the <system.web> element, which can contain numerous subelements used to control how your Web application should behave at runtime. If you have a background in classic ASP, the web.config file should make you quite happy, given that you are not limited to using the IIS manager to alter the behavior of your Web application (which typically required rebooting your app). Under ASP.NET, the web.config file can be modified using any text editor. Table 19-4 outlines the role of the subelements that are defined within the web.config file created by VS .NET.

Table 19-4. Select Elements of a web.config File

Element of web.config File	Meaning in Life
<compilation>	This element is used to enable (or disable) debugging, define the default .NET language used by this Web application, and may optionally define the set of external .NET assemblies that should be automatically referenced (this technique is typically only useful if you are not making use of VS .NET).
<customErrors>	Used to tell the runtime exactly how to display errors that occur during the functioning of the Web app.
<authentication>	A security-related element used to define the authentication mode for this Web application.
<authorization>	Another security-centric element used to define which users can access which resources on the Web server.
<trace>	Used to enable (or disable) tracing support for this Web application.
<sessionState>	Used to control how and where session state data will be stored by the .NET runtime.
<globalization>	Used to configure the globalization settings for this Web application.

A web.config file may contain additional subelements above and beyond the set presented in Table 19-4. A vast majority of these items are security-related, while the remaining items are only useful during advanced ASP.NET scenarios such as creating with custom HTTP headers or custom HTTP modules (not covered here). If you wish to see the complete set of elements that can appear in a web.config file, look up the topic "ASP.NET Settings Schema" using online Help.

NOTE   ASP.NET security issues are also beyond the scope of this text. If you are interested in learning about ASP.NET security, I again point you to *.NET Security* (Bock, Apress 2002).

Enabling Tracing via <trace>

The first aspect of the web.config file we examine is the <trace> sub-element. This XML entity may take any number of attributes to further qualify its behavior, as seen in the following skeleton:

```
<trace enabled="true|false"
       localOnly="true|false"
       pageOutput="true|false"
       requestLimit="integer"
       traceMode="SortByTime|sortByCategory"/>
```

Table 19-5 hits the highlights of each attribute.

Table 19-5. Attributes of the <trace> Element

<trace> Attribute	Meaning in Life
Enabled	Specifies whether tracing is enabled for an application as a whole (the default is false). As you have already seen in the previous chapter, you can selectively enable tracing for a given *.aspx file using the @Page directive.
localOnly	Indicates that the trace information is viewable only on the host Web server and not by remote clients (the default is true).
pageOutput	Specifies how trace output should be viewed.
requestLimit	Specifies the number of trace requests to store on the server. The default is 10. If the limit is reached, trace is automatically disabled.
traceMode	Indicates that trace information is displayed in the order it is processed. The default is SortByTime, but can also be configured to sort by category.

Recall from the previous chapter that individual pages may enable tracing using the <%@Page%> directive. However, if you wish to enable tracing for all pages in your Web application, simply update <trace> as follows:

```
<trace
    enabled="true"
    requestLimit="10"
    pageOutput="false"
    traceMode="SortByTime"
    localOnly="true"
/>
```

Customizing Error Output via <customErrors>

The <customErrors> element can be used to automatically redirect all errors to a custom set of *.html files. This can be helpful if you wish to build a more user-friendly error page than the default supplied by the CLR. In its skeleton form, the <customErrors> element looks like the following:

```
<customErrors defaultRedirect="url" mode="On|Off|RemoteOnly">
   <error statusCode="statuscode" redirect="url"/>
</customErrors>
```

To illustrate the usefulness of the <customErrors> element, assume your ASP.NET Web application has two *.htm files. The first file (genericError.htm) functions as a catch-all error page. Perhaps this page contains an image of your company logo, a link to e-mail the system administrator, and some sort of apologetic verbiage. The second file (Error404.htm) is a custom error page that should only occur when the runtime detects error number 404 (the dreaded resource not found error). Now, if you want to ensure that all errors are handled by these custom pages, you can update your web.config file as follows:

```
<customErrors defaultRedirect = "genericError.htm" mode="On">
     <error statusCode="404" redirect="Error404.htm"/>
</customErrors>
```

Note how the root <customErrors> element is used to specify the name of the generic page for all unhandled errors. One attribute that may appear in the opening tag is mode. The default setting is RemoteOnly, which instructs the runtime *not* to display custom error pages if the HTTP request came from the same machine as the Web server (quite helpful for developers, who would like to see the details). When you set the mode attribute to "on," this will cause custom errors to be seen from all machines (including your development box). Also note that the <customErrors> element may support any number of nested <error> elements to specify which page will be used to handle specific error codes.

To test these custom error redirects, build an *.aspx page that defines two Button widgets and handle their Click events as follows:

```
private void btnGeneralError_Click(object sender, System.EventArgs e)
{
    // This will trigger a general error.
    throw new Exception("General error...");
}
private void btn404Error_Click(object sender, System.EventArgs e)
{
    // This will trigger 404 (assuming there is no file named foo.aspx!)
    Response.Redirect("Foo.aspx");
}
```

Options for Storing State via <sessionState>

By far and away the most powerful aspect of a web.config file is the <sessionState> element. By default, ASP.NET will store session state using an in-process *.dll hosted by the ASP.NET worker process (aspnet_wp.exe). Like any *.dll, the plus side is that access to the information is as fast as possible. However, on the downside, if this AppDomain crashes (for whatever reason) all of the user's state data is destroyed. Furthermore, when you store state data as an in-process *.dll, you cannot interact with a networked Web farm. By default, the <sessionState> element of your web.config file looks like this:

```
<sessionState
        mode="InProc"
        stateConnectionString="tcpip=127.0.0.1:42424"
        sqlConnectionString="data source=127.0.0.1;Trusted_Connection=yes"
        cookieless="false"
        timeout="20"
/>
```

This default mode of storage works just fine if your Web application is hosted by a single Web server. However, under ASP.NET, you can instruct the runtime to host the session state *.dll in a surrogate process named the ASP.NET Session State Server (aspnet_state.exe). When you do so, you are able to offload the *.dll from aspnet_wp.exe into a unique *.exe. The first step in doing so is to start the aspnet_state.exe Windows service. To do so at the command line, simply type:

```
net start aspnet_state
```

Alternatively, you can also start aspnet_state.exe using the Services applet accessed from the Administrative Tools folder of the Control Panel (Figure 19-10).

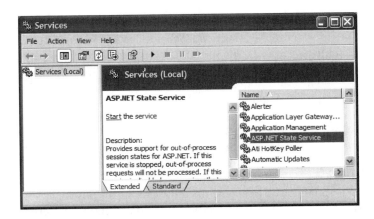

Figure 19-10. The Services applet

The key benefit of this approach is that you can configure aspnet_state.exe to start automatically when the machine boots up using the Properties window. In any case, once the session state server is running, alter the <sessionState> element of your web.config file as follows:

```
<sessionState
        mode="StateServer"
        stateConnectionString="tcpip=127.0.0.1:42424"
        sqlConnectionString="data source=127.0.0.1;Trusted_Connection=yes"
        cookieless="false"
        timeout="20"
/>
```

Here, the mode attribute has been set to StateServer. That's it! At this point the CLR will host session-centric within aspnet_state.exe. In this way, if the AppDomain hosting the Web application crashes, the session data is preserved. Also notice that the <sessionState> element can also support a stateConnectionString attribute. The default TCPIP address value (127.0.0.1) points to the local machine. If you would rather have the .NET runtime use the aspnet_state.exe service located on another networked machine (again, think Web-farms), you are free to update this value.

Finally, if you require the highest degree of isolation and durability for your Web application, you may choose to have the runtime store all your session state data within MS SQL Server. The appropriate update to the web.config file is simple:

```
<sessionState
        mode="SQLServer"
        stateConnectionString="tcpip=127.0.0.1:42424"
        sqlConnectionString="data source=127.0.0.1;Trusted_Connection=yes"
        cookieless="false"
        timeout="20"
/>
```

However, before you attempt to run the associated Web application, you need to ensure that the target machine (specified by the sqlConnectionString attribute) has been properly configured. When you install the .NET SDK (or VS .NET), you will be provided with two files named InstallSqlState.sql and UninstallSqlState.sql, located by default under <drive>:\<%windir%>\Microsoft.NET\Framework\<version>. On the target machine, you must run the InstallSqlState.sql file using a tool such as the SQL Server Query Analyzer (which ships with MS SQL Server).

Once this SQL script has executed, you will find a new SQL Server database has been created (ASPState), which contains a number of stored procedures called by the ASP.NET runtime, as well as a set of tables used to store the session data itself (also, the tempdb database has been updated with a set of tables for swapping purposes). As you would guess, configuring your Web application to store session data within SQL Server is the slowest of all possible options. The benefit is that user-data is as durable as possible (even if the Web server is rebooted).

 NOTE If you make use of the ASP.NET Session State Server or SQL Server to store your session data, you must make sure that any custom types placed in the HttpSessionState object have been marked with the [serializable] attribute! Given this requirement, it is always best practice to always apply the [serializable] attribute to any custom type that will be placed in the HttpSessionState type.

Custom Web Settings via <appSettings>

The final aspect of the web.config file I wish to examine here is the process of storing (and retrieving) custom data. One common use of this technique is to store ADO.NET connection strings. In this way, if you need to alter the connection credentials, you don't have to update or recompile your *.aspx files. Rather, your pages can read the custom XML data at runtime. The first step in doing so is to add a new <appSettings> element in your project's web.config file. This element has two attributes (key and value) that will be used to identify the name and value of the data point. For example:

```
<appSettings>
    <add key = "appConStr"
    value = "server=localhost;uid=sa;pwd=;database=Cars"/>
</appSettings>
```

Programmatically, we can access this value using the AppSettings property of the System.Configuration.ConfigurationSettings type. For example:

```
private void btnReadAppSettings_Click(object sender, System.EventArgs e)
{
    string conStr =
        ConfigurationSettings.AppSettings["appConStr"];
    lblConStringValue.Text = conStr;
}
```

Configuration Inheritance

Last but not least is configuration inheritance. As you learned in the previous chapter, a Web application can be defined as the set of all files contained within a root directory *and any optional subdirectories*. All our example apps in this and the previous chapter have existed on a single root directory managed by IIS (with the optional \bin folder). However, large-scale Web applications tend to define numerous subdirectories off the root, each of which contains some set of related files. Like a traditional desktop application, this is typically done for the benefit of us mere humans, as a hierarchal structure can make a massive set of files more understandable.

When you have an ASP.NET Web application that consists of optional subdirectories off the root, you may be surprised to discover that *each* subdirectory may have its own web.config file! By doing so, you allow each subdirectory to override the settings of a parent directory. If the subdirectory in question does not supply a custom web.config file, it will inherit the settings of the next available web.config file up the directory structure. Thus, as bizarre as it sounds, it is possible to inject an OO-look and feel to a raw directory structure. Figure 19-11 illustrates the concept.

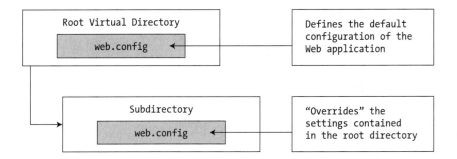

Figure 19-11. Configuration inheritance

Of course, although ASP.NET does allow you to define numerous web.config files for a single Web app, you are not required to do so. In a great many cases, your Web applications function just fine using nothing other than the web.config file located in the root directory of the IIS virtual directory.

That wraps up our examination of ASP.NET. At this point, you should have the tools you need to build Web applications under the .NET platform. To wrap up our voyage, the final chapter examines a related Web-centric topic: XML Web Services.

Summary

In this chapter, you rounded out your knowledge of ASP.NET by examining how to leverage the HttpApplication type. As you have seen, this type provides a number of default event handlers that allow you to intercept various application-and session-level events.

The bulk of this chapter was spent examining a number of state management techniques. Recall that view state is used to automatically repopulate the values of HTML widgets between post backs to a specific page. Next, you checked out the distinction between application-level and session-level data, cookie management, and the ASP.NET application cache. Finally, this chapter examined a number of elements that may be contained in the web.config file.

#### CHAPTER 20

XML Web Services

BACK IN CHAPTER 12, you were introduced to the .NET Remoting layer. As you have seen, this technology is a managed replacement for classic DCOM, which allows any number of .NET-aware machines to exchange information across the wire. While this is all well and good, one possible limitation of this approach to building a distributed system is the fact that all networked machines must have the .NET Framework installed. Therefore, until the .NET platform is completely ported to other non-Windows-based operating systems, it would be next to impossible to pass a CLR type to a .NET-naïve machine.

In contrast to .NET Remoting, XML Web services offer a more agnostic alternative to distributed application development. Simply put, an XML Web service is a unit of code hosted by a Web server (such as Microsoft IIS) that can be invoked using vanilla-flavored HTTP. Furthermore, if the invoked method returns a value to the caller, it is encoded as simple XML. As you would guess, using neutral technologies such as HTTP and XML data representation, XML Web services offer an unprecedented level of operating system, platform, and language interoperability.

In this chapter, you learn how to build XML Web services using the .NET platform, which as you will see is *painfully* simple. In addition, this chapter examines a number of surrounding XML Web service-centric topics such as the Simple Object Access Protocol (SOAP) and the Web Service Description Language (WSDL). Once you have come to understand the composition of an XML Web service, this chapter illustrates how a .NET client application may interact with an XML Web service using a related proxy type.

Understanding the Role of XML Web Services

From the highest level, one can simply define an XML Web service as a unit of code that can be invoked via HTTP requests. Unlike a traditional Web application however, XML Web services are not (necessarily) used to emit HTML back to a browser for display purposes. Rather, an XML Web service exposes the same sort of functionality found in a standard .NET code library, in that it defines computational objects that execute a unit of work for the consumer (e.g., crunch some numbers, read information from a data source, or whatnot), return a result (if necessary), and wait for the next request.

Given this definition, XML Web services may seem to be little more than yet another remoting technology. However, let's think this one through a bit. Historically speaking, accessing remote types required platform-specific (and often language-specific) protocols. For example, DCOM clients communicate with remote COM types using tightly coupled ORPC calls. CORBA and EJB (Enterprise Java Beans) applications also require a specific protocol, and EJB requires a specific language (Java). The basic problem at hand is not the technology themselves, but the fact that each is locked into a specific (often proprietary) wire protocol.

Another fundamental problem with these remoting architectures is that they each require the sender and receiver to understand the same underlying type system. For example, a DCOM client must be able to manipulate COM interfaces, while EJB clients must understand Java agents. Even in the case of .NET Remoting, it is assumed that the client and remote servers are both .NET-aware entities. Given this, it should be obvious that a Java client has little clue what to do with a .NET System.Collections.ArrayList object.

XML Web services provide a way for unrelated platforms, operating systems, and programming languages to exchange information in harmony. As you will see, rather than forcing the caller to understand a specific type system (.NET, COM, J2EE, or whatnot), information is passed between systems via XML data representation. Therefore, as long as the client is able to parse a well-formed XML document, it will be able to map the underlying XML elements into platform and/or language specific types.

In addition to a neutral type system, Web services allow you to invoke methods and properties of a remote object using standard HTTP requests. To be sure, of all the protocols in existence today, HTTP is the one specific wire protocol that all platforms can agree on (after all, HTTP is the backbone of the World Wide Web).

In a nutshell, XML Web services offer a way to let the Web provide information that can be pieced together to build a platform- and language-agnostic distributed system.

XML Web Service Consumers

One aspect of XML Web services that might not be readily understood is the fact that an XML Web service consumer does *not* need to be a traditional Web client. As you will see, console-based and Windows Forms-based clients can use a Web service just as easily. In each case, the XML Web service consumer indirectly interacts with the distant Web service through an intervening proxy type.

The proxy (which is described in detail later in the chapter) looks and feels like the real remote type and exposes the same set of members. Under the hood, however, the proxy's implementation code forwards requests to the XML Web service using standard HTTP. The proxy also maps the incoming stream of XML back into .NET-specific data types (or whatever type system is required by the consumer application). Figure 20-1 illustrates the fundamental nature of XML Web services (do note that the scenarios presented here are *not* all-encompassing).

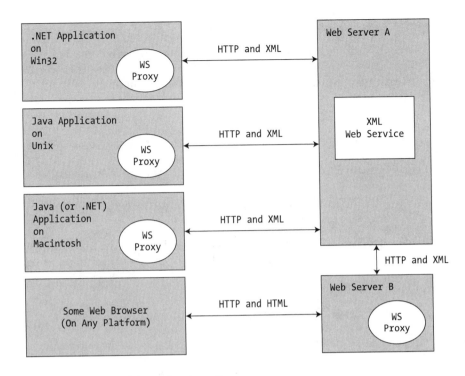

Figure 20-1. XML Web services in action

Again, notice how each consumer application makes use of a language-specific proxy type, which (a) forwards calls to the remote Web service via HTTP, and (b) maps the incoming XML stream back into platform-specific data types. Also note that if the XML Web service client happens to be a Web application (such as an ASP.NET *.aspx file), the Web page itself is the actual client of the Web service. This page may (or may not) make use of the incoming XML data stream to emit an HTML-based UI to the requesting browser.

NOTE   Technically, Internet Explorer 5.0 (and higher) is capable of being the direct client of an XML Web service using WebService behaviors. If you are interested in checking this out, read the article "About the WebService Behavior" online at http://msdn.microsoft.com.

The Building Blocks of an XML Web Service

XML Web services built using the .NET platform are typically hosted by IIS using a unique virtual directory (much like a standard ASP.NET Web application). However, in addition to the managed code that constitutes the exported functionality, an XML Web service requires some supporting infrastructure. Specifically, an XML Web service involves the following key services:

- A discovery service (so clients can resolve the location of the XML Web service)

- A description service (so clients know what the XML Web service can do)

- A transport protocol (to pass the information between the client and the XML Web service)

We'll examine details behind each core requirement throughout this chapter. However, to get into the proper frame of mind, ponder the following overview of each supporting technology.

Previewing XML Web Service Discovery

Before a client can invoke the functionality of a Web service, it must first know of its existence and location. Now, if you are the individual (or company) who is building both the client and XML Web service, the discovery phase is quite simple, given that you already know the location of the Web service in question. However, what if you wish to share the functionality of your Web service with the world at large?

To do this, you have the option of registering your Web service with a UDDI (Universal Description, Discovery and Integration) server. Clients may submit a request to a UDDI catalog to find a list of all Web services that match some search criteria (e.g., "Find me all Web services having to do with financial calculations"). Once you have identified a specific XML Web server from the list returned via the UDDI query, you are then able to investigate its overall functionality. If you like, consider UDDI to be the yellow pages of XML Web services.

In addition to UDDI, an XML Web service built using .NET can be exposed to the masses using DISCO, which is a rather forced acronym standing for Discovery of Web Services. Using a *.disco (or *.vsdisco) file, you are able to advertise the set of XML Web services that are located at a specific URL. For the most part, *.disco/*.vsdisco files are consumed by Visual Studio .NET during the design of a Web service client.

Understand, however, that by default, DISCO functionality is disabled, given the potential security risk of exposing IIS to report the set of all exposed Web services to any interested individual (in fact, the autogenerated *.vsdisco files which used to appear when using VS .NET 2002 are no longer autogenerated). Given these issues, I do not comment on DISCO services for the remainder of this text.

NOTE   If you wish to activate DISCO support for a given Web server, look up the Microsoft Knowledge Base article Q307303 on http://support.microsoft.com.

Previewing XML Web Service Description

Once a client knows the location of a given XML Web service, the client in question must fully understand the exposed functionality. For example, the client must know that there is a method named Foo() that takes three parameters of type {string, bool, int} and returns a custom type named Bar before it can invoke it. As you may be thinking, this is a job for a platform-, language-, and operating system-neutral metalanguage. Specifically speaking, the XML-based grammar used to describe a Web service is termed the Web Service Description Language, or simply WSDL.

The role of WSDL is to describe the functionality of a Web service in a neutral format. In many ways, WSDL is the Web service equivalent of COM-centric type libraries or .NET-centric metadata (recall the Ctrl+M keystroke of ildasm.exe). The distinguishing mark with regard to WSDL syntax is that it describes an XML Web service using the big-string known as XML. Thus, as long as your client can parse a string, it will be able to understand the functionality of a remote Web service.

For the most part, the underlying WSDL can be safely ignored (although the .NET base class libraries do provide a specific namespace devoted to processing WSDL documents). As you will see, the primary consumers of WSDL contracts are proxy generation tools. For example, the wsdl.exe command line utility (as well as the VS .NET Add Web Reference wizard) will generate a C# proxy class based on the data contained in a WSDL document.

Previewing the Transport Protocol

Once the client has created a proxy type to communicate with the remote XML Web service, it is now able to call the exposed Web methods. As mentioned, HTTP is the wire protocol that transmits this data. Specifically however, you can use HTTP GET, HTTP POST, or SOAP to move information between consumers and Web services.

By and large, SOAP will be your first choice, for as you will see, SOAP messages can contain XML descriptions of very complex types (including your custom types as well as serializable types within the .NET libraries). On the other hand, if you make use of the HTTP GET or HTTP POST protocols, you are restricted to a more limited set of core data types. As you would hope, the .NET platform supports all three modes of activation.

The .NET XML Web Service Namespaces

Now that you have an understanding of the role of XML Web services and the surrounding technologies, we can get down to the business of building such a creature using the .NET platform. As you would imagine, the base class libraries define a number of namespaces that allow you interact with each Web service-centric technology (Table 20-1).

Table 20-1. XML Web Service-Centric Namespaces

Web Service-Centric Namespace	Meaning in Life
System.Web.Services	This surprisingly small namespace contains the minimal and complete set of types needed to build a Web service, such as the almighty WebMethodAttribute type.
System.Web.Services.Configuration	These types allow you to configure the runtime behavior of an ASP.NET XML Web service.
System.Web.Services.Description	These types allow you to programmatically interact with the WSDL document that describes a given Web service.
System.Web.Services.Discovery	These types allow a Web consumer to programmatically discover the Web services installed on a given machine.
System.Web.Services.Protocols	This namespace defines a number of types that represent the atoms of the various XML Web service wire protocols (HTTP GET, HTTP POST, and SOAP).

NOTE   All XML Web service-centric namespaces are contained within the System.Web.Services.dll assembly.

Examining the System.Web.Services Namespace

Despite the rich functionality provided by the .NET Web services namespaces, a vast majority of your applications will only require you to directly interact with the types defined in System.Web.Services. As you can see from Table 20-2, the number of types is quite small (which is a good thing).

Table 20-2. Members of the System.Web.Services Namespace

System.Web.Services Type	Meaning in Life
WebMethodAttribute	Adding the [WebMethod] attribute to a method or property in a Web service class type marks the member as invokable via HTTP.
WebService	Defines the (optional) base class for XML Web services built using .NET. If you choose to derive from this base type, your XML Web service will have the ability to retain stateful information.
WebServiceAttribute	The [WebService] attribute may be used to add information to a Web service, such as a string describing its functionality and underlying XML namespace.
WebServiceBindingAttribute	Declares the binding protocol a given Web service method is implementing (HTTP GET, HTTP POST, or SOAP).

The remaining namespaces are typically only of direct use to you if you are interested in manually interacting with a WSDL document, UDDI services, or manipulating the underlying wire protocols. While you will see relevant aspects of these additional namespaces where necessary, consult online Help for complete details of the remaining namespaces if you so choose.

Building an XML Web Service in the Raw

Like any .NET application, XML Web services can be developed manually, without the use of an integrated development environment such as VS .NET. To illustrate, let's get to know the types within the System.Web.Services namespace by building a Web service by hand. Using your text editor of choice, create a new file named HelloWorldWS.asmx and enter the following type definition (by convention, *.asmx is the extension used to mark .NET Web service files):

```
<%@ WebService Language="C#" Class="HelloWS.HelloClass" %>
namespace HelloWS
{
    public class HelloClass
    {
        [System.Web.Services.WebMethod]
        public string HelloWorld()
        { return "Hello!"; }
    }
}
```

For the most part, this *.asmx file looks like any other C# namespace definition. The first noticeable difference is the use of the <%@WebService%> directive, which at minimum must specify the name of the managed language used to build the contained class definition and the name of the class type itself. In addition to the Language and Class attributes, the <%@WebService%> directive may also take Debug attribute (to inform the ASP.NET compiler to emit debugging symbols) and an optional CodeBehind value (which has an identical role to that of the same value used for *.aspx files). Here, we have avoided the use of a code behind file and embedded all required logic directly within HelloWorldWS.asmx.

NOTE The only other directive that may appear in an *.asmx file is <%@Assembly%>, used to mark the names of external assemblies (or file names) that will be used during the ASP.NET compilation cycle. The additional *.aspx directives examined in the previous chapter (such as <%@Import%>) are not valid. Thus, if you would rather not use fully qualified names in your code base (as seen here), simply use the C# "using" keyword.

In addition to the <%@WebService%> directive, the only other distinguishing characteristic of our *.asmx file is the use of the [WebMethod] attribute, which informs the ASP.NET runtime that this method is reachable via incoming HTTP requests.

Creating the IIS Virtual Directory

Now that you have created the HelloWS Web service, the next step is to host this file within a virtual directory. Using the information presented in Chapter 18, create a new virtual directory named HelloWS that maps to the physical folder containing the HelloWorldWS.asmx file (for example, C:\HelloWS).

Testing Your XML Web Service

When you install the .NET Framework, ASP.NET is configured to automatically display a browser-based UI to test installed Web services. When an HTTP request comes in that maps to a given *.asxm file, the ASP.NET runtime makes use of a file named DefaultWsdlHelpGenerator.aspx to create an HTML display that allows you to invoke the Web methods at a given URL (and yes, if you really want to, you can alter the code within this file to suit your needs...edit with care). To illustrate this makeshift client, open your browser of choice and navigate to the HelloWorldWS.asmx file:

```
http://localhost/HelloWS/HelloWorldWS.asmx
```

At this point, you are presented with a list of all Web methods exposed from this URL (Figure 20-2).

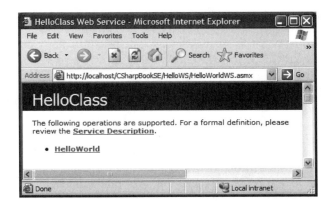

Figure 20-2. Viewing the functionality of the HelloWorldWS Web service

If you click the HelloWorld link, you will be passed to another page that allows you to invoke the [WebMethod] in question. Once you invoke your Web method, you will not be returned a literal .NET-centric System.String, but rather the XML data representation of the textual data returned from the HelloWorld() Web method (Figure 20-3).

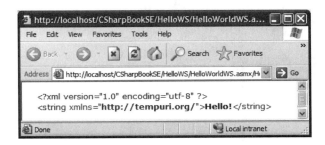

Figure 20-3. Web method return values are expressed in terms of XML.

Although the ASP.NET runtime will dynamically generate an HTML front end to test your Web service, you may wonder what is involved in creating a real client (such as a Windows Forms application). Given that Web methods emit return values via XML, you may fear that you will be required to manually open an HTTP channel and parse the incoming XML tokens back into .NET data types. While you most certainly are free to do so (using types within various .NET namespaces), both .NET SDK and VS .NET provide tools that automate this process. We'll check out client-side functionality later in this chapter.

Viewing the WSDL Contract

As mentioned earlier in this chapter, WSDL is a metalanguage that describes how Web methods can be invoked using the HTTP GET, HTTP POST, and SOAP wire protocols. Notice that when you test a Web services using the autogenerated HTML-based UI, you see a link at the very top of your service's home page named "Service Description." If you click this link, the request is appended with the token "?WSDL." When the ASP.NET runtime receives a request for an *.asmx file tagged with this suffix, it will automatically return the underlying WSDL that describes each Web method.

Once you click this link, you may be alarmed with the verbose nature of WSDL. At this point don't concern yourself with the format of the generated WSDL document. For the time being, just understand that WSDL describes how Web methods can be invoked using each of the current XML Web service wire protocols.

Viewing the Compiled .NET Assembly

As you have just seen, when you deploy your *.asmx files, you are not required to manually compile the code into a .NET *.dll assembly. Rather, when the Web service is first requested, the ASP.NET runtime compiles the *.dll file dynamically. Recall from Chapter 18 that ASP.NET stores compiled *.dlls under the <drive>:\<%windir%>\Microsoft.NET\ Framework\<*version*>\Temporary ASP.NET Files\<*Autogenerated folder names*> subdirectory. Like a compiled ASP.NET Web application, this *.dll can be loaded into ildasm.exe for further exploration (Figure 20-4).

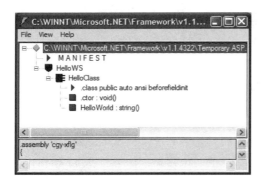

Figure 20-4. Viewing the compiled .NET assembly

Given that we did not deploy a precompiled assembly for the current example, the ASP.NET compiler generated a unique name for the resulting assembly automatically (mine happens to be cgy-xflg.dll). Had we precompiled our code into a more human-readable assembly (such as HelloWorldWS.dll) and deployed this *.dll to a \bin subdirectory under the hosting virtual directory, we would find the shadow copy would sport an identical name.

In addition to the fact that the autogenerated *.dll has no semantic relationship to the name of the original *.asmx file, another issue is the fact that any and all syntactic errors in the *.asmx file are discovered at *runtime* when the ASP.NET compiler kicks in. Had we precompiled the *.asmx file into a .NET assembly, we would be able to squash out any and all typos at *compile* time.

The good news is, when you make use of VS .NET to build your XML Web services, you will always receive a precompiled assembly (placed under the IIS \bin directory) that is named according to your project settings. Given these benefits, I will make use of VS .NET for the remainder of this chapter.

SOURCE CODE   The HelloWorldWS.asmx file is included under the Chapter 20 subdirectory.

Building an XML Web Service Using Visual Studio .NET

Now that you have created an XML Web service by hand, let's see how VS .NET helps get you up and running. Fire up Visual Studio .NET and create a new C# XML Web service project named CalcWebService (Figure 20-5).

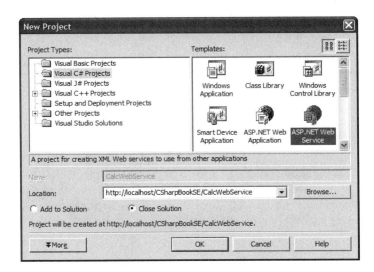

Figure 20-5. Creating a new VS .NET XML Web Service project

Like an ASP.NET application, VS .NET automatically creates a new virtual directory under IIS to host your XML Web service and stores your solution file (*.sln) under the My Documents\ Visual Studio Projects subdirectory.

The Global.asax and Web.config files serve the same purpose as (and look identical to) an ASP.NET application. As you recall from Chapter 19, the Global.asax file allows you to respond to global-level events while web.config allows you to declaratively configure the behavior of your new XML Web service. In addition, VS .NET has created a *.asmx and *.asmx.cs code behind file to which you are able to implement the exposed functionality. Finally, like any .NET application created with VS .NET, you are also provided with the AssemblyInfo.cs file that documents any assembly-level attributes.

The Code Behind File (*.asmx.cs)

When you create a new VS .NET XML Web service project, you will be presented with a design-time component tray that may be used to hold any and all components used by the *.asmx file (such as ADO.NET data components). To view the code behind this design-time template, simply click the "Click here to switch to view code" link to switch to view code link on the designer. Once you do, you will find the following class definition (including a commented-out HelloWorld() Web method, removed for clarity):

```
public class Service1 : System.Web.Services.WebService
{
    public Service1(){  InitializeComponent(); }
    private IContainer components = null;
    private void InitializeComponent() { }
    protected override void Dispose( bool disposing )
    {
        if(disposing && components != null)
        {
            components.Dispose();
        }
        base.Dispose(disposing);
    }
}
```

The only real point of interest is the fact that you derive from a new base class: WebService. You examine the members defined by this type in just a moment. For now, just understand that .NET XML Web services have the *option* of deriving from this base class type. In fact, if you comment out the overridden Dispose() method and derive directly from System.Object, the Web service still functions correctly, as shown here:

```
// I'm still a Web service!
public class Service1 // : System.Web.Services.WebService
{
    public Service1() {  InitializeComponent(); }
    ...
    private void InitializeComponent() { }
    // protected override void Dispose(bool disposing) {...}
}
```

Adding Some Functionality

Rename your initial class type to CalcWS and your initial *.asmx file to CalcWS.asmx. Next, define four Web methods that allow the outside world to add, subtract, multiply, and divide two integers:

```
public class CalcWS : System.Web.Services.WebService
{
    public CalcWS() {  InitializeComponent(); }
...
    [WebMethod]
    public int Add(int x, int y){  return x + y; }
    [WebMethod]
    public int Subtract(int x, int y){  return x - y; }
    [WebMethod]
    public int Multiply(int x, int y){  return x * y; }
    [WebMethod]
    public int Divide(int x, int y)
    {
        // To accommodate all wire protocols, simply return 0
        // (rather than a DivideByZeroException type, which is SOAP-specific).
        if(y == 0)
            return 0;
        else
            return x / y;
    }
}
```

Invoking the CalcWS Web Methods

Testing CalcWS is identical to the process of testing the previous HelloWS XML Web service (using VS .NET, you may run or debug the Web service directly within the IDE). Do note that when you are testing a Web method that requires parameters, the autogenerated HTML UI accounts for each argument (Figure 20-6).

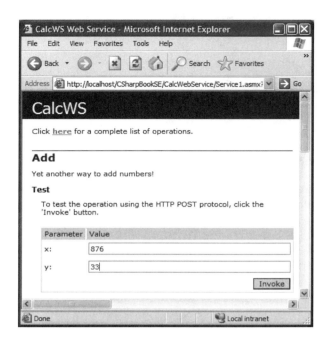

Figure 20-6. Invoking the Add() Web method

Understanding the System.Web.Services.WebService Base Class

As seen during the development of the HelloWS project, .NET Web services are free to derive directly from System.Object. However, by default, Web services developed using Visual Studio .NET automatically derive from the System.Web.Service.WebService base class. This type equips your .NET XML Web service to leverage the same core functionality used by full blown ASP.NET Web apps (Table 20-3).

Table 20-3. Key Members of the System.Web.Services.WebService Type

Property of System.Web.Services.WebService	Meaning in Life
Application	Provides access to the HttpApplicationState type
Context	Provides access to the HttpContext type (which gives you access to the incoming HTTP request and outgoing HTTP response via the Request and Response properties)
Server	Provides access to the HttpServerUtility type
Session	Provides access to the HttpSessionState type for the current session

As you will see, if you wish to build a stateful Web service, you are required to derive from System.Web.Services.WebService, given that this type defines the Application and Session properties. The Context property and Server properties also provide access to the HttpContext and HttpServerUtility types, which allow you to interact with the raw request and response streams (among other things).

Understanding the [WebMethod] Attribute

As noted, the [WebMethod] attribute must be applied to each public method you wish to expose to the outside world through HTTP. Like most attributes, the WebMethodAttribute type may take a number of optional constructor parameters. Table 20-4 lists the core properties of the WebMethodAttribute type.

Table 20-4. Key Members of the WebMethodAttribute Type

WebServiceAttribute Property	Meaning in Life
Description	Used to add a friendly text description of your Web method.
EnableSession	By default, this property is set to true, which configures this method to maintain session state. You may disable this behavior if you set it to false.
MessageName	This property can be used to configure how a Web method is represented in terms of WSDL (typically to avoid name clashes).
TransactionOption	Web methods can function as the root of a COM+ style transaction. This property may be assigned any value from the System.EnterpriseServices.TransactionOption enumeration (which will require you to set a reference to the System.EnterpriseServices.dll assembly).

Documenting a Web Method via the Description Property

The Description property of the WebMethodAttribute type allows you to describe the functionality of a particular Web method. To illustrate, update each of your Web methods with a friendly help string. For example:

```
[WebMethod(Description = "Yet another way to add numbers!")]
public int Add(int x, int y){  return x + y; }
```

If you compile and test once again, you see something like Figure 20-7.

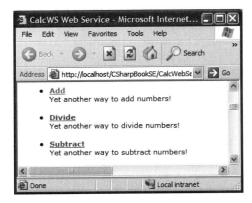

Figure 20-7. Documenting your Web methods

Under the hood, when you set the Description property, the WSDL contract is updated with a new <documentation> element, which can be viewed via the Service Description link of your Web service's home page:

```
<operation name="Add">
    <documentation>Yet another way to add numbers!</documentation>
    <input message="s0:AddSoapIn" />
    <output message="s0:AddSoapOut" />
</operation>
```

As you would guess, it would be completely possible to build a custom utility that reads the value contained within the <documentation> element (for example, an XML Web service-centric object browser). In most cases however, this value will be used by the makeshift browser-based client.

Avoiding WSDL Name Clashes via the MessageName Property

The MessageName property of the System.Web.Services.WebMethod type is of special interest. To illustrate its usefulness, assume your Web calculator now defines an overloaded version of Add() which operates on two floats:

```
[WebMethod(Description = "Add 2 integers.")]
public int Add(int x, int y){  return x + y; }
 [WebMethod(Description = "Add 2 floats.")]
public float Add(float x, float y){  return x + y; }
```

If you recompile your updated class, you will be happy to find you are error-free. However, when you request access to the Web service, you find the following error displayed in the makeshift browser client:

```
System.Exception: Both Single Add(Single, Single) and Int32 Add(Int32, Int32)
use the message name 'Add'.
```

One requirement of WSDL is that each <soap:operation soapAction> element (which is used to define the name of a given Web method) must be uniquely named. However, the default behavior of the ASP.NET WSDL generator is to generate the <soap:operation soapAction> name *exactly* as it appears in the .NET assembly metadata definition (which is why you ended up with two Web methods named Add().)

To resolve the name clash, you can either rename your method (e.g., AddFloats()) or use the MessageName property to establish a unique name within the WSDL document, as shown here:

```
[WebMethod(Description = "Add 2 integers.")]
public int Add(int x, int y){  return x + y; }
 [WebMethod(Description = "Add 2 floats.", MessageName = "AddFloats")]
public float Add(float x, float y){  return x + y; }
```

With this, you can see that each WSDL description is now unique:

```
<operation name="Add">
     <documentation>Add 2 floats.</documentation>
     <input name="AddFloats" message="s0:AddFloatsSoapIn" />
     <output name="AddFloats" message="s0:AddFloatsSoapOut" />
</operation>
<operation name="Add">
     <documentation>Yet another way to add numbers!</documentation>
     <input message="s0:AddSoapIn" />
     <output message="s0:AddSoapOut" />
</operation>
```

As you will see a bit later in this chapter, the client-side proxy type transparently maps these unique WSDL names back into true overloaded Add() methods.

Building Stateful Web Services via the EnableSession Property

As you recall from Chapter 19, the inherited Application and Session properties allow an ASP.NET Web application to maintain stateful data. Web services provide the exact same functionality via the System.Web.Services.WebService base class. For example, assume your CalcWebService maintains an application-level variable (and is thus available to each session) that holds the value of PI, as shown here:

```
public class CalcWebService: System.Web.Services.WebService
{
    // This Web method provides access to an app level variable
    // named SimplePI.
    [WebMethod(Description = "Get app variable")]
    public float GetSimplePI()
    { return (float)Application["SimplePI"]; }
    ...
}
```

The initial value of the SimplePI application variable could be established with the Application_Start() event handler defined in the Global.asax.cs file (recall that the Global class type defines numerous application and session-level event handlers):

```
public class Global : System.Web.HttpApplication
{
...
    protected void Application_Start(Object sender, EventArgs e)
    {
        Application["SimplePI"] = 3.14F;
    }
}
```

In addition to maintaining application-wide variables, you may also make use of the HttpSessionState type (via the inherited Session property) to maintain session-centric information. For the sake of illustration, update the Global.Session_Start() method to assign a random number to each user who is logged on:

```
public class Global : System.Web.HttpApplication
{
...
    protected void Session_Start(Object sender, EventArgs e)
    {
        // To prove session state data is available from a Web service,
        // simply assign a random number to each user.
        Random r = new Random();
        Session["SessionRandomNumber"] = r.Next(1000);
    }
}
```

Now, create a new Web method that returns the user's randomly assigned value:

```
[WebMethod(EnableSession = true,
    Description = "Get your random number!")]
public int GetMyRandomNumber()
{ return (int)Session["SessionRandomNumber"]; }
```

Note that the [WebMethod] attribute has explicitly set the EnableSession property to true. This step is not optional, given that by default, each Web method has session state *disabled*. If you were now to launch two or three browsers (to generate a set of session IDs), you would find that each logged-on user is returned a unique numerical token. For example, client A may receive the following XML:

```
<?xml version="1.0" encoding="utf-8" ?>
<int xmlns="http://www.intertech-inc.com/WebServers">931</int>
```

while client B may find the value 472:

```
<?xml version="1.0" encoding="utf-8" ?>
<int xmlns="http://www.intertech-inc.com/WebServers">472</int>
```

Configuring Session State via web.config

Finally, do be aware that the web.config file may be updated to configure how state is configured for your XML Web service using the <sessionState> element (described in the previous chapter).

```
<sessionState
    mode="InProc"
    stateConnectionString="tcpip=127.0.0.1:42424"
    sqlConnectionString="data source=127.0.0.1;Trusted_Connection=yes"
    cookieless="false"
    timeout="20"
/>
```

Understanding the [WebService] Attribute

In addition to the [WebMethod] attribute, you are also able to qualify the functionality of the Web service itself using the [WebService] attribute. This type defines a few optional properties of interest, the first of which is Namespace.

The WebServiceAttribute.Namespace property can be used to establish the name of the default XML namespace to use within the WSDL document. In a nutshell, XML namespaces are used to scope custom XML elements within a specific group (just like .NET namespaces). By default, the ASP.NET runtime will assign a dummy XML namespace of http://tempuri.org, which can be seen at the home page for a given *.asmx file (Figure 20-8).

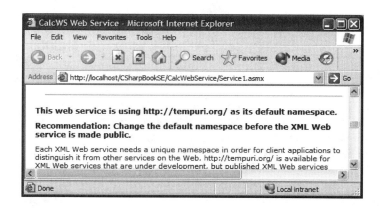

Figure 20-8. The dummy value for your XML namespace is http://tempuri.org.

Before you publish your Web service to the world at large, you should supply a proper namespace that reflects the point of origin. Thus, if you wish to describe and qualify an XML namespace, you can make use of the [WebService] attribute as follows (note that the [WebService] attribute also supports the Description property):

```
[WebService(Description = "The Amazing Calculator Web Service!",
Namespace ="http://www.intertech-inc.com/WebServices")]
public class CalcWS : System.Web.Services.WebService
{... }
```

If you rerun the application, you will find that the warning to replace tempuri.org is no longer present. Furthermore, if you click the Service Description link to view the underlying WSDL, you will find that the TargetNamespace attribute has now been updated with your custom URI.

The final property of the WebServiceAttribute type is Name, which is used to establish the name of the XML Web service exposed to the outside world. By default, the external name of a Web service is identical to the name of the class type itself. However, if you wish to de-couple the .NET class name from the underlying WSDL name, you can update the [WebService] attribute as follows:

```
[WebService(Description = "The Amazing Calculator Web Service!",
    Namespace ="http://www.intertech-inc.com/WebServices",
    Name = "MyWayCoolWebCalculator")]
public class CalcWS : System.Web.Services.WebService
{
    ...
}
```

SOURCE CODE   The files for the CalcWebService project can be found under the Chapter 20 subdirectory.

Exploring the Web Service Description Language (WSDL)

Now that you have seen two XML Web services in action, let's examine some additional syntactic details of WSDL. Recall that WSDL is an XML-based grammar that describes how external clients can interact with the Web methods at a given URL, using each of the supported wire protocols. In many ways a WSDL document can be viewed as a contract between the Web service client and the Web service itself. To this end, it is yet another metalanguage. Specifically, WSDL is used to describe the following characteristics for each exposed Web method:

- The name of the XML Web method

- The number of, type of, and ordering of parameters (if any)

- The type of return value (if any)

- The HTTP GET, HTTP POST, and SOAP calling conventions

In most cases, WSDL documents are generated automatically by the hosting Web server. Recall that when you append the "?WSDL" suffix to a URL that points to an *.asmx file, IIS will emit the WSDL document for the specified XML Web service:

```
http://localhost/SomeWS/theWS.asmx?WSDL
```

As you would expect, this approach is typically all you need to concern yourself with. However, it is also possible to begin a Web service project by building the WSDL document by hand. This approach really highlights the fact that WSDL documents function as a contract between the sender and receiver, and is reminiscent of the process taken by C++ COM developers ("first define the IDL... then implement the coclass"). Once this WSDL document has been created, it may be passed into the wsdl.exe utility to build a client-side proxy file as well as the shell of the server-side *.asmx file.

As you would imagine, taking this approach would require you to have a very intimate view of the WSDL grammar, which is beyond the scope of this chapter. Nevertheless, you'll see numerous examples of working with the wsdl.exe command line tool in the sections that follow. Before that point, however, let's get to know the basic structure of a valid WSDL document.

The Basic Format of a WSDL Document

A valid WSDL document is opened and closed using the root <definitions> element. The opening tag typically defines various xmlns attributes. These qualify the XML namespaces that define various subelements. At minimum, the <definitions> element will specify the namespace where the WSDL elements themselves are defined (http://schemas.xmlsoap.org/wsdl). To be useful, the opening <definitions> tag will also specify numerous XML namespaces that define simple data WSDL types, XML schema, SOAP elements, as well as the target namespace. For example:

```
<?xml version="1.0" encoding="utf-8"?>
<definitions xmlns="http://schemas.xmlsoap.org/wsdl/"
xmlns:soap="http://schemas.xmlsoap.org/wsdl/soap/"
xmlns:s="http://www.w3.org/2001/XMLSchema"
xmlns:s0="http://tempuri.org/"
xmlns:soapenc="http://schemas.xmlsoap.org/soap/encoding/"
xmlns:mime="http://schemas.xmlsoap.org/wsdl/mime/"
targetNamespace="http://tempuri.org/"
xmlns="http://schemas.xmlsoap.org/wsdl/">
</definitions>
```

Within the scope of the root element, you will find five possible subelements. Thus, a bare-bones WSDL document would look something like the following:

```
<?xml version="1.0" encoding="utf-8"?>
<definitions ...>
    <type>
        <!-- List of types exposed from WS ->
    </type>
    <message>
        <!-- Format of the messages ->
    </ message>
    <portType>
        <!-- Port information ->
    </portType>
    <binding>
        <!-- Binding information ->
    </binding>
    <service>
        <!-- Information about the XML Web Service itself ->
    </service>
</definitions>
```

As you would guess, each of these subelements will contain additional elements and attributes to further describe the intended functionality. Let's check out the key nodes in turn.

The <type> Element

First, we have the <type> element, which contains descriptions of any and all custom types exposed from the Web service. You will learn exactly how to expose custom .NET data types via a given Web method a bit later in this chapter. However, for the sake of illustration, assume you have defined a Web method that takes as a parameter a structure named Foo. The Foo structure defines two fields named theInt and theString:

```
public struct Foo
{
    int theInt;
    string theString;
}
```

The underlying <type> element would describe Foo as a <complexType> as follows:

```
<s:complexType name="Foo">
    <s:sequence>
        <s:element minOccurs="1" maxOccurs="1" name="theInt" type="s:int" />
        <s:element minOccurs="0" maxOccurs="1" name="theString" type="s:string" />
    </s:sequence>
</s:complexType>
```

In addition to complex type descriptions, the <type> block also lists any core WSDL data types defined by the http://www.w3.org/2001/XMLSchema XML namespace that have been exposed from the set of Web methods (string, int, float, double, and so forth).

The <message> Element

The <message> element is used to define the format of the request and response exchange for a given Web method. Given that a single Web service allows multiple messages to be transmitted between the sender and receiver, it is permissible for a single WSDL document to define multiple <message> elements.

Regardless of how many <message> elements are defined within a WSDL document, they tend to occur in pairs. The first definition represents the input-centric format of the message, while the second defines the output-centric format of the same message. For example, if you define a single Web method named MyMethod(), which takes no parameters and returns nothing, the SOAP <message> pair could be constructed as follows:

```
<message name="MyMethodSoapIn">
    <part name="parameters" element="sO:MyMethod" />
</message>
<message name="MyMethodSoapOut">
    <part name="parameters" element="sO:MyMethodResponse" />
</message>
```

In reality, <message> elements are not all that useful in and of themselves. However, these message definitions are referenced by other aspects of the WSDL document.

The <portType> Element

The <portType> element defines the characteristics of the various correspondences that can occur between the client and server, each of which is represented by an <operation> subelement. As you would guess, the most common operation is the classic HTTP request/response cycle. Additional operations do exist, however. For example, the one-way operation allows a client to send a message to a given Web server but does not receive a response (sort of a fire-and-forget method invocation). The solicit/response operation allows the *server* to issue a request while the *client* responds (which is the exact opposite of the request/response operation).

To illustrate the format of a possible <operation> subelement, here is the WSDL definition for a traditional request/response operation for the MyMethod() Web method described previously:

```
<portType>
    <operation name="MyMethod">
        <input message="sO:MyMethodSoapIn" />
        <output message="sO:MyMethodSoapOut" />
    </operation>
</portType>
```

Note how the <input> and <output> elements make reference to the related message name defined within the <message> element.

The *<binding>* Element

This element specifies the exact format of the HTTP GET, HTTP POST, and SOAP exchanges. By far and away, this is the most verbose of all the subelements contained in the <definition> root. For example, here is the <binding> element definition that describes how a caller may interact with the MyMethod() Web method using SOAP:

```
<binding name="SomeWSSoap" type="s0:SomeWSSoap">
<soap:binding transport="http://schemas.xmlsoap.org/soap/http" style="document" />
    <operation name="MyMethod">
        <soap:operation soapAction=
            "http://tempuri.org/MyMethod" style="document" />
        <input>
            <soap:body use="literal" />
        </input>
        <output>
            <soap:body use="literal" />
        </output>
    </operation>
</binding>
```

The *<service>* Element

Finally we have the <service> element, which specifies the characteristics of the Web service itself (such as its URL). The chief duty of this element is to describe the set of ports exposed from a given Web server. To do so, the <services> element makes use of any number of <port> subelements (not to be confused with the <portType> element.

Viewing the HelloWS WSDL Document

Now that you have received a high-level tour of the various blocks of information contained in a WSDL document, let's conclude our investigation of WSDL by viewing the WSDL definition for the HelloWS XML Web service created at the onset of this chapter. To do so, navigate to the URL containing the HelloWorldWS.asmx file and click the Service Description link (or simply append "?WSDL" to the URL query string).

As you can see, the root <definitions> element is indeed adorned with numerous XML namespace definitions. The <types> subelement is quite sparse, given that we have defined a single Web method that takes no arguments and returns a simple string type (if you are interested in viewing how parameters are represented in WSDL syntax, pull up the WSDL document for the CalcWebService and check out the description of the Add() Web method):

```
<!-- Definitions of the types -->
<types>
    <s:schema elementFormDefault="qualified" targetNamespace="http://tempuri.org/">
    <s:element name="HelloWorld">
    <s:complexType />
    </s:element>
        <s:element name="HelloWorldResponse">
            <s:complexType>
                <s:sequence>
                    <s:element minOccurs="0" maxOccurs="1"
                        name="HelloWorldResult" type="s:string" />
                </s:sequence>
            </s:complexType>
        </s:element>
    </s:schema>
</types>
```

As mentioned, the role of the <message> element is to describe the characteristics of the HTTP request and response cycle:

```
<!-- Definitions of the messages -->
<message name="HelloWorldSoapIn">
    <part name="parameters" element="s0:HelloWorld" />
</message>
<message name="HelloWorldSoapOut">
    <part name="parameters" element="s0:HelloWorldResponse" />
</message>
```

The <port> and <binding> elements are defined as so:

```
<!-- Port information -->
<portType name="HelloClassSoap">
    <operation name="HelloWorld">
        <input message="s0:HelloWorldSoapIn" />
        <output message="s0:HelloWorldSoapOut" />
    </operation>
</portType>
```

```
<!-- Binding information -->
<binding name="HelloClassSoap" type="s0:HelloClassSoap">
    <soap:binding transport="http://schemas.xmlsoap.org/soap/http"
        style="document" />
    <operation name="HelloWorld">
        <soap:operation soapAction="http://tempuri.org/HelloWorld"
            style="document" />
        <input>
            <soap:body use="literal" />
        </input>
        <output>
            <soap:body use="literal" />
        </output>
    </operation>
</binding>
```

And finally, there is the <service> element, which describes the HelloWS itself:

```
<!-- Definitions of the WS -->
<service name="HelloClass">
    <port name="HelloClassSoap" binding="s0:HelloClassSoap">
        <soap:address location="http://localhost/HelloWS/HelloWorldWS.asmx" />
    </port>
</service>
```

As you can see, WSDL documents tend to be quite verbose. The good news is that you can lead a productive and happy life as a .NET XML Web service developer without becoming an expert in the nuances of WSDL syntax. Although you are always free to create a *.wsdl document by hand, the chances that you will do so are extremely rare. However, having a basic understanding of WSDL will serve you well, especially if you need to tweak the default element definitions emitted by IIS.

NOTE   Recall that the System.Web.Services.Description namespace contains a plethora of types that allow you to programmatically read and manipulate raw WSDL (so check it out if you are so interested).

The wsdl.exe Command Line Utility

Now that you have a better understanding of WSDL's place in the world, you are ready to check out a command-line tool that ships with the .NET SDK named (surprise, surprise) wsdl.exe. In a nutshell, this tool performs two major tasks:

- Generates a server-side file that functions as a skeleton for implementing the XML Web service

- Generates a client-side file that functions as the proxy to the remote XML Web service

Wsdl.exe supports a number of command-line flags. While you may view all possible options by typing **wsdl -?** at the command prompt, Table 20-5 points out some of the more common arguments (do note that each flag supports a shorthand notation as well, which can also be seen via command prompt help).

Table 20-5. Select Flags of wsdl.exe

Wsdl.exe Command-Line Flag	Meaning in Life
/appsettingurlkey	This option instructs wsdl.exe to build a proxy that does not make use of hard-coded URLs. Instead, the proxy class will be configured to read the URL from a client-side *.config file.
/language	Specifies the language to use for the generated proxy class: CS (C#; default) VB (Visual Basic .NET) JS (JScript) VJS (Visual J#). The default is C#.
/namespace	Specifies the namespace for the generated proxy or template. By default your type will not be defined within a namespace definition!
/out	Specifies the file in which to save the generated proxy code. If not specified, the file name is based on the XML Web service name.
/protocol	Specifies the protocol to use within the proxy code. SOAP is the default. However, you can also specify HttpGet or HttpPost to create a proxy that communicates using simple HTTP GET or POST verbs.
/server	Generates an abstract class for an XML Web service based on the WSDL document.

Transforming WSDL into an XML Web Service Skeleton

One interesting use of the wsdl.exe utility is to generate a skeleton class definition in the language of your choice. Once this source code file has been generated, you have a solid starting point to provide the actual implementation of each Web method. To illustrate, open a command window and specify the /server flag, followed by the name of the WSDL document you wish to process. Note that the WDSL document may be contained in a physical *.wsdl file:

```
wsdl /server SimpleHelloWS_wsdl.wsdl
```

or can be obtained dynamically from a given URL via the ?WSDL suffix:

```
wsdl /server http://localhost/helloWS/HelloWorldWS.asmx?WSDL
```

In either case, once the wsdl.exe tool has processed the WSDL elements, you will end up with a C# source code file (if you wish to receive a file written with a different managed language, simply make use of the /language flag):

```
using System.Diagnostics;
using System.Xml.Serialization;
using System;
using System.Web.Services.Protocols;
using System.ComponentModel;
using System.Web.Services;
 [System.Web.Services.WebServiceBindingAttribute
(Name="HelloClassSoap", Namespace="http://tempuri.org/")]
public abstract class HelloClass : System.Web.Services.WebService
{
    [System.Web.Services.WebMethodAttribute()]
    [System.Web.Services.Protocols.SoapDocumentMethodAttribute
    ("http://tempuri.org/HelloWorld",
     RequestNamespace="http://tempuri.org/",
     ResponseNamespace="http://tempuri.org/",
     Use=System.Web.Services.Description.SoapBindingUse.Literal,
     ParameterStyle=System.Web.Services.Protocols.SoapParameterStyle.Wrapped)]
    public abstract string HelloWorld();
}
```

Again, note that the generated class type is simply a shell that you can use to implement the methods of the XML Web service. Notice, for example, that the HelloClass type and HelloWorld() method have both been defined as abstract entities.

Although this is a very interesting feature of the wsdl.exe utility, the chances are that you would rather have this tool go in the other direction and generate a client-side proxy type that will communicate with the remote Web service. You see how to do this very thing in just a moment. But first, let's dive a bit deeper into the wire protocols.

 SOURCE CODE   The SimpleHelloWS_WSDL.wsdl and proxy skeleton files can be found under the Chapter 20 subdirectory.

Revisiting the XML Web Service Wire Protocols

As you know, the purpose of a Web service is to return XML-based data to a consumer, using the HTTP protocol. Specifically, a Web server bundles this data into the body of an HTTP request and transmits it to the consumer using one of three specific techniques (Table 20-6).

Table 20-6. Web Service Wire Protocols

Transmission Protocol	Meaning in Life
HTTP GET	GET submissions append parameters to the query string of the current URL.
HTTP POST	POST transmissions embed the data points into the header of the HTTP message rather than appending them to the query string.
SOAP	SOAP is a wire protocol that specifies how to submit data and invoke methods across the wire using XML.

While each approach leads to the same result (invoking a Web method), your choice of wire protocol determines the types of parameters (and return types) that can be sent between each interested party. The SOAP protocol offers you the greatest form of flexibility, given that SOAP messages allow you to pass complex data types between the caller and XML Web service (as well as binary files). However, for completion let's check out the role of standard GET and POST.

HTTP GET and HTTP POST Messages

Although GET and POST verbs may be familiar constructs, you must be aware that this method of transportation is not rich enough to represent such complex items as structures or classes. When you use GET and POST verbs, you can only interact with Web methods using the types listed in Table 20-7.

Table 20-7. Supported POST and GET Data Types

Supported GET/POST Data Type	Meaning in Life
Enumerations	GET and POST verbs support the transmission of .NET System.Enum types, given that these types are represented as a static constant string.
Simple Arrays	You can construct arrays of any primitive type.
Strings	GET and POST transmit all numerical data as a string token. *String* really refers to the string representation of CLR primitives such as Int16, Int32, Int64, Boolean, Single, Double, Decimal, and so forth.

If you make use of standard HTTP GET or HTTP POST, you are not able to build Web methods that take complex types as parameters or return values (for example, an ADO.NET DataSet or custom structure type). For simple Web services, this limitation may be acceptable. However, if you make use of SOAP messages, you are able to build much more elaborate XML Web services.

SOAP Messages

Although a complete examination of SOAP is outside the scope of this text, understand that SOAP itself does not define a specific protocol and can thus be used with any number of existing Internet protocols (HTTP, SMTP, and others). The general role of SOAP, however, remains the same: Provide a mechanism to invoke methods using complex types in a language- and platform-neutral manner. To do so, SOAP encodes each complex method using SOAP messages.

In a nutshell, a SOAP message defines two core sections. First we have the SOAP envelope, which can be understood as the conceptual container for the relevant information. Second, we have the rules that are used to describe the information in said message (placed into the SOAP body). An optional third section (the SOAP header) may be used to specify general information regarding the message itself such as security or transactional information.

```
<soap:Envelope xmlns:xsi="http://www.w3.org/2001/XMLSchema-instance"
xmlns:xsd="http://www.w3.org/2001/XMLSchema"
xmlns:soap="http://schemas.xmlsoap.org/soap/envelope/">
    <soap:Header>
        <!-- Optional header information -->
    </soap:Header>
    <soap:Body>
        <!-- Method invocation information -->
    </soap:Body>
</soap:Envelope>
```

Viewing a SOAP Message

Like other aspects of WSDL, you are not required to understand the inner details of SOAP to build XML Web services with the .NET platform. However, when you use the makeshift client browser, you are able to view the format of the SOAP message for each exposed Web method. For example, if you were to click the link for the Add() method of the CalcWebService, you would find the following SOAP request:

```
<soap:Envelope xmlns:xsi="http://www.w3.org/2001/XMLSchema-instance"
xmlns:xsd="http://www.w3.org/2001/XMLSchema"
xmlns:soap="http://schemas.xmlsoap.org/soap/envelope/">
  <soap:Body>
    <Add xmlns="http://www.intertech-inc.com/WebServices">
      <x>int</x>
      <y>int</y>
    </Add>
  </soap:Body>
</soap:Envelope>
```

The corresponding SOAP response looks like this:

```
<soap:Envelope xmlns:xsi="http://www.w3.org/2001/XMLSchema-instance"
xmlns:xsd="http://www.w3.org/2001/XMLSchema"
xmlns:soap="http://schemas.xmlsoap.org/soap/envelope/">
  <soap:Body>
    <AddResponse xmlns="http://www.intertech-inc.com/WebServices">
      <AddResult>int</AddResult>
    </AddResponse>
  </soap:Body>
</soap:Envelope>
```

Transforming WSDL into C# Code (Generating a Proxy)

At this point, you are ready to build custom clients that can consume your XML Web services. Although undesirable, it is completely possible to construct a client-side code base that *manually* requests a WSDL definition and *manually* parses each XML node to establish a connection to the remote service. A much-preferred approach is to leverage wsdl.exe to generate a proxy class that maps to the Web methods defined by a given *.asmx file. To do so, specify the name of proxy file to be generated (via the /out flag) and the URL where the WSDL can be obtained:

```
wsdl.exe /out:c:\MyCalcWSProxy.cs
http://localhost/CSharpBookSE/CalcWebService/CalcWS.asmx?WSDL
```

By default, wsdl.exe will generate proxy code written in C#. However, if you wish to obtain proxy code in an alternative .NET language, make use of the /language flag. You should also be aware that by default, wsdl.exe will generate a proxy that communicates with the remote XML Web service using SOAP. If you wish to build a proxy that leverages straight HTTP GET or HTTP POST, you may make use of the /protocol flag.

Investigating the Proxy Code

If you opened up the generated *.cs file, you would find that you are given a class type that derives from System.Web.Services.Protocols.SoapHttpClientProtocol. This base class defines a number of helper functions that will be leveraged within the implementation of the proxy type. Table 20-8 describes some interesting inherited members.

Table 20-8. Core Members of the SoapHttpClientProtocol Type

Inherited Member	Meaning in Life
BeginInvoke()	Starts an asynchronous invocation of the Web method
EndInvoke()	Ends an asynchronous invocation of the Web method
Invoke()	Synchronously invokes a method of the Web service
Proxy	Gets or sets proxy information for making a Web service request through a firewall
Timeout	Gets or sets the timeout (in milliseconds) used for synchronous calls
Url	Gets or sets the base URL to the server to use for requests
UserAgent	Gets or sets the value for the user agent header sent with each request

The constructor of this proxy class hard codes the URL of the remote Web service and stores it in the inherited Url property:

```
[System.Diagnostics.DebuggerStepThroughAttribute()]
[System.ComponentModel.DesignerCategoryAttribute("code")]
[System.Web.Services.WebServiceBindingAttribute(
Name="MyWayCoolWebCalculatorSoap",
Namespace="http://www.intertech-inc.com/WebServices")]
public class MyWayCoolWebCalculator :
    System.Web.Services.Protocols.SoapHttpClientProtocol
{
    public MyWayCoolWebCalculator()
    {
        this.Url = "http://localhost/CSharpBookSE/CalcWebService/CalcWS.asmx";
    }
...
}
```

The generated proxy code defines synchronous and asynchronous members for each Web method defined in the Web service. As you are aware, synchronous method invocations are blocked until the call returns. Asynchronous method inoculations return control to the calling client immediately after sending the invocation request. When the processing has finished, the runtime makes a callback to the client. Here is the synchronous implementation of the Add() method which takes two System.Int32 types (recall that we overloaded this method):

```
[System.Web.Services.Protocols.SoapDocumentMethodAttribute(
"http://www.intertech-inc.com/WebServices/Add",
RequestNamespace="http://www.intertech-inc.com/WebServices",
ResponseNamespace="http://www.intertech-inc.com/WebServices",
Use=System.Web.Services.Description.SoapBindingUse.Literal,
ParameterStyle=System.Web.Services.Protocols.SoapParameterStyle.Wrapped)]
```

```
public int Add(int x, int y)
{
    object[] results = this.Invoke("Add",
        new object[] {x, y});
    return ((int)(results[0]));
}
```

The asynchronous version of this Add() method is represented by the now familiar BeginXXXX() / EndXXX() method pair:

```
public System.IAsyncResult BeginAdd(int x, int y, System.AsyncCallback callback,
    object asyncState)
{
    return this.BeginInvoke("Add",
        new object[] {x, y}, callback, asyncState);
}
public int EndAdd(System.IAsyncResult asyncResult)
{
        object[] results = this.EndInvoke(asyncResult);
        return ((int)(results[0]));
}
```

The remaining proxy methods are implemented more or less the same way. In a nutshell, each synchronous method packages any incoming parameters into a generic array of System.Object types and passes them into the inherited Invoke() method. The return value (if any) is cast into a .NET specific type. The asynchronous methods take a similar approach, however they make use of the inherited BeginInvoke() and EndInvoke() methods.

Wrapping the Proxy Type Within a .NET Namespace

One update you will want to make for the generated proxy file is to wrap the class in a namespace definition, as shown here:

```
namespace CalcWSClient
{
    public class MyWayCoolWebCalculator :
        System.Web.Services.Protocols.SoapHttpClientProtocol
    {...}
}
```

By default, wsdl.exe will not define a specific namespace unless you explicitly specify the /n flag at the command prompt. For example:

```
wsdl.exe /out:c:\MyCalcWSProxy.cs /n:CalcWSClient
http://localhost/CSharpBookSE/CalcWebService/CalcWS.asmx?WSDL
```

Leveraging the Proxy (Synchronous Invocations)

Once you have your proxy file, you can either compile the type into a stand-alone .NET assembly (via csc.exe) or simply include the *.cs file directly in your client application. In either case, you need to explicitly set a reference to the System.Web.Services.dll assembly (given that the proxy code makes use of numerous types defined within this binary).

At this point the client will simply create an instance of the proxy type and call the methods of interest. All of the grunge work of opening an HTTP channel, formatting the SOAP message, and mapping XML to and from .NET data types is handled on your behalf.

Assume you have created a new C# console application project that directly includes the *.cs proxy file and wraps it into the client's namespace. The client code is straightforward:

```
// Don't forget to set a reference to
// System.Web.Services.dll!
using System;
namespace CalcWSClient
{
    class TheClient
    {
        static void Main(string[] args)
        {
            // Exercise the proxy!
            Console.WriteLine("***** The amazing Web Service Client App *****\n");
            MyWayCoolWebCalculator ws = new MyWayCoolWebCalculator();
            Console.WriteLine("2 + 3 = {0}", ws.Add(2, 3));
            Console.WriteLine("23.4 + 33.1 = {0}", ws.Add(23.4F, 33.1F));
            Console.WriteLine("My random number is: {0}",
                ws.GetMyRandomNumber());
            Console.WriteLine("Simple value of PI is: {0}",
                ws.GetSimplePI());
            Console.WriteLine();
        }
    }
}
```

Regarding Overloaded Web Methods

One point of interest is the fact that the overloaded Add() method defined by the Web service indeed is realized by the client as an overloaded method. Recall that WSDL demands a unique name for each method it is describing (therefore, we are required to make use of the MessageName property when applying the [WebService] attribute). However, if you look at the proxy code, you will find that the System.Web.Services.Protocols.SoapDocumentMethodAttribute type maps the overloaded method to the correct underlying WSDL name, for example:

```
[System.Web.Services.Protocols.SoapDocumentMethodAttribute
("http://www.intertech-inc.com/WebServices/Add",
RequestNamespace="http://www.intertech-inc.com/WebServices",
ResponseNamespace="http://www.intertech-inc.com/WebServices",
Use=System.Web.Services.Description.SoapBindingUse.Literal,
ParameterStyle=System.Web.Services.Protocols.SoapParameterStyle.Wrapped)]
public int Add(int x, int y)
{...}
 [System.Web.Services.WebMethodAttribute(MessageName="Add1")]
[System.Web.Services.Protocols.SoapDocumentMethodAttribute
("http://www.intertech-inc.com/WebServices/AddFloats",
RequestElementName="AddFloats",
RequestNamespace="http://www.intertech-inc.com/WebServices",
ResponseElementName="AddFloatsResponse",
ResponseNamespace="http://www.intertech-inc.com/WebServices",
Use=System.Web.Services.Description.SoapBindingUse.Literal,
ParameterStyle=System.Web.Services.Protocols.SoapParameterStyle.Wrapped)]
[return: System.Xml.Serialization.XmlElementAttribute("dddFloatsResult")]
public System.Single Add(System.Single x, System.Single y)
{...}
```

Leveraging the Proxy (Asynchronous Invocations)

As you have seen at numerous points throughout this text, the .NET platform has native support for asynchronous method invocations. The task of asynchronously invoking a method exposed from a given XML Web service under .NET is once again based on the delegate pattern. Thus, if you wish to asynchronously invoke any of the methods exposed by the Calculator XML Web Service, simply leverage the BeginXXX() and EndXXXX() methods.

Recall that when you wish to invoke a method asynchronously, the IAsyncResult interface allows you to gather the method's return value as well as determine if the call has completed. Thus, you may call Add() asynchronously as follows:

```
IAsyncResult result = ws.BeginAdd(30, 21, null , null);
...
if(result.IsCompleted)
    Console.WriteLine("30 + 32 = {0}", ws.EndAdd(result));
```

If you would rather have the XML Web service call back to the client-side code base (rather than poll the method via the IsCompleted property), you can make use of the AsyncCallback delegate:

```
// Assume 'ws' is a static instance of the Calc proxy.
AsyncCallback cb = new AsyncCallback(AdditionDone);
IAsyncResult result = ws.BeginAdd(30, 21, cb, null);
...
public static void AdditionDone(IAsyncResult result)
{
    Console.WriteLine("30 + 32 = {0}", ws.EndAdd(result));
}
```

SOURCE CODE   The CalcWSClient project can be found under the Chapter 20 subdirectory.

Avoiding Hard-Coded Proxy Logic

The default behavior of wsdl.exe is to hard code the URL of the Web service within the proxy's constructor. The obvious drawback to this situation is that if the URL is renamed or relocated, the proxy class must be updated and recompiled. To build a more flexible proxy type, wsdl.exe provides the /appsettingurlkey flag (which may be abbreviated to /urlkey). When you specify this flag at the command line, the proxy's constructor will contain logic that reads the URL using a key contained within a client-side *.config file.

To illustrate, generate a proxy file for the HelloWS Web service created earlier in this chapter (note that HelloURL is just an arbitrary key that will be placed in the *.config file):

```
C:\>wsdl /urlkey:HelloUrl http://localhost/helloWS/helloworldWS.asmx?WSDL
```

If you now check out the default constructor of the proxy, you will find the following logic (note that if the correct key cannot be found, the hard-coded URL will be used as a backup):

```
public HelloClass()
{
    string urlSetting =
        System.Configuration.ConfigurationSettings.AppSettings["HelloUrl"];
    if ((urlSetting != null))
        this.Url = urlSetting;
    else
        this.Url = "http://localhost/helloWS/helloworldWS.asmx";
}
```

The client-side *.config file would look like this:

```
<?xml version="1.0" encoding="utf-8" ?>
<configuration>
    <appSettings>
        <add key="HelloUrl" value="http://localhost/helloWS/helloworldWS.asmx"/>
    </appSettings>
</configuration>
```

SOURCE CODE   The HelloWSClient project can be found under the Chapter 20 subdirectory.

Generating a Proxy with VS .NET

Although wsdl.exe provides a number of command-line arguments that give you ultimate control over how the resulting proxy class will be generated, VS .NET also allows you to quickly generate a proxy file using the Add Web Reference dialog. To activate this tool, simply right-click the References folder of the Solution Explorer. As you can see from Figure 20-9, you are able to obtain references to existing XML Web services located at a variety of locales.

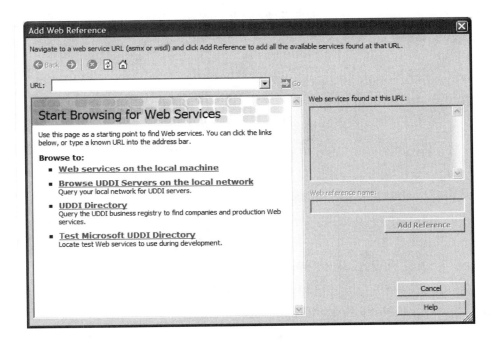

Figure 20-9. The VS .NET Add Web Reference utility

Notice that you are not only able to obtain a list of XML Web services on your local development machine, but you may also query various UDDI catalogs (which we do at the end of this chapter). In any case, once you type a valid URL that points to a given *.wsdl or *.asmx file, your project will contain a new proxy class. Do note that the proxy's namespace (which is based on the URL of origin) will be nested within your client's .NET namespace. Thus, if you added a reference to CalcWS (which is located at http://localhost/CSharpBookSE/CalcWebService/CalcWS.asmx), you would need to specify the following C# using directive:

```
using TheWSClient.localhost;
```

Exposing Arrays of Types from Web Methods

So much for Math 101. The real power of Web services becomes much more evident when you build Web methods that return complex types. To illustrate, let's create a new XML Web service (named CarSalesInfoWS) that is capable of processing arrays, custom UDTs, and ADO.NET DataSets. First, let's examine how to build Web methods that receive and return arrays of information.

Assume you have a Web method named GetSalesTagLines(), which will return an array of strings that represent the current sales for various automobiles. Also assume you have another Web method named SortCarMakes() that allows the caller to pass in an array of unsorted strings and obtain a new array of sorted textual information:

```
namespace CarSalesInfoWS
{
    [WebService(Namespace="http://www.intertech-inc.com/webservices",
     Description="This Web service processes custom types")]
    public class CarSalesInfoService : System.Web.Services.WebService
    {
    ...
        [WebMethod(Description="Get current discount blurbs")]
        public string[] GetSalesTagLines()
        {
            string[] currentDeals = {"Colt prices slashed 50%!",
            "All BMWs come with standard 8-track",
            "Free Pink Caravans...just ask me!"};
            return currentDeals;
        }
        [WebMethod(Description="Sorts a list of car makes")]
        public string[] SortCarMakes(string[] theCarsToSort)
        {
            Array.Sort(theCarsToSort);
            return theCarsToSort;
        }
    }
}
```

Exposing Custom Types from Web Methods

The SOAP protocol is also able to transport XML representations of custom data types (both classes and structures). Interestingly, with the current release of the .NET platform, you are not required to configure these custom types in any way to pass or return custom UDTs. To illustrate, add another Web method named GetSalesInfoDetails(). This method takes no parameters and returns an array of SalesInfoDetails structures:

```
// Helper struct.
public struct SalesInfoDetails
{
    public string info;
    public DateTime dateExpired;
    public string Url;
}
```

The implementation of GetSalesInfoDetails() returns a populated array of this custom UTD as follows:

```
[WebMethod(Description="Get details of current sales")]
public SalesInfoDetails[] GetSalesInfoDetails()
{
    SalesInfoDetails[] theInfo = new SalesInfoDetails[3];
    theInfo[0].info = "Colt prices slashed 50%!";
    theInfo[0].dateExpired = DateTime.Parse("12/02/04");
    theInfo[0].Url= "http://www.CarsRUs.com";
    theInfo[1].info = "All BMWs come with standard 8-track";
    theInfo[1].dateExpired = DateTime.Parse("8/11/03");
    theInfo[1].Url= "http://www.Bmws4U.com";
    theInfo[2].info = "Free Pink Caravans...just ask me!";
    theInfo[2].dateExpired = DateTime.Parse("12/01/09");
    theInfo[2].Url= "http://www.AllPinkVans.com";
    return theInfo;
}
```

A Windows Forms Client

At this point, you can build a client of your choosing. Simply compile the XML Web service project, generate a proxy (a la the Add Web References dialog), and code away. For example, if you have a Windows Forms client application, you could fill a ListBox when you load the main Form with each tag line as follows:

```
private void mainForm_Load(object sender, System.EventArgs e)
{
    CarSalesInfoService ws = new CarSalesInfoService();
    string[] tagLines = ws.GetSalesTagLines();
    foreach(string s in tagLines)
        lstCarSaleTagLines.Items.Add(s);
}
```

You can also get back the array of SalesInfoDetails types in response to a Button Click event as follows:

```
private void btnGetAllDetails_Click(object sender, System.EventArgs e)
{
    CarSalesInfoService ws = new CarSalesInfoService();
    SalesInfoDetails[] theSkinny = ws.GetSalesInfoDetails();
    foreach(SalesInfoDetails s in theSkinny)
    {
        string d = string.Format("Info: {0}\nURL:{1}\nExpiration Date:{2}",
            s.info, s.Url, s.dateExpired);
        MessageBox.Show(d, "Details");
    }
}
```

Exposing Custom Types: The Details

As you have seen, the CarsSalesInfoWS application exposes a Web method that returns an array of SalesInfoDetails structures, which was defined in the server application as so:

```
public struct SalesInfoDetails
{
    public string info;
    public DateTime dateExpired;
    public string Url;
}
```

Again, notice that unlike .NET Remoting, you are not required to mark your custom structures/classes with the [Serializable] attribute. However, if you wish to be more explicit that the SalesInfoDetails type is serialized across the wire as XML, you could update the structure accordingly:

```
[Serializable] public struct SalesInfoDetails
{
    public string info;
    public DateTime dateExpired;
    public string Url;
}
```

One benefit of marking custom types exposed from an XML Web service as serializable is the fact that the same type can be exposed as an MBV type from a .NET Remoting application (where you must mark each MBV type with the [Serializable] attribute).

In either case, however, the .NET runtime will serialize your custom structures and classes using the System.Xml.Serialization.XmlSerializer data type. This type performs the same basic role as the BinaryFormatter and SoapFormatter types (persist a type's state to some stream), however the XmlSerializer can only persist public data and/or private data exposed as public properties. Thus, if the SalesInfoDetails type was updated as follows:

```
[Serializable] public struct SalesInfoDetails
{
    public string info;
    public DateTime dateExpired;
    public string Url;
    private string dealershipName;
}
```

then the dealershipName field would not end up in the resulting XML.

Another point of interest regarding the XmlSerializer is the fact that it allows you to have intimate control over how the type is represented. To illustrate, by default the SalesInfoDetails structure is serialized as so:

```
<SalesInfoDetails>
    <info>Colt prices slashed 50%!</info>
    <dateExpired>2004-12-02T00:00:00.0000000-06:00</dateExpired>
    <Url>http://www.CarsRUs.com</Url>
</SalesInfoDetails>
```

As you can see, each public filed/property becomes a subelement of the root <SalesInfoDetails> element. If you would rather expose each item of the structure as XML properties, you can mock up the structure definitions using attributes found within the System.Xml.Serialization namespace:

```
[XmlRoot]
public struct SalesInfoDetails
{
    [XmlAttribute]public string info;
    [XmlAttribute]public DateTime dateExpired;
    [XmlAttribute]public string Url;
}
```

which would yield the following XML data representation:

```
<SalesInfoDetails info="Colt prices slashed 50%!"
dateExpired="2004-12-02T00:00:00.0000000-06:00"
Url="http://www.CarsRUs.com" />
```

For the most part, you can typically avoid the need to adorn your custom types with XML-centric attributes. However, this can be extremely useful when you need to map the names of a type exposed from an XML Web service into client-side counterparts. As you would hope, the attributes found within the System.Xml.Serialization namespace support various name/value pairs that may be fed into the constructor. If you require such fine tuning, I'll assume you will check out the System.Xml.Serialization namespace at your leisure.

Consuming Custom Types: The Details

When clients set a reference to a Web service that exposes custom types, the proxy class file also contains language definitions for each custom public type. Thus, if you were to examine the client-side representation of this type, you would find the following C# code:

```
[System.Xml.Serialization.XmlTypeAttribute
(Namespace="http://www.intertech-inc.com/webservices")]
public class SalesInfoDetails {
    public string info;
    public System.DateTime dateExpired;
    public string Url;
}
```

Now, understand, of course, that like .NET Remoting, types that are serialized across the wire as XML do not retain implementation logic. Thus, if the SalesInfoDetails structure supported a set of public methods, the proxy generator will fail to account for them (as they are not expressed in the WSDL document in the first place!). However, if you were to distribute a client-side assembly that contained the implementation code of the client-side type, you would be able to leverage the type-specific logic. Doing so, however, would require a .NET-aware machine.

Updating the CarsSalesInfoWS Project

Let's add a final set of Web methods to the CarsSalesInfo application that will illustrate how to leverage CLR types when constructing an XML Web service. Assume you have created another helper structure named Car:

```
public struct Car
{
    public Car(string p, string c, string m)
    {
        petName = p;
        carColor = c;
        carMake = m;
    }
    public string petName;
    public string carColor;
    public string carMake;
}
```

Next, define as private an ArrayList data member (carList) and fill it with some initial cars in the constructor of your Web service, as shown here:

```
public class CarSalesInfoService : System.Web.Services.WebService
{
    private ArrayList theCars = new ArrayList();
    public CarSalesInfoService()
    {
        InitializeComponent();
        theCars.Add(new Car("Biff", "Green", "Firebird"));
        theCars.Add(new Car("Bunny", "Pink", "Colt"));
        theCars.Add(new Car("Chuck", "Red", "BWM"));
        theCars.Add(new Car("Mary", "Red", "Viper"));
        theCars.Add(new Car("Mandy", "Tan", "Golf"));
    }
...
}
```

Now add a method named GetCarList() which returns the entire array of autos. Another method named GetACarFromList() returns a specific car from the array list based on a numerical index. The implementation of each method is simple, as shown here:

```
// Return a given car from the list.
[WebMethod(Description = "Get a specific car from ArrayList")]
public Car GetACarFromList(int carToGet)
{
    if(carToGet <= theCars.Count)
    {
        return (Car) theCars[carToGet];
    }
    throw new IndexOutOfRangeException();
}
// Return the entire set of cars.
[WebMethod(Description = "Get the ArrayList of Cars")]
public ArrayList GetCarList()
{
    return theCars;
}
```

As before, the Car and ArrayList types will be exposed via XML. To wrap things up, here is one final XML Web method that interacts with the Cars database you created during your examination of ADO.NET:

```
// Return all cars in inventory table.
[WebMethod(Description =
    "Returns all autos in the Inventory table of the Cars database")]
public DataSet GetAllCarsFromDB()
{
    // Fill the DataSet with the Inventory table.
    SqlConnection sqlConn = new SqlConnection();
    sqlConn.ConnectionString = "data source=.; initial catalog=Cars;" +
        "user id=sa; password=";
    SqlDataAdapter myDA=
        new SqlDataAdapter("Select * from Inventory", sqlConn);
    DataSet ds = new DataSet();
    myDA.Fill(ds, "Inventory");
    return ds;
}
```

Given that the GetAllCarsFromDB() Web method returns an ADO.NET DataSet (which has already been marked as a serializable type), update the working Windows Forms client to display the results on a DataGrid widget:

```
// Fill data grid.
DataSet ds = ws.GetAllCarsFromDB();
inventoryDG.DataSource = ds.Tables["Inventory"];
```

Figure 20-10 shows the final client-side GUI in action.

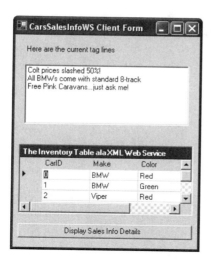

Figure 20-10. A Windows Forms XML Web Service Client application

SOURCE CODE   The CarSalesInfoWS and CarSalesInfoClient projects can be found under the Chapter 20 subdirectory.

Understanding the Discovery Service Protocol (UDDI)

It is a bit ironic that the typical first step taken by a client to chat with a remote Web service is the final topic of this chapter. The reason for such an oddball flow is the fact that the process of identifying if a given Web service exists using UDDI is not only optional, but is unnecessary in a vast majority of cases.

Until XML Web services become the de facto standard of distributed computing (which may take some time), most Web services will be leveraged by companies who are tightly coupled with a given vendor. Given this, the company and vendor at large already know about each other, and therefore have no need to query a UDDI server to see if the Web service in question exists. However, if the creator of an XML Web service wishes to allow the world at large to access the exposed functionality to any number of external developers, the Web service may be posted to a UDDI catalog.

UDDI is an initiative that allows Web service developers to post a commercial Web service to a well-known repository. Despite what you might be thinking, UDDI is not a Microsoft-specific ideal. In fact, IBM (Big Blue) and Sun Microsystems have an equal interest in the success of the UDDI initiative. As you would expect, numerous vendors host UDDI catalogs. For example, Microsoft's official UDDI Web site can be found at `http://uddi.microsoft.com`. The official Web site of UDDI (`http://www.uddi.org`) provides numerous white papers and SDKs that allow you to build up internal UDDI servers.

Interacting with UDDI via VS .NET

Recall that the Add Web Reference dialog box not only allows you to obtain a list of all XML Web services located on your current development machine (as well as a well-known URL), but to submit queries to UDDI servers. Basically, you have the following options:

- Browse for a UDDI server on your internal company intranet.

- Browse the Microsoft-sponsored UDDI production server.

- Browse the Microsoft-sponsored UDDI test server.

To illustrate, assume that you are building an application that needs to discover the current weather forecast on a per ZIP code basis. Your first step would be to query a UDDI catalog with the following question:

- "Do you know of any Web services that pertain to weather data?"

If it is the case that the UDDI server has a list of weather-aware Web services, you are returned a list of all registered URLs that export the functionality of your query. Referencing this list, you are able to pick the specific Web service you wish to communicate with, and eventually obtain the WSDL document that describes the functionality of the weather-centric functionality.

To illustrate, create a brand-new Console application project and activate the Add Web Reference dialog box. Next, select the Test Microsoft UDDI Directory link, which will bring you to the Microsoft UDDI test server. At this point, enter **Weather** as a search criteria (Figure 20-11).

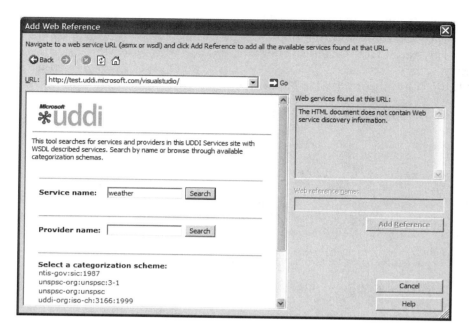

Figure 20-11. Interacting with a UDDI catalog

Once the UDDI catalog has been queried, you will receive a list of all relevant XML Web services (Figure 20-12).

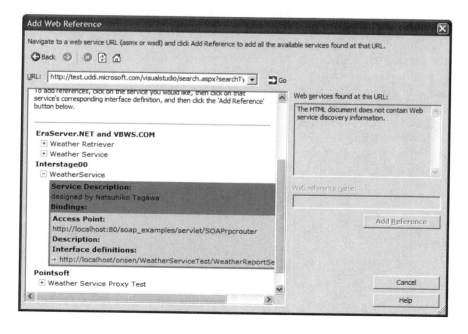

Figure 20-12. Obtaining a list of posted weather-centric Web services

Once you find a posted XML Web service you are interested in programming against, add a reference to your current project. As you would expect, the raw WSDL will be parsed by the tool to provide you with a C# proxy.

NOTE Understand that the UDDI test center is just that. Don't be too surprised if you find a number of broken links. Also be aware that when you query production-level UDDI servers, URLs tend to be much more reliable, given that companies may need to pay some sort of fee to be listed!

Summary

This chapter has exposed you to the core building blocks of .NET Web services. The chapter began by examining the core namespaces (and core types in these namespaces) used during Web service development. As you have seen, Web services developed using the .NET platform require little more than applying the [WebMethod] attribute to each member you wish to expose from the XML Web service type. Optionally, your types may derive from System.Web.Services.WebService to obtain access to the Application and Session properties (among other things). This chapter also examined three key related technologies: a lookup mechanism (UDDI), a description language (WSDL), and a wire protocol (GET, POST, or SOAP).

Once you have created any number of [WebMethod]-enabled members, you can interact with a Web service through an intervening proxy. The wsdl.exe utility generates such a proxy, which can be used by the client like any other C# type. As an alternative to the wsdl.exe command-line tool, Visual Studio .NET offers similar functionality via the Add Web Reference wizard.

Index

Symbols

A

G

Q

R

X